Vietnam

Mason Florence
Robert Storey

LONELY PLANET PUBLICATIONS
Melbourne • Oakland • London • Paris

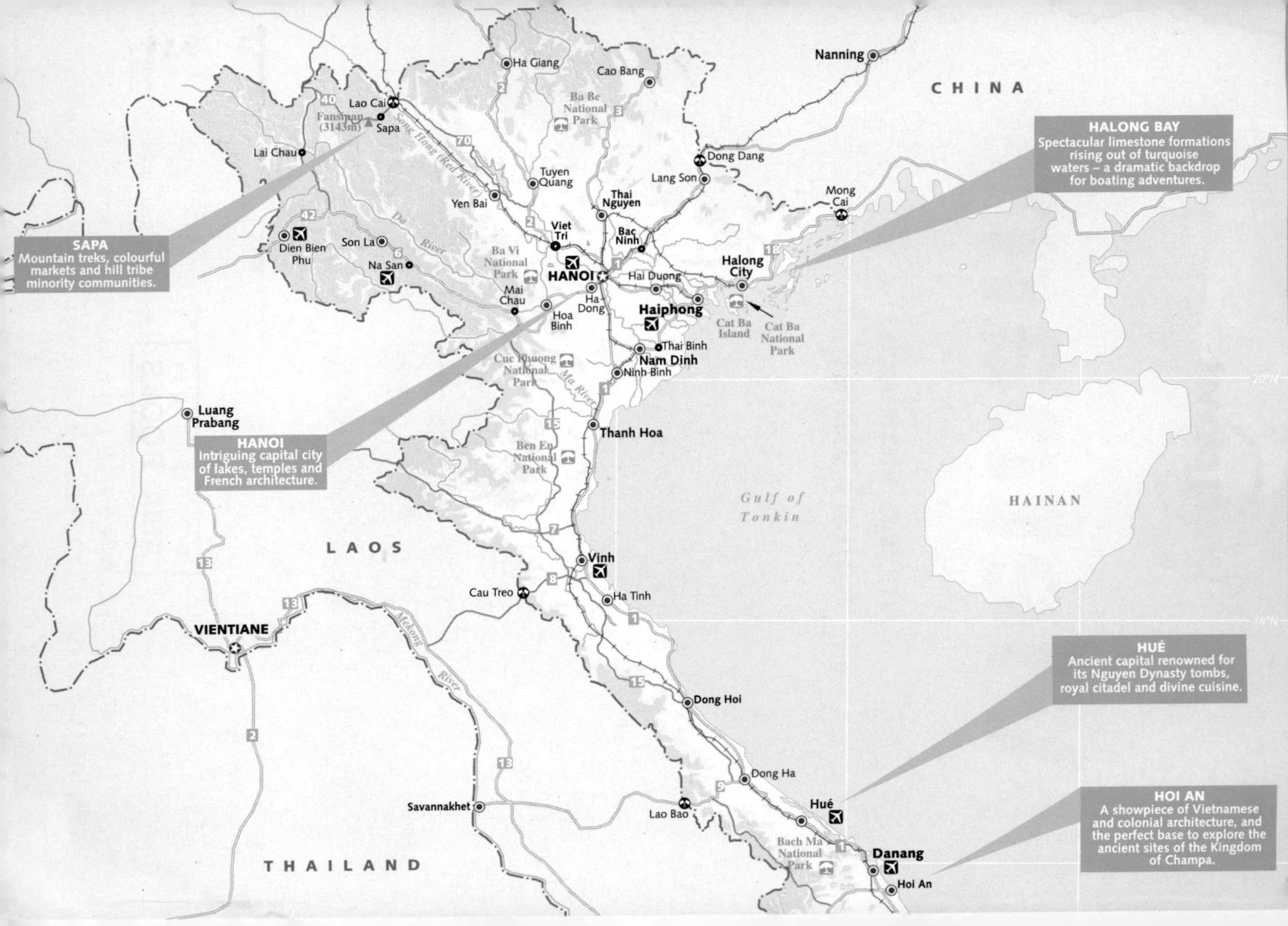
CHINA
LAOS
THAILAND
HAINAN
Gulf of Tonkin
20°N
18°N
HALONG BAY
Spectacular limestone formations rising out of turquoise waters – a dramatic backdrop for boating adventures.
SAPA
Mountain treks, colourful markets and hill tribe minority communities.
HANOI
Intriguing capital city of lakes, temples and French architecture.
HUÉ
Ancient capital renowned for its Nguyen Dynasty tombs, royal citadel and divine cuisine.
HOI AN
A showpiece of Vietnamese and colonial architecture, and the perfect base to explore the ancient sites of the Kingdom of Champa.
Nanning
Ha Giang
Cao Bang
Ba Be National Park
Lao Cai
Fansipan (3143m)
Sapa
Song Hong (Red River)
Lai Chau
Dong Dang
Lang Son
Mong Cai
Tuyen Quang
Yen Bai
Thai Nguyen
Viet Tri
Bac Ninh
Dien Bien Phu
Son La
Da River
Na San
Ba Vi National Park
HANOI
Hai Duong
Halong City
Mai Chau
Ha Dong
Haiphong
Hoa Binh
Cat Ba Island
Cat Ba National Park
Thai Binh
Nam Dinh
Ninh Binh
Cuc Phuong National Park
Ma River
Luang Prabang
Thanh Hoa
Ben En National Park
Vinh
Cau Treo
Ha Tinh
VIENTIANE
Mekong River
Dong Hoi
Dong Ha
Hué
Savannakhet
Lao Bao
Bach Ma National Park
Danang
Hoi An

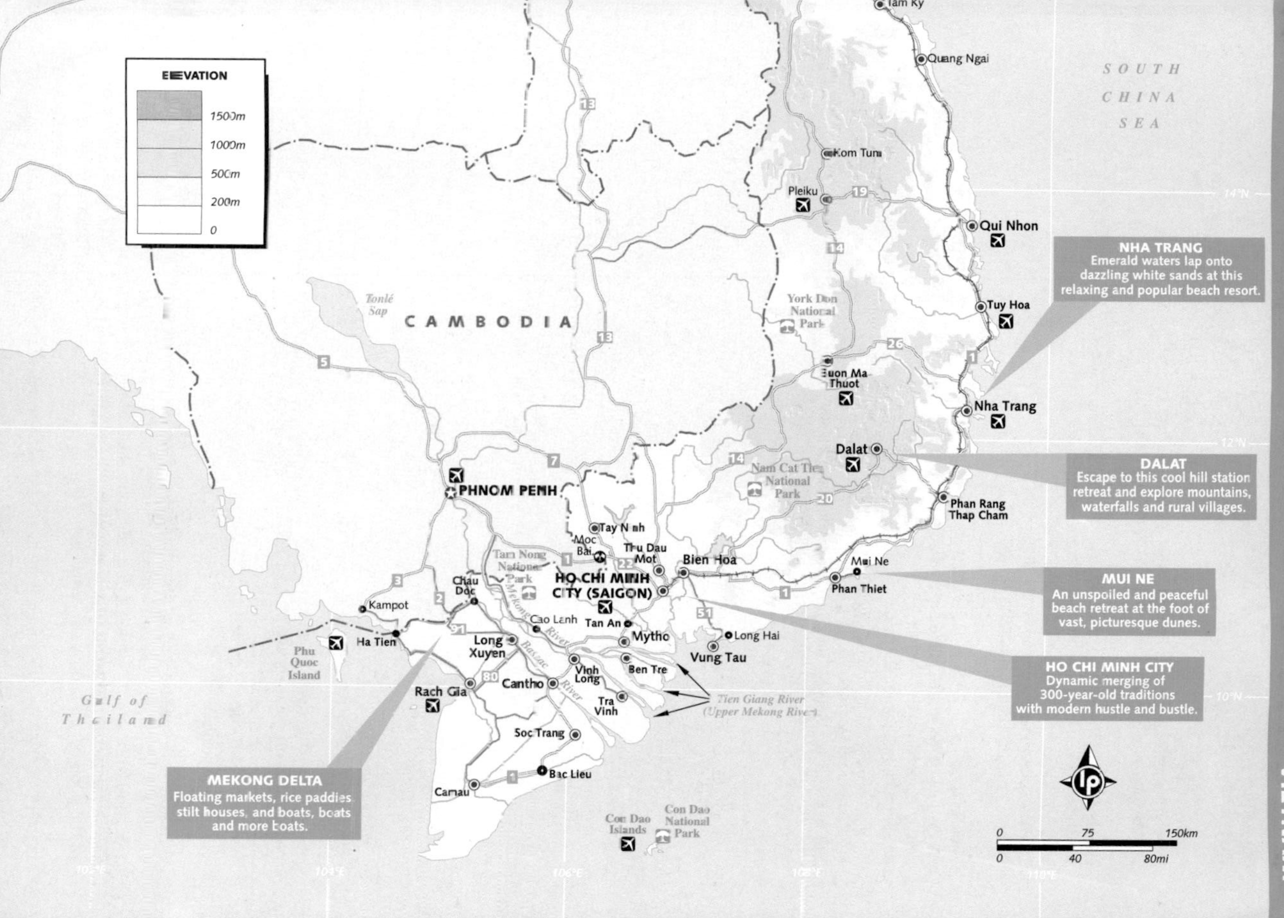
NHA TRANG
Emerald waters lap onto dazzling white sands at this relaxing and popular beach resort.
DALAT
Escape to this cool hill station retreat and explore mountains, waterfalls and rural villages.
MUI NE
An unspoiled and peaceful beach retreat at the foot of vast, picturesque dunes.
HO CHI MINH CITY
Dynamic merging of 300-year-old traditions with modern hustle and bustle.
MEKONG DELTA
Floating markets, rice paddies stilt houses, and boats, boats and more boats.
SOUTH CHINA SEA
Gulf of Thailand
CAMBODIA
Tonlé Sap
PHNOM PENH
HO CHI MINH CITY (SAIGON)
Tam Ky
Quang Ngai
Kom Tum
Pleiku
Qui Nhon
Tuy Hoa
York Don National Park
Buon Ma Thuot
Nha Trang
Dalat
Nam Cat Tien National Park
Phan Rang Thap Cham
Mui Ne
Phan Thiet
Tay Ninh
Moc Bai
Thu Dau Mot
Bien Hoa
Tam Nong National Park
Chau Doc
Kampot
Ha Tien
Phu Quoc Island
Cao Lenh
Tan An
Mytho
Long Hai
Vung Tau
Long Xuyen
Vinh Long
Ben Tre
Rach Gia
Cantho
Tra Vinh
Tien Giang River (Upper Mekong River)
Mekong River
Bassac River
Soc Trang
Bac Lieu
Camau
Con Dao Islands
Con Dao National Park
ELEVATION
1500m
1000m
500m
200m
0
0
75
150km
0
40
80mi
14°N
12°N
10°N
102°E
104°E
106°E
108°E
110°E

Vietnam
6th edition – April 2001
First published – February 1991

Published by
Lonely Planet Publications Pty Ltd ABN 36 005 607 983
90 Maribyrnong St, Footscray, Victoria 3011, Australia

Lonely Planet Offices
Australia Locked Bag 1, Footscray, Victoria 3011
USA 150 Linden St, Oakland, CA 94607
UK 10a Spring Place, London NW5 3BH
France 1 rue du Dahomey, 75011 Paris

Photographs
All of the images in this guide are available for licensing from Lonely Planet Images.
email: lpi@lonelyplanet.com.au

Front cover photograph
Salt field worker, South-Central Coast (Mason Florence)

ISBN 1 86450 189 8

Printed by SNP Offset Sdn Bhd
Printed in Malaysia

Contents – Text

Contents – Maps

MAPS

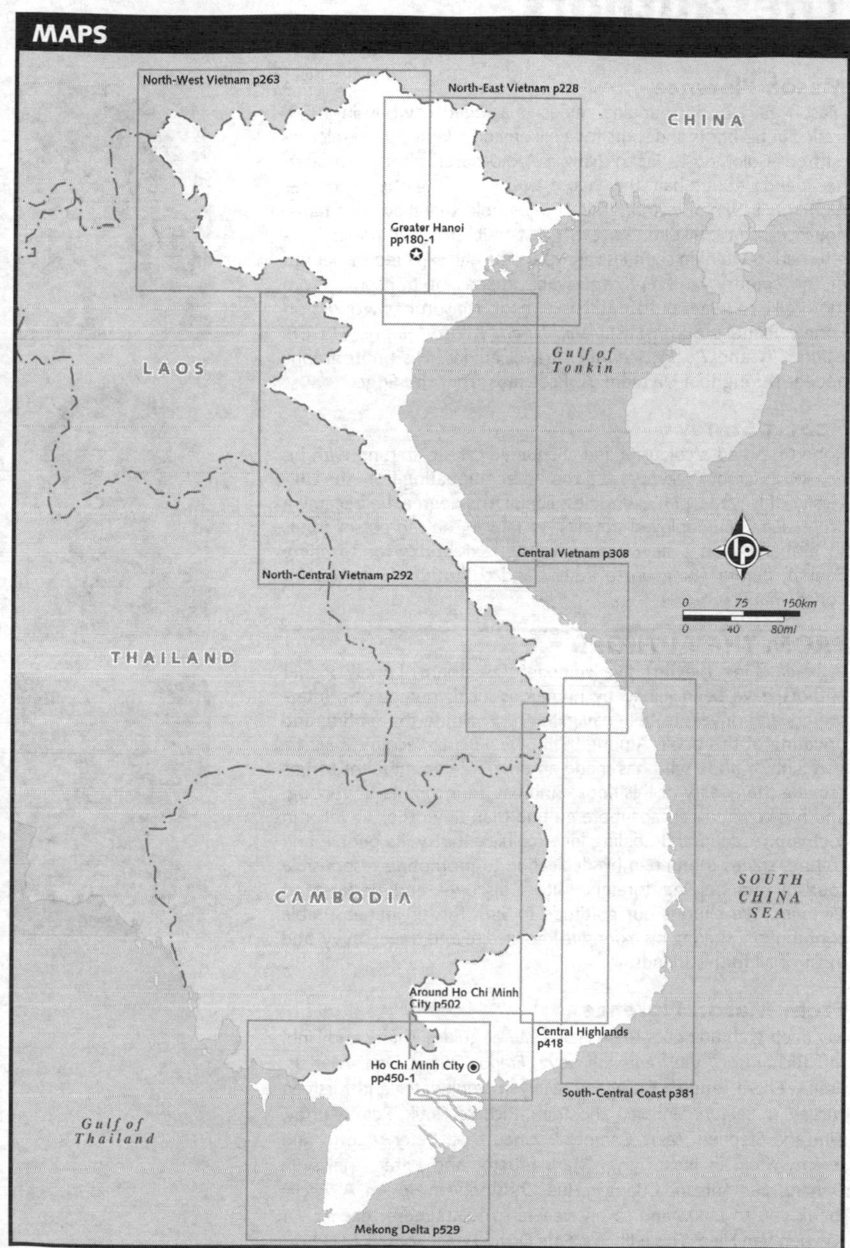
North-West Vietnam p263
North-East Vietnam p228
CHINA
Greater Hanoi pp180-1
LAOS
Gulf of Tonkin
Central Vietnam p308
North-Central Vietnam p292
0 75 150km
0 40 80mi
THAILAND
SOUTH CHINA SEA
CAMBODIA
Around Ho Chi Minh City p502
Central Highlands p418
Ho Chi Minh City pp450-1
South-Central Coast p381
Gulf of Thailand
Mekong Delta p529

The Authors

Mason Florence

Mason gave up his budding career as a rodeo cowboy in 1990, traded in his boots and spurs for a Nikon and a laptop, and relocated from Colorado to Japan. Now a Kyoto-based photo-journalist, he spends about half the year travelling the globe, and free moments in Japan restoring his 300-year-old thatched-roof farmhouse in rural Shikoku. Since his first visit in 1991, Mason has returned to Vietnam countless times, and he has explored the length of the country by every conceivable means of transport; from motorbike to water buffalo to basket boat. Mason has worked on Lonely Planet's *South-East Asia*, *Japan*, *Kyoto*, *Hanoi*, *Ho Chi Minh City* and *Rocky Mountain* travel guides. His photographs appear throughout Vietnam as 'Postcards from the Edge'.

Robert Storey

Robert has had a colourful and chequered career, starting with his first job as a monkeykeeper at a zoo. After graduating from the University of Nevada with a worthless liberal Arts degree, he became a professional, unemployed traveller. In Taiwan, he ran out of funds so embarked on a new career writing text books for teaching English, before going on to author and co-author 13 books for Lonely Planet.

FROM THE AUTHORS

In researching the first five editions of Vietnam, Lonely Planet authors have been joined by numerous local tour guides, interpreters and drivers to help navigate and facilitate the writing and updating of this book. Among them, we wish to recognise Mr Le Van Sinh, a book who has made an ongoing commitment to improving the quality of this book. Sinh has an incurable travel bug, and has covered perhaps more ground than any other traveller in Vietnam. A deep and abiding love for his country, its people and culture, shines through in his dedication to promoting responsible tourism and helping foreign visitors discover and understand Vietnam. We express our gratitude to Sinh for his immeasurable contribution, sharing his extensive knowledge and travel savvy, and most of all for his friendship.

From Mason Florence

My deep gratitude goes to: In Hanoi, stellar guides Thang and Linh, Jeff Richardson, Vinh and the boyz, Fredo, Digby, Dan, Marcus, Jimmy Pham, Andrea Callaghan, Marylin Drinkwater and Kirsteen McLay. In Saigon, Sinhbalo and Tram, Richard Craik, Pete Murray, Kim and Stephen. Marc Campet in Chau Doc, Peter Vidotto and Jeremy Stein in Nha Trang, Mark Proctor and Peter Kneisel in Danang, Lan Anh and Cuong in Hue, Christophe in Hoi An. A special thank you to Luka, and to my venerable Vietnamese teacher, Dr Ngyuen Van Hiep. This edition's 'Safe Driver Prize' goes to Mr Phuc.

This Book

Lonely Planet's first guide to Vietnam started as the Vietnam section of *Vietnam, Laos & Cambodia*, written by Daniel Robinson (Vietnam and Cambodia) and Joe Cummings (Laos). The 2nd edition, dedicated soley to Vietnam, was updated by long-time Lonely Planet author Robert Storey, using material from Daniel Robinson's research. Robert also updated the 3rd and 4th editions. This and the 5th edition were updated by Lonely Planet author and Colorado-escapee, Mason Florence.

From the Publisher

This book was produced in Lonely Planet's Melbourne office. Rachael Antony coordinated the editing, and additional editing and proofing done by an eclectic team of diversely talented individuals: Errol Hunt, Hilary Rogers and Cherry Prior, with guest appearances by Anne Mulvaney, Joanne Newell and Kristin Odijk. Meredith Mail coordinated the cartography, design and layout, with assistance from newcomer Nicholas Stebbing, old timers Chris Thomas and Jack Gavran, and some last-minute help from Chris Love. Quentin Frayne provided the Language chapter, Lara Morcombe took charge of indexing and the charming Kusnander provided the climate chart. LPI provided photographs, Matt King handled illustrations; Martin Harris, Simon Borg, Mick Weldon and Jenny Bowman drew them, and the talented Margaret Jung designed the cover. Anthropologist Philip Taylor from the University of Western Australia updated the History section, and some additional writing was penned by Rachael Antony and Hilary Rogers.

Special thanks for their support, wisdom and advice go to Kristin Odijk, Chris Love, Glenn Beanland, Linda Suttie and Jane Thompson. Also, big thanks to Brian Witty from Community Aid Abroad Tours, Oxfam Australia, Mark Hamman from the University of Queensland for his advice about turtle conservation, Ian Bryson from the Australian National University, David Prater at Pumpkin Press, Markus Madeja in Vietnam, Bruce Evans for his Buddhist expertise and Chris Thomas for going the extra yards. Finally, thanks to Mason Florence, whose madness and mayhem made the process all the more entertaining (hair-raising!).

THANKS
Many thanks to the travellers who used the last edition and wrote to us with helpful hints, advice and interesting anecdotes. Your names appear in the back of this book.

Foreword

ABOUT LONELY PLANET GUIDEBOOKS

The story begins with a classic travel adventure: Tony and Maureen Wheeler's 1972 journey across Europe and Asia to Australia. Useful information about the overland trail did not exist at that time, so Tony and Maureen published the first Lonely Planet guidebook to meet a growing need.

From a kitchen table, then from a tiny office in Melbourne (Australia), Lonely Planet has become the largest independent travel publisher in the world, an international company with offices in Melbourne, Oakland (USA), London (UK) and Paris (France).

Today Lonely Planet guidebooks cover the globe. There is an ever-growing list of books and there's information in a variety of forms and media. Some things haven't changed. The main aim is still to help make it possible for adventurous travellers to get out there – to explore and better understand the world.

At Lonely Planet we believe travellers can make a positive contribution to the countries they visit – if they respect their host communities and spend their money wisely. Since 1986 a percentage of the income from each book has been donated to aid projects and human rights campaigns.

Updates Lonely Planet thoroughly updates each guidebook as often as possible. This usually means there are around two years between editions, although for more unusual or more stable destinations the gap can be longer. Check the imprint page (following the colour map at the beginning of the book) for publication dates.

Between editions up-to-date information is available in two free newsletters – the paper *Planet Talk* and email *Comet* (to subscribe, contact any Lonely Planet office) – and on our Web site at www.lonelyplanet.com. The *Upgrades* section of the Web site covers a number of important and volatile destinations and is regularly updated by Lonely Planet authors. *Scoop* covers news and current affairs relevant to travellers. And, lastly, the *Thorn Tree* bulletin board and *Postcards* section of the site carry unverified, but fascinating, reports from travellers.

Correspondence The process of creating new editions begins with the letters, postcards and emails received from travellers. This correspondence often includes suggestions, criticisms and comments about the current editions. Interesting excerpts are immediately passed on via newsletters and the Web site, and everything goes to our authors to be verified when they're researching on the road. We're keen to get more feedback from organisations or individuals who represent communities visited by travellers.

Lonely Planet gathers information for everyone who's curious about the planet – and especially for those who explore it first-hand. Through guidebooks, phrasebooks, activity guides, maps, literature, newsletters, image library, TV series and Web site we act as an information exchange for a worldwide community of travellers.

Research Authors aim to gather sufficient practical information to enable travellers to make informed choices and to make the mechanics of a journey run smoothly. They also research historical and cultural background to help enrich the travel experience and allow travellers to understand and respond appropriately to cultural and environmental issues.

Authors don't stay in every hotel because that would mean spending a couple of months in each medium-sized city and, no, they don't eat at every restaurant because that would mean stretching belts beyond capacity. They do visit hotels and restaurants to check standards and prices, but feedback based on readers' direct experiences can be very helpful.

Many of our authors work undercover, others aren't so secretive. None of them accept freebies in exchange for positive write-ups. And none of our guidebooks contain any advertising.

Production Authors submit their raw manuscripts and maps to offices in Australia, USA, UK or France. Editors and cartographers – all experienced travellers themselves – then begin the process of assembling the pieces. When the book finally hits the shops, some things are already out of date, we start getting feedback from readers and the process begins again …

WARNING & REQUEST

Things change – prices go up, schedules change, good places go bad and bad places go bankrupt – nothing stays the same. So, if you find things better or worse, recently opened or long since closed, please tell us and help make the next edition even more accurate and useful. We genuinely value all the feedback we receive. Julie Young coordinates a well travelled team that reads and acknowledges every letter, postcard and email and ensures that every morsel of information finds its way to the appropriate authors, editors and cartographers for verification.

Everyone who writes to us will find their name in the next edition of the appropriate guidebook. They will also receive the latest issue of *Planet Talk*, our quarterly printed newsletter, or *Comet*, our monthly email newsletter. Subscriptions to both newsletters are free. The very best contributions will be rewarded with a free guidebook.

Excerpts from your correspondence may appear in new editions of Lonely Planet guidebooks, the Lonely Planet Web site, *Planet Talk* or *Comet*, so please let us know if you *don't* want your letter published or your name acknowledged.

Send all correspondence to the Lonely Planet office closest to you.

Australia: Locked Bag 1, Footscray, Victoria 3011
USA: 150 Linden St, Oakland, CA 94607
UK: 10A Spring Place, London NW5 3BH
France: 1 rue du Dahomey, 75011 Paris

Or email us at: talk2us@lonelyplanet.com.au

For news, views and updates see our Web site: www.lonelyplanet.com

HOW TO USE A LONELY PLANET GUIDEBOOK

The best way to use a Lonely Planet guidebook is any way you choose. At Lonely Planet we believe the most memorable travel experiences are often those that are unexpected, and the finest discoveries are those you make yourself. Guidebooks are not intended to be used as if they provide a detailed set of infallible instructions!

Contents All Lonely Planet guidebooks follow roughly the same format. The Facts about the Destination chapters or sections give background information ranging from history to weather. Facts for the Visitor gives practical information on issues like visas and health. Getting There & Away gives a brief starting point for researching travel to and from the destination. Getting Around gives an overview of the transport options when you arrive.

The peculiar demands of each destination determine how subsequent chapters are broken up, but some things remain constant. We always start with background, then proceed to sights, places to stay, places to eat, entertainment, getting there and away, and getting around information – in that order.

Heading Hierarchy Lonely Planet headings are used in a strict hierarchical structure that can be visualised as a set of Russian dolls. Each heading (and its following text) is encompassed by any preceding heading that is higher on the hierarchical ladder.

Entry Points We do not assume guidebooks will be read from beginning to end, but that people will dip into them. The traditional entry points are the list of contents and the index. In addition, however, some books have a complete list of maps and an index map illustrating map coverage.

There may also be a colour map that shows highlights. These highlights are dealt with in greater detail in the Facts for the Visitor chapter, along with planning questions and suggested itineraries. Each chapter covering a geographical region usually begins with a locator map and another list of highlights. Once you find something of interest in a list of highlights, turn to the index.

Maps Maps play a crucial role in Lonely Planet guidebooks and include a huge amount of information. A legend is printed on the back page. We seek to have complete consistency between maps and text, and to have every important place in the text captured on a map. Map key numbers usually start in the top left corner.

Although inclusion in a guidebook usually implies a recommendation we cannot list every good place. Exclusion does not necessarily imply criticism. In fact there are a number of reasons why we might exclude a place – sometimes it is simply inappropriate to encourage an influx of travellers.

Introduction

Vietnam, a country made famous by war, has a unique and rich civilisation, spectacular scenery and highly cultured, cordial people. While no doubt a long history of wars continues to weigh heavily on the consciousness of all who can remember the years of fighting, the Vietnam of today is a country at peace.

After the reunification of South and North Vietnamese and the beginning of Communist rule in 1975, Vietnam was virtually ostracised by the Western world. But towards the end of the 1980s, the Cold War thawed and the Hanoi government succeeded in reducing Vietnam's international isolation, in part by opening the country's doors to foreign visitors. Not long thereafter, the dramatic collapse of the Eastern Bloc and the ending of the Cambodian civil war greatly reduced tensions in Indochina.

In 1994 the USA finally lifted it's trade embargo against Vietnam – 19 years after the 'American War' ended. In 1995 Vietnam was accepted into the Association of Southeast Asian Nations (ASEAN), thus cementing itself as a regional power. Shortly afterwards Vietnam found itself awash with travellers from both the East and West – for many it was the first opportunity in over a generation to visit a Vietnam at peace with itself and its neighbours. In late 2000, then US President Bill Clinton was the first serving president to visit Vietnam since hostilities between the two countries ceased in 1975. Thus marking the beginning of a new era.

Most visitors to Vietnam are overwhelmed by the sublime beauty of the country's natural setting. The Red River Delta in the north, the Mekong Delta in the south and almost the entire coastal strip are a patchwork of brilliant-green rice paddies tended by peasant women in conical hats. Vietnam's 3451km coastline includes countless unspoiled beaches and a number of stunning lagoons; some sections are shaded by coconut palms and casuarinas, others bounded by seemingly endless expanses of sand dunes or the rugged spurs of the Truong Son Mountains.

Between the two deltas, the coast lining the South China Sea gives way to soaring mountains – the slopes of some are cloaked with rich forests. Slightly farther from the coast are the refreshingly cool plateaus of the Central Highlands, which are dotted with waterfalls. To the north you'll find stunning mountain scenery and Vietnam's most prominent hill tribe minority communities.

Visitors to Vietnam will have their senses thrilled by all its sights, sounds, tastes and smells. There's nothing quite like grabbing a delicious lunch of local delicacies at a food stall deep inside a marketplace, surrounded by tropical fruit vendors and legions of curious youngsters. Or sitting by a

waterfall in the Central Highlands, sipping soda water with lemon juice and watching newlywed couples on their honeymoon tiptoe up to the stream-bank in their 'Sunday finest'. Or being invited by a Buddhist monk to a pagoda to attend prayers conducted, according to Mahayana rites, with chanting, drums and gongs.

Of the 30 or so countries I have been to, Vietnam is easily the most beautiful. I saw more shades of green than I knew existed. Rice fields manually tended from dawn to dusk were always in view as were forest-covered mountains. I also frequently caught glimpses of pristine deserted beaches from the train window as we made our way along the coast…

David Fisher

Fiercely protective of their independence and sovereignty for 2000 years, the Vietnamese are also graciously welcoming of foreigners who come as their guests rather than as conquerors. While relations with the West were obviously strained (to put it mildly) during times of recent war, today the Vietnamese are, almost without exception, extremely friendly to Western visitors (including Americans), regardless of the past, and are supportive of more contact with the outside world.

Visitors to Vietnam today play an important role in conveying the value and potential for international friendship and business relationships.

The astonishing pace of economic development in East Asia has made many countries in the region considerably more expensive, more polluted and less enchanting than they used to be. Rice paddies have given way to industrial estates belching out black smoke; bicycles have been replaced by tour buses; and thatched huts have been bulldozed to make way for office towers and five-star hotels.

Although Vietnam has not yet reached the level of rampant development common to the region, capitalism is no longer a four-letter word here, and private business has mushroomed, adding an atmosphere of hustle and bustle to Ho Chi Minh City, Hanoi and other cities whose resurgent dynamism is reviving the Vietnamese economy.

Red tape kept foreign tourists and investors out for nearly two decades, but visiting has become considerably easier in recent years and the tourist floodgates have opened wide. Already, the relatively short period of economic liberalisation and openness to outsiders has brought dramatic changes.

Consequently, visitors to Vietnam will be intrigued by its dynamic melding of traditional Vietnamese culture, its French colonialist past and Communist legacy, and its current transition as a modern Asian power. While conical hats and rice paddies abound, the Vietnam of today is also where you'll find hip city cafes and nightclubs, a thriving art scene and a decided zest for the future.

Facts about Vietnam

HISTORY

Visitors to Vietnam will notice that, invariably, the major streets of every city and town bear the same two dozen or so names. These are the names of Vietnam's greatest national heroes who, over the last 2000 years, have led the country in its repeated expulsions of foreign invaders and whose exploits have inspired subsequent generations of patriots.

Prehistory

The origins of the Vietnamese people are unknown. Recent archaeological finds indicate that the earliest human habitation of northern Vietnam goes back about 500,000 years. Mesolithic and Neolithic cultures existed in northern Vietnam 10,000 years ago, and may have engaged in primitive agriculture as early as 7000 BC. The sophisticated Bronze Age Dong Son culture emerged sometime around the 3rd century BC.

From the 1st to 6th centuries AD, the south of what is now Vietnam was part of the Indianised kingdom of Funan, which produced notably refined art and architecture. The Funanese constructed an elaborate system of canals that were used for both transportation and the irrigation of wet rice agriculture. The principal port city of Funan was Oc-Eo in what is now Kien Giang Province. Archaeological excavations have yielded evidence of contact between Funan and China, Indonesia, India, Persia and even the Mediterranean. One of the most extraordinary artefacts found at Oc-Eo was a gold Roman medallion dated 152 AD and bearing the likeness of Antoninus Pius. In the mid-6th century, Funan was attacked by the pre-Angkorian kingdom of Chenla, which gradually absorbed the territory of Funan into its own.

The Hindu kingdom of Champa appeared around present-day Danang in the late 2nd century (see the 'Kingdom of Champa' section in the Central Vietnam chapter). Like Funan, it became Indianised (eg, the Chams adopted Hinduism, employed Sanskrit as a sacred language and borrowed heavily from Indian art) through lively commercial relations with India and immigration of Indian literati and priests. By the 8th century, Champa had expanded southward to include what is now Nha Trang and Phan Rang. Champa was a semi-piratic country that lived in part from conducting raids along the entire Indochinese coast; as a result, it was in a constant state of war with the Vietnamese to the north and the Khmers to the west. Brilliant examples of Cham sculpture can be seen in the Cham Museum in Danang.

Chinese Rule (circa 200 BC to AD 938)

When the Chinese conquered the Red River Delta in the 2nd century BC, they found a feudally organised society reliant on slash-and-burn agriculture, hunting and fishing; these proto-Vietnamese also carried on trade with other peoples in the area. Over the next few centuries, significant numbers of Chinese settlers, officials and scholars moved to the Red River Delta, taking over large tracts of land. The Chinese tried to impose a centralised state system on the Vietnamese and forcibly Sinocise their culture, but local rulers tenaciously resisted these efforts.

The most famous act of resistance during this period was the rebellion of the Trung Sisters (Hai Ba Trung). In AD 40, the Chinese executed a high-ranking feudal lord. His widow and her sister rallied tribal chieftains, raised an army and led a revolt that compelled the Chinese governor to flee. The sisters then had themselves proclaimed queens of the newly independent Vietnamese entity. In AD 43, however, the Chinese counterattacked and defeated the Vietnamese; rather than surrender, the Trung Sisters threw themselves into the Hat Giang River.

The early Vietnamese learned a great deal from the Chinese, including the use of metal ploughs and domesticated beasts of burden, and the construction of dikes and irrigation works. These innovations made possible the establishment of a culture based on rice growing, which remains the basis of the Vietnamese way of life to this day. As food became more plentiful, the population grew, forcing the Vietnamese to seek new lands on which to grow rice.

During this era, Vietnam was a key port of call on the sea route between China and India. The Vietnamese were introduced to Confucianism and Taoism by Chinese scholars who came to Vietnam as administrators and refugees. Indians sailing eastward brought Theravada (Hinayana) Buddhism to the Red River Delta while, at the same time, Chinese travellers introduced Mahayana Buddhism. Buddhist monks carried with them the scientific and medical knowledge of the civilisations of India and China; as a result, Vietnamese Buddhists soon counted among their own great doctors, botanists and scholars.

There were numerous major and minor rebellions against Chinese rule – which was characterised by tyranny, forced labour and insatiable demands for tribute – in the 3rd and 6th centuries, but all were crushed. In 679 the Chinese named the country Annam, which means 'the Pacified South'. Ever since this era, the collective memory of those early attempts to throw off the Chinese yoke has played an important role in shaping Vietnamese identity.

Independence from China (10th Century)

The Tang Dynasty in China collapsed in the early 10th century, and in the aftermath the Vietnamese revolted against Chinese rule. In 938, Ngo Quyen finally vanquished the Chinese armies at a battle on the Bach Dang River, ending 1000 years of Chinese rule. Ngo Quyen established an independent Vietnamese state, but after his death, anarchy ruled Vietnam. This was until 968, when the politically astute and powerful Dinh Bo Linh ascended the throne as emperor. Following the custom of the times, he reached an agreement with China: in return for recognition of their de facto independence, the Vietnamese accepted Chinese sovereignty and agreed to pay triennial tribute.

The dynasty founded by Dinh Bo Linh survived only until 980, when Le Dai Hanh overthrew it, beginning what is known as the Early Le Dynasty (980–1009).

Ly Dynasty (1010–1225)

From the 11th to 13th centuries, the independence of the Vietnamese Kingdom (Dai Viet) was consolidated under the emperors of the Ly Dynasty, founded by Ly Thai To. They reorganised the administrative system, founded the nation's first university (the Temple of Literature in Hanoi), promoted agriculture and built the first embankments for flood control along the Red River. Confucian scholars fell out of official favour because of their close cultural links to China; at the same time, the early Ly monarchs, whose dynasty had come to power with Buddhist support, promoted Buddhism.

The Confucian emphasis on educational attainment, ritual performance and government authority reasserted itself with the graduation of the first class from the Temple of Literature in 1075. Following years of classical studies these scholars went into government service, becoming *Quan lai* (mandarins). The basis for the Vietnamese mandarin system of government – whereby the state was run by a scholar class recruited in civil service examinations – dates from this era.

During the Ly Dynasty, the Chinese, Khmers and Chams repeatedly attacked Vietnam, but were repelled, most notably under the renowned strategist and tactician Ly Thuong Kiet (1030–1105), a military mandarin of royal blood who is still revered as a national hero.

Vietnamese conquests of Cham territory, which greatly increased the acreage under rice cultivation, were accompanied by an aggressive policy of colonisation that imposed social structures dominant in the north onto newly settled territories. Potentially the attackers could have benefited from Cham technological and cultural innovations, but instead the Cham civilisation was destroyed. A chain of homogeneous villages were built in its place, which eventually stretched from the Chinese border to the Gulf of Thailand.

Tran Dynasty (1225–1400)

After years of civil strife, the Tran Dynasty overthrew the Ly Dynasty. The Tran increased the land under cultivation to feed the growing population, and improved the dikes on the Red River.

After Mongol warrior Kublai Khan completed his conquest of China in the mid-13th century, he demanded the right to cross Vietnamese territory on his way to attack Champa. The Vietnamese refused this demand, but the Mongols – 500,000 of them – came anyway. The outnumbered Vietnamese under Tran Hung Dao attacked the invaders and forced them back to China, but the Mongols returned with 300,000 men. Tran Hung Dao lured them deep into Vietnamese territory; at high tide he attacked the Mongol fleet as it sailed on the Bach Dang River, ordering a tactical retreat of his forces to lure the Mongols into staying and fighting. The battle continued on for many hours until low tide when a surprise Vietnamese counteroffensive forced the Mongol boats back, impaling them on steel-tipped bamboo stakes set in the river bed the night before. The entire fleet was captured or sunk.

When the Tran Dynasty was overthrown in 1400 by Ho Qui Ly, both the Tran loyalists and the Chams (who had sacked Hanoi in 1371) encouraged Chinese intervention. The Chinese readily complied and took control of Vietnam in 1407, imposing a regime characterised by heavy taxation and slave labour; Chinese culture was forced on the population. The Chinese also took the national archives (and some of the country's intellectuals as well) to China, an irreparable loss to Vietnamese civilisation. Of this period, poet Nguyen Trai (1380–1442) wrote:

> Were the water of the Eastern Sea to be exhausted, the stain of their ignominy could not be washed away; all the bamboo of the Southern Mountains would not suffice to provide the paper for recording all their crimes.

Later Le Dynasty (1428–1524)

Le Loi was born into a large and prosperous family in the village of Lam Son in Thanh Hoa Province and earned a reputation for using his wealth to aid the poor. The ruling Chinese invited him to join the mandarinate, but he refused. In 1418 Le Loi began to organise what came to be known as the Lam Son Uprising, by travelling around the countryside to rally the people against the Chinese. Despite several defeats, he persisted, earning the respect of the peasantry by ensuring that even when facing starvation his guerilla troops did not pillage the land. After his victory in 1428, Le Loi declared himself Emperor Ly Thai To, thus beginning the Later Le Dynasty. To this day, Le Loi is revered as one of Vietnam's greatest national heroes.

After Le Loi's victory over the Chinese, Nguyen Trai, a scholar and Le Loi's companion in arms, wrote his famous *Great Proclamation* (Binh Ngo Dai Cao), extraordinary for the compelling voice it gave to Vietnam's fierce spirit of independence:

> Our people long ago established Vietnam as an independent nation with its own civilisation. We have our own mountains and our own rivers, our own customs and traditions, and these are different from those of the foreign country to the north...We have sometimes been weak and sometimes powerful, but at no time have we suffered from a lack of heroes.

The Later Le Dynasty ruled until 1524 and, nominally, up to 1788. Le Loi and his successors instituted a vast program of agrarian reform and land redistribution. They also launched a campaign to take over Cham lands to the south. In the 15th century Laos was forced into recognising Vietnamese suzerainty.

Under the Later Le Dynasty, an attempt was made to break free of the cultural and intellectual domination of Chinese civilisation. In the realms of law, religion and literature, indigenous traditions came to the fore. The Vietnamese language gained favour among scholars – who had previously disdained it, preferring Chinese – and a number of outstanding works of literature were produced. Legal reforms gave women almost-equal rights in the domestic sphere, but two groups were excluded from full civil rights: slaves (many of them prisoners

Dynasties of Independent Vietnam

dynasty	year
Ngo Dynasty	939–65
Dinh Dynasty	968–80
Early Le Dynasty	980–1009
Ly Dynasty	1010–1225
Tran Dynasty	1225–1400
Ho Dynasty	1400–07
Post-Tran Dynasty	1407–13
Chinese Rule	1414–27
Later Le Dynasty	1428–1524 (nominally until 1788)
Mac Dynasty	1527–92
Trinh Lords of the North	1539–1787
Nguyen Lords of the South	1558–1778
Tay Son Dynasty	1788–1802
Nguyen Dynasty	1802–1945

of war) and, oddly, actors. In the culture of the elite, however, Chinese language and traditions continued to hold sway and neo-Confucianism remained dominant in the areas of social and political morality.

Trinh & Nguyen Lords

Throughout the 17th and 18th centuries, Vietnam was divided between the Trinh Lords, who ruled in the North under the titular kingship of the Later Le monarchs, and the Nguyen Lords, who controlled the South and also nominally recognised the Later Le Dynasty. The Trinh Lords repeatedly failed in attempts to take over areas under Nguyen control, in part because the Portuguese weaponry used by the Nguyen was far superior to the Dutch armaments supplied to the Trinh. During this period the Nguyen extended Vietnamese control into the Khmer territories of the Mekong Delta, populating the area with Vietnamese settlers. Cambodia was finally forced to accept Vietnamese suzerainty in the mid-17th century.

Buddhism enjoyed the patronage and support of both the Trinh and the Nguyen Lords, and many pagodas were built all over the country. However, by this time Vietnamese Buddhism was no longer doctrinally pure, having become intermingled with ancestor worship, animism and popularised Taoism.

Early Contact with the West

According to Chinese records, the first Vietnamese contact with Europeans took place in AD 166 when travellers from the Rome of Marcus Aurelius arrived in the Red River Delta.

The first Portuguese sailors landed in Danang in 1516; they were followed by Dominican missionaries 11 years later. During the next few decades the Portuguese began to trade with Vietnam, setting up a commercial colony alongside those of the Japanese and Chinese at Faifo (present-day Hoi An near Danang).

Franciscan missionaries from the Philippines settled in central Vietnam in 1580, followed in 1615 by the Jesuits who had just been expelled from Japan. In 1637 the Dutch were authorised to set up trading posts in the North and one Le king even took a Dutch woman as one of his six wives. The first English attempt to break into the Vietnamese market ended with the murder of an agent of the East India Company in Hanoi in 1613.

One of the most illustrious of the early missionaries was the brilliant French Jesuit Alexandre de Rhodes (1591–1660). He is most recognised for his work in devising *quoc ngu*, the Latin-based phonetic alphabet in which Vietnamese is written to this day. Over the course of his long career, de Rhodes flitted back and forth between Hanoi, Macau, Rome and Paris, seeking support and funding for his missionary activities and battling both Portuguese colonial opposition and the intractable Vatican bureaucracy. In 1645, he was sentenced to death for illegally entering Vietnam to proselytise, but was expelled instead; two of the priests with him were beheaded.

By the late 17th century most of the European merchants were gone; trade with Vietnam had not proved particularly profitable. But the missionaries remained and the Catholic Church eventually had a greater impact on Vietnam than on any country in Asia except the Philippines, which was ruled by the Spanish for 400 years. The Vietnamese – especially in the North – proved highly receptive to Catholicism, but mass conversions were hindered by the Catholic stand against polygamy and by the opposition of the Vatican to ancestor worship. The Catholic emphasis on individual salvation undermined the established Confucian order, and wary officials of the mandarinate often restricted the activities of missionaries and persecuted their followers. However, despite this friction, the imperial court retained a contingent of Jesuit scholars, astronomers, mathematicians and physicians.

The European missionaries did not hesitate to use secular means to help them achieve their goal – the conversion of all of Asia to Catholicism. Towards this end, French missionaries, who had supplanted the Portuguese by the 18th century, actively campaigned for a greater French political and military role in Vietnam.

Tay Son Rebellion (1771–1802)

In 1765, a rebellion against misgovernment broke out in the town of Tay Son near Qui Nhon. It was led by three brothers from a wealthy merchant family: Nguyen Nhac, Nguyen Hue and Nguyen Lu. By 1773, the Tay Son Rebels (as they came to be known) controlled the whole of central Vietnam and in 1783 they captured Saigon and the rest of the South, killing the reigning prince and his family (as well as 10,000 Chinese residents of Cholon). Nguyen Lu became king of the South while Nguyen Nhac was crowned king of central Vietnam.

Prince Nguyen Anh, the only survivor of the defeated Nguyen clan, fled to Thailand and requested military assistance from the Thais. He also met the French Jesuit missionary Pigneau de Behaine (the Bishop of Adran), whom he eventually authorised to act as his intermediary in seeking assistance from the French. As a sign of good faith, Nguyen Anh sent his four-year-old son Canh with de Behaine to France. The exotic entourage created quite a sensation when it arrived at Versailles in 1787, prompting Louis XVI to authorise a military expedition to Vietnam. Louis XVI later changed his mind, but the bishop managed to convince French merchants in India to buy him two ships, weapons and supplies. With a force of 400 French deserters he had recruited, de Behaine set sail from Pondicherry, India, in June 1789.

Meanwhile, the Tay Son Rebels had overthrown the Trinh Lords in the North and proclaimed allegiance to the Later Le Dynasty. The weak Le emperor, however, proved unable to retain his control of the country and rather than calling on the Tay Son Rebels for help, he turned to the Chinese. Taking advantage of the unstable situation, China sent 200,000 troops to Vietnam under the pretext of helping the emperor. In 1788, with popular sentiment on his side, one of the Tay Son brothers, Nguyen Hue, proclaimed himself Emperor Quang Trung and set out with his army to expel the Chinese. In 1789, Nguyen Hue's armed forces overwhelmingly defeated the Chinese army at Dong Da (near Hanoi) in one of the most celebrated military achievements in Vietnamese history. However, his victory was to be short-lived as he died soon after in 1792.

In the South, Nguyen Anh (a rare surviving Nguyen lord), whose forces were trained by de Behaine's young French adventurers, gradually pushed back the Tay Son. In 1802, Nguyen Anh proclaimed himself Emperor Gia Long, thus beginning the Nguyen Dynasty. When he captured Hanoi, his victory was complete and, for the first time in two centuries, Vietnam was united with Hué as its new national capital.

Nguyen Dynasty (1802–1945)

Emperor Gia Long initiated what historian David Marr has called 'a policy of massive reassertion of Confucian values and institutions' in order to consolidate the dynasty's shaky position by appealing to the conservative tendencies of the elite, who had felt threatened by the atmosphere of reform stirred up by the Tay Son Rebels.

Gia Long also began a large-scale program of public works (dikes, canals, roads, ports, bridges and land reclamation) to rehabilitate the country, which had been devastated by almost three decades of warfare. The Mandarin Road linking Hué to both Hanoi and Saigon was constructed during this period, as were a string of star-shaped citadels – built according to the principles of the French military architect Vauban – in provincial capitals. All these projects imposed a heavy burden on the Vietnamese population in the forms of taxation, military conscription and forced labour.

Gia Long's son, Emperor Minh Mang, worked to consolidate the state and establish a strong central government. Because of his background as a Confucian scholar, he emphasised the importance of traditional Confucian education, which consisted of the memorisation and orthodox interpretation of the Confucian classics and texts of ancient Chinese history. As a result, education and spheres of activity dependent on it stagnated.

Minh Mang was profoundly hostile to Catholicism, which he saw as a threat to the Confucian state, and he extended this antipathy to all Western influences. Seven missionaries and an unknown number of Vietnamese Catholics were executed in the 1830s, inflaming passions among French Catholics who demanded that their government intervene in Vietnam.

Serious uprisings broke out in both the North and the South during this period, growing progressively more serious in the 1840s and 50s. To make matters worse, the civil unrest in the deltas was accompanied by smallpox epidemics, tribal uprisings, drought, locusts and – most serious of all – repeated breaches in the Red River dikes, the result of government neglect.

The early Nguyen emperors continued the expansionist policies of the preceding dynasties, pushing into Cambodia and westward into the mountains along a wide front. They seized huge areas of Lao territory and clashed with Thailand over control of the lands of the weak Khmer Empire.

Minh Mang was succeeded by Emperor Thieu Tri, who expelled most of the foreign missionaries. He was followed by Emperor Tu Duc, who continued to rule according to conservative Confucian precepts and in imitation of Qing practices in China. Both responded to rural unrest with repression.

Emperors of the Nguyen Dynasty

emperor	reign
Gia Long	1802–19
Minh Mang	1820–40
Thieu Tri	1841–47
Tu Duc	1848–83
Duc Duc	1883
Hiep Hoa	1883
Kien Phuc	1883–84
Ham Nghi	1884–85
Dong Khanh	1885–89
Thanh Thai	1889–1907
Duy Tan	1907–16
Khai Dinh	1916–25
Bao Dai	1925–45

French Rule (1859–1954)

Ever since de Behaine's patronage of Nguyen Anh in the late 18th century and his son Canh's appearance at Versailles in 1787, certain segments of French society had retained an active interest in Indochina. But it was not until the Revolution of 1848 and the advent of the Second Empire that there arose a coalition of interests – Catholic, commercial, patriotic, strategic and idealistic (fans of the *mission civilisatrice*) – with sufficient influence to initiate large-scale, long-term colonial efforts. However, for the next four decades the French colonial venture in Indochina was carried out haphazardly and without any preconceived plan. In fact, it was repeatedly on the verge of being discontinued altogether and at times only the insubordinate and reckless actions of a few adventurers kept it going.

France's military activity in Vietnam began in 1847, when the French Navy attacked Danang harbour in response to Thieu Tri's actions against Catholic missionaries. In 1858, a joint military force of 14 ships from France and the Spanish colony of the Philippines stormed Danang after the killing of several missionaries. As disease began to take a heavy toll and the expected support from Catholic Vietnamese failed to materialise, the force left a small garrison in Danang and followed the monsoon winds southward, seizing Saigon in early 1859. Huge quantities of Vietnamese cannons, firearms, swords, saltpetre, sulphur, shot and copper coins were seized; a fire set ablaze in rice storage granaries is said to have smouldered for three years.

The French victory in the 1861 Battle of Ky Hoa (Chi Hoa) marked the beginning of the end of formal, organised Vietnamese military action against the French in the South and the rise of popular guerrilla resistance led by the local scholar-gentry, who had refused en masse to collaborate with the French administration. This resistance took the form of ambushing French river-craft, denying food supplies to French bases and assassinating collaborators.

In 1862, Emperor Tu Duc signed a treaty that gave the French the three eastern provinces of Cochinchina. In addition, missionaries were promised the freedom to proselytise everywhere in the country, several ports were opened to French and Spanish commerce, and Tu Duc undertook to pay a large indemnity. To raise the necessary cash he authorised the sale of opium in the North and sold the monopoly to the Chinese. Additionally, he debased the meritocratic mandarinate by putting lower-ranking mandarinal posts up for sale.

The French offensive of 1867 broke the morale of the resistance, causing the surviving scholar-gentry to flee the delta. Cochinchina became a French colony and the peasantry assumed a position of nonviolent resignation. At the same time, voices among the more educated classes of Vietnamese began to advocate cooperation with, and subordination to, the French, in the interests of continuing technical and economic development.

During this era, the Vietnamese might have been able to reduce the impact of the arrival of the European maritime powers and to retain their independence, but this would have required a degree of imagination and dynamism lacking in Hué. Indeed, until the mid-19th century, the imperial court at Hué, which was dominated by extreme Confucian conservatism, behaved almost as if Europe did not exist, though events such as the Opium War of 1839 in China should have served as a warning. In addition, resistance to colonialism was severely handicapped by an almost total lack of political and economic intelligence about France and the French.

The next major French action came from 1872 to 1874, when Jean Dupuis, a merchant seeking to supply salt and weapons to a Yunnanese general by sailing up the Red River, seized the Hanoi Citadel. Captain Francis Garnier, ostensibly dispatched to reign in Dupuis, instead took over where Dupuis left off. After capturing Hanoi, Garnier's gunboats proceeded to sail around the Red River Delta demanding tribute from provincial fortresses, an activity that ended only when Garnier was killed by the Black Flags (Co Den), a semi-autonomous army of Chinese, Vietnamese and hill tribe troops who fought mostly for booty but resisted the French in part because of a strong antipathy towards Westerners.

These events threw the North into chaos: the Black Flags continued their piratic activities; local bands were organised to take vengeance on the Vietnamese – especially Catholics – who had helped the French; Chinese militias in the pay of both the French and the Nguyen emperors sprang up; Le Dynasty pretenders began asserting their claims; and the hill tribes revolted. As central government authority collapsed and all established order broke down, Tu Duc went so far as to petition for help from the Chinese and to ask for support from the British and even the Americans.

In 1882, a French force under Captain Henri Rivière seized Hanoi, but further conquests were stubbornly resisted by both Chinese regulars and the Black Flags, especially the latter. The following year, Black Flags units ambushed Rivière at Cau Giay, killing him and 32 other Frenchmen, and triumphantly paraded his severed head from hamlet to hamlet.

Meanwhile, only a few weeks after the death of Tu Duc in 1883, the French attacked

Hué and imposed a Treaty of Protectorate on the imperial court. There then began a tragi-comic struggle for royal succession notable for its palace coups, mysteriously dead emperors and heavy-handed French diplomacy. Emperors Duc Duc and Hiep Hoa were succeeded by Kien Phuc, who was followed by 14-year-old Ham Nghi. By the time Ham Nghi and his advisers decided to relocate the court to the mountains and to lead resistance activities from there, the French had rounded up enough mandarin collaborators to give his French-picked successor, Emperor Dong Khanh, sufficient amount of legitimacy to survive.

Ham Nghi held out against the French until 1888 when he was betrayed, captured by the French and exiled then to Algeria. Although the Indochinese Union (made up of Cochinchina, Annam, Tonkin, Cambodia, Laos and the port of Qinzhouwan in China) proclaimed by the French in 1887 effectively ended the existence of an independent Vietnamese state, active resistance to colonialism continued in various parts of the country for the duration of French rule. The establishment of the Indochinese Union ended Vietnamese expansionism and the Vietnamese were forced to give back lands taken from Cambodia and Laos.

Continuing in the tradition of centuries of Vietnamese dynasties, the French colonial authorities carried out ambitious public works, constructing the Saigon-Hanoi railway, as well as ports, extensive irrigation and drainage systems, improved dikes, various public services and research institutes. In order to fund these activities, the government heavily taxed the peasants, devastating the traditional rural economy. The colonial administration also established alcohol, salt and opium monopolies for the purpose of raising revenues. In Saigon, they produced a quick-burning type of opium that helped increase addiction and thus revenues.

And since colonialism was supposed to be a profitable proposition, French capital was invested for quick returns in anthracite coal, tin, tungsten and zinc mines, as well as in tea, coffee and rubber plantations – all of which became notorious for the abysmal wages they paid and their subhuman treatment of Vietnamese workers. Out of the 45,000 indentured workers at one Michelin rubber plantation, 12,000 died of disease and malnutrition between 1917 and 1944.

As land, like capital, became concentrated in the hands of a tiny percentage of the population (in Cochinchina, 2.5% of the population came to own 45% of the land), a sub-proletariat of landless and uprooted peasants was formed. In the countryside these people were reduced to sharecropping, paying up to 60% of their crop in rents. Whereas the majority of Vietnamese peasants had owned their land before the arrival of the French, by the 1930s about 70% were landless. Because French policies impoverished the people of Indochina, the area never became an important market for French industry.

Vietnamese Anti-Colonialism

Throughout the colonial period, the vast majority of Vietnamese retained a strong desire to have their national independence restored. Seething nationalist aspirations often broke out into open defiance of the French, which took forms ranging from the publishing of patriotic periodicals and books to an attempt to poison the French garrison in Hanoi.

The imperial court in Hué, although corrupt, was a centre of nationalist feeling, a fact most evident in the game of musical thrones orchestrated by the French. Upon his death the subservient Dong Khanh was replaced by 10-year-old Emperor Thanh Thai, whose rule the French ended when he was discovered to have been plotting against them. He was deported to the Indian Ocean island of Réunion, where he remained until 1947.

His son and successor, Emperor Duy Tan, was only in his teens in 1916 when he and poet Tran Cao Van planned a general uprising in Hué that was discovered the day before it was scheduled to begin; Tran Cao Van was beheaded and Duy Tan was exiled to Réunion. Duy Tan was succeeded by the docile Emperor Khai Dinh. On his death he was followed by his son, Emperor Bao Dai, who at the time of his accession in 1925, was 12 years old and at school in France.

Some Vietnamese nationalists (such as scholar and patriot Phan Boi Chau, who rejected French rule but not Western ideas and technology) looked to Japan and China for support and political inspiration, especially after Japan's victory in the Russo-Japanese war of 1905 showed all of Asia that Western powers could be defeated. Sun Yatsen's 1911 revolution in China was also closely followed in Vietnamese nationalist circles.

Viet Nam Quoc Dan Dang (VNQDD), a predominantly middle-class, nationalist party modelled after the Chinese Kuomintang (Nationalist Party), was founded in 1927 by nationalist leaders. One of them, Nguyen Thai Hoc, was later guillotined along with 12 comrades in the savage French retribution for the abortive 1930 Yen Bai uprising.

Another source of nationalist agitation was among those Vietnamese who had spent time in France, where they were not hampered by the restrictions on political activity in force in the colonies. In addition, over 100,000 Vietnamese were sent to Europe as soldiers during WWI.

Ultimately, the most successful of the anti-colonialists were the Communists, who were uniquely able to relate to the frustrations and aspirations of the population – especially the peasants – and to effectively channel and organise their demands for more equitable land distribution.

The institutional history of Vietnamese communism – which in many ways is the political biography of Ho Chi Minh (1890–1969; see 'Ho Chi Minh' boxed text later in this section) – is rather complicated. In brief, the first Marxist grouping in Indochina was the Viet Nam Cach Menh Thanh Nien Dong Chi Hoi (Vietnam Revolutionary Youth League), founded by Ho Chi Minh in Canton, China, in 1925. The Revolutionary Youth League was succeeded in February 1930 by the Dang Cong San Viet Nam (Vietnamese Communist Party), a union of three groups effected by Ho that was renamed the Dang Cong San Dong Duong (Indochinese Communist Party) in October 1930. In 1941, Ho formed the Viet Nam Doc Lap Dong Minh Hoi (League for the Independence of Vietnam), much better known as the Viet Minh, which resisted the Japanese (and thus received Chinese and American aid) and carried out extensive political activities during WWII. Despite its broad nationalist program and claims to the contrary, the Viet Minh was, from its inception, dominated by Ho's Communists.

Communist successes in the late 1920s included major strikes by urban workers. During the Nghe Tinh Uprising (1930–1), revolutionary committees (or soviets) took control of parts of Nghe An and Ha Tinh provinces (thus all the streets named 'Xo Viet Nghe Tinh'), but after an unprecedented wave of terror the French managed to re-establish control. A 1940 uprising in the South was also brutally suppressed, seriously damaging the Party's infrastructure. French prisons, filled with arrested cadres, were turned by the captives into revolutionary 'universities' in which Marxist-Leninist theory was taught.

WWII

When France fell to Nazi Germany in 1940, the Indochinese government of Vichy-appointed Admiral Jean Decoux concluded an agreement to accept the presence of Japanese troops in Vietnam. For their own convenience the Japanese, who sought to exploit the area's strategic location and its natural resources, left the French administration in charge of the day-to-day running of the country. The only group that did anything significant to resist the Japanese occupation was the Communist-dominated Viet Minh, which from 1944 received funding and arms from the US Office of Strategic Services (OSS), the predecessor of the CIA. This affiliation offered the Viet Minh the hope of eventual US recognition of their demands for independence; it also proved useful to Ho in that it implied that he had the support of the Americans.

In March 1945, as a Viet Minh offensive was getting under way and Decoux's government was plotting to resist the Japanese – something they hadn't tried in the preceding 4½ years – the Japanese overthrew Decoux,

Ho Chi Minh

Ho Chi Minh – meaning 'Bringer of Light' – is the best known of some 50 aliases assumed by Nguyen Tat Thanh (1890–1969) over the course of his long career. He was founder of the Vietnamese Communist Party and president of the Democratic Republic of Vietnam from 1946 until his death. Born the son of a fiercely nationalistic scholar-official of humble means, he was educated in the Quoc Hoc Secondary School in Hué, before working briefly as a teacher in Phan Thiet. In 1911, he signed on as a cook's apprentice on a French ship, sailing to North America, Africa and Europe. He stopped off in Europe, where, while working as a gardener, snow sweeper, waiter, photo retoucher and stoker, his political consciousness began to develop.

After living briefly in London, Ho Chi Minh moved to Paris, where he adopted the name Nguyen Ai Quoc (Nguyen the Patriot). During this period, he mastered a number of languages (including English, French, German and Mandarin Chinese) and began to write about and debate the issue of Indochinese independence. During the 1919 Versailles Peace Conference, he tried to present an independence plan for Vietnam to US president Woodrow Wilson. Ho was a founding member of the French Communist Party, which was established in 1920. In 1923 he was summoned to Moscow for training by Communist International, which later sent him to Guangzhou (Canton), China, where he founded the Revolutionary Youth League of Vietnam, a precursor to the Indochinese Communist Party and the Vietnamese Communist Party.

During the early 1930s the English rulers of Hong Kong obliged the French government by imprisoning Ho for his revolutionary activities in France, Indonchina, China and Hong Kong. After his release, he travelled to the USSR and China. In 1941 Ho Chi Minh returned to Vietnam – for the first time in 30 years. That same year, at the age of 51, he helped found the Viet Minh Front, the goal of which was the independence of Vietnam from French colonial rule and Japanese occupation. In 1942 he was arrested and held for a year by the Nationalist Chinese. As Japan prepared to surrender in August 1945, Ho Chi Minh led the August Revolution, which took control of much of Vietnam; and it was he who composed Vietnam's Declaration of Independence (modelled in part on the American Declaration of Independence) and read it publicly. His mausoleum was later built nearby.

The return of the French shortly thereafter forced Ho Chi Minh and the Viet Minh to flee Hanoi and take up armed resistance. Ho spent eight years conducting a guerrilla war until the Viet Minh's victory against the French at Dien Bien Phu in 1954. He led North Vietnam until his death in September 1969 – he never lived to see the North's victory over the South. Ho Chi Minh is affectionately referred to as 'Uncle Ho' (Bac Ho) by his admirers.

The Party has worked hard to preserve the image of 'Uncle Ho' who, like his erstwhile nemesis South Vietnamese president Ngo Dinh Diem, never married.

However, a surprise spate of sensationalist stories published in Vietnamese newspapers during the early 1990s alleged that Ho had had numerous lovers, two wives – one French! – and a son born to a Tay minority woman. She later died in mysterious circumstances. Perhaps time will reveal the true story.

imprisoning both his troops and his administrators. Decoux's administration was replaced with a puppet regime – nominally independent within Japan's Greater East-Asian Co-Prosperity Sphere – led by Emperor Bao Dai, who abrogated the 1883 treaty that made Annam and Tonkin French protectorates. During this period, Japanese rice requisitions and the Japanese policy of forcing farmers to plant industrial crops, in combination with floods and breaches in the dikes, caused a horrific famine in which two million of North Vietnam's 10 million people starved to death.

By the spring of 1945 the Viet Minh controlled large parts of the country, particularly in the North. In mid-August, after the atomic bombing of Hiroshima and Nagasaki, Ho Chi Minh formed the National Liberation Committee and called for a general uprising, later known as the August Revolution (Cach Mang Thang Tam), to take advantage of the power vacuum. Almost immediately, the Viet Minh assumed complete control of the North. In central Vietnam, Bao Dai abdicated in favour of the new government (which later appointed him its 'Supreme Adviser', whatever that meant). In the South, the Viet Minh soon held power in a shaky coalition with non-Communist groups. On 2 September 1945, Ho – with American OSS agents at his side and borrowing liberally from the stirring prose of the American Declaration of Independence – declared the Democratic Republic of Vietnam independent at a rally in Hanoi's Ba Dinh Square. During this period, Ho wrote no fewer than eight letters to US president Harry Truman and the State Department asking for US aid, but did not receive replies.

A minor item on the agenda of the Potsdam Conference of 1945 was the procedure for disarming Japanese occupation forces in Vietnam. It was decided that the Chinese Kuomintang would accept the Japanese surrender north of the 16th parallel and the British would do the same south of that line.

When the British arrived in Saigon, chaos reigned with enraged French settlers beginning to take matters into their own hands, and competing Vietnamese groups on the verge of civil war. With only 1800 British, Indian and Ghurka troops at his disposal, British General Gracey ordered the defeated Japanese troops to help him restore order. He also released and armed 1400 imprisoned French paratroopers, who immediately went out on a rampage around the city, overthrowing the Committee of the South government, breaking into the homes and shops of the Vietnamese and indiscriminately clubbing men, women and children. The Viet Minh and allied groups responded by calling a general strike and by beginning a guerrilla campaign against the French. On 24 September, French General Jacques Philippe Leclerc arrived in Saigon, with the declaration that 'We have come to reclaim our inheritance'.

Meanwhile, in Hué, the imperial library was demolished (priceless documents were being used in the marketplace to wrap fish). In the North, 180,000 Chinese Kuomintang troops were fleeing the Chinese Communists and pillaging their way southward towards Hanoi. Ho tried to placate them, but as the months of Chinese occupation dragged on, he decided to accept a temporary return of the French in order to get rid of the anti-Communist Kuomintang who, in addition to everything else, were supporting the Viet Minh's nationalist rivals. Most of the Kuomintang soldiers were packed off to Taiwan. The French were to stay for five years in return for recognising Vietnam as a free state within the French Union.

The British wanted out, the French wanted in, Ho Chi Minh wanted the Chinese to go and the Americans under Truman were not as actively opposed to colonialism as they had been under Franklin Roosevelt. So the French managed to regain control of Vietnam, at least in name. But when the French shelled Haiphong in November 1946 after an obscure customs dispute, killing hundreds of civilians, the patience of the Viet Minh ended. Only a few weeks later fighting broke out in Hanoi, marking the start of the Franco-Viet Minh War. Ho Chi Minh and his forces fled to the mountains, where they would remain for the next eight years.

Franco-Viet Minh War (1946–54)

In the face of Vietnamese determination that their country regain its independence, the French proved unable to reassert their control. Despite massive American aid and the existence of significant indigenous anti-Communist elements – who in 1949 rallied to support Bao Dai's 'Associated State' within the French Union – it was an unwinnable war. As Ho said to the French at the time: 'You can kill 10 of my men for every one I kill of yours, but even at those odds, you will lose and I will win'.

After eight years of fighting, the Viet Minh controlled much of Vietnam and neighbouring Laos. On 7 May 1954, after a 57-day siege, over 10,000 starving French troops surrendered to the Viet Minh at Dien Bien Phu – a catastrophic defeat that shattered France's remaining public support for the war. The next day, the Geneva Conference opened to negotiate an end to the conflict; 2½ months later, the Geneva Accords were signed. This provided for an exchange of prisoners, the temporary division of Vietnam into two zones at the Ben Hai River (near the 17th parallel), the free passage of people across the 17th parallel for a period of 300 days and the holding of nationwide elections on 20 July 1956. In the course of the Franco-Viet Minh War, more than 35,000 French fighters were killed and 48,000 were wounded – Vietnamese casualties were even greater.

South Vietnam

After the signing of the Geneva Accords, the South was ruled by a government led by Ngo Dinh Diem (pronounced 'zee-EM'), a fiercely anti-Communist Catholic whose brother had been killed by the Viet Minh in 1945. His power base was significantly strengthened by some 900,000 refugees – many of them Catholics – who fled the Communist North during the 300-day free-passage period.

In 1955 Diem, convinced that Ho Chi Minh would win an election, refused – with US encouragement – to implement the Geneva Accords; instead, he held a referendum on his continued rule. Diem claimed to have won 98.2% of the vote in an election that was by all accounts rigged (in Saigon, he received a third more votes than there were registered voters!). After Diem declared himself president of the Republic of Vietnam, the new regime was recognised by France, the USA, Great Britain, Australia, New Zealand, Italy, Japan, Thailand and South Korea.

During the first few years of his rule, Diem consolidated power fairly effectively, defeating the Binh Xuyen crime syndicate and the private armies of the Hoa Hao and Caodai religious sects. During a 1957 official visit to the USA, President Dwight Eisenhower called Diem the 'miracle man' of Asia. But as time went on he became increasingly tyrannical in dealing with dissent. Running the government became a family affair (Diem's much-hated sister-in-law became Vietnam's powerful 'first lady' while his father-in-law was appointed US ambassador).

Such blatant nepotism was offensive enough, but worse still, Diem's land-reform program ended up reversing the land redistribution effected by the Viet Minh in the 1940s. The favouritism he showed to Catholics alienated many Buddhists. In the early 1960s, the South was rocked by anti-Diem unrest led by university students and Buddhist clergy, including several highly publicised self-immolations by monks that shocked the world. When Diem used French contacts to explore negotiations with Hanoi, the USA threw its support behind a military coup; in November 1963, Diem was overthrown and killed. He was followed by a succession of military rulers who continued his repressive policies.

North Vietnam

The Geneva Accords allowed the leadership of the Democratic Republic of Vietnam to return to Hanoi and to assert control of all territory north of the 17th parallel. The new government immediately set out to eliminate those elements of the population that threatened its power. A radical land-reform program was implemented, providing about half a hectare of land each to some 1.5 million peasants. Tens of thousands of 'landlords', some with only tiny holdings – and many of whom were denounced to 'security committees' by envious neighbours – were arrested. Hasty 'trials' resulted in 10,000 to 15,000 executions and the imprisonment of 50,000 to 100,000 people. In 1956, the Party, faced with serious rural unrest caused by the program, recognised that the People's Agricultural Reform Tribunals had gotten out of hand and began a 'Campaign for the Rectification of Errors'.

On 12 December 1955, shortly after Diem had declared the South a republic, the USA closed its consulate in Hanoi.

The North-South War

Although there were Communist-led guerrilla attacks on Diem's government during the mid-1950s, the real campaign to 'liberate' the South began in 1959 when Hanoi, responding to the demands of Southern cadres that they be allowed to resist the Diem regime, changed from a strategy of 'political struggle' to one of 'armed struggle'. Shortly thereafter, the Ho Chi Minh Trail, which had been in existence for several years, was expanded. In April 1960, universal military conscription was implemented in the North. Eight months later, Hanoi announced the formation of the National Liberation Front (NLF), whose political platform called for a neutralisation of Vietnam, the withdrawal of all foreign troops and gradual reunification of the North and South. In the South, the NLF came to be known derogatorily as the 'Viet Cong' or just the 'VC'; both are abbreviations for Viet Nam Cong San, which means 'Vietnamese Communist' (today they are no longer considered pejorative). American soldiers nicknamed the VC 'Charlie'.

When the NLF campaign got under way, the military situation of the Diem government rapidly deteriorated. To turn things around, the Strategic Hamlets Program (Ap Chien Luoc) began in 1962. Following tactics employed successfully by the British in Malaya during the 1950s, peasants were forcibly moved into fortified 'strategic hamlets' in order to deny the VC bases of support. The program was widely criticised for incompetence and excessive brutality, and many of the strategic hamlets were infiltrated by the VC and fell under their control. The program was finally abandoned with the death of Diem, but after the war ended the VC admitted that the program had caused them very serious concern and that they had expended a major effort sabotaging it.

And for the South it was no longer just a battle with the VC. In 1964, Hanoi began infiltrating regular North Vietnamese Army (NVA) units into the South. By early 1965, the Saigon government was in desperate straits; desertions from the Army of the Republic of Vietnam (ARVN), whose command was notorious for corruption and incompetence, had reached 2000 per month. The South was losing 500 men and a district capital each week, yet in 10 years only one senior South Vietnamese army officer had been wounded. The army was getting ready to evacuate Hué and Danang, and the central highlands seemed about to fall. The South Vietnamese general staff even prepared a plan to move its headquarters from Saigon to the Vung Tau Peninsula, which was easy to defend and only minutes from ships that could spirit them out of the country. It was at this point that the USA committed its first combat troops.

Enter the Americans

In the 1870s, Emperor Tu Duc sent a respected scholar, Bui Vien, to Washington in an attempt to garner international support to counter the French. Bui Vien met President Ulysses S Grant, but without the proper documents of accreditation he was sent back to Vietnam empty-handed.

The theory rapidly gaining acceptance in the West was that there was a worldwide Communist movement intent on overthrowing one government after another through waging various 'wars of liberation'. Known as the Domino Theory, it gained considerable support after the start of the Korean War in 1950, and the Americans saw France's colonial war in Indochina as an important part of the worldwide struggle to stop Communist expansion. By 1954,

US military aid to the French war effort topped US$2 billion. In 1950, 35 US soldiers arrived in Vietnam as part of the US Military Assistance Advisory Group (MAAG), ostensibly to instruct troops receiving US weapons on how to use them; there would be American soldiers on Vietnamese soil for the next 25 years.

In 1950, the People's Republic of China established diplomatic relations with the Democratic Republic of Vietnam; shortly thereafter, the Soviet Union did the same. Only then did Washington recognise Bao Dai's French-backed government. The circumstances of this event are instructive: though Ho's government had been around since 1945, the USSR didn't get around to recognising it until the Communist Chinese did so, and the US State Department – which at the time was reverberating with recriminations over who was to blame for 'losing China' to Communism – recognised Bao Dai's government as a reaction to these events. From that point on, US policy in Indochina largely became a knee-jerk reaction against whatever the Communists did.

When the last French troops left Vietnam in April 1956, the MAAG, now numbering several hundred men, assumed responsibility for training the South Vietnamese military; the transition couldn't have been neater. The first American troops to die in Vietnam were killed at Bien Hoa in 1959 at a time when about 700 US military personnel were in the country.

As the military position of the South Vietnamese government continued to deteriorate, the US Kennedy administration (1961–3) sent more and more military advisers to Vietnam. By the end of 1963, there were 16,300 US military personnel in the country.

Vietnam became a central issue in the USA's 1964 presidential election. The candidate for the Republican Party, Senator Barry Goldwater of Arizona, took the more aggressive stance – he warned that if elected he would tell Ho Chi Minh to stop the war 'or there won't be enough left of North Vietnam to grow rice on it'. Many Americans, with bitter memories of how Chinese troops came to the aid of North Korea during the Korean War, feared the same would happen again if the USA invaded North Vietnam. The thought of a possible nuclear confrontation with Russia could not be ruled out either. With such horrors in mind, voters overwhelmingly supported Lyndon Baines Johnson.

Ironically, it was 'peace candidate' Johnson who rapidly escalated the USA's involvement in the war. A major turning-point in American strategy was precipitated by the August 1964 Tonkin Gulf Incidents, in which two American destroyers, the *Maddox* and the *Turner Joy*, claimed to have come under 'unprovoked' attack while sailing off the North Vietnamese coast. Subsequent research indicates that the first attack took place while the *Maddox* was in North Vietnamese territorial waters assisting a secret South Vietnamese commando raid and that the second attack simply never took place.

But on Johnson's orders, carrier-based jets flew 64 sorties against the North – the first of thousands of such missions that would hit every single road and rail bridge in the country, as well as 4000 of North Vietnam's 5788 villages. Two American aircraft were lost and the pilot of one, Lieutenant Everett Alvarez, became the first American prisoner of war (POW) of the conflict; he would remain in captivity for eight years.

A few days later, an indignant (and misled) Congress almost unanimously (two senators dissented) passed the Tonkin Gulf Resolution, which gave the president the power to 'take all necessary measures' to 'repel any armed attack against the forces of the United States and to prevent further aggression'. Only later was it established that the Johnson administration had in fact drafted the resolution before the 'attacks' had actually taken place. Until its repeal in 1970, the resolution was treated by US presidents as a blank cheque to do whatever they chose in Vietnam without any congressional control.

As the military situation of the Saigon government reached a new nadir, the first US combat troops splashed ashore at Danang in March 1965, ostensibly to defend Danang air base. But once they had 'American boys' fighting and dying, they had to do everything necessary to protect and support them, including sending over more American boys. By December 1965, 184,300 American military personnel were in Vietnam, and American dead numbered 636. Twelve months later, the totals were 385,300 US troops in Vietnam and 6644 dead. By December 1967, 485,600 US soldiers were in the country and 16,021 had died. In 1967, with South Vietnamese and 'Free World Military Forces' counted in, there were 1.3 million men – one for every 15 people in South Vietnam – under arms for the Saigon government.

By 1966, the failed Strategic Hamlets Program of earlier years was replaced with a policy of 'pacification', 'search and destroy' and 'free-fire zones'. Pacification meant building a pro-government civilian infrastructure of teachers, health-care workers and officials in each village, as well as soldiers to guard them and keep the VC away from the villagers. To protect the villages from VC raids, mobile search and destroy units of soldiers moved around the country (often by helicopter) to hunt bands of VC guerrillas. In some cases, villagers were evacuated so the Americans could use heavy weaponry like napalm, artillery, bombs and tanks in areas that were declared free-fire zones. A relatively little-publicised strategy was dubbed Operation Phoenix, a controversial program run by the CIA and aimed at eliminating VC cadres by assassination, capture or defection.

These strategies were only partially successful – US forces could control the countryside by day while the VC usually controlled it by night. The VC proved adept at infiltrating pacified villages. Although lacking heavy weapons like tanks and aircraft, VC guerrillas still continued to inflict heavy casualties on US and ARVN troops in ambushes and by using mines and booby traps. Although free-fire zones were supposed to prevent civilian casualties, plenty of villagers were nevertheless shelled, bombed, strafed or napalmed to death – their surviving relatives often joined ranks with the VC.

The Turning Point

In January 1968, North Vietnamese troops launched a major attack at Khe Sanh in the Demilitarised Zone. This battle, the single largest of the war, was in part a massive diversion for what was to follow only a week later: the Tet Offensive.

The Tet Offensive marked a crucial turning point in the war. On the evening of 31 January, as the country celebrated the Lunar New Year, the VC launched a stunning offensive in over 100 cities and towns, including Saigon. As the television cameras rolled, a VC commando team took over the courtyard of the central Saigon US embassy building.

The American forces had long been wanting to engage the VC in an open battle rather than a guerrilla war where the enemy couldn't be seen. The Tet Offensive provided them with this opportunity. Though taken by complete surprise (a major failure of US military intelligence), the South Vietnamese and Americans immediately counterattacked with massive firepower, bombing and shelling heavily populated cities as they had the open jungle. The effect was devastating on the VC, but also on the civilian population. In Ben Tre, an American officer bitterly explained that 'we had to destroy the town in order to save it'.

The Tet Offensive killed about 1000 American soldiers and 2000 ARVN troops, but VC losses were more than 10 times higher at approximately 32,000 deaths. In addition, some 500 American and 10,000 North Vietnamese troops had died at the battle of Khe Sanh a week before. According to American estimates, 165,000 civilians also died in the three weeks following the start of the Tet Offensive; two million more became refugees.

The VC only held the cities for three or four days (with the exception of Hué, which they held for 25 days). The surviving VC then retreated to the jungles. They had hoped the offensive would lead to a popular uprising against the Americans and that ARVN forces would desert or switch sides – this did not happen. General William Westmoreland, commander of US forces in

Vietnam, insisted that the uprising had been a failure and a decisive military blow to the Communists (and he was right – by their own admission, the VC never recovered from their high casualties). Westmoreland then asked for an additional 206,000 troops – he didn't get them and was replaced in July by General Creighton W Abrams.

Perhaps the VC lost the battle, but they were far from losing the war. After years of hearing that they were winning, many Americans – having watched the killing and chaos in Saigon on their nightly TV news – stopped believing what they were being told by their government. While US generals were proclaiming a great victory, public tolerance of the war and its casualties reached breaking point. For the VC, the Tet Offensive proved to be a big success after all – it made the cost of fighting the war (both in dollars and in lives) unbearable for the Americans.

Anti-war demonstrations rocked US campuses and spilled out into the streets. Seeing his political popularity plummet in the polls, Johnson decided not to stand for re-election.

Richard Nixon was elected president of the USA, in part because of a promise that he had a 'secret plan' to end the war. Many suspected this would be a military invasion of North Vietnam, but it didn't turn out to be that. The plan, later to be labelled the 'Nixon Doctrine', was unveiled in July 1969 and called on Asian nations to be more 'self-reliant' in defence matters and not expect the USA to become embroiled in future civil wars. Nixon's strategy called for 'Vietnamisation' – making the South Vietnamese military fight the war without American troops.

Nixon Doctrine or not, the first half of 1969 saw still greater escalation of the conflict. In April, the number of US soldiers in Vietnam reached an all-time high of 543,400. By the end of 1969, US troop levels were down to 475,200; 40,024 Americans had been killed in action, as had 110,176 ARVN troops. While the fighting raged, Nixon's chief negotiator, Henry Kissinger, pursued talks in Paris with his North Vietnamese counterpart Le Duc Tho.

In 1969, the Americans began secretly bombing Cambodia. The following year, American ground forces were sent into Cambodia to extricate ARVN units whose fighting ability was still unable to match the enemy's. This new escalation infuriated previously quiescent elements of the American public, leading to even more bitter anti-war protests. The television screens of America were almost daily filled with scenes of demonstrations, student strikes and even deadly acts of self-immolation. A peace demonstration at Kent State University in Ohio resulted in four protesters being shot dead by National Guard troops.

The rise of organisations like 'Vietnam Veterans Against the War' demonstrated that it wasn't just 'cowardly students fearing military conscription' who wanted the USA out of Vietnam. It was clear that the war was ripping the USA apart. Nor were the protests just confined to the USA – huge anti-American demonstrations in Western Europe were shaking the NATO alliance. There was even a Vietnamese peace movement – under great risk to themselves, idealistic young students in Saigon protested against the US presence in their country.

In 1971, excerpts from a scandalous top-secret study of American involvement in Indochina were published in the *New York Times* after a legal battle which went to the US Supreme Court. The study, known as the 'Pentagon Papers', was commissioned by the US Defense Department and detailed how the military and former presidents had systematically lied to Congress and the American public. The Pentagon Papers infuriated Americans and caused anti-war sentiment to reach new heights. The *New York Times* obtained the study from one of its authors, Dr Daniel Ellsberg, who had turned against the war. Ellsberg was subsequently prosecuted for espionage, theft and conspiracy. A judge dismissed the charges after Nixon's notorious 'White House Plumbers' (so called because they were supposed to stop 'leaks') burgled the office of Ellsberg's psychiatrist to obtain evidence.

In the spring of 1972, the North Vietnamese launched an offensive across the

17th parallel; the USA responded with increased bombing of the North and mined seven North Vietnamese harbours. The 'Christmas Bombing' of Haiphong and Hanoi at the end of 1972 was meant to wrest concessions from North Vietnam at the negotiating table. Finally, Kissinger and Le Duc Tho reached agreement. The Paris Agreements, signed by the USA, North Vietnam, South Vietnam and the VC on 27 January 1973, provided for a cease-fire, the establishment of the National Council of Reconciliation and Concord, the total withdrawal of US combat forces and the release of 590 American POWs. The agreement made no mention of approximately 200,000 North Vietnamese troops then in South Vietnam.

Nixon was re-elected president in November 1972, shortly before the Paris peace agreements were signed. By 1973, he became hopelessly mired in the Watergate scandal resulting from illegal activities regarding his re-election campaign. The Pentagon Papers and Watergate contributed to such a high level of public distrust of the military and presidents that the US Congress passed a resolution prohibiting any further US military involvement in Indochina after 15 August 1973. Nixon resigned in disgrace in 1974 and was succeeded by Gerald Ford.

In total, 3.14 million Americans (including 7200 women) served in the US armed forces in Vietnam during the war. Officially, 58,183 Americans (including eight women) were killed in action or are listed as missing in action (MIA). The US losses were nearly double those of the Korean War. Pentagon figures indicate that by 1972, 3689 fixed-wing aircraft and 4857 helicopters had been lost and 15 million tonnes of ammunition had been expended. The direct cost of the war was officially put at US$165 billion, though its true cost to the economy was at least twice that. By comparison, the Korean War had cost America US$18 billion.

By the end of 1973, 223,748 South Vietnamese soldiers had been killed in action; North Vietnamese and VC fatalities have been estimated at one million. Approximately four million civilians – 10% of the population of Vietnam – were killed or injured during the war, many in the North as a result of American bombing. Over 2200 Americans and 300,000 Vietnamese are still listed as MIA (see 'Missing in Action' boxed text in the Central Vietnam chapter).

As far as anyone knows, the Soviet Union and China – who supplied all the weapons to North Vietnam and the VC – did not suffer a single casualty.

Other Foreign Involvement

Australia, New Zealand, South Korea, the Philippines and Thailand also sent military personnel to South Vietnam as part of what the Americans called the Free World Military Forces, whose purpose was to help internationalise the American war effort and thus confer upon its legitimacy. The Korean (who numbered nearly 50,000), Thai and Filipino forces were heavily subsidised by the Americans.

Australia's participation in the conflict constituted the most significant commitment of Australian military forces overseas since the 1940s. At its peak strength, the Australian forces in Vietnam – which included army, navy and air force units – numbered 8300, two-thirds larger than the size of the Australian contingent in the Korean War. Overall, 46,852 Australian military personnel served in Vietnam, including 17,424 draftees; the Australian casualties totalled 496 killed and 2398 wounded.

Most of New Zealand's contingent, which numbered 548 at its high point in 1968, operated as an integral part of the Australian Task Force, which was stationed near Baria (just north of Vung Tau).

The Australian foreign affairs establishment decided to commit Australian troops to America's cause in order to encourage US military involvement in South-East Asia. This, they argued, would further Australia's defence interests by having the Americans play an active role in an area of great importance to Australia's long-term security. The first Australian troops in Vietnam were 30 guerrilla warfare specialists, with experience in Malaya and Borneo, sent to Vietnam in May 1962. Australia announced the commitment of combat units in April 1965, only a few weeks after the first American combat troops arrived in Danang. The last Australian combat troops withdrew in December 1971; the last advisers returned home a year later. The Australian and New Zealand forces preferred to operate independently of US units, in part because they felt the Americans took unnecessary risks and were willing to sustain unacceptably high numbers of casualties.

Royal Thai army troops were stationed in Vietnam from 1967 to 1973; Thailand also allowed the US Air Force to base B-52s and fighter aircraft on its territory. The Philippines sent units for noncombat 'civic action' work. South Korea's soldiers, who operated in the South between 1965 and 1971, were noted for both their exceptional fighting ability and extreme brutality.

Taiwan's brief role was one of the most under-reported facts of the war because it was such an embarrassment. At that time, the United States of America still recognised Taiwan's ruling Kuomintang as the legitimate government of all China. Ever since 1949, when the Kuomintang troops were defeated by the Communists, Taiwan's president Chiang Kaishek had been promising to 'retake the mainland'. When US president Johnson asked Taiwan to supply around 20,000 troops, Chiang was happy to comply, and some troops were immediately dispatched to Saigon. Chiang then rapidly tried to increase the number to 200,000! It soon became apparent that Chiang was planning to use Vietnam as a stepping stone to invade mainland China and draw the USA into his personal war against the Chinese Communists. The USA wanted no part of this and asked Chiang to withdraw his troops from South Vietnam – this was promptly done and the whole incident was hushed up.

It's not generally known that Spain's General Franco – whose regime was regarded by the USA as a bulwark against Communism – supplied about 50 military personnel to the war effort. However, their role was noncombatant.

Fall of the South (1975)

Except for a small contingent of technicians and CIA agents, all US military personnel were out of Vietnam by 1973. The bombing of North Vietnam had ceased and the American POWs were released, but the guerrilla war continued – the only difference was that the fighting had been thoroughly Vietnamised. However, the foreign powers continued to bankroll the war. America supplied the South Vietnamese military with weapons, ammunition and fuel while the USSR and China did the same for the North.

Although the USA had ended its combat role, anti-war organisations such as the Indochina Resource Centre continued to lobby the US government to cut off all financial and military assistance to South Vietnam. They nearly succeeded – the US Senate came within two votes of doing just that. The anti-war lobby did succeed in having funding greatly reduced. In 1975, America gave South Vietnam US$700 million in aid, less than half of what military experts estimated was needed. The South Vietnamese suddenly found they were running desperately low on stocks of ammunition and fuel.

The North Vietnamese were quick to assess the situation. They continued a major military build-up and in January 1975 launched a massive conventional ground attack across the 17th parallel using tanks and heavy artillery. The invasion – a blatant violation of the Paris agreements – panicked the South Vietnamese army and government, which in the past had always depended on the Americans. In March, the NVA quickly occupied a strategic section of the central highlands at Buon Ma Thuot. In the absence of US military support or advice, President Nguyen Van Thieu personally decided on a strategy of tactical withdrawal to more defensible positions. This proved to be a spectacular military blunder. Rather than stand and fight as expected, South Vietnamese troops were ordered to retreat from Central Highland bases at Pleiku and Kon Tum. The totally unplanned withdrawal was a disaster. Retreating ARVN soldiers were intercepted and attacked by the well-disciplined North

Disorderly Departure

One tragic legacy of the American War was the plight of thousands of Amerasians. Marriages, relationships and prostitution between American soldiers and Vietnamese women were common during the war. But when the Americans were rotated home, all too often they abandoned their 'wives' and mistresses, leaving them to raise children who were half white or half black in a society not particularly tolerant of such racial integration.

After reunification, the Amerasians – living reminders of the American presence – were often mistreated by Vietnamese and even abandoned by their mothers and other relatives, forcing them to live on the streets. They were also denied educational and vocational opportunities, and were sadly referred to as 'children of the dust'.

At the end of the 1980s, the Orderly Departure Programme (ODP), carried out under the auspices of the United Nations High Commission for Refugees (UNHCR), was designed to allow for the orderly resettlement in the West (mostly in the USA) of Amerasians and political refugees who otherwise might have tried to flee the country by land or sea. Thousands of Vietnamese and their families were flown via Bangkok to the Philippines, where they underwent six months of English instruction before proceeding to the USA.

Unfortunately, many Amerasian children were adopted by people eager to emigrate, but were then dumped and left to fend for themselves after the family's arrival in the USA. Asian American LEAD (☎ 202-518 6737), 3045 15th St NW, Washington, DC 20009, USA, is an organisation that has been doing good work to train and mentor young Indo-Chinese, especially Amerasian kids and their parents, as they adapt to life in the USA.

The ODP was mainly aimed at the South Vietnamese and failed to stem the flow of refugees from the North. After the Vietnam-China border opened in 1990, many simply took the train to China. From there they only had to take a short boat ride across the Pearl River to Hong Kong to be declared 'boat people'.

However, boarding a ramshackle refugee boat, regardless of whether it was headed for Hong Kong, Malaysia, the Philippines or Australia, was an enormous risk. With little or no supplies, the boats filled to bursting point, and the craft ill-equipped to cope with bad weather, conditions were heinous. Even now many survivors experience psychological trauma stemming from their flight – many boats were attacked by pirates who stole possessions, killed and brutalised passengers and raped the women on board.

As the refugee camps in Hong Kong swelled to bursting point, the public's patience ran out. 'Refugee fatigue' became the buzzword in Hong Kong and the public demanded that something be done.

Since all but a handful of the arrivals were declared to be economic migrants rather than political refugees, the Hong Kong government experimented with forcible repatriation in 1990. This prompted a vehement protest from the USA and the UNHCR. The Hong Kong government backed off temporarily and finally agreed with Vietnam on a program of combined voluntary and forced repatriation. Those willing to return would not be penalised, would get back their citizenship (the previous policy was to strip all refugees of their citizenship, thus rendering them stateless) and would receive a resettlement allowance of US$30 per month, for several months, from the UNHCR.

The voluntary repatriation didn't go quite as planned; some of the volunteers were back in Hong Kong a few months later seeking another resettlement allowance. In such cases, forcible repatriation swiftly followed. The program produced results – by the end of 1992 practically no new Vietnamese refugees arrived in Hong Kong.

Among the thousands of Vietnamese seeking legitimate refuge in Hong Kong was a small hardcore faction of misfits with a criminal past who the Vietnamese government didn't want back. Hong Kong didn't want them either, nor would any Western countries roll out the welcome mat. And so these refugees were stuck in the camps behind razor wire, preying on each other and staging the occasional violent protest over their grim situation. Finally, major riots broke out in the camps in 1995 and 1996, and some of the refugees escaped and could still be hiding in Hong Kong, possibly surviving by theft, smuggling, prostitution and drug dealing.

Vietnamese troops. The withdrawal became a disaster as panicking ARVN soldiers deserted en masse in order to try to save their families.

Whole brigades of ARVN soldiers disintegrated and fled southward, joining the hundreds of thousands of civilians clogging National Highway 1. City after city – Buon Ma Thuot, Quang Tri, Hué, Danang, Qui Nhon, Tuy Hoa, Nha Trang – were simply abandoned by the defenders with hardly a shot fired. So quickly did the ARVN troops flee that the North Vietnamese army could barely keep up with them. The US Congress, fed up with the war and its drain on the treasury, refused to send emergency aid that Nixon – before his resignation – had promised would be forthcoming in the event of such an invasion.

Nguyen Van Thieu, in power since 1967, resigned on 21 April 1975 and fled the country, allegedly taking with him millions of dollars in ill-gotten wealth. He moved to Britain, rather than the USA, and bitterly blamed the Americans for 'abandoning' his regime.

Thieu was replaced by Vice President Tran Van Huong, who quit a week later, turning the presidency over to General Duong Van Minh, who surrendered on the morning of 30 April 1975, after only 43 hours in office, in Saigon's Independence Palace (now Reunification Palace).

The last Americans were evacuated to ships stationed just offshore, transported by helicopter from the US embassy roof just a few hours before South Vietnam surrendered. Thus more than a decade of US military involvement was brought to an end. Throughout the entire episode, the USA had never declared war on North Vietnam.

The Americans weren't the only ones who left. As the South collapsed, 135,000 Vietnamese also fled the country; in the next five years, at least 545,000 of their compatriots would do the same. Those who left by sea would become known to the world as 'boat people'.

Since Reunification

On the first day of their victory, the Communists changed Saigon's name to Ho Chi Minh City. That proved to be only the first change of many.

The sudden success of the 1975 North Vietnamese offensive surprised the North almost as much as it did the South. As a result, Hanoi had not prepared specific plans to deal with the integration of the two parts of the country, whose social and economic systems could hardly have been more different.

The North was faced with the legacy of a cruel and protracted war that had literally fractured the country; there were high levels of understandable bitterness (if not hatred) on both sides, and a mind-boggling array of problems. War damage extended from the unmarked minefields to war-focused, dysfunctional economies, from vast acreages of chemically poisoned countryside to millions of people who had been affected physically or mentally. The country was diplomatically isolated and its old allies were no longer willing or able to provide significant aid. Peace may have arrived, but in many ways the war was far from over.

Until the formal reunification of Vietnam in July 1976, the South was nominally ruled by a Provisional Revolutionary Government. Because the Communist Party did not really trust the Southern urban intelligentsia – even those of its members who had supported the VC – large numbers of Northern cadres were sent southward to manage the transition. This created resentment among Southerners who had worked against the Thieu government and then, after its overthrow, found themselves frozen out of positions of responsibility (even today, most of the officials and police in Saigon are from the North).

After months of debate, those in Hanoi who wanted to implement a rapid transition to socialism (including the collectivisation of agriculture) in the South gained the upper hand. Great efforts were made to deal with the South's social problems: millions of illiterates and unemployed, several hundred thousand prostitutes and drug addicts, and tens of thousands of people who made their living by criminal activities. Many of these people were encouraged to move to the newly collectivised farms in the countryside. This may have had some benefits, but

MATT DARBY

TOM DOWNS

MASON FLORENCE

VERONICA GARBUTT

Faces of Vietnam – fruit seller, fortune teller, hill-tribe lady, a fisherman, his wife and baby.

MATT DARBY

MATT DARBY

MASON FLORENCE

Smiles and skylarks: children at school, on a rainy day excursion, playing on Dad's cyclo.

the results of the transition to socialism were mostly disastrous to the South's economy.

Reunification was accompanied by large-scale political repression. Despite repeated promises to the contrary, hundreds of thousands of people who had ties to the previous regime had their property and homes confiscated and were subsequently rounded up and imprisoned without trial in forced-labour camps euphemistically known as 're-education camps'. Tens of thousands of businesspeople, intellectuals, artists, journalists, writers, union leaders and Buddhist, Catholic and Protestant clergy – some of whom had opposed both Thieu and the war – were held in horrendous conditions.

Some were able to buy themselves out, but most of the wealthy simply had their bank accounts and property confiscated. While the majority of detainees were released within a few years, some (declared to be 'obstinate and counter-revolutionary elements') were to spend the next decade or more in the camps. The purge and terrible economic conditions prompted hundreds of thousands of Southerners to flee their homeland by sea or overland through Cambodia (see the 'Disorderly Departure' boxed text earlier in this section)

The purge affected not only former opponents of the Communists, but also their families. Even today, the children of former counter-revolutionaries can be discriminated against. One way this is done is to deny them a *ho khau*, a sort of residence permit needed for attending school, seeking employment, and owning farmland, a home or a business and so on.

Relations with China to the north and its Khmer Rouge allies to the West were rapidly deteriorating and war-weary Vietnam seemed beset by enemies.

An anti-capitalist campaign was launched in March 1978, during which private property and businesses were seized. Most of the victims were ethnic-Chinese – hundreds of thousands soon became refugees, and relations with China soured further. Meanwhile, repeated attacks on Vietnamese border villages by the Khmer Rouge forced Vietnam to respond. Vietnamese forces entered Cambodia at the end of 1978. They succeeded in driving the Khmer Rouge from power in early 1979 and set up a pro-Hanoi regime in Phnom Penh.

China viewed the attack on its Khmer Rouge allies as a serious provocation. In February 1979, Chinese forces invaded Vietnam and fought a brief, 17-day war before withdrawing.

Khmer Rouge forces, with support from China and Thailand, continued a costly guerrilla war against the Vietnamese on Cambodian soil for the next decade. Vietnam pulled its forces out of Cambodia in September 1989. The Cambodian civil war was officially settled in 1992 and United Nations peace-keeping forces were called in to monitor the peace agreement. Although Khmer Rouge units continue to violate the terms of the peace plan, Vietnam is no longer involved in the conflict. For the first time since WWII, Vietnam is at peace.

Opening the Door

The recent liberalisation of foreign investment laws and the relaxation of visa regulations for tourists seem to be part of a general Vietnamese opening-up to the world.

Sweden, the first Western country to establish diplomatic relations with Hanoi, did so in 1969; since that time, most Western nations have followed suit.

The Soviet Union began its first cautious opening to the West in 1984 with the appointment of Mikhail Gorbachev as Secretary General of the Communist Party. Vietnam followed suit in 1986 by choosing reform-minded Nguyen Van Linh to be General Secretary of the Vietnamese Communist Party. However, dramatic changes in Eastern Europe and the USSR were not viewed with favour in Hanoi. The Vietnamese Communist Party denounced the participation of non-Communists in Eastern Bloc governments, calling the democratic revolutions 'a counterattack from imperialist circles' against socialism.

General Secretary Linh declared at the end of 1989 that 'we resolutely reject pluralism, a multiparty system and opposition parties'. But in February 1990, the government called

'*Doi Moi*' and Beyond

Vietnam surfed the boom transforming much of South-East Asia in the 1990s and experienced first-hand the stresses and pitfalls of globalisation. Like most nations in the region, Vietnam went from heady growth early in the decade to an equally dramatic slowdown. At the beginning of the new millennium many people were still wondering whether the thrilling ride of the early 1990s had been an illusion and what, if anything, could be done to restart the process.

The groundwork for the reforms that enabled Vietnam's growth spurt were laid in the 1980s, but only took effect in 1990. Foreign investment poured in. Small businesses of all kinds reaped the benefits of liberalisation. The cities in particular were a hive of activity. Many people joined the giddy collective leap from agricultural into post-industrial lifestyles, and the rapidly growing service and tertiary sectors soaked up hundreds of thousands of workers.

Zealot-like converts to the newly-acquired language of market economics were plentiful. People from all walks of life seemed confident their lives would improve. And the economy did take off, surpassing most expectations. The World Bank and IMF applauded the liberal reforms as Vietnam posted high growth rates typical of the tiger cub economies. The results were seen as the South's vindication, the triumph of the market over Marx and Mao, reversing the Northern-engineered unification of 1975. Washed in a flood of upbeat hype, Vietnam's transition out of communism seemed forsworn.

The lifting of the US embargo on trading with its former enemy in 1994 was heralded as an historic event. When Pepsi and Coca Cola began their competitive posturing for the huge Vietnamese market, there was a feeling that capitalism had arrived. Yet Vietnam's tide had already turned. The country was full of investors, traders and travellers from Taiwan, South Korea, Hong Kong, Singapore, Indonesia and southern China. No time was wasted in extracting resources at bargain basement prices, flogging off consumer goods, cashing in on cheap labour, sinking capital in quick return ventures and celebrating the good life to be had.

The cultural impacts of Vietnam's regional engagement were significant. In a process better described as 're-Orientalisation' than Westernisation, Vietnam morphed rapidly from East bloc into East Asia. Advertisements for Honda, Daewoo and Cheng Fong brushed aside revolutionary imagery on billboards. Vietnam was quickly overrun with regional popular culture, like the Japanese cartoon 'Doraemon', Canto-pop, karaoke, Korean clothing fashions and Hong Kong martial arts and gangster videos. Television advertisements made in Japan and South Korea for the Thai and Indonesian markets slid between segments of Australian soap operas. When Vietnam joined Association of Southeast Asian Nations (ASEAN) in 1995, it diplomatically cemented a process of regional integration that was already taking place in cultural and economic spheres.

Although the upbeat mood was pervasive, there were clear indicators that Vietnam was not immune to problems associated with headlong growth. The triumph of a new breed of 'red capitalists' dedicated to getting rich was only one aspect of the transforming social landscape. Pronounced differences in the level of economic activity between countryside and city resulted in yawning rural urban differentiation and a flood of migrants to urban centres. With the notable exception of the ethnic Chinese, Vietnam's ethnic minorities, mostly located in remote regions of the country, were locked out of the rewards of 'marketisation'. The South and particularly Ho Chi Minh City sucked up the lion's share of investment and remained Vietnam's capitalist frontier, monopolising the best and the worst of what global re-engagement had to offer. As in the north, prostitution re-emerged as a serious problem. While the growth of the sex industry was partly in response to increasing domestic demand, the industry offended the cultural sensibilities of many Vietnamese. Increasingly shrill complaints were voiced about corruption, which only became more entrenched as efforts to eradicate it remained tokenistic. Vietnam's forests, beaches, rivers and fields were ravaged by seemingly unfettered resource extraction and development: a new biological apocalypse visited on a landscape already battered from war.

'Doi Moi' and Beyond

In the middle of the decade it became common to hear comments made about the negative impacts of the liberal reforms: complaints about mistreatment of factory workers by foreign bosses; worries about Vietnam's increasingly individualistic, culturally rootless, Generation X; anxieties about cultural inundation by 'inappropriate' foreign influences; the resurgence of ritual and popular religious practices denounced in some circles as 'superstitious'; and laments at the relentless commercialisation of the educational and health sectors.

The growing mood of cultural conservatism had political parallels. In 1996 and '97 party conservatives launched campaigns against 'peaceful evolutionism' (the alleged attempt by 'enemies' to subvert socialism) and 'social evils' including prostitution, crime and advertising slogans in foreign languages. Reformists in the politburo were accused of deviations from the communist path. This reactive mood culminated in the 1996 Party Congress, whose main result was stalemate on progressing the reforms.

When financial crisis struck the region, Vietnam was already back-peddling. News reports of the flight of capital had been doing the rounds for some time. A number of big companies had their noses bloodied. No longer was Vietnam thought an easy place to make money. Being less integrated into the global economy than Thailand or Indonesia, the regional meltdown hit Vietnam indirectly when its neighbours' capital was withdrawn. Some thought the crisis was a reason to deepen the reforms. Party conservatives saw it as evidence of the superiority of the communist path.

Apart from impasses at the leadership level, the country was experiencing serious internal problems. Riots broke out in Thai Binh and Dong Nai provinces, the people fed up with their corrupt and undemocratic leaders. The government's response, an anti-corruption drive, achieved little. The prosecution of several high-flying entrepreneurs only depressed local business. Lowered growth rates, rising unemployment, complaints about excessive taxation, a struggling private sector and a stagnant rural economy were further symptoms of the domestic malaise.

By the late 1990s foreign media reportage on Vietnam was very negative. In a notorious piece in the *Economist* entitled 'Good Night Vietnam', the country was portrayed as a land beyond capitalism. Vietnam also received damaging criticism of its repression of religious groups from the United Nations Rapporteur for Religious Intolerance, Abdelfattah Amor, and from Amnesty International, Human Rights Watch and the US State Department for its mistreatment of dissidents.

Despite the bad publicity and poor figures, the country was changing quickly. Although investors had voted with their feet, Vietnam remained a favoured recipient of bilateral and multilateral development aid. Provincial capitals grew steadily, government offices were refurbished, new markets opened, bridges were built and roads widened. Dedicated industrial regions like Binh Duong province in the south boomed rapidly and continued to receive foreign investment. In urban centres there was much greater choice of consumer goods, lifestyles, services for the growing middle class and a boom in domestic tourism. Internet service providers sprang up like mushrooms, not only in tourist areas but to service an increasingly computer-literate urban population.

With the signing of a trade agreement with the USA in 2000, a more optimistic mood began to creep back into the country. There is no doubt that the country will continue to be drawn into global exchanges; however, equally, communism is not going anywhere fast. Big players like the USA who seek to re-engage Vietnam will have to find ways of coming to terms with its political system and confront the kinds of cultural sensitivities and social rifts that have emerged in the country's engagements with the nonsocialist world.

Philip Taylor

Philip Taylor is an anthropologist who has spent over two years in Vietnam. Some of these ideas appear in his book, *Fragments of the Present: Searching for modernity in Vietnam's south*, St Leonards, NSW: Allen and Unwin 2001.

for more openness and criticism. The response came swiftly, with an outpouring of news articles, editorials and letters from the public condemning corruption, inept leadership and the high living standards of senior officials while most people lived in extreme poverty. Taken aback by the harsh criticism, official control over literature, the arts and the media were tightened once again in a campaign against 'deviant ideological viewpoints'. An effort was made to blame public dissatisfaction on foreign imperialists. Interior Minister Mai Chi Tho wrote in the army's newspaper:

> Through modern communications means and newspapers, letters and video tapes brought to Vietnam, they have conducted virulent attacks against Marxism-Leninism and the Party's leadership, blaming all socio-economic difficulties on the Communist Party in order to demand political pluralism, a multiparty system and bourgeois-type democracy.

At age 75, ailing Nguyen Van Linh was replaced as Secretary General in June 1991 by Prime Minister Do Muoi. Regarded as a conservative, Muoi nevertheless vowed to continue the economic reforms started by Linh. At the same time, a major shake-up of the ruling Politburo and Central Committee of the Communist Party saw many members forcibly retired and replaced by younger, more liberal-minded leaders. The sudden collapse of the USSR just two months later caused the government to reiterate its stand that political pluralism would not be tolerated, but at the same time economic reforms were speeded up.

Muoi and Prime Minister Vo Van Kiet visited Beijing in November 1991 to heal Vietnam's 12-year rift with China. The visit was reciprocated in December 1992 when Chinese prime minister Li Peng visited Hanoi. It was all smiles and warm handshakes in front of the cameras, but relations between the countries remain tense. However, trade across the China-Vietnam border (both legal and other-wise) is booming.

Relations with Vietnam's old nemesis, the USA, have also improved over the last decade. In early 1994, the USA finally lifted its economic embargo which had been in place against the old North Vietnam since the 1960s. Thus allowing Vietnam access to loans from the International Monetary Fund (IMF), imported high-tech goods and American companies.

Full diplomatic relations with the USA have been restored. In 2000 US President, Bill Clinton, (who did not fight in the American War) became the first serving president to visit Vietnam in over 25 years. (See 'Doi Moi and Beyond' boxed text in this section for more on recent history.)

GEOGRAPHY

Vietnam stretches over 1600km along the eastern coast of the Indochinese Peninsula (from 8°34' N to 23°22' N). The country's land area is 326,797 sq km, or 329,566 sq km including water. This makes it slightly larger than Italy and a bit smaller than Japan. Vietnam has 3451km of coastline and 3818km of land borders: 1555km with Laos, 1281km with China and 982km with Cambodia.

Vietnamese often describe their country as resembling a bamboo pole supporting a basket of rice on each end. The country is S-shaped, broad in the north and south and very narrow in the centre where at one point it is only 50km wide.

The country's two main cultivated areas are the Red River Delta (15,000 sq km) in the north and the Mekong Delta (60,000 sq km) in the south. Silt carried by the Red River and its tributaries (confined to their paths by 3000km of dikes) has raised the level of the river beds above that of the surrounding plains. Breaches in the levees result in disastrous flooding.

Three-quarters of the country consists of mountains and hills, the highest of which is 3143m-high Fansipan (or 'Phan Si Pan') in the Hoang Lien Mountains in the far northwest. The Truong Son Mountains (Annamite Cordillera), which form the central highlands, run almost the full length of Vietnam along its borders with Laos and Cambodia.

The largest metropolis is Ho Chi Minh City (usually still called Saigon), followed by Hanoi, Haiphong and Danang.

GEOLOGY

There are several notable geological features found in Vietnam, but the most striking by far are the karst formations. Karst consists of irregular limestone in which erosion has produced fissures, sinkholes, caves and underground rivers. The northern part of Vietnam has a spectacular assemblage of these formations, notably around Halong Bay, Bai Tu Long Bay and Tam Coc. At Halong and Bai Tu Long bays, an enormous limestone plateau has gradually sunk into the ocean – the old mountain tops stick out of the sea like vertical fingers pointing towards the sky. At Tam Coc, the karst formations are similar except they are all still above sea level. In the south there is a less impressive collection around the Ha Tien area in the Mekong Delta. The Marble Mountains near Danang in central Vietnam are yet another example.

Not all of Vietnam's mountains are limestone. The coastal ranges near Nha Trang and those at Hai Van Pass (Danang) are composed of granite. The giant boulders littering the hillsides can be quite an impressive sight.

The western part of the central highlands (near Buon Me Thuot and Pleiku) is known for its red volcanic soil, which is extremely fertile. However, the highlands are just that – high above sea level, but mostly flat and not too scenic.

The Mekong River has produced one of the world's great deltas, composed of fine silt that has washed downstream for millions of years. The silt is fertile and supports lush tropical vegetation. The Mekong Delta continues to grow at a rate of about 100m per year, though global warming and a consequent rise in world sea levels could submerge it.

CLIMATE

There are no good or bad seasons for visiting Vietnam. When one region is wet, cold or steamy hot, there is always somewhere else that is sunny and pleasantly warm.

Vietnam has a remarkably diverse climate because of its wide range of latitudes and altitudes. Although the entire country lies in the tropics and subtropics, local conditions vary from frosty winters in the far northern hills to year-round, sub-equatorial warmth in the Mekong Delta. Because about one-third of Vietnam is over 500m above sea level, much of the country enjoys a subtropical or – above 2000m – temperate climate.

Vietnam lies in the East Asian monsoon zone. Its weather is determined by two monsoons that set the rhythm of rural life. The winter monsoon comes from the northeast between October and March bringing wet chilly winters to all areas north of Nha Trang, but dry and warm temperatures to the south. From April or May to October, the south-western monsoon – its winds laden with moisture picked up while crossing the Indian Ocean and the Gulf of Thailand – brings warm, humid weather to the whole country except for those areas sheltered by mountains (such as the central coastal lowlands and the Red River Delta).

Between July and November, violent and unpredictable typhoons often develop over the ocean east of Vietnam, hitting central and northern Vietnam with devastating results.

Most of Vietnam receives about 2000mm of precipitation annually, though parts of the central highlands get approximately 3300mm.

The South

The south, with its sub-equatorial climate, has two main seasons: the wet and the dry. The wet season lasts from May to November (June to August are the wettest months). During this time, there are heavy but short-lived downpours almost daily, usually in the afternoon. The dry season runs from December to April. Late February to May is hot and very humid, but things cool down slightly when the summer rainy season begins.

In Saigon, the average annual temperature is 27°C. In April, daily highs are usually in the low 30s. In January, the daily lows average 21°C. Average humidity is 80% and annual rainfall averages 1979mm. The coldest temperature ever recorded in Saigon is 14°C.

Central Vietnam

The coastal lowlands are denied significant rainfall from the south-western monsoon

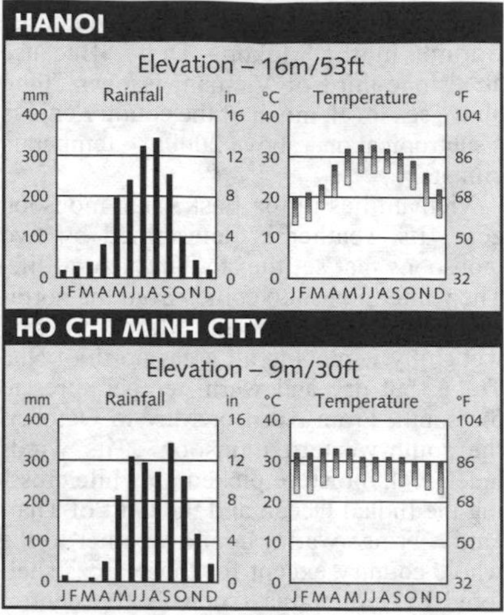

(April or May to October) by the Truong Son Mountains, which are very wet during this period. Much of the coastal strip's precipitation is brought between December and February by the north-eastern monsoon. Nha Trang's long dry season lasts from late January to October, while Dalat's dry season is from December to March. Dalat, like the rest of the central highlands, is much cooler than the Mekong Delta and the coastal strip. From November to March, Dalat's daily highs are usually in the low to mid-20s.

The cold and wet winter weather of the north-central coastal lowlands is accompanied by fog and fine drizzle.

The North

Areas north of the 18th parallel have two seasons: winter and summer. Winter is quite cool and wet, and usually lasts from around November to April. February and March are marked by a persistent drizzling rain that the Vietnamese call 'rain dust' *(crachin)*. The hot summers run from May to October. The north is subject to occasional typhoons during the summer months.

ECOLOGY & ENVIRONMENT

Vietnam's environment is not in the worst shape, but there are some troubling signs. Because Vietnam is a poor, densely populated agricultural country, humans often compete head-on with native plants and animals for the same resources.

Deforestation is perhaps the most serious problem. Originally, almost the whole of Vietnam was covered with dense forests. Since the arrival of the first human beings many millennia ago, Vietnam has been progressively denuded of forest cover. While 44% of the original forest cover was extant in 1943, by 1976 only 29% remained, by 1983 only 24% was left and in 1995 it was down to 20%. Fortunately, recent reforestation projects by the Forest Ministry, including banning of unprocessed timber exports in 1992, have seen a significant rise in forest cover – in early 1998 the coverage was 28%, and a year later in 1999 it was up to 30%.

In addition, the Ministry of Education has made the planting and taking care of trees by pupils part of the curriculum. However, even at this rate, reforestation can not keep up with forest losses.

Each hectare of land stripped of vegetation contributes to the flooding of areas downstream from water catchment areas, irreversible soil erosion (upland soils are especially fragile), the silting up of rivers, streams, lakes and reservoirs, the loss of wildlife habitat and unpredictable climatic changes.

Vietnam has so far suffered little industrial pollution largely because there is little industry. However, the nation's rapid economic and population growth indicates environmental trouble ahead. The dramatic increase in noisy, smoke-spewing motorbikes over the past few years should be taken as a sign of abominations to come.

FLORA & FAUNA

Flora

Despite widespread deforestation, Vietnam's vegetation is what you'd expect to find in a tropical country – abundant and varied.

The remaining forests of Vietnam are estimated to still contain over 12,000 plant species, only 7000 of which have been identified and 2300 of which are known to

Flora & Fauna of Vietnam

Originally Vietnam was virtually covered in forest, from vast mangrove swamps fringing the coast to dense rainforest in the mountainous regions. Over millennia the forests have progressively been pushed back: first by the gradual clearing of land for the cultivation of rice and other crops, and then by a rapidly expanding population and the ravages of war.

Much has been said about the human and economic devastation wrought by the American War, but it was also the most intensive attempt to destroy a country's natural environment – 'ecocide' (see the 'Ecocide' boxed text in the Around Ho Chi Minh City chapter). US forces sprayed 72 million litres of herbicides, known as Agents Orange, White and Blue (after the colour of the canisters they came in), over 16% of South Vietnam to destroy natural cover for Viet Cong (VC) troops.

Although the scars of war can still be seen and much of the damage is irreversible, re-forestation programs have been implemented and today the landscape is showing signs of recovery. Natural forests at higher elevations, such as in the north-west, feature wild rhododendrons, dwarf bamboo and many varieties of orchids; the central coast is drier and features stands of pines; while the river deltas support mangrove forests, which are valuable nurseries for fish and crustaceans as well as feeding sites for many bird species.

Rare and little-known birds previously thought to be extinct are turning up and no doubt more await, particularly in the extensive forests of the Lao border region. For example, Edwards' pheasant, a species previously thought to be extinct in the wild, was recently rediscovered; other rare and endangered species recently spotted by scientific expeditions include the white-winged wood duck and white-shouldered ibis.

Even a casual visitor will notice a few birds: swallows and swifts flying over fields and along watercourses; flocks of finches at roadsides and in paddies; and bulbuls and mynas in gardens and patches of forest. Vietnam is on the East Asian Flyway and is an important stopover for migratory waders en route from Siberian breeding grounds to their Australian winter quarters. A coastal reserve has been established at the Red River mouth for the protection of these birds, including rare species such as the spoon-billed sandpiper and Nordmann's greenshank.

Zoologists have recently seen previously unknown species of large mammals in Vietnam. In 1992 John MacKinnon, who was working for the World Wildlife Fund (now the World Wide Fund for Nature), sighted a large ox at Vu Quang in northern Vietnam. This ox was only the fourth large land mammal to be discovered in the 20th century. In 1994 a hitherto unknown species of muntjac deer was seen near the same site. It is believed that both animals occur in border areas with Laos and Cambodia, from Nghe An to Dak Lak. The scientific and conservation interest of these recent discoveries has not been lost on authorities, and the Vietnam government recently expanded the reserve from 16,000 to 60,000 hectares and banned logging within its boundaries.

Scientists are only beginning to catalogue the country's flora and fauna – visitors are most likely to encounter macaques, rhesus monkey and tree squirrels – however, as research continues, more rare and previously undocumented species should be discovered.

David Andrew

Vu Quang Ox

be useful to humans for food, medicines, animal fodder, wood products and other purposes.

One interesting development in the forestry projects has been the sudden appearance of large tracts of young eucalyptus trees courtesy of Australia.

Fauna

Vietnam has some interesting wildlife, but it is rapidly disappearing. The main cause is the destruction of wildlife habitats, although hunting, poaching and pollution have all taken their toll too.

Because Vietnam includes a wide range of habitats – from equatorial lowlands to high, temperate plateaus and even alpine peaks – its wild fauna is enormously diverse. Vietnam is home to 273 species of mammals, over 800 species of birds (see Books in the Facts for the Visitor chapter for recommended birdwatching guides), 180 species of reptiles, 80 species of amphibians, hundreds of species of fish and thousands of invertebrates.

Endangered Species

Tragically, Vietnam's wildlife is in a precipitous decline as the forest habitats are destroyed and waterways become polluted. In addition, uncontrolled illegal hunting – many people in remote areas have access to weapons left over from the American War – has exterminated local animal populations, in some cases eliminating entire species from the country. Officially, the government has recognised 54 species of mammals and 60 species of birds as endangered. The tapir and Sumatran rhinoceros are already extinct in Vietnam, and there are thought to be fewer than 20 koupreys and between 20 and 30 Javan rhinoceroses left in the country.

Larger animals of special importance in the country's conservation efforts include the elephant, rhinoceros, tiger, leopard, black bear, honey bear, snub-nosed monkey, douc langur (remarkable for its variegated colours), concolour gibbonmacaque, rhesus monkey, serow (a kind of mountain goat), flying squirrel, kouprey (a blackish-brown forest ox), banteng (a kind of wild ox), deer, peacock, pheasant, crocodile, python, cobra and turtle.

It is encouraging that some wildlife seems to be returning to reforested areas. For example, birds, fish and crustaceans have reappeared in replanted mangrove swamps. Areas in which large animals were thought to have been wiped out by war and poaching are proving to be 'hot spots' of biodiversity and abundance. Once-extensive forests are still home to spectacular examples, such as tiger, Asian elephant, clouded leopard and sun bear, although their numbers are dwindling under pressure from hunting and habitat destruction. Unless the government takes immediate remedial measures – including banning the sale and export of tiger skins and ivory – hundreds of species of mammals, birds and plants will become extinct within the next decade. Unfortunately, the impact of mass tourism could speed up the destruction of native species, as one traveller noted:

> The locals sell colourful live coral dredged up from the sea floor, which of course goes white and dead in a few hours anyway. Coral reefs are becoming scarce enough without tourists depleting them further. If you want to take home souvenirs, try to find something else besides coral and rare seashells.

However, Vietnam seems to be the last place in the world where zoologists are discovering previously unknown species of large mammals. None had been found for nearly 50 years until 1992, when a large ox was discovered at Vu Quang. The ox dubbed the Vu Quang ox, is a boldly marked, forest-dwelling herbivore that physically resembles a small antelope, although genetically it appears to be more similar to the ox (see the 'Flora & Fauna of Vietnam' boxed text earlier in this chapter). Around the same time in the early nineties, a small population of the world's rarest rhinoceros, the Javan rhino, was discovered in the Nam Cat Tien National Park, south-west of Dalat. The government is showing enthusiasm for ecological protection and Vietnam today has a surprising amount to offer the visitor interested in wildlife. A total of 87 reserves

National Park Highlights

park	chapter	features	access	best time to visit
Cuc Phuong	North-Central Vietnam	hiking, grottoes endangered primate centre, birdlife, Tonkin rare leaf monkeys	car/motorbike	October to March
Nam Cat Tien	Central Highlands	primates, elephants, birdlife, rhinos, tigers	car/motorbike then boat	November to February
Ba Be	North-East Vietnam	lakes, rainforest, waterfalls, towering peaks, bears, monkeys, birdlife	public transport to Cho Ra, then motorbike/4WD	April to November
Bach Ma	Central Vietnam	hiking, waterfalls, birdlife, tigers, primates	car/motorbike	February to September
Cat Ba	North-East Vietnam	hiking, caves, minority villages, monkeys, boars, deer, waterfowl	minibus/ motorbike	April to August
Yok Don	Central Highlands	ethnic groups, elephant rides, stilt houses	4WD/ motorbike	November to February

cover about 3.3% of Vietnam's land area. Recent moves forward in conservation have included the protection of an area straddling the Vietnamese-Lao border that includes the provinces of Nghe An, Ha Tinh and Quang Binh in Vietnam and Bolikhamsai and Khammuan in Laos as a refuge for the region's biodiversity. This region also includes two of the world's most endangered monkeys, the douc langur and the Ha Tinh langur, and is potentially home to other rare or even undiscovered creatures.

However, travellers are advised not to try to see these rare animals in the wild, as this may put them in even greater peril – many local people believe that tourists want to buy skins and skulls. In general, travellers to Vietnam should not buy products made from wildlife.

Continued habitat destruction and poaching means that many now-rare species are headed for the extinction list. Captive breeding programs may be the only hope for some.

National Parks

Vietnam has 10 national parks and an expanding array of nature reserves well worth exploring. The parks are seldom visited as travellers tend to get stuck on the tourist trail, without the time or wanderlust to explore them. Access can be problematic with some parks hidden in remote areas.

The most interesting and accessible parks are Cat Ba, Ba Be and Cuc Phuong in the North; Bach Ma in the centre; and Nam Cat Tien and Yok Don in the South (see the National Parks table for more details on access). However, the national parks service has plans to improve the existing parks and reserves as well as opening up some new ones. Keep your ears open for news on this.

Cat Ba National Park is a beautiful island and, during the summer months, attracts a steady stream of foreign travellers willing to make the boat journey. Ba Be National Park features spectacular waterfalls and is accessible by rented jeep or motorbike from Hanoi. Cuc Phuong National Park is less visited, but is easily reached from Hanoi and offers great hiking. Bach Ma National Park near Hué is also seldom visited, but is demonstrating good potential for responsible ecotourism. Nam Cat Tien National Park, in the southern part of the central highlands, is relatively easy to reach from Saigon, but still sees very few visitors. Nam Cat Tien is very popular, however, with birdwatchers. Also in the central highlands is Yok Don National Park, which is not particularly scenic but is home to the local minority tribes.

In an attempt to prevent any possible ecological and hydrological catastrophe, the government has been setting aside tens of thousands of square kilometres of forest land with plans to create about 100 protected areas in the form of national parks and nature reserves. Over 40 of these reserves (including the national parks) have already received government approval. Ecologists hope that because tropical ecosystems have a high number of diverse species but low densities of individual species, reserve areas will be large enough to contain viable populations of each of the species. However, there are development interests that are not amenable to increasing the size of Vietnam's national parks and forest reserves – as in the West, even the best-laid plans can sometimes go awry.

Another problem is poaching, and this is one threat that travellers should take seriously. Poachers often carry guns, both for their illegal hunting activities and to drive away any potential witnesses or law enforcement authorities. They are also not above supplementing their income with armed robberies. In particular, the areas near the Cambodian and Lao borders bring a greater risk of getting shot at if you go strolling in the jungle. The government discourages foreign travellers from visiting these remote nature reserves near the border, while scientists seeking permission to visit are usually obliged to take along a few AK-47-toting soldiers for protection. Of course, this doesn't apply to those parts of national parks that see a reasonable amount of tourist traffic.

I met the director of Bach Ma National Park. He expressed his desire to see more visitors to the park, used terms like 'eco-tourism' and explained that overseas interest in Vietnam's national parks program was vital in order to raise the government's commitment. Serious pressures from logging, poaching, agriculture etc, require national and provincial government assistance in overcoming. This will only happen if the park's tourist potential is seen as something worth protecting.

Tim Weisselberg

The parks have the added appeal of being among the few places in Vietnam where tourists are unlikely to be hassled to buy anything.

GOVERNMENT & POLITICS

When it comes to government and politics, Vietnam has a lot of both.

The Socialist Republic of Vietnam (SRV; Cong Hoa Xa Hoi Chu Nghia Viet Nam) came into existence in July 1976 as a unitary state comprising the Democratic Republic of Vietnam (DRV; North Vietnam) and the defeated Republic of Vietnam (RVN; South Vietnam). From April 1975 until the declaration of the SRV, the South had been ruled – at least in name – by a Provisional Revolutionary Government.

Officially, the government espouses a Marxist-Leninist political philosophy. Its political institutions have borrowed a great deal from the Soviet and Chinese models, in particular the ability to create mountains of red tape.

The Orwellian national slogan, which appears at the top of every official document, is *Doc Lap – Tu Do – Hanh Phuc*, based on one of Ho Chi Minh's sayings that means 'Independence – Freedom – Happiness'.

Vietnam's political system is dominated by the two million member Communist

Party (Dang Cong San Viet Nam), whose influence is felt at every level of the country's social and political life.

The leadership of the Communist Party has been collective in style and structure ever since its founding by Ho Chi Minh in 1930. The Party's decentralised structure, though originally necessitated by the difficulty of communications between the Party headquarters and its branches, has allowed local leaders a considerable amount of leeway for initiative. Unfortunately, this has also allowed the development of localised corruption, which Hanoi has had difficulty controlling.

The official media has described a number of cases. In Thanh Hoa Province, local Party chief Ha Trong Hoa turned his police force into a band of Mafia-style gangsters and ruled for years before Hanoi finally stepped in and ousted him. Pham Chi Tin, the son of a high-ranking Communist Party official, was arrested by the military in 1994 after his gang (the Nha Trang police force) terrorised local residents for years – Hanoi took action after he kidnapped a tourist from Hong Kong to extort money from the victim's family. There was a similar crackdown in Vung Tau recently.

Relatively speaking, the policies of the Vietnamese Communist Party have been characterised by a flexible, nondoctrinaire approach.

The most powerful institution in the Party is the Political Bureau (Politburo), which has about a dozen members. It oversees the Party's day-to-day functioning and has the power to issue directives to the government. The Politburo is formally elected by the Central Committee, whose 125 or so full members and about 50 alternate members meet only once or twice a year.

Party Congresses, at which major policy changes are ratified after a long process of behind-the-scenes discussions and consultations, were held in 1935, 1951, 1960, 1976, 1982, 1986, 1991, 1996 and 1997. The last few Party Congresses have reflected intense intra-Party disagreements over the path Vietnamese Communism should take, with changing coalitions of conservatives and dogmatists squaring off against more pragmatic elements. The position of Party Chairman has been left vacant since Ho Chi Minh's death in 1969.

Vietnam's unicameral National Assembly (Quoc Hoi) is the highest legislative authority in the country. Its 500 or so deputies, whose terms last five years, each represent around 100,000 voters. The National Assembly's function is basically to rubberstamp – in most cases unanimously – Politburo decisions and Party-initiated legislation during its biannual sessions, which last about a week.

The Council of State functions as the country's collective presidency. Its members (who numbered 15 at the time of writing) are elected by the National Assembly. The Council of State carries out the duties of the National Assembly when the latter is not in session. The Council of Ministers is another elected by the National Assembly. Its functions are similar to a Western-style cabinet.

During the 1980s and early 1990s thousands of Party members were expelled, in part to reduce corruption (seen by a fed-up public as endemic) and in part to make room for more young people and workers. As in China, Vietnam has been ruled by a gerontocracy. Few high-ranking officials ever retire – they just fade away.

There are 25 official government ministries serving under the command of the men above. Despite official rhetoric about the equality of women, females are underrepresented in the Party, especially at the highest levels (there have been no female members of the Politburo since 1945).

Candidates to the National Assembly and local People's Committees are elected to office. Everyone of voting age (18 years) is required to vote, though proxy-voting is allowed (and is very common). This permits the government to boast that elections produce 100% voter participation, thus conferring legitimacy on the process. Only Party-approved candidates are permitted to run and opposition parties are prohibited. Some independents have appeared on the slate, but they must also have the government's approval to run.

Theoretically the military does not seem to have any direct political role, however, virtually all of Vietnam's high-ranking politicians and officials came from the military.

The government seems to have a hard time deciding how to carve the political turkey. After reunification, the provincial structure of the South was completely reorganised. Then on 1 July 1989, several provinces that were joined after 1975 were split apart. Since then there have been even more splits; the last one was in 1996 when eight new provinces were created, bringing the total to 61. Even the Vietnamese have difficulty keeping up with the redrawing of political boundaries.

Vietnam became a member of the Association of Southeast Asian Nations (ASEAN) in July 1995, and in November of the same year the American President Bill Clinton officially announced US-Vietnamese relations 'normalised'. In July 2000, after more than four years on the drawing board, a historic trade pact was finally signed between former enemies.

ECONOMY

Vietnam is one of the poorest countries in Asia with an estimated per capita income of less than US$300 per year, and hard currency debts of US$1.4 billion (owed mainly to Russia, the IMF and Japan). Unable to repay these loans, Vietnam has been unofficially bankrupt since the 1980s.

An agreement reached in 1996 reduced Vietnam's debt by 50%, with the remainder to be paid off gradually. The country's improving economy increases the possibility that it will meet its obligations to lenders, and that Vietnam will eventually be issuing new bonds overseas.

Despite its hard-working, educated workforce, the country's economy is beset by low wages, poor infrastructure, a trade deficit, unemployment, under-employment and, until recently, erratic runaway inflation (700% in 1986, 30% in 1989, 50% in 1991, 3% in 1996 and 8% in 1998).

The economy was hurt by wartime infrastructure damage (not a single bridge in the North survived American air raids, while in the South many bridges were blown up by the VC), but by the government's own admission the present economic fiasco is the result of the ideologically driven policies that were followed after reunification, plus corruption and the burden of heavy military spending.

Just how the average Vietnamese manages to survive is a mystery. Salaries in Ho Chi Minh City are in the range of US$50 to US$90 per month, but elsewhere they're about half that. You simply can't survive on such wages unless you can grow your own food and build your own house (possible in the countryside, but not in Saigon or Hanoi). So people scrounge on the side, finding some odd job they can do. Many women are forced to resort to part-time prostitution, while government officials and police often turn to corruption.

Although Vietnam and Russia are still officially as close as lips and teeth, Vietnamese from all parts of the country seem to harbour an unreserved hostility towards the few remaining Russian experts in their country. This bitterness is an outgrowth of the widespread belief that Soviet economic policies are to blame for Vietnam's economy going straight down the toilet after reunification.

The once ubiquitous posters of those two white guys, Marx and Lenin, served to underline the foreign origin of much of the Vietnamese Party's unpopular ideology, including collectivisation and centralised planning. Perhaps not that surprisingly, the posters disappeared almost overnight with the Soviet Union's demise in 1991.

Economic Reforms

Vietnam might well have collapsed had it not been for Soviet aid and recent capitalist-style reforms. Vietnam's efforts to restructure the economy really got under way with the Sixth Party Congress held in December 1986. At that time, Nguyen Van Linh (a proponent of reform) was appointed General Secretary of the Communist Party.

Immediately upon the legalisation of limited private enterprise, family businesses began popping up all over the country. But it's the South, with its experience with capitalism, that has the entrepreneurial skills and managerial dynamism needed to effect the reforms. With 'new thinking' in Hanoi now modelling the economic life of the whole country in the mould of the prereunification South, people have been remarking that, in the end, the South won the war.

As a direct result of these economic reforms, Vietnam moved from being a rice importer in the mid-1980s to become the world's second-largest rice exporter in 1997 (after Thailand).

Vietnam's economy started growing in the late 1980s, reversing the trend of the previous decade when it experienced precipitous negative economic growth. But official growth figures don't tell the whole story; there is a significant 'black economy' not recorded in the government's statistics. Indeed, the amount of smuggling going on across the Cambodian-Vietnamese border easily exceeds the official trade between those two countries.

Another fact that the government doesn't like to admit is that the urban economy is improving much faster than the rural economy, widening the already significant gap in Vietnamese standards of living. The Vietnamese government fears what China is already experiencing – a mass exodus of countryside residents into the already overcrowded cities.

Before 1991, Vietnam's major trading partners were the USSR and other members of the Council for Mutual Economic Assistance (COMECON – the Eastern Bloc's equivalent to the European Union). Most of the trade with COMECON was on a barter basis; Vietnam traded its crude oil, wood and sugar cane for refined oil, machinery and weapons. Because the value of Vietnam's agricultural products was not nearly enough to pay for the expensive war toys, the USSR had to subsidise the Vietnamese economy, leaving Vietnam with an enormous rouble-denominated debt.

The disintegration of COMECON and the USSR in 1991 could have brought complete economic collapse to Vietnam. Almost miraculously, this was avoided because Vietnam moved quickly to establish hard currency trade relations with China, Hong Kong, Japan, Singapore, South Korea, Taiwan, Thailand and Western nations. This explains why Vietnamese officials have suddenly become so anxious to do business with the West. Many former Eastern Bloc countries have not fared as well as Vietnam – their economies collapsed along with the USSR.

The transition from an isolated, socialist barter economy to a free market, hard currency trading economy is not complete and has not been easy. Many of Vietnam's manufactured goods (bicycles, shoes, even toothpaste) are of such poor quality that they are practically unsaleable, especially in the face of competition from foreign goods.

One of the first effects of free (or freeish) trade with capitalist countries was the wiping out of many state-run enterprises, leading to job lay-offs and an increase in unemployment. Even Vietnam's sugar-cane growers were hurt – shoddy equipment at state-run refineries produced such a low-quality product that imported refined sugar replaced the domestic product for a while.

The Vietnamese government responded with a number of 'temporary import bans' (protectionism). Such bans theoretically give a boost to struggling domestic industries, but also lead to increased smuggling. Slowly but surely, the country is regaining its ability to compete in foreign markets; low wages and the strong Vietnamese work ethic (when offered incentives) bodes well for Vietnam's export industries.

The more liberal rules have had a dramatic effect on foreign joint-venture operations – foreign investors have been tripping over themselves to get into the country. Some of the most successful joint ventures to date have involved hotels, though some of these 'investments' are clear cases of real-estate speculation (foreigners cannot buy land directly, but businesses with a Vietnamese partner can). The leading foreign investors are the Koreans, Singaporeans and Taiwanese.

Unfortunately, political meddling hasn't stopped completely. The bureaucracy is still plagued by middle-level functionaries with jobs that are essentially worthless (or counterproductive) and should be eliminated.

Such bureaucrats view the reforms as a serious threat and would like to see them fail. Despite recent successes, the reformers still do not have the upper hand.

The Vietnamese bureaucracy, official incompetence, corruption and the ever-changing rules and regulations continue to irritate foreign investors. On paper, intellectual property rights are protected, but enforcement is lax – patents, copyrights and trademarks are openly pirated. Tax rates and government fees are frequently revised without warning. Some municipalities have forced foreign companies to hire employees from state employment agencies, with the only employees available being the 'spoiled brats' of cadres (also see the 'Swords into Market Shares' boxed text in the Ho Chi Minh City chapter).

Economic Backlash

Recalcitrant bureaucrats or not, the reforms have already gained enough momentum to make it hard to imagine reversing them – putting the toothpaste back in the tube might well be impossible. However, there has been a conservative backlash against the reforms. Rather than shrinking, the state sector has been expanding. Various government regulations make it difficult or impossible for private businesses to function except in a joint venture with a state-owned company. Such joint ventures often come to grief and many foreign investors are becoming disillusioned with Vietnam. In 1996, the number of foreign investment projects actually dropped by 17% from the previous year.

One of the most visible signs of the anti-market backlash was the 'social evils' campaign launched with much fanfare in late 1995. Borrowing phrases from China's goofy 'spiritual campaign' of the 1980s, the government declared that evil ideas from the West were 'polluting' Vietnamese society. The pollution would have to be 'cleaned up'. Aside from obvious foreign pollution such as prostitution, drugs and karaoke, one of the major evils identified was the use of English in advertising. Vietnamese police were ordered to destroy English signs – companies like Coca-Cola and Sony watched in disbelief as their multimillion-dollar advertising campaigns were annihilated by enthusiastic vigilantes.

Meanwhile, socially evil foreign video tapes, music tapes, magazines and other paraphernalia were burned in public bonfires. Vietnam's official *Moi* newspaper reported that, 'thanks to education and propaganda, people voluntarily gave up 27,302 video tapes'.

After foreign investors threatened to pull out of the country, the Vietnamese authorities relaxed the rules somewhat. However, the Vietnamese press still rants periodically about social evils and, even now, every business must have a sign in Vietnamese larger than the English sign.

Tourists were also affected by the social evils campaign. During the first half of 1996, the authorities refused all visa extensions. Then during June 1996 (during the Eighth Party Congress), all tourist visas were refused. This brought about the near collapse of the tourist industry, forcing the government to beat a retreat and ease up on the restrictions. The industry didn't start to recover until nearly the end of the year, but overall 1996 tourist-related revenues declined by an estimated 30%. Since then there has been a gradual increase in the number of tourist arrivals to Vietnam. In 1999 the official government estimate was around 1.7 million, though some question the validity of this figure.

Back in 1995, the government promised to open a capital market by year's end, but in the end it just didn't happen and seemed to have been postponed indefinitely. At last, however, in July 2000, Vietnam's first stock market was established in Ho Chi Minh City, a long-awaited prerequisite to future privatisation moves.

Privatisation of large state industries has not yet begun but is being considered. Likely candidates for privatisation would be Vietnam Airlines, the banking industry and telecommunications. Whether or not the generation of socialist leaders can bring themselves to put the state's prime assets on the auction block remains to be seen.

On a more positive note, Vietnam has seen economic growth rates of around 8% to 9% annually in the past few years. Vietnam's joining ASEAN in 1995 was a step that observers claim should greatly benefit its economy and further spur on reforms.

Hanoi is intent on limiting Vietnam's restructuring *(doi moi)* to economic spheres, keeping ideas such as pluralism and democracy from undermining the present power structure. Whether it is possible to have economic liberalisation without a concurrent liberalisation in the political sphere remains to be seen.

Vietnam's role model at the moment seems to be China, where economic liberalisation coupled with harsh political controls seems to be at least partially successful in reviving the economy. The role model of the former Soviet Union – where political liberalisation preceded economic restructuring – is pointed to as an example of the wrong way to reform.

The crippling economic crisis that has gripped Asia in recent years has had a substantial effect on Vietnam. Countless promising joint business ventures, in particular those depending on Asian funding, have collapsed. While many Vietnamese labourers in Korea, for example, have lost their jobs there and are returning home, the closing of Korean and Taiwanese factories in Vietnam has also driven up unemployment on the homefront. Import and export trading too have shown a steady decrease since the late 1990s.

POPULATION & PEOPLE

In 1999 Vietnam's population reached 77.8 million, making it the 13th most populous country in the world. Eighty-four per cent of the population is ethnic-Vietnamese, 2% is ethnic-Chinese and the rest is made up of Khmers, Chams and members of over 50 ethno-linguistic groups.

Vietnam has an average population density of 225 persons per square kilometre, one of the world's highest for an agricultural country. Much of the Red River Delta has a population density of 1000 people per square kilometre or more. Life expectancy is 66 years and infant mortality is 48 per 1000. The rate of population growth is 2.1% per year and, until recently, ideology prevented any effective family planning.

Unfortunately, the 15 years or so during which Vietnam encouraged large families will be a burden for some time to come. The country's population will likely double in the next century before zero population growth can be achieved. The task of reducing population growth is daunting. As elsewhere in the Third World, low education and low incomes tend to encourage large families. Unable to afford modern birth control techniques, most Vietnamese couples still rely on condoms, termination or self-induced miscarriage to avoid unwanted births.

The Vietnamese government takes a carrot and stick approach to family planning. For couples who limit their family size to two children or less, there are promises of benefits in education, housing, health care and employment (though a lack of funding means these promises are often not kept). The stick comes for those who exceed the two child limit. To begin with, the government can deny the third child household registration (needed to obtain an ID card, admission to school and access to various crucial permits). If the parents have a government job, they can be fired. In general, these inducements have succeeded in urban areas – a two child family is now the norm in Hanoi and Saigon. However, family planning campaigns have had only a minor impact on birth rates in rural areas.

Ethnic-Vietnamese

The Vietnamese people (called Annamites by the French) developed as a distinct ethnic group between 200 BC and AD 200 through the fusion of people of Indonesian stock with Viet and Tai immigrants from the north and the Chinese who arrived – along with Chinese rule (circa 200 BC to AD 938) – from the 2nd century BC. Vietnamese civilisation has been profoundly influenced by China and India (via Champa and the Khmers) but the fact that the Vietnamese were never absorbed by China indicates that a strong local culture existed prior to the millennium of Chinese rule.

The Vietnamese have lived for thousands of years by growing rice and, as a result, have historically preferred to settle in lowland areas suitable for rice cultivation. Over the past two millennia, they have slowly pushed southward along the narrow coastal strip, defeating the Chams in the 15th century and taking over the Mekong Delta from the Khmers in the 18th century. The Vietnamese have tended to view highland areas (and their inhabitants) with suspicion.

Vietnamese who have emigrated abroad are known as Viet Kieu (Overseas Vietnamese). They are intensely disliked by the local Vietnamese, who accuse them of being cowardly, arrogant, pampered, privileged and so on. These negative judgments are probably coloured by jealousy. In the 1980s, returning Viet Kieu were often followed by the police and everyone they spoke to was questioned and harassed by the authorities. This has all changed. Indeed, official policy is to welcome the Viet Kieu and encourage them to resettle in Vietnam. Many Viet Kieu are cynical about this. 'They don't want us back, just our money, professional skills and connections' is a comment you're likely to hear in Overseas Vietnamese communities. That the police still often shake down the Viet Kieu for money is not encouraging. The Vietnamese press frequently writes about the importance to the economy of receiving money transfers from relatives abroad.

Ethnic-Chinese

The Hoa (ethnic-Chinese) constitute the largest single minority group in Vietnam. Today, most of them live in the South, especially in and around Saigon's sister city of Cholon. Although most of Vietnam's ethnic-Chinese have lived in Vietnam for generations, historically they have tried to maintain their own Chinese identities, languages, school systems and even citizenship. They have organised themselves into communities known as *bang* (congregations), according to their ancestors' province of origin and dialect. Important bang include Fujian (Phuoc Kien in Vietnamese), Cantonese (Quang Dong in Vietnamese; Guangdong in Chinese), Hainan (Hai Nam), Chaozhou (Tieu Chau) and Hakka (Nuoc Hue in Vietnamese; Kejia in Mandarin Chinese).

During the 1950s, President Diem tried without much success to forcibly assimilate South Vietnam's ethnic-Chinese population. In the North, too, the ethnic-Chinese have resisted Vietnamisation.

The Chinese are well known for their entrepreneurial abilities – before the fall of South Vietnam in 1975, ethnic-Chinese controlled nearly half of the country's economic activity. Historical antipathies between China and Vietnam and the prominence of ethnic-Chinese in commerce have generated a great deal of animosity towards them. In March 1978, the Vietnamese Communists launched a campaign against the 'bourgeois elements' (considered a euphemism for the ethnic-Chinese), which turned into open racial persecution. The campaign influenced China's decision to attack Vietnam in 1979 and caused about one-third of Vietnam's ethnic-Chinese to flee to China and the West. Vietnamese officials now admit that the anti-capitalist and anti-Chinese campaign was a tragic mistake that cost the country heavily.

Other Minorities

Vietnam has one of the most diverse and complex ethno-linguistic mixes in all of Asia. Many of the country's 54 distinct ethnic groups have not-so-distant relations scattered throughout neighbouring Laos, southern China and Cambodia, as well as Thailand and Myanmar (Burma). Most of the Vietnamese ethnic minorities, who are believed to number between six and eight million, reside in the central highlands and the mountainous regions of the north-west, with a smattering along the coastal plains in the South.

Khmers Khmers (ethnic-Cambodians) number about 700,000 and are concentrated in the south-western Mekong Delta. They practise Hinayana (Theravada) Buddhism.

Also see the 'Hill Tribes in Vietnam' section in the North-West chapter and 'The Kingdom of Champa' section in the Central Vietnam chapter.

PHIL WEYMOUTH

JOHN ELK III

NICK WELLMAN

JOHN BORTHWICK

Behind the wheel – bike, trike or bus your way around Vietnam.

MASON FLORENCE

PHIL WEYMOUTH

GLENN BEANLAND

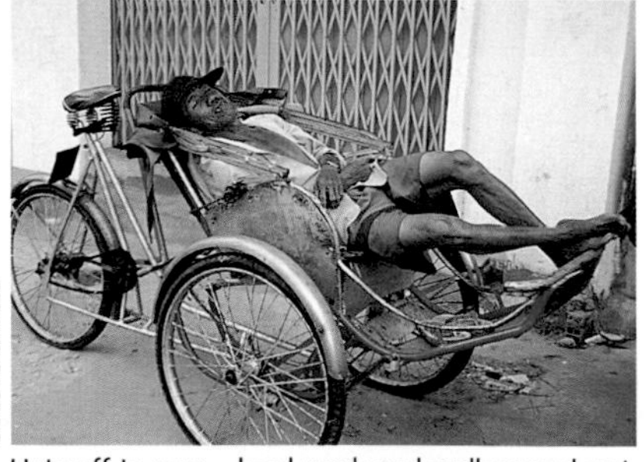

CRAIG PERSHOUSE

JULIA WILKINSON

Hats off to you – hard work and well-earned rest.

Indians Almost all of South Vietnam's Indian population, most of whose roots were in southern India, left in 1975. The remaining community in Saigon worships at the Mariamman Hindu temple and the Central Mosque.

Westerners Vietnam has a handful of ethnic 'Westerners', most of whom are in fact American-Vietnamese, French-Vietnamese or French-Chinese.

EDUCATION

Compared with other Third World countries, Vietnam's population is very well educated. Vietnam's literacy rate is estimated at 82%, although official figures put it even higher (95%). Before the colonial period, the majority of the population possessed some degree of literacy, but by 1939 only 15% of school-age children were receiving any kind of instruction and 80% of the population was illiterate.

During the late 19th century, one of the few things that French colonial officials and Vietnamese nationalists agreed on was that the traditional Confucian educational system, on which the mandarinal civil service was based, was in desperate need of reform. Mandarinal examinations were held in Tonkin until WWI and in Annam until the war's end.

Many of Indochina's independence leaders were educated in elite French-language secondary schools such as the Lycée Albert Sarraut in Hanoi and the Lycée Chasseloup Laubat in Saigon.

Although the children of foreign residents can theoretically attend Vietnamese schools, the majority go to special private academies. These are expensive, but if you're working for a foreign company then it's possible that they will pay the bill.

ARTS

Dance

Not surprisingly, ethnic minorities have their own dancing traditions, which differ sharply from the Vietnamese majority. While in most hill tribes the majority of the dancers are women, a few hill tribe groups allow only the men to dance. A great deal of anthropological research has been carried out in recent years in order to preserve and revive indigenous traditions.

Music

Traditional Though heavily influenced by the Chinese and, in the South, the Khmer and Indianised Cham musical traditions, Vietnamese music has a high degree of originality in style and instrumentation. The traditional system of writing down music and the five note (pentatonic) scale are of Chinese origin. Vietnamese choral music is unique in that the melody must correspond to the tones; it cannot rise during a word that has a falling tone.

There are three broad categories of Vietnamese music:

Folk includes children's songs, love songs, work songs, festival songs, lullabies, lamentations and funeral songs. It is usually sung without instrumental accompaniment.

Classical (or 'learned music') is rather rigid and formal. It was performed at the imperial court and for the entertainment of the mandarin elite. A traditional orchestra consists of 40 musicians. There are two main types of classical chamber music: *hat a dao* (from the North) and *ca Hue* (from central Vietnam).

Theatre includes singing, dancing and instrumentation.

There are music conservatories teaching traditional Vietnamese and Western classical music in Hanoi, Hué and Saigon.

Each of Vietnam's ethno-linguistic minorities also have their own musical traditions that often include distinctive costumes and instruments such as reed flutes, lithophones (similar to xylophones), bamboo whistles, gongs and stringed instruments made from gourds.

Contemporary/Pop Strange as it seems, much of the world's Vietnamese pop music is originally recorded in California by Overseas Vietnamese. One reason Vietnam itself produces relatively few home-grown crooners is that all music tapes are instantly pirated, thus depriving the singing stars of the revenue they would need to survive.

However, works by Overseas Vietnamese are protected by copyright.

The best known of the Overseas Vietnamese singers is Khanh Ly, who left Vietnam in 1975 and today resides in the USA. She is enormously popular both in Vietnam and abroad, and her distinctive, angelic voice sends chills. Though her music is widely available in Vietnam, the Vietnamese government takes a deprecating view of her recently composed lyrics that recall the trials of her life as a refugee.

Vietnam's number one domestic heart throb is Hué-born Quang Linh, a former banker in Hanoi whose early popularity among Saigonese shot him up in the local pop charts. He is adored by Vietnamese of all ages for his radiant love songs.

Other celebrated local pop singers include sex-symbol Phuong Thanh, Vietnam's answer to Madonna (without the dirty dancing). Her likeness is plastered on a variety of paraphernalia (from school notebooks to beer glasses). Phuong Thanh's male equivalent would have to be youth idol Lam Truong.

Of the legion of notable Vietnamese composers, the leader of the pack is Trinh Cong Son, whose lyrics touch on themes of love, war and family. A former literature student from Hué, today he makes his home in Saigon, where he even has his own celebrity restaurant! Over his long career Trinh Cong Son has written over 500 songs, making him perhaps the most prolific Vietnamese composer in history.

Other well-known contemporary composers you are likely to hear the work of are Tran Tien and Thanh Tung.

Literature

Vietnamese literature can be divided into three types:

Traditional oral literature *(truyen khau)* was begun long before recorded history and includes legends, folk songs and proverbs.

Sino-Vietnamese literature *(Han Viet)* was written in Chinese characters *(chu nho)*. It dates from 939 AD, when the first independent Vietnamese kingdom was established. Sino-Vietnamese literature became dominated by Confucian and Buddhist texts and was governed by strict rules of metre and verse.

Modern Vietnamese literature *(Quoc am)* includes anything recorded in *nom* characters or the Romanised quoc ngu script. The earliest extant text written in nom is the late-13th-century *Van Te Ca Sau* (Ode to an Alligator). Literature written in *quoc ngu* has played an important role in Vietnamese nationalism.

One of Vietnam's literary masterpieces, *The Tale of Kieu* (Kim Van Kieu) was written during the first half of the 19th century – a period marked by a great deal of literary activity – by Nguyen Du (1765–1820), a poet, scholar, mandarin and diplomat.

Architecture

The Vietnamese have not been prolific builders like their neighbours the Khmers, who erected the monuments of Angkor in Cambodia, and the Chams, whose graceful brick towers, constructed using sophisticated masonry technology, adorn many parts of the southern half of the country. For more information on Cham architecture see the 'Po Klong Garai' and 'Po Nagar' boxed texts in the South-Central Coast chapter and the 'Kingdom of Champa' section in the Danang chapter.

Most Vietnamese constructions are traditionally made of wood and other materials that are vulnerable to decay in the tropical climate. This, coupled with the fact that almost all stone structures erected by the Vietnamese have been destroyed in countless feudal wars and invasions, means that very little premodern Vietnamese architecture remains.

Plenty of pagodas and temples founded hundreds of years ago are still functioning, but they have usually been rebuilt many times with little concern for making the upgraded structure an exact copy of the original. As a result, many modern elements have been casually introduced into pagoda architecture – the neon haloes for statues of Buddha is one of the most glaring examples.

Because of the Vietnamese custom of ancestor worship, many graves from previous centuries survive today. These include temples erected in memory of high-ranking mandarins, royal family members and emperors.

Memorials for Vietnamese who died in the wars against the Chinese, French and Americans usually contain cement obelisks inscribed with the words *'To quoc ghi cong'* (the country will remember their exploits). Many of the tombstones within the memorials were erected over empty graves; most Viet Minh and Viet Cong dead were buried where they fell.

Painting

Traditional Painting on frame-mounted silk dates from the 13th century. Silk painting was at one time the preserve of scholar-calligraphers, who also painted scenes from nature. Before the advent of photography, realistic portraits for use in ancestor worship were produced. Some of these – usually of former head monks – can still be seen in Buddhist pagodas.

Modern During this century, Vietnamese painting has been influenced by Western trends. Much recent work has had political rather than aesthetic or artistic motives. According to an official account, the fighting of the French and American forces provided painters with 'rich human material: People's Army combatants facing the jets, peasant and factory women in the militia who handled guns as well as they did their production work, young volunteers who repaired roads in record time...old mothers offering tea to anti-aircraft gunners...' – there's lots of this stuff at the Fine Arts Museum in Hanoi.

The recent economic liberalisation has convinced many young artists to abandon the revolutionary themes and concentrate on producing commercial paintings. Some have gone back to the traditional-style silk paintings, while others are experimenting with new subjects. There is a noticeable tendency now to produce paintings of nudes, which might indicate either an attempt to appeal to Western tastes or an expression of long-suppressed desires.

The cheaper stuff (US$10 to US$50) is sent to hotel gift shops and street markets. The higher-standard works are put on display in an array of art galleries where aspiring young artists display their latest works. Typical prices for paintings are in the US$30 to US$50 range, but some artists may ask 10 times that. It's important to know that there are quite a few forgeries around – just because you spot a painting by a 'famous Vietnamese artist' does not mean that it's an original, though it may still be an attractive work of art.

To keep up with the latest in the Vietnamese art world, look for the bi-monthly Asian Art News, a sleek English-language magazine about contemporary art in Asia. It's a great information source and devotes ample attention to Vietnam. For subscription information, contact the magazine at (☎ 852-2522 3443, fax 2521 5268, email asianart@netvigator.com) G/F 28 Arbuthnot Rd, Central Hong Kong.

Sculpture

Vietnamese sculpture has traditionally centred on religious themes and functioned as an adjunct to architecture, especially within pagodas, temples and tombs. Examples of inscribed stelae (carved stone slabs or columns), erected hundreds of years ago to commemorate the founding of a pagoda or important national events, can still be seen (eg, Thien Mu Pagoda in Hué and the Temple of Literature in Hanoi).

The Cham civilisation produced spectacular carved sandstone figures for its Hindu and Buddhist sanctuaries. Cham sculpture was profoundly influenced by Indian art but over the centuries also incorporated Indonesian and Vietnamese elements. The largest single collection of Cham sculpture in the world is at the Cham Museum in Danang.

Lacquerware

The art of making lacquerware was brought to Vietnam from China in the mid-15th century. Before that time, the Vietnamese used lacquer solely for practical purposes (ie, making things watertight). During the 1930s, the Fine Arts School in Hanoi employed several Japanese teachers who introduced new styles and production methods. Their influence is still evident in some Vietnamese lacquerware, especially that made in the North. Although a 1985 government publication declared that 'at present, lacquer painting deals boldly with realistic and revolutionary themes and forges unceasingly ahead', most of the lacquerware for sale is inlaid with mother-of-pearl and appears to be of traditional design.

Lacquer is a resin extracted from the *cay son*, (literally, tree paint). It is creamy white in raw form but is made *son then* (black) or *canh dan* (brown; cockroach wing) by mixing it with resin in an iron container for 40 hours. After an object (traditionally made of teak) has been treated with a fixative, a requisite 10 coats of lacquer is applied. Each coat must be dried for a week and then thoroughly sanded with pumice and cuttlebone before the next layer can be applied. A specially refined lacquer is used for the 11th and final coat, which is sanded with a fine coal powder and lime wash before the object is decorated. Designs may be added by engraving in low relief, by painting or by inlaying mother-of-pearl, egg shell, silver or even gold.

Ceramics

The production of *gom* (ceramics) has a long history in Vietnam. In ancient times, ceramic objects were made by coating a wicker mould with clay and baking it. Later, ceramic production became very refined, and each dynastic period is known for its particular techniques and motifs.

Cinema

One of Vietnam's first cinematographic efforts was a newsreel of Ho Chi Minh's 1945 Proclamation of Independence. Following this, parts of the battle of Dien Bien Phu were restaged for the benefit of movie cameras.

Prior to reunification, the South Vietnamese movie industry concentrated on producing sensational, low-budget flicks. Until recently, most North Vietnamese film-making efforts have been dedicated to 'the mobilisation of the masses for economic reconstruction, the building of socialism and the struggle for national reunification'. Predictable themes include 'workers devoted to socialist industrialisation', 'old mothers who continuously risk their lives to help the people's army' and 'children who are ready to face any danger'.

The relaxation of ideological censorship of the arts has proceeded in fits and starts, but in the last few years the gradual increase in artistic freedoms has affected film-making, as well as many other genres. In the late 1980s and early 1990s, paranoia concerning the radical changes in Eastern Europe caused a return to greater government control of the arts. Today, however, film production in Vietnam has taken a notable swing back to more liberal ways, and Vietnamese and Overseas Vietnamese producers, directors and actors are finally beginning to receive due recognition, both in Vietnam and abroad.

Theatre & Puppetry

These days, the various forms of Vietnamese theatre are performed by dozens of state-funded troupes and companies around the country. Vietnamese theatre integrates music, singing, recitation, declamation, dance and mime into a single artistic whole. There are several basic forms:

Classical theatre is known as *hat tuong* in the north and *hat boi* (songs with show dress) in the south. It is based on Chinese opera and was probably brought to Vietnam by the 13th-century Mongol invaders eventually chased out by Tran Hung Dao. Hat tuong is very formalistic, employing gestures and scenery similar to Chinese theatre. The accompanying orchestra, which is dominated by the drum, usually has six musicians. Often, the audience also has a drum so it too can comment on the onstage action. Hat tuong has a limited cast of typical characters who establish their identities using combinations of make-up and dress that the audience can readily recognise. For instance, red face paint represents courage, loyalty and faithfulness. Traitors and cruel people have white faces. Lowlanders are given green faces; highlanders have black ones. Horizontal eyebrows represent honesty, erect eyebrows symbolise cruelty and lowered eyebrows belong to characters with a cowardly nature. A male character can express emotions (pensiveness, worry, anger etc) by fingering his beard in various ways.

Popular theatre *(hat cheo)* often engages in social protest through satire. The singing and declamation are in everyday language and include many proverbs and sayings. Many of the melodies are of peasant origin.

Modern theatre *(cai luong)* originated in the south in the early 20th century and shows strong Western influences.

Spoken drama *(kich noi* or *kich)*, with its Western roots, appeared in the 1920s. It's popular among students and intellectuals.

Conventional puppetry *(roi can)* and that uniquely Vietnamese art form, **water puppetry** *(roi nuoc)*, draw their plots from the same legendary and historical sources as other forms of traditional theatre. It is thought that water puppetry developed when determined puppeteers in the Red River Delta managed to carry on with the show despite flooding (see the 'Punch & Judy in a Pool' boxed text in the Hanoi chapter). Water puppetry is staged in Saigon, though it's far better known in Hanoi. See Water Puppets under Entertainment in the Hanoi and Ho Chi Minh City chapters for details on where water puppet performances are held.

SOCIETY & CONDUCT

Try to learn about the Vietnamese culture before you arrive and respect cultural differences, rather than trying to change them.

Traditional Culture

Face Having 'big face' is synonymous with prestige, and prestige is particularly important in the Orient. All families, even poor ones, are expected to have big wedding parties and throw their money around like it's water in order to gain face. This is often ruinously expensive, but the fact that the wedding results in bankruptcy for the young couple is far less important than losing face.

Beauty Concepts The Vietnamese consider pale skin to be beautiful. On sunny days trendy Vietnamese women can often be seen strolling under the shade of an umbrella in order to keep from tanning. As in 19th-century Europe, peasants get tanned and those who are wealthier do not. Women who work in the fields will go to great lengths to preserve their pale skin by wearing long-sleeved shirts, gloves, a conical hat and wrapping their face in a towel. To tell a Vietnamese woman that she has white skin is a great compliment; telling her that she has a 'lovely suntan' would be an insult.

Women in Society As in most parts of Asia, Vietnamese women are given plenty of hard work to do, but have little authority at the decision-making level. Vietnamese women proved to be highly successful as guerrillas and brought plenty of grief to US soldiers. After the war, their contribution received plenty of lip-service, but all the important government posts were given to men. In the countryside, you'll see women doing such jobs as farm labour, crushing rocks at construction sites and carrying baskets weighing 60kg. It's doubtful that most Western men are capable of such strenuous activity.

Vietnam's two children per family policy appears to be benefiting women, and more women are delaying marriage to get an education. About 50% of university students are female, but their skills don't seem to be put to much use after graduation.

One of the sadder ironies of Vietnam's recent opening to the capitalist West has been the influx of pimps posing as 'talent scouts'. Promises of lucrative jobs in developed countries are being dangled in front of naive Vietnamese women who only discover upon their arrival abroad that the job is prostitution. With no money to return home, they usually have little choice but to submit. Japanese gangsters have been particularly active in this particular form of job recruitment.

Geomancy Geomancy is the art (or science) of manipulating or judging the environment. The Vietnamese call it *phong thuy*, meaning 'wind water', but many Westerners know it by its Chinese name, *feng shui*.

If you want to build a house or find a suitable site for a grave, you call in a geomancer. The orientation of houses, *dinh* (communal meeting halls), tombs and pagodas is determined by geomancers, which is why cemeteries have tombstones turned every which way. The location of an ancestor's grave is an especially serious matter – if the grave is in the wrong spot or facing the wrong way, there's no telling what trouble the spirits might cause. Ditto for the location of the family altar, which can be found in every Vietnamese home.

Failing businesses may call in a geomancer. Sometimes the solution is to move a door or a window. If this doesn't do the trick, it might be necessary to move an ancestor's grave. Distraught spirits may have to be placated with payments of cash (donated to a temple), especially if one wishes to erect a building or other structure that blocks the spirits' view. The date on which you begin construction of a new building is also a crucial matter.

The concept of geomancy is believed to have originated with the Chinese. Although the Communists (both Chinese and Vietnamese) have disparaged geomancy as superstition, it still has a large influence on people's behaviour.

Curious Looks In urban centres tourists may not rate a second look. But, if you're in the hinterlands and doing something unusual, like writing in a diary – or even if you're just standing there! – many curious people, especially children, may gather round you to watch.

Getting used to this kind of attention can be difficult and stressful for some, however, it's best not to worry about it; after all, they are just curious about you. As a tourist you'll probably spend a lot of time just sitting around looking at people – and taking snapshots. Being stared at is a good chance to see how it feels to be on the other end of 'curious looks'!

No Knock Vietnamese don't share Western concepts of privacy and personal space, so don't be surprised if people walk into your room without knocking. What happens is, you're sitting starkers in your hotel room and the maid unlocks the door and walks in unannounced. If you'd rather not do nude modelling, check to see if there's a bolt on the door that cannot be opened from the outside with a key. Failing that, prop a chair up against the door. Otherwise, just grin and bare it.

Ong Tay & Ba Tay The main reason children shout *Ong Tay!* (Mr Westerner) and *Ba Tay!* (Mrs Westerner) at white Westerners is similar to why people tap on aquarium fish tanks or try to catch the attention of primates at the zoo: they want to be recognised by an exotic being and provoke some kind of reaction.

Often, children will unabashedly come up to you and pull the hair on your arms or legs (they want to test if it's real) or dare each other to touch your skin. Some travellers have been pinched or kicked without provocation, but this is rare.

In the past, the term *Lien Xo!* (Soviet Union) was often shouted at Westerners, all of whom were assumed to be the legendary and very unpopular Russians residing in Vietnam. However, Russian tourists and technical advisers are far less common now – few of them can afford a holiday in Vietnam any more and their technical skills are considered inferior to those available from the West. Therefore, Lien Xo is going out of fashion as an attention-seeking call.

In the markets, vendors may try to woo you by calling you *Dong Chi!* (Comrade) on the assumption that you will find this a kindred term of endearment. Depending on your age and how sloppy you look, a more common name you may be called (not necessarily to your face) is *tay balo* – literally 'Westerner backpack' – a relatively recent and slightly condescending term for scruffy-looking backpackers.

If you are cycling, you may also hear people call *Tay di xe dap* at you, which simply means 'Westerner travelling by bicycle'. While it may seem a strange form of address in the land of bicycles, it's perhaps understandable in a place where locals have only been used to seeing foreigners travelling in Citroëns, followed by jeeps, then black Volgas and now in white Toyotas. Another explanation is that although virtually all Vietnamese ride bicycles, they would never look at one again if they had the means to travel by motorbike or car. They simply do not believe that anyone, let alone a rich foreigner, would choose to travel by bicycle – there is obviously something wrong with such a person.

Lunar Calendar The Vietnamese lunar calendar closely resembles the Chinese one,

Vietnamese Zodiac

If you want to know your sign in the Vietnamese zodiac, look up your year of birth in the following chart (future years are included so you can know what's coming). However, because Vietnamese astrology follows the lunar calendar, the Vietnamese New Year usually falls in late January or early February. Therefore if your birthday is in January it will be included in the Zodiac year before the calendar year of your birth.

Rat	1924	1936	1948	1960	1972	1984	1996
Ox/Cow	1925	1937	1949	1961	1973	1985	1997
Tiger	1926	1938	1950	1962	1974	1986	1998
Rabbit	1927	1939	1951	1963	1975	1987	1999
Dragon	1928	1940	1952	1964	1976	1988	2000
Snake	1929	1941	1953	1965	1977	1989	2001
Horse	1930	1942	1954	1966	1978	1990	2002
Goat	1931	1943	1955	1967	1979	1991	2003
Monkey	1932	1944	1956	1968	1980	1992	2004
Rooster	1933	1945	1957	1969	1981	1993	2005
Dog	1934	1946	1958	1970	1982	1994	2006
Pig	1935	1947	1959	1971	1983	1995	2007

though there are some minor variations. Year one of the Vietnamese lunar calendar corresponds to 2637 BC and each lunar month has 29 or 30 days, resulting in years with 355 days.

Approximately every third year is a leap year; an extra month is added between the third and fourth months to keep the lunar year in sync with the solar year. If this weren't done, you'd end up having the seasons gradually rotate around the lunar year, playing havoc with all elements of life linked to the agricultural seasons. To find out the Gregorian (solar) date corresponding to a lunar date, check any Vietnamese or Chinese calendar.

Instead of dividing time into centuries, the Vietnamese calendar uses units of 60 years called *hoi*. Each hoi consists of six 10-year cycles *(can)* and five 12-year cycles *(ky)*, which run simultaneously. The name of each year in the cycle consists of the can name followed by the ky name, a system that never produces the same combination twice. The 10 heavenly stems of the can cycle are;

giap	water in nature
at	water in the home
binh	lighted fire
dinh	latent fire
mau	wood
ky	wood prepared to burn
canh	metal
tan	wrought metal
nham	virgin land
quy	cultivated land

The 12 zodiacal stems of the ky are as follows:

tý	rat
suu	water buffalo
dan	tiger
mao	cat
thin	dragon
ty	snake
ngo	horse
mui	goat
than	monkey
dau	rooster
tuat	dog
hoi	pig

Thus in 2001 the Vietnamese year is Tan Ty (snake), in 2002 it's Nham Ngo (horse) and in 2003 it's Quy Mui (goat).

Dos & Don'ts

Clothing Please respect local dress standards, particularly at religious sites (avoid wearing shorts or sleeveless tops and always remove your shoes before entering a temple). In general, Vietnamese dress standards are conservative, especially in the countryside. Nude and topless sunbathing is considered *totally* inappropriate, even at beaches and hot-spring resorts.

Greetings The traditional Vietnamese form of greeting is to press your hands together in front of your body and bow slightly. These days, the Western custom of shaking hands has almost completely taken over, but the traditional greeting is still sometimes used by Buddhist monks and nuns – it is proper to respond in kind.

Name Cards Name cards are very popular in Vietnam and, like elsewhere in East Asia, exchanging business cards is an important part of even the smallest transaction or business contact. Get some printed before you arrive in Vietnam and hand them out like confetti. In Bangkok and Hong Kong, machines using the latest laser-printing technology can easily make inexpensive custom-designed business cards in around 20 minutes. You need to put your occupation on your name card; if you don't have one, why not try 'backpacker'?

Deadly Chopsticks Leaving a pair of chopsticks sticking vertically in a rice bowl looks very much like the incense sticks that are burned for the dead. This is a powerful death sign and is not appreciated anywhere in the Orient.

Mean Feet Like the Chinese and Japanese, Vietnamese strictly maintain clean floors and it's usual to remove shoes when entering somebody's home. If you are entering a 'shoes off' home, your host will probably provide a pair of slippers. Shoes must be removed inside most Buddhist temples, but this is not universal so look to see what others do. If a bunch of shoes are piled up near the doorway, you should pay heed.

It's rude to point the bottoms of your feet towards other people; the only exception may be with close friends. When sitting on the floor, you should fold your legs into the lotus position to avoid pointing your soles at others. Most importantly, never point your feet towards anything sacred such as figures of Buddhas or the ancestral shrines found in most homes.

In formal situations, do not sit with your legs crossed when sitting on a chair.

Keep Your Hat in Hand As a form of respect to elderly or other respected people (monks etc), take off your hat and bow your head politely when addressing them. The head is the symbolic highest point in Asia – never pat or touch someone on their head.

Pity the Unmarried Telling the Vietnamese that you are single or divorced and enjoying a life without children may disturb them greatly. Not having a family is regarded as bad luck and such people are to be pitied, not envied. Almost every Vietnamese will ask if you are married and have children. If you are young and single, simply say you are 'not yet married' and that will be accepted. If you are not so young (over 30) and unmarried, it's better to lie. Divorce is scandalous and you'd be better off claiming that your former spouse died.

Show Some Respect In face-conscious Asia, foreigners should pay double attention to showing respect (it's not a bad idea even at home). One expat in Vietnam had this to say on the matter:

> The main reason I write is to plead with you to clearly (in boldface if necessary) and strongly implore your readers to show a little respect for the locals. Fighting over and gloating about ripping off a cyclo driver for US$0.10 is a small 'victory' and shameful thing to do. These people obviously need the money. If nothing else, travellers should at least be cordial and respectful – smile, it works wonders here. What I've seen recently here where I work has made me realise that imperialism is not yet dead. Because of the power of money, some foreigners act like they're inherently superior. The imperialist of old came with a gun and a uniform, the imperialist today comes with a camera.
>
> **Steve McNicholas**

Vernon Weitzel of the Australian National University sends these 10 tips for successfully dealing with Vietnamese officials, business people etc:

- Always smile and be pleasant.
- Don't run around complaining about everything.
- If you want to criticise someone, do it in a joking manner to avoid confrontation.
- Expect delays – build them into your schedule.
- Never show anger – ever! Getting visibly upset is not only rude – it will cause you to lose face.
- Don't be competitive. Treating your interaction as a cooperative enterprise works much better.
- Don't act as though you deserve service from anyone. If you do, it's likely that you will be delayed.
- Don't be too inquisitive about personal matters.
- Sitting and sipping tea and the exchange of gifts (sharing cigarettes, for instance) are an important prelude to any business interaction.
- The mentality of officialdom is very Confucian. Expect astounding amounts of red tape.

RELIGION

Four great philosophies and religions have shaped the spiritual life of the Vietnamese people: Confucianism, Taoism, Buddhism and Christianity. Over the centuries, Confucianism, Taoism and Buddhism have fused with popular Chinese beliefs and ancient Vietnamese animism to form what is known collectively as the Triple Religion, or Tam Giao. Confucianism, more a system of social and political morality than a religion, took on many religious aspects. Taoism, which began as an esoteric philosophy for scholars, then mixed with Buddhism popular among the peasants, and many Taoist elements became an intrinsic part of popular religion. If asked their religion most Vietnamese are likely to say that they are Buddhist, but when it comes to family or civic duties they are likely to follow Confucianism while turning to Taoist conceptions in understanding the nature of the cosmos.

Mahayana Buddhism

The predominant religion in Vietnam is Mahayana Buddhism, called Dai Thua, or Bac Tong (meaning 'From the North' – ie, China), also known as the Greater Wheel school, Greater Vehicle school and Northern Buddhism). The largest Mahayana sect in the country is Zen (Dhyana; Thien in Vietnamese), also known as the school of meditation. Dao Trang (the Pure Land school), the second-largest Mahayana sect in Vietnam, is practised mainly in the South.

Mahayana Buddhism differs from Theravada Buddhism in several important ways. Whereas the Theravada Buddhist strives to become an *arhat* (one who attained nirvana), the Mahayanist ideal is that of the Bodhisattva, one who strives to perfect oneself in the necessary virtues (generosity, morality, patience, vigour, concentration and wisdom), but even after attaining this perfection chooses to remain in the world in order to save others.

Mahayanists consider Gautama Buddha to be only one of the innumerable manifestations of the one ultimate Buddha. These countless Buddhas and Bodhisattvas, who are as numberless as the universes to which they minister, gave rise in popular Vietnamese religion – with its countless Taoist divinities and spirits – to a pantheon of deities and helpers whose aid can be sought through invocations and offerings.

Mahayana Buddhist pagodas in Vietnam usually include a number of elements. In front of the pagoda is a white statue of a standing Quan The Am Bo Tat or Avalokiteçvara Bodhisattva (Hindi), Guanyin (Chinese), or Goddess of Mercy (English). A variation of the Goddess of Mercy shows her with multiple arms and sometimes multiple eyes and ears, permitting her to touch, see and hear all. This version of the Goddess of Mercy is called Chuan De or Qianshou Guanyin (Chinese).

Inside the main sanctuary are representations of the three Buddhas: A Di Da (pronounced **ah**-zee-dah; Amitabha), the Buddha of the Past; Thich Ca Mau Ni (Sakyamuni, or Siddhartha Gautama), the historical Buddha; and Di Lac (pronounced zee-lock; Maitreya), the Buddha of the Future. Nearby are often statues of the eight Kim Cang (Genies of the Cardinal Directions), the La Han (arhats) and various Bo Tat (Bodhisattvas) such as Van Thu (Manjusri), Quan The Am Bo Tat (Avalokiteçvara) and Dia Tang (Ksitigartha).

Pagoda or Temple

Travelling around Vietnam, one continually encounters the terms 'pagoda' and 'temple'. The Vietnamese use these terms somewhat differently to the Chinese and, as a result, there is a bit of confusion (particularly if you've just come from China).

To the Chinese, a *bata* (pagoda) is usually a tall eight-sided tower built to house the ashes of the deceased. A *miao* or *si* (Chinese temple) is an active place of worship.

The Vietnamese regard a pagoda *(chua)* as a place of worship, and it's by no means certain that you'll find a tower to store the ashes of the dearly departed. A *den* (Vietnamese temple) is not really a place of worship, but rather a structure built to honour some great historical figure (Confucius, Tran Hung Dao and even Ho Chi Minh).

The Caodai Temple seems to fall between the cracks. Given the mixture of ideas that is part and parcel of Caodaism, it's hard to say if this is a temple, pagoda, church or mosque.

Sometimes, an altar is set aside for Taoist divinities such as Ngoc Hoang (Jade Emperor) and Thien Hau (Goddess of the Sea or Queen of Heaven). Thien Hau is known as Tin Hau in Hong Kong and Matsu in Taiwan. Every pagoda has an altar for funerary tablets commemorating deceased Buddhist monks (who are often buried in stupas near the pagoda) and lay people.

The function of the *bonze* (Vietnamese Buddhist monk) is to minister to the spiritual needs of the peasantry, but it is largely up to them whether they invoke the lore of Taoism or the philosophy of Buddhism. A monk may live reclusively on a remote hilltop or may manage a pagoda on a busy city street. And they may choose to fulfil any number of functions: telling fortunes, making and selling *fu* (talismans), advising where a house should be constructed (geomancy), reciting incantations at funerals or even performing *cham chu* (acupuncture).

History Theravada Buddhism was brought to Vietnam from India by pilgrims at the end of the 2nd century AD. Simultaneously, Chinese monks introduced Mahayana Buddhism, but this did not become popular with the masses until many centuries later.

Buddhism received royal patronage between the 10th and 13th centuries. This backing included recognition of the Buddhist hierarchy, financial support for the construction of pagodas and other projects, and the active participation of the clergy in ruling the country. By the 11th century, Buddhism had filtered down to the villages and it was proclaimed the official state religion in the mid-12th century.

During the 13th and 14th centuries, Confucian scholars gradually replaced Vietnamese monks as advisers to the Tran Dynasty. The Confucians accused the Buddhists of shirking their responsibilities to family and country with their doctrine of withdrawal from worldly matters. The Chinese invasion of 1414 reinvigorated Confucianism while simultaneously resulting in the destruction of many Buddhist pagodas and manuscripts. The Nguyen Lords (1558–1778), who ruled the southern part of the country, reversed this trend.

A revival of Vietnamese Buddhism spread throughout the country in the 1920s with the creation of Buddhist organisations in various parts of the country. In the 1950s and 60s, attempts were made to unite the various streams of Buddhism in Vietnam. During the early 1960s, South Vietnamese Buddhist monks and lay people played an active role in opposing the regime of Ngo Dinh Diem.

Over the centuries, the Buddhist ideals and beliefs held by the educated elite only superficially touched the rural masses (90% of the population), whose traditions were transmitted orally and put to the test by daily observance. The common people were far less concerned with the philosophy of good government than they were with seeking aid from supernatural beings for problems of the here and now.

Gradually, the various Mahayana Buddhas and Bodhisattvas became mixed up with mysticism, animism, polytheism and Hindu tantrism, as well as the multiple divinities and ranks of deities of the Taoist pantheon. The Triple Religion flourished despite clerical attempts to maintain some semblance of Buddhist orthodoxy and doctrinal purity. Although the majority of the population has only a vague notion of academic Buddhist doctrines, they invite monks to participate in life-cycle ceremonies such as funerals. And Buddhist pagodas have come to be seen by many Vietnamese as a physical and spiritual refuge from an uncertain world.

After 1975, many monks, including some who actively opposed the South Vietnamese government and the war, were rounded up and sent to re-education camps. Temples were closed and the training of young monks was prohibited. In the last few years, most of these restrictions have been lifted and a religious revival of sorts is taking place.

Theravada Buddhism

Theravada Buddhism is called Tieu Thua, or Nam Tong (meaning 'From the South' – ie, India). It's also known as Hinayana, the Lesser Wheel school, the Lesser Vehicle school and Southern Buddhism. It is practised mainly in the Mekong Delta region, mostly by ethnic-Khmers. The most important Theravada sect in Vietnam is the disciplinary school, Luat Tong.

Basically, the Theravada school of Buddhism is an earlier and, according to its followers, less corrupted form of Buddhism than the Mahayana schools found in most of East Asia and Himalayan regions. The Theravada school is called the Southern school because it took the southern route from India through South-East Asia, while the Northern school proceeded north into Nepal, Tibet, China, Korea, Mongolia, Vietnam and Japan. Because the Southern school tried to preserve or limit the Buddhist doctrines to only those canons codified in the early Buddhist era, the Northern school gave Theravada Buddhism the name Hinayana, or Lesser Vehicle. They considered themselves Greater Vehicle because they built upon the earlier teachings, expanding the doctrine to be more responsive to the needs of lay people.

Confucianism

While it is more a religious philosophy than an organised religion, Confucianism (Nho Giao, or Khong Giao) has been an important force in shaping Vietnam's social system and the everyday lives and beliefs of its people.

Confucius (Khong Tu) was born in China around 550 BC. He saw people as social beings formed by society yet capable of shaping their own society. He believed that the individual exists in and for society and drew up a code of ethics to guide the individual in social interaction. This code laid down a person's specific obligations to family, society and the state. Central to Confucianism is an emphasis on duty and hierarchy.

According to Confucian philosophy, which was brought to Vietnam by the Chinese during their 1000 year rule, the emperor alone, governing under the mandate of heaven, can intercede on behalf of the nation with the powers of heaven and earth. Only virtue, as acquired through education, gives one the right (the mandate of heaven) to wield political power. From this it followed that an absence of virtue would result in the withdrawal of this mandate, sanctioning rebellion against an unjust ruler. Natural disasters or defeat on the battlefield were often interpreted as a sign that the mandate of heaven had been withdrawn.

Confucian philosophy in some senses was democratic: as virtue could be acquired only through learning, education rather than birth made a person virtuous. Therefore, education had to be widespread. Until the beginning of this century, Confucian philosophy and texts formed the basis of Vietnam's education system. Generation after generation of young people – in the villages as well as the cities – were taught their duties to family (including ancestor worship) and community and were told that each person had to know their own place in the social hierarchy and should behave accordingly.

A system of government-run civil service examinations selected from among the country's best students those who would join the nonhereditary ruling class, the mandarins. As a result, education was prized not only as the path to virtue, but as a means to social and political advancement. This system helped create the respect for intellectual and literary accomplishment for which the Vietnamese are famous to this day.

The political institutions based on Confucianism finally degenerated and became discredited, as they did elsewhere in the Chinese-influenced world. Over the centuries, the philosophy became conservative and backward-looking. This reactionary trend became dominant in Vietnam in the 15th century, suiting despotic rulers who emphasised the divine right of kings rather than their responsibilities under the doctrine of the mandate of heaven.

Taoism

Taoism (Lao Giao, or Dao Giao) originated in China and is based on the philosophy of Laotse (Thai Thuong Lao Quan). Laotse (literally, The Old One) lived in the 6th century BC. Little is known about Laotse and there is some question as to whether or not he really existed. He is believed to have been the custodian of the imperial archives for the Chinese government and Confucius is supposed to have consulted him.

It is doubtful that Laotse ever intended his philosophy to become a religion. Chang Ling has been credited with formally establishing the religion in 143 BC. Taoism later split into two divisions, the Cult of the Immortals and The Way of the Heavenly Teacher.

Understanding Taoism is not easy. The philosophy emphasises contemplation and simplicity of life. Its ideal is returning to the Tao (the Way – the essence of which all things are made). Only a small elite in China and Vietnam has ever been able to grasp Taoist philosophy, which is based on various correspondences (eg, the human body represents a microcosm of a macro earth) and complementary contradictions *am* and *duong* (Vietnamese equivalents of Yin and Yang). As a result, there are very few pure Taoist pagodas in Vietnam, yet much of Taoist ritualism has been absorbed into Chinese and Vietnamese Buddhism. The Taoist influence you are most likely to notice is the dragons and demons that decorate temple rooftops.

According to the Taoist cosmology, Ngoc Hoang, the Emperor of Jade (Chinese: Yu Huang) whose abode is in heaven, rules over a world of divinities, genies, spirits and demons in which the forces of nature are incarnated as supernatural beings and great historical personages have become gods. It is this aspect of Taoism that has become assimilated into the daily lives of most Vietnamese as a collection of rituals and mystical and animistic beliefs. Much of the sorcery and magic that are now part of popular Vietnamese religion have their origins in Taoism.

Ancestor Worship

Vietnamese ancestor worship, which is the ritual expression of *hieu* filial piety, dates from long before the arrival of Confucianism or Buddhism. Some people consider it to be a religion unto itself.

Ancestor worship is based on the belief that the soul lives on after death and becomes the protector of its descendants. Because of the influence the spirits of one's ancestors exert on the living, it is considered not only shameful for them to be upset or restless, but downright dangerous. A soul with no descendants is doomed to eternal wandering because it will not receive homage.

Traditionally, the Vietnamese venerate and honour the spirits of their ancestors regularly, especially on the anniversary of their death, when sacrifices are offered to both the god of the household and the spirit of the ancestors. To request intercession for success in business or on behalf of a sick child, sacrifices and prayers are offered to the ancestral spirits. The ancestors are informed on occasions of family joy or sorrow, such as weddings, success in an examination or death. Important elements in worship are the family altar, a plot of land whose income is set aside for the support of the ancestors, and the designation of a direct male descendent of the deceased to assume the obligation of upholding the required rituals.

Many pagodas have altars on which memorial tablets and photographs of the deceased are displayed. One may look at the young faces in the photographs and ponder the tragedy of so many people having had their lives cut short. Some visitors wonder if they died as a result of war. The real explanation is less tragic: most of the dead had passed on decades after the photos were taken, but rather than use a picture of an aged, infirm parent, survivors chose a more flattering (though slightly outdated) picture of the deceased in their prime.

Caodaism

Caodaism is an indigenous Vietnamese sect that seeks to create the ideal religion by fusing the secular and religious philosophies of both East and West. It was founded in the early 1920s based on messages revealed in seances to Ngo Minh Chieu, the group's founder. The sect's colourful headquarters is in Tay Ninh, 96km north-west of Saigon. There are currently about two million followers of Caodaism in Vietnam. For more information, see Tay Ninh in the Around Ho Chi Minh City chapter.

Hoa Hao Buddhist Sect

The Hoa Hao Buddhist sect (Phat Giao Hoa Hao) was founded in the Mekong Delta in 1939 by Huynh Phu So, a young man who had studied with the most famous of the region's occultists. After he was miraculously cured of sickness, So began preaching a reformed Buddhism based on the common people and embodied in personal faith rather than elaborate rituals. His philosophies emphasised the need for simplicity in worship and denied the necessity for intermediaries between human beings and the Supreme Being.

In 1940 the French, who called Huynh Phu So the 'mad monk', tried to silence him. When arresting him failed, they committed him to an insane asylum, where he soon converted the Vietnamese psychiatrist assigned to his case. During WWII, the Hoa Hao sect continued to grow and to build up a militia with weapons supplied by the Japanese. In 1947, after clashes between Hoa Hao forces and the Viet Minh, Huynh Phu So was assassinated by the Viet Minh, who thereby earned the animosity of what had by then become a powerful political and military force in the Mekong Delta, especially around Chau Doc. The military power of the Hoa Hao was crushed in 1956 when one of its guerrilla commanders was captured by the Diem government and publicly guillotined. Subsequently, elements of the Hoa Hao army joined the Viet Cong.

Hoa Hao sect followers are thought to number approximately 1.5 million.

Catholicism

Catholicism was introduced into Vietnam in the 16th century by missionaries from Portugal, Spain and France. Particularly active during the 16th and 17th centuries were the French Jesuits and Portuguese Dominicans. Pope Alexander VII assigned the first bishops to Vietnam in 1659 and the first Vietnamese priests were ordained nine years later. According to some estimates, there were 800,000 Catholics in Vietnam by 1685. Over the next three centuries, Catholicism was discouraged and at times outlawed. The first known edict forbidding missionary activity was promulgated in 1533. Foreign missionaries and their followers were severely persecuted during the 17th and 18th centuries.

When the French began their efforts to turn Vietnam into a part of their empire, the treatment of Catholics was one of their most important pretexts for intervention. Under French rule the Catholic Church was given preferential status and Catholicism flourished. Though it incorporated certain limited aspects of Vietnamese culture, Catholicism (unlike Buddhism, for instance) succeeded in retaining its doctrinal purity.

Today, Vietnam has the highest percentage of Catholics (8% to 10% of the population) in Asia outside the Philippines. Many of the 900,000 refugees who fled North Vietnam to the South in 1954 were Catholics, as was the then South Vietnamese president Ngo Dinh Diem. Since 1954 in the North and 1975 in the South, Catholics have faced severe restrictions on their religious activities, including strict limits on the ordination of priests and religious education. As in the former Soviet Union, all churches were viewed as being a capitalist institution and a rival centre of power that could subvert the government.

Since around 1990, the government has taken a more liberal line. There is no question that the Catholic religion is making a comeback, though the old churches have become quite dilapidated and there is a shortage of trained clergy. Also, a lack of funds prevents many churches from doing necessary restoration work, but donations from both locals and Overseas Vietnamese are gradually solving this problem.

Protestantism

Protestantism was introduced to Vietnam in 1911. The majority of Vietnam's Protestants, who number about 200,000, are Montagnards living in the central highlands. Protestants in Vietnam have been doubly unfortunate in that they were persecuted first by Diem and later by the Communists.

Until 1975, the most active Protestant group in South Vietnam was the Christian and Missionary Alliance, whose work went mostly unhindered after Diem's assassination in 1963. After reunification, many Protestant clergymen – especially those trained by American missionaries – were imprisoned. But since 1990, the government has mostly ignored the Protestant church.

Islam

Muslims – mostly made up of ethnic-Khmers and Chams – constitute about 0.5% of Vietnam's population. There were small communities of Malaysian, Indonesian and South Indian Muslims in Saigon until 1975, when almost all of them fled. Today, Saigon's 5000 Muslims (including a handful of South Indians) congregate in about a dozen mosques, including the large Central Mosque.

Arab traders reached China in the 7th century and may have stopped in Vietnam on the way, but the earliest evidence of an Islamic presence in Vietnam is a 10th century pillar inscribed in Arabic, found near the coastal town of Phan Rang. It appears that Islam spread among Cham refugees who fled to Cambodia after the destruction of their kingdom in 1471, but that these converts had little success in propagating Islam among their fellow Chams still in Vietnam.

The Vietnamese Chams consider themselves Muslims, but in practise they follow a localised interpretation, or adaptation of Islamic theology and laws. Their communities have very few copies of the Qur'an and even religious dignitaries can hardly read Arabic. Though Muslims the world over pray five times a day, the Chams pray only on Fridays and celebrate Ramadan (a month of dawn to dusk fasting) for only three days. Their worship services consist of the recitation of a few Arabic verses from the Qur'an in a localised form. Instead of performing ritual ablutions, they make motions as if they were drawing water from a well. Circumcision is symbolically performed on boys at age 15; the ceremony consists of a religious leader making the gestures of circumcision with a wooden knife. The Chams of Vietnam do not make the pilgrimage to Mecca and though they do not eat pork; they do drink alcohol. In addition, their Islam-based religious rituals exist side by side with animism and the worship of Hindu deities. The Chams have even taken the Arabic words of common Qur'anic expressions and turned them into the names of deities.

Cham religious leaders wear a white robe and an elaborate turban with gold, red or brown tassels. Rank is indicated by the length of the tassels.

Hinduism

Champa was profoundly influenced by Hinduism and many of the Cham towers, built as Hindu sanctuaries, contain lingas (phallic symbols of Shiva) that are still worshipped by ethnic-Vietnamese and ethnic-Chinese alike. After the fall of Champa in the 15th century, most Chams who remained in Vietnam became Muslims, but continued to practise various Brahmanic (high-caste Hindu) rituals and customs.

LANGUAGE

Vietnamese is the official language of Vietnam, and it is spoken throughout the country. Dialectical differences are marked between the north, central and southern regions.

There are also dozens of different languages spoken by the various ethnic minorities, particularly in the Central Highlands and the far north of the country. Khmer, the Cambodian language, is spoken in parts of the Mekong Delta, and in addition Laotian and various Chinese dialects can be heard in spots along their respective borders.

The Vietnamese people's knowledge of foreign languages reflects their country's relationship with foreign powers – cordial or otherwise – in recent history.

Much of Vietnam's elder generation still speak French, while many middle-aged Vietnamese speak Russian and other Eastern European languages – many of these people spent time in countries like Russia, Bulgaria and the former East Germany during the Cold War (at least until it thawed in the late 1980s). Today, however, Vietnam's youth has fully embraced the English language. A fair number of young people also study Japanese, French and other Western European languages.

For a good start on basic vocabulary and picking up some conversational Vietnamese, see the Language chapter in the back of this book.

Facts for the Visitor

HIGHLIGHTS

Vietnam offers tremendous variety and can suit many different tastes – it's difficult to say just which places should top your list.

Beach lovers will almost certainly want to check out tranquil Mui Ne Beach, or the bustling party scene further north in Nha Trang. More adventurous beach-goers will appreciate remote Phu Quoc Island.

The splendid rock formations, sea cliffs and grottoes of Halong Bay could easily rate as one of the wonders of the world. Nearby, Cat Ba Island also gets rave reviews from those who make the effort to get there, despite its rapid development. Similar scenery (without the water) can be found at the Perfume Pagoda and in Tam Coc.

Sapa and nearby Bac Ha offer a glimpse of traditional ethnic lifestyles in the mountains along the Chinese border. Mai Chau and myriad other less-travelled parts of the northern mountains offer opportunities to visit ethnic villages and to hike. The rugged overland 'north-west loop' passes through some of Vietnam's most scenic high-country landscape; done by jeep or motorbike, this route ranks among the most memorable for many.

History and architecture buffs will be attracted to Hué and Hoi An, the latter being among the most charming spots in the country. For those fascinated by the American War effort and all its implications, what better place to pursue the topic than the old Demilitarised Zone (DMZ)?

Dalat – with its parklike setting, waterfalls, ethnic minorities and cool mountain climate – is considered the jewel (and the kitsch) of the Central Highlands.

The Mekong Delta is more varied than most people imagine – popular scenic spots include Cantho, Soc Trang and Chau Doc.

And if you've spent enough time admiring Vietnam's landscape, perhaps you'd like to see what lies underneath – there are few better places to do this than in Phong Nha Cave.

Finally, don't forget Vietnam's big cities. Freewheeling Ho Chi Minh City, with its dilapidated colonial elegance, outstanding food and bustling nightlife, is a laboratory for Vietnam's economic reforms. Hanoi, with its monuments, parks, lakes and tree-lined boulevards, is the beguiling seat of power in a country trying to figure out which direction to head.

SUGGESTED ITINERARIES

One Week

The North From Hanoi, make a two-day trip to Halong Bay and/or Mai Chau followed by a day trip to the Perfume Pagoda and/or Tam Coc. Spend the remaining time exploring the delights of the capital.

The South From Ho Chi Minh City, it's possible to do a day trip to the Cu Chi Tunnels, a two- or three- day tour of the Mekong Delta and a one- or two-day trip to the beaches at Vung Tau or Long Hai. The rest of the time can be spent sightseeing, eating, shopping and carousing in Ho Chi Minh City.

Two Weeks

Note that highlights of the following two options can also be combined; a typical whirlwind tour means flying into Ho Chi Minh City and out of Hanoi (or vice-versa), and making a B-line between Hué and Hanoi. Excursion airline tickets allowing such a routing are common, and recommended to avoid backtracking.

The North Follow the above one-week itinerary for the north, then take a spin into the north-west mountains (especially Sapa and Bac Ha) and/or a trip to Cuc Phuong, Ba Be or Cat Ba National Parks.

The South A two-week visit to the south will allow for the one-week itinerary, followed by a loop up to Dalat, and back down to the beaches or Nha Trang and/or Mui Ne Beach. Time permitting, you could then head to Hoi An and fly back to Ho Chi Minh City from Danang or Hué.

One Month

A month is enough time to take in most of the major sights. Starting in the south (this itinerary can also be followed in reverse from Hanoi), follow the two-week itinerary as far as Hoi An or Danang before pressing on to Hué. Many people then take a DMZ tour out of Hué; after that allow some time to cover the ground between here and Hanoi (most skip this part of Vietnam, and opt to spend more time in other more stimulating regions). You'll then have the option of flying out of Hanoi or continuing overland to China.

Two Months

Two months will allow you ample time to see everything in detail. In addition to the preceding suggestions, explore the Mekong Delta more thoroughly, taking in a side trip to lovely Phu Quoc Island. Or spend some days lingering around the beaches and giant sand dunes at Mui Ne Beach (near Phan Thiet), south of Nha Trang. A trip to the western part of the Central Highlands should include a visit to Kon Tum. Don't forget Phong Nha Cave to the north of the DMZ. In the far north, you can explore remote areas such as Dien Bien Phu, Cao Bang and Bai Tu Long Bay.

PLANNING

When to Go

There is no good or bad time to visit Vietnam. When one region is wet, cold or steaming hot, there is always somewhere else that is sunny and pleasant.

Visitors should allow for the fact that during Tet – the colourful Lunar New Year which falls in late January or early February – flights into, out of and around Vietnam are likely to be booked solid. The New Year festival is more than just a one-day event – it continues for at least a week. You are likely to encounter some difficulties booking hotels and flights for at least a week before and after Tet. This festival affects the whole of East Asia during this period (see the 'Tet Festival' special section in this chapter).

Maps

Almost every bookshop in Vietnam can sell you a map of the entire country. Reasonable tourist maps of Ho Chi Minh City, Hanoi, Danang, Hué and a few other major cities are issued within Vietnam in slightly different forms every few years. Unfortunately, maps of smaller towns and cities are practically nonexistent and most Vietnamese have never seen a map of the town they live in.

An oddity found in Vietnam is streets named after momentous historical dates. For example, ĐL 3 Thang 2 (usually written ĐL 3/2) refers to 3 February, the anniversary of the founding of the Vietnamese Communist Party.

Vietnamese street names are preceded with the words *Pho, Duong* and *Dai Lo* – on maps within this book, they appear respectively as P, Đ and ĐL.

Highly detailed topographic maps are produced in Vietnam, but are difficult to find. The government treats them like military secrets – ridiculous in this age of satellite photos. The best examples were made by the Americans during the American War, but they are out of date – towns have changed names and new roads have been built. Gecase Company (a government agency) has produced new ones, but you need special permission to buy them, which may require proof of how you plan to use them and/or reassurance by a local that the maps will not leave the country. However, these maps can sometimes be found on sale from street vendors in Hanoi and Ho Chi Minh City.

If you obtain the necessary permission, you can buy these topographic maps for US$3 each (you must purchase a minimum of 10) at Gecase Company (☎ 845 2670, fax 842 4216) 28 Đ Nguyen Van Troi, Phu Nhuan District in Ho Chi Minh City, close to Vinh Nghiem Pagoda.

Lonely Planet produces the *Vietnam Travel Atlas*, a boon to hikers and cyclists exploring the back country. Nelles has a large fold-up map of Vietnam, Cambodia and Laos.

What to Bring

Bring as little as possible. Many travellers try to bring everything bar the kitchen sink. Keep in mind that you can and will buy things in Vietnam (especially clothing), so don't burden yourself with a lot of unnecessary junk.

Backpacks are the easiest type of bag to carry and a frameless or internal-frame pack is the easiest to manage on buses and trains. Packs that close with a zipper can usually be secured with a padlock. Of course, any pack can be slit open with a razor blade, but a padlock will usually prevent pilfering by hotel staff and baggage handlers at airports. A cable lock or loop cable with lock can be used to secure the backpack on buses and trains (pack snatchers are a serious problem).

A day-pack can be handy, so you can leave your main luggage at the hotel or left-luggage room in the train stations. A belt-pack is OK for maps, extra film and other miscellanea, but don't use it for valuables such as your travellers cheques and passport, as it's an easy target for pickpockets.

If you don't want to use a backpack, a shoulder bag is much easier to carry than a suitcase. Some cleverly designed shoulder bags can also double as backpacks by rearranging a few straps.

Inside? Lightweight and compact are two words that should be etched in your mind when you're deciding what to bring. Dark-coloured clothing is preferred because it doesn't show the dirt – white clothes will force you to do laundry daily. You will, no doubt, be buying clothes along the way – clothing is cheap and abundant in Vietnam and neighbouring countries.

Nylon sports shoes are best – comfortable, washable and lightweight. Sandals are appropriate footwear in the tropical heat – even Ho Chi Minh wore them during his public appearances. Rubber thongs are somewhat less appropriate for formal occasions, but are nevertheless commonly worn in Vietnam.

A Swiss army knife or equivalent comes in handy, but you don't need one with 27 separate functions. Basically, you need one small sharp blade, a can opener and a bottle opener – a built-in magnifying glass or backscratcher probably isn't necessary.

The secret of successful packing is plastic bags or nylon 'stuff bags' – they keep things not only separate and clean, but also dry.

The following is a checklist of things you might consider packing. If you do forget to bring some 'essential' item, it's quite likely it can be bought in Vietnam, at least in Ho Chi Minh City and Hanoi.

Name cards, Swiss army knife, flashlight (and rechargeable batteries), compass, padlock, cable lock (to secure baggage), camera and accessories, ear plugs, alarm clock, sunglasses, hat, sunscreen, leakproof water bottle, cup, plate, fork, spoon, thongs (flip flops), rain jacket or poncho, backpack rain cover, sweater (for winter and air-con bus trips), sewing kit, toilet paper, tampons, condoms, nail clippers, tweezers, mosquito repellent, aspirin, anti-diarrhoea drugs, vitamins, rehydration salts, any special medications you use and a copy of the prescription (see the Health section later in this chapter).

If you'll be doing any cycling, bring all necessary safety equipment (helmet, reflectors, mirrors etc), as well as an inner tube repair kit. Everything you need to know about cycling in Vietnam is covered in Lonely Planet's *Cycling Vietnam, Laos & Cambodia.*

Hill-climbing boots with 25 eyelets on each side may be great for mountain climbing, but you will soon regret wearing them elsewhere. Etiquette requires removal of shoes at private homes, temples and even mini-hotels. This custom, coupled with predominantly hot weather, means thongs (flip-flops) or sandals are more practical. Just make sure that you have a comfortable pair you can walk in that won't fall off when you ride on a motorbike.

If you have particularly large feet, finding shoes that fit can be difficult in Vietnam, but for most Western tourists, this will probably not be a problem.

A final thought: airlines do lose bags from time to time – you have a much better chance of keeping yours if it is tagged with your name and address *inside* the bag as well as outside. Other tags can always fall off or be removed.

RESPONSIBLE TOURISM

The effects of the recent arrival of mass tourism, both positive and negative, are being felt in Vietnam. While positive contributions include dollars flowing into the local economy, the creation of jobs and a growing sense of globalisation, it is important for travellers to recognise and heed the potentially damaging costs of their visit on the country as a whole. Negative effects of tourism, both domestic and international, can be markedly reduced by responsible travel and a general respect for local culture and customs. By minimising negative impact, each visitor can make a difference. Try to be sensitive to local customs and take note of what local people do (for more information, see Society & Conduct in the Facts about Vietnam chapter).

See the 'NGOs in Vietnam' boxed text later in this chapter for a list of organisations that are working towards reducing the impact of tourism on Vietnam's people, their cultural heritage and environment.

Prostitution & Paedophilia

In Asia, the prevalence of prostitution is unfortunate but real, and where there is demand there is usually supply. The 'Social Evils' campaign recently saw the government crack down on the sex industry with heavy penalties, but the problem still remains. Avoid patronising bars etc that offer sex and massage services, such as the 'bar oms', and never buy sexual services.

Not only does prostitution involve adults, but it also concerns a growing number of children. The penalties in Vietnam for paedophiles are severe, and other countries around the world also have very strict laws and reinforcements. As a direct response to this child abuse, a number of countries, including Australia, New Zealand, Germany, Sweden, Norway, France and the USA, now prosecute and punish citizens for paedophilia offences committed abroad.

The sexual exploitation of children is already a significant problem in Asia, please don't let it get a strong foothold in Vietnam. If you see or suspect anything involving minors, please don't just ignore it; if you have any information, ie, the offenders' name and nationality, speak to their embassy. Any details you have can also be passed on to an appropriate organisation such as End Child Prostitution and Trafficking (ECPAT, e ecpat@ecpat.org). This is a global network of organisations that works to stop child prostitution, child pornography and the traffic of children for sexual purposes. ECPAT International is based in Bangkok, or you can find them on the Internet www.ecpat.org.

The Natural Environment

Vietnam has a low level of environmental awareness and responsibility, and many people remain unaware of the implications of littering. Try and raise awareness subtly by example, and dispose of your litter as responsibly as possible.

Vietnam's faunal populations are under considerable threat from domestic consumption and the illegal international trade in animal products (see Flora & Fauna in the Facts about Vietnam chapter). Though it may be 'exotic' to try wild meat such as muntjac, bats, frogs, deer, sea-horses, shark fins and snake (wine) and so on – or to buy

Green Travel

Simple acts can make a big difference. While you're in Vietnam you can help make a positive contribution to the environment. Here's some hints about things you might consider while on holiday (and even when you're at home!):

- Please don't buy souvenirs, or eat meals produced from endangered species and wildlife, including things like turtles and coral.
- Think about taking reusable calico shopping bags and refuse plastic bags whenever possible – they end up clogging waterways.
- Straws get stuck in dolphin's blowholes – consider reusing your straws or drinking from your own cup.
- As an alternative to take away food packaging take a reusable drink bottle and a light-weight aluminium or stainless steel food container (readily available in Western camping stores) – they'll also come in handy on long journeys.
- Using rechargeable batteries for your Walkman etc will cut down on the rubbish you leave behind.

products made from endangered plants and animals – it will indicate your support or acceptance of such practices and add to the demand for them. Politely refuse and explain to your host why.

Forest products such as rattan, orchids and medicinal herbs are under threat and the majority are still collected directly from Vietnam's dwindling forests. However, some of these products can be cultivated, an industry with potential for local people to earn additional income while protecting natural areas are protected from exploitation and degradation.

When visiting coral reefs and snorkelling or diving, or simply boating, be careful not to touch live coral or anchor boats on it, as this hinders the coral's growth. If your tour operator does this, and it's possible to anchor in a sandy area, try to convince the operator to do so and indicate your willingness to swim to the coral. Don't buy coral as a souvenir.

Vietnam is home to a large expanse of limestone or Karst landscape. When visiting limestone caves, be aware that touching the formations hinders growth and turns the limestone black. Don't break off the stalactites or stalagmites as they take lifetimes to regrow. Don't carve graffiti onto limestone formations, cave walls or other rock.

Finally do not remove or buy 'souvenirs' that have been taken from historical sites and natural areas.

TOURIST OFFICES

Vietnam's tourist offices are not like those found in other countries. If you were to visit a government-run tourist office in Australia, Western Europe or Japan you'd get lots of free, colourful, glossy brochures, maps and helpful advice on transport, places to stay, where to book tours and so on. Such tourist offices make no profit – indeed, they can lose money.

Vietnam's tourist offices operate on a different philosophy. They are government-owned enterprises whose primary interests are booking tours and earning a profit. In fact, these 'tourist offices' are little more than travel agencies, but they are among the most profitable hard-currency cash cows the Vietnamese government has. Don't come here looking for freebies; even the colourful brochures and maps – when they have them – are for sale.

Vietnam Tourism and Saigon Tourist are the oldest examples of this genre. However, nowadays every province has at least one such organisation, while larger cities may have dozens of competing government-run 'tourist offices', with each one earning a tidy profit. Many private companies have formed joint ventures with the state-run organisations, thus further diluting any real distinction between these tourist offices and private travel agencies.

Passenger arrivals to Vietnam rose from just 300,000 in 1991 to 1.5 million in 1998, and to 1.7 million in 1999. In late 1999 the Vietnam National Administration of Tourism (VNAT) announced an ambitious tourism promotion campaign under the slogan, 'Vietnam, A Destination for the New Millennium'. Government authorities aimed to attract two million foreign tourists to Vietnam in 2000, hoping to share in the successes of Thailand Tourism Authority's ongoing 'Amazing Thailand' tourism campaign.

Many in the travel industry, however, are sceptical about whether Vietnam, which only opened to tourism in the late 1980s, can handle such an increase of tourists. Critics say the country still lacks some important elements of basic tourist infrastructure, including a tourist police force, and 'real' tourist information offices etc. Well, if you take the campaign slogan at face value, they've got the rest of the millennium to work it out.

VISAS & DOCUMENTS

Passport

A passport is essential. If yours is within a few months of expiration, get a new one – many countries will not issue a visa if your passport has less than six months of validity remaining. Be sure that your passport has at least a few blank pages for visas and entry and exit stamps. It could be very inconvenient to run out of blank pages when you are too far away from an embassy to get a new passport issued or extra pages added.

Losing your passport is very bad news indeed. Getting a new one takes time and money. It's wise to have a driving licence, student card, ID card or something else with your photo on it – some embassies want to see picture ID before issuing a replacement passport. Keeping the original of an old expired passport is also very useful for this purpose.

It certainly helps to keep a separate record of the number and date of issue your passport as well as a photocopy of either it or your birth certificate. While you're compiling that info, add the serial number of your travellers cheques, travel insurance details and US$300 or so as emergency cash (better hotels have a safe for valuables – that may be a good place to keep this stuff).

If you are a national of a country without diplomatic relations with Vietnam and you lose your passport while in the country, the situation is still not hopeless. If the immigration police are unable to locate the passport, you will be issued documents allowing you to leave Vietnam but you may be allowed to stay until your visa (the validity of which is on record with the police) expires.

In Vietnam, it seems that everyone wants to do something with your passport. You will almost always be required to leave your passport with the hotel reception desk (they need it to register your presence with the police), with a travel agency (to get a local travel permit or visa extension) or with bureaucratic ministries of every sort.

Visas

Until recently, visas to Vietnam had to specify exactly where you enter the country and where you exit. Vietnam may have been the only country in the world to slap on this restriction. Thankfully, however, as of January 2000, a new regulation came into place and now all tourist visas are stamped *cau cac cua khau quoc te* (or some variation of this phrase), meaning 'any international border.' This allows you to enter and exit Vietnam at any of the four international airports (in Hanoi, Ho Chi Minh City, Danang and Dalat) or six land borders (one with Cambodia, two with Laos and three with China.

Arranging the necessary paperwork for a Vietnamese visa has become fairly straightforward – the only problem is that it tends to be quite expensive and unnecessarily time-consuming. In most cases you are better off getting your visa from a travel agent rather than the Vietnamese embassy, mainly for the sheer convenience and to avoid queues. The travel agency processing your visa requires a photocopy of your passport and one to three photos (the actual number differs for various countries).

Bangkok has always been considered a convenient place to get visas for Vietnam. Even travel agents in neighbouring countries send the paperwork by courier to Bangkok for processing because it's so much cheaper and efficient than dealing with the local Vietnamese embassy (the one in Beijing is notorious). In Bangkok, single-entry tourist visas cost about US$40 at budget travel agencies. Many travel agencies offer package deals with a visa and return air ticket included (Bangkok–Ho Chi Minh City, returning Hanoi–Bangkok); try around Soi Khao San (Khao San Rd).

See the Internet Resources section later in this chapter for details of Lonely Planet's Web site, which has hot links to the most up-to-date visa information.

Tourist Visas Processing a visa application takes four or five working days in Bangkok (two days for an express visa), five days in Malaysia, five to 10 days in Hong Kong and 10 working days in Taiwan. No-one has yet offered a satisfactory explanation of why it should take so much longer in some countries than in others.

Tourist visas are valid for only a single 30-day stay. To make matters worse, the visa specifies the exact date of arrival and departure. Thus, you must solidify your travel plans well in advance. You cannot arrive even one day earlier than your visa specifies. And if you change your plans and postpone your trip by two weeks, then you'll only have 16 days remaining on your visa instead of 30 days.

Theoretically, you can enter Vietnam with a sponsor's letter and get your visa stamped into your passport on arrival for US$110. In practice, this is more trouble than it's worth. Aside from being expensive, this 'visa on arrival' process is not easy to arrange and is usually only done for group tours. Only a few travel agencies are authorised to do the sponsor's letter, so it simply isn't an option for most travellers. If you do use this procedure, note that you must have the right cash (US dollars in the exact amount) because there is no place to change money before you pass through immigration.

In our experience, personal appearance influences the reception you receive from immigration – if you wear shorts or scruffy clothing, look dirty or unshaven, you can expect problems. You don't need to get all dressed up, but try to look 'respectable'.

Always have some photos with you; immigration police have been known to inexplicably give travellers more forms to fill out and attached photos are required. Of course, there is a photographer right there at the airport to serve you – for a substantial fee.

Business Visas There are several advantages in having a business visa: it is are usually valid for three or six months, can be issued for multiple-entry journeys and will look more impressive when you have to deal with bureaucratic authorities. Also, you are permitted to work if you have a business visa, though doing so will make you subject to taxes and other bureaucratic regulations that change from week to week.

Getting a business visa has now become fairly easy. Some travel agencies that do tourist visas can also do business visas. The main drawback is cost – a business visa costs about four times what you'd pay for a tourist visa. Trying to obtain the visa yourself through a Vietnamese embassy will probably be more trouble than it's worth – you'd better let a travel agent handle it.

It tends to be much easier to apply for a business visa once you are in Vietnam. If approved, most make a short trip abroad to Phnom Penh, Vientiane or Bangkok to pick up the visa from a Vietnamese embassy. It is actually possible to get the visa stamped in Vietnam, but this is far more expensive (it seems that they include the airfare and other expenses you would have incurred on a trip outside Vietnam into the price of the visa).

Student Visas A student visa is something you usually arrange after arrival. It's acceptable to enter Vietnam on a tourist visa, enrol in a Vietnamese language course and then apply at the immigration police for a change in status. Of course, you do have to pay tuition and are expected to attend class. A minimum of 10 hours of study per week is needed to qualify for student status.

Visa Extensions If you've got the dollars, they've got the rubber stamp. In Ho Chi Minh City and Hanoi, visa extensions cost around US$30 but you should probably go to a travel agency to get this taken care of – fronting up at the immigration police yourself usually doesn't work. The procedure takes one or two days. Official policy is that you are permitted one visa extension only, for a maximum of 30 days.

Be alert for sudden unannounced changes to these regulations. In the early 1990s, two visa extensions (60 days) were permitted, then suddenly in 1995 *no* visa extensions were permitted, and since 1996, only one visa extension has been allowed. Sudden and arbitrary changes to the regulations are standard procedure in Vietnam – try not to get caught short.

Usually the extension goes smoothly if you work through a reliable agent who has good connections. The less you personally get involved with the bureaucracy, the better off you are.

In theory, you should be able to extend your visa in any provincial capital. In practice, it goes smoothest in major cities such as Ho Chi Minh City, Hanoi, Danang and Hué, that cater to mass tourism.

I got my visa extension in Vinh, which only cost US$2, but in Ho Chi Minh City I was later told that this was invalid. The police cancelled my first extension, forced me to buy a second one, plus I had to pay a US$10 fine for overstaying 13 days. I also lost three days dealing with the bureaucracy.

Gerhard Heinzel

Officially, the airport immigration police should accept your visa extension regardless of its origin.

Re-Entry Visas It's possible to enter Cambodia, Laos or any other country from Vietnam and then re-enter on your original single-entry Vietnamese tourist visa. However, you must apply for a re-entry visa *before* you leave Vietnam. You'll be given a receipt and confirmation number to pick up the visa in the country you are headed to. If you do not have a re-entry visa, you will have to go through the whole expensive and time-consuming procedure of applying for a new Vietnamese visa.

Re-entry visas are easy enough to arrange in Hanoi or Ho Chi Minh City, but you will almost certainly have to ask a travel agent to do the paperwork for you. Travel agents charge about US$25 for this service and can complete the procedure in one or two days. Although travellers can theoretically secure the re-entry visa without going through a travel agent, the Vietnamese bureaucrats usually thwart such individual efforts.

If you already have a valid business visa that allows you multiple entries for Vietnam, you do not need a re-entry visa.

Travel Permits

Formerly, foreigners had to have *giay phep di lai* (internal travel permits) to travel anywhere beyond the city in which they arrived. From 1975 to 1988, even citizens of Vietnam needed these permits to travel around their own country (to prevent them from fleeing). The central government changed the rules in 1993 and internal travel permits are no longer needed, although the Vietnamese must carry ID cards with them at all times. There have, however, been reports of some con artists who will insist that you still need one and will quite happily sell you a fake 'internal travel permit'.

Although internal travel permits have been abolished, uncertainty still prevails in some small towns and villages. Unfortunately, the police in many places seem to make up their own rules as they go along, no matter what the Interior Ministry in Hanoi says. What this means is that some provincial governments are chasing foreign dollars by charging for local 'travel permits', which consist of a photocopied piece of paper with a policeman's signature on it. The bottom line is that you may have to inquire locally to see if a permit is required.

The main purpose of the permits seems to be to extract cash from foreigners. Some local provincial governments demand that you secure and pay for a permit to visit the surrounding area on your arrival, hire a local guide and rent a car from the local government, even if you've already arrived in an official government rental car!

Places where permits are currently required include Lat Village (near Dalat), minority villages around Buon Ma Thuot and Pleiku, and the remote villages in the mountains of the north. Authorities in Ha Giang Province, for one, are notorious for changing the rules day by day. Even if you are able to secure a travel permit to travel in Ha Giang, there is still a strong possibility that you'll be sent back to Hanoi after you've arrived. Additional information about obtaining these permits is provided in the relevant regional chapters.

However, don't rely solely on the information supplied in this book, because policies do change. We are pleased to report that the need for travel permits is diminishing and there seems to have been some strong pressure applied by Hanoi to stop this nonsense. For the latest scoop, consult a reputable local travel agent.

Travel Insurance

Although you may have medical insurance in your own country, it is probably not valid in Vietnam. A travel insurance policy to cover theft, loss and medical problems is a good idea. Some policies offer lower and higher medical-expense options; the higher ones are chiefly for countries such as the USA, which has extremely high medical costs. There is a wide variety of policies available, so check the small print.

Some policies specifically exclude 'dangerous activities', which can include scuba diving, motorcycling or even trekking. A locally acquired motorcycle licence is not valid under some policies.

You may prefer a policy that pays doctors or hospitals directly rather requiring you to pay on the spot and claim later. If you have to claim later, make sure you keep all documentation. Some policies ask you to call (reverse charges) a centre in your home country where an immediate assessment of your problem is made.

Check that the policy covers ambulances or an emergency flight home.

Driving Licence & Permits

If you plan to drive abroad, get an International Driving Permit from your local automobile association or motor vehicle department before you leave. In many countries, these are valid for only one year, so there's no sense getting one too far in advance of your departure. However, some countries will issue International Driving Permits valid for several years – it depends on where you live. Make sure your licence states that it is valid for motorcycles if you plan to ride one.

Student & Youth Cards

Bona fide full-time students coming from the USA, Australia and Europe can often get some good discounts on international (not domestic) air tickets with the help of an International Student Identity Card (ISIC). To get this card, inquire at your campus.

Student Travel (STA) issues STA Youth Cards, which have some of the same benefits, to persons aged between 13 and 26 years. However, no place in Vietnam issues these cards, nor are they of any use within the country.

International Health Card

An International Health Certificate is useful (though not essential), to record any vaccinations you've had. These can be issued in Vietnam.

Other Documents

If you're travelling with your spouse, a photocopy of your marriage certificate may come in handy should you become involved with the law, hospitals or other bureaucratic authorities.

If you're planning on working or studying in Vietnam, it could be helpful to bring copies of transcripts, diplomas, letters of reference and other relevant professional qualifications.

A collection of passport photos for visas (about 10 should be sufficient) will be useful if you're planning on visiting several countries or if you need to apply for visa extensions or other documents. Of course, you can get these in Vietnam and elsewhere, but they must have a neutral background.

Copies

All important documents (passport data page and visa page, credit cards, travel insurance policy, air/bus/train tickets, driving licence etc) should be photocopied before you leave home. Leave one copy with someone at home and keep another with you, separate from the originals.

It's also a good idea to store details of your vital travel documents in Lonely Planet's free online Travel Vault in case you lose the photocopies or can't be bothered with them. Your password-protected Travel Vault is accessible online anywhere in the world – create it at www.ekno.lonelyplanet.com.

During your time in Vietnam, you are almost certain to encounter various people who want to take your valuable documents away from you. This is particularly true of hotel clerks; they say they need your passport to register you with the police, though in many cases the only motive is to make sure you pay your hotel bill and don't steal the towels. Some hotels will accept photocopies, but most will not. Once you've handed over your passport, you are left with no documentation at all. At least the photocopies give you something to show to the authorities (the police, the railway ticket office, Vietnam Airlines etc) while the hotel holds your original documents. And if worse comes to worse, photocopies are helpful if you need to replace the documents that the hotel or police manage to lose.

If police stop you on the street and ask for your passport, give them the photocopy and explain your hotel has the original.

EMBASSIES & CONSULATES

Vietnamese Embassies & Consulates

Diplomatic representation abroad includes:

Australia
Embassy: (☎ 02-6286 6059, fax 6286 4534) 6 Timbarra Crescent, O'Malley, Canberra, ACT 2603
Consulate: (☎ 02-9327 2539, fax 9328 1653) 489 New South Head Rd, Double Bay, NSW 2028

Cambodia
Embassy: (☎ 05-1881 1804, fax 236 2314) 436 Blvd Preach, Monivong, Phnom Penh

Canada
Embassy: (☎ 613-236 0772, fax 236 2704) 226 Maclaren St, Ottawa, Ontario K2P 0L9

China
Embassy: (☎ 010-532 1125, fax 532 5720) 32 Guanghua Lu, Jianguomen Wai, Beijing
Consulate: (☎ 020-652 7908, fax 652 7808) Jin Yanf Hotel, 92 Huanshi Western Rd
Guangzhou Consulate: (☎ 22-591 4510, fax 591 4524) 15th floor, Great Smart Tower Bldg, 230 Wanchai Rd, Hong Kong

France
Embassy: (☎ 01 44 14 64 00, fax 01 45 24 39 48) 62–6 rue Boileau, Paris 75016

Germany
Embassy: (☎ 228-357021, fax 351866) Konstantinstrasse 37, 5300 Bonn 2

Italy
Embassy: (☎ 06-854 3223, fax 854 8501) 34 Via Clituno, 00198 Rome

Japan
Embassy: (☎ 03-3466 3311, fax 3466 3312) 50–11 Moto Yoyogi-Cho, Shibuya-ku, Tokyo 151
Consulate: (☎ 06-263 1600, fax 263 1770) 10th floor, Estate Bakurocho Bldg, 4-10 Bakurocho, Chuo-ku, Osaka

Laos
Embassy: (☎ 214-13409) 1 Thap Luang Rd, Vientiane
Consulate: (☎ 412-12239, fax 12182) 418 Sisavang Vong, Savannakhet

Philippines
Embassy: (☎ 2-500 364/508 101) 54 Victor Cruz, Malatc, Metro Manila

Thailand
Embassy: (☎ 2-251 7201251 5836) 83/1 Wireless Rd, Bangkok

UK
Embassy: (☎ 0171-937 1912, fax 937 6108) 12–14 Victoria Rd, London W8 5RD

USA
Embassy: (☎ 202-861 0737, fax 861 0917) 1233, 20th St NW, Washington, DC 20036

Embassies & Consulates in Vietnam

With the exception of those for Laos and Cambodia, Hanoi's embassies and Ho Chi Minh City's consulates do very little visa business for non-Vietnamese. You may, however, have several good reasons to visit your own country's embassy.

It's important to realise what your own embassy – the embassy of the country of which you are a citizen – can and can't do to help you if you get into trouble. Generally speaking, it won't be much help in emergencies if the trouble you're in is remotely your own fault. Remember that you are bound by the laws of the country you are in. Your embassy will not be sympathetic if you end up in jail after committing a crime locally, even if such actions are legal in your own country (though they can intervene to make sure that you're being treated fairly).

In genuine emergencies you might get some assistance, but only if other channels have been exhausted. For example, if you need to get home urgently, a free air-ticket is exceedingly unlikely – the embassy would expect you to have insurance. If you have all your money and documents stolen, it might assist with getting a new passport, but a loan for onward travel is out of the question.

Some embassies used to keep letters for travellers or have a small reading room with home newspapers, but these days the mail holding service has mostly been stopped and even newspapers tend to be out of date.

If you're staying a long time in Vietnam, you should register your passport at your embassy (this makes it much easier to issue a new one if yours is lost or stolen). Also consider registering with your embassy if you intend on travelling to more remote areas. Your embassy can also help you obtain a ballot for absentee voting or provide forms for filing income-tax returns. Embassies can also advise business people and will sometimes intervene in trade disputes.

However, remember that the people who work at your embassy are busy – please don't bother them with trivial matters.

The following list has the addresses of some foreign embassies in Hanoi and consulates in Ho Chi Minh City:

Australia
Embassy: (☎ 831 7755, fax 831 7711)
Van Phuc Diplomatic Quarter, Hanoi
Consulate: (☎ 829 6035, fax 829 6031)
The Landmark, 5B Đ Ton Duc Thang, District 1, Ho Chi Minh City

Cambodia
Embassy: (☎ 825 3788, fax 826 5225)
71 Pho Tran Hung Dao, Hanoi
Consulate: (☎ 829 2751, fax 829 2744)
41 Đ Phung Khac Khoan, District 1, Ho Chi Minh City

Canada
Embassy: (☎ 823 5500, fax 823 5333)
31 Pho Hung Vuong, Hanoi
Consulate: (☎ 824 5025, fax 829 4528)
10th floor, Metropolitan Bldg, 235 Đ Dong Khoi, District 1, Ho Chi Minh City

China
Embassy: (☎ 845 3736, fax 823 2826)
46 Pho Hoang Dieu, Hanoi
Consulate: (☎ 829 2457, fax 829 5009)
39 Đ Nguyen Thi Minh Khai, Ho Chi Minh City

France
Embassy: (☎ 825 2719, fax 826 4236)
57 Pho Tran Hung Dao, Hanoi
Consulate: (☎ 829 7231, fax 829 1675)
27 Đ Nguyen Thi Minh Khai, District 1, Ho Chi Minh City

Germany
Embassy: (☎ 845 3836, fax 845 3838)
29 Pho Tran Phu, Hanoi
Consulate: (☎ 829 1967, fax 823 1919)
126 Đ Nguyen Dinh Chieu, District 3, Ho Chi Minh City

Japan
Embassy: (☎ 846 3000, fax 846 3043)
27 Pho Lieu Giai, Hanoi
Consulate: (☎ 822 5314, fax 822 5316) 13–17 ĐL Nguyen Hue, District 1, Ho Chi Minh City

Laos
Embassy: (☎ 825 4576, fax 822 8414)
40 Pho Quang Trung, Hanoi
Consulate: (☎ 829 9272) 93 Đ Pasteur, District 1, Ho Chi Minh City

Netherlands
Embassy: (☎ 843 0605, fax 843 1013)
Block D1, Van Phuc Diplomatic Quarter, Hanoi
Consulate: (☎ 823 5932, fax 823 5934)
Saigon Tower, 29 ĐL Le Duan, District 1, Ho Chi Minh City

New Zealand
Embassy: (☎ 824 1481, fax 824 1480)
32 Pho Hang Bai, Hanoi
Consulate: (☎ 822 6907, fax 822 6905)
5th floor, Yoco Bldg, 41 Đ Nguyen Thi Minh Khai, District 1, Ho Chi Minh City

Philippines
Embassy: (☎ 825 7948, fax 826 5760)
27B Pho Tran Hung Dao, Hanoi

Thailand
Embassy: (☎ 823 5092, fax 823 5088)
63–5 Pho Hoang Dieu, Hanoi
Consulate: (☎ 822 2637, fax 829 1002)
77 Đ Tran Quoc Thao, District 3, Ho Chi Minh City

UK
Embassy: (☎ 825 2510, fax 826 5762)
31 Pho Hai Ba Trung, Hanoi
Consulate: (☎ 829 8433, fax 822 1971)
25 ĐL Le Duan, District 1, Ho Chi Minh City

USA
Embassy: (☎ 843 1500, fax 843 1510)
7 Pho Lang Ha, Hanoi
Consulate: (☎ 822 9433, fax 822 9434)
4 ĐL Le Duan, District 1, Ho Chi Minh City

CUSTOMS

If you enter Vietnam by air, the customs inspection is usually fast and cursory. Unless the x-ray machine indicates that your backpack is filled with guns or heroin, you should get through the whole procedure in minutes.

However, if you enter overland, expect a mild to rigorous search. Your baggage may be completely emptied.

You are permitted to bring in a duty-free allowance of 200 cigarettes, 50 cigars or 250g of tobacco; 2L of liquor; gifts worth up to US$50; and a reasonable quantity of luggage and personal effects. Items that you cannot bring into Vietnam include opium, weapons, explosives and 'cultural materials unsuitable to Vietnamese society'.

During the height of the 'Social Evils' campaign in 1996, a letter was circulated to customs officials stipulating fines of 20 million dong (US$1820) for the import/export of cultural materials relating negatively to Vietnam. That included this guidebook, the popular CD ROM *Vietnam: A Portrait* and all cassette tapes or CDs containing music produced by Overseas Vietnamese. Fortunately, the rule was seldom enforced and the social evils furore seems to have died down now, but it's best to keep such dangerous items out of sight anyway.

Tourists can bring an unlimited amount of foreign currency into Vietnam, but they are required to declare it on their customs form upon arrival. Theoretically, when you leave the country you should have exchange receipts for all the foreign currency you have spent, but in practice the authorities really don't care.

When entering Vietnam, visitors must also declare all precious metals (especially gold), jewellery, cameras and electronic devices in their possession. Customs is liable to tax you on gold bars, jewellery and diamonds – if you don't need this stuff, then don't bring it. Theoretically, declaring your goods means that when you leave, you will have no hassles taking these items out with you. It also means that you could be asked to show these items so that customs officials know you didn't sell them on the black market, though in practice you will seldom be troubled unless you bring in an unreasonable amount of goods or something of great value.

The import and export of Vietnamese currency and live animals is forbidden.

MONEY

Currency

The currency of Vietnam is the dong (abbreviated to a 'd' following the amount). The banknotes come in denominations of 200d, 500d, 1000d, 2000d, 5000d, 10,000d, 20,000d, 50,000d and 100,000d. It can be difficult to get change for the largest notes in small towns, so keep a stack of smaller bills handy.

Now that Ho Chi Minh has been canonised (against his wishes), you'll find his picture on *every* banknote. There are no coins currently in use in Vietnam, though the dong used to be subdivided into 10 *hao* and 100 *xu*. All dong-denominated prices are based on a US$1 =14,000d conversion rate.

In the recent past, many upmarket hotels and restaurants demanded payment in US dollars and would not accept Vietnamese currency. In 1994, the Vietnamese government banned this practice – officially all businesses in Vietnam must advertise and accept payment in dong only. In reality, however, many hotels and businesses still quote prices in US dollars and will 'exchange' on the spot.

We also prefer to quote prices in US dollars; firstly because the Vietnamese themselves often quote prices in dollars; and secondly because dong prices are unwieldy. For example, a night at a mid-range hotel can easily cost over 300,000d and buying a domestic air ticket from Hanoi to Ho Chi Minh City costs 1.9 million dong!

Where prices are quoted in dong we try to give this price and also an approximate dollar equivalent in brackets.

Ultimately, whenever possible, it is best to think in dong, have prices quoted in dong and use dong. This said, it's also advisable to bring a small pocket calculator with you for converting currency, unless of course you are the sort of person who can nonchalantly multiply US$33.50 by 14,095 (and add 10% tax) in your head.

The dong has experienced its ups and downs. Past attempts by the government to solve the country's debt problems with the printing press led to devastating inflation and frequent devaluations. In 1991 the dong lost close to half its value. In 1992 it gained 35% against the US dollar, making it one of the best currency investments of the year! This surge in value was due to the shutting down of the printing presses and the turnaround in Vietnam's chronic trade deficit – in 1992 the country experienced what is believed to be its first trade surplus since reunification. The Asian economic crisis, which wreaked severe havoc on the Thai, Korean and Indonesian currencies in the late 1990s, caused the dong to lose about 15% of its US dollar value.

The Americans introduced Western banking practices to South Vietnam – personal cheques were commonly used for large purchases, at least in Saigon before reunification. When the North took over, cheques, credit cards, South Vietnamese banknotes and South Vietnamese bank accounts became instantly worthless. As the Vietnamese dismantled the banking system, telegraphic transfers into Vietnam became practically impossible, though later a company called Cosevina was set up to allow Overseas Vietnamese to send money to their relatives.

That was then and this is now. Vietnam is trying to rejoin the world's banking system and capitalist-style monetary instruments such as travellers cheques, credit cards, telegraphic transfers and even letters of credit are all experiencing a revival. Domestic personal cheques have still not been reintroduced, but should be coming soon.

Gold is also used extensively, especially for major transactions such as the sale of homes or cars. If you ask someone how much they paid for their house, they will probably tell you how many *taels* of gold.

Exchange Rates

country	unit		dong
Australia	A$1	=	7,610d
Canada	C$1	=	9,315d
China	Y1	=	1,745d
euro	1€	=	12,500d
France	1FF	=	1,900d
Germany	DM1	=	6,390d
Hong Kong	HK$1	=	1,851d
Japan	¥100	=	135d
New Zealand	NZ$1	=	5,760d
Singapore	S$1	=	8,290d
Taiwan	NT$1	=	450d
Thailand	B1	=	330d
UK	UK£	=	20,665d
USA	US$1	=	14,430d

Exchanging Money

Theoretically you can convert French francs, German marks, pounds sterling, Japanese yen and other major currencies, but the reality is that US dollars are still much preferred. Be sure to bring enough US dollars in cash or travellers cheques for your whole visit and keep them in a safe place, eg, in a moneybelt. Try not to keep the whole lot in one place (if the moneybelt goes, everything goes with it). Unless you borrow, or get someone to wire money to you (which is only possible in Ho Chi Minh City and Hanoi), losing your cash could put you in a really bad situation.

Once in Vietnam, beware of counterfeit cash, especially the 20,000d and 50,000d notes. These fakes are imported from China. There shouldn't be any problem if you've changed money in a bank, but out on the free market it's a different story.

It's a good idea to check that the dollars and travellers cheques you bring to Vietnam do not have anything scribbled on them or look too tattered, lest they be summarily rejected by uptight clerks. Ironically, some travellers have had problems changing dollars that looked 'too new' because the bank clerks suspected they were counterfeit!

Vietcombank is another name for the state-owned Bank for Foreign Trade of Vietnam (Ngan Hang Ngoai Thuong Viet Nam). Some other banks can change foreign currency and travellers cheques, but Vietcombank is the most organised. Banking hours are normally from 8 am to 3 pm Monday to Friday, and 8 am to noon on Saturday; most banks also close for 1½ hours during lunch, all day Sunday and on public holidays.

Travellers cheques can be exchanged only at authorised foreign exchange banks. The problem is that not every city (indeed, not every province) has a foreign exchange bank. Outrageously, there are no banks at the border crossings with Cambodia and Laos, nor are there any at Lao Cai and Dong Dang (both major border crossings with China). The only way to change money at these places is on the black market. Furthermore, the Vietcombank branches at Ho Chi Minh City and Hanoi airports only operate during banking hours – they are closed when several flights arrive and depart. Therefore, it's imperative that you do not rely entirely on travellers cheques. Keep a reasonable stash of US dollars cash on hand, in a variety of denominations.

If you only have travellers cheques, you can stock up on US dollars at foreign exchange banks. These banks usually charge a 2% commission to change US dollar travellers cheques into US dollars cash (other banks may charge more). Vietcombank charges no commission if you exchange travellers cheques for dong (but again, other banks do).

Money for Nothing

The dong has certainly had a rocky history. In the days of French Indochina, the local currency was known as the *piastre*. The partitioning of Vietnam in 1954 created separate versions of the dong for North and South Vietnam (they were both called dong). The two currencies were valued the same.

In 1975, US$1 was equal to 450d in South Vietnam. In 1976 the Communist Provisional Revolutionary Government (PRG) cancelled the South Vietnamese dong and issued its own PRG dong. The swap rate between the two dong was not set at 1:1, but rather at 500:1 in favour of the PRG dong. Furthermore, southerners were only permitted to exchange a maximum of 200d per family. This sudden demonetarisation of South Vietnam instantly turned much of the affluent population into paupers and caused the swift collapse of the economy. Those with the foresight to have kept their wealth hidden in gold or jewellery escaped some of the hardships.

In 1977 both the North Vietnamese dong and the PRG dong were done away with and swapped for a reunification dong. In the North the swap was 1:1, but in the South the ratio was 1:1.2. This time the southerners got a slightly better deal, though it was small compensation for the 500:1 loss of the previous year.

The last great attempt at currency swapping was in 1985. Realising that inflation was rapidly eroding the value of the dong, the government decided to solve the problem by reissuing a new dong at a swap ratio of 10:1 in favour of the new dong. This time each family was allowed only 2000d of the new banknotes, though on special application more was allotted. Rather than controlling price increases as the government had hoped, the currency reissue ignited yet another round of hyper-inflation. These days, the old 20d notes are literally not worth the paper they're printed on.

If your travellers cheques are denominated currencies other than US dollars, you may find them difficult to exchange. If you insist, the banks may exchange non-US dollar cheques for dong, but they will charge a hefty commission (perhaps 10%) to protect themselves against any possible exchange rate fluctuations – often they do not know the latest exchange rate for anything but US dollars.

Foreign exchange banks observe all major public holidays. If you arrive during the Lunar New Year, the banks may be closed for three or four days in a row. Try not to get caught short.

You can reconvert reasonable amounts of dong back into dollars on departure without an official receipt, though the definition of 'reasonable' is questionable. Most visitors have had no problem, but having an official receipt should settle any arguments that arise. You cannot legally take the dong out with you.

The relatively low value of Vietnamese banknotes means that almost any currency exchange will leave you with hundreds of banknotes to count; changing US$100 will net you about 1.4 million dong! Notes are usually presented in brick-sized piles bound with rubber bands; counting them is a slow, but necessary, process.

Visa, MasterCard, American Express and JCB cards are now widely acceptable in all major cities and many tourist centres. However, you will usually be charged a 3% commission each time you use a credit card to purchase something or pay a hotel bill; always ask first, as some charge higher commissions than others. Better restaurants do not usually slap on an additional charge.

Getting a cash advance from Visa, MasterCard and JCB is possible at Vietcombank in most cities, as well as at foreign banks such as ANZ in Ho Chi Minh City and Hanoi. Banks generally charge a 3% commission for this service.

There are a few banks in Ho Chi Minh City that have installed Automatic Teller Machines (ATMs) that accept foreign ATM cards, notably ANZ Bank and Hongkong Bank (HSBC). Payment is made in dong *only*, and there is a daily limit of 2,000,000d (US$160). Cash advances for larger amounts of dong, as well as US dollars, are handled at the bank counters during office hours.

Foreigners who spend a lot of time in Vietnam working, doing business or just hanging around, can open bank accounts at Vietcombank. The accounts can be denominated in Vietnamese dong or US dollars. Both demand-deposit and time-deposit accounts are available and interest is paid. Vietcombank can arrange letters of credit for those doing import and export business in Vietnam. It is even possible to borrow money from Vietcombank.

Bear in mind that outside major cities it can be very difficult to find banks that cash travellers cheques, so be sure to change sufficient funds before heading to countryside. US dollars cash is far less of problem to use, but the rates tend to drop the further away you are from the city.

Black Market The black market is Vietnam's unofficial banking system. It's almost everywhere and operates quite openly. Private individuals (taxi drivers etc) and some shops (jewellery stores, travel agencies) will exchange US dollars for dong and vice versa. While the practice is illegal, law enforcement is virtually nonexistent. However, black market exchange rates are usually *worse* than the official exchange rates, so the only advantage is the convenience of changing money when and where you like. Typically you lose from 1% to 5% on black market transactions. In some provincial villages (for example, in Sapa) you can even change travellers cheques on the black market, but you'll have to pay an exorbitant 10% commission.

One of the most common, convenient and generally safe ways of changing US dollars (cash only) to dong is at jewellery stores. Most tend to match the going bank rate (giving a slightly better rate on higher denominations like US$50 and US$100 notes). Count the money at the counter before you leave the store.

If people approach you on the street with offers to change money at rates better than the official bank rate, you can rest assured that you are being set up for a rip-off. *Don't even think about trying it!* Remember, if an offer seems too good to be true, that's because it is.

Security

Vietnam has its fair share of pickpockets, especially in Ho Chi Minh City, Nha Trang, and increasingly, Hanoi. Rather than lose your precious cash and travellers cheques (not to mention your passport), large amounts of money and other valuables should be kept far from sticky fingers. Various devices that usually thwart pickpockets include pockets sewn on the inside of your trousers, Velcro tabs to seal pocket openings, a moneybelt under your clothes or a pouch under your shirt. A vest (waistcoat) worn under your outer jacket will do very nicely only in those rare parts of Vietnam that get cold – this isn't feasible during summer or in the south where it's just too hot to wear an extra layer.

A secret stash of cash (maybe inside your backpack frame?) is a good idea for those special emergencies.

Costs

Vietnam remains one of the best travel bargains in east Asia, and the cost of travelling largely depends on your tastes and susceptibility to luxuries. Ascetics can get by on US$10 a day while a conventional budget traveller can live very well on US$20 to US$25. Transport is likely to be the biggest expense, especially if you rent a car, which many travellers wind up doing. If you opt to travel by bus or train, you can save a considerable sum.

Foreigners are frequently overcharged, particularly when buying souvenirs, and occasionally in restaurants. Rapacious bus and taxi drivers will often bump up their rates to several times the Vietnamese price. However, don't assume that everyone is trying to rip you off – despite severe poverty, many Vietnamese will only ask the local price for most goods and services.

Tipping & Bargaining

Tipping according to a percentage of the bill is not expected in Vietnam, but it is enormously appreciated. For a person who earns US$50 per month, a US$1 tip is about half a day's wages. Upmarket hotels and some restaurants tend to slap a 5% service charge on top of the government's 10% value-added tax (VAT) – this service charge might be considered a mandatory tip, though it's doubtful that much of it reaches the employees. In general, if you stay a couple of days in the same hotel it's not a bad idea to tip the staff who clean your room – US$0.50 to US$1 should be enough.

You should also consider tipping drivers and guides – after all, the time they spend on the road with you means time away from home and family. Ditto if you take a day tour with a group – the guides and drivers are paid next to nothing. Typically travellers on minibus tours will pool together to collect a communal tip to be split between the guide and driver. About US$1 per day (per tourist) is standard. Of course you can give more if you're feeling generous, or if you find a genuine reason not to tip, don't.

It is considered proper to make a small donation at the end of a visit to a pagoda, especially if the monk has shown you around; most pagodas have contribution boxes for this purpose.

Many foreigners just assume that every Vietnamese is out to rip them off. That just isn't true – you needn't bargain for everything. But there are times when bargaining is essential. In touristy areas, postcard vendors have a reputation for charging about five times the going rate. Most cyclo and motorbike drivers also try to grossly overcharge foreigners – find out the correct rate in advance and then bargain accordingly.

Remember, in the Orient, 'face' is important (see Society & Conduct in the Facts about Vietnam chapter). Bargaining should be good-natured – smile, don't get angry or argue. Many Westerners seem to take bargaining too seriously and get offended if they don't get the goods for less than half the original asking price. In some cases you will be able to get a 50% discount or more, at other times this may only be 10%, but by no means should you get angry during the bargaining process. And once the money is accepted, the deal is done – if you harbour hard feelings because you later find out that someone else got it cheaper, the only one you are hurting is yourself.

Taxes

On most goods you pay for, the marked or stated price usually includes any relevant taxes. Value-added tax was implemented in 1999, so don't be surprised to find an extra 10% tacked on to your bill. Some hotels and restaurants may also charge an additional 5% service charge, but this should be stated on the rate sheet or menu (ask if you're not sure).

If you're working in Vietnam, the issue of paying taxes is totally flaky. Normal income taxes are typically 40% to 50% depending on how much you earn. In reality, few Vietnamese report all their income. As a foreign resident, you can theoretically be taxed on your 'worldwide income', which includes money not earned in Vietnam! Needless to say, most expats 'forget' to report their foreign-earned income.

The Vietnamese government is said to be looking at ways to crack down on tax evasion. If the tax collectors really get their act together, it will be a disaster for the economy.

POST & COMMUNICATIONS

Postal Rates

Domestic postal rates are sinfully cheap; a domestic letter costs 400d (US$0.03) to mail.

International postal rates are similar to what you pay in European countries, ie, postcards to Europe or the USA cost about US$0.50 – the exact amount varies continent to continent. While these rates might not seem expensive to you, the tariffs are so out of line with most salaries that locals literally cannot afford to send letters to their friends and relatives abroad. If you would like to correspond with Vietnamese whom you meet during your visit, try leaving them enough stamps to cover postage for several letters, explaining that the stamps were extras you didn't use and would be of no value to you at home. Or buy a bunch of Vietnamese stamps to take home with you and when you write to Vietnamese friends include a few stamps for their replies.

Sending Mail

Post offices all over the country usually keep long hours, about 6 am to 8 pm including weekends and public holidays (even Tet).

Items mailed from anywhere other than large towns and cities are likely to take over a month to arrive at their international destination. Air mail service from Ho Chi Minh City and Hanoi takes approximately five to 10 days to most Western countries provided it readily passes 'security' (ie, it's not considered subversive). The express mail service (EMS) available in Ho Chi Minh City and Hanoi can take as little as four days.

EMS is available to most developed countries and a few less developed ones such as Mozambique and Ethiopia. It's perhaps twice as fast to use EMS rather than regular air mail, and the big advantage is that the letter or small parcel will be registered. There is also domestic EMS between Ho Chi Minh City and Hanoi promising next-day delivery, and this service also exists in some smaller cities such as Danang and Nha Trang. The domestic EMS rates are very reasonable; US$0.35 for a letter weighing under 20g.

Foreigners wishing to send parcels out of Vietnam sometimes have to deal with time-consuming inspections of the contents, but this is happening less frequently now. The most important thing is to keep the parcel small. If it's documents only, you should be OK. Sending out video tapes and the like can be problematic.

Private Couriers Private couriers deliver both international and domestic small parcels or documents. For international service, couriers charge approximately US$35 to US$60 (depending on the destination) for the first 500g and about US$5 to US$15 for each additional 500g. The domestic service tariff is about US$20 for the first 500g and US$5 for each additional 500g.

See the Hanoi and Ho Chi Minh City chapters for listings of private couriers.

Freight Forwarders Planning on shipping home Vietnamese furniture or moving an entire household? For this you need the services of an international mover.

In Vietnam, much of this business goes to Saigon Van (☎ 08 821 3002), 76 Đ Ngo Duc Ke, District 1 in Ho Chi Minh City, or (☎ 04 943 0610), 21 Pho Ngo Van So in Hanoi. This company is associated with the international company Atlas Van Lines.

Another competitor in Hanoi is JVK International Movers (☎ 04 826 0334), 5A Pho Yet Kieu. For shipping services, contact ILM Vietnam Transport (☎ 04 533 0330), 181B Pho Tay Son, Hanoi.

Receiving Mail

Every city, town, village and rural subdistrict in Vietnam has some sort of post office. All post offices are marked 'Buu Dien' – some with bright neon signage.

Mail delivery is mostly reliable and fast. However, this reliability becomes questionable if your envelope or package contains something worth stealing. One of our correspondents in Ho Chi Minh City reports that his mail was opened and newspaper clippings about the Vietnamese economy were removed. Normal letters and postcards should be fine.

Poste restante works well in post offices in Hanoi and Ho Chi Minh City. Elsewhere, it's less certain – the smaller the town the less likely the service will exist. Foreigners have to pay a US$0.04 service charge for each letter they pick up from poste restante.

Receiving even a small package from abroad can cause a headache and large ones will produce a migraine. If you're lucky, customs will clear the package and the post office clerks will simply let you take it away. If you're unlucky, customs will demand an inspection at which you must be present. In that case, the post office will give you a written notice that you must take to the customs office along with your passport. In Ho Chi Minh City, the customs office for incoming parcels is in the rear of the post office building. The procedure requires you to fill out numerous forms, pay some small fees (around US$1 in total) and hand over your passport with the hope that it's eventually returned to you along with the parcel.

continued on page 85

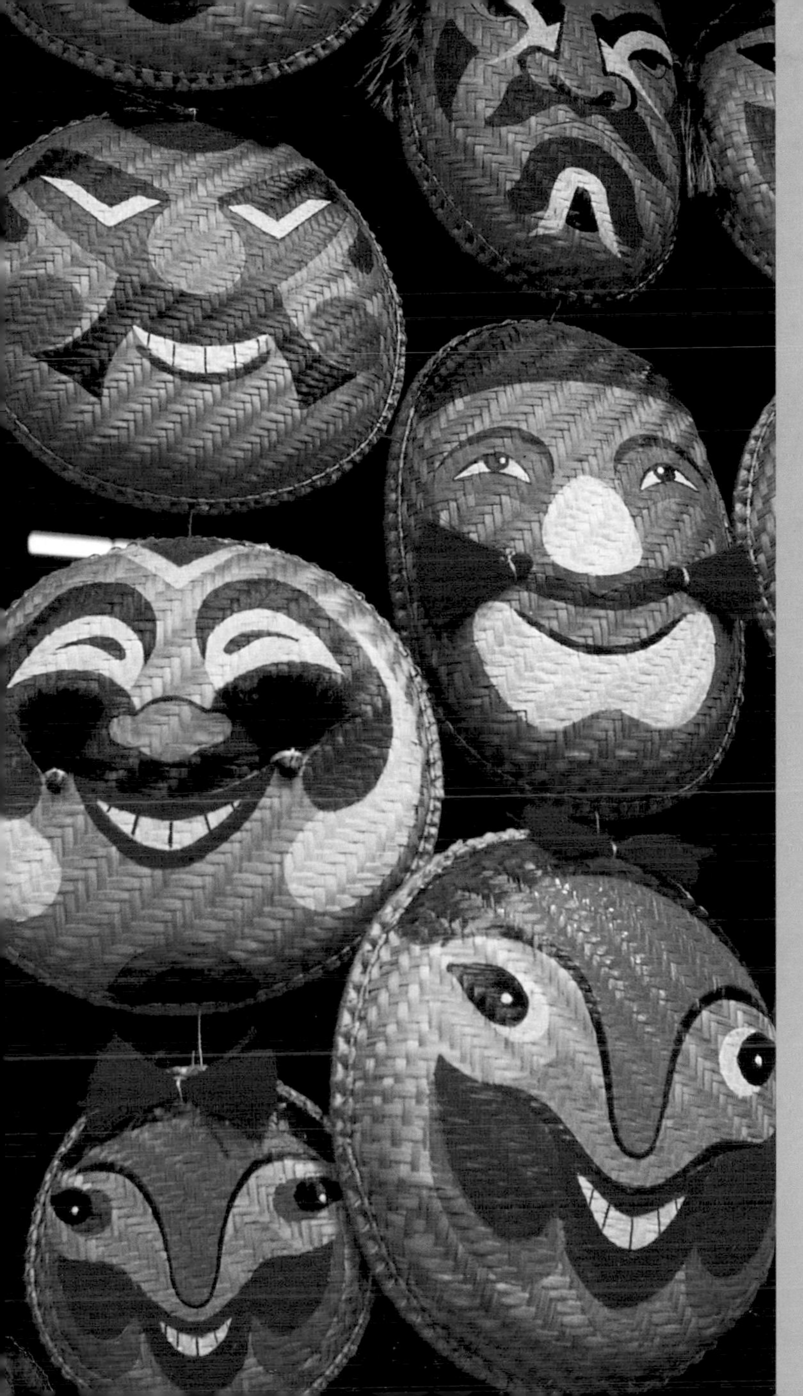

The Tet Festival

MASON FLORENCE

JULIET COOMBE

JOHN BORTHWICK

Title page: Grins and grimaces – Tet festival masks (photograph by Mason Florence).

Top: Incense sticks are hot property during the Tet festival.

Middle: Ghost money offerings to appease the ancestors.

Bottom: Banned substance – firecracker boom sticks.

MASON FLORENCE

The Tet Nguyen Dan (Festival of the First Day) announces Lunar New Year, and is the most important date in the Vietnamese festival calendar. Commonly known as Tet, it is much more than your average Gregorian New Year's celebration; it's a time when families reunite in the hope of good fortune for the coming year and ancestral spirits are welcomed back into the family home. And Tet is everybody's birthday; on this day everyone becomes one year older.

The festival falls some time between 19 January and 20 February on the Western calendar. The exact dates vary from year to year due to differences between the lunar and solar calendars. The first three days after New Year's day are the official holidays but many people take the whole week off, particularly in the south.

Tet rites begin seven days before New Year's Day. This is when the Tao Quan – the three Spirits of the Hearth found in the kitchen of every home – ascend to the heavens to report on the past year's events to the Jade Emperor. Often these kitchen gods are described as a single person and may be called Ong Tao, Ong Lo or Ong Vua Bep. The Tao Quan ride fish on their journey to heaven, so on this day people all over Vietnam release live carp into rivers and lakes. Altars, laden with offerings of food, fresh water, flowers, betel and more live carp for celestial transport, are assembled in preparation for the gods' departure, all in the hope of receiving a favourable report and ensuring good luck for the family in the coming year.

Other rituals performed during pre-Tet week include visiting cemeteries and inviting the spirits of dead relatives home for the celebrations. Absent family members start to make their way home so the whole family can celebrate Tet under the same roof. All loose ends are tied up so that the new year can be started with a clean slate; debts are paid and absolutely everything is cleaned, including ancestors' graves.

Much like the tradition of Christmas trees in the West, Vietnamese homes are decorated with trees at this time. A New Year's tree *(cay neu)* is constructed to ward off evil spirits. Kumquat trees are popular throughout the country, while branches of pink *dao* peach blossoms grace houses in the north, and yellow *mai* apricot blossoms can be found in southern and central Vietnamese homes. For a spectacular sight, go to ĐL Nguyen Hue in Ho Chi Minh City, much of which is taken over by the annual Tet flower market at this time of year. In Hanoi, the area around Pho Hang Dau and Pho Hang Ma is transformed into a massive peach blossom and kumquat tree market. Or be dazzled by the blocked-off streets near the Dong Xuan market, ablaze with red and gold decorations for sale. A few days before the New Year is heralded in, the excitement at these markets is almost palpable as people rush to buy their food and decorations, and motorbikes laden with blossoms and two or three kumquat trees jam the streets.

This is an expensive time of year for most families with so much to buy (the kumquat trees alone cost around US$20). In addition, children

Tao Quan

One legend behind the Tao Quan is based on the story of a woodcutter and his wife. The couple lived happily together until the man was driven to drink through the worry of being unable to provide enough food for them both. He became violent towards his wife and eventually she could no longer bear it and left him. After some time she met and married a local hunter, forgetting the terrors of her previous marriage.

One day, a few days before the Vietnamese New Year, the woman received a beggar at the front door while the hunter was searching for game. She offered the beggar a meal and soon realised that he was her former husband. Panicked by the sound of her current husband returning, she hid the beggar under a pile of hay. The hungry hunter promptly set the hay alight and placed his recently caught game on it to roast, unaware that there was someone there. Fearing that the hunter might kill the woman if he cried out, the beggar remained silently burning to death. The poor woman was torn with grief, realising that her former husband was dying for her sake. With little hesitation, she threw herself onto the fire to die with him. The confused hunter thought that he must have driven her to such desperation, so he too jumped into the fire, unable to contemplate life without her.

All three perished, an act of devotion which so deeply touched the Jade Emperor that he made them gods. In their new role, they were to look out for the wellbeing of the Vietnamese people from the vantage point of the hearth.

are given red envelopes containing substantial amounts of *li xi*, or lucky money. The Vietnamese see all this expense as being necessary to gain favour with the gods for the coming year.

Like special events anywhere, a large part of the celebrations revolve around food. A Tet staple is *banh chung*. These intriguing square parcels are made of fatty pork and bean paste, sandwiched between two layers of glutinous *nep* rice. They're wrapped in green *dong* (a leaf resembling that of a banana tree) and tied with bamboo twine, giving them the appearance of a present. You'll see mountains of them everywhere and will no doubt be invited to taste one. A similar food which is round in shape, *banh day*, is served in the south.

Banh chung is often accompanied by *mang*, a dish made with boiled bamboo shoots and fried pork marinated in *nuoc mam* (fish sauce). Many visitors don't appreciate these dishes but they have a symbolic significance for Vietnamese people, their simple ingredients being reminders of past hard times. For sweets, *mut* – candied fruit such as sugared apples, plums and even tomatoes – is popular. Fresh fruit is another essential element of Tet: red dragon fruit and watermelons are big favourites.

On New Year's Eve, the Tao Quan return to earth. At the stroke of midnight, all problems from the previous year are left behind and jubilant celebrations ensue. The goal seems to be to make as much noise as possible: drums and percussion are popular, and so were firecrackers until their ban in 1995 (although you might still hear recordings of exploding firecrackers blaring from cassette players). Any noise will do really, as long as it provides a suitable welcome back for the gods while scaring off any evil spirits that may be loitering.

The events of New Year's Day are very important as they're believed to affect the course of life in the year ahead. People take extra care not to be rude or show anger. Other no-noes include sewing, sweeping, swearing and breaking things; all acts that might attract bad spirits. Similarly, it's crucial that the first visitor of the year to each household is suitable. They're usually male – best of all is a wealthy married man with several children. Foreigners are sometimes welcomed as the first to enter the house, although not always, so it's wise not to visit any Vietnamese house on the first day of Tet unless you are explicitly invited (and make sure you confirm the time they want you to arrive). Those blacklisted as first visitors include single middle-aged women, and anyone who has lost their job, had an accident or lost a family member during the previous year – all signs of bad luck. Such unfortunates and their families can be ostracised from their community and sometimes stay home during the whole Tet period.

Unique to the south is the Unicorn Dance – a procession led by people carrying brightly coloured square flags followed by the unicorn itself (several men dressed up in tight uniforms) and then another mythical creature called Dia (a man with a moonlike face-mask). At the tail end come the drums and cymbals. The procession begins early on the first morning of Tet, and systematically visits every home and shop in its area, looking for donations. The Vietnamese are generous in their gifts as the unicorn is regarded as a symbol of wealth, peace and prosperity. However, they make the unicorn work for its rewards: homeowners or

Banh Chung

The fable behind banh chung cakes originated with King Hung Vuong the Sixth, who fathered 22 sons, all worthy heirs. In order to select his successor, the king instructed them to search the globe for delicacies unknown to him. Whoever returned with the best dish would rule the kingdom. Twenty-one of them did as they were told, but one young prince, Lang Lieu, remained in the palace with no idea of where to start looking. He was filled with gloom until one night a genie appeared in his dreams. 'Man cannot live without rice', she said, and told him the recipe for banh chung. When the time came for the king to taste the 22 dishes, he was bitterly disappointed with the 21 from the princes who had travelled abroad. Finally he tasted the rice creations of Lang Lieu and was amazed at how delicious they were. When told of the genie's assistance with the recipe, the king was impressed with this divine support and named Lang Lieu his successor.

shopkeepers often present their donations tied to a pole suspended from the 1st floor balcony or window. To reach the gifts, the unicorn is elevated through a human pyramid until it can swallow the prize in its mouth.

In Hanoi, a popular activity during the weeks that follow Tet is *co nguoi*, or human chess. All the human chess pieces come from the same village, Lien Xa, in the northern province of Ha Tay. They're chosen because they're attractive, young, unmarried and have had no recent deaths in their families or other signs of bad luck. The form of chess played is Chinese. Although the pieces and moves are different from Western chess, the objective remains the same: to capture the opposing leader, in this case the 'general'. The final is held at the Temple of De Thich, who was the right-hand man of the Jade Emperor, and the celestial God of Chess.

Apart from New Year's Eve itself, Tet is not a particularly boisterous celebration. It's closer to a Western Christmas day, a quiet family affair. Difficulty in booking transport and accommodation aside, this is an excellent time to visit the country, especially to witness the contrasting frenzied activity before the New Year and the calm (and quiet streets!) afterwards. Wherever you're staying, it's more than likely you'll be invited to join in the celebrations.

New Year's Day is due to fall on the following dates: 24 January 2001, 12 February 2002 and 1 February 2003.

If you are visiting Vietnam during Tet, be sure you learn this phrase: *Chúc mùng nam mói!* (Happy New Year!).

Michelle Bennett

continued from page 80

Your package will then be opened in front of you and inspected, but don't think that's all there is to it. Your parcel then gets packed up again and disappears into some other office along with your forms, passport and another fee. You take a seat in the waiting room, and after a few hours somebody will hopefully call your name. At that point, all your possessions should be returned to you, along with some more forms which you must get stamped before you and your package can leave the building.

If you are particularly unlucky, customs may decide that you must pay import duty. If your parcel contains books, documents, video tapes, computer disks or dangerous goods, it's possible that a further inspection will be required. This could take anywhere from a few days to a few weeks. Presumably, you won't have to spend the entire time in the waiting room while this is being done.

Telephone

Useful Phone Numbers The following phone services are available, but don't be surprised if the person answering only speaks Vietnamese:

Ambulance	☎ 115
Directory Assistance	☎ 116
Fire International Operator	☎ 110
International Prefix	☎ 00
Police	☎ 113
Time Information	☎ 117

Also, every city has a general information service (☎ 1080) that has information on everything from phone numbers and train and plane timetables, to exchange rates and the latest football scores. It even provides marriage counselling or bed time lullabies for your child – no kidding! You can usually be connected to an operator who speaks English or French.

International Calls International telecommunications charges from Vietnam are among the highest in the world, so unless you have some matter of earthshaking importance, it's better to wait until you reach Hong Kong, Bangkok or Singapore to call the loved ones at home. Thankfully email is widely available in Vietnam now.

If you're living in Vietnam, you may be tempted to subscribe to a callback service, which would greatly reduce your phone bill. However, Vietnam is one of the few countries that has made this illegal and there are draconian penalties if you get caught.

International and domestic long-distance calls can be booked at many hotels, but it's expensive. A cheaper alternative is to book long-distance phone calls from the post office. Operator-assisted calls will incur a three-minute charge – even if you only talk for one minute – at an inflated rate. As in most countries, the cheapest way to make a long-distance call is to dial direct.

Foreigners are not permitted to make international reverse-charge (collect) calls. However, Vietnamese nationals can. Why? Because the Directorate General of Posts & Telecommunications (DGPT) earns less from a reverse-charge call than from a call paid for in Vietnam. However, since most Vietnamese cannot possibly afford to pay for an international call, they are permitted to make reverse charge calls to their overseas relatives (the assumption being that those relatives will probably send money).

This means that if your credit cards or travellers cheques are stolen, you are unable to make a collect call to report the loss to the issuing company. At best this is a major nuisance – it could prove disastrous if all your cash is stolen and you need to call abroad for help.

The cheapest and simplest way to make an International Direct Dial (IDD) call is with a telephone card, known as a 'UniphoneKad', available from the telephone company. UniphoneKads can only be used in special telephones that are mainly found in Ho Chi Minh City, usually in the lobbies of major hotels. The cards are issued in four denominations; 30,000d (US$2.30), 60,000d (US$4.60), 150,000d (US$11.50) and 300,000d (US$23). The 150,000d and 300,000d cards can be used to make both domestic and international calls, while the

Provincial Area Codes

no	province	capital	area code
1	LaiChau	Dien Bien Phu	☎023
2	Lao Cai (21)*	Lao Cai	☎020
3	Ha Giang	Ha Giang	☎019
4	Cao Bang	Cao Bang	☎026
5	Lang Son	Lang Son	☎025
6	Quang Ninh	Halong City	☎033
7	Bac Giang (13)	Bac Giang	☎0240
8	Thai Nguyen (20)	Thai Nguyen	☎0280
9	Bac Kan (20)	Bac Kan	☎0281
10	Tuyen Quang	Tuyen Quang	☎027
11	Yen Bai (21)	Yen Bai	☎029
12	Son La	Son Lo	☎022
13	Phu Tho	Viet Tri	☎0210
14	Vinh Phuc	Vinh Yen	☎0211
16	Bac Ninh (13)	Bac Ninh	☎0241
17	Hai Duong	Hai Duong	☎0320
19	Thai Binh (17)	Thai Binh	☎036
20	Hung Yen	Hung Yen	☎0321
21	Ha Tay	Ha Dong	☎034
22	Hoa Binh	Hoa Binh	☎018
23	Ha Nam	Ha Nam	☎0351
24	Nam Dinh	Nam Dinh	☎0350
25	Ninh Binh (18)	Ninh Binh	☎030
26	Thanh Hoa (36)	Thanh Hoa	☎037
27	Nghe An (37)	Vinh	☎038
28	Ha Tinh (38)	Ha Tinh	☎039
29	Quang Binh (39/40)	Dong Hoi	☎052
30	Quang Tri (39/40)	Dong Ha	☎053
31	Thua Thien-Hue (39/40)	Hue	☎054
33	Quang Nam (43)	Tam Ky	☎510
34	Quang Ngai (47)	Quang Ngai	☎055
35	Kon Tum (46)	Kon Tum	☎060
36	Binh Dinh (44)	Qui Nhon	☎056
37	Gia Lai	Pleiku	☎059
38	Phu Yen (45)	Tuy Hoa	☎057
39	Dac Lac (47)	Buon Ma Thuot	☎050
40	Khanh Hoa (45)	Nha Trang	☎058
41	Ninh Thuan	Phan Rang	☎068
42	Lam Dong (49)	Dalat	☎063
43	Binh Phuoc (61)	Dong Xoai	☎0651
44	Tay Ninh (70)	Tay Ninh	☎066
45	Binh Duong (61)	Thu Dau Mot	☎0650
46	Dong Nai(60)	Bien Hoa	☎061
47	Binh Thuan (48)	Phan Thiet	☎062
48	Ba Ria (78)	Vung Tau	☎064
50	Long An (62)	Tan An	☎072
51	Tien Giang (63)	Mytho	☎073
52	Ben Tre (71)	Ben Tre	☎075
53	Tra Vinh	Tra Vinh	☎074
54	Vinh Long (64)	Vinh Long	☎070
55	Dong Thap (66)	Cao Lanh	☎067
56	An Giang (67)	Long Xuyen	☎076
57	Kien Giang	Rach Gia	☎077
58	Cantho (65)	Cantho	☎071
59	Soc Trang	Soc Trang	☎079
60	Bac Lieu (69)	Bac Lieu	☎0781
61	Camau (69)	Camau	☎0780

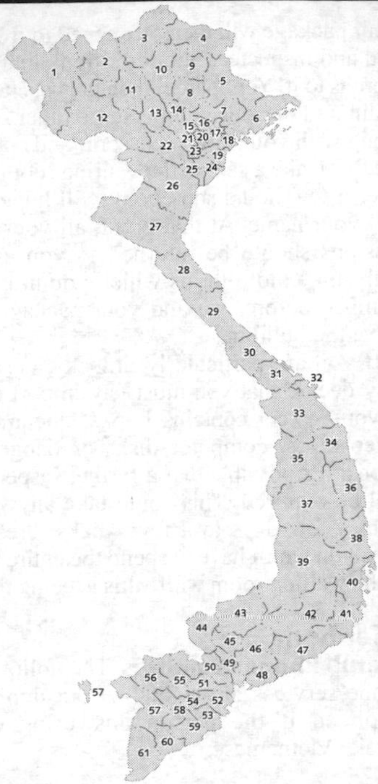

no	municipality	area code
15	Hanoi (29, 30, 31, 32)	☎04
18	Haiphong City (15)	☎031
32	Danang City (43)	☎0511
49	Ho Chi Minh City (Saigon) 50 (govt) 51/55 (private)	☎08

*numbers in brackets represent the vehicle license plate code for each province.

30,000d and 60,000d cards work for domestic calls only.

From our experience, we have found that international calls cost more than the advertised rate (perhaps there is some sort of hidden tax) – this applies even when you use a phone card. There is a 15% discount for calls placed between 11 pm and 7 am and on Sunday and public holidays.

Lonely Planet's eKno Communication Card provides competitive international calls. For information on joining and accessing the service, see the eKno Web site at www.ekno.lonelyplanet.com.

Domestic Calls Except for some special numbers (eg, fire brigade and directory assistance), all phone numbers in Hanoi and Ho Chi Minh City have seven digits. Outside those two cities, phone numbers have six digits.

Area codes in Vietnam are assigned according to province (see the Provincial Area Codes table following).

Local calls can usually be made from any hotel or restaurant phone and are often free – you should, however, confirm this with your hotel so you don't have any unpleasant surprises when you check out.

Domestic long-distance calls are reasonably priced and are cheaper if you dial direct.

Any call between Hanoi and Ho Chi Minh City at the full daytime rate will cost approximately US$0.45 per minute. An operator-assisted call is around US$0.80 per minute and there is a three-minute minimum charge time. You can save up to 20% by calling between 10 pm and 5 am.

Cellular Phones As in other developing countries, Vietnam is putting a lot of money into the cellular network simply because it's cheaper than laying thousands of kilometres of copper or fibre-optic cables. Aside from offering the obvious advantages of portability and convenience, cellular phones bypass Vietnam's decrepit wiring system, which plagues conventional telephone calls with crackling static.

Resident foreigners can apply for a cellular phone in Hanoi, Ho Chi Minh City and other major cities. Foreign tourists can make a cellular call using their own phones provided they are on the GSM system and acquire a card for use in Vietnam.

Rental mobile phones with pre-paid cards recently debuted in Vietnam. Companies offering cellular service are:

Hanoi
VMS MobiFone (☎ 833 4448) 54 Pho Lang Ha
HP (☎ 943 2125) 73 Pho Hue
Ho Chi Minh City
VMS MobiFone (☎ 822 8171) 123 Đ Hai Ba Trung, District 1
Vina Phone (☎ 824 5168) 53C Đ Nguyen Du, District 1
Phones For Rent (mobile ☎ 091-802787)

Fax

Most post offices and hotels offer domestic and international fax, (and telegraph and telex) services. Hotels are likely to charge more than the post office.

If you happen to have your own portable computer with a built-in fax modem, it's tempting to attach it to any available phone line and send a fax. However, this is illegal – the Vietnamese government insists that all fax machines be registered and that includes computer fax modems.

Email & Internet Access

There's nothing like sending a postcard to the folks back home, but travelling with a portable computer is also a great way to stay in touch. But unless you know what you are doing it is fraught with potential problems. If you plan to carry your notebook or palmtop computer with you, remember that the power supply voltage in the countries you visit may vary from that at home, risking damage to your equipment. The best investment is a universal AC adaptor for your appliance, which will enable you to plug it in anywhere without frying the innards. You'll also need a plug adaptor for each country you visit – often it's easiest to buy these before you leave home.

It is only recently that public-access online services have returned to Vietnam. In the summer of 1997, the government authorities, perhaps feeling threatened by the prospect of too much information flowing freely from the outside world, closed down all Internet cafes (and confiscated computers along the way). Fortunately, they have re-emerged, and it seems they're here to stay. Access to online services is now widely available in major tourist centres such as Hanoi, Ho Chi Minh City, Hoi An, Hué, Danang, Nha Trang and Dalat. You'll find everything from trendy cybercafes to computer terminals in the lobbies of hotels and guesthouses. You can also find public Internet access in some Vietnamese post offices.

As most travellers in Vietnam do not have access to a local Internet Service Provider (ISP) dial-up, most rely on cybercafes and other public access points to collect email. In Vietnam, Hotmail tends to download much slower than Yahoo! Mail. However, either can be sluggish, so you may want to bring a book along to read while you surf. To be sure your account is secure after you leave, always sign out and be sure to check that the 'save password' option is *not* checked.

Unfortunately, popular ISPs, such as CompuServe, America Online and Asia Online, do *not* have local nodes in Vietnam. Tech-heads should note that most cafe proprietors will get upset if you try to change the configuration on their computers to receive your mail.

If you use cybercafes, you'll need to carry three pieces of information with you to enable you to access your Internet mail account: your incoming (POP or IMAP) mail server name, your account name and your password. Your ISP or network supervisor will be able to give you these. Armed with this information, you should be able to access your Internet mail account from any net-connected machine in Vietnam, provided it runs some kind of email software (remember that Netscape and Internet Explorer both have mail modules). It pays to become familiar with the process for doing this before you leave home. Another option is to open a free eKno Web-based email account online at www.ekno.lonelyplanet.com. You can then access your mail from anywhere in the world from any net-connected machine running a standard Web browser.

The cost for Internet access ranges from about US$0.01 to US$0.10 per minute, depending on where you are. Printing usually costs between US$0.08 and US$0.16 per page, and scanning also costs about US$0.16 a page.

INTERNET RESOURCES

The World Wide Web is a rich resource for travellers. You can research your trip, hunt down bargain air fares, book hotels, check on weather conditions or chat with locals and other travellers about the best places to visit (or avoid!).

A great place to start is the Lonely Planet Web site (www.lonelyplanet.com). Here you'll find succinct summaries on travelling to most places on earth, postcards from other travellers, and the Thorn Tree bulletin board, where you can ask questions before you go or dispense advice when you get back. You can also find travel news and updates to many of our most popular guidebooks, and the subWWWay section links you to useful travel resources elsewhere on the Web.

Ironically some of the best online information about Vietnam originates in its old nemesis, the USA. Many online authors are Overseas Vietnamese living in the USA and elsewhere. The Internet changes from day to day, so anything we can say about Web sites is likely to become dated fast. However, there are a few good sites worth recommending.

Perhaps the best all-round site on contemporary Vietnam is Destination Vietnam (www.destinationvietnam.com). Published for years in print form, DV has recently made the full shift over to an electronic magazine. It is a one-stop Vietnam information zone covering travel, art, history, culture and even adoption. The site has an online contemporary Vietnamese art gallery, subsections that delve deeper into specific topics and enough interesting links to keep you wired for weeks.

Another excellent place to begin is the well-established Vietnam Adventures Online (www.vietnamadventures.com). It is full of practical travel information and features monthly adventures and special travel deals.

Vietnam Online (www.vietnamonline.com) was launched in 1995 and gets lots of hits. The site is loaded with useful travel lore and boasts good coverage on employment and business opportunities in Vietnam.

Vietnam Now (www.vietnamnow.com) is also dedicated to travel in Vietnam, and has an interesting selection of links and a travellers' message board.

Using the aforementioned sites, you should be able to link to the *Democracy Newsletter*, Miss Vietnam Tet Pageant, Vietnamese photo collections, Vietnamese Professional Society and so on.

BOOKS

To pass the time and preserve your sanity, take at least a few books with you. Purchasing books within Vietnam is a hit or miss (mostly miss) affair.

Your local bookshop or library at home is best placed to advise on the availability of the following recommendations.

Lonely Planet

Cyclists, hikers and other back-country explorers may want to score a copy of Lonely Planet's *Thailand, Vietnam, Laos & Cambodia Road Atlas*.

Our *Vietnamese Phrasebook* is not only educational, but will also give you something to do during those long bus rides.

If you're after the detailed ins and outs of Ho Chi Minh City and Hanoi, there are LP city guides to both *Ho Chi Minh City* and *Hanoi*.

LP's *South-East Asia on a shoestring* has general travel information for the region.

LP's *World Food Vietnam*, is a compact, illustrated guide to eating and drinking your way though Vietnam, and has a handy eating and shopping vocabulary.

Guidebooks

There are a number of locally produced English (and some French) guides for sale at bookshops Vietnam. See Bookshops in the Hanoi and Ho Chi Minh City chapters for where to find them.

Travel

Fragrant Palm Leaves (Parallax Press, 1998) is a remarkable, poetic collection of Zen monk and peace crusader Thich Nhat Hanh's journal entries. Written in the 1960s, he wrote both in Vietnam and in the USA.

Sparring with Charlie: Motorbiking down the Ho Chi Minh Trail by Christopher Hunt is a recent light-hearted travelogue about the modern Vietnam.

In a similar vein is *Ten Years After* by Tim Page. This impressive book boasts '12 months worth of photos taken 10 years after the war'. Page also returned to Vietnam to write *Derailed in Uncle Ho's Victory Garden*.

Vietnam Notebook is an insightful collection of essays by Murray Hiebert, the Hanoi correspondent for the *Far Eastern Economic Review*.

A Dragon Apparent is about author Norman Lewis' fascinating journeys through Vietnam, Laos and Cambodia in 1950.

Karen Muller's *Hitchhiking in Vietnam* (1998) is a travelogue detailing a woman's tumultuous seven-month journey through Vietnam. You can access her Web site by searching the homepage of www.pbs.org.

Wildlife

Useful books about Vietnam's wildlife are few and far between, and unfortunately some of the better Vietnamese language books are out of print. *A Guide to the Birds of Thailand* (Philip Round & Boonsong Lakagul, Saha Kam Bhaet Company, 1991) covers the majority if not all of Vietnam's birds. It's particularly relevant to the bird species in the southern and central regions of Vietnam.

A Field Guide to the Birds of South-East Asia, by Ben King, Martin Woodcock and Edward Dickinson is slightly out of date and difficult to use, but it gives thorough Vietnam coverage. These two books are not available in Vietnam, but you should be able to find them in Bangkok (try Asia Books).

History & Politics

Shadows and Wind, by journalist Robert Templer is a snappily written exploration of contemporary Vietnam, covering everything from Ho Chi Minh personality cults to Vietnam's rock n' roll youngsters.

Vietnam: Politics, Economics and Society by Melanie Beresford gives a good overview of post-reunification Vietnam.

During the colonial period, French researchers wrote quite a number of works on Vietnam's cultural history and archaeology that remain unsurpassed. Several good books on the Chams are *Les États Hinduisés d'Indochine et d'Indonésie* by Georges Coedes (1928), *L'Art du Champa et Son Evolution* by Philippe Stern (1942) and *Le Royaume du Champa* by Georges Maspero (1928). *Les Arts du Champa: Architecture et Sculpture* by Tran Ky Phuong, curator of the Cham Museum in Danang and Vietnam's foremost scholar of the Chams, was published in the early 1990s.

The Birth of Vietnam by Keith Weller Taylor tackles the country's early history under Chinese rule.

The Vietnamese Gulag by Doan Van Toai tells of one man's experiences in the post-reunification re-education camps.

For a very readable account of Vietnamese history from prehistoric times until the fall of Ho Chi Minh City, try Stanley Karnow's *Vietnam: A History*, which was published as a companion volume to the American Public Broadcasting System series *Vietnam: A Television History*.

A number of biographies of Ho Chi Minh have been written, including *Ho Chi Minh: A Political Biography* by Jean Lacouture and *Ho* by David Halberstam.

A most scholarly work on Caodaism is *Caodai Spiritism: A Study of Religion in Vietnamese Society* by Victor L Oliver.

An excellent reference work is *Vietnam's Famous Ancient Pagodas (Viet Nam Danh Lam Co Tu)*, which is written in Vietnamese, English, French and Chinese. The publisher is the Social Sciences Publishing House and you should be able to find copies in Ho Chi Minh City and Hanoi.

Fiction

Perhaps the most popular and best known contemporary Vietnamese author is dissident writer Duong Thu Huong, whose books are now banned in Vietnam for their 'subversive' content. *Paradise of the Blind*, the first Vietnamese novel to be published in the USA, is set in a rural northern village and a Hanoi slum and recalls the lives of three women and the hardships they face over a span 40 years. Huong's *Novel Without A Name* is a captivating story of the horrors and losses of the American War from the perspective of North Vietnamese soldiers. Her latest work, *Memories of a Pure Spring*, tells the powerful tale of a romance between the leader of a wartime musical troupe and a singer in the group he marries.

Pulitzer Prize winning author Robert Owen Butler's *A Good Scent From a Strange Mountain* is a captivating series of 15 stories written from a first person perspective of Overseas Vietnamese living in the southern United States. Butler has been widely praised for his astute understanding of Vietnamese people and culture.

The Sacred Willow by Duong Van Mai Elliot, spans four tumultuous generations of an upper-class Vietnamese family. This enlightening historical memoir traces French colonisation, WWII and the wars with the French and Americans.

Vietnam: A Traveller's Literary Companion is an engaging collection of stories by Vietnamese writers, ranging from folklore and the tragedy of war to love and family ties.

The Other Side of Heaven is a unique and well-balanced anthology of postwar fiction, alternating between Vietnamese and American writers.

Two other laudable collections of contemporary fiction from Vietnamese writers are Le Minh Khue's *The Stars, The Earth, The River*, a set of stories on politics and war told from a female perspective, and *Behind the Red Mist* by Ho Anh Thai, one of Vietnam's most important post-war generation authors.

Graham Greene's 1954 novel *The Quiet American*, which is set during the last days of French rule, is probably the most famous Western work of fiction on Vietnam. Much of the action takes place at Ho Chi Minh City's Continental Hotel and at the Caodai complex in Tay Ninh.

The Lover by Marguerite Duras is a fictional love story set in Saigon during the 1930s, and has been made into a major motion picture.

Hill Tribes

Ethnic Minorities of Vietnam by Dang Nghiem Van presents an English language ethnographic overview of Vietnam's ethnic population and is available in major bookstores in Hanoi and Ho Chi Minh City.

For a deeper study, look for Joachim Schliesinger's two volume *Hill Tribes of Vietnam*. Volume 1 provides an introduction and overview, while Volume 2 introduces detailed profiles of the various hill tribe groups. Asia Books in Bangkok is a good place to look for these titles.

Franco-Viet Minh War

Worthwhile books covering this topic include Peter M Dunn's *The First Vietnam War* and two works by Bernard B Fall: *Street Without Joy: Indochina at War 1946–54* (1961) and *Hell in a Very Small Place: The Siege of Dien Bien Phu* (1967).

American War

What the Americans call the Vietnam War, the Vietnamese call the American War. Whatever you call it, there are whole libraries of books on the topic.

The earliest days of US involvement in Indochina – when the US Office of Strategic Services (OSS; predecessor of the CIA) was providing funding and weapons to Ho Chi Minh at the end of WWII – are recounted in Archimedes L Patti's riveting work *Why Vietnam?*. Patti was the head of the OSS team in Vietnam and was at Ho Chi Minh's side when he declared Vietnam independent in 1945.

The Making of a Quagmire by David Halberstam (1965) is one of the best accounts of America's effort in the war during the early 1960s.

Three of the finest essays on the war are collected in *The Real War* by Jonathan Schell.

An overview of the conflict is provided by George C Herring's *America's Longest War*, 2nd edition.

Fire in the Lake by Francis Fitzgerald (1972) is a superb history of American involvement in Vietnam; it received the Pulitzer Prize, the National Book Award and the Bancroft Prize for History.

Perhaps the best Vietnamese autobiographical account of the war is Le Ly Hayslip's captivating *When Heaven and Earth Changed Places*.

A highly acclaimed biographical account of the US war effort is *A Bright Shining Lie: John Paul Vann & America in Vietnam* by Neil Sheehan; it won both the Pulitzer Prize and the National Book Award.

Another fine biography is Tim Bowden's *One Crowded Hour,* which details the life of Australian film journalist Neil Davis. He was responsible for shooting some of the most famous footage of the war, including that of the North Vietnamese tank crashing through the gate of the Presidential Palace in Saigon in 1975.

Two good accounts of the fall of South Vietnam are *The Fall of Saigon* by David Butler and *55 Days: The Fall of South Vietnam* by Alan Dawson.

Perhaps the best book about the fall is *Decent Interval* by Frank Snepp. Except for pirated editions sold in Vietnam itself, it's out of print and for a very interesting reason. The author was the CIA's chief strategy analyst in Vietnam, but he broke his contract with the CIA by publishing this book (CIA agents are prohibited from publishing anything about their work). The US government sued Snepp and all the royalties that he earned from book sales were confiscated. Copies of the book can still be found in some public libraries.

Brother Enemy by Nayan Chanda is highly recommended. This is not actually a book about the war, but about its immediate aftermath. Chanda was a correspondent for the *Far Eastern Economic Review* and was in Saigon when it fell.

An oft-cited analysis of where US military strategy in Vietnam went wrong is *On Strategy* by Colonel Harry G Summers Jr.

The Pentagon Papers, a massive, top-secret history of the US role in Indochina, was commissioned by Defence Secretary

Robert McNamara in 1967 and published amid a great furore by the *New York Times* in 1971.

A story mostly neglected by writers is the painful experience of the fatherless Amerasian children left behind in Vietnam after 1975. The whole sordid tale is told in unforgettable detail by Thomas Bass in *Vietnamerica*.

The coffee-table book *Requiem* (1997) features a powerful collection of images shot by combat photographers (both foreign and South and North Vietnamese), who died while on assignment in Vietnam and Indochina.

Australia Australia's involvement in the American War is covered in *Australia's Vietnam*, a collection of essays edited by Peter King; *Australia's War in Vietnam* by Frank Frost; Gregory Pemberton's *All the Way: Australia's Road to Vietnam*; and John J Coe's *Desperate Praise: The Australians in Vietnam*.

Soldiers' Experiences One of the finest books about the war is *The Sorrow of War* by Vietnamese writer Bao Ninh. The author fought for North Vietnam, but his book is by no means a piece of anti-American propaganda. On the contrary, he's cynical about the entire war and its avowed goals, and neither side comes out looking very good. The book won a literature prize in Vietnam in 1993, and English-language copies are available in Hanoi and Ho Chi Minh City. However, Vietnamese-language editions of the book are banned in Vietnam!

Viet Cong Memoir by Truong Nhu Tang is the autobiography of a Viet Cong cadre who later became disenchanted with post-1975 Vietnam.

Some of the better books about what it was like to be an American soldier in Vietnam include *Born on the 4th of July* by Ron Kovic; the superb *Dispatches* by Michael Herr; *Chickenhawk* by Robert Mason, a stunning autobiographical account of the helicopter war; *A Rumor of War* by Philip Caputo; and *Nam* by Mark Baker. *A Piece of My Heart* by Keith Walker tells the stories of American women who served in Vietnam.

Chained Eagle by Everett Alvarez Jr, a US pilot who was imprisoned in North Vietnam for 8½ years, recounts the horrors endured by American POWs.

Brothers in Arms by William Broyles Jr is the story of the 1984 visit to Vietnam by an American journalist who served as an infantry lieutenant during the war.

Viet Cong Memoir by Truong Nhu Tang is the autobiography of a Viet Cong cadre who later became disenchanted with post-1975 Vietnam.

FILMS

Contemporary Vietnamese

In recent years Vietnamese cinema has evolved from the realm of propaganda to a world that more closely reflects the lives of modern Vietnamese people and the issues they face. Though strict government control and cultural censorship remain a reality, Vietnamese film makers today operate in a far more tolerant environment, one that has allowed an increase in film production and cinematic achievement.

The flurry of contemporary films by Vietnamese directors span a wide range of themes ranging from warfare to modern romance.

In Nguyen Khac's *The Retired General* (1988), the central character copes with readjusting from his soldierly purpose during the American War to life as a civilian family man; symbolising Vietnam's difficult transition from wartime to the post-war era of new economic reforms.

Returning to Ngo Thuy, a recent production by directors Le Manh Thich and Do Khanh Toan, revisits and pays homage to the women of Ngo Thuy village. In 1971, at the height of the American War, these women were the subject of a widely shown propaganda film aimed at encouraging people to join the war effort.

The period of *doi moi* reforms in the 1980s and 1990s has had a powerful influence on Vietnamese film, in particular the effects of the new market economy on women. Popular subject-matter includes how Vietnamese women contend with the struggle between traditional duty and modern desires. Vu Xuan Hung's *Misfortunes*

End (1996), for example, tells the poignant tale of a Vietnamese silk weaver faced with the reality of being deserted by her two-timing husband for an upwardly mobile business woman.

Dang Nhat Minh is perhaps Vietnam's most prolific film maker. In *The Return* (1993), Minh hones in on the complexities of modern relationships, while his *The Girl on the River* (1987) tells the stirring tale of a female journalist who joins an ex-prostitute in search of a former lover and Viet Cong soldier whose life she had saved, and whose heart she'd been promised. His tragic films like *When The Tenth Morning Comes* (1984) and *Nostalgia For Countryland* (1995) tell of the hardships, suffering and loss the Vietnamese people have endured in the recent past. His latest work, *Hanoi – Winter 1946* (1997), recalls Ho Chi Minh's campaign against the French colonialists.

Though few of Vietnam's domestically produced films ever make it outside Vietnam, young Overseas Vietnamese film directors are steadily carving a niche for themselves in the international film industry and snapping up awards at film festivals worldwide. Sadly, few of these films have been screened in Vietnam.

Tran Anh Hung's touching *The Scent of Green Papaya*, (1993) which was filmed in France, celebrates the coming of age of young peasant girl working as a servant for an affluent Saigon family during the 1950's. *Cyclo*, Tran Anh Hung's visually stunning masterpiece, digs to the core of Ho Chi Minh City's gritty underworld. His latest film, the French-language production *La verticale de l'été* (2000) tells the story of three Hanoian sisters and the borderless bonds of kinship.

Vietnamese-American Tony Bui made a splash in 1999 with his exquisite feature debut *Three Seasons* (1999). Set in present-day Ho Chi Minh City, this beautifully made film weaves together the lives of four unlikely characters and their interplay with an American war veteran (fleshed out on the screen by Harvey Keitel) who comes to Vietnam in search of his long lost, grown-up daughter.

Lesser-known Overseas Vietnamese film makers include Van Phan Sylvian, whose post-war documentary *Goodbye Vietnam* focuses on the hardships of Vietnam's mixed race 'Amerasian' children, left behind by Western soldiers and the discrimination they've had to face at home and abroad.

Contemporary Western Films

The Americans might have lost the American war, but Hollywood has spent the last thirty years claiming a moral victory on screen. The best offerings reflect the futility of war, but rarely offer a balanced portrayal of the Vietnamese people. Instead, the focus is on American soldiers as multiple victims – of the Viet Cong, the American government who sent them to war and cheated them of their youth, and their own society who, sadly, shunned them when they returned – often suffering from extreme mental and physical illnesses.

Director Oliver Stone made the fascinating movie *Heaven and Earth*, adapted from Vietnamese-born American immigrant, Le Ly Hayslip's book *When Heaven and Earth Changed Places*. He also directed *Born on the 4th of July* based on Ron Kovic's book.

Some of the most popular war films include *Rambo*, *Full Metal Jacket*, *Platoon*, *The Deer Hunter*, *Good Morning Vietnam*, *Air America* and *Apocalypse Now*.

French films include colonialist nostalgia *Indochine*, (starring Catherine Deneuve), and director Pierre Schoendoerffer's *Dien Bien Phu* – which examines the human side of the French-Vietnamese war and the last days of French rule. Amazingly, it was filmed in Vietnam with the full cooperation of the Vietnamese government.

CD ROMS

'Passage to Vietnam' is a CD produced by Rick Smolan, who created the famed *Day in the Life* series. It is a collection of beautiful photos and narrative.

NEWSPAPERS & MAGAZINES

The *Vietnam News* is an English-language newspaper published daily. Despite the name, it contains relatively little news about Vietnam – most stories (including the sports section) cover foreign news. If you're desperate for some news of the outside world, it will do in a pinch. It's also good for wrapping fish.

One of Vietnam's best magazines is the monthly *Vietnam Economic Times* (VET). It carries strong analysis and provides a well-rounded monthly news summary. VET's free insert, *The Guide*, is an excellent source of leisure information. The supplement can be picked up in hotels, bars and restaurants in larger cities.

You might also look out for the weekly English-language *Vietnam Investment Review*, a broadsheet newspaper. VIR's free supplement, *Time Out*, may be useful for finding what's going on in Ho Chi Minh City and Hanoi, but its focus is on the expat scene and is of little interest to travellers.

The *Saigon Times* is another weekly magazine heavy on business news, with a few light features worth looking at.

Vietnam Today is a monthly magazine published by Communication Indochine Pty Ltd.

Imported newspapers and magazines are readily available in Ho Chi Minh City, Hanoi and some other large cities. Elsewhere it's slim pickings.

RADIO

The Voice of Vietnam broadcasts on short wave, AM and FM for about 18 hours a day. The broadcasts consist mostly of music, but there are also news bulletins in Vietnamese, English, French and Russian. Don't worry if you miss one bulletin – the same edition is broadcast throughout the day and is also printed in the daily *Vietnam News*.

The first broadcast of the Voice of Vietnam took place in 1945. During the American War, it broadcast a great deal of propaganda programming to the South, including special English programs for American GIs. From 1968 to 1976, the Voice of Vietnam used the transmitters of Radio Havana-Cuba to deliver its message direct to the American people.

Vietnamese domestic national radio broadcasts news and music programs from 7 am until 11 pm. In Ho Chi Minh City, frequencies include 610kHz and 820kHz on the AM band, and 78.5MHz, 99.9MHz and 103.3MHz on the FM band.

Visitors wishing to keep up on events in the rest of the world – and in Vietnam itself – may want to bring along a small short-wave receiver. News, music and feature programs in a multitude of languages can easily be picked up, especially at night.

TV

Vietnamese TV began broadcasting in 1970, and it's fair to say that the content hasn't improved much since then. There are currently three channels in Hanoi and Ho Chi Minh City, and two channels elsewhere. Broadcast hours from Monday to Saturday are 9 to 11.30 am and 7 to 11 pm. On Sunday there is an extra broadcast from 3 to 4 pm. English-language news follows the last broadcast sometime after 10 pm. Sometimes soccer or other sports come on at strange hours, for example 1.30 am.

Satellite TV

Satellite TV is now widely available, which is a boon for some foreign visitors. You're most likely to find it in the better hotels and upmarket pubs. Hong Kong's Star TV is the most popular station, along with CNN, the Sports Channel, CNBC Asia and MTV.

VIDEO SYSTEMS

It's hard to know what is Vietnam's official video standard. That's because most new TVs and video players sold in Vietnam are multistandard: PAL, NTSC and SECAM.

PHOTOGRAPHY & VIDEO

Film & Equipment

Colour print film is widely available, but check the expiry date printed on the box. Avoid buying film from outdoor souvenir stalls – the film may have been cooking in the sun for months. Film prices are perfectly reasonable and you really won't save anything by bringing film from abroad.

Colour slide film can be bought in Hanoi and Ho Chi Minh City, but don't count on it elsewhere. In touristy resorts such as Nha Trang and Halong Bay, you may find slide film in hotel gift shops.

Black and white film is rapidly disappearing, but can still be found in speciality shops. If you really need the stuff then you'd best bring a supply from abroad.

Many tourists travel around Vietnam by van or minibus; the metal floors of these vehicles get very hot, but you might not notice if the vehicle is air-conditioned. Many travellers have roasted their film by placing it in their backpacks and setting the backpack on the floor of the vehicle.

Photo-processing shops have become ubiquitous in places where tourists congregate. Most of these shops are equipped with the latest one-hour, colour-printing equipment. Printing costs are about US$5 per roll depending on the print size you choose. The quality tends to be quite good. Be sure to specify if you want glossy or mat finish on your prints.

Colour slide film can be developed quickly (three hours) in Hanoi and Ho Chi Minh City, but forget it outside of those two cities. Processing costs about US$5 per roll, but most shops do not mount the slides unless you request (and pay for) it. However, our experiences with slides and black and white film have been terrible, in terms of bad development or scratched film, so it's probably best to develop them elsewhere.

Plastic laminating is cheap. Just look for the signs saying 'Ep Plastic'. It's particularly advisable to laminate photos intended as presents to protect them from Vietnam's tropical climate. Unlaminated photos can deteriorate and go mouldy.

Cameras are fairly expensive in Vietnam and the selection is limited – bring one from abroad. Happily, lithium batteries (needed by many of today's point-and-shoot cameras) are available in most cities, though they're scarce in the hinterland.

Restrictions

The Vietnamese police usually don't care what you photograph, but on occasion they get pernickety. Obviously, don't photograph sensitive sites such as airports, seaports, military bases, border checkpoints etc. Photography from aircraft (excepting chartered aircraft) is now permitted. Don't even think of trying to get a snapshot of Ho Chi Minh in his glass sarcophagus!

Perhaps it would be wise to memorise the following message, which appears on signs in various places: '*Cam Chup Hinh Va Quay Video*', which means 'no photography or video taping'.

Some touristy sites charge a camera fee of about US$0.50, or a video fee of US$2 to US$5. If the staff refuse to issue a receipt for the camera fee, then you should refuse to pay – the 'fee' in that case is likely to go into their pocket.

Photographing People

Photographing anyone, particularly hill tribe people, demands patience and the utmost respect for local customs. The beauty and diversity of the Vietnamese people and the scenery provides ample opportunity, but it is important to remember you are just visiting and that not only may your actions be interpreted as rude or offensive, but your behaviour will influence the reception of future visitors. That is not to say that taking pictures is bad, but just keep in mind the various effects a camera can have.

Whatever you do, photograph with discretion and manners. It's always polite to ask first and if the person says no, don't take the photo. A gesture, a smile and a nod are all that is usually necessary. Remember, wherever you are in Vietnam, the people are *not* exotic birds of paradise.

The popular weekend market in Sapa is a good example of where a crowd of camera-toting tourists can appear somewhat overwhelming to the local folk. While the entrepreneurial Hmong do not generally mind being photographed (though buying some handicraft will help facilitate this), other groups in the area such as the Red Dzao tend to be far more camera-shy and have had their fair share of 'must get this shot' photographers literally chasing them through the market!

Like their Japanese and Chinese counterparts, Vietnamese people seems to have a near obsession with collecting hundreds (or thousands) of photos of themselves posing in front of something. The pose is always the same: a stiff, frontal shot, hands at the sides etc. The result is that all of their photos look nearly identical. The purpose of the photos seems to be to prove that they've been to a particular place. Since many Vietnamese cannot afford their own camera, virtually every site with tourist potential has a legion of photographers always ready to snap a few pictures. Some photographers will get the film processed and mail it to their customers, while others will shoot a roll and hand it over unprocessed.

Most Vietnamese cannot understand why Westerners shoot dozens of rolls of film without posing in each and every frame. Furthermore, when Westerners proudly show off their best photographs, Vietnamese look at them and say the photos are 'boring' because there are seldom any people in them.

Airport Security

The dreaded x-ray machines at Vietnam's airports are no longer a problem – the old Soviet-made 'microwave ovens' had a habit of frying your film, but they've been replaced with modern, film-safe equipment imported from Germany. However, it is hazardous if you attempt to film the airport security procedures (the film will most likely be ripped out of your camera).

Of greater concern are the new-fangled, high powered x-ray machines that are gradually being installed in airports in other parts of Asia, Europe and the Americas. To avoid possible x-ray damage from these machines, you should always hand-carry your film, and whenever possible (even if the sign says 'X-ray Safe') insist – politely – on a hand-check.

The authorities seem to be far more sensitive about video tape material than film. Surprisingly, it's more of a problem when exiting the country than entering (logically you would think the opposite). The great stumbling block appears to be what the authorities like to call 'cultural materials'. Video tapes are deemed to be cultural materials that must be screened in advance by 'experts' from the Department of Culture. Fortunately these checks are aimed more at commercial tapes so your holiday footage will probably be excluded.

TIME

Vietnam, like Thailand, is seven hours ahead of Greenwich Mean Time/Universal Time Coordinated (GMT/UTC). Because it is so close to the equator, Vietnam does not have daylight saving time. Thus, without allowing variations for daylight saving, when it's noon in Hanoi or Ho Chi Minh City it is 9 pm the previous day in Los Angeles, midnight in New York, 5 am in London, 1 pm in Perth and 3 pm in Sydney.

ELECTRICITY

Electric current in Vietnam is mostly 220V at 50Hz (cycles), but often you'll still find 110V (also at 50Hz). Unfortunately, looking at the shape of the outlet on the wall gives no clue as to what voltage is flowing through the wires. In the south, most outlets are US-style flat pins. Despite the American-inspired design, the voltage is still likely to be 220V. In the north, most outlets are the Russian-inspired round pins and also usually carry 220V. If the voltage is not marked on the socket try finding a light bulb or appliance with the voltage written on it. Sockets are two-prong only.

Much of the electrical wiring in Vietnam is 'improvised' to say the least. Be especially careful in rural areas – exposed live wires are a fire hazard and offer opportunities to electrocute yourself.

In drought years, power failures increase sharply because hydroelectric power is used. The situation is getting worse as the demand from air-conditioners and power-hungry factories rises. There are plans to build a new power station in the Mekong Delta to alleviate this, but no one is sure just when it will happen. For a long time the north had excess hydroelectric capacity, but consumerism has changed the picture and blackouts can occur in summer when people use their air-conditioners. A new power line, opened in 1994, connects the north and south, and has greatly alleviated the winter electricity shortages that formerly plagued Ho Chi Minh City.

In rural areas, power is often supplied by diesel generators that frequently shut down. This means you should keep your torch handy. More seriously, it also means that there are probably frequent surges in the current. Sensitive electronic equipment should be shielded with a surge suppressor or, better yet, run on rechargeable batteries.

WEIGHTS & MEASURES

The Vietnamese use the international metric system (see the back of this book for a metric conversion table). In addition, two weight measurements have been borrowed from the Chinese: the *tael* and the *catty*. A catty equals 0.6kg (1.32lb). There are 16 taels to the catty, so one tael equals 37.5g (1.32oz). Gold is always sold by the tael.

LAUNDRY

It is usually easy to find a hotel attendant who can get your laundry spotlessly clean for the equivalent of one or two US dollars. There have, however, been a number of reports of gross overcharging at certain hotels, so always ask to see the price list beforehand.

Budget hotels do not have clothes dryers – they rely on the sunshine – so allow at least a day and a half for washing and drying, especially during the wet season.

TOILETS

The issue of toilets and what to do with used toilet paper has caused some concern. As one traveller wrote:

> We are still not sure about the toilet paper...in two hotels they have been angry with us for flushing down the paper in the toilet. In other places it seems quite OK though.

In general, if you see a wastepaper basket next to the toilet, that is where you should throw the toilet paper. The problem is that many hotels' sewage systems cannot handle toilet paper. This is especially true in old hotels where the antiquated plumbing was designed in the pre-toilet paper era. Also, in rural areas there is no sewage treatment plant – the waste empties into an underground septic tank and toilet paper will really create a mess in there. For the sake of international relations, be considerate and throw the paper in the wastepaper basket.

Toilet paper is seldom provided in the toilets at bus and train stations or in other public buildings, though hotels usually supply it. You'd be wise to keep a stash of your own with you at all times while travelling around.

Another thing you should be mentally prepared for is squat toilets. For the uninitiated, a squat toilet has no seat for you to sit on while reading the morning newspaper; it's a hole in the floor. The only way to flush it is to fill the conveniently placed bucket with water and pour it into the hole. While it takes some practise to get proficient at balancing yourself over a squat toilet, at least you don't need to worry if the toilet seat is clean. Furthermore, some experts claim squatting is better for your digestive system.

Better hotels will have Western-style toilets, but squat toilets are the norm in cheaper hotels and public places such as restaurants, bus stations etc.

The scarcity of public toilets seems to be a greater problem for women than for men. Vietnamese males are often seen urinating in public, but this appears to be socially unacceptable for women. Women might find road side toilet stops easier if wearing a sarong.

HEALTH

Travel health depends on your predeparture preparations, your daily health care while travelling and how you handle any medical problem that does develop. While the potential dangers can seem quite frightening, in reality few travellers experience anything more than an upset stomach.

Vietnam's economy has significantly improved recently, which has brought with it some major improvements to the medical situation. In the past, people were frequently malnourished and therefore highly prone to disease – this is not such a huge problem any more. Also, immunisation programs are helping to stop the spread of disease.

Rural areas can still be a problem; although foreigners with cold, hard cash will receive the best treatment available, even bars of gold cannot buy you blood tests and x-rays when the local health clinic doesn't even have a thermometer or any aspirin. If you become seriously ill in rural Vietnam,

Traditional Healing Techniques

There are a number of traditional medical treatments practised in Vietnam. Herbal medicine, much of it imported from China, is widely available and sometimes surprisingly effective. As with Western medicine, self-diagnosis is not advisable – see a doctor. Traditional medicine doctors, also mostly ethnic-Chinese, can be readily found wherever a large Chinese community exists, including Saigon, Hanoi and Hoi An.

If you visit a traditional Chinese-Vietnamese doctor, you might be surprised by what they discover about your body. For example, the doctor will almost certainly take your pulse and then may perhaps tell you that you have a 'slippery' or 'thready' pulse. Traditional doctors have identified more than 30 different kinds of pulses. A pulse could be empty, prison, leisurely, bowstring, irregular or even regularly irregular. The doctor may then examine your tongue to see if it is slippery, dry, pale, greasy, has a thick coating or possibly no coating at all. The doctor, having discovered your ailment, eg, wet heat, as evidenced by a slippery pulse and a red greasy tongue, will prescribe the proper herbs for your condition.

Once you have a diagnosis you may be treated by moxibustion, a traditional treatment whereby various types of herbs, rolled into what looks like a ball of fluffy cotton, are held near the skin and ignited. A slight variation of this method is to place the herb on a slice of ginger and then ignite it. The idea is to apply the maximum amount of heat possible without burning the patient. This heat treatment is supposed to be very good for diseases such as arthritis.

It is common to see Vietnamese people covered with long bands of red welts on their necks, foreheads and backs. Don't worry, this is not some kind of hideous skin disease, but rather a treatment known as *cao gio*, literally 'scrape wind'. In traditional Vietnamese folk medicine, many illnesses are

get to Ho Chi Minh City as quickly as you can. If you need any type of surgery or other extensive treatment, don't hesitate to fly to Bangkok, Hong Kong or another reasonably developed country as soon as possible.

You can buy plenty of dangerous drugs across the counter in Vietnam without a prescription, but you should exercise restraint – some drugs like steroids can make you feel great and then kill you, especially if you have an infection. Remember that drugs may not be of the same strength as in other countries, or may have deteriorated due to age or poor storage conditions. Check the expiry dates on any medicines you buy. Chinese shops often sell herbal medicines imported from China.

If you need some special medication then take it with you.

The addresses and telephone numbers of the best medical facilities in Vietnam can be found under the Information section near the beginning of the Ho Chi Minh City and Hanoi chapters. These are the only two cities where you are likely to find health facilities that come close to meeting developed-country standards.

Predeparture Planning

Immunisations Plan ahead for getting your vaccinations: some of them require more than one injection, while others should not be given together. Note that some should not be given during pregnancy or to people with allergies – discuss this with your doctor.

It is recommended you seek medical advice at least six weeks before travel. Be aware that there is often a greater risk of disease with children and during pregnancy (for more details about the diseases themselves, see the individual disease entries later in this section). Although there are currently no mandatory vaccinations for travellers to Vietnam, it is safer to carry proof of your vaccinations.

For information on current immunisation recommendations for Vietnam, consider emailing the international team of doctors at the Hanoi Family Medical Practice

Traditional Healing Techniques

attributed to 'poisonous wind' *(trung gio)*. The bad, or 'cold' wind can be released by applying eucalyptus oil or tiger balm and scraping the skin with spoons, coins etc, thus raising the welts. The results aren't pretty, but the locals say this treatment is good for the common cold, fatigue, headaches and other ailments. Whether the cure hurts less than the disease is something one can only judge from experience.

Another technique to battle bad breezes is called *giac hoi*. This one employs suction cups, typically made of bamboo or glass, which are placed on the patient's skin. A burning piece of alcohol-soaked cotton is briefly put inside the cup to drive out the air before it is applied. As the cup cools, a partial vacuum is produced, leaving a nasty-looking, but harmless, red circular mark on the skin. The mark goes away in a few days.

Can you cure people by sticking needles into them? The adherents of acupuncture say you can and they have some solid evidence to back them up. For example, some major surgical operations have been performed using acupuncture as the only anaesthetic (this works best on the head). In this case, a small electric current (from batteries) is passed through the needles.

Becoming a human pin cushion might not sound pleasant, but if done properly it doesn't hurt. Knowing just where to insert the needle is crucial. Acupuncturists have identified more than 2000 insertion points, but only about 150 are commonly used. The exact mechanism by which acupuncture works is not fully understood. Practitioners talk of energy channels or meridians that connect the needle insertion point to the particular organ, gland or joint being treated. The acupuncture point is sometimes quite far from the area of the body being treated.

Non-sterile acupuncture needles pose a genuine health risk in this era of the AIDS epidemic. You'd be wise to purchase your own if you wish to try this treatment.

e hfmeprac.kot@fmail.vnn.vn. They can provide the latest scoop on vaccinations, malaria and dengue fever status (in real time), and offer general medical advice regarding Vietnam.

Discuss your requirements with your doctor, but vaccinations you should consider for this trip include the following:

Cholera The current injectable vaccine against cholera is poorly protective and has many side effects, so it is not generally recommended for travellers. However, in some situations it may be necessary to have a certificate, as travellers are very rarely asked by immigration officials to present one, even though all countries and the World Health Organisation (WHO) has dropped cholera immunisation as a health requirement for entry.

Diphtheria & Tetanus Vaccinations for these two diseases are usually combined and are recommended for everyone. After an initial course of three injections (usually given in childhood), boosters are necessary every 10 years.

Hepatitis A Hepatitis A vaccine (eg Avaxim, Havrix 1440 or VAQTA) provides long-term immunity (possibly more than 10 years) after an initial injection and a booster at six to 12 months. Alternatively, an injection of gamma globulin can provide short-term protection against hepatitis A – two to six months, depending on the dose given. It is not a vaccine, but is ready-made antibody collected from blood donations. It is reasonably effective and, unlike the vaccine, it is protective immediately. However, because it is a blood product, there are current concerns about its long-term safety. Hepatitis A vaccine is also available in a combined form, Twinrix, with a hepatitis B vaccine. Three injections over a six-month period are required, the first two providing substantial protection against hepatitis A.

Hepatitis B Travellers who should consider vaccination against hepatitis B include those on a long trip, as well as those visiting countries where there are high levels of hepatitis B infection, where blood transfusions may not be adequately screened or where sexual contact or needle sharing is a possibility. Vaccination involves three injections, with a booster at 12 months. More rapid courses are available if necessary.

Japanese B Encephalitis Consider vaccination against this disease if spending a month or longer in a high-risk area (which includes parts of Vietnam), making repeated trips to a risk area or visiting during an epidemic. It involves three injections over 30 days.

Polio Everyone should keep up to date with this vaccination, it is normally given in childhood. A booster every 10 years maintains immunity.

Rabies Vaccination should be considered by those who will spend a month or longer in a country where rabies is common, especially if they are cycling, handling animals, caving or travelling to remote areas, and for children (who may not report a bite). Pretravel rabies vaccination involves having three injections over 21 to 28 days. If someone who has been vaccinated is bitten or scratched by an animal, they will require two booster injections of vaccine; those not vaccinated will require more.

Tuberculosis The risk of TB to travellers is usually very low, unless you are living with or closely associated with local people in high-risk areas. Vaccination against TB (BCG) is recommended for children and young adults living in these areas for three months or more.

Typhoid Vaccination against typhoid may be required if you are travelling for more than a couple of weeks in most parts of Asia. It is now available either as an injection or as capsules to be taken orally. A combined hepatitis A and typhoid vaccine was launched recently, but availability is limited – check with your doctor to find out its status in your country.

Yellow Fever A yellow fever vaccination is now the only vaccine that is a legal requirement for entry into Vietnam, for travellers over one year of age coming from an infected area (parts of Africa and South America).

Malaria Medication

Antimalarial drugs don't prevent infection, but kill the malaria parasites during their development and significantly reduce the risk of becoming very ill or dying. Expert advice on medication should be sought, as there are many factors to consider, including; the area to be visited, risk of exposure to malaria-carrying mosquitoes, side effects of medication, your medical history, age and whether you are pregnant. Travellers to isolated areas in high-risk regions such as Camau and Bac Lieu provinces and the rural south may like to carry a treatment dose of medication for use if symptoms occur.

Health Insurance

Make sure that you have adequate health insurance. See Travel Insurance under Visas & Documents earlier in this chapter for details.

Travel Health Guides

Lonely Planet's *Healthy Travel Asia* is a handy pocket size and packed with useful information including pretrip planning, emergency first aid, immunisation and disease information and what to do if you get sick on the road.

Lonely Planet's *Travel with Children* includes advice on travel health for younger children. There are also a number of excellent travel health sites on the Internet. The Lonely Planet home page (www.lonelplanet.com) has links to the World Health Organization and the US Centers for Disease Control & Prevention.

Other Preparations

Make sure you're healthy before you start travelling. If you are going on a long trip make sure your teeth are OK. If you wear glasses take a spare pair and your prescription with you. If you require a particular medication, take an adequate supply because it may not be available locally. Take part of the packaging showing the generic name rather than the brand, which will make getting replacements easier. It's a good idea to have a legible prescription or letter from your doctor to show that you legally use the medication to avoid any problems.

Basic Rules

Food There is an old colonial adage which says 'If you can cook it, boil it or peel it you can eat it...otherwise forget it'. Vegetables and fruit should be washed with purified water or peeled where possible. Beware of ice cream sold in the street or anywhere it might have been melted and refrozen; if there's any doubt (eg, a power cut in the last day or two), steer well clear.

Shellfish such as mussels, oysters and clams should be avoided, as well as undercooked meat, particularly in the form of mince. Steaming does not make shellfish safe for eating.

If a place looks clean and well run and the vendor also looks clean and healthy, then the food is probably safe. In general, places that are packed with travellers or locals will be fine, while empty restaurants may be questionable. The food in busy restaurants is cooked and eaten quite quickly, with little standing around and probably without being reheated.

Water The number one rule is *be careful of the water*. Ice can be particularly risky; if you don't know for certain that the water is safe, assume the worst. Reputable brands of bottled water or soft drinks are generally fine, although in some places bottles may be refilled with tap water. Only use water from containers with a serrated seal – not tops or corks. Take care with fruit juice, particularly if water may have been added. Milk should be treated with suspicion as it is often unpasteurised, though boiled milk is fine if it is kept hygienically. Tea or coffee should also be OK, since the water should have been boiled.

Water Purification The simplest way of purifying water is to boil it thoroughly. Vigorous boiling should be satisfactory; however, at high altitude water boils at a lower temperature, so germs are less likely to be killed. Make sure you boil it for longer in these environments.

Consider purchasing a water filter for a long trip. There are two main kinds of filter. Total filters take out all parasites, bacteria and viruses and make water safe to drink. They are often expensive, but they can be more cost effective than buying bottled water. Simple filters (which can even be a nylon mesh bag) take out dirt and larger foreign bodies from the water so that chemical solutions work much more effectively; if water is dirty, chemical solutions may not work at all. It's very important when buying a filter to read the specifications, so that you know exactly what it removes from the water and what it doesn't. Simple filtering will not remove all dangerous organisms, so if you cannot boil water it should be treated chemically. Chlorine tablets will kill many pathogens, but not some parasites, such as giardia and amoebic cysts. Iodine is more effective in purifying water and is available in tablet form. Follow the directions carefully and remember that too much iodine can be harmful.

Everyday Health

Normal body temperature is up to 37°C (98.6°F); more than 2°C (4°F) higher indicates a high fever. The normal adult pulse rate is 60 to 100 per minute (children 80 to 100, babies 100 to 140). As a general rule the pulse increases about 20 beats per minute for each 1°C (2°F) rise in fever.

Respiration (breathing) rate is also an indicator of illness. Count the number of breaths per minute: Between 12 and 20 is normal for adults and older children (up to 30 for younger children, 40 for babies). People with a high fever or serious respiratory illness breathe more quickly than normal. More than 40 shallow breaths a minute may indicate pneumonia.

Medical Problems & Treatment

Self-diagnosis and treatment can be risky, so you should always seek medical help. An embassy, consulate or hotel can usually recommend a local doctor or clinic. Although we do give drug dosages in this section, they are for emergency use only. Correct diagnosis from a qualified physician is vital. In this section we have used the generic names for medications – check with a pharmacist for brands available locally.

Note that antibiotics should ideally be administered only under medical supervision. Take only the recommended dose at the prescribed intervals and use the whole course, even if the illness seems to be cured earlier. Stop immediately if there are any serious reactions and don't use the antibiotic at all if you are unsure that you have the correct one. Some people are allergic to commonly prescribed antibiotics such as penicillin; carry this information (eg, on a bracelet) when travelling.

Environmental Hazards

Heat Exhaustion Dehydration and salt deficiency can cause heat exhaustion. Take time to acclimatise to high temperatures, drink sufficient liquids and do not do anything too physically demanding.

Salt deficiency is characterised by fatigue, lethargy, headaches, giddiness and muscle cramps; salt tablets may help, but adding extra salt to your food is better.

Anhidrotic heat exhaustion is a rare form of heat exhaustion that is caused by an inability to sweat. It tends to affect people who have been in a hot climate for some time, rather than newcomers. It can progress to heatstroke. Treatment involves removal to a cooler climate.

Medical Kit Check List

Following is a list of items you should consider including in your medical kit – consult your pharmacist for brands available in your country.

- ☐ **Aspirin or paracetamol (acetaminophen in the USA)** – for pain or fever
- ☐ **Antihistamine** – for allergies, eg, hay fever; to ease the itch from insect bites or stings; and to prevent motion sickness
- ☐ **Cold and flu tablets, throat lozenges and nasal decongestant**
- ☐ **Multivitamins** – consider for long trips, when dietary vitamin intake may be inadequate
- ☐ **Antibiotics** – consider including these if you're travelling well off the beaten track; see your doctor, as they must be prescribed, and carry the prescription with you
- ☐ **Loperamide or diphenoxylate** –'blockers' for diarrhoea
- ☐ **Prochlorperazine or metaclopramide** – for nausea and vomiting
- ☐ **Rehydration mixture** – to prevent dehydration, which may occur, for example, during bouts of diarrhoea; particularly important when travelling with children
- ☐ **Insect repellent, sunscreen, lip balm and eye drops**
- ☐ **Calamine lotion, sting relief spray or aloe vera** – to ease irritation from sunburn and insect bites or stings
- ☐ **Antifungal cream or powder** – for fungal skin infections and thrush
- ☐ **Antiseptic (such as povidone-iodine)** – for cuts and grazes
- ☐ **Bandages, Band-Aids (plasters) and other wound dressings**
- ☐ **Water purification tablets or iodine**
- ☐ **Scissors, tweezers and a thermometer** – note that mercury thermometers are prohibited by airlines
- ☐ **Sterile kit** – in case you need injections in a country with medical hygiene problems; discuss with your doctor

Heatstroke This serious, occasionally fatal condition can occur if the body's heat-regulating mechanism breaks down and the body temperature rises to dangerous levels. Long, continuous periods of exposure to high temperatures and insufficient fluids can leave you vulnerable to heatstroke.

The symptoms are feeling unwell, not sweating very much (or at all) and a high body temperature (39°C to 41°C or 102°F to 106°F). Where sweating has ceased, the skin becomes flushed and red. Severe, throbbing headaches and lack of coordination will also occur, and the sufferer may be confused or aggressive. Eventually the sufferer will become delirious or convulse. Hospitalisation is essential, but in the interim get victims out of the sun, remove their clothing, cover them with a wet sheet or towel and then fan continually. Give fluids if they are conscious.

Jet Lag Jet lag is experienced when a person travels by air across more than three time zones (each time zone usually represents a one-hour time difference). It occurs because many of the functions of the human body (such as temperature, pulse rate and emptying of the bladder and bowels) are regulated by internal 24-hour cycles. When we travel long distances rapidly, our bodies take time to adjust to the 'new time' of our destination, and we may experience fatigue, disorientation, insomnia, anxiety, impaired concentration and loss of appetite. These effects will usually be gone within three days of arrival, but to minimise the impact of jet lag:

- Rest for a couple of days prior to departure.
- Try to select flight schedules that minimise sleep deprivation; arriving late in the day means you can go to sleep soon after you arrive. For very long flights, try to organise a stopover.
- Avoid excessive eating (which bloats the stomach) and alcohol (which causes dehydration) during the flight. Instead, drink plenty of

noncarbonated, nonalcoholic drinks such as fruit juice or water.
- Avoid smoking.
- Make yourself comfortable by wearing loose-fitting clothes and perhaps bringing an eye mask and ear plugs to help you sleep.
- Try to sleep at the appropriate time for the time zone you are travelling to.

Motion Sickness Eating lightly before and during a trip will reduce your chances of getting motion sickness. If you are prone to motion sickness try to find a place that minimises movement – near the wing on aircraft, close to midships on boats, near the centre on buses. Fresh air usually helps; reading and cigarette smoke don't. Commercial motion-sickness preparations, which can cause drowsiness, have to be taken before the trip commences. Ginger (available in capsule form) and peppermint (including mint-flavoured sweets) are natural preventatives.

Prickly Heat Prickly heat is an itchy rash caused by excessive perspiration trapped under the skin. It usually strikes people who have just arrived in a hot climate. Keeping cool, bathing often, drying the skin and using a mild talcum or prickly heat powder, or resorting to air-conditioning may help.

Sunburn In the tropics, the desert or at high altitude you can get sunburnt surprisingly quickly, even through cloud. Use a sunscreen, a hat, and a barrier cream for your nose and lips. Calamine lotion or a commercial after sun preparation are good for mild sunburn. Protect your eyes with good quality sunglasses, particularly if you will be near water, sand or snow.

Infectious Diseases

Diarrhoea Simple things like a change of water, food or climate can all cause a mild bout of diarrhoea, but a few rushed toilet trips with no other symptoms is not indicative of a major problem.

Dehydration is the main danger with any diarrhoea, particularly in children or the elderly, where dehydration can occur quite quickly. Under all circumstances, *fluid replacement* is the most important thing to remember. Weak black tea with a little sugar, soda water, or soft drinks allowed to go flat and diluted 50% with clean water are all good. With severe diarrhoea a rehydrating solution is preferable to replace minerals and salts lost. Commercially available oral rehydration salts (ORS) are very useful; add them to boiled or bottled water. In an emergency, you can make up a solution of six teaspoons of sugar and a half teaspoon of

Nutrition

If your diet is poor or limited in variety, if you're travelling hard and fast and therefore missing meals, or if you simply lose your appetite, you can soon start to lose weight and place your health at risk.

Make sure your diet is well balanced. Cooked eggs, tofu, beans, lentils and nuts are all safe ways to get protein. Fruit you can peel (bananas, oranges or mandarins, for example) is usually safe and a good source of vitamins. Melons can harbour bacteria in their flesh and are best avoided. Try to eat plenty of grains (including rice) and bread. Remember that although food is generally safer if it is cooked well, overcooked food loses much of its nutritional value. If your diet isn't well balanced or if your food intake is insufficient, it's a good idea to take vitamin and iron pills.

In hot regions such as the Mekong Delta, make sure you drink enough – don't rely on feeling thirsty to indicate when you should drink. Not needing to urinate or voiding small amounts of very dark yellow urine is a danger sign. Always carry a water bottle with you on long trips. Excessive sweating can lead to loss of salt and therefore muscle cramping. Salt tablets are not a good idea as a preventative, but in places where salt is not used much, adding salt to food can help.

salt to a litre of boiled or bottled water. You need to drink at least the same volume of fluid that you are losing in bowel movements and vomiting. Urine is the best guide to the adequacy of replacement – if you have small amounts of concentrated urine, you need to drink more. Keep drinking small amounts often. Stick to a bland diet as you recover.

Gut-paralysing drugs such as loperamide or diphenoxylate can be used to bring relief from the symptoms, although they do not actually cure the problem. Only use these drugs if you do not have access to toilets, that is, if you *must* travel. Note that these drugs are not recommended for children under 12 years.

In certain situations antibiotics may be required: diarrhoea with blood or mucus (dysentery), any diarrhoea with fever, profuse watery diarrhoea, persistent diarrhoea not improving after 48 hours and severe diarrhoea. These suggest a more serious cause of diarrhoea, and in these situations gut-paralysing drugs should be avoided.

In these situations, a stool test may be necessary to diagnose what bug is causing your diarrhoea, so you should seek medical help urgently. Where this is not possible the recommended drugs for bacterial diarrhoea (the most likely cause of severe diarrhoea in travellers) are norfloxacin 400mg twice daily for three days or ciprofloxacin 500mg twice daily for five days. These are not recommended for children or pregnant women. The drug of choice for children is co-trimoxazole with dosage dependent on weight. A five-day course is given. Ampicillin or amoxycillin may be given in pregnancy, but medical care is necessary.

Two other causes of persistent diarrhoea in travellers are giardiasis and amoebic dysentery.

Giardiasis is caused by a common parasite, *Giardia lamblia*. Symptoms include stomach cramps, nausea, a bloated stomach, watery, foul-smelling diarrhoea and frequent gas. Giardiasis can appear several weeks after you have been exposed to the parasite. The symptoms may disappear for a few days and then return; this can go on for several weeks.

Amoebic dysentery, caused by the protozoan *Entamoeba histolytica*, is characterised by a gradual onset of low-grade diarrhoea, often with blood and mucus. Cramping abdominal pain and vomiting are less likely than in other types of diarrhoea, and fever may not be present. It will persist until treated and can recur and cause other health problems.

You should seek medical advice if you think you have giardiasis or amoebic dysentery, but where this is not possible, tinidazole or metronidazole are the recommended drugs. Treatment is a 2g single dose of tinidazole or 250mg of metronidazole three times daily for five to 10 days.

Fungal Infections Fungal infections occur more commonly in hot weather and are usually found on the scalp, between the toes (athlete's foot) or fingers, in the groin and on the body (ringworm). You get ringworm (which is a fungal infection, not a worm) from infected animals or other people. Moisture encourages these infections.

To prevent fungal infections wear loose, comfortable clothes, avoid artificial fibres, wash frequently and dry yourself carefully. If you do get an infection, wash the infected area at least daily with a disinfectant or medicated soap and water, and rinse and dry well. Apply an antifungal cream or powder such as tolnaftate. Try to expose the infected area to air or sunlight as much as possible and wash all towels and underwear in hot water, change them often and let them dry in the sun.

Hepatitis Hepatitis is a general term for inflammation of the liver. It is a common disease worldwide. There are several different viruses that cause hepatitis, and they differ in the way that they are transmitted. The symptoms are similar in all forms of the illness, and include fever, chills, headache, fatigue, feelings of weakness and aches and pains, followed by loss of appetite, nausea, vomiting, abdominal pain, dark urine, light-coloured faeces, jaundiced (yellow) skin and yellowing of the whites of the eyes. People who have had hepatitis should avoid alcohol for some time after the illness, as the liver needs time to recover.

Hepatitis A is transmitted by contaminated food and drinking water. You should seek medical advice, but there is not much you can do apart from resting, drinking lots of fluids, eating lightly and avoiding fatty foods. Hepatitis E is transmitted in the same way as hepatitis A; it can be particularly serious in pregnant women.

There are almost 300 million chronic carriers of hepatitis B in the world. It is spread through contact with infected blood, blood products or body fluids, for example through sexual contact, unsterilised needles and blood transfusions, or contact with blood via small breaks in the skin. Other risk situations include shaving, tattooing or body piercing with contaminated equipment. The symptoms of hepatitis B may be more severe than type A and the disease can lead to long term problems such as chronic liver damage, liver cancer or a long term carrier state. Hepatitis C and D are spread in the same way as hepatitis B and can also lead to long term complications.

There are vaccines against hepatitis A and B, but there are currently no vaccines against the other types of hepatitis. Following the basic rules about food and water (hepatitis A and E) and avoiding risk situations (hepatitis B, C and D) are important preventative measures.

HIV & AIDS Infection with the human immunodeficiency virus (HIV) may lead to acquired immune deficiency syndrome (AIDS), which is a fatal disease. Any exposure to blood, blood products or body fluids may put the individual at risk. The disease is often transmitted through sexual contact or dirty needles – vaccinations, acupuncture, tattooing and body piercing can be potentially as dangerous as intravenous drug use. HIV/AIDS can also be spread through infected blood transfusions.

If you do need an injection, ask to see the syringe unwrapped in front of you, or take a needle and syringe pack with you. Fear of HIV infection should never preclude treatment for serious medical conditions.

Official figures on the number of people with HIV/AIDS in Vietnam are vague. Though health education messages relating to HIV/AIDS can be seen all over Vietnam, the official line is that infection is largely limited to sex workers and drug users. Condoms are widely available all over Vietnam.

Intestinal Worms These parasites are most common in rural, tropical areas. The different worms have different ways of infecting people. Some may be ingested on food such as undercooked meat (eg, tapeworms) and some enter through your skin (eg, hookworms). Infestations may not show up for some time, and although they are generally not serious, if left untreated some can cause severe health problems later. Consider having a stool test when you return home to check for these and determine the appropriate treatment.

Schistosomiasis Also known as bilharzia, this disease is transmitted by minute worms. They infect certain varieties of freshwater snails found in rivers, streams, lakes and particularly behind dams. The worms multiply and are eventually discharged into the water.

The worm enters through the skin and attaches itself to your intestines or bladder. The first symptom may be a general feeling of being unwell, or a tingling and sometimes a light rash around the area where it entered. Weeks later a high fever may develop. Once the disease is established abdominal pain and blood in the urine are other signs. The infection often causes no symptoms until the disease is well established (several months to years after exposure) and damage to internal organs irreversible.

Avoiding swimming or bathing in fresh water where bilharzia is present is the main method of preventing the disease. Even deep water can be infected. If you do get wet, dry off quickly and dry your clothes as well.

A blood test is the most reliable way to diagnose the disease, but the test will not show positive until a number of weeks after exposure.

Sexually Transmitted Infections HIV/AIDS and hepatitis B can be transmitted through sexual contact – see the relevant sections earlier for more details. Other STIs include gonorrhoea, herpes and syphilis; sores, blisters or rashes around the genitals, and discharges or pain when urinating are common symptoms. In some STIs, such as wart virus or chlamydia, symptoms may be less marked or not observed at all, especially in women. Chlamydia infection can cause infertility in men and women before any symptoms have been noticed.

Syphilis symptoms eventually disappear completely, but the disease continues and can cause severe problems in later years. The treatment of gonorrhoea and syphilis is with antibiotics. The different sexually transmitted diseases each require specific antibiotics.

While abstinence from sexual contact is the only 100% effective prevention, using condoms is also effective. Condoms are widely available all over Vietnam, but when purchasing, ensure the package hasn't been stored in the sun as the rubber could have deteriorated.

Typhoid Typhoid fever is a dangerous gut infection caused by contaminated water and food. Medical help must be sought.

During its early stages sufferers may feel they have a bad cold or flu on the way, as early symptoms are a headache, body aches and a fever that rises a little each day until it is around 40°C (104°F) or more. The victim's pulse is often slow relative to the degree of fever present – unlike a normal fever where the pulse increases. There may also be vomiting, abdominal pain, diarrhoea or constipation.

In the second week the high fever and slow pulse continue and a few pink spots may appear on the body; trembling, delirium, weakness, weight loss and dehydration may occur. Complications such as pneumonia, perforated bowel or meningitis may occur.

Insect-Borne Diseases

Filariasis, Lyme disease and typhus are all insect-borne diseases, but they do not pose a great risk to travellers. For more information on these diseases, see Less Common Diseases at the end of this section.

Malaria This serious and potentially fatal disease is spread by mosquito bites. If you are travelling in endemic areas it is extremely important to avoid mosquito bites and to take tablets to prevent this disease. Symptoms range from fever, chills and sweating, headache, diarrhoea and abdominal pains to a vague feeling of ill-health. Seek medical help immediately if malaria is suspected. Without treatment malaria can rapidly become more serious and can be fatal.

If medical care is not available, malaria tablets can be used for treatment. You need to use a malaria tablet that is different from the one you were taking when you contracted malaria. The standard treatment dose of mefloquine is two 250mg tablets and a further two six hours later. For Fansidar, it's a single dose of three tablets. If you were previously taking mefloquine and cannot obtain Fansidar, then other alternatives are Malarone (atovaquone-proguanil; four tablets once daily for three days), halofantrine (three doses of two 250mg tablets every six hours) or quinine sulphate (600mg every six hours). There is a greater risk of side effects with these dosages than in normal use if used with mefloquine, so medical advice is preferable. Be aware also that halofantrine is no longer recommended by the WHO as emergency standby treatment, because of side effects, and should only be used if no other drugs are available.

Travellers are advised to prevent mosquito bites at all times. The main messages are:

- Wear light-coloured clothing, long trousers and long-sleeved shirts.
- Use mosquito repellents containing the compound DEET on exposed areas (prolonged overuse of DEET may be harmful, especially to children, but its use is considered preferable to being bitten by disease-transmitting mosquitoes).
- Avoid perfumes or aftershave.
- Use a mosquito net impregnated with mosquito repellent (permethrin) – it may be worth taking your own.

• Impregnating your clothes with permethrin effectively deters mosquitoes and other insects.

Dengue Fever This viral disease is transmitted by mosquitoes and is fast becoming one of the top public health problems in the tropical world. Unlike the malaria mosquito, the *Aedes aegypti* mosquito, which transmits the dengue virus, is most active during the day, and is found mainly in urban areas, in and around human dwellings.

Signs and symptoms of dengue fever include a sudden onset of high fever, headache, joint and muscle pains (hence its old name, 'breakbone fever') and nausea and vomiting. A rash of small red spots sometimes appears three to four days after the onset of fever. In the early phase of illness, dengue may be mistaken for other infectious diseases, including malaria and influenza. Minor bleeding such as nose bleeds may occur in the course of the illness, but this does not necessarily mean that you have progressed to the potentially fatal dengue haemorrhagic fever (DHF). This is a severe illness, characterised by heavy bleeding, which is thought to be a result of second infection due to a different strain (there are four major strains) and usually affects residents of the country rather than travellers. Recovery even from simple dengue fever may be prolonged, with tiredness lasting for several weeks.

You should seek medical attention as soon as possible if you think you may be infected. A blood test can exclude malaria and indicate the possibility of dengue fever. There is no specific treatment for dengue. Aspirin should be avoided, as it increases the risk of haemorrhaging. There is no vaccine against dengue fever. The best prevention is to avoid mosquito bites at all times by covering up, using insect repellents containing the compound DEET and mosquito nets – see the Malaria section earlier for more advice on avoiding mosquito bites.

Japanese B Encephalitis This viral infection of the brain is also transmitted by mosquitoes. Most cases occur in rural areas, as the virus exists in pigs and wading birds. Symptoms include fever, headache and alteration in consciousness. Hospitalisation is needed for correct diagnosis and treatment. There is a high mortality rate among those who have symptoms; of those who survive, many are intellectually disabled.

Cuts, Bites & Stings

See Less Common Diseases further in this section for details of rabies, which is passed through animal bites.

Cuts & Scratches Wash well and treat any cut with an antiseptic such as povidone-iodine. Where possible avoid bandages and adhesive dressings, which can keep wounds wet. Coral cuts are notoriously slow to heal and if they are not adequately cleaned, small pieces of coral can become embedded in the wound.

Bedbugs & Lice Bedbugs live in various places, but particularly in dirty mattresses and bedding, evidenced by spots of blood on bedclothes or on the wall. Bedbugs leave itchy bites in neat rows. Calamine lotion or a sting relief spray may help.

All lice cause itching and discomfort. They make themselves at home in your hair (head lice), your clothing (body lice) or in your pubic hair (crabs). You catch lice through direct contact with infected people or by sharing combs, clothing and the like. Powder or shampoo treatment will kill the lice and infected clothing should then be washed in very hot, soapy water and left in the sun to dry.

Bites & Stings Bee and wasp stings are usually painful rather than dangerous. However, in people who are allergic to them, severe breathing difficulties may occur and require urgent medical care. Calamine lotion or a sting relief spray will give relief and ice packs will reduce the pain and swelling. There are some spiders with dangerous bites but antivenins are usually available. Scorpion stings are notoriously painful and in some parts of Asia can actually be fatal. Scorpions often shelter in shoes or clothing.

There are various fish and other sea creatures that can sting or bite, or that are dangerous to eat – seek local advice.

Jellyfish Avoid contact with these sea creatures, which have stinging tentacles – seek local advice. Stings from most jellyfish are simply rather painful. Dousing in vinegar will deactivate any stingers that have not 'fired'. Calamine lotion, antihistamines and analgesics may reduce the reaction and relieve the pain; you can also apply an icepack, but be careful not to get any water on the wound it will sting.

Leeches & Ticks Leeches may be present in damp rainforest conditions; they attach themselves to your skin to suck your blood. Trekkers often get them on their legs or in their boots. Salt or a lighted cigarette end will make them fall off. Do not pull them off, as the bite is then more likely to become infected. Clean and apply pressure if the point of attachment is bleeding. An insect repellent may keep them away.

You should always check all over your body if you have been walking through a potentially tick-infested area as ticks can cause skin infections and other more serious diseases. If a tick is found attached, press down around the tick's head with tweezers, grab the head and gently pull upwards. Avoid pulling the rear of the body as this may squeeze the tick's gut contents through the attached mouth parts into the skin, increasing the risk of infection and disease. Smearing chemicals on the tick will not make it let go and is not recommended.

Snakes To minimise your chances of being bitten always wear boots, socks and long trousers when walking through undergrowth where snakes may be present. Don't put your hands into holes and crevices, and be careful when collecting firewood.

Snake bites do not cause instantaneous death and antivenins are usually available. Immediately wrap the bitten limb tightly, as you would for a sprained ankle, and then attach a splint to immobilise it. Keep the victim still and seek medical help, if possible with the dead snake for identification. But don't attempt to catch the snake if there is a possibility of being bitten again. Tourniquets and sucking out the poison are now comprehensively discredited.

Women's Health

Gynaecological Problems Antibiotic use, synthetic underwear, sweating and contraceptive pills can lead to fungal vaginal infections, especially when travelling in hot climates. Thrush or vaginal candidiasis is characterised by a rash, itch and discharge. Nystatin, miconazole or clotrimazole pessaries or vaginal cream are the usual treatment, but some people use a more traditional remedy involving a vinegar or lemon-juice douche, or yoghurt. Maintaining good personal hygiene and wearing loose-fitting clothes and cotton underwear may help prevent these infections.

Sexually transmitted diseases are a major cause of vaginal problems. Symptoms include a smelly discharge, painful intercourse and sometimes a burning sensation when urinating. Medical attention should be sought and male sexual partners must also be treated. For more details see the section on Sexually Transmitted Diseases earlier. Besides abstinence, the best thing is to practise safe sex using condoms.

Pregnancy It is not advisable to travel to some places while pregnant, as some vaccinations normally used to prevent serious diseases are not advisable during pregnancy (eg, yellow fever). In addition, some diseases are much more serious for pregnant women, and may increase the risk of a stillborn child (eg, malaria).

Most miscarriages occur during the first three months of pregnancy. Miscarriage is not uncommon and can occasionally lead to severe bleeding. The last three months should also be spent within reasonable distance of good medical care. A baby born as early as 24 weeks stands a chance of survival, but only in a good modern hospital. Pregnant women should avoid all unnecessary medication, although vaccinations and malarial prophylactics should still be taken where needed. Additional care should be taken to prevent illness and particular attention should be paid to diet and nutrition. Alcohol and nicotine, for example, should be avoided.

Less Common Diseases

The following diseases pose a small risk to travellers, and so are only mentioned in passing. Seek medical advice if you think you may have any of these diseases.

Cholera This is the worst of the watery diarrhoeas and medical help should be sought. Outbreaks of cholera are generally widely reported, so you can avoid such problem areas. Fluid replacement is the most vital treatment – the risk of dehydration is severe as you may lose up to 20L a day. If there is a delay in getting to hospital, then begin taking tetracycline. The adult dose is 250mg four times daily. It is not recommended for children under nine years or for pregnant women. Tetracycline may help shorten the illness, but adequate fluids are required to save lives.

Filariasis This is a mosquito-transmitted parasitic infection found in parts of Asia. Possible symptoms include fever, pain and swelling of the lymph glands; inflammation of lymph drainage areas; swelling of a limb or the scrotum; skin rashes; and blindness. Treatment is available to eliminate the parasites from the body, but some of the damage already caused may not be reversible. Medical advice should be obtained promptly if the infection is suspected.

Rabies This fatal viral infection is found in many countries. Many animals can be infected (such as dogs, cats, bats and monkeys) and it is their saliva which is infectious. Any bite, scratch or even lick from an animal should be cleaned immediately and thoroughly. Scrub with soap and running water, and then apply alcohol or iodine solution. Medical help should be sought promptly to receive a course of injections to prevent the onset of symptoms and death.

Tetanus This disease is caused by a germ that lives in soil and in the faeces of horses and other animals. It enters the body via breaks in the skin. The first symptom may be discomfort in swallowing, or stiffening of the jaw and neck; this is followed by painful convulsions of the jaw and whole body. The disease can be fatal. It can be prevented by vaccination.

Tuberculosis (TB) TB is a bacterial infection usually transmitted from person to person by coughing but which may be transmitted through consumption of unpasteurised milk. Milk that has been boiled is safe to drink, and the souring of milk to make yoghurt or cheese also kills the bacilli. Travellers are usually not at great risk as close household contact with the infected person is usually required before the disease is passed on. You may need to have a TB test before you travel as this can help diagnose the disease later if you become ill.

Typhus This disease is spread by ticks, mites or lice. It begins with fever, chills, headache and muscle pains followed a few days later by a body rash. There is often a large painful sore at the site of the bite and nearby lymph nodes are swollen and painful. Typhus can be treated under medical supervision. Seek local advice on areas where ticks pose a danger and always check your skin carefully for ticks after walking in a danger area such as a tropical forest. An insect repellent can help, and walkers in tick-infested areas should consider having their boots and trousers impregnated with benzyl benzoate and dibutylphthalate.

WOMEN TRAVELLERS

Like Thailand and other predominantly Buddhist countries, Vietnam is in general relatively free of serious hassles for female Western travellers. But it is a different story for some Asian women, particularly those who are young. It is not uncommon for an Asian woman accompanied by a Western male to be mistaken for a Vietnamese prostitute. The fact that the couple could be married (or friends) might not to occur to everyone,

NGOs in Vietnam

Since opening its doors to the world in the late 1980s, Vietnam has welcomed hundreds of local and international nongovernmental organisations (NGOs) aiming to provide support to the country's people, animals and natural environment. Many of these organisations are seeking volunteers and/or donations, but you should always contact them before visiting. The best place to begin is the NGO Resource Centre (☎ 04-832 8570, fax 04-832 8611, ⓔ NGOCentr@netnam.org.vn), Hotel La Thanh, 218 Pho Doi Can, Hanoi, which keeps extensive files on all of the NGOs operating in Vietnam.

The following is a selective list of notable NGOs in Vietnam doing good work, in particular for disadvantaged children.

Christina Noble Children's Foundation (CNCF)
CNCF Vietnam (☎ 08-822 2276, fax 08-822 2276, ⓔ vietnam@cncf.org, or, mamatina@hcm.vnn.vn) 38 D\- Tu Xuong, District 3, Ho Chi Minh City
CNCF UK (☎ 171-233 1413, fax 233 1424, Web site: www.cncf.org) 10 Great George Street, 7th floor, London SW 1P 3AE

CNCF serves children at risk of sexual and economic exploitation who are in need of emergency and long term medical care, nutritional rehabilitation, educational opportunities, vocational training and job placement.

East Meets West
East Meets West, Vietnam (☎ 0511-829 110, fax 0511-821 850, ⓔ emwfvn@dng.vnn.vn, Web site: www.eastmeetswest.org) Postal address: 56 Đ Pasteur, Danang

East Meets West, USA (☎ 510-763-7045, fax 510-763-6545, ⓔ info@eastmeetswest.org, Web site: same as above) Postal address: P.O. Box 29292 Oakland, CA 94604

This humanitarian relief organisation, founded in 1988 by Le Ly Hayslip, whose life story was chronicled in two books she wrote, and later became the subject material for Oliver Stone's film *Heaven and Earth*. Le Ly (who fled Vietnam to the USA) returned to her rural village in Central Vietnam to help heal the wounds of war between the United States and Vietnam, and set into motion what would become one of the most productive NGOs in the country. Today East Meets West provides countless programs for enhancing the education and health of children, building and renovating vital institutions – schools, hospitals, medical and dental clinics, and clean and safe water systems for home and agricultural use.

Education For Development (EFD)
(☎/fax 08-837 1820, ⓔ efd-vn@hcm.vnn.vn) 245 D\- Nguyen Trai, District 1, Ho Chi Minh City

EFD works with street children and working children.

nor does the fact that the woman may not be Vietnamese at all. Asian women travelling in Vietnam with a Western male companion have occasionally reported verbal abuse, although the nasty words are spoken entirely in Vietnamese, which means many women have no idea what insults are being hurled at them.

For racially mixed couples wanting to visit Vietnam, there's no need to be overly paranoid, but a few precautions and words of advice are helpful. Dress 'like a foreigner' – sewing patches on your clothing with Japanese or Chinese characters can work wonders. One traveller got good

NGOs in Vietnam

ETHOS

ETHOS Vietnam (☎/fax 04-718 0040) IPO Box 220, Hanoi, Vietnam
ETHOS UK (☎ 0870-840 8408, fax 840 8409, ⓔ projects@ethos.org.uk, Web site: www.ethos.org.uk) 53 Home Close, Chiseldon, Swindon, Wiltshire, SN4 0ND, England (Registered Charity in England no.1071972)

Ethos works directly with women and children, in their environment, and aims to provide safer, sustainable and healthy lives for families in difficult circumstances.

Frontier-Vietnam

Frontier-Vietnam (ⓔ frontier@netnam.org.vn, website: www.frontier.ac.uk)
Postal address: PO Box 242, GPO Hanoi, Hanoi, Vietnam

Frontier-Vietnam has an ongoing Forest Biodiversity Research Project, which carries out biodiversity and socio-economic surveys of the protected areas of Vietnam. They also have a Medicinal Plants Project in Sapa where they develop environmental education units in local schools and teach ethnic minority farmers how to cultivate and harvest medicinal plants. The Medicinal Plants Centre in Sapa then buys the herbs back from the farmers (and sells them in the cities) thus generating much needed guaranteed income while conserving local biodiversity.

Green Bamboo Shelter

(☎ 08-821 0199) 40/34 D\- Calmette, District 1, Ho Chi Minh City

Green Bamboo provides shelter, food, clothing and protection for street boys, as well as facillitating access to education programs.

KOTO (☎ 04-747 0337/0338, fax 747 0339, ⓔ kotohanoi@hn.vnn.vn) 61 Van Mieu, Dong Da District, Hanoi, Vietnam

KOTO is a street children's NGO-cum-sandwich-shop providing career training and guidance to former street children. Travellers can help out by eating at KOTO (see Places to Eat in the Hanoi chapter).

Saigon Children's Charity (SCC)

(ⓔ scc@hcmc.netnam.vn)

SCC provides education and development programs for disadvantaged children.

UNICEF (☎ 04-826 1170~5, fax 826 2641) 72 Ly Thuong Kiet, Hanoi, Vietnam

results by sewing a Korean flag onto her backpack.

If it comes down to an actual confrontation, *never* get let it get physical. Just give a good shout at the antagonist in any language *other* than Vietnamese – this should make the person realise that they are confronting a foreigner rather than a 'Vietnamese whore', and could actually lead to an apology.

You are not likely to encounter any such harassment. Things have improved recently, this may be due to more and more Vietnamese people being exposed to foreigner visitors and their realisation that there are indeed other Asian women in Vietnam beside the Vietnamese.

GAY & LESBIAN TRAVELLERS

Vietnam is relatively hassle-free place for homosexuals. There are no official laws on same-sex relationships in Vietnam, nor much in the way of official harassment.

However, the government is still notorious for closing down gay venues, and places that get written up in the mass media have a mysterious tendency to be raided soon after. As such, most gay venues keep a fairly low profile. There is, however, a healthy gay scene in Vietnam, especially in Hanoi and Ho Chi Minh City, evident by unabashed cruising around certain lakes in Hanoi and the thriving cafe scene in Ho Chi Minh City.

Common local attitudes suggest a general social prohibition, though the lack of any laws make things fairly safe (even if the authorities do break up a party on occasion). Major headlines were made in 1997 with Vietnam's first gay male marriage, and again in 1998 at the country's first lesbian wedding, in the Mekong Delta. However, displaying peculiar double standards, two weeks later government officials broke up the women's marriage, who signed an agreement promising not to live together again.

With the vast number of same-sex travel partners – gay or otherwise – checking into hotels throughout Vietnam, it is fair to say there is little scrutiny over how travelling foreigners are related. However it would be prudent not to flaunt your sexuality. Likewise with heterosexual couples, passionate public displays of affection are considered a basic no-no. Vietnamese of the same sex, friends and otherwise, can be frequently seen walking hand in hand, so theoretically there is no reason same sex foreign couples wouldn't do the same.

A good idea is to check out the Net. Check out Utopia at www.utopia-asia.com, which is chock-full of information and contacts, including detailed sections on the legality of homosexuality in Vietnam and some local gay terminology.

Douglas Thompson's *The Men of Vietnam* is a comprehensive gay travel guide to Vietnam. The book can be ordered at the above mentioned Internet site.

DISABLED TRAVELLERS

Vietnam is not a particularly good place for disabled travellers, despite the fact that many Vietnamese are disabled as a result of war injuries. Tactical problems include the crazy traffic, a lack of pedestrian footpaths, a lack of lifts in the buildings and the ubiquitous squat toilets.

Potential travellers might try asking for tips or travel suggestions at relevant action groups in their home town (some Vietnam Veteran groups which organise reunion tours to Vietnam might have some good ideas).Or, try visiting the Lonely Planet's Web site and seeking the advice of other travellers via the Thorn Tree (www.lonelyplanet.com.au).

SENIOR TRAVELLERS

Like many Asian countries there is a deep and definite sense of respect for the elderly in Vietnam, though seniors are likely to encounter some mobility problems.

There are no 'senior citizen' discounts for pensioners nor are any international cards officially recognised, but it may be worth flashing your card and seeing what you can get.

TRAVEL WITH CHILDREN

In general, foreign children have a good time in Vietnam mainly because of the overwhelming amount of attention they attract (Vietnamese are big on kids) and the fact that almost everybody wants to play with them!

There is plenty to do in big cities to keep kids interested, though in most smaller towns and rural areas you will probably encounter the boredom factor. The zoos, parks and some of the best ice-cream shops in South-East Asia are recommended. Kids visiting the south should not miss one of Ho Chi Minh City's water parks, while Hanoi's two big must-sees are the circus and water-puppet performances.

continued on page 125

Tastes of Vietnam

GREG ELMS

GARRETT CULHANE

GREG ELMS

Title page: Red hot chilli peppers (photograph by Garrett Culhane).

Top: Time to roll up your sleeves and dig out the nut cracker – yum!

Middle: Rice paper rolls rock!

Bottom: Ubiquitous, nutritious and delicious – pho.

GARRETT CULHANE

One of the delights of visiting Vietnam is the amazing cuisine – there are said to be nearly 500 different traditional Vietnamese dishes – which is, in general, superbly prepared and very reasonably priced. Eating is such an integral part of the culture that a time-honoured Vietnamese proverb, hoc an, hoc noi, dictates that people should 'learn to eat before learning to speak...'

Vietnam is almost completely self-sufficient when it comes to tasty ingredients, and although its cuisine has been subject to colonial influences from the French and Chinese, it retains a unique flavour. This is largely due to the use of the uniquely Vietnamese nuoc mam (fermented fish sauce), an abundance of fresh vegetables and herbs, and the dominance of rice. The proximity of Vietnam to the sea, and having two major deltas within its borders, has ensured the use of fish and seafood in many dishes.

For the full scoop on Vietnamese cuisine, snap up a copy of Lonely Planet's *World Food Vietnam*, a compact but exhaustive guide to the culinary delights of Vietnam.

Utensils

Traditionally Vietnamese cooking was done over the hearth, which was considered to be the most important part of a house. There were no ovens as such, so food was prepared by boiling, steaming, grilling or frying. Thus a traditional kitchen would be equipped with terracotta cooking pots, woks, bamboo chopsticks and utensils and an essential rice cooker. A pestle and mortar would also be used to finely grind herbs and spices.

Most of these utensils are still regularly used in Vietnamese kitchens, although these days gas burners have replaced the hearths. Some restaurants serve food in traditional terracotta pots that resemble samovars with their tops cut off, and put live coals in the centre to keep the food hot while it is being served.

Eating Etiquette

Eating plays a huge role in Vietnamese society and there is certain etiquette involved in the dining experience. Although your hosts will be too polite to actually point out your faux pas, it is worth abiding by certain customs. When invited out to dine, it is polite to bring along a small gift – flowers are suitable but should never be white as this is a death sign.

Unlike the Western practice of each person ordering their own plate of food, dining in most Asian countries is a communal affair. That is, a selection of dishes are put on the table to be shared by a small group. People generally use their own chopsticks to serve themselves from a communal plate of food, although serving spoons or chopsticks may be supplied. Sharing dishes with three or four people ensures that you get to sample several different types of dishes and is a fun and very sociable way to eat – many visitors come to prefer it over Western individualism. If you eat with a group of Vietnamese, you may find that some of your fellow diners pick out the best-looking pieces of food with their chopsticks and put them into your rice bowl – a way of honouring you as a distinguished guest.

No-one will be offended if you ask for a knife and fork, although in some places this may not be an option. Fortunately spoons will usually be provided alongside chopsticks – although it's worth noting that the Vietnamese sip their food from the spoon and never place it directly into their mouth.

The proper way to eat Vietnamese food is to take rice from the large shared dish and put it in your rice bowl. Once you have the rice use your chopsticks to take meat, fish or vegetables from the serving dishes (never pour dipping sauces directly into your bowl). Transfer all food to your rice bowl before eating it and never use the chopsticks to pierce food on communal plates. Holding the rice bowl near your mouth, use your chopsticks to eat. Leaving the rice bowl on the table and conveying your food, precariously perched between chopsticks, all the way from the table to your mouth strikes Vietnamese as odd, though they will be more amused than offended. When passing or taking something always use both hands and it is polite to acknowledge the transaction with a small nod.

All good hosts must feed their guests, even if they're not hungry. In most cases they will try to feed you till you are unable to move, and then they will continue to try and stuff more food into you. It's a good idea to make sure you are really hungry before you arrive and then start feigning satisfaction from the earliest point possible. This way you may only be force-fed an extra one or two helpings over your limit.

If you want to deliver a 'delicious' compliment to the chef, just say *long num*.

Dining Out

You'll never have to look very far for food in Vietnam – restaurants *(nha hang)* of one sort or another seem to be in every nook and cranny. Unless you eat in exclusive hotels or restaurants, Vietnamese food is very cheap. The best bargains can be found at street stalls, most of which are limited to the amount of ingredients they can carry, so tend to specialise in a couple of particular dishes. Wander around until something takes your fancy – a bowl of noodles costs around US$0.50.

Basic restaurants with bamboo and cardboard walls have rice, meat and vegetable meals costing around US$1. Most cafes and decent restaurants can fill your stomach for US$2 to US$5. With the relaxation of laws governing joint ventures, there has been a recent surge of classier Vietnamese restaurants popping up in the cities. Traditional Vietnamese dishes taste all the better for being consumed in ambient French-style courtyards or riverside terraces. However, in classy restaurants the bill can add up fast; be aware that the small snacks that appear on the table will cost you if you indulge (and are charged per person).

Although most serve exclusively Vietnamese food, some cafes can rustle up something Western, but the Vietnamese are much better at producing their food than the Western stuff – the Vietnamese pizza is particularly notorious. But Western restaurants are increasing in number, and the cooks are slowly learning to accommodate Western tastes. Plus, there is a growing wave of expat chefs, notably Italians and French, offering up savoury delights from their home countries.

There are no 'real' hours of business for places to eat, but as a general rule of thumb, cafes (especially travellers cafes) are open most of the day and into the night. Street stalls are open from very early in the morning till late at night. Restaurants will usually open for lunch from about 11 am to 2 pm and for dinner from 5 to 10 pm.

Exotic Meats

It is disturbing to most animal lovers that Fido can wind up on the menu, however, most Vietnamese don't eat dog – it's a specialty item. Dog meat is most popular in the North, where its consumption is believed to bring good fortune (as long as it is only eaten during the second half of the lunar month). To find (or avoid) a restaurant serving dog meat, look for a sign saying *thit cho* (in the north), or *thit cay* (in the south).

Though it may be exotic to try wild meat such as muntjac, bat, frog, deer, sea horse, shark fin and snake, many of these are endangered; eating it will indicate your support and acceptance of such practices and add to the demand for these products.

Fortunately, laws regarding the capture and sale of snakes have made snake meat a rarity. However, you are likely to still see snake, which is believed to have some medicinal properties and is widely touted as being an aphrodisiac. The more poisonous the snake, the worthier its reputation (and the higher the price charged). Cobras are a favourite, though pythons have a lot more meat. Feasting on such delicacies is not cheap and be aware that eating undercooked snake meat can prove dangerous.

One non-endangered animal eaten in the countryside is *chuot dong*, a rice-patty dwelling rodent whose meat tastes 'just like chicken'. Do not confuse these creatures with *chuot cong*, the larger and nastier urban rats similar to those found in cities around the world.

The Bill

Many visitors are surprised to find that most local Vietnamese restaurants do not display prices on the menu at all. This is normal. Vietnamese typically eat out in groups and are charged by the amount ordered to feed the whole group. In the case of no-price menus, you should definitely ask the total price when you place your order. Vietnamese diners know this and will always ask, so don't be shy about speaking up unless you want a shock when the bill finally comes. To get the bill, politely catch the attention of the waiting staff and write in the air as if with a pen on an imaginary piece of paper. Once you have it, check it carefully – overcharging or simple human error is not uncommon when more than one person orders food, or when many items are listed on the bill.

The moist hand towels sealed in plastic that you are given at most restaurants are occasionally free, but typically you'll be charged from US$0.04 to US$0.20 for the pleasure of using them (a small price to pay depending on how dirty your hands are). It is advisable not to wipe your face with these – people have complained of eye irritation, though it's hard to say if this is from bacteria or the chemicals used to clean the towels.

Typical Vietnamese Dishes

On menus, dishes are usually listed according to their main ingredient. For instance, all the chicken dishes appear together, as do all the beef dishes and so on.

One of the most popular dished is Vietnamese spring rolls (*nem*), which are known as *cha gio* (pronounced chow yau) in the south and *nem Sai Gon* or *nem ran* in the north. They are made of rice paper, and are filled with minced pork, crab, vermicelli, *moc nhi* (a kind of edible fungus), onion, mushroom and eggs, and then fried until the rice paper turns a crispy brown. *Nem rau* are vegetable spring rolls.

A variation on the theme are the delicious larger 'fresh' spring rolls called *banh trang* in the south and *banh da* in the north. With these you put the ingredients together yourself and roll your own. The outer shell is a translucent rice crepe. These are excellent, and are typically eaten with a kind of shrimp paste called *mam tep* or *mam tom* – the latter smells stronger.

Other popular dishes available throughout Vietnam include:

Banh cuon – a steamed rice dumpling into which minced pork and moc nhi is rolled, and served with ca cuong, a special type of *nuoc mam* dipping sauce containing a filtered extract from insect semen, which gives the sauce its flowery aroma and pearlike taste

Bo bay mon – sugar-beef dishes

Bun bo – rice vermicelli and vegetables served dry, or with beef soup. The dish originated in Hué, where it is called *bun bo Hué*.

Bun cha – rice vermicelli with roasted pork and vegetables, served with a mixture of vinegar, chilli and sugar

Cha – pork paste fried in fat or broiled over hot coals

Cha ca – filleted fish slices broiled over charcoal, often served with noodles, green salad, roasted peanuts and a sauce made from nuoc mam, lemon and a special volatile oil

Cha que – cha prepared with cinnamon

Chao tom – grilled sugar cane rolled in spiced shrimp paste

Com tay cam – rice with mushrooms, chicken and finely sliced pork flavoured with ginger

Dua chua – bean sprout salad that tastes vaguely like Korean kimchi

Ech tam bot ran – frog meat soaked in a thin batter and fried in oil, usually served with nuoc mam cham and pepper

Gio – lean, seasoned pork pounded into a paste before being packed into banana leaves and boiled

lau – Vietnamese hot pot, popular served with fish (*lau ca*) or goat (*lau de*) or vegetables only (*lau rau*)
Oc nhoi – snail meat, pork, chopped green onion, nuoc mam and pepper rolled up in ginger leaves and cooked in snail shells

There is also a wide variety of Western-style foods available. Excellent French bread is available everywhere – it's best in the morning when it's warm and fresh (baguettes are about US$0.10). Imported French cheese spread can be bought from street stalls for around US$1.50 per pack, and some king of salami or pâté is available.

Rice

The staple of Vietnamese cuisine is plain white rice *(com)* dressed up with a plethora of vegetables, meat, fish and spices. Rice is also used for a variety of byproducts including rice wine and noodles.

The most common style of Vietnamese restaurant, found throughout the country, is known as *com-pho*, literally rice and noodle shop, which is just what they serve. You will see signs reading com-pho everywhere in your travels.

Another common type of rice restaurant is called *com binh dan*, which are inexpensive places that offer an array of fresh meats and vegetables served with steamed rice; there are no menus, just point to order. Most dishes are under US$2.

Noodles

Vietnamese noodle dishes *(pho)* are eaten at all hours of the day, but are a special favourite for breakfast. Most Westerners would prefer their noodles for lunch, and fortunately you can also get bread, cheese and eggs in the morning. Noodles are usually eaten as a soup rather

Hué Cuisine

The historic city of Hué, on the banks of the Perfume River in Central Vietnam, is home to a remarkable tradition of Vietnamese haute cuisine. As the site of the Nguyen Emperors' capital, it is the place where intricate and delicious dishes were developed and prepared. Emperor Tu Duc, who reigned from 1848 to 1883, demanded that his tea be made from dew that had accumulated on leaves overnight. He also expected 50 dishes prepared by 50 cooks to be served by 50 servants at each meal. Ironically, as the size of the servings declined, the time taken to prepare them rose in direct proportion.

His cooks obediently learned sophisticated techniques and presentation skills to keep the king happy. Recipes were passed down from generation to generation, and are the source of some of the delicate combinations of flavours found today.

One excellent place in Hué to sample haute cuisine inspired by these creative traditions is called Tinh Gia Vien (see Places to Eat, North Bank, in the Central Vietnam chapter).

than 'dry' like spaghetti. The noodles served with Vietnamese soups are of three types: white rice noodles *(banh pho)*, clear noodles made from rice mixed with manioc powder *(mien)* and yellow, wheat noodles *(mi)*. Many noodle soups are available either with broth *(nuoc leo)* or without *(kho*, literally 'dry'). Some of the more popular dishes include:

Bun thang – rice noodles and shredded chicken with fried egg and prawns on top, served with a broth made by boiling chicken, dried prawns and pig bones
Canh kho hoa – a bitter soup (said to be especially good for the health of people who have spent a lot of time in the sun)
Mi ga – chicken soup with dry noodles
Mien luon – vermicelli soup with eel seasoned with mushrooms, shallots, fried eggs and chicken
Pho bo – beef noodle soup
Pho ga – chicken soup with rice noodles

Nuoc Mam

Nuoc mam (pronounced nuke mom) is a type of fermented fish sauce – instantly identifiable by its distinctive smell – without which no Vietnamese meal is complete. Though nuoc mam is to Vietnamese cuisine what soy sauce is to Japanese food, many hotel restaurants won't serve it to foreigners, knowing that the odour may drive away their Western customers.

The sauce is made by fermenting highly salted fish in large ceramic vats for four to 12 months. The price of nuoc mam varies considerably according to the quality. Connoisseurs insist the high-grade rocket fuel has a much milder aroma than the cheaper variety, though most foreigners will find it hard to tell the difference.

A more palatable version of fish sauce served in eateries throughout Vietnam is *nuoc mam cham*. This is basically nuoc mam with lime, vinegar, sugar, water, chilli and garlic added, which makes it much more agreeable to Western taste buds.

Nuoc mam actually isn't bad once you get used to it, and in the past some people even took a few bottles home with them in their luggage (God help you if the bottle leaked). However, in accordance with international aviation regulations against taking strong-smelling and corrosive substances on board, nuoc mam recently joined the durian fruit among the food substances banned from Vietnam Airlines. The ban apparently resulted from an incident in which a bottle of the sauce broke on a Vietnam Airline's flight, causing angry protests from perturbed foreign passengers sensitive to its smell.

If nuoc mam isn't strong enough for you, try *mam tom*, a powerful shrimp paste that American soldiers sometimes called 'Viet Cong tear gas'. It's often served with dog meat – foreigners generally find it far more revolting than the dog itself.

Vegetarian Food

Because Buddhist monks of the Mahayana tradition are strict vegetarians (at least they are supposed to be), Vietnamese vegetarian cooking (an chay) has a long history and is an integral part of Vietnamese cuisine. Because it does not include many expensive ingredients, vegetarian food is unbelievably cheap. In some specialty restaurants, chef prepare vegetarian dishes (mostly tofu-based) that bear a remarkable resemblance to common meat dishes.

On full moon (the 15th day of the lunar month) or new moon days (the last day of the lunar month), many Vietnamese and Chinese avoid eating meat or even nuoc mam. On such days, some food stalls, especially in the marketplaces, serve vegetarian meals. To find out when the next new or full moon will be, consult any Vietnamese calendar.

Common vegetarian selections include:

Rau xao hon hop – fried vegetables
Xup rau – vegetable soup

Desserts & Cakes

Vietnamese sweets *(do ngot)* and desserts *(do trang mieng)* are popular everywhere, and are especially prevalent during religious or spiritual holidays and events when traditional cakes (*danh*) come in a wide variety of shapes and flavours.

In addition to the delicious European-style pastries and ice cream found in Vietnam, try to find an opportunity to sample one or more of the following traditional delicacies:

Banh bao – filled Chinese pastry that can most easily be described as looking like a woman's breast, complete with a reddish dot on top. Inside the sweet, doughy exterior is meat, onions and vegetables (it's often dunked in soy sauce)
Banh chung – square cake made from sticky rice and filled with beans, onion and pork, boiled in leaves for 10 hours – a traditional Tet favourite (see 'The Tet Festival' special section in this chapter)
Banh dau xanh – mung bean cake, usually served with hot tea, which 'melts on your tongue'
Banh deo – cake made of dried sticky rice flour mixed with a boiled sugar solution and filled with candied fruit, sesame seeds, fat etc, and eaten during the mid autumn festival
Banh it nhan dau – a traditional Vietnamese treat, this is a gooey pastry made of pulverised sticky rice, beans and sugar. It is steamed (and sold) in a banana leaf folded into a triangular pyramid. You often see it on sale at Mekong Delta ferry crossings
Banh it nhan dua – a variation of the above mentioned pastry, made with coconut instead of beans
Che – highly popular with Hanoians, this is served in a tall ice-cream sundae glass, and typically contains beans, fruit, coconut and sugar; an interesting variety made with pomelo flower is called *che buoi*

Kem dua/kem trai dua – delicious mix of ice cream, candied fruit and the jellylike meat of young coconut served in a baby coconut shell
Mut – candied fruit or vegetables, made with carrot, coconut, kumquat, gourd, ginger root, lotus seeds, tomato etc
Yaourt – little jars or plastic cups of sweetened frozen yoghurt are usually available from ice cream stalls.

Fruit

Fruit *(qua* or *trai)* is available in Vietnam year-round, but many of the country's most interesting specialties have short seasons.

avocado – often eaten in a glass with ice and sweetened with either sugar or condensed milk
cinnamon apple – also known as custard apple, sugar apple and sweetsop, it is ripe when it's very soft and the area around the stem turns blackish
coconut – in their mature state, coconuts are eaten only by children or as jam. For snacking, Vietnamese prefer the soft jellylike meat and fresher milk of young coconuts. The coconuts grown around the Ha Tien area in the Mekong Delta are a special variety with delicious coconut flesh, but no milk.
durian – an enormous watermelon-sized fruit, has bright orange segments with a slightly rubbery texture, and is so smelly that some hotels post signs saying not to eat it in their rooms!
green banana – sold in markets and are usually ripe enough to eat (in fact, they taste better than the yellow ones)
jackfruit – an enormous watermelon-sized fruit, with bright orange segments with a slightly rubbery texture

Ice Cream

Kem (ice cream) was introduced to Vietnam on a large scale by the Americans, who made a reliable supply of the stuff a top wartime priority. The US army hired two American companies, Foremost Dairy and Meadowgold Dairies, to build dozens of ice-cream factories all around the country. Inevitably, local people developed a taste for the product. Even 15 years after bona fide Foremost products ceased to be available in the Socialist Republic, the company's orange-and-white logo was prominently on display in shops selling ice cream. Recently, however, the government has been making an effort to purge the country of these obsolete signs because it wants to encourage these companies to return. Foremost did in fact return to Vietnam in 1994 to set up a new dairy, and was soon followed by American ice-cream mega giants Baskin Robbins and Carvel.

Proving more popular than the American stuff, however, is the laudable, French-run Fanny's Ice Cream (there are branches in several major tourist centres, including Hanoi and Ho Chi Minh City), which whips up delicious homemade flavors using fresh local fruits and even young sticky rice *com*!

longan – small and juicy brown-skinned balls grown all over the Mekong Delta region
lychee – these are larger and sweeter that longans
papaya or ***pawpaw*** – has bright orange flesh that tastes melonlike (the black seeds are said to act as a contraceptive)
pomelo – looks like a huge orange or grapefruit; the skin is greenish and the flesh often has a purple tinge

Drinks

Coffee

Vietnamese coffee is fine stuff. Particularly notable are the beans grown in the Central Highlands area around Buon Ma Thuot. There is, however, one qualifier – you'll probably need to dilute it with hot water. The Vietnamese prefer their coffee so strong and so sweet that it will turn your teeth inside out. Ordering 'white coffee' usually results in a coffee with about 30% to 40% sweet condensed milk. Ovaltine and Milo, which are regarded as desserts rather than drinks, will also be served this way. Those restaurants accustomed to travellers will be prepared with thermos bottles of hot water so you can dilute your coffee (or Ovaltine etc) as you wish. However, restaurants that deal with a mainly Vietnamese clientele will probably be dumbfounded by your request for hot water. You'll also need to communicate the fact that you need a large glass – ultra-sweet coffee is traditionally served in a tiny shot glass, leaving you no room to add any water.

Instant coffee *(ca phe tan* or *ca phe bot)* made its debut in 1996 – a disaster! Many cafes assume Westerners prefer instant coffee because it's 'modern' and comes from the West. You need to communicate the fact that you want fresh-brewed Vietnamese coffee, not imported instant powder. The words for fresh-brewed coffee are *ca phe phin*.

Rather than prepare coffee in a pot, the Vietnamese prefer to brew it right at the table, French-style – a dripper with coffee grounds is placed over the cup and hot water poured in. If you prefer iced coffee, the same method is applied, but with a glass of ice under the dripper. Both the drippers and packaged coffee make inexpensive souvenirs.

Perhaps the highest grade Vietnamese coffee is known as *chon*; these beans are fed to a certain species of weasel and later collected from the weasel's excrement. One place you can try a cup of this stuff (for about US$0.70) is Trung Ngyuen, a popular chain of coffee shops found in Hanoi and Ho Chi Minh City. Trung Ngyuen, consequently, means Central Highlands.

Tea

Vietnamese tea in the south is cheap, but disappointing – the aroma is perfumelike, but the taste sometimes resembles the glue found on postal envelopes. Guests are always served tea (local green tea or Lipton) when visiting a Vietnamese home or business.

Tea grown in the north is much better, but also much stronger – be prepared for a caffeine jolt. The northern tea is similar to Chinese green tea and is almost always sold in loose form rather than teabags. The Vietnamese never put milk or sugar into green tea and will think you're a loony if you do.

Imported tea (in teabag form) can be bought in major cities, but is still rare in rural areas. The price is perfectly reasonable so there's no need to bring it from abroad. Most restaurants can dig up some lemon and sugar for your tea, although milk is not always available.

Mineral Water

The selection of mineral water *(nuoc suoi)* has been expanding rapidly ever since the Vietnamese realised that tourists were willing to pay good money for water sealed in plastic bottles.

High-quality mineral water in large plastic bottles is readily available for under US$1 (see the 'C'est La Vie' boxed text). If you prefer your mineral water with fizzy bubbles, look for Vinh Hao carbonated water (available in the south only). It's normally mixed with ice, lemon and sugar (outstanding!) which is called *so-da chanh*.

Coconut Milk

There is nothing more refreshing on a hot day than fresh coconut milk (nuoc dua). The Vietnamese believe that coconut milk, like hot milk in Western culture, makes you tired. Athletes, for instance, would never drink it before a competition.

The coconuts grown around the Ha Tien area in the Mekong Delta are a special variety with delicious coconut flesh, but no milk.

Soft Drinks

These days nearly all of Vietnam's domestic carbonated soft drinks have been replaced by Coca-Cola and Pepsi. When the US economic embargo was lifted in 1994, Pepsi beat Coca-Cola into the Vietnamese market – a major coup. However, Coca-Cola has hit back hard with a high-pitched sales campaign and seems to have the dominant market share now. Sprite and 7Up are also widely available. Diet drinks can increasingly be found in the supermarkets of large cities.

One excellent domestic soft drink with a pleasant fruit flavour is *nuoc khoang kim boi*; a bottle costs US$0.30.

In addition, the usual fruit juices (*sinh to*), including delicious sugar cane juice, are available throughout Vietnam.

Beer

Saigon Export (yes, they do really export it) and Saigon Lager are two local brands of beer costing about two-thirds the price of the imported brands in cans and about half the price of bottles. Other Vietnamese brands include Castel, Huda (from Hué), Halida, Bia Hanoi and 333 (pronounced ba-ba-ba), as well as dozens of other locally brewed selections.

Nameless regional beers, though watery and often flat, are available in bottles for less than the name brands. One traveller described such 'no-label beers' as being a cross between light beer and iced tea.

Memorise the words *bia hoi*, which means 'draught beer'. There are signs advertising it everywhere and most cafes have it on the menu. The quality varies, but it is generally OK and very cheap (about US$0.25 per litre). Places that serve bia hoi usually also have good, cheap food. *Bia tuoi*, literally 'fresh beer' is similar to bia hoi.

There are a number of foreign brands that are brewed in Vietnam under licence. These include BGI, Carlsberg, Heineken and Vinagen.

Wine

Vietnam produces over 50 varieties of wine *(ruou)*, many of them made from rice. The cheapest rice wines *(ruou de)* are used for cooking – drink them at your peril.

Another Vietnamese specialty is snake wine *(ruou ran)*. This is basically rice wine with a pickled snake floating in it. This elixir is said to have some tonic properties and drinking it is claimed to cure everything from night blindness to impotence (see Exotic Meats earlier in this section).

A variation on the theme is to have the snake killed right at your table and the blood poured into a cup. To get the full health benefits, the Vietnamese recommend that you drink the snake's blood mixed with rice wine and eat the gall bladder raw (delicious!). Connoisseurs of this cuisine also recommend that you put the snake's still-beating heart into a glass of rice wine and 'bottoms up'. This cocktail is believed to work as an aphrodisiac.

For the less adventurous, the imported wine situation is constantly and thankfully improving.

The Vietnamese will have to work on their techniques for distilling champagne. The stuff presently available tastes like it was drained from an old rusty radiator. Occasionally you can find the odd bottle of

C'est la Vie

The Vietnamese are notorious copycats, and the prevailing trend in business is to imitate thy neighbour, rather than create an original niche. This tendency is displayed by restaurants, hotels, street names and tour programs, but perhaps the best example is the bottled water market.

In 1989 La Vie, the famed French mineral-water maker, was the first foreign outfit to set up bottling plants in Vietnam. Since then, strikingly close variations on the trademark red, white and blue label design, as well as variations on the name La Vie, have appeared in all corners of the country.

At last count there were over 20 different spin-offs, including those with nonsense names like La Viei, La Vu, La Vi and La Ve. The best, perhaps, are the those that have meaning in French: slurp down a cold bottle of La Vif (The Lively), La Vide (The Empty) or, brace yourself, La Viole (The Rape).

Russian stuff (some of it very good and cheap) but often these have been sitting in the sun on display racks.

Hard Liquor

Alcoholic beverages (ruou manh) from China are very cheap, taste like paint thinner and smell like diesel fuel. Russian vodka is one of the few things the former USSR has left to export. Locally produced Hanoi Vodka is also available. Nep moi is a smooth, locally produced vodka made from sticky rice.

As in the rest of Asia, the Vietnamese nouveaux riches prefer foreign name brands such as Johnny Walker Black. You can sit in almost any high-class Vietnamese restaurant and watch groups of rosy-cheeked businessmen or government officials polish off bottles of the stuff in no time flat.

continued from page 112

Nature lovers with children can hike in one of Vietnam's expansive national parks or nature reserves. Cuc Phuong National Park (see the North-Central Vietnam chapter) in particular is home to the interesting Endangered Primate Rescue Centre, where you can peek in on efforts being made to protect and breed endangered monkeys. This is a good place to learn first hand about pressures on the evironment and the plight of our furry friends. Babies and unborn children can present their own peculiar problems, Lonely Planet's *Travel with Children* by Maureen Wheeler gives a rundown on health precautions to be taken with kids and advice on travel during pregnancy.

USEFUL ORGANISATIONS

Chamber of Commerce

Vietcochamber, the Chamber of Commerce & Industry, is supposed to initiate and facilitate contacts between foreign business and Vietnamese companies. It may also be able to help with obtaining and extending business visas. Vietcochamber publishes a listing of government companies and its contact details. It has offices in Ho Chi Minh City, Hanoi and Danang.

Nongovernment Organisations

There are various nongovernment organisations (NGOs), including churches, humanitarian aid organisations and the like working in Vietnam. See the 'NGOs in Vietnam' boxed text, following.

DANGERS & ANNOYANCES

Culture Shock

The most dangerous thing in Vietnam is your own psyche. As one traveller noted:

> My first day on landing in Ho Chi Minh City was one of shock and horror. For the first couple of days I thought the whole idea of Vietnam was a terrible mistake. No matter how much reading and research you do prior to arriving, nothing prepares you for the sights, sounds and smells of this place. Three days after arriving I was OK, had settled down and was having a fantastic time.
>
> **Craig McGrath**

Another traveller had this to say:

> Some extremely upsetting sights, sounds and smells in Ho Chi Minh City were a shock, but that was overcome because of the wonderful people. The street kids were an absolute joy. The smiling people, the most hard working and industrious anyone could ever meet, with hope and humour facing their everyday hardships with laughter and companionship – just great.
>
> **Audrey Snoddon**

This is not to say that nothing can go wrong. There are some things you should definitely be concerned about. Just remember, though, that worrying about all the 'problems' you will encounter can do more to ruin your trip than the problems themselves. Just take necessary precautions to guard yourself against the minority of schemers and thieves so you can get back to connecting with the other 99.9% of the population who are genuinely honest and delightful. After all, you're here to have fun!

Theft

The Vietnamese are convinced that their cities are very dangerous and full of criminals. Before reunification, street crime was rampant in the south, especially in Ho Chi Minh City. Motorbike-borne thieves (called cowboys by the Americans) would speed down major thoroughfares, ripping pedestrians' watches off their wrists. Pickpocketing and confidence tricks were also common. Even after the fall of Saigon, a few bold criminals managed to swindle some newly arrived North Vietnamese troops. When a few such outlaws were summarily shot, street crime almost disappeared overnight.

Well, it seems to have reappeared with a vengeance. We have had countless reports of street crime, particularly in Ho Chi Minh City, and regardless of how safe it may seem, you should always exercise caution and common sense. One strong suggestion for Ho Chi Minh City is do not have anything dangling off your body that you are not ready to part with. This includes bags, and any jewellery – even of the costume variety, which might tempt a robber.

Especially watch out for drive-by thieves on motorbikes – they specialise in snatching handbags and cameras from tourists walking in the city and riding in cyclos. Some have become proficient at grabbing valuables from the open window of a car and speeding away with the loot. Foreigners have occasionally reported having their eyeglasses and hats snatched too.

Pickpocketing – often involving kids, women with babies and newspaper vendors – is also a serious problem, especially in tourist areas of Ho Chi Minh City, such as Đ Dong Khoi and the Pham Ngu Lao area. Many of the street kids, adorable as they may be, are very skilled at liberating people from their wallets or whatever else may be in their pocket or handbag. You need to watch very carefully (beware of large groups of children) and in some cases you may have to physically keep the kids at arm's distance.

Of course they're not all bad – there are heaps of kids trying to survive by selling postcards and souvenirs – but some know exactly how to prey on peoples' weaknesses for cute kids.

Letters from travellers such as the following are common:

We didn't have trouble with pickpockets except in Ho Chi Minh City. The children selling postcards will place a postcard filled hand over your fanny pack while expertly unzipping the thing with their free hand. We luckily noticed what was going on before the pack was fully unzipped and contents stolen. However, I recommend fanny pack locks or, better yet, steering clear of children selling post cards.

Dee Mahan

In HCMC another one of our fellow travellers lost his camera while trying to take a picture. The thieves were two young guys on a motorcycle. The idea is to get close enough to the tourist so the passenger can grab anything not properly secured, ie handbags, cameras, sunglasses and even hats!

Another thing to watch are crowds of lovely little children who try and sell postcards, etc. These children work in groups and while the older kids are keeping your attention diverted the smaller kids are able to open the zips on bumbags and empty their contents. These kids are very touchy feely and after a while you become impervious to them touching your arms or rubbing your skin, but keep an eye on them as they are able to steal your watch with amazing ease.

As terrible as all this sounds, as long as you are careful then you should be safe. My trip to Vietnam was one of the greatest trips of my life, and with a certain amount of wariness there are few problems to be encountered.

Matthew Ford

We felt secure at all times. Nobody bothered us. In Ho Chi Minh City, however, I was strongly discouraged from walking around the waterfront even during the day. They told me a robbing technique is to pull your bag while pushing you into the water!

Javier Jimenez

Avoid setting things down while you're eating or at least take the precaution of fastening these items to your seat with a strap or chain. Remember, any luggage that you leave unattended for even a moment may grow legs and vanish.

There are also 'taxi girls' (sometimes transvestites) who approach Western men, give them a big hug and ask if they'd like 'a good time'. Then they suddenly change their mind and depart – along with a wristwatch and wallet.

One of Ho Chi Minh City's latest scams is a well-choreographed routine practiced by local prostitutes – this one is just made to be videotaped. A man is approached on the street by a pair of beautiful women, and the arm of one sweeps down to spontaneously procure an excruciatingly grasp on his testicles! Faced with that spur of the moment consideration for his wallet, or his 'family jewels', most find that before the first soprano note leaves his lips, the castrator's partner will have managed to empty the contents of his pocket. It usually takes several minutes of recovery to realise what happened, and by that time the dynamic duo will be long gone.

We have also had reports of people being drugged and robbed on long-distance public buses. It usually starts with a friendly fellow passenger offering you a free Coke, which turns out to be a chloral-hydrate cocktail. You wake up hours later to find your valuables and new-found 'friend' gone.

Even assuming that you are too wise to accept gifts from strangers, there is at least one other way you can be drugged. One traveller we know well claims that his fellow passenger leaned across him to open a window, while an accomplice took advantage of the diversion to drop some drugs into his water bottle. The lesson seems to be that you shouldn't keep your water bottle where others can easily get their hands on it with the lid firmly on.

Despite all this, don't be overly paranoid. Although crime certainly exists and you need to be aware of it, theft in Vietnam does not seem to be any worse than what you'd expect in a large city anywhere. Don't assume that everyone's a thief – most Vietnamese are poor, but honest.

And finally, there is the problem of your fellow travellers. It's a disgusting reality that a number of backpackers subsidise their journey by ripping off whoever they can, including other backpackers. This is most likely to happen if you stay in a dormitory, though dorms are rare in Vietnam. Perhaps most disturbing are attempts by foreigners to rip off the Vietnamese. There have been reports of backpackers slipping out of restaurants without paying their bills, cheating their guides out of promised pay etc. We know one fellow who deliberately short-changed his driver US$40 because the car's air-conditioner broke down on the last day of the trip. This is pretty sick.

To avoid theft, probably the best advice you can follow is to not bring anything valuable that you don't need. Expensive watches, jewellery and electronic gadgets invite theft – do you really need these things while travelling?

Beggar Fatigue

Just as you're about to dig into the scrumptious Vietnamese meal you've ordered, you feel someone gently tugging on your shirt sleeve. You turn around to deal with this latest 'annoyance' only to find it's a bony, eight-year-old boy holding his three-year-old sister in his arms. The little girl has a distended stomach, her palm is stretched out to you and her hungry eyes are fixed on your plate of steaming chicken, vegetables and rice.

This is the face of poverty. How do you deal with these situations? If you're like most of us, not very well. All of the children and people on the streets selling or begging have found themselves in such a position due to circumstance. It certainly wasn't a choice, and in many cases it still isn't. These people deserve a chance and respect, and it helps to gain a better understanding of the life these people lead and have led.

In a conversation about the issue of post card sellers, a local social worker in Hanoi offered the following insight:

> Like any trade, you learn the most effective ways to achieve good results, and selling on the streets is no different. An innocent or naive foreigner already overcome with guilt by the obvious signs of poverty is usually the target. Street children have become experts in the field of sympathy story telling, their words, actions and tones used have a great affect and generous results. The foreigner is so taken and overwhelmed by the hardships and misfortunes this child is faced with they soon succumb to doing the best they can to help in their given situation, this usually means giving money or material items.
>
> People often feel threatened or uncomfortable with the older boys who are selling on the streets; these boys have usually been selling since they were younger, their selling tool then was their youthfulness and cute childlike behaviour. Adolescence and puberty brings facial hair, broken voices and many other signs of adulthood. The ideal selling tool that once was, has gone; rather than fuss and coo over this individual, people now walk away and seem suddenly afraid. So the older seller feels cheated and hurt, he may become angry and behave in a more aggressive manner because now this is the only way he knows to get attention.
>
> If you do buy books, postcards or souvenirs from street vendors, it is best for all parties involved to avoid handing over more than the standard selling price (in the case of post cards, just check at any local book store). Find out the approximate price first, and don't be afraid to barter. By paying over the odds or handing out money you could actually be contributing to the growing number of street children and the numerous problems they face.

Tuan

Tuan (his name has been changed for the purpose of this book) was a bright eighteen-year-old boy who worked on the streets of Hanoi selling postcards for about four years. He became a well-known face in the area he worked, particularly with a number of expats. Tuan had a physical deformity that attracted a great deal of attention and sympathy over the years. The problem was a curable one, something that is easily resolved in the West, but in Vietnam is almost impossible to fix for someone in the circumstances of a street child.

In addition to being visually eye-catching, like many postcard sellers, Tuan spoke very good English and could easily interact with and charm foreign tourists.

Many street children become great storytellers, realising that hard-luck tales (often exaggerated, though based on reality) are a good way to be given money. It's also a way of attracting the sympathy, attention and affection the children obviously lack and yearn for.

Over the years, a number of foreigners were very taken by Tuan and his problems. While they could do little to solve the underlying social problems that lead to homelessness, in Tuan's case it was clear that some of his problems could be solved with a straightforward trip to the doctor. Consequently, many people gave money to him without hesitation. People would literally hand over one hundred dollars or more and either take him along to a doctor to plan an operation or they would trust him to make the visit himself. The majority of people who assisted Tuan over the years were only visiting the area for a short period of time, so they were unable to follow up their support, or assist Tuan in his treatment.

Children like Tuan have no idea how to be responsible for large amounts of money. They don't get paid large pay-packets – they rely on the goodwill of tourists to pay for over-priced postcards to make enough cash to get through the day. Overcharging foreigners is justified with the belief

How To Help So what can you do to help these street people, many of whom are malnourished and illiterate with no future? It is a difficult question with no simple answer, but if you would like to do something to help, please think before acting.

Many people become overcome with guilt when seeing so much blatant poverty, and desperation tends to bring out peoples' charitable side.

Taking the matter into your own hands by giving out money or gifts to people on the streets can prove to cause more damage than good. The more people are given hand outs, the more reliant and attracted they become to life on the streets. The sooner money becomes too difficult to acquire, people recognise that life on the streets is no longer so fruitful. This will hopefully discourage parents and 'leaders' forcing children and beggars onto the streets and gradually reduce the growing problems.

One way to contribute and help improve the situation is to invest just a few hours to find out about local organisations that work with disadvantaged people; these groups are far more likely to see that contributions are used in the most effective way possible to help those who need it. If you want to give, the most effective way is to seek out those who will use it wisely in your absence. For a list of reputable aid organisations that accept donations, see the 'NGOs in Vietnam' boxed text earlier in this chapter.

In Hanoi, you can visit the NGO Resource Centre (fax 832 8611, e gocentr@netnam.org.vn) in the La Thanh Hotel, 218 Doi Can; here you'll find listings and information on various aid organisations working in Vietnam. In terms of volunteering, always contact the particular group you want to help in advance to find out its needs and requirements; never just show up, as this usually causes more inconvenience than it does help.

Alternatively if you want to do something instant, avoid money and anything that can be sold. Giving money or items that can be sold will be of no benefit, as

Tuan

that all foreigners are rich – what's an extra five dollars to them? The problem is that they become totally dependent on tourists as a source of income.

So what happens with the money? In Tuan's case it sadly led him into a life of drugs. He became a heroin addict. Like other addicts, he was supported through drug rehabilitation, and went through five detoxification programs. Why? The donor helping Tuan was usually unable to go through the program with him and give the support and encouragement he desperately needed. If someone had paid in advance, Tuan would go along for the treatment – although he was addicted, some tiny piece of will seemed to remind him he must stop to survive. But, if Tuan was given the money and responsibility to take himself along to the hospital, as was so often the case, then the money was inevitably used for his next fix.

The problem with most addicts is that after going through the gruelling and lonely ordeal of detoxification, they leave the program and end up back on the streets – exposed to the same street life and drug culture as before. Without proper counselling, guidance or support, these youngsters do not have the strength to walk away and begin their lives over without drugs.

People want to help, but what they don't realise is that sometimes they are actually making the situation far worse, and in Tuan's case creating even bigger problems that did not exist in the first place. If all of those people who had helped Tuan over the years had instead focused their time on seeking out people or local organisations who could have helped, perhaps Tuan would be alive today. Instead Tuan no longer has that chance, as his drug use resulted in him contracting AIDS. In the end, Tuan lost his battle.

(See the 'Beggar Fatigue' and 'NGOs in Vietnam' boxed text this chapter for more information about what you can do to help street children.)

more often than not the parents or a leader is nearby to take away any money or items that are given.

The elderly and, in particular, young children begging will almost always have a parent or leader only a few steps behind them to take away whatever is given or earned. The elderly and the young are easily controlled and are ideal begging tools; people know how much they can make by pushing them into these unfair conditions. Small children are often forced to beg for money, with the cash going towards their parents' drinking and gambling habits rather than food or schooling for the children. Of course, that's if the kids have parents, which many of them don't.

As a rule of thumb, if you are going to give something directly to a beggar, it's better to give food than money; take them to a market or food stall and buy them a nutritious meal or some fruit to be sure they are the only beneficiaries and no harm is done. Even something not so good for their teeth is better than money, as one traveller realised:

I will always remember the beam of delight that came over the face of a hard-bitten child beggar when I offered him a cake similar to the one I was eating.

Gordon Balderston

Message from a Reader Two foreign readers with experience working with projects for street children in Vietnam wrote in with the following recommendations to help debunk some of the 'myths' that tourists often hold regarding the giving of money to child beggars:

Many tourists wish to make random acts of kindness to do good deeds. They wish to enrich the life of a poor child in rags and with stunted growth; they give money or food believing that this is the best way and all they can do to help. However, many do not realise that their act of kindness contributes to dimming the flame of that child's future. Most fail to recognise that when they give money, it:

- spoils the children and makes them reluctant to accept stable but low-paying jobs that give them skills for a more secure future

- may be used for drugs
- reinforces the notion of victimisation and reliance on charity
- will be gone within a day; the majority of street children don't save money, thus it has no long term value
- may be used parents for drinking and gambling.

In addition, the money garnered by the child may be enough to support the family, making the parents feel less responsible; some even stop working to live on the earnings of their children.

Rather than giving money to children, direct the child to a local organisation (such as The Children's Desk in Ho Chi Minh City) where they can be referred to a shelter or to other free services and/or donate to and support legitimate organisations which offer educational and vocational training, free medical services, job placements, etc

Your money will be more wisely spent with greater long-term benefits for street children. However, please be aware that some children may refuse these services because they become addicted to the 'quick money' and lack the necessary (parental) guidance and support to continue their education. The social workers you encounter will have a much greater understanding of the children's background than the average tourist.

If you are interested in volunteering to work with street children for some length of time, organisations usually prefer that you contact them before you leave your home country. They need to organise their programs to accommodate volunteers and to ensure that you will also benefit from the experience. But if you are interested in spending an hour, or a couple of days, you can try your luck at contacting them with some idea in mind (sports, games, making handicrafts, bringing some books for the children to look at, card games, etc).

Tracy Vuong & Tina Russell

Violence

Unlike in many Western cities, recreational homicide is not a popular sport in Vietnam. The country is virtually free of terrorists harbouring a political agenda. Violence against foreigners is extremely rare and is not something you should waste much time worrying about. In general theft is not life-threatening – like most thieves in the world, they are simply after your money and/or valuables.

However, there have been a few rare incidents involving guns, particularly on remote rural roads. One gang terrorised motorists in the Danang area for two years, stopping vehicles and robbing the passengers at gunpoint. After committing over 60 robberies, the gang was caught in mid-1994 and the thieves were sentenced to death. Another gang in the Mekong Delta robbed tourist boats at gunpoint before they were finally caught.

You do see a lot of street arguments between Vietnamese. Usually this takes the form of two young macho types threatening and pushing each other while their respective girlfriends try to separate them. The whole point of the threats and chest thumping is to save face and there is seldom any bloodshed. The cause of these arguments usually has something to do with money, usually as a result of some minor motor vehicle accident and the heated issue of who should pay for the broken headlight or squashed chicken. Such macho posturing is likely to exclude foreigners.

As a good general rule of thumb *do not* get into fights with Vietnamese. Social incorrectness aside, these fights often boil down to strength in numbers and many a macho foreigner has wound up in the hospital after the one little guy he squared off with whistled for his friends who were nearby. If you become embroiled in one of these situations, swallow your pride and find another safer way to vent your frustration.

Scams

Con artists and thieves are, of course, always seeking new tricks to separate naive tourists from their money and are becoming more savvy in their ways. We can't warn you about every trick you might encounter, so perhaps the best advice we can give is to maintain a healthy scepticism (as you would any where else in the world) and be prepared to argue when unnecessary demands are made for your money.

One sound piece of advice is *never* to take up with prostitutes who may chat you up in a bar or on the street – period. Beside the fundamental objections to this, the illegality of it and the obvious health risks involved, there are other serious dangers at hand (like getting ripped-off, for one). The chances of a man 'getting lucky' with a Vietnamese woman who is not a prostitute without a long and proper period of courtship is virtually none. Vietnamese women willing to sleep with a man they hardly know are doing it for money – don't let your ego get in the way.

One traveller wrote:

> I heard about a scam in Ho Chi Minh City – where women go back to hotels with a Western male. Once they are in the hotel room, the local police (are they really police?) knock on the door and demand a bribe to turn a blind eye to the use of a prostitute, even though the male may have thought he had just got lucky and there was no discussion of payment.
>
> **Andrew H**

Beware of a motorbike rental scam that some travellers have encountered in Ho Chi Minh City. What happens is that you rent a bike and the owner supplies you with an excellent lock and suggests you use it. What he doesn't tell you is that he, too, has a key and that somebody will follow you and 'steal' the bike at the first opportunity. You then have to pay for a new bike or forfeit your passport, visa, deposit or whatever security you left with him.

More common is when your motorbike won't start after you parked it in a 'safe' area with a guard. But yes, the guard knows somebody who can repair your bike. The mechanic shows up and goes about reinstalling the parts they removed earlier and now the bike works fine. That will be US$10 please.

Despite an array of scams, however, it is important to keep in mind the Vietnamese are not always out to get you. One concerning trend we're noticing in Vietnam, relative to neighbouring countries such as Thailand and Laos, is a general lack of trust for the locals on the part of foreigners. Some may blame guidebooks in part, for trying to make people aware of all the potential dangers and annoyances you might encounter while travelling; the key is trying to differentiate between who is good and bad and not close yourself off to everyone you encounter.

This is not always easy. Even one of the original authors of this book, a veteran travel writer and Vietnam-hand, was duped by a longtime Vietnamese friend who joined him on the road updating a former edition in 1996. This involved a clever attempt by the author's 'friend', unbeknown to him, to collect fees from hotels and restaurants that wished to be included in this guide!

One final word of advice (this may sound strange coming from the people who write these books); we're seeing an awful lot of travellers in Vietnam with their noses dug too deep inside guidebooks. The paranoia people develop from being hassled so much seems to result in many refusing to believe anyone if it's 'not in the book'. For both better and worse, often it's not. Try to keep an open mind, be aware of what can happen, what things 'should' cost, etc, and use this information in conjunction with your own better judgement.

Undetonated Explosives

Four armies expended untold energy and resources for over three decades mining, booby trapping, rocketing, strafing, mortaring and bombarding wide areas of Vietnam. When the fighting stopped most of this ordnance remained exactly where it had landed or been laid; American estimates at the end of the war placed the quantity of unexploded ordnance at 150,000 tonnes.

Since 1975, about 40,000 Vietnamese have been maimed or killed by this leftover ordnance while clearing land for cultivation or ploughing their fields. While cities, cultivated areas and well-travelled rural roads and paths are safe for travel, straying from these areas could land you in the middle of a minefield that, though known to the locals, may be completely unmarked.

Recent tragedies include the deaths of six children, in August 2000, who were killed when a left-over shell detonated, in Bonh Dinh, Central Vietnam. In 1997, several children were killed by a bomb blast in a school yard in the Nghe An Province.

Never touch any rockets, artillery shells, mortars, mines or other relics of war you may come across. Such objects can remain lethal for decades. In Europe, people are still occasionally injured by ordnance leftover from WWII, and even WWI, and every few years you read about city blocks in London or Rotterdam being evacuated after an old bomb is discovered in someone's backyard.

Especially dangerous are the nasty white phosphorus artillery shells (known to the Americans as 'Willy Peter') in which the active ingredient does not deteriorate as quickly as that in explosives. Upon contact with the air the white phosphorus ignites and burns intensely; if any of it gets on your body it will eat all the way through your hand, leg or torso unless scooped out with a razor blade – this stuff terrifies even the hardiest of scrap-metal scavengers.

Finally, don't climb inside bomb craters – you never know what undetonated explosive device is at the bottom. Remember, one bomb can ruin your whole day.

One US-based organisation worth a mention is Peace Trees Vietnam. This laudable NGO trains Vietnamese military personnel to clear old mine fields; once the bombs are removed, they send teams of former GIs into the areas replant the area with hundreds of new trees. Thus restoring the environment and contributing to improving relations between the two former enemies. You can contact Peace Trees Vietnam, (☎ 202-842 8451), or write to PO Box 10697, Bainbridge, WA 98110, USA.

You can learn more about landmines at the Web site of Nobel Peace Prize winner International Campaign to Ban Landmines (www.icbl.org).

Sea Creatures

If you plan to spend your time swimming, snorkelling and scuba diving, you should be aware of various hazardous creatures that live in the sea. The list of dangerous sea creatures found in Vietnam is extensive and includes sharks, jellyfish, stonefish, scorpion fish, sea snakes and stingrays, to name a few. However, there is little cause for alarm – most of these creatures avoid humans, or humans avoid them, so the actual number of people injured or killed is fairly small. Nonetheless, exercising some common sense is strongly advised.

Jellyfish tend to travel in groups, so as long as you look before you leap into the sea, avoiding them should not be too hard. Make local inquiries – many places have a 'jellyfish season' (usually summer). Stings from most jellyfish are simply painful (see Cuts, Bites & Stings in the Health section earlier this chapter).

Stonefish, scorpion fish and stingrays tend to hang out in shallow water along the ocean floor and can be very difficult to see. One way to protect yourself against these nasties is to wear shoes in the sea. To treat a sting by a stonefish or scorpion fish, immerse the affected area in hot water and seek medical treatment.

All sea snakes are poisonous but are generally nonaggressive. Furthermore, their small fangs are placed towards the rear of the mouth so it's difficult for them to bite large creatures like humans.

Noise

One annoyance that can be insidiously draining on your energy during a trip to Vietnam is noise. At night, there is often a competing cacophony from motorcycles, dance halls, cafes, video parlours, karaoke lounges, restaurants and so on; if your hotel is near any of these (and it's unlikely to be in a totally noise-free zone), sleep may be difficult. In some places, even the ice cream and snack vendors' carts have a booming, distorted portable cassette player attached.

The Vietnamese themselves seem to be immune to the noise. Indeed, a cafe that doesn't have an eardrum-splitting clamour emanating from a loudspeaker will have difficulty attracting customers; that is to say, Vietnamese customers. The foreigners will flee as soon as the sound system is turned on. Those who stay long enough to finish a meal or a cup of coffee will walk away with their heads literally pounding.

Fortunately, most noise subsides around 10 or 11 pm, as few clubs stay open much later than that. Unfortunately, however, the Vietnamese are very early risers; most are up and about from around 5 am onwards. This not only means that traffic noise starts early, but you may to be woken up by the crackle of cafe speakers, followed by very loud (and usually atrocious) karaoke music. It's worth trying to get a room at the back of a hotel, or wherever else the street noise looks likely to be diminished. Other than that, consider bringing a set of earplugs.

LEGAL MATTERS

Civil Law

The French gave the Vietnamese the Napoleonic Code, much of which has still to be repealed, although these laws may conflict with later statutes. From about 1960 to 1975, South Vietnam modified much of its commercial code to resemble that of the USA. Since reunification, Soviet-style laws have been applied to the whole country with devastating consequences for private property owners. The recent economic reforms have seen a flood of new property legislation, much of it the result of advice from the United Nations, International Monetary Fund and other international organisations. The rapid speed at which legislation is being enacted is a challenge for those who must interpret and en force the law.

On paper, it all looks good. In practice, the rule of law barely exists in Vietnam these days. Local officials interpret the law anyway it suits them, often against the wishes of Hanoi. This poses serious problems for joint ventures – foreigners who have gone to court in Vietnam to settle civil disputes have generally fared pretty badly. It's particularly difficult to sue a state-run company, even if that company committed obvious fraud. The government has a reputation for suddenly cancelling permits, revoking licences and basically tearing up written contracts. There is no independent judiciary.

Not surprisingly, most legal disputes are settled out of court. In general, you can accomplish more with a carton of cigarettes and a bottle of good cognac than you can with a lawyer.

Drugs

During the American War, US troops were known to consume large quantities of potent weed, hashish and other stronger recreational chemicals. After 1975, the loss of American customers, plus the Communists' sophisticated police state apparatus and the country's extreme poverty, suppressed the domestic demand for drugs. However, the recent influx of foreign tourists along with economic progress has revived the drug trade. Vietnam has a very serious problem with heroin today and the authorities are not amused.

You may well be approached with offers to buy marijuana and occasionally opium. Giving in to this temptation is risky at best. There are many plain clothes police in Vietnam – just because you don't see them doesn't mean they aren't there. If arrested, you could be subjected to a long prison term and/or a large fine. At the time of writing, 22 Vietnamese and Laotian nationals were on trial for heroin trafficking, with a top judge predicting a possible ten death sentences.

Vietnam's proximity to, and drug trade with, the Golden Triangle means you can expect vigorous luggage searches by customs officials at your next destination. In short, drug use in Vietnam is still a very perilous activity and taking some samples out is even riskier. Nearby Thailand, Malaysia and Indonesia impose life-time prison sentences and the death penalty for drug use and trafficking.

The Police

The problem of police corruption has been acknowledged in official newspapers. One 1998 media report said corruption had increased by over nine times since 1997! The same problems that plague many Third World police forces – very low pay and low levels of education and training – certainly exist in Vietnam. If something does go wrong, or if something is stolen, the police often can't do much more than write a report for your insurance company. Unfortunately, some people have found it necessary to pay a 'tip' for this limited service. The tip can be anything from a pack of Marlboros to US$100.

The government has attempted to crack down hard on the worst abuses. In 1996 one policeman was imprisoned after he shot and killed a motorcyclist who refused to pay an on-the-spot fine for a bogus traffic violation. Hanoi has warned all provincial governments that any police caught shaking down foreign tourists will be fired and arrested, but it is questionable whether this actually happens.

The crackdown has dented the enthusiasm of the police to confront foreigners directly with demands for bribes. However, it has not eliminated the problem altogether. You may be stopped for no apparent reason while riding a motorcycle (or even just riding as a passenger in a car) and have a fine imposed.

Fines are generally negotiable – the bidding may start at US$25, but can be reduced all the way down to US$5. If you refuse to pay the fine, your vehicle could be impounded. In 1998, we were detained by the police in a Mekong Delta city after simply inquiring about the name of a nearby river at the local tourist office. As soon as we pulled away, our car was pulled over for running a traffic light (which did not exist!). We were immediately led to the police station and interrogated for 'drawing maps without a permit'. In the end the US$50 fine was negotiated down to US$30 – without a receipt of course.

With all this having been said, there is really no need for paranoia. The Vietnamese police can be a nuisance and you (or more likely your driver or guide) may have to occasionally pay, but this will rarely cost a lot. To avoid getting upset, you have to do as the Vietnamese do – think of 'fines' as a 'tax'. Remember too that you are not being targeted per se because you are a foreigner; in fact, most cops prefer preying on Vietnamese, who are easier to extort money from.

Foreigners who stay in Vietnam longterm and attempt to do business can expect periodic visits from the police collecting 'taxes' and 'donations'. Often they will direct their requests towards the Vietnamese employees rather than confront a foreign manager directly. The issue is further complicated by the fact that most Vietnamese police (perhaps 75%) wear plain clothes – so are those police really who they say they are? It's just one of those things that makes doing business in Vietnam so exciting. Good luck.

BUSINESS HOURS

Vietnamese rise early (and consider sleeping in to be a sure indication of illness). Offices, museums and many shops open between 7 and 8 am (depending on the season – things open a tad earlier in the summer) and close between 4 and 5 pm. Lunch is taken very seriously and virtually everything shuts down between noon and 1.30 pm. Government workers tend to take longer breaks, so figure on getting nothing done from 11.30 am to 2 pm.

Most government offices are open on Saturday until noon, and are closed all day on Sunday. Most museums are closed on Monday. Temples are usually open all day every day.

Vietnamese tend to eat their meals by the clock, and disrupting someone's meal schedule is considered rude. This effectively means that you shouldn't visit people during lunch (unless invited). It also means that if you hire somebody for the whole day (eg, a cyclo driver, a guide etc) you must take a lunch break by noon and dinner by 5 pm. Delaying the lunch break until 1 pm will earn you a reputation as a sadistic employer.

Many small privately owned shops, restaurants and street stalls stay open seven days a week, often until late at night – they need the money.

PUBLIC HOLIDAYS & SPECIAL EVENTS

Politics affects everything, including public holidays. As an indication of Vietnam's new openness, Christmas, New Year's Day, Tet (Lunar New Year) and Buddha's Birthday were re-established as holidays in 1990 after a 15-year lapse. The following are Vietnam's public holidays:

New Year's Day (Tet Duong Lich) 1 January

Anniversary of the Founding of the Vietnamese Communist Party (Thanh Lap Dang CSVN) 3 February – the Vietnamese Communist Party was founded on this date in 1930

Liberation Day (Saigon Giai Phong) 30 April – the date on which Saigon surrendered is commemorated nationwide as Liberation Day. Many cities and provinces also commemorate the anniversary of the date in March or April of

1975 when they were 'liberated' by the North Vietnamese Army.

International Workers' Day (Quoc Te Lao Dong) 1 May – also known as May Day, this falls back-to-back with Liberation Day, giving everyone a two-day holiday.

Ho Chi Minh's Birthday (Sinh Nhat Bac Ho) 19 May

Buddha's Birthday (Phat Dan) Eighth day of the fourth moon (usually June)

National Day (Quoc Khanh) 2 September – commemorates the proclamation of the Declaration of Independence of the Democratic Republic of Vietnam in Hanoi by Ho Chi Minh in 1945

Christmas (Giang Sinh) 25 December

Special prayers are held at Vietnamese and Chinese pagodas when the moon is full or just the thinnest sliver. Many Buddhists eat only vegetarian food on these days, which, according to the Chinese lunar calendar, fall on the 14th and 15th days of the month and from the last (29th or 30th) day of the month to the first day of the next month.

The following major religious festivals include the lunar date (check against any Vietnamese calendar for the Gregorian dates):

Tet (Tet Nguyen Dan) First to seventh days of the first moon – the Vietnamese Lunar New Year is the most important festival of the year and falls in late January or early February. This public holiday is officially three days, but many people take an entire week off work and few businesses are open (see the 'Tet Festival' section earlier in this chapter).

Holiday of the Dead *(Thanh Minh)* Fifth day of the third moon – people pay solemn visits to graves of deceased relatives, which are specially tidied up a few days before, and make offerings of food, flowers, joss sticks and votive papers.

Buddha's Birth, Enlightenment and Death Eighth day of the fourth moon – this day is celebrated at pagodas and temples which, like many private homes, are festooned with lanterns. Processions are held during the evening. This festival has been redesignated a public holiday.

Summer Solstice Day (Tiet Doan Ngo) Fifth day of the fifth moon – offerings are made to spirits, ghosts and the God of Death to ward off epidemics. Human effigies are burned to satisfy the requirements of the God of Death for souls to staff his army.

Wandering Souls Day (Trung Nguyen) Fifteenth day of the seventh moon – this is the second largest Vietnamese festival of the year. Offerings of food and gifts are made in homes and pagodas for the wandering souls of the forgotten dead.

Mid-Autumn Festival (Trung Thu) Fifteenth day of the eighth moon – this festival is celebrated with moon cakes of sticky rice filled with lotus seeds, watermelon seeds, peanuts, the yolks of duck eggs, raisins, sugar and other such things. For this festival children carry colourful lanterns in the form of boats, unicorns, dragons, lobsters, carp, hares and toads in an evening procession accompanied by the banging of drums and cymbals.

Confucius' Birthday Twenty-eighth day of the ninth moon

ACTIVITIES

Exercise Clubs

The Vietnamese government highly promotes gymnastics, which is a mandatory subject from elementary school to university – a Soviet and Chinese influence. Other popular sports include tennis, badminton, table tennis and handball.

Unless you're working at a school with such facilities, your best bet is to try the exercise clubs at major hotels. Some hotels open their exercise facilities to nonguests for a fee. Depending on the particular hotel, you may be charged a single day's use or monthly membership.

Gambling

The Vietnamese government recently lifted it's 14 year old ban on gambling. Consequently, that most bourgeois of capitalist activities, is staging a comeback. Once again, horse racing is popular in Ho Chi Minh City. Vietnam's first casino since liberation opened in 1994 at Do Son Beach near Haiphong. In the back alleys of large cities, slot machines have popped up inside karaoke clubs and are now legal as 'entertainment devices'.

It's easy to ignore the horse racing, casinos and slot machines if you don't want to play, but you'll have a hard time escaping *xo so*, the state lottery. Touts (mostly children) selling lottery tickets will approach you anytime, anywhere, and they are usually very persistent. If the kids seem miserable, it's not hard to understand – they get to keep only 12% of the face value of each ticket sold; 1% goes to the wholesaler and the other 87% goes to the government.

While your chances of winning are minuscule, hitting the jackpot in the state lottery can make you a dong multimillionaire. The smallest denomination lottery ticket is 2000d (US$0.16), while the largest prize is 50 million dong (US$4000).

The official state lottery has to compete against *danh de*, an illegal numbers game reputed to offer better odds. Two of the most popular forms of illegal gambling are *tu sat* (dominoes) and *choi ga* (cock fighting).

Some of the ethnic-Chinese living in the Cholon district of Ho Chi Minh City are said to be keen mahjong players.

Golf

Mark Twain once said that playing golf was 'a waste of a good walk' and apparently Ho Chi Minh agreed with him. When the French departed Vietnam, Ho's advisers declared golf to be a 'bourgeois practice'. In 1975, after the fall of South Vietnam, golf was banned and all courses were shut down and turned into farming cooperatives. However, times have changed – golf was revived in 1992 and now even government officials can often be seen riding around in electric carts in hot pursuit of a little white ball.

All over East Asia, playing golf can win you considerable points in the 'face game' even if you never hit the ball. For maximum snob value, you need to join a country club, and the fees are outrageously high. In Vietnam, golf memberships start at around US$20,000 or so – Japanese travellers comment that this is incredibly cheap.

Most clubs (not all) will allow you to simply pay a steep guest fee for attacking a golf ball with a No 5 iron. Chances are that you'll have the course to yourself, since most of the members will be back at the clubhouse drinking scotch. Nevertheless, some clubs will require you to be accompanied by a member before they permit you to play.

See the regional chapters for details on individual clubs and courses.

Hash House Harriers

Founded in Malaysia in the mid-1930s, this organisation has slowly spread around the world.

Hash House Harriers is a loosely strung international club that appeals mainly to the young or young at heart. Activities typically include a weekend afternoon easy jogging session followed by a dinner and beer party, which can continue until the wee hours of the morning.

The Hash is very informal. There is no club headquarters and no stable contact telephone or address. Nonetheless, finding the Hash is easy. Some embassy or consulate employees know about it; otherwise look for announcements in the *Vietnam Economic Times*, *Vietnam Investment Review* and expat bars.

There is a mandatory US$5 donation, which entitles you to a free T-shirt and refreshments. All excess funds are donated to local charities.

See the Hanoi and Ho Chi Minh City chapters for more information about the Hash.

Water Sports

With 3451km of mostly tropical coastline, you would imagine Vietnam to be Asia's answer to Queensland, Florida or the Spanish Riviera. Indeed, there are some excellent beaches, though perhaps not quite as many as you'd expect. Part of the reason is that the southern part of the country (which has the best tropical climate and highest population) is dominated by the huge Mekong Delta. While this region is lush, green and lovely, it's also very muddy and the 'beaches' tend to be mangrove swamps. One of the few beach areas in the delta region is Hon Chong, which faces the Gulf of Thailand. Other better beaches can be found on nearby Phu Quoc Island, also in the Gulf of Thailand.

The southernmost sandy beach on the east coast is Vung Tau, a very popular place close to Ho Chi Minh City, which is unfortunately plagued by crowds and polluted water. Fortunately there are other considerably cleaner beaches in the area, such as Long Hai and Ho Coc. Farther north, Mui

Ne Beach is even more beautiful, though getting there from Ho Chi Minh City demands a bit more time. If you're planning to beach-hop up the coast, consider stopping at Ca Na, about halfway between Phan Thiet and Nha Trang. Nha Trang has emerged as Vietnam's premier beach resort, in part because of its offshore islands and scuba diving, and vast accommodation, eating and nightlife offerings.

Heading north towards Danang other good beaches include isolated Doc Let, and the fine sands of Cua Dai, near Hoi An. There are plenty of other beaches to explore along this stretch, mostly undeveloped, but the weather here becomes more seasonal – May to July is the best time, while during the winter powerful rip tides can make swimming dangerous.

The Danang area is blessed with a 30km white sand beach consisting of a variety of Vietnamese names, but known collectively as 'China Beach' in English.

Hué has truly awful winter weather and it just gets worse the further north you go. During the summer though, the beaches are thick with sun-tanned Vietnamese (though few foreigners). The best-known northern beaches are at Cua Lo (near Vinh), Sam Son (near Thanh Hoa) and Do Son (near Haiphong), though these pale in comparison to beaches further south.

Most Vietnamese people love the beach, but have a respectful fear of the sea – they like to wade up to their knees, but seldom dive in and go for a proper swim. The place you are most likely to see Vietnamese actually swimming is in rivers and public swimming pools. Surfing and windsurfing have only recently arrived on the scene, but they are sure to expand.

It is possible to hire snorkelling gear and scuba equipment at several beach resorts, but some warnings are necessary. Sometimes the equipment is good; sometimes it's not – it's not unknown for half-empty tanks of air to be rented out. During squalls, boat operators have occasionally been known to head for shore, leaving hapless divers for lost! Of course, fatal diving accidents can and do occur in developed countries as well, but extra precautions should be taken here. Don't assume that the equipment and training is up to international standards.

For more on beaches see the individual entries under the regional chapters.

LANGUAGE COURSES

If you'd like to learn to speak Vietnamese, courses are now being offered in Ho Chi Minh City, Hanoi and elsewhere. To qualify for student visa status, you need to study at a bona fide university (as opposed to a private language centre or with a tutor). Universities require that you study at least 10 hours per week. Lessons usually last for two hours per day, for which you pay a tuition fee of around US$5.

You should establish early on whether you want to study in northern or southern Vietnam, because the regional dialects are very different. Foreign students who learn Vietnamese in Hanoi and then move to Ho Chi Minh City to find work (or vice versa) have been dismayed to discover that they cannot communicate. But (get ready for this) the majority of the teachers at universities in the south have been imported from the north and will tell you that the northern dialect is the 'correct one'! So even if you study at a university in Ho Chi Minh City, you may find that you need to hire a local private tutor (cheap at any rate) to help rid you of a northern accent.

For further information and contact details to study Vietnamese, see Language Courses in the Hanoi and Ho Chi Minh City chapters.

WORK

From 1975 to about 1990, Vietnam's foreign workers were basically technical specialists and military advisers from Eastern Europe and the now-defunct Soviet Union. The declining fortunes of the former Eastern Bloc have caused most of these advisers to be withdrawn.

Vietnam's opening to capitalist countries has suddenly created all sorts of work opportunities for Westerners. However, don't come to Vietnam looking for big money. The best-paid Westerners living in Vietnam are those working for international organisations, such as the United Nations and embassies, or those hired by private foreign companies attempting to set up joint-venture operations. People with specialist high-technology skills may also find themselves in demand and may be able to secure high pay and cushy benefits.

It's nice work if you can get it, but such plum jobs are thin on the ground. Foreigners who look like Rambo have occasionally been approached by Vietnamese talent scouts wanting to recruit them to work as extras in war movies, but for most travellers, the main work opportunities will be teaching a foreign language.

English is by far the most popular foreign language with Vietnamese students, and about 10% of foreign-language students in Vietnam also want to learn French. Many also want to learn Chinese, but there is a large ethnic-Chinese community in Vietnam so there is little need to import foreign teachers. There is also a limited demand for teachers of Japanese, German, Spanish and Korean.

Government-run universities in Vietnam hire some foreign teachers. Pay is generally around US$2 per hour, but benefits such as free housing and unlimited visa renewals are usually thrown in. Teaching at a university requires some commitment (eg, you may have to sign a one-year contract).

There is also a budding free market in private language centres and home tutoring – this is where most newly arrived foreigners seek work. Pay in the private sector is slightly better – expect about US$3 to US$4 per hour depending on where you teach. However, it is likely that these private schools won't be able to offer the same benefits as a government-run school. You will also need a business visa and in some cases the school may not be able to help you acquire one. A possible way around the visa hurdles is to sign up for Vietnamese language lessons at a university, but be aware that you may actually be expected to attend class and study.

Private tutoring pays even better – around US$5 per hour and more. In this case, you are in business for yourself. The authorities may or may not turn a blind eye to such activities.

Everyone who has become a foreign-language teacher in Vietnam will have a different story to tell. One experienced English teacher in Ho Chi Minh City gave this summation of his experience:

> There are countless schools that are willing to hire you. Pay is around US$4 per hour in Ho Chi Minh City. They tell you a business visa is required for it to be legal, but some will let this slide. I don't advise signing a contract unless the school is *very* reputable (ie, other foreigners are working there and are happy). Agreements mean nothing here. Your salary might be lowered without your consent, you might get underpaid (count the money in that envelope carefully) and you might find upon arriving for class that the director has decided that the lesson you have prepared has been replaced by another. Flakiness abounds on all fronts. The classes are huge (up to 60). You might find yourself yelling into a microphone, competing with the roar of traffic noises a few metres away, and all with the teachers shouting into microphones in the adjoining classrooms. Other than a few token nods to the Asian tradition of respecting teachers, the students are often uncooperative in these huge classes, talking to each other while you're lecturing, arriving late, leaving early etc.
>
> The answer, I find, is to teach privately. The students are much more motivated and respectful, especially if you keep the class size small. Still, there's the flakiness factor. Classes routinely cancel at the last minute with no reason given. Or a group of students might cancel forever with no warning. Everything is subject to change at a moment's notice. Ask for payment two weeks in advance and things go much better, but they'll only agree if they know that you too are reliable and won't abscond. In other words, you have to work a while to build up your reputation. You can make between US$5 and US$10 per hour depending on the number of students in your class and how affluent they are. I have a teaching certificate, but I hardly think it's mandatory – plenty of people find work without one.
>
> The authorities must know what I've been doing all along, but they've never bothered me. I've been working on a tourist visa and have been getting away with it. Other teachers I know have obtained business visas through local companies, whom they basically bribed to exercise their pull with the authorities and say these teachers work for them as 'consultants'.

Finding teaching jobs is quite easy in places such as Ho Chi Minh City and Hanoi, and is sometimes possible in towns that have universities. Pay in the smaller towns tends to be lower and work opportunities are fewer.

Looking for employment is a matter of asking around – jobs are rarely advertised. The longer you stay, the easier it is to find work – travellers hoping to land a quick job and depart two months later will probably be disappointed.

Some Western journalists and photographers manage to make a living in Vietnam by selling their stories and pictures to Western news organisations. If you're lucky enough to land a full-time job with Reuters, that's great; then there are always the domestic English-language media outlets to explore. Most journalists, however, are forced to work freelance and pay can vary from decent to dismal. Be aware though that as a freelancer you won't have any back-up if you get into trouble with the authorities over your work.

For the lowdown on the plight of journalism in Vietnam, check the Web sites for Amnesty International (www.amnestyinternational.org) or International PEN Web site (www.oneworld.org/internatpen)

Volunteer Work

For information on volunteer work opportunities, you may wish to contact the NGO Resource Centre (fax 832 8611, ⓔ gocentr@netnam.org.vn), La Thanh Hotel, 218 Doi Can, Hanoi, which has links with most international NGOs in Vietnam.

Also see the 'NGOs in Vietnam' boxed text earlier in this chapter for leads.

ACCOMMODATION

The tourist boom initially created a shortage of hotel space, but overbuilding and a decline in tourist arrivals has now produced a glut. At the time of writing, there were about a dozen half-finished luxury hotels in Ho Chi Minh City and Hanoi stalled mid-construction – some say they may never be opened. Even the famed Ho Chi Minh City Floating Hotel shut its doors in 1997 and was towed from the Saigon River to Palau in the western Pacific.

In larger cities there is a plentiful supply of international-standard hotel rooms, and prices have dropped considerably lately. This applies across the board, from guesthouses to topnotch hotels. What this means is that travellers are in a better negotiating position. During our last visit rooms could be found in posh four-star hotels (many of which were operating with as low as a 20% occupancy rate) for as little as US$80! In the high seasons, however, you may have to search around, especially in popular places like Hoi An, where there are still not enough rooms to accommodate its large number of visitors.

If there is one thing that budget travellers frequently complain about outside of major tourist centres, it's the cost of the hotels. Most government-run hotels maintain a price differential – foreigners are charged more than Vietnamese (usually double). The theory is that foreigners are richer than local Vietnamese and therefore can afford to pay a premium. This doesn't explain though why some hotels give discounts to Overseas Vietnamese and 'other Asians'.

Another factor to take into account is the taxes. Some hotels levy a room tax of 10%. Ask in advance if the room rate includes tax or not.

There are now regulations requiring hotels and guesthouses to maintain 'acceptable standards' before they can be approved to receive foreign guests (you'd never know it by some of the dumps around). So it is possible that you will front up to what seems like a perfectly serviceable hotel and be refused a room even if the place is empty. In that case, there is little point arguing. The hotel staff won't risk trouble with the police just to accommodate you, though they may refer you elsewhere.

Theoretically, these regulations are meant to protect foreign tourists from staying in dirty and dangerous places. In practice, the motive is often less honourable. In some places, foreigners are simply not allowed to stay in private hotels because these compete with the government-owned ones, even though the private hotels are often of a higher standard. Though a highly unlikely scenario, theoretically if the approved hotels were all full, and you couldn't stay in the unapproved ones, your only choice would be to sleep in the street. The Vietnamese have an expression for sleeping in the street – it's called staying in a 'thousand star hotel'.

Reservations

A 'reservation' means next to nothing unless you've paid for the room in advance. It's possible to arrange this through some travel agencies, but don't expect much at the budget end of the spectrum. However, there is seldom much need for reservations – you can almost always find a place to stay, and moreover, a reservation usually nullifies any chance of negotiating the room tariff. An important exception is during the Tet holiday and the 10-day period immediately following Tet – at that time reservations are recommended.

Camping

Perhaps because so many millions of Vietnamese spent much of the war years living in tents (often either as soldiers or refugees), camping is not the popular pastime it is in the West. Even in Dalat, where youth groups often go for outdoor holidays, very little proper equipment can be hired.

Camping can be difficult for travllers, because in many locations, the local government prohibits foreigners to camp anyway.

The younger generation, however, appears to have discovered a taste for sleeping in tents (just so long as there is karaoke nearby). At beach resorts such as Mui Ne Beach (near Phan Thiet), beachfront camping has become all the rage, and is more affordable than a private bungalow.

The biggest problem with camping is finding a remote spot where curious locals and the police won't create difficulties for you. Some innovative private travel agencies in Ho Chi Minh City and Hanoi offer organised camping trips, especially to national parks. See the relevant Travel Agencies sections in those chapters.

Dormitories

While there are *nha tro* (dormitories) all over Vietnam (especially around train and bus stations), most of these are officially off-limits to foreigners. In this case, the government's motives are not simply to charge you more money for accommodation. There is a significant chance of getting robbed while sleeping in a Vietnamese dorm, and by Western standards many of these places are considered substandard (beds generally consist of a wooden platform and straw mat). Even though budget travellers like to complain about this policy, it's one case where the Vietnamese government is really trying to protect you.

The concept of a relatively upmarket, foreigner-only dorm (furnished with real mattresses) is starting to catch on. Some of these 'dormitories' are actually rooms with just two beds – you share the room with only one other person and still pay only US$2 to US$4 per person. You are most likely to find these in private mini-hotels in areas frequented by budget travellers (Ho Chi Minh City's Pham Ngu Lao area pioneered the concept, but there are dorms in Hanoi, Nha Trang and other backpacker centres). Expect to see more of these places in the future.

Hotels

Most of the *khach san* (large hotels) and *nha khach* or *nha nghi* (guesthouses) are government-owned or joint ventures. There is also a rapidly increasing number of small private hotels, usually referred to as mini-hotels.

There is some confusion over the terms 'singles', 'doubles', 'double occupancy' and 'twins', so let's set the record straight here. A single is a room containing one bed, even if two people sleep in it. If there are two beds in the room, that is a twin, even if only one person occupies it. If two people stay in the same room, that is double occupancy – in most cases, there is no extra charge for this. There is considerable confusion over the term 'doubles' – in some hotels this means twin beds, while in others it means double occupancy. More than a few travellers have paid extra for twin beds when what they really wanted was a bed for two people. It's always a good idea to take a look at the room to make sure that you're getting what you wanted and are not paying extra for something you don't need.

Most hotels now have rooms with a private bathroom – ask first or take a look at the room to be sure. Some hotels have an attached bath, but the toilet is outside (a peculiar arrangement). If your hotel has no hot bath, you can try looking for a local *tam goi* (bathhouse), though these are becoming increasingly rare.

A few hotels might try to charge the foreigners' price for your Vietnamese guide and/or driver as long as they know that you're paying the bill. This is not on – if they stay in a separate room, they should be charged like any local. Don't accept this nonsense from anyone.

The Vietnamese seem to be absolutely obsessed with air-conditioning, which has become a big prestige item. For them, finding a hotel room with air-conditioning seems more important than having a room with an attached bathroom. If you travel with guides, don't be surprised if they ask for an air-con room (which costs three times as much as a room with a fan) and then complain that they couldn't sleep because the room was too cold.

It's a good idea to ask for a receipt when you pay (and save it), especially if you'll be staying for more than a few days. Confusion can arise over how many days you have paid for and how much you still owe. A few hotels are guilty of chaotic bookkeeping (sometimes deliberate), and one shift at the front desk might have no clue about what other shifts have and have not done.

It's important to realise that many hotels have both an upmarket new wing and a squalid old wing, with a wide variation in prices between the two buildings. Furthermore, many Vietnamese hotels offer a wide range of prices within the same building! For example, one hotel in Hanoi we checked into had room prices running from US$6 to US$60! Cheap rooms are almost always on the top floor because few hotels have lifts and guests paying US$60 are not keen on having to walk up seven storeys or more.

Even at the biggest and most expensive hotels, it's possible to get discounts if you're staying long term. For definition's sake, long term can mean three days or more. Booking through some foreign or domestic travel agencies can also net you a discount.

The following are some of the more common hotel names and their translations:

hotel name	english translation
Binh Minh	Sunrise
Bong Sen	Lotus
Cuu Long	Nine Dragons
Doc Lap	Descending Dragon
Hoa Binh	Peace
Huong Sen	Lotus Fragrance
Huu Nghi	Friendship
Thang Long	Ascending Dragon
Thong Nhat	Reunification
Tu Do	Freedom

Hotel Security Hotel security can be a problem. Many hotels post a small sign warning you not to leave cameras, passports and other valuables in your room. Most places have a safety deposit system of some kind, but if you are leaving cash or travellers cheques, be sure to seal the loot in an envelope and have it signed for by the staff.

Some hotel rooms come equipped with a closet that can be locked – if so, use it and take the key with you. You would be very wise to bring a chain with a padlock – this can be used to lock the closet and then you won't have to worry about the employees having keys. If your room or the hotel has a safe, make use of it. A few hotels have a place where you can attach a padlock to the outside of the door rather than using a lock built into the door itself. The hotel will provide you with a padlock, but you'd be wise to bring your own. A combination lock might be more convenient, but make sure it's one that is not easily broken (cheaper ones can be pried apart with a screwdriver).

Beware of hotel rooms with windows or balconies that might allow a thief to enter while you are out. We have heard several reports of theft in this fashion, so when you do go out, be sure to lock all windows and doors.

Police Registration Back in the old days when the Soviets told the Vietnamese how to run their country, all hotel guests had to deposit their passports and/or visas with reception – the staff then had to take these valuable documents over to the police station and register their guests. It was not uncommon for the police to then pay a visit to your hotel room and question you about why you were there, how long would you be staying, where did you come from and where were you going to next, finally terminating the interview by requesting a 'tip'. Your documents would be returned only upon your departure and there was always the concern that they could be 'lost'.

The good news is that the government no longer requires police registration of hotel guests. The bad news is that provincial governments make up their own rules and so little has changed. Though technically you do not need to leave your passport with hotel reception, most hotels will request it anyway as 'security' (ie, to make sure you don't run away without paying).

The regulations are as clear as mud. Each city you visit may have its own arbitrary rules and these rules can change at the drop of a hat. There is no question that most foreigners don't like to see their valuable documents passing through so many hands with the chance that something could get lost.

When you check out of a hotel, you must check your documents very carefully. Be sure that the blue entry card is still together with the passport (you will be required to turn them both over when you check in).

Homestays

It's possible to arrange to stay in the homes of local people, but – depending on the local government – the family may have to register all foreign visitors to their homes, including relatives, with the police. The police can – and often do – arbitrarily deny such registration requests and will force you to stay in a hotel or guesthouse licensed to accept foreigners.

Rental Accommodation

Renting a medium-size house in Ho Chi Minh City costs about US$50 per month for a Vietnamese family. Unfortunately, foreigners cannot do this. The local authorities set the price that foreigners pay and 85% of the rent money goes to the government. Many landlords are unwilling to rent to foreigners because they get so little financial reward and so much unwanted attention from the authorities. Even once you've moved into your new home, the authorities can revoke your right to reside there with no notice at all.

The result is that foreigners are forced to rent high-priced villas or expensive luxury flats. In 1996 Decree 56/CP, which governs the renting of houses to foreigners, was issued by the government. The decree was supposed to streamline rentals, but in fact it hits landlords with new taxes that will cause rents to sharply increase. Protests from important expats (like embassy people and foreign investors) have caused the government to delay implementation of the new regulations. No one is sure how the issue will be resolved, but it seems likely that renting a house in Vietnam is not going to get cheaper anytime soon.

Consequently, many expats wind up living in mini-hotels. Big discounts can be negotiated for long-term stays. It's wise to first live in the hotel for at least one night before agreeing to anything. You'll want to be sure that the place really is clean and quiet with functional plumbing before you hand over a month's rent.

ENTERTAINMENT

Cinemas

Movie theatres are common in nearly all major towns and cities. Many urban maps have *rap* (cinemas) marked with a special symbol.

Films from the former Eastern Bloc have been replaced with Western movies that are either subtitled or dubbed. The dubbed ones are a kick, as most voice-overs are handled by just one person (who by nature can only be male *or* female). Watching Arnold Schwartzenneger speaking in Vietnamese is hard enough to swallow, but try to imagine what it's like when he has a dainty woman's voice!

Regional imports are popular, but Vietnam now produces its own kung fu movies rather than importing them from China, Hong Kong and Taiwan. Love stories also are popular, but Vietnamese censors take a dim view of nudity and sex – murder and mayhem are OK.

Discos

Following reunification, ballrooms and discos were denounced as imperialist dens of iniquity and were shut down by the authorities. Since 1990 they have reopened, though certain forms of dancing (such as Brazil's erotic dance, the lambada) technically remain banned. Hanoi and Ho Chi Minh City are the hot beds for nightclubs – the 'in' place to go seems to change by the week.

Karaoke

Most Westerners find karaoke as appealing as roasted gecko with shrimp paste. Nonetheless, karaoke has taken over Asia and you'll have a hard time avoiding it.

For those unfamiliar with karaoke, it's simply a system where you are supposed to sing along with a video. The words to the song are flashed on the bottom of the screen (a number of languages are possible) and participants are supplied with a microphone. Really fancy karaoke bars have superb audio systems and big-screen video, but no matter how good the equipment, it's not going to sound any better than the ability of the singer. And with a few exceptions, it sounds truly awful. The Vietnamese only enjoy karaoke if it's played at over 150 decibels.

A big warning – many karaoke places have hidden charges, in particular at *karaoke om* joints where young women are provided to 'hold' while you sing. It is best to avoid these type of places. Even at regular karaoke places, the beers might only be US$1 apiece, but there can be a hefty charge for use of the microphone and video tapes. You may well be charged double the Vietnamese rate for an English-language tape. Get this all worked out in advance.

Pubs

Vietnamese-style pubs tend to be karaoke lounges – you know you've assimilated when you start enjoying these places. However, the increasing number of tourists and expats (especially in Hanoi and Ho Chi Minh City) has caused a boom in Western-style pubs. Many of these are husband-wife joint ventures (typically a Western husband and Vietnamese wife). Aside from the Tiger beer, many of these places are quite indistinguishable from their counterparts in London, Berlin, New York or Melbourne. Darts, Mexican food, rock music, oak furniture and CNN can make you forget just where you are.

SPECTATOR SPORTS

Football (soccer) is Vietnam's number one spectator sport and the country has gone hog-wild for the game. During the World Cup or any major European championship game, half of the country stays up all night to watch live games in different time zones around the world. Post-game fun includes hazardous high-speed motorbike cruising in the streets of Hanoi and Ho Chi Minh City.

Tennis has considerable snob appeal – trendy Vietnamese like to both watch and play. The Vietnamese are incredibly skilled at badminton. Other favourites include volleyball and table tennis.

SHOPPING

As a general principal, try to find a shop that does not cater particularly to tourists and that does put price tags on all its items. In touristy areas, items sold with no visible price tags must be bargained for – expect the vendor to start the bidding at two to five times the real price. Tagged items may be negotiable, but more often than not the prices are fixed.

One annoying habit that you'll just have to get used to is the tendency of many vendors to start shoving one item after another into your face and practically forcing you to buy it. They don't give you much chance to look at the items you really want to buy. It's a self-defeating sales tactic, since many foreigners just get flustered and walk away from any shop that does this.

Please don't buy souvenirs taken from historical sites, or made from endangered wildlife such as turtle shells.

Antiques

There are several good shops to hunt for antiques in Hanoi and Ho Chi Minh City, but Vietnam has severe regulations on the export of real antiques, so be sure that what you buy can be taken out of the country legally.

A Vietnamese speciality is the 'instant antique' with a price tag of around US$2 for a teapot or ceramic dinner plate. Of course, it's OK to buy fake antiques as long as you aren't paying genuine antique prices. However, a problem occurs if you've bought an antique (or something that looks antique) and didn't get an official export certificate:

When I was in the airport in Hanoi, a customs officer eyed out two porcelain vases I had bought and told me that I should go to the Department of Culture in Hanoi to have them assessed or pay a fine of US$20. Of course, there was no representative of the Department of Culture at the airport to make such an evaluation, so getting them assessed would require me to miss my flight.

Anna Crawford Pinnerup

Just what happens to confiscated 'antiques' is a good question. Some say that the authorities sell them back to the souvenir shops. You might call it recycling.

Handicrafts

Hot items on the tourist market include lacquerware, mother-of-pearl inlay, ceramics (check out the elephants), colourful embroidered items (hangings, tablecloths, pillow cases, pyjamas and robes), greeting cards with silk paintings on the front, woodblock prints, oil paintings, watercolours, blinds made of hanging bamboo beads (many travellers like the replica of the Mona Lisa), reed mats, carpets, jewellery and leatherwork.

Clothing

Ao dais (the national of dress of both Vietnamese women and men) are a popular item, especially for women. Ready-made ao dais cost from about US$10 to US$20, while the custom-tailored sets are notably more. Prices vary by the store and material used. If you want to buy custom-made clothing for your friends, you'll need their measurements; neck diameter, breast, waist, hip and length (from waist to hem). As a general rule, you get best results when you're right there and are measured by the tailor or seamstress.

Women all over the country wear conical hats, in part to keep the sun off their faces (though they also function like umbrellas in the rain). If you hold a well-made conical hat up to the light, you'll be able to see that between the layers of straw material are fine paper cuts. The best-quality conical hats are produced in the Hué area.

T-shirts are ever popular items with travellers. A printed shirt costs around US$2 while an embroidered design will cost maybe US$3.50. However, don't believe sizes – 'large' in Asia is often equivalent to 'medium' in the West – if you are really large, forget it unless you want to have your shirts individually tailored.

These days more and more hill tribe garb is finding its way to shops in Hanoi and Ho Chi Minh City. It is indeed colourful, but you may need to set the dyes yourself so that those colours don't bleed all over the rest of your clothes.

Stamps

Postage stamps already set in a collector's book are readily available either inside or near the post office in major cities or at some hotel gift shops and bookshops. You can even find stamps from the now-extinct South Vietnamese regime.

Gems

Vietnam produces some good gems, but there are plenty of fakes and flawed gems around. This doesn't mean that you can't buy something if you think it's beautiful, but don't think that you'll find a cut diamond or polished ruby for a fraction of what you'd pay at home. Some travellers have actually thought that they could buy gems in Vietnam and sell these at home for a profit. Such business requires considerable expertise and good connections in the mining industry.

Music

Ho Chi Minh City and Hanoi both have an astounding collection of CDs and audio tapes for sale, most of which are pirated. The majority of Vietnamese hits were originally recorded by Overseas Vietnamese in California and bootlegged in Vietnam. There are also the latest Chinese music tapes from Hong Kong and Taiwan (mostly soft rock). Hard rock from the West is not as popular, but there is a small and devoted core of avant-garde types who like it.

CDs are not yet manufactured in Vietnam, though it seems only a matter of time. Plenty are imported – about 80% of those available are pirated copies from China and are therefore very cheap. The official word is that this illegal practice will be 'cleaned up' by the authorities, but don't hold your breath waiting.

Electronics

Electronic goods sold in Vietnam are actually not such a great bargain. You'd be better off purchasing these in duty-free ports such as Hong Kong and Singapore. However, the prices charged in Vietnam are not bad, mainly due to the black market (smuggling), which also results in 'duty-free' goods.

Only those items imported legally by an authorised agent will include a warranty card valid in Vietnam. Unfortunately, Vietnamese electronics that are not black market are often 'grey market' – that is, imported legally, but by someone other than the authorised importer. This does not circumvent the need to pay import taxes, but it creates a tidy profit for the resellers because they avoid paying commissions to the authorised agent. As with smuggled goods, grey market items are usually sold without a warranty that is valid in Vietnam. However, some electronic goods include an international warranty card, which presumably solves this problem.

War Souvenirs

In places frequented by tourists, it's easy to buy what looks like equipment left over from the American War. However, almost all of these items are reproductions and your chances of finding anything original are slim. Enterprising back-alley tailors turn out US military uniforms, while metalcraft shops have learned how to make helmets, bayonets and dog tags.

The 'Zippo' lighters engraved with 'soldier poetry' seem to be the hottest-selling item. You can pay extra to get one that's been beat up to look like a war relic, or just buy a brand-new shiny one for less money.

One thing you should think twice about purchasing are weapons and ammunition *even if fake*. You may have several opportunities to buy old bullets and dud mortar shells, especially around the area of the old DMZ. Most of these items are either fake or deactivated, but you can occasionally find real bullets for sale with the gunpowder still inside. Real or not, it's illegal to carry ammunition and weapons on airlines and many countries will arrest you if any such goods are found in your luggage.

Getting There & Away

AIR

Airports & Airlines

Ho Chi Minh's Tan Son Nhat Airport is Vietnam's busiest international air hub, followed by Hanoi's Noi Bai Airport. A few international flights also serve Danang.

Vietnam Airlines (Hang Khong Viet Nam) is the nation's state-owned flag carrier, and the majority of flights into and out of Vietnam are joint operations between Vietnam Airlines and foreign companies. The air ticket you purchase might have the words 'Vietnam Airlines' printed on it, but you could actually find yourself flying on Cathay Pacific, Thai Airways International (THAI) or another carrier.

Though most of Vietnam Airlines' aging fleet aircraft has been upgraded to modern French Airbuses and American Boeings, the airline still has some growing up to do. Among its problems are frequent delays and the cancellation of domestic flights (more often than not because not enough seats were sold!), and the dual-tiered pricing system that requires foreigners to pay around double the cost of their already overpriced fares.

While discounted flights can be taken into Vietnam, buying tickets in Vietnam is a total rip-off, and Vietnam Airlines will not allow foreign carriers that fly in and out of Vietnam to undercut their inflated fares. For example, a ticket from Bangkok to Hanoi or Ho Chi Minh City costs about half the price of the ticket in the opposite direction. If Vietnam Airlines would loosen up and not be so greedy, more discount fares would be available both in and out of Vietnam, which would no doubt attract more visitors.

A large number of international flights leaving Hanoi connect through Ho Chi Minh City, but instead of allowing passengers to check in for their international flight in Hanoi, Vietnam Airlines requires passengers to first pay a domestic departure tax, fly to Ho Chi Minh City, claim their bags, wait in line (again) to recheck your bags, then pay an international departure tax before boarding the international flight. Ugh.

Another minor annoyance on Vietnam Airlines is its strict 20kg baggage weight limit (for both domestic *and* international routes); you'll almost surely be forced to pay US$2 per kilogram over the limit, obviously another clever profit-generating tactic for the airline. Keep your baggage locked. Travellers have reported things being pilfered from their luggage on departure.

Bicycles can travel by air. You *can* take them to pieces and put them in a bike bag or box, but it's much easier simply to wheel your bike to the check-in desk, where it should be treated as a piece of baggage. You may have to remove the pedals and turn the handlebars sideways so that it takes up less space in the aircraft's hold; check all this with the airline well in advance, preferably before you pay for your ticket.

In an apparent attempt to give Vietnam Airlines some much needed competition

WARNING

The information in this chapter is particularly vulnerable to change: Prices for international travel are volatile, routes are introduced and cancelled, schedules change, special deals come and go, and rules and visa requirements are amended. Airlines and governments seem to take a perverse pleasure in making price structures and regulations as complicated as possible. You should check directly with the airline or a travel agent to make sure you understand how a fare (and ticket you may buy) works. In addition, the travel industry is highly competitive and there are many lurks and perks.

The upshot of this is that you should get opinions, quotes and advice from as many airlines and travel agents as possible before you part with your hard-earned cash. The details given in this chapter should be regarded as pointers and are not a substitute for your own careful, up-to-date research.

Pacific Airlines commenced operations in 1992. Its domestic and international flight schedule, however, is very limited – the airline only connects Hanoi with Ho Chi Minh City, and Ho Chi Minh City with Taiwan.

Buying Tickets

An air ticket alone can gouge a great slice out of anyone's budget, but you can reduce the cost by finding discounted fares. Stiff competition has resulted in widespread discounting – good news for travellers! But unless you buy carefully, it is still possible to end up paying exorbitant amounts for a journey. It's important to ask what restrictions, if any, apply to your ticket. Many travellers end up changing their route half way through their trip, so think carefully before buying a ticket that is not easily refunded.

For long-term travel, there are plenty of discount tickets which are valid for 12 months, allowing multiple stopovers with open dates. For short-term, travel cheaper fares are usually available by travelling midweek. When you're looking for bargain air fares, go to a travel agent rather than directly to the airline. From time to time, airlines do have promotional fares and special offers, but generally they only sell fares at the official listed price.

One exception is booking on the Internet, and many airlines offer some excellent fares to Web surfers. They may sell seats by auction or simply cut prices to reflect the reduced cost of electronic selling. Many travel agents around the world have Web sites, which can make the Internet a quick and easy way to compare prices, a good start for when you're ready to start negotiating with your favourite travel agency. Online ticket sales work well if you are doing a simple one-way or return trip on specified dates. However, online superfast fare generators are no substitute for a travel agent who knows all about special deals, has strategies for avoiding layovers and can offer advice on everything from which airline has the best vegetarian food to the best travel insurance to bundle with your ticket.

The days when some travel agents would routinely fleece travellers by running off with their money are, happily, almost over. Paying by credit card generally offers protection, as most card issuers provide refunds if you can prove you didn't get what you paid for. Similar protection can be obtained by buying a ticket from a bonded agent, such as one covered by the Air Transport Operators License (ATOL) scheme in the UK. Agents who only accept cash should hand over the tickets straight away and not tell you to 'come back tomorrow'. After you've made a booking or paid your deposit, call the airline and confirm that the booking was made. It's generally not advisable to send money (even cheques) through the post unless the agent is very well established – some travellers have reported being ripped off by fly-by-night mail-order ticket agents.

You may decide to pay more than the rock-bottom fare by opting for the safety of a better-known travel agent. Firms such as STA Travel, which has offices worldwide, Council Travel in the USA and Usit Campus (formerly Campus Travel) in the UK are not going to disappear overnight and they do offer good prices to most destinations.

If you purchase a ticket and later want to make changes to your route or get a refund, contact the original travel agent. Airlines only issue refunds to the purchaser of a ticket – usually the travel agent who bought the ticket on your behalf.

It is difficult to get reservations for flights to/from Vietnam during and around holidays, especially Tet, the Lunar New Year, which falls between late January and mid-February. If you will be in Vietnam during this period (a favourite time for family visits by overseas Vietnamese), make reservations well in advance or you may find yourself marooned in Bangkok on the way in or stranded in Ho Chi Minh on the way out. During other times it shouldn't be too difficult to get a flight out of the country, but it's wise to book your departure at least a few days in advance.

Be aware that Vietnam is not the only country to celebrate the Lunar New Year – it's also *the* major holiday in Singapore, Macau, China, Taiwan and Korea, and is celebrated by sizeable Chinese minorities in

Thailand and Malaysia. Many people hit the road at this time, resulting in overbooked airlines, trains and hotels all over Asia. The chaos begins about a week before Tet and lasts for about two weeks after it.

Student & Youth Fares Full-time students and people under 26 have access to better deals than other travellers. The better deals may not always be cheaper fares, but may include more flexibility to change flights and/or routes. You have to show a document proving your date of birth or a valid International Student Identity Card (ISIC) when buying your ticket and boarding the plane. There are plenty of places around the world where nonstudents can get fake student cards, but if you get caught using a fake card you could have your ticket confiscated.

Frequent Fliers Most airlines (including Vietnam Airlines) offer frequent-flier deals that can earn you a free air ticket or other goodies. To qualify, you have to accumulate sufficient mileage with the same airline or airline alliance. Many airlines have 'blackout periods', or times when you cannot fly for free on your frequent-flier points (Christmas and Tet, for example). The worst thing about frequent-flier programs is that they tend to lock you into one airline, and that airline may not always have the cheapest fares or most convenient flight schedule.

Courier Flights Courier flights are a great bargain if you're lucky enough to find one. Air-freight companies expedite delivery of urgent items by sending them with you as your baggage allowance. You are permitted to bring along a carry-on bag, but that's all. In return, you get a steeply discounted ticket.

There are other restrictions: Courier tickets are sold for a fixed date and schedule changes can be difficult to make. If you buy a return ticket, your schedule will be even more rigid. You need to clarify before you fly what restrictions apply to your ticket, and don't expect a refund once you've paid.

Booking a courier ticket takes some effort. They are not readily available and arrangements have to be made a month or more in advance. You won't find courier flights on all routes either – just on the major air routes.

Courier flights are occasionally advertised in the newspapers, or you could contact air-freight companies listed in the phone book. You may even have to go to the air-freight company to get an answer – the companies aren't always keen to give out information over the phone.

Kelly Monaghan's *Air Courier Bargains* (The Intrepid Traveller), now in its seventh edition, tells you everything you need to know to be an air courier. *Travel Unlimited* (PO Box 1058, Allston, MA 02134, USA) is a monthly travel newsletter based in the USA that publishes many courier flight deals from destinations worldwide. A 12-month subscription to the newsletter costs US$25, or US$35 for readers outside the USA. Another possibility (at least for US residents) is to join the International Association of Air Travel Couriers (IAATC). The membership fee of $45 gets members a bimonthly update of air-courier offerings, access to a fax-on-demand service with daily updates of last-minute specials and the bimonthly newsletter, *Shoestring Traveler*. For more information, contact IAATC (☎ 561-582 8320) or visit its Web site: www.courier.org. However, be aware that joining this organisation is no guarantee that you'll get a courier flight.

Second-hand Tickets You'll occasionally see advertisements on youth hostel bulletin boards and sometimes in newspapers for 'second-hand tickets'. That is, somebody purchased a return ticket or a ticket with multiple stopovers and now wants to sell the unused portion of the ticket.

The prices offered look very attractive indeed. Unfortunately, these tickets, if used for international travel, are usually worthless, as the name on the ticket must match the name on the passport of the person checking in. Some people reason that the seller of the ticket can check you in with his or her passport, and then give you the boarding pass – wrong again! Usually the immigration people want to see your boarding pass, and if it

Air Travel Glossary

Cancellation Penalties If you have to cancel or change a discounted ticket, there are often heavy penalties involved; insurance can sometimes be taken out against these penalties. Some airlines impose penalties on regular tickets as well, particularly against 'no-show' passengers.

Courier Fares Businesses often need to send urgent documents or freight securely and quickly. Courier companies hire people to accompany the package through customs and, in return, offer a discount ticket which is sometimes a phenomenal bargain. However, you may have to surrender all your baggage allowance and take only carry-on luggage.

Full Fares Airlines traditionally offer 1st class (coded F), business class (coded J) and economy class (coded Y) tickets. These days there are so many promotional and discounted fares available that few passengers pay full economy fare.

Lost Tickets If you lose your airline ticket an airline will usually treat it like a travellers cheque and, after inquiries, issue you with another one. Legally, however, an airline is entitled to treat it like cash and if you lose it then it's gone forever. Take good care of your tickets.

Onward Tickets An entry requirement for many countries is that you have a ticket out of the country. If you're unsure of your next move, the easiest solution is to buy the cheapest onward ticket to a neighbouring country or a ticket from a reliable airline which can later be refunded if you do not use it.

Open-Jaw Tickets These are return tickets where you fly out to one place but return from another. If available, this can save you backtracking to your arrival point.

Overbooking Since every flight has some passengers who fail to show up, airlines often book more passengers than they have seats. Usually excess passengers make up for the no-shows, but occasionally somebody gets 'bumped' onto the next available flight. Guess who it is most likely to be? The passengers who check in late.

Promotional Fares These are officially discounted fares, available from travel agencies or direct from the airline.

Reconfirmation If you don't reconfirm your flight at least 72 hours prior to departure, the airline may delete your name from the passenger list. Ring to find out if your airline requires reconfirmation.

Restrictions Discounted tickets often have various restrictions on them – such as needing to be paid for in advance and incurring a penalty to be altered. Others are restrictions on the minimum and maximum period you must be away.

Round-the-World Tickets RTW tickets give you a limited period (usually a year) in which to circumnavigate the globe. You can go anywhere the carrying airlines go, as long as you don't backtrack. The number of stopovers or total number of separate flights is decided before you set off and they usually cost a bit more than a basic return flight.

Transferred Tickets Airline tickets cannot be transferred from one person to another. Travellers sometimes try to sell the return half of their ticket, but officials can ask you to prove that you are the person named on the ticket. On an international flight tickets are compared with passports.

Travel Periods Ticket prices vary with the time of year. There is a low (off-peak) season and a high (peak) season, and often a low-shoulder season and a high-shoulder season as well. Usually the fare depends on your outward flight – if you depart in the high season and return in the low season, you pay the high-season fare.

doesn't match the name in your passport, then you won't be able to board your flight.

Ticketless Travel Ticketless travel, or electronic tickets, whereby your reservation details are contained within an airline computer, is becoming more common. On simple return trips the absence of a ticket can be a benefit – it's one less thing to worry about. However, if you are planning a complicated itinerary that you may wish to amend en route, there is no substitute for the good old paper version.

Travellers with Special Needs

Most international airlines can cater to people with special needs – travellers with disabilities, people with young children and even children travelling alone.

Travellers with special dietary preferences (vegetarian, kosher etc) can request appropriate meals with advance notice. If you are travelling in a wheelchair, most international airports can provide an escort from check-in desk to plane where needed, and ramps, lifts, toilets and phones are generally available.

Airlines usually allow babies up to two years of age to fly for 10% of the adult fare, although a few airlines may allow them to travel free of charge. Reputable international airlines usually provide nappies (diapers), tissues, talcum powder and all the other paraphernalia needed to keep babies clean, dry and half-happy. For children between the ages of two and 12, the fare on international flights is usually 50% of the regular fare or 67% of a discounted fare.

Departure Tax

The departure tax for international flights from Vietnam is US$10, which can be paid in dong or US dollars. Children under two years of age are exempt.

The USA

Discount travel agents in the USA are known as consolidators (although there won't be a sign on the door saying so). San Francisco is the ticket consolidator capital of the USA, although some good deals can be found in Los Angeles, New York and other big cities. Consolidators can be found through the Yellow Pages or the major daily newspapers. The *New York Times*, *Los Angeles Times*, *Chicago Tribune* and *San Francisco Examiner* all produce weekly travel sections in which you will find a number of travel agency ads.

Council Travel, the USA's largest student travel organisation, has around 60 offices; its head office (☎ 800-226 8624) is at 205 E 42 St, New York, NY 10017. Call it for the office nearest you or visit its Web site at www.ciee.org. STA Travel (☎ 800-777 0112, toll free) has offices in Boston, Chicago, Miami, New York, Philadelphia, San Francisco and other major cities. Call for office locations or visit its Web site at www.statravel.com.

At the time of writing, no US air carriers were flying into Vietnam, though Delta Air Lines has begun code sharing with Air France on its flights from Paris to Vietnam.

China Airlines and EVA Airways (both Taiwanese) currently offer the cheapest fares on flights from the USA to Vietnam, all of which transit in Taipei. Low-season San Francisco–Ho Chi Minh City one-way/return tickets are priced around US$500/800; while New York–Ho Chi Minh City costs US$650/950.

Other airlines with routes between the USA and Vietnam include Cathay Pacific Airways (via Hong Kong), Singapore Airlines (via Singapore), Thai Airways International (via Bangkok) Japan Airlines (via Osaka) and Asiana Airlines (via Seoul).

Canada

Canadian discount air-ticket sellers are also known as consolidators and their air fares tend to be about 10% higher than those sold in the USA. The *Globe & Mail, Toronto Star, Montreal Gazette* and *Vancouver Sun* carry travel-agents ads and are a good place to look for cheap fares.

Travel CUTS (☎ 800-667 2887) is Canada's national student travel agency and has offices in all major cities. Its Web address is www.travelcuts.com.

Typical fares for return low/high-season tickets from Toronto are C$2000/3500, or C$1600/2500 from Vancouver.

Australia

Air fares between Australia and Asia are relatively expensive considering the distances flown. Ethnic Vietnamese living in Australia are known to have the inside scoop on ticket discounts.

Cheap flights from Australia to Vietnam generally go via South-East Asian capitals, involving stopovers at Kuala Lumpur, Bangkok or Singapore. If a long stopover between connections is necessary, transit accommodation is sometimes included in the price of the ticket.

Quite a few travel offices specialise in discount air tickets. Some travel agents, particularly smaller ones, advertise cheap air fares in the travel sections of weekend newspapers, such as *The Age* in Melbourne and *Sydney Morning Herald*.

Two well-known agents for cheap fares are STA Travel and Flight Centre. STA Travel (☎ 03-9349 2411) has its main office at 224 Faraday St, Carlton, VIC 3053, and also has offices in all major cities and on many university campuses. Call (☎ 131 776) Australia-wide for the location of your nearest branch or visit STA's Web site at www.statravel.com.au. Flight Centre (☎ 131 600 Australia-wide) has a central office at 82 Elizabeth St, Sydney, and there are also dozens of offices throughout Australia. Its Web address is www.flightcentre.com.au.

Qantas Airways and Vietnam Airlines offer a nine-hour joint service from Melbourne and Sydney to Ho Chi Minh City. Rock-bottom excursion fares from Melbourne hover around A$700/1000 one way/return, or A$800/A$1200 from Sydney. Most flights to Hanoi involve a change of plane in Ho Chi Minh City.

New Zealand

The *New Zealand Herald* has a travel section where travel agents advertise fares. Flight Centre (☎ 09-309 6171) has a large central office in Auckland at National Bank Towers (corner Queen and Darby Sts) and many branches throughout the country. STA Travel (☎ 09-309 0458) has its main office at 10 High St, Auckland, and has other offices in Auckland as well as in Hamilton, Palmerston North, Wellington, Christchurch and Dunedin. Its Web address is www.sta.travel.com.au.

Low season return fares from Auckland to either Ho Chi Minh City or Hanoi, flying with Malaysian Airlines or Thai start from around NZ$1509. In the high season fares start from around NZ$1855.

The UK

Airline ticket discounters are known as bucket shops in the UK. Despite the somewhat disreputable name, there is nothing under-the-counter about them. Discount air travel is big business in London. Advertisements for many travel agents appear in the travel pages of the weekend broadsheets, such as the *Independent on Saturday* and the *Sunday Times*. Look out for the free magazines, such as *TNT*, which are widely available in London – start by looking outside the main railway and underground stations.

For students or travellers under 26, popular travel agencies in the UK include STA Travel (☎ 020-7361 6161), which has an office at 86 Old Brompton Rd, London SW7 3LQ, and also has other offices in London and Manchester. Visit its Web site at www.statravel.co.uk. Usit Campus (☎ 020-7730 3402), 52 Grosvenor Gardens, London SW1W0AG, has branches throughout the UK. The Web address is www.usitcampus.com. Both of these agencies sell tickets to all travellers, but cater especially to young people and students. Charter flights can work out as a cheaper alternative to scheduled flights, especially if you do not qualify for the under 26 and student discounts.

Other recommended travel agencies include Trailfinders (☎ 020-7938 3939), 194 Kensington High St, London W8 7RG; Bridge the World (☎ 020-7734 7447), 4 Regent Place, London W1R 5FB; and Flightbookers (☎ 020-7757 2000), 177–178 Tottenham Court Rd, London W1P 9LF.

There are no direct flights between the UK and Vietnam, but relatively cheap tickets are available via Hong Kong, Bangkok or Kuala Lumpur. Fares from London to Ho Chi Minh City/Hanoi on THAI via Bangkok average UK£550 in the low season (April to June) and UK£750 in the high season (July to August). These fares allow for an open-jaw option, flying into Hanoi and out of Ho Chi Minh City or vice versa. Special offer fares in the low season can be as low as UK£450.

Continental Europe

Though London is the travel discount capital of Europe, there are several other cities where you will find a range of good deals. Generally, there is not much variation in air fare prices for departures from the main European cities. All the major airlines are usually offering some sort of deal, and travel agents generally have a number of deals on offer, so shop around.

Across Europe, many travel agencies have ties with STA Travel, where cheap tickets can be purchased and tickets issued by STA Travel can be altered (usually for a US$25 fee). Outlets in major cities include Voyages Wasteels (☎ 08 03 88 70 04 – this number can only be dialled from within France, fax 01 43 25 46 25), 11 rue Dupuytren, 75006 Paris, France; STA Travel (☎ 030-311 0950, fax 313 0948), Goethestrasse 73, 10625 Berlin, Germany; Passaggi (☎ 06-474 0923, fax 482 7436), Stazione Termini FS, Gelleria Di Tesla, Rome, Italy; and ISYTS (☎ 01-322 1267, fax 323 3767), 11 Nikis St, upper floor, Syntagma Square, Athens, Greece.

France has a network of student travel agencies that can supply discount tickets to travellers of all ages. OTU Voyages (☎ 01 44 41 38 50) has a central Paris office at 39 Ave Georges Bernanos, 75005, and another 42 offices around the country. The Web address is www.otu.fr. Acceuil des Jeunes en France (☎ 01 42 77 87 80), 119 rue Saint Martin, 75004, Paris, is another popular discount travel agency.

General travel agencies in Paris that offer some of the best services and deals include Nouvelles Frontières (☎ 08 03 33 33 33), 5 Ave de l'Opèra, 75001, Web address www.nouvelles-frontieres.com; and Voyageurs du Monde (☎ 01 42 86 16 00) at 55 rue Sainte Anne, 75002.

Belgium, Switzerland, the Netherlands and Greece are also good places for buying discount air tickets. In Belgium, Acotra Student Travel Agency (☎ 02-512 86 07) rue de la Madeline, Brussels, and WATS Reizen (☎ 03-226 16 26) de Keyserlei 44, Antwerp, are both well-known agencies. In Switzerland, SSR Voyages (☎ 01-297 11 11) specialises in student, youth and budget fares. In Zurich, there is a branch at Leonhardstrasse 10 and there are others in most major Swiss cities. The Web address is www.ssr.ch.

In the Netherlands, NBBS Reizen is the official student travel agency. You can find it in Amsterdam (☎ 020-624 09 89) at Rokin 66 and there are several other agencies around the city. Another recommended travel agent in Amsterdam is Malibu Travel (☎ 020-626 32 30) at Prinsengracht 230.

In Greece, check the many travel agencies in Athen's backstreets between Syntagma and Omonia Squares. For student and nonconcession fares, try Magic Bus (☎ 01-323 7471, fax 322 0219).

Asia

Although most Asian countries are now offering fairly competitive air fare deals, Bangkok, Singapore and Hong Kong are still the best places to shop around for discount tickets. Hong Kong's travel market can be unpredictable, but some excellent bargains are available if you are lucky.

Cambodia There are daily flights between Phnom Penh and Ho Chi Minh City (US$113/210 one way/return) on either Royal Air Cambodge or Vietnam Airlines. There is a US$5 airport tax to fly out of Cambodia. One-month visas for Cambodia are available upon arrival at Phnom Penh Airport for US$20.

China China Southern Airlines and Vietnam Airlines fly China-Vietnam routes. The only direct flight between Ho Chi Minh City and mainland China is to Guangzhou (Canton). All other flights are via Hanoi.

Hong Kong After Bangkok, Hong Kong is the second most popular point for departures to Vietnam. The 2½-hour flights between Hong Kong and Ho Chi Minh City run daily. Hanoi–Hong Kong flights also operate daily and take 1¾ hours.

Hong Kong's flag carrier, Cathay Pacific Airways, and Vietnam Airlines offer a joint service between Hong Kong and Ho Chi Minh City with one-way/return fares for US$300/550. There are also direct flights between Hong Kong and Hanoi (US$275/500 one way/return). The most popular ticket is an 'open jaw' deal for US$525 – this allows you to fly from Hong Kong to Ho Chi Minh City and return from Hanoi to Hong Kong (or vice versa).

Hong Kong has a number of excellent, reliable travel agencies and some that are not-so-reliable ones. A good way to check on a travel agent is to look it up in the phone book: fly-by-night operators don't usually stay around long enough to get listed. Many travellers use the Hong Kong Student Travel Bureau (☎ 2730 3269), 8th floor, Star House, Tsimshatsui. You could also try Phoenix Services (☎ 2722 7378), 7th floor, Milton Mansion, 96 Nathan Rd, Tsimshatsui.

Japan Air fares in Japan have dropped substantially in recent years and it has become an OK place to find deals. The cheapest round-trip tickets from Tokyo or Osaka are on Korean Air (via Seoul). A 60-day fixed date return ticket can go for as little as US$375.

Vietnam Airlines shares a daily direct route with Japan Airlines between Osaka and Ho Chi Minh City. Osaka–Ho Chi Minh City flights take approximately 5½ hours and the one-way/return fares cost around US$450/700 (10-day fixed ticket).

Arranging visas in Japan is expensive and time-consuming, and Japanese travel agents charge high prices to process visa applications; consider taking care of your visa somewhere else like Korea.

Korea Korean Air, Asiana Airlines and Vietnam Airlines all fly the Seoul–Ho Chi Minh City route – there's at least one flight per day. There are also direct Seoul-Hanoi flights at least three times weekly. Flying time between Ho Chi Minh City and Seoul is 4¾ hours. The cheapest one-way/return fares are around US$200/350.

A good travel agency for discount tickets, Joy Travel Service (☎ 02 776 9871, fax 756 5342), 10th floor, 24–2 Mukyo-dong, Chung-gu, Seoul, is directly behind Seoul's City Hall.

Laos Lao Aviation and Vietnam Airlines offer joint services between Vientiane and Hanoi (US$88/176 one way/return) or Vientiane and Ho Chi Minh City (US$135/270).

Malaysia Malaysia Airlines and Vietnam Airlines have a joint service from Kuala Lumpur to Ho Chi Minh City (US$115/235 one way/return; two hours). There are also flights from Kuala Lumpur to Hanoi (US$170/340; three hours 10 minutes).

The Philippines Philippine Airlines and Vietnam Airlines fly Manila–Ho Chi Minh City. Economy one-way/return tickets start at US$160/300. Flying time from Manila to Ho Chi Minh is 2½ hours.

Singapore Singapore Airlines and Vietnam Airlines offer a daily joint service on the Ho Chi Minh–Singapore route. The flying time between Singapore and Ho Chi Minh City is two hours. The fare is US$200/US$350 one way/return. Most flights from Singapore continue to Hanoi. The Singapore-Hanoi one-way fare costs around US$240.

In Singapore, STA Travel (☎ 737 7188) Orchard Parade Hotel, 1 Tanglin Rd, offers competitive discount fares for Asian destinations and beyond. Singapore, like Bangkok, has hundreds of travel agents, so you can compare prices on flights. Chinatown Point shopping centre on New Bridge Rd has a good selection of travel agents.

Taiwan The large numbers of Taiwanese who visit Vietnam have made Taiwan a good embarkation point for Vietnam, with frequent flights now offered by four competing airlines. The flight time between Vietnam and Taiwan is around three hours. At the budget end, one-way/return fares are US$350/550.

A long-running discount travel agent with a good reputation is Jenny Su Travel (☎ 02-2594 7733/2596 2263, fax 2592 0068), 10th floor, 27 Chungshan N Rd, Section 3, Taipei.

Thailand Bangkok, only 80 minutes flying time from Ho Chi Minh City, has emerged as the main port of embarkation for air travel to Vietnam.

THAI, Air France and Vietnam Airlines offer daily Bangkok-Ho Chi Minh City services for around US$100 one way; return tickets cost about double this. There are also direct Bangkok-Hanoi flights for roughly the same price.

Many choose an open-jaw ticket that flies people into either Ho Chi Minh City or Hanoi, from where they travel overland before flying back to Bangkok from the other city. These tickets cost around US$220.

Khao San Rd in Bangkok is the budget travellers headquarters. Bangkok has a number of excellent travel agents, but there are also some suspect ones; ask the advice of other travellers before handing over your cash. STA Travel (☎ 02-236 0262), 33 Surawong Rd, is a good and reliable place to start.

LAND

Border Crossings

There are currently six places where foreigners may cross overland into Vietnam.

There are several shared border crossings; one with Cambodia, two with Laos and three with China. There are no legal moneychanging facilities on the Vietnamese side of any of these crossings, so be sure to have some US dollars handy (preferably in small denominations). The black market is also an option, and they will exchange local currencies – Vietnamese dong, Chinese renminbi, Lao kip and Cambodian riel. Still, try to find a bank or legal moneychanger – black marketeers have a well-deserved reputation for short-changing and outright theft.

Vietnamese police at the land border crossings are known to be particularly problematic. Most travellers find that it's much easier to exit Vietnam overland than it is to enter that way. Travellers at the border crossings are routinely asked for an 'immigration fee' and/or a 'customs fee' of some kind. Though of course they know this is illegal, the Vietnamese border guards are accustomed to collecting tourist's money.

Vietnam no longer requires travellers to have a special visa for entering overland. Valid tourist visas allow you to enter and exit Vietnam at any of the official international borders.

Cambodia The only frontier crossing between Cambodia and Vietnam open to Westerners is Moc Bai, which connects Vietnam's Tay Ninh Province with Cambodia's Svay Rieng Province. Other border crossings are considered too risky due to bandits and are currently off limits. There has been talk of the far south-western border in the Chau Doc/Ha Tien area opening to foreign tourists – keep an ear to the ground.

Buses run every day between Phnom Penh and Ho Chi Minh City (via Moc Bai). The easiest and cheapest alternative is the private Sinh Cafe bus, which transports travellers between Ho Chi Minh City and Phnom Penh in one day. Daily departures in either direction are at 8.30 am, and tickets cost just US$6 per person – cheap! Buses departing from Ho Chi Minh City arrive at the border around 11.30 am; after clearing customs you switch to a different bus on the Cambodian side for the final six- to seven-hour ride to the Capital Guesthouse in Phnom Penh.

Another alternative is one of the private buses from the Mobile Petrol Station (☎ 822 2496) at 147 Đ Nguyen Du. Tickets cost 280,000d (US$20) per person. The 16-person air-conditioned Ford vans are a bit more comfortable than the Sinh Cafe buses, and the ride is a straight shot (no changing buses). At the time of writing, departures from Ho Chi Minh City were on Wednesday and Saturday at 6 am, arriving in Phnom Penh at 3 pm, but you should definitely call ahead to check the current schedule.

Another way to get to/from the border is share taxi; these run directly from Ho Chi Minh City to Moc Bai border crossing and cost around US$20 for up to four people. Check at travel agencies/cafes in Ho Chi Minh's Pham Ngu Lao area for recent prices.

Another cheap, if more complicated and time-consuming way, is to board one of the many bus tours heading for the Caodai Great Temple at Tay Ninh. But instead of going to Tay Ninh, get off at Go Dau where the highway forks. There will be motorbike taxis waiting here, and for as little as US$0.50 you can get a ride to the Moc Bai border crossing. You have to walk across the border but you will find air-con share taxis waiting on the Cambodian side to take you to Phnom Penh for about US$5 per person.

To do this overland crossing, you will need a Cambodian visa (which takes seven working days to process) and, if you plan to return, a re-entry visa for Vietnam (you must apply, however, *before* you leave Vietnam). Once the paper work is filed, Vietnamese re-entry visas can be picked up at the Vietnamese embassy in Phnom Penh.

Laos There are two points where you can cross the border overland between Laos and Vietnam – Lao Bao and the Keo Nua Pass. Keep your ears open for news on the Tay Trang border near Dien Bien Phu (northwest Vietnam) opening up to foreigners.

Lao Bao The tiny Vietnamese village of Lao Bao is on National Hwy 9, 80km west of Dong Ha and 3km east of Laos. Just across the border is the southern Lao province of Savannakhet, but there is no town on that side of the border. An international bus runs between Danang (Vietnam) and Savannakhet via Dong Ha and Lao Bao. In Laos, the only place you are likely to board is Savannakhet. The bus is supposed to run on Sunday, Tuesday and Thursday, but this schedule is hardly engraved in stone. The fare from Dong Ha to Savannakhet costs US$15 for foreigners. The bus departs from Danang at 4 am, Dong Ha at 10 am and Lao Bao at 2 pm, arriving in Savannakhet at 7 pm. The border guards here (both Laotian and Vietnamese) have been known to ask for bribes.

There are also local buses that just go to the border from either side. While it's cheaper to get a local bus, rather than the cross-border express, it also involves more hassle. For one thing, there is a 1km walk between the Vietnamese and Laotian border checkpoints. Furthermore, the bus from Dong Ha terminates at Lao Bao, 3km from the actual border checkpoint (though you can cover this by motorbike). The bus from Dong Ha to Lao Bao costs between US$1 and US$4 depending on whether it's 'deluxe' or 'standard'. These buses normally depart twice daily, around early morning and noon – these departure times are approximate because the buses won't leave until they're completely full.

There is no accommodation on the Lao side of the border, but, if you ask nicely, you might be able to sleep in the restaurant there (500m from the border post). To say that the facilities around the border are primitive is an understatement.

Visas for Laos can be obtained in Ho Chi Minh City, Hanoi or Danang. If you have a Vietnamese re-entry visa, it can be amended at the Vietnamese embassy in Vientiane or the Vietnamese consulate in Savannakhet.

The highway on the Lao side of the border crosses the Ho Chi Minh Trail. This is one of the few places where you can actually get a look at it, although there is not a whole lot to see.

Keo Nua Pass Vietnam's National Hwy 8 crosses the border at Keo Nua Pass (734m), known as Cau Treo in Vietnamese.

The nearest Vietnamese city of any importance is Vinh, about 80km from the border and accessible via National Hwy 8. On the Lao side it's about 200km from the border to Tha Khaek, just opposite Kakhon Phanom in Thailand. There is at least one international bus daily, plus local buses that approach the border checkpoint from either side but do not cross.

China The Vietnam-China border crossings hours are 7 am to 4 pm (Vietnam time) or 8 am to 5 pm China time. Set your watch when you cross the border – the time in China is one hour behind Vietnam. Neither country observes daylight-saving time.

There are currently three border checkpoints where foreigners are permitted to cross between Vietnam and China: Friendship Pass, Lao Cai and Mong Cai.

Friendship Pass The busiest border crossing is at the Vietnamese town of Dong Dang, 164km north-east of Hanoi. The closest town on the Chinese side of the border is Pinxiang (about 10km north of the border gate). The crossing point (Friendship Pass) is known as Huu Nghi Quan (Vietnamese) or Youyi Guan (Chinese).

Dong Dang is an obscure town. The nearest city is Lang Son (see the North-East Vietnam chapter), 18km to the south. Buses and minibuses on the Hanoi–Lang Son route are frequent. The cheapest way to cover the 18km between Dong Dang and Lang Son is to hire a motorbike for about US$1.50. There are also minibuses cruising the streets looking for passengers. Just make sure they take you to Huu Nghi Quan – there is another checkpoint, but Huu Nghi Quan is the only point where foreigners can cross. There is a customs checkpoint between Lang Son and Dong Dang, and sometimes there are long delays while the officials thoroughly search the luggage of Vietnamese and Chinese travellers. For this reason, a motorbike might prove faster than a van, since you won't have to wait for your fellow passengers to be searched. Note that this is only a problem when you're heading south towards Lang Son, not the other way.

On the Chinese side, it's a 20-minute drive from the border to Pinxiang by bus or share taxi – the latter costs US$3. Pinxiang is connected by train to Nanning, the capital of China's Guangxi Province. Trains to Nanning depart Pinxiang at 8 am and 1.30 pm. More frequent are the buses (once every 30 minutes), which take four hours to make the journey and cost US$4.

There is a 600m walk between the Vietnamese and Chinese border posts.

There is a twice-weekly international train between Beijing and Hanoi that stops at Friendship Pass. You can board or exit the train at numerous stations in China. The entire Beijing-Hanoi run is 2951km and the journey takes approximately 55 hours, including a three-hour delay (if you're lucky) at the border checkpoint. Schedules change.

A word of advice – because train tickets to China are expensive in Hanoi, some travellers prefer to buy a ticket to Dong Dang, walk across the border and then buy a Chinese train ticket on the Chinese side. However, the Friendship Pass is several kilometres from Dong Dang and you'll have to hire someone to take you there by motorbike. It's a better idea to buy a ticket from Hanoi to Pinxiang, and then get another ticket to Nanning or beyond once you're in Pinxiang.

Lao Cai–Hekou A 762km metre-gauge railway, inaugurated in 1910, links Hanoi with Kunming in China's Yunnan Province. The border town on the Vietnamese side is Lao Cai (294km from Hanoi). On the Chinese side, the border town is Hekou (468km from Kunming).

Vietnamese and Chinese authorities have started a direct international train service between Hanoi and Kunming. Make inquiries for the latest schedule. Domestic trains also run daily on both sides of the border. On the Chinese side, Hekou-Kunming takes approximately 17 hours.

Mong Cai–Dongxing Vietnam's third (but seldom-used) border crossing between Vietnam and China can be found at Mong Cai, in the north-east corner of the country, just opposite the Chinese city of Dongxing. Until recently, only Vietnamese and Chinese citizens could cross here, but the official word is that the border is open. (See the Mong Cai section in the North-East Vietnam chapter for details on this boarder crossing.)

Car & Motorbike

Drivers of cars and riders of motorbikes will need the vehicle's registration papers, liability insurance and an International Driving permit in addition to their domestic licence. You also need a *Carnet de passage en douane*, which is effectively a passport for the vehicle and acts as a temporary waiver of import duty. The *carnet* may also need to specify any expensive spare parts that you're planning to carry with you, such as a gearbox. This is designed to prevent car-import rackets. Contact your local automobile association for details about all documentation.

Liability insurance is not available in advance for many Asian countries but has to be bought when crossing the border. The cost and quality of such local insurance varies wildly, and you will find in some countries that you are effectively travelling uninsured.

Anyone who is planning to take their own vehicle should check in advance what spare parts and petrol are likely to be available.

Bicycle

Cycling is a cheap, convenient, healthy, environmentally sound and above all fun way of travelling. With the loosening of the borders in South-East Asia more and more people are planning overland trips by bicycle. All you need to know about bicycle travel in Vietnam's region is contained in Lonely Planet's *Cycling Vietnam, Laos & Cambodia*.

One note of caution: Before you leave home, go over your bike with a fine-tooth comb and fill your repair kit with every imaginable spare part. As with cars and motorbikes, you won't necessarily be able to buy that crucial gizmo for your machine when it breaks down somewhere in the back of beyond as the sun sets.

San Francisco-based Velo-Asia Cycling Adventures runs exciting cycling tours in Vietnam (see the Organised Tours listing later in this chapter).

SEA

In 1975, unauthorised departure by sea suddenly became very popular among fed-up Vietnamese nationals. Since about 1990, the number of people fleeing the country by boat has been reduced, first by the Orderly Departure Program (see the 'Disorderly Departure' boxed text in the Facts about Vietnam chapter) and later by the opening of the Chinese border (which provided a much safer and easier route out). Nowadays, few Vietnamese have anywhere to flee, as most Western nations are suffering from compassion fatigue and won't grant them refugee status.

For foreign tourists, there are few options to arrive or depart legally by sea. Yachts and fishing boats that have shown up without authorisation in Vietnamese territorial waters have been seized and their crews imprisoned – sometimes for many months – until a satisfactory payment in hard currency has been received by the aggrieved authorities.

Nowadays, however, some luxury (and some not so luxurious) cruise ships dock at Vietnamese ports, notably Ho Chi Minh City, Danang and Haiphong. These same cities are also frequent ports of call for freighters from Singapore, Taiwan and Thailand.

ORGANISED TOURS

Package tours to Vietnam are offered by travel agencies worldwide. Nearly all these tours follow one of a dozen or so set itineraries. Tours booked outside Vietnam are not a total rip-off, given what you get (visa, air tickets, tourist-class accommodation, food, transport, a guide etc), but then again they're not cheap: prices range from about US$500 for a three-day Ho Chi Minh City 'shopping tour' to over US$2000 for a week-long trip flying around the country. Covering the same ground on your own can cost as little as US$20 a day (excluding air fare), but this self-propelled travel involves far more work.

It's quite easy to fly into Vietnam and make all the arrangements there after arrival (see Organised Tours in the Getting Around chapter) and for many this way is more fun. The main thing you gain by booking before arrival is time, and if your time is more precious than money, a prebooked package tour could be right for you.

Almost any reputable travel agency can book you onto a standard mad-dash minibus tour around Vietnam. More noteworthy are the adventure tours arranged for people with a particular passion. These can include speciality tours for cyclists, trekkers, birdwatchers, war veterans, 4WD enthusiasts and Vietnamese cuisine buffs. If you have a particular interest and want to organise a group tour, you might surf, and advertise on, the Internet.

Consider contacting the following speciality travel outfits:

Australia

Community Aid Abroad (CAA), Oxfam Australia (☎ 08-8232 2727, fax: 8232 2808, freecall outside Adelaide: 1800 814 848, ⓔ info@tours.caa.org.au) Specialises in

sustainable, responsible tourism tours – percentage of proceeds supports local CAA aid projects.
Web site: www.caa.org.au/travel

Griswalds Vietnamese Vacations (☎ 02-9564 5040, fax 9564 1373, ⓔ Griswalds@vietnam vacations.com.au) PO Box 501, Leichhardt, NSW 2040. Company motto: 'Your dong is safe in our hands.'
Web site: www.vietnamvacations.com.au

Intrepid Travel (☎ 03-9473 2611, fax 9419 5878) 11 Spring St, Fitzroy, Victoria 3065

Obitours (☎ 02-9954 1399, fax 9954 1655) 3rd floor, 73 Walker St (PO Box 834), North Sydney, NSW 2059

Peregrine *Sydney*: (☎ 02-9290 2770) 5/38 York St, NSW 2000. *Melbourne*: (☎ 03-9662 2800, fax 9663 8618) 258 Lonsdale St, VIC 3000

Travel Indochina (☎ 02-9244 2133, fax 9244 2233, ⓔ travindo@concorde.com.au) 403 George St, Sydney, NSW 2000
Web site: wwwtravelindochina.com.au

Canada

Global Adventures (☎ 800-781 2269/604-940 2220, fax 940 2233) Runs 12-day sea kayaking trips in Halong Bay.
Web site: www.portal.ca/~global

France

Nouveau Monde Voyages (☎ 1 43 29 40 40, fax 1 46 34 19 67) 8 rue Mabillon, Paris 75006

Germany

Geoplan Touristik (☎ 307-954021, fax 954025) Steglitzer Damm 96B, D-12 169, Berlin

The Netherlands

Tradewind Holidays (☎ 20-661 0101, fax 642 0137) PO Box 70449, Amsterdam 1007 KK

New Zealand

Adventure World (☎ 649-524 5118, fax 520 6629) 101 Great South Rd, Auckland

Go Orient Holidays (☎ 649-379 5520, fax 377 0111) 151 Victoria St West, Auckland

Thailand

Asian Trails (☎ 02-658 6080, fax 02-658 6099, ⓔ asiantrails@asiantrails.org) 15th floor, Mercury Tower, 540 Ploenchit Rd, Bangkok 10330
Web site: www.asiantrails.net

The UK

Asian Journeys (☎ 1604-234855, fax 234866) 32 Semilong Rd, Northampton NN2 6BT

The USA

Asia Transpacific Journeys (☎ 800-642 2742) PO Box 1279, Boulder, CO 80306. Offers trekking tours and cycling trips to suit all budgets.
Web site: www.SoutheastAsia.com

Asian Pacific Adventures (☎ 800-825 1680/323-935 3156) 826 South Sierra Bonita Ave, Los Angeles, CA 90036. Arranges cycling trips (not to be confused with the preceding company).

Latitudes-Expeditions East (☎ 800-580 4883/415-398 0458, fax 680 1522) 870 Market St, Suite 482, San Francisco, CA 94102. South-East Asia specialist.
Web site: www.weblatitudes.com

Sea Canoe International Adventures (☎ 800-444 1043, fax 888-824 5621) Offers kayaking trips in Halong Bay.
Web site: www.seacanoe.com

The Global Spectrum (☎ 800-419 4446, ⓔ gspectrum@gspectrum.com) Suite 204, 1901 Pennsylvania Ave NW, Washington, DC 20006

Velo-Asia Cycling Adventures (☎ 415-282-1788, ⓔ info@veloasia.com) A San Francisco–based outfit arranging cycling trips, plus trekking, boating and culinary theme tours.
Web site: www.veloasia.com

Wild Card Adventures (☎ 800-590 3776, fax 360-387 9816, ⓔ swild7@juno.com) 751 Maple Grove Rd, Camano Island, WA 98292. Customised Vietnam travel itineraries, unusual programs and destinations; group size is limited to 10 people.

Vietnam

The following Vietnam-based, foreign-run travel agencies offer a spectrum of upmarket tours throughout Vietnam and Indochina.

Exotissimo

Hanoi: (☎ 04-828 2150, fax 828 2146) 26 Tran Nhat Duat
Web site: www.exotissimo.com

Ho Chi Minh City: (☎ 08-825 1723, fax 829 5800, ⓔ richard@exotissimo.com) 37 Đ Ton Duc Thang, District 1

Phoenix Vietnam (☎ 04-733 6456, fax 733 6457, ⓔ phoenix.vn@fpt.vn) 23, Pho Quan Thanh, Ba Dinh, Hanoi
Web site: www.phoenixvietnam.com

Vidotour (☎ 829 1438, fax 1435, ⓔ vidotour@ bdvn.vnmail.vnd.net) 41 Đ Dinh Tien Hoang, District 1, Ho Chi Minh City

Getting Around

AIR

Vietnam Airlines has a near monopoly on domestic flights, though Pacific Airlines also flies the Hanoi–Ho Chi Minh City (Saigon) route daily.

The Vietnam Airlines booking offices in Ho Chi Minh City and Hanoi are the two busiest in the land. Just before public holidays, buying an air ticket literally requires some strong-arm tactics – the Vietnamese are not big on queuing up and you might experience a struggling mass of elbows, hands and slithering bodies. You can avoid this hassle by purchasing from a less congested booking office. As there are many travel agents around that sell domestic air tickets, there's no real need to go to the airline office at all. The travel agents do not charge any more than the airline – the airline pays a commission to them.

You'll need your passport to make a booking on all domestic flights, and you'll have to show it at the check-in counter and yet again at the security checkpoint. Vietnamese nationals must show their ID cards.

Vietnam Airlines is gradually getting its act together and many (but not all) branch offices accept travellers cheques and credit cards for ticket purchases. The airline has retired all of its ancient Soviet-built fleet (thank God!) and purchased new Western-made aircraft. If you are landing at Hanoi's Noi Bai airport you may still see a handful of the old Tupolov 72s rusting out on the tarmac. Good riddance.

Vasco charters small, fixed-wing aircraft and helicopters. Most of the pilots are Westerners, but the government requires a Vietnamese observer on board. Aerial photography is not permitted unless you have a Ministry of Defence (MOD) photographer, which is an expensive hassle; costs start at US$850 an hour. Contact Vasco in Hanoi or Ho Chi Minh City for details (see under Getting There & Away in the Hanoi and Ho Chi Minh City chapters for Vasco contact details).

All aircraft return to their point of origin on the same day as their departure. (See the 'Domestic Airline Schedules' boxed text in this chapter. It covers all the possible routes available within Vietnam.)

The airlines charge US$10 if you want to refund an unused domestic air ticket. If you bought the ticket from a travel agency, you also lose an additional 5% (the travel-agent's commission).

Northern Flight Service Company (☎ 827 4409, fax 827 2780), at 173 Pho Truong Chinh, offers a helicopter charter service from Hanoi to Halong Bay on Saturday only. The cost for the charter service is $175 per person (paying an extra $20 includes transfers to Hanoi's Gia Lam airport and the harbour in Halong, a four- to five-hour boat ride and lunch in Halong Bay). The

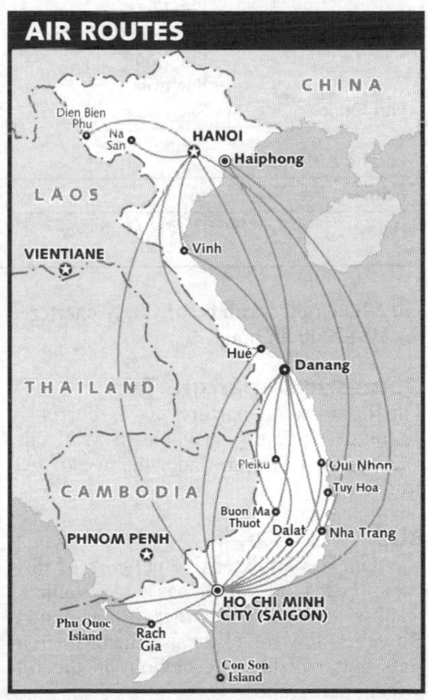

Domestic Airline Schedules (US$)

Vietnam Airlines

from	to	frequency	economy	1st class
Danang	Buon Ma Thuot	3 weekly	42	–
	Haiphong	3 weekly	77	–
	Nha Trang	3 weekly	42	–
	Pleiku	3 weekly	42	–
	Qui Nhon	3 weekly	42	–
	Vinh	3 weekly	54	–
Hanoi	Danang	3 daily	77	92
	Dien Bien Phu	3 weekly	50	–
	Hué	2 daily	77	92
	Son La	2 weekly	42	–
	Nha Trang	1 daily	112	–
Ho Chi Minh City	Buon Ma Thuot	3 weekly	50	–
	Dalat	1 daily	35	–
	Danang	3 daily	77	92
	Haiphong	5 weekly	146	208
	Hanoi	7 daily	146	208
	Hué	1 daily	77	92
	Nha Trang	2 daily	50	–
	Phu Quoc	3 weekly	54	–
	Pleiku	3 weekly	54	–
	Qui Nhon	3 weekly	54	–
	Rach Gia	5 weekly	54	–
Phu Quoc	Rach Gia	2 weekly	35	–

Pacific Airlines

from	to	frequency	economy	1st class
Hanoi	Ho Chi Minh City	1 daily	146	–

same helicopters can be privately chartered for US$2000 an hour.

Domestic Departure Tax

The domestic departure tax is currently 20,000d (US$1.60), payable in local currency only. Children under the age of two are exempt.

BUS

Vietnam has an extensive network of dirt-cheap buses, and other passenger vehicles reach virtually every corner of the country. However, few travellers use them, for reasons that will become obvious in the following paragraphs.

Road safety is not one of Vietnam's strong points. The Vietnamese intercity road network of two-lane highways is becoming more and more dangerous due to the rapid increase in the number of motor vehicles. High-speed, head-on collisions between buses, trucks and other smaller vehicles have become a sickeningly familiar sight on National Hwy 1. Vietnam does not have an efficient emergency rescue system or even a proper ambulance network – if something happens to you out on the road, you could be hours from even rudimentary medical treatment.

If possible, try to travel during daylight hours only. Indeed, many drivers refuse to drive after dark in rural areas because the unlit highways often have huge potholes and lots of bicycles and pedestrians (including dogs and chickens), who seem oblivious to the traffic. However, if you like living dangerously, there are some overnight buses.

Package-tour groups tend to travel on modern, Japanese-made buses with air-con and cushy seats. However, public bus companies never use these because they're too expensive.

Public buses come mainly in four flavours: Korean-made (almost new), Russian-made (circa 1970), US-made (circa 1965) and French-made (antique).

Most comfortable are the Korean-made (usually Hyundai) buses. Many of these are air-con and the seats are reasonably comfortable. You'll find these almost exclusively on very-long-distance routes such as Ho Chi Minh City–Hanoi (a two-day, nonstop drive!). The bad news is these buses are equipped with video-tape players and evil karaoke machines. You can ignore the blood-splattered kung fu videos by closing your eyes (or wearing a blindfold), but you'll need to be deaf to sleep through the karaoke sessions – ear plugs are recommended!

The vast majority of Vietnam's buses are Russian or US made. There is little difference between the two; most seem to have been designed for military use. The Vietnamese have modified the vehicles with fancy paint jobs – a nice touch. Not so nice is the fact that the bus companies have installed many additional seats – you can expect little leg room and much discomfort. You can purchase two tickets, which, theoretically, entitles you to two seats, but you might have to defend your turf when the bus gets packed to overflowing! Many buses are literally standing room only – if you drop dead, you'll never hit the floor. Luggage is stacked wherever it fits, which in many cases means that it gets tied onto the roof. The police frequently stop the buses to cite the drivers for overloading, though after a quick fix (US$5) the bus continues on its way. Another problem is mechanical breakdowns, which occur far too frequently.

The French-made buses are becoming rare, which is not surprising since they are about 50 years old. How the Vietnamese keep the old bangers running is anybody's guess. These museums-on-wheels sputter, creep and crawl along at around 30km/h – don't expect to get anywhere fast. As with the Russian and US buses, you can expect overloading, extreme discomfort and frequent breakdowns. After an eight-hour ride, one traveller put it succinctly when she said 'I feel like a million dong'.

It's fair to say that riding the buses will give you ample opportunity to have 'personal contact' with the Vietnamese people. If you're looking to meet locals, what better way than to have a few sitting on your lap! As one reader says:

> I enjoyed the bus-riding scene, the scenery and the conversations (gesturing) with people. Although I'd rate the conditions as terrible, the riding community suffered, slept and ate together.

Figuring out the bus system is anything but easy. Many cities have several bus stations, and responsibilities are divided according to the location of the destination (whether it is north or south of the city) and the type of service being offered (local or long distance, express or nonexpress).

Most long-distance buses depart in the early morning. Often, half a dozen vehicles heading for the same destination will leave at the same time, usually around 5.30 am. The first thing they do after departure is look for a functioning petrol station (sometimes difficult to find due to power failures) – just why they don't fill the tank the night before has always mystified us.

Overnight buses have begun since curfew regulations were relaxed in 1989, but neither passengers nor drivers are especially fond of travelling all night. Short-distance buses, like service taxis, depart when full (ie, jam-packed with people and luggage). They often operate throughout the day, but don't count on anything leaving after about 4 pm.

Be aware that your luggage can easily be pilfered at toilet stops unless you have a trusted friend watching it or you bring it to the toilet with you. When tied to the rooftop it should be reasonably safe from pilfering,

Passing Water

The engines of many older trucks and buses are equipped with an ingenious gravity-powered heat-dissipation system. This is designed to supplement the radiator, which cannot cope when these ancient vehicles are heavily overloaded (a frequent occurrence), and helps prevent overheating.

A drum attached to the roof of the cab is connected to the engine by a hose. This hose passes by the driver's window, where a stopcock allows the driver to control the water flow. Cold water in the rooftop drum slowly drains into the engine; hot water squirts out the radiator overflow tank. When the drum is empty, the driver simply stops at any of the numerous water-filling stations that line major highways and tops it up.

but it will be exposed to constant road dust and sometimes heavy rain. Do not accept drinks from fellow passengers as there is a chance you may be drugged and robbed.

Reservations & Costs

Buses normally leave early in the morning, so if you don't plan to bargain with the bus driver, show up at the bus station the day before departure and at least *try* to purchase a ticket.

Costs are negligible, though foreigners are typically charged anywhere from twice to 10 times the going rate. Outside of the Mekong Delta and major cities, most ticket offices won't even sell foreigners a normal ticket; rather, they leave you to battle it out with the bus driver. It is helpful to determine the cost of the ticket for Vietnamese before starting these 'negotiations'.

Open Tours

In backpacker haunts throughout Vietnam, you'll see lots of signs advertising 'Open Date Ticket' or just 'Open Ticket'. Basically, this is a bus service catering to foreign budget travellers, not to Vietnamese. These air-con buses run between Ho Chi Minh City and Hanoi and you may enter and exit the bus at any major city along the route. You are not obliged to follow a fixed schedule.

Competition has driven the price of these tours lower and lower – at the time of writing you could buy a ticket all the way from Hanoi to Ho Chi Minh City for just US$33. There are two tickets available: Ho Chi Minh City–Hué for as cheap as US$23 and Hué-Hanoi for as low as US$10. Shorter individual legs cost less. Don't be surprised to find that these prices keep dropping.

As cheap as it is, we are not keen on this deal. Once you've bought the ticket, you're stuck with it. If you're dissatisfied with the service provided, that's too bad. Also, it really isolates you from Vietnam – you should try to have at least some contact with the locals other than the bus driver. Buying minibus tickets all along the way costs a bit more, but you achieve maximum flexibility.

Nevertheless, Open Tickets are a temptation and many people go for them. If you're buying these, we recommend looking for them at cafes in Ho Chi Minh City and Hanoi.

MINIBUS

There are two categories of minibus: public and chartered.

Public Minibuses

The public minibuses (actually privately owned) run like the larger bus services. They depart when full and will pick up as many passengers as possible along the route. They may also drive around town before departure, hunting for additional customers before actually heading out to the highway. Such minibuses will usually become ridiculously crowded as the journey progresses and are not comfortable by any means. The frequent stops to pick up and discharge passengers (and arrange their luggage and chickens) can make for a slow journey. Minibuses congregate near bus stations, though you can often arrange to have one pick you up at your hotel.

Chartered Minibuses

The majority of independent travellers in Vietnam choose this form of transport above all others. Chartered minibuses are just what the name implies. Some cater exclusively to tourists, but well-heeled Vietnamese also travel this way.

This is the deluxe class – air-con is standard and you can be certain of having enough space to sit comfortably. Such luxury, of course, is something you must pay for – prices will be substantially higher than what you'd pay on public buses. Nevertheless, it's still very cheap by any standard.

In places where tourists are numerous, there are bound to be people booking seats on chartered minibuses. Budget hotels and cafes are the best places to inquire about these vehicles. However, there are some unscrupulous cafes that will sell you a tourist-priced ticket and then stick you on a malfunctioning local bus.

If the chartered minibuses cannot fill all the seats, they may still pick up some passengers en route. However, any reputable company puts a limit on the number of passengers – they should pick up no more people than they have empty seats and should not pick up anybody with excessive luggage. If you paid top dollar for a chartered minibus and they still try to pack in a ridiculous number of passengers, you've been had.

TRAIN

The 2600km Vietnamese railway system (Duong Sat Viet Nam) runs along the coast between Ho Chi Minh City and Hanoi, and links the capital with Haiphong and northern towns. While sometimes even slower than buses, trains offer a more relaxing way to get around and more leg and body room than the jam-packed buses. Dilapidated as the tracks, rolling stock and engines may appear, the trains are much safer than the country's kamikaze bus fleet. Furthermore, the railway authorities have been rapidly upgrading the facilities to accommodate tourists –with air-con sleeping berths available on express trains.

One key factor to take into account when deciding whether to go by train or bus is the hour at which the train gets to where you want to go – trying to find a place to stay at 3 am is likely to be very frustrating.

Even the express trains in Vietnam are slow by developed-country standards, but conditions are improving as the tracks and equipment are being upgraded. The quickest rail journey between Hanoi and Ho Chi Minh City takes 32 hours. The slowest express train on this route takes 41 hours.

There are also local trains that only cover short routes like Ho Chi Minh City to Nha Trang. These local trains can crawl along at 15km/h. There are several reasons for the excruciating slowness. There is only one track running between Ho Chi Minh City and Hanoi. Trains can pass each other only at those few points where a siding has been constructed. Each time trains go by each other, one of them has to stop on the prearranged sidetrack and wait for the oncoming train to arrive. If one is late, so is the other. Subsequent trains going in both directions may also be delayed.

Petty crime is a problem on Vietnamese trains, especially if you travel in budget class, where your fellow passengers are likely to be desperately poor. While there doesn't seem to be organised pack-napping gangs, as there are in India, the Vietnamese seem convinced that the young men and boys you see hanging out in the stations and on trains have only larceny on their minds. Thieves have become proficient at grabbing packs through the windows as trains pull out of stations. To protect your belongings, always keep your bag near you and lock or tie it to something, especially at night. If you are riding in a sleeper car, try to secure the bottom berth; bags can be stowed underneath and the only way a thief can get to your stuff is by literally lifting you up. If you must leave your pack for a moment, ask someone who looks responsible to keep an eye on it.

Another hazard is children who frequently throw rocks at the train. Passengers have been severely injured this way and many conductors insist that you keep down the metal window shield for just this reason. Unfortunately, these shields obstruct the view.

There is supposedly a 20kg limit for luggage carried on Vietnamese trains. Enforcement isn't really strict, but if you have too much stuff you might have to send it in the freight car (hopefully on the same train) and pay a small extra charge. This is a hassle that you'll probably want to avoid. Bicycles can also be sent in the freight car. Just make sure that the train you are on has a freight car (most have) or your luggage will arrive later than you do.

Eating is no problem – there are vendors at every station who board the train and practically stuff food, drinks, cigarettes and lottery tickets into your pockets. However, the food supplied by the railway company (free, as part of the cost of the ticket for some long journeys) could be better. It's a good idea to stock up on your favourite munchies before taking a long trip.

Schedules

Odd-numbered trains travel southward; even-numbered trains travel northward. The fastest service is provided by the *Reunification Express*, which runs between Ho Chi Minh City and Hanoi, making only a few short stops en route. If you want to stop at some obscure point between the major towns, you'll have to use one of the slower local trains.

Aside from the main Ho Chi Minh City–Hanoi run, three rail spur lines link Hanoi with the other parts of northern Vietnam. One takes you east to the port city of Haiphong. A second heads north-east to Lang Son, crosses the border and continues to Nanning, China. A third goes north-west to Lao Cai and onwards to Kunming, China.

One of the unfortunate things about the train system is that there is not yet a computerised booking system. This is no problem when you are purchasing tickets in Ho Chi Minh City or Hanoi, but becomes a problem when you want to buy a ticket at some other point along the route. For example, many travellers want to board the *Reunification Express* in Nha Trang and take it to Hué, but the staff at Nha Trang train station aren't always informed about empty seats and thus may not be able to sell you a ticket even when space is available. This is a problem that may be solved eventually.

Four *Reunification Express* trains depart Ho Chi Minh City station between 9 am and 10.30 pm every day. The same number of trains depart Hanoi between 5 am and 6.40 pm daily.

In addition, there are local trains. One train departs Ho Chi Minh City at 6 pm and arrives in Nha Trang at 5.30 am daily. The return service leaves Nha Trang at 6 pm, arriving in Ho Chi Minh City at 4.20 am. There is another local service to Hué departing Ho Chi Minh City at 10 am and returning from Hué at 10.10 am daily.

The train schedule changes so frequently (about every six months) that there's little point in reproducing the whole thing here. The timetables for all trains are posted at major stations and you can copy these down. At one time, free photocopied timetables were also available at some stations but now seem to have vanished – perhaps the railway administration will get smart and start selling these.

It's important to realise that the train schedule is 'bare-bones' during the Tet festival. For example, the *Reunification Express* is suspended for nine days beginning four days before Tet and continuing for four days afterwards.

It's *very* important that you hang onto your ticket until you've exited the train station at your final destination. Some travellers have discarded their tickets while leaving the train only to find that the gatekeepers won't allow them to exit the station without a ticket. In this situation, you could be forced to purchase another ticket at the full price. The purpose of this system is to catch people who have sneaked aboard without paying.

Classes

There are five classes of train travel in Vietnam: hard seat, soft seat, hard sleeper, soft sleeper (normal) and soft sleeper (air-con). Since it's all that the vast majority of Vietnamese can afford, hard seat is usually packed. Hard seat is tolerable for day travel, but overnight it can be even less comfortable than the bus, where at least you are hemmed in and thus propped upright.

Soft-seat carriages have vinyl-covered seats rather than the uncomfortable hard-seat benches.

The *Reunification Express*

Construction of the 1726km Hanoi-Saigon railway – the Transindochinois – began in 1899 (under Governor-General Paul Doumer) and was completed in 1936. In the late 1930s, the trip from Hanoi to Saigon took 40 hours and 20 minutes at an average speed of 43km/h. During WWII, the Japanese made extensive use of the rail system, resulting in Viet Minh sabotage on the ground and US bombing from the air. After WWII, efforts were made to repair the Transindochinois, major parts of which were either damaged or had become overgrown.

During the Franco-Viet Minh War, the Viet Minh engaged in massive sabotage against the rail system. Sometimes they would pry up and carry off several kilometres of track in a single night. In 1948 the French responded by introducing two armoured trains that were equipped with turret-mounted cannon, anti-aircraft machine guns, grenade launchers and mortars (similar trains are used in Cambodia today on the Phnom Penh–Battambang line). The Viet Minh used their bounty to create a 300km network of tracks in an area wholly under their control (between Ninh Hoa and Danang) – the French quickly responded with their own sabotage.

In the late 1950s, the South, with US funding, reconstructed the track between Saigon and Hué, a distance of 1041km. But between 1961 and 1964 alone, 795 Viet Cong attacks were launched on the rail system, forcing the abandonment of large sections of track (including the Dalat spur). A major reconstruction effort was carried out between 1967 and 1969, and three sections of track were put back into operation: one in the immediate vicinity of Saigon, another between Nha Trang and Qui Nhon, and a third between Danang and Hué.

By 1960 the North had repaired 1000km of track, mostly between Hanoi and China. During the US air war against the North, the northern rail network was repeatedly bombed. Even now clusters of bomb craters can be seen around virtually every rail bridge and train station in the north.

After reunification, the government immediately set about re-establishing the Hanoi–Ho Chi Minh City rail link as a symbol of Vietnamese unity. By the time the *Reunification* (Thong Nhat) *Express* trains were inaugurated on 31 December 1976, 1334 bridges, 27 tunnels, 158 stations and 1370 shunts (switches) had been repaired.

Today the *Reunification Express* chugs along at more or less the same speed it did in the 1930s; at an average of 48km/h, it takes between 32 and 41 hours between Hanoi and Ho Chi Minh City, depending on which train you catch.

Hard sleeper has three tiers of beds (six beds per compartment). Because the Vietnamese don't seem to like climbing up, the upper berth is cheapest, followed by the middle berth and finally the lower berth. The best bunk is the one in the middle because the bottom berth is invaded by seatless travellers during the day. There is no door to separate the compartment from the corridor.

Soft sleeper has two tiers (four beds per compartment) and all bunks are priced the same. These compartments have a door. The best trains have two categories of soft sleeper, one with air-con and one without. At present, air-con is only available on the very fastest express train.

Reservations

The supply of train seats is often insufficient to meet demand. Reservations for all trips should be made at least one day in advance. For sleeping berths, you may have to book passage three or more days before the date of travel. Bring your passport and visa when buying train tickets. Though such documents are never checked at bus stations, train personnel may ask to have a look at them.

You do not necessarily need to go to the train station to get your ticket. Many travel agencies, hotels and cafes sell train tickets for a small commission (in most cases, well worth the time and trouble you'll save buying the tickets on your own).

Reunification Express Fares from Hanoi (US$)

Hanoi–Ho Chi Minh City (S3/S5/S7 Trains); 37/39/41 hours

station	distance from Hanoi	hard seat	soft seat	bottom berth	middle berth	top berth	soft sleeper
Nam Dinh	87km	3/3	3/3	5/6	5/5	4/5	5/6
Ninh Binh	115km	4/4	4/4	6/7	6/6	6/6	7/8
Thanh Hoa	1551km	5/6	6/6	9/10	9/9	8/9	10/11
Vinh	319km	9/10	9/10	17/18	15/18	14/15	17/19
Dong Hoi	522km	14/16	16/17	27/29	24/27	22/27	28/32
Dong Ha	622km	17/18	18/20	32/35	27/32	26/29	33/38
Hué	688km	19/20	20/22	35/38	32/35	28/32	36/32
Danang	791km	21/23	23/25	40/44	36/40	33/32	42/36
Quang Ngai	928km	25/27	27/29	47/51	43/49	38/43	49/56
Dieu Tri	1096km	29/32	32/35	55/61	50/55	45/55	57/50
Tuy Hoa	1195km	32/35	35/38	60/66	55/60	53/55	62/72
Nha Trang	1315km	38/41	41/45	72/79	65/72	59/65	75/86
Thap Cham	1408km	41/44	44/48	77/84	70/77	62/70	80/92
HCMC	1726km	46/49	49/54	87/95	78/87	70/78	90/103

Hanoi–Ho Chi Minh City (S1 Express Train); 32 hours

station	distance from Hanoi	soft seat	bottom berth	middle berth	top berth	soft sleeper	air-con soft sleeper
Vinh	319km	12	20	18	17	21	27
Hué	688km	25	41	38	35	45	57
Danang	791km	29	48	44	40	51	66
Dieu Tri	1096km	40	66	61	55	71	91
Nha Trang	1315km	52	85	79	72	93	119
HCMC	1726km	82	103	95	89	111	143

Fares, departure times and durations are the same as those shown above from Ho Chi Minh City to Hanoi on trains S2 (32 hours) and S4/S6/S8 (37/39/41 hours).

If you arrive early (7.30 am, for example) at a train station in central Vietnam, you may be told that all tickets to Hanoi or Ho Chi Minh City are sold out. However, this may simply mean that there are no tickets *at the moment*, but more may become available after 8 pm, when Ho Chi Minh City and Hanoi offices phone through the details of unsold tickets. You don't have to pay a bribe to get these tickets – just be polite and persevere. Buying through a travel agency could eliminate this hassle. Of course, not much can be done if the seats are really sold out.

Reservations can be made only for travel originating from the city where you are booking them from. In Nha Trang, for instance, you can reserve a place to Danang but cannot book passage from Danang to Hué. For this reason – and because train stations are often far from the part of town where you will be staying – it is a good idea to make reservations for onward travel as soon as you arrive in a city.

If you are travelling with a bicycle (for which there is a small surcharge), it may only be possible to get it out of checked baggage at certain stations.

Costs

One disadvantage of rail travel is that, officially, foreigners are supposed to pay a surcharge of around 400% over and above what Vietnamese pay. It works out to about US$100 for a Ho Chi Minh City–Hanoi ticket in a hard-sleeper compartment. This is compared with US$173 to fly the same route.

Some foreigners have managed to pay local prices, but this is almost impossible to do unless you have an Asian face. Even with Asian features, you are supposed to show ID when the ticket is purchased, though a Vietnamese person could buy the ticket for you. The ticket clearly indicates whether you paid foreign or local prices, and the name of the purchaser is also written on the ticket. Most conductors will enforce the rules – if you have blond hair and a big nose, don't think that you're going to fool the conductors into believing you're Vietnamese, even if you do happen to wear a conical hat.

The price for a ticket depends on which train you take: The Ho Chi Minh City–Hanoi run takes 32, 37, 39 or 41 hours – the fastest trains are the most expensive. See the table *Reunification Express* Fares from Hanoi in this chapter.

CAR & MOTORBIKE

The discomfort and unreliability of Vietnam's public transport makes renting a vehicle a popular option. Having your own set of wheels gives you maximum flexibility to visit remote regions and stop where and when you please. The major considerations are safety, the mechanical condition of the vehicle, reliability of the rental agency and your budget.

In general, the major highways are hard surfaced and reasonably well maintained, but seasonal flooding can be a problem. A big typhoon can create potholes the size of bomb craters. In remote areas roads are not surfaced and will become a sea of mud if the weather turns bad – such roads are best tackled with a 4WD vehicle or motorbike. Mountain roads are particularly dangerous – landslides, falling rocks and runaway vehicles can add unwelcome excitement to your journey. The occasional roadside cemetery often indicates where a bus plunged over the edge.

The pumps in petrol stations may say something like 'Regular' or 'Super-Unleaded'. Basically this means nothing except that the machinery was purchased from abroad. However, petrol does have an octane rating – 86 would be low and 95 would be top end, but there can be several gradations in between.

Xang (black-market petrol) and *dau* (oil) is sold in soft drink bottles at little stalls along major roads and highways. In rural areas you'll see the bottles stacked by the roadside next to a stall. In Ho Chi Minh City, it's not permitted to stack bottles of petrol by the roadside, so the vendor places a couple of bricks with a rolled-up newspaper stuck vertically in between. In cities, this is the universal sign indicating petrol for sale. Be forewarned that black-market petrol is often mixed with kerosene (it's cheaper), which is likely to cause engine problems – use in emergencies only. If the vendor claims that bottled petrol costs the same as what you buy in a petrol station, that's a clear warning sign to stay away.

Leaving an unattended vehicle parked out on the street overnight is not wise. If travelling by motorbike you can usually bring it inside the hotel. If travelling by car, it's necessary to find a hotel with a garage or fenced-in compound (many hotels are so equipped). There are also commercial non-hotel garages.

If you're on a motorbike, serious sunburn is a major risk and something you should take care to prevent. The cooling breeze prevents you from realising how badly burned you are getting until it's too late. Cover up exposed skin or wear sunscreen. Bikers also must consider the opposite problem – occasional heavy rains. Rainsuits and ponchos should be carried – especially during the monsoon season. Sun block is somewhat hard to find in Vietnam, but rain gear is readily available.

Road Rules

Basically, there aren't any. The biggest vehicle wins, by default. Be particularly careful about children on the road – you'll find kids playing hopscotch in the middle of a major highway. Many young boys seem to enjoy playing a game of 'chicken' – deliberately sticking their arms and legs in front of fast-approaching vehicles and withdrawing them (hopefully) at the last possible moment. Other children try to entertain themselves by throwing rocks at passing vehicles – make sure you wear a helmet. Livestock on the road are also a menace – hit a cow on a motorbike and you'll both be hamburger.

In cities there is a rule that you cannot turn right on a red light. It's easy to run afoul of this law in Vietnam and the police will fine you for this offence.

If you are involved in an accident, be aware that calling the police is just about the worst thing you can do. The usual response of the police is to impound both vehicles regardless of who caused the accident. You must pay a substantial sum (around US$100 or more) to get the vehicle back. When Vietnamese have an accident, the usual response is for the two drivers to stand in the street and argue with each other for 30 minutes about whose fault it was. Whoever tires of the argument first hands over some money to pay for damages and it's all settled. As a foreigner, you're at a disadvantage in these negotiations. Perhaps it's best to feign some injury (to gain sympathy) but offer to pay for the other driver's minor damages. If none of this works and you are being asked to pay excessive damages, you could always say you want to call the police. Because you are a foreigner, the locals might just believe you're crazy enough to do that, and the negotiations will likely be concluded quickly.

Of course, in the case of a serious accident or death you should contact the nearest police station.

Car Although the police frequently stop drivers and fine them for all sorts of real and imagined offences, we have never seen anybody stopped for speeding. Driving is normally performed Grand Prix style, as if there were some sort of prize for the first car to cross the finish line.

Honking at all pedestrians and bicycles (to warn them of your approach) is considered a basic element of safe driving – larger trucks might as well have a permanent siren attached.

There is no national seat-belt law – indeed, the Vietnamese laugh at foreigners who insist on using seat belts. Actually, you'll be hard-pressed to find a vehicle equipped with seat belts or air bags – most Vietnamese drivers remove these 'nuisance' items.

The law says that you are supposed to turn on your headlights at night. That seems elementary enough, but many people drive at night without lights because they believe that this saves petrol (it doesn't).

Motorbike The legal definition of a moped is any motor-driven, two-wheeled vehicle 50cc or less. Motorbikes are two-wheeled vehicles with engines over 50cc. You won't need an International Driving Licence to drive a moped in Vietnam, but you'll need one with motorbike endorsement to drive a motorbike. Expats remaining in the country over six months are expected to obtain a Vietnamese driving licence. The Vietnamese licence will be valid only for the length of your visa! If you extend your visa, you need to extend your driving licence too.

Technically, the maximum legal size for a motorbike is 125cc. There are indeed larger bikes around – these are classified as 'motorcycles'. To drive a motorcycle, the owner must join a motorcycle association and do voluntary public service work (riding in patriotic parades and sporting events etc). There is an awful lot of bureaucracy involved in owning such a vehicle and riders can expect to be stopped by the police frequently to have their papers checked. Most people who own these road hogs are the sons of high-ranking officials – they apparently find loopholes in the regulations. Some foreigners with diplomatic privileges seem to find a way to skirt the rules too.

The major cities have *giu xe* (parking lots) for bicycles and motorbikes – usually just a roped-off section of sidewalk – which charge US$0.20 to guard your vehicle (bike theft is a major problem). When you pull up, a number will be chalked on the seat or stapled to the handlebars and you'll be handed a reclaim chit. Without it, getting your wheels back may be a real hassle, especially if you come back after the workers have changed shifts. Outside of the designated parking lots, some travellers simply ask a stranger to watch their bikes – this may not always be such a good idea. One traveller wrote:

> We asked some locals to watch our motorbike while we went to explore a beach in a nearby cove. When we returned, we found that our new 'friends' had removed some vital engine components and we had to buy these back from the very people who stole them.

Locals are required to have liability insurance on their motorbikes, but foreigners are not covered and there is currently no way to arrange this. If you want to insure yourself against injury, disfigurement or death, you'll need some sort of travel insurance with a foreign company (be sure that motorbike accidents are not excluded from your policy!). Travel insurance is something that must be arranged before you come to Vietnam. As for liability insurance, consider burning some incense at a local temple.

The government has been talking about requiring the use of safety helmets. However, most Vietnamese disdain wearing them, in part because of the expense and also because of the tropical heat. You can purchase high-quality safety helmets in Ho Chi Minh City and Hanoi for around US$40, or buy a low-quality 'eggshell' helmet for US$20. For the serious biker, bringing a helmet from abroad is the best idea, but make sure it's something that you can tolerate wearing in hot weather. As a last resort, you might consider purchasing a slightly battered US army helmet from the War Surplus Market – the bullet holes provide ventilation!

The law says that a motorbike can carry only two persons, but we've seen up to seven on one vehicle (and they had luggage). In general, this law is enforced in cities but mostly ignored in rural areas.

Rental

Car Drive-yourself rental cars have yet to make their debut in Vietnam, but cars with drivers can be hired from various outlets. Given the low cost of labour, renting a vehicle with a driver and guide is a realistic option even if you're a budget traveller. Split between several people, the cost per day can be very reasonable.

Hanoi and Ho Chi Minh City have an especially wide selection of government bodies, state companies and private concerns that rent out vehicles. The service is offered by various competing agencies, including many provincial tourism authorities and private companies. Bargaining is possible and, when you've completed negotiations, a contract should be signed to prevent any later disputes.

For sightseeing trips around Ho Chi Minh City or Hanoi, a car with driver can also be rented by the day or by the hour (renting by the day is cheaper). For definition purposes, a 'day' is eight hours or less with a total distance travelled of less than 100km. Based on this formula, it costs about US$25 per day (or US$4 per hour) for a Russian car; US$35 per day (US$5 per hour) for a small Japanese car; US$40 per day (US$6 per hour) for a larger, late-model Japanese car; and US$64 per day (US$8 per hour) for a limousine.

Renting a van is worth considering for large groups. Vans hold approximately eight to 12 passengers, so the cost per person works out less than a car. One advantage of vans is that they have high clearance, a consideration on some of the dismal unsurfaced roads.

For the really bad roads of north-west Vietnam, the only reasonably safe vehicle is a 4WD. Without 4WD, the muddy mountain roads can be deadly. The 4WDs come in different varieties – the cheapest (and least comfortable) are Russian-made, while more cushy vehicles are available from Korea and Japan for about twice the price.

With the exception of Russian-built or really old vehicles, most are equipped with air-con. Since air-con cars often cost more to rent, you might make your preferences known early when negotiating a price. Also, it's been our experience that not having an air-conditioner can be an advantage – Vietnamese drivers usually insist on keeping the air-conditioner at full-blast all day, even if it means wearing a winter coat in the tropical heat.

Many travellers have rented cars from private individuals – some have been satisfied and some have not. Some of these self-proclaimed guides with cars offer very low prices, but they have no insurance and by law are not permitted to transport tourists. There have been reports of reckless driving, vehicles in lousy mechanical condition and trouble with the police. It's often better to find companions and rent a car and driver from a reliable company.

Almost all cars are equipped with a cassette tape player. Bring some music tapes or buy them from the local markets and hope your driver, guide and fellow passengers have the same taste in music as you do!

Motorbike Renting a motorbike is now possible from a wide variety of outlets – cafes, travel agencies, motorbike shops, hotels etc. If you don't want to drive yourself, many cyclo (pedicab) drivers are also willing to act as your personal motorbike chauffeur and guide for around US$6 to US$8 per day. However, take care to find someone who you feel is competent and easy to get along with.

How much you pay for a motorbike depends on the engine size. Renting a 50cc moped (the most popular model) is cheap at around US$6 per day, usually with unlimited mileage. Regular motorbikes start from around US$5. The Saigon Scooter Center (☎ 090-845819, ⓔ ssc@hcm.vnn.vn), 175/12 Đ Pham Ngu Lao in Ho Chi Minh City, arranges interesting one-way/drop-off rental options.

A minor complication occurs if the renter requires a deposit or some other security. New motorbikes cost about US$2000, so leaving a deposit to cover its value would not be a trivial lump of cash. Others prefer to hold your passport until you return the bike. There have not been any huge problems with renters losing or refusing to return these items, though you are placing yourself in their hands, plus you really do need your passport with you on the road for checking into hotels.

You should definitely sign some sort of agreement (preferably in English or another language you understand) clearly stating what you are renting, how much it costs, the extent of compensation you must pay if the bike is stolen etc. People in the business of renting out motorbikes are usually equipped with a standard rental agreement.

Most bikes' rear-view mirrors are removed or turned around so that they don't get broken in the handlebar-to-handlebar traffic. This might make sense in Ho Chi Minh City with its continuous close encounters, but have the mirrors properly installed if you're going out on the highway. It's rather important to know when a big truck is bearing down on you from behind.

Purchase

Car Foreigners with resident certificates can purchase a car, but unless you're staying long-term it does not make much sense to do so. Foreign companies can also purchase cars, though companies that do so also usually hire a Vietnamese driver rather than let their foreign employees drive themselves. Special licence plates are affixed to foreign-owned vehicles.

Motorbike Except for bona fide foreign residents, buying a motorbike for touring in Vietnam is technically illegal. However, some travellers have reported that so far the authorities have turned a blind eye to the practice. Apparently, you buy a bike but register it in the name of a trusted Vietnamese friend. Some shops that sell motorbikes will let you keep the bike registered in the shop's name. This requires that you trust the shopkeepers, but in most cases this seems to work out OK.

The big issue is what to do with the bike when you're finished with it. If you return to the city where you originally purchased the bike, you can simply sell it back to the shop you bought it from (at a discount, of

On The Plate

You can learn a great deal about a vehicle by examining its licence plate. Whether you are in a confusing bus station looking for the right bus or hitchhiking and trying to avoid accidentally flagging down an army truck, the following information should prove useful.

First, there are the several types of licence plates. Privately owned vehicles have black digits on a white background. Vehicles with white numbers on a green field are owned by the government, while white on blue are police-owned. Diplomatic cars have the letters NG in red over green numbers on a white field. Other cars owned by foreigners begin with the letters NN and are green-on-white. Military plates have white numbers on red.

The first two numbers on a number plate are the two-digit code assigned to the vehicle's province of origin. Because the vast majority of vehicles in the country are controlled at the provincial level and used to link a given province with other parts of the country, there is usually a 50-50 chance that the vehicle is headed towards its home territory.

The two-digit number codes for most provinces are shown in the 'Province Area Codes' boxed text in the Facts for the Visitor chapter.

course). Another possible solution is to sell it to another foreigner travelling in the opposite direction – notice boards at the cafes in Ho Chi Minh City and Hanoi can be useful in this regard. If you're unlucky, you might have to simply scrap the bike. Given this possibility, it's best not to buy a very expensive motorbike in the first place. But, remember, buying a motorbike is illegal and a crackdown may come at any time.

Japanese-made motorbikes are the best available, but by far the most expensive. The Honda Dream is everyone's favourite for the lowlands – and the most likely to get stolen. A new Dream goes for about US$2300.

The best alternative for the mountains is to buy a 125cc Russian-made Minsk, which sells used for around US$400 to US$450, and brand new for around US$600. It is a powerful bike and it's very easy to find spare parts and mechanics who can do repairs. The Minsk handles particularly well on muddy roads, a significant point in its favour (see the 'Minsk Mania' boxed text in the Hanoi chapter).

A compromise is the Taiwanese-made Bonus. This 125cc bike costs around US$1900 new, and quality is somewhere halfway between a Minsk and a Honda Dream. The bike handles well on paved roads, but poorly in the mud – the Minsk is better for mud-slogging.

There are some other cheap bikes from Eastern Europe, but basically they are junk.

BICYCLE

A great way to get around Vietnam's towns and cities is to do as the locals do: ride a bicycle. During rush hours, urban thoroughfares approach gridlock as rushing streams of cyclists force their way through intersections without the benefit of traffic lights. Riders are always crashing into each other and getting knocked down, but because bicycle traffic is so heavy, they are rarely going fast enough to be injured. In the countryside, Westerners on bicycles are often greeted enthusiastically by locals, who may never have seen a foreigner pedalling around before.

Bicycles are utility vehicles in much of rural Vietnam. To see a bike carrying three pigs or 300kg of vegetables is not unusual. One has to marvel at how people manage to load all these items on the bike and ride it without the whole thing tipping over.

Vietnam is also a possible place for long-distance cycling: much of the country is flat or only moderately hilly, the major roads are of a serviceable standard and the shortage of vehicles makes for relatively light traffic. Bicycles can be transported around the country on the top of buses or in train baggage compartments. Lonely Planet's *Cycling Vietnam, Laos & Cambodia* gives the low-down on cycling through Vietnam.

Groups of Western cyclists have begun touring Vietnam, and there are even tour companies that specialise in bicycling trips (see the Organised Tours section in the Getting There & Away chapter). The flatlands of the Mekong Delta region are a logical place for long-distance riding. The entire coastal route along National Hwy 1 is feasible, but the insane traffic makes it unpleasant and dangerous.

Cycling is probably not a good idea in the winter months north of the old Demilitarised Zone, particularly if you'll be heading from south to north. This is because of the monsoon wind, which blows from north to south – nothing is more depressing than constantly riding into a cold headwind. Doing it from north to south means you'll have the wind to your back, but it will still be cold.

Mountain bikes and 10-speed bikes can be bought at a few speciality shops in Hanoi and Ho Chi Minh City, but you'll probably do better to bring your own if you plan to travel long distance by pedal power. Mountain bikes are definitely preferred – the occasional big pothole or unsealed road can be rough on a set of delicate rims. Basic cycling safety equipment is hardly available in Vietnam: Bring helmets, night lights, front and rear reflectors, leg reflectors and rear-view mirrors. For long-distance riding, pack spare parts such as spokes, tubes, a pump, cables and a water bottle. Bring along some tools: a spoke wrench, a chain tool, a multifunction tool and a small bottle of chain lube. A bell is mandatory – the louder the better. Padded gloves ease the shock of rough roads. A pocket-size inner-tube repair kit is necessary. Don't forget to deflate your tyres before boarding planes, as your bike will probably travel in an unpressurised cabin, which can result in exploded tubes.

Hotels and some travel agencies are starting to get into the business of renting out bicycles. The cost varies but is around US$1 per day or US$0.20 per hour.

There are innumerable roadside bicycle-repair stands in every city and town in Vietnam. Usually, they consist of no more than a pump, an upturned military helmet and a metal ammunition box filled with oily bolts and a few wrenches.

Pumping up a tyre costs US$0.04. Fixing a punctured inner tube should cost about US$0.40 depending on the size of the patch. The common practice is to use 'hot patches', which have to be burned into place – this is more time consuming than using glue, but it makes for a good seal.

Many travellers buy a cheap bicycle, use it during their visit and, at the end, either sell it or give it to a Vietnamese friend. Locally produced bicycles are available starting at about US$30, but are of truly inferior quality. A fairly decent, one-speed, Chinese-made bicycle costs about US$60 to US$80. A Taiwanese-made mountain bike goes for about US$200 and Japanese-made bikes about US$300. You may occasionally find a European bike, including the German-made Mifa (about US$70), Czech-made Eska (US$120) and French-made Peugeot (US$230).

All Vietnamese-made bicycles have the same mixte (unisex) frame, but the various models are equipped with different accessories. The Vietnamese-made frame is quite serviceable, but the locally produced moving parts (including brakes, crank shaft, pedals and gears, as well as tyre inner tubes) should be avoided unless you enjoy frequent visits to bicycle-repair shops.

Although you will often see two Vietnamese riding on a single bike, this is generally *not* a good idea, as one traveller discovered:

> I rented a bike in Saigon and had the splendid idea to carry my friend on the rear bike rack in order to return to the hotel. However, after only 5m, the rear wheel snapped! Back in the bicycle shop (by cyclo), I pretended an accident had occurred, so they charged me only US$3 extra. Conclusion: these cheap Chinese bikes can carry two local people, but apparently not two Westerners.
>
> **Thilo Shönfeld**

HITCHING

Hitching is never entirely safe in any country in the world, and we don't recommend it. Travellers who decide to hitch should understand that they are taking a potentially serious risk. People who do choose to hitch will be safer if they travel in pairs and let someone know where they are planning to go and when they will arrive.

One of the advantages of going from Hanoi to Saigon is that most people are doing just the opposite. Many folks pay for car rides heading north, so it's relatively easy to catch an empty car going south. I'd go to larger hotels, meet the driver the night before and make a private deal (not with the driver's boss). I also tried standing by the roadside and flagging cars down. Some drivers knew what was going on and knew exactly how much to charge. But on certain stretches of highway, traffic of passenger vehicles was light indeed. The best advice in such cases is to start out early.

Ivan Kasimoff

WALKING

You aren't likely to do much long-distance walking in the steamy, tropical lowlands, which are dominated by dense vegetation. However, many spots in the Central Highlands and the far north offer myriad hiking possibilities. Remember that you may need to arrange special permits, especially if you want to spend the night in remote mountain villages where there are no hotels.

One thing to be aware of in the south is that in equatorial regions there is very little twilight and night comes on suddenly without warning. Therefore, you can't readily judge how many hours of daylight remain unless you have a watch. Pay attention to how long you'll need to get back to civilisation – otherwise, be prepared for an impromptu camping trip.

If you'd rather run, not walk, it's interesting to note that long-distance running has made its debut in Vietnam. At the end of the 1980s, someone actually ran from Hanoi to Danang. No wonder the Vietnamese think that foreigners are mad.

BOAT

Vietnam has an enormous number of rivers that are at least partly navigable, but the most important by far is the multibranched Mekong River. Scenic day trips by boat are also possible on rivers in Hoi An, Danang, Hué, Tam Coc and even Ho Chi Minh City, but only in the Mekong Delta are boats used as a practical means of transport.

Boat trips are also possible on the sea – a cruise to the islands off the coast of Nha Trang is a particularly popular trip. Boats are a practical means of getting from the Mekong Delta to Phu Quoc Island. If you visit Halong Bay, a cruise to the offshore islands is practically mandatory.

Pay attention to the condition of the boats. Small boats with small engines (or no engines) are going to be slow. If the water is rough, small boats will bounce around like a cork. Many people enjoy this, but it's not much fun if you're prone to seasickness. Some of the smaller river craft can only accommodate two or three people and you can easily get splashed. Whenever you take such a small boat, it's wise to keep your camera in a plastic bag when not actually in use to protect it from splashes.

In some parts of Vietnam (particularly the Mekong Delta) you'll have to make some ferry crossings. This is no big deal, but a few precautions are called for. Passengers are required to get out of their vehicles before these are driven onto the ferries – be sure that your luggage is secure. Don't stand between parked vehicles on the ferry – they can roll and you could wind up as the meat in the sandwich. Be sure you buy a passenger ticket before boarding – at some ferry crossings, you buy the ticket on one side of the river and have to give it to the gatekeeper on the other side. But on some very small ferries (the ones that do not carry cars) you buy the tickets on board – confusing.

LOCAL TRANSPORT

Bus

Vietnam has some of the worst local innercity bus transport in Asia. The bus systems in Hanoi and Ho Chi Minh City have improved in the past few years but are light years behind Hong Kong and, in general, this is not a practical way to get around. Fortunately, there are many other options.

Taxi

Western-style taxis with meters were introduced to Ho Chi Minh City in 1994 and have spread quickly to other cities.

For details on exactly what is available in each city, see the Getting There & Away and Getting Around sections of each chapter.

Cyclo

The cyclo *(xich lo)*, or pedicab, short for the French *cyclo-pousse*, is the best invention since sliced bread. Cyclos offer easy, cheap and aesthetic transportation around Vietnam's confusing, sprawling cities. Riding these clever contraptions will also give you the moral superiority that comes with knowing you're being kind to the environment – much kinder than all those drivers on whining, smoke-spewing motorbikes.

Groups of cyclo drivers always hang out near major hotels and markets, and many speak at least broken English: In the south, many of the cyclo drivers are former Army of the Republic of Vietnam (ARVN) soldiers. Those who speak English charge a little more than those who don't, but avoiding the language problem may be worth the minor added expense (we're talking peanuts). To make sure the driver understands where you want to go, it's useful to bring a city map with you.

All cyclo drivers are male, although they vary in age from around 15 to perhaps 60 years old. Many of the younger ones are transients from the countryside, coming to Ho Chi Minh City and Hanoi to seek their fortune – with no place to live, they may even sleep in their cyclo (see the 'Life on the Streets' boxed text in the Ho Chi Minh City chapter). Since 1995 the government has required cyclo drivers to obtain a licence which requires passing an exam on traffic-safety laws.

Most cyclo drivers rent out their vehicles for US$1 per day. The more affluent cyclo drivers buy their own vehicle for US$200, but to do so requires that the owner has a residence permit for the place where the cyclo is to be driven – the transients from the countryside are thus excluded from vehicle ownership. Operating a cyclo is often a family business – a father and son take turns so the vehicle gets used 18 hours a day. But driving a cyclo is no way to get rich – the average price charged is around US$0.20 per kilometre – and it's hard work, so it doesn't hurt to tip. Bargaining is almost always necessary: The drivers know that US$1 or its dong equivalent is nothing to most Westerners. If the cyclo drivers waiting outside your hotel want too much, flag down someone else less used to spendthrift tourists. Settle on a fare *before* going anywhere or you're likely to be asked for some outrageous quantity of dong at the trip's end.

I had a fingers bargaining session with a cyclo driver, only to discover at the end of the ride that he was bargaining dollars and I was bargaining dong! He got 10,000d not US$10 – much to his disappointment – but I had to be very forceful to get away with it.

Mike Conrad

We should point out that sometimes these misunderstandings are sincere, not always attempts to cheat you. We know one traveller who had a vociferous argument when he tried to pay his cyclo driver 1000d rather than US$1. In fact, no one – not even a Vietnamese – can hire a cyclo for 1000d and the price really should have been about US$1. Bargaining solely by finger-language is perhaps not such a good idea – since you cannot possibly hold up 10,000 fingers, probably the best solution is to write things down, or ideally learn to say the basic numbers in Vietnamese (this can help immensely in keeping the price under control).

As a basic rule, short rides around town should cost about 5000d. For a long ride, say over 2km or more, you can expect to pay a bit more, but rarely over 10,000d. Cyclo drivers will usually try to demand more, but in most cases politely refusing them and walking away will bring a change of heart. It's a good idea to have your money counted out and ready before getting on a cyclo. It also pays to have the exact change – drivers may claim they cannot change a 10,000d note.

Cyclos are cheaper by time rather than distance. A typical price is US$1 per hour. If this works out well, don't be surprised if the driver comes around to your hotel the next morning to see if you want to hire him again.

We found the best friends we made were the incredibly loyal cyclo drivers in Nha Trang and

Hanoi, who would wait outside your hotel all day to take you anywhere as a 'regular' customer. They were all charming and we were sad to say goodbye to them.

Meriel Rule

There have been some reports of travellers being mugged by their cyclo drivers in Ho Chi Minh City. Typically, what happens is the driver will take a 'shortcut' down a dark alley where some of his accomplices are waiting.

In 1998 a US volunteer doctor on a goodwill visit was found murdered – he was last seen hopping in a cyclo on his way back to his hotel at night. Perhaps the lesson is to use cyclos *only* during the day. So far the problem is limited to Ho Chi Minh City, but there is no guarantee that the problem will not spread in the future. If you are coming home from a bar late at night, take a metre taxi; it will not cost much more than a cyclo, but it is much safer.

Honda Om

The *Honda om* is an ordinary motorbike on which you ride seated behind the driver. In other words, it's a motorbike taxi. Don't expect to find one with a meter – negotiate the price beforehand. The fare is a fraction more than a cyclo for short trips and about the same as a cyclo for longer distances. Getting around this way is quite respectable as long as you don't have a lot of luggage with you.

You'll find plenty of Honda om drivers hanging around markets, hotels and bus stations. They make themselves pretty conspicuous, so they're not hard to find. However, it can be difficult to find one when you're just walking down a street – there is no set procedure for finding a driver willing to transport you somewhere. Just stand by the roadside and try to flag someone down (most drivers can always use some extra cash) or ask a someone local to find a Honda om for you.

Urban Orienteering

Urban orienteering is very easy in Vietnam. Vietnamese is written with a Latin-based alphabet. You can at least read the street signs and maps, even if the pronunciation is incomprehensible! In addition, finding out where you are is easy: Street signs are plentiful, and almost every shop and restaurant has the street name and number on its sign. Street names are sometimes abbreviated on street signs with just the initials ('DBP' for 'Dien Bien Phu' etc).

Most street numbers are sequential, with odd and even numbers on opposite sides of the street, but there are confusing exceptions. In some places, consecutive buildings are numbered 15A, 15B, 15C and so forth, while elsewhere, consecutive addresses read 15D, 17D, 19D etc. Sometimes, especially in Danang and Ho Chi Minh City, two numbering systems – the old confusing one and the new, even-more-confusing one – are in use simultaneously, so that an address may read '1743/697'. In some cases (such as Đuong Lac Long Quan, where Giac Lam Pagoda is in Ho Chi Minh City) several streets, originally numbered separately, have been run together under one name, so that as you walk along the numbers go from one into the hundreds (or thousands) and then start over again.

The Vietnamese post office is comfortable with the English words and abbreviations for street (St), road (Rd) and boulevard (Blvd), but this is not what you'll see on street signs around Ho Chi Minh City. There are several words for 'street', the main ones used in Ho Chi Minh City being Dai Lo (ĐL) and Duong (Đ). In Vietnamese, the word 'street' comes before the name, so Le Duan Blvd becomes Dai Lo Le Duan (or abbreviated ĐL Le Duan). In Hanoi and other cities in northern Vietnam, street names are commonly prefaced with the word 'Pho'.

A few tips: many restaurants are named after their street addresses. For instance, 'Nha Hang 51 Nguyen Hue' (*nha hang* means restaurant) is at 51 Đ Nguyen Hue. If you are travelling by bus or car, a good way to get oriented is to look for the post office – the words following Buu Dien (Post Office) on the sign are the name of the district, town or village you're in.

On maps in this book, Pho is shortened to 'P', Dai Lo to 'ĐL' and Duong to 'Đ'.

Xe Lam

Xe Lams are tiny, three-wheeled trucks used for short-haul passenger and freight transport (similar to the Indonesian *bajaj*). They tend to have whining two-stroke 'lawn mower' engines with no mufflers, and emit copious quantities of blue exhaust smoke, but they get the job done.

Walking

If you don't want to wind up like a bug on a windshield, you need to pay attention to a few pedestrian survival rules, especially on the streets of motorbike-crazed Ho Chi Minh City and Hanoi. Foreigners frequently make the mistake of thinking that the best way to cross a busy Vietnamese street is to run quickly across it. This does not always work, and sometimes it can get you creamed. Most Vietnamese cross the street slowly – very slowly – giving the motorbike drivers sufficient time to judge their position so they can pass to either side of you. They will not stop or even slow down, but they will try to avoid hitting you. Just don't make any sudden moves. Good luck.

> Crossing the street in Saigon is an art. Move slowly and deliberately, never be indecisive or hesitant, unless you see a bus coming, then the above does not apply…RUN!
>
> **Ron Settle**

Mekong Delta Special

Two forms of transport used mostly in the Mekong Delta are the *xe dap loi*, a wagon pulled by a bicycle, and the *xe Honda loi*, a wagon pulled by a motorbike.

ORGANISED TOURS

If you decide to rent a car with driver and guide, you'll have the opportunity to design your own itinerary for what amounts to a private tour for you and your companions. Seeing the country this way is almost like individual travel, except that it's more luxurious, and also offers you the advantage of stopping anywhere along the route for that once-in-a-lifetime photo.

The cost varies considerably. On the high end are tours booked through government travel agencies like Ho Chi Minh City Tourist and Vietnam Tourism. A tour booked with these agencies is about US$50 to US$60 a day for one person (and less each for two or more people because transport and lodging costs can be shared).

This price includes accommodation at a tourist-class hotel, a guide who will accompany you everywhere, a driver and a car. Insist that your guides are fluent in a language you know well. The cost of the car is typically computed on a per-kilometre basis, but it varies depending on what type of vehicle you choose.

When you settle on your itinerary, make sure to get a written copy from the travel agency. If you later find that your guide feels like deviating from what you paid for, that piece of paper is your most effective leverage. If your guide asks for the itinerary, keep the original and give them a photocopy, as there have been reports of guides taking tourists' itineraries and then running the tour their way. One traveller wrote:

> Our guide was incredibly stubborn and arrogant, always thinking that he knew more than us. Whenever we tried to tell him something, he suddenly developed a hearing problem. But whenever he wasn't sure about something (like the location of a hotel, the name of a temple etc), he asked to borrow our Lonely Planet book!

A good guide can be your translator and travelling companion, and can save you as much money as they are costing you (by helping you save money along the way). A bad guide can ruin your trip. If possible, meet and interview your guide before starting out – make sure that this is someone you can travel with.

Agree on the price before beginning the journey. For a good, experienced private guide, US$10 to US$15 per day is a typical rate; it's proper to throw in a bonus at the end of your trip if your guide proved particularly helpful and saved you money.

Less experienced guides (especially students working part-time) can be hired for around US$5 per day. A guide hired from a government-owned travel agency will cost you US$20 per day, of which perhaps only US$5 actually goes into the guide's pocket.

You are usually responsible for private guides' travel expenses – with a guide hired from the government, you need to check. If you can gather up a small group of travellers, the cost of hiring a guide can be shared among all of you. If you are travelling solo, your guide may be able to drive you around on a motorbike, but you should pay for the petrol and parking fees. If the police stop you, do *not* say that this person is your guide, since it is technically illegal for an unlicensed person to work as a guide – instead, say this person is 'just a friend'. If your guide gets fined, you should of course reimburse them – the cost of the 'fine' can usually be bargained down.

The best time to meet guides is usually in the morning – try visiting the travellers cafes around 7 to 9 am. Otherwise, try the evenings – most of the best guides will be working during daytime hours, but they'll be drinking beer in the cafes once the tour is back.

For trips in and around big cities like Ho Chi Minh City and Hanoi, you will often find women working as guides. However, very few women are employed as guides on long-distance trips.

Hanoi

☎ 04 • pop 3,500,000

A city of lakes, shaded boulevards and verdant public parks where jeans-clad young lovers stroll beside their venerable elders practising elegant, slow-motion shadow boxing. Hanoi's prosperous shop owners exemplify Vietnam's new economic reforms while traditional ways along the merchant guild streets in the Old Quarter live on as a reminder of the city's rich cultural heritage.

Hanoi, capital of the Socialist Republic of Vietnam (SRV), is different things to different people. Most foreigners on a short visit find Hanoi to be slow paced, pleasant and even charming. Physically, it's a more attractive city than Ho Chi Minh City – there is less traffic, noise and pollution with more trees and open spaces. Some have called it the Paris of the Orient – which Parisians could consider either an insult or a compliment. Hanoi's centre is an architectural museum piece, its blocks of ochre buildings retaining the air of a provincial French town of the 1930s. The people of Hanoi are known for being more reserved – and at the same time more traditionally hospitable – than their southern compatriots.

Hanoi used to be notorious among travellers as a place to avoid. Many western visitors (both backpackers and businesspeople) were routinely harassed by the police, especially at the airport where officials would arbitrarily detain and fine foreigners as they were trying to leave.

Hanoi's reputation for harassing foreigners and resisting economic reform caused most foreign investment to flow into Ho Chi Minh City and other places in the south. Resistance to reform is strongest among ageing officials, but geriatric revolutionaries in the prime of senility are being forcibly retired. The younger generation – with no romantic attachment to the past – is more interested in the side of the bread that is buttered. Attitudes have changed fast and the Hanoi of today is dramatically different from just a few years ago. Foreigners have returned in the form of tourists, business travellers, students and expatriates. Foreign

Highlights

- Take a walking tour through the historical streets of the bustling Old Quarter.
- Explore Hanoi's intriguing museums, pagodas and the spectacular Temple of Literature.
- Enjoy a performance of the city's famed water puppets.
- See 'Uncle Ho' in the flesh at Ho Chi Minh's Mausoleum.
- Sample the flourishing culinary delights, cafes and nightlife of modern Hanoi.
- Take a day excursion to the outstanding complex of pagodas and Buddhist shrines at the famed Perfume Pagoda.
- Cycle to the excellent Museum of Ethnology, devoted to the culture of Vietnam's ethnic minorities.

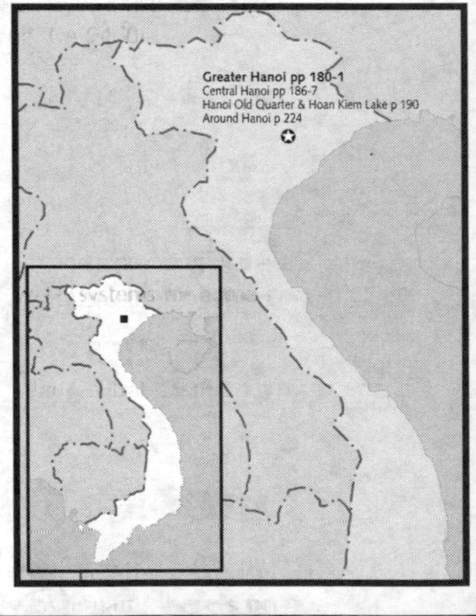

investors are now looking at Hanoi with the same enthusiasm that only a few years ago was reserved exclusively for Ho Chi Minh.

The first beneficiaries of the city's recent economic resurgence have been the shop and restaurant owners. No longer is a shopping trip in Hanoi limited to a large state owned department store specialising in empty shelves. Colour and liveliness has returned to the streets – unfortunately, so has the traffic. Buildings are being repaired and foreign companies are now investing in everything from joint-venture hotels to banks and telecommunications. Hanoi, and the rest of the north, has great potential to develop export-oriented manufacturing industries – a potential now only beginning to be realised.

HISTORY

The site where Hanoi now stands has been inhabited since the Neolithic period. Emperor Ly Thai To moved his capital here in 1010 AD, renaming the site Thang Long (City of the Soaring Dragon). Hanoi served as the capital of the Later Le Dynasty, founded by Le Loi, from its establishment in 1428 until 1788 when it was overthrown by Nguyen Hué, founder of the Tay Son Dynasty. The decision by Emperor Gia Long, founder of the Nguyen Dynasty, to rule from Hué relegated Hanoi to the status of a regional capital.

Over the centuries Hanoi has borne a variety of names, including Dong Kinh (Eastern Capital), from which the Europeans derived the name they eventually applied to all of northern Vietnam, Tonkin. The city was named Hanoi (The City in a Bend of the River) by Emperor Tu Duc in 1831. From 1902 to 1953, Hanoi served as the capital of French Indochina.

Hanoi was proclaimed the capital of Vietnam after the August Revolution of 1945, but it was not until the Geneva Accords of 1954 that the Viet Minh, driven from the city by the French in 1946, were able to return.

During the American War, US bombing destroyed parts of Hanoi and killed many hundreds of civilians; almost all the damage has since been repaired.

One of the prime targets was the 1682m Long Bien Bridge, originally built from 1888 to 1902 under the direction of the same architect who designed Paris's Eiffel Tower. It was once named after the turn-of-the-century French governor general of Indochina, Paul Doumer (1857–1932), who was assassinated a year after becoming President of France. US aircraft repeatedly bombed the strategic bridge, yet after each attack the Vietnamese somehow managed to improvise replacement spans and return it to road and rail service. It is said that when US POW's were put to work repairing the bridge, the US military, fearing for their safety, ended the attacks.

In Hanoi and much of the north Ho Chi Minh created a very effective police state. For four decades locals suffered under a regime characterised by the ruthless police power; anonymous denunciations by a huge network of secret informers; detention without trial of monks, priests, landowners and anyone seen as a potential threat to the government; and the black-listing of dissidents and their children and their children's children. The combined legacy of human rights violations and economic turmoil produced a steady haemorrhage of refugees, even into China despite that country's less-than-impressive human rights record. Ironically, the political and economic situation turned around so sharply in the 1990s that Vietnamese officials now worry about an invasion of refugees from China.

ORIENTATION

Hanoi sprawls along the banks of the Song Hong (Red River), which is spanned by two bridges – the Long Bien Bridge (now used only by nonmotorised vehicles and pedestrians), and, 600m south, the newer Chuong Duong Bridge.

The attractive centre of Hanoi is built around Hoan Kiem Lake. Just north of this lake is the Old Quarter (known to the French as the Cité Indigène). The Old Quarter is characterised by narrow streets whose names change every one or two blocks. Tourists mostly like to base themselves in this part of town.

GREATER HANOI

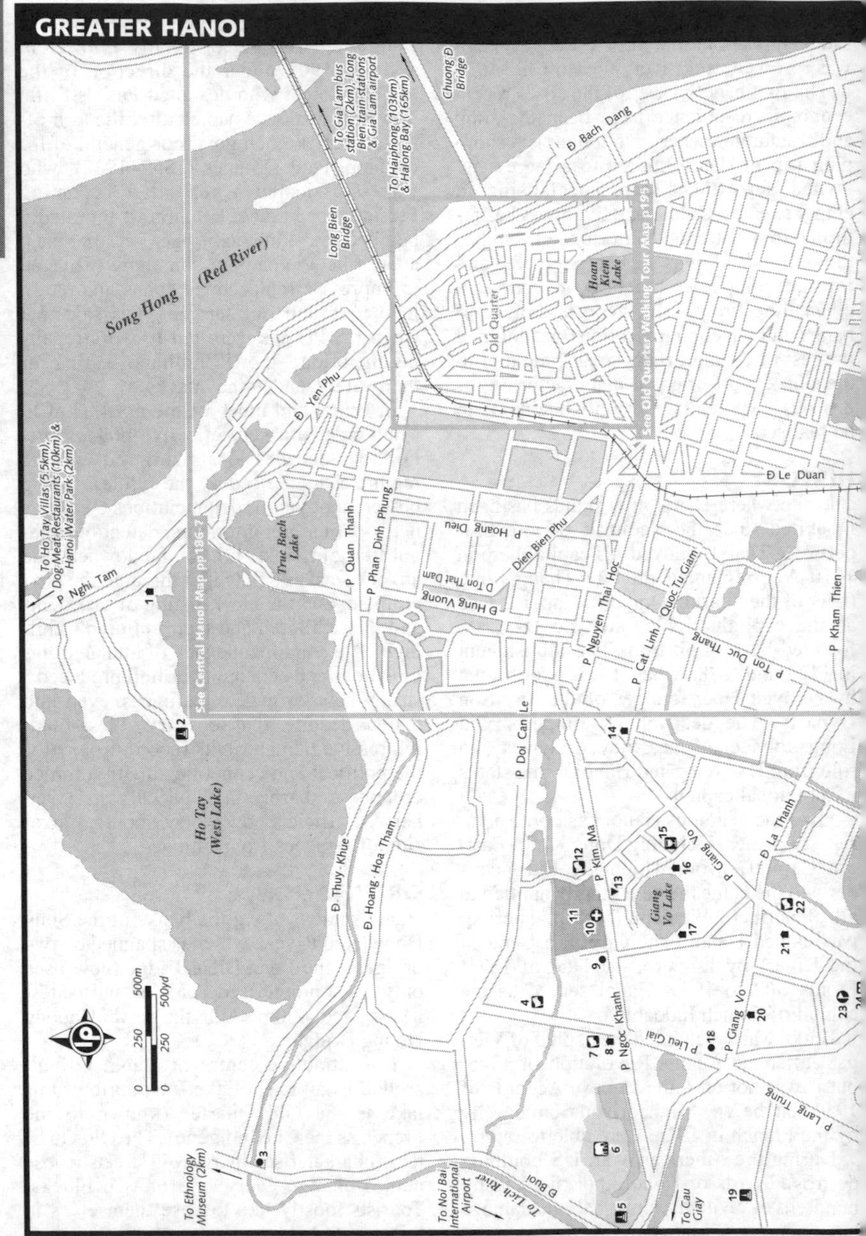

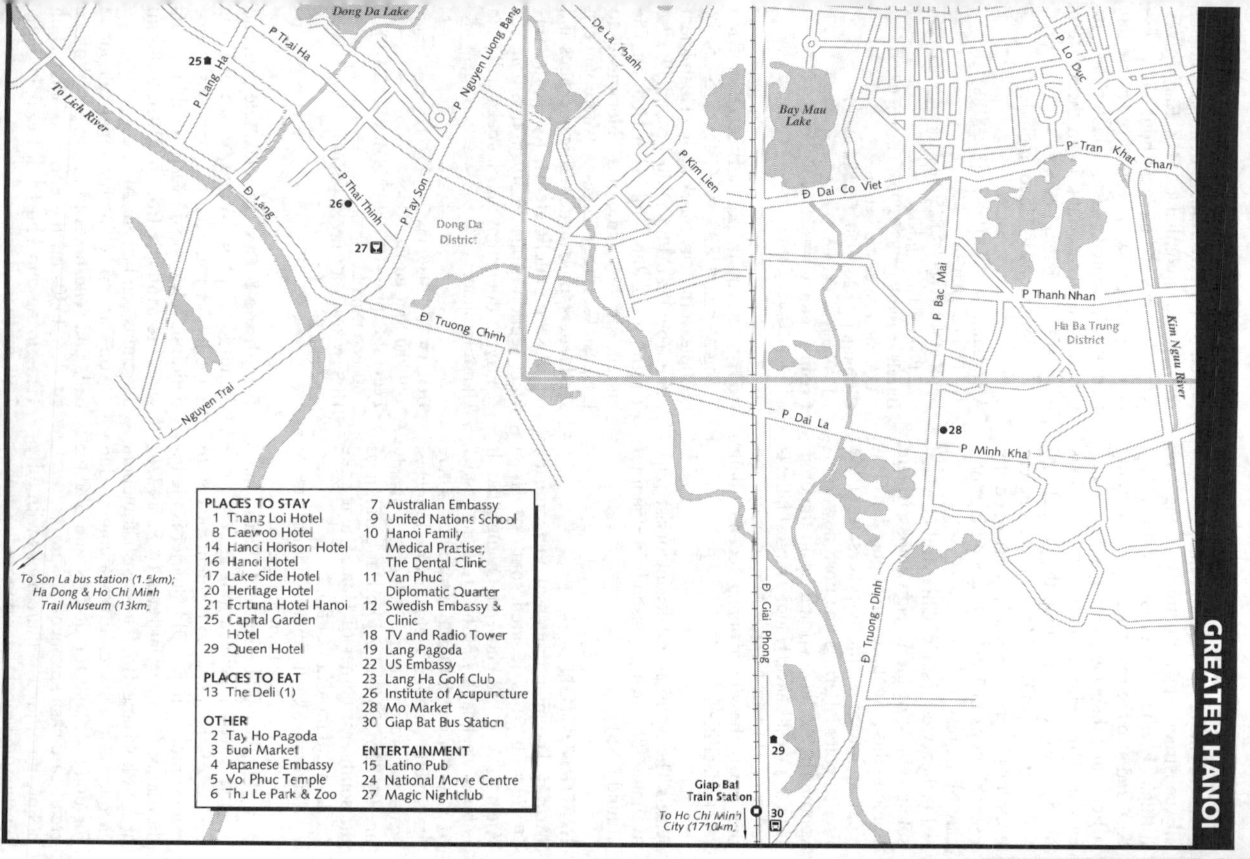
GREATER HANOI
Dong Da Lake
P Trai Ha
P Lang Ha
To Lich River
P Nguyen Luong Bang
De La Thanh
P Kim Lien
Bay Mau Lake
P Lo Duc
P Tran Khat Chan
Đ Dai Co Viet
P Thai Thinh
P Tay Son
Dong Da District
Đ Lang
Đ Truong Chinh
Nguyen Trai
P Bac Mai
P Thanh Nhan
Ha Ba Trung District
Kim Nguu River
P Dai La
P Minh Kha
Đ Giai Phong
Đ Truong Dinh
Giap Bat Train Station
To Ho Chi Minh City (1710km)
To Son La bus station (1.5km); Ha Dong & Ho Chi Minh Trail Museum (13km)
PLACES TO STAY
1 Thang Loi Hotel
8 Daewoo Hotel
14 Hanoi Horison Hotel
16 Hanoi Hotel
17 Lake Side Hotel
20 Heritage Hotel
21 Fortuna Hotel Hanoi
25 Capital Garden Hotel
29 Queen Hotel
PLACES TO EAT
13 The Deli (1)
OTHER
2 Tay Ho Pagoda
3 Buoi Market
4 Japanese Embassy
5 Vo Phuc Temple
6 Thu Le Park & Zoo
7 Australian Embassy
9 United Nations School
10 Hanoi Family Medical Practise; The Dental Clinic
11 Van Phuc Diplomatic Quarter
12 Swedish Embassy & Clinic
18 TV and Radio Tower
19 Lang Pagoda
22 US Embassy
23 Lang Ha Golf Club
26 Institute of Acupuncture
28 Mo Market
30 Giap Bat Bus Station
ENTERTAINMENT
15 Latino Pub
24 National Movie Centre
27 Magic Nightclub

Along the western periphery of the Old Quarter is the ancient Hanoi Citadel, originally constructed by Emperor Gia Long. Unfortunately, the Citadel is now a military base and also the residence of high-ranking officers and their families – in other words, closed to the public. There are ambitious plans, however, to develop the citadel into a tourist attraction. Most of the ancient buildings were tragically destroyed by French troops in 1894 – US bombing took care of the rest.

Further west is Ho Chi Minh's Mausoleum. Most of the foreign embassies are found in this neighbourhood housed in classical architectural masterpieces from the French colonial era. Some posh new joint-venture hotels have sprung up in the area. Ho Tay (West Lake), Hanoi's largest lake, is north of Ho Chi Minh's Mausoleum, and this too is the site of many recently built tourist facilities.

Maps There are several decent tourist maps available for sale at bookshops in Hanoi for around US$1.

INFORMATION

Money The main branch of Vietcombank (☎ 826 8045) is located south of Hoan Kiem Lake at 198 Pho Tran Quang Khai. It is open weekdays 7.30 to 11.30 am, and 1 to 3.30 pm and Saturday mornings. There are several smaller Vietcombank branches scattered around town, including a handy one (☎ 826 8031) at 2 Pho Hang Bai, near the south-east corner of Hoan Kiem Lake (adjacent to the Ciao Cafe).

Vietcombank's former headquarters, at 47–49 Pho Ly Thai To, no longer dishes out dong; but this building, one of Hanoi's most stately, is worth taking a look at.

One of the most convenient places to change money in the Old Quarter is the Industrial & Commercial Bank (☎ 825 4276) at 37 Pho Hang Bo. They cash travellers cheques at the standard 0.5% commission for dong, 1.25% for dollars and 3% for credit-card cash advances.

Foreign or joint-venture banks with fully functioning branches (as opposed to useless representative offices) can be found, but are forced by the government to impose higher fees than Vietcombank. ANZ Bank gives cash advances and has a 24-hour ATM (dispensing dong only) if you have an internationally accepted Visa, MasterCard or Cirrus card. ANZ Bank is on the western edge of Hoan Kiem Lake.

Foreign banks in Hanoi include:

ANZ Bank (☎ 825 8190, fax 825 8188)
14 Pho Le Thai To
Bank of America (☎ 825 0003, fax 824 9322)
27 Pho Ly Thuong Kiet
Barclays Bank (☎ 825 0907, fax 825 0789)
33A Pho Pham Ngu Lao
Citibank (☎ 825 1950, fax 824 3960)
17 Pho Ngo Quyen
Credit Lyonnais (☎ 825 8102, fax 826 0080)
10 Pho Trang Thi

Post The main post office (Buu Dien Trung Vong; ☎ 825 7036, fax 825 3525), occupies a full city block facing Hoan Kiem Lake, (between Pho Dinh Le and Pho Le Thach, at 75 Pho Dinh Tien Hoang). The entrance in the middle of the block leads to the postal services windows where you can send letters, pick up domestic packages and purchase philatelic items; the postal services section is open 6.30 am to 8 pm.

Private document and parcel carriers in Hanoi include:

DHL (☎ 733 2086, fax 775 4672)
49 Pho Nguyen Thai Hoc
Federal Express (☎ 824 9054, fax 825 2479)
6C Pho Dinh Le
UPS (☎ 824 6483, fax 824 6464)
4C Pho Dinh Le

Telephone & Fax The telex, telegram and domestic telephone office (☎ 825 5918) is to the left as you enter the main post office building. Telex and domestic telephone services are available from 6.30 am to 8 pm; telegrams can be sent 24 hours a day.

You can make international telephone calls and send faxes from the postal office (☎ 825 2030) on the corner of Pho Dinh Tien Hoang and Pho Dinh Le; open daily 7.30 am to 9.30 pm.

Email & Internet Access There are many Internet cafes in Hanoi, in particular at backpacker cafes/travel agents on and around Pho Hang Bac (in the Old Quarter). Among these is Classy Zone (☎ 926 0410, ⓔ classyzone@hotmail.com) at 137 Pho Hang Bac. The Emotion Cybernet Café, at 52 Pho Ly Thuong Kiet, is also good and well-established.

The going rate for online access in Hanoi is around 300d to 400d per minute – about US$0.03. 'Ten free minutes online' is the latest tour operator gimmick to attract customers – it beats 'one free Chinese beer'!

Travel Agencies There are plenty of travel agencies in Hanoi, both government and privately owned, which can book tours, provide cars, guides, issue air tickets and arrange visa extensions.

Most budget agencies also double as restaurant/cafes, which offer cheap eats, rooms for rent and Internet access. The mighty alliance between Ho Chi Minh City's Sinh Cafe and state-run Hanoi Toserco captures a large share of the local 'fast-food' tourist market (in particular the dirt-cheap 'open tour' bus tickets which shuttle travellers along Highway 1 between Hanoi and Ho Chi Minh City). The proliferation, however, of 'fake' Sinh cafes in Hanoi has confused more than a few travellers.

The majority of Hanoi's hotels also pedal tours (most of which are farmed out to the agencies listed below), however it is *not* advisable to book trips through hotels. Though the prices are roughly the same (the hotels collecting a sales commission from the agents), booking directly with the tour operators will give a much better idea of what you'll get for your money, who it is you'll be travelling with, and also with how many other people.

There has been a stream of complaints lately about certain budget tour operators in Hanoi. The biggest issue seems to be the gap between what they promise and what they actually deliver. Competition is fierce, and cut-throat price cutting among various tour operators has driven the cost of tours so low that in some cases it has become difficult to provide a satisfactory product. Sometimes the profit margin for the tour operator is so slim the only way for them to make any money is increase the number of customers, and in doing so lower the quality of the tour. You can do the math for yourself. Usually these customers have booked the same tour from a variety of outlets for different prices – usually within a few dollars of each other.

You can indeed buy a two-day/one-night, all-inclusive excursion to Halong Bay for as little as US$16, but do you really care to travel on a 45-seat bus and be herded onto a boat to tour the bay and grottos? One traveller advises:

In Hanoi, I think you should warn your readers about the tour agencies. Most share the same buses and really pack the buses to the brim. Passenger comfort is really a concern.

Hieu Doan

On a recent trip to Halong Bay we witnessed crowds of up to 50 tourists packed onto one boat – not very safe, nor much fun. You can't help wondering if these people, who have spent all the time, money and effort to come to Vietnam, wouldn't prefer to pay a little more to experience something better on their trip? In the long run, the dollars saved will probably not be remembered as much as the quality of the trip itself. In the end it is your choice, but be aware if you always buy the cheapest thing out there, you'll have to share the blame if you don't come away satisfied.

When booking tours in Hanoi, our suggestion would be to ask if the company will definitely be running the tour itself, and whether they pass you on to another company if they don't get a certain number signed up. Particularly if the latter is going to happen, ask if you will still get the same deal you paid for, or will you get the schedule and program that the other company runs? And what are the price differences between the tour you are booking and the one the other company runs?

Meriel Rule

We suggest seeking out tour operators who stick to small groups, and use their own vehicles and guides. One such outfit we've had good experiences with is Handspan Adventure Travel (www.handspan.com), a reputable tour operator that works in conjunction with the Aussie-run Kangaroo Cafe. In addition to the standard tour programs offered elsewhere, they offer trips such as kayaking in Halong Bay and the Da River in the deep north-west. At the time of writing Handspan was the only budget tour agency offering the chance to sleep aboard the boat in Halong Bay, a trip that gets rave reviews from travellers. This company also operates TF Handspan Travel, which focuses on upmarket tours for the local expat community. Also worth a plug in the upmarket bracket is Buffalo Tours, which runs innovative eco-tours throughout Vietnam. Buffalo Tours and Handspan Adventure travel are the most eco-conscious.

New places open all the time, and existing places change, so the following lists are not engraved in stone. With that caveat in mind, shop around, but consider the following places; all agencies are found in the Old Quarter with the exception of the Lotus Café and Orient Café which are on the Central Hanoi map.

Budget Agencies

A to Z Queen Cafe (☎ 826 0860, fax 826 0300, ⓔ queenaz@fpt.vn) 65 Pho Hang Bac; (☎ 826 7356, 934 3728) 50 Hang Be
Explorer Tours (☎ 923 0713, ⓔ explorertours@yahoo.com) 49 Pho Hang Bo
Green Bamboo Tours (☎ 826 8752) 49 Pho Nha Chung
Handspan Adventure Travel (☎ 926 0501, fax 926 0581, ⓔ handspan@hn.vnn.vn) 80 Pho Ma May
Web site: www.handspan.com
Hanoi's Old Quarter Cafe (☎ 926 0313, fax 824 5924, ⓔ oldquarterhn@hn.vnn.vn) 22 Pho Hang Be; (☎ 824 5923, fax 824 5924) 30 Pho Luong Van Can
Kim's Cafe (☎ 824 9049, ⓔ kimscafe@hotmail.com) 79 & 127 Pho Hang Bac
Lotus Café (☎ 826 8642) 42V Pho Ly Thuong Kiet (Lotus Guesthouse)
Love Planet (☎ 828 4864, fax 828 0913, ⓔ loveplanet@hn.vnn.vn) 25 Pho Hang Bac
Old Darling Cafe (☎ 824 3024) 142 Pho Hang Bac; (☎ 828 9977, fax 826 8148, ⓔ theolddarlingtravel@mail.com) 4 Pho Hang Quat
Orient Cafe (☎ 824 7390) 53 Pho Tran Hung Dao
Rainbow Tours (☎ 826 8752, fax 928 5487, ⓔ cuong@fpt.vn) 42 Pho Nha Chung
Romantic Travellers Cafe (☎ 828 9236, ⓔ romantic.darling@fpt.vn) 24 Pho Hang Non
Real Darling Cafe (☎ 826 9386, fax 825 6562) 33 Pho Hang Quat
Red River Tours (☎ 826 8427, fax 828 7159, ⓔ redrivertours.hn.vn@ftp.vn) 73 Pho Hang Bo
Web site: www.redriverstours.com
Sinh Cafe (☎ 828 7552, fax 822 6055) 18 Pho Luong Van Can; (☎ 934 0535) 56 Pho Hang Be; (☎ 926 0038) 52 Pho Hang Bac

Mid-Range & Top-End Agencies

Ann Tours (☎ 822 0018, fax 832 3866) 26 Pho Yet Kieu
Buffalo Tours (☎ 828 0702, fax 826 9370, ⓔ buffalo@netnam.org.vn) 11 Pho Hang Muoi
Diethelm Travel (☎ 934 4844, fax 934 4850, ⓔ dtvl@netnam.vn) 44B Pho Ly Thuong Kiet
Exotissimo Travel (☎ 828 2150, 828 2146) 26 Pho Tran Nhat Duat
Phoenix Vietnam (☎ 733 6456, fax 733 6457, ⓔ phoenix.vn@fpt.vn) 23 Pho Quan Thanh, Ba Dinh
TF Handspan Travel (☎ 926 0444, fax 926 0445, ⓔ linh@handspan.com) 36 Pho Nguyen Huu Huan

Motorbiking Speciality Tours Motorbiking Vietnam's 'deep north' is an unforgettable ride. For those seeking true adventure there is just no better way to go. If you are not confident in riding a motorbike yourself, it's not expensive to hire someone to drive one for you. Four-wheel-drive jeep trips in the north are also highly recommended, though the mobility of travelling on two wheels is unrivalled.

While it is possible to organise a motorbiking trip on your own, a guide can make the trip run smoothly, find secret road routes, and open doors you could never touch from the cursory scan of a map. Motorbikes are easily hired in Hanoi, and if you book a guided trip the operator can assist you in finding the right one at the right price. The ultimate vehicle to look for is the Russian Minsk (also see the 'Minsk Mania' boxed text). For information about motorbike rental, see the Getting Around section later in this chapter.

Minsk Mania

MИHCK

Among the 300-odd members of Hanoi's free-wheelin' Minsk Club, few had ever even *heard* of a Minsk motorbike before coming to Vietnam. These days, however, owning the Belarussian wonderbike is the latest craze among Hanoi's eclectic expat community, and the club roster continues to expand.

The 125cc Russian-made Minsk is pre-WWII in design, just like a Volkswagon. This means the bike is simple and robust, and does not require a rocket scientist to repair it. In the rugged mountains of Vietnam, the Minsk rules supreme; every mechanic knows how to fix one, and parts can be found everywhere (even in the most-rural areas).

Minsks pack the kind of power you'll need in the mountains, plus they're light enough to be carried by two people across rivers and rocky terrain. They might spew a bit of smoke, but the mystique of riding a Minsk is something even Harley Davidson devotees might not understand.

The Minsk Club promotes motorbiking in Vietnam, sharing travel information, and hosts a variety of activities like parties, *bia hoi* meetings and occasional rallies. All are welcome in the cult and at its events. You don't have to be an expat, nor ride a Minsk for that matter (though you may feel like the black sheep without one?). Girls needn't be shy – one-third of the Minsk Club members are women.

Just when you think you may just be the first foreigner to stumble upon a remote corner of Nowheresville, Vietnam, don't be surprised to spot a sticker with the cryptic Minsk logo somewhere within view. The Minsk Club is everywhere and they're known to leave their mark.

There are a handful of companies in Hanoi running motorbiking speciality tours, with a growing contingent of free-wheeling guides who know the roads and ways of the wild northern territory. Foreign guides charge considerably more than a local Vietnamese guide, but readers reports say they are worth every dong. Based on a group of four people, you can expect to pay around US$50 per day per person for an all-inclusive tour (providing motorbike rental, tour guide, food, drinks and accommodation).

One such outfit is Association Bourlingue (☎/fax 928 1734, e fredo-binh@hn.vnn.vn), run by Fredo (or Binh in Vietnamese), a French-Vietnamese expat and one of Hanoi's top foreign motorbike guides. He speaks French, English and Vietnamese, and also has Vietnamese guides on call. The base of operations for Fredo's clan is at Bar Le , 2A Pho Ta Hien, in the Old Quarter.

Other praiseworthy foreign guides well worth tracking down are Digby and Dan, two adventure-craving, *bia hoi* connoisseurs hailing from Oz and the UK, respectively. They can be reached on ☎ 091-524658, or at their Web site: www.motorbikingvietnam.com.

Another good place to inquire about motorbiking trips with local Vietnamese guides is the above mentioned Handspan Adventure Tours.

Bookshops If you're out of reading material, Hanoi's a good chance to stock up; in the Old Quarter, the Thang Long Bookshop (☎ 825 7043) at 53–55 Pho Trang Tien, a short walk from Hoan Kiem Lake, is one of the biggest and best bookshops in town.

There's also an interesting used-book shop with a wide selection of paperbacks, mostly in English, but some in French and other languages, on the second floor of the Love Planet Café (☎ 828 4864), at 25 Pho Hang Bac.

For French books, try the Librairie Vietnamienne Francophone (☎ 825 7376), 64 Pho Trang Tien, near the corner with Pho Hang Bai.

A block away in the central area, the air-conditioned Hanoi Bookstore (Hieu Sach Hanoi; ☎ 824 1616), 34 Pho Trang Tien, also has a decent collection of imported news magazines and a selection of imported classical novels in English.

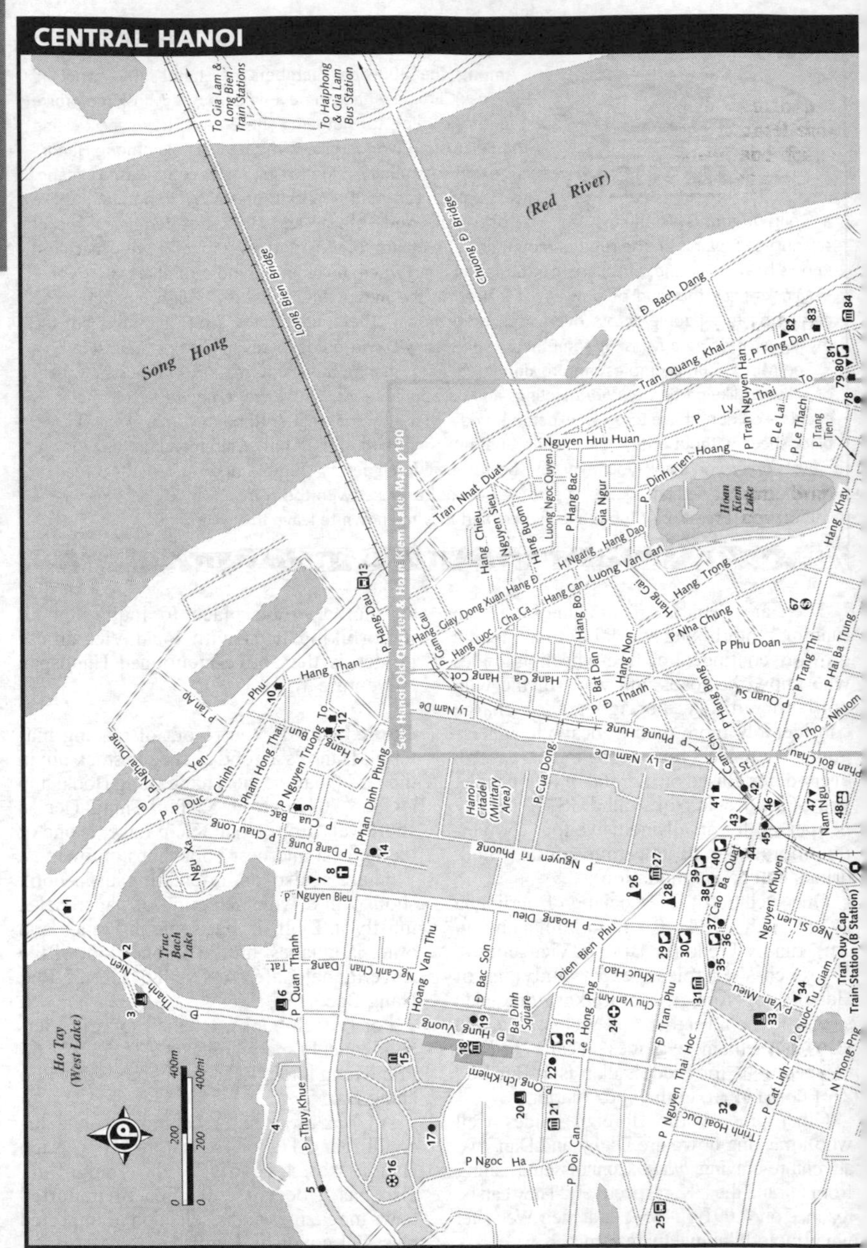
CENTRAL HANOI
To Gia Lam & Long Bien Train Stations
To Haiphong & Gia Lam Bus Station
(Red River)
Song Hong
Long Bien Bridge
Chuong Đ Bridge
Đ Bach Dang
Tran Quang Khai
P Tong Dan
See Hanoi Old Quarter & Hoan Kiem Lake Map p190
Nguyen Huu Huan
Tran Nhat Duat
P Ly Thai To
P Tran Nguyen Han
P Le Lai
P Le Thach
P Trang Tien
Dinh Tien Hoang
Hoan Kiem Lake
Hang Khay
Hang Chieu
Nguyen Sieu
Hang Buom
Luong Ngoc Quyen
P Hang Bac
Gia Ngu
Hang Dao
Hang Can
Luong Van Can
Hang Giay
Dong Xuan
Hang Luoc
Cha Ca
Hang Bo
Hang Gai
Hang Trong
Hang Cot
Hang Ga
Bat Dan
Hang Non
P Nha Chung
P Phu Doan
P Trang Thi
P Hai Ba Trung
P Quan Su
P Tho Nhuom
Phan Boi Chau
P Hang Bong
P Đ Thanh
Ly Nam De
P Phung Hung
P Ly Nam De
P Hang Dau
Hang Than
Phu
P Tan Ap
P Nghia Dung
Yen
Phu
Đ
P Duc Chinh
Pham Hong Thai
P Nguyen Truong To
Hang Bun
P Cua Bac
P Chau Long
P Dang Dung
P Phan Dinh Phung
Ngu Xa
Hanoi Citadel (Military Area)
P Cua Dong
P Nguyen Tri Phuong
P Hoang Dieu
Dien Bien Phu
Cao Ba Quat
Cam Chi
St
Nam Ngu
Nguyen Khuyen
Ngo Si Lien
Tran Quy Cap Train Station (B Station)
P Nguyen Bieu
P Quan Thanh
Truc Bach Lake
Thanh Nien
Đ
Dang Tat
Ng Canh Chan
Hoang Van Thu
Đ Bac Son
Hung Vuong
Ba Dinh Square
Khuc Hao
Chu Van An
Le Hong Png
Đ Tran Phu
P Nguyen Thai Hoc
P Van Mieu
P Quoc Tu Giam
N Thong Png
P Cat Linh
Trinh Hoai Duc
P Ong Ich Khiem
P Doi Can
P Ngoc Ha
Đ Thuy Khue
Ho Tay (West Lake)
0 200 400m
0 200 400mi
1 2 3 4 5 6 7 8 9 10 11 12 13 14 15 16 17 18 19 20 21 22 23 24 25 26 27 28 29 30 31 32 33 34 35 36 37 38 39 40 41 42 43 44 45 46 47 48
67
78 79 80 81 82 83 84

CENTRAL HANOI

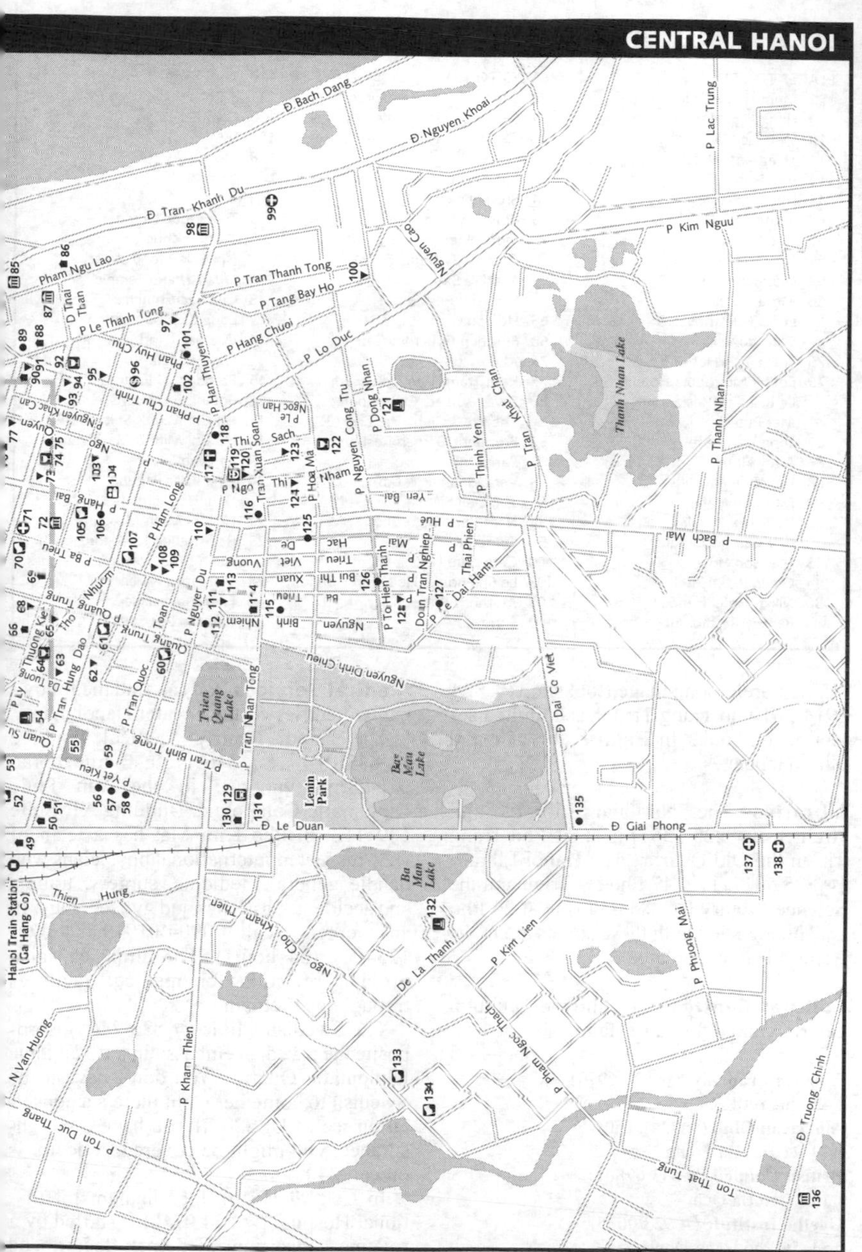

CENTRAL HANOI

PLACES TO STAY
1 Meritus Westlake
9 Hang Nga Hotel
10 Viet Bac Hotel
11 Thien Thai Hotel
12 Anh Hotel II
41 Dream 2 Hotel
49 Mango Hotel
50 Hotel 30/4
51 Thu Do Hotel
53 Guoman Hotel
66 Melia Hotel
69 Lotus Guesthouse & Café (tours)
76 Trang Tien Hotel
79 Sofitel Metropole Hotel; Le Beaulieu Restaurant; Met Pub
83 Tong Dan Hotel
86 Army Hotel
88 Hanoi Opera Hilton
90 Dan Chu Hotel
102 De Syloia Hotel; Cay Cau Restaurant
113 Madison Hotel
114 Green Park Hotel
130 Nikko Hotel Hanoi; Benkay Restaurant

PLACES TO EAT
2 Shrimp Cakes Restaurant
4 Seafood Restaurants
7 Seasons of Hanoi
34 Koto
43 Luna d'Autunno
44 Brother's Cafe
46 Kinh Do Cafe
47 Indochine
62 Com Chay Nang Tam
63 Mekki's Bar; Lan Anh Restaurant
65 Hoa Sua
68 Emotion Cybernet Cafe
73 Al Fresco's
77 Kem Trang Tien Ice Cream
80 Diva; Au Lac; Club Opera; The Press Club; The Deli (3)
82 President Garden Restaurant
91 Paris Deli
93 Verandah Bar & Cafe
94 The Deli (2)
95 Nam Phuong
97 Emperor
100 Café Que Huong
103 Le Splendide; Hoa Binh Hotel
108 Mother's Pride
109 Soho
110 Tiem Pho
111 Il Grillo
120 Com Duc Vien
123 Ky Y
128 Momiji

OTHER
3 Tran Quoc Pagoda
5 Đ Thuy Khue (speciality food street)
6 Quan Thanh Temple
8 Cua Bac Church
13 Long Bien bus station
14 Cua Bac (Northern Gate of Old Citadel)
15 Presidential Palace
16 Botanical Gardens
17 Ho Chi Minh's Stilt House
18 Ho Chi Minh's Mausoleum
19 Ba Dinh Square
20 One Pillar Pagoda; Dien Huu Pagoda
21 Ho Chi Minh Museum
22 Registration Desk for Ho Chi Minh's Mausoleum
24 Vietnam - Korea Friendship clinic
25 Kim Ma Bus Station

The Foreign Language Bookshop (☎ 824 8914), 61 Pho Trang Tien, has a limited selection of books in English, French and other languages.

Libraries The National Library and Archives (☎ 825 3357) is at 31 Pho Trang Thi in the Old Quarter. The Hanoi Library (☎ 825 4817) is at 47 Pho Ba Trieu and the Science Library (☎ 825 2345) is at 26 Pho Ly Thuong Kiet; both these streets are in the Central Hanoi map area.

Cultural Centres The following cultural centres can be found in Hanoi.

Alliance Francaise (☎ 826 6970)
42 Pho Yet Kieu
American Club (☎ 824 1850)
19–21 Hai Ba Trung
British Council (☎ 843 6780)
18B Cao Ba Quat
Goethe Institute (☎ 923 0035)
54–56 Pho Hang Dong

Medical Services You can find the following two entries on the Greater Hanoi map.

The Hanoi Family Medical Practice (☎ 843 0748, fax 846 1750, ⓔ hfmedprac.kot@fmail.vnn.vn), in the Van Phuc Diplomatic Compound, Building A1, Suite 109–112 on Pho Kim Ma, has a team of well-respected international physicians who handle general medicine, surgery, trauma and accident, obstetrics and gynaecology. In an emergency, call ☎ 090-401919 or ☎ 090-1234911 (24 hours). The clinic can also provide referrals for medical facilities throughout Vietnam.

The Swedish Clinic (☎ 825 2464) is opposite the Swedish embassy in the Van Phuc Diplomatic Quarter. You don't have to be Swedish to come here, but there's a consultation fee of US$80. If you have travel insurance, you might be covered. A doctor is on call 24 hours.

In Central Hanoi, the Vietnam International Hospital (☎ 574 0740) is staffed by a rotating consortium of French doctors and

CENTRAL HANOI

26 Flag Tower
27 Army Museum
28 Lenin Monument
31 Fine Arts Museum
32 Hanoi Stadium
33 Temple of Literature
35 Deja Vu
38 British Council
42 Cam Chi (speciality food street)
45 Cua Nam Market
54 Ambassadors' Pagoda
55 Friendship Cultural Hall
56 Alliance Française de Hanoi
57 Hanoi College of Fine Art & Gallery
58 Ann Tours
59 Vietnam Airlines
67 Credit Lyonnais Bank
71 International SOS Clinic
72 Women's Museum
75 American Club
78 Hanoi Bookstore (Hieu Sach Hanoi); Singapore Airlines
84 Revolutionary Museum
85 History Museum; Vietnamese Language Centre
87 Geology Museum
96 Vietcombank
98 Border Guard Museum
99 Friendship Hospital
101 Mai Gallery
106 Immigration Police Office
112 Song Hong Art Gallery
115 Institute of Traditional Medicine
116 Hom Market
117 Ham Long Church
118 Hanoi Gormet
121 Hai Ba Trung Temple
124 Hanoi Star Mart
125 Pho Mai Hac De (speciality food street)
126 Pho To Hien Thanh (speciality food street)
127 Dong Son Gallery
129 Kim Lien Bus Depot (City Buses)
132 Kim Lien Pagoda
135 Hanoi University & Vietnamese Language Centre
136 Air Force Museum
137 Vietnam International Hospital
138 Bach Mai Hospital

ENTERTAINMENT

48 Fanslands Cinema; Tam Tu
64 Pear Tree Pub
74 Spotted Cow
89 Opera House
92 Camellia Café & Bar
104 Thang 8 Cinema
119 Youth Theatre
122 Apocalypse Now
131 Central Circus

EMBASSIES

23 Canadian Embassy
29 Chinese Embassy
30 Singaporean Embassy
36 Belgian Embassy
37 Korean Embassy
39 German Embassy
40 Danish Embassy; Swiss Embassy
52 Egyptian Embassy
60 Lao Embassy– Consular Section
61 Cambodian Embassy
70 UK Embassy
81 Italian Embassy
105 New Zealand Embassy
107 French Embassy; French clinic
133 Philippine Embassy
134 Thai Embassy

also offers 24-hour emergency service (☎ 547 1111). Just next door is the Bach Mai Hospital (Benh Vien Bach Mai; ☎ 869 3731) on Pho Giai Phong. It has an international department where doctors speak English.

The International SOS Clinic (☎ 934 0555, fax 934 0556) is at 31 Pho Hai Ba Trung. Resident foreigners can contact SOS for information about a long-term medical and emergency evacuation plan.

The Friendship Hospital (Benh Vien Huu Nghi; ☎ 825 2231), 1 Pho Tran Khanh Du, has excellent up-to-date equipment and the doctors speak English. This place does mostly diagnostic work – surgery and extensive treatment should be done elsewhere.

The French embassy (☎ 825 2719), 49 Pho Ba Trieu, operates a 24-hour clinic for French nationals only.

In the Old Quarter, The Viet Duc Hospital (Benh Vien Viet Duc; ☎ 825 3531), 40 Pho Tranh Thi, is open 24 hours and can do emergency surgery. Doctors speak English, French and German.

If you don't have insurance, the Vietnam-Korea Friendship clinic (☎ 843 7231) at 12 Chu Van An is reputed to be the least expensive medical facility in Hanoi that maintains a high international standard. The clinic is headed up by Dr Lee, a Harvard-educated specialist in tropical diseases.

For tooth problems, The Dental Clinic (☎ 846 2864, mobile ☎ 090-401919, fax 823 0281) is in building A2 in the Van Phuc Diplomatic Quarter, 101–102 Pho Kim Ma (adjacent to the aforementioned Hanoi Family Medical Practice on Greater Hanoi Map).

Grand Dentistry (☎ 824 5772), 10 Pho Ngo Duc Ke, is staffed by American dentists. There are also dentists on call at the Vietnam International Hospital and SOS.

For traditional Vietnamese medicine, see the 'Massage' section later this chapter.

LAKES, TEMPLES & PAGODAS

Hoan Kiem Lake

Hoan Kiem Lake is an enchanting body of water right in the heart of Hanoi. Legend

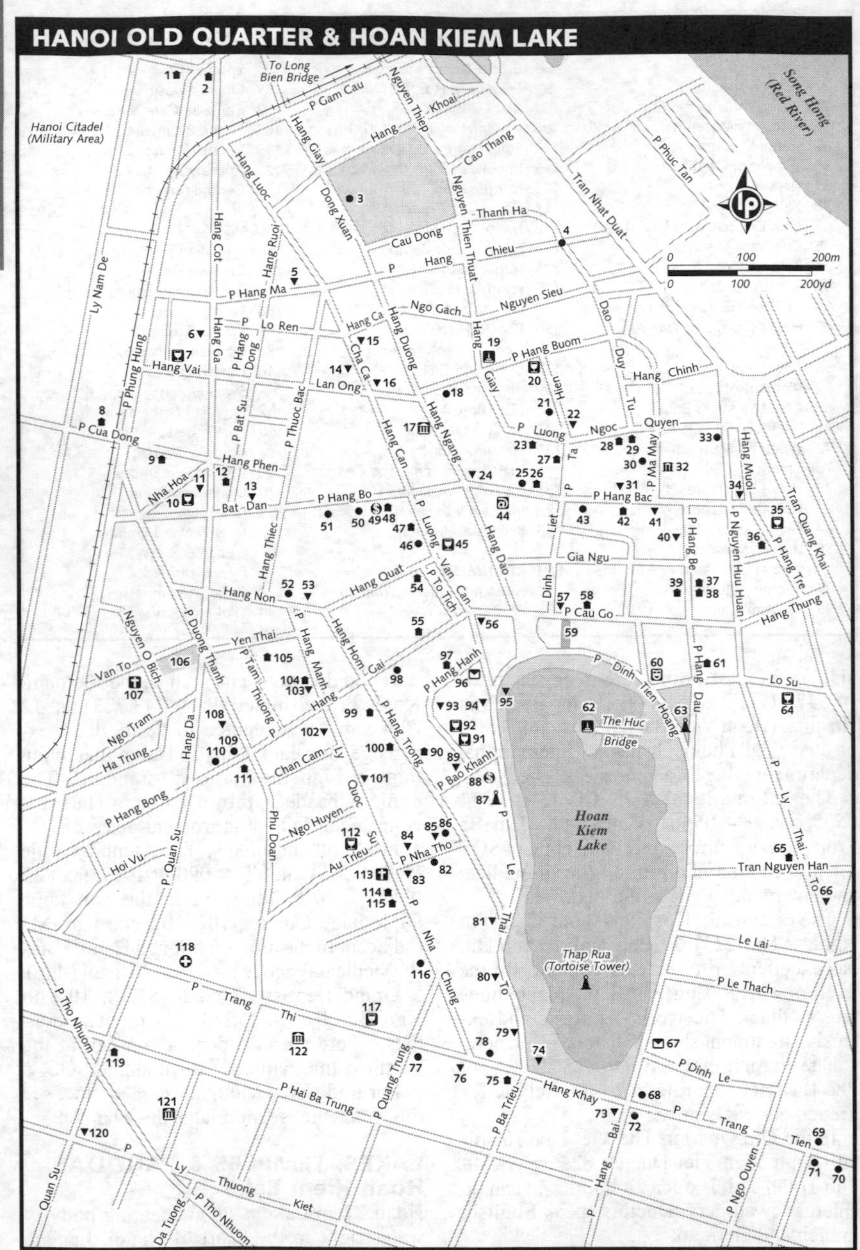
HANOI OLD QUARTER & HOAN KIEM LAKE
To Long Bien Bridge
Hanoi Citadel (Military Area)
Song Hong (Red River)
P Gam Cau
Hang Khoai
Nguyen Thiep
Hang Giay
Hang Luoc
Dong Xuan
Cao Thang
Nguyen Thien Thuat
Thanh Ha
Tran Nhat Duat
P Phuc Tan
Cau Dong
P Hang Chieu
Hang Cot
Hang Ruoi
Ly Nam De
P Hang Ma
Ngo Gach
Nguyen Sieu
Dao Duy Tu
Hang Ca
P Lo Ren
Hang Ga
P Hang Dong
Hang Duong
P Phung Hung
Hang Vai
Cha Ca
Lan Ong
Hang Giay
P Hang Buom
Hien
Hang Chinh
P Bat Su
P Thuoc Bac
Hang Ngang
Hang Can
P Luong Ngoc Quyen
P Cua Dong
Hang Phen
Nha Hoa
Bat Dan
P Hang Bo
Ta Hien
P Ma May
Hang Muoi
P Hang Bac
Tran Quang Khai
P Luong Van Can
Hang Dao
Dinh Liet
P Hang Be
P Nguyen Huu Huan
P Hang Tre
Gia Ngu
Hang Thiec
Hang Quat
P To Tich
Hang Non
P Cau Go
Hang Thung
Nguyen O Bich
P Duong Thanh
Yen Thai
P Hang Manh
Hang Hom
P Tam Thuong
Van To
Hang Gai
P Hang Hanh
P Dinh Tien Hoang
P Hang Dau
Lo Su
Ngo Tram
Hang Da
The Huc Bridge
Ha Trung
Chan Cam
Ly Quoc Su
P Hang Trong
P Bao Khanh
P Ly Thai To
P Hang Bong
Ngo Huyen
Phu Doan
Hoan Kiem Lake
Hoi Vu
Au Trieu
P Nha Tho
P Le Thai To
P Quan Su
Tran Nguyen Han
P Nha Chung
Le Lai
Thap Rua (Tortoise Tower)
P Le Thach
P Tho Nhuom
P Trang Thi
P Dinh Le
P Quang Trung
P Ba Trieu
Hang Khay
P Hai Ba Trung
P Trang Tien
P Hang Bai
P Ngo Quyen
P Ly Thuong Kiet
Quan Su
Da Tuong
P Tho Nhuom
0 100 200m
0 100 200yd

HANOI OLD QUARTER & HOAN KIEM LAKE

PLACES TO STAY
1 Chains First Eden Hotel
2 Galaxy Hotel
8 Viet Anh Hotel
9 Asia Hotel
12 Stars Hotel
23 Prince Hotel (1)
26 Prince Hotel (2)
27 Thuy Nga Guesthouse; Prince Cafe & Internet
28 Van Xuan Hotel
29 Camilla Hotel
36 Royal Hotel; Club Monaco
37 Classic Street Hotel
38 Anh Sinh Hotel
39 Queen 2; Hanoi Spirit Club
42 A to Z Queen Cafe (tours)
47 Hong Ngoc Hotel 3
48 Hoa Linh Hotel
54 Real Darling Cafe (tours)
55 Trang An Hotel
58 Thang Long Hotel I & II
61 Salute Hotel
75 Thuy Nga Hotel
90 Tu Do (Freedom) Hotel
97 Win Hotel
99 Lucky Hotel
100 Huyen Trang Hotel
104 Hong Ngoc Hotel 1
105 Thu Giang Guesthouse; Manh Dung Guesthouse
111 Diamond Hotel
114 Spring Hotel
115 Nam Phuong Hotel (1)
119 Somerset Grand Hanoi; Red Onion Bistro

PLACES TO EAT
5 Thang Long
6 Thanh Van
11 Cha Ca 66
13 La Dolce Vita
14 Cha Ca La Vong
15 Baan Thai Restaurant
16 Tuyet Nhung
22 Little Hanoi (1)
24 Old Darling Café (tours)
31 Sinh Cafe
34 Trung Nguyen coffee shop
40 Tandoor
41 Love Planet
53 Tin Tin Bar & Cafe
56 Little Hanoi (2)
57 Smiling Café
66 Khazana
73 Ciao Café
74 Dak Linh Cafe
76 Saigon Sakura
79 Fanny's Ice Cream
80 Il Padrino
81 Green Ho Guom
83 Mediterraneo Restaurant; La Salsa Tapas Bar
84 Moca Cafe
85 La Brique
89 Kangaroo Cafe; Nam Phuong Hotel (2)
93 Le Cafe des Arts
94 Mama Rosa
95 Dinh Lang Restaurant; Thuy Ta Cafe
101 Pepperonis Pizza & Cafe
102 Pho Bo Dac Biet
103 Hanoi Garden
108 Cyclo Bar & Restaurant
120 San Ho Restaurant

OTHER
3 Dong Xuan Market
4 Cua O Quan Chuong (Old East Gate)
10 Bia Hoi Ha Chau Quan
17 Memorial House
18 Trang An Gallery
19 Bac Ma Temple
21 The Furniture Gallery
25 Vietnamese House
30 Handspan Adventure Travel; Tamarind Café & Fruit Juice Bar
32 House at 87 Ma May
33 TF Handspan Travel
43 Kim's Cafe
44 Kim Tours; Classy Zone Internet Service
46 Hanoi's Old Quarter Cafe; Sinh Cafe
49 Industrial & Commercial Bank
50 Explorer Tours
51 Red River Tours
52 Romantic Travellers' Cafe
59 Trung Tam Thuong Mai Supermarket
62 Ngoc Son Temple
63 Martyrs' Monument
65 Hanoi Star Mart; Energy Hotel
67 Main Post Office
68 Librairie Vietnamienne Francophone (French-language bookshop)
69 Nam Son Gallery
70 Hanoi Studio
71 Van Gallery
72 Thang Long Bookshop
77 Vietnam Airlines Minibus Stop
78 Green Bamboo Tours
82 Indochine House Antiques
86 La Boutique and the Silk
87 Le Thai To Statue
88 ANZ Bank
96 Post Office
98 Co Xanh Gallery
106 Hang Da Market
107 Protestant Church
109 Salon Natasha
110 Apricot Gallery
112 Church Cafe Bia Hoi
113 St Joseph Cathedral
116 Rainbow Tours
118 Viet Duc Hospital
121 Hoa Lo Prison Museum
122 National Library & Archives

ENTERTAINMENT
7 The Modern Toast
20 Bar Le Maquis; Association Bourlingue (motor bike guides)
35 Highway #4
45 Jazz Club
60 Water Puppet Theatre
64 R & R Tavern
91 Golden Cock
92 Polite Pub
117 New Century Nightclub

has it that in the mid-15th century, Heaven gave Emperor Ly Thai To (Le Loi) a magical sword which he used to drive the Chinese out of Vietnam. One day after the war, while out boating, he came upon a giant golden tortoise swimming on the surface of the water; the creature grabbed the sword and disappeared into the depths of the lake. Since that time, the lake has been known as Ho Hoan Kiem (Lake of the Restored Sword) because the tortoise restored the sword to its divine owners.

The forlorn Thap Rua (Tortoise Tower), topped with a red star, on an islet in the middle of the lake, is often used as an emblem of Hanoi. Every morning around 6 am, local residents can be seen doing their traditional morning exercises, jogging and playing badminton around this lake.

Ngoc Son Temple

Ngoc Son (Jade Mountain) Temple, founded in the 18th century, is on an island in the northern part of Hoan Kiem Lake (see Old Quarter map). Surrounded by water and shaded by trees, it is a delightfully quiet place to rest. The temple is dedicated to the scholar Van Xuong, General Tran Hung Dao (who defeated the Mongols in the 13th century) and La To, patron saint of physicians.

Ngoc Son Temple is reached via the red painted, wooden The Huc (Rising Sun) Bridge, which was constructed in 1885. To the left of the gate stands an obelisk whose top is shaped like a paintbrush. The temple is open daily from 8 am to 5 pm; the entrance fee is 12,000d (US$0.85).

One Pillar Pagoda

Hanoi's famous One Pillar Pagoda (Chua Mot Cot) was built by the Emperor Ly Thai Tong, who ruled from 1028 to 1054. According to the annals, the heirless emperor dreamed that he had met Quan The Am Bo Tat (Goddess of Mercy), who, while seated on a lotus flower, handed him a male child. Ly Thai Tong then married a young peasant girl he met by chance and had a son and heir by her. To express his gratitude for this event, he constructed the One Pillar Pagoda in 1049.

The One Pillar Pagoda, built of wood on a single stone pillar 1.25m in diameter, is designed to resemble a lotus blossom, symbol of purity, rising out of a sea of sorrow. One of the last acts of the French before quitting Hanoi in 1954 was to destroy the One Pillar Pagoda; the structure was rebuilt by the new government. The pagoda is on Pho Ong Ich Kiem near Ho Chi Minh's Mausoleum.

Dien Huu Pagoda

The entrance to Dien Huu Pagoda is a few metres from the staircase of the One Pillar Pagoda (Central Hanoi map). This small pagoda, which surrounds a garden courtyard, is one of the most delightful in Hanoi. The old wood and ceramic statues on the altar are distinctively northern. An elderly monk can sometimes be found performing acupuncture on the front porch.

Temple of Literature

The Temple of Literature (Van Mieu) is a pleasant retreat from the streets of Hanoi. It was founded in 1070 by Emperor Ly Thanh Tong, who dedicated it to Confucius (in Vietnamese, Khong Tu) in order to honour scholars and men of literary accomplishment.

The temple constitutes a rare example of well-preserved traditional Vietnamese architecture and is well worth a visit.

Vietnam's first university was established here in 1076 to educate the sons of mandarins. In 1484 Emperor Le Thanh Tong ordered that stelae be erected in the temple premises recording the names, places of birth and achievements of men who received doctorates in each triennial examination, commencing in 1442. Though 116 examinations were held between 1442 and 1778, when the practice was discontinued, only 82 stelae are extant. In 1802 Emperor Gia Long transferred the National University to his new capital, Hué. Major renovations were carried out here in 1920 and 1956.

The Temple of Literature is made up of five separate courtyards divided by walls. The central pathways and gates between them were reserved for the king. The walkways on one side were solely for the use of administrative mandarins; while those on the other side were for military mandarins.

The main entrance is preceded by a gate on which an inscription requests that visitors dismount their horses before entering. Khué Van Pavilion, at the far side of the second courtyard, was constructed in 1802 and is a fine example of Vietnamese architecture. The 82 stelae, considered the most precious artefacts in the temple, are arrayed to either side of the third enclosure; each one sits on a stone tortoise.

continued on page 197

Hanoi's Old Quarter

MASON FLORENCE

JOHN ELK III

JULIET COOMBE

Title page: Blow your own trumpet – pick up a pipe in Hanoi's Old Quarter (photograph by John Elk III).

Top: Incense is commonly found on altars in temples, homes and businesses.

Middle: Go crazy – get something for everyone with souvenir shopping.

Bottom: Learning the tricks of the trade in the Old Quarter.

JOHN ELK III

Hanoi's Old Quarter, or 36 Pho Puong (36 Streets), with over a thousand years of history, remains one of Vietnam's most lively and unusual places, where you can buy anything from a gravestone to silk pyjamas.

Hanoi's commercial quarter evolved alongside the Red River and the smaller To Lich River, which once flowed through the city centre to create an intricate network of canals and waterways teeming with boats. As the waters could rise as high as 8m during the monsoon, dikes, which can still be seen today along Tran Quang Khai, were constructed to protect the city.

Exploring the maze of back streets is fascinating; some streets open up while others narrow down into a warren of smaller alleys. The area is known for its tunnel, or tube, houses – so called because their small frontages hide very long rooms. These tunnel houses were developed to avoid taxes based on the width of their frontage onto the street. By feudal law, houses were also limited to two storeys and, out of respect for the king, could not be taller than the Royal Palace. These days there are taller buildings (six to eight storeys high) but there are no real high rise buildings.

ght: Walk or bike your way along the narrow laneways of the Old Quarter.

In the 13th century, Hanoi's 36 guilds established themselves here with each taking a different street (hence the name 36 Streets). *Hang* in Vietnamese means 'merchandise' and is usually followed by the name of the product that was traditionally sold in that street. Thus, Pho Hang Gai translates as 'Silk Street' (see the boxed text 'Meaning of the 36 Streets' for others, however these days the street name may not necessarily correspond to what is sold there.

Opportunities to lighten your load of dong are almost endless and as you wander around you'll find wool clothes, cosmetics, fake Ray Ban sunglasses, luxury foods, printed T-shirts, musical instruments, plumbing supplies, herbal medicines, gold and silver jewellery, religious offerings, spices, woven mats and much, much more (see also the Shopping section in this chapter).

Some of the more specialised streets include Pho Hang Quat which has red candlesticks, funeral boxes, flags and other temple items; and Pho Hang Gai which is somewhat more glamorous with silk, embroidery, lacquerware, paintings and water puppets – the silk sleeping bag liners and elegant Vietnamese *ao dai* are very popular with travellers. Finally, no trip to the Quarter would be complete without a trip to Dong Xuan market, on Pho Hong Khoi and Pho Dong Xuan, which was rebuilt after a 1994 fire.

A stroll through the historic Old Quarter can last anywhere from a few minutes to the better part of a day, depending on your pace and how well you navigate the increasing motor traffic plaguing the streets. However long, or whatever detours you might take, the following course will provide you with a good dose of Vietnamese culture, and some insight into the country's long history.

A logical starting point is the **Ngoc Son Temple** in the northern end of **Hoan Kiem Lake**. After crossing back over the bright red **Huc Bridge**, stop for a quick look at the **Martyrs' Monument**, erected to those who died in fighting for Vietnam's independence. Head north on Pho Hang Dau past the **Water Puppet Theatre** (see the 'Punch & Judy in a Pool' boxed text in this chapter) and you'll soon be surrounded by shoe shops selling every shape, size and style, demonstrating how serious Hanoians are about their footwear. Crossing over Pho Cau Go, pop into the colourful **flower market** which occupies the narrow eastern terminus of Pho Gia Nhu.

Back on Pho Hang Be, continue north to the 'T' intersection with Pho Hang Bac. Near here are several shops that carve intricate **gravestones** (most bearing an image of the deceased) by hand. A short detour north on Pho Ma May will lead you to the **Memorial House** at number 87 (see the main text entry earlier in this chapter), an exquisite Chinese merchant's home that was recently restored and opened as a museum.

Return to Pho Hang Bac and head west past a strip of snazzy **jewellery shops**, then right onto Pho Hang Ngang past a row of **clothing shops**, and right again onto Pho Hang Buom; this will take you past the small **Bach Ma Temple** (White Horse Temple). As you pass the pagoda, with its red funeral palanquin, look for its white-bearded temple guards,

1 Ngoc Son Temple
2 The Huc Bridge
3 Martyrs' Monument
4 Water Puppet Theatre
5 Shoe Shops
6 Flower Market
7 Gravestones
8 House at 87 May
9 Jewellery Shops
10 Clothing Shops
11 Bach Ma Temple
12 Cua O Quan Chuong (Old East Gate)
13 Straw Mats & Rope
14 'Ghost Money'
15 Blacksmiths
16 Herb Sellers
17 Towel Shops
18 Tin Box Makers
19 Mirrors
20 Buddhist Alters & Statues
21 Leather Shops
22 St Joseph Cathedral
23 Cafes

who spend their days sipping tea. Legend has it that Ly King used the pagoda to pray for assistance in building the city walls because they persistently collapsed, no matter how many times he rebuilt them. His prayers were finally answered when a white horse appeared out of the temple and guided him to the site where he could safely build his walls. Evidence of his success is still visible at Cua O Quan Chuong, the quarter's well-preserved **Old East Gate** at the eastern end of Pho Hang Chieu, near the intersection with Pho Tran Nhat Duat.

Head west, back along Pho Hang Chieu past a handful of shops selling **straw mats and rope** to reach one of the most interesting streets, Pho Hang Ma (literally 'counterfeit street'), where imitation **'ghost money'** is sold for burning in Buddhist ceremonies – it even has US$5000 bills! Loop around and follow your ears to the sounds of

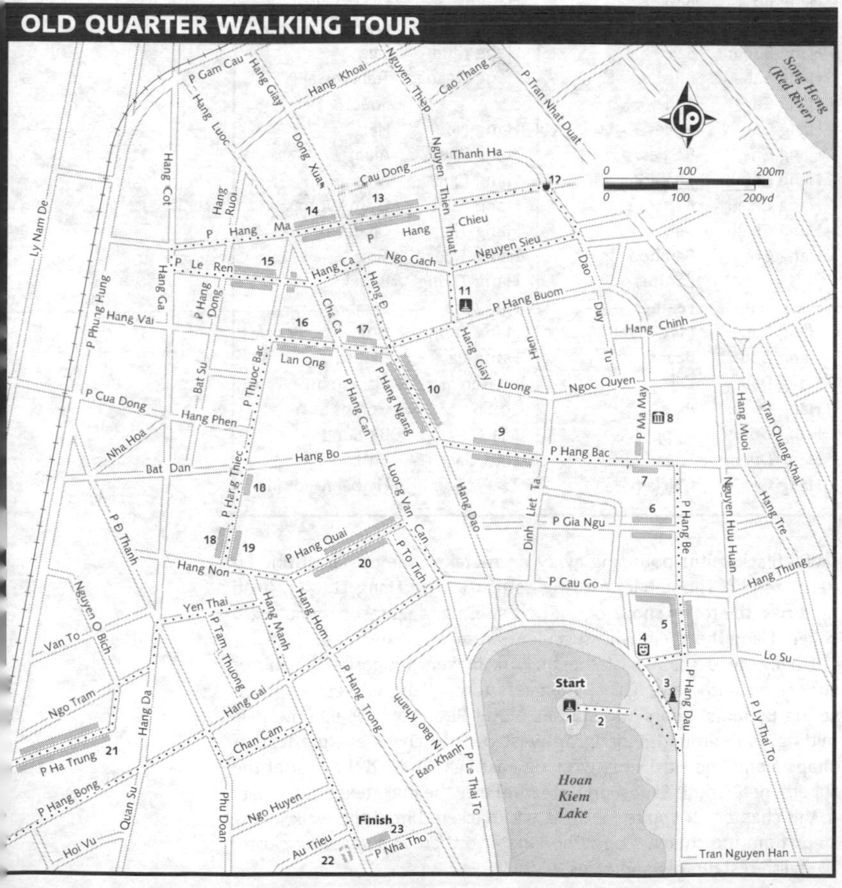

OLD QUARTER WALKING TOUR

Meaning of the 36 Streets

street name	description	street name	description
Bat Dan	Wooden Bowls	Hang Gai	Hemp
Bat Su	China Bowls	Hang Giay	Paper
Cha Ca	Roasted Fish	Hang Giay	Shoes
Chan Cam	String Instruments	Hang Hanh	Onions
		Hang Hom	Cases
Cho Gao	Rice Market	Hang Huong	Incense
Gia Ngu	Fishermen	Hang Khay	Trays
Hai Tuong	Sandals	Hang Khoai	Sweet Potato
Hang Bac	Silversmiths	Hang Luoc	Comb
Hang Be	Rafts	Hang Ma	Votive Papers
Hang Bo	Basket	Hang Mam	Pickled Fish
Hang Bong	Cotton	Hang Manh	Bamboo Screens
Hang Buom	Sails	Hang Muoi	Salt
Hang But	Brushes	Hang Ngang	Transversal Street
Hang Ca	Fish		
Hang Can	Scales	Hang Non	Hats
Hang Chai	Bottles	Hang Phen	Alum
Hang Chi	Threads	Hang Quat	Fans
Hang Chieu	Mats	Hang Ruoi	Clam Worms
Hang Chinh	Jars	Hang Than	Charcoal
Hang Cot	Bamboo Lattices	Hang Thiec	Tin
		Hang Thung	Barrel
Hang Da	Leather	Hang Tre	Bamboo
Hang Dao	(Silk) Dyer	Hang Trong	Drum
Hang Dau	Beans	Hang Vai	Cloth
Hang Dau	Oils	Lo Ren	Blacksmiths
Hang Dieu	Pipes	Lo Su	Coffins
Hang Dong	Copper	Ma May	Rattan
Hang Duong	Sugar	Ngo Gach	Bricks
Hang Ga	Chicken	Thuoc Bac	Herbal Medicine

skilful **blacksmiths** pounding away on metal on the corner of Pho Lo Ren and Pho Thuoc Bac. Moving south on Pho Hang Duong, head right past the **towel shops** onto Pho Lan Ong, a fantastic row of **herb sellers** filling the street with succulent aromas.

Finally, head south past the **tin box makers** (opposite the **mirror shops**) on Pho Hang Thiec, then left toward the interesting shops selling **Buddhist altars and statues** along Pho Hang Quai. Time permitting, loop around and zigzag west over to check out the **leather shops** along Pho Ha Trung, working east again to end the tour at the superb, neo-Gothic **St Joseph Cathedral** (see the main text entry earlier in this chapter). If you're feeling a bit knackered from the walk, a few steps from the church along Pho Nha Tho there is an alluring cluster of stylish **restaurants and cafes**.

continued from page 192

The Temple of Literature is 2km west of Hoan Kiem Lake (see Central Hanoi map). The complex, which is 350m by 70m, is bounded by Pho Nguyen Thai Hoc, Pho Ton Duc Thang, Pho Quoc Tu Giam and Pho Van Mieu. Enter from Pho Quoc Tu Giam. It is open Tuesday to Sunday from 7.30 to 6 pm (8 am to 5 pm from November to March); the entrance fee is 12,000d (US$0.85).

If you're looking for a great place to eat near this site, try Koto, just across the road on Pho Van Mieu (see Places to Eat later in this chapter).

Ho Tay

Two legends explain the origins of Ho Tay (West Lake), also known as the Lake of Mist and the Big Lake. According to one legend, Ho Tay was created when the Dragon King drowned an evil nine-tailed fox in his lair, which was in a forest on this site. Another legend relates that in the 11th century, a Vietnamese Buddhist monk, Khong Lo, rendered a great service to the emperor of China, who rewarded him with a vast quantity of bronze from which he cast a huge bell. The sound of the bell could be heard all the way to China, where the Golden Buffalo Calf, mistaking the ringing for its mother's call, ran southward, trampling on the site of Ho Tay and turning it into a lake.

In reality, the lake was created when the Song Hong (Red River) overflowed its banks. Indeed, Song Hong has changed its course numerous times, alternately flooding some lands and creating new ones though silt build up. The flood problem has been partially controlled by building dikes. The highway along the east side of Ho Tay is built upon one.

The lake was once ringed with magnificent palaces and pavilions. These were destroyed in the course of various feudal wars. The circumference of West Lake is about 13km.

The **Tran Quoc Pagoda** is on the shore of Ho Tay just off Đ Thanh Nien, which divides Ho Tay from Truc Bach Lake. A stele here dating from 1639 tells the history of this site. The pagoda was rebuilt in the 15th century and again in 1842. There are a number of monks' funerary monuments in the garden. This is one of the oldest pagodas in Vietnam.

On the south side of the lake is a popular strip of outdoor seafood restaurants (see Places to Eat later in this chapter) while the north side has been ear-marked for the development of luxurious villas and hotels.

Truc Bach Lake

Truc Bach (White Silk) Lake is separated from Ho Tay by Đ Thanh Nien, which is lined with flame trees. During the 18th century, the Trinh lords built a palace on this site; it was later transformed into a reformatory for deviant royal concubines, who were condemned to weave a very fine white silk.

The **Quan Thanh Temple** (Den Quan Thanh) is on the shore of Truc Bach Lake near the intersection of Đ Thanh Nein and Pho Quan Thanh (see Central Hanoi map). The temple, shaded by huge trees, was established during the Ly Dynasty (1010 to 1225) and was dedicated to Tran Vo (God of the North), whose symbols of power are the tortoise and the snake. A bronze statue and bell here date from 1677.

Tay Ho Pagoda

The Tay Ho Pagoda (Phu Tay Ho) is the most popular spot for worship in Hanoi. Throngs of people come here on the first and 15th day of each lunar month in the hopes of decreasing risk and receiving good fortune. (See Greater Hanoi map).

Ambassadors' Pagoda

The Ambassadors' Pagoda (Quan Su; ☎ 825 2427) is the official centre of Buddhism in Hanoi, attracting quite a crowd – mostly old women – on holidays. During the 17th century, there was a guesthouse here for the ambassadors of Buddhist countries. Today, there are about a dozen monks and nuns at the Ambassadors' Pagoda. Next to the pagoda is a store selling Buddhist ritual objects.

The Ambassadors' Pagoda is at 73 Pho Quan Su (between Pho Ly Thuong Kiet and Pho Tran Hung Dao – see Central Hanoi map); it is open to the public daily from 7.30 to 11.30 am and 1.30 to 5.30 pm.

Hai Ba Trung Temple

The Hai Ba Trung Temple, founded in 1142, is 2km south of Hoan Kiem Lake on Pho Tho Lao (see Central Hanoi map). A statue here shows the two Trung sisters (1st century AD) kneeling with their arms raised, as if to address a crowd. Some people say the statue shows the sisters, who had been proclaimed queens of the Vietnamese, about to dive into a river. They are said to have drowned themselves rather than surrender following their defeat at the hands of the Chinese.

Ho Chi Minh's Mausoleum

In the tradition of Lenin and Stalin before him and Mao after him, the final resting place of Ho Chi Minh is a glass sarcophagus set deep in the bowels of a monumental edifice that has become a site of pilgrimage. Ho Chi Minh's Mausoleum – built despite the fact that his will requested cremation – was constructed between 1973 and 1975 of native materials gathered from all over Vietnam; the roof and peristyle are said to evoke either a traditional communal house or a lotus flower – to many tourists it looks like a cold concrete cubicle with columns. High-ranking party and government leaders stand in front of the mausoleum when reviewing parades or ceremonies taking place on the grassy expanses of Ba Dinh Square.

Ho Chi Minh's Mausoleum is open from 8 to 11 am Tuesday to Thursday and weekends; entry is free. The mausoleum is closed for three months a year (usually from 5 September to early December) while Ho Chi Minh's embalmed corpse goes to Russia for maintenance. Unlike the Vietnamese, foreigners do not have to queue but can go directly to the registration desk about 300m west of here at 5 Pho Ngoc Ha (see Central Hanoi map).

Photography is permitted outside the building but not inside. All visitors must register and leave their bags and cameras at a reception hall in the block next to Pho Chua Mot Cot. Despite what the clerk may say, you do *not* have to pay for this service. Soundtracks for a 20-minute video about Ho Chi Minh are available in Vietnamese, French, English, Khmer, Lao, Russian and Spanish.

Honour guards will accompany you as you march in single file from the reception area to the mausoleum entrance. Inside the building, more guards regaled in snowy-white bleached military uniforms are posted at intervals of five paces, giving an eerily authoritarian aspect to the macabre spectacle of the embalmed, helpless body with its wispy white hair. The whole place has a 'sanitised for your protection' atmosphere.

The following rules are strictly applied to all visitors to the mausoleum:

- People wearing shorts, tank-tops etc will not be admitted.
- Nothing (including day packs and cameras) may be taken into the mausoleum.
- A respectful demeanour must be maintained at all times.
- For obvious reasons of decorum, photography is absolutely prohibited inside the mausoleum.
- It is forbidden to put your hands in your pockets.
- Hats must be taken off inside the mausoleum building.

Many of the visitors are groups of students, and it's interesting to watch their reactions to Ho. Most show deep respect and admiration for Ho. Though the Vietnamese as a whole are mostly disappointed with Communism, few – at least the younger generation – show any hostility or bitterness towards Ho himself. He is seen as the liberator of the Vietnamese people from colonialism, and Vietnam's subsequent economic and political mismanagement are viewed as the misdoings of Ho's comrades and successors. Of course, this view is reinforced by the educational system which only emphasises Ho's deeds and accomplishments.

If you're lucky, you'll catch the 'Changing of the Guard' outside Ho's Mausoleum – the pomp and ceremony displayed here rivals the British equivalent at Buckingham Palace.

Ho Chi Minh's Stilt House

Behind Ho Chi Minh's Mausoleum is a stilt house (Nha San Bac Ho) where Ho lived on and off from 1958 to 1969. The house is built in the style of Vietnam's ethnic minorities, and has been preserved just as Ho left it. It's set in a well-tended garden next to a carp-filled pond. Just how much time Ho actually spent here is questionable – the house would have made a tempting target for US bombers had it been suspected that Ho could be found here.

Near Ho's stilt house is the Presidential Palace, a beautifully restored colonial building constructed in 1906 as the Palace of the Governor General of Indochina. The palace is now used for official receptions.

Entry costs 3000d (US$0.25); see the Central Hanoi map.

Thu Le Park & Zoo

Thu Le Park and Zoo (Bach Thu Thu Le), with its expanses of shaded grass and ponds, is 6km west of Hoan Kiem Lake (see the Greater Hanoi map).

St Joseph Cathedral

Stepping inside the Old Quarter's neo-Gothic St Joseph Cathedral (inaugurated in 1886) is like being instantly transported to medieval Europe. The cathedral is noteworthy for its square towers, elaborate altar and stained-glass windows. The first Catholic mission in Hanoi was founded in 1679. The cathedral stands at the west end of Pho Nha Tho, or 'Church Street', which has developed into a fashionable strip of restaurants, cafes and boutiques.

The main gate to St Joseph Cathedral is open daily from 5 to 7 am and 5 to 7 pm, when Masses are held. Guests are welcome at other times of the day, but must enter the cathedral via the compound of the Diocese of Hanoi, the entrance to which is a block away at 40 Pho Nha Chung. After walking through the gate, go straight and then turn right. When you reach the side door to the cathedral, ring the small bell high up to the right-hand side of the door to call the priest to let you in.

MUSEUMS

In addition to the usual two-hour lunch break, it's worth noting that many of Hanoi's museums are closed on Monday.

Memorial House

The delightful house at **87 Pho Ma May**, north of Hoan Kiem Lake in the Old Quarter, is definitely worth visiting. This thoughtfully restored, traditional Chinese-style dwelling is sparsely decorated, and gives an excellent idea of how local merchants used to live in the Old Quarter. The restoration of the house was carried out in cooperation with the city of Toulouse, France, and completed in October, 1999. While there are many such houses open to the public in Hoi An, there is little, if anything, else like it in Hanoi.

The house is open from Monday to Friday from 9 to 11.30 am and 2 to 5 pm; entry costs 3000d (US$0.25).

There is another less interesting **Memorial House** two blocks west of here at 48 Pho Hang Ngang. This one was where Ho Chi Minh is said to have drafted Vietnam's Declaration of Independence in 1945. It was closed at the time of writing, but may be reopened as a museum in the future.

Ho Chi Minh Museum

The Ho Chi Minh Museum (Bao Tang Ho Chi Minh) is divided into two sections, 'Past' and 'Future'. You start in the past and move to the future by walking in a clockwise direction downwards through the museum, starting at the right-hand side of the top of the stairs. The displays are modern and all have a message (eg peace, happiness, freedom).

It's probably worth taking an English-speaking guide since some of the symbolism is hard to figure out (did Ho Chi Minh have a cubist period?). The 1958 Ford Edsel bursting through the wall (a US commercial failure to symbolise their military failure) is a knockout.

The museum is the huge cement structure next to Ho Chi Minh's Mausoleum (see Central Hanoi map). Photography is forbidden – you must leave bags and cameras at reception upon entry.

The museum is open daily from 8 to 11 am and 1.30 to 4.30 pm. Entry costs 6000d (US$0.45).

History Museum

The History Museum (Bao Tang Lich Su), once the museum of the École Française d'Extrême Orient, is one block east of the Municipal Theatre at 1 Pho Pham Ngu Lao

Radio Hanoi & Jane Fonda

Those old enough to remember the American War may recall the radio broadcasts from Hanoi that were made by the high profile American film actor Jane Fonda in 1972. Fonda, perhaps the most famous anti-war activist of the time, actually made only one live broadcast over Radio Hanoi, her famous speech directed to US pilots involved in the war. Subsequent broadcasts played over the radio were tape-recorded speeches and conversations made during her stay in North Vietnam. Fonda was not the only US civilian to visit Hanoi during the war, but she was certainly the most famous.

As a direct result of Jane Fonda's visit, Representative Ichord, chairman of the US House Internal Security Committee at the time, proposed an amendment to the 1950 Internal Security Act to make it illegal for any US citizen to visit a country at war with the USA. The Ichord Amendment – which later came to be known as the 'Jane Fonda Amendment' – never passed.

Her visit continues to stir emotions to this very day. Even as late as 1984 the Justice Department looked into whether Fonda should be prosecuted.

There are those who say that she was simply exercising her right to freedom of speech in speaking out against a war which she thought was morally wrong. A widely circulated photograph of Jane Fonda sitting behind an anti-aircraft gun wearing a North Vietnamese helmet outraged many Americans, even those who opposed the war, however Fonda also made a sincere effort to visit the captured American pilots at the nearby 'Hanoi Hilton' prison (see the Hoa Lo Prison entry in this chapter), but her request was rejected by North Vietnamese authorities.

An act of treason? Or a heartfelt wish to speak out against an unjust war? You be the judge. Here's the transcript of her speech:

This is Jane Fonda. During my two-week visit in the Democratic Republic of Vietnam, I've had the opportunity to visit a great many places and speak to a large number of people from all walks of life – workers, peasants, students, artists and dancers, historians, journalists, film actresses, soldiers, militia girls, members of the women's union, writers.

I visited the (Dam Xuac) agricultural co-op, where the silk worms are also raised and thread is made. I visited a textile factory, a kindergarten in Hanoi. The beautiful Temple of Literature was where I saw traditional dances and heard songs of resistance. I also saw an unforgettable ballet about the guerrillas training bees in the South to attack enemy soldiers. The bees were danced by women, and they did their job well.

In the shadow of the Temple of Literature I saw Vietnamese actors and actresses perform the second act of Arthur Miller's play *All My Sons*, and this was very moving to me – the fact that artists

(Central Hanoi map). This elegant, ochre-coloured structure was the brainchild of French architect Ernest Hebrard and was built between 1925 and 1932. Hebrard was among the first in Vietnam to incorporate a blend of Chinese and French design elements in his creations, and this particular building remains one of Hanoi's most stunning architectural showpieces.

Exhibits include artefacts from Vietnam's turbulent past including; prehistory (Palaeolithic and Neolithic periods); proto-Vietnamese civilisations (1st and 2nd millennia BC); the Dong Son culture (3rd century BC to 3rd century AD); the Oc-Eo (Funan) culture of the Mekong Delta (1st to 6th century AD); the Kingdom of Champa (2nd to 15th century); the Khmer kingdoms; various Vietnamese dynasties and their resistance to Chinese attempts at domination; the struggle against the French; and the history of the Communist Party. The museum is open Friday to Wednesday from 8.15 to 11.45 am and 1.30 to 5 pm; entry is 10,000d (US$0.80).

Radio Hanoi & Jane Fonda

here are translating and performing American plays while US imperialists are bombing their country.

I cherish the memory of the blushing militia girls on the roof of their factory, encouraging one of their sisters as she sang a song praising the blue sky of Vietnam – these women, who are so gentle and poetic, whose voices are so beautiful, but who, when American planes are bombing their city, become such good fighters.

I cherish the way a farmer evacuated from Hanoi, without hesitation, offered me, an American, their best individual bomb shelter while US bombs fell near by. The daughter and I, in fact, shared the shelter wrapped in each others arms, cheek against cheek. It was on the road back from Nam Dinh, where I had witnessed the systematic destruction of civilian targets – schools, hospitals, pagodas, the factories, houses, and the dike system.

As I left the United States two weeks ago, Nixon was again telling the American people that he was winding down the war, but in the rubble-strewn streets of Nam Dinh, his words echoed with sinister (words indistinct) of a true killer. And like the young Vietnamese woman I held in my arms clinging to me tightly – and I pressed my cheek against hers – I thought, this is a war against Vietnam perhaps, but the tragedy is America's.

One thing that I have learned beyond the shadow of a doubt since I've been in this country is that Nixon will never be able to break the spirit of these people; he'll never be able to turn Vietnam, North and South, into a neo-colony of the United States by bombing, by invading, by attacking in any way. One has only to go into the countryside and listen to the peasants describe the lives they led before the revolution to understand why every bomb that is dropped only strengthens their determination to resist.

I've spoken to many peasants who talked about the days when their parents had to sell themselves out to landlords as virtually slaves, when there were very few schools and much illiteracy, inadequate medical care, when they were not masters of their own lives.

But now, despite the bombs, despite the crimes being created – being committed against them by Richard Nixon, these people own their own land, build their own schools – the children learning, literacy – illiteracy is being wiped out, there is no more prostitution as there was during the time when this was a French colony. In other words, the people have taken power into their own hands, and they are controlling their own lives.

And after 4000 years of struggling against nature and foreign invaders – and the last 25 years, prior to the revolution, of struggling against French colonialism – I don't think that the people of Vietnam are about to compromise in any way, shape or form about the freedom and independence of their country, and I think Richard Nixon would do well to read Vietnamese history, particularity their poetry, and particularly the poetry written by Ho Chi Minh.

Fine Arts Museum

The Fine Arts Museum (Bao Tang My Thuat) is housed in the former French Ministry of Information. Here you can see some very intricate sculptures, paintings, lacquerware, ceramics and other traditional Vietnamese fine arts. Some reproductions of antiques are on sale here, but be sure to ask for a certificate to clear these goods through customs when you leave Vietnam.

The Fine Arts Museum is at 66 Pho Nguyen Thai Ho (on the corner with Pho Cao Ba Quai), across the street from the back wall of the Temple of Literature; see the Central Hanoi map. It is open Tuesday to Sunday from 8 am until noon and 1 to 4 pm; entry costs 10,000d (US$0.80).

Women's Museum

The excellent Women's Museum (Bao Tang Phu Nu) at 36 Pho Ly Thuong Kiet gets good reviews from travellers. There's the inevitable tribute to women soldiers, but, fortunately, there's much more than that. On the 4th floor you can see different costumes worn by the 54 minority groups in Vietnam. This is one place where many of the exhibits have English explanations.

The museum is open from 8 am to 4 pm daily, and entrance costs 10,000d (US$0.80). See the Central Hanoi map.

Geology Museum

The Geology Museum (Bao Tang Dia Chat) tells the story of the geologic processes that created such breathtaking spots as Halong Bay; however, most of the explanations are in Vietnamese.

It's located at 6 Pho Pham Ngu Lao (see Central Hanoi map), and is open from 8 am to noon and 1.30 to 4.30pm from Monday to Saturday; but don't be surprised if it's closed during 'opening hours'; entry is free.

Army Museum

The Army Museum (Bao Tang Quan Doi), on Pho Dien Bien Phu, is open daily. Outside, Soviet and Chinese weaponry supplied to the North are displayed alongside French and US-made weapons captured in the Franco–Viet Minh and American wars. The centrepiece is a Soviet-built MiG-21 jet fighter, triumphant amid the wreckage of French aircraft downed at Dien Bien Phu, and a US F-111. The displays include scale models of various epic battles from the long military history of Vietnam, including Dien Bien Phu and the capture of Saigon. It's open Tuesday to Sunday, 8 to 11.30 am and 1.30 to 4.30 pm; entry is 10,000d (US$0.80).

Next to the Army Museum is the hexagonal Flag Tower, which has become one of the symbols of Hanoi. See Central Hanoi map.

Hoa Lo Prison Museum

This provocative site (☎ 934 2253), at 1 Pho Hoa Lo on the corner with Pho Hai Ba Trung, is all that remains of the former Hoa Lo Prison, ironically nicknamed the 'Hanoi Hilton' by US POWs during the American War. Those incarcerated at Hoa Lo included Pete Peterson, who would later become the first US Ambassador to Vietnam following the re-establishment of diplomatic ties between the two countries in 1995.

The vast prison complex itself was built by the French in 1896. Originally intended to house around 450 inmates, records indicate that by the 1930s there were close to 2000 prisoners inside! The prison was recently razed to the ground to make room for a modern skyscraper, though the building at the front of the site has been thoughtfully preserved and restored as a museum (look for the sign over the gate reading 'Maison Centrale'). There are some English and French labels corresponding with the displays, and you may be able to find an English-speaking guide on site.

The bulk of the exhibits relate to the prison's use up to the mid-1950s, focusing on the Vietnamese struggle for independence from France. Notable tools of torture on display in the dark chambers include an ominous French guillotine which was used to behead Vietnamese revolutionaries during the colonial period.

There are also mug shots on display of Americans and Vietnamese who served time at Hoa Lo. Propaganda photos of cheerful-looking American prisoners (showing how well the Vietnamese hosts treated their guests) are shown with a placard reading:

> From August 5, 1964 to January 24, 1973, US government carried out two destruction wars by air and navy against Northern Vietnam. The Northern Army and people brought down thousands of aircrafts and captured hundreds of American pilots. Part of these pilots were detained in Hoa Lo Prison by our Ministry of Interior. Though having committed untold crimes on our people, but American pilots suffered no revenge once they were captured and detained. Instead they were well treated with adequate food, clothing and shelter. According to the provisions of Paris Agreement, our government had in March 1973 returned all captured pilots to the US government.

The museum is open from 8 to 11 am and 1 and 4 pm; entry is 10,000d (US$0.80).

Revolutionary Museum

The Revolutionary Museum (Bao Tang Cach Mang), at 25 Pho Tong Dan, creatively presents the history of the Vietnamese Revolution. It's near the History Museum, see the Central Hanoi map.

The museum is open from Tuesday to Friday from 8 to 11.30 am and 1 to 4 pm, and Saturday mornings. Admission costs 10,000d (US$0.80).

Air Force Museum

This is one of the larger museums in the country and, though seldom visited by foreigners, it's very worthwhile if you are a war history or aircraft buff.

The Air Force Museum (Bao Tang Khong Quan) has many of its exhibits outdoors. This includes a number of Soviet-built MiG fighters, reconnaissance planes, helicopters and anti-aircraft equipment. Inside the museum hall are other weapons, including mortars, machine guns and some US-made bombs (hopefully defused). There is a partially truncated MiG with a ladder – you can climb up into the cockpit and have your photo taken. The museum has other war memorabilia, including paintings of obvious Soviet design and portraits of Ho Chi Minh.

The Air Force Museum, on Đ Truong Chinh in the Dong Da District (far southwest – see the Central Hanoi map), is open daily from 8 to 11 am and 1 to 5 pm. Entry costs 5000d (US$0.40).

Border Guard Museum

The Border Guard Museum (Bao Tang Bien Phong) at 2 Pho Tran Hung Dao is dedicated to those friendly boys in uniform you encountered at the airport or border crossing. Theoretically, it's open 8 to 11 am Monday to Saturday, but it's often shut; entry is free. See Central Hanoi map.

ACTIVITIES

Swimming

Several upmarket hotels have swimming pools, but for hotel guests' and members' use only. For the general public, the Army Hotel (☎ 826 5540), near the History Museum, charges US$4 for day use of their pool (towels provided). The Ho Tay Villas (☎ 825 8241) out by West Lake has the best deal charging US$1 per day. Also by West Lake is the Thang Loi Hotel, which has a swimming pool open to the public for US$1 on weekdays, or US$2 on weekends.

Following in the footsteps of Ho Chi Minh City, the recently-completed **Hanoi Water Park** (☎ 753 2757) is about 5km from city centre (see Greater Hanoi map) and offers the usual variety of pools, slides and splashing opportunities. Entry costs 50,000d (US$4) for those over 110cm-tall, or 30,000d (US$2.50) for shorter people. Go figure.

You can get to the water park by bicycle, motorbike or meter taxi.

Fitness Clubs

A number of international hotels open their exercise centres to the public for a fee. Top of the market is the Clark Hatch Fitness Centre (☎ 826 6919 ext 8881) in the Sofitel Metropole Hotel. Similar is the Daewoo Hotel Fitness Centre (☎ 835 1000) and Meritus Lifestyle Club (☎ 823 8888). The Hanoi Club (☎ 823 8115), 76 Pho Yen Phu, offers a full service fitness centre.

Golf

King's Valley is an 18-hole golf course 45km west of Hanoi, close to the base of Ba Vi Mountain (see Around Hanoi map). Membership is a whopping US$5000, but the club is open to visitors.

On the western side of Hanoi, but still within the city limits, is the Lang Ha Golf Club (☎ 835 0908), 16A Pho Lang Ha, opposite the TV tower (Greater Hanoi map). Basically, this is just a driving range – you'll have to go to King's Valley if you want to pursue a white ball over hills and fields. The driving range is open daily to members and non-members alike from 6 am to 10 pm.

Hash House Harriers

Expats in Hanoi who belong to this organisation get together once weekly on Saturday afternoon for a run, fun and drinking party. The venue and exact time changes, so check for notices at expat pubs, like the Spotted Cow.

Massage

The government has severely restricted the number of places licensed to give massages because of the concern that naughty 'extra services' might be offered. At the present time, you can get a good legitimate massage at the Hoa Binh Hotel, Dan Chu Hotel and Thang Loi Hotel for about US$4 to US$6 per hour. The upmarket Guoman, Sofitel Metropole Hotel and Nikko Hotels charge around US$10 or US$20 per hour for this service.

You might also see what's on offer at the Institute of Traditional Medicine (☎ 943 1018) at 26–29 Pho Nguyen Binh Khiem, or the Institute of Acupuncture (☎ 853 3881) at H3 Pho Vinh Ho, Pho Thai Thinh, see the Greater Hanoi map.

Beauty Salons

Many of Vietnam's city beauty salons offer – ahem – 'extra services' as standard. If you feel in need of sprucing, a good, legitimate hairdresser is Deja Vu Salon (☎ 823 3439), at 29 Pho Cao Ba Quat. It's run by a friendly, English-speaking stylist named Vu who has earned a steady following among Hanoi's expat community.

His salon maintains a high international standard and hairdressing prices are reasonable at US$9/10 for men/women (including a hair wash, head massage, cut, blow dry and finish). Manicures and pedicures cost US$4.

LANGUAGE COURSES

There are professionally taught courses at the Vietnamese Language Centre (☎ 826 2468) at Hanoi Foreign Language College (Dai Hoc Ngoai Ngu), a branch of Hanoi National University. The main campus is 9km from central Hanoi, but there is a smaller campus closer to the city centre in the History Museum compound at 1 Pho Pham Ngu Lao.

Tuition varies depending on class size, but should be no more than US$7 per session for individual tutoring. There is a dormitory for foreign students where you can stay for around US$200 per month. The Vietnamese embassy in your home country should be able to provide you with more detailed information.

ORGANISED TOURS

There are many tours available, both day and overnighters. Travellers' cafes and budget tour agencies generally offer the best deals (see Travel Agents earlier in this chapter).

SPECIAL EVENTS

Tet, the Vietnamese Lunar New Year, falls in late January or early February (see 'The Tet Festival' special section in the Facts for the Visitor chapter). A flower market is held during the week preceding Tet on Pho Hang Luoc. A two-week flower exhibition and competition, beginning on the first day of the new year, takes place in Lenin Park. On the 13th day of the first lunar month boys and girl in Lim village (Ha Bac Province), engage in *hat doi*, a traditional game in which groups conduct a sung dialogue with each other; other activities include chess and cock fighting. Wrestling matches are held on the 15th day of the first lunar month at Dong Da Mound, site of the uprising against Chinese invaders led by Emperor Quang Trung (Nguyen Hue) in 1788.

Vietnam's National Day, 2 September, is celebrated at Ba Dinh Square (the expanse of grass in front of Ho Chi Minh's Mausoleum) with a rally and fireworks; boat races are held on Hoan Kiem Lake.

PLACES TO STAY

The majority of Hanoi's budget accommodation is within 1km of Hoan Kiem Lake. Unlike Ho Chi Minh City's Pham Ngu Lao district, where the cheapies are lined up wall-to-wall, lodgings here are more scattered, though they're mostly in and around the traditional Old Quarter.

There are several budget places around with both dorm beds and cheap rooms (under US$10), but for between US$10 and US$15 you can choose from a wide selection of 'mini-hotels' with clean, air-con rooms – some even offer satellite TV.

In the US$20 to US$50 range there is usually little to justify the price difference between the cheaper mini-hotels in town, though there are a few exceptions.

If you are willing to shell out between US$50 and US$100, however, it is possible to stay in posh four-star hotels that in cities like Hong Kong or Bangkok would cost around double. Keep an eye out in *Vietnam*

News, *The Guide* and *Time Out* for the latest deals.

Places to Stay – Budget

Old Quarter Popular with budget travellers is the friendly Thu Giang Guesthouse (☎ 828 5734, e thuyhan00@hotmail.com, 5A Pho Tam Thuong), tucked away in a narrow alley between Pho Yen Thai and Pho Hang Gai. Modest air-con rooms with private bathroom rent for US$6/7. If they are full, you can try one of the neighbours such as the family-run Manh Dung Guesthouse (☎ 826 7201, fax 824 8118, c manhdung@vista.gov.vn, 2 Pho Tam Thuong) which charges the same and has Internet facilities.

The family-run ***Thuy Nga Guesthouse*** *(☎ 826 6053, fax 828 2892, 24C Ta Hien)* is a bright and airy, six-room place where rooms cost US$8/$9 (with balcony).

Stars Hotel *(☎ 828 1911, 828 1928, 26 Pho Bat Su)* has received a steady stream of positive reports for clean, comfortable rooms and friendly service. Rates for air-con rooms are US$10 to US$15; nicer rooms have balconies.

A to Z Queen Cafe *(☎ 826 0860, fax 825 0000, e queenaz@fpt.vn, 65 Pho Hang Bac)* has very basic fan doubles with shared bath for US$4/6. The ***Queen 2*** *(☎ 826 7356, fax 824 7183, 50 Pho Hang Be)* – formerly the *Binh Minh Hotel* – has dorm beds costing US$2.50/3, fan doubles at US$6/7, and air-con rooms for US$8 to US$12. Just across the street, the ***Anh Sinh Hotel*** *(☎/fax 824 2229, 49 Pho Hang Be)* charges around the same.

Real Darling Cafe *(☎ 826 9386, fax 825 6562, e Darling_Cafe@hotmail.com, 33 Pho Hang Quat)* advertises itself as 'probably the best tourist cafe in Hanoi'. Singles/doubles cost US$5/6; dorm beds are US$3.

Thang Long Hotel I *(☎ 824 5712, fax 824 5502, 52 Pho Cau Go)* is an older mini-hotel close to the northern end of Hoan Kien Lake. Rooms are small, and have fridge, telephone, private toilet and satellite TV. Fan doubles cost US$6 to US$8, twins/doubles/triples with air-con cost from US$10 to US$15. There's a nearly identical set up at the nearby ***Thang Long Hotel II*** *(☎ 826 2330, fax 824 5502, 62 Pho Cau Go)*.

Diamond Hotel *(☎ 828 6708, fax 824 6331, 95 Pho Hang Bong)* is bit dated, but strives to maintain an international standard. Small air-con rooms rent for US$10, and larger corner doubles go for US$20. The hotel is well-located, and has an elevator.

Prince Hotel (1) *(☎ 828 0155, fax 828 0156, e ngodzung@hn.vnn.vn, 51 Pho Luong Ngoc Quyen)* is recommended. Small rooms cost US$15, and spacious doubles decorated with Chinese-style furniture are US$20 (with balcony). Just next door, the ***Prince Cafe*** *(☎ 828 1893, e huuthang@hn.vnn.vn, 53 Pho Luong Ngoc Quyen)* rents clean budget rooms for US$6, or US$10 with balcony. Try not to get confused, but there is yet *another* ***Prince Hotel*** (2) *(☎ 926 0150, fax 926 0149, 88 Pho Hang Bac)* around the block, this one also good. Rates are US$10 to US$20 for clean, air-con doubles with bath tubs and satellite TV.

Spring Hotel *(☎ 826 8500, fax 826 0083, 8 Pho Nha Chung)* a well-located mini-hotel, costs US$10 with shared bathroom, or US$15 to US$30 with attached toilet.

The attractive ***Asia Hotel*** *(☎ 826 9007, fax 824 5184, 5 Pho Cua Dong)* has a warm atmosphere and offers singles for $10/12, or US$18/20 for doubles.

The ***Nam Phuong Hotel*** (1) *(☎ 824 6894, 26 Pho Nha Chung)* is near St Joseph's Cathedral. It's basic, but rooms are bright and airy and the staff are helpful. Fan rooms start at US$7, or US$8 with air-con.

A second ***Nam Phuong Hotel*** (2) *(☎ 825 8030, fax 825 8964, 16 Pho Bao Khanh)* – this one just next door to the popular Kangaroo Cafe – charges US$10 to US$25.

Van Xuan Hotel *(☎ 824 4743, fax 824 6475, 15 Pho Luong Ngoc Quyen)* is state-run with air-con doubles for US$10. A room with private bath and balcony costs US$15 to US$25. There is also an in-house sauna and massage service.

Next door to the Van Xuan is the popular ***Camilla Hotel*** *(☎ 828 3583, 13 Pho Luong Ngoc Quyen)*, where doubles cost US$12 to US$25.

Central Hanoi Area Just north of the Old Quarter, the Viet Bac Hotel (☎ 828 3242, fax 828 1225, 23 Pho Hang Than) is an oldie, but a goodie. Clean rooms are good value at US$8 to US$26.

Travellers say good things about the friendly ***Tong Dan Hotel*** *(☎ 825 2219, fax 825 5354,* e *tongdanhotel@hn.vnn.vn, 210 Pho Tran Quang Khai/17 Pho Tong Dan)*, also known as *Nam Phuong Hotel*, it's east of Hoan Kiem Lake near the Red River. Their motto is 'More than a hotel, it's a home!' Well-appointed rooms cost US$10 to US$20. You can enter the hotel on Pho Tran Quang Khai or Pho Tong Dan; upper floor rooms on the Pho Tong Dan side overlook the American ambassador's residence.

The six-room ***Dream 2 Hotel*** *(☎ 828 7045, fax 828 7472, 3B Pho Tong Duy Tan)* is a standard mini-hotel, but it's clean and on a quiet street between the Old Quarter and Ho Chi Minh's Mausoleum. Air-con doubles cost US$13, or US$15 with a balcony.

Lotus Guesthouse *(☎ 934 4197, fax 826 8642, lotus-travel@hn.vnn.vn, 42V Pho Ly Thuong Kiet)* is friendly, quiet and clean with a cosy in-house cafe. Dorm beds cost US$4, rooms cost US$6 to US$15.

Opposite the Hanoi train station, ***Hotel 30/4*** *(☎ 826 0807, fax 822 1818, 115 Pho Tran Hung Dao)* is named after 30 April 1975, the date when the North Vietnamese entered Saigon. Not surprisingly, it's state-owned. Large echo-chamber rooms cost US$7 to US$10, or US$15 with private bath. The in-house Green Tomato Restaurant is worth a try.

A few steps away from the 30/4 is the huge old ***Thu Do Hotel*** *(☎ 825 2288, fax 826 1121, 109 Pho Tran Hung Dao)*, where singles/doubles with attached bath cost just US$7/14.

Near the train station, the aging ***Mango Hotel*** *(☎ 824 3704, fax 824 3966, 118 Pho Le Duan)* has spacious grounds. Its restaurant has a reputation as a good place for Vietnamese wedding banquets. Singles/doubles cost US$10/12.

Another worth considering is the ***Trang Tien Hotel*** *(☎ 825 6115, fax 825 1416, 35 Pho Trang Tien)*. Doubles cost US$15 to US$25 – which is decent value considering the location.

Places to Stay – Mid-Range

Old Quarter A short stroll north-west from Hoan Kiem Lake, the ***Hong Ngoc Hotel 1*** *(☎ 828 5053, fax 828 5054, 34 Pho Hang Manh)* is pleasant and the friendly staff aim to please. Double rooms are spacious, decorated with reproduction Chinese antiques, and cost US$20 to US$35. Similar standards are found at the nearby ***Hong Ngoc Hotel 3*** *(☎ 826 7566, fax 824 5362, 14 Pho Luong Van Can)* rates range from US$15 to US$$30.

The attractive ***Classic Street Hotel*** *(☎ 825 2421, fax 934 5920, 41 Pho Hang Be)* is a new Old Quarter hotel with a stylish milieu of old Hanoi. All rooms have air-con and satellite TV. Standard rooms are US$18, or US$25/35 for deluxe rooms (including breakfast).

Salute Hotel *(☎ 825 8003, fax 934 3607, 7 Pho Hang Dau)* is another classy joint with a sleek marble facade, an elevator, and friendly staff. Rooms cost US$16 to US$40.

Lucky Hotel *(☎ 825 1029, fax 825 1731,* e *luckyhotel@hn.vnn.vn, 12 Pho Hang Trong)* offers clean air-con doubles for US$20 and US$30, and spacious suites for US$45 (including breakfast). The hotel has a lift, and rooms feature satellite TV with movie channels. There is a similar set up just down the street at the ***Huyen Trang Hotel*** *(☎ 826 8480, fax 824 7449,* e *huyetrang@fpt.vn, 36 Pho Hang Trong)*, where rooms are done up with Chinese-style furnishings.

The smaller ***Tu Do Hotel*** *(☎ 826 7119, fax 824 3918, freedomhotel@hn.vnn.vn, 45 Pho Hang Trong)* – known in English as the *Freedom Hotel* – has 12 decent rooms with air-con and satellite TV. Singles/doubles cost US$15/US$20 to US$30.

Trang An Hotel *(☎ 826 8982, fax 825 8511, 58 Pho Hang Gai)* is a friendly mini-hotel near the north-west corner of Hoan Kiem Lake. It's located on 'silk street,' and even has a boutique in the lobby. Rates range from US$15 to US$25.

Chains First Eden Hotel *(☎ 828 3896, fax 828 4066,* e *cfeden@hn.vnn.vn, 3A*

Pho Phan Dinh Phung) is near the Old Quarter, west of the Long Bien Bridge. This large business hotel has a health club, business centre, sauna, satellite TV, and Chinese-Vietnamese restaurant. Double rooms cost from US$35 to US$89.

Very close by is the popular ***Galaxy Hotel*** *(☎ 828 2888, fax 828 2466, ⓔ galaxyhtl@netnam.org.vn, 1 Pho Phan Dinh Phung)*, a clean and well-appointed lodging choice with a business centre, an attractive cafe-restaurant and satellite TV in all rooms. Singles/doubles cost US$40/45.

The ***Thuy Nga Hotel*** *(☎ 934 1256, fax 934 1262, thuyngahotel@hn.vnn.vn, 4 Pho Ba Trieu)* is a good mini-hotel near the south-west corner of Hoan Kiem Lake, but it's pricey for the standard. Rooms rent for US$40 to US$70.

Viet Anh Hotel *(☎ 846 8525, fax 824 3198, 22 Pho Cua Dong)* is an attractive new mini-hotel north-west of the Old Quarter. Rooms in back cost US$20, but are dark and windowless; front rooms with balconies are a much better deal at US$22.

The friendly ***Win Hotel*** *(☎ 826 7150, fax 824 7448, 34 Pho Hang Hanh)* is set amid a slew of local cafes on 'coffee street' and has spiffy rooms for US$20 to US$30.

Central Hanoi Area The new ***Thien Thai Hotel*** *(☎ 823 7126, fax 823 6917, 45 Pho Ngyuen Truong To)*, or the *Paradise Hotel*, is a spiffy-looking place with a colonial motif. All rooms have balconies, and cost from US$20, including breakfast – good value. If it's full, consider the nearby ***Anh Hotel II*** *(☎ 843 5141, fax 843 0618, 43 Pho Nguyen Truong To)*, a smaller place with singles/doubles starting from US$20/30.

Hang Nga Hotel *(☎ 843 7777, fax 843 7779, 65 Pho Cua Bac)*, north-west of the Old Quarter, rents ship-shape rooms from US$25 to US$70. Rooms on the top floor have a view of West Lake; there's an elevator to reach them.

Army Hotel *(Khach San Quan Doi, ☎ 825 2896, fax 825 9276, 33C Pho Pham Ngu Lao)* is indeed owned by the army but looks nothing like a barracks. It's a popular place for tour groups and has its own gym and salt-water swimming pool. Rates range from US$35 to US$50.

Madison Hotel *(☎ 822 8164, fax 822 5533, 16 Pho Bui Thi Xuan)* is just east of Thien Quang Lake. The management advertises this as Hanoi's first 'boutique hotel' – a flaky description, but it's still quite nice. Rooms are US$30 to US$45, including breakfast.

A short walk from Lenin Park, the ***Green Park Hotel*** *(☎ 822 7725, fax 822 5977, greenpark@hn.vnn.vn, 48 Pho Tan Nhan Tong)* is, well, big and green. If you can handle the colour scheme, it's not a bad place to stay. Rooms cost US$40 to US$75, but a 30% discount is typically offered. There are good views from the top-floor restaurant.

Dan Chu Hotel *(☎ 825 4937, fax 826 6786, ⓔ danchu@hn.vnn.vn, 29 Pho Trang Tien)*, once called the *Hanoi Hotel*, was built in the late 19th century. Room rates have risen considerably since then; rooms cost US$35 to US$75 (breakfast included). The Dan Chu also runs an attractive ***villa*** a few hundred metres away at 4 Pho Pham Su Manh.

Greater Hanoi Area Just to the west of Ho Chi Minh's Mausoleum is the ***Heritage Hotel*** *(☎ 834 4727, fax 834 3882, 80 Pho Giang Vo)*. This very business-oriented Singapore joint-venture hotel has doubles from US$90 to US$130.

The old ***Thang Loi Hotel*** *(☎ 829 4211, fax 829 3800)* is nicknamed the *Cuban Hotel* because it was built, in the mid-1970s, with Cuban assistance. The floor plan of each level is said to have been copied from a one-storey Cuban building, which explains the doors that lead nowhere. Around the main building are bungalows. The hotel is built on pylons over Ho Tay, and is surrounded by attractive landscaping and a swimming pool. The hotel also boasts tennis courts, a sauna and a massage service. Excepting the massage, all this cushy comfort will cost you from around US$40. The hotel is on Duong Yen Phu, 3.5km from the city centre.

The ***Ho Tay Villas*** *(Khuy Biet Thu Ho Tay, ☎ 0804 7772, fax 823 2126)* is now a tourist hotel, but unfortunately the facilities and service have taken a nose dive lately. It was previously the Communist Party Guesthouse. The spacious villas, set on Ho Tay, were once the exclusive preserve of top party officials; but now visitors bearing US dollars are welcome to avail themselves of the facilities. Even if you don't stay, it's instructive to visit to see how the 'people's representatives' lived in one of Asia's poorest countries. The hotel is 5.5km north of central Hanoi. Rooms are range from US$30 to US$120.

Places to Stay – Top End

Old Quarter The ***Royal Hotel*** *(☎ 824 4233, fax 824 4234, 20 Pho Hang Tre)*, north-east of Hoan Kiem Lake is proud of its luxury business facilities. Rooms cost US$50 to US$90 inclusive of breakfast. It's on the pricey side for the standard, but hotel guests have free entry to the popular in-house nightclub, Monaco Club.

Central Hanoi Area The ***De Syloia Hotel*** *(☎ 824 5346, fax 824 1083, 17A Pho Tran Hung Dao)* is an elegant boutique hotel with a French theme. Rooms here cost US$50 to US$70. There is a fitness centre and sauna here, and the in-house Vietnamese restaurant, Cay Cau, is recommended.

The stately ***Guoman Hotel*** *(☎ 822 2800, fax 822 2822, guomanhn@hn.vnn.vn, 83A Pho Ly Thuong Kiet)* maintains an international four-star standard. It's located about 1km south-west of Hoan Kiem Lake. Facilities include a sleek health club, 24-hour cafe and two fine bars. Rates range from US$52 to US$80.

The giant ***Sofitel Metropole Hotel*** *(☎ 826 6919, fax 826 6920, 15 Pho Ngo Quyen)* is one of Vietnam's great luxury hotels. This place has a French motif that just won't quit – close the curtains and you'll think you're in Paris. Facilities include a swimming pool, fitness centre, sauna and beauty parlour, but (blessedly) no karaoke. Doubles cost US$120 to US$500.

Hanoi Opera Hilton *(☎ 933 0500, fax 933 0530, 1 Le Thanh Tong)* commands a prime location beside Hanoi's grand Opera House. It looks dazzling from the outside, and is everything you'd expect from a Hilton in terms of facilities, service and food, but the colour-scheme on the interior is nauseating. Just say 'no' to lime green. Rates are in the US$100 to US$200 range.

Melia Hotel *(☎ 934 3343, 934 3344, 44B Pho Ly Thuong Kiet)* is the opposite of the Hilton. It is the ugliest new sky-scraper in Hanoi – looks like a candy cane – but thankfully, once you are inside the place it is blissfully tasteful. Rates are US$88 to US$138.

The ***Meritus Westlake*** *(☎ 823 8888, fax 829 388, 1 Đ Thanh Nien)* is a gigantic Singaporean joint venture boasting every possible amenity, including South-East Asia's first all-weather swimming pool (it has a retractable roof). Rates range from US$200 to US$1000 for the Presidential Suite.

Greater Hanoi Area The snazzy ***Hanoi Horison Hotel*** *(☎ 733 0808, fax 733 0688, 40 Pho Cat Linh)* features a tasteful towering brick smokestack in front, preserved from an old brick factory which once stood on the site. Rooms cost US$95 to US$200. It also has an excellent health club and swimming pool.

Fortuna Hotel Hanoi *(☎ 831 3333, fax 831 3300, 6B Pho Lang Ha)* is a big, snazzy Singaporean joint venture with an in-house bowling alley! Rates are US$50 to US$90.

Daewoo Hotel *(☎ 831 5000, fax 831 5010)* in the Daeha Centre (west Hanoi) is the city's largest and most expensive hotel. The style at this South Korean joint venture is most definitely *not* French colonial. The hotel is a 15-storey behemoth and offers everything you could want in life, including a swimming pool, nightclub, health club, business centre and three restaurants. Budget rooms are US$199, and suites go for up to a cool US$1500.

Places To Stay – Rental

As elsewhere in Vietnam, the budget end of the market is served by mini-hotels. Look around for the best deal and don't be afraid to negotiate.

There are around 5000 expats living in Hanoi (about three times that many live in

DIY catering at Hanoi's food stores.

Street food – fresh, hot, spicy

A cyclo rider uses a second set of handles to pull his load through the market.

Small scale entrepreneur

Hanoi's famous water puppets

MANFRED GOTTSCHALK

Landmark – St Joseph Cathedral

JOHN ELK III

Detail from prayer hall, Temple of Literature

RICHARD I'ANSON

Information overload – Hanoi's street signs.

JOHN ELK III

A moment of repose by Hoan Kiem Lake.

MASON FLORENCE

Tran Quoc Pagoda

Ho Chi Minh City). Well-heeled foreigners with big budgets typically live in fancy apartments which command high rents. A typical luxury two-bedroom flat leases for US$800 to US$3000 per month. Those of us who are more budget constrained can find a good private air-con room in a local guest-house or mini-hotel for around US$200 to US$300 a month.

The ***Somerset Grand Hanoi*** *(☎ 934 2342, fax 822 1968, 49 Pho Hai Ba Trung)* is a modern sky-scraper built on the site of the former Hoa Lu POW prison (see Old Quarter map). One-, two- and three-bedroom flats go for between US$85 and US$135 per night – decent value if you consider guests have easy access to a swimming pool, health club and sauna, and the Red Onion, one of Hanoi's best restaurants. Their Web site is www.somerset.com.

PLACES TO EAT

In recent years Hanoi has undergone a miraculous transformation from a culinary wasteland to a premier world city for eating and drinking. The city boasts everything from cheap backpacker joints (yes, *more* banana pancakes) to exquisite Vietnamese restaurants and a growing legion of chic cafes.

You can combine food for the body with food for the soul at Hoa Sua restaurant and Koto (later in this section) – both are recommended for their excellent food and vocational training programs for street kids.

Restaurants, bars and cafes have a strong tendency to change names, location, management, etc, so keep an eye out in *The Guide* and *Time Out* for current listings.

Travellers Cafes

The budget end of the food business is dominated by cafes preparing a variety of Vietnamese and western dishes. Aside from the food, these are good places to look for cheap rooms, surf the Internet, meet other travellers and arrange tours. You can find the usual backpacker cuisine (banana pancakes, milkshakes, cakes and coffee), as well as Vietnamese favourites like spring rolls. Rather than listing them all here again, check out the budget Travel Agents section earlier in this chapter; any of the ones on the list will do.

Just off the west shore of Hoan Kiem Lake is the friendly ***Kangaroo Cafe*** *(☎ 828 9931, e kangaroo@hn.vnn.vn, 18 Pho Bao Khanh)*, run by zany Australian expats, Max & Aaron. 'Mad Max' bears an uncanny resemblance to American movie-star Tom Selleck, helping him to land a variety of roles in locally produced films and serial dramas. The cafe is the shop front for Griswalds Vietnamese Vacations, an Aussie-based tour company that specialises in small group boutique tours to Vietnam, making it a good place to look for travel advice. They serve excellent Western food (and mugs of good coffee) at Vietnamese prices.

Also in the Old Quarter, the ***Tin Tin Bar & Cafe*** *(☎ 826 0326, 14 Pho Hang Non)* makes good pizza, crepes, fried rice, burgers and so on.

To the north end of Hoan Kiem Lake, the ***Smiling Cafe*** *(☎ 825 1532, 100 Pho Cau Go)* has a great 2nd-floor balcony to relax and study the Hanoi traffic from.

Vietnamese

Old Quarter *Little Hanoi* (1) *(☎ 926 0168, 25 Pho Ta Hien)* is a cosy eatery worth seeking out. It's cheap, friendly, and popular with backpackers. A few minutes walk away, near the north-west corner of Hoan Kiem Lake, there is an unrelated place called ***Little Hanoi*** (2) *(☎ 928 5333, 21 Pho Hang Gai)*. This one is more of an open-air cafe, serving a mix of Vietnamese food and deli sandwiches.

Hanoi Garden *(☎ 824 3402, 36 Pho Hang Manh)* a fine choice for lunch or dinner, serves southern Vietnamese-meals at reasonable prices (set menus for about US$4) and has indoor and outdoor courtyard seating.

A slightly lower-budget place for good Vietnamese food is the ***Dinh Lang Restaurant*** *(☎ 828 6290)*. It offers great views over Hoan Kiem Lake, and also hosts traditional music nightly. It's right above the bustling ***Thuy Ta Cafe*** *(☎ 828 8148, 1 Pho Le Thai To)*.

One of Hanoi's most famous food specialities is *cha ca*, perhaps best thought of as sumptuous little fish hamburgers.

The best known cha ca restaurant in town is ***Cha Ca La Vong*** *(☎ 825 3929, 14 Pho Cha Ca)*, though some say it's over-rated, and over-priced. Other worthy (and cheaper) places to try this local delicacy include ***Cha Ca 66*** *(☎ 826 7881, 66 Pho Hang Ga)* and ***Thang Long*** *(☎ 824 5115, 40 Pho Hang Ma)*.

On Pho Cha Ca, ***Tuyet Nhung*** *(☎ 828 1164)* is a good place to sample *banh cuon*, which it defines as 'rolled rice paper with grilled meat and belostomatid sauce' (just imagine a tasty dumpling with a fried onion garnish). The cost is 5000d (US$0.40) a portion, or 9000d served with *cha* (pork roll). Another good place for banh cuon is ***Thanh Van*** *(14 Hang Ga)*.

For a good bowl of beef noodle soup *(pho bo)*, try ***Pho Bo Dac Biet*** *(2B Pho Ly Quoc Su)*.

Central Hanoi Area ***Soho*** *(☎ 826 6555, 57 Pho Ba Trieu)* is a stylish but casual Vietnamese restaurant located about 1km south of Hoan Kiem Lake. You might try their signature dish, Franco-Vietnamese bouillabaisse, or check the daily specials board. You can sit indoors or outside on the pleasant veranda.

Tiem Pho *(48–50 Pho Hué)* serves up great chicken noodle soup *(pho ga)*, and keeps late hours.

Vietnamese – Gourmet

Central Area ***Brothers Cafe*** *(☎ 733 3866, 26 Pho Nguyen Thai Hoc)* is a remarkable eatery set in the rear courtyard of an elegantly restored, 250-year-old Buddhist temple. The nightly dinner buffet (US$10 per person, including one drink) is very reasonable; their US$5 lunch special is a bargain. The 'one with nature' atmosphere created by the owner Khai (founder of the trendy boutique Khai Silk) is simply serene.

Emperor *(☎ 826 8801, 18B Pho Le Thanh Tong)* is another indoor-outdoor restaurant with a stunning traditional atmosphere and cosy Chinese-style furniture. They serve great Vietnamese cuisine, and there's also a stylish bar with a pool table. Fine French food is available in the attached villa at the front.

Club Opera *(☎ 824 6950, 59 Pho Ly Thai To)*, just across from the Sofitel Metropole Hotel, serves delicious Vietnamese fare in a cosy European atmosphere. The restaurant features an ever-changing menu of delicious seasonal dishes, and presents live traditional music on Friday, Saturday and Sunday from 7.30 to 9.30 pm.

Seasons of Hanoi (☎ 843 5444, 95B Pho Quan Thanh) is yet another excellent choice for *haute* Vietnamese cuisine. It is housed in a classic French villa and tastefully decorated with an eclectic collection of Vietnamese and colonial-era antiques.

Nam Phuong *(☎ 824 0926, 19 Pho Phan Chu Trinh)* is an elegant setting for authentic Vietnamese cuisine, and like Seasons, above, occupies a charming villa. Nam Phuong also features live traditional music, as well as an impressive wine list.

Also housed in a restored villa is ***Indochine*** *(☎ 824 6097, 16 Pho Nam Ngu)*, where authentic Vietnamese food is served by waiting staff in traditional dress. Lunch is from 11 am; dinner from 5.30 pm.

Com Duc Vien *(☎ 943 0081, 13 Pho Ngo Thi Nham)* is a classic villa in which to sample fine Vietnamese food.

Vegetarian

The ***Tamarind Cafe & Fruit Juice Bar*** *(☎ 926 0580, 80 Pho Ma May)* is a newly-opened cafe-restaurant in the heart of the Old Quarter. It serves Asian-style vegetarian dishes and fresh fruit smoothies (drink in or take-away). You'll find it at the same address as Handspan Adventure Travel.

In the central area, about 1km south-west of Hoan Kiem Lake, the smoke-free ***Com Chay Nang Tam*** *(☎ 826 6140, 79A Pho Tran Hung Dao)* is a Hanoi institution. It is famed for delicious vegetarian creations that are named for, and look remarkably like, meat dishes – something which some vegetarians might find confronting, but it's an ancient Vietnamese tradition to make guests feel at home. Try the superb 'fried snow balls'.

International

The ***Red Onion Bistro*** *(☎ 934 2342, 49 Pho Hai Ba Trung)* is one of Hanoi's true gems. Bobbie Chinn, the talented, California-reared chef, keeps customers coming back with creative Asian 'fusion cooking'. Recommended are his authentic Thai curries, superb salads and *anything* on the menu with salmon. Save room for dessert – the warm chocolate pudding is tantalising. Red Onion is on the fourth floor of the Somerset Grand Hanoi building.

Old Quarter The ***Cyclo Bar & Restaurant*** *(☎ 828 6844, 38 Pho Duong Thanh)* is worthy of a plug for creative design alone. They serve up respectable Vietnamese and French food to customers seated in actual cyclos (cleverly transformed into tables). Their US$4 set lunch is good value.

Pepperonis Pizza & Cafe *(☎ 928 5246, 29 Pho Ly Quoc Su)* has pizzas for just US$1.25 to US$4 and pasta dishes for US$1.60. Another casual spot for pizzas and pasta is ***Mama Rosa*** *(☎ 825 8057, 6 Pho Le Thai To)*, just across from the lakeside Thuy Ta Cafe. Both these pizza joints can deliver.

Green Ho Guom *(☎ 828 8806, 32 Pho Le Thai To)* is a spacious and funky place with live music and noisy karaoke. It serves Vietnamese and Western dishes at reasonable prices.

Central Area Highly recommended for lunch (and well worth supporting) is the open-air ***Hoa Sua*** *(☎ 824 0448, 81 Pho Tho Nhuom)*, a successful goodwill project which takes in and trains a steady stream of needy street children (with few other educational opportunities) for culinary careers – they have turned out hundreds of professional chefs. There is excellent French and Vietnamese food, and the pastries from the bakery here are superb.

Al Fresco's *(☎ 826 7782, 23L Pho Hai Ba Trung)* is a delightful Aussie-run eatery dishing up fantastic pizzas, Tex-Mex, juicy ribs and salads. Prices are reasonable and the portions are gigantic. Come hungry. Or work up an appetite.

Sea Food

Old Quarter *La Brique (☎ 928 5638, 6 Pho Nha Tho)* is a pleasant spot along the trendy strip by St Joseph's Cathedral. It was opened by Ali, a French-Algerian writer, who presents a simple but excellent selection of local seafood specialties. The fish wrapped in banana leaf is divine. The exposed brick walls of this one-time wholesale fish market give the place its name.

San Ho Restaurant *(☎ 822 2184, 58 Pho Ly Thuong Kiet)* is set in an attractive villa and is known as one of the best seafood restaurants in Hanoi.

Central Area If you can ignore the pitiful sight of the caged bears on display, the food at the ***Sam Son Seafood Market*** *(☎ 825 0780, 77 Pho Doc Bac)*, a giant fish market-cum-restaurant on the banks of the Red River is delicious.

The ***Shrimp Cakes Restaurant*** *(Nha Hang Banh Tom Hotay; ☎ 825 7839, 1 Đ Thanh Nien)* specialises in, surprise, shrimp cakes. It is located on the shores of Truc Bach Lake, and though the food has been good in the past, reviews of late are mixed. There have also been complaints about inflated prices for foreigners.

Italian

Old Quarter There are loads of Italian restaurants in Hanoi to choose from. The following are the most authentic and are run by bona fide Italianos.

La Dolce Vita *(☎ 828 6411, 10 Pho Bat Dan)* – also known as *Bat Dan Cafe* – is right in the heart of the Old Quarter. Photographer/chef Gino makes excellent pastas and salads at reasonable prices and offers a wide selection of board games.

Il Padrino *(☎ 828 8449, 42 Pho Le Thai To)* is a stylish little ristorante just across from Hoan Kiem Lake. 'The Godfather' does killer pizzas and caffeine addicts will welcome their *real* Italian coffee.

For more good pastas and some of the best pizza this side of Bangkok, try ***Mediterraneo Restaurant*** *(☎ 826 6288, 23 Pho Nha Tho)* near St Joseph's Cathedral.

Central Area The latest arrival on Hanoi's burgeoning ristorante scene is the cosy, indoor-outdoor ***Luna d'Autunno*** *(☎ 823 7338, 11B Dien Bien Phu)*, or the *Autumn Moon*. The artsy decor is enticing, and dishes are eclectic Italian. Live Jazz is performed on Friday nights, followed by classical piano music Saturdays.

Il Grillo *(☎ 822 7720, 116 Pho Ba Trieu)* is an excellent upmarket option done up in a classic Italian tavern motif. The congenial proprietors serve savoury dishes and offer up the best selection of Italian wines in Vietnam.

French

In the Old Quarter, try ***Le Cafe des Arts*** *(☎ 828 7207, 11B Pho Bao Khanh)*, a casual French/Vietnamese-run place modelled on a Parisian brasserie. It serves up good 'anytime food' and hosts a rotating series of art exhibitions and cultural events.

In the central area, Hanoi's best upmarket French restaurant is ***Le Beaulieu Restaurant*** *(☎ 826 6919 ext 8028, 15 Pho Ngo Quyen)*, in the elegant Sofitel Metropole Hotel. It offers savoury, authentic French cooking and a romantic atmosphere. Another option for fine French fare in Central Hanoi is ***Le Splendide*** *(☎ 826 6087, 44 Pho Ngo Quyen)*, in the Hoa Binh Hotel.

Another snazzy choice is the ***President Garden Restaurant*** *(☎ 825 3606, 14 Pho Tong Dan)*.

Asian

Good Chinese food in Hanoi tends to be pricey, and the best stuff is usually at upmarket hotels like Nikko, Melia and Hanoi Hotel.

Old Quarter There is excellent Thai food at ***Baan Thai Restaurant*** *(☎ 828 1120, 3B Pho Cha Ca)* which has a handy photo-illustrated menu.

For good North Indian food in a pleasant atmosphere, look for ***Khazana*** *(☎ 824 1166, 41B Pho Ly Thai To)*. ***Tandoor*** *(☎ 824 5359, 24 Pho Hang Be)* makes up for a lack of atmosphere with its food. Both of these places are run by Indian expats, and serve reasonably priced lunch specials.

Despite the cheesy name, ***Saigon Sakura*** *(☎ 825 7565, 17 Pho Trang Thi)* dishes up good Japanese fare.

Central Area Hanoi's resident Japanese agree that Nikko Hotel's ***Benkay Restaurant*** can't be beat. A less expensive, but excellent option is ***Ky Y*** *(☎ 978 1386, 29 Pho Phu Dong Thien Vuong)* which serves fresh sushi and sashimi for lunch and dinner from Monday to Saturday.

Another possibility is ***Momiji*** *(☎ 821 6033, 322 Pho Ba Trieu)*. The Vietnamese owner here spent some years living in Japan.

For authentic Malaysian food, look no further than ***Mother's Pride*** *(☎ 825 6334, 14-16 Pho Ba Trieu)* – also known as *Thu Thuy Asian Food*.

For delicious Thai food, try ***Tam Tu*** *(☎ 825 1682, 84 Pho Ly Thuong Kiet)*.

Speciality Food Streets

If you would like to combine eating with exploration, the following food streets can be found on the Central Hanoi map.

Cam Chi Cam Chi is about 500m north-east of Hanoi train station. It's a very small street – basically an alley – crammed full of lively ***street stalls*** serving budget-priced, delicious food. Forget about English menus and don't expect comfortable seating. Still, where else can you have a small banquet for US$2? The derivation of 'Cam Chi' (meaning forbidden to point), dates from centuries ago. It is said that the street was named as a reminder for local residents to keep their curious fingers in their pockets when the King and his entourage made their way through this neighbourhood.

Pho Mai Hac De This food street, located in the south-central area, has several blocks of ***restaurants*** running south from the northern terminus at Pho Tran Nhan Tong.

Đ Thuy Khue On the south bank of Ho Tay, Đ Thuy Khue features a strip of 30 odd ***outdoor seafood restaurants*** with pleasant lakeside seating. These places are highly popular with locals, and the level of competition is evident by the daredevil touts who literally throw themselves in front of oncoming traffic to steer people to their tables. You can eat well here for about US$6 per person.

Pho To Hien Thanh This street runs in an east-west direction, and also specialises in small ***seafood restaurants***. It's south of the city centre, just east of Bay Mau Lake.

Pho Nghi Tam Approximately 10km north of central Hanoi, Pho Nghi Tam has a 1km stretch with about 60 ***dog-meat restaurants*** (see Greater Hanoi map). The street runs along the embankment between Ho Tay (West Lake) and Song Hong (Red River). Even if you have no interest in eating dog meat, it's interesting to cruise this stretch of road on the last evening of the lunar month. Hanoians believe that eating dog meat in the first half of the lunar month brings bad luck – consequently, these restaurants are deserted at that time and most shut down. Business picks up in the second half of the lunar month and the last day is particularly auspicious – the restaurants are packed. Cruise by in the evening and you'll see thousands of motorbikes parked here. As you drive along, hawkers practically leap out in front of you to extol the virtues of their particular canine specialties.

Delicatessens & Self-Catering

Old Quarter ***Trung Tam Thuong Mai*** *(7 Pho Dinh Tien Hoang)* is a supermarket well-stocked with imported Western junk food and drinks. You can enter by the lake or in back.

Central Area ***Koto*** *(☎ 747 0338, ⓔ koto hanoi@hn.vnn.vn, 61 Pho Van Mieu)* is a praiseworthy grassroots effort providing career training and guidance to former street children. Founded by Jimmy Pham, a warm-hearted Vietnamese-Australian, Koto stands for 'Know One, Teach One'. They make delicious sandwiches, real coffees, fruit shakes and other healthy dishes in a classic Chinese-style atmosphere. Koto is open for breakfast (good buffets), lunch and dinner, and is located just around the corner from the Temple of Literature (well worth stopping in to eat before or after you tour the site).

The Deli (1) *(☎ 846 0007, 18 Pho Tran Huy Lieu)*, out of town near Giang Vo Lake, and ***The Deli*** (2) *(☎ 934 2335, 13B Pho Ha Ba Trung)* whip up tasty sandwiches for about US$1.20. Independent of these two, there is a third place calling itself ***The Deli*** (3) *(☎ 934 0888, 59A Pho Ly Thai To)*, this one at The Press Club. It's a first-rate bakery-deli with both eat-in and take-out service; they knock 50% off the price of bakery goods after 6 pm.

Paris Deli *(☎ 934 5269, 2 Pho Phan Chu Trinh)* is a Parisian-style cafe-restaurant opposite the Hanoi Opera House. They serve excellent baguette sandwiches and pastries, and also deliver.

Hanoi Gormet *(☎ 943 1009, 1B Pho Ham Long)* is the most chic deli in town. It has fine imported meats and every European fix – at a price.

More determined self-caterers can buy fresh vegetables at the ***Hom Market*** just south of the city centre near the intersection of Pho Hué and Pho Tran Xuan Soan.

Hanoi Star Mart *(☎ 822 5999, 60 Pho Ngo Thi Nham)* is one of the best mini-supermarkets in town. There is a smaller branch next to the Energy Hotel at 30 Pho Ly Thai To.

Cafes

Old Quarter ***Dak Linh Cafe*** *(☎ 828 7043)* offers a prime patio-setting on the south-west shore of Hoan Kiem Lake, the ***Ciao Cafe*** *(☎ 934 1494, 2 Pho Hang Bai)* nearby attracts a local crowd.

Moca Cafe *(☎ 825 6334, 14–16 Pho Nha Tro)* is a spacious cafe-restaurant near St Joseph's Cathedral. They do espresso, cappuccinos and lattes for about US$1.50.

Popular Ho Chi Minh City cafe chain ***Trung Nguyen*** *(☎ 926 0473, 20 Pho Hang Mam)* serves real Vietnamese coffee from the Central Highlands. The second- and third-floor balconies are a good place to watch the world go by.

Central Area ***Au Lac*** *(☎ 825 7807, 57 Pho Ly Thai To)* is set in the pleasant front courtyard of a French villa opposite the Sofitel Hotel. It serves excellent light food and the coffee is among Hanoi's best. A few steps away is another lovely French-style place, ***Diva*** *(☎ 934 4088)* which is owned by a former Miss Vietnam and offers both indoor and outdoor seating.

For some of the best yoghurt, French pastries and coffee in Vietnam, visit the ***Kinh Do Cafe*** *(☎ 825 0216, 252 Pho Hang Bong)* near the city centre. Their breakfasts are outstanding.

Ice Cream Shops

The best ice cream joint in town is ***Fanny's Ice Cream*** *(☎ 828 5656, 48 Pho Le Thai To)*, just across from the Hoan Kiem lakefront in the Old Quarter. It serves great 'Franco-Vietnamese' ice cream, and if you are there in right season don't miss the *com*, a delightful local flavour extracted from young sticky rice.

The most popular ice cream with local Hanoians is at ***Kem Trang Tien*** *(54 Pho Trang Tien)*, between the Opera House and Hoan Kiem Lake. Just look for the mob on the sidewalk lined up to take away sticks of the tasty treat (US$0.30). There is also an attached indoor cafe here where you can relax in air-con comfort.

Pub Grub

In the Old Quarter try ***La Salsa*** *(☎ 828 9052, 25 Pho Nha Tho)* a French/Canadian-run tapas bar on the trendy strip by St Joseph's Cathedral. The food is excellent and it's proving to be very popular with both tourists and local expats.

In the central area, the British-run ***Verandah Bar & Cafe*** *(☎ 825 7220, 9 Pho Nguyen Khac Can)* is located in a stylish French villa. It's perhaps more cafe than bar, and they serve good Sunday brunches. The menu includes chicken enchiladas, smoked salmon and quiche. You can sit by the bar or out on the verandah.

Met Pub *(☎ 826 6919 ext 8857)* is in the new annexe of the Sofitel Metropole Hotel. It's a lovely place with fine food and Hanoi's best beer selection, but it's also very expensive.

Mekki's Bar *(☎ 826 7552)* at the Lan Anh Restaurant is a bar/restaurant run by an Algerian man and his Vietnamese wife. They serve a wide variety of French, Middle Eastern and Vietnamese dishes.

In the Greater Hanoi area, just 30m in front of the Hanoi Hotel is the ***Latino Pub*** *(☎ 846 0836, 102 C8 Pho Giang Vo)*. The menu includes Tex-Mex food and Latin American dishes. The Vietnamese owner lived abroad for a while and speaks fluent Spanish.

ENTERTAINMENT

Pubs

Old Quarter ***Bar Le Maquis*** *(☎ 828 2598, 2A Pho Ta Hien)* is a cosy little speakeasy tucked away in the Old Quarter. It's run by a French-Vietnamese motorcycle guide named Fredo-Binh, and attracts an well-rounded mix of expats, travellers and motorbiking afficionados. Le Maquis is one of the few places you'll find in the Old Quarter that stays open after 11 pm.

Highway #4 *(5 Pho Hang Tre)*, is a popular gathering point for members of Hanoi's notorious Minsk Club. This is the place to discover the mystical, medicinal, healing (and intoxicating) qualities of *ruou*, Vietnamese rice wine - consider sampling the fragrant, fruit-flavoured varieties. The bar boasts a rugged mountain decor and is an excellent place to find information on motorbiking Vietnam. Highway #4 is north-east of Hoan Kiem Lake, near the junction of Pho Hang Mam, on the east side of Pho Hang Tre.

The Modern Toast *(☎ 828 3305 46 Pho Hang Vai)* is another recommended Old Quarter pub, and one of the only places in Vietnam where you are likely to hear Tom Waits on the stereo. It's a stylish little place run by an Irishman named Kevin, which could explain why the beer prices are so low.

The unforgettably named ***Golden Cock*** *(☎ 825 0499, 5 Pho Bao Khanh)* is an open-minded expat favourite. Next door to the 'GC' is the popular ***Polite Pub*** *(☎ 825*

0959), which is known to keep late hours. Pho Bao Khanh is near the north-west corner of Hoan Kiem Lake.

The ***R&R Tavern*** *(☎ 971 0498, 47 Pho Lo Su)* is run by a mellow American called Jay (with his Vietnamese wife), who can regale you with friendly conversation and South-East Asia's best selection of Grateful Dead classics. They also serve up home-cooked meals and if you're stumbling home in the wee hours, or just an early riser, try the *real* buttermilk pancakes for breakfast.

Central Area The ***Camellia Cafe & Bar*** *(☎ 933 1233, 5 Pho Hai Ba Trung)*, a block south of the Hanoi Opera House, is the city's after, after hours hangout. Run by a young Japanese hipster called Kazu, the Camellia attracts a broad swathe of Hanoi's emerging trendies from necktied expats to Vietnamese go-go girls and grunge heads; after 4 am the cast of characters is straight out of the Rocky Horror Picture Show. It never closes.

The legendary ***Apocalypse Now*** *(☎ 971 2783, 5C Pho Hoa Ma)* – same family as the one in Ho Chi Minh City – is best on weekends and is known for loud and raucous music. Apocalypse opens at 5 pm and closes when the last customers trickle away.

The ***Spotted Cow*** *(☎ 824 1028, 23C Pho Hai Ba Trung)* is a very popular Aussie-run pub featuring intellectually-stimulating leisure activities such as darts and frog-racing.

Cafe Que Huong *(☎ 971 1444, 42 Pho Tang Bat Ho)* offering stylish villa surroundings and three fine pool tables, sees a good mix of foreigners and Vietnamese.

Live Jazz

Jazz Club by Quyen Van Minh *(Cau Lac Bo, ☎ 825 7655, 31–33 Pho Luong Van Can)* is *the* place in Hanoi to catch hot live jazz (well, mostly jazz). Bar owner Minh teaches saxophone at the Hanoi Conservatory and moonlights here, jamming with a variety of musicians from his students and his talented son to top-notch international jazz players. Bands perform nightly from 8.30 to 11.30 pm. The club is located near the north-west corner of Hoan Kiem Lake (see Old Quarter map).

Traditional Music

In the Old Quarter, the new ***Hanoi Spirit Club*** *(☎ 826 7356, 50 Pho Hang Be)* – part of the Queen 2 budget travellers' hostel – stages free traditional music nightly.

Some of the best places to catch live traditional music are upmarket Vietnamese restaurants in the central area, like ***Club Opera***, ***Nam Phuong***, ***Indochine*** or ***Cay Cau*** (in the De Syloia Hotel).

There is also live music performed daily at the ***Temple of Literature***.

Nightclubs

If you want to see how fashionable Vietnamese yuppies 'do the hustle', there are several local discos to check out. These places have a strong tendency to change with the wind, so ask around for what's hot or not during your visit. Most clubs have a cover charge of around US$4.

In the Old Quarter, ***New Century Nightclub*** *(☎ 928 5285, 10 Pho Trang Thi)* is all the rage. This place is right out of New York, London or Paris.

Club Monaco is another popular spot with local Hanoians. It's in the Royal Hotel, close to the Chuong Duong Bridge.

The spacious, ***Magic Nightclub*** *(☎ 563 0257, 3 Pho Thai Thinh)* is far from the city centre, but a cool dance place entered via a boardwalk of arcade games. Being Japanese-run, it has Karaoke rooms. (See Greater Hanoi map).

Cinemas

The ***National Movie Centre*** *(☎ 514 1114, 87 Pho Lang Ha)* is the newest and best venue to catch foreign films in Hanoi (see Greater Hanoi map).

In central Hanoi, ***Fanslands Cinema*** *(☎ 825 7484, 84 Pho Ly Thuong Kiet)* also offers Western movies, while French speakers might check out the ***Alliance Française de Hanoi*** *(☎ 826 6970, 42 Pho Yet Kieu)*.

Thang 8 Cinema *(Pho Hang Bai)*, opposite the Immigration Police Office, also shows foreign films.

Punch & Judy in a Pool

The ancient art of water puppetry *(roi nuoc)* was virtually unknown outside of northern Vietnam until the 1960s. Depending on which story you believe, it originated with rice farmers who spent much of their time in flooded fields and either saw the potential of the water surface as a dynamic stage or adapted conventional puppetry during a massive flood of the Red River Delta. Whatever the true history, it is at least 1000 years old.

The farmers carved the puppets from water-resistant fig tree timber *(sung)* in forms modelled on the villagers themselves, animals from their daily lives and more fanciful mythical creatures such as the dragon, phoenix and unicorn. Performances were usually staged in ponds, lakes or flooded paddy fields.

Ancient scholarly references to water puppetry indicate that during the Ly and Tran dynasties (1010–1400) water puppetry moved from being a simple pastime of villagers to formal courtly entertainment. The art form then all but disappeared, until interest was rekindled by the opening of the Municipal Water Puppet Theatre in Hanoi.

Contemporary performances use a square tank of waist-deep water for the 'stage'; the water is murky to conceal the mechanisms that operate the puppets. The wooden puppets can be up to 50cm long and weigh as much as 15kg; they're painted with a glossy vegetable-based paint. Each lasts only about three to four months if used continually, so puppet production provides several villages outside Hanoi with a full-time industry.

Eleven puppeteers, trained for a minimum of three years, are involved in each performance. They stand in the water behind a bamboo screen and have traditionally suffered from a host of water-borne diseases – these days they wear waders to avoid this nasty occupational hazard.

Some puppets are simply attached to a long pole while others are set on a floating base which in turn is attached to a pole. Most have articulated limbs and heads, some also have rudders to help

Opera House

The magnificent 900-seat ***Hanoi Opera House*** *(☎ 825 4312)*, which faces east up Pho Trang Tien, was built in 1911, its painstaking three-year renovation was recently completed. It was from a balcony on this building that a Viet Minh-run committee of citizens announced that it had taken over the city on 16 August 1945. Periodic performances are held here in the evenings. The theatre's Vietnamese name, Nha Hat Lon, appropriately translates to 'House Sing Big'. Check the listings in *The Guide* or *Time Out* to find out if anything is happening here during your stay. (See Central Area map.)

Circus

One Russian entertainment tradition which has survived and thrived in Vietnam is the circus. Many of the performers – gymnasts, jugglers, animal trainers – at Hanoi's ***Central Circus*** (Rap Xiec Trung Uong) were originally trained in Eastern Europe, though today's new recruits learn their skills from their Vietnamese elders. The circus has nightly performances from Tuesday to Sunday from 8 to 10 pm in a huge tent near the northern entrance to Lenin Park (Cong Vien Le Nin); see the Central Area map. There is a special show staged for children on Sunday mornings at 9 am. Entry is US$2.50.

Water Puppets

This fantastic art form (see the 'Punch & Judy in a Pool' boxed text) originated in northern Vietnam, and Hanoi is the best place to see it. Just on the shore of Hoan Kiem Lake is the ***Municipal Water Puppet Theatre*** *(Roi Nuoc Thang Long, ☎ 824 9494, 57B Pho Dinh Tien Hoang)*. Performances are held daily from 8 to 9.15 pm. Admission is US$1.60, or US$3.20 for the best seats and a take-home cassette of the music. See Old Quarter map.

SHOPPING

Whether or not you wish to buy anything, your first encounter will likely be with the

Punch & Judy in a Pool

guide them. There can be as many as three poles attached to one puppet, and in the darkened auditorium it looks as if they are literally walking on water.

The considerable skills required to operate the puppets were traditionally kept secret and passed only from father to son; never to daughters through fear that they would marry outside the village and take the secrets with them.

The music, which is provided by a band, is as important as the action on stage. The band includes wooden flutes (sao), gongs (cong), cylindrical drums (trong com), bamboo xylophones and the fascinating single-stringed dan bau. The body of the dan bau is made of the hard rind of the bau, a Chinese cucumber, and produces a range of haunting notes through the use of a 'whammy bar', a flexible bamboo stem attached to one end of the soundbox which alters the tension on the string.

The performance consists of a number of vignettes depicting pastoral scenes and legends that explain the origins of various natural and social phenomena from the formation of lakes to the formation of nation states. One memorable scene is a wetly balletic depiction of rice farming in which the rice growing looks like accelerated film footage and the harvesting scenes are frantic and graceful. Another tells of the battle between a fisherman and his prey which is so realistic it appears as if a live fish is being used. There are also fire-breathing dragons (complete with fireworks), a slapstick cat-and-mouse game between a jaguar, a flock of ducks and the ducks' keeper, and a flute playing boy riding a buffalo.

The performance is unquestionably entertaining. The water puppets are both curiously amusing and graceful, and the water greatly enhances the drama by allowing the puppets to appear and disappear as if by magic. Spectators in the front row seats can expect a bit of splashing.

children who sell postcards and maps. Of course, they are found all over the country, but in Hanoi many are orphans who have a special card to prove it, which they will immediately show to foreigners. They are also the most notorious overchargers, asking about triple the going price. A reasonable amount of bargaining is called for.

Market

In the Old Quarter, the three-storey **Dong Xuan Market** is 900m north of Hoan Kiem Lake. The market burned down in 1994, killing five people (all of whom had entered the building after the fire started to either rescue goods or steal them). The market has now been re-built and is a tourist attraction in its own right. There are hundreds of stalls here, employing around 3000 people.

Hang Da Market is relatively small, but good for imported foods, wine, beer and flowers. The 2nd floor is good for fabric and ready-made clothing. The market is very close to St Joseph Cathedral.

In the central area, **Hom Market** is on the north-east corner of Pho Hué and Pho Tran Xuan Soan. It's a good general-purpose market with lots of imported food items.

Cua Nam Market is a few blocks north of the Hanoi train station. The market itself is of no great interest (except maybe for the flowers), but Đ Le Duan between the market and the train station is a treasure trove of household goods, including electronics, plasticware and the like. It's a particularly good shopping area if you're setting up a residence in Hanoi.

In the greater Hanoi region, **Mo Market** is far to the south of the central area on Pho Bac Mai and Pho Minh Khai. It's not a place for tourism, as the main products are fresh meat, fish and vegetables, but may be of interest to expats who prefer to do their own cooking.

Buoi Market out in the far north-west part of town is notable for live animals (chickens, ducks etc), but also features ornamental plants. You can probably find better quality ornamental plants for sale at the gardens in front of the Temple of Literature.

Shops

Around Pho Hang Bong and Pho Hang Gai, just north-west of Hoan Kiem Lake, are plenty of shops selling souvenir T-shirts and Viet Cong headgear. T-shirts are either printed or embroidered. It might be worth noting, however, that neither Ho Chi Minh T-shirts nor VC headgear are very popular apparel with Vietnamese refugees and certain war veterans living in the West. Wearing such souvenirs while walking down a street in Los Angeles or Melbourne might offend someone, possibly endangering your relationship with the Overseas Vietnamese community, as well as your dental work.

Pho Hang Gai and its continuation, Pho Hang Bong, are a good place to look for embroidered tablecloths, T-shirts and wall hangings. Pho Hang Gai is also a good place to have clothes custom-tailored. Take a look along Pho Hang Dao (just north of Hoa Kiem Lake) for souvenir Russian-made watches.

La Boutique and the Silk (☎ 928 5368), located near St Joseph's Cathedral at 6 Pho Nha Tho, is well worth stopping by. It's run by a Frenchman whose original designs are inspired by Vietnamese ethnic minority costumes. He also imports high quality, Lao silk.

Another place in vogue for silk clothing is Khai Silk (☎ 825 4237, ⓔ khaisilk@fpt.vn), at 96 Pho Hang Gai. The proprietor, Khai, is fluent in French and English, and the clothes are modern and Western in design. There are also Khai Silk branches in the posh Sofitel Metropole and Nikko Hotels.

If you don't make it up to Sapa, there is a wide selection of ethnic minority garb and handicrafts available in Hanoi; a stroll along Pho Hang Bac or Pho To Tich will turn up close to a dozen places.

There is an outstanding shoe market along Pho Hang Dau at the north-east corner of Hoan Kiem Lake; however, it's difficult to find large sizes for big Western feet.

For the best in bootleg CDs (usually about US$2), there are several shops along Pho Hang Bong, including Tu Lap (☎ 826 1974) at No 36A.

On Pho Trang Tien you'll find many shops willing to make dirt-cheap eyeglasses in a mere 10 minutes.

Stamp collectors should try the philatelic counter at the GPO (in the main postal services hall).

Galleries

Aspiring young artists display their works in Hanoi's private art galleries in hopes of attracting a buyer. The highest concentration of upmarket galleries is on Pho Trang Tien, between Hoan Kiem Lake and the Opera House – just stroll down the strip.

Most art galleries have some English-speaking staff, and are open daily until 8 or 9 pm. Prices range from a few dollars into the thousands, and polite bargaining is the norm. Some popular galleries include:

Apricot Gallery (☎ 828 8965)
40B Pho Hang Bong
Co Xanh Gallery (☎ 826 7116)
51 Pho Hang Gai
Dong Son Gallery (☎ 821 8876)
47 Pho Le Dai Hanh
Hanoi Studio (☎ 934 4433)
13 Pho Trang Tien
Mai Gallery (☎ 825 1225)
3B Phan Huy Chu
Nam Son Gallery (☎ 826 2993)
41 Pho Trang Tien
Salon Natasha (☎ 826 1387)
30 Pho Hang Bong
Song Hong Art Gallery (☎ 822 9064)
71A Pho Nguyen Du
Trang An Gallery (☎ 826 9480)
15 Pho Hang Buom
Van Gallery (☎ 934 6197)
25-27 Pho Trang Tien

Handicrafts & Antiques

There are quite a number of stores in Hanoi offering new and antique Vietnamese handicrafts (lacquerware, mother-of-pearl inlay, ceramics, sandalwood statuettes etc), as well as watercolours, oil paintings, prints and assorted antiques (real and fake). Pho Hang Gai, Pho To Tich, Pho Hang Khai and Pho Cau Go are good areas for souvenir hunting.

In the Old Quarter, Indochine House (☎ 824 8071) is a fashionable gallery offering an interesting mix of authentic Vietnamese antiques and reproduction furniture. It's located at 13 Pho Nha Tho, near St Joseph's Cathedral.

Furniture Gallery (☎ 826 9769) is an enormous warehouse of antiques, paintings, furniture and handicrafts. It's at 8B Pho Ta Hien (see Old Quarter map).

Not far from Furniture Gallery at 92 Hang Bac is Vietnamese House (☎ 826 2455), a small but attractive shop dealing in a hodge-podge of old and new treasures.

There is a strip of antique shops on Duong Le Duan, across from the Nikko Hotel (see Central Area map), but most tend to be over-priced.

GETTING THERE & AWAY

Air

Hanoi has fewer direct international flights than Ho Chi Minh City, but with a change of aircraft in Hong Kong or Bangkok you can get to almost anywhere. As time goes on, more and more air carriers are flying directly into Hanoi. For details on international flights, see the Getting There & Away chapter. Hanoi booking offices for international airlines follow:

Aeroflot (☎ 825 6742, fax 824 9411)
4 Pho Trang Thi
Air France (☎ 825 3484/824 7066, fax 826 6694) 1 Pho Ba Trieu
Cathay Pacific Airways (☎ 826 7298, fax 826 7709) 49 Hai Ba Trung
China Airlines (☎ 824 2688, fax 824 2588)
18 Pho Tran Hung Dao
China Southern Airlines (☎ 826 9233/826 9234)
Binh Minh Hotel, 27 Pho Ly Thai To
Czech Airlines (☎ 845 6512, fax 846 4000)
102 A2 Van Phuc Diplomatic Quarter
Japan Airlines (☎ 826 6693, fax 826 6698)
1 Pho Ba Trieu
Lao Aviation (☎ 826 6538, fax 822 9951)
41 Pho Quang Trung
Malaysia Airlines (☎ 826 8820, 826 8821, fax 824 2388) 15 Pho Ngo Quyen
Pacific Airlines (☎ 851 5356, fax 851 5350)
100 Pho Le Duan
Singapore Airlines (☎ 826 8888, fax 826 8666)
17 Pho Ngo Quyen
Thai Airways (☎ 826 6893, fax 826 7934)
44B Pho Ly Thuong Kiet
Vasco (☎ 827 1707, fax 827 2705)
Gia Lam airport
Vietnam Airlines (☎ 942 0848, fax 942 0846)
94 Pho Tran Quoc Toan

Pacific Airlines is the only company besides Vietnam Airlines to offer domestic flights. Both companies charge exactly the same fares on domestic flights, but Pacific Airlines is cheaper on its scant international routes. For details of domestic flights, see the Getting Around chapter.

Bus

Hanoi has several main bus stations and each one serves a particular area.

In the central area, Kim Ma bus station (Ben Xe Kim Ma) is opposite 166 Pho Nguyen Thai Hoc (on the corner of Pho Giang Vo). This is where you get buses to the north west part of Vietnam, including Pho Lu and Dien Bien Phu. Tickets should be purchased the day before departure.

Gia Lam bus station (Ben Xe Gia Lam) is where you catch buses to points north-east of Hanoi. This includes Halong Bay, Haiphong and Lang Son (near the China border). The bus station is 2km north-east of the centre – you have to cross the Red River to get there. Cyclos won't cross the bridge so you need to get there by motorbike or taxi.

Also in that area, Giap Bat bus station (Ben Xe Giap Bat) serves points south of Hanoi, including Ho Chi Minh City. The station is 7km south of the Hanoi train station on Đ Giai Phong.

Son La bus station (Ben Xe Son La), south-west of Hanoi at Km 8, Pho Nguyen Trai (near Hanoi University), also has buses to the north-west (Hoa Binh, Mai Chau, Son La, Tuan Giao, Dien Bien Phu and Lai Chau).

Train

The main Hanoi train station (Ga Hang Co; ☎ 825 3949) is at 120 Đ Le Duan, at the western end of Pho Tran Hung Dao; Trains from here go to destinations south. The ticket office is open from 7.30 to 11.30 am and 1.30 to 3.30 pm only and there is a special counter where foreigners can purchase tickets. It's often best to buy tickets at least one day before departure to ensure a seat or sleeper.

Where you purchase the ticket is not necessarily where the train departs. Just behind the main station on Đ Le Duan is Tran Quy

Cap station (or 'B station') on Pho Tran Qui Cap (☎ 825 2628) for northbound trains. The B station is a two-block walk from the front station entrance.

To make things even more complicated – some northbound (Viet Tri, Yen Bai, Lao Cai, Lang Son) and eastbound (Haiphong) trains depart from both Gia Lam and Long Bien (☎ 826 8280) train stations (both are across the bridge on the east side of the Red River). Some of the local southbound trains leave from the Giap Bat train station (about 7km south of Hanoi train station). Be sure to ask just where you need to go to catch your train; you can try phoning for information, but don't expect much help (even if are lucky enough to get through).

For more information on trains see the Getting There & Away chapter. For information on trains to Haiphong, see the Haiphong section in the North-East Vietnam chapter.

Minibus

Tourist-style minibuses can be booked through most hotels and cafes. Popular destinations include Halong Bay and Sapa.

There are frequent minibuses throughout the day to Haiphong from Gia Lam bus station. Services begin around 5 am and the last bus leaves Hanoi about 6 pm. These minibuses depart when full (and they really mean 'full'). They typically cost around US$3 to US$5 per person. In Haiphong, you catch the minibuses at the Tam Bac bus station.

Car & Motorbike

To hire a car with a driver, contact a hotel, travellers' cafe or travel agency. The main roads in the north-east are generally OK, but in parts of the north-west they are awful. For this reason, you may need a high clearance vehicle or a 4WD.

The average cost for a six-day trip in a Russian jeep is US$180 (including jeep, driver and petrol). You should inquire about who is responsible for the driver's room and board – some travellers don't mind picking up his meals (most hotels have a room set aside for drivers so you won't need to worry about this cost).

For a fancier Japanese or Korean 4WD you are looking at paying around double the cost of a Russian jeep, but if you can afford the comfort, why not have it? Land distances from Hanoi are as follows:

destination	distance (km)
Ba Be National Park	240
Bac Giang	51
Bac Ninh	29
Bach Thong (Bac Can)	162
Cam Pha	190
Cao Bang	272
Da Bac (Cho Bo)	104
Danang	763
Dien Bien Phu	420
Ha Dong	11
Ha Giang	343
Hai Duong	58
Haiphong	103
Halong City	165
Hoa Binh	74
Ho Chi Minh City	1710
Hué	658
Lai Chau	490
Lang Son	146
Lao Cai	294
Ninh Binh	93
Sapa	324
Son La	308
Tam Dao	85
Thai Binh	109
Thai Nguyen	73
Thanh Hoa	175
Tuyen Quang	165
Viet Tri	73
Vinh	319
Yen Bai	155

A long-distance journey from Hanoi into the mountainous hinterland of the north is exciting, though slightly risky in terms of traffic accidents and definitely tiring. You probably wouldn't want to do it during the coldest months (January and February), and in mid-summer you have to contend with occasionally heavy rains. Despite such annoyances, many travellers prefer motorbike travel to all other forms of transport.

If you plan to tour the north by bike, see the Motorbiking Specialty Tours section under Travel Agents earlier in this chapter.

There are several good outfits who can arrange guides, rentals and help with itinerary planning.

The 125cc Russian-made Minsk (also see the 'Minsk Mania' boxed text earlier in this chapter) is the best overall bike for touring the north – you will need that kind of power for the mountainous regions.

Quality of rental bikes can be extremely variable, so try to find a reputable dealer. Hanoi's expat community seems to agree that Phung Duc Cuong has got the best bikes in Hanoi; to contact him inquire at Bar Le Maquis or Highway #4 (see the Pubs section under Entertainment). Cuong rents, repairs, buys and sells Minsks.

The daily rental cost for a Minsk is around US$5; you may be able to find them for a dollar or so cheaper, but beware of the quality. If you intend to buy a Minsk, remember that is not necessarily better to buy a new one. Used bikes have been tested, and a well-maintained second-hand bike is often more reliable, and definitely cheaper, than purchasing something new.

There are dozens of motorbike shops along Pho Hué where you can inquire about purchasing a machine. These shops also sell good-quality helmets.

GETTING AROUND

To/From the Airport

Hanoi's Noi Bai airport is about 35km north of the city and the journey can take from 45 minutes to an hour. The airport freeway is one of the most modern roads in Vietnam (although you'll see oxen herded by farmers dressed in rags crossing it). It's also interesting to see how the freeway suddenly terminates in the suburbs north of Hanoi.

Vietnam Airlines minibuses between Hanoi and Noi Bai airport charge US$3 a seat. Coming from the airport, the driver will drop you at the Vietnam Airlines office at 1 Pho Quang Trung. From here it is a short walk north into the Old Quarter, or you can hire one of the countless cyclo or motorbike drivers to deliver you to your hotel. A ride from here to any place in the city centre should not cost more than 5000d per person; if you can't agree on the fare, just start to walk away – the drivers will likely have a change of heart.

The minibus service works OK but beware of the usual scams, especially at the airport:

> The official airport minibus seems open to fiddling. We got a ticket from the kiosk inside the airport building, but the driver wanted us to pay him again personally. On the way back, we bought our tickets off the driver, but they didn't look very 'new'.
>
> **B Bolton**

Also, be warned that occasionally local touts (well-dressed and posing as employees of Vietnam Airlines) board the official minibuses. They are skilled at befriending newly arrived passengers, and by the time you reach the city will offer to recommend a 'good, cheap hotel'. If you want to avoid the sales pitch, just tell whoever that you've already got a hotel reservation (even if you don't). One would hope that it is above Vietnam Airlines to allow 'friends' of drivers to pull this scam on their vehicles, but that's wishful thinking.

Getting to the airport from town, you can take one of the minibuses that depart roughly every half-hour from opposite the same Vietnam Airlines office on Pho Quang Trung. It's best – though not essential – to book the day before. Tickets are sold inside the booking office.

Airport Taxi (☎ 873 3333) charges US$10 for a taxi ride to or from Noi Bai airport. They do *not* require that you pay the toll for the bridge which must be crossed en route. Some other taxi drivers require that you pay the toll, so ask first.

At the airport itself, find the taxi booking desk, where the price is only US$10, but beware of this scam: after buying a ticket you may well be escorted to the minibus (which only costs US$1.60). Out in the car park, taxis can be negotiated for whatever the market will bear (usually around US$10), but you are better off using the official airport taxi for the same price.

In central Hanoi, there is always a collection of taxi drivers just outside the Vietnam Airlines office – it won't take much effort to find one. Don't pay more than US$10, including the toll.

There are share cabs/private minibuses from travellers' cafes for about US$2.

Bus

There are 13 bus lines in Hanoi, though they are numbered one to 14 (route No 13 was axed). Figuring out exactly where the buses go can be a challenge, and service on some of the lines is infrequent. Still, when it comes to economy, only walking is cheaper. Bus fares are typically US$0.10 to US$0.20 depending on the route.

Bus lines were previously shown in red on Hanoi tourist maps, but this is no longer the case as the number of routes has proliferated to the point where it became quite unmanageable. So far, nobody has published a bus-route guide with maps and information on bus stops. Until that happens, we offer the following guide to Hanoi's bus system:

1 **Ha Dong – Yen Phu** Nguyen Trai, Nguyen Luong Bang, Kham Thien, Nguyen Thuong Hien, Yet Kieu, Quan Su, Hang Da, Hang Cot, Hang Dau
2 **Ha Dong – Bac Co** Nguyen Trai, Nguyen Luong Bang, Ton Duc Thang, Nguyen Thai Hoc, Hai Ba Trung, Phan Chu Trinh, Bac Co
3 **Giap Bat – Gia Lam bus station** Vong, Kim Lien bus station, Hanoi train station, Tran Hung Dao, Phan Chu Trinh, Bac Co, Tran.Quang Khai, Long Bien bus station, Gia Lam bus station
4 **Long Bien bus station – Giap Bat train station** Long Bien bus station, Nguyen Huu Huan, Phan Chu Trinh, Lo Duc, Mai Dong, Nguyen Thi Minh Kahi, Mo Market, Truong Dinh, Duoi Ca (Giap Bat train station)
5 **Nhon – Phan Chu Trinh** Nhon, Cau Dien, Cau Giay, Kim Ma bus station, Nguyen Thai Hoc, Tran Phu, Cua Nam, Hai Ba Trung, Phan Chu Trinh
6 **Long Bien bus station – Ngoc Hoi** Long Bien bus station, Nguyen Huu Huan, Ly Thai To, Co Tan, Phan Chu Trinh, Le Van Huu, Nguyen Du, Le Duan, Kim Lien bus station, Giai Phong, Duoi Ca, Van Dien, Ngoc Hoi
7 **Bo Ho – Cua Nam – Cau Giay** Bo Ho, Hang Gai, Hang Bong, Dien Bien Phu, Le Hong Phong, Doi Can, Buoi, Cau Giay
8 **Long Bien bus station – Mo Market** Long Bien bus station, Hang Dau, Hang Can, Bo Ho, Dinh Tien Hoang, Ba Trieu, Le Dai Hanh, Bach Mai, Mo Market
9 **Long Bien bus station – Cau Bieu**
10 **Bac Co – Yen Vien** Bac Co, Tran Quang Khai, Tran Nhat Duat, Long Bien bus station, Gia Lam bus station, Yen Vien
11 **Kim Lien bus station – Phu Thuy**
12 **Giap Bat – Kim Ma** Kim Lien bus station, Trung Tu, Chua Boc, Thai Ha, Lang Ha, Giang Vo, Kim Ma bus station
14 **Nghia Do – Bo Ho** Nghia Do, Hoang Hoa Tham, Phan Dinh Phung, Hang Cot, Hang Luoc, Luong Van Can, Bo Ho

Taxi

There are several companies in Hanoi offering metered taxi services. All charge similar rates. Flagfall is US$1, which takes you 2km, every kilometre thereafter costs between US$0.45 and US$0.60 depending on which company you choose. Competitors in this business include:

Airport Taxi	☎ 873 3333
City Taxi	☎ 822 2222
Red Taxi	☎ 856 8686
Taxi PT	☎ 856 5656
Viet Phuong Taxi	☎ 828 2828

Cyclo

The cyclos in Hanoi are wider than the Ho Chi Minh City variety, making it possible for two people to fit in one vehicle and share the fare. One common cyclo driver's ploy when carrying two passengers is to agree on a price, and then *double* it upon arrival gesturing 'no, no, no ... that was per person'.

In any case, you should not pay more than 5000 dong (US$0.40) per person for a trip in the city centre. Longer rides (for example from the Old Quarter to Ho Chi Minh's Mausoleum) can be as much as double that. Try to negotiate in dong, not dollars. You'll also find that a little bit of Vietnamese goes a long way when talking about prices.

The cyclo drivers in Hanoi are even less likely to speak English than in Ho Chi Minh City, so take a map of the city with you. And finally, some travellers have reported communication problems:

We felt that we were ripped off on more than one occasion in 'misunderstandings' with cyclo drivers. Once we had a really unpleasant time when one young man tried to extort US$15 from us for a 30-minute ride for two.

Barbara Case

Motorbike

You won't have any trouble finding a motorbike taxi *(xe om)* – just stroll along any major street and you'll get an offer every 10 seconds.

The cost should be around the same as a cyclo – 5000d per person maximum for a lift in the city centre, or 10,000d for longer rides.

Though many travellers have rented motorbikes and scooters to tour Hanoi, it is *not* recommended to drive in the city. The main reason for this is the extreme danger for someone who is not accustomed to Vietnamese driving style, not to mention dealing with the hassles of traffic, parking, etc It's also easy to unknowingly violate rules, but the police will happily remind you (the reminder will cost around US$5 without receipt, US$25 with).

If you are set on exploring Hanoi on two wheels, do it on a bicycle.

Bicycle

The best way to get around Hanoi is by bicycle. Many hotels and cafes offer these for rent. Bike rentals cost about US$1.

If you want to purchase your own set of wheels, Pho Ba Trieu and Pho Hué are the best places to look for bicycle shops (see Central Hanoi map).

Around Hanoi

MUSEUM OF ETHNOLOGY

The praiseworthy Vietnam Museum of Ethnicity (☎ 756 2193), Đ Nguyen Van Huyen, was designed with the help of the Musee del'Homme in Paris. It is well worth the trip to observe the depth of Vietnam's cultural diversity. The museum features an astounding collection of art and everyday objects with some 15,000 artefacts gathered from throughout Vietnam.

It has excellent maps and the displays are well labelled in Vietnamese, French and English. Interesting dioramas portray a typical village market, the making of conical hats and a Tay shamanic ceremony, while videos show the real life contexts. Visitors can also enter a traditional Black Thai house reconstructed within the museum. There is also a centre for research and conservation and staff regularly collaborate with ethnographers and scholars from Japan, France, the Netherlands, Canada, USA and other countries. A craft shop here – affiliated with Craft Link, a fair trade organisation – sells books, postcards and arts and crafts from ethnic communities.

Getting There & Away

The museum is on Đ Nguyen Van Huyen in the Cau Giay District, about 7km from the city centre. It's open Tuesday to Sunday from 8.30 to 5.30 pm; entry is US$0.80

The best way to get there is by rented bicycle (about a 30-minute ride). If you're short of time or energy, a motorbike taxi should cost around 20,000d, or 50,000d round-trip (including waiting time). An air-con meter taxi costs around 40,000d each way.

HO CHI MINH TRAIL MUSEUM

The Ho Chi Minh Trail Museum is out on Highway 6, about 13km south-west of Hanoi. It can be combined with a day trip to handicraft villages (see later in this section).

PERFUME PAGODA

The Perfume Pagoda (Chua Huong) is about 60km south-west of Hanoi by road. The pagoda is a highlight of the Hanoi area and should not be missed. The fun boat trip along the scenic waterways takes about three hours. A word of warning: bring good walking shoes! The path to the top is steep in places and if it's raining the ground can get *very* slippery.

The Perfume Pagoda itself is a complex of pagodas and Buddhist shrines built into the limestone cliffs of Huong Tich Mountain (Mountain of the Fragrant Traces). Among the better known sites here are Thien Chu (Pagoda Leading to Heaven);

Giai Oan Chu (Purgatorial Pagoda), where the faithful believe deities purify souls, cure sufferings and grant offspring to childless families; and Huong Tich Chu (Pagoda of the Perfumed Vestige).

Great numbers of Buddhist pilgrims come here during a festival that begins in the middle of the second lunar month and lasts until the last week of the third lunar month (usually corresponding to March and April). Pilgrims and other visitors spend their time here boating, hiking and exploring the caves. Weekends also tend to draw crowds, as one pair of travellers reported:

Avoid Sundays! This is the busiest day for locals – we had the misfortune of travelling there on a Sunday and ended up in a mob of thousands of locals pushing and shoving on the stairs leading to the temple. We were very disappointed after having spent all the time in transit.

Martin & Christina Semler

Getting There & Away

Getting to the pagoda requires a journey first by road and then by river.

If you want to do the river trip, which is highly recommended, you will need to travel from Hanoi by car for two hours to My Duc, then take a small boat rowed by

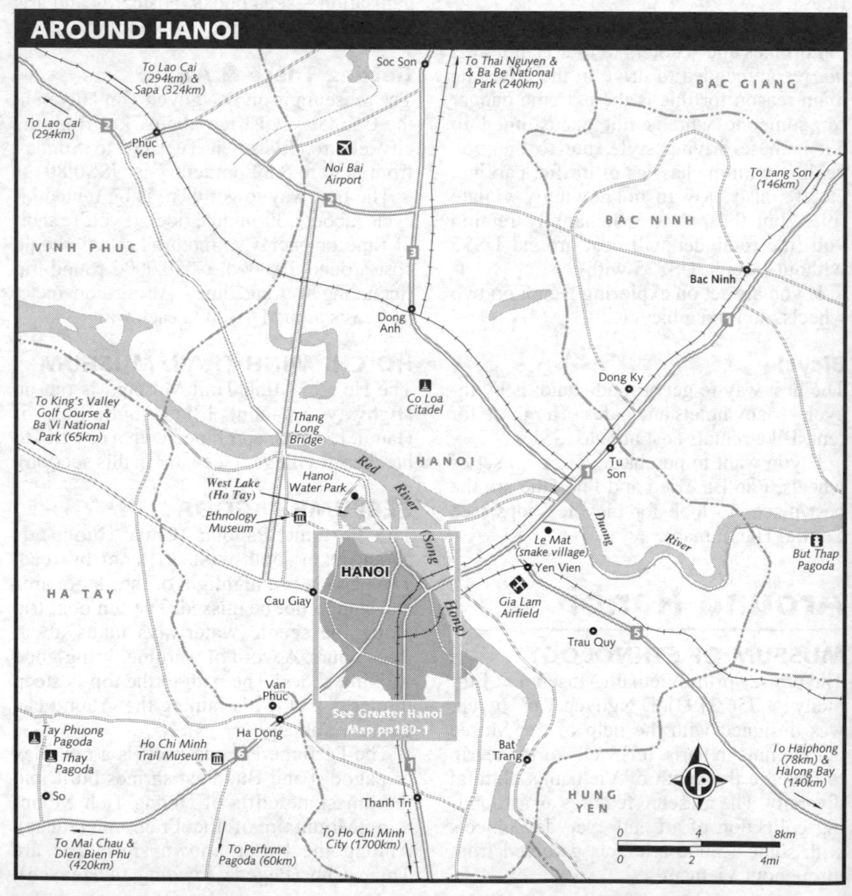

two women for 1½ hours to the foot of the mountain.

The main pagoda area is about a 4km (two-hour) walk up from where the boat lets you off. The scenery is comparable to Halong Bay, although you are on a river rather than the sea. The combined fee for the boat journey and general admission ticket is US$7. The return trip to your vehicle is also by rowboat.

Most of the travellers' cafes offer inexpensive tours to the pagoda. You can find day trips as cheap as US$9 or US$10, inclusive of transport, guide and lunch (drinks excluded). For a better quality tour (meaning smaller group and a more comfortable vehicle) expect to spend around US$14 to US$16.

THAY & TAY PHUONG PAGODAS

Thay Pagoda (the Master's Pagoda), also known as Thien Phuc (Heavenly Blessing), is dedicated to Thich Ca Buddha (Sakyamuni, the historical Buddha) and 18 *arhats* appear on the central altar. On the left is a statue of the 12th-century monk Tu Dao Hanh, the 'Master' after whom the pagoda is named; on the right is a statue of King Ly Nhan Tong, who is believed to have been a reincarnation of Tu Dao Hanh. In front of the pagoda is a small stage built on stilts in the middle of a pond; water-puppet shows are staged here during festivals.

The pagoda's annual festival is held from the fifth to the seventh days of the third lunar month. Pilgrims and other visitors enjoy watching water puppet shows, hiking and exploring caves in the area.

Tay Phuong Pagoda (Pagoda of the West), also known as Sung Phuc Pagoda, consists of three parallel single-level structures built on a hillock said to resemble a buffalo. The 76 figures carved from jackfruit wood, many from the 18th century, are the pagoda's most celebrated feature. The earliest construction here dates from the 8th century.

Getting There & Away

The pagodas are about 40km south-west of Hanoi in Ha Tay Province. Hanoi's cafes catering to budget travellers can arrange combined day tours of the Thay and Tay Phuong pagodas.

VAN PHUC & BUT THAP PAGODAS

Van Phuc Pagoda, surrounded by hills considered noteworthy for their beauty, was founded in 1037 AD. It is 27km south-east of Hanoi.

But Thap Pagoda, also known as Ninh Phuc Pagoda, is known for its four-storey stone stupa dedicated to the monk Chuyet Cong. The pagoda's date of founding is uncertain, but records indicate that it was rebuilt in the 17th and 18th centuries; the layout of the structure is traditional.

HANDICRAFT VILLAGES

There are numerous villages surrounding Hanoi which specialise in particular cottage industries. Visiting these villages can make a rewarding day trip, though you'll need a good guide to make the journey worthwhile.

Bat Trang is known as the 'ceramic village'. You can see artisans create superb ceramic vases and other masterpieces in their kilns. It's hot sweaty work, but the results are superb. Bat Trang is 13km south-east of Hanoi.

So is known for its delicate noodles. The village even produces the flour from which the noodles are made. The flour is made from yams and cassava (manioc) rather than wheat. So is in Ha Tay Province, about 25km south west of Hanoi.

Van Phuc is a silk village. You can see silk cloth being produced on a loom. Many of the fine silk items you see on sale in Hanoi's Pho Hang Gai originate here. Van Phuc is 8km south-west of Hanoi in Ha Tay Province.

Dong Ky was at one time known as the 'firecracker village'. Prior to 1995 (when the government banned firecrackers) there was always a firecracker festival in Dong Ky. A competition for the loudest firecracker once resulted in the building of a gargantuan 16m long firecracker.

With the firecracker industry now extinguished, the village survives by producing beautiful traditional furniture inlaid with mother-of-pearl. If you wish, you can have handcrafted furniture custom-made here and exported directly to your address abroad. Arranging the payments may prove a bit tricky if you're leaving Vietnam before the final product is produced and shipped. Dong Ky is 15km north-east of Hanoi.

Other handicraft villages in the region produce conical hats, delicate wooden bird cages and herbs.

LE MAT

Le Mat is called the 'snake village.' The locals raise snakes for the upmarket restaurants in Hanoi, and for producing medicinal spirits. Fresh snake cuisine and snake elixir is available at this village, and for around US$6 or US$8 you can try a set course consisting of snake meat prepared in around 10 different ways. Of the 25 or so snake restaurants in the village, consider trying ***Phong Do*** *(☎ 827 3244)*, or ***Phong Do II*** *(☎ 827 1091)*. On the 23rd day of the third lunar month is the very interesting Le Mat Festival, featuring 'snake dances' and other activities.

Le Mat is 7km north-east of central Hanoi.

CO LOA CITADEL

Co Loa Citadel (Co Loa Thanh), the first fortified citadel recorded in Vietnamese history, dates from the 3rd century BC. Only vestiges of the massive ancient ramparts, which enclosed an area of about 5 sq, remain. Co Loa became the national capital during the Ngo Quyen reign (939–44AD). In the centre of the citadel are temples dedicated to King An Duong Vuong (ruled 257–208 BC), who founded the legendary Thuc Dynasty, and his daughter My Nuong (Mi Chau). When My Nuong showed her father's magic crossbow trigger – which made the Vietnamese king invincible in battle – to her husband (who was the son of a Chinese general), he stole it and gave it to his father. With its help, the Chinese were able to defeat An Duong Vuong and his forces, depriving Vietnam of its independence.

Co Loa Citadel is 16km north of central Hanoi in Dong Anh district.

BA VI NATIONAL PARK

☎ 034

Ba Vi National Park (☎ 881082) is centred around scenic Ba Vi Mountain (Nui Ba Vi) and attracts Hanoi expats looking for a Sunday escape from the city. The park has over 2000 flowering plants, 12 of which have been classified as rare and precious – so please don't pick any of the flowers or plants. There are also reportedly 12 species of mammal living in the park but human encroachment on the area has made the chances of seeing any of them pretty rare.

There are hiking opportunities through the forested slopes of the mountain and anyone who climbs up to the summit will be rewarded with a spectacular view of the Red River valley from the summit (elevation 1287m).

The ***Ba Vi Guesthouse*** *(☎ 881198)* in the park rents fan rooms with bath for US$6, or US$8 with air-con. Prices go up about US$2 per room on weekends.

Warning: you must have your passport with you to check into the guesthouse here; one traveller we met was sent back to Hanoi because he had forgotten to bring it along.

Ba Vi National Park is about 65km west of Hanoi. Contact Handspan Adventure Travel or Buffalo Tours (see the list of travel agents earlier in this chapter) for information and current tour programs.

North-East Vietnam

Dominated by the Red River basin and the sea, the fertile north-east is the cradle of Vietnamese civilisation. Much of Vietnamese history, not all of it happy, was made here. In particular, Vietnam had less than cordial relations with the Chinese, who invaded in the 2nd century BC and stayed for about 1000 years. Indeed, the last invasion took place as recently as 1979 (see Mong Cai later in this chapter).

On a more positive note, this part of Vietnam is showing some real economic potential. Much investor interest centres on Haiphong, Vietnam's largest seaport. However, it's the scenery – not history, politics and economics – that is the major tourist drawcard here. In particular, the spectacular coastline of Halong Bay, Bai Tu Long Bay and Cat Ba Island offer some of nature's most bizarre geologic displays. Add to that such interesting side attractions as Ba Be Lakes, the mountains around Cao Bang plus the region's accessibility to China, and it's not hard to see why Vietnam's north-east is a major magnet for visitors.

Highlights

- Cruise the emerald waters of Halong Bay and explore some of the 3000-plus islets and grottoes of this magnificent Unesco World Heritage site.
- Relax on the beaches of Cat Ba Island, or trek through its scenic and untamed national park.
- Discover the lakes, rivers, waterfalls and caves in Ba Be National Park from the comfort of a boat.

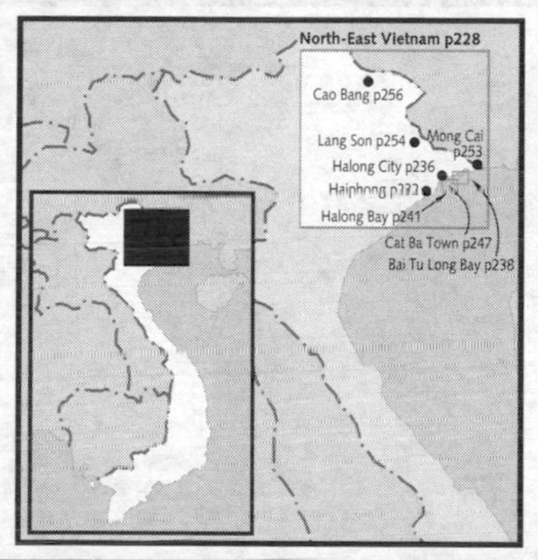

TAM DAO HILL STATION

• elevation 930m

Much of Tam Dao Hill Station was founded by the French in 1907. It was a popular place of escape from the heat of the Red River Delta, and became known to them as the Cascade d'Argent (Silver Cascade). Unfortunately, the grand old colonial villas are run-down and many have been replaced by politically correct, Soviet-inspired, concrete-box architecture. A belated effort to restore the colonial villas is now underway.

Hanoi residents sometimes call Tam Dao 'the Dalat of the north'. This has more to do with its high elevation and cool climate than any resemblance to Dalat. The problem with Tam Dao is that it's very small, still developing, and there just isn't that much to see and do here. Most visitors quickly grow bored, however at least a couple of travellers seemed to enjoy it:

> This place is really damp: we had to scrape the mushrooms off our sheets, and clothes will stay wet. Perhaps we went at the wrong time of year, but in early April the clouds just drift right in through the open windows into your room…Tam Dao has no nightlife, but for sheer atmosphere you can't beat it. There is a grand stone staircase at the back leading up to a radio transmitter. Over towards the waterfall another path comes out on a wide area of ruins and great balustrades looking over the valley. It's like Babylon or something. The people are very friendly and there are not many tourists… We went to Tam Dao to watch birds, and it is an excellent place to do so.
>
> **Tim Woodward & Phaik Hua Tan**

The drive to get there is very picturesque. If you're living in Hanoi and would like to find a summer weekend retreat, it might be worth heading up for the cool weather and a change of pace, or for the annual Halloween party held here on or around 31 October. However, travellers with limited time will almost certainly prefer to spend their precious holidays relaxing somewhere else.

The three summits of Tam Dao Mountain, all about 1400m in height, are visible to the north-east of the hill station. Many hill tribe people live in the Tam Dao region, though the communities are less prominent than they used to be.

Though logging (both legal and otherwise) has had a serious impact on the environment, the relative dampness makes the Tam Dao area particularly rich in flora and fauna. In 1994 a previously unknown species of flying (actually gliding) tree frog in the *Polypedates* genus was discovered in the jungle of the park.

Remember that it is cool up in Tam Dao and that this part of Vietnam has a distinct winter. Don't be caught unprepared. Generally the best times to visit are from late April to mid-October. As with other popular sites in Vietnam, weekends can be

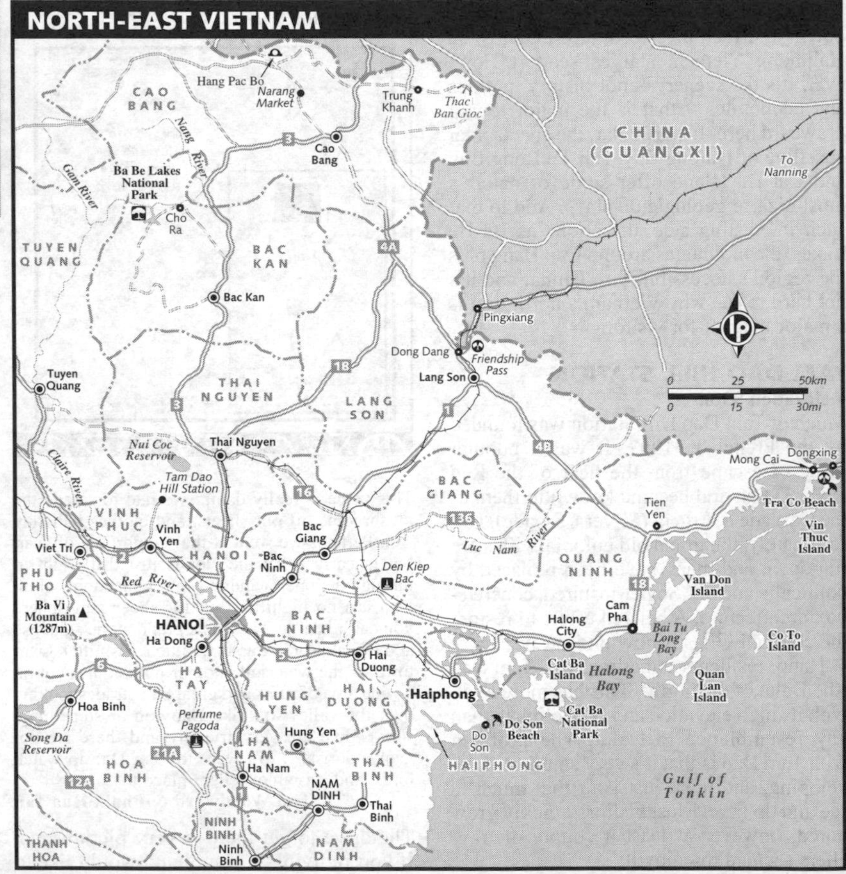

packed with domestic tour groups, so try to visit during the week if possible.

Places to Stay & Eat

There are several hotels in Tam Dao, most charging from US$8 to US$12, including the ***Trade Union Hotel*** *(☎ 824247)*, a huge state-run concrete building with twins/triples costing US$10/12.

The fanciest place in the area is modern ***Cay Thong*** *(☎/fax 824256)*, which charges from US$15 to US$45 for twins. The name means 'pine tree'.

There are heaps of ***restaurants***, but they are generally expensive – ask for prices first. The restaurants all have the same menu, written in the same handwriting. The chief items are fried or grilled deer, roast squirrel and roast silver pheasant. The latter delicacy is not yet considered an endangered species, but may be soon, so please don't order it!

Getting There & Away

Tam Dao National Park is 85km north-west of Hanoi in Vinh Phuc Province. Public transport is likely to be a problem. First, you must take a bus from Kim Ma bus station (west of the city centre) to Vinh Yen – the last one leaves at 1 pm. From there you must hire a motorbike (about US$2) or taxi for the 24km single-lane track that leads up to Tam Dao. There is a toll for using this road – about 5000d (US$0.40) for motorbikes, or 20,000d (US$1.60) for cars.

Probably the easiest way to reach Tam Dao is to simply rent your own motorbike in Hanoi and drive yourself.

Taxi drivers typically ask something like US$40 to bring you to Tam Dao from Hanoi, and perhaps US$30 to come back and pick you up a few days later. It should be possible to bargain something cheaper and if you're going to Cao Bang or Ba Be Lakes, you could easily arrange a stopover in Tam Dao for a little extra money.

THAI NGUYEN

• pop 171,400 • elevation 300m

There isn't a whole lot in Thai Nguyen to hold your interest, but there are a couple of lightweight sightseeing attractions in the area that just might be worth visiting if you have time.

Should you decide to break here for the night, there are a handful of reasonable hotels on the main drag.

Bao Tang Van Hoa Cac Dan Toc

The only really worthwhile thing to see in town is the Bao Tang Van Hoa Cac Dan Toc (Museum of the Cultures of Vietnam's Ethnic Groups). It is the largest Montagnard (hill tribes) museum in Vietnam and is well worth a visit if you are in the area. The giant pastel-pink building houses a wide array of colourful exhibits representing the 50-odd hill tribes residing in Vietnam.

The museum is open Tuesday to Sunday from 8 to 11 am and 2 to 4.30 pm. Entry costs US$0.80. There is an interesting English booklet on the displays available for US$2.

Getting There & Away

Thai Nguyen is 76km north of Hanoi, and the road there is in good nick.

Buses and minibuses to Thai Nguyen depart from Hanoi's Gia Lam station.

The Hanoi–Thai Nguyen train leaves once a day at 1.40 pm, arriving at 4.30 pm.

AROUND THAI NGUYEN

Phuong Hoang Cave

Phuong Hoang Cave is one of the largest and most accessible caverns in northern Vietnam (Phuong Hoang means Phoenix). There are four main chambers, two of which are illuminated by the sun when the angle is correct. Most of the stalactites and stalagmites are still in place, although quite a few have been broken off by thoughtless souvenir hunters. Like many caves in Vietnam, this one served as a 'hospital' – the euphemism for an ammunition depot. If you want to see anything, you'd best bring a good torch (flashlight).

The cave is a 40km ride over a bumpy road from Thai Nguyen on a motorbike.

Nui Coc Reservoir

A now popular scenic spot is Nui Coc Reservoir, 25km west of Thai Nguyen. By world standards it's not an impressive body of water, but it's a major drawcard for city-bound Hanoi residents looking to get away from it all. On summer weekends it can get particularly crowded. You can leave the water-skis at home, but you'll have plenty of opportunities to take a touristy boat trip. A one-hour, circular tour of the lake is de rigueur – cost depends on the size of the boat and number of passengers. Small boats costing US$11 per hour have a maximum capacity of 12 people (safe capacity of around 10). Larger boats costing US$25 per hour can hold up to 60 people. Guides are included, but there is an 'admission fee' of 6000d (US$0.45), plus another 6000d if you chose to swim in the lake's swimming pool.

If you wish to stay at Nui Coc Reservoir, rooms at the trade union-run ***Nui Coc Hotel*** *(☎ 825312)* cost from US$11 to US$22.

The reservoir can be reached by motorbike from Thai Nguyen.

DEN KIEP BAC

This temple is perhaps of more interest to domestic travellers than foreigners. Indeed, to the Vietnamese it is something of a hallowed shrine.

Den Kiep Bac (Kiep Bac Temple) is dedicated to Tran Hung Dao (1228–1300; born Tran Quoc Tuan). He was an outstanding general of renowned bravery whose armies defeated 300,000 Mongol invaders in the mid-1280s. Second only to Ho Chi Minh, he is a revered Vietnamese folk hero.

The temple was founded in 1300 and built on the site where Tran Hung Dao is said to have died. The temple was built not only for the general, but also to honour other notable members of his family. One was the general's daughter, Quyen Thanh, who married Tran Nhat Ton, the person credited with founding the Vietnamese sect of Buddhism called Truc Lam.

There is a Tran Hung Dao Festival held at Den Kiep Bac every year from the 18th to the 20th day of the eighth lunar month. You should expect to encounter heaps of souvenir vendors at the entrance, though they are not permitted inside the temple. You should consider purchasing incense from them – it's considered proper to burn a few sticks in Tran Hung Dao's honour, though international travellers may be excused from this requirement.

Den Kiep Bac is in Hai Duong Province, 80km from Hanoi and 49km from Bac Ninh, and can easily be visited on the way to Haiphong or Halong Bay.

CON SON

This is another place primarily of interest to Vietnamese rather than foreigners. Con Son (in Hai Duong Province, about 100km east of Hanoi) was home to Nguyen Trai (1380–1442), famed Vietnamese poet, writer and general. Nguyen Trai assisted emperor Le Loi in his successful battle against the Chinese Ming dynasty in the 13th century.

Con Son has a temple honouring Nguyen Trai. It's atop a mountain (a 600 step climb to reach it) so you'll get some exercise if you visit. Alternatively you can take another route past a spring. The mountain is covered with pines and makes for pleasant walking. There's a reasonably large lake nearby and, on the opposite side, there's a standard, Communist-inspired war memorial.

The well-maintained ***Con Son Hotel*** *(☎ 882240, fax 882630)* has twin rooms costing US$15 to US$20. You can eat at this hotel only if you order meals in advance, or you can go 4km to the town of Sao Do, which has a few restaurants.

Near the shore of the lake, the ***Con Son Trade Union Guesthouse*** *(☎ 882289)* is run by the military and has rooms for US$15 and US$20, though these prices are negotiable.

HAIPHONG

☎ 031 • pop 1,667,600

By expanding the city limits, Haiphong has become Vietnam's third most populous city (in reality Danang has a higher population). It is the north's main industrial centre and one of the country's most important seaports.

The French took possession of Haiphong – then a small market town – in 1874. The city soon developed and became a major port industrial concerns were established here in part because of its proximity to coal supplies.

One of the immediate causes of the Franco–Viet Minh War was the infamous French bombardment of the 'native quarters' of Haiphong in 1946, in which hundreds of civilians were killed and injured (a contemporary French account estimated civilian deaths at than 6000).

Haiphong came under US air and naval attacks between 1965 and 1972. In May 1972 President Nixon ordered the mining of Haiphong harbour to cut the flow of Soviet military supplies to North Vietnam. As part of the Paris cease-fire accords of 1973, the USA agreed to help clear the mines from Haiphong harbour – 10 US navy minesweepers were involved in the effort.

Since the late 1970s Haiphong has experienced a massive exodus, including many ethnic-Chinese refugees, who have taken much of the city's fishing fleet with them.

In spite of being a major port and one of Vietnam's largest cities, Haiphong today is a relatively sleepy place with little traffic and many beautiful French-colonial buildings. A Haiphong travel pamphlet suggests the town's current touristic ambitions may be at odds with its Socialist heritage:

> Nowadays Haiphong is one of the creative and active cities in the socialist construction and in the defence of the socialist country. The people in Haiphong are sparing no effort to build it both into a modern port city with developed industry and agriculture and a centre of import and export, tourism and attendance and at the same time an iron fortress against foreign invasion.

While it may not be worth a special trip, Haiphong makes a reasonable stopover en route to/from Cat Ba Island or Halong Bay. In general the city is far less postcard-vendor/shoeshine-boy ridden than Hanoi, though you should take usual caution around the train station and ferry landing:

> Beware! By far our most unpleasant experience in Vietnam was at the ferry port in Haiphong. A group of schoolgirls by the pier ostensibly selling postcards and giving 'friendly advice' were suspiciously, but almost convincingly, enthusiastic in trying to persuade us *not* to take the ferry to Hon Gai. They claimed that 'there's no place to stay' in Hon Gai. They almost succeeded in stopping the four of us from having what turned out to be a wonderful experience. They and their 'student' friend (a young man in his early 20s) wanted us to go in a minibus to who-knows-where instead. I'll leave it to the readers to imagine what their purpose might have been, but we all felt ill at ease and our sixth senses told us something was wrong.
>
> **John Holton**

Information

Travel Agencies Haiphong's Vietnam Tourism (☎ 842957, fax 842974), 12 Pho Le Dai Hanh, is ready, willing and able to take your money if you'd like to book a trip to Cat Ba or Halong Bay. Don't expect too much in the way of information though.

Money Vietcombank (☎ 842658, fax 841117), 11 Pho Hoang Dieu, is not far from the post office.

Post & Communications The grand, old, yellow main post office on the corner with Pho Hoang Van Thu is at 3 Pho Nguyen Tri Phuong.

Laundry Do Thanh, on Pho Ly Tu Trong (just around the corner from the Navy Hotel), offers a good laundry and dry cleaning-service.

Emergency If you need medical treatment, you'd do better to get yourself to Hanoi. Otherwise, some places to try include the Benh Vien Dong Y (Traditional Medicine Hospital), on Pho Nguyen Duc Canh, and the Benh Vien Viet-Tiep (Vietnam-Czech Friendship Hospital), on Pho Nha Thuong.

Du Hang Pagoda

Du Hang Pagoda, at 121 Pho Chua Hang, was founded three centuries ago. Though it has been rebuilt several times, it remains a good example of traditional Vietnamese architecture and sculpture.

Hang Kenh Communal House

Hang Kenh Communal House on Pho Hang Kenh is known for its 500 relief sculptures

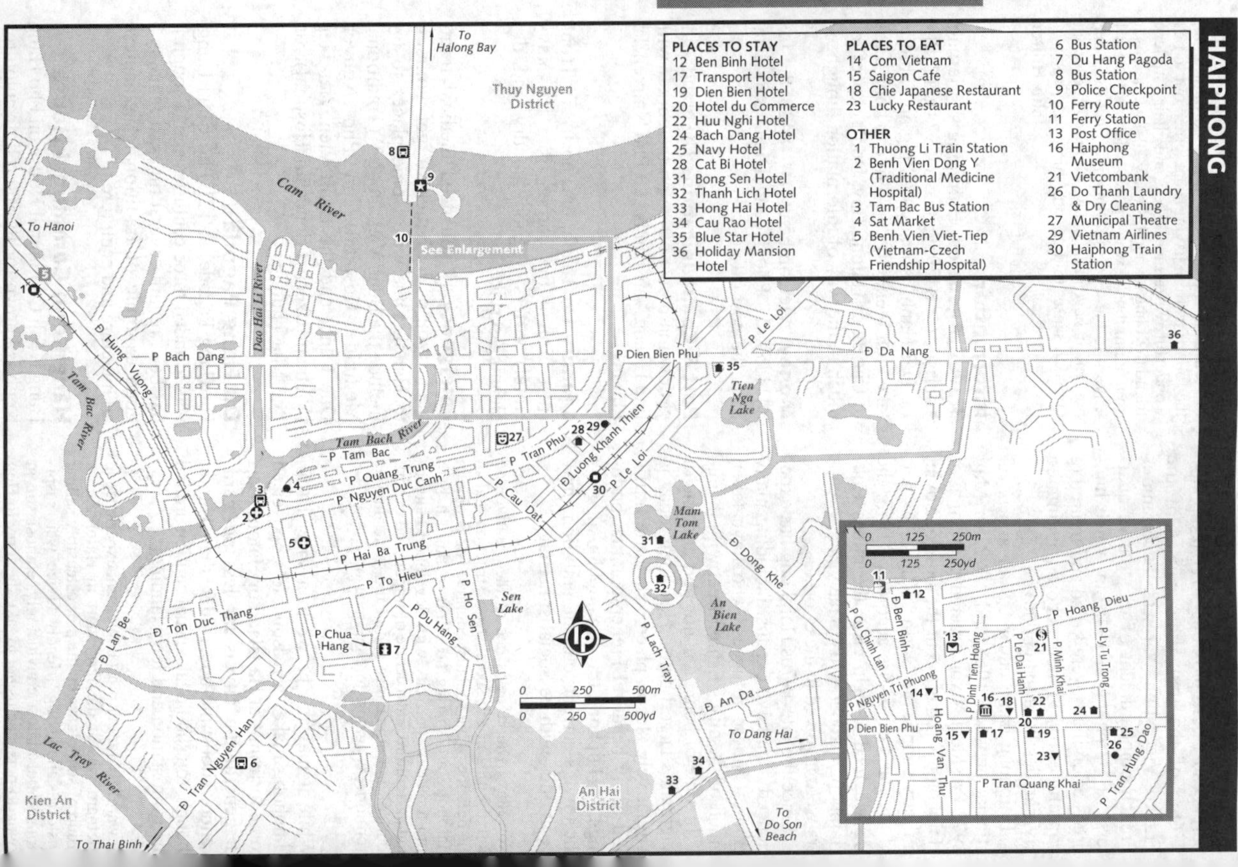
HAIPHONG
PLACES TO STAY
12 Ben Binh Hotel
17 Transport Hotel
19 Dien Bien Hotel
20 Hotel du Commerce
22 Huu Nghi Hotel
24 Bach Dang Hotel
25 Navy Hotel
28 Cat Bi Hotel
31 Bong Sen Hotel
32 Thanh Lich Hotel
33 Hong Hai Hotel
34 Cau Rao Hotel
35 Blue Star Hotel
36 Holiday Mansion Hotel
PLACES TO EAT
14 Com Vietnam
15 Saigon Cafe
18 Chie Japanese Restaurant
23 Lucky Restaurant
OTHER
1 Thuong Li Train Station
2 Benh Vien Dong Y (Traditional Medicine Hospital)
3 Tam Bac Bus Station
4 Sat Market
5 Benh Vien Viet-Tiep (Vietnam-Czech Friendship Hospital)
6 Bus Station
7 Du Hang Pagoda
8 Bus Station
9 Police Checkpoint
10 Ferry Route
11 Ferry Station
13 Post Office
16 Haiphong Museum
21 Vietcombank
26 Do Thanh Laundry & Dry Cleaning
27 Municipal Theatre
29 Vietnam Airlines
30 Haiphong Train Station
To Halong Bay
Thuy Nguyen District
Cam River
Dao Hai Li River
Tam Bach River
Tam Bac River
Lac Tray River
To Hanoi
To Thai Binh
To Do Son Beach
To Dang Hai
Kien An District
An Hai District
Tien Nga Lake
Mam Tom Lake
An Bien Lake
Sen Lake
See Enlargement
Đ Hung Vuong
P Bach Dang
P Tam Bac
P Quang Trung
P Nguyen Duc Canh
P Hai Ba Trung
P To Hieu
P Chua Hang
P Du Hang
P Ho Sen
P Cau Dat
P Tran Phu
Đ Luong Khanh Thien
P Le Loi
P Dien Bien Phu
Đ Da Nang
Đ Dong Khe
P Lach Tray
Đ An Da
Đ Ton Duc Thang
Đ Lan Be
Đ Tran Nguyen Han
P Hoang Dieu
P Ly Tu Trong
P Minh Khai
P Le Dai Hanh
P Dinh Tien Hoang
Đ Ben Binh
P Cu Chinh Lan
P Nguyen Tri Phuong
P Hoang Van Thu
P Dien Bien Phu
P Tran Quang Khai
P Tran Hung Dao
0 125 250m
0 125 250yd
0 250 500m
0 250 500yd

in wood and is well worth a visit. The surrounding area was once part of the village of Kenh.

Hang Kenh Tapestry Factory

Founded around 70 years ago, the Hang Kenh Tapestry Factory produces wool tapestries for export.

Dang Hai Flower Village

Flowers grown at Dang Hai, which is 5km from Haiphong, are sold on the international market.

Places to Stay

The ***Thanh Lich Hotel*** *(☎ 847361, fax 847361, 47 Pho Lach Tray)* is the cheapest place in town; the only real drawback of staying here, however, is that it's over 1km from the city centre. Still, you can get there cheaply by cyclo or motorbike taxi. Fan rooms cost US$6 with shared bath or US$10 with private bath. There is a restaurant inside the park-like compound. Next door is the newer ***Bong Sen Hotel***, but for the money it charges you're better off staying in town.

The ***Transport Hotel*** *(Khach San Giao Thong, ☎ 745118, fax 745375, 103 Pho Dien Bien Phu)* is appropriately entered through a large parking garage. The rooms are a bit dingy, but cheap at US$9 with air-con and a fridge.

The ***Dien Bien Hotel*** *(☎ 745264, fax 754743, 67 Pho Dien Bien Phu)* has a name that will probably not enthral many French travellers, but the rooms are OK, and cost US$15 and US$20.

Directly across the street is the French-era ***Hotel du Commerce*** *(☎ 842706, fax 842560, 62 Pho Dien Bien Phu)*. The tariff is US$11 to US$25.

Next door to the Hotel du Commerce is the snazzy, big, three-star ***Huu Nghi Hotel*** *(☎ 823310, fax 823245)*, with well appointed rooms for US$50 to US$300.

The ***Bach Dang Hotel*** *(☎ 842444, fax 841625, 42 Pho Dien Bien Phu)* underwent a recent renovation and spruced up a minimalist approach to decorating. Rooms cost US$20 to US$35.

The ***Cat Bi Hotel*** *(☎ 846306, fax 845181, 30 Pho Tran Phu)* is a standard minihotel close to the train station. Rooms cost US$18 to US$35.

Just across from the ferry station is the enormous ***Ben Binh Hotel*** *(Nha Khach Ben Binh, ☎ 842260, fax 842524, 6 Đ Ben Binh)* – budget rooms are scruffy at US$15, though the larger, spiffier US$25 rooms are good value.

The spacious ***Navy Hotel*** *(Khach San Hai Quan, ☎ 823713, fax 842278, 27C Pho Dien Bien Phu)* may appeal to visiting seafarers. Rooms cost from US$20 to US$60 for a palatial suite complete with kitchen and dining room – impressive.

About 2km south of the city centre, on the road to Do Son Beach, is the ***Cau Rao Hotel*** *(☎ 847021, fax 847586, 460 Đ Lach Tray)*. It's a quiet and pleasant place, but not much English is spoken. Doubles cost US$10 to US$25.

The eight-room ***Blue Star Hotel*** *(☎ 852038, fax 826414, 34B Đ Da Nang)* is a large five-storey place in the quiet, eastern part of town. Good air-con rooms cost from US$22.

Still farther out on the eastern periphery is the luxurious ***Holiday Mansion Hotel*** *(☎ 845667, fax 845668, Đ Da Nang)*. The price range here is US$15 to US$40.

Places to Eat

Haiphong is noted for its excellent fresh seafood, which is available from most ***hotel restaurants***.

Com Vietnam *(☎ 841698, 4 Pho Hoang Van Thu)*, not far from the post office, is a pleasant little Vietnamese restaurant with reasonable prices. Ditto for the ***Lucky Restaurant*** *(☎ 842009, 22-B2 Pho Minh Khai)*.

Some expats in Haiphong congregate at the loungey ***Saigon Cafe***, which features live music in the evenings. It's at the corner of Pho Dien Bien Phu and Pho Dinh Tien Hoang.

For good Japanese fare, try ***Chie*** *(☎ 823327, 64 Pho Dien Bien Phu)*. Meals cost about US$5, and the friendly Vietnamese staff welcome customers with a vigorous Japanese 'Irashaimase!' greeting.

Getting There & Away

Air Vietnam Airlines flies the Haiphong-Ho Chi Minh City route five times weekly and the Haiphong-Danang route three times a week.

Bus Haiphong has several long-distance bus stations. For Bai Chay (in Halong Bay) the station is in the Thuy Nguyen District (northern bank of the Cam River). To reach it, you must take a ferry. Bus departures are infrequent (there is only one bus scheduled daily), although minibuses will make the run when demand is sufficient. Buses for Bai Chay leave Haiphong around 9 am. Departure from Bai Chay is around noon. The one-way fare is US$4.

Hoang Long Transport has air-con Hanoi-Haiphong buses (US$1.80, two hours) departing from Hanoi's Kim Ma bus station every half-hour from about 5 am to 6 pm. In Haiphong, get these buses at the Tam Bac bus station.

Train Haiphong is not on the main line between Hanoi and Ho Chi Minh City, but there is a spur line connecting it to Hanoi. There is one express train daily to/from Hanoi's B station and several others from Hanoi's Long Bien station (on the eastern side of the Red River). Hard seat tickets cost US$4.

The train from Hanoi's B station departs at 6.15 am and arrives in Haiphong at 8 am. The train departs Haiphong at 6.10 pm and arrives in Hanoi at 8.55 pm.

The trains from Long Bien station depart at 9.20 am, 2.55 pm and 5.45pm; they take about 2¾ hours to Haiphong. For the return trip, trains depart Haiphong at 6.10 and 8.15 am and 2.35 pm.

There are two train stations within the city limits of Haiphong. The Thuong Li train station is in the western part of the city, far from the centre. The Haiphong train station is right in the city centre; this is the last stop for the train coming from Hanoi and is where you should get off.

Car & Motorbike Haiphong is 103km from Hanoi on Highway 5. A new expressway (Vietnam's first) between the two cities was completed in 1999.

Boat The two ferries of interest to travellers are the hydrofoils going to Cat Ba Island, and slow boats to Hon Gai (see Getting There & Away entries in the Halong Bay special section for details).

Getting Around

Haiphong is serviced by VP Taxi (☎ 828282), which offers metered, air-con taxis. There are also plenty of cyclos cruising around town.

DO SON BEACH

☎ 031 • pop 30,000

The palm-shaded beach at Do Son, 21km south-east of central Haiphong, is a popular seaside resort and a favourite of Hanoi's expat community. The hilly, 4km-long promontory ends with a string of islets. The peninsula's nine hills are known as Cuu Long Son (Nine Dragons).

The resort is not all it's cracked up to be, or rather it's more cracked up than it used to be. Many of the hotels are looking rather dog-eared.

The town is famous for its ritual **buffalo fights** which are held annually on the 10th day of the eighth lunar month, the date on which the leader of an 18th-century peasant rebellion was killed here.

More recently, the town has become famous for the first **casino** to open in Vietnam since 1975. This joint venture between the government and a Hong Kong company started operations in 1994. Foreigners are welcome to lose their fortunes here, but Vietnamese are barred from entering the casino

HALONG CITY

☎ 033 • pop 149,900

The majority of food, accommodation and other life-support systems for Halong Bay are to be found in the dismal town of Halong City, the capital of Quang Ninh Province and Vietnam's latest sin city (the number of signs advertising 'Thai Massage' gives a good indication of the prostitution market). In recent years this once-peaceful outpost has been developed into a 'pleasure den' for package tourists (both domestic and international, with a large following of border-hopping Chinese).

Unless you plan to partake in the sleazy joys of this poor attempt at replicating Thailand's Pattaya, there is *no* good reason to visit Halong City, other than as a launch pad for boats. This is one place where you'll be thankful for arriving on a group tour. A growing cartel of persistent young Mafia thugs who control the flow of local tourist dollars will make trying to get a fair price on a hotel, meal or self-booked boat trip into Halong Bay a real nightmare – they won't give up until you make a booking that they can get a commission from, meaning you pay more than you should. At least if you are on a tour from Hanoi, you will be spared the riffraff, and spending a night in purgatory should not be the end of the world. Better yet, consider a tour on which you can sleep aboard a boat in the bay.

If you are hellbent on travelling independently to Halong Bay from Hanoi, it is advisable to give Halong City a miss and make a beeline to less hassle-ridden Cat Ba Island (see the Halong Bay special section), where you can also arrange interesting boat trips.

Orientation

Halong City is bisected by a bay, and for travellers the most important district (on the western side) is called Bai Chay. Accommodation can be found on both sides of the bay, but Bai Chay is more scenic, closer to Hanoi and much better endowed with hotels and restaurants. Bai Chay is also where the majority of tourist boats are moored.

A short ferry ride (US$0.04) across the bay takes you to the Hon Gai district (also spelled Hong Gai). Hon Gai is the main port district and exports coal (a major product of this province), which means this area is a bit dirty, but at least there is some local flavour. The ferry from Haiphong docks in Hon Gai, so if you arrive late, you may find it easier (and definitely more peaceful) to spend the night there before crossing to Bai Chay the next morning. Motorbike drivers on both sides will take you from either ferry landing into town for about US$0.15.

District names are important – most long-distance buses will be marked 'Bai Chay' or 'Hon Gai' rather than 'Halong City'.

Information

There is an office of Quang Ninh Tourist (☎ 846350, fax 846319) on the main road in Bai Chay. This agency owns several hotels, and can inform you about boat tours and the like.

Money Vietcombank has a branch in Hon Gai, which is inconvenient, as most tourists stay in Bai Chay on the other side of the bay.

Email & Internet Access Internet access is available at the Emotion Cybernet Cafe (☎ 847354, ⓔ Emotioncafe@hn.fpt.vn), right on the main drag in Bai Chay. The cost is 600d/minute.

Beaches

The 'beaches' around Halong City are basically mud and rock – a problem the authorities are trying to 'correct'. A Taiwanese company has a built two beaches in Bai Chay with imported sand, but they are not at all attractive for swimming. The nearby boardwalk is attractive enough, but as one traveller noted:

> Halong City is dreadful. Full of new hotels and restaurants with depressingly repetitive food. The promenade is a bad imitation of the French Riviera and the boat trips are a rip-off.
>
> **Antonio Vivaldi & Gabriella Paradisi**

Places to Stay

The majority of visitors stay in Bai Chay. There are more than 100 hotels here and keen competition keeps prices down (if you can avoid the commission-seeking touts), though you will probably have to pay more in the peak summer travel season or during Tet.

Bai Chay The heaviest concentration of hotels is in town in the aptly named 'hotel alley'. This is where you'll find countless minihotels, most of them nearly identical. Expect to pay something like US$10 to US$12 for a double room with private bath and air-con.

A couple of hillside hotels with views of the bay provide an interesting alternative. The clean, cheap and friendly ***Bong Lai Hotel*** *(☎ 845658)* has fan rooms for US$8, or US$11 with air-con. Air-con rooms at the nearby ***Hai Long Hotel*** *(☎ 846378, fax 846171)* are priced at US$15.

Back down at the waterfront and close to the ferry landing is the ***Van Hai Hotel*** *(☎ 846403, fax 846115)*. It's a state-run place that looks good on the outside, but actually is in pretty poor condition and isn't worth the money. Rooms cost US$25 to US$30 and include breakfast.

If you're looking for something fancy, right by the car ferry landing is the snazzy ***Halong Plaza Hotel*** *(☎ 845810, fax 846867)*. Rooms cost from US$98 to US$260.

The majority of the other hotels are strung out for 2km along the main road heading west of town (towards Hanoi). Most accommodation here consists of large, expensive, state-run hotels.

Thanh Nien Hotel *(☎ 846715, fax 846226)* is in a busy location right on the beachfront and houses a popular restaurant. Rooms with airconditioning cost US$20 including breakfast.

Vuon Dao Hotel *(☎ 846452, fax 846287)* is a state-run behemoth, but offers nice views of the bay. Rooms cost from US$35. Yet another state-run monstrosity, this one popular with Chinese visitors, is the ***Suoi Mo Hotel*** *(☎ 846381, fax 846729)* which charges US$25 to US$35. Both these hotels are just off the main road to Hanoi.

The glitzy ***Heritage Halong Hotel*** *(☎ 846888, fax 846718)* is a huge upmarket Singaporean joint venture with rooms priced from US$110 to US$250. It was built right in front of (and stole the prime views from) the sleepy ***Bien Dong Hotel*** *(☎ 846677, fax 847635)*, where air-con twins run US$25, including breakfast.

Nearby is the ***Halong Hotel*** *(☎ 846320, fax 846318)*, which is divided into four buildings with prices running from US$20 up to US$110.

Just to the western side of the Halong Hotel is the three-star ***Halong Bay Hotel*** *(☎ 845209, fax 846856)*. This Vietnam Tourism joint venture has rooms priced from US$55 to US$105.

Hon Gai There are fewer places to stay here, but the demand is low (and there are fewer

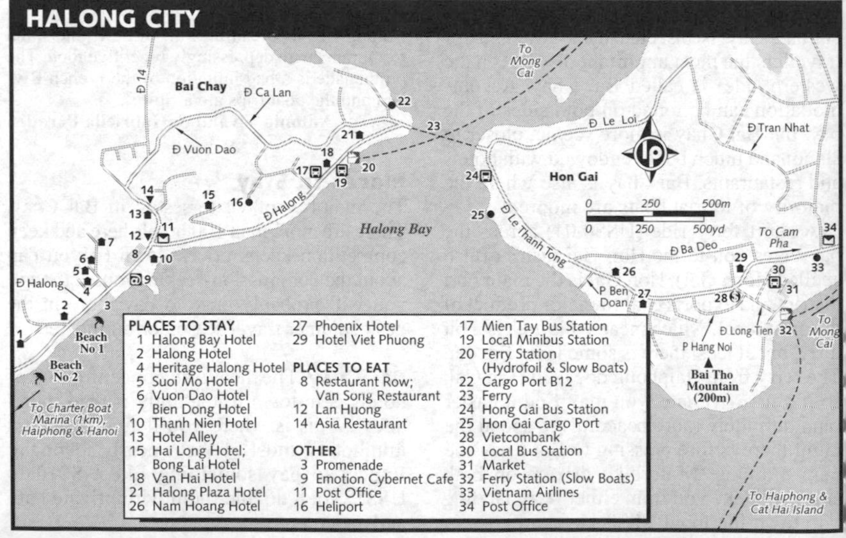

touts) so prices have remained cheap. The hotels are clustered mainly along Đ Le Thanh Tong, which runs on an east-west axis, as well as tucked away on Pho Hang Noi.

Hotel Viet Phuong *(☎ 826197),* on Đ Le Thanh Tong, has decent air-con rooms for US$8. It advertises 'commodious comfortable rooms with propitious parking'!

The ***Phoenix Hotel*** *(☎ 827236, 169 Đ Le Thanh Tong)* is a cosy little family run place charging US$8 for rooms with a fan or US$11 with air-con.

Nam Hoang Hotel *(☎ 824889, 153 Đ Le Thanh Tong)* charges US$9 for basic air-con doubles.

Places to Eat

Except for minihotels, most hotels have restaurants. If you're on a tour, it's likely that meals will be included.

For independent travellers, the area just west of central Bai Chay contains a solid row of cheap ***restaurants***, all of which are OK. The owner of the ***Van Song Restaurant*** here speaks fluent French.

For a less expensive, more local scene, check out the nearby ***Lan Huong***, where customers sit on plastic chairs outside on the footpath.

We can also endorse the ***Asia Restaurant*** *(☎ 846927)* on the 'hotel alley' slope. The owner, Mr Vinh, speaks excellent German (he formerly ran a restaurant in East Berlin) and some English. The Vietnamese food here is very good and prices are reasonable.

In Hong Gai, check out the string of local eateries along Pho Ben Doan.

Getting There & Away

Bus Hoang Long Transport has air-con Hanoi Halong City (Bai Chay) buses (US$2, four hours) departing from Hanoi's Kim Ma bus station around every hour from 5 am to 6 pm. In Halong City, you catch Hanoi-bound buses from Mien Tay bus station (ben xe) in Bai Chay.

Buses to Haiphong take approximately two hours.

Buses to north-east destinations (such as Mong Cai on the China border) leave from the Hon Gai bus station.

Car & Motorbike Halong City is 160km from Hanoi, 55km from Haiphong and 45km from Cam Pha. The one-way trip from Hanoi to Halong City takes about three hours by car.

Boat There are daily slow-boats connecting Hon Gai with Haiphong (US$3.50, three hours). Boats depart Haiphong at 6 and 11 am and 1.30 and 4 pm. Return boats leave Hon Gai at 6, 8.30 and 11 am and 4 pm.

Another slow boat connecting Hon Gai to Cat Hai Island leaves at 12.30 pm daily (US$2, two hours). This trip offers decent views of Halong Bay. From Cat Hai you can hop on another small ferry to get to Cat Ba Island (see Cat Ba Island in the Halong Bay special section for more information). There are also direct boats from Hong Gai to Cat Ba Island leaving at 1 pm and costing US$2.

There are both hydrofoil and slow ferry services linking Bai Chay and the Mong Cai area, near the Chinese border, and slow ferry from Hong Gai to Mong Cai (see the Mong Cai section later in this chapter for details).

BAI TU LONG BAY

There's more to north-east Vietnam than Halong Bay. The sinking limestone plateau, which gave birth to the bay's spectacular islands, continues some 100km to the Chinese border. The area immediately north-east of Halong Bay is known as Bai Tu Long Bay.

Bai Tu Long Bay is every bit as beautiful as its famous neighbour. Indeed, you could say it's more beautiful since it has scarcely seen any tourist development. Visitors of any kind are rare, but this will no doubt change – already some of the tourist cafes in Hanoi have made some pioneering forays into this uncharted region. Hopefully the coming hotel, restaurant and souvenir shop boom will be handled more tastefully here than at Halong Bay (but don't count on it).

Charter boats can take you to Bai Tu Long Bay from Halong Bay; a boat for 20 passengers costs US$10 per hour and the one-way journey takes about five hours. An alternative is to travel overland to Cai Rong from where you can take a public ferry to some of the remote outlying islands or charter a boat.

At the time of writing there had not yet been any reported incidents of piracy involving international travellers at Bai Tu Long Bay. This is not surprising, since there have been scarcely any visitors to rob. However, security could become a problem if tourists start visiting en masse. Halong Bay had serious problems with piracy until the authorities cracked down with regular police patrol boats. Don't be too surprised if history repeats itself here.

Van Don Island

Also known as Cam Pha, this is the largest and most developed island in the archipelago, though the potential for mass tourism has yet to be realised. Van Don is reminiscent of Cat Ba Island before the hotel building boom in the late 1990s.

Cai Rong is the main town on the island, which is about 30km in length and 15km across at the widest point. Bai Dai (Long Beach) is aptly named, though the sand is yellowish. Just offshore, however, there are rock formations similar to those in Halong Bay, and a number of white-sand beaches in site (looks like a prime place for kayaking). At the time of writing a new hotel was being constructed right on Long Beach.

Places to Stay & Eat It's pleasant to stay near Cai Rong pier on the south-eastern edge of town. About 100m before the pier is the ***Hung Toan Hotel*** *(☎ 874220)*. The three rooms on the top floor are best – they share a huge balcony that affords superb views of Bai Tu Long Bay. Twins cost US$8 to US$10.

The ***Duyen Huong Guesthouse*** *(☎ 874 113)* is a clean little place also worth recommending. Rooms with attached bath and hot water cost just US$4. Two of the rooms in the rear overlook the pier.

Nha Hang Huong Que *(☎ 874126)* is a basic guesthouse/restaurant; one room on the second storey overlooks the bay.

NORTH-EAST VIETNAM

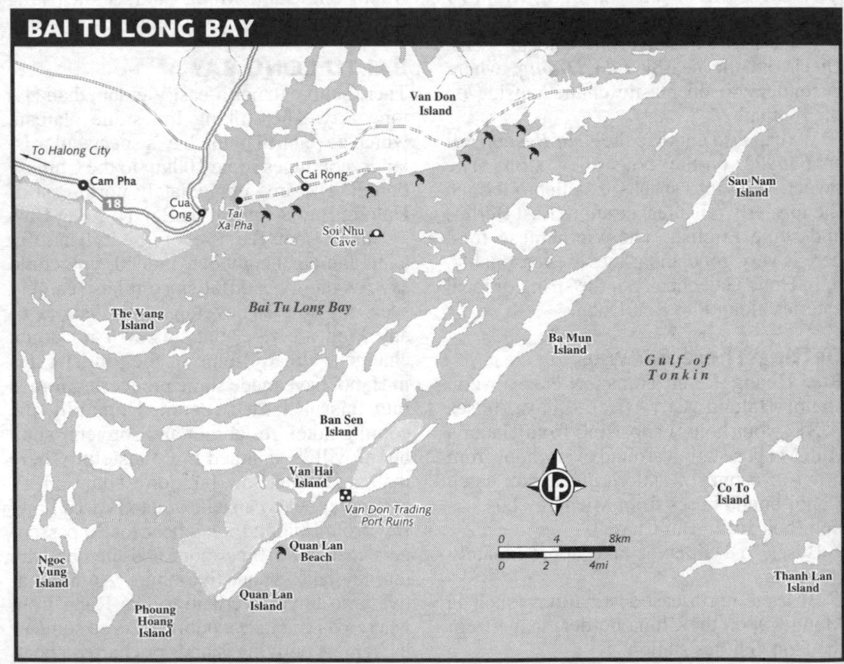

Nightly rates are US$4. The nearby ***Thanh Thao*** (☎ *874380)* is also very basic and charges the same.

The ***Phuc Loc Guesthouse*** *(☎ 874156)* is in the centre, almost opposite the market. The rooms aren't bad, but check the plumbing – not all of the ancient Soviet toilets are in working condition. A twin room costs US$4/5 without/with air-con.

Phan Tuyet is the largest restaurant on the island and serves good food. Another nearby choice serving edible Vietnamese food is ***Kim Liem***.

Getting There & Away Van Don Island is so close to the Vietnamese mainland that some day a bridge surely will be built. For the moment, the island's inhabitants rely on two rickety old ferries that run between Cua Ong Pha (Cua Ong Pier; on the mainland) and Tai Xa Pha (Tai Xa Pier; on Van Don Island). The passenger ferry (which also carries bicycles, motorbikes and chickens) runs every 30 minutes while the car ferry runs every two hours (both operate from 6 am to 6 pm). The journey takes 30 minutes.

Frequent buses run between Hon Gai (Halong City) and Cua Ong bus station (☎ 874074), 1km from the pier. A few other (rare) buses run directly between Van Don Island and Hon Gai, Haiphong and Hanoi; departures tend to be very early in the morning, usually around 5 am.

If you didn't take a direct bus, you can pay US$0.50 for a motorbike to take you the 7km between Cua Ong Pha and Cua Ong town.

Cai Rong Pha (Cai Rong Pier) is just on the edge of Cai Rong town. This is where you catch boats to the outlying islands. You can also charter a boat from here to Hon Gai or Bai Chay for around US$10 per hour (the one-way journey takes five hours).

Quan Lan Island

This place has the most potential as a beach resort. The main attraction is a beautiful, 1km long **white-sand beach** shaped like a crescent moon. The water is clear blue and the waves are suitable for surfing. The best time to play in the water is from about May to October – winter is too chilly. However, at present there are no tourist facilities.

There is a special event Hoi Cheo Boi (**Rowing Boat Festival**) held here from the 16th to the 18th day of the sixth lunar month. It's the biggest festival in the bay area, and thousands of people turn out to see it.

The north-eastern part of the island has some battered ruins of the old Van Don Trading Port. There is little to show that this was once part of a major trading route between Vietnam and China. Deep water ports such as Haiphong and Hon Gai long ago superseded these islands in importance.

Even during the festival, Quan Lan Island is totally lacking in tourist facilities. There are neither hotels nor restaurants. However, this may change as travel agencies in Hanoi and Halong Bay are considering running tours to the island.

A ferry service between Quan Lan and Van Don Islands runs daily. From Van Don to Quan Lan the boat leaves at 3 pm and from Quan Lan to Van Don departure is at 7 am; so in other words a trip to the island requires an overnight stay (and as there are no hotels, you'll have to camp, bringing all your own gear and supplies). The one-way fare is 20,000d (US$1.60) and the journey takes two hours.

Van Hai Island

Ancient Chinese graves have been found here, indicating that this region has seen considerable maritime trade. There are many good beaches, but a sand-mining pit (used to make glass) is destroying the place.

Ban Sen Island

Also known as Tra Ban Island, this is the closest major island to Van Don Island, making it easy to visit and a good place to get away from it all (there are almost no tourist facilities).

Boats leave Ban Sen Island daily at 7 am, arriving at Van Don Island between 8 and 8.30 am. Going the other way, boats depart Van Don Island at 2 pm and arrive on the north side of Ban Sen Island between 3 and 3.30 pm. The one-way fare is 15,000d (US$1.10).

Thanh Lan Island

This hilly island, reaching up to 190m, has a few flat spots available allowing the locals to cultivate rice and vegetables.

Co To Island

In the north-east, Co To Island is the farthest inhabited island from the mainland. The highest peak reaches a respectable 170m. There are numerous other hills with a large lighthouse atop one of them. The coastline is mostly cliffs or large rocks, but there's at least one fine sandy beach. Fishing boats usually anchor just off here, and you can walk to some of them during low tide.

There is a small and very basic ***guesthouse*** *(☎ 889156)* on the island charging just US$0.50 per person. The phone is actually the neighbour's number, so it may take a minute or two to get someone on the line.

Ferries bound for Co To Island depart Van Don Island on Monday, Wednesday and Friday at unspecified times – check the schedule in Cai Rong. They return from Co To Island on Tuesday, Thursday and Friday. There are no boats on Sunday. The one-way fare is 30,000d (US$2.40) and the journey takes about five hours (depending on the wind).

MONG CAI

pop 48,100

Mong Cai is located on the Chinese border in the extreme north-eastern corner of Vietnam. Previously the border gate (Cua Khau Quoc Te Mong Cai) was only open to Vietnamese and Chinese, but today it is one of six official international overland border crossings in Vietnam.

So few travellers come and go this way that we have yet to meet someone who has entered or exited Vietnam here, but after repeated inquiries the Vietnamese border guards assured us that foreigners holding a valid passport and tourist visa *can* indeed cross here.

One would be hard-pressed to say that Mong Cai is an attractive place. For the Vietnamese the big attraction here is a chance to purchase low-priced (and low-quality) Chinese-made consumer goods. Chinese tourists find little to buy in Mong Cai, but they seem to enjoy the low-cost Vietnamese food, booze and women.

Lots of cars are exported to China via Mong Cai, not because the Vietnamese are known for producing great cars, but because many Japanese and Korean companies have established assembly plants in Vietnam, while they have shunned China.

If you've been learning to speak Chinese, you'll find plenty of opportunity to practice in Mong Cai. Many hotels, restaurants and shops are staffed by Vietnamese who can speak at least basic Chinese. Furthermore, about 70% of the stalls are run by Chinese who cross the border daily to flog their wares. This explains why the market shuts so early (3 pm) – the Chinese have to head across the border before it closes at 4 pm. It also means you won't have any problem spending Chinese yuan if you have them.

Other than the bustling markets (which aren't all that wonderful) and the prospect of crossing the border, Mong Cai has little of interest tourists. The town is dusty and the buildings are ramshackle. Dongxing (on the Chinese side) is even worse.

History

Mong Cai is a free-trade zone with plenty of frenetic activity in the city's booming markets. It wasn't always so. From 1978 to 1990, the border was virtually sealed. How two former friends became such bitter enemies and 'friends' again is an interesting story.

China was a good friend of North Vietnam from 1954 (when the French left) until the late 1970s. But their relations began to sour shortly after reunification as the Vietnamese government became more and more friendly with China's rival, the USSR. There's good reason to believe that Vietnam was simply playing them off against each other, while receiving aid from both.

In March 1978 the Vietnamese government launched a campaign in the south against 'commercial opportunists', seizing private property in order to complete the country's 'socialist transformation'.

continued on page 252

Halong Bay

CRAIG PERSHOUSE

MATT DARBY

Title page: View of UNESCO heritage listed Halong Bay (photograph by Mark Kirby).

Top: Halong Bay is famous for its limestone formations, caves and grottos.

Bottom: Board a boat, or jaunt on a junk and enjoy the bay's aquamarine waters – don't forget your sunscreen!

MARK KIRBY

Magnificent Halong Bay, with its 3000-plus islands rising from the clear, emerald waters of the Gulf of Tonkin and covering an area of 1500 sq km, is one of the natural marvels of Vietnam. In 1994 Halong Bay was designated as Vietnam's second United Nations Educational, Scientific and Cultural Organization (Unesco) World Heritage site. Visitors have compared the area's magical landscape of limestone islets to Guilin in China and Krabi in southern Thailand. These tiny islands are dotted with innumerable beaches and grottoes created by wind and waves.

As the number one tourist attraction in the north-east, Halong Bay draws a steady stream of visitors year-round. During February, March and April, Halong Bay and Cat Ba Island's weather is often cold and drizzly, and the ensuing fog can make visibility low, although the temperature rarely falls below 10°C. During the summer months, tropical storms are frequent.

Besides the breathtaking vistas, visitors to Halong Bay come to explore the countless caves (some of which are beautifully illuminated for the sake of tourists). There is only one proper beach in Halong Bay, called Titop Beach. Over in Lan Ha Bay (off Cat Ba Island) the opposite

HALONG BAY

Hoang Tan
Tuan Chau Island
Halong City
To Haiphong
To Cam Pha
18
Hang Dau Go
To Haiphong
Halong Bay
Cat Hai
Phu Long
Cat Ba Island
Ra Luan Commune
Bo Nau Grotto
Hien Hao Commune
Trung Trang Cave
Cat Ba National Park
Viet Hai Commune
Xuan Dam Commune
Tran Chau Commune
Gulf of Tonkin
Cat Ba
Lan Ha Bay
Dau Be Island
0 5 10km
0 2.5 5mi
Approximate Scale

is true; Lan Ha boasts over 100 beaches, but almost no caves at all.

Ha long translates literally as 'where the dragon descends into the sea'. Legend has it that the islands of Halong Bay were created by a great dragon who lived in the mountains. As it ran towards the coast, its flailing tail gouged out valleys and crevasses; as it plunged into the sea, the areas dug up by the tail became filled with water, leaving only the high land visible.

The dragon may be legend, but sailors in the Halong Bay region have often reported sightings of a mysterious marine creature of gargantuan proportions known as the Tarasque. More paranoid elements of the military suspect it's an imperialist spy submarine, while eccentric travellers believe they have discovered Vietnam's version of the Loch Ness monster. Meanwhile, the monster, or whatever it is, continues to haunt Halong Bay, unfettered by the marine police, Vietnam Tourism and the immigration authorities. Enterprising Vietnamese boat owners have made a cottage industry out of the creature, offering cash-laden tourists the chance to rent a junk and pursue the Tarasque before he gets fed up and swims away.

Dragons aside, the biggest threat to the bay may be from souvenir-hunting tourists. Rare corals and seashells are rapidly being stripped from the seafloor, while stalactites and stalagmites are being broken off from the caves. These items get turned into key rings, paperweights and ashtrays, which are on sale in the local souvenir shops. You might consider the virtue of not buying these items and spending your cash instead on postcards and silk paintings.

Grottoes

Due to the rock type of Halong Bay's islands, the area is dotted with thousands of caves of all sizes and shapes.

Hang Dau Go (Grotto of Wooden Stakes), known to the French as the Grotte des Merveilles (Cave of Marvels), is a huge cave consisting of three chambers, which you reach via 90 steps. Among the stalactites of the first hall, scores of gnomes appear to be holding a meeting. The walls of the second chamber sparkle if bright light is shone on them. The cave derives its Vietnamese name from the third of the chambers, which is said to have been used during the 13th century to store the sharp bamboo stakes that Vietnamese folk hero and war general Tran Hung Dao planted in the bed of the Bach Dang River to impale Mongolian general Kublai Khan's invasion fleet.

Drum Grotto is so named because when the wind blows through its many stalactites and stalagmites, visitors think they hear the sound of distant drumbeats. Other well-known caves in Halong Bay include the Grotto of Bo Nau, the 2km-long Hang Hanh Cave and Hang Ca, where inside the cave is a quiet lake that locals dive for oysters.

The newest and most spectacular caves area is the Thien Cung Caves (a World Heritage Site), which only opened in May 1998. Unlike most caves one visits, there are comparatively few stalagmites and stalactites, but masses of 'cauliflower' formations, many of which are beautifully illuminated. En route to the caves small boats draw up alongside trying to sell fish, shells and (sadly) coral.

Linda Reed

Islands

Some tourist boats stop at Deu (also called Reu) Island, which supports an unusual species of monkey distinguished by their red buttocks. A few travellers also visit Ngoc Vung Island, which has a red brick lighthouse.

Tuan Chau Island (5km west of Bai Chay) is one of the few islands in Halong Bay that has seen any development. Ho Chi Minh's former summer residence is here. Currently there are three villas and a restaurant. In 1997 the government revealed plans to build a US$100 million resort complex here, complete with hotels, villas and a golf course.

Getting There & Away

For most travellers, it's well worth booking a one- or two-night Halong Bay tour at a cafe or hotel in Hanoi. These trips are very reasonably priced, starting from as low as US$12 to US$16 per person on a jam-packed 45-seat bus, and rising to the US$30 to US$35 range for a small-group tour, on which you can sleep out on the bay on a boat (recommended). Most tours include transport, meals, accommodation and boat tours of Halong Bay. Drinks are generally extra.

You really couldn't do it any cheaper by travelling there on your own, and the hassle factor in Halong City, the main launch point for boat tours of Halong Bay, is high enough to make your hair turn grey. But for those who prefer independent travel, there are buses direct to Halong City from Hanoi, as well as ferries from Haiphong. (For further information on Halong City, see the North-East Vietnam chapter.) A better independent travel option is to get to Cat Ba Island (see later in this special section), from where you can also include Halong Bay on a chartered boat trip.

If you book a tour, there is always a small chance that the boat-trip portion may be cancelled due to bad weather. This may entitle you to a partial refund, but remember that the boat trip is only a small portion of the cost of the journey (it's hotels, food and transport along the way that really add up). Depending on the number of people in your group, you probably won't get back more than US$5 to US$10 if the boats don't sail.

Air HeliJet has a helicopter flight from Hanoi departing at 8 am and returning at 3.30 pm every Saturday. The US$195 fare includes a four-hour boat trip and lunch. Bookings can be made at the Sofitel Metropole Hotel (☎ 04-826 6919 ext 8046).

There are also chartered helicopter flights from Hanoi to Halong Bay costing US$100 per person one way. This service is offered by Vasco (☎ 04-827 1707, fax 827 2705), which operates out of Hanoi's Gia Lam airport.

There is yet another competitor in this business, North SFC (☎ 04-852 3451, fax 852 1523), 173 Đ Truong Chinh, Hanoi.

Getting Around

Air If you've got cash to burn, Vasco's helicopters (see under Getting There & Away earlier) can be chartered for whirlwind tours of the bay. Of course, it's hard to imagine how you'll see the grottoes from a helicopter unless the pilots are really skilled.

Boat You won't see much unless you take a boat tour of the islands and their grottoes. If you do end up travelling independently to Halong City, cruises for a few hours up to a whole day are offered by private boat owners, travel agencies and hotels in Bai Chay. Competition is fierce, but overcharging and high-pressure sales tactics are still the norm in Bai Chay.

Since the area is large, it's advisable to take a fast boat in order to see more. The rare but romantic junks are very photogenic (indeed, videogenic) and can be hired as well. However, junks are so slow on a calm day that they hardly seem to be moving at all.

You needn't rent a whole boat for yourself – there are plenty of other travellers, Vietnamese and international, who wouldn't mind getting together a small sightseeing group. A small boat can hold six to 12 people and costs around US$6 per hour. Mid-sized boats (the most popular ones) take around 20 passengers and cost US$15 per hour. Larger boats can hold 50 to 100 people and cost US$25 per hour.

All tourist boats are inconveniently located at a marina about 2km west of central Bai Chay.

In the past there were stories of armed pirate-style robberies from small boats – the overseas passengers lost all their money, passports etc. This has been cracked down upon. Still, be careful with your valuables. Snatch-and-run-style theft is still a possibility, much like the motorbike 'cowboys' in Saigon (see the boxed text 'Warning' in this special section).

CAT BA ISLAND

☎ 031 • pop 12,000

Cat Ba is the largest island in the Halong Bay vicinity. **Lan Ha Bay**, off the east side of the island, is especially scenic and offers numerous beaches to explore. While the vast majority of Halong Bay's islands are uninhabited vertical rocks, Cat Ba has a few tiny **fishing villages** and a fast-growing town. The terrain is too rocky for agriculture: Most residents earn their living from the sea while others cater to the tourist trade. Life has always been hard here and, not surprisingly, many Cat Ba residents joined the exodus of Vietnamese 'boat people' in the 1970s and 1980s. Although the island lost much of its fishing fleet this way, the overseas Vietnamese have sent back large amounts of money to relatives on the island, thus financing the new hotels and restaurants that you'll see.

There is very little motorised traffic and, indeed, very few roads. Compared with the tourist carnival at Bai Chay, Cat Ba is still relatively laid-back, despite about a 10-fold increase in hotel rooms (and karaoke machines!) since 1996.

WARNING

It's common practice to take a swim during a boat trip. If you do go swimming, it is wise to have someone (hopefully trustworthy) watch your valuables while you are cavorting in the water. One traveller warned:

Sometimes a boat approaches and offers fish and crabs, but beware – these people may be robbers! They grabbed the bag of an English guy (with his passport, money and cheques) and disappeared. Our tourist boat was slow and couldn't catch that fast boat. Two travellers we met reported that the crew of their boat stole some small things while they were swimming.

Pat Sanders

About half of Cat Ba Island (which has a total area of 354 sq km) and 90 sq km of the adjacent waters were declared a national park in 1986 to protect the island's diverse ecosystems. These include subtropical evergreen forests on the hills, freshwater swamp forests at the base of the hills, coastal mangrove forests, small freshwater lakes and coral reefs. Most of the coastline consists of rocky cliffs, but there are a few sandy **beaches** tucked into small coves. The main beaches are Cai Vieng, Hong Xoai Be and Hong Xoai Lon.

There are numerous lakes, waterfalls and grottoes in the spectacular limestone hills, the highest of which rises 331m above sea level. The growth of the vegetation is stunted near the summits because of high winds. The largest permanent body of water on the island is **Ech Lake**, which covers an area of three hectares. Almost all of the surface streams are seasonal; most of the island's rainwater flows into caves and follows underground streams to the sea, creating a shortage of fresh water during the dry season. Although parts of the interior of the island are below sea level, most of the island is between 50m and 200m in elevation.

The waters off Cat Ba Island are home to 200 species of fish, 500 species of molluscs and 400 species of arthropods. Larger marine animals in the area include seals and three species of dolphins.

Stone tools and bones left by humans who lived here between 6000 and 7000 years ago have been found at 17 sites on the Island. The most thoroughly studied site is **Cai Beo Cave**, discovered by a French archaeologist in 1938, which is 1.5km from Cat Ba town.

Trung Trang Cave is easily accessible, however you will need a torch (flashlight) if you want to see anything. The cave is just south of the park entrance along the main drag. Entry costs US$1.

Ho Chi Minh himself paid a visit to Cat Ba Island on 1 April 1951, and there is a large annual festival on the island to commemorate the day. A **monument** to Uncle Ho stands on Mountain No 1, the hillock across from the pier in Cat Ba town.

The best weather on Cat Ba Island is from late September to November, particularly the latter, when the air and water temperature is mild and skies are mostly clear. December to February is cooler, but still pleasant. From February to April rain is common. The summer months from June through August are hot and humid.

Cat Ba National Park

Cat Ba National Park is home to 32 types of mammals – including François monkeys, wild boar, deer, squirrels and hedgehogs – and over 70 species of birds have been sighted, including hawks, hornbills and cuckoos. Cat Ba lies on a major migration route for waterfowl (ducks, geese and shore birds) who feed and roost in the mangrove forests and on the beaches. The 745 species of plants recorded on Cat Ba include 118 timber species and 160 plants with medicinal value. There are currently around 45 park rangers stationed here to protect the flora and fauna.

Admission to the park is US$1; the services of a guide cost US$5 per day regardless of group size. A guide is not mandatory, but is definitely recommended – otherwise, all you are likely to see is a canopy of trees. The guide will take you on a walk through a cave – bring a torch – then on to a mountain peak. However the guide stops just short of the summit because they're afraid tourists will fall on the last section of slippery rocks (apparently an overseas tourist filed a lawsuit after falling). The last part of the walk is rather hairy, but push on to the summit if you like (at your own risk) – many say the views are worth it.

There is a *very* challenging 18km (five to six hour) hike through the park that many enjoy. You need a guide, bus transport to the trailhead and a boat to return – all of this can be easily arranged at the hotels in Cat Ba. The hike includes a visit to Viet Hai, a remote minority village. If you're planning on doing this hike, equip yourself with proper hiking shoes, a raincoat and a generous supply of water (at least 3L) plus some food, as there are no opportunities (yet) to buy supplies en route. This is *not* an easy walk, though there are shorter options that are less hard-core. Camping is allowed in the park, but you'll need to bring your own gear.

Two caves in the national park are open to visitors. One has been preserved in its natural state, while the other has historical significance – it served as a secret, bomb-proof hospital during the American War. You have to pay an additional US$1 fee to visit the Trung Trang Cave.

To reach the national park headquarters at Trung Trang, take a minibus from one of the hotels in Cat Ba (US$0.50, 30 minutes). All restaurants and hotels should be able to sell you minibus tickets. Another option is to hire a motorbike for about 15,000d (US$1.10) one way.

The park is home to a unique species of tree called Cay Kim Gao (for aspiring horticulturists the Latin name is *Podocarpus fleuryi hickel).* In ancient days kings and nobles would eat only with chopsticks made from this timber; anything poisonous it touches turns the light-coloured wood to black!

Beaches

The white-sand Cat Co beaches (called simply Cat Co 1 and Cat Co 2) make a great place to lounge around for the day. They are about 1km from Cat Ba town and can be reached on foot or by motorbike for about 3000d (US$0.25). There is a 5000d (US$0.40) entry fee to the beaches.

The two beaches are separated by a small hillock that can be climbed over in about 20 minutes. Most, however, take the easier route along a new, 700m, wooden seaside walkway (around the mountain). Cat Co 2 is the less busy and more attractive of the two, and also offers simple accommodation and camping.

On weekends the beaches fill up with Vietnamese tourists (and become messy with litter), but during the week the crowds diminish.

Places to Stay

Over the past several years Cat Ba's accommodation offerings have risen to over 40 hotels and guesthouses, feeding both an expanding domestic and foreign tourist market. Until recently there was just a handful of places to stay, no electricity, and mostly intrepid travellers.

Since being 'discovered' by Hanoi residents, however, Cat Ba has turned into a highly popular summer getaway, filling up on weekends and holidays (this is of course when the karaoke machines are in full gear). Still, Cat Ba is a far more pleasant place to stay than Halong City for anyone planning to tour Halong Bay.

In May 1998 the island was finally hooked up to the national power grid, which brings with it such modern amenities as air-con, satellite TV and hot water. The good news is the departure of the noisy generators, which used to rattle so loud that having a conversation over dinner was a challenge. The bad news is the clamour of the generators has been replaced with off-tune melodies flowing from a plethora of open-air karaoke joints. The authorities in Haiphong permitted the plaguing of the peaceful island with karaoke as long as it was not behind closed doors and was over by midnight. The theory was this would prevent prostitution from penetrating the town (the move has clearly been met with little success).

Places to Stay – Budget

Most of island's hotels are on the waterfront in Cat Ba town. The ones to the east (that is, the ones not built right up against the hillside) tend to offer better cross breezes and less of the seedy, karaoke–call girl scene.

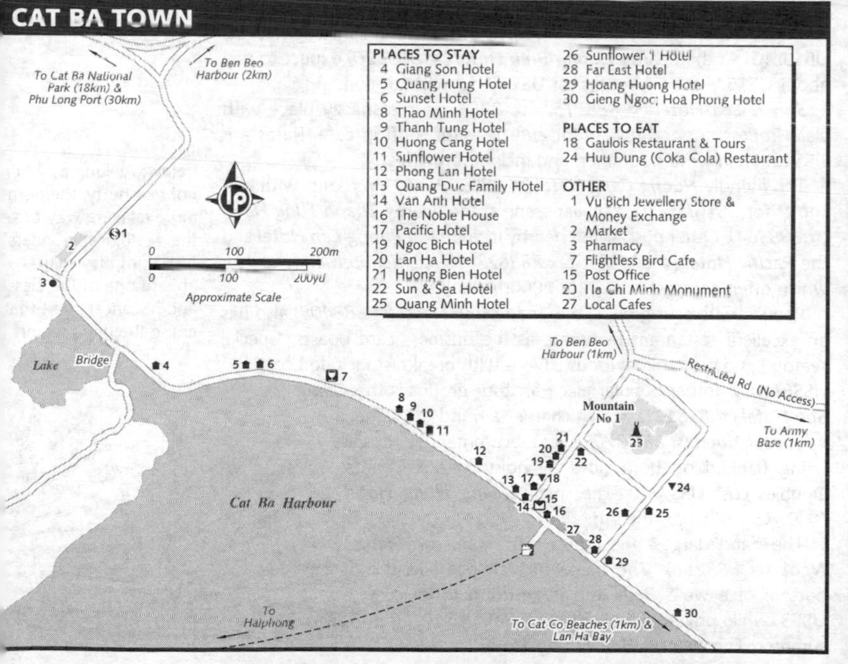

Room rates fluctuate greatly between high-season summer months (May to September) and the slower winter months (October to April). When choosing a hotel avoid ones advertising 'karaoke' – they tend to be brothels.

Quang Duc Family Hotel *(☎ 888231, fax 888423)* is Cat Ba's original 'family hotel' and worthy of a plug. Twins cost US$10/12 in winter/summer, and come furnished with air-con and satellite TV. Next door, the ***Van Anh Hotel*** *(☎ 888201)* has air-con rooms with two or three beds costing US$12/15 in winter/summer.

Also recommended is the ***Hoang Huong Hotel*** *(☎ 888274)*, where twins with fan cost US$6/10 or, with air-con US$8/12. There is a good indoor/outdoor restaurant on the ground level, as well as Internet access.

Across the way is the ***Far East Hotel*** *(☎ 888555, fax 888570)*, also called *Vien Dong*. Winter/summer rates are US$7/9 with fan or US$10/12 with air-con.

Sunflower Hotel *(☎ 888215, fax 888451, ⓔ sunflowerhotel@hn.vnn.vn)* has an open-air billiards bar on the seventh-floor rooftop with a great view of the harbour. Winter rates are US$12/15 for fan/air-con rooms; they're about US$2 more in summer. French and English are spoken. Rates at the newer ***Sunflower 1 Hotel*** are similar, while across the road at the ***Quang Minh Hotel*** *(☎ 888229, fax 888570)*, basic but bright and airy rooms rent for US$8/12 with fan/air-con.

The ***Lan Ha Hotel*** *(☎ 888299)* has fan twins for US$4/5 in winter/summer. The neighbouring ***Ngoc Bich Hotel*** is similar, and costs US$5/10. At the nearby ***Huong Bien Hotel*** *(☎ 888620)* expect to pay about US$5/6 for fan rooms, or US$10/12 with air-con.

Sun & Sea Hotel *(☎ 888315, fax 888475)* is a snazzy place with clean rooms, a good restaurant and pleasant rooftop cafe. Rates are US$12/17 in winter/summer, and include breakfast.

The friendly ***Huong Cang Hotel*** *(☎ 888399)* has fan rooms with balconies for US$6/10. It's a similar scene at the nearby ***Thanh Tung Hotel*** *(☎ 888364)*. Other possibilities nearby include the ***Phong Lan Hotel*** and the ***Pacific Hotel*** *(☎ 888331, fax 888623, ⓔ pacifichotel@hn.vnn.vn)*, which offers Internet access for 2000d/minute.

Popular with tour groups, the ***Thao Minh Hotel*** *(☎ 888408)* also has an excellent restaurant featuring, as the business card boasts, 'special seafood and wild animal foods'. Twins with breakfast included cost US$8/10. Another popular place for tour groups is the ***Giang Son Hotel*** *(☎ 888121)*, which charges around the same.

Sunset Hotel *(☎ 888 370)* is also recommended, despite being flanked on both sides by noisy karaoke joints. Doubles cost US$7/10. The small ***Quang Hung Hotel*** *(☎ 888222)* charges the same.

The island's largest guesthouse is the state-run ***Gieng Ngoc*** *(☎ 888286)*. The name means 'pearl at the bottom of a well'. Beds in a large dorm room cost US$3, while private doubles/triples cost US$12/16 in summer. The nearby ***Hoa Phong Hotel*** *(☎ 888412)*

Below: As long as you'r not in a hurry, there's n more relaxing way to se the geological wonders of Halong Bay than aboard one of the classi and historical junks that cruise the bay's waters.

offers summer twins/triples for US$10/12, or a 'family' room with six beds for US$16. Knock off about 30% in winter.

If you want to avoid the hoopla in town, consider spending the night at the simple two-room ***guesthouse*** over on Cat Co Hai (Cat Co Beach No 2). The room tariff is just US$3.20. The manager also rents out tents (US$2) for guests to ***camp*** on the beach.

If you really want to get away from it all, the national parks department recently built a basic four-room ***beach guesthouse*** (US$10/room) on the nearby island of Cat Dua (Pineapple Island). It is also possible to camp on the beach provided you bring your own gear. Except for the local park rangers, the island is uninhabited, that is unless you count the wild deer, monkeys and snakes! There is no electricity (generator only), and no restaurants, so you'll need to prepare all provisions on Cat Ba Island. Cat Dua is about 30 minutes by boat from Cat Ba Town; there is no public ferry, so you must arrange a private boat to take you over and pick you up. Either decide on a day/time to return with the boat driver, or if you have a Vietnamese mobile phone you can call for pick up. A boat, able to carry about 15 people, should cost about US$6 one way. To make arrangements, speak to Mr Phuc at the Quang Duc Family Hotel.

Places to Stay – Mid-Range

At the time of writing ***The Noble House*** *(☎ 888363)*, a new Aussie-managed hotel was under construction just across from the boat pier. With all the trimmings and bay views from the rooms, it promises to be Cat Ba's most luxurious accommodation. Expect rates to be around US$20 to US$50 in winter, and slightly more in summer.

Places to Eat

The friendly ***Huu Dung Restaurant*** has some of the best fresh seafood in town. It is affectionately known as the *Coka Cola Restaurant* (the red-tile roof of the open-air wooden building is painted like a Coke billboard). Travellers rave about the spring rolls, fried cuttlefish, battered shrimp and the house special, whole fish.

Another excellent place to eat is the ***Gaulois Restaurant*** *(☎ 888482)*. The delightful owners, Mr Thanh and his wife Tram, serve up delicious Vietnamese and backpacker fare, and can also arrange tours and provide the latest travel information. The menu is illustrated with photos.

There is a strip of small outdoor ***cafes*** opposite the ferry landing where you can grab a coffee or snack while waiting for the ferry to leave.

Floating Restaurants There are numerous 'floating' seafood restaurants just offshore in the Cat Ba town harbour. There have been several reports of overcharging, so be sure to work out the price, as well as the cost of a boat to get you out there and back, in advance. One traveller commented:

When you go to the floating restaurants agree upon a price up front for the food…most of the menus have no price and as with most places in Vietnam, if you're a tourist, they'll try and hit you with crazy prices. We ended up paying ridiculous amounts of money in the restaurant. If we didn't pay them, the boat driver would not take us back to the island.

Paul Jaines

A better alternative is a floating restaurant called ***Xuan Hong*** *(☎ 888485)*, which is a few kilometres away, moored just off shore at Ben Beo Harbour. The water is cleaner on this part of the island, the fish is tastier, and rip-offs are less prevalent (though you should always keep an eye out to be sure). Xuan Hong is a fascinating fish farm–cum–restaurant where you can tread on the edges of the large fish cages and get a close look at the workings of the 'farm'. You know the fish is fresh when it is plucked from the cages *after* you've ordered (aspiring sushi chefs should bring their own knife)!

Ask Mr Phuc at the Quang Duc Family Hotel to help make arrangements (he turned us on to the place). If you don't speak Vietnamese, it is best to go here with a local who can help with the ordering and negotiation (seafood prices are by the kilogram, and you'll need to be sure the amount you ordered is what actually reads on the scale). Menu choices (and average prices) include shrimp (160,000d/kg), shark (100,000/kg), muscles (110,000d/kg), crab (55,000d/kg) and 'cat's eye' snails (10,000d/kg). These prices include the preparation.

Entertainment

Thankfully there are alternatives to the lewd karaoke-massage scene. The ***Flightless Bird Cafe*** *(☎ 888517)* is one. Run by a congenial expat New Zealander named Graeme and his Vietnamese wife Nu, this stylish cafe-bar is a great place for drinks, darts, good music and movies. There is a pleasant second-floor balcony overlooking the harbour. At the time of writing the cafe was only open in the evenings, but the proprietors had plans for serving a Western 'all-day breakfast'.

Getting There & Away

Cat Ba Island is 40km east of Haiphong and 20km south of Halong City. A great innovation for getting there are the 75-seat and 108-seat

Feeling Queasy

The seas, especially those between Cat Hai Island and Cat Ba town can get pretty rough (yes, even in the hydrofoils). The stretch between Cat Hai and Phu Long port is smoother, and is a very short hop. If you are prone to sea sickness, come prepared. Even if you aren't, bring a poncho just in case your neighbour is. Transparent plastic bags are provided to let you know exactly what all the seasick-prone people sitting around you had for lunch. Seats in the rear of the hydrofoil are the least bumpy.

Russian-built hydrofoils. These air-conditioned water rockets reduce the Haiphong–Cat Ba journey to just 45 minutes and 1¼ hours respectively. The fare for foreigners is 90,000d (US$7). The hydrofoil currently runs once daily in each direction; from Haiphong to Cat Ba at 9 am, with a return trip at 4 pm. Why they leave at the same time and do not stagger the departures is a true mystery. Be aware, however, that the schedule is highly subject to change. In general, but especially during the peak summer season weekend, you should book tickets in advance.

Slow boats take about 2½ hours and cost 70,000d (US$5.50) per person. Schedules are in a constant state of flux, so make inquiries locally.

An alternative way to reach Cat Ba is via the island of Cat Hai, which is closer to Haiphong. A boat departs Haiphong and makes a brief stop in Cat Hai, before continuing to the port of Phu Long on Cat Ba Island. There is also a 12.30 pm slow boat from Hon Gai (Halong City), which takes about two hours to Cat Hai, from where it's possible to catch another boat across to Phu Long port (US$0.60, 20 minutes).

There plenty of slow, chartered tourist boats making the run from Halong City to Cat Ba Island. Check with the cafes and travel agencies in Hanoi about tour options. Such trips generally include all transport, accommodation, food and a guide, but ask to make sure.

Be aware – there is more than one pier on Cat Ba Island. One is in Cat Ba town (which is where most travellers want to go) and the other is at Phu Long, some 30km away. From Phu Long, motorbike drivers will be waiting to whisk you away on battered Russian minsks for the 30km ride to the centre of town (or about 15km to the Cat Ba National Park) for about US$4. There is also a public bus (US$1.60) meeting the boats, but this takes considerably more time getting you to your hotel.

Getting Around

Rented bicycles are a great way to explore the island. Several of the hotels can find you a Chinese junker, or inquire at the Flightless Bird Cafe about mountain-bike rentals.

Minibuses (always with driver) are easily arranged. Motorbike rentals (either with or without driver) are available from most of the hotels, as are some rental bicycles. If you're heading out to the beaches or national park, pay the US$0.15 parking fee to make sure your vehicle is still there when you return: There have been reports of theft and vandalism.

You'll have plenty of offers to take a trip around Cat Ba fishing harbour in a small rowboat for around US$1.50. One enterprising fellow sits in his paddleboat and calls out to every foreigner the only English sentence he knows: 'Hello how are you I'm fine thank you very much'.

Tours of the island and national park, boat trips around Halong Bay, and fishing trips are being peddled by nearly every hotel and restaurant in Cat Ba town. Prices depend on the number of people, but typical prices are US$8 for day trips and US$20 for a two-day/one-night trip.

We are able to endorse a few reliable tour operators including Mr Phuc at the Quang Duc Family Hotel, and Mr Thanh at the Gaulois Restaurant. They can arrange interesting boat/trekking trips.

continued from page 240

The campaign hit the ethnic-Chinese particularly hard. It was widely assumed that the Marxist-Leninist rhetoric veiled ancient Vietnamese antipathy towards the Chinese.

The anti-capitalist and anti-Chinese campaign caused up to 500,000 of Vietnam's 1.8 million ethnic-Chinese to flee the country. Those in the north fled overland to China, while those in the south left by sea. Creating Chinese refugees in the south proved to be lucrative for the government – to leave, refugees typically had to pay up to US$5000 each in 'exit fees'. In Ho Chi Minh City, Chinese entrepreneurs had that kind of money, but refugees in the north were mostly dirt-poor.

In response, China cut all aid to Vietnam, cancelled dozens of development projects and withdrew 800 technicians. Vietnam's invasion of Cambodia in late 1978 was the final straw: Beijing – alarmed because the Khmer Rouge was its close ally and worried by the huge build-up of Soviet military forces on the Chinese-Soviet border – became convinced that Vietnam had fallen into the Russian camp, which was trying to encircle China with hostile forces.

In February 1979 China invaded northern Vietnam 'to teach the Vietnamese a lesson'. Just what lesson the Vietnamese learned is not clear, but the Chinese learned that Vietnam's troops – hardened by many years of fighting the US – were no pushovers. Although China's forces were withdrawn after 17 days and the operation was officially declared a 'great success', most observers soon realised that China's People's Liberation Army (PLA) had been badly mauled by the Vietnamese. It is believed to have suffered 20,000 casualties in 2½ weeks of fighting. Ironically, China's aid to Vietnam was partially responsible for China's humiliation.

Officially, these 'misunderstandings' are considered ancient history – trade across the Chinese-Vietnamese border is booming and both countries publicly profess to be 'good neighbours'. In practice, China and Vietnam remain highly suspicious of each other's intentions. Continued conflicts over who owns oil-drilling rights in the South China Sea is an especially sore point. China has neither forgiven nor forgotten its humiliation at the hands of the Vietnamese and has relentlessly been building up its military ever since. Thus, the border area remains militarily sensitive, though the most likely future battleground is at sea.

If you visit China and discuss this border war, you will almost certainly be told that China acted in self-defence because the Vietnamese were launching raids across the border and murdering innocent Chinese villagers. Virtually all Western observers, from the US government's Central Intelligence Agency to historians, consider China's version of events to be nonsense. The Chinese also claim they won this war – nobody outside of China believes that either.

You'd hardly know these tensions exist when you visit Mong Cai. This town appears to be the most popular border crossing for Vietnamese and Chinese nationals.

Information

Travel Agencies OSC Hai Phong Tourist (☎ 883506) is a place to rent cars, motorbikes and hire tour guides. With the requisite visas, staff can arrange trips to China.

The hydrofoil ticket office (☎ 883988) is beside the Nha Nghi Binh Dan (guesthouse).

Money Vietcombank is in the centre of town; travellers cheques can be cashed here.

Emergency If you need to purchase any medical supplies, there a **pharmacy** across from the Tiem An Viet-Trung Restaurant.

Places to Stay

Nha Nghi Hai Thinh *(☎ 882254)* offers basic fan rooms with attached toilet and hot water from US$5. There's a pool table on the ground floor. A similar standard prevails at the ***Nha Nghi Hai Dang*** *(☎ 881555)*, where in place of a pool table you'll find a toy store!

Viet Thai Hotel *(☎ 881070, fax 881100)* is a newly restored place not far from the border gate. Fan/air-con rooms cost US$9/11. A block away and charging the same is the attractive ***Truong Minh Hotel*** *(☎ 883368)*. The ***Thang Loi Hotel*** *(☎ 881002)* charges US$9 to $12 for air-con comfort, while the ***Cong Nghe Hotel*** *(☎ 883011, fax 882012)* has US$9 air-con rooms.

Opposite the bus station, the ***Thien Huong Hotel*** *(☎ 882429)* and ***Nha Nghi Cao Son*** both look nice. Rates are around US$11 to US$16.

Places to Eat

The fanciest place to dine in Mong Cai is the ***Nha Hang Le Huy*** *(☎ 887125)*, opposite the Thuong Mai Hotel. It does Vietnamese and Chinese dishes.

For overpriced Vietnamese food masquerading as authentic Chinese food, look for ***Tiem An Viet-Trung***. It is actually Chinese run, and there is no English menu.

A third option is the ***Hoa Phuong Restaurant*** *(☎ 831515)*, whose name means 'Flame Flower'.

Delicious dumpling-like *banh cuon* (steamed rice pancake) is served in the morning in the south part of town near the river. A strip of ***restaurants*** in the east of town on Pho Hung Vuong serve *com-pho* (rice-noodle soup).

Getting There & Away

Bus Mong Cai is 360km from Hanoi. You'll pass plenty of coal mines en route – your face (and lungs) will receive a fine coating of black coal dust before the journey is completed. Just pity the folks who live here and have to breathe this in every day.

Buses to/from Hanoi (US$5, 10 hours) leave two or three times a day, in the early morning. A scant few buses also connect Mong Cai and Haiphong (US$4, eight hours).

Buses are frequent between Mong Cai and Hon Gai (Halong City). They leave approximately every 30 minutes between 5.30 am and 5.30 pm (US$3, six hours).

Mong Cai–Lang Son is a five-hour journey. However, buses on this route only leave once or twice a day (if at all) and only in the early morning. Much of the road is unpaved – expect plenty of dust or mud.

Boat Two high-speed hydrofoils run between Mong Cai and Bai Chay (Halong City) daily, taking just three hours en route. From Bai Chay departures are at 7 am and 1 pm, and back from Mong Cai shuttle vans leave the hydrofoil ticket office in town at

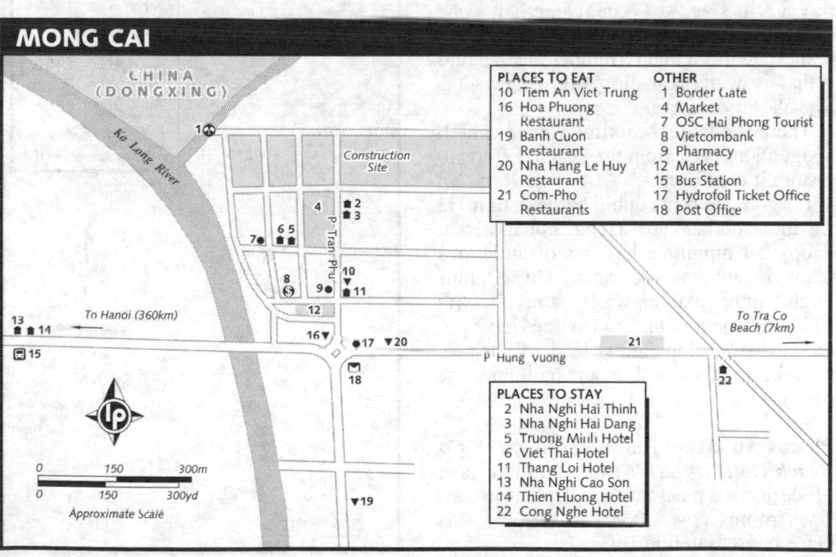

8.30 am and 2.30 pm. The cost is US$12, and includes a van/boat ride between Mong Cai and the pier, and Van Gia Island (where the boats actually depart from).

There is also a large daily slow ferry between Hon Gai and Mong Cai, The boat starts in Haiphong at 6 pm, leaves Hon Gai at 9 pm and finally arrives in Mong Cai the next morning between 3 am and 5 am. The same boat makes the return trip from Mong Cai to Hon Gai at 10 am, docking in Hon Gai at 6 pm. The cost is US$6.

It is possible to charter a boat from Van Don Island to Mong Cai; captains in Van Don ask about US$150/200 one way/return. The one-way trip takes six hours.

AROUND MONG CAI

Tra Co Beach

Seven kilometres to the south-east of Mong Cai is Tra Co, an oddly shaped peninsula widely touted as a beach resort. Despite a considerable public-relations effort, the beach at Tra Co is a disappointment: the sand is dull and hard-packed. Indeed, you can easily drive a conventional car on the beach (and many people do so).

The most impressive thing about this beach is its size. At 17km in length, it's one of the longest stretches of sandy beachfront real estate in Vietnam. Another neat feature is that the water is shallow, allowing waders to walk far offshore.

There is a large, beautiful, ruined church about 500m back from the beach. Efforts to restore it continue.

It's going to be an uphill battle to turn Tra Co into another Nha Trang, but the local People's Committee has lots of ambitious plans to increase tourism. These plans might not be total hogwash – after all, with China just next door, Tra Co does have potential to develop into a land of casinos, karaoke lounges and steam bath/massage parlours.

Places to Stay The motel-like ***Tra Co Beach Hotel*** (☎ *881264*) is next to the post office and is a pleasant enough place to stay. Twin rooms cost US$10 to US$15. This place boasts satellite TV.

Across the street is the less interesting ***Dai Duong Mini-Hotel*** (☎ *881140*). At least it's cheap – twins, complete with satellite TV, cost from US$6 to US$10.

Two other nearby options to consider are the ***Tra Long Hotel*** (☎ *881131*), with fan rooms for US$6, and the larger ***Sao Bien Hotel*** (☎ *881243*), with US$7 fan rooms and air-con twins for US$10 to US$14.

LANG SON

pop 62,300 • elevation 270m

The capital of mountainous Lang Son Province, Lang Son is in an area populated largely by Montagnards (Tho, Nung, Man and Dzao), many of whom continue their traditional way of life. There are also caves 2.5km from Lang Son, near the village of Ky Lua. However, the real drawcard is neither Montagnards nor caves, but Lang Son's role as a trading post and crossing point into China. However, the border is actually in Dong Dang, 18km to the north.

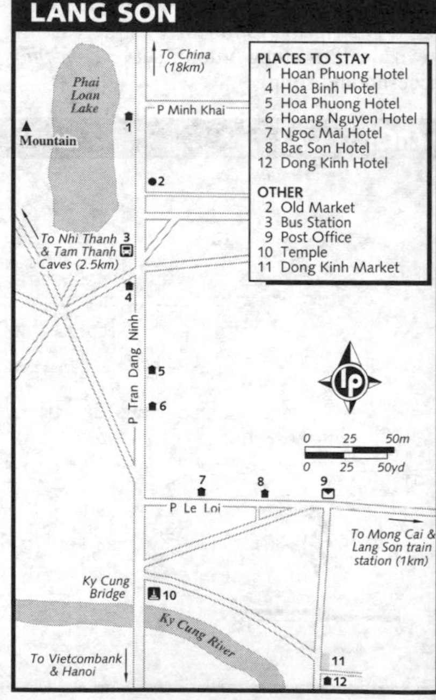

Lang Son was partially destroyed in February 1979 by invading Chinese forces; the ruins of the town and the devastated frontier village of Dong Dang were often shown to foreign journalists as evidence of Chinese aggression. Although the border remains heavily fortified, Sino-Vietnamese trade appears to be in full swing again.

Orientation

Lang Son is bisected by the Ky Cung River. Most hotels and the post office are on the northern shore, but Vietcombank is on the southern side. On the western side of town are mountains riddled with attractive caves.

Tam Thanh & Nhi Thanh Caves

There are two large and beautiful caves just 2.5km from the centre and both are illuminated, which makes for easy exploration.

Tam Thanh Cave is excellent. A notable feature is a 'bottomless pond'. Its name is Am Ty (Hell) – an indication of just how deep it is. The cave also has a viewing point (a natural 'window') presenting a sweeping view of the surrounding rice fields. There is also a place where dripping water is collected in a basin – drinking from here is claimed to do wonders for your health

The Ngoc Tuyen River flows through Nhi Thanh Cave, which has excellent stalactites and stalagmites, giving added charm.

Places to Stay

The privately owned, friendly ***Hoang Nguyen Hotel*** *(☎ 870349, 84 Pho Tran Dang Ninh)* is clean, pleasant and has US$10 to US$15 twins. Next door, the ***Hoa Phuong Hotel*** *(☎ 871233, 92 Pho Tran Dang Ninh)* has similar standards (except for the giant girlie posters in the lobby) and prices.

The ***Hoa Binh Hotel*** *(☎ 870807, 127 Pho Tran Dang Ninh)* is a relatively new place with rates from US$10 to US$12. The similar ***Hoan Phuong Hotel*** *(☎ 870488, 299 Pho Tran Dang Ninh)* costs the same.

Ngoc Mai Hotel *(☎ 871837, 25 Pho Le Loi)* has nice rooms with TV (Vietnamese and Chinese channels only) costing US$15 to US$20.

The ***Bac Son Hotel*** *(☎ 871849, 41 Pho Le Loi)* is in a beautiful colonial building. Twins cost US$25, which includes breakfast. This state-run place is often full.

Near the Dong Kinh Market is the new, all air-con ***Dong Kinh Hotel*** *(☎ 870166, fax 875461)*. Deluxe doubles for foreigners cost US$20. Triples are US$14 (Russian air-con) or US$18 (Japanese air-con).

Places to Eat

Both Pho Tran Dang Ninh and Pho Le Loi are thick with good local restaurants. *Pho chua* (a noodle dish) is the budget speciality of Lang Son. If you'd prefer to eat upmarket, check out the *vit quay* (roast duck) or *lon quay* (suckling pig).

Shopping

The Dong Kinh Market is a four-storey Aladdin's den of cheap goods (that break easily) from China.

Getting There & Away

Buses to Lang Son depart Hanoi's Long Bien bus station at about 6 am. The journey takes roughly five hours.

Two daily trains run between Hanoi and Dong Dang (via Lang Son; see the Getting There & Away chapter).

Getting Around

The usual motorbike taxis can be found almost anywhere, but are especially abundant around the post office and the market.

On Pho Tran Dang Ninh, you'll see minibuses looking for passengers heading to the border at Dong Dang.

CAO BANG

pop 45,500 • elevation 700m

The dusty capital of Cao Bang Province, Cao Bang town is 300m above sea level and has a pleasant climate. The main reason to come here is to make excursions into the surrounding scenic countryside. This is the most beautiful mountain area in the north-east and is worth exploring.

While in Cao Bang town, climb the hill leading up to the War Memorial. There are great views from the summit.

Information

Cao Bang Tourist (☎ 852245) is inside the Phong Lan Hotel and, when the staff are present, can arrange cars, 4WDs and guides for visiting the outlying districts.

There is no foreign exchange bank in Cao Bang.

Places to Stay & Eat

The nicest hotel in town is the 11-room ***Huong Thom Hotel** (☎ 855888)*, near the market, which charges US$15 including breakfast. Some rooms have river views.

***Phong Lan Hotel** (☎ 852260),* on Đ Nguyen Du, is a dreary, state-run hotel, but has some of the cheapest rooms in town and an OK restaurant. Doubles cost US$8 to US$20.

The ***Phuong Dong Guesthouse** (☎ 853178),* on Đ Pac Bo, is clean enough and not bad value at US$10 to US$12 a room.

The ***Bang Giang Hotel** (☎ 853431),* near the bridge in the north of town, is an enormous hotel with bright cheery rooms. Rooms on the upper floors in the rear of the building have sweeping views overlooking the river. Twins cost US$20.

The ***Duc Trung Mini-Hotel** (☎ 853424)* is a small, privately owned place on a quiet street at the southern edge of town. It's not a bad place, if you can just ignore the stuffed black bear in the lobby. Twins are US$15.

The ***People's Committee Guesthouse** (Nha Khach UBND, ☎ 851023)* has good rooms priced from US$6 to US$20.

Beside the hotel restaurants, there are plenty of good ***food stalls*** near the market.

Getting There & Away

Cao Bang is 272km north of Hanoi, along Highway 3. This is a sealed road, but due to the mountainous terrain, Cao Bang–Hanoi is a full day's drive. There are several direct buses daily from Hanoi (10 hours) and Thai Nguyen. A daily bus to/from Lang Son takes seven hours.

You can approach Cao Bang from either Halong Bay or Mong Cai, by taking Hwy 4B (which is mostly a rough dirt road).

Cao Bang has ambitious plans to open an airport, but no word yet as to when.

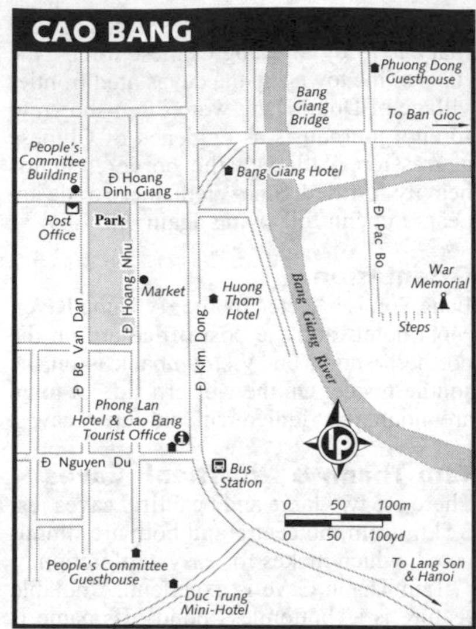

AROUND CAO BANG

Ban Gioc

This scenic spot sees very few visitors. The name Ban Gioc is derived from the Montagnard languages spoken in the area, and is sometimes spelled Ban Doc.

Thac Ban Gioc This waterfall is the largest (although not the highest) in the country. The vertical drop is only 53m, with an approximate 300m span. The water volume varies considerably between the dry and rainy seasons – the falls are most impressive from May to September.

The falls have three levels, creating a sort of giant staircase. It's a beautiful sight and should not be missed if you've time to make the journey.

The falls are fed by the Quay Son River, which marks the border with China. There's been a major build-up of tourist facilities on the Chinese side in recent years, but almost nothing on the Vietnamese side. The falls are actually in Vietnam, and many Chinese sneak across for a better view.

There is no official border checkpoint here and the area is only loosely patrolled. Despite this, a police permit is needed to

The Legend of the Lakes

The charming setting of Thang Hen wouldn't be complete without a depressing legend to go along with it. It seems that there was a very handsome and clever young man named Chang Sung. His mother adored him and deemed that he should become a mandarin and then marry a beautiful girl.

Under Confucian tradition, the only way to become a mandarin was to pass a competitive examination – Chang Sung, being a clever boy, sat the exam and passed. He received an official letter bearing the good news and ordering him to report to the royal palace just one week later.

With her son virtually guaranteed admission to mandarinhood, Mama launched Phase II of her plan – a beautiful girl, Biooc Luong (Yellow Flower), was chosen to marry Chang Sung and a big wedding was hastily arranged.

Chang Sung couldn't have been happier, in fact, he and Biooc were having such a great time on their honeymoon, he forgot all about his crucial appointment at the royal palace until the night before the deadline.

Knowing how disappointed Mama would be if he missed his chance to be a mandarin, Chang Sung summoned magical forces to help him hop in great leaps and bounds to the palace. Unfortunately, he messed up the aerodynamics and leapt 36 times, with no control over his direction or velocity, and wound up creating 36 craters, finally landing at the top of Ma Phuc Pass, where he died of exhaustion and became a rock. The craters filled up with water during the rainy season and became the 36 lakes of Thang Hen. No doubt Mama was proud of his civil engineering works, but still disappointed that Chang Sung didn't become a mandarin.

visit – you cannot simply rent a motorbike and go on your own. The permit (US$4) can be organised through travel agencies in Hanoi or hotels in Cao Bang, though you actually pick the permit up in Trung Khanh.

The road between Cao Bang and Trung Khanh is in good nick, but brace yourself for bumps on the last 27km to the waterfall.

Nguom Ngao Cave The main entrance to this cave is 2km from the waterfall, just off the road to Cao Bang. Actually, there are two main entrances – it's customary to enter by one and exit by the other. The cave is enormous (about 3km long) and one branch reaches almost all the way to the waterfalls where there is a 'secret' entrance.

To explore the cave you need a guide – fortunately they are readily available. They are paid a pittance and won't accept tips (that will probably change), but you might consider offering them cigarettes and a share of your picnic lunch.

Lights have been installed in the cave and the generators are turned on whenever tourists show up. The US$1 entrance fee helps pay the fuel and maintenance cost of the lighting system. Just to be safe, bring a torch – the generator could cut off suddenly without warning. Alternatively, you can always find your way out if you can locate the generator cable.

Places to Stay & Eat There are no hotels on the Vietnamese side of the border. Unless you want to try camping (and you'll have to bring your own gear), you'll have to stay in Trung Khanh, 27km from the falls. The only accommodation is the ***People's Committee Guesthouse*** *(Nha Khach UBND)*, in the centre of town. Rooms are dormitory-style with four to five beds and they cost US$4 each. The facilities are basic and the place is pretty dirty.

There is limited food available in Trung Khanh, but nothing at all in Ban Gioc. You'd be wise to prepare at least a picnic lunch for the trip to the waterfall and caves, and it wouldn't be a bad idea to bring some extra food and drink just in case you're delayed by a vehicle breakdown – otherwise, you'll be foraging for nuts and berries.

Getting There & Away Ban Gioc is 85km from Cao Ban, and the mountainous journey takes about four hours. There is currently no public transport going to Ban Gioc.

The scenery along the route is impressive, and the last 10km along the Quay Son River is particularly spectacular.

Thang Hen Lake

This is a large lake that can be visited year-round; however, what you get to see varies according to the seasons. During the rainy season (May to September) 36 lakes in the area are separated by convoluted rock formations. In the dry season, most of the lakes, except Thang Hen itself, are dry. However, during this time of year the lake level drops low enough to reveal a large cave, which can be explored by bamboo raft.

As yet there are no restaurants or hotels at Thang Hen, nor is there any public transport. To get there you'll need a 4WD or motorbike (though with new road improvements a regular car may be able to make the trip). From Cao Bang drive 20km to the top of Ma Phuc Pass. From there carry on for 1km to the fork in the highway – take the left branch and go another 4km. It's close enough to be visited as a day trip.

Hang Pac Bo

Hang Pac Bo (which means Water Wheel Cave) is just 3km from the Chinese border. The cave and the surrounding area is sacred ground for Vietnamese revolutionaries. On 28 January 1941, Ho Chi Minh re-entered Vietnam here after living abroad for 30 years. His purpose in returning to his native land was to lead the revolution that he had long been planning.

For almost four years Ho Chi Minh lived in this cave, writing poetry while waiting for WWII to end. The reason for remaining so close to China was to allow him to flee across the border if French soldiers discovered his hiding place. Ho named the stream in front of his cave Lenin Creek and a nearby mountain Karl Marx Peak.

In Tay, one of Vietnam's minority languages, *pac bo* means 'water wheel' – so called because there's a spring here.

Narang Market

This is one of the best markets in the provinces. Most of the vendors and customers are local Montagnard groups including the Nung, Tay and H'mong.

Other Montagnard Markets

In Cao Bang Province, Kinh (ethnic-Vietnamese) are a distinct minority. The largest ethnic groups are the Tay (46%), Nung (32%), H'mong (8%), Dzao (7%), Kinh (5%) and Lolo (1%). Intermarriage, mass education and 'modern' clothing is gradually eroding tribal and cultural distinctions.

Most of Cao Bang's Montagnards remain blissfully naive about the ways of the outside world. Cheating in the marketplace, for example, is virtually unknown and even tourists are charged the same price as locals without bargaining. Whether or not this innocence can withstand the onslaught of mass tourism remains to be seen.

The following big Montagnard markets in Cao Bang Province are held every five days, according to lunar calendar dates:

Trung Khanh 5th, 10th, 15th, 20th, 25th and 30th day of each lunar month

Tra Linh 4th, 9th, 14th, 19th, 24th and 29th day of each lunar month

Nuoc Hai 1st, 6th, 11th, 16th, 21st and 26th day of each lunar month

Nagiang 1st, 6th, 11th, 16th, 21st and 26th day of each lunar month; held 20km from Hang Pac Bo in the direction of Cau Bang and attracting Tay, Nung and H'mong

BA BE NATIONAL PARK

• elevation 145m

Ba Be National Park (Vuon Quoc Gia Ba Be), sometimes referred to as Ba Be Lakes (the park's main feature), in Bac Kan Province was established in 1992 as Vietnam's eighth national park. This beautiful region covers more than 23,000 hectares and boasts waterfalls, rivers, deep valleys, lakes and caves set amid towering peaks. The surrounding area is home to members of the Tay minority, who live in stilt homes.

It's a tropical rainforest area with over 400 named plant species. The government subsidises the villagers not to cut down the

The Legend of Widow's Island

A tiny islet in the middle of Ba Be Lakes is the source of a local legend. The Tay people believe that what is a lake today was once farmland, and in the middle was a village called Nam Mau.

One day, the Nam Mau residents found a buffalo wandering in the nearby forest. They caught it, butchered it and shared the meat. However, they didn't share any with a certain lonely old widow.

Unfortunately for the villagers, this wasn't just any old buffalo. It belonged to the river ghost. When the buffalo failed to return home, the ghost went to the village disguised as a beggar. He asked the villagers for something to eat, but they refused to share their buffalo buffet and ran the poor beggar off. Only the widow was kind to him and gave him some food and a place to stay for the night.

That night the beggar told the widow to take some rice husks and sprinkle them on the ground around her house. Later in the evening, it started to rain, and then a flood came. The villagers all drowned, the flood washed away their homes and farms, thus creating Ba Be Lakes. Only the widow's house remained, which is now the present-day Po Gia Mai (Widow's Island).

trees. The 300 wildlife species in the forest include bears, monkeys, birds, butterflies and other insects. Hunting is forbidden, but fishing is permitted (for villagers only).

This region is surrounded by steep mountains up to 1554m high. The 1939 *Madrolle Guide to Indochina* suggests getting around Ba Be Lakes 'in a car, on horseback, or, for ladies, in a chair', meaning, of course, a sedan chair.

Ba Be (Three Bays) is in fact three linked lakes, which have a total length of 8km and a width of about 400m. The deepest point in the lakes is 35m, and there are nearly 50 species of freshwater fish.

Two of the lakes are separated by a 100m-wide strip of water called Be Kam, sandwiched between high walls of chalk rock. The Nang River is navigable for 23km between a point 4km above Cho Ra and the **Thac Dau Dang** (Dau Dang Waterfall), which consists of a series of spectacular cascades between sheer walls of rock.

An interesting place is **Hang Puong** (Puong Cave). The cave is about 30m high and 300m long, and completely passes through a mountain. A navigable river flows through the cave, making for an interesting boat trip. However, the many bats living in the cave generate some powerful odours.

Dao Dang Falls (or Hua Tang Falls in Tay) is a series of rapids spread over 1km. Just 200m below the rapids is a very small Tay village called Hua Tang.

Renting a boat is de rigueur, and costs US$2.30 per hour. The boats carry about eight people, and you should allow at least seven hours to take in most sights. The boat men are known to go slow to get more money, but short of screaming 'faster, faster!' there is not much you can do. Just enjoy the ride. An optional guide (recommended) costs US$10 per day. The boat dock is about 2km from park headquarters.

A US$2.50 entrance fee is payable at a checkpoint on the road into the park (about 2km before park headquarters).

An English-narrated video tape about the park is sold at the visitors centre for US$8.

Bring cash with you (US dollars) as travellers cheques are not accepted here.

Places to Stay & Eat

Just by the park headquarters *(☎ 876131)* are three accommodation options. The seven basic, shared-bath triples in the decidedly dingy ***old wing*** cost US$10. For US$15 you can take a room in a basic, but attractive minority-style wooden ***house***. For US$20 try a room in the spiffy ***new wing***, across the road, with attached bath and hot water (electricity is supplied by a generator from 6 pm to 11 pm only). Meals can be ordered in the park for around US$2.

In Cho Ra, 18km from the lakes, is the ***Ba Be Hotel*** *(☎ 876115)*. It charges US$15 per fan room. The people here can also arrange cheap boat trips to the national park. The boats can carry about 15 people and cost US$16 for a full day (plus the US$5 park entry fee). There are a few basic noodle joints in town.

It may be possible to stay in ***stilt houses*** at the nearby Tay hamlet of Pac Ngoi. The village, on the bank of the river leading into the lake, has about 200 residents living in some 40 stilt houses. To stay, you will need to arrange a permit through the park staff, though local police in the area are known to be fickle about issuing these.

Food is available in the village, including fresh fish from the lake, and prices here are reasonable.

Perhaps the best option is to book an organised tour with the park staff. They can arrange a pleasant three-day/two-night trip in the park, which includes the major sights and one night at Pac Ngoi. The cost for the tour depends on the number of people, but ranges from US$25 to US$40 per person. Some Hanoi tour operators can help you make the booking, or you can contact the park headquarters directly.

Getting There & Away

Ba Be National Park is in Bac Kan Province not far from the borders of Cao Bang Province and Tuyen Quang Province. The lakes are 240km from Hanoi, 61km from Bac Kan (also known as Bach Thong) and 18km from Cho Ra.

Most visitors to the national park get there by chartered vehicle from Hanoi. From Bac Kan onwards the road gets rough, the last 50km particularly so, and should only be attempted with a 4WD, high-clearance vehicle or a powerful motorbike.

Chartering a 4WD from Hanoi to the park should cost about US$200, depending on how long you stay. The one-way journey from Hanoi takes about eight hours; most travellers allow three days and two nights for the entire excursion.

Reaching the park by public transport is possible, but not easy: Take a bus from Hanoi to Bac Kan and from there another bus to Cho Ra; in Cho Ra you will have to get a motorbike (about US$1.50) to do the last 18km, unless you are willing to walk it.

Some cafes in Hanoi offer tours for around US$60. Inquire at Buffalo Tours or Handspan Adventure Travel (see the list of travel agents in the Hanoi chapter).

North-West Vietnam

North-west Vietnam offers travellers some of the country's most spectacular scenery. The mountainous areas are home to many distinct hill tribes, some still living as they have for generations, despite ever-increasing Vietnamese and Western influences.

Hwy 6 winds through beautiful mountains and high plains inhabited by Montagnards (notably the Black Thai, White Thai and H'mong). The Thai are most numerous in the lower lands, where they cultivate tea and fruit and live in attractive stilt houses. The hardy H'mong live in the bleaker highlands over 1000m.

Hwy 6 is mostly bitumen surface from Hanoi to Dien Bien Phu – but the road is a thrill! Even more exciting is Hwy 32 – between Dien Bien Phu and Lai Chau – a dangerous cliffhanger frequently wiped out by landslides. This road is so rough it can jar the fillings out of your teeth. The ensuing stretch from Lai Chau into Sapa is bumpy in places, but offers some of the best mountain vistas in South-East Asia.

The north-west roads are improving bit by bit. However, if you suffer from vertigo, backache or (God forbid) haemorrhoids, you might want to stick to shorter trips. Many travel only as far as Mai Chau or Son La, or Sapa in the other direction, before turning back. Given the state of the roads, this is not surprising.

The most interesting (and hair-raising) journey of all is the 'north-west loop'. Head for Mai Chau, followed by Son La and Dien Bien Phu, then north to Lai Chau, Sapa, Lao Cai and back to Hanoi. The loop route requires a 4WD or motorbike, and you should allow at least a week for this trip.

Highlights

- Hit the road by jeep, motorbike or bicycle and take in some of South-East Asia's most breathtaking mountain scenery.
- Trek to highland villages and learn about hill-tribe communities.
- Make the challenging ascent up Fansipan, the highest peak in Vietnam.

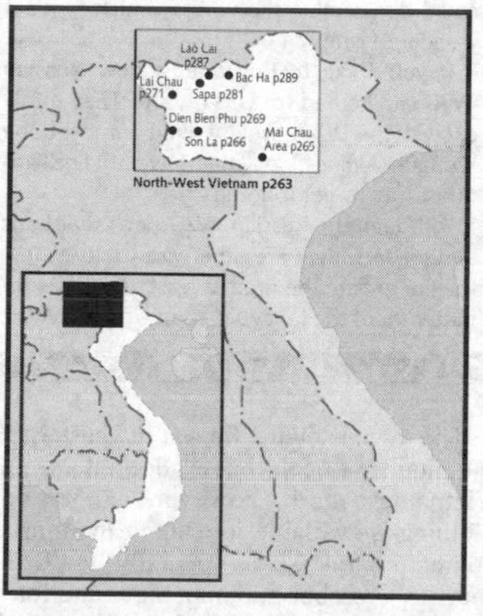

Warning

In the entire north-west of Vietnam, there are very few legal places to cash travellers cheques, and credit cards are of little use. You can cash travellers cheques at some hotels in Sapa, but you will be charged a steep 10% commission. It's easier to swap US dollars for Vietnamese dong, but you'd be wise to complete all your money-changing transactions before leaving Hanoi. The situation is a bit ridiculous given the number of tourists who pass through here now, but that's the reality.

HOA BINH

☎ 008 • pop 75,000 • elevation 200m

The city of Hoa Binh (Peace), the capital of Hoa Binh Province, is 74km south-west of Hanoi. This area is home to many hill-tribe people, including H'mong and Thai. Hoa Binh can be visited on an all-day excursion from Hanoi, or as a stop on the long drive towards Dien Bien Phu.

One for the Road

Russian 4WDs, based on the latest 1950s technology, are still being manufactured and used in Vietnam. There has been absolutely no change in design for the past 40 years, with the exception of the door handles – the new ones are made of plastic and break more easily than the old metal ones. Obviously intended for the Russian climate, the windows do not even open (a horror in summer). You can get a nice breeze if you put the top down, but it's quite a complex procedure. By contrast, with a spanner and a screwdriver you could disassemble the whole vehicle – it's a wonder of simplicity.

If you'd like to buy one, a new Russian 4WD can be had for US$21,000. They easily exceed the 20kg weight limit imposed by Vietnam Airlines, so you'll have to find another way to get it home.

Although the Russian 4WDs lack seat belts and rollbars, they are otherwise pretty safe – they negotiate the mud at least as well as (or better than) the fancy Japanese-made 4WDs.

The town is on the flats at the base of the mountains. Locals have adopted modern Vietnamese garb, however, Montagnard clothing is available for sale in the market, some in large sizes specially made for tourists. Crossbows, opium pipes and lots of other Montagnard paraphernalia can be bought in the market or at the Hoa Binh Hotel souvenir shop.

Information

Hoa Binh Tourist (☎ 854374) no longer has a walk-in office, but the sales and marketing department can be contacted by telephone.

Places to Stay & Eat

The ***Hoa Binh I Hotel*** *(☎ 852051)* is in Montagnard stilt-house style with nontraditional amenities like hot water and TV. Modern intrusions aside, we must admit it's one of the better hotels in north-west Vietnam. The rooms cost US$33. Just opposite is the ***Hoa Binh II Hotel*** *(☎ 852001, fax 854372)*, which charges US$35.

Many ***com-pho places*** line Hwy 6. The popular local eatery ***Quyet Gio*** *(☎ 852956)* does good, cheap Vietnamese food.

SONG DA RESERVOIR

Close to Hoa Binh is a large dam on the Da River (Song Da), which is Vietnam's largest reservoir. The flooding of the Da River has displaced a large number of farmers for about 200km upstream. The dam is part of a major hydroelectric scheme that generates power for the north. In 1994, a 500kV power line was extended from this area to the south, freeing Saigon from the seasonal power shortages that often blacked out the city for up to three days at a time.

Though the dam is just 5km from Hoa Binh, it's best to visit the reservoir by taking a spur road that cuts off from Hwy 6 at Dong Bang Junction (60km from Hoa Binh). From Dong Bang Junction it's just a short drive to Bai San Pier, where you catch boats to the **Ba Khan Islands**. The islands are the tops of submerged mountains and the visual effect is like a freshwater version of Halong Bay. The return trip to the islands takes three hours and costs US$30, but each boat can seat 10 passengers.

Another possible trip is to take a boat to Phuc Nhan village, which is home to members of the Dzao tribe. The return trip costs US$15. The boat leaves you at a pier from where it's a steep 4km uphill walk to the village. If you'd like to stay in the village, you can take the boat one way for US$10 and get a return boat to Bai San Pier the next day.

The last option is to charter a boat from Bai San Pier to Hoa Binh (60km). This costs US$120, but the boat holds 10 people.

MAI CHAU

☎ 018 • pop 47,500 • elevation 300m

This is one of the closest places to Hanoi where you can see a 'real' Montagnard village. Mai Chau is rural with no real town centre – rather, it's a collection of villages, farms and huts spread out over a large area. It's a beautiful area, and most people here are ethnic White Thai, said to be distantly related to tribes in Thailand, Laos and China.

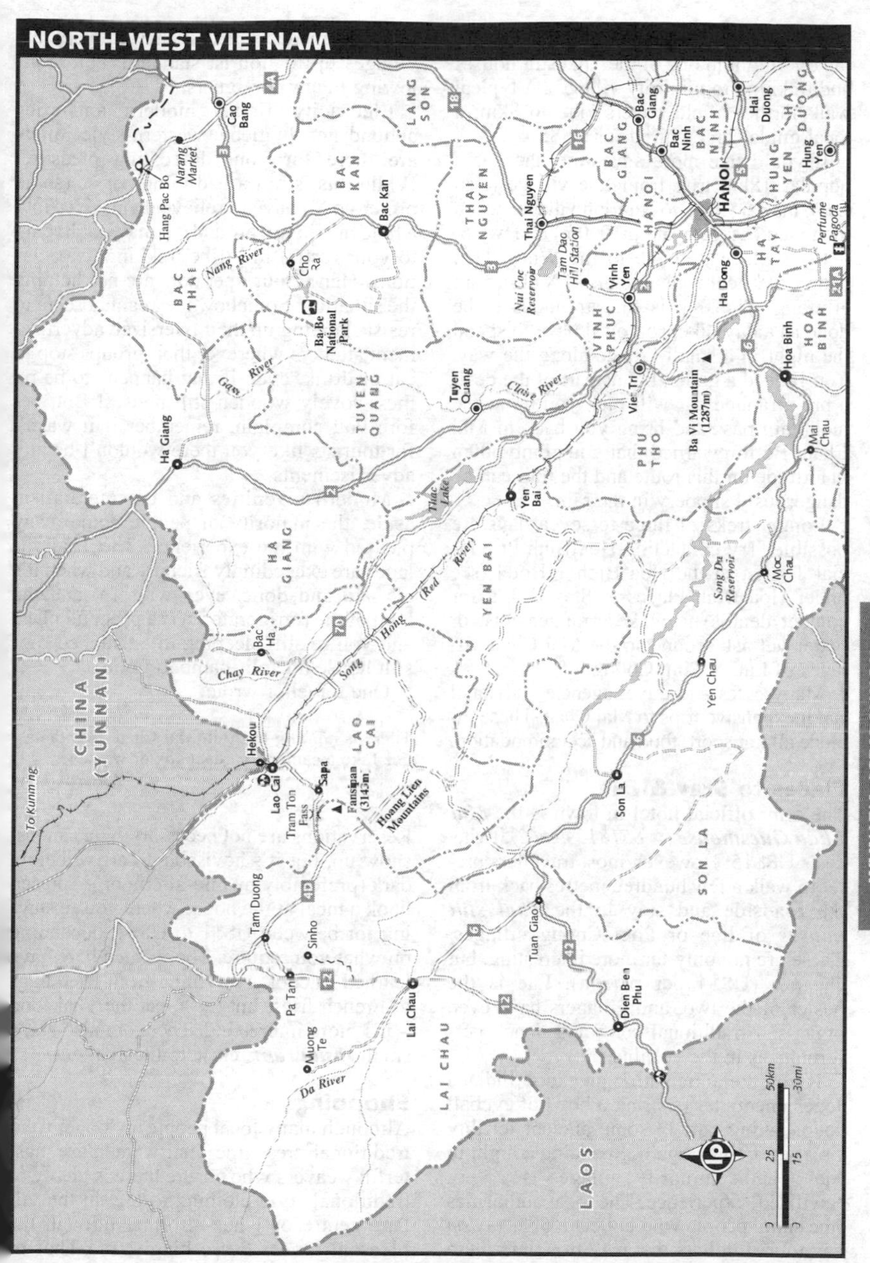
NORTH-WEST VIETNAM
CHINA (YUNNAN)
LAOS
To Kunming
Cao Bang
Narang Market
Hang Pac Bo
Bac Kan
Cho Ra
Ba Be National Park
Nang River
Gam River
BAC THAI
BAC KAN
LANG SON
THAI NGUYEN
Thai Nguyen
BAC GIANG
Bac Giang
Bac Ninh
BAC NINH
Hai Duong
HAI DUONG
HUNG YEN
Hung Yen
HANOI
Ha Dong
HA TAY
Perfume Pagoda
Tam Dao Hill Station
Nui Coc Reservoir
Vinh Yen
VINH PHUC
Viet Tri
PHU THO
Ba Vi Mountain (1287m)
Hoa Binh
HOA BINH
Tuyen Quang
TUYEN QUANG
Clear River
Ha Giang
HA GIANG
Thac Ba Lake
Yen Bai
YEN BAI
Song Hong (Red River)
Song Da Reservoir
Mai Chau
Moc Chau
Bac Ha
Chay River
Hekou
Lao Cai
LAO CAI
Sapa
Fansipan (3143m)
Tram Ton Pass
Hoang Lien Mountains
Yen Chau
Son La
SON LA
Tuan Giao
Dien Bien Phu
Tam Duong
Sinho
Pa Tan
Lai Chau
LAI CHAU
Muong Te
Da River
0 25 50km
0 15 30mi

Interesting things to do here include staying overnight in one of the Thai stilt houses and trekking to minority villages. A typical walk farther afield covers 7km to 8km; a local guide can be hired for US$5.

If you'd like more adventure, there is a popular 18km trek from Lac village (Ban Lac), in Mai Chau, to Xa Linh village, near a mountain pass (elevation 1000m) on Hwy 6.

Lac village is home to the White Thai people, while the inhabitants of Xa Linh are H'mong. The trek is too strenuous to be done as a day hike, so you'll have to spend the night in a small village along the way. You'll need a guide, but as part of the deal, a pre-arranged car will pick you up at the mountain pass and bring you back to Mai Chau. Be forewarned that you climb 600m in altitude on this route and the trail can be dangerously slippery in the rain.

Longer treks of three to seven days are possible. Try contacting Hoa Binh Provincial Tourist in the Hoa Binh 1 Hotel (see under Hoa Binh Places to Stay & Eat for contact details) to make arrangements, or better yet ask around in the Mai Chau villages of Lac or Pom Coong.

Many cafes and travel agencies in Hanoi run inexpensive trips to Mai Chau. These include all transport, food and accommodation.

Places to Stay & Eat

The only official hotel in town is the ***Mai Chau Guesthouse*** *(☎ 851812 ext 62)*, twins costs US$15. However, most travellers prefer to walk a few hundred metres back from the roadside and stay in the ***Thai stilt houses*** of Lac or Pom Coong villages. These are not only far more interesting, but cheaper (US$4 per person). Lac is the busier of the two, and villagers have even organised traditional song and dance performances in the evenings.

If you are anticipating an exotic Indiana Jones encounter (sharing a bowl of eyeball soup, taking part in some ancient fertility ritual etc), think again. Spending a night in Mai Chau's minority villages is a very 'civilised' experience. The local authorities (the same people who collect a 50% tax on any tourist dollars that may flow into these villages) made sure that they brought the villages up to 'tourist standard' before allowing in any foreigners.

Electricity flows, modern amenities abound and hygienic western-style toilets are there for your defecating pleasure. While this is not a bad thing per se (some prefer not to have to relieve themselves into a hole dug in the ground), it may not live up to your rustic 'hill-tribe trekking' expectations. Hanoi tour operators are not helping the situation: Somehow they cannot seem to resist slapping up their oversized advertisement stickers wherever their groups stop to eat or drink, even if that happens to be on these lovely wooden stilt houses! But, before you complain, remember if it wasn't for tourists like you there wouldn't be any advertisements.

Modern amenities and commercialism aside, the majority of people come away pleased with the experience. The Thai villages are exceedingly friendly and when it's all said and done, even with TV and the hum of the refrigerator, it *is* a peaceful place and you're still sleeping in a thatched-roof stilt house on split-bamboo floors.

One traveller wrote:

> There is *nothing* to do in Mai Chau. It is fantastic. Take a camera, cards, book or whatever.
>
> **Annette Low**

Reservations are not necessary; you can just show up, but it's advisable to arrive before dark (preferably by mid-afternoon). You can book a meal at the house where you're staying for between US$1 to US$4, depending on what you require. The women here have learned to cook everything from fried eggs to French fries, but try to eat the Thai food – it's more interesting. There are also some small ***restaurants*** close to the market.

Shopping

Although many local people no longer wear traditional dress, the Thai women are masterful weavers who ensure there is plenty of traditional-style clothing to buy in the village centre or when strolling through the pleasant lanes. Refreshingly, the Thai of

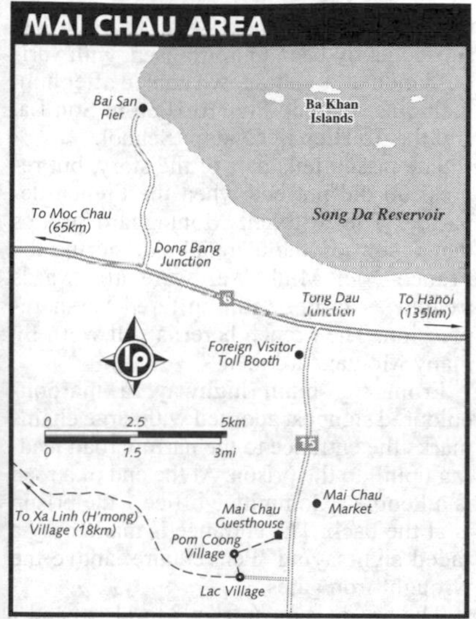

Mai Chau are not nearly as aggressive as their H'mong counterparts in Sapa. Polite bargaining is the norm.

Getting There & Away

Mai Chau is 135km from Hanoi and just 6km south of Tong Dau junction on Hwy 6 (the Hanoi–Dien Bien Phu route).

You'll be hard-pressed to find any direct public transport to Mai Chau from Hanoi; however, buses to nearby Hoa Binh are plentiful. From Hoa Binh you can either get a local bus or hire a motorbike taxi to Ma Chau.

As you enter Mai Chau, there is a barricade across the road. All foreigners must stop here and pay an admission toll of US$0.50, though riding in on the public bus seems to grant you an exemption.

MOC CHAU

☎ 022 • pop 113,100 • elevation 1500m

This highland town produces some of Vietnam's best tea and is a good place to stock up. The surrounding area is also home to several ethnic minorities including Green H'mong, Dzao, Thai and Muong.

Moc Chau boasts a pioneer dairy industry started in the late 1970s with Australian and, later, UN assistance. The pastoral scenes look like something right out of the Netherlands or New Zealand (if you ignore the barren 'slash and burn' hillsides). The dairy provides Hanoi with such delectable luxuries as fresh milk, sweetened condensed milk and little tooth-rotting sweet bars called *banh sua* (milk cake).

Not surprisingly, Moc Chau is a good place to sample fresh milk and yoghurt. Try the dairy shops lining Hwy 6 as it passes through Moc Chau.

If you plan to spend the night, the ***Duc Dung Guesthouse*** *(☎ 866181)*, about 100m off Hwy 6 in the middle of town, is the place to stay. Rooms cost US$8 to US$10 and its restaurant is recommended.

Moc Chau is 200km from Hanoi, and the journey takes roughly six hours by private car. The road is in good condition, so there's no need for a 4WD. It's another 120km from Moc Chau to Son La.

YEN CHAU

☎ 022 • pop 50,800

This small agricultural district is very well known for its fruits. Apart from bananas, the fruits are seasonal – mango harvesting takes place in May and June, longans in July and August and custard apples in August and September.

The mangoes, in particular, are considered to be some of the best in Vietnam, though overseas travellers may find them disappointing at first. This is because they are small and green rather than big, yellow and juicy as in the tropical south. However, many Vietnamese prefer the somewhat tart taste and aroma of the green ones. The colour doesn't give a clue as to when the fruit is ripe, so you may need to ask for a local's 'expert' advice on a mango's ripeness.

Yen Chau is 260km from Hanoi, approximately eight hours by car. Yen Chau to Son La is another 60km.

SON LA

☎ 022 • pop 61,600

Son La, capital of a province of the same name, makes a good overnight stop for travellers doing the run between Hanoi and

Dien Bien Phu. While not one of Vietnam's highlights, the scenery isn't bad and there is certainly enough to see and do to keep you occupied for a day.

The area is populated mainly by Montagnards, notably the Black Thai, Meo, Muong and White Thai.

Vietnamese influence in the area was minimal until this century; from 1959 to 1980 the region was part of the Tay Bac Autonomous Region (Khu Tay Bac Tu Tri).

Old French Prison & Museum

Son La was once the site of a French penal colony in which anticolonial revolutionaries were incarcerated. It was destroyed by the infamous 'off-loading' of unused ammunition by US warplanes returning to their bases after bombing raids on Hanoi and Haiphong.

The Old French Prison (Nha Tu Cu Cua Phap) has been partially restored in the interests of historical tourism. Rebuilt turrets and watchtowers stand guard over the remains of cells, inner walls and a famous lone surviving peach tree. The tree, which blooms with traditional Tet flowers, was planted in the compound by To Hieu, a former inmate from the 1940s. To Hieu has subsequently been immortalised, with various landmarks about town named after him, including a street, Pho To Hieu in Son La, and the To Hieu Secondary School.

The prison tells part of the story, but repression did not end when the French departed. The different Montagnard groups that fought on the colonial side during the Franco–Viet Minh War were afterwards treated as traitors and suffered harsh repression. The French beret is still worn by many Montagnard men.

From the main highway, a maroon-coloured signpost adorned with large chains marks the entrance to the narrow road leading uphill to the prison. At the end of a road is a People's Committee office – the prison is at the back. The entrance is marked by a faded sign saying 'Penitentaire' above the wrought-iron gates.

The prison is open from 7 to 11 am and 1 to 5 pm daily. Entrance costs 10,000d (US$0.80), and the price of the ticket gains you entry to the adjoining museum. Though neglected, there are some interesting hill-tribe displays and a good birds-eye view of the prison from upstairs.

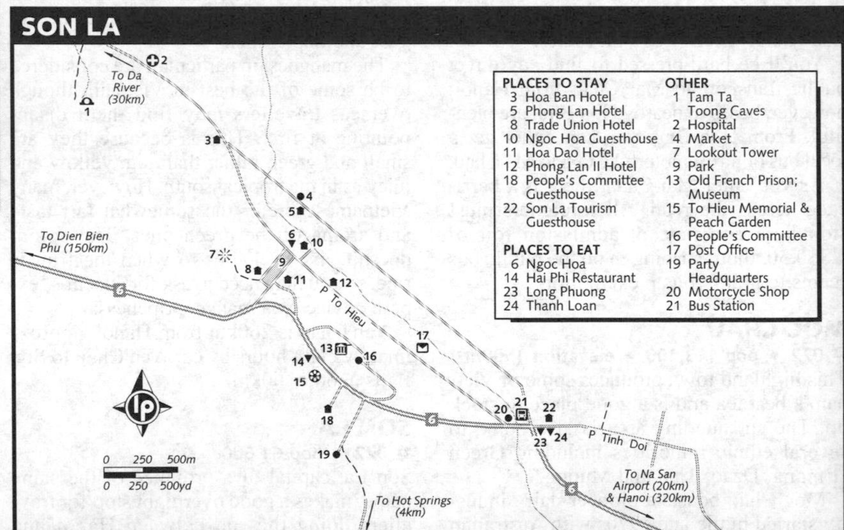

Lookout Tower

This tower offers a sweeping overview of Son La and the surrounding area. The climb is steep and takes about 20 minutes, but the view from the top is well worth it. Photography of the scenery is permitted, but the guards will get uptight if you try to photograph the installations, which serve both telecommunications and military purposes.

The stone steps leading up to the tower are immediately to the left of the Labour Federation Guesthouse.

Market

You can find a small selection of colourful woven shoulder bags, scarves, clothing and other Montagnard crafts at Son La's market.

Tam Ta Toong Caves

There are many caves in the region, but Tam Ta Toong Caves have long been the most accessible from Son La. At the time of writing, however, access was being denied due to fears of people contaminating the waters (the caves are the main water source for Son La). Inquire at your hotel if the caves have been reopened or not.

There are actually two caves here – one dry and one partially flooded. The dry cave is uninteresting, but ironically has an entrance gate and you need permission and a guide to enter. Both can be had for a price – inquire at hotels in town if interested. The flooded cave is adjacent to the dry one, but is more fun and no permit or guide is required. A small adjacent irrigation dam supplies the water that has flooded the cave. The cave goes back about 100m into the hillside. You should find a raft moored at the cave entrance plus an attendant who can take you inside for a negotiable fee. Bring a torch (flashlight).

Tam Ta Toong Caves are a few kilometres north-west of town. Along the highway past the hospital, a bridge crosses a creek just before the pavement ends. Turn left onto an unsealed country road about 20m before the bridge. Head along the track by the creek (which is actually the outflow from the flooded cave) for about 450m, crossing the creek once along the way. An aqueduct crosses the track – turn left and follow the aqueduct to the flooded cave's entrance, which is surrounded by an ugly barbed-wire fence. The dry cave is reached by following the track on the right of the flooded cave up the hill a short distance.

Hot Springs

An enjoyable few hours can be spent strolling through some Thai villages south of town followed by a dip in the Suoi Nuoc Nong hot springs. The facilities here are sadly rather run-down, but the waters are said to do magic for your skin.

The communal pool is free, but you can fork out 5000d (US$0.40) for a tiny cubicle of a room with a private bath tub. Although children can frolic nude in the public pool, it's definitely *not* acceptable for adults. Westerners, in particular, can expect to be the centre of wide-eyed attention.

To get there, start at the signpost with the chains (the same one which marks the French Prison turn-off), take the road that heads south (opposite direction of the prison). The road leads past the party headquarters building, after which the pavement ends. From here it's 5km to a handful of very basic, small bathing huts right beside the track; a couple of communal cement pools lay just behind. A motorbike or high-clearance vehicle can navigate the road, but during the wet season it becomes a muddy quagmire.

Places to Stay

Almost all travellers journeying between Hanoi and Dien Bien Phu (or vice versa) spend the night in Son La.

For a state-run place, the ***Trade Union Hotel*** *(Khach San Cong Doan, ☎ 852244, fax 855312)* is a rare gem. The staff are exceedingly friendly and prices are reasonable. Large twins with hot water cost US$10 to US$20, including breakfast.

Though not as friendly as the folks at the Trade Union Hotel, the recently renovated ***People's Committee Guesthouse*** *(Nha Khach Uy Ban Nhan Dan Tinh Son La, ☎ 852080)* is good value. Air-con rooms cost US$15.

The ***Son La Tourism Guesthouse*** *(Nha Khach Du Lich Son La,* ☎ *852702)*, almost directly across the road from the long-distance bus station, is starting to show its age. Rooms cost US$6 to US$9.

The ***Hoa Dao Hotel*** *(☎ 853823, fax 853712)*, or 'Peach Blossom Hotel,' offers decent rooms with breakfast for US$15. The other upmarket establishment is the ***Hoa Ban Hotel*** *(☎ 854600, fax 852712)*. Prices are US$15 to US$20. The hotel is known for its good restaurant.

One of the newest places in town is the spiffy ***Ngoc Hoa Guesthouse*** *(☎ 853993)*. The per-person rate in a six-bed dorm is US$3, or it's US$12 for a private double.

The ***Phong Lan Hotel*** *(☎ 853516)* has fan rooms costing US$12 and air-con twins from US$20 to US$30 (breakfast included). The ***Phong Lan II Hotel*** *(☎ 852318)* charges US$15 for a room with air-con and a bath.

Places to Eat

There are a couple of good restaurants across from the Son La Tourism Guesthouse. The highest standard is at ***Long Phuong*** *(☎ 852339)*, a good place to sample bitter *mang dang* (bamboo shoots), a speciality of the Thai minority people. For good basic *com-pho* (rice-noodle soup), try ***Thanh Loan*** or ***Ngoc Hoa***, just around the corner from the guesthouse sharing the same name.

The ***Hai Phi Restaurant*** dishes up Son La's speciality – *lau* (goat meat). Try the highly prized *tiet canh*, a bowl of goat's-blood curd dressed with a sprinkling of peanuts and veggies. Or go for the more conventional, but tasty, goat-meat steamboat.

Getting There & Away

Son La's airport is called Na San and is 20km from Son La along the road towards Hanoi. Flights to/from Hanoi run twice weekly, if at all.

Buses take from 12 to 14 hours to travel between Hanoi and Son La, assuming there are no serious breakdowns. From Son La to Dien Bien Phu is another 10 hours.

Son La lies 320km from Hanoi and 150km from Dien Bien Phu. The Hanoi–Son La run typically takes 10 hours. Son La to Dien Bien Phu is another six hours.

TUAN GIAO

☎ 023 • pop 94,900 • elevation 600m

This remote town is at the junction of Hwy 42 to Dien Bien Phu (three hours, 80km) and Hwy 6A to Lai Chau (four hours, 98km). Most travellers approach from Son La (three hours, 75km) and Hanoi (13 hours, 406km). These driving times assume you are travelling by car or motorbike – for public buses, multiply travel time by at least 1.5.

Not many people spend the night unless they are running behind schedule and can't make it to Dien Bien Phu, though if you are taking your time through the north-west it makes a logical place to stop for the night.

Places to Stay & Eat

The ***Thuong Ngiep Hotel*** *(☎ 862613)* is a relatively new place with fan rooms costing US$4 with shared bath, or US$9 with attached bath. It's about 150m from the main junction in the direction of Lai Chau.

The ***People's Committee Guesthouse*** *(Nha Khach Uy Ban Nhan Dan Huyen, ☎ 862391)* can also provide basic accommodation. Rooms in the dingy B-block cost just US$3. For the newer A-block, rates are US$5 with shared bath, or US$8 to US$12 with private bath. The guesthouse is set back behind the post office.

The best place to eat in town – there aren't many – is the ***Hoang Quat Restaurant*** *(☎ 862582)*, about 300m from the junction toward Dien Bien Phu.

DIEN BIEN PHU

☎ 023 • pop 22,400

Dien Bien Phu was the site of that rarest of military events – a battle that can be called truly decisive. On 6 May 1954, the day before the Geneva Conference on Indochina was set to begin half a world away, Viet Minh forces overran the beleaguered French garrison at Dien Bien Phu after a 57-day siege, shattering French morale and forcing the French government to abandon its attempts to re-establish colonial control of Indochina.

Dien Bien Phu, the capital of Dien Bien District of Lai Chau Province (population 545,000), is in one of the most remote parts of Vietnam. The town is 34km from the Lao border in the flat, heart-shaped Muong Thanh Valley, which is about 20km long and 5km wide and surrounded by steep, heavily forested hills. The area is inhabited by Montagnard people, most notably the Thai and H'mong. The government has been encouraging ethnic-Vietnamese to settle in the region and populate the relatively new provincial capital. They currently comprise about one-third of the Muong Thanh Valley's total population of 60,000.

For centuries, Dien Bien Phu was a transit stop on the caravan route from Myanmar and China to northern Vietnam. Dien Bien Phu was established in 1841 by the Nguyen Dynasty to prevent raids on the Red River Delta by bandits.

In early 1954 General Henri Navarre, commander of the French forces in Indochina, sent a force of 12 battalions to occupy the Muong Thanh Valley to prevent the Viet Minh from crossing into Laos and threatening the former Lao capital of Luang Prabang. The French units, which had about 30% ethnic-Vietnamese members, were soon surrounded by a Viet Minh force under General Vo Nguyen Giap consisting of 33 infantry battalions, six artillery regiments and a regiment of engineers. The Viet Minh force, which outnumbered the French by five to one, was equipped with 105mm artillery pieces and anti-aircraft guns, carried by porters through jungles and across rivers in an unbelievable feat of logistics. The guns were emplaced in carefully camouflaged positions dug deep into the hills that overlooked the French positions.

A failed Viet Minh human-wave assault against the French was followed by weeks of intense artillery bombardments. Six battalions of French paratroops were parachuted into Dien Bien Phu as the situation worsened, but bad weather and the Viet Minh artillery, impervious to French air and artillery attacks, prevented sufficient French reinforcements and supplies from arriving. An elaborate system of trenches and tunnels allowed Viet Minh soldiers to reach French positions without coming under fire. The French trenches and bunkers were overrun after deciding against using US conventional bombers – and a Pentagon proposal to use tactical atomic bombs. All 13,000 men in the French garrison were either killed or taken prisoner; Viet Minh casualties were estimated at 25,000. The site of the battle is now marked by the **Dien Bien Phu Museum** (☎ 824971).

The **bunker headquarters** of the French commander, Colonel Christian de Castries, has been re-created, and there are old French

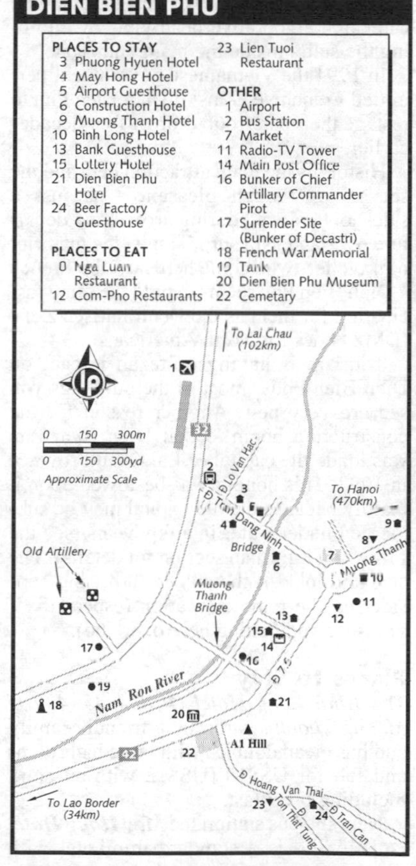

tanks and artillery pieces nearby. One of the two landing strips used by the French is extant. The old **Muong Thanh Bridge** is preserved and closed to motorised traffic. Near the south end of the bridge (though not much more than a crater in the ground overgrown with weeds) is the bunker where Chief Artillery Commander Pirot committed suicide.

There is a **monument** to Viet Minh casualties on the site of the former French position known as Eliane (A1 Hill), where bitter fighting took place. A **memorial** to the 3000 French troops buried under the rice paddies was erected in 1984 on the 30th anniversary of the battle. The **Dien Bien Phu Cemetery** has a remarkably stylish design, and you can catch a good overhead view by climbing the stairs inside the main entry gate.

In 1994 the Vietnamese government permitted French veterans of Dien Bien Phu to restage their paratroop drop of four decades earlier.

History is the main attraction here and the scenery – though pleasant – is just a sideshow enjoyed during arrival and departure overland. Not surprisingly, the majority of travellers who come here now are French – Dien Bien Phu seems to hold the same fascination for them as the Demilitarised Zone (DMZ) does for North Americans.

Tourism is having quite an impact on Dien Bien Phu – most of the buildings you see are very new. Another reason for the construction boom is that Dien Bien Phu was made the capital of Lai Chau Province in 1993. This honour was bestowed upon it mainly because the old capital may be submerged under water in a few years (see the following Lai Chau section for details). The size and look of the city is surprising considering the remote location (especially if you survived getting here overland).

Places to Stay

The ***Binh Long Hotel*** *(☎ 824345, 429 Đ Muong Thanh),* is run by a friendly family and has clean doubles with large bathrooms and fan for US$10 (US$12 with air-con), including breakfast.

Near the bus station the ***May Hong Hotel*** *(☎ 826300)* is a standard minihotel with twins for US$10 including breakfast. Similar rates apply at the ***Phuong Huyen Hotel*** *(☎ 824460, fax 824708)*, but no breakfast is served.

The ***Muong Thanh Hotel*** *(☎ 826719, fax 826720)* is the nicest place in town, but it's often full with tour groups (book ahead). It has a swimming pool, large restaurant, karaoke and 'Thai Massage', plus caged wild animals on display out the back. Twins with attached bath cost US$12 to US$20, including breakfast.

The large, state-run ***Dien Bien Phu Hotel*** *(☎ 825103, fax 825467)* is centrally located and charges around the same, but the facilities are not as nice.

Other accommodation in town comes care of the local airline, bank, lottery commission, construction ministry and – get this – the beer brewery!

The ***Bank Guesthouse*** *(☎ 825852, fax 826016)* has decent rooms behind a large bank building for US$8. Similar standards prevail at the ***Lottery Hotel*** around the corner. The ***Construction Hotel*** *(☎ 824386)* is right by the river and also charges US$8.

Our personal favourite, the ***Beer Factory Guesthouse*** *(Nha May Bia, ☎ 824635)*, has basic rooms from US$6 to US$12. The best part is the attached *bia hoi* pub.

Places to Eat

The best eatery in town is the ***Lien Tuoi Restaurant*** *(☎ 824919)*, on Đ Hoang Van Thai about 400m from the Dien Bien Phu Museum. The menu is in English and French. There are private dining rooms on the 2nd floor.

Nga Luan Restaurant on Đ Muong Thanh, serves a good mix of standard Vietnamese fare.

Beside the restaurants in some hotels, there are a couple of decent local ***com-pho joints*** halfway between the market and Bank Guesthouse on Đ 7.5.

Getting There & Away

The overland trip to Dien Bien Phu can be more intriguing than the actual battlefield sites for which the town is so famous. Of course, you miss out on this if you fly.

The Lao border is only 34km from Dien Bien Phu and there is much speculation about this crossing being opened to foreign tourists. For now, thanks to efforts at keeping a squeeze on the drug-smuggling industry, it's all talk. Nevertheless, keep your ear to the ground – the authorities may just give us a pleasant surprise.

Air Vietnam Airlines usually runs flights between Dien Bien Phu and Hanoi three times a week. The schedule varies according to demand, with the majority of the flights during July and August.

Vietnam Airlines has a booking desk (☎ 824692, fax 826060) at the Airport Guesthouse. It's open from 7.30 to 11.30 am and 1.30 to 4.30 pm daily.

The airport is 1.5km from Dien Bien Phu along the road towards Lai Chau.

Bus There is a direct bus service between Hanoi and Dien Bien Phu. Although the bus is cheap, it's not really much fun. Buses are so packed that the only scenery you get to admire is the armpit of the person sitting next to you. Furthermore, the buses we've seen do not look particularly safe. If overloaded vehicles, bad roads and bad brakes worry you, consider flying or travelling overland by 4WD or motorbike.

Car & Motorbike The 470km drive from Hanoi to Dien Bien Phu on Highways 6 and 42 takes 16 hours (if you're lucky). Conceivably it could be done in a single direct journey, but almost everyone stays overnight in Son La. You certainly wouldn't want to attempt this road in the dark!

LAI CHAU

☎ 023 • pop 19,600 • elevation 600m

This small town is nestled in a beautiful valley carved from spectacular mountains by the Da River, but beneath Lai Chau's beauty lies a difficult existence for locals. Despite a marked increase in tourist numbers, unfortunately tourist dollars land in the hands of a precious few. For the rest of Lai Chau it's a hard living, even for the local gold-panners.

Far from busy trade routes, normal commerce is limited and the town has only been really successful in harvesting particularly valuable cash crops. These include opium and timber. Needless to say, opium harvest-

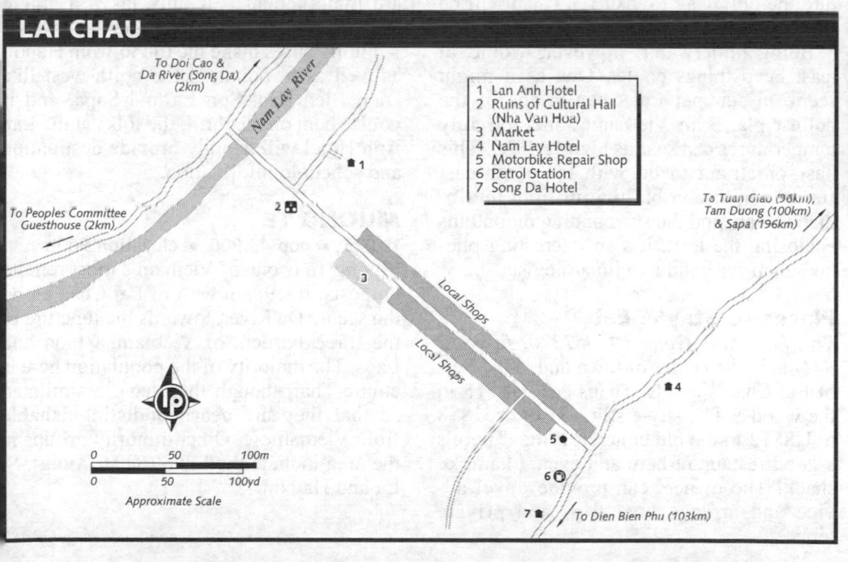

NORTH-WEST VIETNAM

ing does not find favour with the central government. No doubt some is exported directly to China, Thailand and possibly even some Western countries, but a good portion of it may be supplying junkies in Saigon. The government has been trying to discourage the Montagnards from producing opium poppies.

If the opium business is falling on hard times, the same must be said for the timber industry. In recent years the forest cover has been reduced and flooding has increased dramatically. Around 140 people lost their lives in 1990 in a devastating flood on the Da River that swept through the narrow valley. An even worse flood in 1996 killed 100 people and cut all roads into town for two months.

It seems that floods could become a permanent feature of Lai Chau. The government has planned to place a dam in the Ta Bu area (just above the current Song Da Reservoir). For this reason the provincial capital was transferred from Lai Chau to Dien Bien Phu in 1993. If and when this comes to pass (not before 2010), this will be the largest hydroelectric station in South-East Asia. It also could mean that in the future the only way to visit Lai Chau will be by submarine.

Being underwater, however, would at least keep things cooler. Odd as it might seem, in summer Lai Chau is one of the hottest places in Vietnam. June and July temperatures can soar as high as 40°C. This has something to do with the south-east summer monsoon blasting in from the Indian Ocean, and the surrounding mountains enclosing the heat. It's an interesting phenomenon for budding climatologists.

Places to Stay & Eat

The ***Lan Anh Hotel*** *(☎ 852370, fax 852 341)* is in the centre of town and is the best of Lai Chau's hotels. Twins cost US$15 in the woodsy Thai-style stilt houses or US$8 to US$12 in the old concrete wing. There's a good restaurant here and even a karaoke shack! The owners can provide travel advice and arrange boat trips and private tours.

Another decent option is the ***Song Da Hotel*** *(☎ 852527),* which is also central, on the road to/from Dien Bien Phu. Basic twin rooms cost US$8.

In the opposite direction, the ***Nam Lay Hotel*** *(☎ 852346)* is set slightly above the main road. Beds in dorm-style rooms (shared bathroom) cost just US$3, while twins cost US$6.

The bottom of the barrel is the ***People's Committee Guesthouse*** *(Nha Khach UBND),* in an old French-style building 2km from town. The place is an absolute dump. There are no showers and the toilets look like they haven't been cleaned since the French colonial era. All this luxury costs US$8 to US$15 – a ridiculous rip-off.

Getting There & Away

Make local inquiries to find out which roads (if any) are open. The shortest approach is on Hwy 6 from Tuan Giao (four hours, 93km). Most travellers will arrive from Dien Bien Phu (4½ hours, 103km). The road from Lai Chau to Sapa and Lao Cai (eight hours, 180km) is perhaps the most beautiful drive in Vietnam, but it's bumpy. Remember that all of the above travel times are hypothetical – it only takes a single landslide to cause considerable delays.

Public buses make the run to/from Hanoi, as well as to points in the north-west like Dien Bien Phu, Son La and Sapa, and if you're bent on the thrill, the folks at the Lan Anh Hotel will happily provide destination and schedule information.

MUONG TE

☎ 023 • pop 43,900 • elevation 900m

Muong Te is one of Vietnam's most remote outposts. It's 98km west of Lai Chau along the scenic Da River, towards the juncture of the three borders of Vietnam, China and Laos. The majority of the population here is ethnic-Thai, though they have assimilated so that they are nearly indistinguishable from Vietnamese. Other minority groups in the area include the Lahu (Khau Xung), Si La and Ha Nhi.

continued on page 280

Hill Tribes in Vietnam

LIZ THOMPSON

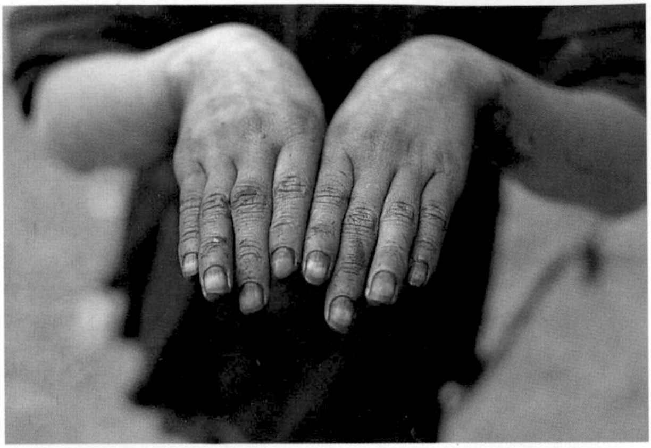

MASON FLORENCE

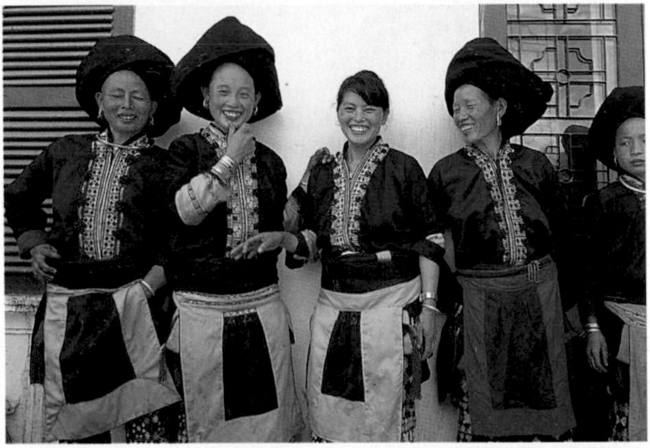

MASON FLORENCE

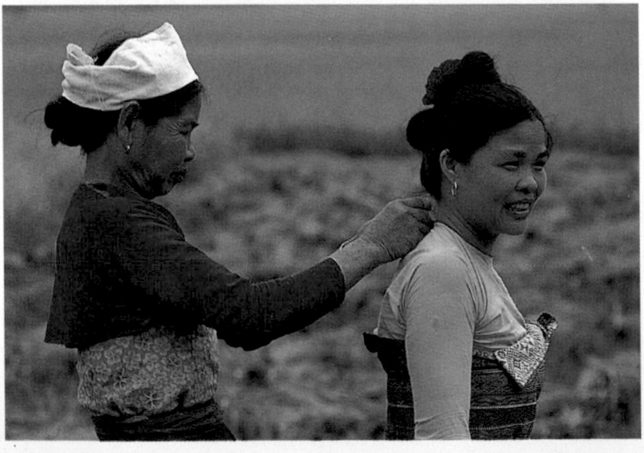

Title page: All the colour of a psychedelic rainbow – hill tribe ladies trading at Bac Ha's Sunday market (photograph by CK Barnes).

Top: Indigo girls – local dyes leave their mark.

Middle: Local women in Tam Duong have a laugh with – or at! – LP author Mason Florence.

Bottom: Keeping up appearances in Mai Chau.

CK BARNES

While the ethnic-Vietnamese and Chinese live mainly in urban centres and coastal areas, the remaining people, an estimated 10% of Vietnam's total population, live primarily in the high country. While several of these groupings represent about a million people, others are feared to have dwindled to as few as 100.

The most prominent of these communities reside in the north-west, in the plush mountain territory along the Lao and Chinese borders, while most of the tribes in the central highlands and the south can be quite difficult to distinguish, at least for foreign visitors, from other Vietnamese.

The French dubbed the hill-tribe peoples 'Montagnards' – highlanders or mountain people – and this name is still used when speaking in French or English. The Vietnamese generally refer to them as moi, a derogatory term meaning 'savages', which unfortunately reflects all-too-common popular attitudes. The present government, however, prefers to use the term 'national minorities'. Some have lived in Vietnam for thousands of years, while others have migrated into the region over the past few centuries. The areas inhabited by each community are often delimited by altitude, with more recent arrivals settling at higher elevations.

Historically, the highland areas were allowed to remain virtually independent as long as their leaders recognised Vietnamese sovereignty and paid tribute and taxes. The 1980 Constitution abolished two such regions established in the northern mountains in 1959.

Over the last century the Montagnards have been pushed into increasingly smaller territories; under French rule, many found themselves dispossessed by French plantations that sprung up all over the highlands. Surrounded by plantations, denied access to their traditional hunting and agricultural grounds, many found themselves forced into plantation labour. Plantation owners also 'imported' lowlander Vietnamese labourers – further displacing the Montagnards.

Attempts by the ethnic-Vietnamese to subjugate the highlanders were met with active resistance (see the 'FULRO' boxed text in the Central Highlands chapter). During the American war the Montagnards occupied the strategic position of what became known as the Ho Chi Minh trail. Consequently, both the Communists and the USA actively recruited Montagnard fighters from the central highlands. Familiarity with the territory meant Montagnards were particularly adept at guerilla war techniques. US officials estimate that around 200,000 Montagnards died during the American War. After the North Vietnamese took over, many who fought beside the South Vietnamese and American forces were punished, imprisoned or executed for being on the losing side. The Vietnamese government only recently lifted special restrictions against US tourists wanting to visit hill tribe areas around Dalat, out of paranoia that the CIA could still be trying to recruit locals.

Most hill-tribe communities share a rural, agricultural lifestyle with similar village architecture and traditional rituals alongside a long history of intertribal warfare. Many are seminomadic, cultivating crops such as 'dry' rice and using slash-and-burn methods, which have taken a heavy toll on the environment. Because such practices destroy the ever-dwindling forests, the government has been trying to encourage the hill tribes to adopt more settled agriculture techniques, often at lower altitudes, with wet (paddy) rice and cash crops such as tea, coffee and cinnamon. Still, some see this as yet another attempt by the government to 'integrate' the Montagnards into mainstream society. Despite the allure of benefits like subsidised irrigation, better education and health care, a long history of independence coupled with a general distrust of the ethnic-Vietnamese majority keeps many away from the lowlands.

As in other parts of Asia, the culture of many of Vietnam's ethnic minorities is slowly giving way to a variety of outside influences. Symbolic is the fact that few still dress in traditional clothing. Most who do are found in the remote villages of the far north, and even there it is often only the women who do so, while the men more typically have switched over to Vietnamese or Western-style clothes. While factors such as the introduction of electricity, modern medicine and education do create advantages, unfortunately it has also contributed to the abandonment of many age-old traditions.

A more recent, and perhaps equally threatening, outside influence is tourism. With further exposure to lowlanders, a developing trend towards commercialism, and growing numbers of people travelling to see hill-tribe regions, the situation will likely worsen. The influence of tourism, in Sapa for instance, has resulted in some children expecting hand-outs of money or sweets.

Vietnam's minorities have substantial autonomy and, though the official national language is Vietnamese, children still learn their local languages (see the Language chapter for useful phrases). Taxes are supposed to be paid, but Hanoi is far away and it seems that, as long as they don't interfere with political agendas, the Montagnards can live as they please. Police officers and members of the army in minority areas are often members of local tribal groups, and the National Assembly in Hanoi has representation by a good number of ethnic minorities.

While there may be no official discrimination system, cultural prejudice against hill-tribe people helps ensure they remain at the bottom of the educational and economic ladder. Despite improvements in rural schooling, there are few employment opportunities. Life expectancy is low and child mortality rates are high. Those who live closer to urban centres and the coast fare better, thanks to better access to medical and education facilities.

Tay

Population 1.2 million
Provinces Bac Can, Ba[c] Giang, Cao Bang, Lang Son, Quang Ninh, Tha[i] Nguyen

The Tay, the most populous of the hill tribes, live at low elevations and valleys in the northern provinces. They adhere closely to Vietnamese beliefs in Buddhism, Confucianism and Taoism, but they also worship genies and local spirits. Since they developed their own script in the 16th century, Tay literature and arts, including music, folk songs, poems and dance, have gained substantial renown. The Tay are known for their abilities in cultivating wet rice, tobacco, fruit, herbs and spices.

They traditionally live in wooden stilt houses, though a long history of proximity to the ethnic-Vietnamese has seen a gradual change to more typical Vietnamese brick and earthen housing. Tay people wear distinctive indigo-blue and black-dyed clothes, and often don head wraps of the same colours. They sometimes carry machete-like farming tools in belt sheaths.

Thai

Population 1 million+
Provinces Hoa Binh, Lai Chau, Nghe An, Son La

Like the Tay, the Thai originated in southern China before settling along fertile riverbeds, once used for irrigation purposes. Theories vary on the Thai's relationship to the Thais of Siam (Thailand), as do references to colours in the subgroups, such as the Red, Black and White Thai. Some contend that the colours correspond to those of the women's skirts, while others believe the names come from the nearby Black and Red Rivers. The Black Thai are predominant in Son La while the White Thai are concentrated in Hoa Binh. Black Thai women usually wear vibrantly coloured blouses and headgear, while the White Thai tend to dress in less-colourful or modern clothing. Most Thai men dress as the ethnic-Vietnamese do.

Villages typically have 40 to 50 bamboo-stilt households. The Thai, using a script developed in the 5th century, have produced literature ranging from poetry and love songs to folk tales. Those staying overnight in the village of Ban Lac (see the Mai Chau section of the North-West Vietnam chapter) should be able to catch a performance of some of the Thai's renowned music and dance.

Muong

Population 900,000+
Provinces Hoa Binh, Thanh Hoa

Found predominantly in Hoa Binh Province, the male-dominated Muong live in *quel* (small stilt-house hamlets), grouped into *muong*. Each muong is overseen by *lang*, a hereditary noble family. Though their origins lie close to the ethnic-Vietnamese and nowadays they are difficult to distinguish, the Muong have a culture similar to the Thai.

They are known for producing folk literature, poems and songs, much of which has been translated into Vietnamese. Musical instruments such as the gong, drums, pan pipes, flutes and two-stringed violin are popular with the Muong. Like the ethnic-Vietnamese, they too cultivate rice in paddies, in the past sticky rice was a staple part of their diet.

Muong women wear long skirts and short vest-like blouses while the men traditionally wear indigo tops and trousers.

Nung

Population 700,000
ovinces Bac Thai, Cao ng, Ha Bac, Lang Son, Tuyen Quang

Concentrated into small villages, Nung homes are typically divided into two sections, one to serve as living quarters and the other for work and worship. From their deep ancestral worship to traditional festivities, the Nung are spiritually and socially similar to the Tay. Nung brides traditionally command high dowries from prospective grooms and tradition dictates inheritance from father to son, a sign of Chinese influences.

Tread Lightly – Responsible Tourism

For the world's indigenous people, tourism is a mixed blessing. The tourism industry (Lonely Planet included) and countries like Vietnam, Thailand and Australia promote images of indigenous people and their distinctive cultures to attract tourists to holiday destinations.

Studies show indigenous cultures are a major drawcard for travellers and attract substantial revenue, yet little of it directly benefits these minority groups, who are often among their country's poorest and most disadvantaged.

Hill-tribe communities in Vietnam have generally not initiated tourist activities, are not the major economic beneficiaries of it, are unable to stop it and have little say in its management.

Studies by the Oxford Committee for Famine Relief (Oxfam) in Vietnam suggests tourism can bring many benefits to its highland communities, including: cross-cultural understanding; improved infrastructure like roads; cheaper market goods; and tourist dollars supporting handicraft industries and providing employment opportunities for locals as guides and hospitality workers.

However, there are also negative side-effects. Tourism creates or contributes to: overtaxing of natural resources, for instance, agricultural land is turned over to build hotels, and precious water supplies are diverted to tourists taking showers; increased litter and pollutants; dependency on tourist dollars; proliferation of drug use and prostitution; and erosion of local values and practices.

If you choose to travel to these regions, the good news is, as a tourist you can make a positive contribution and ensure that the benefits of your stay outweigh the costs. We hope you find this guide useful.

Travel

- Travel in small, less disruptive groups.
- Stay, eat and travel with local businesses to ensure your dollar spreads further and stays within the region.
- Try to book tours with responsible tourism outlets who employ hill-tribe people (preferably in meaningful work) or contribute to community welfare.

Behaviour

- Be polite and respectful.
- Dress modestly: A sarong is acceptable for public bathing and toilet stops.
- Minimise your litter – if you trek overnight take out your rubbish with you.
- Do not urinate or defecate near villagers' households; bury faeces.
- Do not take drugs – young children tend to imitate tourists' behaviour. In neighbouring Thailand drug addiction and HIV infections are decimating hill-tribe populations – similar problems are expected to emerge in Vietnam.

Tread Lightly – Responsible Tourism

- Do not engage in sexual relationships with local people, including prostitutes – in recent years a hill-tribe mother and her child, who was born with Western features and skin tone, have been ostracised by their community.
- Try to learn something about the community's culture and language and teach something good about yours.

Shopping

- Haggle politely and always pay the agreed (and fair) price for goods and services.
- Do not ask to buy a villager's personal household items or the jewellery or clothes they are wearing – they may feel obliged to sell them to please you, but actually need it themselves. There are plenty of items made for tourists that you can buy instead.
- Don't buy village treasures, such as altar pieces (even if offered for sale) – these are valuable to the community and should stay there. Besides, it is illegal to take these items out of Vietnam.

Photographs

- Do not photograph without first asking permission – this includes children. Some minority people (particularly the Dao people) believe the camera will capture their spirit. Do not photograph altars.
- If you take a picture, please do it quickly and avoid using a flash. It is polite to send copies (if possible) – if you promise to do so, keep your word.

Gifts

- Do not give children sweets or money; it encourages begging and paves the way for prostitution for 'gifts' and money. Sweets also contribute to tooth decay.
- Do not give clothes – communities are self-sufficient; don't create expensive (and unnecessary) consumer desires.
- Don't give medicines – It erodes traditional healing practices and the medicine may not be correctly administered.
- Individual gifts create jealousy and create expectations. Instead make donations of picture books, basic first-aid equipment or cash to the local school, medical centre or community fund. Other appropriate gifts are pictures you have taken of the community, postcards of your home country and of yourself and/or family.
- No matter how poor they are, villagers are extremely hospitable, however, feeding a guest can result in food shortages. If you accept an invitation to share a meal, be sure to bring a generous contribution, such as rice, tea, or other locally available foodstuffs with you.

Compiled with assistance from Community Aid Abroad – Oxfam Australia

Most Nung villages still have medicine men who are called upon to help get rid of evil spirits and cure the ill. Their astute gardening skills are known to reap a wide range of crops like vegetables, fruit, spices and bamboo. The Nung are also known for their handicrafts such as bamboo furniture, basketry, silverwork and paper making. The Nung wear primarily black and indigo clothing with head dresses.

H'mong

Population 550,000+
Provinces Cao Bang, Ha Giang, Lai Chau, Lao Cai, Nghe An, Tuyen Quang, Son La, Yen Bai

Since migrating from China in the 19th century, the H'mong have grown to become one of the largest and most underprivileged of the ethnic groups in Vietnam.

The H'mong live at high altitudes and cultivate dry rice, vegetables, fruit and medicinal plants (including opium), and raise pigs, cows, chickens and horses. The H'mong are found throughout South-East Asia and many have also fled Vietnam to Western countries as refugees.

There are several groups within the H'mong, including, Black, White, Red, Green and Flower, each of which bears their own subtle variation on traditional dress. One of the easiest to recognise are the Black Hmong, who wear indigo dyed linen clothing (which gives off a practically metallic shine) with women typically wearing skirts, aprons, wrap-on leggings and a cylindrical hat. The Flower H'mong men wear dark black and blue. The women wear slightly more elaborate outfits than the Black H'mong, usually with a plaid wool headdress. H'mong women typically wear large silver necklaces and clusters of silver bracelets and earrings.

Jarai

Population 190,000+
Provinces Dac Lac, Gia Lai, Khanh Hoa, Phu Yen

The Jarai are the most populous minority in the Central Highlands, especially around Pleiku. Villages are often named for a nearby river, stream or tribal chief, and a nha-rong (a large stilt house; a kind of community centre) is usually found in the centre. Jarai women typically propose marriage to men through a matchmaker, who delivers the prospective groom a copper bracelet. Animistic beliefs and rituals still abound, and the Jarai pay respect to their ancestors and nature through a host of yang (genie). Popular spirits include Po Teo Pui (King of Fire) and Po Teo La (King of Water), who are summoned to bring forth rain.

Perhaps more than any of Vietnam's other hill tribes, the Jarai are renowned for their indigenous musical instruments, from stringed 'gongs' to bamboo tubes, which act as wind flutes and percussion. Jarai women typically wear sleeveless indigo blouses and long skirts.

Bahnar

Population 135,000
Provinces Kon Tum, Binh Dinh, Phu Yen

The Bahnar are believed to have migrated long ago to the central highlands from the coast. They are animists and worship trees such as the banyan and ficus. The Bahnar keep their own traditional calendar, which calls for 10 months of cultivation, with the remaining two months set aside for social and personal duties, such as marriage, weaving, buying and selling food and wares, ceremonies and festivals.

Traditionally, a ceremony was held when babies reached one month of age; their ears were blown into and their lobes were pierced, thus making the child officially a member of the village. Those who died without such holes were believed to be taken to a land of monkeys by a black-eared goddess called Duydai. The Bahnar are renowned for their skilled wood carvings, especially those used to decorate village funeral homes. They wear similar dress to the Jarai.

Sedang

Population 95,000+
Provinces Kon Tum, Quang Ngai, Quang Nam

Native to the central highlands, the Sedang have relations stretching as far as Cambodia. Like many of their neighbours, the Sedang have been adversely affected by centuries of war and outside invasion. The Sedang do not carry family names, and there is said to be complete equality between the sexes. The children of one's siblings are also given the same treatment as one's own, creating a strong fraternal tradition. Although most Sedang spiritual and cultural ceremonies relate to agriculture, they still practice unique customs, such as grave-abandonment, sharing of property with the deceased and giving birth at the forest's edge. Sedang women traditionally wear long skirts and a sarong-like top wrap.

Dao

Population 470,000+
Provinces Chinese and Lao border areas, Sapa

The Dao (or Zao) are one of Vietnam's largest ethnic groups and they live predominantly in the north-western provinces along the borders with China and Laos. The Dao practice ancestor worship of spirits known as 'Ban Ho' and hold elaborate rituals with sacrifices of pigs and chickens. The Dao's close proximity to China explains the common use of traditional Chinese-influenced medicine and the similarity of the Nom Dao script to Chinese characters.

The Dao are famous for their elaborate dress; women's clothing typically features elaborate weaving and silver-coloured beads and coins (the wealth of a woman is said to be in the weight of coins she carries). Long locks of hair are tied up into a large red or embroidered turban.

Ede

Population 24,000+
Provinces Gia Lai, Kon Tum, Dac Lac

The polytheist Ede live communally in beamless, boat-shaped longhouses on stilts. About a third of these homes, which frequently accommodate large extended families, are for communal use, with the rest partitioned into smaller quarters to give privacy to married couples. The Ede people are matrilineal, like the Jarai: The families of Ede girls make proposals of marriage to men and, once wed, the couple resides with the wife's family. Children bear the mother's family name. Inheritance is also reserved solely for women, in particular the youngest daughter of the family. Ede women generally wear colourfully embroidered vests with copper and silver jewellery and beads.

continued from page 272

Apart from a small Sunday market and some nearby villages, there is not much to see or do in Muong Te. There are also a scant few outside visitors (which for some makes it an appealing place to be). The only accommodation in town is the shabby ***People's Committee Guesthouse***, which also has a small restaurant.

Even if you're not planning to visit, you might take the Muong Te turn-off along Route 12 (about 7km outside of Lai Chau) from where you'll soon reach a rickety wooden suspension bridge worth a look (or even a crossing for Indiana Jones wannabes).

If you continue for about 8km beyond this bridge, there is a peculiar historical relic to see: an ancient poem carved in stone by 15th-century Emperor Le Loi, who had succeeded in expelling the Chinese from the region. The 'poem' was left as a warning for any other potential invaders not to mess with Le Loi. The translation from Chinese reads:

Hey! The humble, coward and frantic rebels, I come here to counter-attack for the sake of the border inhabitants. There existed the betrayed subjects since the beginning of the human's history. The land is no longer dangerous. The plants' figures, the whisper of the wind, and even the singing of the songbirds startle the mean enemy. The nation is now integrated and this carved poem – an amulet for Eastern peace of the country.

An Auspicious Day of December, The Year of the Pigs (1432)

To find this spine-chilling vestige, look for the narrow flight of steps marked by a small stone placard reading 'Di Tich Lich Su – Bia Le Loi' on the roadside overlooking the river.

SINHO

☎ 023 • pop 56,200 • elevation 1054m

Sinho is a scenic mountain village with a large percentage of ethnic minorities. There is a colourful Sunday market here, though the dingy ***People's Committee Guesthouse*** is the only hotel in town.

Sinho is a 38km climb on an abysmal dirt road off Route 12; the turn-off is about 1km north of the village of Chan Nua, on the road from Lao Cai. Sinho can also be reached by a challenging trek from the town of Tam Duong.

TAM DUONG

☎ 023 • pop 94,400

This remote town lies between Sapa and Lai Chau. While the town is nothing special, it's the usual lunch stop of travellers making this trip by 4WD. When the road gets particularly bad after a heavy rain, the 'lunch stop' may turn into an 'overnight stop', or even 'turn-around point'.

The local market, about midway through town on Hwy 12, is worth a visit. The majority of people are Montagnards from nearby villages, although the ethnic-Vietnamese are still the largest single group. If you're not rushing to get to Sapa or Lai Chau, it is a definite possibility to base yourself in Tam Duong for a few days and explore the surrounding area.

The drive from Tam Duong to Sapa along Route 4D, threading the Fansipan Mountain Range and the China border, is perhaps the most beautiful stretch of road in Vietnam.

Places to Stay & Eat

The ***Phuong Thanh Hotel*** *(☎ 875158)* is a popular place with basic fan rooms costing US$10. The two rooms at the back offer nice views.

Clean rooms at the friendly ***Tam Duong Hotel*** *(☎ 875288)* cost US$8.

The best food in town can be found at the friendly, family-run ***Tuan Anh***.

Other nearby com-pho spots like ***Phuong Thanh*** should be OK too. Be aware that ***Kieu Trinh*** is known for its canine fare.

SAPA

☎ 020 • pop 36,200 • elevation 1650m

The premier destination of north-west Vietnam, Sapa is a hill station built in 1922. It lies in a beautiful valley close to the border with China. The whole area has spectacular scenery – frequently shrouded in mist and home to diverse hill-tribe communities.

In the past, getting here from Hanoi was not easy due to bad roads. Other historical

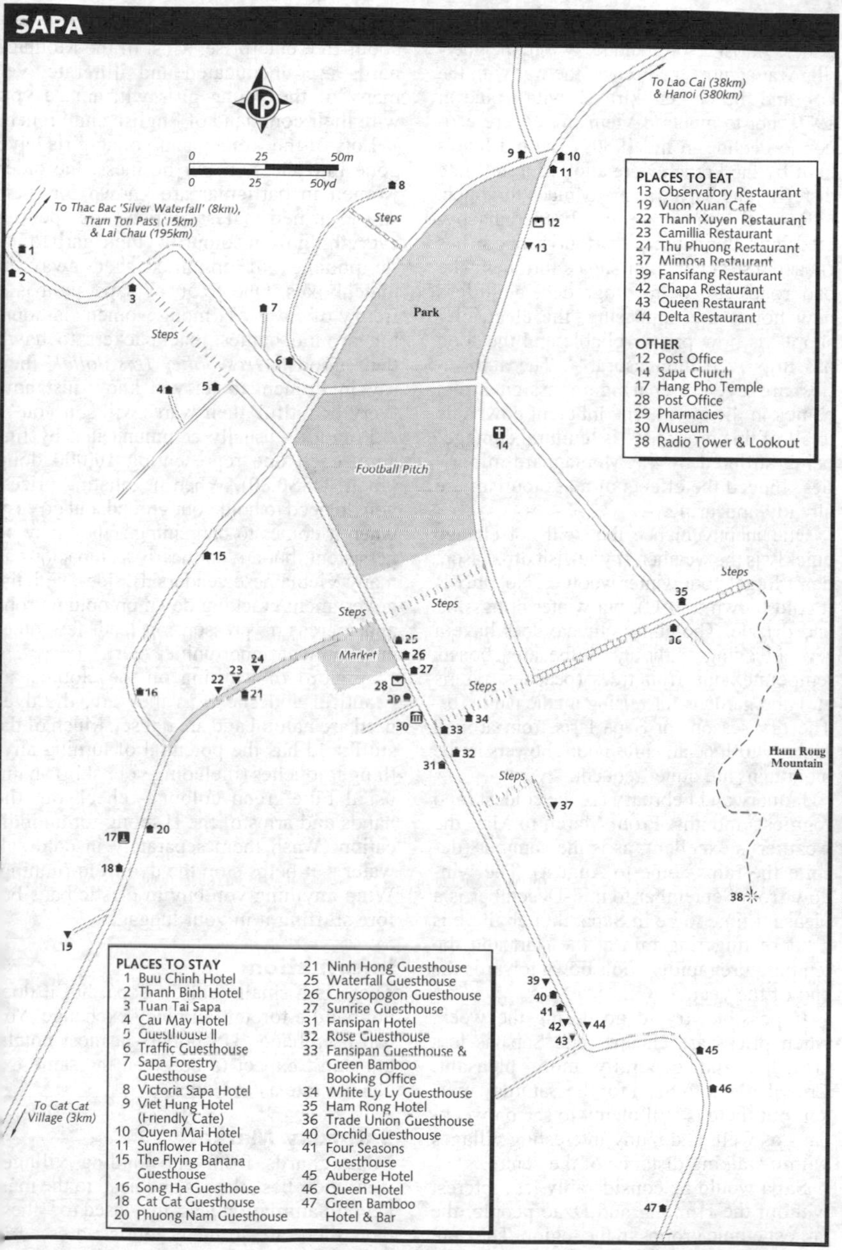

SAPA

To Lao Cai (38km) & Hanoi (380km)

0 25 50m

0 25 50yd

To Thac Bac 'Silver Waterfall' (8km), Tram Ton Pass (15km) & Lai Chau (195km)

Steps

Park

Football Pitch

Market

Ham Rong Mountain

To Cat Cat Village (3km)

PLACES TO EAT

13 Observatory Restaurant
19 Vuon Xuan Cafe
22 Thanh Xuyen Restaurant
23 Camillia Restaurant
24 Thu Phuong Restaurant
37 Mimosa Restaurant
39 Fansifang Restaurant
42 Chapa Restaurant
43 Queen Restaurant
44 Delta Restaurant

OTHER

12 Post Office
14 Sapa Church
17 Hang Pho Temple
28 Post Office
29 Pharmacies
30 Museum
38 Radio Tower & Lookout

PLACES TO STAY

1 Buu Chinh Hotel
2 Thanh Binh Hotel
3 Tuan Tai Sapa
4 Cau May Hotel
5 Guesthouse II
6 Traffic Guesthouse
7 Sapa Forestry Guesthouse
8 Victoria Sapa Hotel
9 Viet Hung Hotel (Friendly Cafe)
10 Quyen Mai Hotel
11 Sunflower Hotel
15 The Flying Banana Guesthouse
16 Song Ha Guesthouse
18 Cat Cat Guesthouse
20 Phuong Nam Guesthouse
21 Ninh Hong Guesthouse
25 Waterfall Guesthouse
26 Chrysopogon Guesthouse
27 Sunrise Guesthouse
31 Fansipan Hotel
32 Rose Guesthouse
33 Fansipan Guesthouse & Green Bamboo Booking Office
34 White Ly Ly Guesthouse
35 Ham Rong Hotel
36 Trade Union Guesthouse
40 Orchid Guesthouse
41 Four Seasons Guesthouse
45 Auberge Hotel
46 Queen Hotel
47 Green Bamboo Hotel & Bar

reasons that prevented Sapa from becoming a slick tourist resort include: WWII, the guerrilla war against the French, the war with the US, and the border skirmish with China in 1979, not to mention Vietnam's severe economic decline in the 1980s. The old hotels built by the French were allowed to fall into disrepair and Sapa was pretty much forgotten.

Recently, the place has been rediscovered, and the subsequent tourist boom has caused a sea change in Sapa's fortunes. The bad roads are being upgraded, countless new hotels are appearing, the electricity supply is now pretty reliable and the food has improved immeasurably. The authorities are even preparing to assign street names in the town! One inherent downside to all of this prosperity is 'cultural damage' being suffered by the Montagnard minorities. Indeed the effects of mass tourism are already appearing.

One inconvenience that will not change quickly is the weather. If you visit off-season, don't forget your winter woollies. Not only is it cold (down to 0°C), but winter brings fog and drizzle. The chilly climate does have a few advantages, though – the area boasts temperate-zone fruit trees (peaches, plums etc) and gardens for raising medicinal herbs. The dry season for Sapa lasts from around January to June and afternoon showers in the mountains are quite frequent.

January and February are the coldest (and foggiest) months. From March to May the weather is excellent, as is the summer (despite the rains; June to August). The window from September to mid-December is a pleasant time to be in Sapa, though there is a bit of lingering rain at the start and the temperature rapidly cools down towards the end of the year.

If possible, try to go during the week, when prices are cheaper and Sapa is less crowded and generally more pleasant. Crowds flock to Sapa for the Saturday market, but there is still plenty to see on weekdays as well, and many interesting villages within walking distance of the centre.

Sapa would be considerably less interest without the H'mong and Dzao people, the largest ethnic groups in the region. They are mostly very poor, but are rapidly learning about free enterprise. Most of the Montagnards are uneducated and illiterate, yet many of the young girls will amaze you with their command of English and French.

Lots of the women and young girls have gone into the souvenir business; the older women in particular are known for their strong-armed sales tactics and peddle everything from colourful ethnic garb to little pouches of opium stashed away in matchboxes. One frequent Sapa sight is a frenzy of elderly H'mong women clamouring around hapless backpackers to hawk their goods. '*Tres Jolie, Tres Jolie!*' they say in French, to let you know just how 'very beautiful' their wares will suit you.

Pricing is usually communicated by fingers, each one representing 10,000 dong (about US$0.80). When negotiating prices, you do need to hold your ground, but go easy when it comes to bargaining – they may be persistent, but are not nearly as rapacious as many Vietnamese vendors. Besides, with the government cracking down on opium crops and increasing pressure on land, few other employment opportunities exist.

A word of warning on the clothes: as beautiful and cheap as they are, the dyes used are natural and are not set. Much of the stuff sold has the potential of turning anything it touches (including your skin) an unusual blue/green colour – check out the hands and arms of the H'mong for an indication. Wash them separately in cold salt water – it helps stop the dye from running. Wrap anything you buy in plastic bags before stuffing it in your luggage.

Information

There is a small bank in Sapa, but it does not handle foreign-currency exchange. You can use/change US dollars at most hotels, but don't expect to be given the same exchange rate as in Hanoi.

Saturday Market

Montagnards from surrounding villages wear their best clothes and head to the market on Saturday, at least they used to – these days there are so many tourists dressed in souvenir H'mong clothing that you have to wonder who's kidding who.

The market is a big magnet for organised tours from Hanoi and many of them plan their visit so that they arrive on Friday night. If you'd rather enjoy Sapa at a more sedate pace, avoid the Saturday market.

Sapa Museum

Displays at the tiny Sapa Museum centre on costumes of the regional ethnic minorities. The museum seems to open only on weekends, but it is worth sticking your head in to check if it's open during the week. Perhaps more interesting is to take a stroll out to some of the villages where there are living, breathing people inside the clothes.

Entry costs 5000d (US$0.40).

Fansipan

Surrounding Sapa are the Hoang Lien Mountains, nicknamed the Tonkinese Alps by the French. These mountains include Fansipan, which at 3143m is Vietnam's highest. The summit towers above Sapa, although it is often obscured by clouds and is occasionally dusted by snow. The peak should be accessible year-round to anyone who is in good shape and properly equipped, but don't underestimate its difficulty. It is very wet and usually cold, so you must be prepared. (See the Health section in the Facts for the Visitor chapter for advice about rural health.) The climbers are primarily tourists.

Fansipan is 9km from Sapa and can only be reached on foot. The terrain is rough and adverse weather is frequent. Despite the short distance, the round trip usually takes three to five days; some very fit and experienced hikers have made it in two days, but this is rare. After the first morning you won't see any more villages; just the forest, striking mountain vistas, and perhaps some local wildlife like monkeys, mountain goats and birds.

No ropes or technical climbing skills are needed, just endurance. There are no mountain huts or other facilities along the way (yet), so you need to be self-sufficient. This means taking a sleeping bag, waterproof tent, food, stove, raincoat or poncho, compass and other miscellaneous survival gear. The question arises – can camping equipment be rented in Sapa? Yes, some is available, but it's not always good quality and you're best off bringing your own gear.

Hiring a reputable guide is vital, and unless you are a seriously experienced mountaineer, finding porters to carry your gear is also strongly recommended. There have been reports of self-propelled hikers getting themselves *very* lost, and even guides who have abandoned their group part way!

Good places to inquire about trekking guides include the Viet Hung Hotel/Friendly Cafe, Chapa Restaurant, Green Bamboo booking office (in the Fanispan Hotel) and Auberge Hotel.

Allow about US$15 a day for the guide (per group), US$10 per day for a porter (this fee will look like a bargain once you're climbing!), and around US$2 a day for food. You are also required to purchase a US$5 permit to climb the mountain.

Fansipan's summit is accessible year-round, though weatherwise the best time for making the ascent is from mid-October to mid-December, and again in March (when the wild flowers are in bloom).

Tram Ton Pass

If you travel along the Sapa–Lai Chau road, you will cross this pass on the north side of Fansipan, 15km from Sapa. At 1900m, this is the highest mountain pass in Vietnam. Aside from magnificent views, the bizarre thing is how dramatically the climate changes. On the Sapa side of the mountain you can often expect cold, foggy and generally nasty weather. Drop down a few hundred metres below the pass on the Lai Chau side and it will often be sunny and warm. Ferocious winds come ripping over the pass, which is not surprising given the temperature differences – Sapa is the coldest place in Vietnam and Lai Chau is the warmest. Tram Ton Pass is the dividing line between two great weather fronts – who says you can't see air?

Just alongside the road about 5km back towards Sapa is Thac Bac, the Silver Waterfall.

Having a height of 100m, it's a big one, but climbing up alongside it can be dangerous. In the winter dry season it may be reduced to a trickle, but can be magnificent in the rainy season.

You can easily get to Tram Ton Pass by motorbike.

Places to Stay

A warning is in order concerning the possibility of carbon-monoxide poisoning in Sapa. One traveller described her experience:

In Sapa – which is bone-chillingly cold in winter – there are many new private hotels popping up. In order to attract customers, they are advertising and telling people that they have heaters in the rooms. The heaters usually turn out to be a small pot with pieces of burning charcoal. These pots create a deadly smoke that can cause illness or death. With this smoke and the new hotels, which are tightly sealed and not regulated very well by authorities, many travellers have become sick and some have had very close calls.

Two women who were staying in a room across from me had a very scary experience. They fell asleep with this charcoal burner in their room. My roommate and I heard a moaning coming from their room and opened the door to see if they were OK. The women could not move or speak. One woman's body had stiffened so that she couldn't unlock her muscles and joints. She could only move her eyes and moan. After a frightening 30 minutes, a doctor came and rubbed some herbal medicine on some specific points of their bodies. In another 15 minutes, they were able to speak and move a little. They were terribly weak and ill for the rest of the night.

Chris Conley

NORTH-WEST VIETNAM

If you're on a tour booked through a cafe or travel agency in Hanoi, your accommodation presumably will be pre-arranged for you. However, self-propelled travellers need to exercise caution. Prices fluctuate wildly according to the volume of tourist traffic. On weekends prices can skyrocket, with an US$8 room going for as much as US$25, if you can find one at all. Needless to say, it's wise to avoid holidays and weekends, especially if you haven't got something pre-booked. Mid-week there should be no problem, especially during the icy winter.

In 1990 there was just one place to stay in Sapa, the dilapidated Peoples' Committee Guesthouse. Now there are roughly 50 lodging options, from a solid string of cheap guesthouses to a luxury resort.

Lamentably, the majority of Sapa's villa-hotels are owned and run by the government, meaning restoration efforts have fallen far short of their potential. Still, they are atmospheric. Worse are the characterless new minihotels popping up and plaguing the town with noisy karaoke. Construction is continuing full bore.

Places to Stay – Budget

The popular ***Viet Hung Hotel*** *(☎ 871313, fax 871684, ⓔ hung.nv@fpt.vn)* is also known as the Friendly Cafe. It's a venerable budget-travellers' place, with basic, but clean and airy rooms. There have been several good reports on trekking guides based here, and the congenial owner Mr Hung is a prime source of travel advice. Rooms cost US$5 to US$10; some have balconies and fireplaces.

The friendly ***Cat Cat Guesthouse*** *(☎ 871387, ⓔ catcat@fpt.vn)* gets rave reviews from guests and has sweeping views from the front terrace and some of the rooms. Winter rates are from US$4 to US$10; summer rates are US$12 to US$15.

The ***Auberge Hotel*** *(☎ 871871/871243, fax 871666, ⓔ aubergesapa@hotmail.com)* is notable for its valley views and bonsai garden. Doubles, some with fireplaces, cost US$6 to US$12. The restaurant is recommended and it's a good place to find travel information.

Just next door to the Auberge is the ***Queen Hotel*** *(☎ 871301, fax 871282)*, another friendly place offering rooms with great views and fireplaces for US$4 to US$10.

Just below the market, ***Ninh Hong Guesthouse*** *(☎ 871334, ⓔ ninhhongsapa@yahoo.com)* receives plenty of good reports from travellers. The owner, Mrs Hong, ensures the family run atmosphere, and is one of Sapa's only female trekking guides. Basic rooms cost just US$3 to US$5.

Four Seasons Guesthouse *(☎ 871308)* has a pleasant rear balcony from which t enjoy the scenery and charges US$12 for clean doubles. Rooms next door at ***Orchid Guesthouse*** *(☎ 871475)* cost US$4 in winter and US$8 to US$10 in summer.

Song Ha Guesthouse *(☎ 871273)* is set in an attractive villa and is worthy of a plug. Rooms cost US$4 and US$5 in winter and US$10 to US$15 in summer.

On the road down to the Cat Cat Guesthouse, the ***Phuong Nam Guesthouse*** *(☎ 871286)* has simple rooms for US$5 to US$10 and a makeshift terrace cafe out back.

Cau May Hotel *(☎ 871293)* is a quiet place set back from the road with some views. Rooms cost US$9 for up to three people.

If you're after that worn French-villa charm, ***White Ly Ly Guesthouse*** *(☎ 871289)* costs US$12 for a double. The nearby ***Trade Union Guesthouse*** *(☎ 871315)* occupies five separate villas. Rooms cost US$13 to US$25. Another partially refurbished French villa, ***Traffic Guesthouse*** *(☎ 871364)* charges US$6 in winter and US$12 in summer.

The friendly state-run ***Sapa Forestry Guesthouse*** *(☎ 871230)* is perched on a quiet hill above the football pitch and charges US$12 for doubles and triples.

The Flying Banana Guesthouse *(☎ 871580, fax 871444)* is a fairly standard minihotel, but it's family run and friendly. Rooms here cost US$6 to US$12.

The larger ***Fansipan Hotel*** *(☎ 871398)* has seen better days, and the white bathroom-tile exterior is anything but aesthetic. Doubles cost US$12; a room with five beds cost US$20. Some of the rooms at the rear have valley views.

The family run ***Thanh Binh Hotel*** *(☎ 871250)* is a friendly place. Basic rooms in this old villa share a balcony around the building and cost US$8 in winter and US$10 in summer.

Tuan Tai Sapa *(☎ 871766)* is a newer place with seven spotless rooms renting for US$7 each.

Places to Stay – Mid-Range

The ***Buu Chinh Hotel*** *(☎ 871389, fax 871332)* is owned by the postal service and is housed in a woodsy, Swiss chalet–style building. Rooms are clean and all have balconies and satellite TV. The room rate is US$20 year-round.

The ***Quyen Mai Hotel*** *(☎ 871450)* is OK as far as hotels with karaoke go. Twins cost US$10 to US$16 and triples cost US$12 to US$24.

The state-run ***Ham Rong Hotel*** *(☎ 871 251, fax 871303)* is made up of three French villas, rooms cost US$15 to US$25. Look for the black satellite TV dish in the courtyard.

The ***Green Bamboo Hotel*** *(☎ 871214)* is a recent construction in French-villa style with fine views and a popular bar. Rates are US$15 to US$25.

Places to Stay – Top End

For the ultimate lodging experience, the luxurious ***Victoria Sapa Hotel*** *(☎ 871522, fax 871539, ⓔ victoriasapa@fpt.vn)* has it all – tastefully decorated rooms, sweeping views from the restaurant, two bars, a heated indoor swimming pool, fitness centre and tennis court. Rates are moderate for this calibre of resort: superior/deluxe rooms cost US$82/100; six-bed family studios go for US$147; and the two luxury suites cost US$180. Rates include breakfast, tax and service.

Hotel guests can travel between Hanoi and Lao Cai in the resort's ***Victoria Express*** *(Hanoi, ☎ 04-933 0318, fax 933 0319, ⓔ victoria@fpt.vn; Ho Chi Minh City (☎ 08-990 1350, fax 990 0229)*, with luxurious, private train carriages (with private dining car) attached to the regular train. Round-trip per person fares are US$50 (weekdays) or US$75 (weekends) in a four-bunk cabin, and US$80 (weekdays) or US$120 (weekends) in a two-bunk cabin. The hotels' vans shuttle guests between Lao Cai and Sapa for US$12 return. Visit its Web site at www.victoriahotels-asia.com.

Places to Eat

The centrally located ***Mimosa Restaurant*** *(☎ 871377)* is a superb, cosy, family run eatery. It does great barbecue beef, wild boar and venison, as well as pizza, pasta and a variety of Asian selections.

The ***Observatory Restaurant*** (☎ *871504*) is a Sapa institution. Its set dinner course is an irrefutable bargain at US$0.80 (the price has not changed since 1990!). It's also a great place to pick up takeaway picnic lunches before heading out on a walk.

The ***Camillia Restaurant***, near the market, boasts one of the most extensive menus in north-west Vietnam. The ***Thanh Xuyen*** and ***Thu Phuong*** restaurants, on either side of the Camillia, are also good.

The ***Auberge Hotel*** is a good breakfast spot, and also has a set vegetarian menu.

The ***Delta Restaurant*** (☎ *871799*), Sapa's first and only Italian restaurant, does good pizzas and pastas.

There are a string of popular eateries worth checking out near the bottom of the main drag (south of the stairs leading down to the market).

The ***Chapa Restaurant*** (☎ *871245*, e *chapatour@fpt.vn*) is a true travellers' cafe with the usual banana pancakes and spring rolls. If you peek in the front door, the place may appear full but there are more tables in the room upstairs and also on the rooftop! Chapa is also a good place to book trekking tours.

Others to consider nearby include the ***Queen Restaurant*** and ***Four Seasons Guesthouse Restaurant*** – both of them are good. The ***Fansifang Restaurant*** is the place to relieve any sudden cravings for antelope.

If you're looking for a place to enjoy a coffee without the locals trying to sell you ethnic apparel, you might check out the rooftop of the ***Vuon Xuan Cafe***, on the road heading down to Cat Cat Village.

Entertainment

Considering the number of travellers to Sapa, organised entertainment is relatively scarce. Mostly it's a cosy cafe scene at the various guesthouses.

The first Western-style watering hole to open in Sapa is at the ***Bamboo Bar*** at the Green Bamboo Hotel – there's a free traditional hill-tribe music and dance show from 8.30 to 10.30 pm Friday and Saturday.

For a more 'civilised' drink, there are two cosy bars at the stylish ***Victoria Sapa Hotel***. Drinks cost a bit more than elsewhere in town, but the atmosphere is hard to beat.

Getting There & Away

Sapa's proximity to the border region makes it a possible first or last stop for travellers crossing between Vietnam and China.

The gateway to Sapa is Lao Cai, 38km away on the Chinese border. Minibuses make the trip (about two hours), but do not run on any particular schedule. However, the minibuses do wait in Lao Cai for the train that arrives from Hanoi. The price for the minibus averages about US$2 per person depending on how many people they squeeze on board. Some of the 'buses' are also pick-up trucks, where passengers ride in the back – this is not so great, as the mountain weather is often foul.

Locals are also very willing to drive you up the mountain to Lao Cai by motorbike for US$5, but travellers have reported problems with drivers taking them halfway and then asking for more money to complete the journey. If you don't cough up the cash, they threaten to leave you stranded.

The advertised rate on minibus services for Sapa–Bac Ha (110km) is around US$12 per person; departure from Sapa is at 6 am and from Bac Ha at 1 pm. For Sapa-Hanoi it's US$18 per person; departure is around 5 am, the trip takes about 12 hours.

Driving a motorbike from Hanoi to Sapa is feasible, but it's a very long trip – start early. The total distance between Hanoi and Sapa is 380km. The last 38km is straight uphill – unless you've been training for the Olympics, it's hell on a bicycle.

Cafes in Hanoi offer weekend trips to Sapa for around US$40. This is probably the most hassle-free way to do the journey, but many prefer to do it on their own.

Once in Sapa, most of the hotels can organise treks and local transport. Purchasing train tickets in Sapa costs a bit more than at the station in Lao Cai, but ensures you a seat on the train. The Green Bamboo booking office, near the market, can organise tickets. Guests at the Victoria Sapa Hotel will likely want to take advantage of its luxury *Victoria Express* carriages attached to the regular trains between Hanoi and Lao Cai. See the Places to Stay section for details

Getting Around
The best way to get around Sapa is to walk. If you've got only an hour or so to kill, it is worthwhile following the steps up to the Sapa radio tower; the views of the valley from here are breathtaking.

For excursions farther out, you can hire a self-drive motorbike for about US$6 a day, or take one with a driver for about US$10.

LAO CAI
☎ 020 • pop 35,100 • elevation 650m

Lao Cai is the major town at the north-west end of the rail line and right on the Chinese border. The town was razed in the Chinese invasion of 1979, so most of the buildings are new.

Needless to say, the border crossing here slammed shut during the 1979 war – it reopened in 1993. Nevertheless, the Vietnamese border guards are still suspicious of foreigners and every backpacker gets treated like a potential spy. Ironically, Chinese citizens can cross the border easily without the need for a passport or visa and are permitted to stay in Vietnam for 15 days.

Despite the scowling guards and vigorous luggage searches, Lao Cai is a major destination for travellers journeying between Hanoi and Kunming in China (or Sapa and Kunming). But Lao Cai is no place to linger – don't bother spending the night if you don't have to.

Orientation & Information
The border town on the Chinese side is called Hekou – you'd have to be an enthusiast of Chinese border towns to want to hang out here. It's separated from Vietnam by a river and a bridge – you must pay a small toll to cross.

There is a bank on the Lao Cai side of the river (right near the bridge) that will do foreign exchange, but it's cash transactions only (no travellers cheques or credit cards). Over on the Chinese side you can cash travellers cheques as long as it's not a bank holiday. It's best to have a ready supply of US dollars handy just in case. Be wary of black marketeers, especially on the Chinese side – they frequently short-change tourists. If you do black market dealings, it's best to change only small amounts.

Places to Stay
In Hekou, budget accommodation is available at the old ***Hekou Hotel***. Somewhat nicer is the ***Dongfeng Hotel***. Another place is the ***Guoji Gongyu Hotel***, just opposite the border gate.

In Lao Cai, closest to the border gate is ***Song Hong Guesthouse*** (*☎ 830004*). Some

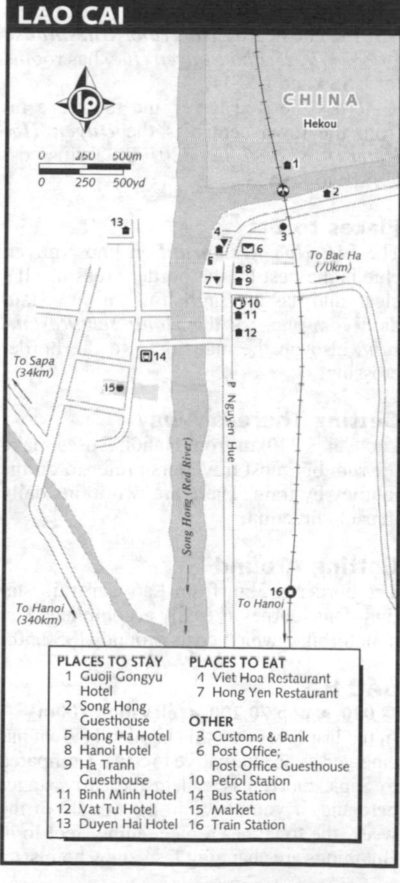

NORTH-WEST VIETNAM

of the 14 rooms have air-con and a nice view of the river and China. Rates are US$10 to US$12.

Hong Ha Hotel *(☎ 830007)* is a relatively large but lacklustre place. Doubles/triples cost US$12/15. The in-house restaurant specialises in animal intestines (heart, liver, kidney, etc).

Hanoi Hotel *(☎ 832486, fax 832 488)* is small with an upstairs restaurant. Air-con rooms cost US$13.

The ***Vat Tu Hotel*** *(☎ 831540)* is farthest from the border and offers twin rooms for US$10 to US$14.

The ***Binh Minh Hotel*** *(☎ 830085, 39 Pho Nguyen Hue)* charges US$12 to US$15. The nearby ***Ha Tranh Guesthouse*** *(☎ 832179, 27 Pho Nguyen Hue)* has rooms for US$9 and US$11.

Across the Red River and therefore far from the town centre is the ***Duyen Hai Hotel*** *(☎ 822086, fax 820172)*. Twins cost US$10 to US$23.

Places to Eat

The ***Viet Hoa Restaurant*** on Pho Nguyen Hue is the best by the border crossing. It's clean and has an English menu. For standard com-pho, try the ***Hong Yen Restaurant***, also on the main drag to the border crossing.

Getting There & Away

Lao Cai is 340km from Hanoi. Buses make the run, but most travellers prefer to do the journey by train. There are two trains daily in each direction.

Getting Around

The border is 3km from Lao Cai train station. This journey is easily accomplished on a motorbike, which costs around US$0.50.

BAC HA

☎ 020 • pop 70,200 • elevation 700m

In the last few years this highlands town has emerged as an alternative to Sapa. Compared to Sapa, tourism is still in the early stages here and, if you arrive in the middle of the week, the town has a nice, empty feel to it. But things are changing fast – new hotels are opening and restaurants are learning how to make banana pancakes.

One thing perhaps slowing down the tourist boom is the loudspeakers on a hill overlooking the town. These relay the clamorous and crackly Voice of Vietnam from 5 to 6 am, and again from 6 to 7 pm every day. If it's any consolation, they used to broadcast *continuously* from 5 am to 9 pm! There is a movement under way by some hotel owners to get these turned off completely, a plea we can only hope will triumph over the din. Until a few years ago, Sapa was similarly bombarded until the local authorities realised it was driving away the tourists.

The highlands around Bac Ha are about 900m above sea level, making it somewhat warmer than Sapa. There are 10 Montagnard groups living around Bac Ha – Flower H'mong, Dzao, Giay (Nhang), Han (Hoa), Xa Fang, Lachi, Nung, Phula, Thai and Thulao – plus the Kinh (ethnic-Vietnamese).

One of Bac Ha's main industries is the manufacture of alcoholic brews (rice wine, cassava wine and corn liquor). The corn stuff produced by the Flower H'mong is so potent it can ignite! Bac Ha is the only place in Vietnam where you'll find this particular ferment. Harvesting opium also used to be a major source of revenue, but the government put a stop to that several years ago.

Keep a torch (flashlight) handy if you wander around town in the evening – Bac Ha's electric power supply isn't very stable and sudden blackouts are a common occurrence. One nice thing about the power failures is that they silence (temporarily) those loudspeakers.

Plum Blossoms

There are many plum trees around Bac Ha and in spring the countryside is white with blossom. The trees bloom in early May. June and July produces some of the best eating plums.

Ban Pho Village

If you want to see what a Montagnard village looks like, this is your chance. The villagers live simply – don't expect bright

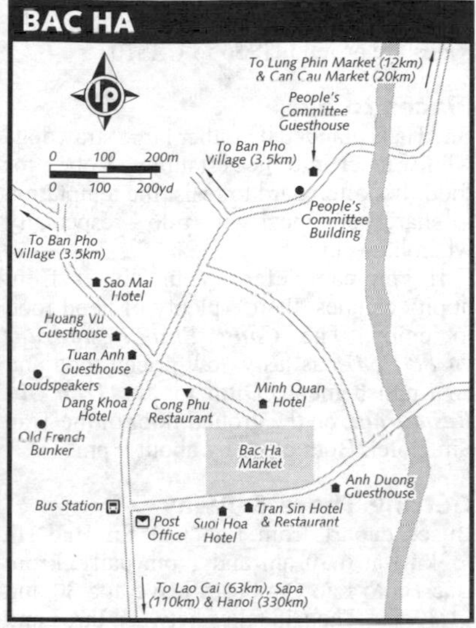

lights and loud music. Indeed, don't even expect electricity. The H'mong villagers are extremely hospitable and probably some of the kindest people you'll meet in Vietnam. If you visit around noon you may be invited to lunch, though that can be a mixed blessing.

H'mong cuisine is particularly memorable – they like to flavour their food with raw pig's blood! They also eat something that I could only describe as 'guts soup'. If you want to visit their homes, it's best to do so just after they've all eaten. If you visit during meal times, then you are obligated to eat – no excuses about not being hungry!
Another warning, at least for men – the H'mong are heavy drinkers. If you are toasted, then you must empty your glass. After the market closes, it's not unusual to see a procession of H'mong women heading home, each one leading a horse behind her with her drunken husband slumped over the saddle.

Vincent Clemente

A polite way to refuse is to tap on your stomach (as if you are not feeling well) or just smile while saying 'no thanks'. If you accept it is polite to reciprocate with an offer a gift of fruit or something. (See the 'Hill Tribes in Vietnam' special section in this chapter.)

Ban Pho is a 7km return trip from Bac Ha. You can take a loop route to get there and back.

Markets

There are several interesting markets around Bac Ha, all within about 20km of each other. You'll see plenty of Flower H'mong – so-called because the women embroider flowers on their colourful skirts. Items on sale include water buffaloes, pigs, horses and chickens. Tourists, however, seem to stick to buying handicrafts.

Bac Ha Market This lively and crowded concrete bazaar is the main market in Bac Ha proper. It's dominated by the Flower H'mong, but these days, the number of tourists is quickly catching up.

The market mainly operates on Sunday.

Can Cau Market This is one of Vietnam's most fascinating open-air markets. It's 20km north of Bac Ha and just 9km south of the Chinese border. Can Cau attracts a large number of Chinese traders, evidenced by the booming dog trade here.

The market runs only on Saturday and getting there is a rough ride. The road leading to Can Cau is pitiless; without a 4WD or strong two-wheeled transport, don't even think about it.

Lung Phin Market This market is between Can Cau market and Bac Ha town, about 12km from the town. It's less busy here than at the other markets, and runs on Sunday.

Places to Stay

Theoretically you should try to find a place to stay as far away as possible from those loudspeakers, but most of the hotels are near the noisy centre of town. The situation could change quickly, but it's fair to say that for now there is no quiet place to stay in Bac Ha.

As in Sapa, room rates tend to increase on weekends, when tourists come to town for the Sunday market. Sunday nights are hardest to find a room.

The ***Sao Mai Hotel*** *(☎ 880288, fax 880285)* is a popular place to stay and the rooms are clean and pleasant. The hotel has three sections: an older concrete building and two recently built wooden houses. Rates are US$8 to US$20. There is a cosy restaurant/bar with outdoor seating under the plum trees. During the busy weekends the friendly owner organises traditional music performances in the bar.

The ***Dang Khoa Hotel*** *(☎ 880290)*, in the centre of town, boasts satellite TV in the lobby. It's a bit run-down, but the adjacent extension with 10 new rooms looks promising. Rooms cost US$5 to US$8.

The ***Hoang Vu Guesthouse*** *(☎ 880264)* is a friendly place charging a flat rate of US$10. Nearby is the newer, family-run ***Tuan Anh Guesthouse*** *(☎ 880377)*, which has five rooms and is a tad cheaper at US$8.

The ***Tran Sin Hotel*** *(☎ 880240)* is near the market. Rooms cost US$10 to US$15. Just next door to the Tran Sinh, the ***Suoi Hoa Hotel*** *(☎ 880370)*, or 'Flower Stream Hotel', has 13 rooms and similar rates. Also in the same price range is the ***Minh Quan Hotel*** *(☎ 880222)*. It's the newest hotel in town and offers a nice view over the Bac Ha market.

The friendly ***Anh Duong Guesthouse*** *(☎ 880329)* offers the advantage of being close to the market, yet far enough from the main road and loudspeakers to be quiet. Rooms cost US$8 to US$12.

The ***Peoples' Committee Guesthouse*** *(☎ 880438)*, housed in an old French colonial-style building and former palace of the local H'mong king, is very basic; only a few of the rooms offer mattresses on the beds. Rates are around US$6 to US$10.

Places to Eat

Bac Ha is plagued by rather large stray dogs who wander into the restaurants to beg for food. It's often hard to resist the temptation to share your meal with fido – especially when he weighs 80kg.

If you can defend your dinner from uppity canines, there's plenty of good food to enjoy. The ***Cong Phu Restaurant*** *(☎ 880254)* has tasty, low-priced food and an English menu. Ditto for the ***Tran Sin Restaurant***, on the ground floor of the Tran Sin Hotel. Both close by about 9 pm.

Getting There & Away

Buses depart from Lao Cai for Bac Ha (63km) at 6.30 am and 1 pm daily. From Bac Ha to Lao Cai buses leave at 5.30 and 11.30 am. The trip takes between three and five hours depending on pick-ups along the way and costs US$1.20. The road is well maintained and the rural scenery is lovely.

Locals on motorbikes are also willing to make the Lao Cai–Bac Ha run for about US$5, or even Sapa–Bac Ha (110km) for US$12. Sunday minibus tours from Sapa to Bac Ha have also started, and cost around US$12 including transportation, guide and trekking to a minority village. On the way back to Sapa it is possible to hop off in Lao Cai and catch the night train back to Hanoi.

Bac Ha is 330km (10 hours) from Hanoi. Some cafes in Hanoi offer four-day bus trips to Bac Ha for around US$60, usually with a visit to Sapa included.

North-Central Vietnam

The north-central region is one of the poorest areas of Vietnam, and perhaps the least visited by foreign tourists. Most travellers make a beeline between Hue and Hanoi by bus, train or air, choosing to spend more time in places Hoi An, Hué and points in the far south or north.

Moreover, as several important sites including Tam Coc, Hoa Lu, Phat Diem and Cuc Phuong National Park are within just a couple of hours from Hanoi, travellers have the option of visiting on day excursion from the capital. The beaches of north-central Vietnam, though popular with domestic tourists, pale in comparison to those in the centre and along the south-central coast.

Highlights

- Visit Tam Coc, the beautiful 'Halong Bay on the rice fields' near Ninh Binh.
- Make a forest trek or visit the Endangered Primate Rescue Centre at Cuc Phuong National Park.
- Explore the magnificent Phong Nha Cave, with its thousands of underground passageways.
- Go temple-hopping in the ancient capital of Hoa Lu.
- Visit the impressive Sino-Vietnamese Phat Diem Cathedral.

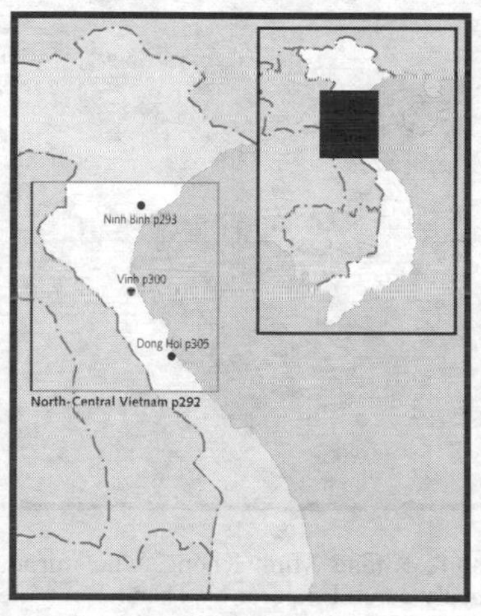

History

The region's historical importance dates back to the 10th century, when the country's capital was at Hoa Lu, with its magnificent temples set amid a beautiful rural landscape of limestone cliffs and rice paddies.

In the 13th and 14th centuries, the Tran Dynasty kings ruled from the capital of Thang Long (present day Hanoi). This was the only period in Vietnamese history when the heirs to the throne semisucceeded their fathers, taking over the official role of king while the older generation shared power in a second unofficial capital in Tuc Mac, about 5km from Nam Dinh. By doing so, the tradition of feuding brothers killing each other off for the throne was quelled, making the Tran Dynasty one of the most politically stable and prosperous periods in Vietnamese history.

During the American War, north-central Vietnam suffered great damage from US bombing, notably in Thanh Hoa.

THAI BINH

☎ 036 • pop 135,000

Few travellers visit Thai Binh because it's not on National Highway 1. You're only likely to come here if you're following the spur route that connects Ninh Binh to Haiphong.

If you miss Thai Binh, you haven't really missed much. The only sight of interest around here is nearby Keo Pagoda. It's easy to catch a motorbike from Thai Binh to the pagoda, which costs about 10,000d.

Keo Pagoda

Keo Pagoda (Chua Keo) was founded in the 12th century to honour Buddha and the

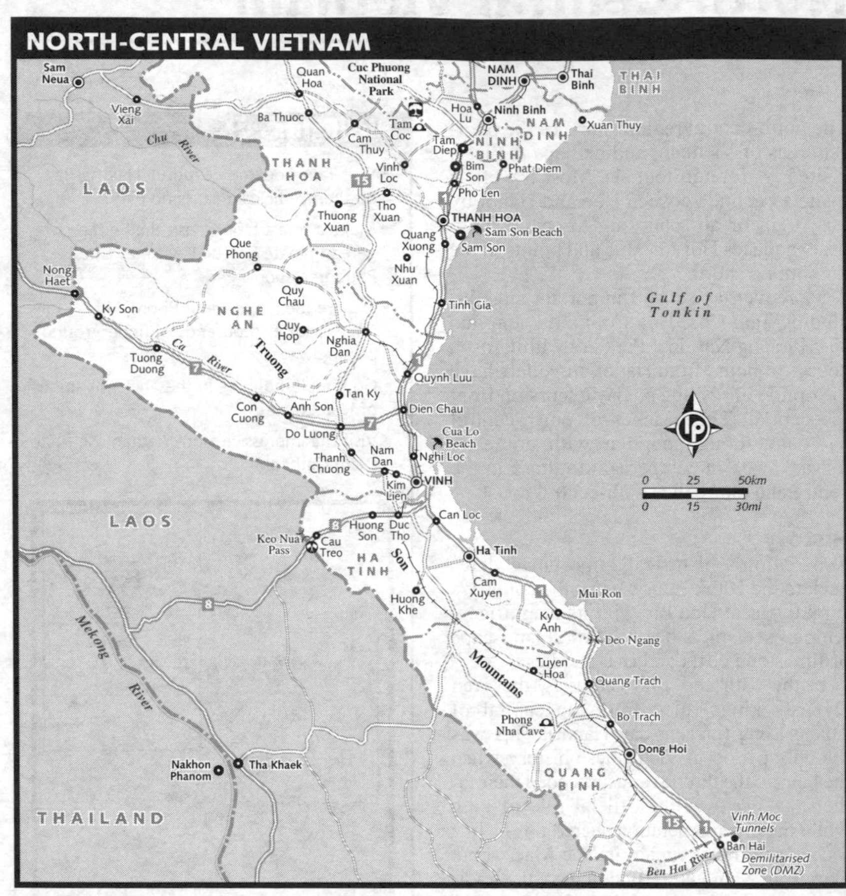

monk Khong Minh Khong, who miraculously cured Emperor Ly Thanh Ton (ruled 1128–38) of leprosy. The finely carved wooden bell tower is considered a masterpiece of traditional Vietnamese architecture. The nearby dike is a good place to get a general view of the pagoda complex.

Keo Pagoda is in Thai Binh Province, 9.5km from the town of Thai Binh.

NINH BINH

☎ 030 • pop 53,000

Ninh Binh has evolved into a major travel centre in recent years. Its sudden transformation from sleepy hamlet to tourist magnet has little to do with Ninh Binh itself, but rather with its proximity to nearby Tam Coc (9km), Hoa Lu (12km) and Cuc Phuong National Park (45km).

Although it is certainly possible to visit these sights as a day trip from Hanoi, many travellers chose to overnight in Ninh Binh or the national park to appreciate the scenery at a more leisurely pace.

Places to Stay & Eat

Thanh Thuy's Guesthouse (☎ *871811, 128 Đ Le Hong Phong*) is run by Mr Tuc and his wife Thuy, who both speak English, German and French, and are well known for their cooking. Basic fan rooms cost US$3 to US$6, air-con raises the tab from US$8 to US$15.

Another family-run, backpacker favourite is the ***Thuy Anh Mini-Hotel*** (☎/fax *871602, 55A Đ Truong Han Sieu*). The rooms are spotless and cost US$7 to US$25. The ***restaurant*** here is superb, and the helpful owners aim to please; they can book tours of the area, rent motorbikes and bicycles, and give you instructions on where to go and what to see.

Just across Đ Tran Hung Dao from the Thuy Anh is the private ***Star Hotel*** (☎ *871522, fax 871200, 267 Đ Tran Hung Dao*), a popular place with dormitory beds for just US$2, and rooms for US$5 to US$20.

Queen Mini-Hotel (☎ *871874*) is just 30m from Ninh Binh train station, and rooms cost US$6 to US$8. There is no restaurant, but ***meals*** can be prepared on request. The English-speaking staff are also helpful with arranging motorbike rentals and tours.

Hoa Lu Hotel (☎ *871217, fax 874126*) is the largest hotel in Ninh Binh. It's 300m north of town on D Tran Hung Dao, and has doubles for US$25 to US$35.

On the way to the hotel, ***Hoa Lu Restaurant*** will keep you from starving, but that's about all we can say.

The state owned ***Trang An Hotel*** (☎ *874742, fax 871200*) is a snazzy place with air-con rooms for US$20. It's on the corner of Đ Tran Hung Dao and Đ Le Hong Phong.

An alternative to staying in town is the pleasant, suburban ***Van Xuan Inter-Hotel Complex*** (☎ *860648, fax 860647*). The hotel is about halfway out on the road to Hoa Lua, and you would be best off staying here with your own transport. Large air-con rooms with satellite TV cost US$25.

Getting There & Away

Bus Ninh Binh is 93km south-west of Hanoi. Regular public buses leave almost hourly from the southern bus terminal in Hanoi and make the 2½ hour run for US$1.60. The bus station in Ninh Binh is across the Van River from the post office.

Ninh Binh is also a hub on the north-south 'open tour' bus route, which drops off and picks up passengers at the Thuy Anh or Star hotels. Seats on a comfortable air-con bus to/from the Old Quarter in Hanoi cost around US$3.

Train Ninh Binh is a scheduled stop for the *Reunification Express* trains travelling between Hanoi and Saigon (see the Getting Around chapter).

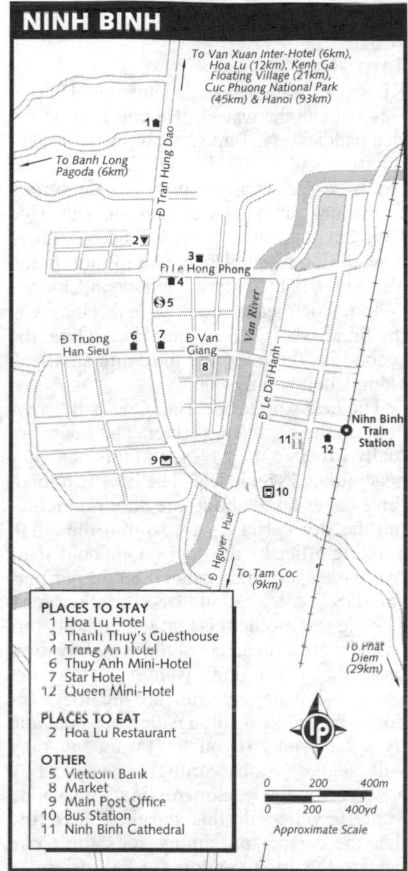

AROUND NINH BINH

☎ 030

Tam Hoc

Known to travellers as Vietnam's 'Halong Bay without the water', 'Halong Bay on the rice paddies' etc, Tam Coc boasts breathtaking scenery. While Halong Bay (see the North-East Vietnam chapter) has huge rock formations jutting out of the sea, Tam Coc has them jutting out of the rice paddies. There is a striking resemblance here to Guilin and Yangshuo, both major attractions in China.

Tam Coc means 'three caves'. Hang Ca, the first cave, is 127m long; Hang Giua, the second is 70m long; the third and smallest, Hang Cuoi, is only 40m.

The best way to see Tam Coc is by rowboat on the Ngo Dong River. The boats actually row into the caves, and this is a very peaceful and scenic trip. The boat trip to all three caves takes about three hours, including the stops. Tickets are sold at the small booking office by the docks. One boat seats two passengers and costs US$3.50 per person (US$2 entry fee and US$1.50 boat fee). The biggest problem is that the boat owners hassle you almost constantly to buy embroidery – if you don't want it, just say no.

Another annoying scam are the boat vendors who paddle up alongside your boat and try to sell drinks. If you don't want any, they will 'suggest' (rather strongly) that you buy a Coke for the person rowing your boat. Many travellers do this and then later find that the oarsperson simply sells the Coke back to the drink vendors for half price.

Even on cloudy days, bring sun screen and a hat or umbrella to protect your skin – there's no shade in the boats. Alternatively, rent an umbrella at the pier for US$0.50.

About 2km past Tam Coc is Bich Dong, another cave with a built-in temple. Getting there is easy enough by river or road; however, many travellers shun the place because of the very aggressive souvenir vendors (mostly children). Admission to the **cave temples** is US$1.50.

There are many restaurants at Tam Coc, including the excellent ***Anh Dzung Restaurant*** (☎ *860230*).

In the area behind the restaurant is Van Lan village, which is famous for its embroidery. Here you can watch the local artisans make napkins, tablecloths, pillowcases, T-shirts etc. Of course, a lot of these items wind up being sold on Hanoi's Pho Hang Gai, but it's cheaper to buy them here directly from the person who creates them. The village has a better selection and slightly lower prices than those available from the boat vendors.

Getting There & Away Tam Coc is 9km south-west of Ninh Binh. Follow National Highway 1 south and turn west at the Tam Coc turn-off. Budget cafes in Hanoi book day trips to Tam Coc, the fast-food version going for about US$12, or something closer to US$20 with a smaller group, comfortable vehicle and professional guide.

Hoa Lu

The scenery here resembles nearby Tam Coc, though Hoa Lu has an interesting historical twist. Hoa Lu was the capital of Vietnam during the Dinh Dynasty (968–80) and

Life on the Mekong River.

Early Le Dynasty (980–1009). The site was a suitable choice for a capital city due to its proximity to China and the natural protection afforded by the region's bizarre landscape.

The ancient citadel of Hoa Lu, most of which has been destroyed, covered an area of about 3 sq km. The outer ramparts encompassed temples, shrines and the palace where the king held court. The royal family lived in the inner citadel.

Yen Ngua mountain provides a scenic backdrop for Hoa Lu's two remaining temples. The first temple, **Dinh Tien Hoang**, was restored in the 17th century and is dedicated to the Dinh Dynasty. Out the front is the stone pedestal of a royal throne; inside are bronze bells and a statue of Emperor Dinh Tien Hoang with his three sons. The second temple, **Le Dai Hanh** (or Duong Van Nga), commemorates the rulers of the Early Le Dynasty. Inside the main hall are an assortment of drums, gongs, incense burners, candle holders and weapons; to the left of the entrance is a sanctuary dedicated to Confucius. You must climb about 200 steps to reach the sanctuaries, but your efforts will be rewarded with great views.

There is a US$2 entry fee to Hoa Lu. There are Vietnamese-speaking guides at the temples who work for free (but you should offer a tip). Alternatively, you can hire an English-speaking guide, which will cost an outrageous US$15 per group.

Getting There & Away Hoa Lu is 12km north of Ninh Binh. There is no public transport, so most travellers get there by bicycle, motorbike or car. Hanoi cafes may be able to organise a tour to get you here.

Banh Long Pagoda

While not spectacular, this Buddhist pagoda is only 6km from Ninh Binh and worth at least a quick look. From National Highway 1 (Đ Tran Hung Dao in Ninh Binh), turn west on the road between the Hoa Lu Restaurant and the Hoa Lu Hotel.

Kenh Ga Floating Village

In Kenh Ga (Chicken Canal), chickens may not be a prominent part of the villagers' lives, but the canal certainly is. Everyone in Kenh Ga lives on boats floating on the Hoang Long River. About the only other place in Vietnam where you can see anything like this is in the Mekong Delta. On the other hand, nowhere in the Mekong Delta will you find as stunning a mountain backdrop as you find at Kenh Ga. Another difference – people in Kenh Ga row boats with their feet.

This is one of the best places in northern Vietnam to see river life. People here seem to spend most of their lives floating on water – children even commute to school by boat.

The village has a **hot spring** (Suoi Nuoc Nong), where you can take a bath by pouring hot water over yourself with a bucket. There is a US$0.25 fee for entry to the springs.

From the pier, you can hire a rowboat to take you to/from the village for US$5 (these boats can only hold three people). For a more extensive look at the river, you can hire a motor launch – the tour covers about 6km and costs US$7 (these boats can hold 10 people).

The locals are very friendly. The children gleefully shout *'tay oi'* (Westerner) at every tourist they see, even Vietnamese tourists!

Getting There & Away Kenh Ga Floating Village is 21km from Ninh Binh. Follow National Highway 1 north for 11km, then it's a 10km drive west to reach the boat pier.

PHAT DIEM

Phat Diem (Kim Son) is the site of a **cathedral** remarkable for its vast dimensions and unique Sino-Vietnamese architecture. During the French era, the cathedral was an important centre of Catholicism in the north, and there was a seminary here. The 1954 division of Vietnam caused Catholics to flee to the south en masse, and the cathedral was closed. It is now functional again, and there are also several dozen other churches in the Phat Diem district. Current estimates are that about 120,000 Catholics live in the area.

The vaulted ceiling is supported by massive wood columns almost 1m in diameter and 10m tall. In the lateral naves, there are a number of curious wood and stone sculptures. The main altar is made of a single block of granite. The outside of the church reaches a height of 16m.

The cathedral complex comprises a number of buildings; the main one was completed in 1891. The whole project was founded by a Vietnamese priest named Six, whose tomb is in the square fronting the cathedral. Behind the main building is a large pile of limestone boulders – Father Six piled them up to test whether the boggy ground would support his planned empire. Apparently the test was a success.

Opposite the main entrance at the back of the cathedral is the bell tower. At its base lie two enormous stone slabs, one atop the other. Like all the other big carved stones here, these were transported from some 200km away with only rudimentary gear. What's interesting about these massive stone slabs is that their sole purpose was to provide a perch for the mandarins to sit and observe (no doubt with great amusement) the rituals of the Catholics at mass.

Atop the cathedral's highest tower is such an enormous bell that Quasimodo's famous chimer at Notre Dame pales in comparison. This bell, and all the other heavy metal, was pushed and pulled to the cathedral's top via an enormous earth ramp. After construction was completed, the dirt was spread around the church grounds to make the whole site about 1m higher than the surrounding terrain. This has, no doubt, offered important protection against floods.

Near the main cathedral is a small chapel built of large carved stone blocks, and inside it's as cool as a cave. Also not far from the cathedral is a covered bridge dating from the late 19th century.

Hoards of Vietnamese tourists come to this place, few of whom are Catholic, but many are extremely curious about churches and Christianity in general. As one reader observed:

> I went to a cathedral for midnight mass on Christmas Eve and found a number of Vietnamese and foreigners huddled on the front pews. Their presence seemed to provide great entertainment for the several thousand Vietnamese onlookers packed into the back of the building. There was a constant buzz of excitement among the rubbernecks, and a massive crush to the middle and even some pillar scaling feats were in order to get a better view. The priest interrupted the service several times to try to control the crowd. In between we were able to catch a few lines of the Vietnamese priest delivering his sermon first in Vietnamese, then French and finally English. Trilingual and very impressive, though his strong French accent made his English difficult to understand. I wasn't surprised to learn that some cathedrals in the south now only permit their congregation members to enter the building for Christmas midnight mass. Apparently, the priests issue members-only passes for the event.

Getting There & Away

Phat Diem is 121km south of Hanoi and 29km south-east of Ninh Binh. There are direct buses from Ninh Binh to Phat Diem, and making the trip by motorbike is also feasible.

There are no regular tours to Phat Diem, though any of the budget agents in Hanoi should be able offer a customised day trip if you are keen on doing the trip by private car, with or without a guide.

CUC PHUONG NATIONAL PARK

☎ 030

Cuc Phuong National Park, established in 1962, is one of Vietnam's most important nature reserves. Ho Chi Minh personally took time off from the war in 1963 to dedicate this, Vietnam's first national park. He offered a short dedication speech:

> Forest is gold. If we know how to conserve it well, it will be very precious. Destruction of the forest will lead to serious effects on both life and productivity.

The national park is 70km from the sea and covers an area about 25km in length and 11km in width, covering land in the provinces of Ninh Binh, Hoa Binh and Thanh Hoa. The elevation of the park's highest peak, Dinh May Bac (Silver Cloud Peak) is 648m. At the park's lower elevations, the climate is subtropical. (The stone tools of prehistoric humans have been discovered in Con Moong Cave, one of the park's many grottoes).

Though wildlife has suffered a precipitous decline in Vietnam in recent decades, the park's 222 sq km of primary tropical forest remain home to an amazing variety of animal and plant life, including over 2000 species of flora from 217 families and 749 genera; 1800 species of insect from 30 orders and 200 families; 320 species of bird; 36 types of bats; 70 species of mammal; and 80 species of reptile.

An extraordinary variety of life forms exist in the park, including several species discovered here, such as a tree known as *Bressiaopsis cucphuongensis* and the endemic red-bellied squirrel *Callosciurus erythrinaceus cucphuongensis*. The Rhesus macaque (*Macaca mullata*) can sometimes be seen in the forests. Sadly, once common spotted deer (*Cervus nippon*) are extinct in the wild, but some 3000 survive captive breeding programs in Vietnam (some of them in Cuc Phuong).

The best time of year to visit the park is in the dry months from October to March. April to June become increasingly hot and wet, and from July to September the rains arrive bringing *lots* of leeches with them. Visitors in April and May should be blessed with the chance to see literally millions of small white butterflies that breed here.

Excellent hiking opportunities abound in the park and you could spend days trekking through the forest. Popular trails include one to a massive 1000 year old tree, and to Kanh, a Muong village. Park staff can provide you with basic maps to find the well-marked trailheads. However, a guide is recommended for day trips and mandatory for longer treks; it is foolish and risky to attempt a trek alone through the dense jungle.

There are three-day treks to Muong villages that can be arranged through travel agencies in Hanoi and Ninh Binh. The 80 or so rangers here are very eco-conscious and are keen to protect wildlife from poaching and trees from illegal logging. A few hundred metres from the park's headquarters is a breeding and research centre for spotted deer. Attempts are being made to reintroduce them into areas from which they were previously annihilated. Believe it or not, there is also an experiment to determine if the deer can be bred for commercial meat production, as well as for their antlers.

Poaching and habitat destruction is a constant headache for the rangers. Many native species, such as the black bear, wild cats, birds and reptiles, have perished in the park as a result of human impact. Episodes of violence have erupted between the Muong and park rangers who have tried to stop people from logging in the park. The government has responded by relocating the villagers to another area further from the park's boundary. However, the high birth rate among the minorities in this area assures that future conflicts are inevitable.

The park is also home to a unique species of tree called Cay Kim Gao (for aspiring horticulturists, the Latin name is *Podocarpus fleuryi hickel*). In ancient days, kings and noble people would only eat with chopsticks made from this lumber – it was said that anything poisonous it touches turns the light coloured wood to black! These chopsticks make a nice souvenir.

Entry to the park is US$5.

Endangered Primate Rescue Center

One of the highlights of a visit to Cuc Phuong is the Endangered Primate Rescue Center. The facility, run by German biologists and local Vietnamese, is a laudable endeavour to improve the wellbeing of Vietnam's monkeys.

What started out as a small scale operation in 1995, with just a handful of primates, has grown into a highly productive centre, where today about 85 creatures are being cared for, studied and bred. There are currently 13 different species of gibbon and langur monkey on site (including four types of langur that only exist here).

The langur, an endemic species, resembles the gibbon, but grows a longer tail. There are estimated to be only about 20 of this species remaining in the wild today – 'wild' being in Cuc Phuong National Park and the surrounding area.

All animals in the centre were either rescued from illegal traders (mostly on their way to China), or bred in captivity. Such rare monkeys are big business and one can fetch anywhere between US$200 and US$600 from buyers looking to cash in on their 'medicinal worth', be it for gall stone relief or as an aphrodisiac. Tragically, the black market demand has driven several such species straight into extinction.

There have also been cases of feeble-minded humans attempting to keep these animals as pets, which they soon discover is next to impossible. The dietary requirements of langurs are highly restrictive; they survive exclusively on fresh-cut leaves (their digestive systems will not tolerate anything else). By unknowingly feeding the monkeys anything other than the correct foliage, people usually discover they've murdered their new 'pet' before they can even show it off to their friends.

Thankfully, giant steps are being taken to curb the illegal trading and to protect the langurs that still exist. Cooperation by Vietnamese authorities, and the staff at the centre, has resulted in incredible successes. One of the larger aims of the centre is to breed rare monkeys in captivity, with the hope of eventually re-introducing them back into their natural habitat. At the time of writing, hunting pressures were still too high to release them into the wild, but as a preliminary step, some gibbons and a group of Hatinh langurs were released into a two hectare, semi-wild area.

Though officially off limits to nonstaff members, it is possible to visit the centre. The best time is generally from about 9 to 11 am, or between 2 and 3 pm. It goes without saying, but visiting the centre demands the utmost respect for both the animals and the staff. Once inside the station, please follow instructions and do not get any stupid ideas about throwing a Snickers bar into the cages!

There is currently no charge to visit the centre, but you might consider purchasing some postcards or a poster – you'll see that the money is going to a very good cause. Some travellers have even contacted the centre in advance offering to bring much needed supplies from abroad. There *is* a possibility of voluntary work here, but without some real background in primate welfare (no, this does *not* constitute having watched *Gorillas in the Mist*), chances are slim.

For more information you can try their somewhat temperamental Web site www.primatecenter.com.

Places to Stay & Eat

Park headquarters charges US$10 for a few basic ***rooms*** in a Muong-style house (shared toilet and cold showers). Overpriced (but sterile) rooms in the ***park guesthouse*** cost US$25, but at this price many opt to stay in Ninh Binh. ***Meals*** are available at both these places for overnight guests. Reservations can be made by contacting Cuc Phuong National Park, (☎ 030-846006) Nho Quan District, Ninh Binh Province, or its Hanoi office (☎ 04-829 2604) at 1 Pho Doc Tan Ap, Hanoi.

Getting There & Away

Cuc Phuong National Park is 45km from Ninh Binh. The turn-off from National Highway 1 is north of Ninh Binh, and follows the road the same highway that goes past the Kenh Ga Floating Village. There is no public transport on this route.

THANH HOA

☎ 037

Thanh Hoa is the capital of Thanh Hoa Province. The only feature of real interest is a large and attractive church on the northern outskirts of town.

Thanh Hoa Province was the site of the Lam Son Uprising (1418–28), in which Vietnamese forces, led by Le Loi (who later became Emperor Ly Thai To) expelled the Chinese and re-established the country's independence.

Muong and Red Tai (Thai) hill tribes live in the western part of the province.

Thanh Hoa Tourist (☎ 852298/852517) at 298 Đ Quang Trung is the official government tourist authority for Thanh Hoa Province.

Places to Stay & Eat

Thanh Hoa Hotel (*☎ 852517, fax 853963, 25A Đ Quang Trung*) is on the west side of the highway in the centre of town. Rooms cost US$10 to US$35. Pacific Airlines has a booking counter in the hotel.

The family-run ***Loi Linh Hotel*** (☎ *851667, 22 Đ Tran Phu*) has air-con rooms for US$14.

Soup shops, ***cafes*** and a few ***restaurants*** can be found along National Highway 1, especially near the southern entrance to town.

Getting There & Away

Thanh Hoa is a stop for the *Reunification Express* trains (see the Getting Around chapter). The city is 502km from Hué, 139km from Vinh and 153km from Hanoi by road.

SAM SON BEACH

☎ 037

Sam Son is possibly the most popular beach resort in the north. It's too far from Hanoi for day-trippers, but during summer the place is chock-a-block with weekenders escaping the oven-hot capital. During the winter, Sam Son is pretty much deserted and only a few of the hotels bother to stay open.

There are in fact two beaches here, separated by a rocky headland. The main beach on the north side of the headland is where you'll find all the ugly high-rise hotels. The southern beach is mostly undeveloped, but it can still fill up with picnickers. The headland itself offers some decent **hiking** and scenic views, though the promontory has a military base and a sign (in English) telling you to keep out. The rest of the headland is a park and is open to the public.

The area is notable for its **pine forests**, enormous granite boulders and sweeping views. The Co Tien Pagoda can also be found in the park.

Places to Stay

Most of Sam Son's ugly state-run hotels offer luxury hotel prices without the luxury. Be aware that prices tend to go up between June and August (high season for domestic tourists). It's possible to negotiate discounts in winter, though there's not much point visiting at that time.

The mammoth-sized ***Huong Bien Hotel*** (☎ *821272*) has basic twin rooms from US$8 to US$25. Don't confuse this place with the dilapidated two-storey hotel by the same name next door.

Along similar lines, the private and smaller ***Hoa Dang Hotel*** (☎ *821288*), has rooms from US$18 to US$22.

The ***Hoa Hong 1 Hotel*** (☎ *821505*) has air-con rooms for US$18.

Getting There & Away

Thanh Hoa is the provincial capital and nearest main road and railway junction to Sam Son Beach. It's a pretty unexciting town, but it's only 16km from Sam Son, a short enough trip by motorbike.

VINH

☎ 038 • pop 201,900

The port city of Vinh is the capital of Nghe An Province. Apart from lashings of dreary Soviet-style architecture, there is almost nothing of interest in the city itself, but there are a few sights in the surrounding area. Vinh's economic fortunes have recently been greatly improved by the sharp increase in traffic on National Highway 1. For travellers, the town is a convenient place to stop for the night if you are on the overland route between Hué and Hanoi. Vinh is also an essential transit point if you're heading overland to/from Tha Khaek in Laos.

Nghe An and neighbouring Ha Tinh provinces have been lumped with poor soil and some of the worst weather in Vietnam; the area frequently suffers from severe floods and devastating typhoons. The locals say, 'The typhoon was born here and comes back often to visit'. The summers are very hot and dry, while in winter the cold and rain are made all the more unpleasant by biting winds from the north.

As a result of the poor climate and many years of half-baked collectivised farming policies, Nghe An and Ha Tinh provinces are among the most destitute regions in Vietnam. The recent economic reforms have greatly improved things, but nobody has yet figured out a way to reform the lousy weather.

History

Vinh's recent history has not been the happiest. It was a pleasant citadel-city during colonial days, but was destroyed in the early 1950s as a result of French aerial bombing and the Viet Minh's scorched-earth policy. Vinh was later devastated by a huge fire.

The Ho Chi Minh Trail began in Nghe An Province, and much of the war *matériel* transported on the Ho Chi Minh Trail was shipped via the port of Vinh. Not too surprisingly, the US military obliterated the city in hundreds of air attacks and naval artillery bombardments from 1964 to 1972, which left only two buildings intact. The Americans paid a high price for the bombings – more US aircraft and pilots were shot down over Nghe An and Ha Tinh provinces than over any other part of North Vietnam. The heavy loss of planes and pilots was one reason why the USA later brought in battleships to pound North Vietnam with artillery shells fired from offshore.

Orientation

As National Highway 1 enters Vinh from the south, it crosses the mouth of the Lam River (Ca River), also known as Cua Hoi Estuary. Street address numbers are often not used in Vinh.

Information

Travel Agencies The government-owned Nghe An Tourist (Cong Ty Du Lich Nghe

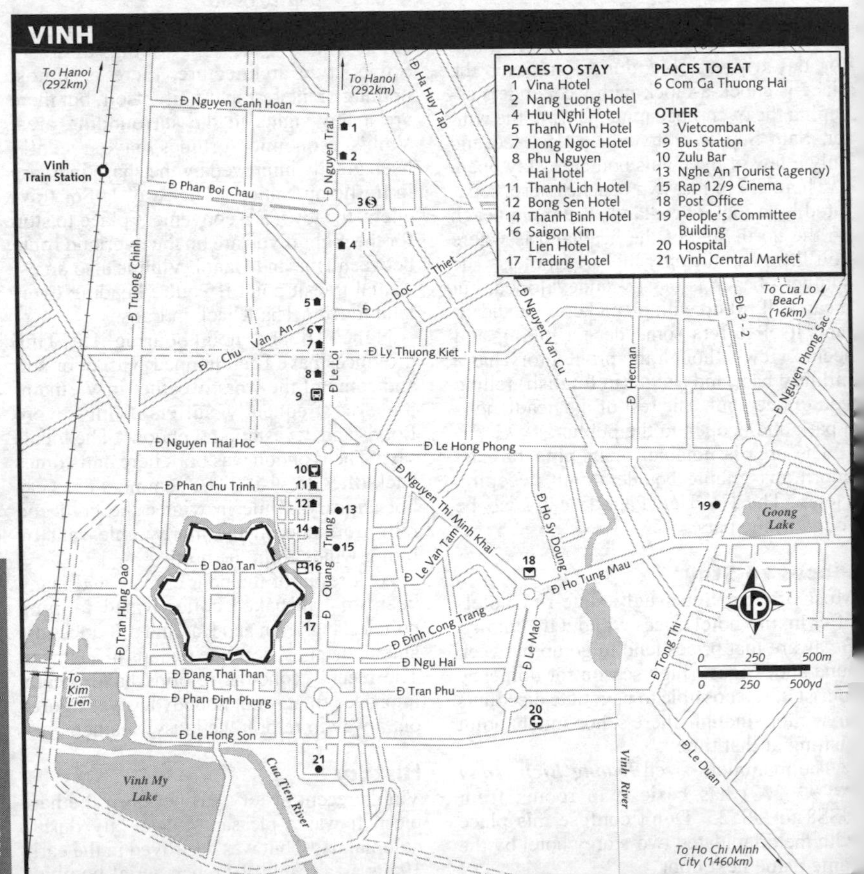

An) is on Đ Quang Trung just to the north of Rap 12/9 cinema.

Money Vietcombank (Ngan Hang Ngoai Thuong Viet Nam) is near the corner of Đ Le Loi and Đ Nguyen Si Sach.

Post The main post office is on Đ Nguyen Thi Minh Khai, near the corner of Đ Dinh Cong Trang. It is open daily from 6.30am to 9 pm.

Medical Services The general hospital is on the corner of Đ Tran Phu and Đ Le Mao.

Places to Stay

Thanh Binh Hotel (☎ *842512, 33 Đ Quang Trung*) is large, renovated and state-run, with rooms US$10 to US$20.

Bong Sen Hotel (☎ *844397, 39 Đ Quang Trung*) is an established cheapie, with doubles from US$7 to US$12.

Vina Hotel (☎ *846990, 9 Đ Nguyen Trai*) has pretty standard rooms with attached bath from US$10 to US$14.

Thanh Lich Hotel (☎ *844961, 49 Đ Quang Trung*) appeals more to Vietnamese tastes than to tourists. The blasting karaoke could raise the dead. Otherwise, rooms are clean enough to justify the US$10 to US$16 price tag.

If you don't mind paying a little extra for the luxury of satellite TV, the ***Phu Nguyen Hai Hotel*** (☎ *848429, fax 832014,* ⓔ *ctpnh@hn.vnn.vn, 81 Đ Le Loi*) is a new and snazzy place worth checking into. Rates are US$20 to US$35.

Also consider the modern ***Hong Ngoc Hotel*** (☎ *841314, fax 841229, 99 Đ Le Loi*). Comfortable rooms with satellite TV and bathtubs cost US$15 and US$25.

Nang Luong Hotel (☎ *844788, 2 Đ Nguyen Trai*) is an old but friendly place. Rooms all have satellite TV and cost US$15 to US$34.

Huu Nghi Hotel (☎ *844633*) on Đ Le Loi is a large, aging upmarket place where rooms with satellite TV cost from US$25 to US$70; breakfast is included.

Trading Hotel aka *Khach San Thuong Mai* (☎ *830211, fax 830393, 19 Đ Quang Trung*) gets the nod from business travellers. It's a newer place with the requisite satellite TV. Doubles cost US$20 to US$35.

Saigon Kim Lien Hotel (☎ *838899, fax 838898,* ⓔ *sgklna@hn.vnn.vn, 25 Đ Quang Trung*) is the largest hotel in Vinh and has everything: air-con, hot water, foreign exchange service, travel agent, restaurant, satellite TV, massage services, the whole lot. All this luxury costs from US$30 to US$70.

Places to Eat

Vinh Market (Cho Vinh) carries the usual plethora of household goods, and there are ***food stalls*** around the back. The market is at the end of Đ Cao Thang, which is the southern continuation of Đ Quang Trung.

For good Chinese-style chicken dishes, look for ***Com Ga Thuong Hai*** (*99 Đ Le Loi*), just next door to the Hong Ngoc Hotel. The restaurant name means Rice Chicken Shanghai.

If you poke around town, it won't be long before you notice the peanut candies on sale almost everywhere. There are at least three different kinds, each one outstanding. You'll find plenty of similar-looking candies elsewhere in Vietnam, but the Vinh varieties are far and away the best. This stuff is export quality (even though it doesn't get exported) and is highly addictive. If you're on a diet, don't even stop in Vinh.

Entertainment

Vinh is not exactly known for its raging nightlife, which is probably the reason why a British expat decided to open the funky ***Zulu Bar*** (☎ *848997, 51 Đ Quang Trung*). Vinh's first (and *only*) Western-style watering hole, this unique little haven is the antithesis to the run-of-the-mill karaoke joints in town, and the place to be if you're overnighting in Vinh.

Getting There & Away

Air The Vietnam Airlines booking office is in the Huu Nghi Hotel. It's possible to fly to Vinh.

Bus The most exciting news for travellers was the opening of the Cau Treo border with

Laos at Keo Nua Pass, 80km from Vinh (see the Getting There & Away chapter).

Vinh bus station (Ben Xe Vinh) is on Đ Le Loi about 1km north of Vinh Market; the ticket office is open from 4.30 am to 5 pm daily. Buses to Buon Ma Thuot, Danang, Hanoi and Saigon depart daily at 5 am; irregular express buses to Hanoi leave at other times of the day as well.

Train Vinh train station, or Ga Vinh, (☎ 824 924) is 1km west of the intersection of Đ Le Loi and Đ Phan Boi Chau, 1.5km north of Vinh Market. The *Reunification Express* stops here (see the Getting Around chapter).

Car & Motorbike Road distances from Vinh are as follows:

Danang	468km
Dong Hoi	197km
Hanoi	292km
Hué	363km
Lao border	87km
Thanh Hoa	139km

Getting Around

Motorbike taxis charge about US$0.50 to most places in town.

Despite its small size, Vinh has three taxi companies: Phu Nguyen Taxi (☎ 833333), Quynh Ha Taxi (☎ 858585) and Viet Anh Taxi (☎ 843999).

AROUND VINH

☎ 038

Cua Lo Beach

This is one of the three major beach resorts in the northern half of the country (which isn't saying much). The other two are at Sam Son and Do Son.

The beach here is actually not bad – there's white sand and clean water, and a grove of pine trees along the shore provides some shade and a wind break. But as a resort area, Cua Lo is far behind Vung Tau, Mui Ne or Nha Trang. Nevertheless, if you're in the area and the weather is suitably warm and dry, Cua Lo could be worth a visit to cool off.

Places to Stay Hotel rates drop considerably during the winter months – the name of the game is negotiation (but do so politely). During the summer peak season there is little latitude for bargaining.

Hon Ngu Hotel (☎ *824127, fax 824446*) is a big white high rise facing the beach. Run by the army with military cleanliness, prices range from US$20 to US$50.

Pacific Hotel (☎ *824164*) is another big high rise with ocean views near the beach. Doubles cost from US$15 to US$50.

Just next door, the private ***Loc Anh Guesthouse*** (☎ *824558*) charges US$12 to US$25.

Further north along the beach is ***Guesthouse of Cua Lo Town*** *aka Nha Khach Thi Cua Lo* (☎ *824541*). Prices in high season are US$18 to US$35.

Getting There & Away Cua Lo is 16km north-east of Vinh and can be reached easily by motorbike and taxi.

Kim Lien

Just 14km north-west of Vinh is **Ho Chi Minh's birthplace** of Sen Village, within Kim Lien. The house in which he was born in 1890 is maintained as a sacred shrine, and is a favourite pilgrimage spot for Vietnamese tourists.

Ho's childhood home is a simple farmhouse made of bamboo and palm leaves, reflecting his humble background. Ho was raised here until 1895, when the family sold this house and moved to Hué so that Ho's father could study.

In 1901, Ho's family returned and bought a house in Kim Lien proper, 2km from Sen Village (Ho remained in Hué so that he could attend secondary school).

Close to the Kim Lien house is a **museum** (☎ *825110*). Both of Ho's houses and the museum are open to the public from 6.30 to 11 am and 2 to 5.30 pm from Tuesday to Sunday. Admission to the houses is free, but you are obliged to buy a bouquet of flowers from the reception desk and place them by the alter.

A placard inside the house tells some of the life story of Ho's mother (Hoang Thi Loan) and his father (Nguyen Sinh Sac)

Betel Nut

One thing you'll undoubtedly see for sale at street stalls everywhere in Vietnam is betel nut. This is not a food – swallow it and you'll be sorry! The betel nut is in fact the seed of the betel palm (a beautiful tree, by the way) and is meant to be chewed. The seed usually has a slit in it and is mixed with lime and wrapped in a leaf. Like tobacco, it's strong stuff that you can barely tolerate at first, but eventually become addicted to.

The first time you bite into betel nut, your whole face gets hot – chewers say it gives them a buzz. Like chewing tobacco, betel nut causes excessive salivation and betel chewers must constantly spit. The reddish-brown stains you see on footpaths are not blood, but betel-saliva juice. Years of constant chewing cause the teeth to become stained progressively browner, eventually becoming nearly black.

Unfortunately, all explanations are in Vietnamese and no English-speaking guides are available.

At the car park by the museum are quite a few vendors plugging the peanut candies for which Vinh is famous. If you haven't bought any yet, this is as good a place as any.

There is no public transport to Kim Lien, but it's easy enough to hire a motorbike or taxi in Vinh.

HA TINH

☎ 039

Ha Tinh lies on the highway between Dong Hoi and Vinh. There is nothing to see here, but you can stay if you're too tired to push on along National Highway 1. Ha Tinh also has a Vietcombank (☎ 856775) at 6 Đ Phan Dinh Phung where you can change money.

Places to Stay & Eat

Ha Tinh's cheapest accommodation is the aging ***Kieu Hoa Hotel*** (*☎ 855658*). It's on the west side of the highway, slightly north of the TV tower. Rooms cost US$17 to US$20.

On the south side of Ha Tinh (and west side of the highway) is ***Nha Khach Huong Thuy*** (*☎ 885412*). The staff speak good English and rooms cost US$15 to US$20.

On the west side of Đ Tran Phu (National Highway 1) opposite the huge TV tower is the ***Binh Minh Hotel*** (*☎ 856825*). Rooms are OK at US$20 and US$30.

DEO NGANG

Deo Ngang (Ngang Pass) is a mountainous coastal area that constitutes the easternmost section of the Hoanh Son Mountains (Transversal Range), which stretches from the Lao border to the sea along the 18th parallel. Until the 11th century, the range formed Vietnam's frontier with the Kingdom of Champa. Later, the French used it as the border between their protectorates of Annam and Tonkin; Annam Gate (Porte d'Annam) is still visible at Ngang Deo from National Highway 1.

The Hoanh Son Mountains now demarcate the border between Quang Binh Province and Ha Tinh Province. There are a number of islands offshore.

Hoanh Son Hotel, just north of the pass and right beside the beach, is a clean place to stay. Rooms cost US$10 with air-con. The hotel also has a ***restaurant*** and the staff are very friendly.

PHONG NHA CAVE

Formed approximately 250 million years ago, Phong Nha Cave is the largest and most beautiful known cave in Vietnam. Located in the village of Son Trach, (55km north-west of Dong Hoi) it was designated as a UNESCO World Heritage Site in 2000. It's remarkable for its thousands of metres of **underground passageways** and **river caves** filled with abundant stalactites and stalagmites.

Only recently has anyone made a thorough, documented exploration of the cave. In 1990, a British caving expedition explored 35km of the cave and made the first reliable map of Phong Nha's underground (and underwater) passageways. They discovered that the main cavern is nearly 8km long, with 14 other caves nearby.

Phong Nha means Cave of Teeth and Wind, but, unfortunately, the 'teeth' (or stalagmites) that were by the entrance are no longer there. Once you get further into the cave, it's mostly unspoiled. There's also a newly discovered dry cave just above the mountain containing Phong Nha Cave. You can walk to it from the entrance to Phong Nha Cave (about ten minutes) – look for the sign to Tien Son at the foot of the stairs.

The Chams used the cave's grottoes as Buddhist sanctuaries in the 9th and 10th centuries; the remains of their altars and inscriptions can still be seen. Vietnamese Buddhists continue to venerate these sanctuaries, as they do other Cham religious sites, so behave respectfully. Also, remember, this is a World Heritage Site, so please do not to remove any stalactites or stalagmites as souvenirs.

In more recent times, the cave was used as a hospital and ammunition depot during the American War. The entrance shows evidence of fighter aircraft attacks. That US warplanes spent considerable time bombing and strafing the Phong Nha area is not surprising – this was one of the key entrance points to the Ho Chi Minh Trail. Some overgrown remains of the trail are still visible, though you'll need a guide to point them out to you.

Entry to the cave costs 15,000d (about US$1), and you can expect to pay about US$1 per person for the mandatory boat ride to reach the cave.

You can inquire at the hotel about booking a vehicle to Phong Nha Cave, but be prepared to bargain. Budget travellers will probably find it more economical to launch their cave explorations from Dong Hoi (20km south of Bo Trach).

Places to Stay & Eat

The only place to stay near the cave itself is the bare bones ***Phong Nha Guesthouse*** (☎ *675016*), located right at the landing where you catch boats to the cave. Dorm beds cost US$1.50 and private fan rooms US$8.

Another option to consider, about 30km from the cave, is ***Da Nhay Hotel*** (☎ *052-866041*), adjacent to a quiet beach about 10km north of Bo Trach (also called Hoan Lao). The hotel has small but comfortable rooms costing US$20.

There is currently only one ***restaurant*** in Son Trach itself, and it's not exactly five star. The sign out the front simply says *Com-Pho* (Rice-Noodles).

Getting There & Away

The Phong Nha Reception Department (☎ 823424) in Son Trach village has overall responsibility for tourist access to the cave (which is a polite way of saying it has a monopoly). At this office you must buy your admission ticket (US$6 per person). You can (and should) rent a generator and lantern here for an additional US$6 (per group), otherwise you won't see much. You should still bring a torch (flashlight) in case the generator fails.

The actual cave entrance is 3km from Son Trach and can only be reached by boat. You book the boat at the Phong Nha Reception Department. The boat can hold about six passengers and the one-way ride takes 30 minutes. Overall, you'll probably spend about two hours on the whole excursion. Unless you have special permission, you are only permitted to explore the first 600m of the cave.

There is no public transport to Son Trach, but hotels and some travel agencies in nearby towns offer transport.

The Phuong Dong Hotel in Dong Hoi (55km from Son Trach) offers transport for US$50 for 10 people (see the Dong Hoi section following).

By contrast, the Da Nhay Hotel near Bo Trach (only 30km from Son Trach) is far more expensive, charging US$120 for 12 persons; however, it also has a car for hire that can carry four persons (US$40). Not surprisingly, it gets few customers, so there may be latitude here for bargaining.

The Le Loi Hué Hotel in Hué (220km from Son Trach) charges US$90 for a car that carries four persons, or US$10 to US$15 per person for a minibus that can carry nine to 12 passengers.

You can travel by public bus to Bo Trach, where you will find motorbike taxis at the bus station. You should be able to negotiate a trip to Son Trach for around US$5 and the drivers will wait for you while you visit the cave.

DONG HOI

☎ 052 • pop 93,500

The fishing port of Dong Hoi is the capital of Quang Binh Province. Important archaeological finds from the Neolithic period have been made in the vicinity. During the American War, the city suffered extensive damage from US bombing. When travelling on National Highway 1 north of the DMZ, note the old French bunkers and US bomb craters lining the route; they're especially prolific near road and rail bridges. The Vietnam-Cuba Hospital is 1km north of town and the Nhat Le River flows along the east side of town.

Usually travellers spend the night in Dong Hoi only if they wish to visit Phong Nha Cave (see Phong Nha Cave section earlier in this chapter for details). The cave is 55km from Dong Hoi, so it can be visited as a day trip. Some hotels in Dong Hoi book trips to the cave.

Dong Hoi is 166km from Hué, 94km from Dong Ha, 197km from Vinh and 489km from Hanoi.

Beaches

Most of Quang Binh Province is lined with sand dunes and beaches. These spread for dozens of kilometres north of town and on a long spit of sand south of town. Nhat Le Beach is at the mouth of the Nhat Le River, about 2.5km from central Dong Hoi. Another bathing site in the region is Ly Hoa Beach.

Places to Stay

The best places to stay are on the west bank of the Nhat Le River, just east of National Highway 1.

One of the nicest places in town is the new ***Huong Quyen Hotel*** (☎ *825260, fax 825261, 18 Đ Quang Trung*) further along Đ Hung Vuong. Fan doubles go for US$10, or US$15 for up to five guests. Air-con rooms cost US$13 to US$15.

Another new place is the large ***Phong Nha Hotel*** (☎ *824971, fax 824973, 5 Đ Truong Phap*), close to Nhat Le Beach, which charges US$15 to US$40.

Thanh My Guesthouse (☎ *821026*) on Đ Nguyen Du charges US$7 to US$14 for basic rooms.

The largest of the riverside hotels is the ***Nhat Le Hotel*** (☎ *822180, 16 Đ Quang Xuan Ky*). Rooms cost from US$7 to US$20.

The ***Phuong Dong Hotel*** (☎ *822276, fax 822404, 20 Đ Quach Xuan Ky*) has several standards of room, for US$10 to US$35. This place also books day trips by car or van to Phong Nha Cave.

Another block to the north is ***Huu Nghi Hotel*** (☎ *822567*) on Đ Quach Xuan Ky. This place has river views and rooms from US$20 to US$35.

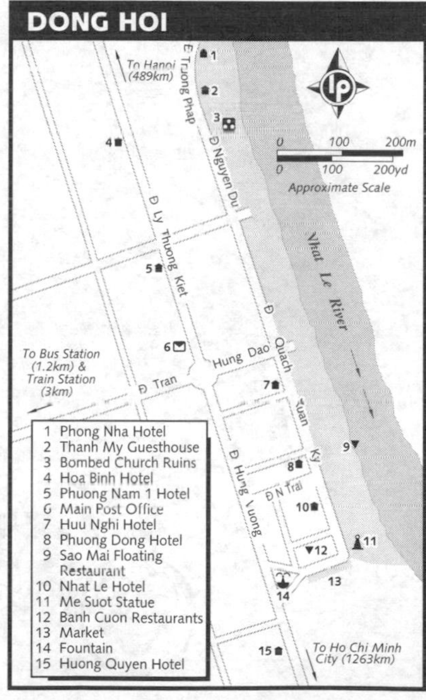

Hoa Binh Hotel (☎ *822347*) on Đ Ly Thuong Kiet is a four-storey building, making it a veritable skyscraper by Dong Hoi standards. Unfortunately, it's starting to fall into disrepair, but that hasn't caused the prices to drop. Rooms cost US$25 and US$30.

Phuong Nam 1 Hotel (☎ *823194*) on Đ Ly Thuong Kiet is an old place with some decaying architectural elegance. Rooms cost from US$20.

Places to Eat

For good seafood at reasonable prices, the ***Sao Mai Floating Restaurant***, moored on the Nhat Le River, makes for an atmospheric dining choice.

For something a bit more casual, there is a cluster of good local ***restaurants*** near the market specialising in dumpling-like *banh cuon*. Try the variation stuffed with wild boar meat!

Getting There & Away

Bus Dong Hoi is on National Highway 1 and is serviced by regular bus traffic.

Train Dong Hoi is a stop for the *Reunification Express* train (see the Getting Around chapter).

Car & Motorbike Road traffic between the towns of Dong Ha and Dong Hoi is light, especially after the early morning 'rush hour'.

Central Vietnam

From 1954 to 1975, the Ben Hai River served as the demarcation line between the Republic of Vietnam (RVN; South Vietnam) and the Democratic Republic of Vietnam (DRV; North Vietnam). On either side of the river was an area 5km wide known as the Demilitarised Zone (DMZ).

The DMZ itself and areas to the south saw plenty of action and experienced a high military presence during the American War. However, the area is still home to some of the most interesting sights Vietnam has to offer. As you head south from the DMZ you reach the historic towns of Hué and Hoi An, two of the most relaxed places you'll find.

Hué, the most historically interesting city in Vietnam, served as Vietnam's political capital from 1802 to 1945 under the 13 emperors of the Nguyen Dynasty. The province of Quang Nam, bordering the municipality of Danang, contains Vietnam's most important Cham sites – including My Son and Tra Kieu (Simhapura) – which have become popular stomping grounds for tourists. Side trips to places like the Marble Mountains and China Beach also continue to draw a steady trickle of travellers. While the once bustling city of Danang is rather quiet these days, the Cham Museum there is topnotch.

The old port of Hoi An (Faifo) has a great deal of rustic charm and is an ideal spot in Vietnam to relax and appreciate what life must have been like in centuries gone by.

Highlights

- Make a day-long pilgrimage into the former battlefields of the Demilitarised Zone (DMZ).
- Take a dragon-boat cruise along the scenic Perfume River and soak in the atmosphere of one of the majestic Royal Tombs.
- Wander along nature walks and explore old French-villa ruins in spectacular Bach Ma National Park
- Linger in the old-world atmosphere of charming Hoi An.
- Make an excursion to the extraordinary Cham ruins at My Son.
- Take in Vietnam's pre-eminent collection of Cham statues at the Cham Museum in Danang.
- Catch some rays on famous China Beach, saving time to explore the canyons and caves of the mystical Marble Mountains

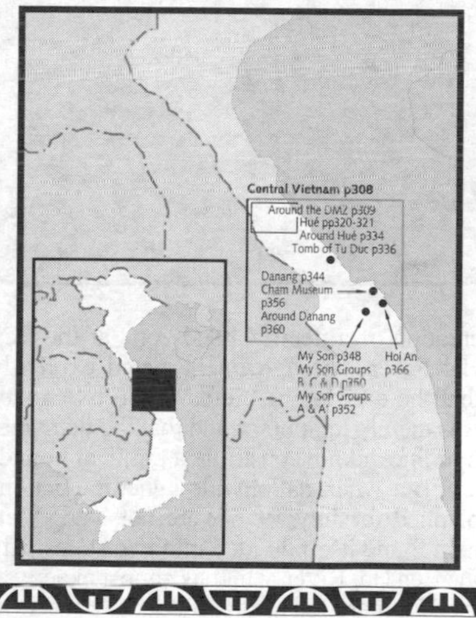

DMZ

The idea of partitioning Vietnam had its origins in a series of agreements concluded between the USA, UK and the USSR at the Potsdam Conference, held in Berlin in July 1945. For logistical and political reasons, the Allies decided that the Japanese occupation forces to the south of the 16th parallel would surrender to the British while those to the north would surrender to the Kuomintang (Nationalist) Chinese army led by Chiang Kaishek.

In April 1954, in Geneva, Ho Chi Minh's government and the French agreed to an armistice; among the provisions was the

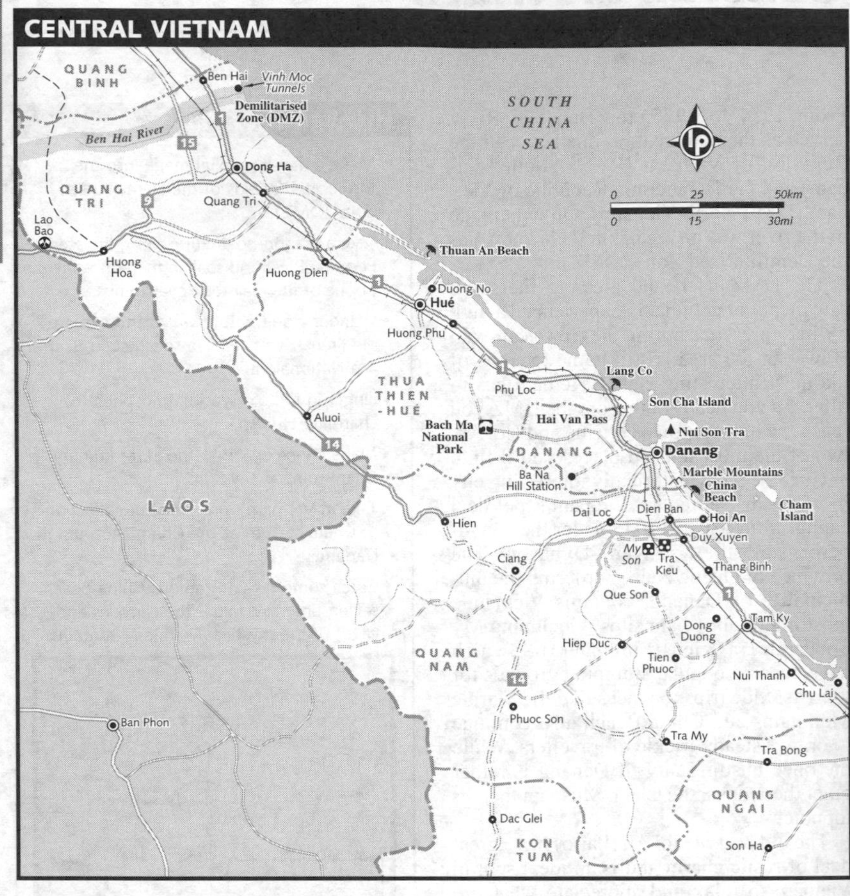

creation of a demilitarised zone at the Ben Hai River. The agreement stated explicitly that the division of Vietnam into two zones was merely temporary and that the demarcation line did not constitute a political boundary. But when nationwide general elections planned for July 1956 were not held, Vietnam found itself divided into two states with the Ben Hai River, which is almost exactly at the 17th parallel, as their de facto border.

During the American War, the area just south of the DMZ was the scene of some of the bloodiest battles of the conflict. Quang Tri, the Rockpile, Khe Sanh, Lang Vay and Hamburger Hill became household names in the USA as, year after year, TV pictures and casualty figures provided Americans with their evening dose of war.

Since 1975, 5000 people have been injured or killed in and around the DMZ by mines and ordnance left over from the war. Despite the risk, impoverished peasants still dig for chunks of leftover metal to sell as scrap, for which they are paid a pittance.

Orientation

The old DMZ extends from the coast westward to the Lao border; National Highway

9 (Quoc Lo 9) runs more or less parallel to the DMZ about 10km to the south. The 'Ho Chi Minh Trail' (Duong Truong Son) – actually a series of roads, trails and paths – ran between North and South Vietnam (perpendicular to Highway 9) through the Truong Son Mountains and western Laos; it was used by the Viet Cong (VC) to transport troops and equipment.

To disrupt the flow of troops and supplies along the Ho Chi Minh Trail, the Americans established a line of bases along Highway 9, including (from east to west) Cua Viet, Gio Linh, Dong Ha, Con Thien, Cam Lo, Camp Carroll, the Rockpile, Ca Lu, Khe Sanh and Lang Vay.

The old bases along Highway 9 can be visited as a day trip. The road leading south-east from the Dakrong Bridge goes to the Ashau Valley (site of the infamous Hamburger Hill) and Aluoi. With a 4WD it is possible to drive the entire 60 rough kilometres from Aluoi to Hué. One traveller wrote in and described the barren landscape around these parts:

> The area is absolutely barren – hardly any shrubs manage to survive in the burned soil, which refuses to recover. The people make a living from scrap-metal collecting, selling drinks and food to the few visitors coming here, and putting entrance fees into their own pockets. The region is poverty stricken, and be prepared to have about a dozen or more people fighting between themselves to sell you a Coke or some fruit. Here even a 50d note can still be seen! When driving through the DMZ, countless unnamed graves are scattered about, part of Vietnam's 300,000 MIAs (soldiers 'missing in action'). Near the Doc Mieu Base there were signs of recent diggings, part of the search for US MIAs.

Information

You will require the services of a good guide to fully appreciate the DMZ. After all, this is a historical place and understanding the significance of each site requires some explanation (and a good

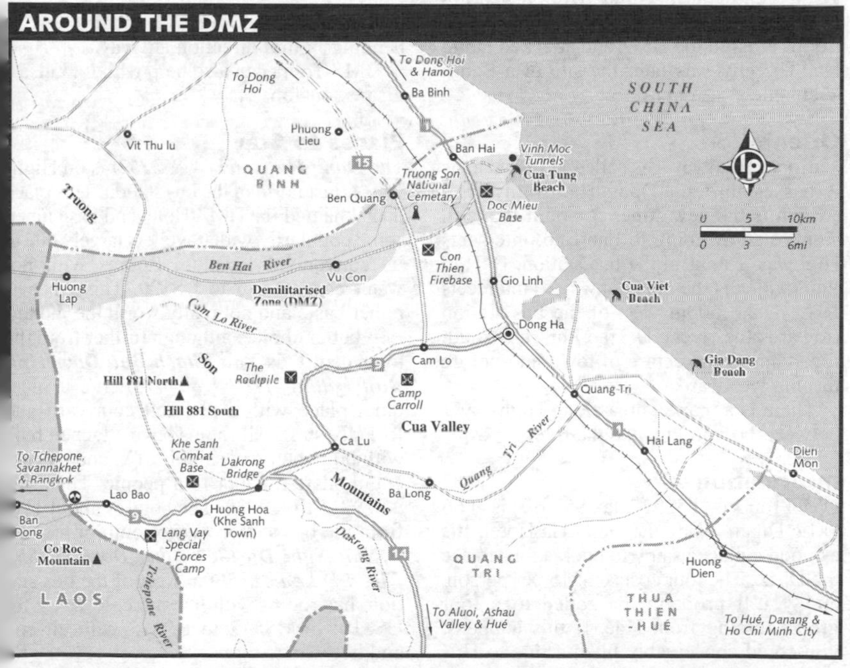

imagination). A guide is also necessary to find many of the sites, since most are unmarked, and it's easy to get lost in the labyrinth of dirt tracks.

Day tours are most readily available in Hué. You can make bookings at almost any hotel or cafe in town. There are actually only a few agencies running the tours, so no matter where you sign up you'll still wind up as part of a group.

Expect to pay around US$11 to US$15 for a day-long outing into the DMZ. Most of these tours have English-speaking guides, but some speak French. You should make your linguistic preferences known at the time you book the trip.

DONG HA

☎ 053 • pop 65,200

Dong Ha, the capital of recently reconstituted Quang Tri Province, is at the intersection of National Highways 1 and 9. Dong Ha served as a US marine command and logistics centre during 1968–69. In the spring of 1968, a division of North Vietnamese troops crossed the DMZ and attacked Dong Ha. The city was later the site of a South Vietnamese army base.

Orientation

National Highway 1 is called Đ Le Duan as it passes through Dong Ha. Highway 9 (which is the new American-built branch), signposted as going to Lao Bao, intersects Highway 1 next to the bus station. Đ Tran Phu (which is the old Highway 9) intersects Đ Le Duan 600m west of the bus station (towards the river). Đ Tran Phu runs south for 400m to the centre of town and before turning westward.

There is a market area along Highway 1 between Đ Tran Phu and the river.

Information

DMZ Tours (☎ 852927, fax 851617) is at 66 Đ Le Duan, inside the Dong Ha Hotel. It's as good a place as any to book a tour to see the DMZ. The tour costs US$15 per person, and you'll probably be added to a tour group coming from Hué. If this happens, you could conceivably hitch a ride to Hué at the end of the tour with them if you're heading in that direction anyway.

DMZ Tours can also help with Lao visas, visa extensions etc.

> **Warning**
>
> The war may be over, but death and injury are still fairly easy to come by in the old Demilitarised Zone. At many of the places listed in this section you will find live mortar rounds, artillery projectiles and mines strewn about. Watch where you step. As tempted as you might be to collect souvenirs, *never* touch any leftover ordnance. If the locals have not carted it off for scrap it means that even they are afraid to disturb it. White phosphorus shells – whose contents burn fiercely when exposed to air – are remarkably impervious to the effects of prolonged exposure and are likely to remain extremely dangerous for many more years. If one of these shells happens to explode while you're playing with it, your whole trip will be ruined – and don't expect a refund from Vietnam Tourism.
>
> In short, be careful. Don't become a candidate for plastic surgery – or worse, a statistic!

Places to Stay

The ***Dong Ha Hotel*** *(☎ 852262)* is on Highway 1, just north of the bus station. This place is nicknamed the DMZ Hotel and has gained some popularity with travellers largely due to its convenient location. Rooms with hot water cost US$15 to US$20. This place is rather basic and not really worth the money.

A better choice, although further from the town centre, is ***Nha Khach Buu Dien Tinh Buu Quang Tri*** *(☎ 854418)*. It's a nice quiet place with a pleasant courtyard and friendly staff. All rooms have attached bath with hot water and satellite TV, and can accommodate three or four people. The price is US$15 to US$20. The hotel is about 1km from the bus station to the south of town.

Nha Nghi Du Lich Cong Doan *(☎ 85.744, 4 Đ Le Loi)*, 500m west of the bus station, has rooms with fan and cold water for US$10; or US$12 to US$15 with air-con and hot water.

***Thanh Tinh Hotel** (☎ 852236, fax 852850, 220 Đ Le Duan)* rents basic doubles/triples with air-con and hot water for US$15/20. Be sure to ask for a room on the 2nd or 3rd storey – they are cleaner and newer.

The snazziest accommodation in Dong Ha is the new ***Hieu Giang Hotel** (☎ 855036, fax 856859, 183 Đ Le Duan)*, located right where Highway 9 intersects Highway 1. Singles cost US$19 to US$35, and doubles US$22 to US$40.

Places to Eat

Beside the dining rooms in Dong Ha's ***hotels*** (most of which are mediocre), there are a slew of roadside ***com pho restaurants*** along Highway 1, in particularly in the vicinity of the bus station, and the intersection of Highway 9.

Just next door to Thanh Tinh Hotel is a large, clean and excellent restaurant called ***Tan Chau 2***.

Getting There & Away

Bus The Dong Ha bus station (Ben Xe Khach Dong Ha) is near the intersection of Highways 1 and 9 at 122 Đ Le Duan. Vehicles to Hué depart approximately hourly between 7 am and 5 pm, and take about 70 minutes. There are buses to Khe Sanh every half-hour from 5.30 am to 6 pm; change buses in Khe Sanh for Lao Bao, and ride out the last 18km to the border. Buses also link Dong Ha with Danang, Con Thien, Cua and Ho Xa (along Highway 1, about 13km west of Vinh Moc).

Buses from Hué to Dong Ha depart from An Hoa bus station.

Train Dong Ha train station (Ga Dong Ha) is a stop for the *Reunification Express* trains (see the Train section in the Getting Around chapter).

To get to the train station from the bus station, head 1km south-east on Highway 1. The train station is 150m across a field to the right (south-west) of the highway.

Car & Motorbike You can expect to pay about US$10 for a *xe om* (motorbike taxi) to/from Dong Ha and the Lao border at Lao Bao. Road distances from Dong Ha are:

Ben Hai River	22km
Danang	190km
Dong Hoi	94km
Hanoi	617km
Ho Chi Minh City	1169km
Hué	72km
Khe Sanh	65km
Lao Bao (Lao border)	80km
Savannakhet, Laos (Thai border)	327km
Truong Son National Cemetery	30km
Vinh	294km
Vinh Moc	41km

QUANG TRI

☎ 053 • pop 15,400

The town of Quang Tri, 59km north of Hué and 12.5km south of Dong Ha, was once an important citadel city. In the spring of 1972, four divisions of North Vietnamese regulars backed by tanks, artillery and rockets poured across the DMZ into Quang Tri Province in what became known as the Eastertide Offensive. They laid siege to the city of Quang Tri, shelling it heavily before capturing it along with the rest of the province. During the next four months, the city was almost completely obliterated by South Vietnamese artillery and massive carpet-bombing by US fighter-bombers and B-52s. The South Vietnamese army suffered 5000 casualties in the rubble-to-rubble fighting to retake the city.

Today, there is little to see in the town of Quang Tri except a memorial and a few remains of the moat, ramparts and gates of the citadel, which once served as South Vietnamese army headquarters. The citadel is 1.6km from Highway 1 on Đ Le Duan, which runs perpendicular to the highway. The ruined, two-storey building between the highway and the bus station used to be a Buddhist high school.

Along Highway 1 near the turn-off to Quang Tri is the skeleton of a church – it's definitely worth taking a look inside. It gives you the chills to see the bullet holes and know that a deadly fight between US forces and the VC took place here.

Cua Viet Beach, once the site of an important American landing dock, is a decent swimming beach, 16km north-east of Quang

Stress

A growing number of war veterans (mostly Americans, but some Australians) are returning to Vietnam. Many psychologists who deal with the long-term effects of war believe that going back can help groups of veterans confront the root causes of Post-Traumatic Stress Disorder (PTSD).

It should be added that many Vietnamese suffer from PTSD too, although unfortunately few have the opportunity (or means) to consult a psychologist.

Tri. There are plans to build a major port here to handle import and export materials from Laos and northern Thailand. Another beach called Gia Dang is 13km east of town, but neither of these, in fact, are worth going out of your way to find. Most travellers wait to get a bit further south to Thuan An Beach (near Hué) or China Beach (near Danang).

Getting There & Away

The bus station is on Đ Le Duan (Quang Tri's main north-south street), 600m from Highway 1. Buses to An Cuu bus station in Hué leave between 5 am and noon, and to Hué's Dong Ba bus station around 6 am. The daily bus to Khe Sanh leaves at about 8 am, and there is also a service to Ho Xa departing around 7 am.

VINH MOC TUNNELS

The remarkable tunnels of Vinh Moc are yet another monument to the tenacity of the North Vietnamese to persevere and triumph – at all costs and despite some incredible sacrifices – in the American War. A visit to the tunnels can be combined with bathing at the beautiful beaches that extend for many kilometres to the north and south of Vinh Moc.

The 2.8km of tunnels here, all of which can be visited, are the real thing and unadulterated for viewing by tourists (unlike the tunnels at Cu Chi). Vinh Moc's underground passageways are also larger and taller than those at Cu Chi, which makes for an easier (and less creepy) visit.

Local authorities, who prefer not to lose any travellers in the maze of forks, branches and identical weaving passageways, are adamant that visitors enter the tunnels only if accompanied by a local guide. It may also set your mind at rest to know that the tunnels have been chemically treated to keep snakes away.

The entrance fee, which includes entry into the on-site museum, is US$2 per person or US$1.50 per person with a group. There are lights installed inside the tunnels, but you should bring a torch (flashlight) anyway as the electricity supply has been known to fail unexpectedly.

History

In 1966 the Americans began a massive aerial and artillery bombardment of North Vietnam. Just north of the DMZ, the villagers of Vinh Moc found themselves living in one of the most heavily bombed and shelled pieces of land on the planet. Small family shelters could not withstand this onslaught and villagers either fled or began tunnelling by hand into the red clay earth.

Of course, the VC found it useful to have a base here and encouraged the villagers to stay. After 18 months of work (during which the excavated earth was camouflaged to prevent its detection from the air), an enormous VC base was established underground. Civilians were employed in the digging and were accommodated in new underground homes. Whole families lived here and some babies were even born in the tunnels.

Later, the civilians and VC were joined by North Vietnamese soldiers whose mission was to keep communications and supply lines to nearby Con Co Island open. A total of 11,500 tonnes of military supplies reached Con Co Island and a further 300 tonnes were shipped to the South, thanks to the Vinh Moc Tunnels.

Other villages north of the DMZ also built tunnel systems, but none were as elaborate as Vinh Moc. The poorly constructed tunnels of Vinh Quang village (at the mouth of the Ben Hai River) collapsed after repeated bombing, killing everyone inside.

The tunnel network at Vinh Moc remains essentially as it looked in 1966, though some of the 12 entrances – seven of which exit onto the palm-lined beach – have been retimbered and others have become overgrown with foliage. The tunnels were built on three levels ranging from 15m to 26m below the crest of the bluff.

The tunnels were repeatedly hit by American bombs, but the only ordnance that posed a real threat was the feared 'drilling bomb'. Only once did such a bomb score a direct hit, but it failed to explode and no one was injured; the inhabitants adapted the bomb hole for use as an air shaft. Occasionally the mouths of the complex that faced the sea were hit by naval gunfire.

Getting There & Away

The turn-off to Vinh Moc from Highway 1 is 6.5km north of the Ben Hai River in the village of Ho Xa. Vinh Moc is another 13km east from Highway 1.

Offshore is Con Co Island, which during the war was an important supply depot. Today the island, which is ringed by rocky beaches, houses a small military base. The trip from Vinh Moc to Con Co takes 2½ to three hours by motorised fishing boat, but the island isn't really set up for visitors.

HUONG HOA (KHE SANH TOWN)

Set amid beautiful hills, valleys and fields at an elevation of about 600m, the town of Khe Sanh is a pleasant district capital. The town is known for its coffee plantations, which were originally cultivated by the French.

Many of the inhabitants are Bru (Van Kieu) tribespeople who have moved here from the surrounding hills, you'll notice many of the women smoking long-stemmed pipes.

The town has now been officially renamed Huong Hoa, but the Western world will forever remember it as Khe Sanh.

Places to Stay

About the only reason for staying here is if you're planning to hit the road to Laos the next morning. At the time of writing the ***People's Committee Guesthouse*** *(☎ 880563)* was the sole option. Rooms cost around US$10.

Getting There & Away

Khe Sanh bus station is on Highway 9, 600m south-west (towards the Lao frontier) of the triangular intersection where the road to Khe Sanh Combat Base branches off. Buses to Dong Ha depart at 7 am and around noon, while the daily bus to Hué leaves at 7 am. There are two buses a day to Lao Bao; the first leaves at 6 am and the second whenever it is full. The ticket window is only open from 6 to 7 am, but after it's closed you can buy tickets on board the buses themselves.

KHE SANH COMBAT BASE

This is the site of the most famous siege (and one of the most controversial battles) of the American War in Vietnam. Khe Sanh sits silently on a barren plateau surrounded by vegetation-covered hills often obscured by mist and fog. It is hard to imagine as you stand in this peaceful, verdant land – with the neat homes and vegetable plots of local people all around – that in early 1968 the bloodiest battle of the war took place here. Approximately 500 Americans (the official figure of 205 was arrived at by statistical sleight of hand), 10,000 North Vietnamese troops and uncounted civilian bystanders died amid the din of machine guns and the fiery explosions of 1000kg bombs, white-phosphorus shells, napalm, mortars and artillery rounds of all sorts.

There's not much left, but some little things help you visualise what the history books say happened here. The outline of the airfield remains distinct (to this day nothing will grow on it). In places, the ground is literally carpeted with bullets and rusting shell casings. And all around are little groups of local people digging holes in their relentless search for scrap metal (once, locals say proudly, they unearthed an entire bulldozer!). The US MIA Team has visited the area countless times to search for the bodies of Americans who disappeared during the fierce battles in the surrounding hills. Most remains they find are Vietnamese.

Missing in Action

An issue that continues to plague relations between the USA and Vietnam is that of US military personnel officially listed as 'missing in action' (MIA). There are still over 2000 American soldiers officially 'unaccounted for' and many of their families are adamant that their loved ones are still alive in secret prison camps deep in the jungles of Vietnam. POW-MIA groups in the USA continue to lobby Congress to 'do something'. It's a highly emotive issue, sometimes cleverly exploited by US politicians. 'No compromise', they insist, 'until Vietnam accounts for every one of the MIAs'.

Others believe the POW-MIA groups are flogging a dead horse. The figure of 2265 MIAs is almost certainly too high. About 400 flight personnel were killed when their planes crashed into the sea off the coast of Vietnam, others died when their aircraft went down in flames or in ground combat – the tropical jungle quickly reclaims a human corpse. However, when Vietnam returned the last 590 American POWs, 37 soldiers believed to have been captured were not among them. The Vietnamese government adamantly denies that there are MIAs still in Vietnam, but the credibility of their government officials has to be questioned in view of their poor human rights' record. On the other hand, it would make no logical sense for Vietnam to continue holding US POWs.

Not much is said about the 300,000 Vietnamese who are also MIAs – they are difficult to identify because they didn't wear ID tags. However, the Vietnamese do feel just as strongly about their MIAs, particularly as they consider it their duty to perform ancestor worship – a difficult task without a corpse.

In the meantime, MIA teams continue to comb the Vietnamese countryside – at an ongoing cost of millions and millions of dollars to American taxpayers. Hawaii-based US troops are still in the field.

History

Despite opposition from marine corps brass to General William Westmoreland's attrition strategy (they thought it futile), the small US Army Special Forces (Green Beret) base at Khe Sanh, built to recruit and train local tribespeople, was turned into a marine stronghold in late 1966. In April 1967 there began a series of 'hill fights' between US forces and the well dug-in North Vietnamese army infantry who held the surrounding hills. In only a few weeks, 155 marines and perhaps thousands of North Vietnamese were killed. The fighting centred on hills 881 South and 881 North, both of which are about 8km northwest of Khe Sanh Combat Base.

In late 1967, American intelligence detected the movement of tens of thousands of North Vietnamese regulars armed with mortars, rockets and artillery into the hills around Khe Sanh. The commander of the US forces in Vietnam, Westmoreland became convinced that the North Vietnamese were planning another Dien Bien Phu (the decisive battle in the Franco–Viet Minh War in 1954). This was an illogical analogy given American firepower and the proxim ity of Khe Sanh to supply lines and othe American bases. President Johnson himsel became obsessed by the spectre of Die Bien Phu: to follow the course of the battle he had a sand-table model of the Khe San plateau constructed in the White House sit uation room and he took the unprecedente step of requiring a written guarantee fror the Joint Chiefs of Staff that Khe San could be held.

Westmoreland, determined to avoid an other Dien Bien Phu at all costs, assemble an armada of 5000 planes and helicopters an increased the number of troops at Khe San to 6000. He even ordered his staff to study th feasibility of using tactical nuclear weapon:

The 75-day siege of Khe Sanh began o 21 January 1968 with a small-scale assau on the base perimeter. As the marines ar the South Vietnamese Rangers braced for full-scale ground attack, Khe Sanh becam the focus of global media attention. It wa the cover story for both *Newsweek* and *Li* magazines and appeared on the front pag of countless newspapers around the worl

Missing in Action

Investigative crews carry out assessments, based on wartime records and interviews with local villagers; once they have enough evidence to warrant a search, a recovery team conducts an on-site excavation. Any remains discovered are flown to the Central Identification Laboratory, Hawaii (CILHA) for forensic identification analysis based on dental records and DNA.

Many Vietnamese are also employed in the search teams, with 75% of their salaries going to the government. Not surprisingly, the Vietnamese government is in no hurry to see the MIA teams leave, despite the Americans raising this issue in diplomatic negotiations. The fact that the MIA teams have been digging through Vietnamese cemeteries looking for American bones has also irritated many locals who would prefer to see their dead rest in peace.

Some Vietnamese sense an opportunity in the MIA issue and regularly approach the US representatives and the occasional backpacker (some believe all Westerners have great influence with the US government!) with 'information' on the whereabouts of US MIA remains in the hope of a cash reward, free landscaping (care of the excavation teams) or even an immigration visa to the USA – despite their persistence, there are no rewards offered for information.

Meanwhile, the whole sad saga continues to play itself out. When private POW-MIA groups started circulating photographs showing US soldiers being held prisoner in a Vietnamese camp, there was a flurry of official investigations. The photos proved to be fakes. But groups such as the National League of Families of American Prisoners and Missing in SouthEast Asia were very effective at stalling the US government's attempts to forge diplomatic relations with Vietnam. Despite protests, diplomatic relations were finally established in 1995, and serving US President Bill Clinton visited Vietnam in 2000.

During the next two months, the base was subject to continuous ground attacks and artillery fire. US aircraft dropped 100,000 tonnes of explosives on the immediate vicinity of Khe Sanh Combat Base. The expected attempt to overrun the base never came and, on 7 April 1968 after heavy fighting, US army troops reopened Highway 9 and linked up with the marines to end the siege.

It now seems clear that the siege of Khe Sanh, in which an estimated 10,000 North Vietnamese died, was merely an enormous diversion intended to draw US forces and the attention of their commanders away from South Vietnam's population centres in preparation for the Tet Offensive, which began a week after the siege started. At the time, however, Westmoreland considered the entire Tet Offensive to be a 'diversionary effort' to distract attention from Khe Sanh!

A few days after Westmoreland's tour of duty in Vietnam ended in July 1968, American forces in the area were redeployed. Policy, it seemed, had been reassessed and holding Khe Sanh, for which so many men had died, was deemed unnecessary. After everything at Khe Sanh was buried, trucked out or blown up – nothing recognisable that could be used in a North Vietnamese propaganda film was to remain – US forces up and left Khe Sanh Combat Base under a curtain of secrecy. The American command had finally realised what a marine officer had expressed long before: 'When you're at Khe Sanh, you're not really anywhere. You could lose it and you really haven't lost a damn thing'.

Getting There & Away

To get to Khe Sanh Combat Base from Khe Sanh bus station, head 600m towards Dong Ha then turn north-west at the triangular intersection. The base is 2.5km further, on the right-hand side of the road.

OTHER MILITARY SITES

Many of the battlefields and former military bases of the DMZ became household names throughout the world. The following include such sites, although nowadays often all that remains is a bomb crater or fields where cows now graze.

Doc Mieu Base

Doc Mieu Base, next to Highway 1 on a low rise 8km south of the Ben Hai River, was once part of an elaborate electronic system (McNamara's Wall, named after the US Secretary of Defence 1961–68) intended to prevent infiltration across the DMZ. Today, it is a lunar landscape of bunkers, craters, shrapnel and live mortar rounds. Bits of cloth and decaying military boots are strewn about on the red earth. This devastation was created not by the war, but by scrap-metal hunters, who have found excavations at this site particularly rewarding.

Ben Hai River

Twenty-two kilometres north of Dong Ha, Highway 1 crosses the Ben Hai River – once the demarcation line between North and South Vietnam – over the decrepit Hien Luong Bridge. Until 1967 (when it was bombed by the Americans), the northern half of the bridge that stood on this site was painted red, while the southern half was yellow. Following the signing of the Paris cease-fire agreements in 1973, the present bridge and the two flag towers were built. A typhoon knocked over the flagpole on the northern bank of the river in 1985.

Cua Tung Beach

Cua Tung Beach, a long, secluded stretch of sand where Vietnam's last emperor, Bao Dai, used to vacation – is just north of the mouth of the Ben Hai. There are beaches on the southern side of the Ben Hai River as well. Every bit of land in the area not levelled for planting is pockmarked with bomb craters of all sizes. Offshore is Con Co Island, which can be reached by motorised boat; the trip takes about 2½ hours.

There are no buses to Cua Tung Beach, which can be reached by turning right (east) off Highway 1 at a point 1.2km north of the Ben Hai River. Cua Tung Beach is about 7km south of Vinh Moc via the dirt road that runs along the coast.

Truong Son National Cemetery

Truong Son National Cemetery is a memorial to tens of thousands of North Vietnamese soldiers from transport, construction and anti-aircraft units who were killed in the Truong Son Mountains (the Annamite Cordillera) along the Ho Chi Minh Trail. There are row after row of white tombstones stretch across the hillsides and the cemetery is maintained by disabled war veterans.

The soldiers are buried in five zones according to the part of Vietnam they came from; each zone is further subdivided into provinces. The gravestones of five colonels and seven decorated heroes (Trung Ta and Dai Ta represent the ranks of the 'martyrs'), including one woman, are in a separate area. Each headstone bears the inscription 'Liet Si', which means 'Martyr'. The remains of soldiers interred here were originally buried near the spot where they were killed and were brought here after reunification. Many graves are empty, simply bearing the names of a small portion of Vietnam's 300,000 MIAs.

On the hilltop above the sculpture garden is a three-sided stele. One face has engraved tributes from high-ranking Vietnamese leaders to the people who worked on the Ho Chi Minh Trail. At the bottom is a poem by the poet To Huu. Another side tells the history of the May 1959 Army Corps (Doang 5.59), which is said to have been founded on Ho Chi Minh's birthday in 1959 with a mission to construct and maintain a supply line to the South. The third side lists the constituent units of the May 1959 Army Corps, which eventually included five divisions. The site where the cemetery now stands was used as a base of the May 1959 Army Corps from 1972 to 1975.

The road to Truong Son National Cemetery intersects Highway 1, 13km north of Dong Ha and 9km south of the Ben Hai River; the distance from the highway to the cemetery is 17km.

A rocky cart path, that is passable (but just barely) by car, links Cam Lo (on Highway 9) with Truong Son National Cemetery (18km). The road passes rubber plantations and also the homes of the Bru tribal people who cultivate, among other crops, black pepper.

Con Thien Firebase

In September 1967, North Vietnamese forces, backed by long-range artillery and rockets, crossed the DMZ and besieged the US marine corps base of Con Thien, which was established to stop infiltrations across the DMZ and to form part of McNamara's Wall.

The Americans responded with 4000 bombing sorties (including 800 by B-52s), during which more than 40,000 tonnes of bombs were dropped on the North Vietnamese forces around Con Thien, transforming the gently sloping brush-covered hills that surrounded the base into a smoking moonscape of craters and ashes. The siege was lifted, but the battle had accomplished its real purpose: to divert US attention from South Vietnam's cities in preparation for the Tet Offensive. The area around the base is still considered too dangerous even for scrap-metal hunters to approach.

Con Thien Firebase is 10km west of Highway 1 and 7km south of Truong Son National Cemetery along the road linking Highway 1 with the cemetery. Concrete bunkers mark the spot a few hundred metres to the south of the road where the base once stood.

Six kilometres towards Highway 1 from Con Thien (and 4km from the highway) is another US base, C-3, the rectangular ramparts of which are still visible just north of the road. It is inaccessible due to mines.

Camp Carroll

Established in 1966, Camp Carroll was named after a US marine corps captain who was killed while trying to seize a nearby ridge. The gargantuan 175mm cannons at Camp Carroll were used to shell targets as far away as Khe Sanh. In 1972 the South Vietnamese commander of Camp Carroll, Lieutenant Colonel Ton That Dinh, surrendered and joined the North Vietnamese army.

These days there is not that much to see at Camp Carroll, except for a few overgrown trenches and the remains of their timber roofs. Bits of military hardware and lots of rusty shell casings litter the ground. The concrete bunkers were destroyed by local people seeking to extract the steel reinforcing rods to sell as scrap; concrete chunks from the bunkers were hauled off for use in construction. Locals prospecting for scrap metal can point out the remains of the base.

The area around Camp Carroll now belongs to the State Pepper Enterprises (Xi Nghiep Ho Tieu Tan Lam). The pepper plants are trained so that they climb up the trunks of jackfruit trees. There are also rubber plantations nearby. The road to Camp Carroll leads on to the fertile Cua Valley, once home to a number of French settlers.

The turn-off to Camp Carroll is 5km west of Cam Lo, 24km north-east of Dakrong Bridge and 37km east of the Khe Sanh bus station. The base is 3km from Highway 9.

The Rockpile

The Rockpile was named after what can only be described as a 230m-high pile of rocks. There was a US marine corps lookout on top of the Rockpile and a base for American long-range artillery was nearby.

Today there isn't much left of the Rockpile except for souvenir vendors. The local tribal people, who live in houses built on stilts, engage in slash-and-burn agriculture.

The Rockpile is 26km west of Dong Ha on Highway 9.

Dakrong Bridge

Dakrong Bridge, crossing the Dakrong River (also known as the Ta Rin River) 3km east of the Khe Sanh bus station, was built during 1975–76 with assistance from the Cuban government. A number of the local tribespeople openly carry assault rifles (for hunting) left over from the war; this is against the law, but the government seems unwilling or unable to do anything about it.

The road that heads south-east from the bridge to Aluoi passes by the stilted homes of the Brus and was once a branch of the Ho Chi Minh Trail.

Aluoi

Aluoi is approximately 65km south-east of Dakrong Bridge and 60km to the west of Hué. There are a number of waterfalls and cascades in the surrounding area. Tribes living in the mountainous Aluoi area include the Ba Co, Ba Hy, Ca Tu and Taoi. US Army Special Forces bases in Aluoi and Ashau were overrun and abandoned in 1966; the area then became an important transhipment centre for supplies coming down the Ho Chi Minh Trail.

Among the better known military sites in the vicinity of Aluoi are landing zones Cunningham, Erskine and Razor, as well as Hill 1175 (west of the valley) and Hill 521 (in Laos). Further south in the Ashau Valley is Hamburger Hill (Apbia Mountain). In May 1969, American forces on a search-and-destroy operation near the Lao border fought in one of the fiercest engagements of the war, suffering many terrible casualties (hence the name). In less than a week of fighting, 241 American soldiers died at Hamburger Hill – a fact that was very well publicised in the American media. A month later, after the American forces withdrew from the area to continue operations elsewhere, the hill was reoccupied by the North Vietnamese army.

Lang Vay Special Forces Camp

In February 1968, Lang Vay (Lang Vei) Special Forces Camp, established in 1962, was attacked and overrun by North Vietnamese infantry backed by nine tanks. Of the base's 500 South Vietnamese, Bru and Montagnard defenders, 316 were killed. Ten of the 24 Americans at the base were killed and 11 were wounded.

All that remains of dog-bone-shaped Lang Vay base are the overgrown remains of numerous concrete bunkers. Locals can show you around.

The base is on a ridge south-west of Highway 9, between Khe Sanh bus station (9.2km) and Lao Bao (7.3km).

LAO BAO

☎ 053

Lao Bao is on the Tchepone River (Song Xe Pon), which marks the Vietnam-Laos border. Towering above Lao Bao on the Lao side of the border is Co Roc Mountain, once a North Vietnamese artillery stronghold.

Two kilometres from the border post is Lao Bao Market, where Thai goods smuggled through the bush from Laos are readily available. Merchants accept either Vietnamese dong or Lao kip.

Getting There & Away

The town of Lao Bao is 18km west of Khe Sanh, 80km from Dong Ha, 152km from Hué, 46km east of Tchepone (Laos), 250km east of Savannakhet (also in Laos, on the Thai frontier) and 950km from Bangkok (Thailand, via Ubon Ratchathani). The Lao Bao border is open for crossing in either direction, provided you have a visa. As more and more travellers enter/exit Vietnam overland, Lao Bao is becoming an important border crossing for trade and tourism between Thailand and central Vietnam. See the Getting There & Away chapter for more information about crossing the border at Lao Bao.

HUÉ

☎ 054 • pop 286,400

Traditionally, Hué has been one of Vietnam's main cultural, religious and educational centres. Today, its main attractions are the splendid tombs of the Nguyen emperors (see the special section 'The Royal Tombs' later in this chapter), several notable pagodas and the remains of the Citadel. Also, as the locals will no doubt tell you repeatedly, the women of Hué are renowned for their beauty.

Tourism just may have saved Hué's cultural sites from oblivion. Between 1975 and 1990, all the old buildings were regarded as politically incorrect, signs of the 'feudal Nguyen Dynasty'. Everything was left to decay. It was only in 1990 that the local government recognised the tourist potential of the place and declared these sites 'national treasures'. In 1993 the complex of monuments in Hué was designated a UNESCO World Heritage Site, and restoration and preservation work continues.

Most of the city's major sights have an admission charge of 55,000d (about US$4), often with an additional charge for video cameras.

History

The citadel city of Phu Xuan was originally built in 1687 at Bao Vinh Village, 5km north-east of present-day Hué. In 1744 Phu Xuan became the capital of the southern part of Vietnam, which was under the rule of the Nguyen lords. The Tay Son Rebels occupied the city from 1786 until 1802, when it fell to Nguyen Anh. He crowned himself Emperor Gia Long, thus founding the Nguyen Dynasty, which ruled the country – at least in name – until 1945.

In 1885, when the advisers of 13-year-old Emperor Ham Nghi objected to French activities in Tonkin, French forces encircled the city. Unwisely, the outnumbered Vietnamese forces launched an attack; the French responded mercilessly. According to a contemporary French account, the French forces took three days to burn the imperial library and remove from the palace every object of value, including everything from gold and silver ornaments to mosquito nets and toothpicks. Ham Nghi fled to Laos, but was eventually captured and exiled to Algeria. The French replaced him with the more pliable Dong Khanh, thus ending any pretence of genuine Vietnamese independence.

The city's present name evolved from its former name, Thanh Hoa. The word *hoa* means 'peace' or 'harmony' in Vietnamese. The city has been called Hué for over two centuries now.

Hué was the site of the bloodiest battles of the 1968 Tet Offensive and was the only city in South Vietnam to be held by the Communists for more than a few days. While the American command was concentrating its energies on relieving the siege of Khe Sanh, North Vietnamese and VC troops skirted the American stronghold and walked right into Hué, South Vietnam's third-largest city. When the Communists arrived, they hoisted their flag from the Citadel's Flag Tower, where it flew for the next 25 days; the local South Vietnamese governmental apparatus completely collapsed.

Immediately upon taking Hué, Communist political cadres implemented detailed plans to liquidate Hué's 'uncooperative' elements. Thousands of people were rounded up in extensive house-to-house searches conducted according to lists of names meticulously prepared months before. During the 3½ weeks Hué remained under Communist control, approximately 3000 civilians – including merchants, Buddhist monks, Catholic priests, intellectuals and a number of travellers, as well as people with ties to the South Vietnamese government – were summarily shot, clubbed to death or buried alive. The victims were buried in shallow mass graves, which were discovered around the city over the next few years.

When South Vietnamese army units proved unable to dislodge the occupying North Vietnamese and VC forces, General Westmoreland ordered US troops to recapture the city. During the next few weeks, whole neighbourhoods were levelled by VC rockets and American bombs. In 10 days of bitter combat, the VC were slowly forced into a retreat from the 'New City'. During the next two weeks, most of the area inside the Citadel (where two-thirds of the population lived) was battered by the South Vietnamese air force, US artillery and brutal house-to-house fighting. Approximately 10,000 people died in Hué during the Tet Offensive. Thousands of VC troops, 400 South Vietnamese soldiers and 150 American marines were among the dead, but most of those killed were civilians.

Long after the American War ended, one American veteran is said to have returned to Hué and, upon meeting a former VC officer, commented that the USA never lost a single major battle during the entire war. 'You are absolutely correct', the former officer agreed, 'but that is irrelevant, is it not?'.

Orientation

The city of Hué lies along either side of the Perfume River. The north side of the river has the Citadel and a few places to stay making for a pleasant and quiet stop. However, it is the south side that has most facilities and a greater selection of hotels and restaurants. The island on which Phu Cat and Phu Hiep subdistricts are located can be reached by crossing the Dong Ba Canal near Dong Ba Market.

Maps Decent tourist maps of Hué and its environs are sold around town for about US$1.

HUÉ

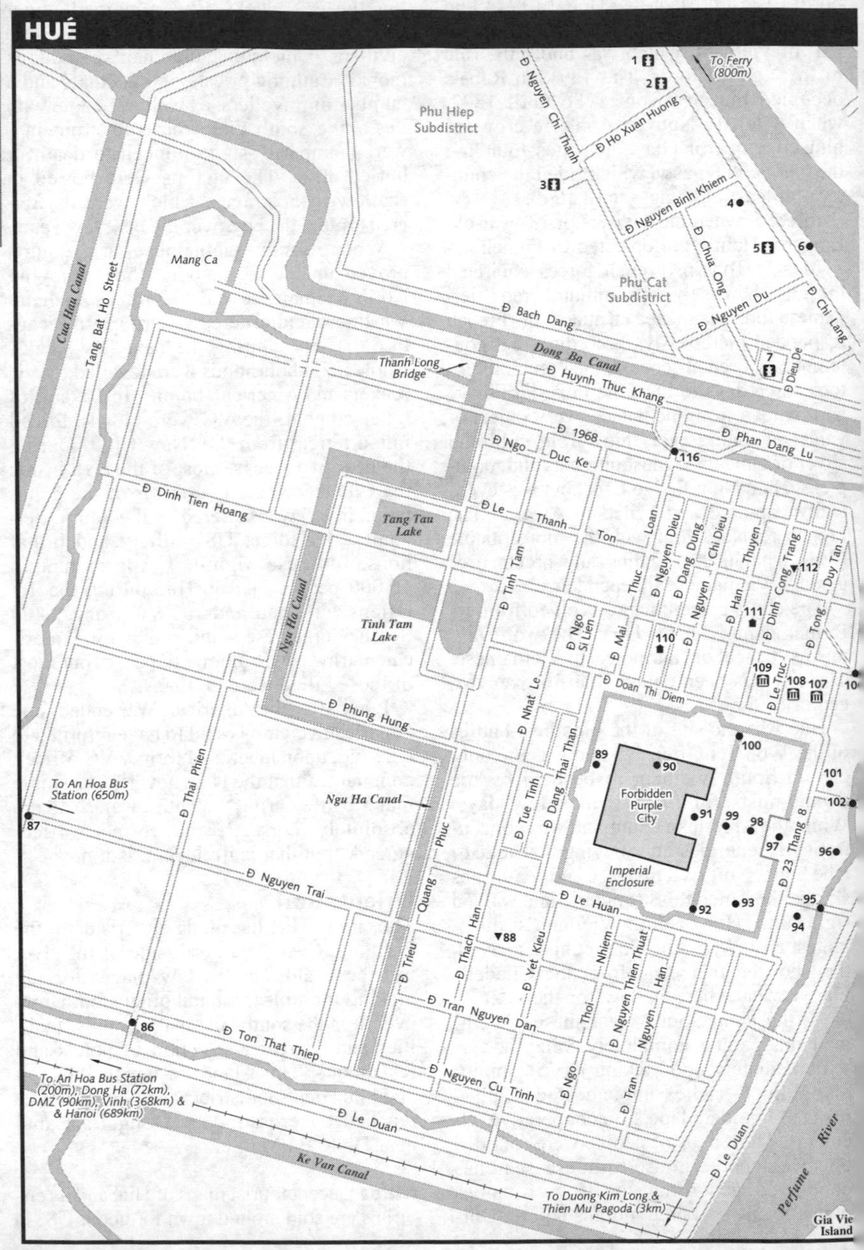

To Ferry (800m)
Phu Hiep Subdistrict
Đ Nguyen Chi Thanh
Đ Ho Xuan Huong
Đ Nguyen Binh Khiem
Đ Chua Ong
Phu Cat Subdistrict
Đ Nguyen Du
Đ Chi Lang
Đ Dieu De
Mang Ca
Cua Hau Canal
Tang Bat Ho Street
Đ Bach Dang
Dong Ba Canal
Thanh Long Bridge
Đ Huynh Thuc Khang
Đ 1968
Đ Phan Dang Lu
Đ Ngo Duc Ke
Đ Dinh Tien Hoang
Đ Le Thanh Ton
Tang Tau Lake
Tinh Tam Lake
Đ Tinh Tam
Đ Mai Thuc Loan
Đ Nguyen Dieu
Đ Dang Dung
Đ Nguyen Chi Dieu
Đ Han Thuyen
Đ Dinh Cong Trang
Đ Tong Duy Tan
Đ Ngo Si Lien
Đ Le Truc
Đ Doan Thi Diem
Ngu Ha Canal
Đ Phung Hung
Đ Nhat Le
Đ Tue Tinh
Đ Dang Thai Than
Forbidden Purple City
Imperial Enclosure
To An Hoa Bus Station (650m)
Đ Thai Phien
Đ Quang Phuc
Đ 23 Thang 8
Đ Nguyen Trai
Đ Le Huan
Đ Trieu
Đ Thach Han
Đ Yet Kieu
Đ Thoi Nhiem
Đ Nguyen Thien Thuat
Đ Nguyen Han
Đ Tran Nguyen Dan
Đ Ton That Thiep
Đ Nguyen Cu Trinh
Đ Ngo
Đ Tran
Đ Le Duan
To An Hoa Bus Station (200m), Dong Ha (72km), DMZ (90km), Vinh (368km) & Hanoi (689km)
Ke Van Canal
To Duong Kim Long & Thien Mu Pagoda (3km)
Perfume River
Gia Vien Island
1 2 3 4 5 6 7
86 87 88 89 90 91 92 93 94 95 96 97 98 99 100 101 102
107 108 109 110 111 112 116

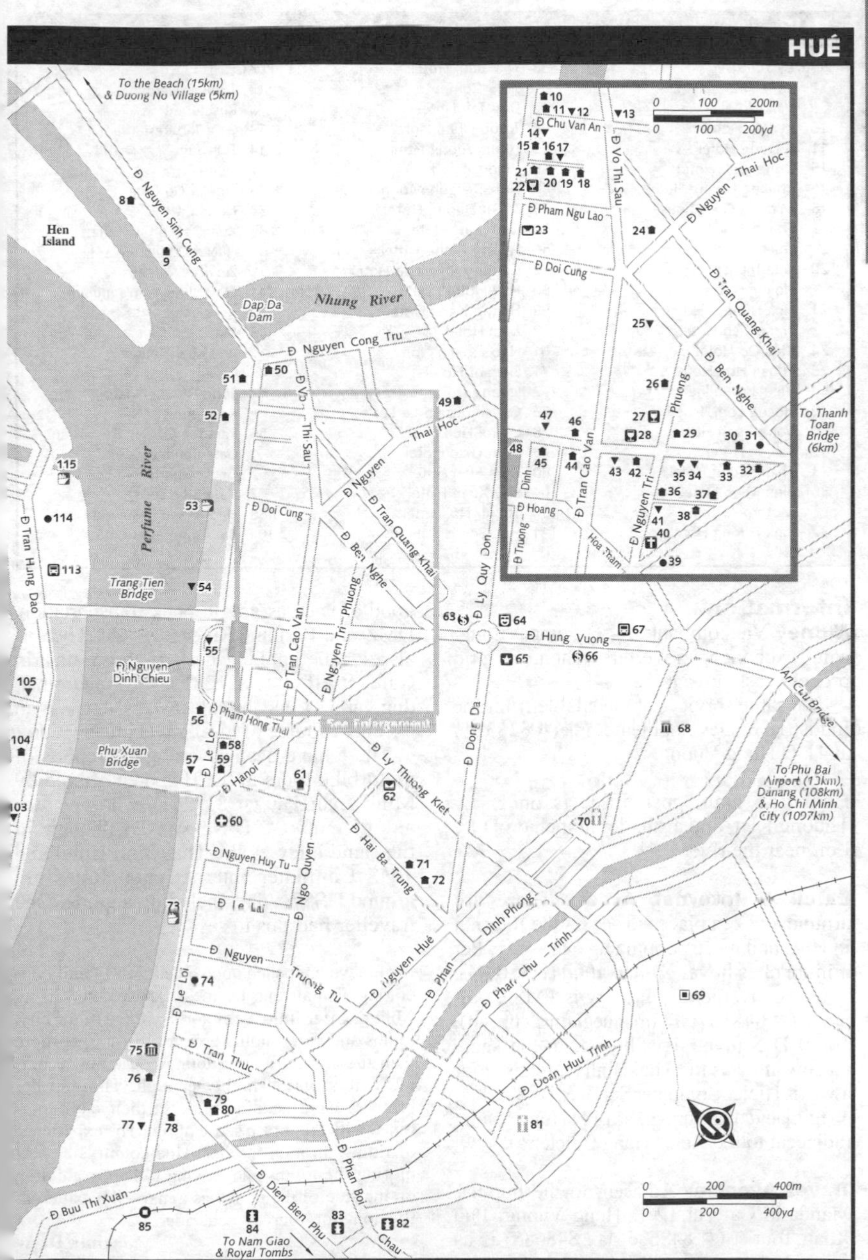
HUÉ
To the Beach (15km) & Duong No Village (5km)
Đ Nguyen Sinh Cung
Hen Island
Nhung River
Dap Da Dam
Đ Nguyen Cong Tru
Perfume River
Trang Tien Bridge
Đ Tran Hung Dao
Đ Nguyen Dinh Chieu
Phu Xuan Bridge
Đ Pham Hong Thai
Đ Le Loi
Đ Hanoi
Đ Vo Thi Sau
Đ Doi Cung
Đ Nguyen Thai Hoc
Đ Tran Quang Khai
Đ Ben Nghe
Đ Tran Cao Van
Đ Nguyen Tri Phuong
See Enlargement
Đ Ly Quy Don
Đ Hung Vuong
Đ Dong Da
Đ Ly Thuong Kiet
Đ Hai Ba Trung
Đ Nguyen Huy Tu
Đ Le Lai
Đ Ngo Quyen
Đ Nguyen Truong To
Đ Nguyen Hue
Đ Phan Dinh Phung
Đ Phan Chu Trinh
Đ Tran Thuc
Đ Doan Huu Trinh
Đ Dien Bien Phu
Đ Phan Boi Chau
Đ Buu Thi Xuan
To Nam Giao & Royal Tombs
An Cuu Bridge
To Phu Bai Airport (13km), Danang (108km) & Ho Chi Minh City (1097km)
To Thanh Toan Bridge (6km)
Đ Chu Van An
Đ Pham Ngu Lao
Đ Dinh Hoang
Đ Truong Dinh
Hoa Tham
0 100 200m
0 100 200yd
0 200 400m
0 200 400yd

HUÉ

PLACES TO STAY
8 Song Huong Hotel
9 Vida Hotel
10 Ky Lan Hotel
11 A Dong Hotel
15 Dong Kinh Hotel
16 Phuong Hoang Hotel
18 Mimosa Guesthouse
19 Thanh Thuy's Guesthouse
20 Guesthouse Hoang Huong
21 Hoa Hong 1 Hotel; Trang Tien Hotel
24 Kinh Do Hotel
26 Thuan Hoa Hotel & Vietnam Airlines
29 Hoang Long Hotel
30 Vong Canh Hotel
32 Saigon Hotel
33 Thang Long Hotel
36 Binh Minh Hotel; Motorbike Tours
37 Binh Duong Hotel
38 Thai Binh Hotel; TMS Computer
42 Duy Tan Hotel
44 Truong Tien Hotel
45 Hung Vuong Hotel
46 L'Indochine Hotel
48 Hotel Saigon Morin
49 Thien Duong Hotel
50 Cuu Long Hotel
51 Huong Giang Hotel
52 Century Riverside Hotel
56 Hué Hotel
58 Hoang Ngoc Hotel
59 Mini Hotel 18
61 Ngo Quyen Hotel
71 Elegant Hotel
72 Huong Dung Hotel
76 Guesthouse 5 Le Loi
78 Le Loi Hué Hotel
79 Nam Giao Hotel
80 Dien Bien Hotel
104 Phu Xuan Hotel
110 Thanh Noi Hotel
111 Hoa Sen Hotel

PLACES TO EAT
12 Tropical Garden Restaurant
13 Ong Tao Restaurant
14 Tinh Tam
17 Dong Tam
25 Stop & Go Cafe
34 News Cafe
35 Xuan Trang Cafeteria; Hi.Net Computer Services
41 Omar Khayyam's Indian Restaurant
43 Mandarin Café; Phu Xuan Tourist
47 Cafes
54 Song Huong Floating Restaurant
55 Paradise Garden Restaurant; Cafe Rendezvous
57 Cercle Sportiff
77 Cafe 3 Le Loi
88 Huong Sen Restaurant
103 Ba Nhon Restaurant

Information

Money Vietcombank, 54 Đ Hung Vuong, can exchange travellers cheques and process cash advances.

The same services are available from the Industrial & Development Bank (☎ 823361) at 41 Đ Hung Vuong.

Post The main post office is on Đ Ly Thuong Kiet, and a smaller branch on Đ Le Loi, near the river.

Email & Internet Access There are around a dozen places to access the Internet in Hué, and more popping up every day. Per minute rates hover around 400d (US$0.03).

One convenient spot to try is TMS Computer (☎ 848531, ⓔ tmshue@dng.vnn.vn), 10/10 Đ Nguyen Tri Phuong, in the same narrow alley as the Thai Binh Hotel. Not far away is HiNet Computer Services (☎ 829004, ⓔ tg.man@dng.vnn.vn) at 14 Đ Hung Vuong (adjacent to the Xuan Trang Cafeteria).

Travel Agencies Adjacent to the popular Mandarin Cafe at 12 Đ Hung Vuong, Phu Xuan Tourist (☎ 848686, fax 848685) is as good a place as any to book transportation, DMZ and Perfume River tours etc. There is also a tour booking desk at the Mandarin Cafe itself (☎ 821281, ⓔ mandarin@dng.vnn.vn), and the cafe owner, Mr Cu, is an excellent source of local travel information.

There have been several good reports of motorbike tours in the Hué area offered by Minh Toan Thu (☎ 832241), who operates an office at 10/2 Đ Nguyen Tri Phuong, in the same alley as the Thai Binh Hotel and TMS Computer Internet cafe. Rates are around US$7 a day, including a guide. One traveller had this to say:

> In Hué we happened upon a delightful family operating a small tour business. These enterprising siblings offer full-day motorbike tours of the city, tombs and surrounding area for just a little more than the cost of a river tour. We cannot recommend this option highly enough. Thu and her brothers have genuine pride in their city, combined with an impish sense of fun. The experience of riding through the lush Hué countryside, exploring the tombs and waving to happy children on the side of the road was a marvellous alternative to a hot, touristy boat ride.
>
> **Jacinta Drew**

HUÉ

105 Lac Thanh Restaurant; Lac Thien Restaurant; Lac Thuan
112 Tinh Gia Vien

OTHER
1 Chua Ong; Chaozhou Pagoda
2 Chua Ba
3 Tang Quang Pagoda
4 Hall of the Cantonese Chinese Congregation
5 Chieu Ung Pagoda
6 Former Indian Mosque
7 Dieu De National Pagoda
22 DMZ Bar & Cafe
23 Post Office
27 Apocalypse Now
28 Brown Eyes Bar; Motobike Tours
31 Dai Ly Thuoc Tay Pharmacy
39 Vietnam Airlines
40 St Xavier Church
53 Tourist Boat Landing
60 Hué General Hospital
62 Post Office
63 Industrial & Commercial Bank
64 Municipal Theatre
65 Police Headquarters
66 Vietcombank
67 An Cuu Bus Station
68 An Dinh Palace
69 Tomb of Duc Duc
70 Notre Dame Cathedral
73 Perfume River Boat Cruises
74 National School
75 Ho Chi Minh Museum
81 Phu Cam Cathedral
82 Linh Quang Pagoda; Phan Boi Chau's Tomb
83 Tu Dam Pagoda
84 Bao Quoc Pagoda
85 Hué Train Station
86 Chanh Tay Gate
87 Nha Do Gate
89 Hoa Binh Gate
90 Royal Library
91 Halls of the Mandarins
92 Chuong Duc Gate
93 Nine Dynastic Urns
94 Nine Holy Cannons (Five Elements)
95 Quang Duc Gate
96 Flag Tower
97 Ngo Mon Gate
98 Trung Dao Bridge
99 Thai Hoa Palace
100 Hien Nhon Gate
101 Nine Holy Cannons (Four Seasons)
102 Ngan Gate
106 Thuong Tu Gate
107 Military Museum
108 Natural History Museum
109 Imperial Museum
113 Dong Ba Bus Station
114 Dong Ba Market
115 Dock
116 Dong Ba Gate

Medical Services Hué General Hospital (Benh Vien Trung Uong Hué, ☎ 822325) is at 16 Đ Le Loi close to Phu Xuan Bridge.

Dr Ngo Quang Phong, the chief doctor at the Century Riverside Hotel, has been recommended by travellers. He can be seen at the hotel (☎ 823390), 49 Đ Le Loi, or at his private clinic (☎ 821061), 117/7 Đ Ba Trieu.

Dai Ly Thuoc Tay (☎ 823361), 33 Đ Hung Vuong, near the junction of Đ Ben Nghe, is a good pharmacy.

Immigration Police Visa extensions can be processed at the immigration police office on Đ Ben Nghe.

Citadel

Construction of the moated Citadel (Kinh Thanh), which has a 10km perimeter, was begun in 1804 by Emperor Gia Long on a site chosen by geomancers. The Citadel was originally made of earth, but earlier in the 19th century, tens of thousands of workers laboured to cover the ramparts, built in the style of the French military architect Vauban, with a layer of bricks 2m thick.

The emperor's official functions were carried out in the Imperial Enclosure (Dai Noi, or Hoang Thanh), a citadel-within a-citadel with 6m-high walls 2.5km in length. The Imperial Enclosure has four gates, the most famous of which is Ngo Mon Gate. Within the Imperial Enclosure is the Forbidden Purple City, which was reserved for the private life of the emperor.

Three sides of the Citadel are straight; the fourth is rounded slightly to follow the curve of the river. The ramparts are encircled by a zigzag moat, which is 30m across and about 4m deep. In the northern corner of the Citadel is Mang Ca Fortress, once known as the French Concession, which is still used as a military base. The Citadel has 10 fortified gates, each reached via a bridge across the moat.

Wide areas within the Citadel are now devoted to agriculture, a legacy of the destruction of 1968.

Flag Tower The 37m-high Flag Tower (Cot Co), also known as the King's Knight, is Vietnam's tallest flagpole. Erected in 1809 and extended in 1831, a terrific typhoon (which devastated the whole city) knocked it down in 1904. The tower was rebuilt in 1915, only to be destroyed again in 1947. It was erected once again, in its present form, in 1949. During the VC occupation of Hué in 1968, the National Liberation Front flag flew defiantly from the tower for 3½ weeks.

Nine Holy Cannons Located just inside the Citadel ramparts near the gates to either side of the Flag Tower, the Nine Holy Cannons, symbolic protectors of the palace and kingdom, were cast from brass articles captured from the Tay Son Rebels. The cannons, which were cast on the orders of Emperor Gia Long in 1804, were never intended to be fired. Each is 5m long, has a bore of 23cm and weighs about 10 tonnes. The four cannons near Ngan Gate represent the four seasons, while the five cannons next to Quang Duc Gate represent the five elements: metal, wood, water, fire and soil.

Ngo Mon Gate The principal entrance to the Imperial Enclosure is Ngo Mon Gate (Noontime Gate), which faces the Flag Tower. It is open from 6.30 am to 5.30 pm; the entrance fee for foreigners is US$4.

The central passageway with its yellow doors was reserved for use by the emperor, as was the bridge across the lotus pond. Everyone else had to use the gates to either side and the paths around the lotus pond.

On top of the gate is Ngu Phung (Belvedere of the Five Phoenixes), where the emperor appeared on important occasions, notably for the promulgation of the lunar calendar. Emperor Bao Dai ended the Nguyen Dynasty here on 30 August 1945 when he abdicated to a delegation sent by Ho Chi Minh's Provisional Revolutionary Government. The middle section of the roof is covered with yellow tiles; the roofs to either side are green.

Thai Hoa Palace Built in 1803 and moved to its present site in 1833, Thai Hoa Palace (Palace of Supreme Harmony) is a spacious hall with an ornate roof of huge timbers supported by 80 carved and lacquered columns. Accessible from Ngo Mon Gate via Trung Dao Bridge, it was used for the emperor's official receptions and other important court ceremonies, such as anniversaries and coronations. During state occasions, the king sat on his elevated throne and received homage from ranks of mandarins. Nine stelae divide the bi-level courtyard into separate areas for officials in each of the nine ranks of the mandarinate; administrative mandarins stood to one side and military mandarins stood to the other.

There is now a souvenir shop here, and a music ensemble dressed in traditional outfits will often perform imperial music for a donation of about US$1.

Halls of the Mandarins The buildings in which the mandarins prepared for court ceremonies, held in Can Chanh Reception Hall, were restored in 1977. The structures are directly behind Thai Hoa Palace on either side of a courtyard, where there are two gargantuan bronze cauldrons *(vac dong)* dating from the 17th century.

Nine Dynastic Urns The Nine Dynastic Urns *(dinh)* were cast in 1835–36. Traditional ornamentation was then chiselled into the sides of the urns, each dedicated to a different Nguyen sovereign. The designs, some of which are of Chinese origin and date back 4000 years, include the sun, moon, meteors, clouds, mountains, rivers and various landscapes. About 2m in height and weighing 1900kg to 2600kg each, the urns symbolise the power and stability of the Nguyen throne. The central urn, which is the largest and most ornate, is dedicated to Gia Long.

Forbidden Purple City The Forbidden Purple City (Tu Cam Thanh) was reserved for the personal use of the emperor. The only servants allowed into the compound were eunuchs, who would pose no threat to the royal concubines.

The Forbidden Purple City was almost entirely destroyed during the Tet Offensive. The area is now given over to vegetable plots, between which touch-sensitive mimosa plants flourish. The two-storey Royal

Library (Thai Binh Lau) has been partially restored. The foundations of the Royal Theatre (Duyen Thi Duong), begun in 1826 and later home of the National Conservatory of Music, can be seen nearby.

Tinh Tam Lake In the middle of Tinh Tam Lake, which is 500m north of the Imperial Enclosure, are two islands connected by bridges. The emperors used to come here with their retinues to relax.

Tang Tau Lake An island in Tang Tau Lake, which is north of Tinh Tam Lake, was once the site of a royal library. It is now occupied by a small Hinayana (Theravada, or Nam Tong) pagoda, called Ngoc Huong Pagoda.

Museums

The beautiful hall that houses the Imperial Museum (Bao Tang Co Vat) was built in 1845 and restored when the museum was founded in 1923. The walls are inscribed with poems written in Vietnamese script *(nom)*. The most precious artefacts were lost during the American War, but the ceramics, furniture and royal clothing that remain are well worth a look.

On the left side of the hall is a royal sedan chair, a gong and a musical instrument consisting of stones hung on a bi-level rack. On the other side of the hall is the equipment for a favourite game of the emperors – the idea was to bounce a stick off a wooden platform into a tall, thin jug. The Imperial Museum is at 3 Đ Le Truc and is open daily from 6.30 am to 5.30 pm.

The building across the street was once a school for princes and the sons of high-ranking mandarins. Behind the school is the Military Museum, with its usual assortment of American and Soviet-made weapons, including a MiG 17. Nearby is the small Natural History Museum.

Ho Chi Minh Museum On display at the Ho Chi Minh Museum (Bao Tang Ho Chi Minh) at 9 Đ Le Loi are photographs, some of Ho's personal effects, and documents relating to his life and accomplishments.

Places of Worship

Thien Mu Pagoda The Thien Mu Pagoda (also known as Linh Mu Pagoda), built on a hillock overlooking the Perfume River, is one of the most famous structures in Vietnam. The existing 21m-high octagonal tower, the seven-storey Thap Phuoc Duyen, was constructed under the reign of Emperor Thieu Tri in 1844 and has become the unofficial symbol of the city of Hué. Each of the seven storeys is dedicated to a *manushi-buddha*. (Also see the 'Thien Mu Pagoda' boxed text in this section).

Thien Mu Pagoda was originally founded in 1601 by the Nguyen lord Nguyen Hoang, governor of Thuan Hoa Province. According to legend, a Fairy Woman (Thien Mu) appeared and told the people that a lord would come to build a pagoda for the country's prosperity. On hearing that, Nguyen Hoang ordered a pagoda to be constructed here. Over the centuries, the pagoda's buildings have been destroyed and rebuilt several times.

To the right of the tower is a pavilion containing a stele dating from 1715. It is set on the back of a massive marble turtle, a symbol of longevity. To the left of the tower is another six-sided pavilion, this one sheltering an enormous bell, Dai Hong Chung, which was cast in 1710 and weighs 2052kg; it is said to be audible 10km away. In the main sanctuary, in a case behind the bronze laughing Buddha, are three statues: A Di Da, the Buddha of the Past; Thich Ca, the historical Buddha (Sakyamuni); and Di Lac Buddha, the Buddha of the Future.

Thien Mu Pagoda is on the banks of the Perfume River, 4km south-west of the Citadel. To get there (a nice bicycle ride), head south-west (parallel to the river) on riverside Đ Tran Hung Dao, which turns into Đ Le Duan after you pass Phu Xuan Bridge. Cross the railway tracks and keep going on Đ Kim Long. Thien Mu Pagoda can also be reached by rowing boat. Entry is free.

Bao Quoc Pagoda Last renovated in 1957, Bao Quoc Pagoda (Pagoda Which Serves the Country) was founded in 1670 by Giac Phong, a Buddhist monk from

Thien Mu Pagoda

The Thien Mu Pagoda is home to the Austin motorcar made famous by Thich Quang Duc's self-immolation in 1963.

The Thien Mu Pagoda just outside Hué was a hotbed of anti-government protest during the early 1960s. Surprisingly, it also became a focus of protest in the 1980s when someone was murdered near the pagoda and anti-Communist demonstrations started here, closing traffic around Phu Xuan Bridge. Monks were arrested and accused of disturbing the traffic and public order. Things have calmed down and a small group of monks, novices and nuns now live at the pagoda.

Behind the main sanctuary of the Thien Mu Pagoda is the Austin motorcar, which transported the monk Thich Quang Duc to the site of his 1963 self-immolation.

Thich Quang Duc travelled to Saigon and publicly burned himself to death to protest the policies of President Ngo Dinh Diem. A famous photograph of his act was printed on the front pages of newspapers around the world. His death soon inspired a number of other self-immolations.

Many Westerners were shocked less by the suicides than by the reaction of Tran Le Xuan (Madame Nhu, the president's notorious sister-in-law), who happily proclaimed the self-immolations a 'barbecue party' and said, 'Let them burn and we shall clap our hands'. Her statements greatly added to the already substantial public disgust with Diem's regime; the US press labelled Madame Nhu the 'Iron Butterfly' and 'Dragon Lady'. In November, both President Diem and his brother Ngo Dinh Nhu (Madame Nhu's husband) were assassinated by Diem's own military. Madame Nhu was outside the country at the time.

A memorial to Thich Quang Duc (Dai Ky Niem Thuong Toa Thich Quang Duc) can be found at the intersection of Đ Nguyen Dinh Chieu and Đ Cach Mang Thang Tam, around the corner from the Xa Loi Pagoda, in Ho Chi Minh City.

China. It was given its present name in 1824 by Emperor Minh Mang, who later celebrated his 40th birthday here in 1830. A school for training monks was opened here in 1940 and the orchid-lined courtyard behind the sanctuary is still a quiet place where students gather to study.

The central altar in the main sanctuary contains three identical Buddha statues, which represent (from left to right) Di Lac, Thich Ca and A Di Da, behind which is a memorial room for deceased monks. Around the main building are monks' tombs, including a three-storey, red-and-grey stupa built for the pagoda's founder.

Bao Quoc Pagoda is on Ham Long Hill in Phuong Duc District. To get there, head south from Đ Le Loi on Đ Dien Bien Phu and turn right immediately after crossing the railway tracks.

Tu Dam Pagoda This pagoda, which is about 400m south of Bao Quoc Pagoda on the corner of Đ Dien Bien Phu and Đ Tu Dam, is one of Vietnam's best known pagodas. Unfortunately, the present buildings are recent additions that date from as recently as 1936.

Tu Dam Pagoda was founded around 1695 by Minh Hoang Tu Dung, a Chinese monk. It was given its present name by Emperor Thieu Tri in 1841. It was here that the Unified Vietnamese Buddhist Association was established at a meeting in 1951. During the early 1960s, Tu Dam was a major centre of the Buddhist anti-Diem and anti-war movement, and in 1968 it became the scene of heavy fighting, scars of which remain.

Today, Tu Dam Pagoda, home to a handful of monks, is the seat of the provincial Buddhist Association. The peculiar bronze Thich Ca Buddha in the sanctuary was cast locally in 1966.

Just east of the pagoda down Đ Tu Dam is **Linh Quang Pagoda** and the tomb of the scholar and anti-colonialist revolutionary Phan Boi Chau (1867–1940).

Notre Dame Cathedral Notre Dame Cathedral (Dong Chua Cuu The) at 80 Đ Nguyen Hué is an impressive modern building combining the functional aspects of a European cathedral with traditional Vietnamese elements, including a distinctly oriental spire. At present, the huge cathedral, which was constructed between 1959 and 1962, has 1600 members. The two French-speaking priests hold daily masses at 5 am and 5 pm with an extra 7 am service on Sunday; children's catechism classes are also conducted on Sunday mornings. Visitors who find the front gate locked should ring the bell of the yellow building next door.

Phu Cam Cathedral Construction of Phu Cam Cathedral began in 1963 and was halted in 1975 before completion of the bell tower. It is the eighth church to be built on this site since 1682 and the Hué diocese, which is based here, hopes eventually to find the funds to complete the structure. Phu Cam Cathedral is at 20 Đ Doan Huu Trinh, at the southern end of Đ Nguyen Truong To. Masses are held at 5 am and 6.45 pm daily (at 5 and 7 am and 2 and 7 pm on Sunday).

St Xavier Church This Catholic church was built around 1915. From the outside it looks derelict, but the inside is well maintained and has a functioning electric organ.

Realise that this is not a tourist attraction as such, but an active place of worship. There is no admission charge, but you might want to make a small donation to help maintain the place.

St Xavier Church is south-west of the Binh Minh Hotel on Đ Nguyen Tri Phuong. You can ask to be let in at the building at the rear. Some of the caretakers speak French, though not much English.

Dieu De National Pagoda The entrance to Dieu De National Pagoda (Quoc Tu Dieu De), built under Emperor Thieu Tri's rule (1841–47), is along Dong Ba Canal at 102 Đ Bach Dang. It is one of the city's three 'national pagodas' (pagodas that were once under the direct patronage of the emperor). Dieu De is famous for its four low towers, one to either side of the gate and two flanking the sanctuary. There are bells in two of the towers; the others contain a drum and a stele dedicated to the pagoda's founder.

During the regime of Ngo Dinh Diem (ruled 1955–63) and through the mid-1960s, Dieu De National Pagoda was a stronghold of Buddhist and student opposition to the South Vietnamese government and the war. In 1966 the pagoda was stormed by police, who confiscated the opposition movement's radio equipment and arrested many monks, Buddhist lay people and students. Today, a handful of monks live at the pagoda.

The pavilions on either side of the entrance to the main sanctuary contain the 18 La Ha, whose rank is just below that of Bodhisattva, and the eight Kim Cang, protectors of Buddha. In the back row of the main dais is Thich Ca Buddha flanked by two assistants, Pho Hien Bo Tat (to his right) and Van Thu Bo Tat (to his left).

Former Indian Mosque Hué's Indian Muslim community constructed this mosque at 120 Đ Chi Lang in 1932. The structure was used as a house of worship until 1975, when the Indian community fled. It is now a private residence.

Chieu Ung Pagoda Chieu Ung Pagoda (Chieu Ung Tu), opposite 138 Đ Chi Lang, was founded by the Hainan Chinese Congregation in the mid-19th century and rebuilt in 1908. It was last repaired in 1940. The pagoda's sanctuary retains its original ornamentation, which is becoming faded but mercifully unaffected by the third-rate modernistic renovations that have marred other such structures. The pagoda was built as a memorial to 108 Hainan merchants who were mistaken for pirates and killed in Vietnam in 1851.

Tang Quang Pagoda Tang Quang Pagoda (Tang Quang Tu), down the alley opposite 80 Đ Nguyen Chi Thanh, is the largest of the three Hinayana pagodas in Hué. Built in 1957, it owes its distinctive architecture to Hinayana Buddhism's historical links to Sri Lanka and India (rather than China). The pagoda's Pali name, Sangharansyarama (Light Coming from the Buddha), is inscribed on the front of the building.

National School

The National School (Quoc Hoc) at 10 Đ Le Loi is one of the most famous secondary schools in Vietnam. It was founded in 1896 and run by Ngo Dinh Kha, the father of South Vietnamese president Ngo Dinh Diem, and many of the school's pupils later rose to prominence in both North and South Vietnam. Numbered among the National School's former students are General Vo Nguyen Giap, strategist of the Viet Minh victory at Dien Bien Phu and North Vietnam's long-serving deputy premier, defence minister and commander-in-chief; and Pham Van Dong, North Vietnam's prime minister for over a quarter of a century; Secretary General and former Prime Minister Do Muoi. Even Ho Chi Minh attended the school briefly in 1908.

The school was given a major renovation in 1996 to celebrate its 100th anniversary and a statue of Ho Chi Minh was erected. The National School and the neighbouring Hai Ba Trung Secondary School cannot be visited until after classes finish, which is at about 3 pm.

Assembly Halls

Hall of the Cantonese Chinese Congregation Founded almost a century ago, the Hall of the Cantonese Chinese Congregation (Chua Quang Dong) is located opposite 154 Đ Chi Lang. Against the right-hand wall is a small altar holding a statue of Confucius (Khong Tu) with a gold beard. On the main altar is red-faced Quan Cong (in Chinese: Guangong) flanked by Trung Phi (left) and Luu Bi (right). On the altar to the left is Laotse with disciples to either side. On the altar to the right is Phat Ba, a female Buddha.

Chua Ba Chua Ba, across the street from 216 Đ Chi Lang, was founded by the Hainan Chinese Congregation almost a century ago. It was damaged in the Tet Offensive and was subsequently reconstructed. On the central altar is Thien Hau Thanh Mau, the Goddess of the Sea and Protector of Fishermen and Sailors. To the right is a glass case in which Quan Cong sits flanked by his usual companions, the mandarin general Chau Xuong (to his right) and the administrative mandarin Quang Binh (to his left).

Chua Ong Chua Ong, opposite 224 Đ Chi Lang, is a large pagoda founded by Hué's Fujian Chinese Congregation during the reign of Vietnamese emperor Tu Duc (ruled 1848–83). The building was severely damaged during the Tet Offensive when an ammunition ship blew up nearby. A gold Buddha sits in a glass case opposite the main doors of the sanctuary. The left-hand altar is dedicated to Thien Hau Thanh Mau and she is flanked by her two assistants, 1000-eyed Thien Ly Nhan and red-faced Thuan Phong Nhi, who can hear for 1000 miles. On the altar to the right is Quan Cong.

Next door is a pagoda of the Chaozhou Chinese Congregation (Tieu Chau Tu).

Thanh Toan Bridge

If you missed the famous Japanese bridge in Hoi An, or prefer the less beaten track, there is another classic covered footbridge about 7km east of central Hué well worth seeking out. Thanh Toan Bridge is architecturally similar to its cousin in Hoi An, though it receives far less visitors (it's mostly used by local villagers for naps in the shady walkway).

The bridge is best reached by motorbike or bicycle. Finding it is a bit tricky, but tolerable if you consider getting lost part of the excursion. Head north for a few hundred metres on Đ Ba Trieu (from the roundabout near the An Cuu bus station) until you see a sign to the Citadel Hotel. Turn right here and follow the delightful (and bumpy) dirt road for another 6km past villages, rice paddies and several pagodas until you reach the bridge.

Places to Stay – Budget

A good place to find basic, cheap rooms near the river is in the narrow alley off Đ Le Loi between Đ Pham Ngu Lao and Đ Chu Van An. Possibilities include ***Guesthouse Hoang Huong*** *(☎ 828509, 46/2 Đ Le Loi)*,which has dorm beds for US$2, singles for US$4 to US$6, and air-con rooms from US$7 to US$10.

The friendly ***Mimosa Guesthouse*** *(☎ 828068, fax 823858, 46/6 Đ Le Loi)* is run by Mr Tran Van Hoang, a former French teacher and author of several books written in French. Rates are US$8 to US$15 for air-con rooms.

The small, family-run ***Thanh Thuy's Guesthouse*** *(☎ 824585, 46/4 Đ Le Loi)* has air-con singles/doubles from US$7/8.

The ***Phuong Hoang Hotel*** *(☎ 826736, fax 828999, 48/3 Đ Le Loi)* – also known as the *Phoenix Hotel* – has air-con rooms with satellite TV (some with river views) from US$15 to US$30.

The ***Binh Duong Hotel*** *(☎/fax 833298, ⓔ binhduong@dng.vnn.vn, 10/4 Đ Nguyen Tri Phuong)* is tucked into a narrow alley in the city centre and is usually chock-a-block with Japanese backpackers. Dorm beds are US$2.50 or US$3, fan singles are US$5 or US$6, fan/air-con doubles are US$8/10, and it costs US$15 for an air-con room with balcony and bath tub. The hotel offers self-service laundry facilities.

Just across the alley, the popular ***Thai Binh Hotel*** *(☎ 828058, fax 832867, ⓔ ksthaibinh@dng.vnn.vn, 10/9 Đ Nguyen Tri Phuong)* has a new and an old wing. Standard rooms cost US$10 to US$15; deluxe rooms with balconies cost US$20 to US$25 and include breakfast. All rooms have satellite TV.

Another family-run place that gets very good reviews from travellers is the pleasant ***Binh Minh Hotel*** *(☎ 825526, fax 828362, ⓔ binhminhhue@dng.vnn.vn, 12 Đ Nguyen Tri Phuong)*. Rooms cost US$8 to US$30. Those staying in US$15 and up rooms can be served breakfast on their balcony.

Close to the river, a relatively new and friendly place worth trying is the ***Hoang Ngoc Hotel*** *(☎ 824785, fax 845996, 3 Đ Truong Dinh)*. Fan singles cost US$6, while air-con doubles are US$10 to US$15.

The ***Duy Tan Hotel*** *(☎ 825001, fax 826477, ⓔ hoqkbon@dng.vnn.vn, 12 Đ Hung Vuong)* is in a good central location with plenty of parking available. Rates are reasonable from US$8 to US$20 for large air-con rooms with balconies.

The friendly ***A Dong Hotel*** *(☎ 824148, fax 828074, ⓔ adongcoltd@dng.vnn.vn, 18 Đ Chu Van An)* is decent value with singles at US$10 and US$15, and doubles for US$15 to US$25.

Le Loi Hué Hotel *(☎ 822153, fax 824527, 2 Đ Le Loi)* is enormous. It's also been enormously successful at attracting backpackers thanks to low prices, good rooms and its location only a 100m walk from the train station. Satellite TV is on tap, and it's also a good place for booking cars, taxis and tours. Rooms cost US$6 to US$40.

Also near the train station, ***Dien Bien Hotel*** *(☎ 821678, fax 821676, 3 Đ Dien Bien Phu)* offers singles/doubles with fan for US$8/10 and with air-con for US$15/20. Next door is the similarly priced but less spacious ***Nam Giao Hotel*** *(☎ 825736)*.

The ***Hoang Long Hotel*** *(☎ 828235, fax 823858, 20 Đ Nguyen Tri Phuong)* is a strange hodge-podge of concrete, marble and tile. Air-con doubles cost US$8 to US$20, and triples go for US$25. Some rooms have balconies.

Thang Long Hotel *(☎ 826462, fax 826 464, 16 Đ Hung Vuong)* is not overly friendly. Fan rooms cost US$6, or US$10 to US$20 with air-con.

The ***Hung Vuong Hotel*** *(☎ 823866, fax 825910, 2 Đ Hung Vuong)* is centrally located, set back off the main road. Air-con rooms, some with balconies, cost US$12 to US$65. The nearby ***Truong Tien Hotel*** *(☎ 823127, fax 847225, ⓔ truongtien@dng.vnn.vn, 8 Đ Hung Vuong)* is a no-fills, motel-style place with rooms from US$8 to US$20.

Vong Canh Hotel *(☎ 824130, fax 826798, 25 Đ Hung Vuong)* is near the post office. The private management is anxious to please. Rooms with a fan cost US$8, or US$10 to US$25 with air-con. Just across the road, prices are similar at the older ***Saigon Hotel***.

Ngo Quyen Hotel *(☎ 823278, fax 823502, 11 Đ Ngo Quyen)* is a large, old and elegant place with that 'seen better days' appearance. Doubles cost US$13 to US$30.

Song Huong Hotel *(☎ 823675, fax 825796, 51–66 Đ Nguyen Sinh Cung)* is an older, state-run place in the north-east part of town (across Dap Da Dam). Fan doubles/triples/quads cost just US$5/6/12, while air-con rooms are US$15 to US$20. Better rooms have IDD phones and satellite TV.

Near the river, the ***Hué Hotel*** *(☎ 823513, fax 824806, 15 Đ Le Loi)* has mediocre government-owned accommodation charging US$10/20 for fan/air-con rooms.

The ***Mini Hotel 18*** *(☎ 823720, fax 825814, 18 Đ Le Loi)* is another, smaller, state-owned place near the river. Reasonable air-con twins cost US$12 to US$15.

The ***Cuu Long Hotel*** *(☎ 828240, 80 Đ Le Loi)* is a basic mini-hotel with air-con rooms from US$8 to US$12.

The popular ***Thanh Noi Hotel*** *(☎ 522478, fax 527211, ⓔ thanhnoi@dng.vnn.vn, 3 Đ Dang Dung)* boasts an ideal location on the historic north bank of Hué (near the Forbidden Purple City). The quiet, tree-shaded compound has its own restaurant, ample parking and an 'intelligent swimming pool' with water jets. Air-con rooms cost US$12 to US$30. Internet access is available in the lobby.

Places to Stay – Mid-Range & Top End

The ***Elegant Hotel*** *(☎ 825973, fax 825972, 33 Đ Hai Ba Trung)* is also known as the *Thanh Lich Hotel*. It's a bit away from the river, but well appointed and reasonably priced. Swish looking singles/doubles with nice balconies, satellite TV, mini bar and bath tubs rent for US$25/30. There is a similar standard next door at the ***Huong Dung Hotel***.

The all air-con ***Thien Duong Hotel*** *(☎ 825976, fax 828233, 33 Đ Nguyen Thai Hoc)* is an older, but very friendly place that gets good reviews. Fan rooms cost US$8, while air-con ranges from US$10 to US$25. The name means 'Paradise Hotel'.

Phu Xuan Hotel *(☎ 527512, 27 Đ Tran Hung Dao)*, an older place near Phu Xuan Bridge, is one of the few hotels on the north bank of the Perfume River. Air-con rooms rent for US$16 to US$19.

Further in on the north bank is ***Hoa Sen Hotel*** *(☎ 525997, 33 Đ Dinh Cong Trang)*, in a very quiet setting among the trees. Rooms cost US$15 to US$25.

The unique ***Vida Hotel*** *(☎ 826145, fax 826147, 31 Đ Nguyen Sinh Cung)* seems to have been roughly modelled on a Swiss chalet. It's in the north-east area beyond Dap Da Dam. Simple, but clean twins with air-con and satellite TV cost US$20 to US$40, the better rooms offering river views.

Guesthouse 5 Le Loi *(☎ 822155, fax 828816, 5 Đ Le Loi)* is housed in a stately old villa. There are some nice river views and lovely gardens. Doubles cost US$20 to US$75.

Kinh Do Hotel *(☎ 823566, fax 821190, 1 Đ Nguyen Thai Hoc)* is a large old place with satellite TV and ample parking, with rooms for US$15 to US$20.

Thuan Hoa Hotel *(☎ 822553, fax 822470, 7 Đ Nguyen Tri Phuong)* looks like a large bank and has an intriguing, glossy brochure that reads, 'Come and have a touch with us and you will enjoy life more'. Touching one of its rooms will cost US$25 and US$50, with satellite TV.

The ***Trang Tien Hotel*** *(☎ 822128, fax 826772, 46A Đ Le Loi)* is a basic place charging US$15 to US$30 for air-con rooms.

L'Indochine Hotel *(☎ 826070, fax 826 074, 3 Đ Hung Vuong)* is an attractive choice, and well located. Rooms cost US$25 to US$60, including breakfast.

The ***Ky Lan Hotel*** *(☎ 826556, 58 Đ Le Loi)* is a medium-sized place sporting black-tinted windows. Air-con doubles/triples cost US$8/10 to US$15/20.

The ***Century Riverside Hotel*** *(☎ 823390, fax 823399, 49 Đ Le Loi)* is a grand place on the shore of the Perfume River. Luxury like this comes at a price – in this case between US$65 and US$170.

The ***Huong Giang Hotel*** *(☎ 822122, fax 823102, e hghotel@dng.vnn.vn, 51 Đ Le Loi)* is another giant place on the river, this one decorated with a tasteful Asian decor. Accommodation costs US$50 to US$230 and it's worth the price. The hotel also has a cheap annexe across the road called the ***Dong Kinh Hotel*** – it's the only lime-green building on the block.

The luxurious ***Hotel Saigon Morin*** *(☎ 823526, fax 825155, e sgmorin@dng.vnn.vn, 30 Đ Le Loi)* occupies an entire city block near the south bank of the Perfume River. The hotel offers all the trimmings and features three restaurants, a lovely courtyard cafe/bar and a swimming pool in the shape of a gourd. Standard rooms cost US$50 or US$60, deluxe rooms US$80 or US$100 and suites US$180 to US$300.

Places to Eat

Hué is a famed culinary city and has set the trends for central Vietnamese cooking. See the 'Tastes of Vietnam' special section earlier in the book for leads on what to try.

South Bank There is a solid string of popular budget cafes worth checking out along Đ Hung Vuong. The competition is fierce and the prices low. The cafes are good places to meet people and swap travellers' tales.

Mandarin Cafe *(☎ 821281, e mandarin@dng.vnn.vn, 12 Đ Hung Vuong)* is a magnet for travellers and tends to stay open late. The sign outside reads 'Lauded in Lonely Planet...', so we figure it can't be that bad? The BLTs, potato salad and trademark banana pancakes are recommended. The cheerful owner Mr Cu speaks English well and is full of useful travel advice.

The unique, indoor-outdoor ***Stop & Go Cafe*** *(☎ 889106, 4 Đ Ben Nghe)* is worthy of a plug. It is run by friendly Mr Do, a silver-haired painter and freelance tour guide, who ensures the cafe's artsy, bohemian air. The house specialities are *banh khoai* (5000d), a kind of omelette purported to put lead in your pencil, and *nem lui* (3000d), delicious grilled spring roll kebabs that you roll yourself in rice paper with lettuce and cucumber and dip into peanut sauce. Yum.

The ***Xuan Trang Cafeteria*** *(☎ 832480, 14A Đ Hung Vuong)* is another highly recommended place for cheap and excellent food. Just next door is the equally popular ***News Cafe***.

In the same area you'll find authentic curries and *nan* at ***Omar Khayyam's Indian Restaurant*** *(☎ 821616, 10 Đ Nguyen Tri Phuong)*.

Also worth seeking out is the pleasant ***Tropical Garden Restaurant*** *(☎ 847143, 5 Đ Chu Van An)*. You can dine in the attractive main building, or outdoors in a delightful, shaded garden. It specialises in central Vietnamese cuisine, and offers tempting set courses from US$5 to US$18. A la carte selections are in the US$2 range.

Another option nearby is the ***Ong Tao Restaurant*** *(☎ 823031, 9B Đ Chu Van An)*, which serves a wide range of local dishes, though the atmosphere is nothing to write home about.

For a slightly more upmarket dining experience, try the pleasant ***Paradise Garden Restaurant*** *(Đ Nguyen Dinh Chieu)*, on the riverfront near Hotel Saigon Morin. The grilled chicken on lemon leaves and the sauteed crab and mushrooms is highly recommended.

The ***Song Huong Floating Restaurant*** *(☎ 823738)* is a pleasant spot on the bank of the Perfume River, just north of Trang Tien Bridge. The food is OK, but most people come to enjoy the river breeze and romantic atmosphere.

There is a cafe on the grounds of ***Le Loi Hué Hotel***, and ***Cafe 3 Le Loi***, just across the street, also dishes up fine food at reasonable prices.

Vegetarian food, which has a long tradition in Hué, is prepared at ***pagodas*** for consumption by the monks. Small groups of visitors might be invited to join the monks for a meal. Stalls in the ***markets*** serve vegetarian food on the first and 15th days of the lunar month.

Down a narrow alley, ***Dong Tam*** *(☎ 828 403, 48/7 Đ Le Loi)* has some of the best Vietnamese vegetarian fare in town, and prices are cheap. Another good vegie alternative is the excellent ***Tinh Tam*** *(4 Đ Chu Van An)*, just around the block.

North Bank ***Lac Thanh Restaurant*** *(☎ 524674, 6A Đ Dinh Tien Hoang)* is a fashionable gathering spot for travellers. The congenial owner, Mr Lac, is deaf and mute so everything is communicated with sign language. However, his daughter, Lan Anh, speaks English well. This is among the best spots in Hué to trade stories and advice with fellow travellers.

Right next door the ***Lac Thien Restaurant*** has sort of cloned Lac Thanh's motif. Six deaf people working here also produce fine food, plus an entertaining atmosphere. In true Vietnamese fashion, yet a *third* clone called ***Lac Thuan*** recently appeared on the other side of Lac Thanh.

Highly recommended is the garden setting at ***Tinh Gia Vien*** *(☎ 522243, 20/3 Đ Le Thanh Ton)*, known for serving dishes in the traditional style of Hué's imperial court. Master chef Madame Ha's artistic presentation of the food is reason enough to visit. Excellent set-course meals cost US$6 to US$10 per person.

Also within the Citadel is ***Huong Sen Restaurant*** *(42 Đ Nguyen Trai)*, near the corner of Đ Thach Han. This 16-sided pavilion, built on pylons in the middle of a lotus pond, is open from 9 am to midnight. You can't beat the atmosphere.

Ba Nhon Restaurant *(☎ 823853, 29 Đ Le Duan)* is actually inside a tourist bus station. It has good Vietnamese food at low prices, but won't win any awards for hygiene or decor. You can peek into the outdoor kitchen and try pointing to what you like best.

Backpackers on a tight budget might explore the ***Dong Ba Market*** (see Shopping in this section). Food here is so cheap they might as well give it away. Nevertheless, it's good quality. The only real problem will be finding comfortable chairs (or, for that matter, any chairs) so you can sit down and enjoy your meal.

Entertainment

The ***DMZ Bar & Cafe*** *(44 Đ Le Loi)* is a popular eating, pool-shooting and dance spot for expats and travellers in the evening.

Nearly across from the Mandarin Cafe on Đ Hung Vuong, ***Brown Eyes Bar*** is a recent arrival that also attracts customers with its pool table.

Apocalypse Now *(☎ 820152, 7 Đ Nguyen Tri Phuong)* has the music, and revelry of its sister bars in Ho Chi Minh City and Hanoi, but overpriced drinks and reports of an 'aggressive atmosphere' could keep people away.

There are, of course, more peaceful evenings to be spent lingering in the ***cafes*** that line the streets.

Shopping

Hué is known for producing the finest conical hats in Vietnam. The city's speciality is 'poem hats' which, when held up to the light, reveal black cut-out scenes that are sandwiched between the layers of translucent palm leaves.

Hué is also home to one of the largest and most beautiful selections of rice paper and silk paintings available in Vietnam, but the prices quoted are usually inflated to about four times the real price. You can often negotiate a 50% discount simply by starting to walk away from a souvenir stall.

Dong Ba Market, on the north bank of the Perfume River a few hundred metres north of Trang Tien Bridge, is Hué's largest market where anything and everything can be bought. It was rebuilt after much of the structure was destroyed by a typhoon in 1986.

Getting There & Away

Air The Vietnam Airlines booking office (☎ 823249), 12 Đ Hanoi, is open Monday to

Saturday from 7 to 11 am and 1.30 to 5 pm. There is also a booking office (☎ 824709) in the Thuan Hoa Hotel. Several flights a day connect Hué to Ho Chi Minh City and Hanoi.

Bus Hué has three main bus stations: An Cuu, near the roundabout at the south-eastern end of Đ Hung Vuong, which serves southern destinations; An Hoa, north-west of the Citadel on Highway 1, serving northern destinations; and Dong Ba, a short-haul bus station next to Dong Ba Market. A minor bus station is Nguyen Hoang, which only has buses to Quang Tri Province.

Minibus Hué is a major target for tourist minibus companies and most backpackers travel this way. A popular run is the Hué–Hoi An minibus, which also stops in Danang. Tickets for the minibuses are sold at some hotels or the Sinh Cafe booking desk at the Mandarin Cafe – staff will tell you where the minibuses pick up from. Departure from either end is twice daily at 8 am and 1 pm, and there is usually a scenic, 10-minute stop at Lang Co Beach and Hai Van Pass. Hué–Hoi An or Hué-Danang tickets cost US$3.

Train Hué train station (Ga Hué, ☎ 822175) is on the south bank at the south-west end of Đ Le Loi. The ticket office is open from 7.30 am to 5 pm.

The *Reunification Express* trains stop in Hué. For information on ticket prices and schedules, see under the Train section in the Getting Around chapter.

Car & Motorbike Road distances from Hué are as follows:

Ben Hai River	94km
Danang	108km
Dong Ha	72km
Dong Hoi	166km
Hanoi	689km
Ho Chi Minh City	1097km
Lao Bao (Lao border)	152km
Quang Tri	56km
Savannakhet, Laos (Thai border)	400km
Vinh	368km

Getting Around

To/From the Airport Hué is served by Phu Bai airport, once an important American air base, which is 14km south of the city centre. Taxi fares there are typically US$8. Share taxis at the airport cost as little as US$2 – inquire at hotels to find these vehicles. Vietnam Airlines runs its own minibus from its office to the airport a couple of hours before flight time – these cost US$2 per person.

Cyclo & Motorbike A typical scene in Hué is a foreigner walking down the street with two cyclos and a motorbike in hot pursuit, the drivers yelling 'hello cyclo' and 'hello motorbike' and the foreigner yelling 'no, no!'.

Self-drive motorbikes can be hired from Lac Thanh Restaurant and some hotels. A 70cc to 100cc bike goes for US$5 to US$7 per day. For guided motorbike tours see Travel Agents under Information.

Bicycle If it's not raining, the most pleasant way to tour the Hué area is by two-wheeled pedal power. Many hotels rent bicycles for about US$1 per day or US$0.20 per hour.

Taxi Co Do Taxi (☎ 830830) has Japanese air-conditioned vehicles with meters.

Boat Boat rides down the Perfume River are highly recommended. Tours typically take in the tombs of Tu Duc, Thieu Tri, Minh Mang (see the special section 'The Royal Tombs') and Thien Mu Pagoda. Many restaurants and hotels catering to travellers arrange these boat tours. Prices vary, but are generally around US$2 per person. The journey takes about six hours and usually runs from 8 am to 2 pm.

Many sights in the vicinity of Hué, including Thuan An Beach, Thien Mu Pagoda and several of the Royal Tombs, can be reached by river. Rates for chartering a boat depend on size – a 15-person boat can be hired for US$15 per hour while a large boat capable of holding 30 passengers goes for US$25 to US$30 per hour.

If you'd rather not book through hotels and want to do it yourself, look for boats at the dock near Dong Ba Market or Dap Da Dam (just east of Huong Giang Hotel).

AROUND HUÉ

☎ 054

Duong No Village

The peaceful village of Duong No makes for a refreshing little excursion from Hué. The main attraction here is the well-preserved, modest home where Ho Chi Minh lived from 1898 to 1900. Today the house is open as a kind of **museum**. Opening hours are from 7 to 11 am and 1.30 to 5 pm, closed Monday and Tuesday, and entry is free.

Duong No, 6km east of Hué, can easily be reached by rented bicycle or motorbike.

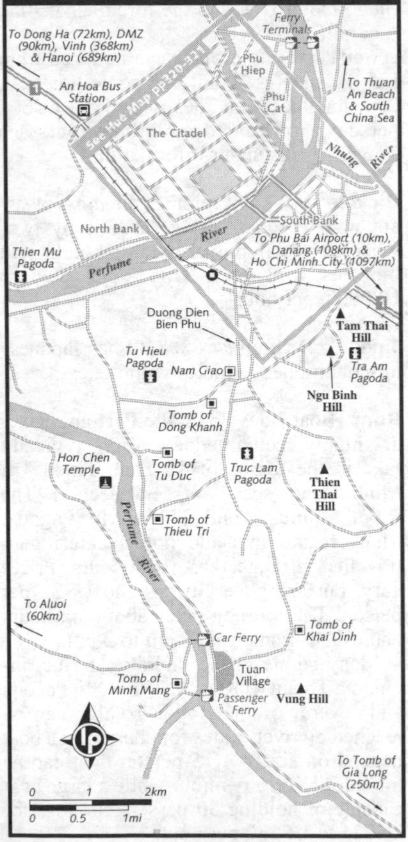

AROUND HUÉ

Thuan An Beach

Thuan An Beach (Bai Tam Thuan An), 13km north-east of Hué, is on a splendid lagoon near the mouth of the Perfume River. In the past this beach earned itself a reputation for hosting some of the most rapacious vendors in Vietnam, but the situation seems to have improved these days.

BACH MA NATIONAL PARK

☎ 054

Bach Ma, a French-era hill station known for its cool weather, is 1200m above sea level, but only 20km from Canh Duong Beach. The French started building villas here in 1930; by 1937 the number of holiday homes had reached 139. It became known as the 'Dalat of Central Vietnam'. Most of the visitors were high-ranking French VIPs. Not surprisingly the Viet Minh tried hard to spoil the holiday – the area saw some heavy fighting in the early 1950s.

Bach Ma has a stunning vista across the coastline near Hai Van Pass, which the Americans used to their advantage – during the war, US troops turned the area into a fortified bunker. The VC did their best to harass the Americans, but couldn't dislodge them. When the war ended, Bach Ma was soon forgotten and the villas abandoned; today, they are in total ruin – only a few stone walls remain, including those of a post office, church and hospital. Between the eerie remains, and memories of the American War, spooky stories abound among locals here who maintain the park is a ghost town (it just may well be!).

In 1991, 22,000 hectares of land were set aside as a nature preserve and designated Bach Ma National Park (Vuon Quoc Gia Bach Ma). Efforts are now fast under way to regenerate patches of forest that were destroyed by clear-cutting and defoliation during the American War.

continued on page 340

THE ROYAL TOMBS

The tombs (lang tam) of the rulers of the Nguyen Dynasty (1802–1945) are extravagant mausoleums constructed along the banks of the Perfume River. Situated between seven and 16km south of Hué (see the Around Hué map), they are open from 6.30 am to 5.30 pm daily (7 am to 5 pm in winter), and the entrance fee for most is 55,000d (US$4).

Although all are unique in structure and design, most of the mausoleums consist of five parts:

- A stele pavilion in which the accomplishments, exploits and virtues of the deceased emperor are engraved on a marble tablet. The testaments were usually written by the dead ruler's successor (though Tu Duc chose to compose his own).
- A temple for the worship of the emperor and empress. In front of each altar, on which the deceased rulers' funerary tablets were placed, is an ornate dais that once held items the emperor used every day: his tea and betel nut trays, cigarette cases etc, most of which have disappeared.
- A sepulchre, usually inside a square or circular enclosure, where the emperor's remains are buried.
- An honour courtyard paved with dark-brown *bat trang* bricks, along the sides of which stand stone elephants, horses, and civil and military mandarins. The civil mandarins wear square hats and hold the symbol of their authority, an ivory sceptre; the military mandarins wear round hats and hold swords.
- A lotus pond surrounded by frangipani and pine trees.

Almost all the tombs, which are in walled compounds, were planned by the Nguyen emperors during their lifetimes. Many of the precious ornaments that once reposited in the tombs disappeared during Vietnam's wars.

Nam Giao

Nam Giao (Temple of Heaven) was once the most important religious site in all Vietnam. It was here that every three years, the emperor solemnly offered elaborate sacrifices to the All-Highest Emperor of the August Heaven (Thuong De). The topmost esplanade, which represents Heaven, is round; the middle terrace, representing Earth, is square, as is the lowest terrace.

After reunification, the provincial government erected – on the site where the sacrificial altar once stood – an obelisk in memory of soldiers killed in the war against the South Vietnamese government and the Americans. There was strong public sentiment in Hué against the obelisk and the Hué Municipal People's Committee finally tore it down in 1993.

Tomb of Dong Khanh

Emperor Dong Khanh, nephew and adopted son of Tu Duc, was placed on the throne by the French after they captured his predecessor, Ham

Nghi. Predictably, Dong Khanh proved docile; he ruled from 1885 until his death three years later.

Dong Khanh's mausoleum, the smallest of the Royal Tombs, was built in 1889. It is about 5km from the city.

Tomb of Tu Duc

The majestic and serene tomb of Emperor Tu Duc is set amid frangipani trees and a grove of pines. Tu Duc designed the exquisitely harmonious tomb, which was constructed between 1864 and 1867, for use both before and after his death. The enormous expense of the tomb and the forced labour used in its construction spawned a coup plot that was discovered and suppressed in 1866.

It is said that Tu Duc, who had the longest reign of any Nguyen monarch (1848–83), lived a life of truly imperial luxury (also see the special section 'Tastes of Vietnam' in the Facts for the Visitor chapter). Though Tu Duc had 104 wives and countless concubines, he had no offspring. One theory has it that he became sterile after contracting smallpox.

Tu Duc's tomb, which is surrounded by a solid octagonal wall, is entered from the east via Vu Khiem Gate. A path paved with bat trang tiles leads to Du Khiem Boat Landing, which is on the shore of Luu

1 Le Thien Anh Tomb
2 Chap Khiem Temple
3 Kien Phuc's Tomb
4 Tu Duc's Tomb
5 Half Moon Lake
6 Stele Pavilion
7 Honour Courtyard
8 Minh Khiem Chamber
9 Luong Khiem Temple
10 On Khiem Palace
11 Hoa Khiem Temple
12 Le Khiem House
13 Phap Khiem House
14 Khiem Cung Gate
15 Du Khiem Boat Landing
16 Xung Khiem Pavilion
17 Harems
18 Deer Raising Garden
19 Chi Khiem Temple
20 Vu Khiem Gate

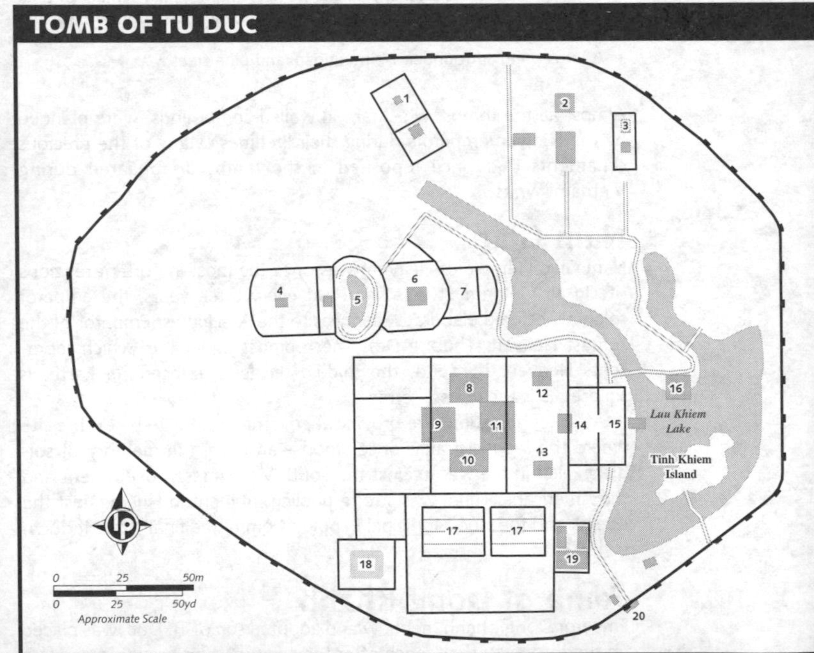

Khiem Lake. From the boat landing, Tinh Khiem Island, where Tu Duc used to hunt small game, is to the right. Across the water to the left is Xung Khiem Pavilion, where the emperor would sit among the columns, with his concubines, composing or reciting poetry. The pavilion, built over the water on piles, was restored in 1986.

Across Khiem Cung Courtyard from Du Khiem Boat Landing are steps leading through Khiem Cung Gate to Hoa Khiem Temple, where Emperor Tu Duc and Empress Hoang Le Thien Anh are worshipped. Before his death, Tu Duc used Hoa Khiem Temple as a palace, staying here during his long visits to the complex.

The temple contains a number of interesting items, including a mirror used by the emperor's concubines; a clock and other objects given to Tu Duc by the French; the emperor and empress's funerary tablets; and two thrones, the larger of which was for the empress (Tu Duc was only 153cm tall).

Minh Khiem Chamber, just to the right behind Hoa Khiem Temple, was originally built for use as a theatre. Tu Duc's mother, the Queen Mother Tu Du, is worshipped in Luong Khiem Temple, directly behind Hoa Khiem Temple.

Back down at the bottom of the stairway, the brick path continues along the shore of the lake to the Honour Courtyard. Across the lake from the courtyard are the tombs of Tu Duc's adopted son, Emperor Kien Phuc (who ruled for only seven months, 1883–84), and Empress Le Thien Anh, Tu Duc's wife. After walking between the honour guard of elephants, horses and diminutive civil and military mandarins (the stone mandarins were made even shorter than the emperor), you reach the masonry Stele Pavilion, which shelters a massive stone tablet weighing about 20 tonnes. It took four years to transport the stele, the largest in Vietnam, from the area of Thanh Hoa, 500km to the north. Tu Duc drafted the inscriptions on the stele himself in order to clarify certain aspects of his reign. He freely admitted that he had made mistakes and chose to name his tomb Khiem, which means 'modest'. The two nearby towers symbolise the emperor's power.

Tu Duc's sepulchre, enclosed by a wall, is on the other side of a half-moon-shaped lake. In fact, Tu Duc was never actually interred here. The site where his remains were buried (along with great treasure) is not known. Because of the danger of grave robbers, some extreme measures were taken to keep the location secret – every one of the 200 servants who buried the king was beheaded.

Tu Duc's tomb is about 6km south of Hué on Van Nien Hill in Duong Xuan Thuong Village. Admission costs US$2.

Tomb of Thieu Tri

Construction of the tomb of Thieu Tri, who ruled from 1841 to 1847, was completed in 1848. It is the only Royal Tomb not enclosed by a wall. Thieu Tri's tomb has a similar layout to Minh Mang's tomb, but is smaller (see the Tomb of Minh Mang in this section). Thieu Tri's tomb is about 7km from Hué.

Tomb of Khai Dinh

The gaudy and crumbling tomb of Emperor Khai Dinh, who ruled from 1916 to 1925, is perhaps symptomatic of the decline of Vietnamese culture during the colonial period. Begun in 1920 and completed in 1931, the grandiose concrete structure is completely unlike Hué's other tombs, being a synthesis of Vietnamese and European elements. Even the stone faces of the mandarin honour guards are endowed with a mixture of Vietnamese and European features.

After climbing 36 steps between four dragon banisters, you reach the first courtyard, flanked by two pavilions. The Honour Courtyard, with its rows of elephants, horses and civil and military mandarins, is 26 steps further up the hillside. In the centre of the courtyard is an octagonal Stele Pavilion.

Up three more flights of stairs is the main building, Thien Dinh, which is divided into three halls. The walls and ceiling are decorated with murals of the 'Four Seasons', the 'Eight Precious Objects', the 'Eight Fairies', and other designs made out of colourful bits of broken porcelain and glass embedded in cement. Under a graceless, 1-tonne, concrete canopy is a gilt bronze statue of Khai Dinh in royal regalia. Behind the statue is the symbol of the sun. The emperor's remains are interred 18m below the statue. Khai Dinh is worshipped in the last hall.

The tomb of Khai Dinh is 10km from Hué in Chau Chu Village.

Tomb of Minh Mang

Perhaps the most majestic of the Royal Tombs is that of Minh Mang, who ruled from 1820 to 1840. Renowned for its architecture, which harmoniously blends into the natural surroundings, the tomb was planned during Minh Mang's lifetime and built between 1841 and 1843 by his successor.

The Honour Courtyard is reached via three gates on the eastern side of the wall: Dai Hong Mon (Great Red Gate; centre), Ta Hong Mon (Left Red Gate; left); and Huu Hong Mon (Right Red Gate; right). Three granite staircases lead from the courtyard to the square Stele Pavilion, Dinh Vuong. Nearby there once stood an altar on which buffaloes, horses and pigs were sacrificed.

Sung An Temple, dedicated to Minh Mang and his empress, is reached via three terraces and Hien Duc Gate. On the other side of the temple, three stone bridges span Trung Minh Ho (Lake of Impeccable Clarity). The central bridge, Cau Trung Dao, constructed of marble, was used only by the emperor. Minh Lau Pavilion stands on the top of three superimposed terraces representing the 'three powers': the heavens, the earth and water. Visible to the left is the Fresh Air Pavilion; the Angling Pavilion is to the right.

From a stone bridge across crescent-shaped Tan Nguyet Lake (Lake of the New Moon), a monumental staircase with dragon banisters leads to the sepulchre, which is surrounded by a circular wall symbolising the sun. In the middle of the enclosure, reached through a bronze door, is the emperor's burial place, a mound of earth covered with mature pine trees and dense shrubbery.

The tomb of Minh Mang, which is on Cam Ke Hill in An Bang Village, is on the west bank of the Perfume River, 12km from Hué. To get there, take a boat across the river from a point about 1.5km west of Khai Dinh's tomb and south of the village. Visitors have reported gross overcharging by the boat operator. Alternatively, walk along the river a bit to the north and you'll find a number of smaller boats willing to take you across for less.

Tomb of Gia Long

Emperor Gia Long, who founded the Nguyen Dynasty in 1802 and ruled until 1819, ordered the construction of his tomb in 1814. According to the royal annals, the emperor himself chose the site after scouting the area on elephant-back. The rarely visited tomb, which is presently in a state of ruin, is 14km south of Hué on the west bank of the Perfume River.

continued from page 334

There are 124 wildlife species living within the boundaries of the park, including tigers and several types of monkey. Thirty-one species of snake have been found (a handful of which are poisonous).

Tragically many animals, like the white ox (*bo tot* in Vietnamese; *bos gaurus* in Latin) and wild buffalo (*trau rung* in Vietnamese; *bubalus bubalus* in Latin) are already extinct. There is still a ray of hope that with enforced protection from poachers, the herds of wild elephant (now on the Lao side of the border) that used to roam the forests here will return to seek the sanctuary of Bach Ma.

A recent victory came with the discovery in 1996 of a previously unknown antelope-like creature called the *sao la (pseudoryx nghetinhensis)*. Footprints and horns have been found in the Bach Ma domain.

As most of the park's resident wildlife is nocturnal, sightings demand a great deal of effort and patience. Feasibility studies are now under way for building viewing towers in the park. Bach Ma is also, however, a birdwatchers' paradise, and plenty of feathered friends can be spotted in the forest. Of the 800-odd species of bird known to inhabit Vietnam, the park is home to some 330.

More than 1150 species of plant life have also been discovered in the park, though this figure is estimated to be just half of the actual number.

About 850 ethnic minority people inhabit the park area. There are also 40 park rangers, including a mobile team that patrols the six stations around the park's periphery, and another at the summit.

It was not until March 1998 that Bach Ma National Park began receiving visitors. Despite its youth, efforts are laudable and park staffers are hard at work protecting the area, working on community development and promoting sustainable eco-tourism.

You currently need a guide to visit the park (☎ 871258, fax 871299); these can be hired for US$12 a day per group at the visitors centre. There are young rangers who speak English well and interesting displays, which includes a huge crate of confiscated hunting and cutting tools, weaponry and the remains of a crashed helicopter.

There are abundant hiking opportunities through beautiful forests on well-groomed nature trails. One track takes you to Hai Vong Dai, a famous viewing point from where you can see the ocean. Other highlights include Do Quyuen Waterfall (a 300m drop) and Tri Sao Waterfall. Near the park entrance is Da Duong Waterfall, and near Km 7 there are good swimming holes on the Pheasant Trail. The park's highest peak – which can be climbed – is 1450m above sea level. From the peak of the Summit Trail there are sweeping 360° views across the stone remains of villas dotted around the nearby hills.

Bach Ma's weather is very foggy and wet from July to February, and the rains that arrive in October and November bring plenty of leeches. Still, these winter months are not out of the question for visiting. The best time to visit Bach Ma is from February to September, particularly between March and June – admittedly a small window of opportunity.

Admission to the park costs US$2.

Places to Stay & Eat

A pleasant ***guesthouse*** *(☎/fax 871330)* rebuilt from one of the old French ruins (actually one of Emperor Bao Dai's) sits in the middle of the park. To reserve accommodation contact the guesthouse directly or call the park headquarters. Rooms with four beds cost US$8 downstairs, or US$10 upstairs with the best views.

The fact that they have restored one villa doesn't mean there will be more. Besides costs (estimated at around US$60,000 to restore one villa), there are concerns about the environment. As one ranger put it, 'We don't want to turn the park into a city in the mountains'. Rather, the park staff are focusing their efforts on constructing camp sites and there is talk of more 'eco-lodges'.

The ***ruins*** also make a good camping ground, though there are proper sites such as the ***camping grounds*** near the park gate and Da Duong Waterfall. Tents can be hired for US$4 (four to six people) and US$5 (1 to 12 people). At the time of writing, rental sleeping bags were still on the rangers' shopping list.

There is a basic ***canteen*** near the gate serving food and those wishing to dine at the ***summit*** can make advance orders to eat here.

Getting There & Away

Bach Ma is 28km west of Lang Co and 45km south-west of Hué. The narrow road into the park was originally built by the French in 1932, was rebuilt in 1993 and recently underwent further upgrading. Today it is sealed nearly all the way to the summit.

The entrance and visitors centre is at Km 3 of the summit road, which starts at the town of Cau Hai on Highway 1. It's another meandering 16km from the gate to the summit, and unless you are willing to walk it, you'll need to hire private transport from the park. Eight-passenger Russian 4WDs rent for around US$20 per day (US$24 overnight) and Japanese 4WDs cost US$24/28 per day/overnight.

SUOI VOI SPRINGS

About 15km north of Lang Co Beach (see its entry following) is the inland turn-off to Elephant Springs (Suoi Voi), a secluded recreation area where one could easily spend a day traipsing through the forest and swimming in cool, crystal-clear streams. It's a pleasant detour and recommended for motorbikers and cyclists who are braving their way north or south along Highway 1.

The main springs, a short walk from the parking area about 1km from the entry gate, feature huge boulders (one in the shape of an elephant's head) and the stunning backdrop of Bach Ma Mountain Range in the distance. Further exploration will lead to less-populated swimming holes, including the Vung Do Pool, about 200m beyond the main area.

Foreign visitors here are scarce (most seem to be rushing in one direction or another along the coast), and on weekdays you may have the whole place to yourself. Weekends, however, are jam-packed with Vietnamese, notably young couples exploring the birds and bees.

To reach the springs from Highway 1, look for a large faded sign reading 'Suoi Voi'. You will see the 19th-century Thua Lau Church just ahead of you after making the turn off to the west. From here follow the dirt road for a few kilometres to the entry gate.

You'll need to buy an entry ticket here (US$0.15), and also pay for parking (bicycles US$0.08, motorbikes US$0.25 and cars US$0.80). Hold onto your ticket as you may be asked to show it more than once. There are some basic ***food stalls*** near the springs, but you're best off bringing a picnic lunch.

About another 15km north of this turn-off is the village of Cau Hai, and the turn-off to reach Bach Ma National Park (see Around Hué earlier in this chapter).

LANG CO BEACH

☎ 054

Lang Co is a pretty, island-like stretch of palm-shaded sand with a crystal-clear, turquoise-blue lagoon on one side and many kilometres of beachfront facing the South China Sea on the other. It's a tranquil spot where lots of travellers make a lunch stop and some spend the night. If you're travelling on one of the 'open tours' along the coast, this makes a fine place to hop off for a night or two (depending, of course, on the season).

The beach here is best enjoyed between April and July. From late August till November rains are frequent, and during the chilly months from December to February it may serve best as just a lunch stop.

There are spectacular views of Lang Co, just north of Hai Van Pass, from both Highway 1 and trains linking Danang and Hué.

Places to Stay & Eat

In a shaded, garden-like compound close to the beach, the large ***Lang Co Hotel*** *(☎ 874426)* run by the government trade union is recommended. The friendly manager, Mr Quang, speaks English well and has plans to run boat trips on the lagoon, as well as tours to Bach Ma National Park. Bicycles rent for just 5000d (US$0.40) a day. Double rooms with fan and shared bath are only US$4, or US$6 with attached bath.

Triples/quads cost US$8/10. Air-con doubles/triples with hot water and private bath cost US$12/15. There is a good beachfront seafood restaurant called ***Hai Duong*** on site.

The Thanh Tam Seaside Resort (☎ 874456), is about one kilometre north of Lang Co Hotel. Beachfront rooms cost US$10 to US$18. The outdoor terrace restaurant used to be good, but at the time of writing we received reports suggesting standards had sharply declined, with even running water lacking. Another guest reported dodgy happenings after dark, advising travellers to limit their visits here to lunch time.

At the time of writing there was a new resort under construction a few hundred metres north of here.

Getting There & Away

Train Lang Co train station, served by non-express trains, is 3km from the beach. Finding someone to take you from the train station to the beach by motorbike shouldn't be difficult.

Car & Motorbike Lang Co is 35km north of Danang over an extremely mountainous section of Highway 1.

DANANG

☎ 0511 • pop 1,100,000

Back in the heady days of the American War, Danang was often referred to as the 'Saigon of the North'. This cliche held a note of both praise and condemnation – like its big sister to the south, Danang was notable for its booming economy, fine restaurants, busy traffic and glittering shops. 'Entertaining the military' was also a profitable business – bars and prostitution were major service industries. As in Saigon, corruption also ran rampant.

Liberation arrived in 1975, promptly putting a sizeable dent in the nightlife. Even today, Danang is a pretty laid-back city, though Vietnam's recent economic liberalisation has helped Danang regain some of its former glory.

Danang is Vietnam's fourth-largest city. It also marks the northern limits of Vietnam's tropical zone and boasts a pleasant year-round climate (nearby Hué is much colder in winter).

Despite the bad rap this place gets from some, Danang is a pleasant enough place to stop off. It is far more relaxed than Ho Chi Minh City or Hanoi, and has some rewarding sights both within the town and the surrounding areas.

History

Danang, known under the French as Tourane, succeeded Hoi An as the most important port in central Vietnam during the 19th century.

In late March 1975, Danang, the second-largest city in South Vietnam, was the scene of utter chaos. Saigon government forces were ordered to abandon Hué, while Quang Ngai had fallen to the Communists, cutting South Vietnam in two. Desperate civilians tried to flee the city, as soldiers of the disintegrating South Vietnamese army engaged in an orgy of looting, pillage and rape. On 29 March 1975, two truckloads of Communist guerrillas, more than half of them women, drove into what had been the most heavily defended city in South Vietnam and, without firing a shot, declared Danang 'liberated'.

Almost the only fighting that took place as Danang fell was between South Vietnamese soldiers and civilians battling for space on flights and ships out of the city. On 27 March, the president of World Airways, Ed Daly, ignoring explicit government orders, sent two 727s from Saigon to Danang to evacuate refugees. When the first plane landed, about a thousand desperate and panicked people mobbed the tarmac. Soldiers fired assault rifles at each other and at the plane as they tried to shove their way through the rear door. As the aircraft taxied down the runway trying to take off, people climbed up into the landing-gear wells and someone threw a hand grenade, damaging the right wing.

Those who managed to fight their way aboard, kicking and punching aside anyone in their way, included over 200 soldiers, mostly members of the elite Black Panthers company. The only civilians on board were two women and one baby – and the baby was only there because it had been thrown aboard by its desperate mother, who was left on the tarmac. Several of the stowaways in the wheel wells couldn't hold on and, as the plane flew southward, TV cameras on the second 727 filmed them falling into the South China Sea.

Orientation

Danang is on the western bank of the Han River. The eastern bank is accessible via new Song Han Bridge or Nguyen Van Troi Bridge further south. It is a long, thin peninsula, at the northern tip of which is Nui Son Tra, named 'Monkey Mountain' by the Americans. Though it has long been a closed military area, local authorities are considering opening the area to tourism. China Beach and the Marble Mountains lie south of the city and Hai Van Pass overlooks it from the north.

Information

Travel Agencies Almost everything can be arranged at local travel agencies, including car rentals, boat trips, visa extensions and a trekking journey to the nearby Ba Na Hill Station, or further afield in Bach Ma National Park.

Dana Tours (☎ 822516, fax 824023, ⓔ danamarle@dng.vnn.vn) at 95 Đ Hung Vuong, Danang's main tour agency, has an enlightened attitude relative to most state-run tour companies, and it's a good place to ask about tours.

Tan Hong Tour Agency (☎ 826242, fax 829350), 98 Đ Phan Chu Chinh, is another good place for booking plane tickets, getting Laos visas and the like.

An Phu Tourist (☎ 818366, fax 864011) is located at 147 Đ Le Loi.

Hoa Binh Tourist (☎ 827183) at 316 Đ Hoang Dieu and on Đ Tran Phu (☎ 830976), just beside Vietnam Airlines.

Money Vietcombank is at 140 Đ Le Loi near the corner of Đ Hai Phong. If you're staying in the northern end of town, the VID Public Bank at 2 Đ Tran Phu can change travellers cheques (no cash advances yet).

Another place to change money and get cash advances is the Danang Commercial Joint Stock Bank, just across Đ Hung Vuong from Dana Tours.

Email & Internet Access There is Net access in Danang for around 600d to 1000d a minute. Places to check email include the Bamboo Bar (see Entertainment) and Christie's Restaurant (see Places to Eat). Christie's usually has the latest travel scoop, and Mark, the Australian proprietor, is full of useful travel advice.

Foreign Consulates One particularly useful consulate is the Lao consulate, 12 Đ Tran Qui Cap, at the northern end of town. Opening hours are Monday to Friday from 8 to 11.30 am and 2 to 4.30 pm.

Medical Services Danang's most advanced medical facility is Hospital C (Benh Vien C; ☎ 822480) at 35 Đ Hai Phong.

Another respectable place is the Vinh Toan Hospital (☎ 892920) on Đ Le Duan.

Places of Worship

Danang Cathedral Danang Cathedral (Chinh Toa Da Nang), known to locals as Con Ga Church (Rooster Church) because of the weathercock on top of the steeple, was built for the city's French residents in 1923. Today, it serves a Catholic community of 4000. The cathedral's architecture is well worth a look, as are the medieval-style stained-glass windows of various saints.

Next door to the cathedral are the offices of the diocese of Danang and the St Paul Convent. About 100 nuns – who wear white habits in summer and black habits in winter – divide their time between here and another convent building across the Han River.

Danang Cathedral is on Đ Tran Phu across from the Green Bamboo 2 Hotel. Masses are held from Monday to Saturday at 5 am and 5 pm, and on Sunday at 5 and 6.30 am and 4.30 pm.

Caodai Temple The Caodai Temple (Thanh That Cao Dai), built in 1956, is the largest such structure outside the sect's headquarters in Tay Ninh (see the Around Ho Chi Minh City chapter). There are

DANANG

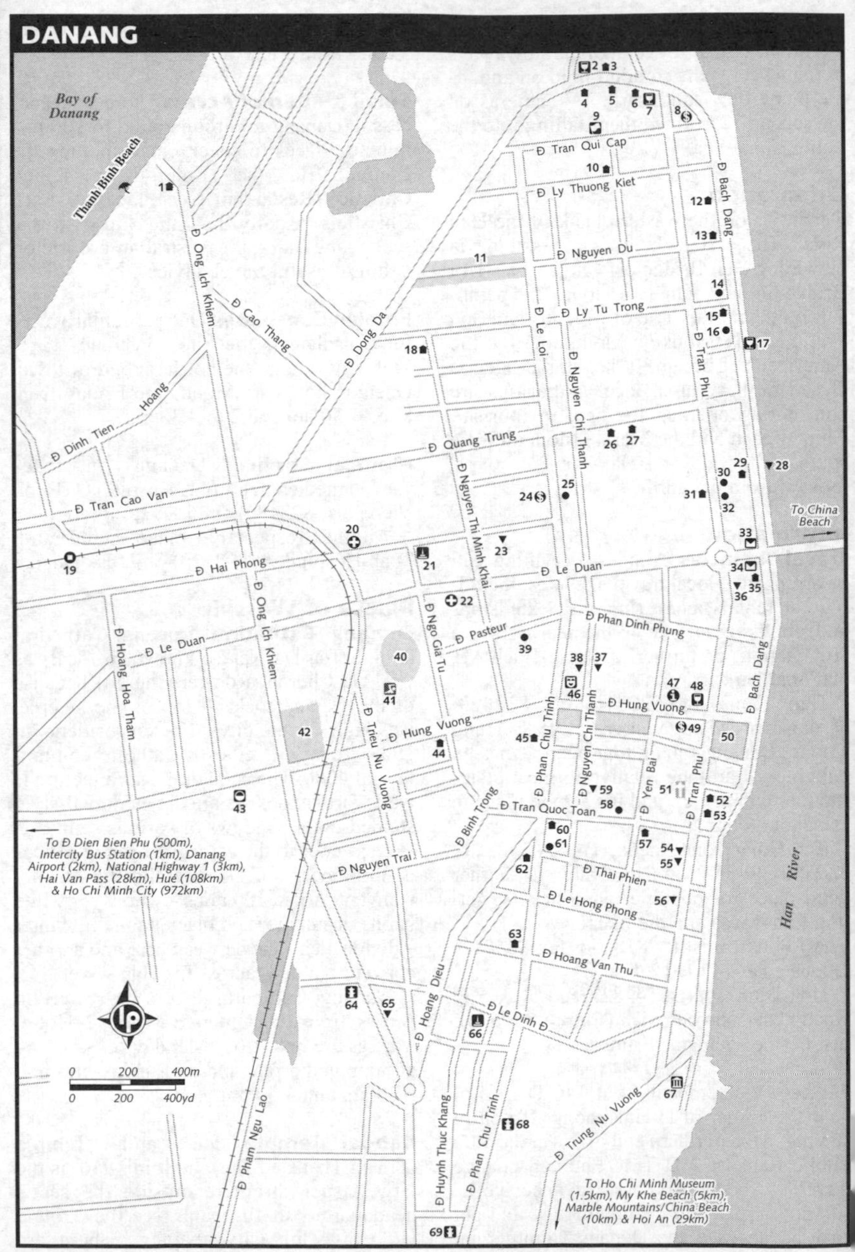

Bay of Danang
Thanh Binh Beach
Đ Tran Qui Cap
Đ Ly Thuong Kiet
Đ Bach Dang
Đ Nguyen Du
Đ Ong Ich Khiem
Đ Cao Thang
Đ Dong Da
Đ Ly Tu Trong
Đ Le Loi
Đ Nguyen Chi Thanh
Đ Tran Phu
Đ Dinh Tien Hoang
Đ Quang Trung
Đ Nguyen Thi Minh Khai
Đ Tran Cao Van
To China Beach
Đ Hai Phong
Đ Le Duan
Đ Phan Dinh Phung
Đ Ngo Gia Tu
Đ Pasteur
Đ Hoang Hoa Tham
Đ Hung Vuong
Đ Phan Chu Trinh
Đ Trieu Nu Vuong
Đ Yen Bai
Đ Tran Quoc Toan
Đ Binh Trong
To Đ Dien Bien Phu (500m), Intercity Bus Station (1km), Danang Airport (2km), National Highway 1 (3km), Hai Van Pass (28km), Hué (108km) & Ho Chi Minh City (972km)
Đ Nguyen Trai
Đ Thai Phien
Đ Le Hong Phong
Han River
Đ Hoang Van Thu
Đ Hoang Dieu
Đ Le Dinh Đ
0 200 400m
0 200 400yd
Đ Trung Nu Vuong
Đ Huynh Thuc Khang
Đ Phan Chu Trinh
Đ Pham Ngu Lao
To Ho Chi Minh Museum (1.5km), My Khe Beach (5km), Marble Mountains/China Beach (10km) & Hoi An (29km)

DANANG

PLACES TO STAY
1 Thanh Binh Guesthouse
3 Harmony Hotel
4 Saigon Tourane Hotel
5 Danang Hotel (Old Wing)
6 Danang Hotel (New Wing)
10 Thu Bon Hotel
12 Thuan An Hotel
13 Elegant Hotel
15 Song Han Hotel
18 Hai Van Hotel
26 Royal Hotel
27 Ami Hotel
29 Bach Dang Hotel
31 Binh Duong Mini-Hotel
35 Riverside Hotel
44 Hoa Sen Hotel
45 Thanh Thanh Hotel
52 Daesco Hotel
53 Green Bamboo 2 Hotel
57 Dai A Hotel
60 Orient Hotel
62 Pacific Hotel
63 Green Bamboo 1 Hotel

PLACES TO EAT
23 My Quang Restaurant
28 Hanakim Dinh Restaurant
36 Com Chay Nga My Vegetarian Restaurant
37 Hong Ngoc Restaurant
38 Hoang Ngoc Restaurant
54 Tiem An Binh Dan Restaurant
55 Tu Do Restaurant; Kim Do Restaurant
56 Tien Hung
59 Phu Lu Restaurant
65 Huong Thien Vegetarian Restaurant

OTHER
2 Cafe Lien
7 Free Time Bar
8 VID Public Bank
9 Lao Consulate
11 Market
14 Linh Cafe
16 Courthouse
17 Bamboo Bar; Mien Trung & Thoi Dan Restaurants
19 Danang Train Station
20 Hospital C
21 Caodai Temple
22 Vinh Toan Hospital
24 Vietcombank
25 An Phu Tourist
30 Hoa Binh Tourist
32 Vietnam & Pacific Airlines Booking Office
33 Post Office (Domestic)
34 Post Office (International)
39 East Meets West Foundation
40 Danang Stadium
41 Swimming Pool
42 Con Market
43 Short-Haul Pickup Truck Station
46 Municipal Theatre
47 Dana Tours
48 The Cool Spot Bar; Christie's Restaurant
49 Danang Commercial Joint Stock Bank
50 Han Market
51 Danang Cathedral
58 Tan Hong Tour Agency
61 Bookshop
64 Phap Lam Pagoda
66 Cao Dai Temple
67 Cham Museum
68 Tam Bao Pagoda
69 Pho Da Pagoda

50,000 Caodais in Quang Nam and Danang Provinces – 20,000 in Danang itself. The temple is across the street from Hospital C on Đ Hai Phong. As with all Caodai temples, prayers are held four times a day at 6 am, noon, 6 pm and midnight.

The left-hand gate to the complex, marked 'Nu Phai', is for women; the right-hand gate, marked 'Nam Phai', is for men. The doors to the sanctuary are also segregated: women to the left, men to the right and priests of either sex through the central door. Behind the main altar sits an enormous globe with the 'divine eye', symbol of Caodaism, on it.

A sign reading 'Van Giao Nhat Ly', which means 'All religions have the same reason', hangs from the ceiling in front of the altar. Behind the gilded letters is a picture of the founders of five of the world's great religions. From left to right they are: Mohammed; Laotse (wearing blue robes cut in the style of the Greek Orthodox); Jesus (portrayed as he is in French icons); Buddha (who has a distinctly South-East Asian appearance); and Confucius (looking as Chinese as could be).

Portraits of early Caodai leaders, dressed in turbans and white robes, are displayed in the building behind the main sanctuary. Ngo Van Chieu, founder of Caodaism, is shown standing wearing a pointed white turban and a long white robe with blue markings.

Phap Lam Pagoda Phap Lam Pagoda (Chua Phap Lam, also known as Chua Tinh Hoi) is opposite 373 Đ Ong Ich Khiem. Built in 1936, this pagoda has a brass statue of Dia Tang, the King of Hell, near the entrance. Several monks live here.

Tam Bao Pagoda The main building of Tam Bao Pagoda (Chua Tam Bao) at 253 Đ Phan Chu Trinh is topped with a five-tiered tower. Only a few monks live at this large pagoda, which was built in 1953.

Pho Da Pagoda This pagoda (also called Pho Da Tu), across from 293 Đ Phan Chu

Trinh, was built in 1923 in a traditional architectural configuration. Today, about 40 monks, most of them young, live and study here. Local lay people and their children participate actively in the pagoda's lively religious life.

Ho Chi Minh Museum

The Ho Chi Minh Museum (Bao Tang Ho Chi Minh) has three sections: a museum of military history in front of which American, Soviet and Chinese weaponry is displayed; a replica of Ho Chi Minh's house in Hanoi (complete with a small lake); and, across the pond from the house, a museum about Uncle Ho.

The replica house is a must-see for anyone who won't make it to the bona fide 'Ho House' in Hanoi (or to one of the other many reproductions scattered throughout the country).

Of all the photos of Ho Chi Minh you'll see, the one at this museum with Ho in red against a white background bears a most uncanny resemblance to America's famous 'Uncle Co' – the great patriot Colonel Sanders himself – and certainly brings out some cravings for KFC.

The museum, on Đ Nguyen Van Troi 250m west of Đ Nui Thanh (see the Around Danang map), is open Tuesday to Sunday from 7 to 11 am and 1 to 4.30 pm.

Boat Trips

The Thuy Tu River north of Danang (near Hai Van Pass) has clean water and is good for boating. Some boats leave from the village of Nam O, which is famous for *nuoc mam* (fish sauce).

There is another local speciality here called *goi ca*, which is fresh, raw fish fillets marinaded in a special sauce and coated in a spicy powder – something like Vietnamese sushi. There are also sandy river beaches here that are fine for swimming. You might also ask about night cruises on the Han River in Danang.

The Bamboo Bar (see Entertainment) can organise boat trips to islands and beaches, as well as **fishing trips**. The cost for five people, including lunch, is about US$30. Christie's Restaurant (see Places to Eat) can also arrange trips on request.

Places to Stay

The following listings are clustered around central Danang. For information on beachside accommodation, see the following Around Danang section.

Places to Stay – Budget

Budget travellers usually stay in hotels at the northern tip of the Danang Peninsula. The adjacent cargo shipping terminal is a bit of an eyesore, but it's quieter than the traffic-clogged city centre about 2km to the south.

The ***Danang Hotel – Old Wing*** *(☎ 823258, 3 Đ Dong Da)* is a total dump, but still popular with backpackers. Spartan fan/air-con rooms cost US$5/8. The building was constructed in the late 1960s to house American military personnel and it hasn't seen much improvement since. Things are slightly better at the adjacent ***Danang Hotel – New Wing*** *(☎ 834662, fax 823431)*, which is plush, with rooms from US$16 to US$40.

Thuan An Hotel *(☎ 820527, Đ Bach Dang)* is a good riverfront mini-hotel with fan singles/doubles for US$5/6, or US$12 to US$16 with air-con.

The ***Harmony Hotel*** *(☎ 829146, fax 829145, 20 Đ Dong Da)* is decent value with large air-con single/double/triples for US$10/12/15.

Thanh Thanh Hotel *(☎ 821230, fax 829886, 50 Đ Phan Chu Trinh)* is an OK place, but the seedy karaoke/massage scene puts many people off. Fan rooms cost US$8 to US$10, or US$14 to US$30 with air-con.

The ***Pacific Hotel*** *(☎ 822137, fax 822921, 92 Đ Phan Chu Trinh)* is across the street from the much pricier Orient Hotel. It's an old place, but not bad. Twins cost US$25 to US$40.

Dai A Hotel *(☎ 827532, fax 825760, 27 Đ Yen Bai)* is a relatively new, all air-con place. Rooms cost US$12 to US$45.

Hai Van Hotel *(☎ 821300, fax 821300, 2 Đ Nguyen Thi Minh Khai)* is an old place, with large rooms from US$8 to US$20.

continued on page 354

KINGDOM OF CHAMPA

The kingdom of Champa flourished from the 2nd to the 15th centuries. It first appeared around present-day Danang and later spread south to what is now Nha Trang and Phan Rang. Champa became Indianised through commercial relations with India: the Chams adopted Hinduism, employed Sanskrit as a sacred language and borrowed from Indian art.

The Chams, who lacked enough land for agriculture along the mountainous coast, were semi-piratic and conducted attacks on passing trading ships. As a result, they were in a constant state of war with the Vietnamese to the north and the Khmers to the west. The Chams successfully threw off Khmer rule in the 12th century, but were entirely absorbed by Vietnam in the 17th century.

The Chams are best known for the many brick sanctuaries (Cham towers) they constructed throughout the south. The greatest collection of Cham art is in the Cham Museum in Danang (see the boxed text titled 'Cham Museum' in this chapter). The major Cham site is at My Son (near Danang), and other Cham ruins can be found in Nha Trang and Phan Rang-Thap Cham (see the South-Central Coast chapter). These more-southern Cham ruins belonged to a slightly different group of Chams who followed Muslim doctrines.

My Son

One of the most stunning sights in the Hoi An area is My Son, Vietnam's most important Cham site, and as of 2000 a UNESCO World Heritage Site. During the centuries when Tra Kieu (then known as Simhapura) served as the political capital of Champa, My Son was the site of the most important Cham intellectual and religious centre, and also may have served as a burial place for Cham monarchs. My Son is considered to be Champa's counterpart to the grand cities of South-East Asia's other Indian-influenced civilisations: Angkor (Cambodia), Bagan (Myanmar), Ayuthaya (Thailand) and Borobudur (Java).

The monuments are set in a verdant valley surrounded by hills and overlooked by massive Cat's Tooth Mountain (Hon Quap). Clear streams (perfect for a dip) run between the structures and past nearby coffee plantations.

My Son became a religious centre under King Bhadravarman in the late 4th century and was occupied until the 13th century – the longest period of development of any monument in South-East Asia (by comparison, Angkor's period of development lasted only three centuries, as did that of Bagan). Most of the temples were dedicated to Cham kings associated with divinities, especially Shiva, who was regarded as the founder and protector of Champa's dynasties.

Champa's contact with Java was extensive. Cham scholars were sent to Java to study and there was a great deal of commerce between the two empires – Cham pottery has been found on Java and, in the 12th century, the Cham king wed a Javanese woman.

Varning

uring the American Var, the hills and valleys ound My Son were extensively mined. During ine-clearing operations 1977, six Vietnamese ppers were killed here. day, grazing cows are metimes blown up, so the years pass and the or beasts clear the ines one by one, the ls around here are becoming less and less safe. All the same, it's commended that you not stray from the arked paths.

Because some of the ornamentation work at My Son was never finished, archaeologists know that the Chams first built their structures and only then carved decorations into the brickwork. Researchers have yet to figure out for certain how the Chams managed to get the baked bricks to stick together. According to one theory, they used a paste prepared with a botanical oil indigenous to central Vietnam. During one period in their history, the summits of some of the towers were covered with a layer of gold.

During the American War, the My Son region was completely devastated and depopulated in extended bitter fighting. Finding it to be a convenient staging ground, VC guerrillas used My Son as a base; in response the Americans bombed the monuments. Traces of 68 structures have been found, of which 25 survived repeated pillaging in previous centuries

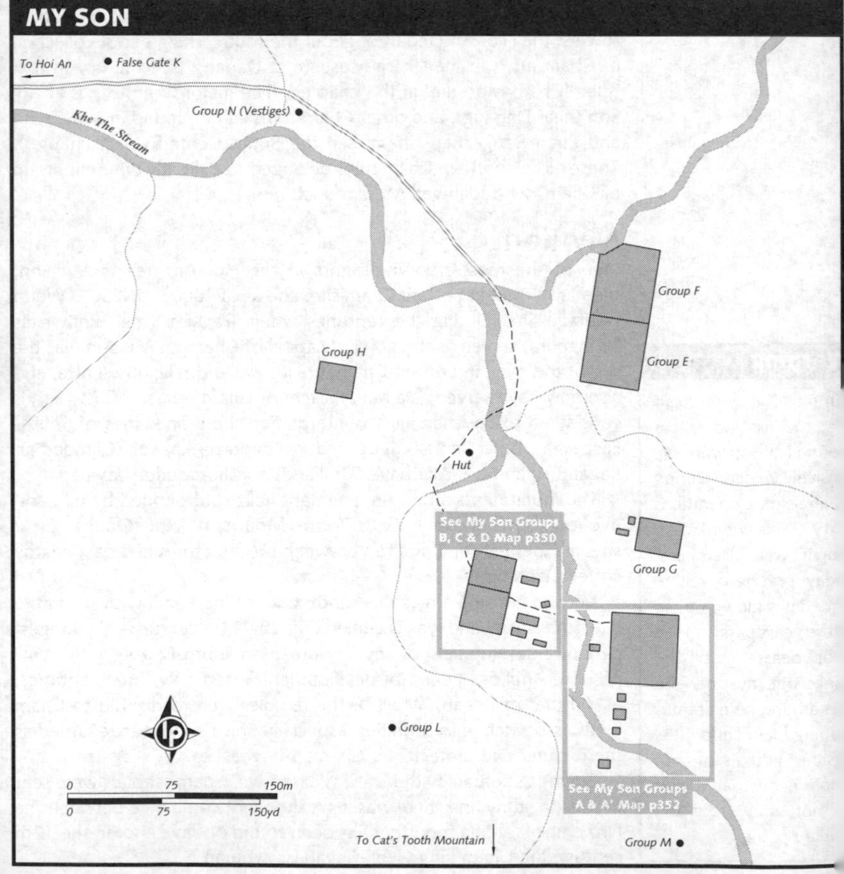

by the Chinese, Khmer and Vietnamese. The American bombings spared about 20 of these, some of which sustained extensive damage. Today, Vietnamese authorities are attempting to restore the remaining sites.

Elements of Cham civilisation can still be seen in the life of the people of Quang Nam, Danang and Quang Ngai Provinces, whose forebears assimilated many Cham innovations into their daily lives. These include techniques for pottery making, fishing, sugar production, rice farming, irrigation, silk production and construction.

Entry costs 50,000d (US$4), which includes local transport from the parking area to the sites (about 1km). On our last visit, staff at the official ticket office tried to resell us tickets that had already been hole-punched, an obvious ploy to pocket the money. Apparently UNSECO officials are not policing the situation, but we can only hope that My Son's recent World Heritage recognition will lead to less of this sort of riff-raff. Ditto for the low-level of security at the parking areas.

By departing from Hoi An at about 5 am, you will arrive to wake up the gods (and the guards) for the sunrise and could be leaving just as the tour groups reach the area! Remember that it is strictly forbidden to climb on the ancient structures.

The Site

Archaeologists have divided My Son's monuments into 10 main groups, lettered A, A', B, C, D, E, F, G, H and K. Each structure has been given a name consisting of a letter followed by a number.

The first structure you encounter along the trail is the false gate K, which dates from the 11th century. Between K and the other groups is a coffee plantation begun in 1986; peanuts and beans are also grown among the bushes.

Group B The main sanctuary (kalan), **B1**, was dedicated to Bhadresvara, which is a contraction of the name of King Bhadravarman, who built the first temple at My Son, combined with '-esvara,' which means Shiva. The first building on this site was erected in the 4th century, destroyed in the 6th century and rebuilt in the 7th century. Only the 11th-century base, made of large sandstone blocks, remains; the brickwork walls have disappeared. The niches in the wall were used to hold lamps (Cham sanctuaries had no windows). The linga (stylised phallus representing Shiva) inside was discovered during excavations in 1985, 1m below its current position.

B5, built in the 10th century, was used for storing sacred books and precious ritual objects (some made of gold), which were used in ceremonies performed in B1. The boat-shaped roof (the 'bow' and 'stern' have fallen off) shows the influence of Malayo-Polynesian architecture. Unlike the sanctuaries, this building has windows. The fine Cham masonry inside is original. Over the window on the wall facing B4 is a brick bas-relief of two elephants under a tree with two birds in it.

The ornamentation on the exterior walls of **B4** is an excellent example of a Cham decorative style, typical of the 9th century, said to resemble worms. This style is unlike anything found in other South-East Asian cultures.

B3 has an Indian-influenced pyramidal roof typical of Cham towers. Inside **B6** is a bath-shaped basin for keeping sacred water that was poured over the linga in B1; this is the only known example of Cham basin.

B2 is a gate. Around the perimeter of Group B are small temples (B7–B13) dedicated to the gods of the directions of the compass *(dikpalaka)*.

Group C The 8th-century **C1** was used to worship Shiva portrayed in human form (rather than in the form of a linga, as in B1). Inside is an altar where a statue of Shiva, now in the Cham Museum in Danang, used to stand. On either side of the stone doorway you can see, bored into the lintel and the floor, the holes in which two wooden doors once swung. Note the motifs, characteristic of the 8th century, carved into the brickwork of the exterior walls.

Group D Building D1, once a mandapa (meditation hall), is now used as a storeroom. It is slated to become a small museum of Cham sculpture. Objects to be displayed include a large panel of Shiva dancing on

MY SON GROUPS B, C & D

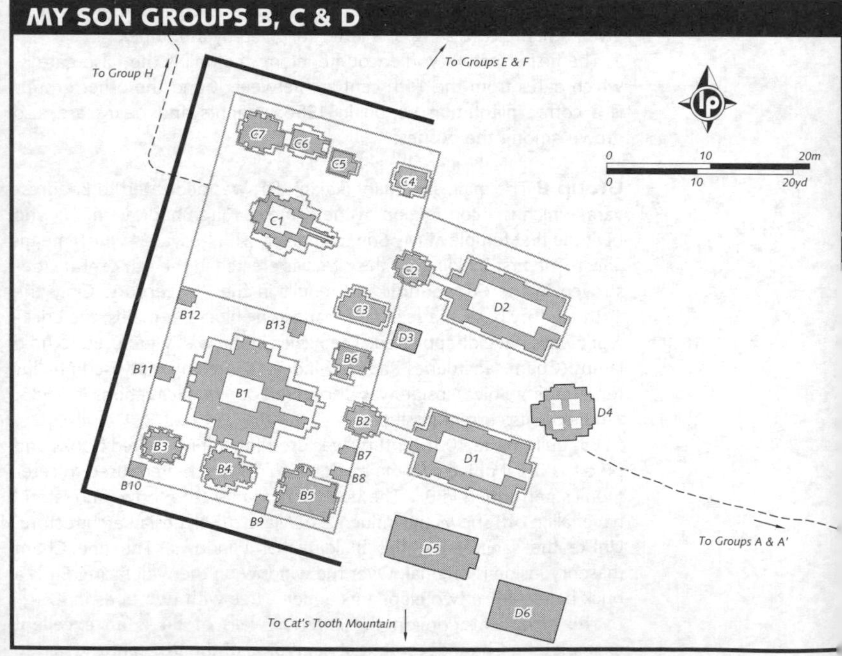

a platform above the bull Nandin: to Shiva's left is Skanda (under a tree), his son Uma, his wife and a worshipper; to Shiva's right is a dancing saint and two musicians under a tree, one with two drums, the other with a flute. The display will also include a finely carved lion – symbol of the power of the king (the lion was believed to be an incarnation of Vishnu and the protector of kings) – whose style belies Javanese influence.

Group A The path from groups B, C and D to Group A leads eastward from near D4.

Group A was almost completely destroyed by US attacks. According to locals, massive A1, considered the most important monument at My Son, remained impervious to aerial bombing and was finally finished off by a helicopter-borne sapper team. All that remains today is a pile of collapsed brick walls. After the destruction of A1, Philippe Stern, an expert on Cham art and curator of the Guimet Museum in Paris, wrote a letter of protest to President Nixon, who ordered US forces to continue killing the VC, but not to do any further damage to Cham monuments.

A1 was the only Cham sanctuary with two doors. One faced the east, direction of the Hindu gods; the other faced west towards groups B, C and D and the spirits of the ancestor-kings that may have been buried there. Inside A1 is a stone altar pieced together in 1988. Among the ruins, some of the brilliant brickwork, which is of a style typical of the 10th century, is still visible. At the base of A1 on the side facing A10 (decorated in 9th-century style) is a carving of a worshipping figure, flanked by round columns, with a Javanese kala-makara (sea-monster god) above. There may be some connection between the presence of this Javanese motif and the studies in Java of a great 10th-century Cham scholar. There are plans to partially restore A1 and A10 as soon as possible.

Other Groups Dating from the 8th century, **Group A'** is at present overgrown and inaccessible. **Group E** was built during the 8th to 11th centuries, while **Group F** dates from the 8th century. **Group G**, which has been damaged by time rather than war, dates from the 12th century. There are long-term plans to restore these monuments.

Tra Kieu (Simhapura)

Tra Kieu, formerly called Simhapura (Lion Citadel), was the first capital city of Champa, serving in that capacity from the 4th through to the 8th centuries. Today, nothing remains of the ancient city except the rectangular ramparts. A large number of artefacts, including some of the finest carvings in the Cham Museum in Danang, were found here.

You can get a good view of the city's outlines from the Mountain Church (Nha Tho Nui), on the top of Buu Chau Hill in Tra Kieu. This modern, open-air structure was built in 1970 to replace an earlier church destroyed by time and war. A Cham tower once stood on this spot.

The Mountain Church is 6.5km from Highway 1 and 19.5km from the beginning of the footpath to My Son. Within Tra Kieu, it is 200m from the morning market (Cho Tra Kieu) and 550m from Tra Kieu Church.

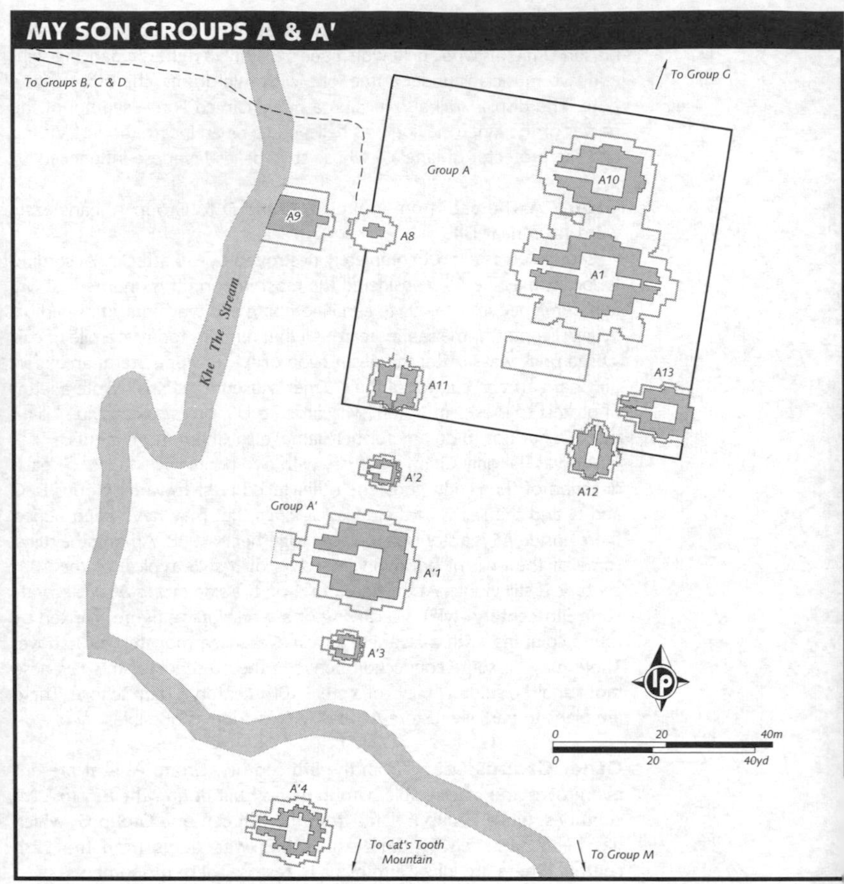

Tra Kieu Church

Tra Kieu Church (Dia So Tra Kieu), which serves the town's Catholic population of 3000, was built a century ago (although the border of the semicircular patio, made of upturned artillery shells, was added later). A priest here, interested in Cham civilisation, has amassed a collection of Cham artefacts found by local people. A 2nd-floor room in the building to the right of the church opened as a museum in 1990. The round ceramic objects with faces on them, which date from the 8th to the 10th century, were affixed to the ends of tile roofs. The face is of Kala, the God of Time. Tra Kieu Church is 7km from Highway 1 and 19km from the trail to My Son. It is 150m down an alley opposite the town's Clinic of Western Medicine (Quay Thuoc Tay Y), 350m from the morning market and 550m from the Mountain Church.

Dong Duong (Indrapura)

The Cham religious centre of Dong Duong (formerly called Indrapura) was the site of an important Mahayana Buddhist monastery, the Monastery of Lakshmindra-Lokeshvara, founded in 875 AD. Dong Duong also served as the capital of Champa from 860 to 986 AD, until the capital was transferred to Cha Ban (near Qui Nhon). Tragically, as a result of the devastation wrought by the French and American wars, only part of the gate to Dong Duong remains.

Places to Stay

The nearest hotels are in Hoi An and Danang.

Getting There & Away

Minibus Numerous hotels in Hoi An can book a day trip to My Son that includes a stop-off at Tra Kieu. At US$6 per person, you could hardly do it cheaper unless you walked. The minibuses depart from Hoi An at 8 am and return at 2 pm.

Honda Om It's possible to get to the sites by rented motorbike. We have had numerous complaints from travellers that their rented motorbikes were vandalised by the locals at My Son, who then asked about US$25 to repair the damage they caused. The police are supposed to have cracked down on this, but we suggest caution nonetheless. It may be better to have somebody else drive you on their motorbike and ask them to wait for you. Dong Duong is 21km from My Son as the crow flies and 55km from Danang.

continued from page 346

Some of the more well-heeled backpackers like the ***Ami Hotel*** *(☎ 824494, fax 825532, 7 Đ Quang Trung)*, which is owned by the local petroleum company. It has fan rooms for US$10, or rooms with air-con and satellite TV from US$12 to US$25.

The all air-con ***Binh Duong Mini-Hotel*** *(☎ 821930, fax 827666, 30–32 Đ Tran Phu)* is a standard mini-hotel known for its friendly service. It has rooms for US$10 to US$35.

The huge ***Thanh Binh Guesthouse*** *(☎ 823014, 5 Đ Ong Ich Khiem)* is right on Thanh Binh Beach, known for its crowds, litter and polluted water. This place is reserved for Vietnamese workers on organised union vacations, but it rents rooms to foreigners for US$6 to US$20 – few take advantage of the offer.

Places to Stay – Mid-Range & Top End

The ***Hoa Sen Hotel*** *(☎ 824505, fax 829001, 101–105 Đ Hung Vuong)* is relatively close to the train station and just a few blocks from Con Market (Cho Con). It's a newer mini-hotel, with rooms from US$12 to US$40. The lobby walls are decorated with provocative quotations.

Thu Bon Hotel *(☎ 821101, fax 822854, 10 Đ Ly Thuong Kiet)* is an older place, but not a bad place to stay. The price is OK for this standard of accommodation – rooms with air-con and satellite TV cost US$22 to US$28, including breakfast.

The ***Elegant Hotel*** *(☎ 892893, fax 835179, ⓔ elegant@dng.vnn.vn, 22A Đ Bach Dang)* lives up to its name. Well-kept rooms with satellite TV cost US$35 to US$140, including breakfast. There's a good in-house restaurant and 24-hour room service.

The ***Song Han Hotel*** *(☎ 822540, fax 821109, 36 Đ Bach Dang)* is right on the Han River and offers good views. This place has fairly basic rooms with satellite TV renting from US$16 to US$55. Massage service is available here.

Close to the top of top-end accommodation in Danang is the stylish ***Saigon Tourane Hotel*** *(☎ 821021, fax 895285, ⓔ sgtouran@dng.vnn.vn, 14A Đ Tran Qui Cap – 5 Đ Dong Da)*. Well-appointed rooms cost US$60 to US$150, including tax, service and breakfast. There is a pleasant rooftop terrace restaurant overlooking the river.

The three-star ***Royal Hotel*** *(☎ 823295, fax 827279, ⓔ royalhotel@dng.vnn.vn, 17 Đ Quang Trung)* is a stylish place featuring an in-house Japanese restaurant serving *ramen* (noodle soup). Twins with all the trimmings cost from US$45, or US$65 for a suite.

The ***Bach Dang Hotel*** *(☎ 823649, fax 821659, 50 Đ Bach Dang)* is a large place that boasts river views from upper-floor rooms. Rates, on the pricey side considering the age of this place, are US$18 to US$50.

Also offering river views is the ***Riverside Hotel*** *(Khach San Tien Sa; ☎ 832591, fax 832593, 68 Đ Bach Dang)*. Rooms cost US$55 to US$120, but 30% discounts are standard.

The new ***Green Bamboo 2 Hotel*** *(☎ 822722, fax 824165, ⓔ bamboogreen@dng.vnn.vn, 177 Đ Tran Phu)* is conveniently located near the centre of town, across the road from Danang Cathedral. Singles/doubles cost US$35/40. The ***Green Bamboo 1 Hotel*** *(☎ 822996, fax 822998, 158 Đ Phan Chu Trinh)* is also new and charges around the same.

The ***Orient Hotel*** *(Khach San Phuong Dong; ☎ 822185, fax 822854, ⓔ phdong@dng.vnn.vn, 97 Đ Phan Chu Trinh)* features an elegant, wood-panelled lobby and slightly over-priced rooms. Rooms with satellite TV start from US$35/45; rates include breakfast.

The ***Daesco Hotel*** *(☎ 892807, 892988, ⓔ daescohotel@dng.vnn.vn, 155 Đ Tran Phu)* is definitely a business travellers' place. Facilities include a fitness centre with sauna/steam bath, bar and restaurant. Rates are US$35 to US$70.

Places to Eat

Christie's Restaurant *(☎ 824040, fax 829323/826645, ⓔ christies@hotmail.com, 112 Đ Tran Phu)* is a pleasant 2nd-storey cafe-restaurant run by an Australian expat named Mark. They dish up good burgers, pizzas and pasta, as well as Japanese and Vietnamese food. There is a book exchange, Western newspapers and satellite TV, plus email service. It's is open daily from 10 am to 10 pm.

Hoang Ngoc Restaurant *(106 Đ Nguyen Chi Thanh)* is a pleasant place with great service and outstanding food. The lively owner, Mr Hoang, is a gem. You can try his speciality, sea slug, which tastes much better than it sounds. Just across the street is the ***Hong Ngoc Restaurant*** *(193 Đ Nguyen Chi Thanh)*, an obvious spin-off.

Phu Lu Restaurant *(225 Đ Nguyen Chi Thanh)* does not offer much in the way of atmosphere, but it does do excellent Chinese food.

Hanakim Dinh Restaurant *(15 Đ Bach Dang)* is a Japanese joint-venture. This riverside restaurant resembles a ship, and caters mainly to Asian tour groups. Two other places on the river, near the Bamboo Bar, serving Vietnamese, Chinese and Western dishes include ***Mien Trung*** *(9 Đ Bach Dang)* and ***Thoi Dai*** *(☎ 826404, 5 Đ Bach Dang)*.

Huong Thien Vegetarian Restaurant *(Quan Chay Huong Thien; 391 Đ Ong Ich Khiem)* is an inexpensive local restaurant serving excellent vegetarian dishes, some resembling meat in appearance. The restaurant is near Phap Lam Pagoda, about 1km from the city centre. There is also good vegie fare at ***Com Chay Nga My Vegetarian Restaurant*** *(53 Đ Tran Phu)*.

Near the Caodai Temple, the popular ***My Quang Restaurant*** *(1A Đ Hai Phong)* serves casual Vietnamese food.

Tu Do Restaurant *(☎ 821869, 172 Đ Tran Phu)* has an extensive menu, the service is punctilious and the food is, in fact, quite good, but some of the prices are a lot higher than you'd expect to pay. Next door is ***Kim Do Restaurant***, a slightly fancier place where the food is excellent, but almost ridiculously expensive. Nearby is ***Tiem An Binh Dan Restaurant*** *(174 Đ Tran Phu)*, a modest place with reasonable prices.

A cheap and excellent place to sample dumpling-like *banh cuon* is ***Tien Hung***, about 100m south of Tu Do Restaurant on Đ Tran Phu.

Entertainment

The Cool Spot Bar *(☎ 824040, 112 Đ Tran Phu)*, not far from the river near the corner of Đ Hung Vuong, is a happening bar with moderate prices and a pool table.

The rustic ***Bamboo Bar*** *(☎ 837175, ⓔ bamboo_dn@dng.vnn.vn, 5 Đ Bach Dang)* is an excellent riverside place to enjoy drinks, a game of pool or some light pub grub on the outdoor terrace. This is a lovely place to watch the evening light fade over the river. The friendly owners here speak English, French and German, and can help organise boat tours and motorbike rentals.

There are also a string of cafe/bars in the northern end of town that make good places for pub grub and drinks. ***Cafe Lien*** *(☎ 895422, ⓔ hailien@dng.vnn.vn, 20 Đ Dong Da)* has low prices, friendly staff, plus this is one place where you never know who you'll meet.

An entertaining local character is Lien, who runs a cafe near the Danang Hotel. She can arrange car and motorbike hire and she will sometimes accompany you on day trips as a guide. A foreign resident with business interests in Danang told me that she was also a police informant and knew everything that was happening in the immediate vicinity of the cafe.

One evening when I was having a beer in the cafe, a blond-haired, blue-eyed and fair-skinned traveller sat down at a nearby table. I judged him to be German or Scandinavian. 'I think you are from Israel', Lien said to him. He was absolutely astonished. 'How do you know that?' he asked her. Lien first gave him a conspiratorial look and then smiled. Finally, she whispered, 'I know everything'.

Ian McVittie

Just up the street, Lien's sister runs ***Linh Cafe*** *(☎ 820401, 34 Đ Bach Dang)*, where there is more Western food and a pool table. A similar scene goes on at the nearby ***Free Time Bar***.

Shopping

Han Market (Cho Han) is at the intersection of Đ Hung Vuong and Đ Tran Phu. Unusually, this market stays open late and is a fine place for a casual stroll or shop in the evenings.

Cham Museum

The best sight in Danang city has to be the Cham Museum (Bao Tang Cham). Founded in 1915 by the École Française d'Extrême Orient, the open-air collection of Cham sculpture is the finest in the world. Many of the sandstone carvings (altars, lingas, garudas, ganeshas, and images of Shiva, Brahma and Vishnu) are breathtaking; making this a place you can easily visit again and again.

A trilingual guidebook, Museum of Cham Sculpture – Danang (Bao Tang Dieu Khac Cham Da Nang; Foreign Languages Publishing House, Hanoi, 1987), on the museum written by its director, Tran Ky Phuong, Vietnam's most eminent scholar of Cham civilisation, provides excellent background on the art of Champa; it also includes some details on the museum's exhibits. The book is usually on sale at the entrance.

It is well worth finding a knowledgeable guide (a scarce commodity in these parts) to show you around. Chances are you can find Mr Nguyen Phu Luy (aka Monsieur Louis), a friendly old man who spends his retired days here befriending foreigners to guide through the displays. He speaks

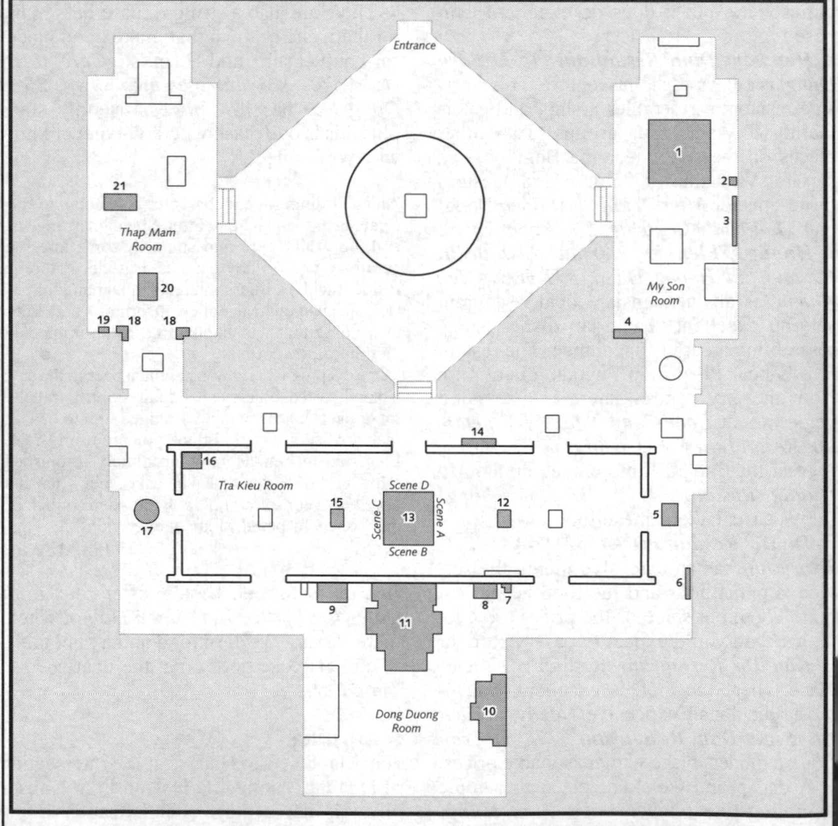

Cham Museum

excellent French and relatively good English, and is highly knowledgeable on Cham art. If you do decide to accept his, or any other guide's services, agree on a price before you begin, as some guides have been known to overcharge people.

The museum's artefacts, which date from the 7th to 15th centuries, were discovered at Dong Duong (Indrapura), Khuong My, My Son, Tra Kieu (Simhapura), Thap Mam (Binh Dinh) and other sites, mostly in Quang Nam and Danang Provinces. The museum's rooms are named after the localities in which the objects displayed in them were found.

The four scenes carved around the base of the 7th-century Tra Kieu Altar tell part of the Ramayana epic and are influenced by the Amaravati style of South India. Scene A (16 characters) tells the story of Prince Rama, who broke the sacred bow (Rudra) at the citadel of Videha, thus winning the right to wed King Janak's daughter, Princess Sita.

Scene B (16 characters) shows the ambassadors sent by King Janak to Prince Rama's father, King Dasaratha, at Ayodhya. The emissaries inform King Dasaratha of the exploits of his son, present him with gifts and invite him to Videha to celebrate his son's wedding.

Scene C (18 characters) shows the royal wedding ceremony (including three of Prince Rama's brothers, who are marrying three of Princess Sita's cousins).

In Scene D, 11 apsaras (heavenly maidens) dance and present flowers to the newlyweds under the guidance of the two gandhara musicians who appear at the beginning of Scene A.

The museum, is located near the corner of Đ Trung Nu Vuong and Đ Bach Dang. It is open daily from 8 to 11 am and 1 to 5 pm.

Admission will cost you US$1.60 – but make sure you hand over the money to an authorised member of the museum staff in the ticket booth and not some entrepreneurial gardener.

no	artefact	original site	construction period
1	My Son Altar	My Son,	8th-9th century
2	Ganesha (seated elephant)	My Son	8th-9th century
3	Birthday of Brahma	My Son	8th-9th century
4	Polo players	Thach An	7th century
5	Altar ornaments	Khuong My	10th century
6	The Goddess Sarasvati	Chanh Lo	11th century
7	Vishnu	Tra Kieu	10th century
8	A deity	Dong Duong	9th-10th century
9	A deity	Dong Duong	9th-10th century
10	Dong Duong Altar ornaments	Dong Duong	9th-10th century
11	Dong Duong Altar	Dong Duong	9th-10th century
12	Linga		
13	Tra Kieu Altar	Tra Kieu	7th century
14	Dancing Shiva	Phong Le	10th century
15	Linga		
16	Dancing female apsaras	Quang Nam-Danang Province	10th century
17	Altar ornaments	Binh Dinh	12th-14th century
18	Lions	Thap Mam	12th-14th century
19	Shiva	Thap Mam	12th-14th century
20	The elephant-lion Gajasimha	Thap Mam	12th-14th century
21	The sea monster Makara	Thap Mam	12th-14th century

The Con Market (Cho Con) is Danang's largest, but functions mostly during the daytime. This huge, colourful market has a selection of just about everything sold in Vietnam: household items, ceramics, fresh vegetables, stationery, cutlery, fruit, flowers, polyester clothes etc.

If you've been on the road for a while and are hard up for reading material, the bookshop next to the Orient Hotel sells *Time* and *Newsweek*.

Getting There & Away

Air During the American War, Danang had one of the busiest airports in the world. Business declined sharply when the war ended, but Danang still distinguishes itself by having one of Vietnam's three international airports. Recently direct flights from Bangkok, Hong Kong and Singapore were re-established. Still, most international flights from Danang fly via Ho Chi Minh City, though you can complete your immigration and customs formalities in Danang.

Vietnam Airlines (☎ 822094), 35 Đ Tran Phu, has an extensive schedule to/from Danang (see the boxed text 'Domestic Airline Schedules' in the Getting Around chapter).

The local Vietnam Airlines reservation inquiries number is ☎ 811111. Telephone bookings are not possible yet, but calling can save a bit of legwork when checking on flights.

Bus The Danang intercity bus station (Ben Xe Khach Da Nang) is about 3km from the city centre on the thoroughfare known, at various points along its length, as Đ Hung Vuong, Đ Ly Thai To and Đ Dien Bien Phu (see the Around Danang map). The ticket office for express buses is west of town, across the street from 200 Đ Dien Bien Phu; it is open from 7 to 11 am and 1 to 5 pm.

Bus services run to Buon Ma Thuot, Kon Tum, Dalat, Vinh, Gia Lai, Haiphong, Hanoi, Ho Chi Minh City, Hon Gai, Lang Son, Nam Dinh and Nha Trang. Most buses depart around 5 am.

There is also a new loop bus route with hourly services covering suburban Danang. Look for the large, red and white buses and sheltered bus stops in town. A convenient stop for Hoi An buses (US$0.40) is across from the Municipal Theatre on Đ Phan Chu Trinh; buses to the base of Hai Van Pass can be boarded on Đ Bach Dang, just south of the bridge.

There are also buses between Danang and Savannakhet in Laos via Dong Ha and the Lao Bao border crossing (see the Getting There & Away chapter).

Minibus Most travellers prefer to stay in Hoi An rather than Danang, so Hoi An has better minibus services. Nevertheless, it is possible to get a seat on an upmarket minibus in Danang. Check at Cafe Lien for information on the minibuses to Hué and Nha Trang.

There is also a daily minibus service between Danang and Hoi An. The bus leaves Danang at 8 am and returns at 5 pm, depending on demand (they always require a minimum of four passengers). Tickets cost US$3 one way or $5.50 return.

Train The Danang train station (Ga Da Nang) is about 1.5km from the city centre on Đ Hai Phong at the northern end of Đ Hoang Hoa Tham. The train ride to Hué is one of the nicest in the country (although the drive up and over Hai Van Pass is also spectacular).

Northbound, the quickest train takes about 3¼ hours to reach Hué; local trains take about six hours. Watch your belongings as you pass through the pitch-black tunnels.

Danang is, of course, served by all *Reunification Express* trains (see the Train section in the Getting Around chapter).

Car & Motorbike The simplest way to get to Hoi An is to hire a car for around US$10 or a motorbike for around US$8 from a local travel agency, Cafe Lien or the Danang Hotel (new wing). For a slightly higher fee you can ask the driver to stop off and wait for you while you visit the Marble Mountains and China Beach. You can also reach My Son by motorbike (US$12) or car (US$35), with the option of being dropped off in Hoi An on the way back if you don't wish to return to Danang.

Road distances from Danang are:

Hanoi	764km
Ho Chi Minh City	972km
Hoi An	30km
Hué	108km
Lao Bao	350km
Nha Trang	541km
Quang Ngai	130km
Qui Nhon	303km
Savannakhet, Laos	500km

Getting Around

To/From the Airport Danang's airport is just 2km west of the city centre, close enough to reach by cyclo in 15 minutes.

Motorbike & Cyclo Danang has plenty of motorbike taxis and cyclo drivers; take the usual caution and be prepared to bargain the fare.

Self-drive motorbikes can be rented at the Bamboo Bar.

Taxi Airport Taxi (☎ 825555) and Dana Taxi (☎ 815815) provide modern vehicles with air-con and meters.

Boat Inquire at Christie's Restaurant or the Bamboo Bar about chartered boat trips in the area.

AROUND DANANG

☎ 0511

Tombs of Spanish & French Soldiers

Spanish-led Filipino and French troops attacked Danang in August 1858, ostensibly to end the mistreatment of Vietnamese Catholics and Catholic missionaries by Emperor Tu Duc's government. The city quickly fell, but the invaders had to contend with cholera, dysentery, scurvy, typhus and mysterious fevers. By the summer of 1859, the number of invaders that had died of illness was 20 times the number that had been killed in combat. Many of these soldiers are buried in a chapel (Bai Mo Phap Va Ta Ban Nha) about 15km north of the city. The names of the dead are written on the walls.

To get there, cross the Song Han Bridge and turn left onto Đ Ngo Quyen (see the Around Danang map). Continue north to Tien Sa Port (Cang Tien Sa). The chapel, a white building, stands on the right on a low hill about 500m past the gate of the port.

Thanh Binh Beach

Thanh Binh Beach is only a couple of kilometres north-west of central Danang. It is often crowded, notwithstanding the fact that the water is not the cleanest. To get there, head all the way to the northern end of Đ Ong Ich Khiem.

Nam O Beach

Nam O Beach is on the Bay of Danang about 15km north-west of the city. The small community of Nam O has supported itself for years by producing firecrackers. Unfortunately, since the ban on firecrackers by the government in 1995, the community has fallen on hard times. However, the resourceful locals have recently gone into making nuoc mam (fish sauce) instead – and while it's not as profitable as firecrackers, it's better than nothing.

China Beach

China Beach, made famous in the American TV series of the same name, stretches for many kilometres north and south of the Marble Mountains. During the American War, US soldiers were airlifted here for 'rest and relaxation', often including a picnic on the beach. For some, it was their last meal before their return to combat by helicopter.

The jumbo beach stretches some 30km south from Son Tra (Monkey) Mountain almost all the way to Hoi An. It has become a very popular seaside escape for both domestic and foreign tourists, and is now home to one of Vietnam's plushest resort hotels.

Though the entire stretch of ocean front is collectively known as 'China Beach', it is worth noting that the name is a recent creation. The beachfront here is, in fact, divided into sections, each with its own local name.

The most populated areas are My Khe Beach (where the Americans did most of their R&R), and the tract of seashore by the

Non Nuoc Seaside Resort. Here you can expect an onslaught of vendors flogging 'China Beach' baseball caps, woodcarvings of Buddha, jade bracelets, new antiques and other tourist paraphernalia, but there are plenty of other peaceful, secluded areas to explore along the coastline.

Many people insist that My Khe Beach (Bai Tam My Khe) was the 'real' China Beach of wartime fame and that the 'present' China Beach is a fake. My Khe is about 6km by road from central Danang. The beach is reputed to have a dangerous undertow, especially in winter. However, it is safer than the rest of China Beach – the bulk of Son Tra Mountain protects it from winds causing rough surf.

The best time for swimming along Danang's beaches is from May to July, when the sea is at its calmest. During other times the water can get rough; lifeguards only patrol Non Nuoc, My An and sometimes My Khe beaches. In December 1992, China Beach was the site of the first international surfing competition to be held in Vietnam.

Ironically, the dangerous winter surf goes hand-in-hand with large breakers, which are

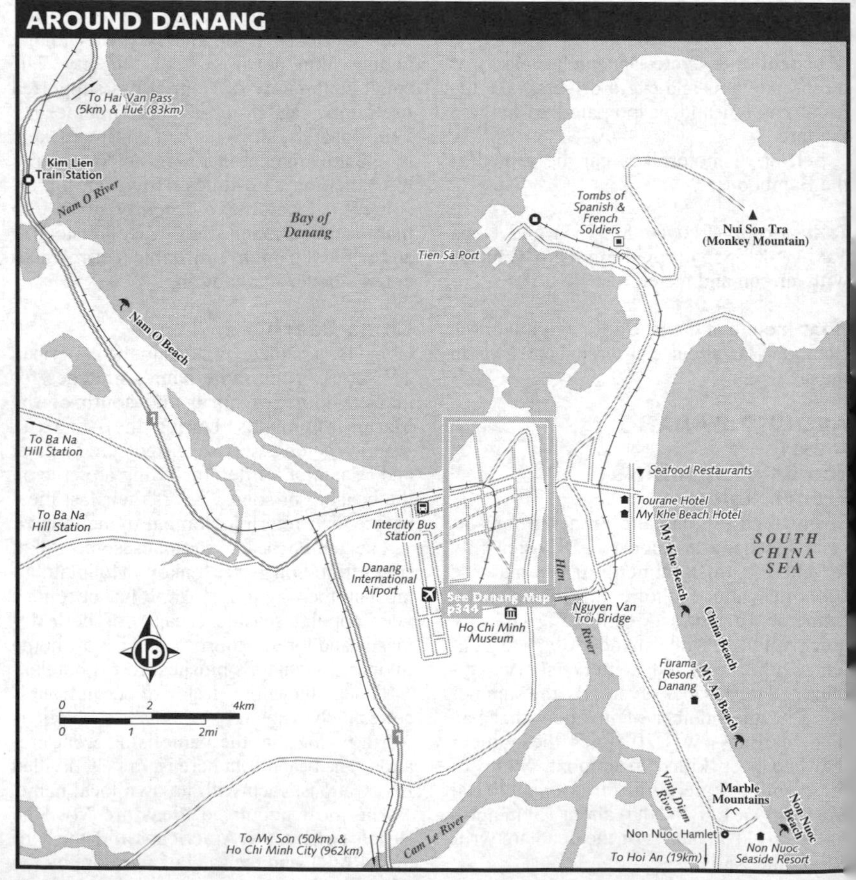

ideal for surfing – assuming that you know what you're doing. The surf can be very good from around mid-September to December, particularly in the morning when wind conditions are right.

Places to Stay & Eat The Russian-built ***Non Nuoc Seaside Resort*** *(☎ 836215, fax 836335)* is worth checking into. The place is an old concrete block, and rooms are nothing to write home about, but it's cheap and within crawling distance of the beach. Singles/doubles with fan are US$8/10, and air-con rooms (some with ocean views) cost US$11 to US$18. The hotel has two ***restaurants*** – the in-house one is OK but the beachfront one (shaped like the conning tower of a submarine) is a highlight.

On the way to the Non Nuoc Seaside Resort you'll pass the ***Dong Hai Seaside Resort*** *(☎ 961009)*, which has very basic rooms in cute little brick cottages from US$8. Another place you'll see is the aging ***China Beach Mini-Hotel*** *(☎ 836066, fax 836691)*, which charges US$10 for air-con rooms with cold water only, or US$12/15 for singles/doubles with hot water.

Another cheap spot right on the beach is the aging ***My Khe Beach Hotel*** *(☎ 836125, fax 836123)*. Single/double/triple budget rooms start at US$8/10/12, but rise to US$30 in the hotel's new wing. There is a very good ***restaurant*** here as well, which offers email service, and donates 10% of its proceeds to a local charity.

The new ***Tourane Hotel*** *(☎ 932666, fax 844328, ⓔ tourinco@dng.vnn.vn)* is an attractive choice just across from the beach. Rooms are in contemporary French-style villas, and cost US$40 to US$70, including breakfast, tax and service. There is a tennis court, ***restaurant*** and bar on the grounds.

Danang's luxury hotel scene is dominated by the ***Furama Resort Danang*** *(☎ 847333, fax 847666, ⓔ furamadn@hn.vnn.vn)*. Perched upon its own private slice of China Beach, this stylish resort features Danang's best diving facility, a putt-putt golf range and a freshwater swimming lagoon. Rooms cost US$140 to US$400; tack on another 15% for service and tax.

On the spur road leading to the Furama Resort is the ***Hoang Kim Hotel*** *(☎ 847111, fax 847112, 27 Đ Ho Xuan Huong)*, a decent mini-hotel just a few hundred metres from the beach. Air-con rooms cost US$12 to US$22.

My Khe Beach is the place to go for seafood. A short walk north of My Khe Beach Hotel are a string of ***seafood restaurants*** with open decks overlooking the ocean. The best of the lot is ***Loi Restaurant*** *(☎ 831088)*. The boss, Mary Ann – she was given her English name by an American soldier when she was a child – speaks good English.

Getting There & Away To get to My Khe Beach from central Danang, cross the Song Han Bridge and head toward the sea. Pickup trucks to China Beach (Bai Tam Non Nuoc) depart when full from the short-haul pickup truck station on Đ Hung Vuong in Danang.

To reach the Non Nuoc Seaside Resort by private transport, head towards the Marble Mountains (see the following entry) and turn left into Non Nuoc Hamlet. Follow the road past the largest mountain around to the right (almost parallel to the beach). Before you hit the sand, turn right towards the casuarina grove (and away from the beach) and follow the road around to the left.

Marble Mountains

The Marble Mountains consist of five stone hillocks, once islands, made of marble. Each is said to represent one of the five elements of the universe and is named accordingly: Thuy Son (Water), Moc Son (Wood), Hoa Son (Fire), Kim So (Metal or Gold) and Tho Son (Earth). The largest and most famous, Thuy Son, has a number of natural *dong* (caves) in which Buddhist sanctuaries have been built over the centuries. When the Champas ruled this area, these same caves were used as Hindu shrines. Thuy Son is a popular pilgrimage site, especially on days of the full and sliver moons and during Tet.

A torch (flashlight) is useful inside the caves. Local children have learned that foreign tourists buy souvenirs and leave tips for

'Mad Jack' Percival in Danang

In May 1845, Captain John 'Mad Jack' Percival sailed the USS Constitution into Turon Bay (Danang) and dropped anchor. He was a full year from Boston on a goodwill tour to show the American flag and look for coal. The aging ship was in dire need of provisions.

At the time a fort commanded both the harbour entrance and the mouth of the Han River. Percival's first order of business was to bury a Seaman Cook – dead from dysentery – in a pristine cove beside the hill fort.

On the third day Percival saluted the fort with six cannon and received a single shot in return. He dispatched a longboat into the town to make arrangements for reprovision. The exchanges were curt. The Americans found the emperor's representatives evasive.

Emperor Thieu Tri had reason to be cautious. China had been forced by British gunboats to open its ports three years earlier. Thieu Tri knew that France was anxious to join its rivals in the China trade. Vietnam – with its splendid harbour at Danang – would be a perfect platform. An armed frigate in the harbour was a cause for concern no matter whose flag the French flew.

On the fourth day, during a return visit to the ship by local authorities, a Chinese interpreter smuggled aboard a note. It was a plea for help from an imprisoned French missionary named LeFevre, who was under sentence of death for plotting against the emperor.

That was enough to get Mad Jack out of his cabin: A Christian prelate was held by 'barbarians'. Interpreting his benign brief rather broadly, Percival led an armed column back to town and delivered a withering note to the Mandarins, demanding release of LeFevre. To show his resolve, he took three hostages and returned to the ship. He gave the Vietnamese a 24-hour ultimatum: release the missionary or he would seize the harbour forts and snatch all the shipping he could lay his hands on.

Anchored off the fort were three armed junks. Percival sent a party of longboats to capture them.

unsolicited guided tours, so you are not likely to begin your visit alone. The local government adopted a regulation (which it sternly enforces) that the children cannot take tips, but can only sell you souvenirs. This seems counterproductive; most travellers would rather tip the kids for the guided tours than buy the crappy souvenirs. In general, the kids are good-natured and some of the caves are difficult to find without their assistance.

Of the two paths leading up Thuy Son, the one closer to the beach (at the end of the village) makes for a better circuit once you get up the top. So, unless you want to walk the following route in reverse, don't go up the staircase with concrete kiosks. A 10,000d (US$0.80) admission fee is collected at either entrance.

At the top of the staircase (from where Cham Island is visible) is a gate, Ong Chon, which is pockmarked with bullet holes. Behind Ong Chon is Linh Ong Pagoda. As you enter the sanctuary, look to the left to see a fantastic figure with a huge tongue. To the right of Linh Ong are monks' quarters and a small orchid garden.

Behind Linh Ong a path leads left through two short tunnels to several caverns known as Tang Chon Dong. There are a number of concrete Buddhas and blocks of carved stone of Cham origin in these caves. Near one of the altars is a flight of steps leading up to another cave, partially open to the sky, with two seated Buddhas in it.

To the left of the small building left of Linh Ong (ie, immediately to the left as you enter Ong Chon Gate) is the main path to the rest of Thuy Son. Stairs off the main pathway lead to Vong Hai Da, a viewpoint for a brilliant panorama of China Beach and the South China Sea.

The stone-paved path continues to the right and into a canyon. On the left is Van Thong Cave. Opposite the entrance is a cement Buddha, behind which a narrow passage leads up to a natural chimney open to the sky.

After you exit the canyon and pass through a battle-scarred masonry gate,

'Mad Jack' Percival in Danang

During the night, soldiers from the fort reboarded the junks – not to free them – but to punish the captains for dereliction. The unlucky commanders were flogged, yoked and tied to the mast. One had his eyes shut with pitch, with the emperor's seal stamped in the tar.

The Vietnamese ignored Percival's ultimatums. So Mad Jack raged against the inner harbour. He sent his longboats chasing deep up the Han spilling Vietnamese sailors into the river. American Marines – armed with musket and cutlass – went ashore against soldiers and civilians alike.

But Percival still needed to reprovision. Knowing this, the Mandarins countered his ultimatums with a deal of their own: Release the three officials and you may continue to take on stores. Then we will give you LeFevre.

The approaches to the forts were patiently reinforced. Vietnamese soldiers marched beneath colourful battle pennants along the riverbanks in ever increasing numbers. More ships – armed and fitted – appeared in the harbour. The Constitution was outgunned and out-manoeuvred. Neither Percival's reckless posturing nor the threat of two decks of cannon had made an impression on the Vietnamese.

Finally, Percival pulled anchor before dawn on 26 May and sailed from Danang. He fired a final salvo at a harbour island and the rounds fell short. He never saw LeFevre, but he left with his stores fully replenished.

In 1849 President Taylor sent a note of apology to Thieu Tri. He deplored the incident and prayed that 'no more blood be spilled between our two peoples'.

Percival – rebuked by the Navy – retired to Massachusetts. His 16 days in Danang slipped from sight. The next hostile Americans who ventured into Danang, 120 years later, could have profited from Mad Jack's experience.

Peter Kneisel

rocky path to the right goes to Linh Nham, a tall chimney-cave with a small altar inside. Nearby, another path leads to Hoa Nghiem, a shallow cave with a Buddha inside. But if you go down the passageway to the left of the Buddha you come to cathedral-like Huyen Khong Cave, lit by an opening to the sky. The entrance to this spectacular chamber is guarded by two administrative mandarins (to the left of the doorway) and two military mandarins (to the right).

Scattered about the cave are Buddhist and Confucian shrines; note the inscriptions carved into the stone walls. On the right a door leads to two stalactites dripping water that local legend describes as coming from heaven. Actually, only one stalactite drips; the other one supposedly ran dry when Emperor Tu Duc touched it. During the American War, this chamber was used by the VC as a field hospital. Inside is a plaque dedicated to the Women's Artillery Group, which destroyed 19 US aircraft as they sat at a base below the mountains in 1972.

Just to the left of the battle-scarred masonry gate is Tam Thai Tu, a pagoda restored by Emperor Minh Mang in 1826. A path heading obliquely to the right goes to the monks' residences, beyond which are two shrines. From there a red dirt path leads to five small pagodas. Before you arrive at the monks' residences, stairs on the left-hand side of the path lead to Vong Giang Dai, which offers a fantastic 180° view of the other Marble Mountains and the surrounding countryside. To get to the stairway down, follow the path straight on from the masonry gate.

Non Nuoc Hamlet

Non Nuoc Hamlet is on the southern side of Thuy Son and is a few hundred metres west of My An Beach. The marble carvings made here by skilled (and not-so-skilled) artisans would make great gifts if they didn't weigh so much. Even so, it can still be entertaining to watch the carvers at work.

The town has been spruced up for tourism. During the war, the Americans referred to the shantytown near here as 'Dogpatch', named after a derelict town in the comic strip *Lil Abner*. Most of the residents living there at the time were refugees fleeing the fighting in the surrounding countryside.

Getting There & Away

Pickup Truck Pickup trucks to the Marble Mountains (Ngu Hanh Son), Non Nuoc Hamlet and nearby China Beach (Bai Tam Non Nuoc) leave when full from the short-haul pickup truck station in Danang. The trip takes about 20 minutes.

Car & Motorbike The 11km route from Danang to the Marble Mountains passes by the remains of a huge 2km-long complex of former American military bases; aircraft revetments are still visible.

The Marble Mountains are 19km north of Hoi An along the 'Korean Highway'.

Boat It is possible to get to the Marble Mountains from Danang by chartered boat. The 8.5km trip up the Han and Vinh Diem Rivers takes about 1¼ hours.

HAI VAN PASS

Hai Van (Sea Cloud) Pass crosses over a spur of the Truong Son Mountain Range that juts into the South China Sea. About 30km north of Danang, Highway 1 climbs to an elevation of 496m, passing south of the Ai Van Son peak (1172m). It's an incredibly mountainous stretch of highway with spectacular views. The railway track, with its many tunnels, goes around the peninsula, following the shoreline to avoid the hills.

In the 15th century, Hai Van Pass formed the boundary between Vietnam and the Kingdom of Champa. Until the American War, the pass was heavily forested. At the summit is an old French fort, later used as a bunker by the South Vietnamese army and the Americans.

If you visit in winter, you may find that the pass serves almost as a visible dividing line between the climates of the north and the south. Acting as a virtual wall, the pass protects the area to the south from the fierce 'Chinese winds' that sweep in from the north-east. From about November to March the exposed north side of the pass (including Lang Co Beach) can be uncomfortably wet and chilly, while just to the south (on the beaches around Danang and Hoi An) it's warm and dry. Of course, variations in this weather pattern occur but in general, when the winter weather is lousy in Hué, it's good in Danang.

Most buses make a 10-minute rest stop at the top of the pass. You'll have to fight off a rather large crowd of persistent souvenir vendors. You would be wise not to agree to change money with anyone on the pass – dollars for dong, dong for dollars, you're more than likely to get short changed.

In June 2000, construction began on a US$150 million tunnel under Hai Van Pass to facilitate traffic flow. The project is estimated to take four years.

BA NA HILL STATION

☎ 0511

Ba Na, the 'Dalat of Danang Province', is a hill station along the crest of Mt Ba Na (Nui Chua), which rises 1485m above the coastal plain. The 360° view is truly spectacular and the air is fresh and cool: when it's 36°C on the coast, it's likely to be between 15°C and 26°C in Ba Na. Rain often falls at altitudes between 700m and 1200m above sea level, but around the hill station itself the sky is usually clear. Mountain paths in the area lead to a variety of waterfalls and viewpoints.

Ba Na was founded in 1919 for use by French settlers. Until WWII, the French travelled the last 20km up the rough mountain road by sedan chair! Of the 200-odd villas that originally stood, a large number of tattered (and photogenic) ruins remain. The provincial government has high hopes of once again making Ba Na a magnet for tourists, and so far seems to be doing a good job at attracting both Vietnamese and foreigners accommodation are the same for travellers and Vietnamese – a relative rarity in Vietnam.

Places to Stay & Eat

The new ***Ba Na Resort*** *(☎ 818055/746447, fax 712307, ⓔ danamarle@dng.vnn.vn)* consists of a 30-room hotel and two types of bungalows. Double rooms cost US$15. Forty simple bungalows, accommodating two guests each, cost just US$6/8. Deluxe bungalows for up to four people have hot water and cost US$20/30 on weekdays/weekends.

There is a large ***restaurant*** at the resort with pleasant outdoor terrace seating (for up to 400 people to handle peak season weekend crowds).

Getting There & Away

By road, Ba Na is 42km west of Danang; 27km as the crow flies.

Until recently the road to Ba Na was in such bad condition that only a motorbike or 4WD could make it all the way; if you took a car you had to walk the last 6km. Major road repairs, however, were completed in 1999, and now it is possible to drive all the way up.

Local buses go from Danang to the bottom of the access road (10,000d), from where shuttle buses take passengers up the mountain for another 15,000d.

There is a new tourist ropeway that whisks visitors up from a free parking lot along the access road. Tickets cost 25,000d up, 20,000d down, or 35,000d round-trip. Many give the ropeway a miss, choosing to drive right up to the parking lot at the top (5000d per car).

An interesting detour on the way to Ba Na is the waterfall at Suoi Mo (Dream Springs). To get there, turn right near the bridge at the bottom of the mountain and continue for 2km. There is a 3000d entry fee, but parking is free. There are no facilities at Suoi Mo.

HOI AN

☎ 0510 • pop 75,800

Hoi An is a picturesque riverside town 30km south of Danang. Most visitors agree it is the most enchanting place on the coast and is one city worth lingering in.

Known as Faifo to early Western traders, it was one of South-East Asia's major international ports during the 17th, 18th and 19th centuries. In its heyday, Hoi An, a contemporary of Macau and Melaka, was an important port of call for Dutch, Portuguese, Chinese, Japanese and other trading vessels. Vietnamese ships and sailors based in Hoi An sailed to all sections of Vietnam, as well as Thailand and Indonesia. Perhaps more than any other place in Vietnam, Hoi An retains a sense of history that grows on you the more you explore it.

Every year during the rainy season, in particular the months of October and November, Hoi An has problems with flooding, especially near the waterfront. The greatest flood ever recorded in Hoi An took place in 1964, when the water reached all the way up to the roof beams of the houses.

Though Hoi An has yet to become a UNESCO World Heritage Site, preservation efforts are well up to par. Several historical structures are open for public viewing, a number of streets in the centre of town are off-limits to motor traffic, and building alteration and height restrictions are well enforced. If only Hanoi would follow suit in the historic Old Quarter.

Despite the number of tourists who come to Hoi An, it is still a very conservative town, and visitors should dress modestly when touring the sites.

'Hoi An Legendary Night' takes place on the 14th day of every lunar month (full moon) from 5.30 to 10 pm. This colourful monthly event features traditional food, song and dance, and games along the lantern-lit streets in the town centre.

History

Recently excavated ceramic fragments from 2200 years ago constitute the earliest evidence of human habitation in the Hoi An area. They are thought to belong to the late-Iron Age Sa Huynh civilisation, which is related to the Dong Son culture of northern Vietnam.

From the 2nd to the 10th centuries, when this region was the heartland of the Kingdom of Champa – when the Cham capital of Simhapura (Tra Kicu) and the temples of Indrapura (Dong Duong) and My Son were built (see the special section 'Kingdom of Champa') – there was a bustling seaport at Hoi An. Persian and Arab documents from the latter part of the period mention Hoi An

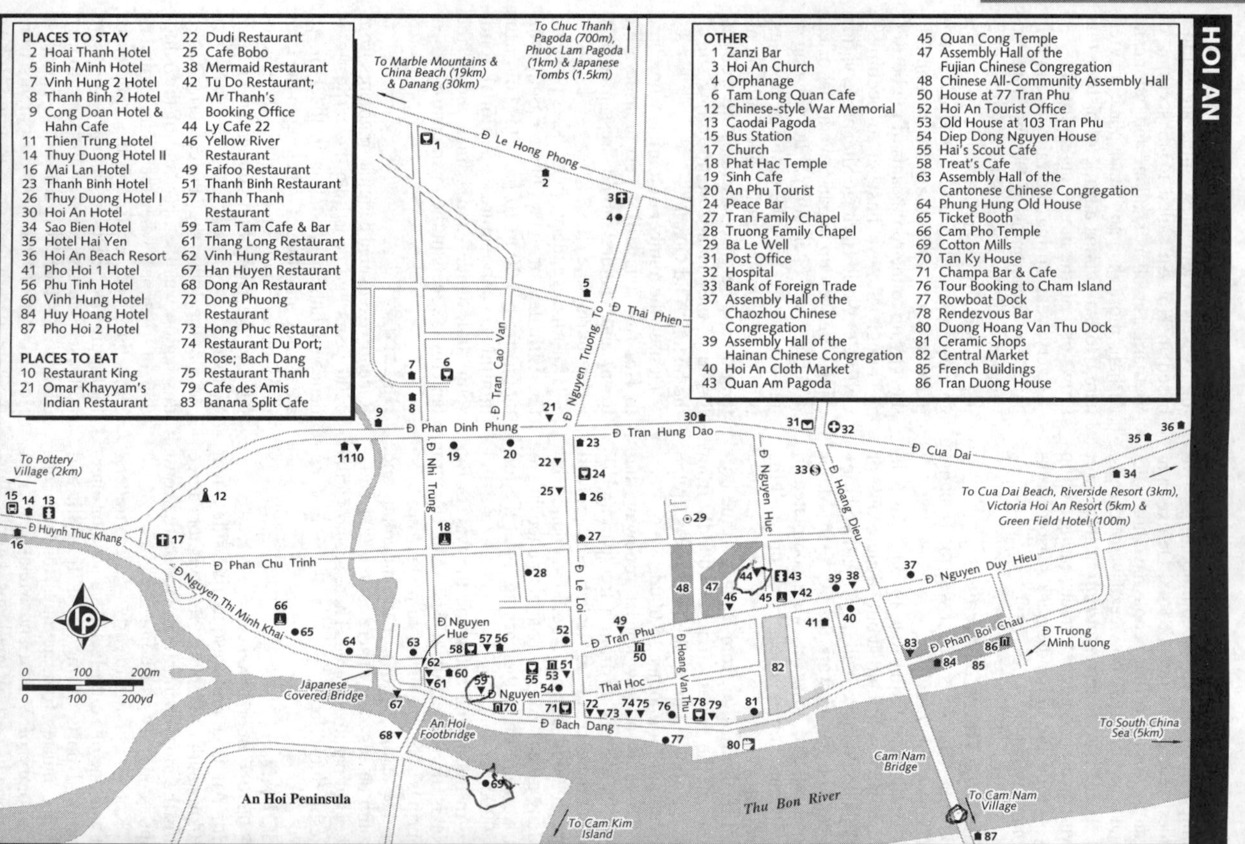
HOI AN
PLACES TO STAY
2 Hoai Thanh Hotel
5 Binh Minh Hotel
7 Vinh Hung 2 Hotel
8 Thanh Binh 2 Hotel
9 Cong Doan Hotel & Hahn Cafe
11 Thien Trung Hotel
14 Thuy Duong Hotel II
16 Mai Lan Hotel
23 Thanh Binh Hotel
26 Thuy Duong Hotel I
30 Hoi An Hotel
34 Sao Bien Hotel
35 Hotel Hai Yen
36 Hoi An Beach Resort
41 Pho Hoi 1 Hotel
56 Phu Tinh Hotel
60 Vinh Hung Hotel
84 Huy Hoang Hotel
87 Pho Hoi 2 Hotel
PLACES TO EAT
10 Restaurant King
21 Omar Khayyam's Indian Restaurant
22 Dudi Restaurant
25 Cafe Bobo
38 Mermaid Restaurant
42 Tu Do Restaurant; Mr Thanh's Booking Office
44 Ly Cafe 22
46 Yellow River Restaurant
49 Faifoo Restaurant
51 Thanh Binh Restaurant
57 Thanh Thanh Restaurant
59 Tam Tam Cafe & Bar
61 Thang Long Restaurant
62 Vinh Hung Restaurant
67 Han Huyen Restaurant
68 Dong An Restaurant
72 Dong Phuong Restaurant
73 Hong Phuc Restaurant
74 Restaurant Du Port; Rose; Bach Dang
75 Restaurant Thanh
79 Cafe des Amis
83 Banana Split Cafe
OTHER
1 Zanzi Bar
3 Hoi An Church
4 Orphanage
6 Tam Long Quan Cafe
12 Chinese-style War Memorial
13 Caodai Pagoda
15 Bus Station
17 Church
18 Phat Hac Temple
19 Sinh Cafe
20 An Phu Tourist
24 Peace Bar
27 Tran Family Chapel
28 Truong Family Chapel
29 Ba Le Well
31 Post Office
32 Hospital
33 Bank of Foreign Trade
37 Assembly Hall of the Chaozhou Chinese Congregation
39 Assembly Hall of the Hainan Chinese Congregation
40 Hoi An Cloth Market
43 Quan Am Pagoda
45 Quan Cong Temple
47 Assembly Hall of the Fujian Chinese Congregation
48 Chinese All-Community Assembly Hall
50 House at 77 Tran Phu
52 Hoi An Tourist Office
53 Old House at 103 Tran Phu
54 Diep Dong Nguyen House
55 Hai's Scout Café
58 Treat's Cafe
63 Assembly Hall of the Cantonese Chinese Congregation
64 Phung Hung Old House
65 Ticket Booth
66 Cam Pho Temple
69 Cotton Mills
70 Tan Ky House
71 Champa Bar & Cafe
76 Tour Booking to Cham Island
77 Rowboat Dock
78 Rendezvous Bar
80 Duong Hoang Van Thu Dock
81 Ceramic Shops
82 Central Market
85 French Buildings
86 Tran Duong House
To Marble Mountains & China Beach (19km) & Danang (30km)
To Chuc Thanh Pagoda (700m), Phuoc Lam Pagoda (1km) & Japanese Tombs (1.5km)
To Pottery Village (2km)
To Cua Dai Beach, Riverside Resort (3km), Victoria Hoi An Resort (5km) & Green Field Hotel (100m)
To South China Sea (5km)
To Cam Nam Village
To Cam Kim Island
Đ Le Hong Phong
Đ Thai Phien
Đ Nguyen Truong To
Đ Tran Cao Van
Đ Phan Dinh Phung
Đ Tran Hung Dao
Đ Cua Dai
Đ Nhi Trung
Đ Huynh Thuc Khang
Đ Phan Chu Trinh
Đ Nguyen Thi Minh Khai
Đ Le Loi
Đ Nguyen Hue
Đ Hoang Dieu
Đ Nguyen Duy Hieu
Đ Tran Phu
Đ Hoang Van Thu
Đ Phan Boi Chau
Đ Truong Minh Luong
Thai Hoc
Đ Nguyen Hue
Đ Nguyen
Đ Bach Dang
Japanese Covered Bridge
An Hoi Footbridge
Cam Nam Bridge
Thu Bon River
An Hoi Peninsula
0 100 200m
0 100 200yd

as a provisioning stop for trading ships. Archaeologists have uncovered the foundations of numerous Cham towers around Hoi An (the bricks and stones of the towers were reused by Vietnamese settlers).

In 1307 the Cham king married the daughter of a Vietnamese monarch of the Tran Dynasty, presenting Quang Nam Province to the Vietnamese as a gift. When the Cham king died, his successor refused to recognise the deal and fighting broke out; for the next century, chaos reigned. By the 15th century, peace had been restored, allowing normal commerce to resume. During the next four centuries, Chinese, Japanese, Dutch, Portuguese, Spanish, Indian, Filipino, Indonesian, Thai, French, English and American ships called at Hoi An to purchase high-grade silk (for which the area is famous), fabrics, paper, porcelain, tea, sugar, molasses, areca nuts, pepper, Chinese medicines, elephant tusks, beeswax, mother-of-pearl, lacquer, sulphur and lead.

The Chinese and Japanese traders sailed south in the spring, driven by winds out of the north-east. They would stay in Hoi An until the summer, when southerly winds would blow them home. During their four month sojourn in Hoi An, the merchants rented waterfront houses for use as warehouses and living quarters. Some traders began leaving full-time agents in Hoi An to take care of off-season business affairs. This is how the foreigners' colonies got started, although the Japanese ceased coming to Hoi An after 1637 when the Japanese government forbade all contact with the outside world.

Hoi An was the first place in Vietnam to be exposed to Christianity. Among the 17th-century missionary visitors was the French priest Alexandre de Rhodes, who devised the Latin-based *quoc ngu* script for the Vietnamese language.

Hoi An was almost completely destroyed during the Tay Son Rebellion in the 1770s and 1780s, but was rebuilt and continued to serve as an important port for foreign trade until the late 19th century, when the Thu Bon River (Cai River), which links Hoi An with the sea, silted up and became too shallow for navigation. During this period Danang (Tourane) began to eclipse Hoi An as a port and centre of commerce. In 1916 a rail line linking Danang with Hoi An was destroyed by a terrible storm; it was never rebuilt.

During French colonisation Hoi An served as an administrative centre. During the American War, the city remained almost completely undamaged.

Hoi An was the site of the first Chinese settlement in southern Vietnam. The town's Chinese congregational assembly halls *(hoi quan)* still play a special role among southern Vietnam's ethnic-Chinese, some of whom come to Hoi An from all over to participate in congregation-wide celebrations. Today, 1300 of Hoi An's population of 75,800 are ethnic-Chinese. Relations between ethnic-Vietnamese and ethnic-Chinese in Hoi An are excellent, partly because the Chinese here have become assimilated to the point where they even speak Vietnamese among themselves.

Information

Travel Agencies Though there are official, government-sponsored tourist offices in town that theoretically book tours (like the Hoi An Tourist Office on the corner of Đ Tran Phu and Đ Le Loi), you are probably better off looking elsewhere.

The following private agencies all run tours, arrange transportation and can help with visa extensions (typically costing US$15 to US$17 for two weeks, or US$25 to US$30 for one month):

An Phu Tourist (☎ 862643, fax 864011, ⓔ anphu18@hotmail.com) 29 Đ Phan Dinh Phung
branch office: (☎ 861447) 141 Đ Tran Phu
Hanh Cafe (☎ 862370) 50 Phan Dinh Phung (Cong Doan Hotel)
Mr Thanh's Booking Office (☎ 8622228) 22 Đ Tran Phu
Sinh Cafe (☎ 863948, ⓔ quanghuy.ha@dng.vnn.vn) 37 Đ Phan Chu Trinh

One local freelance guide we can personally recommend is Madame Thi, one of Hoi An's only female tour guides; look for her at the Faifoo Restaurant, 104 Đ Tran Phu.

Architecture of Hoi An

A number of Hoi An's wooden buildings date from the first part of the 19th century or earlier, giving imaginative visitors the feeling that they have been transported back a couple of centuries to a time when the wharf was crowded with sailing ships, the streets teemed with porters transporting goods to and from warehouses and traders from a dozen countries haggled in a babble of different languages.

Because Hoi An was relatively untouched by the American War, it serves as a museum piece of Vietnamese history. At the time of writing, over 800 structures of historical significance have been officially identified in Hoi An. These structures can be categorised into nine types:

- Houses and shops
- Wells
- Family chapels for ancestor worship
- Pagodas
- Vietnamese and Chinese temples
- Bridges
- Communal buildings
- Assembly halls of various Chinese congregations
- Tombs (Vietnamese, Chinese and Japanese; no original European tombs survive)

Many of Hoi An's older structures exhibit features of traditional architecture rarely seen today. As they have for centuries, some shopfronts (which are open during the day to display their wares) are shuttered at night by the shopkeeper inserting horizontal planks into grooves cut into the columns

Money The Bank of Foreign Trade on Đ Hoang Dieu can exchange both cash and travellers cheques. Cash advances on credit cards are also given here.

Post The post office is on the north-west corner of Đ Ngo Gia Tu and Đ Tran Hung Dao.

Email & Internet Access Little Hoi An has a surprising number of places to get an online fix. There are at least six easy-to-spot places along Đ Le Loi and Đ Tran Phu, most charging around 300d per minute.

Medical Services The hospital is opposite the post office at 10 Đ Tran Hung Dao.

Japanese Covered Bridge

The famed Japanese Covered Bridge (Cau Nhat Ban, or Lai Vien Kieu) connects 155 Đ Tran Phu with 1 Đ Nguyen Thi Minh Khai. The first bridge on this site was constructed in 1593. It was built by the Japanese community of Hoi An to link them with the Chinese quarters across the stream. The bridge was provided with a roof so it could be used as a shelter from both the rain and sun.

The Japanese Covered Bridge is very solidly constructed; apparently the original builders were worried about the threat of earthquakes. Over the centuries, the ornamentation of the bridge has remained relatively faithful to the original Japanese design, reflecting the Japanese preference for understatement, which contrasts greatly with the Vietnamese and Chinese penchant for wild decoration. The French flattened out the roadway to make it more suitable for their motorcars, but the original arched shape was restored during major renovation work carried out in 1986.

Built into the northern side of the bridge is a small temple, Chua Cau. The writing over the door is the name given to the bridge in 1719 to replace the name meaning Japanese Bridge. The new name, Lai Vien Kieu (Bridge for Passers-By from Afar) never quite caught on.

Architecture of Hoi An

that support the roof. Some of the buildings' roofs are made up of thousands of brick-coloured *am* and *duong* (yin and yang) roof tiles – so called because of the way the alternating rows of concave and convex tiles fit snugly together. During the rainy season, the lichens and moss that live on the tiles spring to life, turning entire rooftops bright green.

A number of Hoi An's houses have round pieces of wood with an am and duong symbol in the middle surrounded by a spiral design over the doorway. These 'watchful eyes' *(mat cua)* are supposed to protect the residents of the house from coming to any harm.

Hoi An's historic structures are gradually being restored and there is a sincere effort being made to preserve the unique character of the city. The local government has put some thought into this – old houses must be licensed for restoration work and it must be done in a tasteful manner. The government certifies the historical significance of buildings – at present, there are four categories.

Assistance in historical preservation is being provided to local authorities by the Archaeological Institute in Hanoi, the Japan-Vietnam Friendship Association, and experts from Europe and Japan. The Old Town section of Hoi An is now closed to motor vehicles – a first in Vietnam.

There is a US$4 ticket that you must buy to get into some of the historical buildings. This ticket entitles you to visit four major sights that you select from a list on the ticket. If you want to see more (even if it is only one more sight), you will have to buy another US$4 ticket.

Many of the house owners also charge for the invasion of their privacy – as much as US$3 for a guided tour of the building – but this is negotiable. The government permits this on the basis that the funds will be used for renovation of the homes rather than going towards the purchase of TVs and new motorbikes (although this is good in theory, it is a difficult policy to enforce).

According to legend, there once lived an enormous monster called Cu, whose head was in India, its tail in Japan and its body in Vietnam. Whenever the monster moved, terrible disasters such as floods and earthquakes befell Vietnam. This bridge was built on the monster's weakest point – its 'Achilles' heel', so to speak – killing it. But the people of Hoi An took pity on the slain monster and built this temple to pray for its soul.

The entrances of the bridge are guarded by a pair of monkeys on one side and a pair of dogs on the other. According to one story, these animals were popularly revered because many of Japan's emperors were born in years of the dog and monkey. Another tale relates that construction of the bridge started in the year of the monkey and finished in the year of the dog.

The stelae listing Vietnamese and Chinese contributors to a subsequent restoration of the bridge are written in Chinese characters *(chu nho)*, the nom script not yet having become popular in these parts.

Tan Ky House

The Tan Ky House (☎ 861474) at 101 Đ Nguyen Thai Hoc was built two centuries ago as the home of a well-to-do ethnic-Vietnamese merchant. The house has been lovingly preserved and today looks almost exactly as it did in the early 19th century.

The design of Tan Ky House shows evidence of the Japanese and Chinese influence on local architecture. Japanese elements include the crabshell-shaped ceiling (in the section immediately before the courtyard), which is supported by three progressively shorter beams one on top of the other. There are similar beams in the salon. Under the crabshell ceiling are carvings of crossed sabres enwrapped by a ribbon of silk. The sabres symbolise force; the silk represents flexibility.

Chinese poems written in inlaid mother-of-pearl are hung from a number of the columns that hold up the roof. The Chinese characters on these 150-year-old panels are formed entirely of birds gracefully portrayed in various positions of flight.

The courtyard has four functions: to let in light; to provide ventilation; to bring a glimpse of nature into the home; and to collect rainwater and provide drainage. The stone tiles covering the patio floor were brought from Thanh Hoa Province in north-central Vietnam. The carved, wooden balcony supports around the courtyard are decorated with grape leaves – a European import and further evidence of the unique mingling of cultures that took place in Hoi An.

The back of the house faces the river. In the past, this section of the building was rented out to foreign merchants.

That the house was a place of commerce, as well as a residence, is indicated by the two pulleys attached to a beam in the storage loft just inside the front door.

The exterior of the roof is made of tiles; inside, the ceiling consists of wood. This design keeps the house cool in summer and warm in winter. The floor tiles were brought from near Hanoi.

Tan Ky House is a private home but is open to visitors for a small fee. The owner, whose family has lived here for seven generations, speaks fluent French and English. The house is open every day from 8 am to noon and 2 to 4.30 pm.

Diep Dong Nguyen House

The Diep Dong Nguyen House was built for a Chinese merchant, an ancestor of the present inhabitants, in the late 19th century. The front room on the ground floor was once a dispensary for *thuoc bac* (Chinese medicine); the medicines were stored in the glass-enclosed cases lining the walls. The owner's private collection of antiques, which includes photographs, porcelain and furniture, is on display upstairs. The objects are not for sale! Two of the chairs were once lent by the family to Emperor Bao Dai.

The house, which is at 80 (by the new numbering system) or 58 Đ Nguyen Thai Hoc (by the old system), is open daily from 8 am to noon and 2 to 4.30 pm.

House at 77 Tran Phu

The private house at 77 Đ Tran Phu is about three centuries old. There is some especially fine carving on the wooden walls of the rooms around the courtyard, on the roof beams and under the crabshell roof (in the salon next to the courtyard). Note the green ceramic tiles built into the railing around the courtyard balcony. The house is open to visitors for a small fee.

Tran Duong House

There is a whole city block of colonnaded French buildings on Đ Phan Boi Chau between Nos 22 and 73, among them the 19th-century home of Mr Tran Duong. Mr Duong, a friendly retired mathematics teacher, speaks English and French, and is happy to explain the history of the 62m-long house and its contents to visitors. There is no entrance fee, but contributions are, let's just say, encouraged by the owner. You'll find the house at 25 Đ Phan Boi Chau.

Assembly Halls

Cantonese Chinese Congregation The Assembly Hall of the Cantonese Chinese Congregation, founded in 1786, is at 176 Đ Tran Phu and is open daily from 6 to 7.30 am and 1 to 5.30 pm. The main altar is dedicated to Quan Cong. Note the long-handled brass 'fans' to either side of the altar. The lintel and door posts of the main entrance and a number of the columns supporting the roof are made of single blocks of granite. The other columns were carved out of the durable wood of the jackfruit tree. There are some interesting carvings on the wooden beams that support the roof in front of the main entrance.

Chinese All-Community The Chinese All-Community Assembly Hall (Chua Ba), founded in 1773, was used by all five Chinese congregations in Hoi An: Fujian, Cantonese, Hainan, Chaozhou and Hakka. The pavilions off the main courtyard incorporate 19th-century French elements.

The main entrance is on Đ Tran Phu opposite Đ Hoang Van Thu, but the only way in these days is around the back at 31 Đ Phan Chu Trinh.

Fujian Chinese Congregation This assembly hall was founded as a place to hold community meetings. Later, it was transformed into a temple for the worship of Thien Hau, the deity who was born in Fujian Province. The triple gate to the complex was built in 1975.

The mural near the entrance to the main hall on the right-hand wall depicts Thien Hau, her way lit by lantern light, crossing a stormy sea to rescue a foundering ship. On the wall opposite is a mural of the heads of the six Fujian families who fled from China to Hoi An in the 17th century following the overthrow of the Ming Dynasty.

The second-to-last chamber contains a statue of Thien Hau. To either side of the entrance stand red-skinned Thuan Phong Nhi and green-skinned Thien Ly Nhan. When either sees or hears sailors in distress, they inform Thien Hau, who sets off to effect a rescue. The replica of a Chinese boat along the right-hand wall is in 1:20 scale. The four sets of triple beams that support the roof are typically Japanese.

The central altar in the last chamber contains seated figures of the heads of the six Fujian families. The smaller figures below them represent their successors as clan leaders. In a 30cm-high glass dome is a figurine of Le Huu Trac, a Vietnamese physician renowned in both Vietnam and China for his curative abilities.

Behind the altar on the left is the God of Prosperity. On the right are three fairies and smaller figures representing the 12 'midwives' *(ba mu)*, each of whom teaches newborns a different skill necessary for the first year of life: smiling, sucking, lying on their stomachs and so forth. Childless couples often come here to pray for offspring. The three groups of figures in this chamber represent the elements most central to life: ancestors, children and financial wellbeing.

The middle altar of the room to the right of the courtyard commemorates deceased leaders of the Fujian congregation. On either side are lists of contributors – women on the left and men on the right. The wall panels represent the four seasons.

The Fujian assembly hall, opposite 35 Đ Tran Phu, is open from 7.30 am to noon and 2 to 5.30 pm. It is fairly well lit and can be visited after dark. Shoes should be removed upon mounting the platform just past the naves.

Hainan Chinese Congregation This assembly hall was built in 1883 as a memorial to the 108 merchants from Hainan Island who were mistaken for pirates and killed in Quang Nam Province during the reign of Emperor Tu Duc. The elaborate dais contains plaques in their memory. In front of the central altar is a fine gilded woodcarving of Chinese court life.

The Hainan Congregation Hall is at the east end of Đ Tran Phu, near the corner of Đ Hoang Dieu.

Chaozhou Chinese Congregation The Chaozhou Chinese in Hoi An built their congregational hall in 1776. There is some outstanding woodcarving on the beams, walls and altar. On the doors in front of the altar are carvings of two Chinese girls wearing their hair in the Japanese manner.

The assembly hall is opposite 157 Đ Nguyen Duy Hieu (near the corner with Đ Hoang Dieu).

Places of Worship

Quan Cong Temple Quan Cong Temple, also known as Chua Ong, is at 24 Đ Tran Phu (according to the new numbering system) and 168 Đ Tran Phu (according to the old). Founded in 1653, this Chinese temple is dedicated to Quan Cong, whose partially gilt statue – made of papier-mache on a wood frame – is in the central altar at the back of the sanctuary. On the left is a statue of General Chau Xuong, one of Quan Cong's guardians, striking a tough-guy pose. On the right is the rather plump administrative mandarin Quan Binh. The life-size white horse recalls a mount ridden by Quan Cong until he was given a red horse of extraordinary endurance, representations of which are common in Chinese pagodas.

Stone plaques on the walls list contributors to the construction and repair of the temple. Check out the carp-shaped rain spouts on the roof surrounding the courtyard. The carp, a symbol of patience in Chinese mythology, is a popular symbol in Hoi An.

Shoes should be removed when mounting the platform in front of the statue of Quang Cong.

Truong Family Chapel The Truong Family Chapel (Nha Tho Toc Truong), founded about two centuries ago, is a shrine dedicated to the ancestors of the ethnic-Chinese Truong family. A number of the memorial plaques were presented by emperors of Vietnam to honour members of the Truong family who served as local officials and as mandarins at the imperial court. To get there, turn into the alley next to 69 Đ Phan Chu Trinh.

Tran Family Chapel At 21 Đ Le Loi, at the intersection with Đ Phan Chu Trinh (north-east corner), is the Tran Family Chapel. This house for worshipping ancestors was built about 200 years ago with donations from family members. The Tran family traces its origins to China and moved to Vietnam around 1700. The architecture of the building reflects the influence of Chinese and Japanese styles. The wooden boxes on the altar contain the ancestors' stone tablets featuring chiselled Chinese characters.

Gate of Ba Mu Pagoda Though Ba Mu Pagoda, founded in 1628, was demolished by the South Vietnamese government during the 1960s to make room for a three-storey school building, the gate (Phat Tu) remains standing. Enormous representations of pieces of fruit form part of the wall between the two doorways. The gate is opposite 68 Đ Phan Chu Trinh.

Caodai Pagoda Serving Hoi An's Caodai community, many of whom live along the path out to the Japanese tombs, is the small Caodai Pagoda (built in 1952) between Nos 64 and 70 Đ Huynh Thuc Khang (near the bus station). One priest, who grows sugar and corn in the front yard to raise some extra cash, lives here.

Hoi An Church The only tombs of Europeans in Hoi An rest in the yard of the Hoi An Church, on the corner of Đ Nguyen Truong To and Đ Le Hong Phong. This modern building was constructed to replace an earlier structure at another site – several 18th-century missionaries were exhumed from the original site and reburied here.

Chuc Thanh Pagoda The Chuc Thanh Pagoda, founded in 1454 by Minh Hai, a Buddhist monk from China, is the oldest pagoda in Hoi An. Among the antique ritual objects still in use are several bells, a stone gong two centuries old and a carp-shaped wooden gong said to be even older. Today, several elderly monks live here.

In the main sanctuary, gilt Chinese characters inscribed on a red roof beam give details of the pagoda's construction. An A Di Da Buddha flanked by two Thich Ca Buddhas sits under a wooden canopy on the central dais. In front of them is a statue of a boyhood Thich Ca flanked by his servants.

To get to Chuc Thanh Pagoda, go all the way to the end of Đ Nguyen Truong To and turn left. Follow the sandy path for 500m.

Phuoc Lam Pagoda Phuoc Lam Pagoda was founded in the mid-17th century. The head monk at the end of that century was An Thiem, a Vietnamese prodigy who became a monk at the age of eight. When he was 18, the king drafted An Thiem's brothers into his army to put down a rebellion. An Thiem volunteered to take the places of the other men in his family and eventually rose to the rank of general. After the war, he returned to the monkhood, but felt guilty about the many people he had slain. To atone for his sins, he volunteered to clean the Hoi An Market for 20 years. When that time was up, he was asked to come to Phuoc Lam Pagoda as head monk.

To reach Phuoc Lam Pagoda, continue past Chuc Thanh Pagoda for 350m. The path passes by an obelisk erected over the tomb of 13 ethnic-Chinese decapitated by the Japanese during WWII for resistance activities.

Japanese Tombs

The tombstone of the Japanese merchant Yajirobei, who died in 1647, is clearly inscribed with Japanese characters. The stele, which faces north-east towards Japan, is held in place by the tomb's original covering, made from an especially hard kind of cement, the ingredients of which include powdered seashells, the leaves of the *boi loi* tree and cane sugar. Yajirobei may have been a Christian who came to Vietnam to escape persecution in his native land.

To get to Yajirobei's tomb, head north to the end of D Nguyen Truong Tu and follow the sand path around to the left (west) for 40m until you get to a fork. The path that continues straight on leads to Chuc Thanh Pagoda, but you should turn right (northward). Keep going for just over 1km, turning left (to the north) at the first fork and left (to the north-west) at the second fork. When you arrive at the open fields, keep going until you cross the irrigation channel. Just on the other side of the channel turn right (south-east) onto a raised path. After 150m, turn left (north-east) into the paddies and walk another 100m. The tomb, which is on a platform bounded by a low stone wall, stands surrounded by rice paddies.

The tombstone of a Japanese named Masai, who died in 1629, is a few hundred metres back towards Hoi An. To get there, turn left (south-east) at a point about 100m towards town from the edge of the rice fields. The tombstone is on the right-hand side of the trail about 30m from the main path.

For help in finding the Japanese tombs, show the locals the following words: 'Ma Nhat' (or 'Mo Nhat'), which mean Japanese tombs.

There are more Japanese tombs in Duy Xuyen district, across the delta of the Thu Bon River.

Places to Stay

Tiny Hoi An gets packed in the peak travel seasons – August to October and December to February. Unlike much of the rest of Vietnam, where the overbuilding of hotels has caused mass vacancies and cheaper prices, Hoi An is the one spot that still faces a room shortage. During the high season, hundreds of Hoi An visitors typically need to head up to Danang just to find a room. Though the situation is gradually changing, it is still advisable to book ahead.

Most travellers seem to want to find a room right in the town centre, so not surprisingly these fill up quickly. Yet the quieter and more spacious hotels tend to be on the outskirts of town. Considering how small Hoi An is and how easily you can walk around, there should be no great compulsion to find a place in the bustling heart of town.

Listed below are 'standard' rates; expect most of these to skyrocket during the busy months, especially November to January.

Set down a quiet alley, the friendly ***Pho Hoi 1 Hotel*** *(☎ 861633, fax 862626, 7/2 Đ Tran Phu)* is a pleasant choice. Fan/air-con doubles cost US$8/20. Also recommended, the snazzier ***Pho Hoi 2 Hotel*** *(☎ 862262, fax 862626)*, across Cam Nam Bridge on the bank of the Thu Bon River. Fan rooms cost US$8 to US$15, while air-con rooms cost US$15 to US$35. Top-class rooms have great balconies with river views and satellite TV. These two places are also called the *Faifoo 1* and *2*.

The pleasant ***Huy Hoang Hotel*** *(☎ 861453, fax 863722, 73 Đ Phan Boi Chau)* is also by Cam Nam Bridge and has a lovely riverside garden to sit and sip coffee. Fan rooms cost US$10 to US$15, or US$15 to US$20 with air-con. Two rooms with river views rent for US$30.

The atmospheric ***Vinh Hung Hotel*** *(☎ 861621, fax 861893, ⓔ vinhhung.ha@dng.vnn.vn, 143 Đ Tran Phu)* is housed in a classic Chinese trading house. Standard air-con rooms cost US$15, or US$20 upstairs. For US$30 to US$45 you can stay in one of three rooms decorated with antiques and beautiful canopy beds (unless you're a heavy sleeper, try to avoid the one directly above the reception desk). Rates include breakfast.

Keeping things Chinese, the attractive new ***Vinh Hung 2 Hotel*** *(☎ 863717, fax 864094, ⓔ quanghuy.ha@dng.vnn.vn, Đ Nhi Trung)* is a larger place featuring a swimming pool in the central courtyard. Fan rooms rent for US$15, or US$20 to US$35 with air-con.

Also Chinese in style is the nearby ***Phu Tinh Hotel*** *(☎ 861297, fax 861757, 144 Đ*

Tran Phu). Twins with fan are US$10 or US$12, or US$15 to US$18 with air-con and bath.

The family-run ***Thanh Binh Hotel*** *(☎ 861740, fax 864192, 1 Đ Le Loi)* is close to the town centre and a popular choice. Twins with fan cost US$8, or US$12 to US$20 with air-con. The new ***Thanh Binh 2 Hotel*** *(☎ 863715, fax 864192, Đ Nhi Trung)* is a larger place with singles from US$12 to US$20, and doubles and triples from US$20 to US$30.

Thien Trung Hotel *(☎ 861720, fax 863799, 63 Đ Phan Dinh Phung)* is an older, motel-style place. It's good if you're travelling by car as it has ample parking. Rooms cost US$10 to US$15.

Thuy Duong Hotel I *(☎ 861574, 11 Đ Le Loi)* has fan rooms with outside/inside toilet for US$8/9. Air-con rooms cost US$15 to US$20. The pleasant ***Thuy Duong Hotel II*** *(☎ 861394, fax 861330, 68 Đ Huynh Thuc Khang)*, right between the bus station and a small Caodai pagoda, charges US$12 for fan rooms, and US$15 with air-con.

Mai Lan Hotel *(☎ 861792, fax 862126, 87 Đ Huynh Thuc Khang)* is a decent-looking place opposite the bus station. Rooms cost US$8 with fan, or US$10 with air-con.

Binh Minh Hotel *(☎ 861943, 12 Đ Thai Phien)* has twins with fan for US$7 to US$10, or US$15 with air-con. Being a little further from the town centre means it's often not very full.

The pleasant ***Cua Dai Hotel*** *(☎ 862231, fax 862232, ⓔ cuadaihotel@dng.vnn.vn, 18 Đ Cua Dai)* is an attractive option because it's in a semi-rural area, yet still close enough to allow you to walk to the town centre. Air-con singles/twins cost US$20/25, including breakfast.

Nearby is the friendly ***Hotel Hai Yen*** *(☎ 862445, fax 862443, ⓔ kshaiyen@dng.vnn.vn, 22A Đ Cua Dai)*. Standard rooms are equipped with air-con, satellite TV and bath tubs, and cost US$25. Spacious suites decorated with Chinese reproduction furniture cost US$50.

Also in the neighbourhood is the ***Sao Bien Hotel*** *(Sea Star Hotel; ☎ 861589, fax 861382, 15 Đ Cua Dai)*, which has twins for US$10 to US$25.

On the northern outskirts of town, the huge, state-run ***Hoai Thanh Hotel*** *(☎ 861242, fax 861135, 23 Đ Le Hong Phong)* has fan/air-con rooms from US$14/20. Shelling out US$28 to US$35 earns you the right to watch satellite TV.

The government-owned ***Hoi An Hotel*** *(☎ 861373, fax 861636, 6 Đ Tran Hung Dao)* is a grand, colonial-style building and one of the largest hotels in Vietnam. Room rates range widely – US$20 to US$100.

Cong Doan Hotel *(☎ 826370, fax 861899, ⓔ hatradeunion@dng.vnn.vn, 50 Đ Phan Dinh Phung)*, or *Trade Union Hotel*, is another state-run hotel. It is not very attractive, but will do if everything else is full. Rooms with fan cost US$7 to US$8, or US$10 with air-con.

Green Field Hotel *(☎ 863484, fax 863136, 1C Đ Cua Dai)* – or Dong Xanh in Vietnamese – is a bit of a walk east of the town centre. Rooms with fan cost US$8 to US$15, or US$16 to US$25 with air-con.

At time of writing, three new upmarket places were under construction just outside Hoi An. The stylish ***Victoria Hoi An Resort*** and state-run ***Cua Dai Tourist Village*** are both on Cua Dai Beach, while the ***Riverside Resort*** is between Hoi An and the beach.

Places to Eat

Hoi An's contribution to Vietnamese cuisine is *cao lau*, which is doughy flat noodles mixed with croutons, bean sprouts and greens topped off with pork slices. It is mixed with crumbled, crispy rice paper immediately before eating. You'll see cao lau listed on menus all over Hoi An, which is the only place genuine cao lau can be made because the water used in its preparation must come from the Ba Le Well. The well itself, which is said to date from Cham times, is square in shape. To get there, turn down the alleyway opposite 35 Đ Phan Chu Trinh and hang a right before reaching number 45/17.

Another Hoi An speciality is fried *wonton* and you can find this in most local eateries. ***Ly Cafe 22*** *(☎ 861603, 22 Đ*

Nguyen Hue), a true Hoi An institution, has some of the best wontons (and other dishes) in town. The restaurant opens around 6.30 am, closes when empty and is nearly always crowded.

There are heaps of restaurants on Đ Nguyen Hue, Đ Tran Phu and Đ Bach Dang where you can enjoy a leisurely meal or linger over drinks. Many cuisines are available, including Western (banana pancakes, spaghetti and pizza), Vietnamese, Chinese and vegetarian, for reasonable prices.

Faifoo Restaurant *(☎ 861548, 104 Đ Tran Phu)* is another place serving excellent Vietnamese food, including the ubiquitous cao lau. A huge dinner costs US$3. Ask for Madame Thi, who is an excellent local tour guide.

The delightful ***Yellow River Restaurant*** *(☎ 861053, 38 Đ Tran Phu)* boasts a warm, Chinese-style atmosphere and excellent food. Other Chinese-looking places include the ***Thanh Thanh Restaurant*** and ***Tu Do Restaurant***, both on Đ Tran Phu, and the ***Thanh Binh Restaurant*** on Đ Le Loi.

The ***Mermaid Restaurant*** *(☎ 861527, 2 Đ Tran Phu)* also dishes up great food, including late breakfasts.

There have also been good reports on both ***Thang Long Restaurant*** *(☎ 861944, 136 Đ Nguyen Thai Hoc)* and the indoor-outdoor ***Vinh Hung Restaurant*** *(☎ 862 203, 147B Đ Tran Phu)*.

Some other popular spots for traditional and good backpacker cuisine include ***Cafe Bobo*** and the excellent ***Dudi Restaurant***, both on Đ Le Loi.

Restaurant King *(63 Đ Phan Dinh Phung)*, next to Thien Trung Hotel, is a small, unassuming place that specialises in delicious Hué food (try the spring rolls).

The Đ Bach Dang riverfront is a virtual eating arcade. ***Restaurant Du Port*** *(☎ 861786, 70 Đ Bach Dang)* gets good marks, or you might choose the nearby ***Rose*** or ***Bach Dang*** restaurants. ***Cafe des Amis*** *(☎ 861360, 52 Đ Bach Dang)* has a good set meal that changes every day.

Also notable on the riverside is ***Hong Phuc Restaurant*** *(☎ 862567, 86 Đ Bach Dang)*, known for its 'fish wrapped in banana leaf'. Aussies and Kiwis should feel right at home as the staff insist on calling everyone 'mate'!

Just next door, and also worth trying, is the ***Dong Phuong Restaurant***. Another riverfront dig is ***Restaurant Thanh*** *(76 Đ Bach Dang)*, which serves seafood, pizza and vegetarian food.

Han Huyen Restaurant is also nicknamed the *Floating Restaurant* (it is moored on the riverside). Considering how flood-prone this river is, it's not a bad idea. Just across the footbridge, the ***Dong An Restaurant*** has pleasant tables out on the riverside.

Cloned direct from the beaches of Nha Trang, the ***Banana Split Cafe*** *(☎ 861136, 53 Đ Hoang Dieu)* is where sweet-tooths can relieve any sudden cravings for ice cream, fresh fruit juices and, of course, banana splits.

Omar Khayyam's Indian Restaurant *(14 Đ Phan Dinh Phung)* does authentic curries.

One more fine dining option for *real* Western food is the ***Tam Tam Cafe & Bar*** (see its entry following).

Entertainment

The praiseworthy ***Tam Tam Cafe & Bar*** *(☎ 862212, fax 862207, e tamtam.ha@dng.vnn.vn, 110 Đ Nguyen Thai Hoc)* is upstairs in a thoughtfully restored tea warehouse. This most unexpected retreat is run by an expat Frenchman. There is excellent French and Italian food, a wide range of wine, salads, and a billiard table, a balcony for summer dining and a collection of over 400 CDs. The Aussie steaks washed down with a frosty draught BGI are popular. There is also a simple bar menu for light bites.

Another popular watering hole that get good reports is ***Treat's Café*** *(☎ 861125, 158 Đ Tran Phu)*. It is a spacious place with a pleasant restaurant-cafe on the 2nd storey. The congenial young owner Treat has nicknamed the place the *Same Same But Different Cafe*, and is known for his generous happy hour.

The ***Peace Bar*** *(Đ Le Loi)* is another fashionable backpackers hangout with a wide selection of Western CDs to choose from.

If you're more into the World Music scene, check out the new ***Zanzi Bar*** *(☎ 864400,*

53–54 Đ Nhi Trung) in the northern part of town near Đ Le Hong Phong.

Hai's Scout Cafe *(☎ 863210, 98 Đ Nguyen Thai Hoc)* is a dimly lit local cafe with a pleasant courtyard. It serves sandwiches, light meals, and real cappuccinos and lattes. You can enter the cafe on Đ Nguyen Thai Hoc or Đ Tran Phu.

The ***Rendezvous Bar*** is a small riverfront pub with a pool table.

The ***Champa Bar & Cafe*** *(☎ 861159, 75 Đ Nguyen Thai Hoc)* offers two pool tables, musical 'hits from the 1960s, 1970s, 1980s and 1990s', and traditional music shows staged in the house theatre nightly (Monday to Saturday). The show varies slightly on alternate nights, lasts from 9 to 10 pm and costs US$3. You might also inquire about Champa's Excursions on the Cultural Boat tour programs.

An interesting little cafe worth seeking is the Chinese-style ***Tam Long Quan*** *(☎ 862113, 48/10 Đ Tran Cao Van)*, tucked into a narrow alley near the Vinh Hung 2 Hotel. It is run by Mr Ngo Thi Hai, a local kung-fu master, who has the place decorated with various weaponry and an impressive collection of hand-carved wooden sculptures. At the time of writing staff were learning to make crepes and cakes from a young Frenchman living with the family.

Shopping

Hoi An is a shoppers' Mecca, though lamentably the air of commercialism has been increasingly taking a toll on the mellowed charm of the town. Still, Hoi An is nowhere near as overwhelming as many other tourist centres in Vietnam, and as it has developed as a direct result of us being there, perhaps we ought not complain?

Hoi An is known for its production of cotton cloth. All over the city there are cotton mills with rows of fantastic wooden looms that make a rhythmic 'clackety-clack, clackety-clack' sound as a whirring, cycloidal drive wheel shoots the shuttle back and forth under the watchful eyes of the machine attendant. The elegant technology used in building these domestically produced machines dates from the Industrial Revolution. Indeed, this is what mills in Victorian England must have looked like.

Tailor-made clothing is one of Hoi An's specialities and in the space of just a few years the number of tailor shops has grown from a handful to over 200 shops! (See the boxed text 'Sewing up a Storm' in this section.) Recommending one tailor over another is indeed a difficult proposition, and with so many tailors competing for limited tourist dollars, touts are out in full force (most of them cute young girls who use the 'What's your name? – Where are you from? – Would you like to come and see my auntie's shop?' approach). In fact, the tailors are all rather similar, and most of them should be fine whether you're looking for alterations or a whole new wardrobe. For a look at the various materials available locally, take a peak at the Hoi An Cloth Market on Đ Tran Phu.

One accoutrements connoisseur, however, had this to say:

> The clothes-making scene here is enticing but our advice is to keep it simple...and stick to local styles. Use the models that are on display and get copies made. You'll get better results – and count on some adjustments.
>
> **Heather Merriam**

The presence of numerous tourists has turned the fake antique business into Hoi An's major growth industry. Theoretically you could find something here that is really old, but it's hard to believe that all the genuine stuff wasn't scooped up long ago.

On the other hand, there is some really elegant artwork around, even if it was made only yesterday. Paintings are generally the mass-produced kind of stuff, but are still hand painted; for a few US dollars you can't complain.

Woodcarvings are also a local speciality. Cross Cam Nam Bridge to Cam Nam Village, a lovely spot where some woodcarvings are made. Across the An Hoi footbridge is the An Hoi Peninsula, which is known for its boat factory and mat-weaving factories.

There are lovely blue and white ceramic goods for sale at a strip of small shops along the Đ Bach Dang riverfront.

Sewing Up a Storm

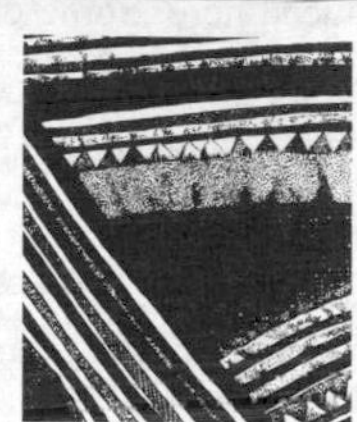

From dawn until dusk, the whirring of sewing machines resounds through historic Hoi An. The town itself is a virtual treasure trove with fabric of every type to be found all over – in some places stacked to the ceilings of the various cloth shops.

Spending a morning being pampered in any of the dressmakers' shops in and around the market is a great experience. Choose your new wardrobe from endless rolls of material and, for a little over the cost of the cloth, you'll soon have tailor-made shirts, trousers, dresses and skirts.

A completely new fitted wardrobe, including material, can cost as little as US$100: an evening dress starts at around US$15, a summer dress at US$8 and a suit at US$20.

Incredibly, the master tailors here can whip together anything from slinky silk pyjamas to a formal Japanese kimono, and are even able to copy designs straight out of fashion magazines – anything from a copy of a designer ball gown to a top city slicker suit in less than a couple of hours. Whether silk, cotton, linen or synthetic, people rave about the clothes they had made in Hoi An.

When buying silk it is important to ascertain that the material is real silk and not 'Vietnamese silk' – a term often used to describe polyester and other synthetic fabrics that look and feel like silk. The only real test is with a cigarette or match (synthetic fibres melt and silk burns), but be careful not to set the shop on fire! Ask for a cut-off sample of the material you are thinking of buying and go outside to test it if you're concerned about its authenticity.

It is also important to check the seams of the finished garment, a single set of stitching along the inside edges will soon cause fraying and, in many cases, great big gaping holes. All well-tailored garments have a second set of stitches (known in the trade as blanket stitching), which binds the edge, oversewing the fabric so fraying is impossible. Ask the person tailoring the outfit to use the same colour cotton as the material – otherwise they will use white cotton throughout. Where possible, also insist on the clothes being lined, as it helps them move and fall in the right direction

A few hours after your initial consultation, when you will be measured from every angle, you can return for your final fitting session and adjustments. Your only concern will be whether to carry your new gear around or make a dash to the post office to send it home.

Juliet Coombe

Getting There & Away

Bus The Hoi An bus station is 1km west of the centre of town at 74 Đ Huynh Thuc Khang. Truck buses from here go to Dai Loc (Ai Nghia), Danang, Quang Ngai, Que Son, Tam Ky and Tra My. Services to Danang cost 20,000d (US$1.60) and begin at 5 am; the last Danang bus departs in the late afternoon.

Minibus Virtually every hotel in Hoi An can sell you a minibus ticket to either Nha Trang or Hué. The Hoi An–Hué minibus goes through Danang and you can be dropped off there if you like. The fare to Nha Trang is around US$8, to Hué is US$4, Danang is US$2 and My Lai is US$6.

Car & Motorbike There are two land routes from Danang to Hoi An. The shorter way is via the Marble Mountains (11km) from where you continue south for another 19km. Alternatively, head south on Highway 1 and, at the signposted intersection 27km from the city, turn left and Hoi An is 10km to the east.

The going rate for a motorbike taxi between Danang and Hoi An is about 30,000d (US$2.40).

Boat Small, motorised ferries leave Hoi An for nearby districts and Cham Island from the landing at the end of Đ Hoang Van Thu. There are daily boats to Cham Island (usually departing between 7 and 8 am), and also to Duy Xuyen (leaving around 5 am). There is also frequent service to Cam Kim Island.

Getting Around

Anywhere within town can be reached on foot. To go further afield, rent a bicycle for US$1 per day or a motorbike for US$5/10 per day without/with driver. Inquire at your hotel, or try Mr My at Cafe Bobo.

Boat A paddle-boat trip on the Thu Bon River (Cai River) – the largest in Quang Nam Province – is recommended. A simple rowing boat with oarsperson costs something like US$2 per hour, and one hour is probably long enough for most travellers. With a motor launch it may be possible to take an all-day boat ride all the way to Tra Kieu (Simhapura) and the My Son area.

Boats that carry up to five people can also be hired to visit area handicraft and fishing villages; expect to pay around US$4 per hour. Look for the boats near the rowboat dock, and across from the Rose restaurant.

AROUND HOI AN

Cua Dai Beach

The fine sands of palm-lined Cua Dai Beach (Bai Tam Cua Dai) are popular but can often be deserted. During the full moon, people hang out until late at night. Fresh seafood and refreshments are sold in the shaded kiosks. Purchasing food or drinks here earns you the right to lounge in one of the cosy deck chairs. Look for a kiosk keeper named Mr My – he has had several recommendations for tasty seafood, cold beer and the fact that he does *not* overcharge travellers (unlike most vendors on the beach).

Cua Dai Beach is 5km east of Hoi An on Đ Cua Dai, which is the continuation of Đ Tran Hung Dao and Đ Phan Dinh Phung. The road passes shrimp-hatching pools built with Australian assistance.

Cam Kim Island

The master woodcarvers, who in previous centuries produced the fine carvings that graced the homes of Hoi An's merchants and the town's public buildings, came from Kim Bong Village on Cam Kim Island. These days, most of the woodcarvings on sale in Hoi An are produced here. Some of the villagers also build wooden boats.

To reach the island, catch one of the frequent boats from the Đ Hoang Van Thu Dock.

Cham Island

Cham Island (Culao Cham) is 21km from Hoi An in the South China Sea. The island is famous as a source of swifts' nests, which are exported to Hong Kong, Singapore and elsewhere for use in bird's-nest soup.

Scuba diving is one possible form of entertainment here. You can get a permit for fishing.

The Cham Island festival is kind of like a blessing of the fleet. It marks the start of the fishing season. It's held yearly, though the exact date isn't fixed. When I attended, it was held on 29 March, which is Danang's liberation day, which was also Easter and possibly significant on the lunar calendar too. They had dragon boat races, coracle races (without paddles, the drivers bounce the coracles along), a tug-of-war, and a religious part with monks, incense and offerings.

Mark Procter

Getting There & Away A motorised ferry to Cham Island's two fishing villages departs from the Đ Hoang Van Thu Dock at about 7 am and the one-way journey takes three hours. The boat returns in the afternoon.

You might also check with tour operators in Hoi An to see what kind of trips are being offered to Cham Island. One place to inquire is at the small booking office near the intersection of Đ Bach Dang and Đ Hoang Van Thu.

Thanh Ha

Thanh Ha, sometimes called the 'pottery village', is 3km west of Hoi An. In the recent past there were many pottery factories here, but the pottery industry has been in decline. Still, some artisans are employed in this hot, sweaty work. The locals don't mind if you visit their factories to watch them at work, though they'd be happier if you bought something in exchange for showing you around.

TAM KY

☎ 0510

Tam Ky, the capital of Quang Nam Province, is a nondescript town on the highway between Chu Lai and Danang. However, travellers are drawn to the Cham towers at nearby Chien Dang (Chien Dang Cham), which is located 5km north of Tam Ky, 69km north of Quang Ngai and 62km south of Danang.

The three towers are enclosed by a wall. A broken stele here dates from the 13th-century reign of King Harivarman. Many of the Cham statues you can see on display at Chien Dang were collected from other parts of the country after the American War and show signs of war-related damage.

Places to Stay

The ***Tam Ky Hotel*** *(Khach San Tam Ky)* is on Highway 1 in the centre of town. This is the only hotel in Tam Ky that can accommodate travellers.

CHU LAI

About 30km north of Quang Ngai, the buildings and concrete aircraft revetments of the huge American base at Chu Lai stretch along several kilometres of sand to the east of Highway 1.

During the war, a huge shantytown made of packing crates and waste tin from canning factories developed next to the base. The inhabitants of the shantytown supported themselves by providing services to the Americans: doing laundry, selling soft drinks and engaging in prostitution.

Nowadays, despite the obvious dangers, collecting and selling scrap metal from abandoned ordnance has become a thriving local industry.

South-Central Coast

This section covers the littoral provinces of Binh Thuan, Ninh Thuan, Khanh Hoa, Phu Yen, Binh Dinh and Quang Ngai. The cities, towns, beaches and historical sites in this region, most of which are along National Highway 1, referred to by many foreign tourists as the 'Ho Chi Minh Trail' (the real one is actually farther inland), are listed from north to south.

The southernmost province, Binh Thuan, is one of the most arid regions of Vietnam (particularly north of Phan Thiet). The nearby plains, dominated by rocky, roundish mountains, support some marginal irrigated rice agriculture. Some of Vietnam's most beautiful beaches are scattered out along the coast, and there are many ruins of Cham culture. There is also easy access in and out of the mountainous regions inland from several points along the coast (see the Central Highlands chapter later in the book).

Highlights

- Soak up the sun and enjoy the sea on peaceful Mui Ne Beach, near Phan Thiet.
- Visit some of the area's impressive Cham ruins, notably at Phan Rang and Thap Cham.
- Go island-hopping or scuba diving in the turquoise waters off Nha Trang.

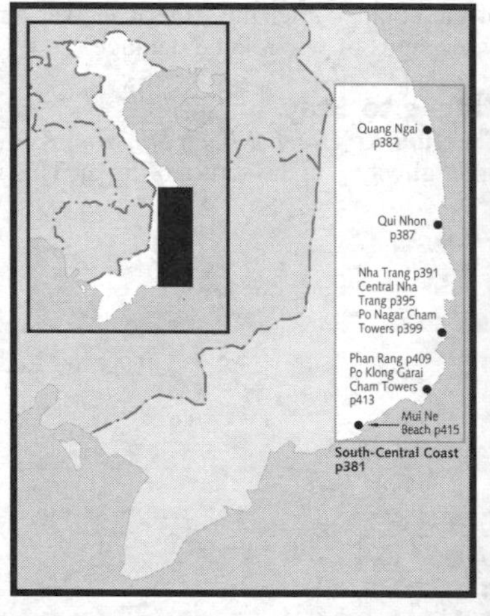

QUANG NGAI

☎ 055 • pop 108,200

Quang Ngai, the capital of Quang Ngai Province, is something of a backwater. Built on the south bank of the Tra Khuc River (known for its oversized water wheels), the city is about 15km from the coast. The city and province of Quang Ngai are also known as Quang Nghia; the name is sometimes abbreviated to Quangai.

Even before WWII, Quang Ngai was an important centre of resistance to the French. During the Franco–Viet Minh War, the area was a Viet Minh stronghold. In 1962, the South Vietnamese Government introduced its ill-fated Strategic Hamlets Program to the area. Villagers were forcibly removed from their homes and resettled in fortified hamlets, infuriating and alienating the local population and increasing popular support for the Viet Cong (VC). Some of the bitterest fighting of the American War took place in Quang Ngai Province.

Son My subdistrict, 14km north of Quang Ngai, was the scene of the infamous My Lai Massacre of 1968, in which hundreds of civilians were slaughtered by American soldiers. A memorial has been erected on the site of the killings.

As a result of the wars, very few older bridges in Quang Ngai Province remain intact. At many river crossings, the rust-streaked concrete pylons of the old French bridges, probably destroyed by the Viet Minh, stand next to the ruins of their replacements, blown up by the VC.

Orientation

National Highway 1 is called Đ Quang Trung as it passes through Quang Ngai. The train station is 3km west of the town centre on Đ Hung Vuong.

Information

Post & Communications The main post office is 150m west of Đ Quang Trung on the corner of Đ Hung Vuong and Đ Phan Dinh Phung.

Places to Stay

If you're looking for peaceful night's sleep, try the ***Hotel 502*** *(☎ 822656, 28 Đ Hung Vuong)*. It's in a courtyard down a quiet alley. Clean rooms start at US$6 with fan, or cost US$9 to US$12 with air-con.

Kim Thanh Hotel *(☎ 823471, 19 Đ Hung Vuong)* seems fairly well attuned to the backpacker market and has doubles going for US$13 to US$18.

Just down the road, the small ***Vietnam Hotel*** *(☎ 823610, 41 Đ Hung Vuong)* could be very handy, should you suddenly forget what country you're travelling in. Fan rooms here cost US$6 to US$8, or US$12 with air-con.

The ***Hoa Vien Hotel*** *(☎ 823455, 12 Đ Phan Chu Trinh)* is another good place. Large rooms with air-con and hot water are available for US$15.

Dung Hung Hotel *(☎ 821704)* is on the busy central artery of town. Rooms cost US$4 with fan and cold water, or US$7 to US$10 with air-con.

The ***Central Hotel*** *(☎ 829999, fax 822460, ⓔ Central@dng.vnn.vn 784 Đ Quang Trung)* is the classiest accommodation option in Quang Ngai. Located at the southern end of town, double rooms in this fancy pleasure palace cost US$35 to US$60, or US$80 for a suite. Facilities include a tennis court and swimming pool.

My Tra Hotel *(☎ 842985, fax 842980)* is another upmarket place, though is not as good value as the Central Hotel. Rooms range from US$30 to US$40 with breakfast included, and suites go for US$105. It's on the northern outskirts of town, just across the Tra Khuc River.

The ***Government Guesthouse*** *(Đ Pham Dinh Phung)* has basic rooms for around US$15.

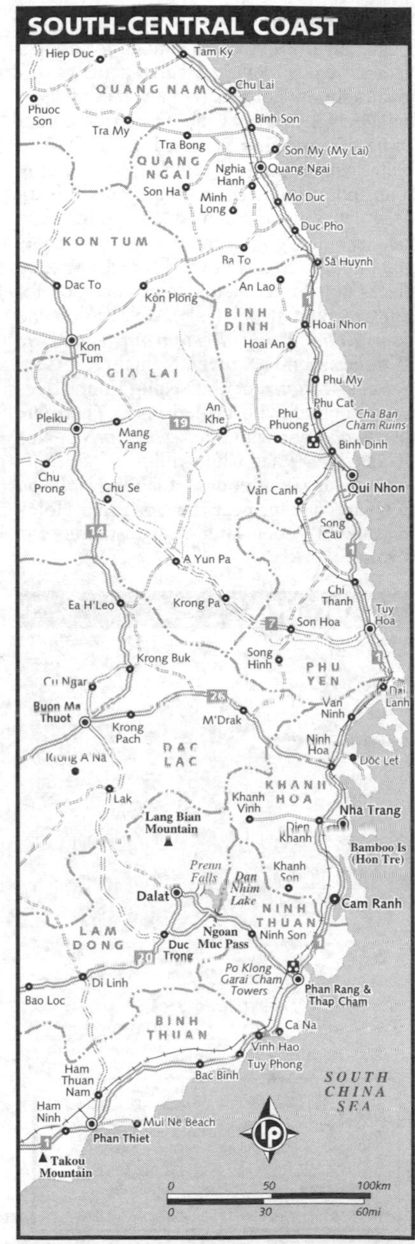

Places to Eat

Quang Ngai Province is famous for a local delicacy called *com ga*, which actually originates further north at Tam Ky. It consists of boiled chicken over yellow rice (the colour comes from being steamed with chicken broth) with a mint leaf garnish, plus egg drop soup and pickled vegies on the side. It is indeed delicious and something any chicken lover should try. At about US$0.50 per plate, you might even have two. There are several places in town to try this treat (just look for signs reading 'Com Ga'). We recommend both ***Bong Hong Restaurant*** and ***Hue Restaurant*** on Đ Nguyen Nghiem.

Bang Restaurant on Đ Hung Vuong does good noodles with grilled pork. There are also two very cheap rice ***restaurants*** at Nos 30 and 34 Đ Phan Chu Trinh.

If you arrive after dark, the ***food stalls*** on Đ Quang Trung, near the Song Tra Hotel, tend to stay open later than restaurants in town.

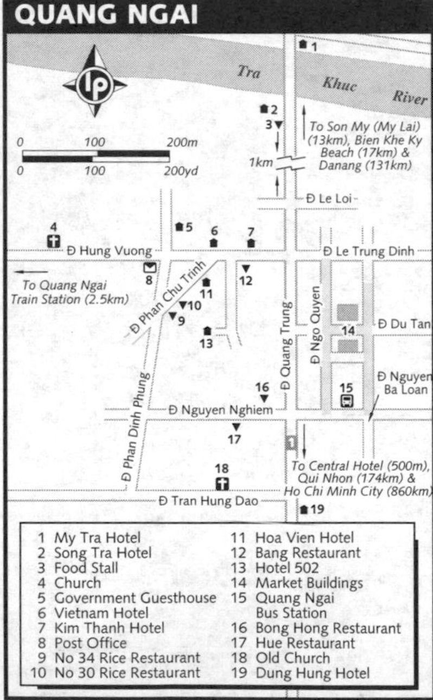

Getting There & Away

Bus Quang Ngai bus station (Ben Xe Khach Quang Ngai) is opposite 32 Đ Nguyen Nghiem, about 100m east of Đ Quang Trung (National Highway 1). Buses from here go to Buon Ma Thuot (and other places in Dak Lak Province), Dalat, Danang, Hoi An, Kon Tum, Pleiku, Nha Trang, Qui Nhon and Ho Chi Minh City.

Minibus There are now some tourist minibuses between Quang Ngai and Hoi An for around US$5. Quang Ngai is 100km from Hoi An; the ride takes about two hours.

Train The Quang Ngai train station (Ga Quang Nghia or Ga Quang Ngai) is 3km west of the centre of town. To get there, take Đ Hung Vuong west from Đ Quang Trung (National Highway 1) and continue going in the same direction after the street name changes to Đ Nguyen Chanh. At 389 Đ Nguyen Chanh (which you'll come to as Đ Nguyen Chanh curves left), continue straight on down a side street. The train station is at the end of the street.

Reunification Express trains stop at Quang Ngai – see the Train section in the Getting Around chapter.

Car & Motorbike Road distances from Quang Ngai are 131km to Danang, 860km to Ho Chi Minh City, 412km to Nha Trang and 174km to Qui Nhon.

AROUND QUANG NGAI

Son My (My Lai)

The site of the My Lai Massacre is 14km from central Quang Ngai. To get there from town, head north (towards Danang) on Đ Quang Trung (National Highway 1) and cross the long bridge over the Tra Khuc River. Metres from the northern end of the bridge, you will come to a triangular concrete stele indicating the way to the Son My Memorial. Turn right (eastward, parallel to the river) on the dirt road and continue for 12km. The road to Son My passes through particularly beautiful countryside with rice paddies, manioc patches and vegetable gardens shaded by casuarinas and eucalyptus trees.

The Son My Memorial is set in a park where Xom Lang sub-hamlet once stood (see the 'My Lai Massacre' boxed text later in this chapter). Around it, among the trees and rice paddies, are the graves of some of the victims, buried in family groups. Near the memorial is a **museum**, which was opened in 1992; admission is US$0.80.

If you don't have a car, the best way to get to Son My District from Quang Ngai is to hire a motorbike taxi *(Honda om)* near the bus station or along D Quang Trung.

Bien Khe Ky Beach

Bien Khe Ky Beach (Bai Bien Khe Ky) is a long, secluded beach of fine sand 17km from Quang Ngai and several kilometres east of the Son My Memorial. The beach stretches for many kilometres along a long, thin casuarina-lined spit of sand. It is separated from the mainland by Song Kinh Giang, a body of water about 150m inland from the beach.

SA HUYNH

☎ 055

Sa Huynh is a little seaside town with a beautiful semicircular beach bordered by rice paddies and coconut palms. The town is also known for its salt marshes and salt-evaporation ponds.

Archaeologists have unearthed remains of the Dong Son Civilisation dating from the 1st century AD in the vicinity of Sa Huynh.

Places to Stay & Eat

There is only one place to stay, the crumbling concrete ***Sa Huynh Hotel*** *(☎ 860311, fax 822836)*, which is right on the beach. Other than the pleasant beachside setting, there's little to recommend this place. Singles with fan cost US$8 to US$10, fan doubles are US$12 to US$13; air-con rooms are US$12 to US$18.

The state-run ***restaurant*** on the hotel grounds is depressing and the service is poor. Fortunately, there are a number of small ***roadside restaurant-cafes*** a few hundred metres away, out on National Highway 1. One of the best is called ***Vinh***.

Getting There & Away

Train Some nonexpress trains stop at the Sa Huynh train station (Ga Sa Huynh), but it will be slow going.

Car & Motorbike Sa Huynh is on National Highway 1 about 114km north of Qui Nhon and 60km south of Quang Ngai.

QUI NHON

☎ 056 • pop 231,300

Qui Nhon (or Quy Nhon) is the capital of Binh Dinh Province and one of Vietnam's more active second-string seaports. The beaches in the immediate vicinity of the city are nothing special, however Qui Nhon is a convenient – though somewhat disappointing – place to break the long journey from Nha Trang to Danang. The town used to be more prosperous a few years ago, when smuggling imported goods by sea was the chief industry – that business has now moved up north to the Chinese border.

There are some Cham towers along National Highway 1 about 10km north of the Qui Nhon turn-off.

During the American War, there was considerable South Vietnamese, American, VC and South Korean military activity in the Qui Nhon area. Refugees dislocated by the fighting and counter-insurgency programs built whole slums of tin and thatch shacks around the city. During this period, the mayor of Qui Nhon, hoping to cash in on the presence of American troops, turned his official residence into a large massage parlour.

Orientation

Qui Nhon is on the coast 10km east of National Highway 1. The big highway junction where you turn off to Qui Nhon is called the Ba Di Bridge Crossroad (Nga Ba Cau Ba Di).

Qui Nhon proper is on an east-west oriented peninsula shaped like the nose of an anteater. The tip of the nose (the port area) is closed to the public. The Municipal Beach is on the peninsula's southern coast.

From the Municipal Beach, Cu Lao Xanh Island is visible offshore. Due east of the beach (to the left as you face the water) you can see, in the distance, an oversize statue

My Lai Massacre

Son My subdistrict was the site of the most horrific war crimes committed by American troops during the American War. The My Lai Massacre consisted of a series of atrocities carried out all over Son My subdistrict, which is divided into four hamlets, only one of which is named My Lai. The largest mass killing took place in Xom Lang (Thuan Yen) subhamlet, where the Son My Memorial was later erected.

Son My subdistrict was a known VC stronghold, and it was widely believed that villagers in the area were providing food and shelter to the VC (if true, the villagers would have had little choice – the VC was known for taking cruel revenge on those who didn't 'cooperate'). Just whose idea it was to 'teach the villagers a lesson' has never been determined. What is known is that several American soldiers had been killed and wounded in the area in the days preceding the 'search-and-destroy operation' that began on the morning of 16 March 1968.

The operation was carried out by Task Force Barker – three companies of American infantry. At about 7.30 am – after the area around Xom Lang had been bombarded with artillery, and the landing zone raked with rocket and machine-gun fire from helicopter gunships – Charlie Company (commanded by Captain Ernest Medina) landed by helicopter. They encountered no resistance during the 'combat-assault', nor did they come under fire at any time during the entire operation; but as soon as their sweep eastward began, so did the atrocities.

As Lieutenant William Calley's 1st Platoon moved through Xom Lang, they shot and bayoneted fleeing villagers, threw hand grenades into houses and bomb shelters, slaughtered livestock and burned dwellings. Somewhere between 75 and 150 unarmed villagers were rounded up and herded to a ditch, where they were mowed down by machine-gun fire.

of Tran Hung Dao erected on a promontory overlooking the fishing village of Hai Minh.

The streets around Lon Market constitute Qui Nhon's town centre.

Information

Money Vietcombank (☎ 822266), or the Bank of Foreign Trade (Ngan Hang Ngoai Thuong), is at 148 Đ Le Loi on the corner of Đ Tran Hung Dao.

Travel Agencies Binh Dinh Tourist (☎ 822940) is located at 266 Đ Phan Boi Chau. It offers tour programs to area sites including the Cham ruins of Thap Doi, Cha Ban and Duong Long.

Emergency The General Hospital is opposite 309 Đ Nguyen Hue.

Long Khanh Pagoda

Long Khanh Pagoda, Qui Nhon's main pagoda, is down an alley opposite 62 Đ Tran Cao Van and next to 143 Đ Tran Cao Van. A 17m-high Buddha (built in 1972) is visible from the street, and presides over a lily pond strongly defended (against surprise attack?) by barbed wire. To the left of the main building is a low tower sheltering a giant drum; to the right, its twin contains an enormous bell, which was cast in 1970.

The main sanctuary was completed in 1946 but was damaged during the Franco–Viet Minh War; repairs were completed in 1957. In front of the large copper Thich Ca Buddha (with its multicoloured neon halo) is a drawing of multiarmed and multieyed Chuan De (the Goddess of Mercy); the numerous arms and eyes mean she can touch and see all. There is a colourfully painted Buddha at the edge of the raised platform. In the corridor that passes behind the main altar is a bronze bell that dates from 1805, and has Chinese inscriptions on it.

Under the eaves of the left-hand building of the courtyard, behind the sanctuary, hangs a blow-up of the famous photograph of the monk Thich Quang Duc. In the photo, he is immolating himself in Saigon

My Lai Massacre

In the next few hours, as command helicopters circled overhead and American navy boats patrolled offshore, the 2nd Platoon (under Lieutenant Stephen Brooks), the 3rd platoon (under Lieutenant Jeffrey La Cross) and the company headquarters group also committed unspeakable crimes. At least half a dozen groups of civilians, including women and children, were assembled and executed. Villagers fleeing towards Quang Ngai along the road were machine-gunned, and wounded civilians (including young children) were summarily shot. As these massacres were taking place, at least four girls and women were raped or gang-raped by groups of soldiers.

One soldier is reported to have shot himself in the foot to get himself out of the slaughter; he was the only American casualty in the entire operation. Troops who participated were ordered to keep their mouths shut, but several disobeyed orders and went public with the story after returning to the USA. When it broke in the newspapers, it had a devastating effect on the military's morale and fuelled further public protests against the war. Unlike WWII veterans, who returned home to parades and glory, soldiers coming home from Vietnam often found themselves ostracised by their fellow citizens and taunted as 'baby killers'.

A cover up of the atrocities was undertaken at all levels of the American army command, eventually leading to several investigations. Lieutenant Calley was made chief ogre and was court-martialled and found guilty of the murders of 22 unarmed civilians. He was sentenced to life imprisonment in 1971 and spent three years under house arrest at Fort Benning, Georgia, while appealing his conviction. Calley was paroled in 1974 after the US Supreme Court refused to hear his case. Calley's case still causes controversy – many claim that he was made a scapegoat due to his low rank, and that officers much higher up ordered the massacres. What is certain is that he didn't act alone.

in June 1963 to protest the policies of the Diem regime. The second level of the two-storey building behind the courtyard contains memorial plaques for deceased monks (on the middle altar) and lay people.

Long Khanh Pagoda was founded around 1700 by a Chinese merchant, Duc Son (1679–1741). The seven monks who live here preside over the religious affairs of Qui Nhon's relatively active Buddhist community. Single-sex religion classes for children are held on Sunday.

Beaches

Qui Nhon Municipal Beach, which extends along the southern side of the anteater's nose, consists of a few hundred metres of sand shaded by a coconut grove. The nicest section of beach is across from the Quy Nhon Hotel, but it has become increasingly dirty. Farther west, the shore is lined with the boats and shacks of fishing families.

A longer, quieter bathing beach begins about 2km south-west of the Municipal Beach. To get there, follow Đ Nguyen Hue away from the tip of the peninsula westward. Part of the seafront near here is lined with industrial plants, some of which belong to the military.

Zoo

Binh Dinh–Xiem Riep–Ratanakiri Zoo, whose inhabitants include monkeys, crocodiles, porcupines and bears, is named after the two Cambodian provinces the animals came from. The uncharitable might classify the animals here as war booty (or prisoners of war). The zoo is at 2B Đ Nguyen Hue.

Lon Market

Lon Market (Cho Lon), Qui Nhon's central market, is a large modern building enclosing a courtyard in which fruits and vegetables are sold.

Leper Hospital

This is not a tourist attraction but visitors are welcome, especially if they make a small donation or purchase a few basic items from the locals. As leper hospitals go, this one is highly unusual. Rather than being a depressing place, it's a sort of model village where infected patients live together with their families in well-kept, small houses. According to their abilities, the patients work in repair-oriented businesses or small craft shops. The hospital grounds are so well maintained that it looks a bit like a resort.

The leper hospital is out on the western end of Đ Nguyen Hue.

Places to Stay

The old ***Bank Hotel*** *(☎ 823591, fax 821013, 257 Đ Le Hong Phong)* has budget rooms with fan and hot bath for US$10. Luxuries such as air-con push up the price from US$15 to US$25.

Thanh Binh Hotel *(☎ 822041, fax 827569, 6 Đ Ly Thuong Kiet)* is a nicer choice, and charges from US$8 to US$18 in the old wing, or US$20 to US$40 in the fancy new wing.

Dien Anh Hotel *(☎ 822876, fax 822869, 298 Đ Phan Boi Chau)* is owned by the local movie studio and attracts aspiring actors. Fan single/doubles cost US$9/10, or US$13/15 with air-con.

Hoang Kim Hotel *(☎ 828768, fax 823826, 369 Đ Le Hong Phong)* – also called the *Golden Age Hotel* – is a centrally located place with rooms from US$8/12 with fan/air-con.

Dong Phuong Hotel *(☎ 822915, 60 Đ Mai Xuan Thuong)* is another concrete box. Accommodation costs US$5 to US$18 – the pricier rooms have hot bath showers. It is known for its massage service.

Anh Thu Mini-Hotel *(☎ 821168, fax 823043, 54 Đ Mai Xuan Thuong)* is getting run-down, but is notable for having motorbikes for rent. Rooms with air-con and bath rent for US$10/13.

One block from the city beach is the friendly ***Hai Ha Mini-Hotel*** *(☎ 891295, 892300, 5 Đ Tran Binh Trong)*. Nice air-con rooms cost US$25.

Facing the beach, the ***Phuong Mai Hotel*** *(☎ 822921, 18 Đ Nguyen Hue)* has a certain derelict charm. All rooms have private baths, though with cold water only. Doubles cost US$10.

Quy Nhon Hotel *(☎ 822401, fax 821162, e hotelquynhon@dng.vnn.vn, 8 Đ Nguyen Hue)* is directly opposite the city beach. Judging from the hotel's brochures, it seems that the management believes the Qui Nhon Municipal Beach and Quy Nhon Hotel are Vietnam's answer to the French Riviera and Club Med. However, Club Med is not exactly shaking in its boots. Room rates are US$14 to US$60, which might sound reasonable until you look at what you're getting.

Two possible choices west of the city centre are the ***Seagull Hotel*** *(☎ 846473, fax 846926, e ks.haiau@dng.vnn.vn, 489 Đ An Duong Vuong)*, and the military-owned ***Binh Duong Hotel*** *(☎ 846267, fax 846558, 489 Đ An Duong Vuong)*. Rates at the Seagull are US$20 to US$45 (including breakfast), and US$18 to US$30 at the Binh Duong.

Places to Eat

Dong Phuong Restaurant, on the ground floor of the Dong Phuong Hotel, serves reasonably good Vietnamese food and a few Western dishes.

A better bet is to head for the local point-and-eat ***com binh dan restaurants*** near the Bank Hotel.

Nearby, there are tasty bakery items and excellent ice cream at ***Kem Bach Ngoc Nha***.

There's a handful of good ***noodle soup shops*** serving *pho* near the corner of Đ Phan Boi Chau and Đ Mai Xuan Thuong.

Getting There & Away

Air Vietnam Airlines flights link Ho Chi Minh City with Qui Nhon five times weekly. There are also flights to/from Danang three times weekly.

Phu Cat airport is 36km north of Qui Nhon. For airline passengers, transport to and from Phu Cat is provided by Vietnam Airlines.

In Qui Nhon, the Vietnam Airlines' booking office (☎ 822953) is near the Thanh Binh Hotel in the building next to 30 Đ Nguyen Thai Hoc.

Bus Qui Nhon bus station or Ben Xe Khach Qui Nhon (☎ 822246) is opposite 543 Đ

Tran Hung Dao (across from the corner with Đ Le Hong Phong).

There are express buses to Buon Ma Thuot, Dalat, Danang, Dong Hoi, Hanoi, Hué, Nha Trang, Ninh Binh, Quang Tri, Ho Chi Minh City, Thanh Hoa and Vinh.

Train The nearest the *Reunification Express* trains get to Qui Nhon is Dieu Tri, 10km from the city. Qui Nhon train station or Ga Qui Nhon (☎ 822036) is at the end of a 10km spur line off the main north-south track. Only two very slow local trains stop at Qui Nhon train station and they are not worth bothering with – get yourself to/from Dieu Tri by taxi or motorbike.

Tickets for trains departing from Dieu Tri can be purchased at the Qui Nhon train station, though if you arrive in Dieu Tri by train, your best bet is to purchase an onward ticket before leaving the station. There is also a ticket office near the Bank Hotel. (For ticket prices, see the Train section in the Getting Around chapter.)

Car & Motorbike Road distances from Qui Nhon are 677km to Ho Chi Minh City, 238km to Nha Trang, 186km to Pleiku,

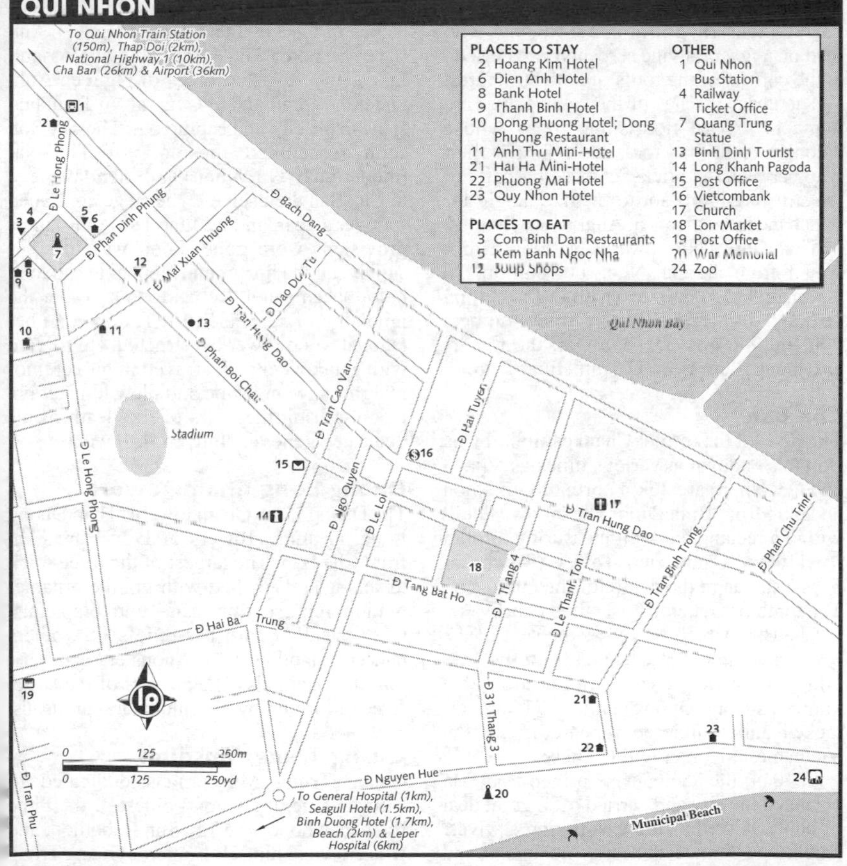

198km to Kon Tum, 174km to Quang Ngai and 303km to Danang.

AROUND QUI NHON

There are half a dozen or so groups of Cham structures in the vicinity of Qui Nhon.

Thap Doi

The two Cham towers of Thap Doi have curved pyramidal roofs rather than the terracing typical of Cham architecture. The larger tower, whose four granite doorways are oriented towards the cardinal directions, retains some of its ornate brickwork and remnants of the granite statuary that once graced its summit. The dismembered torsos of *garuda* (Sanskrit; griffin-like sky beings who feed on *naga*, or divine serpents) can be seen at the corners of the roofs of both structures.

The upper reaches of the small tower are home to several flourishing trees, whose creeping tendrilous roots have forced their way between the bricks, enmeshing parts of the structure in the sort of netlike tangle for which the monuments of Angkor are famous.

Thap Doi is 2km towards National Highway 1 from the Qui Nhon bus station. To get there, head out of town on Đ Tran Hung Dao and turn right between street numbers 900 and 906 onto Đ Thap Doi; the towers are about 100m from Đ Tran Hung Dao.

Cha Ban

The ruins of the former Cham capital of Cha Ban (also known at various times as Vijaya and Qui Nhon) are 26km north of Qui Nhon and 5km from Binh Dinh. The city was built within a rectangular wall measuring 1400m by 1100m. Canh Tien Tower (Tower of Brass) stands in the centre of the enclosure. The tomb of General Vu Tinh is nearby.

Cha Ban, which served as the seat of the royal government of Champa from the year 1000 (after the loss of Indrapura, also known as Dong Duong) until 1471, was attacked and plundered repeatedly by the Vietnamese, Khmer and Chinese.

In 1044, the Vietnamese prince Phat Ma occupied the city and carried off a great deal of booty as well as the Cham king's wives, harem and female dancers, musicians and singers. Cha Ban was under the control of a Khmer overseer from 1190 to 1220.

In 1377, the Vietnamese were defeated and their king was killed in an attempt to capture Cha Ban. The Vietnamese emperor Le Thanh Ton breached the eastern gate of the city in 1471 and captured the Cham king and 50 members of the royal family. During this, the last great battle fought by the Cham, 60,000 Chams were killed and 30,000 more were taken prisoner by the Vietnamese.

During the Tay Son Rebellion, Cha Ban served as the capital of the region of central Vietnam, and was ruled by the eldest of the three Tay Son brothers. The capital was attacked in 1793 by the forces of Nguyen Anh (later Emperor Gia Long), but the assault failed. In 1799, the forces of Nguyen Anh, under the command of General Vu Tinh, laid siege to the city and captured it. The Tay Son soon reoccupied the port of Thi Nai (modern-day Qui Nhon) and then lay siege to Cha Ban themselves. The siege continued for over a year, and by June 1801, Vu Tinh's provisions were gone. Food was in short supply; all the horses and elephants had long before been eaten. Refusing to consider the ignominy of surrender, Vu Tinh had an octagonal wood tower constructed. He filled it with gunpowder and, arrayed in his ceremonial robes, went inside and blew himself up. Upon hearing the news of the death of his dedicated general, Nguyen Anh wept.

Duong Long Cham Towers

The Duong Long Cham towers (Thap Duong Long, meaning Towers of Ivory) are 8km from Cha Ban. The largest of the three brick towers is embellished with granite ornamentation representing naga and elephants. Over the doors are bas-reliefs of women, dancers, standing lions, monsters and various other animals. The corners of the structure arc formed by enormous dragon heads.

Quang Trung Museum

Quang Trung Museum is dedicated to Nguyen Hue, the second-oldest of the three brothers who led the Tay Son Rebellion, and who crowned himself Emperor Quang Trung in 1788. In 1789 Quang Trung led the campaign that overwhelmingly defeated a Chinese invasion of 200,000 troops near Hanoi. This epic battle is still celebrated as one of the greatest triumphs in Vietnamese history. Quang Trung died in 1792 at the age of 40.

During his reign, Quang Trung was something of a social reformer. He encouraged land reform, revised the system of taxation, improved the army and emphasised education, opening many schools and encouraging the development of Vietnamese poetry and literature. Indeed, Communist literature often portrays him as the leader of a peasant revolution whose progressive policies were crushed by the reactionary Nguyen Dynasty, which came to power in 1802 and was overthrown by Ho Chi Minh in 1945.

The Quang Trung Museum, 48km from Qui Nhon, is known for its demonstrations of *binh dinh vo*, a traditional martial art that is performed with a bamboo stick.

Getting There & Away To get there, take National Highway 19 east towards Pleiku. The museum is about 5km off the highway (the turn-off is sign posted) in the Tay Son District, known for the production of a wine made from sticky rice.

Vinh Son Falls

Vinh Son Falls is 18km off National Highway 19, which links Binh Dinh and Pleiku.

SONG CAU

☎ 057

The village of Song Cau is an obscure place that you could easily drive past without ever noticing, but it's worth stopping if you have the time. Near the village is an immense bay, a beautiful rest stop that attracts both foreign and domestic tourists.

Tourists doing the Nha Trang–Hoi An run often make a stopoff for brunch in Song Cau, and some visitors decide to spend the night. Song Cau is along a notorious stretch of National Highway 1 dubbed the 'happy 16 kilometres' by Vietnamese long-distance truck drivers. It was so named for the vast number of taxi girls along the stretch who ply their trade by the roadside.

A good thing to do here is take a boat trip around the bay. The Bai Tien Restaurant-Hotel can help arrange a boat for six people that costs about 30,000d per hour. There are some lovely secluded beaches in the area, including Bai Tro (Tro Beach), which can be reached by boat, or a scenic drive south of Song Cau through rice fields, fish farms and over rickety wooden bridges. Ask for directions at the restaurant.

Places to Stay & Eat

The ***Bai Tien Restaurant-Hotel*** *(☎ 870207)* offers doubles with hot water for US$12. This privately run hotel and restaurant complex is built on stilts over a fish farm on the bay, which makes for an attractive setting.

About 100m south of here is another ***seafood restaurant*** also worth trying.

Getting There & Away

Song Cau is 170km north of Nha Trang and 43km south of Qui Nhon. Highway buses can drop you off and pick you up here (with luck), but most travellers will probably arrive by chartered minibus.

TUY HOA

☎ 057 • pop 185,700

Tuy Hoa, the capital of Phu Yen Province, is a nondescript little town on the coast between Dai Lanh Beach and Qui Nhon. The highway crosses a huge river on the south side of town. The river is navigable and justifies Tuy Hoa's existence – there isn't much else to the place, not even a good beach. One minor attraction is the Nhan Cham Tower, perched on a hill in the southern part of town, just off National Highway 1.

The main appeal of Tuy Hoa to travellers is that it has decent accommodation, which could be useful if you get a late start heading north or south along National Highway 1.

Phu Yen Tourist or Cong Ty Du Lich Phu Yen (☎ 823353), 137 Đ Le Thanh Ton, is the provincial tourist office.

Places to Stay & Eat

The ***Huong Sen Hotel*** *(☎ 823775, fax 823460)* and attached ***restaurant*** is a large place near the centre of town. Room rates cost US$12 with fan, or US$12 to US$20 for air-con.

A cheaper option is the old state-run ***Hong Phu Hotel*** (☎ *824349*), about 500m north of the bus station. Fan rooms cost US$4 to US$6, or US$9 with air-con.

Getting There & Away

The odd thing about Tuy Hoa is that there is an airport. Vietnam Airlines operates two flights weekly between Tuy Hoa and Ho Chi Minh City.

You can also reach Tuy Hao by bus or local train.

DAI LANH BEACH

☎ 058

Semicircular, casuarina-shaded Dai Lanh Beach is another beautiful spot 83km north of Nha Trang and 150km south of Qui Nhon on National Highway 1. At the southern end of the 1km-long beach are a few decent places to stay and eat.

About 1km south of Dai Lanh Beach is a vast sand-dune causeway worth exploring; it connects the mainland to Hon Gom, a mountainous peninsula almost 30km in length. The main village on Hon Gom is Dam Mon (known to the French as Port Dayot), which is on a sheltered bay facing the island of Hon Lon.

At the northern end of Dai Lanh Beach is Dai Lanh Promontory (Mui Dai Lanh), named Cap Varella by the French.

Places to Stay & Eat

The friendly ***Coma Restaurant*** at the southern end of the beach rents two-person tents for US$2.50 a night.

Mid-way down the beach, the ***Thuy Ta Restaurant*** (☎ *842117*) also has tents for rent, as well some ultra-simple straw-roof beach bungalows with brick floors and fans for US$8.

Both places charge US$0.16 for the use of cold showers.

Getting There & Away

Dai Lanh Beach runs along National Highway 1, so any vehicle travelling along the coast between Nha Trang and Tuy Hoa (or Qui Nhon) will get you there. The coastal scenery is stunning, in particular north of Dai Lanh Beach.

Local trains stop directly across from the beach.

WHALE ISLAND

The ***Whale Island Resort*** (☎/*fax 840501,* ⓔ *decouvrir@fmail.vnn.vn or decouvrirvn@saigonnet.vn*) is a peaceful, French-run beach retreat established on Whale Island (Port Dayot). There is no electricity on the island, so at least you are assured it's a (quiet) karaoke-free zone.

In order to reach Whale Island, follow National Highway 1 to Van Ninh, 60km north of Nha Trang and 64km south of Thy Hoa. From here, boats make the two-hour trip to the island.

DOC LET BEACH

☎ 058

Some call this the most spectacular beach in Vietnam, and it would be hard to argue with them. The beach is long and wide, with chalk-white sand and shallow water. Yet despite its beauty, Doc Let gets relatively few visitors, though this is starting to change (try to avoid weekends). From all appearances, it seems that an earlier attempt was made at tourist development, but this was abandoned and most of the buildings are falling apart. However, there still is one functioning ***restaurant*** and guesthouse.

Places to Stay

The ***Doc Let Hotel*** is an unimpressive Vietnamese hotel, but there are also six beach bungalows here. Rooms in the hotel cost US$8, while it's only US$6 to rent a whole bungalow. There is no hot water or air-con

Getting There & Away

Doc Let Beach is on a peninsula to the north of Nha Trang. There is no public transport to this spot, so you need to hire a vehicle To get here, drive 30km north of Nha Trang on National Highway 1. Just north of Ninh Hoa is a petrol station and a fork in the road. You take the right fork (east) and continue for 10km past photogenic salt field until you reach the beach. A sign in English marks the turn-off.

NHA TRANG

☎ 058 • pop 315,200

Nha Trang, the capital of Khanh Hoa Province, has one of the nicest municipal beaches in all of Vietnam. Club Med hasn't arrived yet – there are still no Monte Carlo-style casinos – but the resort town has rapidly developed into a place for sun and fun. Nevertheless, this area has the potential to become another flashy resort like Thailand's Pattaya Beach (dread the thought) – Nha Trang is a place to come and party. If you are after something more tranquil, consider Mui Ne Beach to the south.

The clear turquoise waters around Nha Trang make for excellent fishing, snorkelling and scuba diving. The only time you aren't likely to enjoy these pursuits is in the off-season months of November and December, when the rains come. During heavy rains, water levels rise in the two rivers at either end of the 6km beach; the tides carry fresh water into the bay, which can turn the water a murky brown. Most of the year, however, the water is turquoise, like in the tourist brochures.

The service on the beach is incredible – massage, lunch, cold beer, manicure, beauty treatments. Of late, lots of 'massage' signs have been popping up around town, a sure sign that more visitors are expected.

Nha Trang's dry season, unlike that of Ho Chi Minh City, runs from June to October. The wettest months are October and November, but rain usually falls only at night or in the morning.

The combined fishing fleet of Khanh Hoa Province and neighbouring Phu Yen Province numbers about 10,000 trawlers and junks; they are able to fish during the 250 days of calm seas per year. The area's sea-food products include abalone, lobster, prawns, cuttlefish, mackerel, pomfret, scallops, shrimps, snapper and tuna. Exportable agricultural products from the area include cashew nuts, coconuts, coffee and sesame seeds. Salt production is also large, employing over 4000 people.

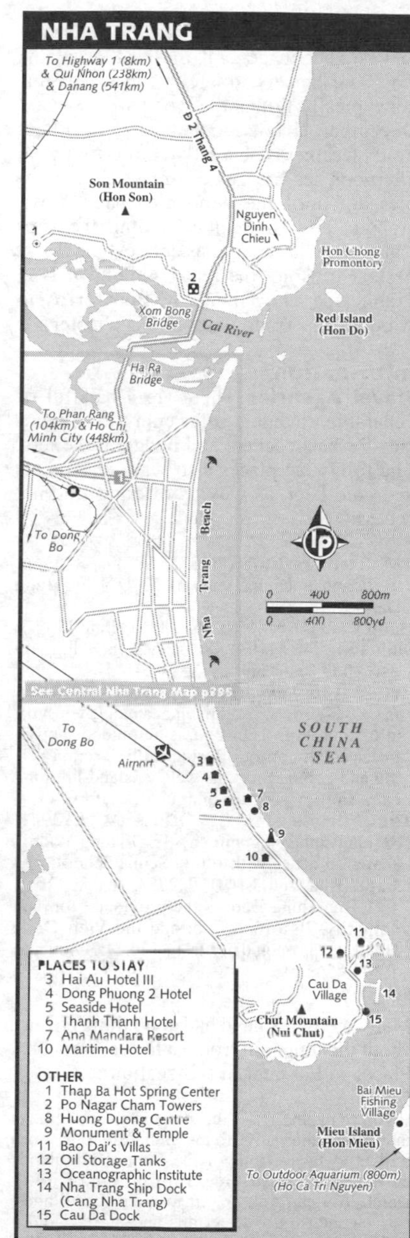

Weather patterns vary greatly from year to year, but in general the best season is from late January to late October. November typically brings the worst weather and December is not much better. The best beach weather is generally before 1 pm; the afternoon sea breezes can make things unpleasant until the wind dies back down around 8 pm. Although well within the tropical zone, Nha Trang has cool evenings.

Boat trips are the real highlight of Nha Trang (see The Islands & Boat Trips in Around Nha Trang, later in this chapter).

Information

Travel Agencies There are a handful of venerable travellers cafes cum travel agencies for backpackers and budget travellers. The following places also serve cheap eats and cold beer, as well as offering Internet access:

TM Brothers Cafe (☎ 814556, fax 815366, ⓔ hoanhaont@dng.vnn.vn) 22 Đ Tran Hung Dao
Hanh Cafe (☎ 814227) 26 Đ Tran Hung Dao
Sinh Cafe (☎ 811981, ⓔ sinhcafent@dng.vnn.vn) 10 Đ Biet Thu
Action And Adventure or AAA (☎ 810630, fax 827436, ⓔ haison.aaa@dng.vnn.vn), at 62 and 98 Đ Tran Phu, is an outdoor activities specialty outfit offering sailing, scuba diving and fishing tours, as well as island-hopping excursions, river trips and jungles safaris.
The Mimosa Tourist Office (☎ 812951, ⓔ nhuttrinh@dng.vnn.vn), 15 Đ Hung Vuong, shares an office with Jimily Scuba School.
Khanh Hoa Tourist (☎ 822753, fax 824206), 1 Đ Tran Hung Dao, is the provincial tourism authority. Its office is beside the Vien Dong Hotel and is open daily from 7 to 11.30 am and 1.30 to 5 pm.

Many travellers have had good things to say about the tours run from Cafe des Amis (see Places to Eat later in this section):

If you're in Nha Trang, heading north or south, an interesting alternative to the Sinh Cafe tourist bus trail is to take a tour of the Central Highlands en route to Hoi An, Hué, Ho Chi Minh City or Dalat. You can trek or raft to minority villages, ride elephants, see waterfalls and more. I did a tour with Vu from Cafe des Amis. He is reliable, trustworthy, and a nice guy. He sits down with you and explains the possible routes, and arranges everything for you at a very reasonable price.

Caprice Olsthoorn, 1999

Bookshops Mr. Lang's Book Exchange, which is outdoors near the War Memorial on Đ Tran Phu, stocks a good collection of books in a variety of languages.

Money Vietcombank (☎ 822720), 17 Đ Quang Trung, is open from 7.30 to 11 am and 1.30 to 4 pm Monday to Friday.

Post The main post office is on the corner of Đ Le Loi and Đ Pasteur, near the northern end of Nha Trang Beach. It's open every day from 6.30 am to 8 pm.

For night owls, the post office at 50 Đ Le Thanh Ton is open 24 hours.

Email & Internet Access Internet access and email services are available from 7 am to 9 pm at the main post office, and across the road at the Internet Services Centre (☎ 826065, ⓔ teltic@dng.vnn.vn), 2 Đ Le Loi, for 600d (US$0.4) per minute.

Some hotels, such as the O-Sin Hotel and Post Hotel, also offer Internet access.

Hon Chong Promontory

Hon Chong is a narrow granite promontory that juts out into the turquoise waters of the South China Sea. The views of the mountainous coastline north of Nha Trang and nearby islands are certainly fine, but unfortunately, the place seems to have been taken over by souvenir kiosks that block most of the view.

To the north-west is Nui Co Tien (Fairy Mountain) with three summits believed to resemble a reclining female fairy (see the 'Fairy Romance' boxed text following).

To the north-east is Hon Rua (Tortoise Island), which really does resemble a tortoise. The two islands of Hon Yen are off in the distance to the east.

Beaches

Coconut palms provide shelter for both bathers and strollers along most of Nh

Fairy Romance

There is a gargantuan handprint on the massive boulder balanced at the tip of the Hon Chong Promontory. According to local legend, a drunk male giant fairy made it when he fell while spying a female fairy bathing nude at Bai Tien (Fairy Beach) – the point of land closest to Hon Rua. Despite the force of his fall, the giant managed to get up and eventually catch the fairy. The two began a life together, but the gods soon intervened and punished the male fairy, sending him off to a 're-education camp' (evidently a post-1975 version of the story) for an indefinite sentence.

The love-sick female fairy waited patiently for her husband to come back, but after a very long time, despairing that he might never return, she lay down in sorrow and turned into Nui Co Tien (Fairy Mountain). The peak on the right is supposed to be her face, gazing up towards the sky; the middle peak is her breasts; and the summit on the left (the highest) forms her crossed legs.

When the giant male fairy finally returned and saw what had become of his wife, he prostrated himself in grief next to a boulder leaving his handprint on it. He, too, turned to stone and can be seen to this day.

Trang's 6km of beachfront. Beach chairs are available for rent – you can just sit and enjoy the drinks and light food that beach vendors have on offer. About the only time you need to move is to use the toilet or when the tide comes up. The water is remarkably clear.

Hon Chong Beach (Bai Tam Hon Chong) is a series of beaches that begin just north of Hon Chong Promontory; fishing families live here among the coconut palms, but the refuse makes the place unsuitable for swimming or sunbathing. Behind the beaches are steep mountains, whose lower reaches support crops that include mangoes and bananas.

About 300m south of Hon Chong (ie, towards Nha Trang) and a few dozen metres from the beach is tiny Hon Do (Red Island), which has a Buddhist temple on top.

Hon Chong is 3.5km from central Nha Trang. From the Po Nagar towers, head north on Đ 2 Thang 4 for 400m. Just before 15 Đ 2 Thang 4, turn right onto Đ Nguyen Dinh Chieu and follow the road for about 700m.

Louisiane Cafe The Louisiane Cafe (☎ 812948) is a large and pleasant beachfront place resembling a Western-style beach club. This attractive, thoughtfully landscaped facility is done in a stylish Mediterranean blue motif. The best thing about Louisiane Cafe is that it is free – well, almost. Guests can indulge themselves in use of the swimming pool and beach chairs here in exchange simply for patronising the restaurant, bakery or bar. In the daytime, vendors are not permitted on the private beach, a restriction you'll come to appreciate with time.

Pasteur Institute

Nha Trang's Pasteur Institute (☎ 822406, fax 824058), 10 Đ Tran Phu, was founded in 1895 by Dr Alexandre Yersin (1863–1943), who was – from among the tens of thousands of colonists who spent time in Vietnam – probably the Frenchman most loved by the Vietnamese. Born in Switzerland of French and Swiss parents, Dr Yersin came to Vietnam in 1889 after working under Louis Pasteur in Paris. He spent the next four years travelling throughout the central highlands and recording his observations. During this period, he came upon the site of what is now Dalat and recommended to the government that a hill station be established there. Dr Yersin also introduced rubber and quinine-producing trees to Vietnam.

In 1894, while in Hong Kong, he discovered the rat-borne microbe that causes bubonic plague.

Today, the Pasteur Institute in Nha Trang coordinates vaccination and hygiene programs for the country's southern coastal region. Despite its minuscule budget and antiquated equipment (the labs look much as they did half a century ago), the institute produces vaccines (eg, rabies, diphtheria, pertussis, typhoid) and carries out research in microbiology, epidemiology and virology. Vietnam's two other Pasteur Institutes are in Ho Chi Minh City and Dalat.

Dr Yersin's library and office are now a museum located on the second floor; items on display include laboratory equipment (such as his astronomical instruments) and some of his personal effects. There is a picture of Dr Yersin above the door to the veranda. The model boat was given to him by local fishermen with whom he spent a great deal of his time.

The Institute library (closed to the public), which is located across the landing from the museum, houses many of Dr Yersin's books as well as modern scientific journals. At his request, Dr Yersin was buried near Nha Trang.

The museum is open from 7 to 11.15 am and 2 to 4.30 pm, closed Saturday afternoon and Sunday. Entry costs US$2.

Long Son Pagoda

Aside from the beach, the most impressive sight in Nha Trang is Long Son Pagoda (also known as Tinh Hoi Khanh Hoa Pagoda and An Nam Phat Hoc Hoi Pagoda). It's about 500m west of the train station opposite 15 Đ 23/10. The pagoda, which has resident monks, was founded in the late 19th century and has been rebuilt several times over the years. The entrance and roofs are decorated with mosaic dragons constructed of glass and bits of ceramic tile. The main sanctuary is an attractive hall adorned with modern interpretations of traditional motifs. Note the ferocious nose hairs on the colourful dragons wrapped around the pillars on either side of the main altar.

At the top of the hill behind the pagoda is a huge white Buddha (Kim Than Phat To), seated on a lotus blossom, visible from all over the city. The platform around the 14m-high figure, which was built in 1963, has great views of Nha Trang and nearby rural areas. As you approach the pagoda from the street, the 152 stone steps up the hill to the Buddha begin to the right of the structure. You should take some time to explore off to the left, where there's an entrance to another impressive hall of the pagoda.

Nha Trang Cathedral

Nha Trang Cathedral, built in the French Gothic style and complete with medieval-looking stained glass windows, stands on a small hill overlooking the train station. It was constructed of simple cement blocks between 1928 and 1933. Today, the cathedral is the seat of the bishop of Nha Trang. In 1988, a Catholic cemetery not far from the church was disinterred to make room for a new train station building. The ashes were brought to the cathedral and reburied in cavities behind the wall of plaques lining the ramp up the hill

Masses are held everyday. If the main gate on Đ Thai Nguyen is closed, go up the ramp opposite 17 Đ Nguyen Trai, which leads to the back of the building.

Oceanographic Institute

The Oceanographic Institute or Vie Nghiem Cuu Bien (☎ 590036), founded i 1923, is housed in a grand French-colonia building 6km south of Nha Trang's mai post office in the port district of Cau D (also called Cau Be). It has an aquarium *(h ca)* and specimen room open to the public it also has a library. The 23 tanks on th ground floor are home to a variety c colourful live specimens of local marin life, including seahorses. It is open dai from 7.30 am to noon, and 1 to 4.30 pn entry is US$0.40.

Behind the main building and across th volleyball court is a large hall filled wi 60,000 dead sea-life specimens, includir stuffed sea birds and fish, corals and th corporeal remains of other marine creatur preserved in glass jars.

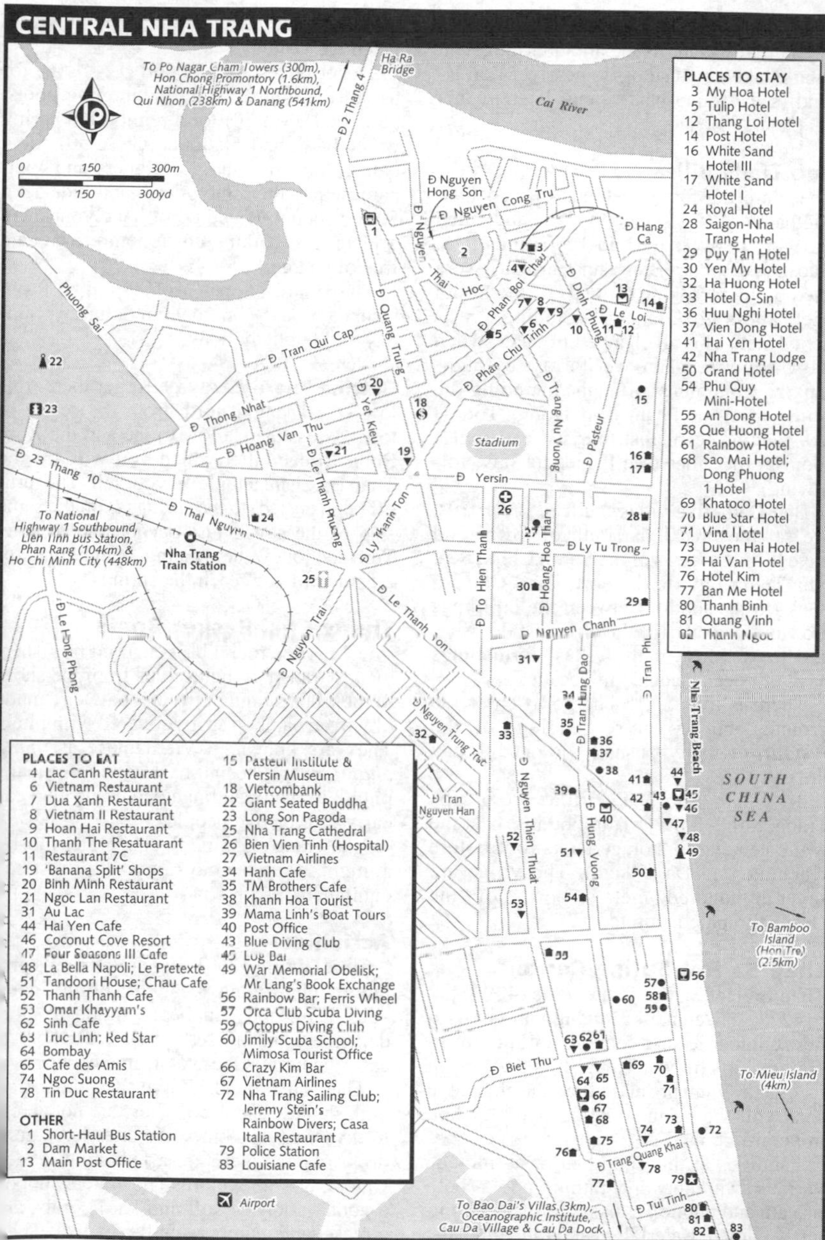

SOUTH-CENTRAL COAST

As nice as the Oceanographic Institute is, if you really want to see an aquarium, you should take a boat across to nearby Mieu Island (see Around Nha Trang, later in this chapter).

Bao Dai's Villas

These are the former retreats of Bao Dai, Vietnam's own 'last emperor' (he abdicated in 1945). Between the mid-1950s and 1975, Bao Dai's Villas (Biet Thu Cau Da) were used by high-ranking officials of the South Vietnamese government, including President Thieu. This all changed in 1975, when the villas were taken over for use by high-ranking Communist officials, including the prime minister Pham Van Dong. Today, low-ranking 'capitalist tourists' can rent a room in the villas (see Places to Stay, following).

Bao Dai's five villas, built in the 1920s, are set on three hills south of town, and have brilliant views of the South China Sea, Nha Trang Bay (to the north) and Cau Da dock (to the south). Between the buildings are winding paths lined with tropical bushes and trees. Most of the villas' furnishings have not been changed in decades.

There is a US$0.15 charge to enter the grounds, but if you're heading for the ***restaurant***, there is usually no need to pay the entry fee.

To get to Bao Dai's Villas from Nha Trang, turn left off Đ Tran Phu just past the white cement oil storage tanks (but before reaching Cau Da village). The villas are several hundred metres north of the Oceanographic Institute.

Thap Ba Hot Spring Center

Thap Ba Hot Spring Center (☎ 514099, fax 514278, ⓔ saomaitk21@dng.vnn.vn) is a new outdoor leisure complex on the northern outskirts of Nha Trang. It is the first of its kind in Vietnam, and offers the chance to soak your bones in soothing pools of hot, mineral-rich mud.

Facilities at this suburban oasis include various swimming and bathing pools (both private and public), a massage service, butterfly garden, waterfall, restaurant and cafe. Lodging facilities were under construction when we visited.

Ticket prices are 15,000d (US$1.10) for use of the mineral water swimming pools, 25,000d (US$1.80) for a regular hot spring water bath, and 50,000d (US$3.50) for a bath in mineral mud. Foreigners and Vietnamese pay the same prices, and kids get a 50% discount. If you don't have your own, a towel and bathing costume are provided free of charge.

The centre is open from 8 am to 8 pm weekdays, and 7 am to 9 pm Saturday, Sunday and public holidays.

Getting There & Away To get there, follow Đ 2 Thang 4 north from the centre of town. Cross the Ha Ra Bridge and the Xom Bong Bridge, after which you will see the Thap Ba Cham temple on your left. The turn-off (sign posted) to the springs is on the same side of the street, just beyond the pagoda. Turn and follow the winding, bumpy road for 2.5km until you reach the springs.

Thung Chai Basket Boats

The 2m-wide round baskets used by fishermen to transport themselves from the shore to their boats (and between boats) are made of woven bamboo strips covered with pitch. They are known in Vietnamese as *thung chai* (*thung* means basket, *chai* means pitch). Rowed standing up, a thung chai can carry four or five people.

Nha Trang's fishing fleet operates mostly at night, using the days in port for rest and equipment repair.

Activities

Scuba Diving Nha Trang is Vietnam's premier scuba diving locale. Visibility averages 15m, and can be as much as 30m depending on the season (late October to early January is the worst time of year).

There are around 25 dive sites in the area, both shallow and deep. There are no wrecks to dive on (yet), but some sites have good drop-offs and there are a few small underwater caves to explore. The waters support a good variety of soft and hard corals, and a reasonable number small reef fish. The are a few resident sharks, including grey nurse sharks and a white-tip shark named 'Eric'. Whale sharks have also been known to pass through, and sting-rays are a common sight.

A full-day outing including boat transport, two dives and lunch typically costs between US$40 and US$60. Most dive operators also offer a range of dive courses, including a Discover Diving program for uncertified, first-time divers to experience the thrill under the supervision of a qualified dive master.

It is difficult to recommend one dive operator over another, so our best advice is to shop around, speak to a few different operators, and use your better judgement. With that caveat in mind, consider the following outfits:

Jeremy Stein's Rainbow Divers (☎ 829946, fax 811223, ⓔ rainbowdivers@hotmail.com), located at the Sailing Club, is run by Briton Jeremy Stein (a dead ringer for Chuck Norris). Web site: www.divevietnam.com

Jimily Scuba School (☎ 812983), at 15 Đ Hung Vuong, is French-Swiss run and offers non-divers a chance to cruise aboard the boat for US$12 including breakfast, lunch, a soft drink and snorkelling gear. There is a branch at the Louisiane Cafe.

Blue Diving Club (☎ 825390, fax 816088, ⓔ bluedivingclub@hotmail.com), at 40 Đ Tran Phu, is opposite the Hai Yen Hotel. French-British owned and operated, Blue Diving has been in town since 1995.

Octopus Diving Club (☎ 810629, fax 827436, ⓔ haison.aaa@dng.vnn.vn), at 62 Đ Tran Phu, is a French-run dive shop right across from the beach.

Orca Club (☎ 811375, fax 811374, ⓔ vietravel.diving@dng.vnn.vn), at 58 Đ Tran Phu, is Vietnamese run, and part of a company called Vietravel.

Coco Dive Center (☎ 812900, fax 810444, ⓔ cocodive@dng.vnn.vn), at 44 Đ Tran Phu, was recently opened by Minh Xuan, Vietnam's first and only PADI Instructor, champion swimmer and local karate champion.
Web site: www.dvdesign.com/cocodive/

Places to Stay

Nha Trang is a trendy place for both domestic and foreign tourists, with the result that there are around 100 hotels to choose from. Several of the state-run hotels occupying prime beachfront property have become markedly run-down, and are really no longer worth considering. For the same money, you can do much better at one of the newer private mini-hotels, which even if not on the beach, will be within a few minutes' walk.

For a quieter beach accommodation alternative to Nha Trang, see the Whale Island section earlier in this chapter.

Places to Stay – Budget

The ***Hotel O-Sin*** *(☎ 825064, fax 824991, ⓔ osinhotel@hotmail.com, 4 Đ Nguyen Thien Thuat)* has earned itself a steady following for its good, cheap rooms. Dorm beds cost just US$2, fan rooms cost US$5 to US$7 and rooms with air-con go for US$8 or US$9.

Another place with a dorm is ***Sao Mai Hotel*** *(☎ 827412, 99 Đ Nguyen Thien Thuat)*. Beds cost US$3, or US$6/7 for fan rooms (US$10/12 with air-con).

Yen My Hotel *(☎ 829064, ⓔ yenmyhotel@hotmail.com, 22 Đ Hoang Hoa Tham)* is a good budget place run by a very friendly man named Mr Duan. Rooms cost US$5 to US$8 with fan, or US$8 to US$12 with air-con.

Another friendly spot worthy of a plug is the new ***An Dong Hotel*** *(☎ 814079, 31 Đ Nguyen Thien Thuat)*. Clean and comfortable fan rooms cost US$8 to US$12, or US$10 to US$18 with air-con.

Blue Star Hotel *(☎ 826447, 1B Đ Biet Thu)* is close to the beach and has received several good reports from travellers. Rates are US$7 with hot water and fan, US$10 for an air-con doubles and triples, and US$12 for a room with a balcony and bathtub.

The ***Tulip Hotel*** *(☎ 821302, 30 Đ Hoang Van Thu)* is a friendly place with dorm beds for US$3, nice double rooms for US$8 with fan, and US$12 to US$20 for air-con.

Hai Van Hotel *(☎ 825139, 115A Đ Nguyen Thien Thuat)* is a friendly place not far from the beach. Fan rooms rent for US$7, or US$10 with air-con.

There is a nearly identical setup across the road at the ***Hotel Kim*** *(☎ 810402, ⓔ kimhotel@dng.vnn.vn, 124 Đ Nguyen Thien Thuat)*.

Po Nagar Cham Towers

The Cham towers of Po Nagar, also known as Thap Ba (the Lady of the City), were built between the 7th and 12th centuries. The site was used for Hindu worship as early as the 2nd century AD. Today, both ethnic-Chinese and Vietnamese Buddhists come to Po Nagar to pray and make offerings according to their respective traditions. This site has a continuing religious significance, so remove your shoes before entering.

The towers serve as the Holy See honouring Goddess Yang Ino Po Nagar, the Goddess of the Dua (Liu) clan which ruled over the southern part of the Cham Kingdom covering Kauthara and Pan Duranga (present day Khanh Hoa and Thuan Hai provinces). The original wooden structure was razed to the ground by attacking Javanese in AD 774 and was replaced by a stone and brick temple (the first of its kind) in 784. There are many stone slabs found throughout the complex, most of which relate to history or religion, and provide great insight into the spiritual life and social structure of the Chams.

Originally the complex covered an area of 500 sq metres and there were seven or eight towers, four of which remain. All the temples face east, as did the original entrance to the complex, which is to the right as you ascend the hillock. In centuries past, a person coming to pray passed through the pillared *mandapa* (meditation hall), 10 pillars of which can still be seen, before proceeding up the staircase to the towers.

The 23m-high **North Tower** (Thap Chinh), with its terraced pyramidal roof, vaulted interior masonry and vestibule is a superb example of Cham architecture. One of the tallest Cham towers, it was built in AD 817 by Pangro, a minister of King Harivarman I, after the original temples here were sacked and burned. The raiders also carried off a *linga* (a stylised phallic symbol representing Shiva) made of precious metal. In AD 918 King Indravarman III placed a gold mukha-linga in the North Tower, but it too was taken, this time by the Khmers. This pattern of statues being destroyed or stolen and then replaced continued for some time until 965, when King Jaya Indravarman I replaced the gold mukha-linga with the stone figure of Uma – a *shakti*, or feminine manifestation of Shiva – which remains to this day.

Above the entrance to the North Tower, two musicians flank a dancing four-armed Shiva, one of whose feet is on the head of the bull Nandin. The sandstone doorposts are covered with inscriptions, as are parts of the walls of the vestibule. A gong and a drum stand under the pyramid-shaped ceiling of the antechamber. In the 28m-high pyramidal main chamber, there is a black stone statue of the goddess Uma (in the shape of Bhagavati) with 10 arms, two of which are hidden under her vest; she is seated leaning back against some sort of monstrous animal.

The **Central Tower** (Thap Nam) was built partly of recycled bricks in the 12th century on the site of a structure dating from the 7th century. It is less finely constructed than the other towers and has little ornamentation; the pyramidal roof lacks terracing or pilasters, although the interior altars were once covered with silver. There is a linga inside the main chamber. Note the inscription on the left-hand wall of the vestibule.

The **South Tower** (Mieu Dong Nam), at one time dedicated to Sandhaka (Shiva), still shelters a linga. The richly ornamented **North-West Tower** (Thap Tay Bac) was originally dedicated to Ganesha. The pyramid-shaped summit of the roof of the North-West Tower has disappeared. The **West Tower**, of which almost nothing remains, was constructed by King Vikrantavarman during the first half of the 9th century. Near the North Tower is a small **museum** with a few mediocre examples of Cham stonework; the explanatory signs are in Vietnamese only. At one time there was a small temple on this site. If you are heading north, be sure to visit the Cham Museum in Danang, which has an extensive and fine collection of Cham statuary (see the Central Vietnam chapter).

The towers of Po Nagar stand on a granite knoll 2km north of Nha Trang on the left bank of the Cai River. To get there from Nha Trang, take Đ Quang Trung (which becomes Đ 2 Thang 4) north across Ha Ra Bridge and Xom Bong Bridge, which span the mouth of the Cai River.

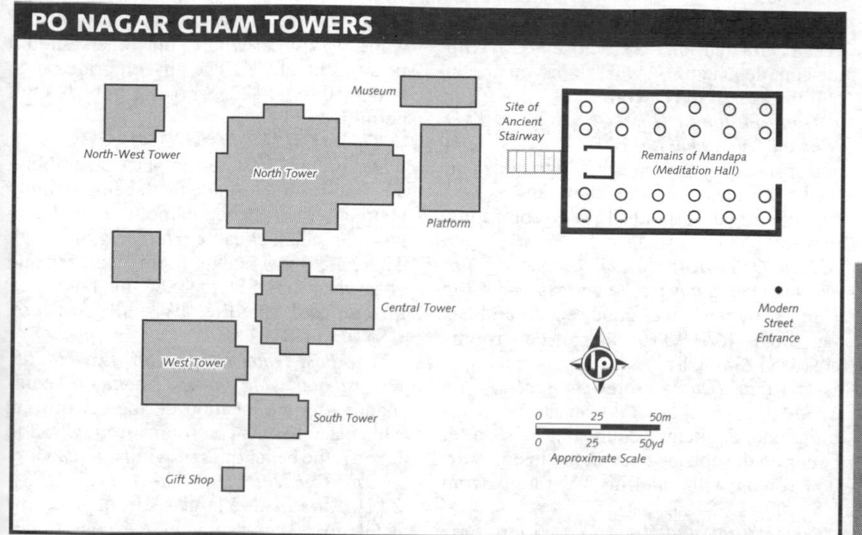

Huu Nghi Hotel *(☎ 826703, fax 827416, 3 Đ Tran Hung Dao)* is another time-honoured backpackers' haunt. Singles/doubles/ triples here range from US$5/7/9 to US$13/15/19.

The friendly ***Ha Huong Hotel*** *(☎ 512069, ⓔ hahuongnt@dng.vnn.vn, 26 Đ Nguyen Trung Truc)* is a quiet street about five minutes' walk from the beach. Rooms are clean, and cost just US$6 with fan and hot water, or US$8 to US$15 with air-con, satellite TV and a balcony.

My Hoa Hotel *(☎ 810111, fax 827554, ⓔ myhoahotel@dng.vnn.vn, 7 Đ Hang Ca)* is a friendly place across the road from the popular Lac Canh Restaurant. Dorm beds cost US$5, or US$7 to US$10 for a private fan room (air-con costs US$12 to US$20).

There is a decent trio of oceanfront mini-hotels side by side on Đ Tran Phu. At No 84, ***Thanh Binh*** *(☎ 825203)* has fan/air-con rooms from US$6/10, and the ***Quang Vinh*** *(☎ 822536)* at 84A charges the same. ***Thanh Ngoc*** *(☎ 825194)* at 84B has fan doubles for US$7 (US$10 with air-con), and fan/air-con triples for US$15/20.

The all-air-con ***Duyen Hai Hotel*** *(☎ 811548, 72–74 Đ Tran Phu)* is a short crawl from the Sailing Club and has rooms for US$11 to US$18.

The ***Royal Hotel*** *(☎ 822298, 822385, 40 Đ Thai Nguyen)* is opposite the train station. Fan singles/doubles/triples cost US$3/5/7, or US$11 for a room that can accommodate seven bodies (in case you brought the family). Standard air-con doubles cost US$7 to US$10.

The ***Grand Hotel*** aka *Nha Khach 44 (☎ 822445, fax 825395)* is a huge beachfront place housed in a stately (but faded and crying out to be restored) French colonial-style building. Rooms with air-con and hot water cost US$9 to US$20, but there are some cheaper prison cells with fan only in a separate wing starting at US$4.

Places to Stay – Mid-Range

The ***Rainbow Hotel*** *(☎ 810501, fax 810030, ⓔ rainbowhotel@dng.vnn.vn, Đ 8 Biet Thu)* is a snazzy new place housed in a pastel-green building not far from the beach – it's hard to miss. Rates are US$15 to US$25.

Dong Phuong 2 Hotel *(☎ 814580, fax 825986, ⓔ dongphuongnt@dng.vnn.vn, 96A6/1 Đ Tran Phu)* is a large and quiet place set back off of main road. Rooms cost US$8 with fan, or US$15 to US$25 with air-con (depending on what floor you are on and the size of the balcony).

Dong Phuong 1 Hotel *(☎ 828247, 103 Đ Nguyen Thien Thuat)* is older, but has clean and spacious rooms featuring high beds and the thickest mattresses in Nha Trang – good for enjoying the satellite TV. Air-con rooms rent for US$15 to US$20.

Phu Quy Mini-Hotel *(☎ 810609, fax 812954, ⓔ phuquyhotel@dng.vnn.vn, 54 Đ Hung Vuong)* receives good reports and has fan rooms for US$10, and air-con rooms cost US$15 to US$18.

The ***Que Huong Hotel*** *(☎ 825047, fax 825344, 60 Đ Tran Phu)* boasts a swimming pool and tennis court, but looks a bit better on the outside than on the inside. Air-con rooms with satellite TV range from US$50 to US$100.

The ***White Sand Hotel I*** *(☎ 825861, fax 810449, 14 Đ Tran Phu)* is a cosy place near the beach. Basic air-con doubles are US$14 to US$20.

The recently renovated ***White Sand Hotel III*** *(☎ 825953, 12 Đ Tran Phu)* next door is slightly nicer and charges the same.

South of town, ***Thanh Thanh Hotel*** *(☎ 824657, 98A Đ Tran Phu)* has balconies overlooking the sea. Rooms are US$10 with fan, US$12 to US$15 with air-con, and US$20 with a sea view.

Next door, the ***Seaside Hotel*** *(☎ 821178, fax 821325, 96B Đ Tran Phu)* has satellite TV. Air-con rooms cost from US$15 to US$35.

A bit further south is the navy-run ***Maritime Hotel*** aka *Khach San Hang Hai, (☎ 331135, fax 881134, 34 Đ Tran Phu)*, which was built to resemble a ship (and it almost does). Budget fan rooms cost just US$3, and air-con rooms range from US$12 to US$20.

The ***Vina Hotel*** *(☎ 823099, fax 825137, 66 Đ Tran Phu)* is known for its satellite TV, bathtubs, massage services and a sickly-looking stuffed deer guarding the reception desk. Rates here are US$12 to US$20.

Khatoco Hotel *(☎ 823723, fax 821925, 9 Đ Biet Thu)* is run by the local tobacco company. Anti-smoking activists will probably want to stay elsewhere, but others should find this hotel OK. The air-con price range is US$10 to US$22. Smoking in bed is not permitted.

Thang Loi Hotel *(☎ 822241, fax 821905, 4 Đ Pasteur)* is a state-run place resembling a US-style motel. Aside from being built on a street with a French name, the hotel also has a French nickname *(Hotel La Fregate)*. There are a few budget rooms with fan and cold water for US$6 to US$8, but hot water, air-con and satellite TV will cost you US$10 to US$22.

The ***Post Hotel*** *(☎ 821250, fax 824205, ⓔ posthotel@dng.vnn.vn, 2 Đ Le Loi)* commands a prime location on the beachfront. This place has air-con rooms from US$8 to US$27, the better ones providing a sea view.

Duy Tan Hotel *(☎ 822671, fax 825034, 24 Đ Tran Phu)* is a large seafront place that is OK for a state-run hotel. Air-conditioned singles/doubles start at US$16/21.

The large old ***Vien Dong Hotel*** *(☎ 821606, fax 821912, 1 Đ Tran Hung Dao)* has long been a travellers' favourite. It has a swimming pool, photoprocessing facilities and bicycle rentals. Singles/doubles/triples start at US$21/26/31. According to the hotel's pamphlet, 'Weapons and objects with offensive smell should be kept at the reception desk'.

The even larger ***Hai Yen Hotel*** *(☎ 822828, fax 821902, 40 Đ Tran Phu)*, whose name means 'sea swift', is notable for its swimming pool and balcony sea views. All rooms have air-con, hot water and satellite TV. Prices range from US$8 to US$52, inclusive of service, tax and breakfast.

Ban Me Hotel *(☎ 829500, fax 810035, 3/3 Đ Tran Quang Khai)* is a large place just a few hundred metres walk from the beach. Clean air-con singles/doubles/triples with satellite TV cost US$18/20/25; suites go for US$28 to US$33. Rates include breakfast.

Furthest from the town centre is ***Bao Dai's Villas*** *(☎ 590148, fax 590146)*, near Cau Da on the coast 6km south of the train station. The spacious top-end rooms are classic, with high ceilings, huge bathrooms and prime views of the bay. This is whe

Vietnam's ruling elite has rested itself since the days of French rule. Rooms cost US$25 to US$80, including breakfast. There is a private beach below the hotel with a good restaurant and another restaurant up top with fine views of the bay.

Places to Stay – Top End

The ***Ana Mandara Resort*** (*☎ 829829, fax 829629, ⓔ resvana@dng.vnn.vn*) is a gorgeous set of open timber-roofed beach villas south of town. This exquisite resort offers every possible luxury and is hands-down Nha Trang's classiest accommodation offering. All this does come at a price, however – nightly rates range from US$137 to US$300, plus 15% tax and service. The pricier villas are more deluxe and closer to the sea.

The ***Nha Trang Lodge*** (*☎ 810500, fax 828800, ⓔ nt-lodge@dng.vnn.vn, 42 Đ Tran Phu*) has 13 floors, making it one of Nha Trang's tallest high rises. This glittering luxury tower offers rooms for US$50 to US$145.

Another skyscraper is the ***Saigon-Nha Trang Hotel*** (*☎ 810500, fax 828800, ⓔ nt-lodge@dng.vnn.vn, 42 Đ Tran Phu*) a glitzy yet sterile joint venture between Saigon Tourist and the Japanese. Facilities include a health club and swimming pool. Rates range from US$60 to US$120 – tack on 15% for tax and service.

Places to Eat

Nha Trang is naturally a seafood haven, and there are a wide variety of excellent eateries to keep you busy for weeks. If you've been enjoying the fresh baguettes in Vietnam, you're in for a treat. Nha Trang has its own unique variety of French bread, a heavier loaf which is closer in consistency (and taste) to a New York City hot pretzel. Proud locals say the bread is more filling for Nha Trang's hard-working fishermen.

Beach Area ***La Bella Napoli*** (*☎ 829621*) on Đ Tran Phu serves up *real* Italian food in a delightful terrace setting overlooking the beach. The congenial owners Marinella and Gigi specialise in home-cooked southern Italian dishes, fresh seafood and great brick-oven pizzas.

A few steps away from La Bella Napoli, ***Le Pretexte*** (*☎ 815964*) is an excellent choice for authentic French cuisine. Here too there is a pleasant beachfront setting.

Casa Italia Restaurant (*☎ 826528*), yet another authentic Italian ristorante, is located at the ***Nha Trang Sailing Club*** (*☎ 826528, 72–4 Đ Tran Phu*). They serve excellent pastas, fine wine, and have a fresh seafood corner as well. The beachside restaurant at the Sailing Club serves both Vietnamese and Western dishes. You can choose from a selection of fresh seafood from a traditional Vietnamese boat and have it cooked in front of you.

The ***Louisiane Cafe*** (see the Beaches section earlier) is a stylish beachfront locale for wining and dining.

Right on the beach opposite the Hai Yen Hotel is the ***Hai Yen Cafe*** and ***Coconut Cove Resort***. Both are outdoor places with thatched sun roofs to offer protection from the elements. Sandwiched between these two is the ***Log Bar***, and a few steps away is the ***Four Seasons III Cafe***.

There is excellent vegetarian fare at the popular ***Cafe des Amis*** (*☎ 813009, 13 Đ Biet Thu*), a few minutes' walk from the beach. The walls here are covered with an interesting collection of works by Vietnamese painters. This is also a recommended place to inquire about jeep/motorbike tours into the Central Highlands.

Across the road there is excellent seafood as at the no-frills ***Red Star*** (*☎ 812790, 14 Đ Biet Thu*), as well as the close-by ***Truc Linh*** (*☎ 825742, 12B Đ Biet Thu*). Try the crab or clams with ginger, lemongrass & chilli, or the fish hot pot.

Ngoc Suong (*☎ 827030, 16 Đ Tran Quang Khai*) is another good seafood spot to consider, as is ***Tin Duc***, just across the road.

The Indian food is worth a try at ***Bombay*** (*15 Đ Biet Thu*).

Other options for Indian include ***Omar Khayyam's*** (*☎ 821426, 24C Đ Nguyen Thien Thuat*), as well as ***Tandoori House*** on Đ Hung Vuong. Just next door to here is the ***Chau Cafe***.

Thanh Thanh Cafe *(☎ 824413, 10 Đ Nguyen Thien Thuat)* is a travellers' cafe serving pizza, Vietnamese dishes and standard backpacker fare.

Central Area One of the best local eateries in town is the ***Lac Canh Restaurant*** *(11 Đ Hang Ca)*, a block east of Dam Market. Beef, squid, giant shrimps, lobsters and the like are grilled right at your table.

Hoan Hai Restaurant *(6 Đ Phan Chu Trinh)* is near Lac Canh. The menu contains delicious marinated beef, vegetarian dishes and some of the best spring rolls in Vietnam.

Thanh The Restaurant *(☎ 821931, 3 Đ Phan Chu Trinh)*, just across the street, also does Vietnamese, Chinese and European-style food.

For cheap and excellent vegetarian food, try tiny ***Au Lac***, near the corner of Đ Hoang Hoa Tham and Đ Nguyen Chanh.

If you're craving an authentic German sausage, the expat-run ***Restaurant 7C*** *(☎ 828243, 7C Đ Le Loi)* serves up excellent bratwurst and schnitzel, plus home-baked brown bread and fresh shark from the waters off Nha Trang. Prices are reasonable. 7C is a short walk from the main post office.

The ***Vietnam Restaurant*** *(23 Đ Hoang Van Thu)* is a good spot popular with locals and, if you can manage without an English menu, is recommended.

There is more of a tourists' scene happening at the nearby ***Vietnam II Restaurant***.

The ***Dua Xanh Restaurant*** *(☎ 823687, 23 Đ Le Loi)* is a nice spot with many seafood dishes. There are outdoor garden tables, and more tables indoors. Leave room for dessert.

Then there's ***Dam Market*** itself, which has a collection of stalls in the covered semicircular food pavilion. Vegetarian food can be found here.

For great ice cream, try one of the ***'Banana Split' shops*** at the roundabout where Đ Quang Trung meets Đ Le Thanh Ton. 'No 58' and 'No 60' are long time rivals, evidenced by their strong-arm tactics for luring customers inside.

Warning!

Although Nha Trang is generally a safe place, be very careful at night, especially on the beach. The best advice, in fact, is to stay off the beach after dark. We have heard countless stories of thievery and rip-offs, mostly instigated by quick-witted prostitutes who canvass the beach. One witness wrote:

> One thing to watch in Nha Trang are the girls who ply their trade along the beachfront after dark. One fellow traveller was walking down the street when a prostitute leapt out from behind a tree and started running her hands all over him. When he finally got away from her he found that the wallet from his backpack and money he had on him was gone.
>
> **Matthew Ford**

Entertainment

Most tourists tend to congregate at the Aussie-run ***Nha Trang Sailing Club*** *(☎ 826528, 72 Đ Tran Phu)* on the beach.

Just up the beach, the ***Rainbow Bar*** draws in a steady stream of backpackers.

The cosy ***Crazy Kim Bar*** *(☎ 816072, 93 Đ Nguyen Thien Thuat)* is a funky little pub worth seeking out. It's run by a Vietnamese-Canadian woman named Kim, who opened the bar as a vehicle in her commendable 'Hands off the Kids!' campaign, which is working to thwart the growing problem of paedophilia which has begun to plague Nha Trang. Proceeds from the sale of booze (try the killer cocktail buckets!) and tee-shirts go towards the cause.

South of town is the Huong Duong Centre, also known as Paradise Village. Inside you'll find the ***Hexagone Disco***, which is open from 8 pm until sunrise.

For something a bit more cultural, there are free ethnic minority song and dance performances nightly at ***Vien Dong Hotel*** *(☎ 821606, 1 Đ Tran Hung Dao)*. The show starts at 7.30 pm and is a good way to start off your evening.

Shopping

Along with Hanoi, Ho Chi Minh City and Hoi An, Nha Trang has emerged as a rea-

Bird's-Nest Island

Salangane Island (Hon Yen or Dao Yen) is the name applied to two lump-shaped islands visible from Nha Trang Beach. These and other islands off Khanh Hoa Province are the source of Vietnam's finest *salangane* (swift) nests. The nests are used in bird's-nest soup as well as in traditional medicine, and are considered an aphrodisiac. It is said that the extraordinary virility of Emperor Minh Mang, who ruled Vietnam from 1820 to 1840, was derived from the consumption of salangane nests.

The nests, which the salanganes build out of their silklike salivary secretions, are semioval and about 5cm to 8cm in diameter. They are usually harvested twice a year. Red nests are the most highly prized. Annual production in Khanh Hoa and Phu Yen provinces is about 1000kg. At present, salangane nests fetch US$2000 per kilogram in the international marketplace!

There is a small, secluded beach at Salangane Island. The 17km trip out to the islands takes three to four hours by small boat from Nha Trang.

The best place to inquire about boats is at travellers cafes in Nha Trang, such as TM Brothers, Hanh Cafe and Sinh Cafe.

sonable place to look for art. Though actual galleries are scant, there are a growing number of local painters and photographers who display their work on the walls of Nha Trang's resorts, restaurants, cafes and bars.

There are quite a number of shops selling beautiful seashells (and items made from seashells) near the Oceanographic Institute in Cau Da village. As a glossy tourist brochure put it, 'Before leaving Nha Trang, tourists had better call at Cau Da to get some souvenirs of the sea…for their dears at home'. The environmentally conscious may choose to resist the temptation and take photos instead.

Getting There & Away

Air Vietnam Airlines (☎ 826768, fax 825956), at 91 Đ Nguyen Thien Thuat, has flights connecting Nha Trang with Ho Chi Minh City twice daily. There are also flights to/from Hanoi once daily and flights to/from Danang four times a week.

Bus Express and regular buses depart from Mien Dong bus station in Ho Chi Minh City to Nha Trang. The express bus trip takes 11 to 12 hours.

Lien Tinh bus station or Ben Xe Lien Tinh (☎ 822192) on Đ 23/10, is Nha Trang's main intercity bus terminal, and is 500m west of the train station. Nonexpress buses from Lien Tinh bus station go to: Bao Loc, Bien Hoa (11 hours), Buon Ma Thuot (six hours), Dalat (six hours), Danang (14 hours), Di Linh, Ho Chi Minh City (12 hours), Phan Rang (2½ hours), Pleiku (10 hours), Quang Ngai and Qui Nhon (seven hours). The short haul bus station (see map) is for local routes only.

Minibus The preferred option, chartered minibuses are easy to book at most places where travellers congregate.

Train Hotels and travellers cafes all book train tickets, and it's worth paying the small commission to use these booking services.

The Nha Trang train station or Ga Nha Trang (☎ 822113), overlooked by the nearby cathedral, is across the street from 26 Đ Thai Nguyen; the ticket office is open between 7 am and 2 pm only.

Nha Trang is well served by express trains connecting Hanoi and Ho Chi Minh City, and a daily local train between Ho Chi

Long Thanh – Photographer

MASON FLORENCE

Of the 500-odd members of the National Association of Photographers, most are based in Hanoi or Ho Chi Minh City, and in this day and age, most choose colour film as their medium. Long Thanh, a photographer born in Nha Trang in 1951, is a rare exception.

A family man, Long Thanh has managed, with limited resources and a geographical disadvantage, to establish himself as Nha Trang's most acclaimed local shutterbug. He has been taking pictures since the 1960s, when at the age of 13 he learned to use a camera while working in a local photo shop. Since then he has not stopped shooting, nor has he abandoned his home town of Nha Trang to seek big-city stardom.

A true purist, Long Thanh religiously uses black-and-white film, and laments the fact that so many great photographers prefer to shoot in colour. He works out of a makeshift darkroom in his simple kitchen, mixes his own chemicals, and awaits the day when professional quality black & white photographic paper will be sold in Vietnam (for now, he relies on friends from abroad to keep him stocked).

Long Thanh's powerful images capture the heart and soul of Vietnam. Among his most compelling works, *Under Rain* is a perfectly timed shot of two young girls caught in a sudden downpour with a mysterious beam of sunlight streaming down from above. *Afternoon Countryside* is another rare scene – a boy dashing across the backs of a herd of water buffalos submerged in a lake outside Nha Trang. Perhaps his most striking image of all is *Young Mother, Young Son*, which portrays a bare-breasted elderly woman, her wrinkled skin like leather, sharing a moment of peace with her tiny grandson.

Though he has shown his photos in group exhibitions abroad nearly 50 times, and had his first international solo exhibition in Hamburg, Germany in 1999, Long Thanh's talents remain relatively undiscovered outside Vietnam. Visitors to Nha Trang, however, can view his photos on the walls of the popular Sailing Club, which features an ongoing exhibition of his work.

If you've got the time, it may be possible to visit Long Thanh's home/studio and talk photography; that is, however, if he is not out on the road looking to capture the next great shot (inquire at the Sailing Club). Long Thanh is an incurable traveller, and has been known to happily accompany new friends on excursions into the Vietnamese countryside. For fellow photographers, who could be a better travel companion?

'Under Rain' by Long Thanh

Minh City and Nha Trang (see the Train section in the Getting Around chapter near the beginning of this book).

Car & Motorbike Road distances from Nha Trang are: 205km to Buon Ma Thuot; 541km to Danang; 448km to Ho Chi Minh City; 104km to Phan Rang; 424km to Pleiku; 412km to Quang Ngai; and 238km to Qui Nhon.

A series of roughly parallel roads head inland from near Nha Trang, linking Vietnam's deltas and coastal regions with the central highlands.

Getting Around

To/From the Airport The airport is on the southern side of town and is so close to many of the hotels that you can actually walk. Cyclos can get you to the airport for about US$1.

Taxi Nha Trang Taxi (☎ 824000) and Khanh Hoa Taxi (☎ 810810) have air-con cars with meters.

Bicycle Most major hotels have bicycle rentals. The cost is around US$1 per day.

AROUND NHA TRANG

The Islands & Boat Tours

Khanh Hoa Province's 71 offshore islands are renowned for the remarkably clear water surrounding them. A trip to these islands is one of the main reasons for visiting Nha Trang, so try to schedule at least one day for a boat journey.

In the interests of environmental preservation, when booking a boat tour you might consider asking if the captain anchors his boat to a bouy, as opposed to dropping anchor directly on the coral:

> The coral was beautiful, but many of us were very disturbed to see that most of the boats – and there were many – were throwing their anchors directly onto the coral – destroying it and leaving it to die. Others were doing the right thing, and attaching (themselves) to buoys that were permanently fixed. The coral is constantly being broken, and its hard to say how long the anchoring area can sustain the damage.
>
> This is an instance where travellers may be able to have a positive impact on the environment of the countries they are travelling through – instead of the reverse. The tour boats depend on travellers, and enough of us pressure them to stop killing coral, maybe they'll stop.
>
> **Peter Foggitt, Australia**

Of course, when booking a tour through a hotel or tourist operator it's hard to know if you'll get a truthful or informed answer to this question. What we suggest is if you do take a tour and it looks as though the captain is about to drop anchor on the coral that you very politely suggest he attaches the boat to a buoy instead. You should also take it up with the actual boat operators – Mama Hanh is the most influential person in the boating business.

The hottest ticket is Mama Hanh's trademark 'Green Hat Boat Tours'. Mama Hanh is a Nha Trang legend who went from running a tiny seafood shack on the beach (when we first met her in 1991) to operating a flotilla of island-hopping party boats.

Mama Hanh's tours seem to get more rave reviews from travellers than anything else on the coast. From guzzling fruit wine at the impromptu 'floating bar' to deck-side dancing, how she does it (seven days a week!) is a biological mystery. A word to the wise: *do not* try and out-party Mama Hanh, or you may end up having your stomach pumped. As one pair of survivors recalled:

> By the end of raging all day in the sun we were completely wiped out. On the minibus from the wharf back to town everyone was half passed out, one poor German gal was vomiting out the window, and there was Mama Hanh, cigarette in one hand and a freshly opened beer in the other, whistling her way home.
>
> **Geoff L'Abbe & Yumi Tsukasaki**

Of course all of this fun in the sun, let's just say, might not be the best environment for families with children (unless you've got a good response ready for when your kid asks 'What kind of cigarette *is* that Mum?'). While no-one is forced to partake in the inebriation (some even view it as a spectator sport), this tour is definitely *not* recommended for recovering alcoholics. If the cultural fanfare of the Mama Hanh experience does not sound up your alley, there are other more orthodox boat tours around. You might check out one outfit called Mama Linh's; apparently Mama Linh herself has pulled up stakes and gone to America, but her boat still sails.

Virtually every hotel in town books Mama Hanh's and other island tours. You can also pay more for a less crowded and more luxurious boat that takes you to more islands. Indeed, you'll have to do this if you want to get in much snorkelling. The place to charter boats is at the Cau Da dock south of Nha Trang. If you're not with an organised group, you'd better book the day before or go to Cau Da dock early in the morning – by 10 am all the boats are gone. Another attractive alternative is joining up with one of the local dive boats – inquire at Jimily Scuba School.

At some of the fishing villages on the islands, shallow water prevents the boats from reaching shore. In this case, you must walk perhaps several hundred metres across floats – a careful balancing act. The floats were designed for Vietnamese, and weightier Westerners might get wet – take care with your camera. Nevertheless, it's all good fun and a visit to these fishing villages is highly recommended.

Mieu Island Also called Tri Nguyen Island, Mieu Island is touted in tourist literature as the site of an 'outdoor aquarium' (Ho Ca Tri Nguyen). In fact, the 'aquarium' is an important fish-breeding farm, where over 40 species of fish, crustaceans and other marine creatures are raised in three separate compartments. There is a ***cafe*** built on stilts over the water. Ask around for canoe rentals.

The main village on Mieu Island is Tri Nguyen. Bai Soai is a gravel beach on the far side of Mieu Island from Cau Da. There are a few ***bungalows*** on the island which rent for US$6, but these are very rustic.

Most people will take some sort of boat tour booked through a hotel, cafe or Khanh Hoa Tourist. Impoverished and less hurried travellers might catch one of the regular ferries that go to Tri Nguyen village from Cau Da dock.

Bamboo Island Several kilometres from the southern part of Nha Trang Beach is Bamboo Island (Hon Tre), the largest island in the Nha Trang area. Tru Beach (Bai Tru) is at the northern end of the island. All kinds of boats can be hired to take you here.

Ebony Island Also called Hon Mun, Ebony Island is just south-east of Bamboo Island and is known for its snorkelling. To get here, you'll probably have to hire a boat.

Hon Tam South-west of Bamboo Island, Hon Tam is close to shore and costs just 2000d to get to, but the beach is dirty and there's not much else to see.

Hon Mot This tiny island is sandwiched neatly between Ebony Island and Hon Tam. This is another great place for snorkelling.

Monkey Island Called Hon Lao in Vietnamese, Monkey Island is named after its large contingent of resident monkeys, and has become a big hit with tourists. Most of the monkeys have grown quite accustomed to receiving food handouts from the tourists, providing ample opportunity to take a memorable photo. However, these are wild monkeys, not zoo animals – you should not make any attempt to pet them, shake hands or pick them up. Some travellers have been scratched and bitten when they attempted to embrace their new-found friends.

Aside from being unwilling to cuddle, the monkeys are materialistic. They will grab the sunglasses off your face or snatch a pen from your shirt pocket and run off. So far, we haven't heard of monkeys slitting open travellers' handbags with a razor blade, but you do need to be almost as careful with your valuables here as you do on the streets of Ho Chi Minh City!

Monkey Island is 12km north of Bamboo Island, and one-day boat tours can easily be arranged in Nha Trang. A faster way to get here is to take a motorbike or car 15km north of Nha Trang on National Highway 1 – near a pagoda and the pleasant ***Nha Trang Restaurant*** is a place where boats will ferry you to the island in fifteen minutes for

US$3. Other destinations from here include Hoa Lan Springs on Hon Heo (Heo Island; US$2.80, 45 minutes), and Hon Thi (Thi Island; US$1.60, 20 minutes).

Dien Khanh Citadel

The citadel dates from the 17th-century Trinh Dynasty. It was rebuilt by Prince Nguyen Anh (later Emperor Gia Long) in 1793 during his successful offensive against the Tay Son Rebels. Only a few sections of the walls and gates are extant. Dien Khanh Citadel is 11km west of Nha Trang near the villages of Dien Toan and Dien Thanh.

Ba Ho Falls

Ba Ho Falls (Suoi Ba Ho), with its three waterfalls and three pools, is in a forested area about 20km north of Nha Trang and about 2km west of Phu Huu Village. The turn off National Highway 1 is just north of a restaurant called ***Quyen***.

Fairy Spring

The enchanting little Fairy Spring (Suoi Tien) seems to pop out of nowhere as you approach it. Like a small oasis, the spring is decorated with its own natural garden of tropical vegetation and smooth boulders.

You'll need to rent a motorbike or car to reach the spring. Driving south on National Highway 1, you come to a spot 17km from Nha Trang where there is a sign posted to your left (east side of the highway). Turn off the highway here and go through the village. The road twists and winds its way for 8km through the hills until it reaches a valley. Just as the road starts to get bad, you come upon the spring. You'll probably see some other vehicles parked here as it's a popular spot with locals.

CAM RANH BAY

☎ 058

Cam Ranh Bay is an excellent natural harbour 56km north of Phan Rang & Thap Cham. The Russian fleet of Admiral Rodjestvenski used it in 1905 at the end of the Russo-Japanese War, as did the Japanese during WWII, when the area was still considered an excellent place for tiger hunting. In the mid-1960s, the Americans constructed a vast base here, including an extensive port, ship-repair facilities and an airstrip.

After reunification, the Russians and their fleet came back, enjoying far better facilities than they had found seven decades before. For a while this became the largest Soviet naval installation outside the USSR.

Despite repeated requests from the Russians, the Vietnamese refused to grant them permanent rights to the base. Then in 1988 Mikhail Gorbachev offered to abandon the installation if the Americans promised to do the same with their six bases across the South China Sea in the Philippines. The following year, however, the Vietnamese, evidently annoyed with the Soviets, appeared to offer the Americans renewed use of Cam Ranh Bay. The Soviet presence at Cam Ranh Bay was significantly reduced in 1990 as part of the Kremlin's cost cutting measures. With the collapse of the Soviet Union in 1991 and the end of the Cold War, the USA did close its bases in the Philippines in 1991 (or, more accurately, the Filipino Senate unceremoniously told the Americans to leave).

Subsequent economic problems have forced the Russians to vastly cut back on their overseas military facilities. However, there are still about 200 to 300 Russian personnel based here, but only two or three ships will be docked at any given time.

Of course, just because the USA and former USSR no longer compete for turf does not mean that there is no need for a military base at Cam Ranh Bay. The Vietnamese are growing increasingly nervous about China's intentions. The Chinese have been rapidly and relentlessly building up their naval facilities in the South China Sea – in 1988, and again in 1992, China seized several islands claimed by Vietnam. In 1995 the Chinese navy seized some more islands claimed by the Philippines. The day may soon come when the Vietnamese will want the facilities at Cam Ranh Bay for their own military use.

The Russian government has informed the Vietnamese of a willingness to permanently withdraw from the bases whenever

Dragon Fruit

The south-central coast is best known for its excellent seafood, but a really exotic treat is green dragon fruit *(thanh long)*. This fruit, which is the size and shape of a small pineapple and has a smooth magenta skin, grows only in the coastal areas south of Nha Trang. Its delicious white meat is speckled with black seeds, and tastes a bit like kiwi fruit. Green dragon fruit grows on a kind of creeping cactus – said to resemble a green dragon – that climbs up the trunks and branches of trees and flourishes on parched hillsides that get very little water. Thanh long is in season from May to September and can be purchased at nearly any local fruit market in the area. The fruit is also exported to Ho Chi Minh City, and even abroad (it fetches a high price in Taiwan), but it is cheapest and freshest at the source. Locals often make a refreshing drink out of crushed green dragon fruit, ice, sugar and sweetened condensed milk. It's also used to make jam.

Vietnam repays its debts. The Vietnamese owe about 30 billion roubles to the former Soviet Union. The Russians are insisting that they should be repaid at the exchange rate in effect at the time of the loans, which was one rouble to one US dollar. The Vietnamese insist that they wish to repay the loan at the current exchange rate – of 20 to 30 roubles to the dollar! The two sides remain far apart on the issue, but until it's resolved, Cam Ranh Bay remains the last hurrah for the Russian navy in Asia.

There are beautiful beaches around Cam Ranh Bay – indeed, Americans stationed here during the war sometimes called it Vietnam's Hawaii. However, as long as this area remains a military base, it isn't likely to develop into a tourist resort. Some American military veterans have managed to tour the facilities at Cam Ranh Bay on organised tours arranged through government-owned travel agencies.

Places to Eat

There are some terrific seafood places along National Highway 1 right beside the '63km to Nha Trang' and '41km to Phan Rang' marker. One such place still fashionable with travellers is ***Ngoc Suong Seafood Restaurant*** *(☎ 854603)*. This is a favourite lunch stop on the Dalat-Nha Trang run.

PHAN RANG & THAP CHAM

☎ 068 • pop 143,700

The twin cities of Phan Rang and Thap Cham, which are famous for their production of table grapes, are in a semi-arid region. The sandy soil supports scrubby vegetation; local flora includes poinciana trees and prickly-pear cacti with vicious thorns. Many of the houses on the outskirts of town are decorated with Greek-style grape trellises.

The area's best known sight (and one of Vietnam's better-known attractions) is the group of Cham towers known as Po Klong Garai, from which Thap Cham (Cham Tower) derives its name (see the 'Po Klong Garai Cham Towers' boxed text, following). You can see Cham towers dotted about the countryside 20km north of Phan Rang.

Ninh Thuan Province is home to tens of thousands of descendants of the Cham people, many of whom live in and around Phan Rang & Thap Cham.

Orientation

National Highway 1 is Phan Rang's main commercial street (called Đ Thong Nhat). Thap Cham, about 7km from Phan Rang, is strung out along National Highway 20, which heads west from Phan Rang towards Ninh Son and Dalat.

Information

The main post office is in the north of town. Internet access is available for 500d per minute from 7 am to 5 pm Monday to Friday.

Po Ro Me Cham Tower

Po Ro Me Cham Tower (Thap Po Ro Me), among the newest of Vietnam's Cham towers, is about 15km south of Phan Rang on a rocky hill 5km west of National Highway 1. The ruins are very interesting, but are also very difficult to reach. The 'road' is a dirt track that can only be negotiated by motorbike or on foot.

The road to take is between km 1566 and 1567 from National Highway 1. We did cross small Cham hamlets, which were nice to go through. Following the image of a small distant tower, we took a road that became a path, and then less than that. Even the motorbike almost did not make it. And after about 2km of the hill, that was it – not even a tiny path to follow. Our poor old bike could not survive the rocks and cactus and died (again!). We finally walked up the hill (great snakes!). That was magic. The feeling of being completely alone on that small hill, with only the distant sound of bells around a cow's neck and nobody around for many kilometres (amazing after weeks in Saigon), was indescribable. At the bottom of the tower are long stairs. The single tower was closed, but still worth the hill climb to get there. It is decorated with beautiful stone statues and there are two Nandin statues just before the entrance. Thank you for at least mentioning its existence, even if we were probably the only foreigners to reach it this year.

Genevieve Mayers

The kalan, which is decorated with numerous paintings, has two inscribed doorposts, two stone statues of the bull Nandin, a basrelief representing a deified king in the form of Shiva and two statues of queens, one of whom has an inscription on her chest. The towers are named after the last ruler of an independent Champa, King Po Ro Me (ruled 1629–51), who died as a prisoner of the Vietnamese.

Tuan Tu Hamlet

There is a minaretless Cham mosque, closed to visitors, in the Cham hamlet of Tuan Tu (population 1000). This Muslim community is governed by elected religious leaders (Thay Mun), who can easily be identified by their traditional costume, which includes a white robe and an elaborate white turban with red tassels. In keeping with Islamic precepts governing modesty, Cham women often wear head coverings and skirts. The Cham, like other ethnic minorities in Vietnam, suffer from discrimination and are even poorer than their ethnic-Vietnamese neighbours.

To get to Tuan Tu Hamlet, head south from Phan Rang along National Highway 1. Go 250m south of the large bridge to a small

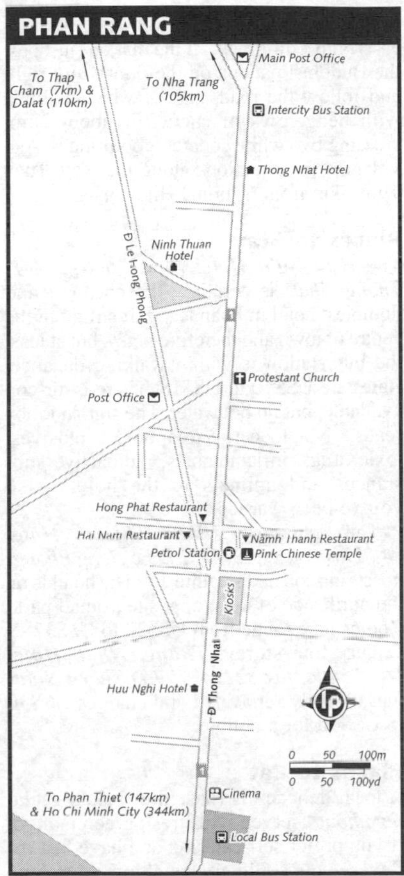

SOUTH-CENTRAL COAST

bridge. Cross it and turn left (to the southeast) onto a dirt track. At the market (just past the Buddhist pagoda on the right), turn right and follow the road, part of which is lined with hedgerows of cacti, for about 2km, crossing two white concrete footbridges. Ask villagers for directions along the way. Tuan Tu is 3km from National Highway 1.

Places to Stay

The ***Huu Nghi Hotel*** *(☎ 822606, 354 Đ Thong Nhat)* is certainly the cheapest and dumpiest hotel in Phan Rang. It's right in the centre of town and therefore noisy, but at least the bus station is within walking distance. Rates are US$10 to US$18. There is air-con available, but no hot water. The sign in lobby reads: 'Not to carry weapons, explosives, toxic drugs, inflammables, radioactive substances and animals in the hotel' – so you've been warned.

The pleasant ***Ninh Thuan Hotel*** *(☎ 827100, fax 822142, 1 Đ Le Hong Phong)* boasts air-con and satellite TV. The hotel is on the north side of town opposite a small park. Rooms here range from US$22 to US$37.

The four-storey ***Thong Nhat Hotel*** *(☎ 825406, fax 822943, 99 Đ Thong Nhat)* was recently renovated and charges US$30 to US$40 for a double.

Places to Eat

A local delicacy is roasted or baked gecko *(ky nhong)* served with fresh green mango. If you prefer self-catering and have fast reflexes, you could try catching your own gecko off the ceiling in your hotel room.

Some good, centrally located places to eat Vietnamese dishes include the ***Hong Phat Restaurant***, ***Hai Nam Restaurant*** and ***Nam Thanh Restaurant***.

Phan Rang is the grape capital of Vietnam. ***Stalls*** alongside National Highway 1 on the south side of town sell fresh grapes, grape juice and dried grapes (too juicy to be called raisins).

Getting There & Away

Bus Buses from Ho Chi Minh City to Phan Rang & Thap Cham depart from Mien Dong bus station.

Phan Rang intercity bus station (Ben Xe Phan Rang) is on the northern outskirts of town opposite 64 Đ Thong Nhat.

The local bus station is at the southern end of town across the street from 426 Đ Thong Nhat.

Train The Thap Cham train station is about 6km west of National Highway 1, within sight of Po Klong Garai Cham towers.

Car & Motorbike Phan Rang is 344km from Ho Chi Minh City, 147km from Phan Thiet, 105km from Nha Trang and 110km from Dalat.

Ninh Chu Beach

If you have your own wheels, you can get away from the traffic around National Highway 1 at Ninh Chu Beach (Bai Tam Ninh Chu), 7km south of Phan Rang. The beach is OK, but the sand is a dark yellow and the water lacks the beautiful turquoise hues of Nha Trang. The ***Ninh Chu Hotel*** *(☎ 873900)* near the beach has rooms from US$11 to US$25.

CA NA

☎ 068

During the 16th century, princes of the Cham royal family would fish and hunt tigers, elephants and rhinoceroses here. Today, Ca Na is better known for its turquoise waters lapping against white-sand beaches dotted with huge granite boulders – it's a beautiful and relaxing spot, but lacks the isolated tropical beach feeling further south at Mui Ne (it's tough to ignore the rumble of trucks drifting over from nearby National Highway 1). Rau Cau Island is visible offshore.

The terrain is studded with magnificent prickly-pear cacti. A small pagoda on the hillside makes for an interesting, but steep, climb over the boulders.

Farther afield is Tra Cang Temple, located about midway between Ca Na and Phan Rang. Unfortunately, you have to sidetrack over an abysmal dirt road to reach it. Many ethnic-Chinese from Cholon visit the temple.

Places to Stay & Eat

The ***Ca Na Hotel*** *(☎ 861342)* is notable for its beach bungalows. Rooms in the ancient concrete hotel near the highway cost US$10 to US$12; a much better choice are the quiet bungalows on the beach for US$15.

Prices are similar at the nearby ***Haison Hotel*** *(☎ 861312, fax 861339)*, a motel-style place across from the Lac Son Pagoda. It's close to the highway, but air-con rooms are spiffy and cost US$15.

Both hotels have decent ***restaurants*** that are popular lunch spots on the Ho Chi Minh City–Nha Trang route.

Getting There & Away

Ca Na is 114km north of Phan Thiet and 32km south of Phan Rang. Many long-haul buses cruising National Highway 1 can drop you here. No train service is available.

VINH HAO

Vinh Hao is an obscure town just off National Highway 1 between Phan Thiet and Phan Rang. The town's only claim to fame is its famous mineral waters, which are bottled and sold all over Vietnam. If you spend any length of time in the country, you are almost certain to sip a bottle of Vinh Hao. The Vietnamese claim that Vinh Hao mineral water is exported (but they don't say to where).

PHAN THIET

☎ 062 • pop 168,400

Phan Thiet is traditionally known for its *nuoc mam* (fish sauce) and fishing industry, though today tourism is playing an increasingly larger role in the local economy. The population includes descendants of the Cham, who controlled this area until 1692. During the colonial period, the Europeans lived in their own segregated ghetto stretching along the north bank of the Phan Thiet River, while the Vietnamese, Cham, Southern Chinese, Malays and Indonesians lived along the south bank.

Besides golfing, there is little to do in Phan Thiet itself, and the beaches are nowhere near as nice as at Mui Ne Beach, 11km away (see the following section).

Orientation

Phan Thiet is built along both banks of the Phan Thiet River, also known as the Ca Ti River and the Muong Man River. National Highway 1 runs right through town; south of the river, it is known as Đ Tran Hung Dao, while north of the river it is called Đ Le Hong Phong.

Information

The Hotel 19-4 offers tours of the area – you can also book cars and arrange guides here.

Phan Thiet Beach

To get to Phan Thiet's beachfront, turn east at Victory Monument, an arrow-shaped concrete tower with victorious cement people at the base.

Fishing Harbour

The river flowing through the centre of town creates a small fishing harbour, which is always chock-a-block with boats. It makes for charming photography.

Golf Course

The Ocean Dunes Golf Course (☎ 822393) is near the beachfront by the Novotel. To drum up business, reasonably priced golf package tours from Ho Chi Minh City (as inexpensive as US$82.50, which includes one round of golf, one night at the upmarket Novotel, breakfast and an after-round massage!) are offered. There is also a minibus shuttle service between the golf course and Ho Chi Minh City. For information, contact the Hotel Sofitel Plaza in Ho Chi Minh City(☎ 08-823 5506, ⓔ nnguyen@hcm.vnn.vn). Its Web site is at www.vietnamgolfresorts.com.

Places to Stay

Unless you are bypassing Mui Ne beach and just looking for place to sleep, don't bother staying in Phan Thiet. Hotels here are not cheap, and tend to be noisy.

The ***Phan Thiet Hotel*** *(☎ 821695, fax 817139, 40 Đ Tran Hung Dao)* is right in the centre of town. It a bit old and musty, and the on-the-highway location is anything but aesthetic. Air-con doubles cost US$10/12, or US$13/17 for triples.

Po Klong Garai Cham Towers

Phan Rang & Thap Cham's most famous landmark is Po Klong Garai, also known as Po Klong Girai (*girai* means dragon). The four brick towers were constructed at the end of the 13th century, during the reign of the Cham monarch Jaya Simhavarman III. The towers were built as Hindu temples and stand on a brick platform at the top of Cho'k Hala, a crumbly granite hill covered with some of the most ornery cacti this side of the Rio Grande.

Over the entrance to the largest tower (the *kalan*, or sanctuary) is a carving of a dancing Shiva with six arms. This bas-relief is known locally as Po Klaun Tri – the Guardian of the temple tower – and is famous for its beauty. Note the inscriptions in the ancient Cham language on the doorposts. These tell of past restoration efforts and offerings of sacrifices and slaves made to the temple towers.

Inside the vestibule is a statue of the bull Nandin (also known as the Kapil Ox), symbol of the agricultural productivity of the countryside. To ensure a good crop, farmers would place an offering of fresh greens, herbs and areca nuts in front of Nandin's muzzle.

Under the main tower is a *mukha-linga*, a linga (a stylised phallus, which symbolises maleness and creative power and represents the Hindu god Shiva) with a painted human face on it. A wooden pyramid has been constructed above the mukha-linga.

Inside the tower, opposite the entrance to the kalan, you can get a good look at some of the Cham's sophisticated masonry technology; the wooden columns that support the lightweight roof are visible. The structure attached to it was originally the main entrance to the complex.

Po Klong Garai towers are one of the most enduring sights of southern Vietnam serving as a testament to the construction skills of the Cham masons.

On a nearby hill is a rock with an inscription from the year 1050, commemorating the erection of a linga by a Cham prince.

On the hill directly south of Cho'k Hala is a concrete water tank built by the Americans

The ***Hotel 19-4*** *(☎ 825216, fax 825184, 1 Đ Tu Van Tu)* is an enormous old place on the north side of town. Rooms with fan and hot bath are US$11. Air-con costs US$13 or, for a larger room, US$18. Opposite is the mini-hotel-style ***Thanh Cong Hotel*** *(☎ 825016, fax 823905, 49–51 Đ Tran Hung Dao)*. Rooms with fan and cold bath is US$5, or US$8 to US$11 with air-con and hot water.

Another option is the luxurious ***Novotel Ocean Dunes Resort*** *(☎ 822393, fax 825682, 1 Đ Ton Tuc Thang)*. Rates range from US$119 to US$174 (but are usually discounted 50%). To get to the hotel, turn towards the sea (east) at the Victory Monument. Facilities include a golf course, several restaurants, a swimming pool, private beach, tennis courts and a fitness centre.

Po Klong Garai Cham Towers

in 1965. It is encircled by French pillboxes, built during the Franco–Viet Minh War to protect the nearby rail yards. To the north of Cho'k Hala, you can see the concrete revetments of Thanh Son Airbase, used since 1975 by the Soviet-built MiGs of the Vietnamese air force.

The Kate New Year is celebrated at the towers in the seventh month of the Cham calendar (around October in the Gregorian calendar). The festival commemorates ancestors, Cham national heroes and deities such as the goddess Po Ino Nagar, who assisted the Chams with their farming.

On the eve of the festival, a procession guarded by the mountain people of Tay Nguyen carries King Po Kloong Garai's clothing to the accompaniment of traditional music. The procession lasts until midnight. The following morning the garments are carried to the tower, once again accompanied by music along with banners, flags, singing and dancing. Notables, dignitaries and village elders follow behind. This colourful ceremony continues into the afternoon.

The Cham's New Year celebrations then carry on for the rest of the month, as they attend parties and visit friends and relatives. The Cham also use this time to pray for good fortune.

Po Klong Garai is located several hundred metres north of National Highway 20, at a point 7km from Phan Rang towards Dalat. The towers are on the opposite side of the tracks to Thap Cham train station.

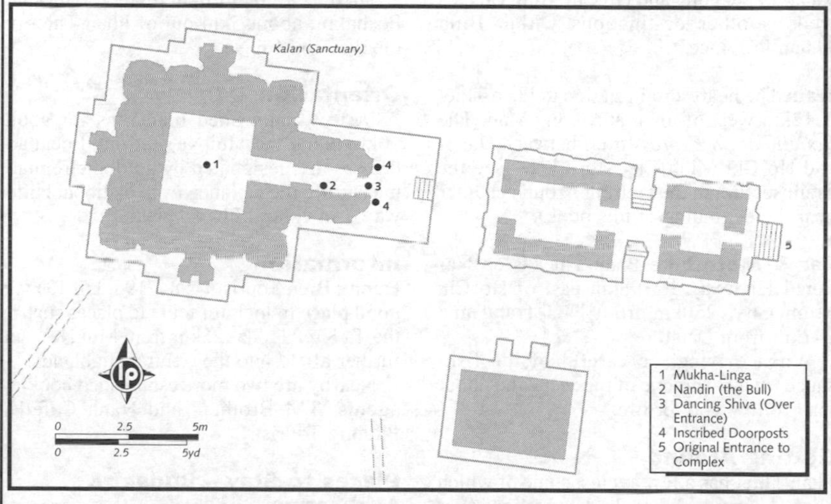

Near the Novotel are two new places worth checking out, the ***Doi Duong Hotel*** *(☎ 822108, fax 825858, 403 Đ Vo Thi Sau)* which charges from US$18 to US$32, and the ***Binh Minh Hotel*** *(☎ 823344, fax 823354, 405 Đ Vo Thi Sau)*, rooms cost from US$8 with fan, or US$12 to US$18 (air-con).

The stylish ***Victoria Phan Thiet Resort*** *(☎ 847170, fax 847174, ⓔ victoriapt@hcm.vnn.vn)* is an upmarket resort at the beach, 9km from Phan Thiet town. It's a beautiful place with sea view cottages furnished to a 'T' (satellite TV, mini-bar, room safes – you get the picture). There are two restaurants, two bars and a fine swimming pool. Rates range from US$80 to US$150 (including tax and service) and yes, credit cards are accepted.

Places to Eat

One good eatery is the friendly ***Hoang Yen Restaurant*** *(☎ 821614, 51 Đ Tran Hung Dao)* about mid-way through Phan Thiet. It is very popular with tour groups passing through town.

Getting There & Away

Bus Buses from Ho Chi Minh City to Phan Thiet depart from Mien Dong bus station.

Phan Thiet bus station (Ben Xe Binh Thuan) is on the northern outskirts of town on Đ Tu Van Tu, just past 217 Đ Le Hong Phong (National Highway 1). The station is open from 5.30 am to 3.30 pm; tickets should be purchased the day before departure.

There are buses to Bien Hoa, Long Khanh, Madagoui, Mui Ne Beach, Phan Rang, Phu Cuong and Ho Chi Minh City, as well as other destinations within Binh Thuan Province.

Train The nearest train station to Phan Thiet is 12km west of town at Muong Man. The *Reunification Express* train between Hanoi and Ho Chi Minh City stops here (see the Train section in the Getting Around chapter near the beginning of this book).

Car & Motorbike Phan Thiet is on National Highway 1, 198km east of Ho Chi Minh City, 250km from Nha Trang and 247km from Dalat.

When driving, be careful of the fish-sauce trucks – hit one of these and the odour may follow you for life.

Getting Around

Phan Thiet has a few cyclos, some of which always seem to be at the bus station. (For transport to Mui Ne Beach, see the following section.)

MUI NE BEACH

☎ 062

Peaceful Mui Ne Beach has emerged as a highly popular alternative to the hoopla further south at Vung Tao. This beautiful beach is 200km from Ho Chi Minh City, and 22km east of Phan Thiet on Route 706, near a fishing village at the tip of Mui Ne Peninsula.

Mui Ne is famous for its enormous sand dunes. These have been a favourite subject matter for many a Vietnamese photographer, including some who sit camel-like on the blazing hot sand for hours waiting for the winds to sculpt the dunes into that perfect 'Kodak moment'.

Also of interest is the **Fairy Spring** (Suoi Tien) which is really a stream that flows through a patch of dunes with interesting sand and rock formations. It's a beautiful trek to follow from the sea to its source, though it might be wise to hire a local guide. You can do the trek barefoot, but if you're heading out into the big sand dunes, this is out of the question (unless you have leather soles on your feet); sandals are even questionable during the midday sun.

There is a small **Cham tower** called Thap Poshaknu about 5km out of Phan Thiet on the way to Mui Ne.

Orientation

A narrow palm-lined road runs for about 10km along the Mui Ne seafront. Local addresses are designated by a kilometre mark measuring the distance from National Highway 1 in central Phan Thiet.

Information

Huong Bien Tourist (☎ 847195, km 13) is a good place to look for tours to places such as the Ta Ku Pagoda (25km from Mui Ne), and further afield into the Central Highlands.

Nearby are two more established booking agents, TM Brothers and Hanh Cafe/Ha Phuong Tourist.

Places to Stay – Budget & Mid-range

Small Garden aka *Vuon Nho (☎ 874012, km 11)* is run by Walter, a Swiss, and his Vietnamese wife Trang. Guests can sleep in a communal house, in the open-air gazebo, or on the beach for US$6 per person. Bungalows with private bath rent for US$25. It's a great spot, though there have been a few complaints from travellers about the 'surly staff'.

Full Moon Resort *(☎ 847008, km 13)* is a pleasant place with simple bungalows decorated with sea shells and split coconuts. Rates here range from US$15 to US$40 including breakfast. They also have tents for US$5.

Next door is ***Mai Khanh*** *(☎ 847177)*, which has very basic fan rooms for US$15/20 as well as bungalows and air-con rooms for US$25.

And next door is the sleek ***Vietnam-Austria House*** *(☎ 847047, km13.5)*, run by an Austrian man and his Vietnamese wife. Squeaky-clean rooms in a modern villa cost US$15/20, or US$25 for a wooden bungalow.

The ***Bien Da*** *(☎ 816619, km 12)* is better known for its open-air restaurant, but also has bamboo bungalows costing US$9 for up to four people.

Close by, the beautifully landscaped ***Bamboo Village Seaside Resort*** *(☎ 847007, fax 847095, ⓔ Dephan@netnam2.org.vn, km 11.8)* has attractive bungalows for US$41 to US$57 (US$49 to US$69 from 21 December to 1 May). There is a swimming pool and a good restaurant on the premises. Check out the Web site www.vietnam-tourism.com/muine for more information.

Huong Bien Mui Ne Resort *(☎ 847258, fax 847338, ⓔ ntd_hbmn@hcm.vnn.vn, km 18)* offers ultra-basic bungalows for US$8 (shared toilet and bath), and simple air-con rooms for US$18 (cold water) and US$22 (hot water). Tents rent for US$4.

Nearby, the friendly ***Nam Duong Hotel*** *(☎ 847441, ⓔ namduong@hcm.vnn.vn, km 19)* – also called the *Indonesia Hotel* – has windowless rooms in a bamboo long house that rent for US$5, or US$11 for rooms of a better standard.

Eschewing the bamboo motif, the ***Palmira Resort*** *(☎ 847004, fax 847006, ⓔ cocogarden@palmiraresort.com, km 11)* offers villa-style accommodation in a pastel motif that just won't quit. Budget rooms are good value at US$25 for three people. Air-con garden-villa rooms rent for US$35, or US$39 to US$59 for villas on the beach-front. All rooms have IDD phones and satellite TV, and rates include tax and service, as well as breakfast in the shade of the pleasant 'coco garden'. Facilities include two restaurants, four bars, a huge swimming pool, tennis courts, a sauna, a fitness room, billiards, table soccer and a kiddie play area. The Web site is at www.palmiraresort.com.

Places to Stay – Top End

Coco Beach *(☎ 847111, fax 847115, ⓔ paradise@cocobeach.net, km 12.5)* – also

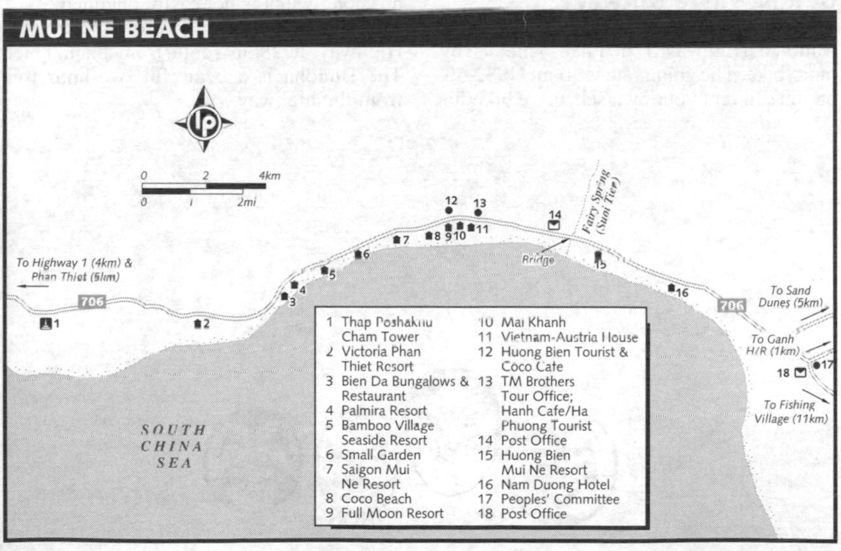

known as *Hai Duong Resort* – is run by Jutta and Daniel, a delightful German/French couple. It is a lovely spot with swaying palm trees and white sand. The beach is private, so vendors won't congregate around you. Thatched-roof bungalows cost US$65 (US$80 from mid-November to mid-April) and villas are US$130 (US$160). Rates include breakfast, tax and service. Activities include windsurfing, sailing, water-skiing, fishing and snorkelling. The Web site is at www.cocobeach.net.

Another upmarket option is the snazzy ***Saigon Mui Ne Resort*** *(☎ 847303, fax 847307, km 12.2)* set in a large, well-manicured compound decorated in a woodsy, ethnic style. Bungalows cost US$50 and villas are US$65; rates include tax and breakfast.

Places to Eat

Most of the beach resorts also double as restaurants. There are also ***local seafood places*** along the beach.

Coco Cafe, attached to Huong Bien Tourist, serves cold drinks, fruit shakes and ice cream.

Getting There & Away

To best way to reach Mui Ne Beach from National Highway 1 in Phan Thiet is by motorbike. The going rate is about US$2.50, or you can rent your own self-drive bike for US$6 a day (ask at the Hoang Yen Restaurant). Between 8.30 am and 4 pm, a local bus makes trips between Phan Thiet bus station and Mui Ne, but it is irregular and slow.

These days many, of the 'open tour' buses cruising National Highway 1 make a detour to Mui Ne.

Getting Around

Mui Ne is small enough to reach most places on foot. You can also rent bicycles to explore the area at most hotels along the beach.

TAKOU MOUNTAIN

What makes this mountain interesting is not its great height, but rather a white reclining Buddha (Tuong Phat Nam). At a length of 49m, this is the largest reclining Buddha in Vietnam. There are several monks in residence nearby.

The pagoda was constructed in 1861 during the Nguyen Dynasty. The reclining Buddha is much more recent, having been built in 1972. The site has become an important pilgrimage centre for Vietnamese Buddhists, many of whom spend the night in the pagoda's dormitory. Unfortunately, foreigners can't stay overnight without police permission, which is not easily obtained.

Takou Mountain is just off of National Highway 1, 28km south from Phan Thiet. The Buddha is a beautiful two-hour trek from the highway.

Central Highlands

The Central Highlands cover the southern part of the Truong Son Mountain Range (Annamite Cordillera) and include the provinces of Lam Dong, Dac Lac (Dak Lak), Gia Lai and Kon Tum. The region, which is home to many highland minority groups, or Montagnards, is renowned for its cool climate, mountain scenery, innumerable streams, lakes and waterfalls.

Although the population of the Central Highlands is only 3.5 million, the area has always been considered strategically important. During the American War, considerable fighting took place around Buon Ma Thuot, Pleiku and Kon Tum.

The western region of the Central Highlands along the border with Cambodia and Laos is a vast, fertile plateau with red volcanic soil. The good soil and sparse population has not gone unnoticed – the government has targeted the area for a massive resettlement program. Most of the new settlers are farmers from the crowded Red River Delta area in the north of the country. The government-financed scheme is mostly successful, though the local hill tribes might be less than thrilled by the sudden influx of northern Vietnamese.

The western highlands area has lost much of its natural beauty. Some remnant forests remain, but most of the trees were either destroyed by Agent Orange during the American War or have been stripped to make way for agriculture. The only thing that really adds a bit of colour to this part of Vietnam are the Montagnards, particularly in the Kon Tum area.

With the exception of Lam Dong Province (where Dalat is), the Central Highlands was closed to foreigners, until 1992. Even Westerners with legitimate business in the area were arrested and sent back to Ho Chi Minh City (Saigon). This extreme sensitivity stemmed partly from the limited nature of central government control in remote areas, as well as a concern that secret 're-education camps' (rumoured to be hidden in the region) would be discovered and publicised.

The situation has changed. Almost all of the Central Highlands is open to foreigners now, however travel permits are still needed for certain areas.

Highlights

- Visit the old French hill station of Dalat, where pine-forested hills, cultivated valleys, lakes and waterfalls meet Vietnamese kitsch.
- Explore the Bahnar and Jarai hill tribe villages around Buon Ma Thuot, Pleiku and Kon Tum.
- Get off the beaten track and into the wilds of Nam Cat Tien or Yok Don national parks.

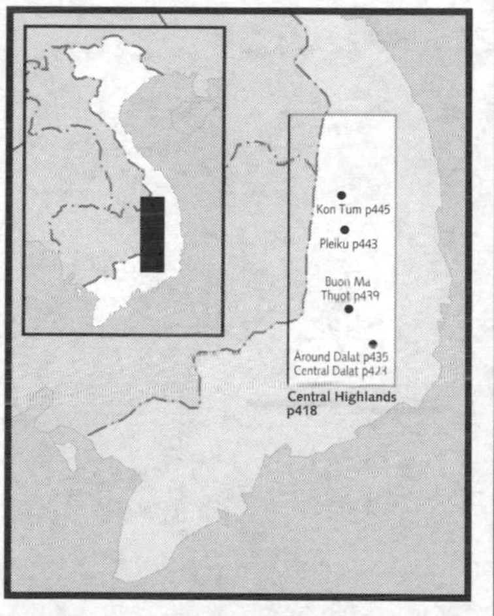

LANGA LAKE

The Ho Chi Minh City–Dalat road (Highway 20) spans this reservoir, which is crossed by a bridge (see the Around Ho Chi Minh City map). Lots of floating houses

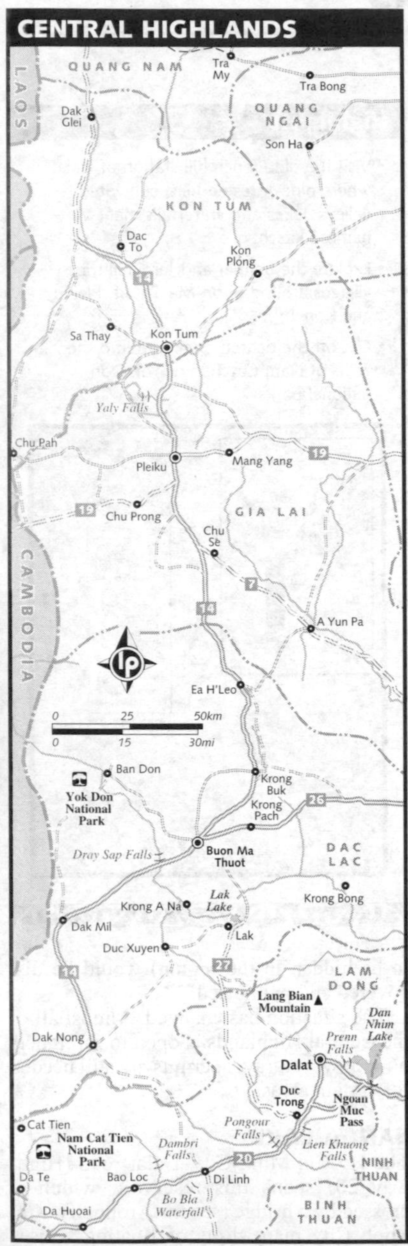

can be seen here, all built since 1991. The whole point behind living in a floating house is to harvest the fish underneath. It's a very scenic spot for photography, although the local children have become very pushy beggars – a consequence of tourists feeding them sweets.

Most tourist minibuses on the Ho Chi Minh City–Dalat road make a 10-minute stop at Langa Lake.

DINH QUAN

There are volcanic craters near the obscure town of Dinh Quan on Highway 20 (see the Around Ho Chi Minh City map). All three volcanoes are now extinct, but are nonetheless very impressive. The craters date from the late Jurassic period, about 150 million years ago.

You can't see many of the craters from the highway – you have to do a little walking. One crater is on the left-hand side of the road, about 2km south of Dinh Quan, and another on the right-hand side of the road around 8km beyond Dinh Quan (toward Dalat).

LAVA TUBES

A little bit beyond the volcanic craters in the direction of Dalat are underground lava tubes. These rare caves were formed as the surface lava cooled and solidified, while the hotter underground lava continued to flow, leaving a hollow space.

Lava tubes are rare in Vietnam and differ sharply in appearance from liestone caves (the latter are formed by underground springs). While limestone caves have abundant stalactites and stalagmites, the walls of lava caves are smooth.

The easiest way to find the lava tubes is to first find the teak forest on Highway 20 between the 'km 120' and 'km 124' markers. The children who live around the forest can point you to the lava tubes' entrances. However, you are strongly advised *not* to go into the tubes by yourself.

It's best to have a guide and, furthermore, inform someone responsible where you are going. You definitely need to bring a torch (flashlight).

NAM CAT TIEN NATIONAL PARK

☎ 061 • elevation 700m

Straddling the border of three provinces – Lam Dong, Dong Nai and Song Be – Nam Cat Tien National Park is just 150km from Ho Chi Minh City, and 40km from Buon Ma Thuot. Nam Cat Tien was hit hard with defoliants during the American War, but the large old-growth trees survived and the smaller plants have recovered. Just as importantly, the wildlife has made a comeback. The area is said to be home to the Javan rhino, considered the rarest mammal in existence. Leopards are also believed to live in the park, while another rare creature found here is a type of wild ox called a gaur. The jungles here support a very healthy population of monkeys and an astounding variety of bird life (avid bird watchers flock here from around the world). Leeches are another less desirable member of the local fauna – come prepared.

Elephants also roam the park, but their presence has caused some controversy. In the early 1990s, the area just outside of Nam Cat Tien was visited by a herd of 10 hungry elephants, in search of food. The creatures fell into an abandoned bomb crater left over from the American War. Local villagers took pity on the elephants and proceeded to dig a ramp to rescue them. Tragically, since then 28 villagers have been killed by rampaging elephants. Theoretically, the problem could have been 'solved' by shooting the elephants, but the Vietnamese government wasn't willing to risk the wrath of international environmental organisations. None of these organisations, however, have came up with the funds for relocating the elephants, some of which were finally removed to zoos. In the longer term, such conflicts will likely be repeated – with increasing competition between Vietnam's growing population and wildlife for the same living space.

Jeeps can rented for US$12 (return) to visit Crocodile Swamp (Bau Sau). It is a 9km drive from the park headquarters, and you'll need to trek the last 4km to the swamp. The walk takes about three hours roundtrip. It may be possible for small groups (four people or less) to spend the night at the ranger post here – a good place to view wildlife that come to drink in the swamp.

Admission to the park costs 40,000d (US$2.85).

Places to Stay & Eat

There are ***bungalows*** *(☎ 791228, fax 791227)* for rent near the park headquarters. Fan triples cost US$10, or US$2 more with aircon. There is also a small ***restaurant*** nearby.

Getting There & Away

The most common approach to the park is from Highway 20, which connects Dalat with Ho Chi Minh City. To reach the park, you have to follow a narrow 24km road which branches west from Highway 20 at Talai Junction (Nga Ban Talai) – the road to the park is signposted at the junction. Another approach is to take a boat across Langa Lake and then hike from there. Dalat Tourist has so far ignored the area, which would normally be a blessing, but you do really need a guide if you want to trek in this remote spot.

Some travel agencies in Ho Chi Minh City have periodically offered customised tours to Nam Cat Tien. However, the tours do not depart on any fixed schedule and good guides are hard to find. You are better off getting to the park on your own and making arrangements with the rangers once you are there.

BAO LOC

☎ 063 • elevation 850m

The town of Bao Loc (also known as B'Lao) is a convenient place to break the trip between Ho Chi Minh City and Dalat. Highway 20 is called Đ Tran Phu as it passes through town. Tea, mulberry leaves (for the silkworm industry) and silk are the major local industries.

Bao Loc Church

Bao Loc Church is several hundred metres towards Dalat along the highway from the Bao Loc Hotel. A new second church stands just next door. Mass is held on Sunday.

Tea Factories

If you've ever wondered how tea is prepared, you might try getting someone to show you around one of Bao Loc's many tea-processing plants. The largest is Nha May Che 19/5, which is 2km towards Dalat from the Bao Loc Hotel. The factory, which produces tea for export, is on the top of a low hill next to a modern yellow water tower. The second-largest tea factory is named 28/3. A joint Vietnamese and Soviet concern named Vietso (formerly Bisinée) is another place where you might inquire.

Places to Stay & Eat

The ***Bao Loc Hotel*** *(☎ 864107, 795 Đ Tran Phu)* was built in 1940, and finally renovated in 1999. Room rates range from US$7 to US$15. There is also a decent ***restaurant*** attached.

About 800m south of the Bao Loc Hotel on the main highway is the reasonable ***Hong Hoang Hotel*** *(☎ 863117)*, which has rooms for US$10 to US$14.

Thanh Van 1 Hotel *(☎ 863005, 65 Đ Le Hong Phong)* is another option. Rooms here rent for US$14 to US$18.

The pleasant, three-star ***Viseri Hotel*** *(☎ 864150, fax 864430)* is right on the lakeside and charges US$25 to US$33 including breakfast.

Lien Do Restaurant *(☎ 864113, 462 Đ Tran Phu)* is a popular stop for tour groups. For a more local scene, look for the ***restaurants*** across the road from the Bao Loc Church.

Getting There & Away

Bus The bus station is 2km from the Bao Loc Hotel.

Car & Motorbike Bao Loc is 177km north-east of Ho Chi Minh City, 49km west of Di Linh and 131km south-west of Dalat.

DAMBRI FALLS

This is one of the highest (90m) and most magnificent waterfalls in Vietnam – and easily accessible. The views are positively breathtaking – the steep walk up the path to the top of the falls will almost certainly take your breath away (unless you opt to ride the new cable car for US$0.40).

If you continue walking upstream from the top of the falls you reach 'Monkey Island,' a mini-zoo filled with monkeys and reindeer (admission US$0.15).

Dambri Falls is close to Bao Loc in an area populated chiefly by Montagnards. Near Bao Loc, you turn off the main highway and follow the road for 18km. As you're driving towards the falls you can see plentiful tea and mulberry plantations; the high peak off to your right is May Bay Mountain.

There is an admission fee of US$0.50 to visit the falls. The ***Dambri Restaurant***, which adjoins the car park, is cheap and good.

DI LINH

The town of Di Linh (pronounced 'zee-ling'), also known as Djiring, is 1010m above sea level. The area's main product is tea, which is grown on giant plantations founded by the French. The Di Linh Plateau, sometimes compared to the Cameron Highlands of Malaysia, is a great place for day hikes. Only a few decades ago, the region was famous for its tiger hunting.

Bo Bla Waterfall

The 32m-high Bo Bla Waterfall is 7km south-west of town, close to Highway 20.

Getting There & Away

Di Linh is 226km north-east of Ho Chi Minh City and 82km south-west of Dalat on the main Ho Chi Minh City–Dalat highway. The town is 96km from Phan Thiet by a secondary road.

Pongour Falls

Pongour Falls, the largest in the Dalat area, is about 55km towards Ho Chi Minh City from Dalat and 7km off the highway. During the rainy season, the falls form a full semicircle. Admission costs US$0.40.

Gougah Falls

Gougah Falls is approximately 40km from Dalat towards Ho Chi Minh City. It is only 500m from the highway so it's easy to get to. Admission costs US$0.20.

Lien Khuong Falls

At Lien Khuong Falls, the Dan Nhim River, 100m wide at this point, drops 15m over an outcrop of volcanic rock. The site, which can be seen from the highway, is 25km towards Ho Chi Minh City from Dalat. Lien Khuong Falls is not far from Lien Khuong airport.

Lien Khuong Falls is not just one, but a number of falls close to the road which are very nice to climb around in. There is a waterfall where you can crawl under the rocky outcrop. The falls are not commercialised –there's not even a sign by the road.

Per Arenmo

DAN NHIM LAKE

Dan Nhim Lake (elevation 1042m) was created by a dam built between 1962 and 1964 by Japan as part of its war reparations. The huge Dan Nhim hydroelectric project supplies electricity to much of the south.

The lake is often used by Ho Chi Minh City movie studios for filming romantic lakeside scenes. The lake's surface area is 9.3 sq km.

The power station is at the western edge of the coastal plain. Water drawn from Dan Nhim Lake gathers speed as it rushes almost a vertical kilometre down from Ngoan Muc Pass in two enormous pipes.

It is said that the forested hills around Dan Nhim Lake are fine for hiking and that there is good fishing in the area. Unfortunately, the local cops are not likely to allow you to wander around without a permit from Dalat Tourist (see the Dalat section).

Getting There & Away

Dan Nhim Lake is about 38km from Dalat in the Don Duong District of Lam Dong Province. As you head towards Phan Rang & Thap Cham, the dam is about a kilometre to the left of the Dalat–Phan Rang highway. The power station is at the base of Ngoan Muc Pass near the town of Ninh Son.

NGOAN MUC PASS

Ngoan Muc Pass (altitude 980m), known to the French as Bellevue Pass, is about 5km towards Phan Rang & Thap Cham from Dan Nhim Lake and 64km west of Phan Rang. On a clear day, you can see all the way across the coastal plain to the Pacific Ocean, an aerial distance of 55km. As the highway winds down the mountain in a series of switchbacks, it passes under the two gargantuan water pipes – still guarded by armed troops in concrete fortifications – that link Dan Nhim Lake with the hydroelectric power station.

To the south of the road (to the right as you face the ocean) you can see the steep tracks of the *crémaillère* (cog railway) linking Thap Cham with Dalat (see the following Dalat section).

Sites of interest at the top of Ngoan Muc Pass include a waterfall next to the highway, pine forests and the old Bellevue train station.

DALAT

☎ 063 • pop 129,400 • elevation 1475m

The jewel of the Central Highlands, Dalat is in a temperate region dotted with lakes, waterfalls, evergreen forests and gardens. The cool climate and the park-like environment make this one of the most delightful cities in all of Vietnam. It was once called Le Petit Paris and to this end there is a miniature replica of the Eiffel Tower behind the central market. Dalat is by far Vietnam's most popular honeymoon spot. It's also the favourite haunt of Vietnamese artists and avant-garde types who have made this their permanent home. It's also (hopefully) the final word in Vietnamese kitsch.

Local industries include growing garden vegetables and flowers (especially beautiful hydrangea flowers). The flowers and vegies are sold all over southern Vietnam. But the biggest contribution to the economy of Dalat is tourism (over 300,000 domestic tourists visit every year). The downside is that the locals are trying to create circus-style 'tourist attractions', complete with sailboats, mini-zoos, balloons for the kiddies and Vietnamese dressed as bunny rabbits.

The Dalat area was once famous for its big-game hunting and a 1950s brochure boasted that 'a two hour drive from the town leads to several game-rich areas abounding in deer, roes, peacocks, pheasants, wild boar, black bear, wild caws, panthers, tigers, gaurs and elephants'. So successful were the hunters that all of the big game is now extinct. However, you will get a whiff of Dalat's former glory by viewing some of the 'souvenirs' about town:

> What will stick in my mind most is the appalling stuffed animals they seem so fond of in Dalat. These seem to have spread all over Vietnam, but the citizens of Dalat in particular, have taken taxidermy to new lows. We had a terrible fit of the giggles as we left the Ho Chi Minh Mausoleum in Hanoi when the thought surfaced of what the Dalat animal stuffers could have done with Ho Chi Minh if the stuffing contract hadn't been given to the Russians.
>
> **Tony Wheeler**

The city's population includes about 5000 members of ethno-linguistic hill tribes, of which there are said to be some 33 distinct communities in Lam Dong Province. Members of these 'hill tribes' (who still refer to themselves by the French word *montagnards*, or 'highlanders') can occasionally be seen in the market places in their traditional dress. Hill tribe women of this area carry their infants on their backs in a long piece of cloth worn over one shoulder and tied in the front.

There is a New Economic Zone (a planned rural settlement where southern refugees and people from the overcrowded north were semi-forcibly resettled after reunification) 14km from Dalat in Lam Ha District; it has a permanent population of about 10,000.

Dalat is often called the City of Eternal Spring. The average maximum daily temperature here is a cool 24°C and the average minimum daily temperature is 15°C. The dry season runs from December to March. Even during the rainy season, which lasts more or less from April to November, it is sunny most of the time.

History

The local area has been home to various Montagnard groups for centuries. The first European to claim they had 'discovered' the site of Dalat was Dr Alexandre Yersin, (a protege of Louis Pasteur – the first person to identify the plague bacillus), in 1893. The city itself was established in 1912 and quickly became popular with Europeans as a cool retreat from the sweltering heat of the coastal plains and the Mekong Delta. In the local Lat language, Da Lat means 'River of the Lat Tribe'.

During the American War Dalat was, by the tacit agreement of all parties concerned, largely spared the ravages of war. Indeed, it seems that while South Vietnamese army officers were being trained at the city's Military Academy and affluent officials of the Saigon regime were relaxing in their villas, Viet Cong (VC) cadres were doing the same thing not far away in *their* villas. Dalat fell to North Vietnamese forces without a fight on 3 April 1975. There is no problem with leftover mines and ordnance in the Dalat area.

Orientation

Dalat's sights are very spread out. The city centre is around Rap 3/4 cinema (named after the date on which Dalat was liberated in 1975), which is up the hill from the central market building. Xuan Huong Lake is a prominent landmark on the southern side of town.

Information

Travel Agencies Dalat's tourist offic cum travel agency is Dalat Touris (☎ 821351, fax 822661, ⓔ dalattouris .com). You'll find its main office is at 35 Tran Hung Dao, but for booking tours c vehicle rentals, visit their booking offic Dalat Toserco (☎ 822125, fax 82833(ⓔ dalattours.com) in the Thuy Tien Hotel a 7 Đ 3 Thang 2, near the city centre.

Also see Adventure Sports later in th section.

Money The place to change both cash ar travellers cheques is the Agriculture Ba of Vietnam (Ngan Hang Nong Nghiep Vie nam). It's on Đ Nguyen Van Troi right in th central area of town.

Post & Communications The post offi is across the street from the Novotel Dalat 14 Đ Tran Phu. In addition to postal servic the post office has international telegrap telex, telephone, fax and email facilities.

CENTRAL HIGHLANDS

A better place to check on your email is the Viet Hung Cafe (☎ 835737, e vaquan@hcm.vnn.vn) at 7 Đ Nguyen Chi Thanh. The friendly owner Mr Quan is a local motorbike driver and an excellent source of travel information for Dalat and the Central Highlands.

Xuan Huong Lake

Xuan Huong Lake in the centre of Dalat was created by a dam in 1919. It is named after a 17th-century Vietnamese poet known for her daring attacks on the hypocrisy of social conventions and the foibles of scholars, monks, mandarins, feudal lords and kings. The lake is circumnavigated by a path.

Paddleboats that look like giant swans can be rented near Thanh Thuy Restaurant, which is 200m north-east of the dam. A golf course occupies 50 hectares on the northern side of the lake near the Flower Gardens. The majestic hilltop Hotel Sofitel Dalat Palace overlooks Xuan Huong Lake from the south.

Crémaillère Railway

About 500m east of Xuan Huong Lake is a train station and, although you aren't likely

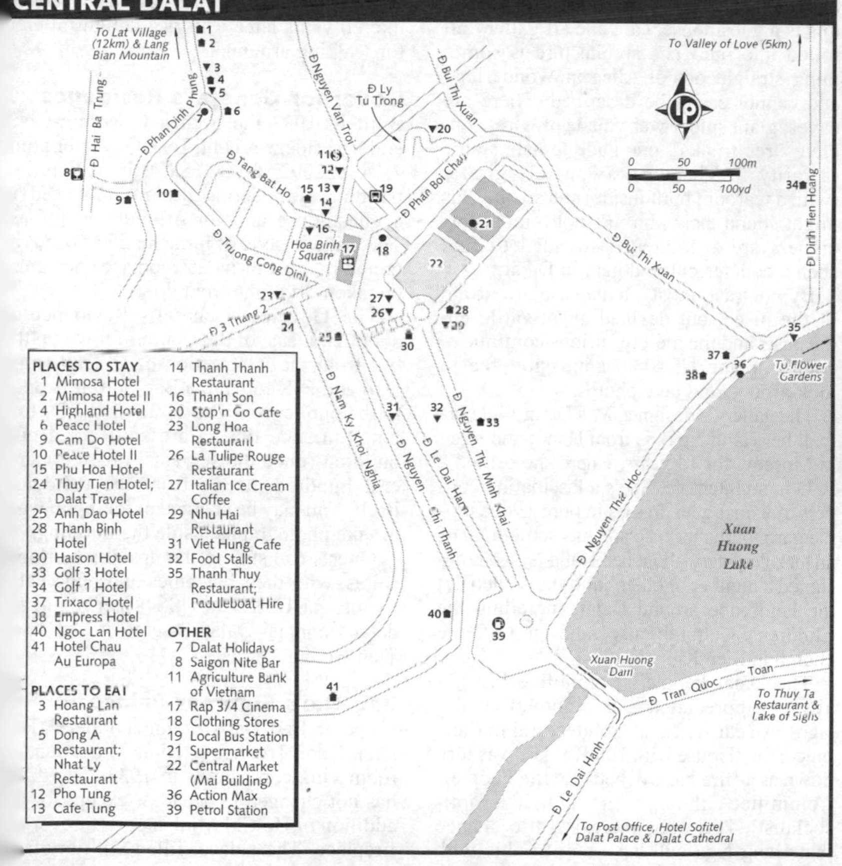

to arrive in Dalat by train, the station is worth a visit. The crémaillère (cog railway) linked Dalat and Thap Cham from 1928 to 1964, when it was closed because of VC attacks. The line has been partially repaired and is now operated as a tourist attraction. You can't get to anywhere useful (like Ho Chi Minh City) on this train, but you can ride 8km down the tracks to Trai Mat Village and back again. The fee for this journey is US$4 for the round trip and a platform ticket costs US$0.30.

Hang Nga Guesthouse & Art Gallery

Nicknamed 'the Crazy House' by locals, this is a guesthouse, cafe and art gallery all rolled into one. The architecture is something straight out of Alice in Wonderland and cannot easily be described. There are caves, giant spider webs made of wire, concrete 'tree trunks', one nude female statue (a rarity in Vietnam), a concrete giraffe (with a tearoom built inside) and so on. This might sound tacky, but it's not – most foreigners are absolutely astounded to find such a counter-cultural gem in Dalat.

By contrast, most Vietnamese are afraid of the place, but devoted avant-garde enthusiasts and the merely curious continue to cough up the US$0.30 admission fee to look around and take photos.

The gallery's designer, Mrs Dang Viet Nga (call her Hang Nga), is from Hanoi and lived in Moscow for 14 years, where she earned a PhD in architecture. She's a fascinating conversationalist who dresses in pure 1960s hippie garb, burns incense and has something of an air of mystery about her. Hang Nga has designed a number of other buildings which dot the landscape around Dalat, including the Children's Cultural Palace and the Catholic church in Lien Khuong.

The Dalat People's Committee has not always appreciated such innovative designs. An earlier Dalat architectural masterpiece, the 'House with 100 Roofs', was torn down as a 'fire hazard' because the People's Committee thought it looked 'anti-socialist'. However, there is little chance that Hang Nga will have any trouble with the authorities – her father, Truong Chinh, was Ho Chi Minh's successor. He served as Vietnam's second president from 1981 until his death in 1988.

The Hang Nga Guesthouse & Art Gallery (☎ 822070) is about 1km south-west of Xuan Huong Lake. The official address is 3 Đ Huynh Thuc Khang.

French District

The area between the Rap 3/4 Cinema and Đ Phan Dinh Phung hasn't changed much since the French departed. If, in the year 1934, someone had evacuated a provincial town in France and repopulated it with Vietnamese, this is what it would have looked like 20 years later. This is a delightful area for walking around.

Governor-General's Residence

Built in 1933 the French Governor-General's Residence (Dinh Toan Quyen or Dinh 2; ☎ 822092, fax 825885), is a dignified building of modernist design, now used as a guesthouse and for official receptions. The original style of furnishing has been retained in most of its 25 rooms. Shoes must be taken off at the front door.

The Governor-General's Residence is about 2km east of the centre of town up the hill from the intersection of Đ Tran Hung Dao and Đ Khoi Nghia Bac Son; it is open to the public from 7 to 11 am and 1.30 to pm. Entrance tickets are sold at an out building (once the servants' quarters) several hundred metres from the residence itself. You may be charged extra if you want to take photographs inside the building.

Guests can stay in the upstairs bedroom suites, with their balconies and huge bathrooms, for US$27 to US$40 per night; for details contact Dalat Toserco in the Th Ṭien Hotel.

Bao Dai's Summer Palace

Emperor Bao Dai's Summer Palace (B Dien Quoc Truong, or Dinh 3) is a tan, room villa constructed in 1933. The dec has not changed in decades, except for the addition of Ho Chi Minh's portrait over the fireplace. The palace, filled with artefa from decades and governments past, is extremely interesting.

For instance, the engraved-glass map of Vietnam was given to Emperor Bao Dai in 1942 by Vietnamese students in France. In Bao Dai's office, the life-size white bust above the bookcase is of Bao Dai himself; the smaller gold and brown busts are of his father, Emperor Khai Dinh. Note the heavy brass royal seal (on the right) and military seal (on the left). The photographs over the fireplace are of (from left to right) Bao Dai, his eldest son, Bao Long (in uniform), and Empress Nam Phuong, who died in 1963.

Upstairs are the royal living quarters. The room of Bao Long, who now lives in England, is decorated in yellow, the royal colour. The huge semicircular couch was used by the emperor and empress for family meetings, during which their three daughters were seated in the yellow chairs and their two sons in the pink chairs. Check out the ancient tan Rouathermique infra-red sauna machine near the top of the stairs.

Bao Dai's Summer Palace is set in a pine grove 500m south-east of the Pasteur Institute, which is on Đ Le Hong Phong, 2km south-west of the city centre. The palace is open to the public from 7 to 11 am and 1.30 to 4 pm and shoes must be removed at the door. The entry fee for foreigners is US$0.40, plus and extra charge for cameras and videos.

Tourists can stay here for US$40 per person per night; for more information contact Dalat Toserco.

Flower Gardens

The Dalat Flower Gardens (Vuon Hoa Dalat; ☎ 822151) were established in 1966 by the South Vietnamese Agricultural Service and renovated in 1985. Flowers represented include hydrangeas, fuchsias and orchids *(hoa lan)*. Most of the latter are in special shaded buildings off to the right from the entrance. The orchids are grown in blocks of coconut palm trunk and in terracotta pots with lots of ventilation holes.

Several monkeys live in cages on the grounds of the Flower Gardens – some feeble-minded tourists enjoy tormenting the monkeys by throwing rocks and lit cigarettes, but those clever monkeys have learned to throw them back.

Near the gate you can buy *(cu ly)*, reddish-brown animal-shaped pieces of fern stems whose fibres are used to stop bleeding in traditional medicine. One traveller said:

> For kitsch, visit the Flower Gardens. I can't describe them, just go there – a marvel!

The Flower Gardens front Xuan Huong Lake at 2 Đ Phu Dong Thien Vuong, which leads from the lake to Dalat University; they are open from 7.30 am to 4 pm. Ticket sales are suspended for a while around noon. Entry costs US$0.30.

Dalat University

Dalat is actually something of an education centre. The reason for this is the climate – before air-conditioning, Dalat was one of the few places in Vietnam where it was possibly to study without working up a sweat. Therefore, a number of educational institutions were located in town, with Dalat University being the most famous.

Dalat University was founded as a Catholic university in 1957 by Hue Archbishop Ngo Dinh Thuc, older brother of President Ngo Dinh Diem (assassinated in 1963), with the help of Cardinal Spelman of New York. The university was seized from the church in 1975 and closed, but it reopened two years later as a state-run institution.

There are presently more than 1200 students from south-central Vietnam studying here, but they all live in off-campus boarding houses. The university library contains 10,000 books, including some in English and European languages.

Dalat University is at 1 Đ Phu Dong Thien Vuong (corner with Đ Dinh Tien Hoang). The 38-hectare campus can easily be identified by the red-star-topped triangular tower. The red star is stuck over the cross which was originally erected by the church. The fact that the cross was never actually removed has led some to speculate that the church may some day get the campus returned to it.

Foreign visitors are generally welcome to visit the campus.

It Could Be You

Asians love to gamble, and the Vietnamese are no exception. Lottery madness has swept Vietnam, particularly in the south (the rage has yet to consume hill tribes in the northern provinces), with tickets being issued in some 40 different provincial areas.

Tickets come in three basic varieties, each costing 2000d (US$0.15). The most popular style is roughly fashioned on paper currency and features chic 1970s motifs like cherry-red sports cars, flowers or voluptuous Vietnamese supermodels. Less popular are instant tickets, sealed in a perforated paper packet and checked on the spot with the vendors who hold the day's winning numbers. Finally there are instant win scratch cards, which are most popular in the central provinces and typically decorated with exotic African wildlife.

Tickets are primarily pedalled on the street by young kids, who clear a 10% commission on each ticket sold (less than US$0.01). Daily winning numbers, announced each afternoon, can be checked with the vendors (earning you the unspoken obligation to buy another one) or in local newspapers the following day. Cash prizes, determined by winning numbers sequentially matching the six digit number on your ticket, max out at 50 million dong (US$360). Winners have one month to make claims.

While Vietnam's lottery is a legitimate, government sanctioned cash cow, frequently reported ticket forgeries, as well as occasional printing mistakes, add a whole other element to the game.

Former Petit Lycee Yersin

The Former Petit Lycee Yersin at 1 Đ Hoang Van Thu is now a cultural centre (☎ 822511) run by the provincial government. Music lessons in electric and acoustic guitar, piano, violin, clarinet, saxophone etc are held here, making this a good place to meet local musicians. It's been reported that a new music centre opened in the French District on Đ Tang Bat Ho.

Valley of Love

Named the Valley of Peace by Emperor Bao Dai, the Valley of Love (Thung Lung Tinh Yeu, or Vallee d'Amour in French), had its name changed in 1972 (the year Da Thien Lake was created) by romantically minded students from Dalat University.

The place has taken on a carnival atmosphere; tourist buses line up to regurgitate visitors and boats line up to accommodate them. Get into the spirit with some aquatic activities. Paddleboats cost US$0.50 per hour, 15-person canoes cost US$4 per hour and obnoxious noise-making motorboats cost US$5 for a whirlwind tour of the lake.

This is a good place to see the 'Dalat cow boys'. The 'cowboys' are in fact Vietnames guides dressed as American cowboys come back in another year and they'll hav the Montagnards dressed up as Indians We've also seen locals dressed as bears; ca Mickey Mouse and Donald Duck costume be far behind? The cowboys rent horses t tourists for US$5 (and up) per hour and ca take you on a guided tour around the lak The Dalat cowboys and 'bears' expect cas if you take their picture – they want abo US$0.30 per photo.

Refreshments and local delicacies (jam candied fruits) are on sale at the looko near where the buses disgorge tourists.

The Valley of Love is 5km north of Xu Huong Lake on Đ Phu Dong Thien Vuon The entrance fee is US$0.40.

Cam Ly Falls

Cam Ly Falls, opened as a tourist site 1911, is one of those must-see spots for d mestic visitors. The grassy areas around t 15m-high cascades are the habitat of hors and Dalat cowboys. Many of the cowbo you see around here aren't guides but tourists – for a fee you can get dressed as a cowboy and have your photo taken. The waterfall (entry US$0.40) is between numbers 57 and 59 on Đ Hoang Van Thu; it is open from 7 am to 6 pm.

Tomb of Nguyen Huu Hao

Nguyen Huu Hao, who died in 1939, was the father of Nam Phuong, Bao Dai's wife. He was the richest person in the Go Cong District of the Mekong Delta. Nguyen Huu Hao's tomb is on a hilltop 400m west of Cam Ly Falls.

Places of Worship

Lam Ty Ni Pagoda This pagoda, also known as Quan Am Tu, was founded in 1961. The decorative front gate was constructed by the pagoda's one monk, Vien Thuc, an industrious man who learned English, French, Khmer and Thai at Dalat University. During his 35 years here, he has built flower beds and gardens in several different styles, including a miniature Japanese garden complete with a bridge. Nearby are trellis-shaded paths decorated with hanging plants. Signs list the Chinese name of each garden. Vien Thuc also built much of the pagoda's wooden furniture.

But more than the pagoda and its gardens the attraction here is Mr Thuc himself and his mind-boggling collection of self-brushed art works. It would be a gross understatement to call him prolific. By his own estimates he has churned out more than 100,000 works of art, piles and piles of which hang in and around the pagoda (even out in the rain!).

So industrious is this eccentric local celebrity, that since he began selling his paintings to tourists he has become, some say, the wealthiest person in Dalat. Judging by the astounding number of 'instant paintings' he sells, you could believe it. The one-time hermit monk has today earned himself the esteemed title of 'the business monk' by local motorbike guides (many of whom resent his financial success, not to mention having to wait for hours while their customers linger at the pagoda).

Paintings sell anywhere from a dollar or two to whatever smooth-talking Mr Thuc can get you for. These days the monk is saving those dollars while he waits for his first passport to be processed and his long-awaited around-the-globe journey to begin. His plans include visiting travellers who have been to see him (and the homes where so many of paintings hang). He says he needs 'at least US$30,000' for the journey, and seems to be doing a damn good job of raising the funds.

Mr Thuc's legendary status has already made him the subject of much rumour and myth. Not long ago we received a sorrowful letter to inform us of his untimely death (he got a good chuckle out of this one!). Commercialised or not, he is certainly a interesting man and provides a most unusual encounter. Be aware that the monk's popularity has sailed to such highs that these days there is a steady stream of visitors at the pagoda, so many that he often needs to lock the pagoda gate just to have time to eat!

Lam Ty Ni Pagoda is about 500m north of the Pasteur Institute at 2 Đ Thien My. A visit here can easily be combined with a stop at Bao Dai's Summer Palace.

Linh Son Pagoda Linh Son Pagoda was built in 1938. The giant bell is said to be made of bronze mixed with gold, its great weight making it too heavy for thieves to carry off. Behind the pagoda are coffee and tea plants tended by the 15 monks, who range in age from 20 to 80, and half a dozen novices.

One of the monks here has led a fascinating life, whose peculiar course reflects the vagaries of Vietnam's modern history. Born in 1926 of a Japanese father and a Vietnamese mother, during WWII he was pressed into the service of the Japanese occupation forces as a translator. He got his high-school degree from a French-language Franciscan convent in 1959 at the age of 35. His interest later turned to American literature, in which he received a master's degree (his thesis was on William Faulkner) from Dalat University in 1975. The monk speaks at least half a dozen East Asian and European languages fluently.

Linh Son Pagoda is about 1km from the town centre on Đ Phan Dinh Phung; the official street address is 120 Đ Nguyen Van Troi.

Dalat Cathedral Dalat Cathedral, which is on Đ Tran Phu next to the Novotel Dalat, was built between 1931 and 1942 for use by French residents and holidaymakers. The cross on the spire is 47m above the ground. Inside, the stained-glass windows bring a hint of medieval Europe to Dalat. The first church built on this site (in the 1920s) is to the left of the cathedral; it has a light-blue arched door.

There are three priests here. Masses are held at 5.30 am and 5.15 pm (Sunday at 5.30 and 7 am, and 4 pm). The parish's three choirs (one for each Sunday Mass) practice on Thursday and Saturday from 5 to 6 pm.

Vietnamese Evangelical Church Dalat's pink Evangelical Church, the main Protestant church in the city, was built in 1940. Until 1975, it was affiliated with the Christian and Missionary Alliance. The serving minister here was trained at Nha Trang Bible College.

Since reunification, Vietnam's Protestants have been persecuted even more than Catholics, in part because many Protestant clergymen were trained by American missionaries. Although religious activities at this church are still restricted by the government, Sunday is a busy day with Bible study, worship and a youth service.

Most of the 25,000 Protestants in Lam Dong Province, who are served by more than 100 churches, are hill tribe people. Dalat's Vietnamese Evangelical Church is one of only six churches in the province whose membership is ethnic-Vietnamese.

The Vietnamese Evangelical Church is 300m north of Rap 3/4 at 72 Đ Nguyen Van Troi.

Domaine de Marie Convent The pink tile-roofed structures of the Domaine de Marie Convent (Nha Tho Domaine), constructed between 1940 and 1942, were once home to 300 nuns. Today, the eight remaining nuns support themselves by making ginger candies and selling the fruit grown in the orchard out the back.

Suzanne Humbert, wife of Admiral Jean Decoux, Vichy-French Governor-General of Indochina from 1940 to 1945, is buried at the base of the outside back wall of the chapel. A benefactress of the chapel, she was killed in a car accident in 1944.

Masses are held in the large chapel Monday to Friday at 5.30 am and on Sunday at 5.30 am and 4.15 pm.

The Domaine de Marie Convent is on a hilltop at 6 Đ Ngo Quyen, which is also called Đ Mai Hac De. The French-speaking nuns are pleased to show visitors around and explain their social work for orphans, homeless and handicapped children. A shop sells handicrafts made by the children and nuns.

Du Sinh Church This church was built in 1955 by Catholic refugees from the north. The four-post, Sino-Vietnamese-style steeple was constructed at the insistence of a Hué-born priest of royal lineage. The church is on a hilltop with beautiful views in all directions, making this a great place for a picnic.

To get to Du Sinh Church, go 500m southwest along Đ Huyen Tran Cong Chua from the former Couvent des Oiseaux, which is now a teachers' training high school.

Thien Vuong Pagoda This pagoda, also known simply as Chua Tau (the Chinese pagoda), is popular with domestic tourists especially ethnic-Chinese. Set on a hilltop amid pine trees, the pagoda was built by the Chaozhou Chinese Congregation. Tho Da the monk who initiated the construction of the pagoda in 1958, emigrated to the USA there are pictures of his 1988 visit on display. The stalls out the front are a good place to buy local candied fruit and preserves.

The pagoda itself consists of three yellow buildings made of wood. In the first building is a gilded, wooden statue of Ho Phap one of the Buddha's protectors. On the other side of Ho Phap's glass case is gilded wooden statue of Pho Hien, a helpe of A Di Da Buddha (the Buddha of the Past). Shoes should be removed before entering the third building, in which there are three 4m-high standing Buddhas donated by a British Buddhist and brought from Hong Kong in 1960. Made of gilded sandalwood and weighing 1400kg each, the figures – said to be the largest sandalwood statues in Vietnam – represent Thich Ca Buddha (the historical Buddha Sakyamuni; in the centre); Quan The Am Bo Tat (Avalokiteçvara, the Goddess of Mercy; on the right); and Dai The Chi Bo Tat (an assistant of A Di Da; on the left).

Thien Vuong Pagoda is about 5km southeast of the centre of town on Đ Khe Sanh.

Minh Nguyet Cu Sy Lam Pagoda A second Chinese Buddhist pagoda, Minh Nguyet Cu Sy Lam Pagoda, is reached by a path beginning across the road from the gate of Thien Vuong Pagoda. It was built by the Cantonese Chinese Congregation in 1962. The main sanctuary of the pagoda is a round structure constructed on a platform representing a lotus blossom.

Inside the pagoda (remove shoes before entering) is a painted cement statue of Quan The Am Bo Tat flanked by two other figures. Notice the repetition of the lotus motif in the window bars, railings, gateposts etc. There is a giant red gourd-shaped incense burning oven near the main sanctuary. The pagoda is open all day and entry is free.

u Nu Pagoda Also known as Chua Linh hong, Su Nu Pagoda is a Buddhist nunnery built in 1952. The nuns here – who, in accordance with Buddhist regulations, are ald – wear grey or brown robes except hen praying, at which time they wear saffron attire. Men are allowed to visit, but nly women live here. The nunnery is open l day, but it is considered impolite to come ound lunch time, when the nuns sing their ayers a cappella before eating. Across the iveway from the main buildings and set nong tea plants is the grave marker of ad nun Thich Nu Dieu Huong.

Su Nu Pagoda is about 1km south of Đ Thai To at 72 Đ Hoang Hoa Tham.

Hiking & Cycling

The best way to enjoy the forests and cultivated countryside around Dalat is by foot, horseback or bicycle. Some suggested routes include:

- Heading out on Đ 3 Thang 4, which becomes Highway 20, to the pine forests of Prenn Pass and Quang Trung Reservoir.
- Going via the Governor-General's Residence and up Đ Khe Sanh to Thien Vuong Pagoda.
- Taking Đ Phu Dong Thien Vuong from Dalat University to the Valley of Love.
- Going out to Bao Dai's Summer Palace and from there, after stopping at Lam Ty Ni Pagoda, heading via Đ Thien My and Đ Huyen Tran Cong Chua to Du Sinh Church.

Adventure Sports

Outdoorsy types and thrill-seekers will want to check out the activities offered by Action Max, an adventure sports outfit which offers paragliding, canyoning and treks to minority villages in the area surrounding Dalat. It has knowledgeable English- and French-speaking guides (it's run by Didier, a Frenchman) leading everything from low-impact hikes to technical rock climbing. The Action Max office (☎ 836135, e tvm46@hotmail.com) is at 2 Đ Nguyen Thai Hoc.

Another contender in the adventure sports game is Dalat Holidays (☎ 829422, e langbian@hcm.vnn.vn), located at 73 Đ Truong Cong Dinh.

Golf

The Dalat People's Committee set up a joint venture with a Hong Kong company to renovate the old golf course once used by Bao Dai, the last Vietnamese emperor. The course has been renamed Dalat Pines. Visitors can play here for US$25 to US$35 per day.

Places to Stay

Due to its popularity with domestic tourists, Dalat has an extensive network of excellent hotels to suit all budgets.

Demand is particularly heavy on Saturday night. During the high season (June and July) or Tet, accommodation can be tight. Dalat Tourist can help with arranging accommodation in some of Dalat's posh ***villas***, including Bao Dai's Summer Palace and the Governor-General's Residence.

Unless you like icy showers, make sure they have hot water before you check in. If there is a power failure, the hot water will be off too, but in that case some hotels will boil water on a gas stove and give it to you in a bucket. No hotels in cool Dalat have air-conditioning and it's hard to imagine why anyone would want it!

Budget Cheap hotels currently in vogue with budget travellers include the following.

The ***Highland Hotel*** *(☎ 823738, 90 Đ Phan Dinh Phung)* right in the heart of Dalat. It's a good budget place with singles for US$4 and US$5 and doubles for US$6 and US$7.

Backpackers have long been fond of the ***Peace Hotel*** *(☎ 822787, 64 Đ Truong Cong Dinh)*. Twins are US$8 to US$15. The ***Peace Hotel II*** *(☎ 822982, 67 Đ Truong Cong Dinh)* charges US$8 to US$12.

The recently renovated ***Mimosa Hotel*** *(☎ 822656, 170 Đ Phan Dinh Phung)* is an old Dalat budget institution offering singles for US$7, or US$8 to US$15 for twins. ***Mimosa Hotel II*** *(☎ 822180, 118 Đ Phan Dinh Phung)*, also called the *Thanh The Hotel*, has singles for US$5 to US$8 and doubles go for US$10 to US$15.

Thanh Binh Hotel *(☎ 822909, 40 Đ Nguyen Thi Minh Khai)* is a good budget hotel right across the street from the central market building. Singles are US$6 to US$8 and twins US$10 to US$12.

Cam Do Hotel *(☎ 822732, 81 Đ Phan Dinh Phung)* is a standard backpackers' special. Singles/doubles/triples cost US$8/10/15.

Phu Hoa Hotel *(☎ 822194, 16 Đ Tang Bat Ho)* is an old, but still reasonably pleasant, place in the centre. Rates for singles are US$7 and doubles are US$10 to US$12.

Trixaco Hotel *(☎ 822789, 7 Đ Nguyen Thai Hoc)* is a fine place with nice views of Xuan Huong Lake. Singles are US$8 and twins are US$10 to US$30.

Haison Hotel *(☎ 822622, fax 822623, 1 Đ Nguyen Thi Minh Khai)* is a spiffy place across the roundabout from the central market building. The hotel advertises its 'elegant and cosy dancing hall' and 'urbane service staff'. Room rates including breakfast are US$7 to US$12 for singles, US$12 to US$25 for doubles.

Thuy Tien Hotel *(☎ 821731, 822482)* is in the heart of the old French section at the corner of Đ 3 Thang 2 and Đ Nam Ky Khoi Nghia. Singles cost US$8 to US$12 and twins are US$12 to US$15.

Truong Nguyen Mini-Hotel *(☎ 821772, 7A Đ Hai Thuong)* is one of the few private hotels which can accept foreign guests. Singles are US$8 and twins cost US$15 to US$20.

Lam Son Hotel *(☎ 822362, 5 Đ Hai Thuong)* is 500m west of the centre of town in an old French villa. This large, quiet place is good value if you don't mind the 10-minute walk to the town centre. Singles are US$8 to US$10 and twins cost US$12 to US$14. The management is very friendly and travellers give it favourable comments.

Mid-Range Recommended is the friendly family-run ***Hotel Chau Au Europe*** *(☎ 822870, fax 824488, 76 Đ Nguyen Chi Thanh)*. The tariff here is US$15 for single and US$20 to $25 for doubles.

The three-star ***Lavy Hotel*** *(☎ 825465, fax 825466, 20 Đ Hung Vuong)* has single for US$30 to US$50 and doubles priced a US$40 to US$60.

Anh Dao Hotel *(☎ 822384, fax 823 570, 50 Hoa Binh Square)* is up the hill from the central market building on Đ Nguyen Chi Thanh. Singles here are US$15 to US$2 and doubles cost US$25. Breakfast is included in the tariff.

Ngoc Lan Hotel *(☎ 822136, fax 82403, 42 Đ Nguyen Chi Thanh)*, this big old place overlooking the petrol station and the lake has been fully renovated, along with the prices; singles are US$25 to US$30, and doubles are US$30 to US$40; all prices include breakfast.

Hang Nga Guesthouse *(☎ 822070, 3 Huynh Thuc Khang)* is a most amazing place – unique in Vietnam if not the world. This exotic guesthouse is actually an gallery of sorts and a cafe. Hotel rooms are built inside artificial tree trunks and caves. The owner, Hang Nga, is the daughter of a former president of Vietnam. Twin rooms cost US$29 to US$54; quads run at US$74 and US$84.

Villa Hoang Hau *(☎ 821431, fax 822333, 8A Đ Ho Tung Mau)* is an excellent little private hotel just south of Xuan Huong Lake. Twins cost US$20 to US$30.

Duy Tan Hotel *(☎ 822216, 82 Đ 3 Thang 2)* on the corner with Đ Hoang Van Thu, is notable for the fenced-in car park which reassures Americans and Aussies accustomed to motel-style travel. Singles are US$20 to US$30 and twins cost US$25 to US$35.

Golf 1 Hotel *(☎ 824082, fax 824945, 11 Đ Dinh Tien Hoang)* is on the edge of the Dalat golf course. It's a lovely place with doubles costing US$30 to US$50. The ***Golf 2 Hotel*** *(☎ 826031, fax 820532, 114 Đ 3 Thang 2)* is another snazzy place with rates from US$25 to US$35, including breakfast. The mammoth ***Golf 3 Hotel*** *(☎ 826042, fax 830 396)* is central at 4 Đ Nguyen Thi Minh Khai. Room rates are from US$32 to US$70. There is a good restaurant on the ground level, a bar on the basement level and a rooftop cafe commanding great views of Dalat.

Empress Hotel *(☎ 833888, fax 829399, 5 Đ Nguyen Thai Hoc)* is an elegant new place set on Xuan Huong Lake – the views are great. This hotel has some of the most beautiful rooms in Dalat. Rates range from US$60 to US$100, including breakfast.

Minh Tam Villas *(☎ 822447, fax 824420, 20A Đ Khe Sanh)* is 3km out of town and there are good views of the surrounding landscape from here. The house originally belonged to a French architect who sold it to a well-to-do Vietnamese family in 1954. It underwent several major renovations and in 1975 was 'donated' to the victorious Communist government. The chalet-style A-frame villas were added later. Twin rooms in the main house cost US$35 to US$45, while smaller (and nicer) cottages go for US$25.

Many of Dalat's 2500 chalet-style ***villas*** also can be rented and there is a whole neighbourhood of villas near the Pasteur Institute including ***Bao Dai's Summer Villa***. The prime villas are along the ridge south of Đ Tran Hung Dao and are simply called the ***Tran Hung Dao Villas***.

Top End ***Hotel Sofitel Dalat Palace*** *(☎ 825444, fax 825666, 12 Đ Tran Phu)* is a grand old place built between 1916 and 1922. Panoramic views of Xuan Huong Lake can be enjoyed in the hotel's expansive ground-floor public areas, where one can sit in a rattan chair sipping tea or soda while gazing out through a wall of windows. There are tennis courts nearby. Major renovation work has turned this into Dalat's premier luxury accommodation. The tariff ranges from US$169 to a cool US$414.

Another vintage hostelry is the large ***Novotel Dalat*** *(☎ 825777, fax 825888, 7 Đ Tran Phu)*, nearly opposite the Sofitel. The building was built in 1932 as the Du Parc Hotel and has also undergone extensive renovation work. Today it too retains much of the original French colonial air (despite the franchisy name). Published rates are US$119 to US$189, though rooms have been offered for as low as US$60.

Places to Eat

Local Specialities Dalat is a paradise for lovers of fresh garden vegetables, which are grown locally and sold all over the south. The abundance of just-picked peas, carrots, radishes, tomatoes, cucumbers, avocados, green peppers, lettuce, Chinese cabbage, bean sprouts, beets, green beans, potatoes, corn, bamboo shoots, garlic, spinach, squash and yams makes for meals unavailable anywhere else in the country. Persimmons and cherries are in season from November to January. Apples are known here as *bom*, after the French *pomme*. Because of fierce competition in the domestic tourism market, restaurant prices are very reasonable.

The Dalat area is justifiably famous for its strawberry jam, dried blackcurrants and candied plums and peaches, all of which can be purchased from ***food stalls*** in the market area just west of Xuan Huong Lake. Other local delicacies include avocado ice cream, sweet beans *(mut dao)* and strawberry, blackberry and artichoke extracts (syrups for making drinks). The strawberry extract is great in tea. The region also produces grape, mulberry and strawberry wines. Artichoke tea, another local speciality, is made from the root of the artichoke plant. Most of these products can be purchased at the ***central market*** and at ***stalls*** in front of Thien Vuong Pagoda.

Dau hu, a type of pudding common in China, is also one of Dalat's specialities. Made from soy milk, sugar and a slice of ginger, dau hu is sold by itinerant women ***vendors*** who walk around carrying a large bowl of the stuff and a small stand suspended from either end of a bamboo pole.

Street Market The stairway down to Đ Nguyen Thi Minh Khai turns into a big food stall area in the late afternoon and early evening. Women sell all sorts of pre-cooked home made dishes or prepare them on a portable charcoal stove. The prices are amazingly cheap. Of course, other vendors with more permanent stalls in the market sell similar things, but at higher prices. Most of the people doing business on these stairs are minority people; one thing that should become immediately obvious is how much poorer than the ethnic-Vietnamese they are. These people sell their goods in early morning or late afternoon because during the day the police chase them away.

Restaurants European fare can be had at ***La Tulipe Rouge Restaurant*** *(1 Đ Nguyen Thi Minh Khai)*. ***Thanh Thanh Restaurant*** *(4 Đ Tang Bat Ho)* is an upmarket eatery with fine French food. Even more upscale is the ***Thuy Ta Restaurant*** *(2 Đ Yersin)* which is built on pilings over Xuan Huong Lake.

Across from the Phu Hoa Hotel on Đ Tang Bat Ho, ***Thanh Son*** dishes up tempting fare including its house specialty, clay pot stews.

Hoang Lan Restaurant on Đ Phan Dinh Phung has excellent food in the budget range. ***Long Hoa Restaurant*** on Đ 3 Thang 2 is also in vogue with travellers.

A good all-round place to eat is the ***Dong A Restaurant*** *(☎ 821033, 82 Đ Phan Dinh Phung)*. This place dishes up Vietnamese, Chinese, Western and vegetarian cuisine. The sweet 'n' sour soup is good and can be ordered vegetarian-style or with eel, pork or fish. Just next door is ***Nhat Ly Restaurant***, which is equally good (and cleaner).

Pho Tung is on the other side of Rap 3/4 cinema from the central market building; it is not a bad restaurant and has an outstanding bakery. It's difficult to resist all those delectable pastries and cakes in the windows – close your eyes as you walk by or else break out some dong and pig out.

If it's fresh Vietnamese vegetables you're craving, the place to find them is the ***Nhu Hai Restaurant*** on the traffic circle in front of the central market building. They also do good meat dishes.

Vegetarian There are also vegetarian ***food stalls*** (signposted *'com chay'*, meaning 'vegetarian food') in the market area west of Xuan Huong Dam. All serve delicious 100% vegetarian food prepared to resemble and taste like traditional Vietnamese meat dishes.

Cafes The coffee and cake in Dalat is some of the best in Vietnam and a visit to any of the town's finer cafes should make you an instant addict. At some you can order simple meals and breakfast.

Stop'n Go Cafe *(☎ 828458, 2A Đ Ly Tu Trong)* is Dalat's avant-garde hang-out. Mostly drinks are served, but you can also buy 'breakfast' at anytime. Check out the book of poems and the paintings for sale.

Cafe Tung *(6 Khu Hoa Binh Square)* was a famous hang-out of Saigonese intellectuals during the 1950s. Old-timers swear that the place remains exactly as it was when they were young. As it did then, Cafe Tung serves only tea, coffee, hot cocoa, lemon soda and orange soda to the accompaniment of mellow French music. This is a marvellous place to warm up and unwind on a chilly evening.

The specialities at the ***Viet Hung Ca***[illegible] *(Kem Viet Hung)* are ice cream and iced coffee. The cafe has entrances across from 22 Nguyen Chi Thanh and on Đ Le Dai Han[illegible]

Entertainment

Dalat's only real bar is the ***Saigon Nite B***[illegible] *(☎ 820 007, 11A Hai Ba Trung)*. Run zany Mr Dung and his friendly daughter, this lively little place has a billiards table and tempting happy hour from 5 to 8 pm.

The busy ***market*** area just to the west of Xuan Huong Dam provides another form of entertainment. This is where you can hang out, drinking coffee and chatting with the locals.

Shopping

In the past few years, the Dalat tourist kitsch-junk market has really come into its own. Without any effort at all, you'll be able to find that special something for your loved ones at home – perhaps a battery-powered stuffed koala that sings *Waltzing Matilda* or a lacquered alligator with a light bulb in its mouth.

In addition to these useful items, Dalat is known for its *kim mao cau tich*, a kind of fern whose fibres are used to stop bleeding in traditional Chinese medicine. The stuff is also known as *cu ly* (animals) because the fibrous matter is sold attached to branches pruned to resemble reddish-brown hairy animals. Tourists from Taiwan and Hong Kong seem to love this stuff.

The hill tribes of Lam Dong Province make handicrafts for their own use only – but just wait, Dalat Tourist will get them too. Lat products include dyed rush mats and rice baskets that roll up when empty. Koho and Chill people produce the split-bamboo baskets used by all the Montagnards in this area to carry things on their backs. The Chill also weave cloth, including the dark blue cotton shawls worn by some Montagnard women.

The hill tribe people carry water in a hollow gourd with a corn-cob stopper that is sometimes wrapped in a leaf for a tighter fit. A market for such goods has not yet developed so there are no shops in town selling them. If you are interested in Montagnard handicrafts, you might ask around at Chicken Village (see later), or Lat Village (12km north of Dalat).

Hoa Binh Square and the adjacent central market building is one big buy and sell, making this one of the best places in Vietnam to pick up clothing at a good price.

Getting There & Away

Air Vietnam Airlines has daily services connecting Dalat and Ho Chi Minh City (see the Getting Around chapter).

In mid-2000, Dalat's newly upgraded Lien Khuong airport (30km south of the city) became Vietnam's fourth international airport, and a direct Dalat-Singapore route was inaugurated by Vietnam Airlines.

The Vietnam Airlines office in Dalat (☎ 822895) is located at 40 Đ Ho Tung Mao, next to the Hotel Sofitel Dalat Palace.

Bus Regulations prohibiting foreigners from riding on the public buses have been lifted. However, it is cheaper and easier to use the private tourist minibuses (see the following section).

Buses depart from (and arrive at) the long-distance bus station (Ben Xe Khach Noi Thanh) to/from Ho Chi Minh City, Nha Trang, Hué, Hanoi and Buon Ma Thuot. This bus station is 1km due south of Xuan Huong Lake, next to the cable car station, where you get cable cars to Thien Vuong Pagoda.

In Ho Chi Minh City, buses to Dalat depart from the Van Thanh bus station.

Minibus It's easy enough to book a seat on a tourist minibus. In Ho Chi Minh City, this is most readily accomplished at the travellers' cafes around Đ Pham Ngu Lao. In Nha Trang, almost any hotel can sell you a minibus ticket to Dalat. To leave Dalat, you can purchase a minibus ticket at most of the hotels – which are authorised to accept foreign guests.

Car & Motorbike From Ho Chi Minh City, taking the inland route to Dalat via Bao Loc and Di Linh is faster than the coastal route via Ngoan Muc Pass. Road distances from Dalat are:

Danang	746km
Di Linh	82km
Nha Trang	205km
Phan Rang & Thap Cham	101km
Phan Thiet	247km
Ho Chi Minh City	308km

There are roads connecting Dalat to Buon Ma Thuot and other parts of the Central Highlands.

Getting Around

Private vehicles are forbidden to carry foreigners, so you must rent them from Dalat Tourist. Dalat is much too hilly for cyclos.

To/From the Airport You will need to take a government taxi (about US$20) to Lien Khuong airport. An alternative is to make the trip by motorbike, which should cost around US$5.

Motorbike Motorbikes are a popular way of touring the Dalat environs. Drivers riding vintage Russian and East German motorbikes are *everywhere* and can be hired for about US$8 per day. These can be flagged down around the central market area or by the Phu Hoa Hotel, but don't worry about looking; they'll find you.

Bicycle Pedal power is great way of seeing Dalat, but the hilly terrain and long distances between the sights make it both time and energy consuming. Still, if you're not in a rush and have the stamina, it's a good option. Several hotels in town rent bikes for about US$2 per day.

AROUND DALAT

Lake of Sighs

The Lake of Sighs (Ho Than Tho) is a natural lake enlarged by a French-built dam; the forests in the area are hardly Dalat's finest. There are several small restaurants up the hill from the dam. Horses can be hired near the restaurants for US$4 an hour.

According to legend, Mai Nuong and Hoang Tung met here in 1788 while he was hunting and she was picking mushrooms. They fell in love and sought their parents' permission to marry. But at that time Vietnam was threatened by a Chinese invasion and Hoang Tung, heeding Emperor Quang Trung's call-to-arms, joined the army without waiting to tell Mai Nuong. Unaware that he was off fighting and afraid that his absence meant that he no longer loved her, Mai Nuong sent word for him to meet her at the lake. When he did not come she was overcome with sorrow and, to prove her love, threw herself into the lake and drowned. Thereafter, the lake has been known as the Lake of Sighs.

The Lake of Sighs is 6km north-east of the centre of Dalat via Đ Phan Chu Trinh. There is an admission fee of US$0.30.

Prenn Pass

The area along Highway 20 between Dalat and Datanla Falls is known as Prenn Pass. The hillsides support mature pine forests while the valleys are used to cultivate vegetables. This is a great area for hiking and horse-riding, but make local inquiries before heading out to be sure that there will be no problems with the police.

Prenn Falls

This is one of the largest and loveliest falls in the Dalat area, but is starting to suffer the effects of commercial exploitation.

Prenn Falls (elevation 1124m) consists of a 15m free fall over a wide rocky outcrop. A path goes under the outcrop, affording a view of the pool and surrounding rainforest through the curtain of falling water. An ominous sign of possible kitschy horrors to come is the 'Dalat Tourist Sailboats' now plying the waters of the tiny pool at the waterfall's base.

After a rainstorm the waterfall becomes a raging brown torrent (deforestation and the consequent soil erosion are responsible for the coffee colour). Refreshments are sold at kiosks near the falls. The park around the falls was dedicated by the Queen of Thailand in 1959.

The entrance to Prenn Falls is near the Prenn Restaurant, which is 13km from Dalat towards Phan Rang & Thap Cham. Entry costs US$0.50.

Quang Trung Reservoir

Quang Trung Reservoir (Tuyen Lam Lake) is an artificial lake created by a dam in 1980. It is named after Emperor Quang Trung (also known as Nguyen Hue), a leader of the Tay Son Rebellion. The area is being developed for tourism; there are several cafes near

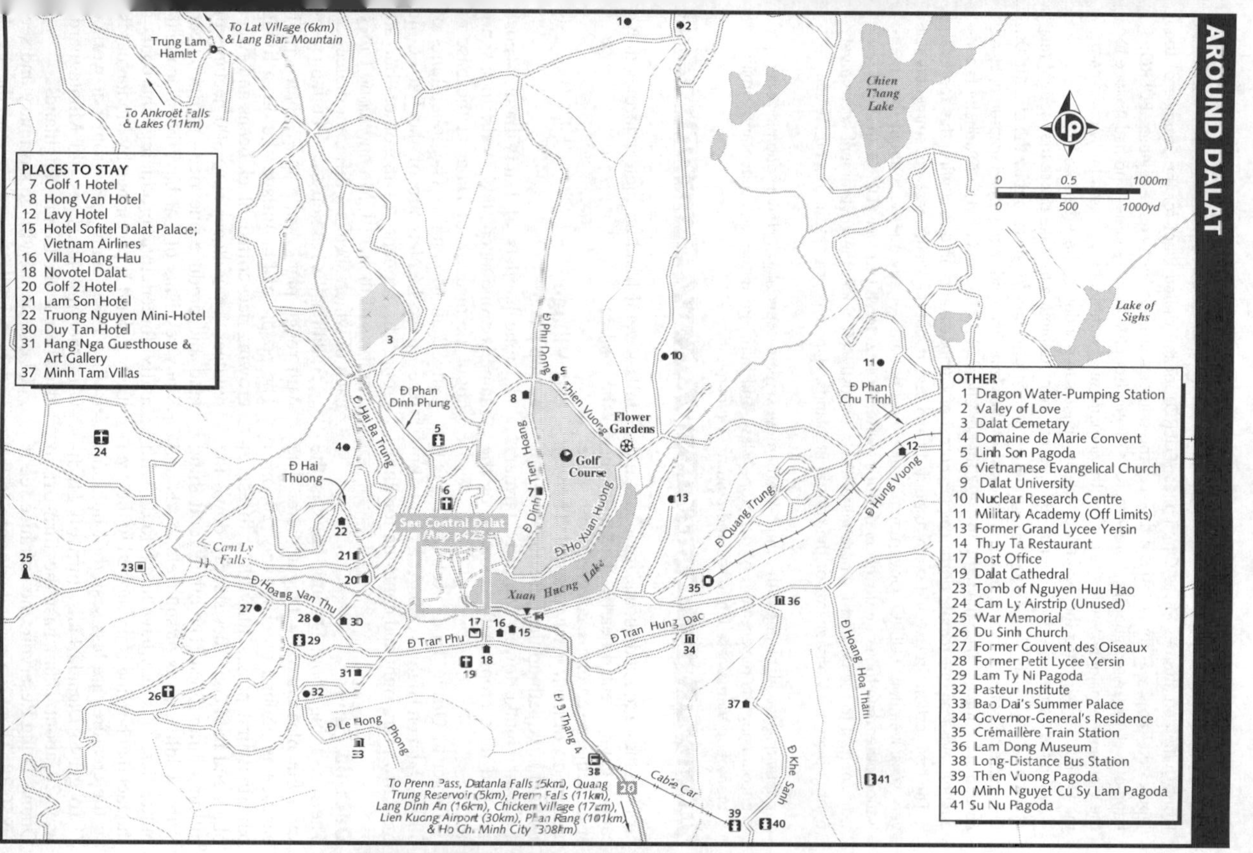

CENTRAL HIGHLANDS

FULRO

Front Unifié de Lutte des Races Opprimées (FULRO), or the United Front for the Struggle of the Oppressed Races, was for decades a thorn in the side of successive Vietnamese regimes. FULRO, a band of well-organised guerrillas, drew recruits mainly from the Montagnards, who had no love for the Vietnamese majority. While the old South Vietnamese government suppressed the Montagnards, the US military exploited their valuable skills in jungle survival during the American War.

When the Communists took over in 1975, rather than attempting to make peace they sought retribution against FULRO. The guerrillas continued their insurrection for years, but by the mid-1980s, they were considered a spent force, with most of their guerrilla bands either dead, captured, living abroad or having given up the fight. In 1992 the surrender of a lone band of FULRO adherents conducting raids from the remote north-eastern corner of Cambodia appeared to confirm this appraisal.

The insurrection issue would seem to be dead and buried, but the Vietnamese government is still very sensitive about FULRO. Government guides will not answer any questions about the organisation other than to assure travellers that it's 'perfectly safe' to visit former FULRO areas.

In contrast to the far north, where minorities are mostly left alone, the government keeps a very tight grip on the Montagnards of the central highlands. Hanoi's policies in this region include:

- populating the highlands with ethnic-Vietnamese settlers, especially in New Economic zones
- encouraging the replacement of traditional slash-and-burn agriculture with sedentary farming
- promoting Vietnamese language and culture (Vietnamisation).

far from the dam. Paddleboats, rowboats and canoes can be rented nearby. The hillscape around the reservoir is covered with pine trees, most of them newly planted. There is a switchback path up the hill south-west of the water intake tower. Minority farmers live and raise crops in the vicinity of the lake.

To get to Quang Trung Reservoir, head out of Dalat on Highway 20. At a point 5km from town turn right and continue for 2km.

Datanla Falls

The nice thing about Datanla Falls is the short but pleasant walk to get there. The cascade is 350m from Highway 20 on a path that first passes through a forest of pines and then continues steeply down the hill into a rainforest. The other good thing is the wildlife – lots of squirrels, birds and butterflies. This may have much to do with the fact that hunting is prohibited in the area so the creatures are less scared of humans.

To get to Datanla Falls, turn off Highway 20 about 200m past the turn-off to Quang Trung Reservoir; the entrance fee is US$0.30. There is a second entrance to the falls several hundred metres farther down the road.

Lat Village

• pop 6,000

The nine hamlets of Lat Village, whose name is pronounced 'lak' by the locals, are about 12km north of Dalat at the base of Lang Bian Mountain. The inhabitants of five of the hamlets are of the Lat ethnic group; the residents of the other four are members of the Chill, Ma and Koho tribes, each of which speaks a different dialect.

Traditionally, Lat houses are built on piles with rough plank walls and a thatch roof. The people of Lat Village eke out a living growing rice, coffee, black beans and sweet potatoes. The villages have 300 hectares of land and produce one rice crop per year. Many residents of Lat have been economically forced into producing charcoal, a lowly task often performed by Montagnards. Before 1975, many men from Lat worked with the Americans, as did Montagnards elsewhere in the Central Highlands.

Classes in the village's primary and secondary schools, successors of the École

Franco-Koho established in Dalat in 1948, are conducted in Vietnamese rather than the tribal languages. Lat has one Catholic church and one Protestant church. A Koho-language Bible (Sra Goh) was published by Protestants in 1971; a Lat-language Bible, prepared by Catholics, appeared the following year. Both Montagnard dialects, which are quite similar, are written in a Latin-based script.

To visit the village, you must first obtain a US$4 permit. Inquire at Dalat Toserco, 7 Đ 3 Thang 2. If you've already booked a day tour, the permit can be arranged by the tour operator.

There are no restaurants in Lat, just a few ***food stalls***.

To get to Lat from Dalat, head north on Đ Xo Viet Nghe Tinh. At Trung Lam Hamlet there is a fork in the road marked by a street sign. Continue straight on (north-west) rather than to the left (which leads to Suoi Vang, the Golden Stream, 14km away). By bicycle, the 12km trip from Dalat to Lat takes about 40 minutes. On foot, it's a two-hour walk.

Lang Bian Mountain

Lang Bian Mountain (also called Lam Vien Mountain) has five volcanic peaks ranging in altitude from 2100m to 2400m. Of the two highest peaks, the eastern one is known to locals by the woman's name K'Lang; the western one bears a man's name, K'Biang. The upper reaches of the mountain are forested. Only half a century ago, the verdant foothills of Lang Bian Mountain, now defoliated, sheltered wild oxen, deer, boars, elephants, rhinoceroses and tigers.

The hike up to the top of Lang Bian Mountain, from where the views are truly spectacular, takes three to four hours from Lat Village. The path begins due north of Lat and is easily recognisable as a red gash in the green mountainside.

You do not need a permit to visit Lang Bian Mountain, though taking a guide along will make the trip more interesting. Consider contacting Action Max (see the earlier Dalat section) to see what outdoor programs they are offering to Lang Bian.

Ankroët Falls & Lakes

The two Ankroët Lakes were created as part of a hydroelectric project. The waterfall (Thac Ankroët) is about 15m high. The Ankroët Lakes are 18km north-west of Dalat in an area inhabited by hill tribes.

Chicken Village

This village has become very popular with travellers because it's conveniently on the Dalat–Nha Trang highway, 17km from Dalat.

Home to the Koho minority, to a certain extent the Koho have been assimilated into Vietnamese society. For example, they no longer live in stilt houses and they wear Vietnamese-style clothing (although very ragged). Nevertheless, they have a lifestyle all their own and it could be worth a stopover if you're heading to Nha Trang anyway.

This place takes its name from a huge concrete statue of a chicken which sits squarely in the centre of the village. We questioned the villagers extensively to learn the history behind this unusual statue and were surprised to find that most had no idea or else refused to discuss when the statue was built or why. It certainly has no religious significance to the villagers. Finally we heard this story from a local woman:

> When a couple gets married here, it's the bride's family who must pay for the engagement ring and wedding party. Her family is also supposed to present the groom's family with a gift. We had a sad case many years ago where the man's family demanded a special gift, a chicken with nine fingers. No one had ever seen such a chicken, but there were rumours that these could be found in the mountains. So the girl went to the mountains to search for one. Unfortunately, her effort was in vain and she died in the wilderness. The villagers were stricken with grief by this senseless tragedy and the girl was made into a hero.
>
> There was fighting in this area during the war and after liberation the government wanted to give the locals some sort of gift. The villagers asked if they could commemorate the brave young girl who died for love. The government officials were touched by this tragic story and complied with the wishes of the villagers. So the concrete chicken was built.

The story does sound a bit far-fetched and one local man had a somewhat different tale to tell. He claims that after the Communist victory in 1975, the villagers retreated to the woods and adopted nomadic slash-and-burn agriculture because of attempts to enforce farm collectivisation. Many of the men went into the illegal timber harvesting business, which did quite a bit of damage to the region's forests.

The government then granted them several redeeming concessions to entice them to relocate to their permanent village site. After they returned, the government thought of building some sort of memorial, possibly a statue of Ho Chi Minh. It was finally decided that the huge concrete chicken would be most appropriate because it would commemorate the hard-working peasants. After all, what better way to symbolise the chicken farmers than to build a statue of a chicken?

The residents of Chicken Village are extremely poor, but we were surprised to find no beggars at all. This is particularly remarkable given the large number of tourists who stop here. We'd like to suggest that you do *not* give sweets or money to the children – if you want to help the villagers, there are a couple of shops where you can buy simple things like drinks, biscuits and such. There are also beautiful weavings for sale near the highway.

BUON MA THUOT

☎ 050 • pop 186,600 • elevation 451m

Buon Ma Thuot (or Ban Me Thuot), is the capital of Dac Lac Province and the largest town in the western highlands. Before WWII, the city was a centre for big-game hunting, but the animals have all but disappeared (along with most of the region's rainforest).

The region's main crop is coffee, which is grown on plantations run by German managers who are said to be as imperiously demanding as their French predecessors. It's the coffee industry which accounts for Buon Ma Thuot's current prosperity.

A large percentage of the area's population is made up of Montagnards. The government's policy of assimilation has had its effect in that nearly all the Montagnards now speak Vietnamese quite fluently.

The rainy season around Buon Ma Thuot lasts from April to November, though downpours are usually short. Because of its lower elevation, Buon Ma Thuot is warmer and more humid than Dalat, it is also very windy.

Buon Ma Thuot is the gateway to Yok Don National Park and even a possible back door to Nam Cat Tien National Park. However, most travellers approach Nam Cat Tien from the Dalat side. If you could find a good guide, visiting the coffee plantations and processing plants could be interesting, but good guides are as scarce as snow storms in Buon Ma Thuot.

Information

Travel Agencies Dak Lak Tourist (☎ 852108, fax 852865), the provincial tourism authority, is in a dilapidated building at 3 Đ Phan Chu Trinh next to the modern Thang Loi Hotel. Be prepared to pay high prices for guides who may speak only Vietnamese and lose their way while 'guiding' you. This agency knows little about the one and only thing in Buon Ma Thuot that really interests tourists – the coffee industry.

Travel Permits Permits are still required to visit minority villages in the surrounding area. See Dak Lak Tourist to get these valuable bits of paper. You do *not* need a travel permit for Buon Ma Thuot itself.

Money Vietcombank at 62 Đ Nguyen Tat Thanh is rather inconveniently a few kilometres from the town centre in the direction of the bus station.

Ethnographic Museum

There are said to be 31 distinct ethnic groups in Dac Lac Province, and the museum is one place to get some understanding of these disparate groups. Don't expect too much – there seem to be more minority exhibits in the adjacent souvenir shop than in the museum itself. Displays at the museum feature traditional Montagnard dress as well as agricultural implements, fishing gear, bows and arrows, weaving looms and musical instruments. There is a photo collection with explanations about the history ical contacts between the Montagnards and the majority Vietnamese – some of the history is plausible, some is pure fiction.

The Ethnographic Museum (☎ 850426) is in the former reception of the Bao Dai Villas at the corner of Đ Nguyen Du and Đ Le Duan. It's open Monday to Saturday from 7 to 11 am, and 1.30 to 5 pm. Entry costs US$0.80.

Revolution Museum

The Buon Ma Thuot Revolution Museum is at 1 Đ Le Duan. The entrance fee is US$1, or US$8 for a group.

Victory Monument

You can hardly miss this place, as it dominates the central square of town. The victory monument commemorates the events of 10 March 1975, when VC and North Vietnamese troops 'liberated' the city. It was this battle that triggered the complete collapse of South Vietnam.

Places to Stay

The ***Guesthouse 43*** *(☎ 853921, 43 Đ Ly Thuong Kiet)* has cheap fan rooms at US$4 to US$6 (toilet outside). The ***Hong Kong Hotel*** *(☎ 852630, 35 Đ Hai Ba Trung)* has

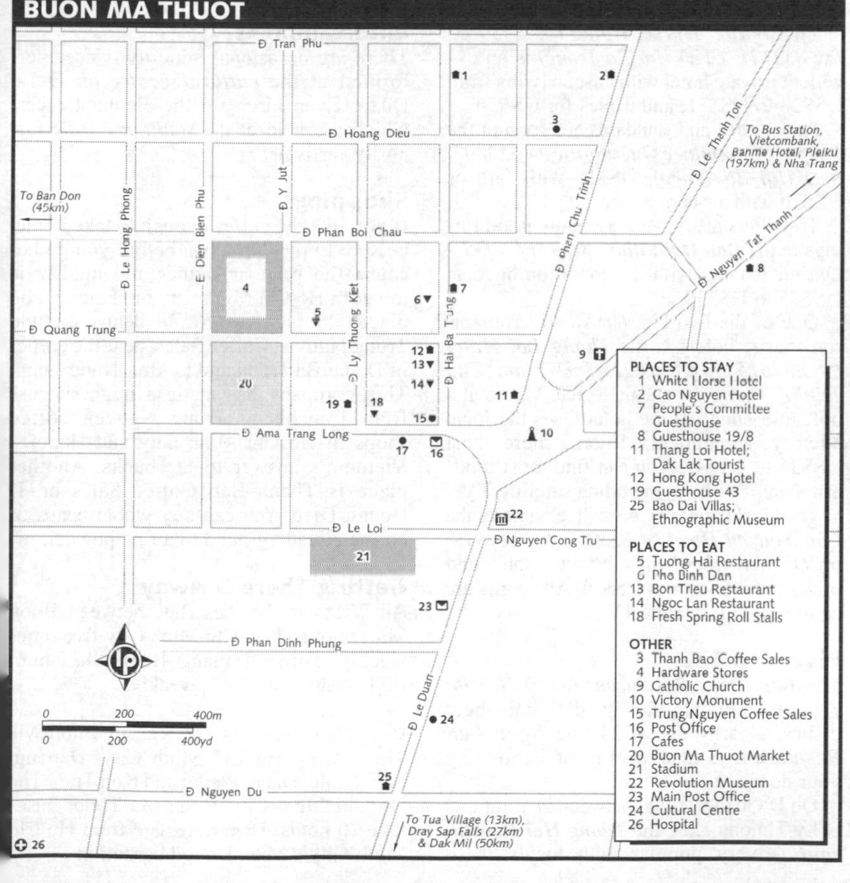

a sign outside in English saying 'Popular'. This grubby place has fan singles/twins for US$8/10, or US$12 with air-con.

A nicer choice is the ***Guesthouse 19/8*** *(☎ 869211, 18A Đ Nguyen Tat Thanh)*, north-east of the Victory Monument. Rates are US$15 with fan, or US$20 with air-con.

Banme Hotel *(☎ 851001)* is about 3km north of the centre, but within walking distance of the bus station. This is a motel-style place, an important consideration if you want a secure parking place overnight. From the centre, you can catch a motorbike to the hotel for around US$0.40. Rooms with fan and hot water cost US$8 to US$12. An air-con room is US$20 (breakfast included).

The ***White Horse Hotel*** *(☎ 853963, fax 852121, 61 Đ Hai Ba Trung)* is an excellent private hotel with air-con twins from US$28 to US$31, and triples for US$36.

Room rates and standards are good at the ***People's Committee Guesthouse*** *(☎ 852407, 8 Đ Hai Ba Trung)*, US$15 with fan, or US$20 with air-con.

Travellers also give reasonably good ratings to the ***Bao Dai Villas*** *(☎ 852177, Đ Le Duan)*. Rooms with air-conditioning cost US$15 to US$30.

One of the two big, classy government-run tourist hotels is the ***Thang Loi Hotel*** *(☎ 857615, fax 857622, 3 Đ Phan Chu Trinh)*. *Thang loi* means 'victory', so it's not surprising that the hotel faces the local Victory Monument. Rooms here cost US$35 to US$45. You can find most modern amenities here, including satellite TV.

The local People's Committee operates the ***Cao Nguyen Hotel*** *(☎ 855960, fax 851912, 65 Đ Phan Chu Trinh)*. It's luxurious, and prices are US$45 and US$50. All rooms are equipped with satellite TV.

Places to Eat

The ***Bon Trieu Restaurant*** *(33 Đ Hai Ba Trung)* is known for its delicious beef dishes. Nearby at No 24, the ***Ngoc Lan Restaurant*** is also worthy of depositing your dong.

On Đ Quang Trung, between Đ Y Jut and Đ Ly Thuong Kiet, the ***Tuong Hai Restaurant*** is very popular with locals. Also known for its top-notch beef noodle soup, is ***Pho Binh Dan*** on Đ Hai Ba Trung.

For excellent fresh spring rolls *(nem ninh hoa)*, head for the ***stalls*** at 20–22–26 Đ Ly Thuong Kiet.

Buon Ma Thuot is justifiably famous for its coffee, which is the best in Vietnam. As usual, the Vietnamese serve it so strong it will make your hair stand on end, and typically in a very tiny cup that allows you no room to add water or milk. Most coffee shops in Buon Ma Thuot also throw in a free pot of tea (awful stuff) – be sure you don't mistake it for water and use it to dilute your coffee!

Entertainment

There are occasional minority dances performed at the ***cultural centre*** on Đ Le Duan. Even rarer are the elephant races, which are held at the ***stadium*** during minority festivals.

Shopping

If you like the coffee enough to take home, be sure to pick up a bag before you go because the price is higher and quality is lower in Ho Chi Minh City or Hanoi. Good places to pick up coffee beans include Trung Nguyen Coffee Sales, near the corner of Đ Hai Ba Trung and Đ Ama Trang Long. This company has made a huge success from franchising Trung Nguyen coffee shops in Ho Chi Minh City and Hanoi – Vietnam's answer to Starbucks. Another place is Thanh Bao Coffee Sales on Đ Hoang Dieu. You can buy whole beans or coffee already ground to a fine powder.

Getting There & Away

Air Vietnam Airlines flies between Buon Ma Thuot and Ho Chi Minh City five times weekly. Direct Danang–Buon Ma Thuot flights run three times weekly.

Bus There are bus services to Buon Ma Thuot from Ho Chi Minh City, Danang, Nha Trang, Dalat, Pleiku and Kon Tum. The Ho Chi Minh City–Buon Ma Thuot buses take 20 hours. Departures are from Ho Chi Minh City's Mien Dong bus station.

Car & Motorbike The road linking the coast with Buon Ma Thuot intersects Highway 1 at Ninh Hoa (160km from Buon Ma Thuot), which is only 34km north of Nha Trang (see South-Central Coast map). The road is surfaced and in good condition, though a bit steep. Buon Ma Thuot to Pleiku is 197km on an excellent highway.

There is a road connecting Buon Ma Thuot with Dalat (via Lak Lake), but it's in horrid condition and you can expect a muddy quagmire if it's been raining. It's recommended for sturdy motorbikes or 4WDs only.

AROUND BUON MA THUOT

Dray Sap Falls

Dray Sap Falls, about 27km from Buon Ma Thuot, is in the middle of a hardwood rainforest. Entry to see the falls costs US$0.80.

Tua Village

The Rhade (or Ede) hamlet of Tua is 13km from Buon Ma Thuot. The people raise animals and grow manioc (cassava), sweet potatoes and maize. This village has become one of the most heavily 'Vietnamesed' in the region, but along with the loss of cultural identity it has earned a higher standard of living.

Rhade society is matrilineal and matrilocal (centred on the household of the wife's family). Extended families live in longhouses – each section of which houses a nuclear family. Each longhouse is presided over by a man, often the husband of the senior woman of the family. The property of the extended family is owned and controlled by the oldest woman in the group.

The religion of the Rhade is animistic. In the past century many Rhade have converted to Christianity.

Yok Don National Park

☎ 050

The largest of Vietnam's national parks, Yok Don encompasses 58,200 hectares and there are plans to expand to 100,000. The tourist action centres on Ban Don Village in Ea Sup District, 45km north-west of Buon Ma Thuot.

Yok Don is home to nearly 70 animal species, 38 of which are listed as endangered in Indochina, and 17 of those species endangered worldwide. The park habitat accommodates some 200 different species of bird. In recent years previously unknown animals like the *Canisauvus*, a wild dog species, have been discovered in the park.

There are about 17 ethnic groups here. The locals are mostly M'nong, a matrilineal tribe in which the family name is passed down through the female line and children are considered members of their mother's family. The M'nong are known for their fiercely belligerent attitude towards other tribes in the area, as well as towards ethnic-Vietnamese.

The M'nong hunt wild elephants using domesticated elephants, dozens of which live in Ban Don. You are *not* permitted to photograph the elephants, as it would hurt the local postcard industry. For an unreasonable US$60, you can arrange a four-hour elephant ride through some beautiful forests. You must book these trips through Dak Lak Tourist in Buon Ma Thuot – you cannot simply turn up.

A traditional activity here involves tourists drinking wine from a communal jug. Everyone gathers around the wine jug and drinks at the same time through very long straws – it makes for good photos.

You'll need a 4WD or motorbike to reach Ban Don, and you can expect the road to be nearly impassable if it's been raining. In Ban Don you can contact Banmeco Travel Agency or Buon Don Tourist (☎ 798119) to inquire about local accommodation and tour programs in and around the park. There is a 13th-century Cham tower 36km north of Ban Don at Ya Liao.

Places to Stay The ***Yok Don Guesthouse*** *(☎ 853110)* lacks hot water, but what do you want for US$10? You'd do better to stay in the nearby ***stilt houses*** – it's cheap (US$5.50 per person), and definitely more aesthetic.

Another option is to overnight in the ***bungalows*** out on nearby Aino Island.

Lak Lake

Lak Lake (Ho Lak) is about 50km south of Buon Ma Thuot. Emperor Bao Dai built a

CENTRAL HIGHLANDS

small palace here, but it is now a ruin. Nevertheless, the lake views are fantastic and the climb up the adjacent hills is well worthwhile. The nearby M'nong village is a unique experience.

From Lak Lake it is possible to reach Dalat (148km) on Route 27, a breathtaking road through the forest. Outside of the dry season you will need a 4WD or motorbike to get there.

You can stay in stilt houses for US$5 overnight. Two-hour elephant rides can be arranged for around US$30.

PLEIKU

☎ 059 • pop 141,700 • elevation 750m

Pleiku (or Playcu) is the major market town of the western highlands, but as a tourist destination most call it 'a hole'. More than 140,000 souls live here now and the population is rapidly growing. The city is 785m above sea level, which makes the climate cool. It's warmer than Dalat, but windier.

In February 1965, the VC shelled a US compound in Pleiku killing eight Americans. Although the USA already had over 23,000 military advisers in Vietnam, their role was supposed to be non-combatant at that time. The attack on Pleiku was used as a justification by President Johnson to begin a relentless bombing campaign against North Vietnam and the rapid build-up of American troops.

When American troops departed in 1973, the South Vietnamese continued to keep Pleiku as their main combat base in the area. When these troops fled the advancing VC, the whole civilian population of Pleiku and nearby Kon Tum fled with them. The stampede to the coastline involved over 100,000 people, but tens of thousands died along the way.

The departing soldiers torched Pleiku, but the city was rebuilt in the 1980s with assistance from the Soviet Union. As a result, the city has a large collection of ugly, Soviet-style buildings and lacks much of the colour and antiquity you find elsewhere in Vietnamese towns. Hopefully, the recent inflow of tourist dollars will bring some badly needed improvements to the architecture, as well as the local economy, but for now Pleiku is a pretty monotonous town.

The Jarai minority live in the Pleiku area and have an unusual burial custom. Each deceased gets a portrait carved from wood and for years relatives bring them food. The grave is set up as a miniature village with several people buried in one graveyard. After seven years, the grave is abandoned.

Information

Travel Agencies The Gia Lai Tourist (☎/fax 824891) is alongside the Hung Vuong Hotel, 215 Đ Hung Vuong. It offers a wide variety of tours including trekking, elephant riding and programs catering to war veterans. There are some very good guides working for this company, though it's not certain they are worth the high prices you must pay for them (90% of which goes to the government).

Travel Permit While you do not need a permit to stay overnight in Pleiku itself, or to travel the major highways, you do need one to visit hill tribe villages in Gia Lai Province. The permits will cost you money (the exact amount dependent on where you want to go) and you may be forced to hire a guide, car and driver in Pleiku even if you already have your own vehicle. You can figure on all this costing something like US$50 per day, but at least you get much better guides than are available in Buon Ma Thuot. However, the high prices put off many travellers, who usually just skip Pleiku entirely and head north to Kon Tum, where the authorities are more hospitable.

If you want a travel permit, you need to visit the already-mentioned Gia Lai Tourist. Do *not* go to the police station – travellers who have done so have received a rather rude reception.

Sea Lake

Bien Ho, or Sea Lake, is a deep mountain lake about 7km north of Pleiku. It is believed to have been formed from a prehistoric volcanic crater. Both the lake itself and the surrounding area boast beautiful scenery, making it a pleasant day excursion from Pleiku.

Yaly Falls

Sadly, this place is probably no longer worth visiting. Yaly Falls was once the largest waterfall in the Central Highlands and a hot destination for tourists. However, a new hydroelectric scheme has sucked away most of the water and there is only a trickle left. During a heavy rain it might still look impressive, but otherwise all you are going to see is a damp cliff in the forest.

Places to Stay

The place most successful at attracting the backpacker set is ***Thanh Lich Hotel*** *(☎ 824 674, 86 Đ Nguyen Van Troi)*. Fan rooms here cost US$7 to US$10, or US$22 with air-con.

The recently renovated ***Vinh Hoi Hotel*** *(☎ 824644, fax 871305, 39 Đ Tran Phu)* may be Pleiku's nicest accommodation choice. Budget rooms with fan and cold water cost just US$7. Rooms with air-con and hot water range from US$22 to US$24.

The ***Ialy Hotel*** *(☎ 824843, fax 827619, 89 Đ Hung Vuong)* is a decent choice. Rooms with air-con and hot water cost US$13 to US$25.

The ***Movie Star Hotel*** *(Khach San Dien Anh; ☎ 823855, fax 823700, 6 Đ Vo Thi Sau)* is Pleiku's most charming accommodation and a big hit with travellers. Rooms with fan are US$10. Rooms with air-con come in three standards costing US$18, US$20 and US$25; try to avoid the blaring TV noise on the 1st floor.

The ***Hung Vuong Hotel*** *(☎ 824270, 215 Đ Hung Vuong)* is the closest to the bus station but a bit close to the road and consequently noisy. Basic twin rooms cost US$10 to US$25.

The ***Pleiku Hotel*** *(☎ 824628, fax 822 151, Đ Le Loi)* is a big state-run monolith and the Stalinesque architecture is impressive. Rates are US$11 for a fan room, or US$27 to US$31 with air-con and hot water.

Places to Eat

You'll be hard pressed to find a satisfying meal anywhere in Pleiku, but one of the best is ***Thanh Restaurant*** at Đ 80 Hai Ba Trung.

The Chinese family-run ***My Tam Restaurant*** is a hit with locals and has perhaps the best fried chicken in the Central Highlands.

Entertainment

Pleiku is anything but an entertainment Mecca, though for a kick you might head

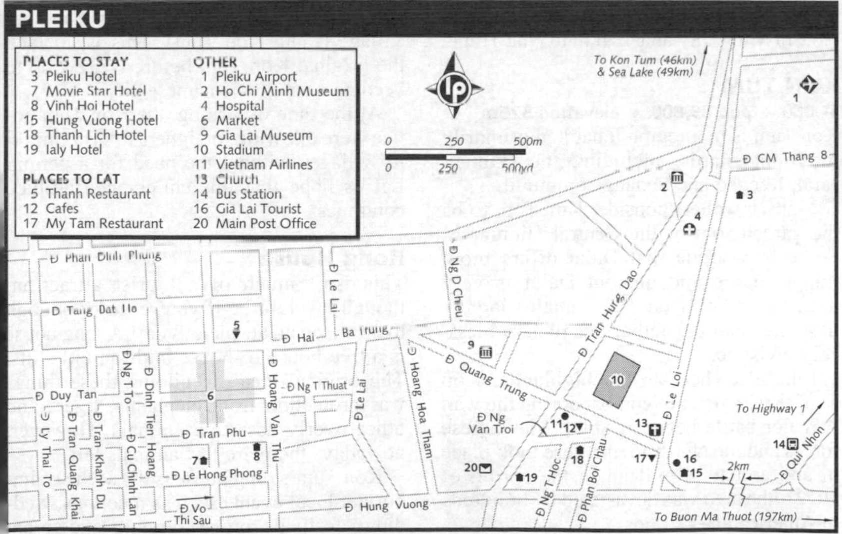

for the *cafes* across from the Thanh Lich Hotel. The strong coffee around here is akin to rocket fuel, and if that doesn't lift you, the hits-from-the-70s music selection just might. There's nothing like a good dose of caffeine and ABBA to help keep awake.

Getting There & Away

Air The local Vietnam Airlines office (☎ 823058, 825893) is located at 55 Đ Quang Trung, near the corner of Đ Tran Hung Dao.

There are flights connecting Pleiku to Ho Chi Minh City and Danang. The direct flight between Pleiku and Hanoi has been suspended for years – if you want to fly that way you must transit in Danang.

Bus There are bus services to Pleiku from most coastal cities between Nha Trang and Danang.

Car & Motorbike Pleiku is linked by road to Buon Ma Thuot (197km), Qui Nhon (186km via An Khe), Kon Tum (49km) and Cambodia's Ratanakiri Province (via Chu Nghe). There is a particularly barren stretch of land on the road from Buon Ma Thuot, probably the result of Agent Orange use and overlogging.

Road distances from Pleiku are 550km to Ho Chi Minh City and 424km to Nha Trang.

KON TUM

☎ 060 • pop 89,800 • elevation 525m

Kon Tum is in a region inhabited primarily by Montagnards, including the Bahnar, Jarai, Rengao and Sedang communities.

Many travellers consider Kon Tum to be the garden spot of the Central Highlands. Some may argue that Dalat offers more things to see and do, but Dalat is very touristy. So far, Kon Tum remains largely unspoiled and the authorities remain blessedly invisible.

Like elsewhere in the highlands, Kon Tum saw its share of combat during the war. A major battle between South Vietnamese forces and the North Vietnamese took place in and around Kon Tum in the spring of 1972 – the area was devastated by hundreds of American B-52 raids.

Information

Travel Agencies Kon Tum Tourist (☎ 863 336, fax 862122) is at 168 Đ Ba Trieu. There is also a branch office inside the Dakbla Hotel.

Money There is *no* place to cash travellers cheques in Kon Tum. The nearest place to accomplish this is in Pleiku.

Montagnard Villages

There are quite a few Montagnard villages all around the edges of Kon Tum. Montagnard-watching seems to be a favourite 'sport' of travellers on 'snap-shot safari'. Please remember to treat the locals with respect. Some travellers seem to think that the hill tribe people are running around 'costumes' for the benefit of photographers – this, of course, is not the case. In general, the local tribes welcome tourists, but only if you are not too intrusive into their lifestyle.

Some of the small villages (or perhaps we should say 'neighbourhoods') are on the periphery of Kon Tum and you can even walk to them from the centre. There are two Bahnar villages, simply called Lang Bana in Vietnamese: one is on the east side of town, the other on the west side.

On the east side of Kon Tum is Kon Tum Village (Lang Kon Tum). This is, in fact, the original Kon Tum before it grew up to become a small Vietnamese city.

At the time of writing, the Kon Tum police were allowing foreigners to visit minority villages without the need for a permit. Let us hope that this enlightened attitude continues.

Rong House

This isn't much of a tourist attraction, though it might be if you're lucky enough to arrive on an auspicious day. A rong house is a tree house or house built on tall stilts. The original idea of building these things was protection from elephants, tigers and other overly assertive animals. However, nowadays there are few animals left.

Kon Tum's rong house is the scene of important local events such as meetings, weddings, festivals, prayer sessions and so on.

If you happen to stumble upon one of these activities in progress, it could indeed be interesting. It's worth remembering that uninvited guests are not *always* welcome at weddings.

Nguc Kon Tum

This is an abandoned prison compound on the western side of Kon Tum. The prisoners incarcerated here were VC and all were freed in 1975 when the war ended.

This was one of the more famous prisons run by the South Vietnamese; VC who survived their internment here were made into heroes after liberation. Having a politically correct background was (and still is) very important in post-war Vietnam – many of the high-ranking officers who are *now* in the military were former prisoners at Nguc Kon Tum. ARVN soldiers who were prisoners of the VC have not fared so well.

Nguc Kon Tum is currently open to the public and you can wander inside and have a look. Unfortunately, no effort is being made to preserve the place, nor are there any guides available to explain the historical significance of what you are looking at. Apparently the local tourism authorities have not quite grasped the economic potential of this would-be war museum.

Dak To & Charlie Hill

This obscure outpost, 42km north of Kon Tum, was a major battlefield during the American War. In 1972, the area was the scene of intense fighting and was one of the last big battles before American troops pulled out.

Dak To has become popular with visiting groups of American veterans, but you probably won't find much of interest if you're not a war buff. More intriguingly, those few VC veterans with sufficient free time and money also like to come here to stir their memories.

About 5km south of Dak To is Charlie Hill. The hill was a fortified ARVN stronghold before the VC tried to overrun it. The South Vietnamese officer in charge, Colonel Ngoc Minh, decided that he would neither surrender nor retreat and the battle became a fierce fight to the death. Unusually for a guerrilla war, this was a prolonged battle. The VC laid siege to the hill for 1½ months before they managed to kill Colonel Minh and 150 ARVN troops who made their last stand here.

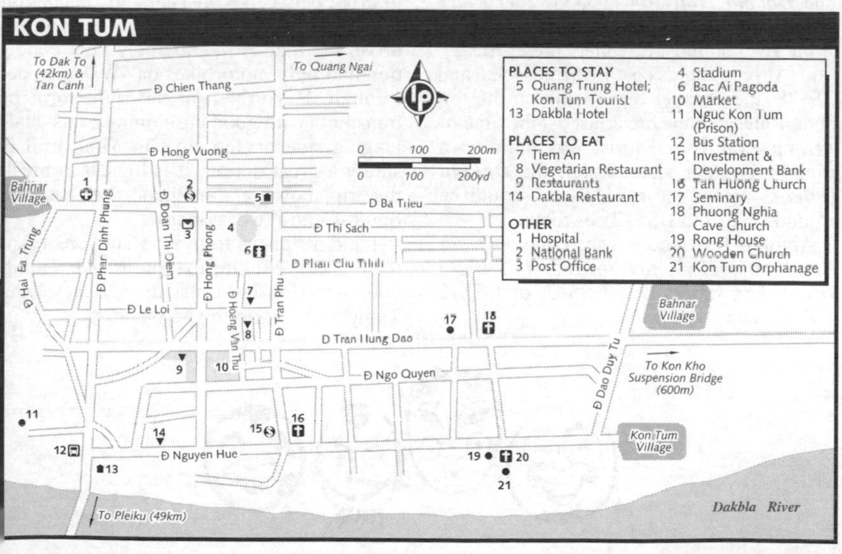

Although largely forgotten in the west, the battle is well known even now in Vietnam. The reason for this is largely because the fight was commemorated by a popular song, *Nguoi O Lai Charlie* (The People Stayed in Charlie).

Not surprisingly, the hill was heavily mined during the war and is still considered unsafe to climb.

The newly built rong house in Dak To is worth seeking out.

Kon Tum Orphanage

A short walk from the town centre, this delightful orphanage makes for a great place to visit. Staff here are welcoming of visitors, who come to share some time with the adorable resident children. If you plan to visit you should consider making a donation to the orphanage; canned food, clothing or toys for the kids would be appropriate, and monetary contributions are of course appreciated.

The orphanage is just behind the wooden church on Đ Nguyen Hue. From here, you can continue east to visit nearby minority villages.

Places to Stay

The ***Dakbla Hotel*** *(☎ 863333, 2 Đ Phan Dinh Phung)* is relatively attractive and next to the river so most travellers prefer to stay here. Air-con rooms cost US$15, US$26 and US$28, the cheaper ones being on the top floor. Rates include breakfast. At the time of writing Kon Tom Tourist was building a slightly cheaper sister hotel, the ***Dakbla Hotel 2***, across the road. Rates should be around US$10 to US$12 per room.

An oldie but goodie is the ***Quang Trung Hotel*** *(☎ 862249, fax 862122, 168 Đ Ba Trieu)*. Fan rooms cost US$13, or US$18 with air-con.

Places to Eat

Dakbla Restaurant *(168 Đ Nguyen Hue)* has good food and reasonable prices, so it tends to draw the most travellers.

Crowded with locals eating *lau* and drinking beer is ***Tiem An*** *(78 Đ Le Loi)*. Across the road there is a good ***vegetarian restaurant*** at 33 Đ Le Loi.

Getting There & Away

Bus Buses connect Kon Tum to Danang, Pleiku and Buon Ma Thuot. One traveller, however, had this to say:

> A trip to the highlands town of Kon Tum is definitely worth it, if only to escape the Sinh Cafe tourist trail on the coast. However, travellers should be aware of the sign at the bus station that clearly states that foreigners can't be sold tickets. This of course means that on the bus the fare is as high as the conductor wants it to be.
>
> **Todd Griffin**

Car & Motorbike The fastest approach to Kon Tum from the coast is on Highway 19 between Qui Nhon and Pleiku. Highway 14 between Kon Tum and Buon Ma Thuot is also in good nick.

Looking at a map, it might seem feasible to drive between Kon Tum and Danang on Highway 14. Although this is a beautiful drive, the road is in extremely poor condition and only motorbikes or 4WDs can get through. If you've got the right form of transport (with good cushioning), this challenging ride on the Ho Chi Minh trail is surely a great option. It is logical to break the trip, however, in Phuoc Son (see the South-Central Coast map).

Land distances from Kon Tum are 49km to Pleiku, 246km to Buon Ma Thuot, 896km to Ho Chi Minh City, 436km to Nha Trang and 198km to Qui Nhon.

Ho Chi Minh City

☎ 08 • pop 4,858,000

In this, the largest of Vietnam's cities, you'll see the hustle and bustle of Vietnamese life everywhere, and there is something invigorating about it all. Contrasting images of the exotic and mundane abound. There are the street markets, where bargains are struck and deals are done; the pavement cafes, where stereo speakers fill the surrounding streets with a melodious thumping beat; and the sleek new cafes and pubs, where tourists chat over beer, pretzels, coffee and croissants. A young office worker manoeuvres her Honda Dream through rush-hour traffic, long hair flowing, high heels working the brake pedal. The sweating Chinese businessman chats on his cellular phone, cursing his necktie in the tropical heat. A desperate beggar suddenly grabs your arm, rudely reminding you that this is still a developing city despite the trimmings.

The city churns, ferments, bubbles and fumes. Yet within this teeming 300 year old metropolis are timeless traditions and the beauty of an ancient culture. In the pagodas monks pray and incense burns. Artists create masterpieces on canvas or in carved wood. Puppeteers entertain children in the parks, while in the back alleys where tourists seldom venture, acupuncturists treat patients and students learn to play the violin. A seamstress carefully creates an *ao dai*, the graceful Vietnamese costume that could make the fashion designers of Paris envious.

Actually, Ho Chi Minh City is not so much a city as a small province covering an area of 2029 sq km stretching from the South China Sea almost to the Cambodian border. Rural regions make up about 90% of the land area of Ho Chi Minh City and hold around 25% of the municipality's population. The other 75% is crammed into the remaining 10% that constitutes the urban centre.

The city centre is still unofficially called 'Saigon'. But officially, Saigon refers only to District 1, which is one small piece of the municipal pie. Southerners certainly prefer the name Saigon, but northerners tend to toe the official line. Most government officials are from the north, so if you have to deal with bureaucracy it's best to say Ho Chi Minh City.

To the west of the city centre is District 5, the huge Chinese neighbourhood called Cholon, meaning 'Big Market', a good indication of the importance the Chinese have traditionally played in Vietnam's economy. However, Cholon is decidedly less Chinese

Highlights

- Encounter Saigon traffic head on from the seat of a cyclo pedicab.
- Visit some of the city's myriad museums and sprawling parks.
- Admire the elaborate Chinese pagodas in Cholon.
- Explore the city's endless culinary possibilities.
- Splish-splash a day away at the Saigon Water Park.

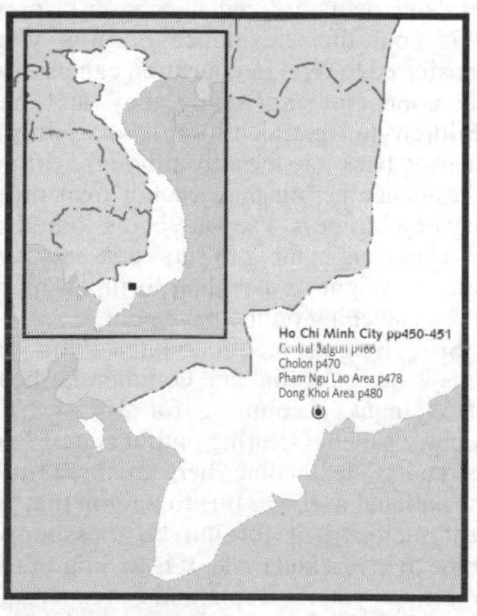

than it used to be, largely thanks to the anticapitalist, anti-Chinese campaign of 1978–79 which caused many ethnic Chinese to flee the country, taking with them their money and entrepreneurial skills. Many of these refugees are now returning (with foreign passports) to explore investment possibilities and Cholon's hotels are once again packed with Chinese-speaking businesspeople.

Officially, greater Ho Chi Minh City claims a population of close to five million. Six to seven million may be the real figure. The government census-takers only count those who have official residence permits, but probably one-third of the population lives here illegally. Many of these illegal residents actually lived in Saigon prior to 1975, but their residence permits were transferred to rural re-education camps after liberation. Not surprisingly, they (and their children and grandchildren) have simply sneaked back into the city, although without a residence permit they cannot own property or a business. They are being joined by an increasing number of rural peasants who come to Saigon to seek their fortune – many end up sleeping on the pavement.

Still, Saigon accommodates them all. This is the industrial and commercial heart of Vietnam, accounting for 30% of the country's manufacturing output and 25% of its retail trade. Incomes here are three times the national average. It is to Saigon that the vast majority of foreign businesspeople come to invest and trade. It is to Saigon that ambitious young people and bureaucrats – from the north and south – gravitate to make a go of it.

Explosive growth is making its mark in new high-rise buildings, joint-venture hotels and colourful shops. The downside is the sharp increase in traffic, pollution and other urban ills. Still, Saigon's neoclassical and international-style buildings, and pavement kiosks selling French rolls and croissants, give certain neighbourhoods an attractive, vaguely French atmosphere. The Americans left their mark on the city too, at least in the form of some heavily fortified apartment blocks and government buildings.

Saigon hums and buzzes with the tenacious will of human beings to survive and improve their lot. It is here that the economic changes sweeping Vietnam – and their negative social implications – are most evident.

History

Saigon was captured by the French in 1859, becoming the capital of the French colony of Cochinchina a few years later. In 1950, the author Norman Lewis described Saigon as follows: 'its inspiration has been purely commercial and it is therefore without folly, fervour or much ostentation ... a pleasant, colourless and characterless French provincial city'. The city served as the capital of the Republic of Vietnam from 1956 until 1975, when it fell to advancing North Vietnamese forces.

Cholon rose to prominence after Chinese merchants began settling there in 1778 and, despite the mass migrations after 1975, still constitutes the largest ethnic-Chinese community in Vietnam.

Orientation

Ho Chi Minh City (Thanh Pho Ho Chi Minh) is divided into 16 urban districts (*quan*, derived from French *quartier*) and five rural districts *(huyen)*. District 1 corresponds to Saigon proper and District 5 is Cholon.

Information

Travel Agencies Saigon Tourist is Ho Chi Minh City's official government-run travel agency. It owns, or is a joint-venture partner in, over 70 hotels and numerous restaurants around town, plus a car rental agency, the Vietnam Golf and Country Club and tourist traps like Binh Quoi Tourist Village.

Vietnam Tourism is the national government's tourist agency, it's open 7.30 to 11.30 am and 1 to 4.30 pm Monday to Saturday.

There are plenty of other travel agencies in Saigon, virtually all of them joint ventures between government agencies and private companies. These places can provide cars, book air tickets and extend your visa. Competition between the private agencies is keen, and you can often undercut Saigon Tourist's tariffs by 50% if you shop around

Visit several tour operators to see what's being offered. They're all fairly similar in their tour programs and price. Most of the guides around are excellent and standards are ever-improving. The best way to find out the latest is to speak with other travellers who have just arrived back from a tour.

Two good newcomers on the budget tour scene are Delta Adventure Tours and Tometeco/Pro Tour; both organise innovative, small group Mekong Delta tours that stand apart from the standard delta excursions by offering walks and cycling. Delta Adventure Tours (the Pham Ngu Lao branch of Saigon Tourist) is run by Kim and Stephen, an Overseas Vietnamese (Viet Kieu) couple who returned from the US a few years ago.

Sinhbalo Adventures is the brainchild of Vietnam travel guru Le Van Sinh. In addition to the standard routes, it organises special interest tours such as 'deep Mekong Delta', remote hill tribe trekking, birdwatching in national parks and motorbiking the Ho Chi Minh Trail.

The following agencies should be used as a starting point only:

Budget Agencies

Ben Thanh Tourist/Buffalo Tours (☎ 886 0365, fax 836 1953) 45 Đ Bui Vien, District 1
Delta Adventure Tours (☎ 836 8542, e sgnkimcafe@hotmail.com) 187A–195 D Pham Ngu Lao, District 1
Fiditourist (☎ 835 3018) 195 Đ Pham Ngu Lao, District 1
Kim Travel (☎/fax 835 9859, e cafekim@hcm.vnn.vn) 268 Đ De Tham, District 1
Linh Cafe (☎ 836 7016/836 0643) 291 Đ Pham Ngu Lao, District 1
Sinh Cafe (☎ 836 7338, fax 836 9322) 248 Đ De Tham, District 1
Tometeco/Pro Tour (☎/fax 837 3716, e pro_tours@yahoo.com) 40 Đ Bui Vien, District 1

Mid-Range & Top-End Agencies

Ann Tours (☎ 833 2564, fax 832 3866) 58 Đ Ton That Tung, District 1
Asian Trails (☎ 822 0649, fax 822 0650, e asiantrails@hcm.vnn.vn) 41 Đ Dinh Tien Hoang, District 1
Atlas Tours (☎ 822 4122, fax 829 8604) 164 Đ Nguyen Van Thu, District 1
Exotissimo (☎ 825 1723, fax 829 5800, e info@exotissimo.com, www.exotissimo.com) Saigon Trade Center, 37 Đ Ton Duc Thang, District 1
Phoenix Vietnam (☎ 824 4282, fax 824 4286, e phoenix.vn.sgn@hcm.fpt.vn) 8A/10B1 Đ Thai Van Lung, District 1
Saigon Tourist (☎ 829 8129, fax 822 4987) 49 Đ Le Thanh Ton, District 1
Sinhbalo Adventures (☎/fax 836 7682, e sinhbalo@hcm.vnn.vn, www.sinhbalo.com) 43 Đ Bui Vien, District 1
Travel Indochina (☎ 845 5080, fax 845 5079) 157 Đ Huynh Van Banh, Phu Nhuan District
Vidotour (☎ 829 1438, fax 829 1435, e vidotour@fmail.vnn.vn) 41 Đ Dinh Tien Hoang, District 1
Vietnam Tourism (☎ 829 1276, fax 829 0775) 69–71 Đ Nam Ky Khoi Nghia, District 3

Nam Duong Travel Agency (☎ 836 9630, fax 836 9632) at 213 Đ Pham Ngu Lao specialises in domestic and international air fares. Just up the street is the Saigon Railways Tourist Services ticket office.

Motorbiking Speciality Tours The Saigon Scooter Center (☎ 090-845819, e ssc@hcm.vnn.vn), 175/12 Đ Pham Ngu Lao, offers travellers the chance to hit the road by classic scooter or motorbike. It offers customised Vietnam itineraries and the flexibility of one-way trips with pick-up/drop-off in Saigon or Hanoi. Details about the tours, including programs in the Mekong Delta and Central Highlands, can be found on the SSC Web site: www.saigonscootercentre.com.

Money There is a bank just outside the airport exit which gives the official exchange rate. Have sufficient US dollar notes in small denominations to get yourself into the city, in case the bank is closed.

Vietcombank (☎ 829 7245, fax 823 0310), also known as the Bank for Foreign Trade of Vietnam, occupies two adjacent buildings at the intersection of Đ Ben Chuong and Đ Pasteur. The east building is for foreign exchange and it is worth a visit just to see the stunning ornate interior. It's open 7 to 11.30 am and 1.30 to 3.30 pm

HO CHI MINH CITY

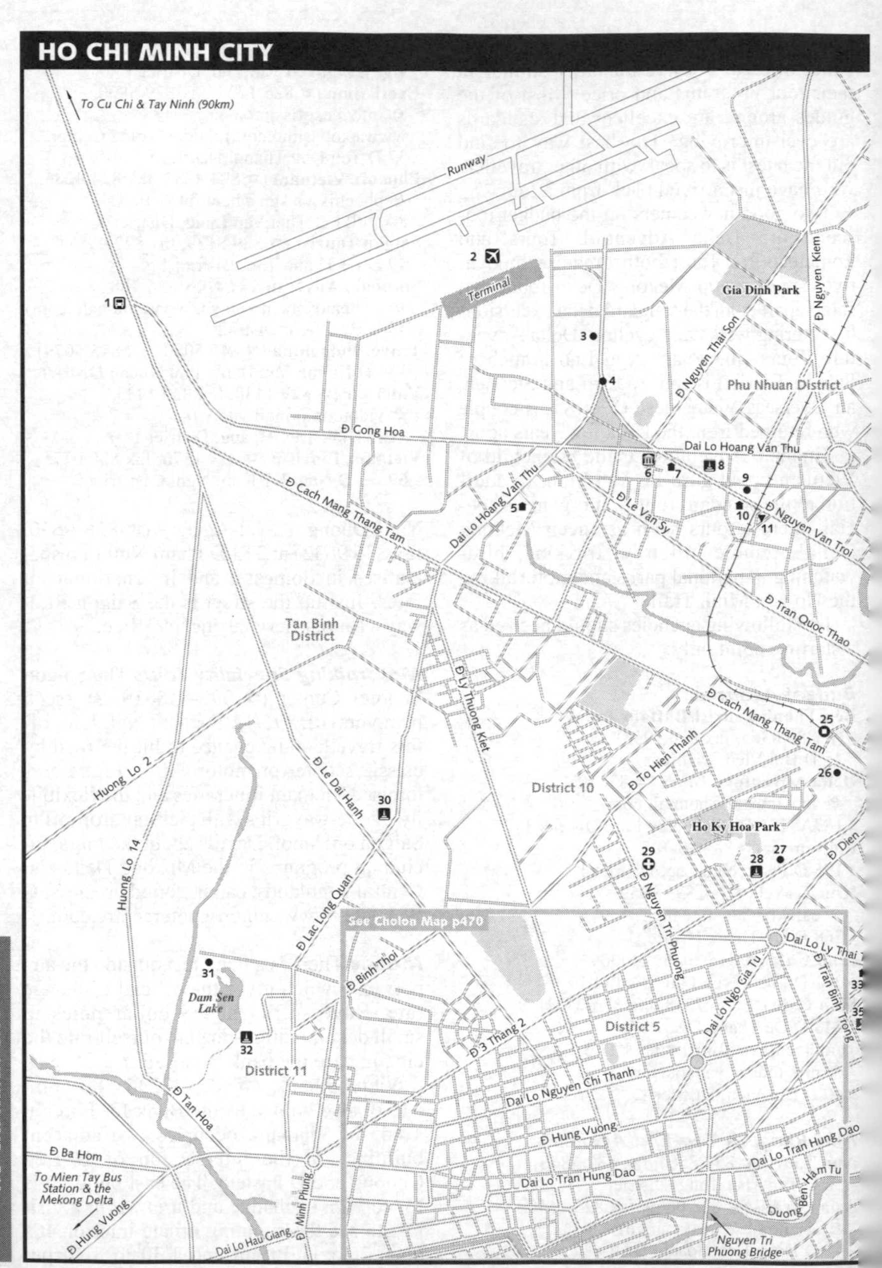

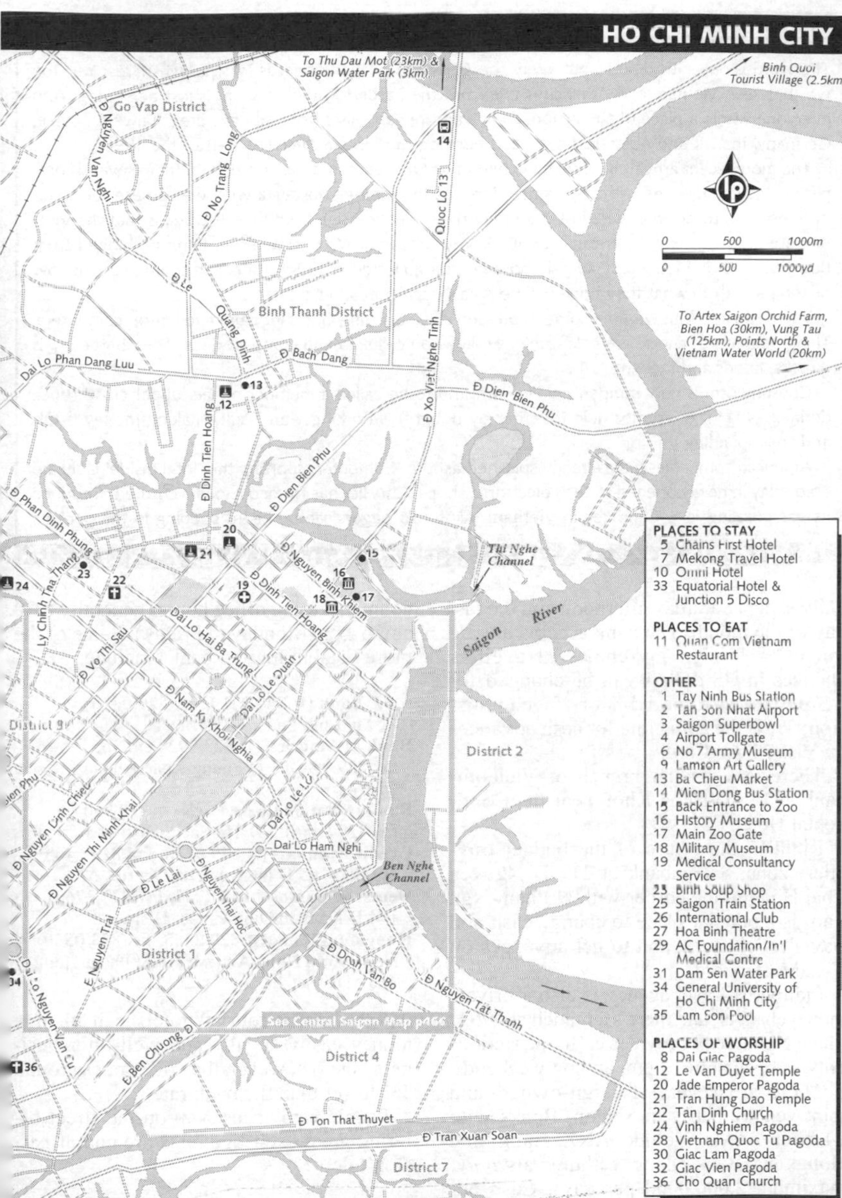
HO CHI MINH CITY
To Thu Dau Mot (23km) & Saigon Water Park (3km)
Binh Quoi Tourist Village (2.5km)
Go Vap District
Binh Thanh District
To Artex Saigon Orchid Farm, Bien Hoa (30km), Vung Tau (125km), Points North & Vietnam Water World (20km)
Thi Nghe Channel
Saigon River
District 2
District 1
District 4
District 7
Ben Nghe Channel
See Central Saigon Map p466
To Can Gio (50km)
PLACES TO STAY
5 Chains First Hotel
7 Mekong Travel Hotel
10 Omni Hotel
33 Equatorial Hotel & Junction 5 Disco
PLACES TO EAT
11 Quan Com Vietnam Restaurant
OTHER
1 Tay Ninh Bus Station
2 Tan Son Nhat Airport
3 Saigon Superbowl
4 Airport Tollgate
6 No 7 Army Museum
9 Lamson Art Gallery
13 Ba Chieu Market
14 Mien Dong Bus Station
15 Back Entrance to Zoo
16 History Museum
17 Main Zoo Gate
18 Military Museum
19 Medical Consultancy Service
23 Binh Soup Shop
25 Saigon Train Station
26 International Club
27 Hoa Binh Theatre
29 AC Foundation/Int'l Medical Centre
31 Dam Sen Water Park
34 General University of Ho Chi Minh City
35 Lam Son Pool
PLACES OF WORSHIP
8 Dai Giac Pagoda
12 Le Van Duyet Temple
20 Jade Emperor Pagoda
21 Tran Hung Dao Temple
22 Tan Dinh Church
24 Vinh Nghiem Pagoda
28 Vietnam Quoc Tu Pagoda
30 Giac Lam Pagoda
32 Giac Vien Pagoda
36 Cho Quan Church

Swords into Market Shares

The word is out – it's time to put away the guns and beat the swords into ploughshares. Yes, the war between Vietnam and America is over, but the battle for market share is just beginning. And everyone wants a piece of the action. Joint-venture capitalists from Japan, Korea, Taiwan, France, Germany, the UK and Australia have been flocking to Vietnam since the start of the 1990s.

The more recent arrivals in town have been the Americans and they bring with them several competitive advantages. As with the French, there is this strange nostalgia with Vietnamese for doing business with those who were just yesterday their enemy. Aside from that, the fact is that the Vietnamese love anything American – be it Mickey Mouse or Michael Jackson. Long prohibited from doing business in Vietnam by a US-imposed embargo (lifted in 1994), American companies are now beating a path to what they hope will be Asia's newest economic tiger.

The new American warriors come in pressed suits, carrying Gucci luggage and laptop computers. Their weapons of choice are cola drinks, Hollywood celluloid and compact discs. Their battle cry is 'Stocks, bonds and rock 'n' roll!'.

Consumerism is now rampant in Vietnam and to be called a member of the 'upper crust' (once defined as 'a lot of crumbs held together by dough') is no longer an insult. Making money is OK and so is spending it.

American companies have already splashed ashore. Computers sporting the 'Intel Inside' label are on display in newly opened hi-tech electronic shops. Chrysler has formed a joint-venture to produce its gas-guzzling Jeep Cherokee in Vietnam. Motorola pagers can be heard beeping in the pockets

daily except Saturday afternoon and the last day of the month. The bank accepts a wide range of foreign currencies. Travellers cheques in US dollars can be changed for US dollars cash for 1.5% or 2% commission; 3% is the going rate for cash advances on Visa/MasterCard.

There is a smaller branch of Vietcombank at 175 Đ Dong Khoi, near the Continental Hotel.

Right in the centre of the budget travellers zone, Sacombank at 211 Đ Nguyen Thai Hoc (on the corner with Đ Pham Ngu Lao) is a popular place to change cash and travellers cheques, and to get advances on Visa/MasterCard.

Fiditourist travel agency is also a private moneychanger, and there's a branch at 195 Đ Pham Ngu Lao. It provides cash transactions only, is open until 10 pm, and on weekends.

There are several foreign-owned and joint-venture banks in Saigon. Banks with 24-hour ATMs include ANZ Bank and Hongkong Bank (dong withdrawals *only*; maximum 2,000,000d per day). Cash advances for larger amounts of dong, as well as US dollars, can be handled at the bank counters during office hours (generally 8.30 am to 4 pm Monday to Friday). Some of the more notable foreign banks include:

ANZ Bank (☎ 829 9319, fax 829 9316) 11 Me Linh Square, District 1
Bank of America (☎ 829 9928 ext 155, fax 829 9942) 1 Đ Phung Khac Khoan, District 1
Banque Nationale de Paris (☎ 829 9504, fax 829 9486) 2 Đ Thi Sach, District 1
Crédit Lyonnais (☎ 829 9226, fax 829 6465) 4th floor, 65 Đ Nguyen Du, District 1
Deutsche Bank (☎ 822 2747, fax 822 2760) 174 Đ Nguyen Dinh Chieu, District 3
Hongkong Bank (☎ 829 2288, fax 823 0530) New World Hotel Annexe, 75 Đ Pham Hong Thai, District 1

All the major tourist hotels can change money easily, legally and well after business hours; however, they offer rates around 5% lower than the bank rate.

People who accost you on the street offering great exchange rates are con artists. Don't do it!

Post Saigon's French-style main post office (Buu Dien Thanh Pho Ho Chi Minh), with

Swords into Market Shares

and handbags of the Vietnamese well-to-do. Pepsi was the first American soft drink vendor to return to Vietnam, but Coke was not far behind.

American fast food should find a ready market among Vietnam's trendy urban elite. McDonald's – when it finally opens Vietnam – will be an instant hit. That is, of course, if nobody clones the name first. Saigon has already seen a chain of fake 7-Elevens come and go.

Foreign investors, for their part, are displeased with the lack of protection for intellectual property rights. Trademarks, patents and copyrights are violated with impunity by the Vietnamese. The proliferation of pirated music tapes and fake Rolex watches are potential bones of contention. Nothing is sacred – Lonely Planet too has problems with high quality photocopies of this guidebook and others being circulated throughout Vietnam. Even downsized copies of the Statue of Liberty have popped up in Vietnam's newest avant-garde cafes. Vietnamese who know their history point out that the original Statue of Liberty was a gift to America from France – 'Why then' they ask, 'shouldn't we have one too?'. Why not indeed?

On the other hand, the Vietnamese government has so far refused anyone permission to capitalise on Ho Chi Minh's name. A proposed American joint-venture called 'Uncle Ho's Hamburgers' flew like a lead balloon, though Kentucky Fried Chicken did managed to enter Vietnam and has successfully franchised. The Vietnamese joint-venture partner, however, was not amused when the American business rep pointed out that Ho Chi Minh does vaguely resemble Colonel Sanders. 'No' said the frowning Vietnamese, 'Ho Chi Minh was a general'.

its glass canopy and iron frame, is at 2 Cong Xa Paris, right next to Notre Dame Cathedral. Built between 1886 and 1891, it is by far the largest post office in Vietnam. Under the benevolent gaze of Ho Chi Minh, you'll be charged exorbitant rates for international telecommunications services. The staff at the information desk (☎ 829 6555, 829 9615), to the left as you enter the building, speak English. Postal services are available 7.30 am to 7.30 pm daily. To your right as you enter the building is the poste restante counter. Pens, envelopes, aerograms, postcards and stamp collections are sold at the counter to the right of the entrance and outside the post office along Đ Nguyen Du.

The District 1 post office (☎ 829 9086), which serves central Saigon, is on ĐL Le Loi near the intersection with Đ Pasteur.

A convenient post office (☎ 886 0050) for the Pham Ngu Lao area is at 17 Đ Bui Vien. It's open 7 am to 10 pm daily. There is another small post office on Đ Pham Ngu Lao, west of Đ De Tham on the corner of Do Quang Doa.

A number of private carriers operate from or near the main post office. The DHL counter (☎ 823 1525, fax 845 6841) is inside the post office. Around the corner at 80C Đ Nguyen Du is Airborne Express (☎ 829 2976, fax 829 2961), and UPS (824 3597, fax 824 3596) is just next door at No 80. Federal Express (☎ 829 0995, fax 829 0477) at 146 Đ Pasteur is attached to the Rex Hotel.

Telephone International phone calls can be made from post offices and better hotels. At the post office don't get tricked into paying more than you should for your local calls. These cost US$0.08 only and not the US$1 the employee behind the desk may tell you.

Fax Faxes can be sent to you at post offices (fax 829 8540/829 8546; US$0.60) and delivered to your hotel for a small charge. The fax should clearly indicate your name, hotel phone number and the address of the hotel (including your room number).

Email & Internet Access Internet access is widely available in Ho Chi Minh City. The largest concentration of Internet cafes is in the Pham Ngu Lao area. There are over

20 places along Đ Pham Ngu Lao, Đ De Tham and Đ Bui Vien – just stroll around and take your pick. Most places charge just 200d to 300d per minute, though there are places charging as low as 100d (less than US$0.01!) a minute.

An option closer to the centre of town is Tin Cafe (☎ 822 9786, ⓔ PQHOI@bdvn.vnmail.vnd.net), 2A ĐL Le Duan. It's a pleasant place to check mail or surf the Net over a cappuccino, and is open 7.30 am to 10.30 pm daily.

Bookshops The best area to look for maps, books and stationery is along the north side of ĐL Le Loi, between the Rex Hotel and Đ Nam Ky Khoi Nghia. There are many small, privately run shops, and the large government-run Saigon Bookstore (☎ 829 6438), at 60–62 ĐL Le Loi is just a stone's throw from the Rex Hotel.

Viet My Bookstore (☎ 822 9650), 41 Đ Dinh Tien Hoang, District 1, has a number of imported books and magazines published in English, French and Chinese.

Fahasa (☎ 822 4670), 185 Đ Dong Khoi, District 1 and (☎ 822 5446), 40 ĐL Nguyen Hue, are two of the better government-run bookshops. You should at least manage to find a good dictionary or some maps here, as well as general books in English and French.

Also worth a look is Bookazine (☎ 829 7455), 28 Đ Dong Khoi. It's open 8 am to 10 pm daily.

The cosy Tiem Sach Bookshop at 20 Đ Ho Huan Nghiep has a massive library of mostly used English and French titles. The shop is open 8.30 am to 10 pm daily and doubles as the Bo Gio cafe.

Xunhasaba (☎ 823 0724, fax 824 1321), which is the Vietnamese acronym for State Enterprise for Export & Import of Books & Periodicals, has an outlet at 25B Đ Nguyen Binh Khiem, District 1.

On Đ De Tham in the Pham Ngu Lao area are a handful of shops dealing in used paperbacks and bootleg CDs, where you can also swap books. Also on Đ Pham Ngu Lao is Anh Khoa Bookshop, which sells some English books and various stationery goods.

War of the Names

One of the primary battlegrounds for the hearts and minds of the Vietnamese people during the last four decades has been the naming of Vietnam's provinces, districts, cities, towns, streets and institutions. Some places have been known by three or more names since WWII and, in many cases, more than one name is still used.

Urban locations have borne: French names (often of the generals, administrators and martyrs who made French colonialism possible); names commemorating the historical figures chosen for veneration by the South Vietnamese government; and the alternative set of heroes selected by the Hanoi government. Buddhist pagodas have formal names as well as one or more popular monikers. Chinese pagodas bear various Chinese appellations – most of which also have Vietnamese equivalents – based on the titles and celestial ranks of those to whom they are consecrated. In the highlands, both Montagnard and Vietnamese names for mountains, villages and so on are in use. The differences in vocabulary and pronunciation between the north, centre and south sometimes result in the use of different words and spellings (such as 'Pleiku' and 'Playcu').

When French control of Vietnam ended in 1954, almost all French names were replaced in both the North and the South. For example, Cap St Jacques became Vung Tau, Tourane was rechristened Danang and Rue Catinat in Saigon was renamed Đ Tu Do (Freedom) – since reunification it has been known as Đ Dong Khoi (Uprising). In 1956, the names of some of the provinces and towns in the South were changed as part of an effort to erase from popular memory the Viet Minh's anti-French exploits, which were often known by the places where they took place. The village-based southern Communists, who by this time had gone underground, continued to use the old designations and boundaries in running their regional, district and village organisations. The peasants quickly adapted

Libraries The Municipal Library is at 34 D Ly Tu Trong. Nearby at 69 Đ Ly Tu Trong is the General Sciences Library with a total of 500 seats in its reading rooms.

Laundry Almost every hotel does laundry, but check the cost beforehand, to avoid confusion when you go to pay the bill. Most hotels have a price list.

Medical Services There are several foreign doctors resident in Saigon providing medical and surgical services.

The Western medical team at the 24-hour AC Foundation/International Medical Center (☎ 865 4025, fax 864 2788, ⓔ fac@hcm.vnn.vn), 520 Đ Nguyen Tri Phuong, District 10, a nonprofit organisation, bills itself as the least expensive Western health care centre in Vietnam.

The Medical Consultancy Service (☎/fax 822 8440, 090-805495/090-920641, ⓔ medicis@hcm.vnn.vn), Fidi House, 3F, 2E Nguyen Thanh Y, District 1, also provides 24-hour service, seven days a week. The clinic has foreign-trained doctors who speak English, German, French and Italian.

SOS International (clinic ☎ 829 8424, 24-hour emergency ☎ 829 8520, fax 829 8551), 65 Đ Nguyen Du, District 1, has a medical services program (including dental treatment) for resident expats.

The Emergency Centre (☎ 829 2071), 125 ĐL Le Loi, District 1, operates 24 hours. Doctors speak English and French.

The Pasteur Institute (☎ 820 0739), 167 Đ Pasteur, District 3, has good facilities for medical tests. You must be referred here by a doctor.

Cho Ray Hospital (Benh Vien Cho Ray; ☎ 855 4137, fax 855 7267), with 1000 beds, is one of the largest medical facilities in Vietnam. It's at 201 ĐL Nguyen Chi Thanh, District 5, and there is a section for foreigners on the 10th floor. About one-third of the 200 doctors speak English and there are 24-hour emergency facilities.

Pharmacies are everywhere. One good one is at 678 Đ Nguyen Dinh Chieu, District 3. The owner speaks excellent English

War of the Names

to this situation, using one set of names for where they lived when dealing with the Communists and a different set of names when talking to representatives of the South Vietnamese government.

Later, US soldiers in Vietnam gave nicknames (such as China Beach near Danang) to places whose Vietnamese names they found inconvenient or difficult to remember or pronounce. This helped to make a very foreign land seem a bit more familiar.

After reunification, the first order of Saigon's provisional municipal Military Management Committee was to change the name of the city to 'Ho Chi Minh City', a decision confirmed in Hanoi a year later. The new government immediately began changing street names considered inappropriate – a process which is still continuing – and renamed almost all the city's hotels, dropping English and French names in favour of Vietnamese ones. The only French names still in use are those of Albert Calmette (1893-1934, developer of a tuberculosis vaccine), Marie Curie (1867-1934, who won the Nobel Prize for her research into radioactivity), Louis Pasteur (1822-95, chemist and bacteriologist) and Alexandre Yersin (1863-1943, discoverer of the plague bacillus).

All this renaming has had mixed results. Streets, districts and provinces are usually known by their new names. As if navigating your way around Saigon wasn't confusing enough, in 1999 when the municipal Peoples' Committee set out to name 25 new city streets, they also decided to *rename* another 152! This makes using anything but the latest street maps a risky proposition, though fortunately most of important streets in the city centre have not changed name, and tourist maps of the city are also updated annually.

Most residents of Ho Chi Minh City still prefer to call the place Saigon, especially since Ho Chi Minh City is in fact a huge area that stretches from near Cambodia all the way to the South China Sea.

and French. There are also a couple of pharmacies in the backpacker centre on Đ De Tham where the staff are accustomed to serving travellers.

Dental care is available at the Dental Clinic Starlight (☎ 822 2433, 24-hour emergency ☎ 090-834901), 10C Đ Thai Van Lung, District 1, and Grand Dentistry (☎ 824 5772), 10 Đ Ngo Duc Ke, District 1.

Photo Processing These days Saigon is well endowed with labs which can process colour print film in about an hour. These are easy to spot (look for the Fuji and Kodak signage), with several popular ones along ĐL Nguyen Hue between the Rex Hotel and the Saigon River. Photo Nhu (☎ 836 8093), at 231 Đ Pham Ngu Lao, is very good.

Visa Extensions The Immigration Police Office (Phong Quan Ly Nguoi Nuoc Ngoai; ☎ 839 2221), 254 Đ Nguyen Trai, is open 8 to 11 am and 1 to 4 pm. Most probably, you will be told to use the services of a private agency. Most travel agencies can arrange visa extensions.

Dangers & Annoyances Saigon is the most theft-ridden of any city in Vietnam, so don't become a statistic. See Dangers & Annoyances in the Fact for the Visitor chapter for advice on how to avoid street crime.

Walking Tour

Ho Chi Minh City's immense sprawl makes it somewhat impractical to see all of it on foot, though a one-day walking tour of the city centre, District 1, is certainly possible (and recommended).

The Pham Ngu Lao area makes a good starting point. Follow Đ Nguyen Thai Hoc to the mammoth New World Hotel, turn right and follow Đ Le Lai a few minutes north to the vast indoor **Ben Thanh Market**. The market is at its bustling best in the morning.

After exploring the market, cross the large roundabout, where you'll see a statue of Tran Nguyen Han on horseback. One short block south, on Đ Pho Duc Chinh, is the praiseworthy **Fine Arts Museum**. After touring the exhibits, zigzag west to ĐL Ham Nghi and turn north again on Đ Ton That Dam to stroll through the colourful outdoor **street market**. At the northern terminus turn west at the 'T' on Đ Huyen Thuc Khang to Đ Pasteur and out to ĐL Le Loi, the large boulevard leading to the grand and thoughtfully restored **Municipal Theatre**.

From the theatre, head up ĐL Le Loi, and turn left at the Rex Hotel up ĐL Nguyen Hue. At the northern end is the old **Hôtel de Ville**. You'll have to admire it from the outside because it's now home to the local People's Committee – requests to visit the interior are usually refused. However, a one-block walk south on Đ Le Thanh Ton will bring you to the **Museum of Ho Chi Minh City**, where visitors are warmly received.

The popular **War Remnants Museum** (closed 11.45 am to 1.30 pm) is just a few blocks to the north-west (technically in District 3) along Đ Nam Ky Khoi Nghia then left on Đ Vo Van Tan. Nearby is **Reunification Palace** (closed 11 am to 1 pm).

Later in the afternoon you can stroll north along ĐL Le Duan, stopping to look at **Notre Dame Cathedral** and the impressive French-style **post office**. At the end of the boulevard are the **zoo & botanical garden**, in the grounds of which is the excellent **History Museum**. Just across from the main gate you'll find the quiet **Ho Chi Minh Military Museum**.

A few blocks to the north-west along Đ Nguyen Binh Khiem will bring you to the **Jade Emperor Pagoda**, a colourful way to end your tour. By this time you will most likely be tired enough to head for your hotel, take a shower, enjoy a cold drink and prepare yourself for tackling the nightlife of Ho Chi Minh City.

MUSEUMS

War Remnants Museum

Once known as the Museum of Chinese and American War Crimes, the museum's name was changed to avoid offending Chinese and American tourists. However, the pamphlet handed out at reception pulls no punches: it's entitled 'Some Pictures of US Imperialists Aggressive War Crimes in Vietnam'.

The War Remnants Museum (☎ 829 0325) is now the most popular museum in Saigon with Western tourists. Many of the atrocities documented here were well publicised in the West, but rarely do Westerners have the opportunity to hear the victims of the USA's military actions tell their own story.

US armoured vehicles, artillery pieces, bombs and infantry weapons are on display in the yard. There is also a guillotine which the French used to deal with Viet Minh 'troublemakers'. Many of the photographs illustrating US atrocities are from US sources, including photos of the infamous My Lai Massacre. There is a model of the notorious tiger cages used by the South Vietnamese military to house Viet Cong (VC) prisoners on Con Son Island. There are also pictures of deformed babies, their birth defects attributed to the widespread spraying of chemical herbicides by the Americans. An adjacent room has exhibits displaying 'counter-revolutionary war crimes' committed by saboteurs within Vietnam after 1975. Counter-revolutionaries are portrayed as being allied with both the US and Chinese imperialists.

Despite the relative one-sidedness of the exhibits, there are few museums in the world which drive home so well the point that warfare is horribly brutal and that many of the victims are civilians. Even those who adamantly supported the war will have a difficult time not being horrified by the photos of children mangled by American bombing, napalming and artillery shells. There are also scenes of torture – it takes a strong stomach to look at these. You'll also have a rare chance to see some of the experimental weapons used in the war, which were at one time military secrets, such as the 'flechette' (an artillery shell filled with thousands of tiny darts).

The War Remnants Museum is in the former US Information Service building at 28 Đ Vo Van Tan (at the intersection with Đ Le Qui Don). Opening hours are 7.30 to 11.45 am and 1.30 to 4.45 pm daily and entry costs US$0.80. Explanations are in Vietnamese, English and Chinese.

Museum of Ho Chi Minh City

Housed in a grey, neoclassical structure built in 1886 and once known as Gia Long Palace (and more recently the Revolutionary Museum), the Museum of Ho Chi Minh City (☎ 829 9741) is a singularly beautiful and amazing building. The museum displays artefacts from the various periods of the Communist struggle for power in Vietnam. The photographs of anticolonial activists executed by the French appear out of place in the gilded, 19th-century ballrooms, but then again the contrast gives a sense of the immense power and complacency of colonial France. There are photos of Vietnamese peace demonstrators in Saigon demanding that US troops get out, and a dramatic suicidal photo of Thich Quang Duc; the monk who made global headlines when he burned himself to death, in protest against the policies of President Ngo Dinh Diem, in 1963 (also see the 'Thien Mu Pagoda' boxed text in the Central Vietnam chapter).

The information plaques are in Vietnamese only, but some of the exhibits include documents in French or English, and many others are self-explanatory if you know some basic Vietnamese history (see History in the Facts about Vietnam chapter). The exhibitions cover the various periods in the city's 300-year history.

Among the most interesting artefacts on display is a *ghe* (a long, narrow rowing boat) with a false bottom in which arms were smuggled. Nearby is a small diorama of the Cu Chi Tunnels. The adjoining room has examples of infantry weapons used by the VC and various captured South Vietnamese and American medals, hats and plaques. A map shows Communist advances during the dramatic collapse of South Vietnam in early 1975. There are also photographs of the liberation of Saigon.

Deep beneath the building is a network of reinforced concrete bunkers and fortified corridors. The system, branches of which stretch all the way to Reunification Palace, included living areas, a kitchen and a large meeting hall. In 1963, President Diem and his brother hid here before fleeing to Cha Tam Church (see the Cha Tam Church entry later). The network is not currently open to the public because most of the tunnels are flooded, but if you want to bring a torch (flashlight), a museum guard might show you around.

In the garden behind the museum is a Soviet tank, an American Huey UH-1 helicopter and an anti-aircraft gun. In the garden fronting Đ Nam Ky Khoi Nghia is more military hardware, including the American-built F-5E jet used by a renegade South Vietnamese air force pilot to bomb the Presidential Palace (now Reunification Palace) on 8 April 1975.

The museum is at 65 Đ Ly Tu Trong, one block east of Reunification Palace. It is open 8 to 11.30 am and 2 to 4.30 pm Tuesday to Sunday. Admission is US$0.80.

History Museum

The History Museum (Vien Bao Tang Lich Su; ☎ 829 8146), built in 1929 by the Société des Études Indochinoises, is just inside the main entrance to the zoo on Đ Nguyen Binh Khiem. The museum has an excellent collection of artefacts illustrating the evolution of the cultures of Vietnam, from the Bronze Age Dong Son civilisation (13th century BC to 1st century AD) and the Oc-Eo (Funan) civilisation (1st to 6th centuries AD), to the Chams, Khmers and Vietnamese. There are many valuable relics taken from Cambodia's Angkor Wat.

At the back of the building on the 3rd floor is a research library (☎ 829 0268; open Monday to Saturday) with numerous books on Indochina from the French period.

The museum is open 8 to 11.30 am and 1 to 4 pm Tuesday to Sunday. Admission costs US$0.80.

Ho Chi Minh Museum

This museum (Khu Luu Niem Bac Ho; ☎ 829 1060) is in the old customs house at 1 Đ Nguyen Tat Thanh, District 4, just across Ben Nghe Channel from the quayside end of ĐL Ham Nghi. Nicknamed the 'Dragon House' (Nha Rong), it was built in 1863. The tie between Ho Chi Minh and the museum building is tenuous: 21-year-old Ho, having signed on as a stoker and galley-boy on a French freighter, left Vietnam from here in 1911, beginning 30 years of exile in France, the Soviet Union, China and elsewhere.

The museum houses many of Ho's personal effects, including some of his clothing (he was a man of informal dress), sandals, his beloved American-made Zenith radio and other memorabilia. The explanatory signs in the museum are in Vietnamese, but if you know something about Ho (see the 'Ho Chi Minh' boxed text in the Facts about Vietnam chapter, you should be able to follow most of the photographs and exhibits.

The museum is open 7.30 to 11.30 am and 1.30 to 9 pm daily.

Ho Chi Minh Military Museum

The Ho Chi Minh Military Museum is just across Đ Nguyen Binh Khiem (on the corner of ĐL Le Duan) from the main gate of the zoo. US, Chinese and Soviet war material is on display outdoors, including a Cessna A-37 of the South Vietnamese air force and a US-built F-5E Tiger with the 20mm nose gun still loaded. The tank on display is one of the tanks which broke into the grounds of Reunification Palace on 30 April 1975.

Fine Arts Museum

This classic yellow and white building, with some modest Chinese influence, houses one of the more interesting collections in Vietnam. If you are not interested in the collection, just enter to view the huge hall with its Art Nouveau windows and floors. On the 1st floor is officially accepted contemporary art. Most of it is just kitsch or desperate attempts to master abstract art, but occasionally something brilliant is displayed here. Most of the recent art is for sale and prices are fair.

The 2nd floor displays old politically correct art. Some of it is pretty crude – pictures of heroic figures waving red flags, children with rifles, a wounded soldier joining the Communist Party, innumerable tanks and weaponry, grotesque Americans and God-like reverence for Ho Chi Minh. Neverthe-less, it's worth seeing because Vietnamese

Whitewashing Nature

Visitors to Ho Chi Minh City have often wondered why the lower parts of all the trees are painted white. Theories posited by tourists have included that the paint:

1) protects the trees from termites;
2) protects the trees from Agent Orange;
3) protects the trees from urine damage;
4) is some government official's idea of Art Nouveau; or
5) is an ancient Vietnamese tradition.

It turns out that the mystery of the white trees has a much simpler explanation – they are painted white so people don't bump into them at night!

artists managed not to be as dull and conformist as their counterparts in Eastern Europe. Once you've passed several paintings and sculptures of Uncle Ho, you will see that those artists who studied before 1975 managed to somehow transfer their own aesthetics into the world of prescribed subjects. Most impressive are some drawings of prison riots in 1973. Also on the 2nd floor are some remarkable abstract paintings.

The 3rd floor has a good collection of older art, mainly Funan Oc-Eo sculptures strongly resembling styles of ancient Greece and Egypt. You will also find here the best Cham pieces outside of Danang. Also interesting are the many pieces of Indian art, such as stone statues of elephant heads. Some pieces clearly originated in Angkor culture.

The cafe in the garden in front of the museum is a preferred spot for elderly gentlemen to exchange stamp collections and sip iced tea.

The Fine Arts Museum (Bao Tang My Thuat; ☎ 822 2577) is at 97A Đ Pho Duc Chinh, District 1. It's open 7.45 to 11.15 am and 1.30 to 4.15 pm Monday to Saturday. Admission is US$0.40.

No 7 Army Museum

Out near the airport is the No 7 Army Museum (Bao Tang Luc Luong Vu Trang Mien Dong Nam Bo; ☎ 842 1354), 247 ĐL Hoang Van Thu, Ward 1, Tan Binh District. Despite the fancy exterior, it's an unimpressive display. The main feature is yet another statue of Ho Chi Minh, though there is a small collection of tanks behind the main building. There are a few photos from the French-era Viet Minh battles. Visitors are few, and it is often closed during opening hours (7.30 to 11 am and 1.30 to 5 pm Monday to Saturday). Admission is free.

Ton Duc Thang Museum

This small, seldom-visited museum (Bao Tang Ton Duc Thang; ☎ 829 4651) is dedicated to Ton Duc Thang, Ho Chi Minh's successor as president of Vietnam, who was born in Long Xuyen, An Giang Province, in 1888. He died in office in 1980. Photos and displays illustrate his role in the Vietnamese Revolution, including the time he spent imprisoned on Con Dao Island.

The museum is on the waterfront at 5 Đ Ton Duc Thang, half a block north of the Tran Hung Dao statue. It is open 8 to 11 am and 2 to 6 pm Tuesday to Sunday. Admission is US$0.80.

REUNIFICATION PALACE

It was towards this building – then known as Independence Palace, or the Presidential Palace – that the first Communist tanks in Saigon rushed on the morning of 30 April 1975. After crashing through the wrought-iron gates – in a dramatic scene recorded by photojournalists and shown around the world – a soldier ran into the building and up the stairs to unfurl a VC flag from the 4th floor balcony. In an ornate 2nd-floor reception chamber, General Minh, who had become head of state only 43 hours before, waited with his improvised cabinet. 'I have been waiting since early this morning to transfer power to you,' Minh said to the VC officer who entered the room. 'There is no question of your transferring power,' replied the officer. 'You cannot give up what you do not have.'

Reunification Palace (Hoi Truong Thong Nhat) is one of the most fascinating sights in Saigon, both because of its striking modern architecture and the eerie feeling you get as you walk through the deserted halls. The building, once the symbol of the South Vietnamese government, is preserved almost as it was on that day in April 1975 when the Republic of Vietnam, which hundreds of thousands of Vietnamese and 58,183 Americans had died trying to save, ceased to exist. Some recent additions include a statue of Ho Chi Minh and a viewing room where you can watch a video of Vietnamese history in a variety of languages. The national anthem is played at the end of the tape and you are expected to stand up – it would be rude not to.

In 1868 a residence for the French governor general of Cochinchina was built on this site, and gradually expanded to become Norodom Palace. When the French departed, the palace became home for South Vietnamese president Ngo Dinh Diem. So hated was Diem that his own air force bombed the palace in 1962 in an unsuccessful attempt to kill him. The president ordered a new residence to be built on the same site, this time with a sizable bomb shelter in the basement. Work was completed in 1966, but Diem did not get to see his dream house because he was murdered by his own troops in 1963. The new building was named Independence Palace and was home to South Vietnamese president Nguyen Van Thieu until his hasty departure in 1975.

The Norodom Palace, designed by Paris-trained Vietnamese architect Ngo Viet Thu, is an outstanding example of 1960s architecture. It has an airy and open atmosphere and its spacious chambers are tastefully decorated with the finest modern Vietnamese art and crafts. In its grandeur, the building feels worthy of a head of state.

The ground-floor room with the boat-shaped table was often used for conferences. Upstairs, in the Presidential Receiving Room (the one with the red chairs in it, called in Vietnamese Phu Dau Rong, or the Dragon's Head Room), the South Vietnam president received foreign delegations. The president sat behind the desk; the chairs with dragons carved into the arms were used by his assistants. The chair facing the desk was reserved for foreign ambassadors. Next door is a meeting room. The room with gold-coloured chairs and curtains was used by the vice president. You can even sit in the former president's chair and have your photo taken.

In the back of the structure is the president's living quarters. Check out the model boats, horse tails and severed elephants' feet. On the 3rd floor there is a card-playing room with a bar and a movie-screening chamber. This floor also boasts a terrace with a heliport – there is still a moribund helicopter parked here, but it costs US$1 to walk around on the helipad. The 4th floor has a dance hall and casino.

Perhaps most interesting of all is the basement with its network of tunnels, telecommunications centre and war room (with the best map of Vietnam you'll ever see pasted on the wall). One tunnel stretches all the way to Gia Long Palace, now the Revolutionary Museum.

Reunification Palace is open to visitors from 7.30 to 11 am and 1 to 4 pm daily, except when official receptions or meetings are taking place. English- and French-speaking guides are on duty during these hours. The visitors office (☎ 829 0629) and entrance is at 106 Đ Nguyen Du. The entrance fee for travellers is US$1 (free for residents).

PEOPLE'S COMMITTEE BUILDING

Saigon's gingerbread Hôtel de Ville, one of the city's most prominent landmarks, is now the somewhat incongruous home of the Ho Chi Minh City People's Committee. It was built between 1901 and 1908 after years of the sort of architectural controversy peculiar to the French. Situated at the north-western end of ĐL Nguyen Hue and facing towards the river, the former hotel is notable for its gardens, ornate facade and elegant interior lit with crystal chandeliers. It's easily the most photographed building in Vietnam. At night, the exterior is usually covered with thousands of geckos feasting on insects.

Unfortunately, you'll have to content yourself with admiring the exterior only. The building is not open to the public and requests by tourists to visit the interior are rudely rebuffed.

ZOO & BOTANICAL GARDEN

The Zoo and Botanical Garden (Thao Cam Vien) make pleasant places for a relaxing stroll under the giant tropical trees that thrive amid lakes, lawns and flowerbeds. Unfortunately, the zoo facilities are a bit run-down, but gradually improving.

The Botanical Garden, founded in 1864, was one of the first projects undertaken by the French after they established Cochinchina as a colony. It was once one of the finest such gardens in Asia, but this is certainly no longer true. The emphasis now is on the fun fair, with kiddie rides, fun house, miniature train, house of mirrors etc.

The zoo's main gate is on Đ Nguyen Binh Khiem on the corner of ĐL Le Duan. There is another entrance on Đ Nguyen Thi Minh Khai near the bridge over Thi Nghe Channel.

Just inside the main gate is the **Temple of King Hung Vuong**. The Hung kings are said to be the first rulers of the Vietnamese nation, having established their rule in the Red River region before it was invaded by the Chinese.

PLACES OF WORSHIP

Greater Ho Chi Minh City

Giac Lam Pagoda Giac Lam Pagoda dates from 1744 and is believed to be the oldest pagoda in greater Ho Chi Minh City. The last reconstruction here was in 1900, so the architecture, layout and ornamentation remain almost unaltered by the modernist renovations that have transformed so many of Vietnam's religious structures. Ten monks live at this Vietnamese Buddhist pagoda, which also incorporates aspects of Taoism and Confucianism. It is well worth the trip out here from central Saigon, as one couple observed:

> It's incredibly beautiful and best of all we met Dat Le Tan, a caretaker who worked as an interpreter for the US Army between 1968 and 1975. While we were at Giac Lam, it began pouring down rain. He invited us to stay until the rain had stopped, made us tea and sat down to talk to us. We were also joined by some students, who are attracted to the compound because of the peace and quiet – they can settle down there to do some serious study without distraction. For us, Giac Lam was one of the highlights of Saigon.
>
> **Debbie Hanlon & Paul Fewster**

To the right of the gate to the pagoda compound are the ornate tombs of venerated monks. The *bo de* (bodhi, or pipal) tree in the front garden was the gift of a monk from Sri Lanka. Next to the tree is a regular feature seen in Vietnamese Buddhist temples, a gleaming white statue of Quan The Am Bo Tat (Avalokiteçvara, Guanyin in Chinese, the Goddess of Mercy) standing on a lotus blossom, a symbol of purity.

The roof line of the main building is decorated both inside and outside with unusual blue-and-white porcelain plates. Through the main entrance is a reception hall lined with funeral tablets and photos of the deceased. Roughly in the centre of the hall, near an old French chandelier, is a figure of 18-armed Chuan De, another form of the Goddess of Mercy. Note the carved hardwood columns which bear gilded Vietnamese inscriptions written in *nom* characters. The wall to the left is covered with portraits of great monks from previous generations. Their names and other biographical information are recorded on the vertical red tablets in gold nom characters. A box for donations sits nearby. Shoes should be removed when passing from the rough red floor tiles to the smaller, white-black-grey tiles.

On the other side of the wall from the monks' funeral tablets is the main sanctuary, which is filled with countless gilded figures. On the dais in the centre of the back row sits A Di Da (pronounced 'AH-zee-dah'), the Buddha of the Past (Amitabha). To his right is Kasyape and to his left Anand; both are disciples of the Thich Ca Buddha (the historical Buddha Sakyamuni, whose real name was Siddhartha Gautama). Directly in front of A Di Da is a statue of the Thich Ca Buddha, flanked by two guardians. In front is a tiny figure of the Thich Ca Buddha as a child. As always, he is clothed in a yellow robe.

The fat laughing fellow, seated with five children climbing all over him, is Ameda. To his left is Ngoc Hoang, the Taoist Jade Emperor, who presides over a world of innumerable supernatural beings. In the front row is a statue of the Thich Ca Buddha with two Bodhisattvas on each side. On the altars along the side walls of the sanctuary are various Bodhisattvas and the Judges of the 10 Regions of Hell. Each of the judges is holding a scroll resembling the handle of a fork.

The red and gold Christmas tree-shaped object is a wooden altar bearing 49 lamps and 49 miniature statues of Bodhisattvas. People pray for sick relatives or ask for happiness by contributing kerosene for use in the lamps. Petitioners' names and those of ill family members are written on slips of paper, which are attached to the branches of the 'tree'.

The frame of the large bronze bell in the corner looks like a university bulletin board because petitioners have attached to it lists of names: those of people seeking happiness and those of the sick and the dead, placed there by relatives. It is believed that when the bell is rung, the sound will resonate to the heavens above and the underground heavens below, carrying with it the attached supplications.

Prayers here consist of chanting to the accompaniment of drums, bells and gongs and they follow a traditional rite seldom performed these days. Prayers are held daily from 4 to 5 am, 11 am to noon, 4 to 5 pm and 7 to 9 pm.

Giac Lam Pagoda is about 3km from Cholon at 118 Đ Lac Long Quan in the Tan Binh District. Beware: the numbering on Đ Lac Long Quan is extremely confusing, starting over from '1' several times and at one point jumping to four digits. In many places, odd and even numbers are on the same side of the street.

The best way to get to Giac Lam from Cholon is to take ĐL Nguyen Chi Thanh or ĐL 3/2 to Đ Le Dai Hanh. Head north-west on Đ Le Dai Hanh and turn right onto Đ Lac Long Quan. Walk 100m and the pagoda gate will be on your left. It is open to visitors from 6 am to 9 pm.

Giac Vien Pagoda Giac Vien Pagoda is architecturally similar to Giac Lam. Both share an atmosphere of scholarly serenity, though Giac Vien, which is right next to Dam Sen Lake in District 11, is in a more rural setting. Giac Vien Pagoda was founded by Hai Tinh Giac Vien about 200 years ago. It is said that Emperor Gia Long, who died in 1819, used to worship at Giac Vien. Today, 10 monks live here.

The pagoda is in a relatively poor part of the city. Because of the impossibly confusing numbering on Đ Lac Long Quan, the best way to get there from Cholon is to take ĐL Nguyen Chi Thanh or ĐL 3/2 to Đ Le Dai Hanh. Turn left (south-west) off Đ Le Dai Hanh onto Đ Binh Thoi and turn right (north) at Đ Lac Long Quan. The gate leading to the pagoda is at 247 Đ Lac Long Quan.

Pass through the gate and go several hundred metres down a potholed, dirt road, turning left at the 'T' and right at the fork. You will pass several impressive tombs of monks on the right before arriving at the pagoda itself.

The first chamber as you enter the pagoda is lined with funeral tablets. At the back of the second chamber is a statue of Hai Tinh Giac Vien, holding a horse-tail swatch. The nearby portraits are of his disciples and successors as head monk. A donation box sits to the left of the statue. Opposite Hai Tinh Giac Vien is a representation of 18-armed Chuan De, who is flanked by two guardians.

The main sanctuary is on the other side of the wall behind the Hai Tinh Giac Vien statue. A Di Da is at the back of the dais. Directly in front of him is the Thich Ca Buddha flanked by his disciples Anand (on the left) and Kasyape (on the right). To the right of Kasyape is the Ti Lu Buddha; to the left of Anand is the Nhien Dang Buddha. At the foot of the Thich Ca Buddha is a small figure of Thich Ca as a child. Fat, laughing Ameda is seated with children climbing all over him; on either side of him stand guardians. In the front row of the dais is Thich Ca with two Bodhisattvas on each side.

In front of the dais is a fantastic brass incense basin with fierce dragon heads emerging from each side. On the altar to the left of the dais is Dai The Chi Bo Tat, on the altar to the right is Quan The Am Bo Tat. The Guardian of the Pagoda is against the wall opposite the dais. Nearby is a 'Christmas tree' similar to the one in Giac Lam Pagoda. Lining the side walls are the Judges of the 10 Regions of Hell (holding scrolls) and 18 Bodhisattvas.

Giac Vien Pagoda is open 7 am to 7 pm, but come before dark as the electricity is often out. Prayers are held daily from 4 to 5 am, 8 to 10 am, 2 to 3 pm, 4 to 5 pm and 7 to 9 pm.

Jade Emperor Pagoda The Jade Emperor Pagoda (known in Vietnamese as Phuoc Hai Tu and Chua Ngoc Hoang), built in 1909 by the Cantonese (Quang Dong) Congregation, is truly a gem of a Chinese temple. It is one of the most spectacularly colourful pagodas in Saigon, filled with statues of phantasmal divinities and grotesque heroes. The pungent smoke of burning joss sticks fills the air, obscuring the exquisite woodcarvings decorated with gilded Chinese characters. The roof is covered with elaborate tilework. The statues, which represent characters from both the Buddhist and Taoist traditions, are made of reinforced papier mache.

As you enter the main doors of the building, Mon Quan, the God of the Gate, stands to the right in an elaborately carved wooden case. Opposite him, in a similar case, is Tho Than (Tho Dia), the God of the Land. Straight on is an altar on which are placed, from left to right, figures of: Phat Mau Chuan De, mother of the five Buddhas of the cardinal directions; Dia Tang Vuong Bo Tat (Ksitigartha), the King of Hell; the Di Lac Buddha (Maitreya), the Buddha of the Future; Quan The Am Bo Tat; and a bas-relief portrait of the Thich Ca Buddha. Behind the altar, in a glass case, is the Duoc Su Buddha, also known as the Nhu Lai Buddha. The figure is said to be made of sandalwood.

To either side of the altar, against the walls, are two especially fierce and menacing figures. On the right (as you face the altar) is a 4m-high statue of the general who defeated the Green Dragon. He is stepping on the vanquished dragon. On the left is the general who defeated the White Tiger, which is also being stepped on.

The Taoist Jade Emperor, Ngoc Hoang, draped in luxurious robes, presides over the main sanctuary. He is flanked by the 'Four Big Diamonds' (Tu Dai Kim Cuong), his four guardians, so named because they are said to be as hard as diamonds. In front of the Jade Emperor stand six figures, three to each side. On the left is Bac Dau, the Taoist God of the Northern Polar Star and God of Longevity, flanked by his two guardians; and on the right is Nam Tao, the Taoist God of the Southern Polar Star and God of Happiness, also flanked by two guardians.

In the case to the right of the Jade Emperor is 18-armed Phat Mau Chuan De. Two faces, affixed to her head behind each ear, look to either side. On the wall to her right, at a height of about 4m, is Dai Minh Vuong Quang, who was reincarnated as Sakyamuni, riding on the back of a phoenix. Below are the Tien Nhan, literally the 'god-persons'.

In the case to the left of the Jade Emperor sits Ong Bac De, a reincarnation of the Jade Emperor, holding a sword. One of his feet is resting on a turtle while the other rests on a snake. On the wall to the left of Ong Bac De, about 4m off the ground, is Thien Loi, the God of Lightning, who slays evil people. Below Thien Loi are the military commanders of Ong Bac De (on the lower step) and Thien Loi's guardians (on the upper step). At the top of the two carved pillars that separate the three alcoves are the Goddess of the Moon (on the left) and the God of the Sun (on the right).

Quan Am Thi Kinh

Quan Am Thi Kinh was a woman unjustly turned out of her home by her husband. She disguised herself as a monk and went to live in a pagoda, where a young woman accused her of fathering her child. She accepted the blame – and the responsibility that went along with it – and again found herself out on the streets, this time with her 'son'. Much later, about to die, she returned to the monastery to confess her secret. When the emperor of China heard of her story, he declared her the Guardian Spirit of Mother and Child.

It is believed that she has the power to bestow male offspring on those who fervently believe in her and as such is extremely popular with childless couples.

Out the door on the left-hand side of the Jade Emperor's chamber is another room. The semi-enclosed area to the right (as you enter) is presided over by Thanh Hoang, the Chief of Hell; to the left is his red horse. Of the six figures lining the walls, the two closest to Thanh Hoang are Am Quan, the God of Yin (on the left), and Duong Quan, the God of Yang (on the right). The other four figures, the Thuong Thien Phat Ac, are gods who dispense punishments for evil acts and rewards for good deeds. Thanh Hoang faces in the direction of the famous Hall of the 10 Hells. The carved wooden panels lining the walls graphically depict the varied torments awaiting evil people in each of the 10 Regions of Hell. At the top of each panel is one of the Judges of the 10 Regions examining a book in which the deeds of the deceased are inscribed.

On the wall opposite Thanh Hoang is a bas-relief wood panel depicting Quan Am Thi Kinh standing on a lotus blossom. On the panel, Quan Am Thi Kinh is shown holding her 'son'. To her left is Long Nu, a very young Buddha who is her protector. To her right is Thien Tai, her guardian spirit, who knew the real story all along (see the 'Quan Am Thi Kinh' boxed text in this section). Above her left shoulder is a bird bearing prayer beads.

To the right of the panel of Quan Am Thi Kinh is a panel depicting Dia Tang Vuong Bo Tat, the King of Hell.

On the other side of the wall is a fascinating little room in which the ceramic figures of 12 women, overrun with children and wearing colourful clothes, sit in two rows of six. Each of the women exemplifies a human characteristic, either good or bad (as in the case of the woman drinking alcohol from a jug). Each figure represents one year in the 12-year Chinese calendar. Presiding over the room is Kim Hoa Thanh Mau, the Chief of All Women.

Off to the right of the main chamber, stairs lead up to a 2nd-floor sanctuary and balcony.

The Jade Emperor Pagoda is at 73 Đ Mai Thi Luu in a part of the city known as Da Kao (or Da Cao). To get there, go to 20 Đ Dien Bien Phu and walk half a block northwestward.

Dai Giac Pagoda This Vietnamese Buddhist pagoda is built in a style characteristic of pagodas constructed during the 1960s. In the courtyard, under the unfinished 10-level, red-pink tower inlaid with porcelain shards, is an artificial cave made of volcanic rocks in which there is a gilded statue of the Goddess of Mercy. In the main sanctuary, the 2.5m gilt Buddha has a green neon halo, while below, a smaller white reclining Buddha (in a glass case) has a blue neon halo. Dai Giac Pagoda is at 112 Đ Nguyen Van Troi, 1.5km towards the city centre from the gate to the airport.

Vinh Nghiem Pagoda Vinh Nghiem Pagoda, inaugurated in 1971, is noteworthy for its vast sanctuary and eight-storey tower each level of which contains a statue of the Buddha. It was built with help from the Japan-Vietnam Friendship Association which explains the presence of Japanese elements in its architecture. At the base of the tower (which is open only on holidays) is a shop selling Buddhist ritual objects. Behind the sanctuary is a three-storey tower which serves as a repository for carefully labelled ceramic urns containing the ashes of peopl who have been cremated. The pagoda is just off Đ Nguyen Van Troi in District 3 and is open 7.30 to 11.30 am and 2 to 6 pm daily.

Le Van Duyet Temple This temple is dedicated to Marshal Le Van Duyet (pronounced 'Zyet'; 1763–1831), who is buried here with his wife. The marshal was a South Vietnam general and viceroy who helped put down the Tay Son Rebellion and reunify Vietnam. When the Nguyen Dynasty came to power in 1802, he was elevated by Emperor Gia Long to the rank of marshal. Le Van Duyet fell into disfavour with Gia Long's successor, Minh Mang, who tried him posthumously and desecrated his grave. Emperor Thieu Tri, who succeeded Minh Mang, restored the tomb, thus fulfilling a prophesy of its destruction and restoration. Le Van Duyet was considered a national hero in the South before 1975, but is disliked by the Communists because of his involvement in the expansion of French influence.

The temple itself was renovated in 1937 and has a distinctly modern feel to it, though since 1975 the government has done little to keep it from becoming dilapidated. Among the items on display are a portrait of Le Van Duyet, some of his personal effects (including European-style crystal goblets) and other antiques. There are two wonderful life-size horses on either side of the entrance to the third and last chamber, which is kept locked.

During celebrations of Tet and the 30th day of the seventh lunar month (the anniversary of Le Van Duyet's death), the tomb is thronged with pilgrims. Vietnamese used to come here to take oaths of good faith if they could not afford the services of a court of justice. The tropical fish are on sale to visitors. The caged birds are bought by pilgrims and freed to earn merit. The birds are often recaptured (and liberated again).

Tran Hung Dao Temple This small temple is dedicated to Tran Hung Dao, a national hero who in 1287 vanquished an invasion force, said to have numbered 300,000 men, which had been dispatched by the Mongol emperor Kublai Khan. The temple is at 36 Đ Vo Thi Sau, a block north-east of the telecommunications dishes that are between Đ Dien Bien Phu and Đ Vo Thi Sau.

The public park between the antenna dishes and ĐL Hai Ba Trung was built in 1983 on the site of the **Massiges Cemetery**, burial place of French soldiers and settlers. The remains of French military personnel were exhumed and repatriated to France. The tomb of the 18th-century French missionary and diplomat Pigneau de Béhaine, Bishop of Adran, which was completely destroyed after reunification, was also here.

The temple is open 6 to 11 am and 2 to 6 pm Monday to Friday.

Cho Quan Church Built by the French about 100 years ago, Cho Quan Church is one of the largest churches in Saigon. It's the only church we've seen in the city where the figure of Jesus on the altar has a neon halo. The view from the belfry is worth the steep climb. The church is at 133 Đ Tran Binh Trong (between ĐL Tran Hung Dao and Đ Nguyen Trai). It's open 4 to 7 am and 3 to 6 pm Monday to Saturday, and 4 to 9 am and 1.30 to 6 pm Sunday. Sunday masses are held at 5, 6.30 and 8.30 am, and 4.30 and 6 pm.

Central Saigon

Notre Dame Cathedral Built between 1877 and 1883, Notre Dame Cathedral is set in the heart of Saigon's government quarter. The cathedral is on Đ Han Thuyen, facing Đ Dong Khoi. It has a neo-Romanesque form and two 40m-high square towers, tipped with iron spires, that dominate the city's skyline. In front of the cathedral (in the centre of the square bounded by the main post office) is a statue of the Virgin Mary. If the front gates are locked try the door on the side of the building that faces Reunification Palace.

Unusually, this cathedral has no stained-glass windows. The glass was a casualty of fighting during WWII. A number of foreign travellers worship here and the priests are allowed to add a short sermon in French or English to their longer presentations in Vietnamese. The 9.30 am Sunday mass might be the best one for tourists to attend.

CENTRAL SAIGON

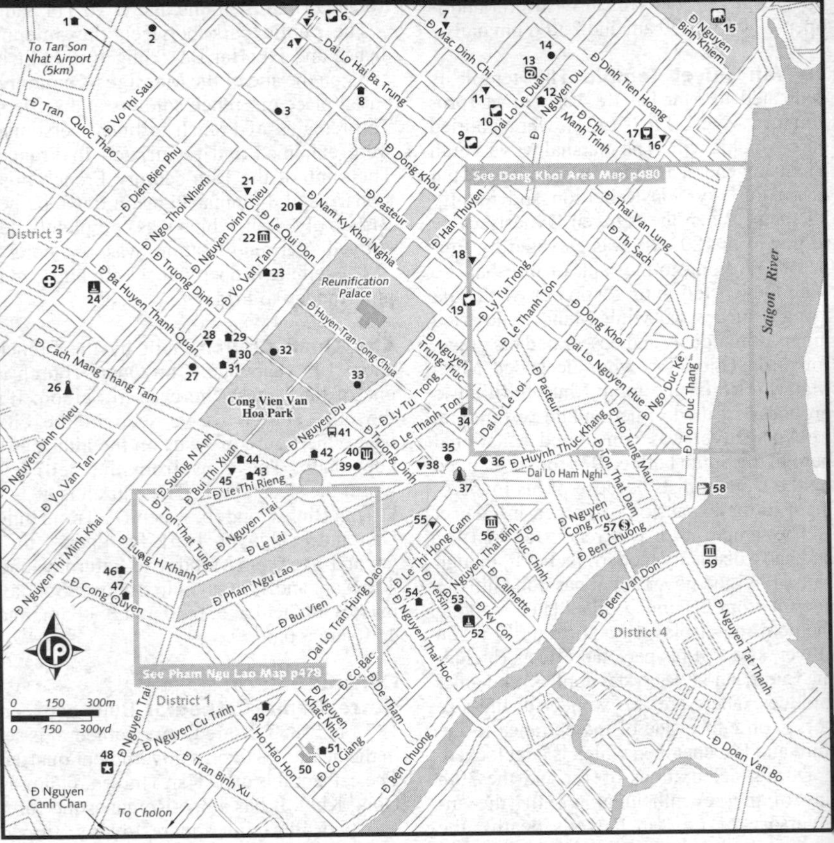

Xa Loi Pagoda Xa Loi Vietnamese Buddhist Pagoda, built in 1956, is famed as the repository of a sacred relic of the Buddha. In August 1963, truckloads of armed men under the command of President Ngo Dinh Diem's brother, Ngo Dinh Nhu, attacked Xa Loi Pagoda, which had become a centre of opposition to the Diem government. The pagoda was ransacked and 400 monks and nuns, including the country's 80-year-old Buddhist patriarch, were arrested. This raid and others elsewhere helped solidify opposition among Buddhists to the Diem regime, a crucial factor in the US decision to support the coup against Diem. This pagoda was also the site of several self-immolations by monks protesting against the Diem regime and the American War.

Women enter the main hall of Xa Lo Pagoda by the staircase on the right as yo come in the gate; men use the stairs on th left. The walls of the sanctuary are adorne with paintings depicting the Buddha's life

Xa Loi Pagoda is in District 3 at 89 Đ B Huyen Thanh Quan, near Đ Dien Bien Ph It is open 7 to 11 am and 2 to 5 pm daily. monk preaches every Sunday from 8 to 1 am. On days of the full moon and ne

CENTRAL SAIGON

PLACES TO STAY
1 Saigon Lodge Hotel
8 Que Huong (Liberty) Hotel
12 Hanoi Sofitel Plaza Saigon
20 Victory Hotel
23 International Hotel
29 Bao Yen Hotel
30 Chancery Saigon Hotel
31 Saigon Star Hotel
34 Tan Loc Hotel
42 Hoang Gia Hotel
43 Oriole Hotel
44 Rang Dong Hotel
46 Empress Hotel
47 Hoang Yen Mini-Hotel
49 Metropole Hotel
50 Guesthouse District
51 Miss Loi's Guesthouse
54 Hanoi Hotel

PLACES TO EAT
4 Tib Cafe
5 L'Etoile Restaurant
7 Hoa Vien Restaurant
11 Ciao Cafe
16 The Sushi Bar
18 La Bibliotheque
21 ABC Restaurant
28 Tandoor Indian Restaurant
38 Bavaria Restaurant
45 Annie's Pizza
55 Tin Nghia Vegetarian Restaurant

OTHER
2 Pasteur Institute
3 Ho Chi Minh City Association of Fine Arts
6 Cambodian Consulate
9 French Consulate
10 US Consulate
13 Tin Cafe; Viet My Bookshop
14 The Home Zone; Vidotour
15 Zoo & Botanical Garden
17 No 5 Ly Tu Trong
19 Lao Consulate
22 War Remnants Museum
25 Dien Bien Phu Hospital
26 Thich Quang Duc Memorial
27 Vinh Loi Gallery
32 Worker's Club
33 Conservatory of Music
35 Ben Thanh Market
36 Emergency Centre
37 Tran Nguyen Han Statue
39 Bicycle Shops
41 Bus Stop (to Cambodia)
48 Immigration Police Office
53 Dan Sinh Market
56 Fine Arts Museum; Blue Space Gallery
57 Vietcombank
58 Ferries across Saigon River & to Mekong Delta
59 Ho Chi Minh Museum

PLACES OF WORSHIP
24 Xa Loi Pagoda
40 Mariamman Hindu Temple
52 Phung Son Tu Pagoda

moon, special prayers are held from 7 to 9 am and 7 to 8 pm.

Phung Son Tu Pagoda Phung Son Tu Pagoda, built by the Fujian Congregation in the mid-1940s, is more typical of Saigon's Chinese pagodas. The interior is often hung with huge incense spirals that burn for hours. Worshippers include both ethnic-Chinese and ethnic-Vietnamese. Phung Son Tu is dedicated to Ong Bon, Guardian Spirit of Happiness and Virtue, whose statue is behind the main altar in the sanctuary. On the right-hand side of the main hall is the multi-armed Buddhist Goddess of Mercy. This pagoda is only 1km from central Saigon at 338 Đ Yersin.

Mariamman Hindu Temple This is the only Hindu temple still in use in Saigon, and is a little piece of southern India in the centre of Saigon. Though there are only 50 to 60 Hindus in Saigon – all of them Tamils – this temple, known in Vietnamese as Chua Ba Mariamman, is also considered sacred by many ethnic-Vietnamese and ethnic-Chinese. Indeed, it is reputed to have miraculous powers. The temple was built at the end of the 19th century and dedicated to the Hindu goddess Mariamman.

The lion to the left of the entrance used to be carried around Saigon in a street procession every autumn. In the shrine in the middle of the temple is Mariamman, flanked by her guardians – Maduraiveeran (to her left) and Pechiamman (to her right). In front of the figure of Mariamman are two *lingas* (phallic symbols). Favourite offerings placed nearby often include joss sticks, jasmine, lilies and gladioli. The wooden stairs, on the left as you enter the building, lead to the roof, where you'll find two colourful towers covered with innumerable figures of lions, goddesses and guardians.

After reunification, the government took over the temple and turned part of it into a factory for joss sticks. Another section was occupied by a company producing seafood for export – the seafood was dried in the sun on the roof. The whole temple is to be returned to the local Hindu community.

Mariamman Temple is only three blocks west of Ben Thanh Market, at 45 Đ Truong Dinh. It is open 7 am to 7 pm daily. Take off your shoes before stepping onto the slightly raised platform.

Saigon Central Mosque Built by South Indian Muslims in 1935 on the site of an earlier mosque, the Saigon Central Mosque is an immaculately clean and well-kept island of calm in the middle of the bustling Dong Khoi area. In front of the sparkling white and blue structure at 66 Đ Dong Du, with its four nonfunctional minarets, is a pool for ritual ablutions required by Islamic law before prayers. Take off your shoes before entering the sanctuary.

The simplicity of the mosque is in marked contrast to the exuberance of Chinese temple decorations and the rows of figures, facing elaborate ritual objects, in Buddhist pagodas. Islamic law strictly forbids using human or animal figures for decoration.

Only half a dozen Indian Muslims remain in Saigon; most of the community fled in 1975. As a result, prayers – held five times a day – are sparsely attended except on Friday, when several dozen worshippers (mainly non-Indian Muslims) are present.

There are 12 other mosques serving the 5000 or so Muslims in Saigon.

Cholon

An Quang Pagoda An Quang Pagoda gained some notoriety during the American War as the home of Thich Tri Quang, a powerful monk who led protests against the South Vietnamese government in 1963 and 1966. When the war ended, you would have expected the Communists to be grateful. Instead, he was placed under house arrest and later thrown into solitary confinement for 16 months. Thich Tri Quang was eventually released and is said to still be living at An Quang Pagoda.

An Quang Pagoda is on Đ Su Van Hanh, near the intersection with Đ Ba Hat, in District 10.

Tam Son Hoi Quan Pagoda This pagoda, known to the Vietnamese as Chua Ba Chua, was built by the Fujian Congregation in the 19th century and retains most of its original rich ornamentation. The pagoda is dedicated to Me Sanh, the Goddess of Fertility. Both men and women – but more of the latter – come here to pray for children.

To the right of the covered courtyard is the deified general Quan Cong with his long black beard; on either side he is flanked by two guardians, the mandarin general Chau Xuong on the left (holding a weapon) and the administrative mandarin Quan Binh on the right. Next to Chau Xuong is Quan Cong's sacred red horse.

Behind the main altar (directly across the courtyard from the entrance) is Thien Hau, the Goddess of the Sea, who protects fisherfolk and sailors. To the right is an ornate case in which Me Sanh, in white, sits surrounded by her daughters. In the case to the left of Thien Hau is Ong Bon. In front of Thien Hau is Quan The Am Bo Tat, enclosed in glass.

Across the courtyard from Quan Cong is a small room containing ossuary jars and memorials in which the dead are represented by their photographs. Next to this chamber is a small room containing the papier-mache head of a dragon of the type used by the Fujian Congregation for dragon dancing.

Tam Son Hoi Quan Pagoda is at 118 Đ Trieu Quang Phuc, close to 370 ĐL Tran Hung Dao.

Thien Hau Pagoda Thien Hau Pagoda (also known as Ba Mieu, Pho Mieu and Chua Ba) was built by the Cantonese Congregation in the early 19th century. The pagoda, one of the most active in Cholon, is dedicated to Thien Hau (also known as Tuc Goi La Ba). It is said that Thien Hau can travel over the oceans on a mat and ride the clouds to wherever she pleases. Her mobility allows her to save people in trouble on the high seas.

Thien Hau is very popular in Hong Kong (where she's called Tin Hau) and in Taiwan (where her name is Matsu). This might explain why Thien Hau Pagoda is included on so many tour group agendas.

Though there are guardians to either side of the entrance, it is said that the real protectors of the pagoda are the two land turtles who live here. There are intricate ceramic friezes above the roof line of the interior courtyard. Near the huge braziers are two miniature wooden structures in which a small figure of Thien Hau is paraded around on the 23rd day of the third lunar month. On the main dais are three figures of Thien Hau, one behind the other, all flanked by two servants or guardians. To the left of the dais is a bed for Thien Hau. To the right is a scale-model boat and on the far right is the Goddess Long Mau, Protector of Mothers and Newborns.

Thien Hau Pagoda is at 710 Đ Nguyen Trai and is open from 6 am to 5.30 pm.

Nghia An Hoi Quan Pagoda Nghia An Hoi Quan Pagoda, built by the Chaozhou Chinese Congregation, is noteworthy for its gilded woodwork. There is a carved wooden boat over the entrance and, inside to the left of the doorway, is an enormous representation of Quan Cong's red horse with its groom. To the right of the entrance is an elaborate altar in which a bearded Ong Bon stands holding a stick. Behind the main altar are three glass cases. In the centre is Quan Cong and to either side are his assistants, Chau Xuong (on the left) and Quan Binh (on the right). To the right of Quan Binh is an especially elaborate case holding Thien Hau.

Nghia An Hoi Quan Pagoda is at 678 Đ Nguyen Trai (not far from Thien Hau Pagoda) and is open from 4 am to 6 pm.

Cholon Mosque The clean lines and lack of ornamentation of the Cholon Mosque are in stark contrast to nearby Chinese and Vietnamese Buddhist pagodas. In the courtyard is a pool for ritual ablutions. Note the tile *mihrab* (the niche in the wall indicating the direction of prayer, which is towards Mecca). The mosque was built by Tamil Muslims in 1932. Since 1975, it has served the Malaysian and Indonesian Muslim communities.

Cholon Mosque is at 641 Đ Nguyen Trai and is open all day Friday and at prayer times on other days.

Quan Am Pagoda Quan Am Pagoda was founded in 1816 by the Fujian Congregation. The temple is named for Quan The Am Bo Tat, the Goddess of Mercy.

This is the most active pagoda in Cholon and the Chinese influence is obvious. The roof is decorated with fantastic scenes, rendered in ceramic, from traditional Chinese plays and stories. The tableaux include ships, houses, people and several ferocious dragons. The front doors are decorated with very old gold and lacquer panels. On the walls of the porch are murals in slight relief picturing scenes of China from the time of Quan Cong. There are elaborate woodcarvings on roof supports above the porch.

Behind the main altar is A Pho, the Holy Mother Celestial Empress, gilded and in rich raiment. In front of her, in a glass case, are three painted statues of Thich Ca Buddha, a standing gold Quan The Am Bo Tat, a seated laughing Ameda and, to the far left, a gold figure of Dia Tang Vuong Bo Tat (King of Hell).

In the courtyard behind the main sanctuary, in the pink-tile altar, is another figure of A Pho. Quan The Am Bo Tat, dressed in white embroidered robes, stands nearby. To the left of the altar is her richly ornamented bed. To the right of the altar is Quan Cong, flanked by his guardians. To the far right, in front of another pink altar, is the black-faced judge Bao Cong.

Quan Am Pagoda is at 12 Đ Lao Tu, one block off Đ Chau Van Liem.

Phuoc An Hoi Quan Pagoda Phuoc An Hoi Quan Pagoda, built in 1902 by the Fujian Congregation, is one of the most beautifully ornamented pagodas in Saigon. Of special interest are the many small porcelain figures, the elaborate brass ritual objects and the fine woodcarvings on the altars, walls, columns and hanging lanterns. From outside the building you can see the ceramic scenes, each containing innumerable small figurines, which decorate the roof.

To the left of the entrance is a life-size figure of the sacred horse of Quan Cong. Before leaving on a journey, people make offerings to the horse. They then stroke the horse's mane and ring the bell around its neck. Behind the main altar, with its stone

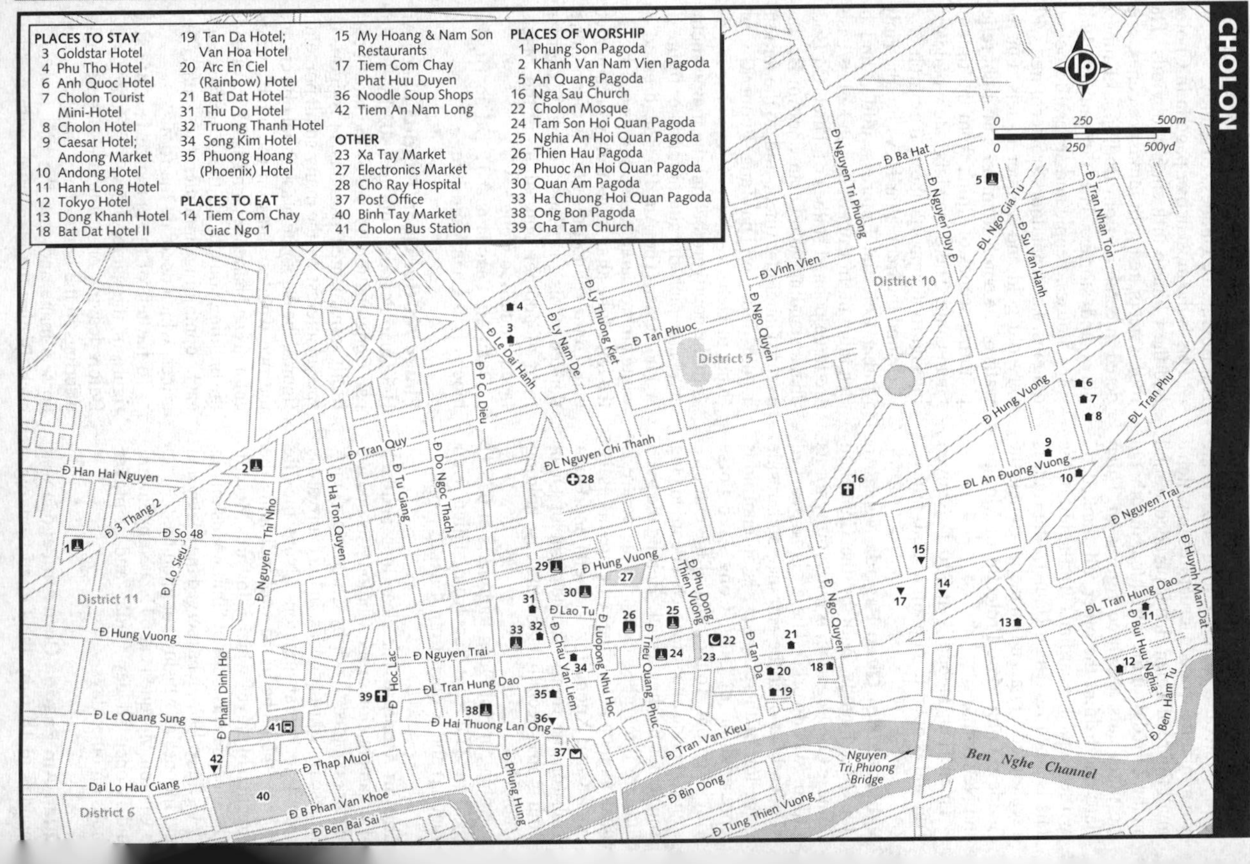
CHOLON
PLACES TO STAY
3 Goldstar Hotel
4 Phu Tho Hotel
6 Anh Quoc Hotel
7 Cholon Tourist Mini-Hotel
8 Cholon Hotel
9 Caesar Hotel; Andong Market
10 Andong Hotel
11 Hanh Long Hotel
12 Tokyo Hotel
13 Dong Khanh Hotel
18 Bat Dat Hotel II
19 Tan Da Hotel; Van Hoa Hotel
20 Arc En Ciel (Rainbow) Hotel
21 Bat Dat Hotel
31 Thu Do Hotel
32 Truong Thanh Hotel
34 Song Kim Hotel
35 Phuong Hoang (Phoenix) Hotel
PLACES TO EAT
14 Tiem Com Chay Giac Ngo 1
15 My Hoang & Nam Son Restaurants
17 Tiem Com Chay Phat Huu Duyen
36 Noodle Soup Shops
42 Tiem An Nam Long
OTHER
23 Xa Tay Market
27 Electronics Market
28 Cho Ray Hospital
37 Post Office
40 Binh Tay Market
41 Cholon Bus Station
PLACES OF WORSHIP
1 Phung Son Pagoda
2 Khanh Van Nam Vien Pagoda
5 An Quang Pagoda
16 Nga Sau Church
22 Cholon Mosque
24 Tam Son Hoi Quan Pagoda
25 Nghia An Hoi Quan Pagoda
26 Thien Hau Pagoda
29 Phuoc An Hoi Quan Pagoda
30 Quan Am Pagoda
33 Ha Chuong Hoi Quan Pagoda
38 Ong Bon Pagoda
39 Cha Tam Church
0 250 500m
0 250 500yd
District 5
District 6
District 10
District 11
Ben Nghe Channel
Nguyen Tri Phuong Bridge
Đ Ba Hat
Đ Nguyen Tri Phuong
Đ Nguyen Duy Đ
ĐL Ngo Gia Tu
Đ Su Van Hanh
Đ Tran Nhan Ton
Đ Vinh Vien
Đ Ngo Quyen
Đ Tan Phuoc
Đ Ly Thuong Kiet
Đ Ly Nam De
Đ Le Dai Hanh
Đ P Co Dieu
Đ Hung Vuong
ĐL Tran Phu
ĐL An Duong Vuong
Đ Nguyen Trai
Đ Huynh Man Dat
ĐL Tran Hung Dao
Đ Bui Huu Nghia
Đ Ben Ham Tu
ĐL Nguyen Chi Thanh
Đ Tran Quy
Đ Do Ngoc Thach
Đ Tu Giang
Đ Ha Ton Quyen
Đ Han Hai Nguyen
Đ 3 Thang 2
Đ So 48
Đ Lo Sieu
Đ Nguyen Thi Nho
Đ Lao Tu
Đ Chau Van Liem
Đ Luopong Nhu Hoc
Đ Trieu Quang Phuc
Đ Phu Dong Thien Vuong
Đ Tan Da
Đ Hoc Lac
Đ Hai Thuong Lan Ong
Đ Pham Dinh Ho
Đ Le Quang Sung
Đ Thap Muoi
Dai Lo Hau Giang
Đ B Phan Van Khoe
Đ Ben Bai Sai
Đ Phung Hung
Đ Tran Van Kieu
Đ Bin Dong
Đ Tung Thien Vuong

and brass incense braziers, is Quan Cong, to whom the pagoda is dedicated. Behind the altar to the left is Ong Bon and two servants. The altar to the right is occupied by representations of Buddhist (rather than Taoist) personages. In the glass case are a plaster Thich Ca Buddha and two figures of the Goddess of Mercy, one made of porcelain and the other cast in brass.

Phuoc An Hoi Quan Pagoda is at 184 Đ Hung Vuong, near the intersection with Đ Thuan Kieu.

Ong Bon Pagoda Ong Bon Pagoda (also known as Chua Ong Bon and Nhi Phu Hoi Quan) was built by the Fujian Congregation and is dedicated to Ong Bon, Guardian Spirit of Happiness and Virtue. The wooden altar is intricately carved and gilded.

As you enter the pagoda, there is a room to the right of the open-air courtyard. In it, behind the table, is a figure of Quan The Am Bo Tat in a glass case. Above the case is the head of a Thich Ca Buddha.

Directly across the courtyard from the pagoda entrance, against the wall, is Ong Bon, to whom people come to pray for general happiness and relief from financial difficulties. He faces a fine, carved wooden altar. On the walls of this chamber are rather indistinct murals of five tigers (to the left) and two dragons (to the right).

In the area on the other side of the wall with the mural of the dragons is a furnace for burning paper representations of the wealth people wish to bestow upon deceased family members. Diagonally opposite is Quan Cong flanked by his guardians Chau Xuong (to his right) and Quan Binh (to his left).

Ong Bon Pagoda is at 264 DL Hai Thuong Lai Ong, which runs parallel to ĐL Tran Hung Dao. It's open 5 am to 5 pm.

Ha Chuong Hoi Quan Pagoda This typical Fujian pagoda is dedicated to Thien Hau, who was born in Fujian. The four carved stone pillars, wrapped in painted dragons, were made in China and brought to Vietnam by boat. There are interesting murals to either side of the main altar. Note the ceramic relief scenes on the roof.

The pagoda becomes extremely active during the Lantern Festival, a Chinese holiday held on the 15th day of the first lunar month (the first full moon of the new lunar year).

Ha Chuong Hoi Quan Pagoda at 802 Đ Nguyen Trai.

Cha Tam Church It is in Cha Tam Church that President Ngo Dinh Diem and his brother Ngo Dinh Nhu took refuge on 2 November 1963 after fleeing the Presidential Palace during a coup attempt. When their efforts to contact loyal military officers (of whom there were almost none) failed, Diem and Nhu agreed to surrender unconditionally and revealed where they were hiding.

The coup leaders sent an M-113 armoured personnel carrier to the church and the two were taken into custody. But before the vehicle reached central Saigon, the soldiers had killed Diem and Nhu by shooting them at point-blank range and then repeatedly stabbing their bodies.

When news of the deaths was broadcast on radio, Saigon exploded into rejoicing. Portraits of the two were torn up and political prisoners, many of whom had been tortured, were set free. The city's nightclubs, closed because of the Ngos' conservative Catholic beliefs, reopened. Three weeks later, US president John F Kennedy was assassinated. As Kennedy's administration had supported the coup against Diem, some conspiracy theorists have speculated that he was killed by Diem's family in retaliation.

Cha Tam Church, built around the turn of the 19th century, is an attractive white and pastel-yellow structure. The statue in the tower is of François Xavier Tam Assou (1855–1934), a Chinese-born vicar apostolic (delegate of the pope) of Saigon. Today, the church has a very active congregation of 3000 ethnic-Vietnamese and 2000 ethnic-Chinese.

Vietnamese-language Masses are held Monday to Saturday at 5.30 am and on Sunday at 5.30 and 8.30 am and 3.45 pm. Masses in Chinese are held Monday to Saturday at 5.30 pm and on Sunday at 7 am and 5 pm. Cha Tam Church is at 25 Đ Hoc Lac, at the western end of ĐL Tran Hung Dao.

Khanh Van Nam Vien Pagoda Built between 1939 and 1942 by the Cantonese Congregation, Khanh Van Nam Vien Pagoda is said to be the only Taoist pagoda in Vietnam. The number of true Taoists in Saigon is said to number only 4000, though most Chinese practice a mixture of Taoism and Buddhism.

A few metres from the door is a statue of Hoang Linh Quan, chief guardian of the pagoda. There is a Yin and Yang symbol on the platform on which the incense braziers sit. Behind the main altar are four figures: Quan Cong (on the right) and Lu Tung Pan (on the left) represent Taoism; between them is Van Xuong representing Confucianism; and behind Van Xuong is Quan The Am Bo Tat.

In front of these figures is a glass case containing seven gods and one goddess, all of which are made of porcelain. In the altars to either side of the four figures are Hoa De (on the left), a famous doctor during the Han Dynasty, and Huynh Dai Tien (on the right), a disciple of Laotse (Thai Thuong Lao Quan in Vietnamese).

Upstairs is a 150cm-high statue of Laotse. Behind his head is a halo consisting of a round mirror with fluorescent lighting around the edge.

Off to the left of Laotse are two stone plaques with instructions for inhalation and exhalation exercises. A schematic drawing represents the human organs as a scene from rural China. The diaphragm, agent of inhalation, is at the bottom. The stomach is represented by a peasant ploughing with a water buffalo. The kidney is marked by four Yin and Yang symbols, the liver is shown as a grove of trees and the heart is represented by a circle with a peasant standing in it, above which is a constellation. The tall pagoda represents the throat and the broken rainbow is the mouth. At the top are mountains and a seated figure representing the brain and the imagination, respectively.

The pagoda operates a home for 30 elderly people who have no families. Each of the old folk, most of whom are women, have their own wood stove made of brick and can cook for themselves. Next door, also run by the pagoda, is a free medical clinic which offers Chinese herbal medicines and acupuncture treatments to the community. If you would like to support this worthy venture you can leave a donation with the monks.

The pagoda is open 6.30 am to 5.30 pm daily and prayers are held from 8 to 9 am. To reach the pagoda, turn off Đ Nguyen Thi Nho (which runs perpendicular to Đ Hung Vuong) between numbers 269B and 271B; the address of the pagoda is 46/5 Đ Lo Sieu.

Phung Son Pagoda Phung Son Pagoda (also known as Phung Son Tu and Chua Go) is extremely rich in statuary made of hammered copper, bronze, wood and ceramic. Some statues are gilded while others, beautifully carved, are painted. This Vietnamese Buddhist pagoda was built between 1802 and 1820 on the site of structures from the Oc-Eo (Funan) period, contemporaneous with early centuries of Christianity. The foundations of Funanese buildings have been discovered here.

Once upon a time, it was decided that Phung Son Pagoda should be moved to a different site. The pagoda's ritual objects – bells, drums, statues – were loaded onto the back of a white elephant, but the elephant slipped because of the great weight and all the precious objects fell into a nearby pond. This event was interpreted as an omen that the pagoda should remain at its original location. All the articles were retrieved except for the bell, which locals say was heard ringing whenever there was a full or new moon, until about a century ago.

The main dais, with its many levels, is dominated by a gilded A Di Da Buddha seated under a canopy flanked by long mobiles resembling human forms without heads. A Di Da is flanked by Quan The Am Bo Tat (on the left), and Dai The Chi Bo Tat (on the right). To the left of the main dais is an altar with a statue of Bodhidharma, who brought Buddhism from India to China. The statue, which is made of Chinese ceramic, has a face with Indian features.

As you walk from the main sanctuary to the room with the open-air courtyard in the middle, you come to an altar with four statues on it, including a standing bronze Thich

Ca Buddha of Thai origin. To the right is an altar with a glass case containing a statue made of sandalwood, and claimed to be Long Vuong (Dragon King), who brings rain. Around the pagoda building are a number of interesting monks' tombs.

Phung Son Pagoda is in District 11 at 1408 ĐL 3/2. Prayers are held three times a day from 4 to 5 am, 4 to 5 pm and 6 to 7 pm. The main entrances are locked most of the time because of problems with theft, but the side entrance (to the left as you approach the building) is open from 5 am to 7 pm.

PARKS

Cong Vien Van Hoa Park

Next to the old Cercle Sportif, an elite sporting club during the French period, the bench-lined walks of Cong Vien Van Hoa Park are shaded with avenues of enormous tropical trees.

This place still has an active sports club, although now you don't have to be French to visit. There are 11 tennis courts, a swimming pool and a clubhouse, all of which have a grand colonial feel about them. There are Roman-style baths with a coffee shop overlooking the colonnaded pool.

The tennis courts are available for hire at a reasonable fee. Hourly tickets are on sale for use of the pool and you can even buy a bathing costume if you don't have one. The antique dressing rooms are quaint, but there are no lockers. Other facilities include a gymnasium, table tennis, weightlifting, wrestling mats, and ballroom dancing classes.

In the morning, you can often see people here practising the art of *thai cuc quyen*, or slow-motion shadow boxing (see the 'Thai Cuc Quyen' boxed text).

Within the park is a small-scale model of Nha Trang's Cham towers.

Cong Vien Van Hoa Park is adjacent to Reunification Palace. There are entrances across from 115 Đ Nguyen Du and on Đ Nguyen Thi Minh Khai.

Ho Ky Hoa Park

Ho Ky Hoa Park, whose name means Lake and Gardens, is a children's amusement park in District 10 just off ĐL 3/2. It is behind Vietnam Quoc Tu Pagoda. There are paddleboats, rowing boats and sailboats for hire. Fishing is allowed in the lakes and a small swimming pool is open to the public for part of the year. The cafes are open year-round and there are also two arcades of Japanese video games. Within the park boundaries is a rather expensive hotel. Ho Ky Hoa Park is open 7 am to 9.30 pm daily and is crowded on Sundays.

BINH SOUP SHOP

It might seem strange to introduce a noodle soup restaurant as a sight, but there is more to this shop than just the soup. The Binh Soup Shop was the secret headquarters of the VC in Saigon. It was from here that the VC planned its attack on the US embassy and other places within Saigon during the Tet Offensive of 1968. One has to wonder how many American soldiers ate here completely unaware that the staff were all VC infiltrators.

The Binh Soup Shop (☎ 844 3775) is at 7 Đ Ly Chinh Thang, District 3. By the way, the soup isn't bad. The shop starts serving *pho* (Vietnam's 'breakfast of champions') to hungry customers at 6 am.

ARTEX SAIGON ORCHID FARM

There are a number of orchid farms (Vuon Cay Kieng) in suburban Ho Chi Minh City, with most concentrated in the Thu Duc District. Artex Saigon Orchid Farm, east of Saigon, is the largest of them all, with 50,000 plants representing 1000 varieties. It is primarily a commercial concern, but visitors are welcome to stop by to relax in the luxurious garden.

Founded in 1970 the farm makes its real profit not from flower sales, but by selling orchid plants, which take six years to mature and are thus very expensive. In addition to varieties imported from overseas, the farm has a collection of orchids native to Vietnam. Ask to see the orange-yellow Cattleya orchid variety called Richard Nixon; it has another variety named for Joseph Stalin. The nurseries are at their most beautiful just before Tet, when demand for all sorts of flowers and house plants reaches its peak. After Tet, the place is bare.

Thai Cuc Quyen

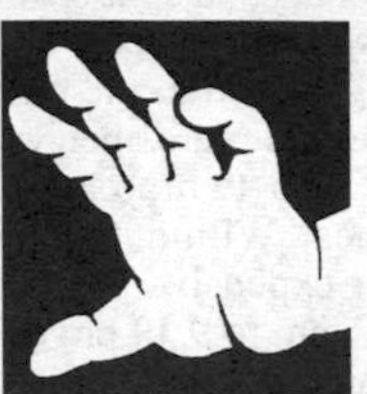

Thai cuc quyen, or slow motion shadow boxing, has in recent years become quite trendy in Western countries. It has been popular in Vietnam for centuries, but it originated in China, where it is known as *taijiquan*. It is basically a form of exercise, but is also considered to be an art and a form of martial arts related to Chinese *kung fu*. Kung fu differs from thai cuc quyen in that the former is performed at much higher speed and with the intention of doing bodily harm. Kung fu also often employs weapons. Thai cuc quyen is not a form of self-defence, but it does employ similar movements to kung fu.

Thai cuc quyen has different styles, and is very popular among old people and young women who believe it will help keep their bodies beautiful. The movements are supposed to develop the breathing muscles, promote digestion and improve muscle tone.

A modern innovation is to perform thai cuc quyen movements to the thump of disco music. Westerners find it remarkable to see a large group performing slow motion movements in the park at the crack of dawn to the steady beat of disco music supplied by a portable cassette player.

Thai cuc quyen and all manner of exercises are customarily done just as the sun rises, which means that if you want to see or participate in them, you have to get up early. In Saigon, the best place to see thai cuc quyen is at Cong Vien Van Hoa Park or the Cholon district where there is a large ethnic-Chinese population.

Artex Saigon Orchid Farm (☎ 896 6686) is 15km from Saigon in Thu Duc District, a rural part of Ho Chi Minh City, on the way to Bien Hoa. The official address is 5/81 Xa Lo Vong Dai, but this highway is better known as Xa Lo Dai Han, the 'Korean Highway', because it was built by Koreans. At Km 14 on Xa Lo Dai Han there is a two-storey police post. Turn left (if heading out of Saigon towards Bien Hoa), continue 300m and turn left again to reach the farm.

BINH QUOI TOURIST VILLAGE

Built on a small peninsula in the Saigon River, the Binh Quoi Tourist Village (Lang Du Lich Binh Quoi; ☎ 899 1831) is a slick tourist trap operated by Saigon Tourist. Backpackers are few, but upmarket tourists get carted out here by the busload and some city-weary locals also seem to like it.

The village is essentially a park featuring boat rides, water-puppet shows, a restaurant, a swimming pool, tennis courts, a camping ground, a guesthouse, bungalows and amusements for the kids. The park puts in a plug for Vietnam's ethnic minorities by staging traditional-style minority weddings accompanied by music. There are some alligators kept in an enclosure for viewing. River cruises can be fun – the smaller cruise boats have 16 seats and the larger ones have 100 seats.

Next door to the water-puppet theatre, you can make bookings for the local nightlife, including dinner cruises and shows.

Binh Quoi Bungalows *(☎ 899 1831/899 4103)* is perhaps one of the better-value places to stay here. Built on stilts above the water, the bungalows give you a taste of traditional river life in the Mekong Delta, but with air-conditioning and tennis courts. The standard price range is US$10 to US$18. It's worth asking for a room with good views of the river.

Binh Quoi Tourist Village is 8km north of central Saigon in the Binh Thanh District. The official address is 1147 Đ Xo Viet Nghe Tinh. You can get there by cyclo, motorbike or taxi. A much slower alternative is to charter a boat from the Me Linh Square area on the Saigon River.

SAIGON WATER PARK

And now for something different. The Saigon Water Park (☎ 897 0456) is a giant oasis in the suburbs of Saigon. This refreshing complex on the banks of the

Saigon River is chock-full of pools and water rides: loop-the-loop slides, a children's wading pool and even a 'wave pool'.

This Australian-built leisure land is the perfect antidote for anyone who needs to cool down from an overdose of pagodas and museums. Except for the weekend crowds, there is absolutely nothing traditionally Vietnamese about the place, right down to the real live lifeguards whistling out their *Baywatch* fantasies. Anyone with kids and a half-day to spare will quickly come to appreciate this wet and wonderful playground on a sweltering Saigon day. Bring a waterproof camera. There is also a restaurant here with fine views over the river.

The park is open 9 am to 5 pm Monday to Friday, 9 am to 8 pm Saturday and 8 am to 8 pm on Sunday and public holidays. The best time to avoid the crowds is between 11 am and 2 pm on weekdays (most Vietnamese stay out of the midday sun) – but this is also the best time of day to get sunburnt.

The all-you-can-splash and slide entry fee is 60,000d (US$4.30), or 35,000d for a 'swim-only' ticket (access to swimming pools, but not water slides). Children (defined as people under 1.1m in height) pay 35,000d (US$2.50).

Saigon Water Park is on Đ Kha Van Can, in the Thu Duc District (near Go Dua Bridge). It's too far for cyclos, but you can take a meter taxi for about US$4, or catch a shuttle bus (once every half-hour) from Ben Thanh Market for US$0.40.

Since people began flocking to Saigon Water Park, others have followed suit. Now there are several other water parks, including Vietnam Water World (near Saigon Water Park), Sharks (in Cholon) and another in Dam Sen Park.

ACTIVITIES

Swimming

If you don't make it to Saigon Water Park or one of its recent clones, there are several fine swimming pools at plush tourist hotels. You needn't stay at these hotels to use the facilities, but you must pay an admission fee of US$5 to US$10 per day. Hotels offering access to their pools include the Embassy (not so good), Omni, Equatorial, Metropole, Palace and Rex. About the only major hotel which does not offer public access to its pool is the New World.

There are a number of public pools where Vietnamese go and some of the newer ones are in very good condition. These pools charge by the hour and this works out to be very cheap if you're staying only a short time. One such place is the Olympic-sized Lam Son Pool (☎ 358028), 342 Đ Tran Binh Trong, District 5 – the weekday charge is around US$0.50 per hour, US$1 on weekends. For US$1.50 per hour you can visit the pool at the Workers' Club, 55B Đ Nguyen Thi Minh Khai, District 3.

The International Club (☎ 865 7695), 285B Đ Cach Mang Thang Tam, District 10, also has an excellent outdoor swimming pool, as well as sauna and steam rooms, an exercise gym and beauty salon inside. The bizarre interior of the place resembles an old hotel, but it is very popular with expats and attracts a good number of Asian businessmen looking to wind down from the stresses of corporate Vietnam. Entry to the pool costs US$1.50 weekdays and US$2.25 on weekends. There is also a massage service, and a US$9 ticket entitles you to a 45-minute rubdown and all-day use of the club's facilities. The management here is serious about keeping its massage legitimate: the rules posted in the massage rooms state clearly that 'all club employees, male and female, are required to wear underwear at all times'!

Massage

Perhaps the best rub-down in town is at the Vietnamese Traditional Medicine Institute (☎ 839 6697), 185 Đ Cong Quyen, District 1, very close to the Pham Ngu Lao area. Here you can enjoy a no-nonsense massage performed by well-trained blind masseuses. The cost is just US$2 per hour (air-con comfort will set you back an extra dollar). There is also a sauna room available for US$1.50 per hour. Walk-in service is from 9 am to 8 pm daily.

Most upmarket hotels offer some kind of massage service (some more legitimate than others).

Bowling

The Saigon Superbowl (☎ 885 0188, fax 845 8119) is near the airport at A43 Đ Truong Son, Tan Binh District. There are 32 lanes here, as well as a video game arcade and shops. Bowling costs US$3 (US$4 after 5 pm). Shoe rental is US$0.50.

The Bowling Centre (☎ 864 3784) is in the International Club at 285B Đ Cach Mang Thang Tam, District 10. There are 12 lanes here and 65 video game machines. It's open 10 am to midnight daily.

Golf

The Vietnam Golf and Country Club (Cau Lac Bo Golf Quoc Te Viet Nam) is another cash cow of Saigon Tourist. The course was the first in Vietnam to provide night golfing under floodlights. The club (☎ 832 2084, fax 832 2083), 40–42 Đ Nguyen Trai, Thu Duc District, is in Lam Vien Park, about 15km east of central Saigon. Membership starts at US$5000 to US$60,000, but paying visitors are welcome. The driving range costs US$10, or you can play a full round for US$50. Other facilities include tennis courts and a swimming pool.

The Rach Chiec Driving Range (☎ 896 0756) is a good place to practice your swing. A one-month membership costs US$70 and gets progressively cheaper the longer you join for. Clubs (US$4 to US$6) and shoes (US$6) are available to rent, and an instructor can be hired for US$12 per hour. The range is open 6 am to 10 pm daily. It's in An Phu Village, a 20-minute drive north along Highway 1 from central Saigon.

Hash House Harriers

This organisation meets once a week for a jogging session followed by a drinking session. The times and meeting places change, as do the people organising it. Look for the latest announcements in expat pubs around town, like Underground and No 5 Ly Tu Trong or in local magazines like *The Guide* and *Time Out*.

LANGUAGE COURSES

The vast majority of foreign-language students enrol at the General University of Ho Chi Minh City (Truong Dai Hoc Tong Hop), 12 Đ Binh Hoang, District 5. It's near the south-west corner of ĐL Nguyen Van Cu and ĐL Tran Phu.

PLACES TO STAY – BUDGET

Different categories of travellers have staked out their own turf in Saigon. Budget travellers tend to congregate around the Pham Ngu Lao area at the western end of District 1; this has by far the widest availability of cheap accommodation. Travellers with a little more cash to spare prefer the more upmarket hotels concentrated around Đ Dong Khoi, on the eastern side of District 1. French travellers seem to have an affinity for District 3. Cholon attracts plenty of Hong Kongers and Taiwanese.

Touts from private hotels hang around the airport looking for business. Taxi drivers will often shove hotel name cards into your hands. If the hotels weren't paying sizable commissions, the touts wouldn't bother.

Another problem is touts in the Pham Ngu Lao area, who watch for tourists and then hurry ahead and dive into the hotel to ask for a commission. If they don't get it, they can create a big argument, causing considerable hassle for both the tourists and hotel owners.

If you don't really know where you want to stay, but you're limited by your budget, it's not a bad idea to take a meter taxi into Pham Ngu Lao and proceed on foot. If you don't want to lug your bags around (which also makes you a prime target for cyclo drivers and touts) consider dropping your gear at one of the travellers cafes and setting out on foot. Most won't mind keeping an eye on it for you and they'll be happy to show you the tour programs they have on offer.

Another alternative is to email or fax ahead for reservations – most hotels will fetch you at the airport for around US$5, or if you're staying a few nights usually for free. You lose any potential walk-in negotiating power, but at least it's hassle-free.

Pham Ngu Lao Area

Đ Pham Ngu Lao, Đ De Tham and Đ Bui Vien form the half-rectangle which is the heart of the budget-traveller haven. These streets and the adjoining alleys, collectively known as 'Pham Ngu Lao', contain a treasure trove of cheap accommodation and cafes catering to the bottom end of the market. At last count there were close to 100 places to stay in the area.

Unfortunately, a major construction project is under way to redevelop the northern side of Đ Pham Ngu Lao into the enormous Saigon Commercial Centre. It is estimated that construction will take about four years and will generate a considerable amount of dust and noise.

The low-budget ***Bich Thuy Guesthouse*** *(☎ 836 9953, 5 Đ Do Quang Doa)*, also known as *Friendly Guesthouse*, is run by friendly Mr Phuc, a veteran tourist driver. It's a very basic, eight-room place. Dorm beds cost US$3, or US$5 for a private fan room. There is one room with air-con for US$7. Breakfast is complimentary.

The first place in this neighbourhood to offer dormitory accommodation was ***Tan Thanh Thanh Hotel*** *(☎ 837 3595, fax 836 7027, ⓔ tanthanhthanh@hcm.fpt.vn, 205 Đ Pham Ngu Lao)*. Dorm beds start at US$3 and private rooms range from US$5 to US$10. Guests are served a complimentary breakfast.

Warm-hearted Madam Cuc's ***Hotel 64*** *(☎ 836 5073, fax 836 0658, 64 Đ Bui Vien)* is excellent. One reader called this place the 'Hilton of backpacker guesthouses'. The same folks run the excellent ***Hotel 127*** (☎ 836 8761, fax 836 0658, ⓔ *guesthouse127@bdvn.vnd.net 127 Đ Cong Quyen)*. Both places have been recently renovated and provide a welcoming reception. Spotless rooms cost US$8 to US$20.

A couple of doors down from Hotel 64, ***Hotel 70*** *(☎ 836 5649, fax 836 9569, 70 Đ Bui Vien)* also keeps a high standard and charges around the same prices. The nearby ***Minh Chau Guesthouse*** *(☎/fax 836 7588, ⓔ minhchauhotel@hcm.vnn.vn, 75 Đ Bui Vien)* is slightly lower key, and offers email service in the lobby.

Travellers have good things to say about ***Mai Phai Hotel*** *(☎ 836 5868, fax 837 1575, ⓔ maiphaihotel@saigonnet.vn, 209 Đ Pham Ngu Lao)*. It's a snappy-looking mini-hotel where rooms cost US$12 to US$30 with all the trimmings (air-con, IDD phones, satellite TV). It also has a lift.

Just next door is the pleasant and friendly ***Hotel 211*** *(☎ 836 7353, fax 836 1883, 211 Đ Pham Ngu Lao)*. Dorm beds are US$3, while rooms cost US$7/8 with fan or US$10/12 with air-con. All rooms have private bath with hot water.

Quyen Thanh Hotel *(☎ 836 8570, fax 836 9946, 212 Đ De Tham)* has air-con rooms from US$15 and larger fully equipped rooms for US$20. There is an excellent souvenir shop on the ground floor.

Other good places on Đ De Tham include ***Hotel 265*** *(☎ 836 1883, 265 Đ De Tham)*, with dorm beds for US$3 and air-con rooms from US$10/12. Practically next door is the equally good ***Le Le 2*** *(☎ 836 8585, fax 836 8787)* with air-con comfort for US$8 to US$15. Ditto for the ***Peace Hotel*** *(☎ 837 2025, fax 836 8824, 272 Đ De Tham)* across the street.

Dong A-1 Hotel *(☎ 836 8614, fax 836 8753, ⓔ dahotel@saigonnet.vn, 131 Đ Bui Vien)* is a good-looking place. Air-con rooms equipped with satellite TV range from US$8 to US$20.

Nhat Thai Hotel *(☎ 836 0184, 373/10 Đ Pham Ngu Lao)* is an older place down a tiny alley behind the Thai Binh Market. Rooms with air-con (some with balconies) are US$10. There is a similar standard a few doors down at the ***Coco Loco Guesthouse*** *(☎ 837 2647, 373/2 Pham Ngu Lao)*.

Just one block north-west of Thai Binh Market is ***Huong Yen Mini-Hotel*** *(☎ 839 1348, fax 829 8540, 83A Đ Bui Thi Xuan)*, where the owner speaks French. Singles/twins are US$16/21 and the tariff includes breakfast.

About 100m south of Đ Pham Ngu Lao is Đ Bui Vien, which is rapidly being transformed into a solid string of guesthouses and mini-hotels. Try 'mini-hotel alley', flanked by (and addressed as an extension of) Đ Bui Vien and Đ Pham Ngu Lao, with more than a dozen places, all virtually identical. Most are family-run and the price range is US$6 to US$10 for fan rooms, US$12 to US$18 for bigger air-con rooms (some with balconies).

Bi Saigon and ***Bee Saigon*** *(☎ 836 0678, fax 836 7947, both at 185/26 Pham Ngu Lao)* have received good reports. French travellers gravitate to the nearby ***Mini-Hotel Cam*** *(☎ 836 7622, 40/31 Đ Bui Vien).*

A quieter alternative about 10 minutes' walk from the Pham Ngu Lao area is a string of fine guesthouses on an alley connecting Đ Co Giang and Đ Co Bac (see the Central Saigon map). This area is far enough away for you not to have to deal with touts every time you step outside.

The first hotel to appear here, and probably still the best, is ***Miss Loi's Guesthouse*** *(☎ 835 2973, 178/20 Đ Co Giang).* Fan rooms cost US$8 to US$10 and air-con rooms are US$12 to US$15. Zany Miss Loi throws in breakfast free and even has her own in-house beauty salon! Many of her neighbours are jumping into this business and the area seems destined to develop into another backpackers haven. To reach these guesthouses walk south-west on Đ Co Bac and turn left after you pass the *nuoc mam* (fish sauce) shops.

There are several more options on the streets splintering off from the roundabout with the mounted horseman statue near the New World Hotel. Consider ***Oriole Hotel*** *(☎ 832 3494, fax 839 5919, 74 Đ Le Thi Rieng)*, a friendly mini-hotel with comfortable air-con rooms from US$12 to US$20.

Cholon (District 5)

Just up the street is ***Truong Thanh Hotel*** *(☎ 855 6044, 111–117 Đ Chau Van Liem).* It's definitely a budget place. Rooms with fan cost from US$4 to US$6, while air-con costs US$10.

Phuong Hoang Hotel *(☎ 855 1888, fax 855 2228, 411 ĐL Tran Hung Dao)* is in an eight-storey building (Also known as *Phoenix Hotel)*, in central Cholon. Rooms with fan/air-con cost US$10/16.

Tan Da Hotel *(☎ 855 5711, 17–19 Đ Tan Da)* is close to the upmarket Arc En Ciel

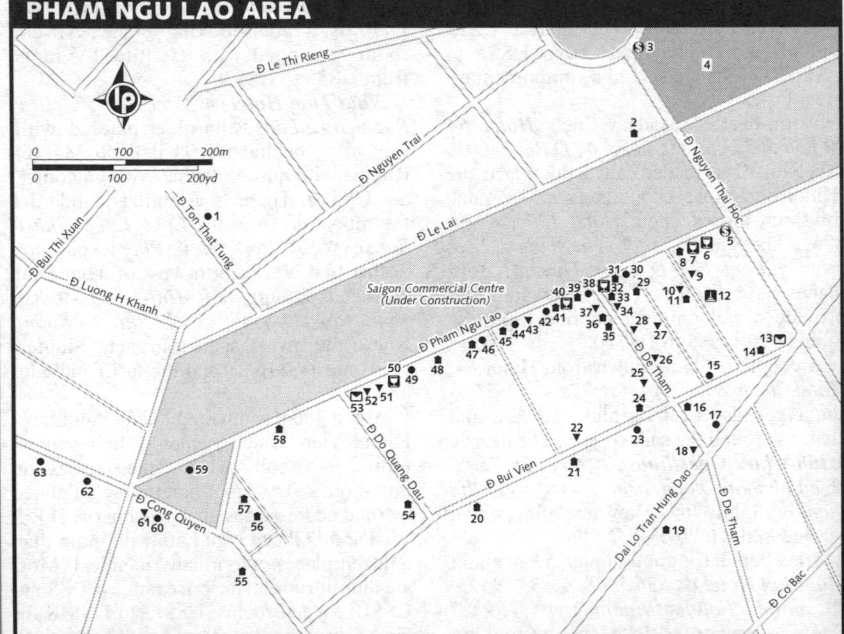

Hotel. Rooms at *Tan Dan Hotel* with fan/air-con cost US$10/16.

***Bat Dat Hotel II** (☎ 855 5902, 41 Đ Ngo Quyen)* is the cheap cousin of the nearby pricey Bat Dat Hotel. Air-con twins are US$11 to US$15.

PLACES TO STAY – MID-RANGE

Pham Ngu Lao Area

Pham Ngu Lao boasts a good number of slightly upmarket places which cater both to backpackers who don't mind shelling out a bit more for a nice room, and moneybags who prefer to be where the action is without sacrificing comfort.

Room rates at the attractive ***Hanh Hoa Hotel** (☎ 836 0245, fax 836 1482, 237 Đ Pham Ngu Lao)* range from US$20 to US$35 – decent value. This is one of the few places in the area featuring satellite TV.

Another hotel which has managed to inch its way into backpacker central is the sleek ***Le Le Hotel** (☎ 836 8686, fax 836 8787, 171 Đ Pham Ngu Lao)*. This place has an elevator and satellite TV. Rooms cost US$12 to US$40.

***Giant Dragon Hotel** (☎ 836 4759, fax 836 7279, 173 Đ Pham Ngu Lao)* has plush rooms with satellite TV, costing US$20 to US$35.

***Rang Dong Hotel** (☎ 832 2106, fax 839 3318, 81–83 Đ Cach Mang Thang Tam)* is sizable and reasonably priced, from US$25 to US$50.

***Empress Hotel** (☎ 832 2888, fax 835 8215, 136 Đ Bui Thi Xuan)* is a snazzy place where twins cost US$30 to US$60.

***Liberty 4 Hotel** (☎ 836 5822, fax 836 5435, 265 Đ Pham Ngu Lao)* offers excellent views from its 9th floor restaurant. Rooms are nice, but it's questionable whether they're worth the price – US$25 to US$60.

Nearby is the three-star ***Vien Dong Hotel** (☎ 836 8941, fax 836 8812, 275A Đ Pham Ngu Lao)*, with budget rooms costing US$25 and deluxe suites US$50, including breakfast, tax and service charges. Amenities include a rooftop restaurant, a restaurant serving halal Muslim food, and a nightclub.

Also in the neighbourhood is the friendly, neon-lit ***Tan Kim Long Hotel** (☎ 836 8136,*

PHAM NGU LAO AREA

PLACES TO STAY
- 2 Palace Saigon Hotel
- 4 New World Hotel
- 8 Le Le Hotel; Giant Dragon Hotel
- 11 Hotel Linh Linh
- 14 Hong Kong Mini-Hotel
- 16 Quyen Thanh Hotel
- 19 Windsor Saigon Hotel
- 20 Dong A-1 Hotel
- 21 Minh Chau Guesthouse
- 24 Hotel 64; Hotel 70
- 29 Bi Saigon; Bee Saigon
- 31 Liberty 3 Hotel
- 33 Peace Hotel; Bin Cafe
- 35 Hotel 265
- 36 Le Le 2 Hotel
- 39 Tan Thanh Thanh Hotel
- 41 Hotel 211; Mai Phai Hotel
- 45 Hanh Hoa Hotel
- 47 Liberty 4 Hotel
- 48 Vien Dong Hotel
- 54 Bich Thuy Guesthouse
- 55 Guesthouse 127
- 56 Nhat Thai Guesthouse
- 57 Coco Loco Guesthouse
- 58 Tan Kim Long Hotel

PLACES TO EAT
- 9 Margherita Restaurant
- 10 Bodhi Tree Vegetarian Restaurant
- 18 The Sandwich Box (Cafe Van)
- 22 Pho Bo Noodle Shop
- 25 Cafe 333
- 26 Sasa Cafe; Cappuccino; Lucky; Shanti Indian Restaurant
- 27 Thuong Chi Restaurant; Mini-Hotel Cam
- 34 Kim Cafe; Kim Travel
- 37 Saigon Cafe
- 43 Lac Thien Restaurant
- 51 Kim's Cafe & Bar
- 52 Linh Cafe
- 61 Dinh Y Restaurant

OTHER
- 1 Ann Tours
- 3 Hongkong Bank (HSBC)
- 5 Sacombank
- 6 Long Phi Bar
- 7 Backpacker Bar
- 12 Chua An Lac Temple
- 13 Post Office
- 15 Tometeco/Pro Tour
- 17 Cong Nhan Cinema
- 23 Sinhbalo Adventures/ Ben Thanh Tourist
- 28 Sinh Cafe
- 30 Delta Adventure Tours
- 32 Allez Boo Bar (bar)
- 38 Fiditourist; Currency Exchange
- 40 Guns & Roses Bar
- 42 Nam Duong Travel Agency
- 44 Photo Nhu
- 46 Anh Khoa Bookshop
- 49 Saigon Railways Tourist Services
- 50 Bar Rolling Stones (bar)
- 53 Post Office
- 59 Thai Binh Market
- 60 Traditional Massage Institute
- 62 Hanoi Mart
- 63 Co-op Mart

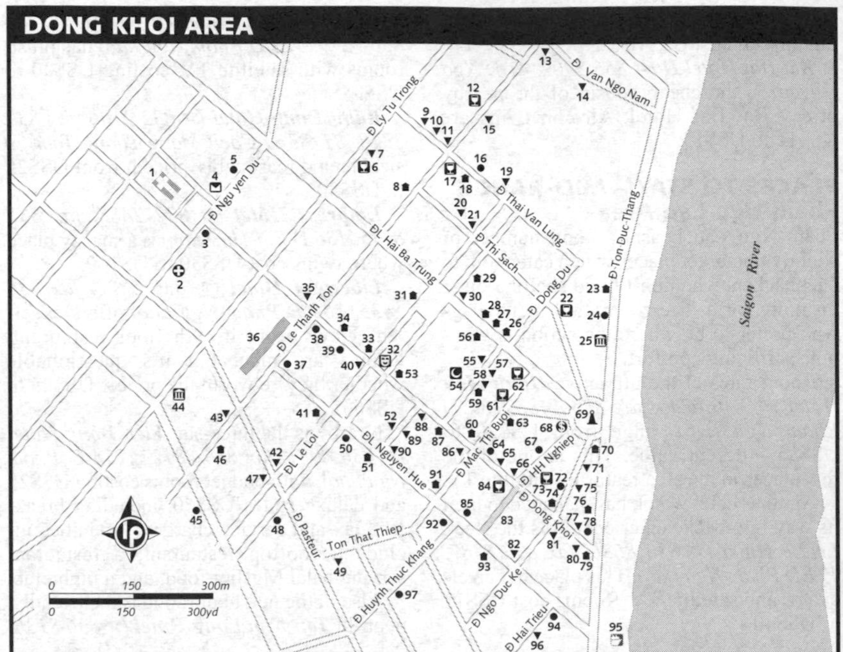

fax 836 8230, 365 Đ Pham Ngu Lao), where singles/doubles cost US$15/20.

A short walk south of Đ Bui Vien is the debonair ***Windsor Saigon Hotel*** *(☎ 836 7848, fax 836 7889, 193 ĐL Tran Hung Dao)*. It has all amenities, including a white stretch Cadillac limo! The fancy Four Seasons Restaurant here gets good reviews as does the excellent bakery/deli offering pastries, fine wine, cheese and *real* sausages. Room rates range from US$40 for 'studios' to US$70 for 'apartments'.

Not far from the Windsor, ***Hanoi Hotel*** *(☎ 821 0799, fax 821 3535, 3 Đ Trinh Van Can)* has rooms costing US$20 to US$40 with bath tubs, satellite TV and two telephones (one in the bathroom).

Also in the neighbourhood, ***Metropole Hotel*** *(☎ 832 2021, fax 832 2019, 148 ĐL Tran Hung Dao)* is an older, but fancy place with rates from US$40 to US$70.

Virtually next door to the posh New World Hotel is ***Palace Saigon Hotel*** *(☎ 833 1353/835 9421, 82 Đ Le Lai)*. It has doubles for US$20 to US$30.

Dong Khoi Area

One of the better deals in the city centre is ***Khach San Dien Luc*** *(☎ 822 9058, fax 822 9385, 5/11 Đ Nguyen Sieu)*. It has the sterility and look of a new hospital, but belongs to the Ministry of Energy (the agency responsible for the frequent power blackouts that grip Vietnam). Rooms cost US$15 to US$25 (they get cheaper as you go upstairs) and feature IDD phones and satellite TV.

Bach Dang Hotel *(☎ 825 1501, fax 823 0587, 33 Đ Mac Thi Buoi)* is a bright and airy place in a prime position near the Saigon River. Rooms cost US$39 to US$45, and have satellite TV.

Nam Phuong Hotel *(☎ 822 4446, fax 829 7459, 46 ĐL Hai Ba Trung)* has clean rooms, weary guests will be thankful for the lift (a rarity in such tall, thin mini-hotels). Rooms cost US$28 to US$40.

DONG KHOI AREA

PLACES TO STAY

8 Spring Hotel
18 Orchid Hotel
23 Saigon Marriot Hotel
26 NY Kim Phuong Hotel
27 Fimex Hotel
28 Nam Phuong Hotel
29 Khach San Dien Luc
31 Park Hyatt Hotel (Under Construction)
33 Continental Hotel
34 Asian Hotel
41 Rex Hotel
46 Norfolk Hotel
51 Kim Do Hotel
53 Caravelle Hotel
56 Bong Sen Annexe
59 Saigon Hotel
60 Huong Sen Hotel
63 Bach Dang Hotel
70 Renaissance Riverside Hotel
74 Grand Hotel
76 Riverside Hotel
79 Majestic Hotel
87 Bong Sen Hotel & Mondial Hotel
91 Palace Hotel
93 Saigon Prince Hotel

PLACES TO EAT

7 Bo Tung Xeo Restaurant
9 Sapa; Why Not?
10 Chao Thai Restaurant
11 Indian Heritage Restaurant
13 Hoi An Restaurant
14 Mandarine Restaurant
15 Ashoka Indian Restaurant
19 Bibi's
20 Mogambo's Cafe
21 Camargue Restaurant
30 Kem Bach Dang
35 Chi Lang Cafe
40 Givral Restaurant
42 Kem Bach Dang
43 Rex Garden Restaurant
47 Kem Bach Dang
49 Fanny's Ice Cream
52 Lemon Grass; Globo; Augustin
55 Tan Nam Restaurant
57 Cafe Latin; Indochine House Antiques
58 Dong Du Cafe
65 Gartenstadt Restaurant; Cool Restaurant
66 Paloma Cafe
71 La Fourchette Restaurant
75 Restaurants 19 & 13
77 Moonfish Cafe
80 Maxim's Dinner Theatre; Vietsilk
81 Paris Deli
82 Santa Lucia Restaurant
86 Vietnam House
88 Brodard Café
89 Angkor Encore Restaurant
90 Ciao Cafe
96 Urvashi Indian Restaurant

OTHER

1 Notre Dame Cathedral
2 SOS International; Thai Airways
3 Metropolitan Building
4 Main Post Office
5 UPS; EMS; Airbourne Express
16 Dental Clinic Starlight
24 Landmark Building; Le Caprice Restaurant
25 Ton Duc Thang Museum
36 Hôtel de Ville (People's Commitee)
37 Vietnam Airlines
38 Saigon Tourist
39 Fahasa Bookshop
44 Museum of Ho Chi Minh City
45 Saigon Intershop & Minimart
48 Saigon Centre; Java Cafe; Paris-Deli; Post Office
50 Tax Department Store
54 Saigon Central Mosque; Indian Canteen
64 Cathay Pacific
67 Tiem Sach Bookshop; Bo Gio Café (ice cream)
68 ANZ Bank
69 Me Linh Square & Tran Hung Dao Statue
72 Grand Dentistry
73 Tropical Rainforest Nightclub
78 Pacific Airlines
83 Pedestrian Shopping Mall
84 Underground Bar & Restaurant
85 Fahasa Bookshop
92 Sun Wah Tower
94 Harbour View Tower (Office Building)
95 Hydrofoils to Vung Tao & Mekong Delta; Small boats for hire
97 Huynh Thuc Khang Street Market

ENTERTAINMENT

6 Blue Gecko Bar & Restaurant
12 Tex Mex Cantina
17 Sheridan's Irish House; Am Tra Chinese Restaurant
22 Apocalypse Now
32 Municipal Theatre
61 Hard Rock Cafe
62 Wild West Saloon

Moving further into the centre, ***Saigon Hotel*** (☎ *829 9734, fax 829 1466, 47 Đ Dong Du)* is a huge motel-looking place (run by Saigon Tourist) just across the street from the Saigon Central Mosque. Doubles cost US$39 to US$79. Deluxe rooms and suites come equipped with satellite TV.

Kim Do Hotel (☎ *822 5914, fax 822 5915, 133 ĐL Nguyen Hue)* is another fancy pleasure dome brought to you by Saigon Tourist. Rates are US$40 to US$100. It's fair to say you get what you pay for here.

The contemporary ***Asian Hotel*** (☎ *829 6979, fax 829 7433, 146–150 Đ Dong Khoi)* is a fine place to stay and is notable for its in-house restaurant. Single/double rooms start from US$30/40.

Bong Sen Hotel (☎ *829 1516, fax 829 8076, 117–123 Đ Dong Khoi)*, or Lotus Hotel, is affectionately called 'the BS' by travellers. It offers air-con twins for US$56 to US$185 and has the distinction of being one of the only hotels in Vietnam which had raised its prices since we last visited.

Bong Sen Annexe *(☎ 823 5818, fax 823 5816, 61–63 ĐL Hai Ba Trung)* is an attractive choice offering slightly more reasonable rates. Economy singles/doubles cost US$40/56, city-view rooms are US$50/65 and 'junior suites' are US$70/85.

Fimex Hotel *(☎ 822 0082, fax 822 0085, 40–42 ĐL Hai Ba Trung)* is a nice new mini-hotel with rates from US$18 to US$30 including tax, service and breakfast. A similar place worth considering is ***NY Kim Phuong Hotel*** *(☎ 824 4290, fax 822 1647, 22 ĐL Hai Ba Trung)*, just down the street. Standard rooms go for US$25, and deluxe rooms for US$28 to US$45. Rates include breakfast and a 'fruit bucket'.

Huong Sen Hotel *(☎ 829 1415, fax 829 0916, 66–70 Đ Dong Khoi)* has a decent in-house restaurant on the 6th floor and charges US$20 to US$35 for twin rooms.

Spring Hotel *(☎ 829 7362, fax 822 1383, 44–46 Đ Le Thanh Ton)* is a rather attractive place with a subtle Japanese feel to it. Doubles range from US$25 to US$59. The tariff includes breakfast at the in-house restaurant.

Orchid Hotel (☎ 823 1809, fax 829 2245, 29A Đ Don Dat), on the corner of Đ Thai Van Lang, is another good place with an array of amenities including karaoke and 24-hour room service. Singles/doubles range from US$25/30 to US$40/50 for suites.

Tan Loc Hotel *(☎ 823 0028, fax 829 8360, 177 Đ Le Thanh Ton)* has twins costing US$22 to US$35 – decent value. Breakfast is complimentary.

District 3

This district attracts a large number of French travellers, possibly because of its French-style architecture. On the north side of Cong Vien Van Hoa Park is ***Bao Yen Hotel*** *(☎ 829 9848, 9 Đ Truong Dinh)*. Prices are a very reasonable US$12 to US$15 and all rooms have air-con.

One place which gets the thumbs up from French travellers is ***Guesthouse Loan*** *(☎ 844 5313)*. This place is also known as *No 3 Ly Chinh Thang Hotel*, which is also its address. Prices are US$14 to US$16 and all rooms have air-con and hot water.

Que Huong Hotel *(☎ 829 4227, fax 829 0919, 167 ĐL Hai Ba Trung)*, also known as *Liberty Hotel*, is two blocks from the French consulate. Singles/doubles cost US$25/30, and suites go for US$45. The lunch buffet in the ground-floor restaurant is good value at US$2.

Victory Hotel *(☎ 823 1755, fax 829 9604, 14 Đ Vo Van Tan)* is just one block northwest of Reunification Palace and is in far better shape than the palace itself. Rates are US$28 to US$60.

Saigon Star Hotel *(☎ 823 0260, fax 823 0255, 204 Đ Nguyen Thi Minh Khai)* is modern and luxurious. It features satellite TV, two restaurants and a coffee shop, the Moonlight Karaoke Club and a business centre with email services. Rates are typically from US$30 to US$40, including breakfast. The nearby all-suite ***Chancery Saigon Hotel*** *(☎ 829 9152, fax 825 1464, e chancery@hcm.vnn.vn, 196 Đ Nguyen Thi Minh Khai)* has a slightly higher standard and charges from US$40 to US$60.

On the road to the airport is ***Saigon Lodge Hotel*** *(☎ 823 0112, fax 825 1070, 215 Đ Nam Ky Khoi Nghia)*. This place boasts the usual hotel amenities, plus satellite TV and halal food. Twins are US$32 to US$40.

International Hotel *(☎ 829 0009, fax 829 0066, 19 Đ Vo Van Tan)* maintains plush standards; rooms are US$30 to US$50 including breakfast.

Cholon (District 5)

The five-storey ***Dong Khanh Hotel*** *(☎ 835 2410, 2 ĐL Tran Hung Dao)* is the pride and joy of Saigon Tourist. Single/doubles cost from US$25/35.

The ***Tokyo Hotel*** *(☎ 835 7558, fax 835 2505, 106–108 Đ Tran Tuan Khai)* has all the modern conveniences at nice prices, plus friendly staff. Doubles cost US$28 to US$50.

Equatorial Hotel *(☎ 839 0000, fax 839 0011, 242 Đ Tran Binh Trong)* is one of Cholon's plushest accommodation options. Rooms are US$55 to US$65.

Arc En Ciel Hotel *(☎ 855 4435, fax 855 0332, 52–56 Đ Tan Da)* is a prime venue for tour groups from Hong Kong and Taiwan, and includes the Rainbow Disco Karaoke

Singles/doubles cost from US$25/35. The hotel is on the corner of ĐL Tran Hung Dao.

A near neighbour to the Arc En Ciel is ***Van Hoa Hotel*** *(☎ 855 4182, fax 856 3118, 36 Đ Tan Da)*. It looks like a good place and rooms cost US$18 to US$25.

Bat Dat Hotel *(☎ 855 1662, 238–244 ĐL Tran Hung Dao)* is across from the Arc En Ciel. This formerly cheap hotel is now plush and offers twins from US$30 to US$40.

Hanh Long Hotel *(☎ 835 1087, fax 835 0742, 1027 ĐL Tran Hung Dao)* is a decent choice – the name means 'happy dragon'. Rooms are US$20 to US$32.

Regent Hotel *(☎ 835 3548, fax 835 7094, 700 ĐL Tran Hung Dao)* is a joint Viet-Thai venture. Facilities are excellent. Rooms are US$26 to US$45.

Cholon Hotel *(☎ 835 7058, fax 835 5375, 170–174 Đ Su Van Hanh)* is good value. The desk clerks speak English and Chinese. Squeaky-clean singles/twins cost US$18.

Next door is the privately owned ***Cholon Tourist Mini-Hotel*** *(☎ 835 7100, fax 835 5375, 192–194 Đ Su Van Hanh)*. It's of a high standard and caters to the Taiwanese market. Rooms cost US$22/28.

Next to Cholon Tourist, ***Anh Quoc Hotel*** *(☎ 835 9447, fax 839 6872, 196 Đ Su Van Hanh)* has decent air-con rooms for US$15.

Andong Hotel *(☎ 835 2001, 9 ĐL An Duong Vuong)*, right at the intersection of ĐL Tran Phu, is a clean place. All rooms have hot water, telephone, air-con and refrigerator. Twins cost US$20 to US$25.

Right inside Andong Market is ***Caesar Hotel*** *(☎ 835 0677, fax 835 0106, 34–36 ĐL An Duong Vuong)*, a slick Taiwanese joint venture. To get there it's probably easiest to ask taxis or cyclos to take you to the market. Rooms are US$28 to US$40.

District 11

About 1km north of central Cholon is ***Phu Tho Hotel*** *(☎ 855 1309, fax 855 1255, 527 Đ 3/2)*. The price range is US$22 to US$40, with breakfast. There is a huge restaurant here with built-in karaoke facilities.

Goldstar Hotel *(☎ 856 3606, fax 855 1644, 174–176 Đ Le Dai Hanh)* is spotlessly clean and singles/doubles are US$18/20. All rooms have private bath, refrigerator and air-con, and the upper floors give a good view of the Saigon Race Track.

Tan Binh & Phu Nhuan Districts

These are the areas out towards the airport in the northern part of the city.

Almost within walking distance of the airport is ***Mekong Travel Hotel*** *(☎ 844 1024, fax 844 4809, 243A ĐL Hoang Van Thu)*. Single/twin rooms in this sleek place are US$25/35. It's certainly one of the better deals near the airport.

Omni Hotel *(☎ 844 9222, fax 844 9200, 251 Đ Nguyen Van Troi)* is the most posh accommodation in the area. This place has everything from room safes to a florist and health club. The price for all this comfort is around US$50 to US$80.

Chains First Hotel *(☎ 844 1199, fax 844 4282, 18 Đ Hoang Viet)* boasts coffee shop, gift shop, tennis courts, sauna, massage services, three restaurants, swimming pool, business centre and a free airport shuttle service. Single/twin rooms start at US$30/50, including breakfast and a basket of fruit.

PLACES TO STAY – TOP END

Pham Ngu Lao Area

The enormous ***New World Hotel*** *(☎ 822 8888, fax 823 0710, 76 Đ Le Lai)* is a slick luxury tower and one of the most upmarket hotels in Saigon. The clientele tends to be mainly Chinese-speaking tour groups from Hong Kong and Taiwan, but anyone with hard currency is welcome. Rates start at US$65 and creep right up to the presidential suite, which goes for a cool US$850.

Dong Khoi Area

One of Saigon's most historic lodgings is the venerable ***Continental Hotel*** *(☎ 829 9201, fax 824 1772, 132–134 Đ Dong Khoi)*, the setting for much of the action in Graham Greene's well-known novel *The Quiet American*. The hotel dates from the turn of the 19th century and received its last renovation in 1989, at the hands of its current owner, Saigon Tourist. The Continental charges US$70 to US$140, which includes breakfast and fruit.

Another classic central hotel is the giant ***Rex Hotel*** (*☎ 829 6043, fax 829 6536, 141 ĐL Nguyen Hue*). Its ambience of mellowed kitsch dates from the time it put up US military officers. Twins and suites cost US$79 to US$760. Amenities include a large gift shop, a tailor, unisex beauty parlour, photocopy machines, massage service, acupuncture, a swimming pool on the 6th floor, an excellent restaurant on the 5th floor and a coffee shop on the ground floor. There are great views from the 5th floor rooftop veranda, which is decorated with caged birds and potted bonsai bushes shaped like animals.

The enormous and posh ***Caravelle Hotel*** (*☎ 823 4999, fax 824 3999, 19 Lam Son Square*) sits on a prime piece of real estate once occupied by the Catholic Diocese of Saigon. Rooms at this snazzy place range from US$120 for a standard to US$800 for luxurious suites.

Majestic Hotel (*☎ 829 5514, fax 829 5510, 1 Đ Dong Khoi*) is right on the Saigon River. Following a major renovation it can truly reclaim its title as one of the city's most majestic hotels. One guest wrote: 'The Majestic wins hands-down for class and bygone days atmosphere'. Prices are US$70 to US$100, and suites cost US$150.

Aptly named, ***Grand Hotel*** (*☎ 823 0163, fax 823 5871, 12 Đ Ngo Duc Ke*), formerly (Dong Khoi Hotel), is a pleasant choice. This recently renovated landmark building is notable for its spacious suites with 4.5m-high ceilings and French windows. It's on the corner of Đ Dong Khoi, and rates range from US$45 to US$150.

Palace Hotel (*☎ 822 2316, fax 824 4229, 56–64 ĐL Nguyen Hue*), whose Vietnamese name Huu Nghi means 'friendship', offers superb views from the 14th-floor restaurant and 15th-floor terrace. Rates range from US$40 to US$165 with breakfast. The Palace has an imported-food shop, a dance hall, bar and a small swimming pool on the 16th floor.

In the same neighbourhood is ***Saigon Prince Hotel*** (*☎ 822 2999, fax 824 1888, 63 ĐL Nguyen Hue*). Glittering, luxury twins cost US$90 to US$215, plus 15% for tax and service. Local expats say it has the best massage service in town.

Norfolk Hotel (*☎ 829 5368, fax 829 3415, 117 Đ Le Thanh Ton*) is an Australian joint venture and is popular with business travellers. All rooms boast satellite TV and a minibar. Twins cost US$85 to US$150, plus tax and service, but including breakfast.

Riverside Hotel (*☎ 822 4038, fax 825 1417, 18 Đ Ton Duc Thang*) is very close to the Saigon River. This old colonial building has been renovated and now features a good restaurant and bar. Doubles cost US$40 to US$120.

Don't confuse the above with the new ***Renaissance Riverside Hotel*** (*☎ 822 0033, fax 823 5666, 8–15 Đ Ton Duc Thang*), a glitzy skyscraper which, as the name suggests, also overlooks the river. Rates range from US$70 to US$155. A bit further up Đ Ton Duc Thang is the brand-new ***Saigon Marriot Hotel***. Rates were not available at the time of writing.

The 291-room ***Hotel Sofitel Plaza Saigon*** (*☎ 824 1555, fax 824 1666, 17 ĐL Le Duan*) is among the newest and sleekest of Saigon's posh hotels. There are two fine in-house restaurants, L'Elysee Bar which has a delightful terrace, and a rooftop swimming pool. Rates start at a modest US$200 and climb to US$1450 for the presidential suite.

PLACES TO STAY – RENTAL

There are some 15,000 expats living in Saigon, but even with these numbers, there still there does not appear to be a shortage of good-quality rental accommodation.

Unfortunately, living cheaply is not easy. Unless you marry a Vietnamese national and move in with the family, there isn't much chance of you renting a worker's flat (US$50 per month). Unfortunately, the police will not permit it.

The budget market is served chiefly by the mini-hotels scattered all around town. Discounts can be negotiated for long-term rentals at almost any hotel; expect to pay somewhere between US$200 and US$300 per month for a decent air-con room. If you've got a big budget, but don't need a large space, even the big five-star luxury hotels offer steep discounts to long-termers. The name of the game is negotiation.

Expats with a liberal budget have two basic options – villas or specially built luxury flats. Villas seem more popular and Saigon has a large supply. Villas which can be rented by foreigners typically cost from US$1000 to US$3000 a month. Real estate agents who cater to the expat market advertise in the *Vietnam Economic Times* and *Vietnam Investment Review*.

PLACES TO EAT

Both Vietnamese and Western food are widely available in Saigon and English menus are common. Central Saigon is the place to look for fine Western and Vietnamese food. Cholon's speciality is Chinese food.

Vietnamese – Budget

Bo Tung Xeo Restaurant *(☎ 825 1330, 31 Đ Ly Tu Trong)* is a indoor-outdoor eatery in the city centre, popular with locals, which serves amazingly cheap and tasty Vietnamese BBQ. The house speciality is tender marinated beef (about US$2 a portion, including a salad) which you grill over charcoal right at your table. There are also good seafood dishes on the menu, and the cheerful staff speak English.

Along Đ Ngo Duc Ke, near the river in District 1, is a strip of excellent restaurants serving good, cheap Vietnamese food. At No 19, ***Restaurant 19*** *(☎ 829 8882)* serves a very tasty variation on Hanoi's *cha ca* fish cakes and good Thai dishes as well. Nearby, ***Restaurant 13*** is highly popular with locals and expats alike.

For Hué-style Vietnamese fare, ***Tib Cafe*** *(187 ĐL Hai Ba Trung)* in District 3 makes a good choice for dinner. In the Pham Ngu Lao area there are also cheap and excellent Hué-style dishes at ***Thuong Chi*** *(40/29 Đ Bui Vien)*.

Vietnamese – Mid-Range & Top End

Compared to what you'll pay for fine Vietnamese food abroad, Saigon's better Vietnamese restaurants are a relative bargain. It's possible to eat like a king (it's worth splurging once in a while) in a fancy upmarket restaurant for around US$10 to US$20 or so per person. Aspiring interior designers will enjoy checking out the woodsy, ethnic decor at many of the better places.

Mandarine *(☎ 822 9783, 11A Đ Ngo Van Nam)* is perhaps the best Vietnamese restaurant in the city centre. The selection of fine, traditional dishes drawing from southern, central and northern Vietnamese cooking styles is superb, and the pleasant decor and live traditional music performances make it an all-round good bet. A house speciality worth trying is the Hanoi-style *cha ca*.

Just down the street (and run by the same people) is ***Hoi An*** *(☎ 823 1049, 11 Đ Le Thanh Ton)*, a lovely, Chinese-style place decorated in a classical, antique motif. Here they specialise in central Vietnamese and imperial Hué-style dishes.

Lemon Grass *(☎ 822 0496, 4 Đ Nguyen Thiep, District 1)* is another favourite in the centre of town. You'd be hard-pressed to find anything bad on the menu, so if you can't decide what to order just pick something at random. Two women in traditional clothing play musical instruments while you eat.

Other popular (and slightly cheaper) places with traditional decor and fine food in the Dong Khoi area include ***Tan Nam Restaurant*** *(☎ 829 8634, 60–62 Đ Dong Du, District 1)* and ***Cool*** *(☎ 829 1364, 30 Đ Dong Khoi, District 1)*, where there is an ethnic feel and plenty of plant life to enrich the air. The Vietnamese name is Kinh Bac.

Vietnam House *(☎ 829 1623, 93–95 Đ Dong Khoi)* is on the corner of Đ Mac Thi Buoi. The food and decor are Vietnamese-style. The restaurant is open from 10 am until midnight.

If you're out by the airport, ***Quan Com Vietnam*** *(☎ 844 4236, 173 Đ Nguyen Van Troi)* is another good place to sample fine Vietnamese fare.

Chinese

Cholon is the place to eat Chinese food. Two highly popular indoor/outdoor restaurants where you can do so are ***Nam Son*** *(520 Đ Nguyen Trai)* and nearby ***My Huong***

(131 Đ Nguyen Tri Phuong). Both serve all kinds of good food, including superb noodle soup with duck.

Tiem An Nam Long, near the Binh Tay Market on the corner of Đ Hau Giang and Đ Pham Dinh Ho, is noteworthy for tasty wok-fried dishes and sidewalk seating. There is an English menu with no prices, but everything is cheap – most dishes cost under US$2.

Tiem Com Chay Phat Huu Duyen *(527 Đ Nguyen Trai)* is a small, popular Chinese vegetarian restaurant near the southern end of Đ Phuoc Hung. Its open 7.30 am to 10 pm.

Tiem Com Chay Giac Ngo 1 *(124 Đ Nguyen Tri Phuong)* also dishes up excellent vegetarian food and has an English menu.

Am Tra *(☎ 823 0973, 19 Đ Le Thanh Ton)* might just be the only Chinese restaurant in the world combined with an Irish Pub!

Thai & Japanese

Chao Thai *(☎ 824 1457, 16 Đ Thai Van Lung, District 1)* is the best of Saigon's Thai restaurants, both for food and atmosphere. Its US$6.50 lunch set is a good value.

The Sushi Bar *(2 Đ Le Thanh Ton)* serves – guess what? And it's good.

Indian

Some of the best Indian food in District 1 is at ***Urvashi*** *(☎ 821 3102, 27 Đ Hai Trieu)*. Here they prepare a variety of Indian cooking styles and the US$4 Thali lunch set menu is a guaranteed filler.

Also central, ***Indian Heritage*** *(☎ 823 4687, 26A Đ Le Thanh Ton)* serves an excellent lunch buffet for US$5. Just across the street is ***Ashoka*** *(☎ 823 1372, 17A/10 Đ Le Thanh Ton, District 1)*, another moderately priced Indian restaurant with a lunch buffet and halal food. Also recommended for North Indian dishes is ***Tandoor (☎ 824 4839, 103 Đ Vo Van Tan, District 3)***.

For really cheap Indian food, you have to go the atmospheric, cult-like ***canteen*** *(66 Đ Dong Du)* behind the Saigon Central Mosque (opposite the Saigon Hotel).

French

Restaurant Bibi *(☎ 829 5783, 8A/8D2 Đ Thai Van Lung)* is a great place for casual French bistro fare in District 1. The bright Mediterranean decor creates a pleasant atmosphere to dine in.

Just next door to the famed Lemon Grass Restaurant is ***Augustin*** *(☎ 829 2941, 10 Đ Nguyen Thiep)*. It's a popular spot serving bistro-style food. Many consider it Saigon's best, cheap French restaurant.

Another excellent choice in District 1 for authentic, yet inexpensive French food is ***La Fourchette*** *(☎ 836 9816, 9 Đ Ngo Duc Ke)*.

Camargue *(☎ 824 3148, 16 Đ Cao Ba Quat)* is housed in a stunning restored villa with a tropical open-air terrace. The menu includes a variety of gourmet dishes complimented by a well-appointed wine list. Camargue, also home to trendy ***Vasco's Bar***, is a short walk from the Municipal Theatre.

If you prefer a fancy French restaurant, ***Le Caprice*** *(☎ 822 8337, 5B Đ Ton Duc Thang)* is a very high-class place on the top floor of the Landmark building; the views are stunning and so are the prices.

L'Etoile *(☎ 829 7939, 180 ĐL Hai Ba Trung, District 1)* serves terrific French food, but doesn't get the crowds it used to.

Brodard Café *(☎ 822 3966, 131 Đ Dong Khoi)* is an oldie but goodie. This place is known for good French food and its prices are OK. It's on the corner of Đ Nguyen Thiep, in District 1.

International

Encore Angkor *(☎ 822 6278, 5 Đ Nguyen Thiep, District 1)*, right in the city centre, may be the only restaurant in Vietnam specialising in Cambodian-inspired Khmer cuisine. This stylish little bistro is run by Daniel Hung, a French photographer born to Khmer/Vietnamese parents, who serves beautifully presented traditional Khmer dishes at very reasonable prices.

Moonfish Cafe *(☎ 823 8822, 6 Đ Dong Khoi)* is a chic and stylish cafe-bistro near the Saigon River doing fusion cooking, real coffees and fresh pastries.

Annie's Pizza *(☎ 839 2577, 21 Đ Bui Thi Xuan)* does the best peperoni and mozzarella in town. If you don't feel like trekking over there (it's near the large New World Hotel) just phone for a home delivery.

The long-standing ***Givral Restaurant*** *(☎ 829 2747, 169 Đ Dong Khoi)*, across the street from the Continental Hotel, has excellent selections of cakes, home-made ice cream and yoghurt. This Japanese joint venture also does kotobuki-style pastries. Aside from the junk food, there's French, Chinese, Vietnamese and Russian cuisine on the menu.

A stone's throw from the Rex Hotel, ***Rex Garden Restaurant*** *(☎ 824 2799, 86 Đ Le Thanh Ton, District 1)* is in an attractive setting and serves good Vietnamese and French dishes. You can dine in air-con comfort, or outside surrounded by views of past and present – on one side an army tank and on the other a row of tennis courts where Saigon's nouveaux-riches swat at little yellow balls in the heat.

Maxim's Dinner Theatre *(☎ 829 6676, 15 Đ Dong Khoi)*, next to the Majestic Hotel, is very much what the name implies – a restaurant with live musical performances. The menu includes Chinese and French food. The sea slug and duck web has disappointed a few travellers, but the creme caramel and vanilla souffle should not be missed. Maxim's is open 11 am to 11 pm, but is usually empty until dinner. Reservations are recommended on weekends.

La Bibliotheque *(☎ 822 2931, 84A Đ Nguyen Du)*, a Saigon institution near the Notre Dame Cathedral, is housed in the home of local personality Madame Dai, who keeps an excellent library of antique books (hence the name of the restaurant) and serves fine French and continental dishes.

The popular Swiss-Vietnamese run ***Sapa Restaurant & Bar*** *(☎ 829 5754, 26 Đ Thai Van Lung, District 1)* is a fine place to sample bona fide Swiss cuisine or relax over a drink. The menu features schnitzel and cheese fondue. Next door to Sapa at No 24, the French-run ***Why Not?*** *(☎ 822 6138)* is worth checking out for good European food or a game of darts.

Some of the best authentic Italian food in town is found at the atmospheric ***Santa Lucia*** *(☎ 822 6562, 14 ĐL Nguyen Hue)* in central District 1.

For good German fare in the same area, check out ***Gartenstadt*** *(☎ 822 3623, 34 Đ Dong Khoi)*, a popular expat business lunch spot. ***Bavaria*** *(☎ 822 2673, 20 Đ Le Anh Xuan)*, near the New World Hotel, is another worthy German restaurant and Bavarian-style pub.

Back in the centre, ***Mogambo's Cafe*** *(☎ 825 1311, 20 Đ Thi Sach)* is noted for its Polynesian decor and juicy burgers. This place is a restaurant, pub and hotel.

One of the trendiest bar/restaurants in the Dong Khoi area is ***Globo Cafe*** *(☎ 822 8855, 6 Đ Nguyen Thiep, District 1)*. It does good French and Italian dishes, including praiseworthy pizzas. Not far away is ***Cafe Latin*** *(☎ 822 6363, 25 Đ Dong Du)*, Vietnam's first tapas bar. There is a superb wine collection and fresh bread baked daily. The attached ***Billabong Restaurant*** is notable for Aussie food and other international cuisine.

Both of the central locations of ***Ciao Cafe*** *(☎ 822 9796, 21–23 Đ Nguyen Thi Minh Khai;* and *☎ 825 1203, 72 ĐL Nguyen Hue)* do good pizza, spaghetti, sandwiches, cakes, pastries and ice cream.

Paloma Cafe *(☎ 829 5813, 26 Đ Dong Khoi)* is a stylish place with wooden tables, white tablecloths, polished silverware, aggressive air-conditioning and waiters who need to be tipped. Judging from the crowd that packs in every night, they must be doing something right – it's very popular with young, fashion-conscious Vietnamese.

Also popular with young Vietnamese is Saigon's only Czech restaurant, ***Hoa Vien*** *(☎ 825 8605, 30 Đ Mac Dinh Chi)* in District 1. The big drawcard is the draught Pilsner Urquell beer.

For a good late-night bowl of noodles in District 3, try the trendy ***ABC Restaurant*** *(☎ 823 0388, 172H Đ Nguyen Dinh Chieu)*. It's open until about 3 am.

Vegetarian

On the first and 15th days of the lunar month, food stalls around the city – especially in the markets – serve vegetarian versions of meaty Vietnamese dishes. While these stalls are quick in serving customers, a little patience is required – good home-cooking takes time, but it's worth the wait.

The largest concentration of vegetarian restaurants is in and around the Pham Ngu Lao area.

Bodhi Tree *(☎ 837 1910, 174/6 Đ Pham Ngu Lao)* is in a narrow alley two streets east of Đ De Tham. Its food is excellent and very cheap. One neighbour has cleverly opened up a place with the exact same name.

The owners of ***Tin Nghia*** *(☎ 821 2538, 9 ĐL Tran Hung Dao)* are strict Buddhists. This simple establishment is about 200m from Ben Thanh Market. It serves an assortment of cheap and delicious traditional Vietnamese food prepared without meat, chicken, fish or egg. Instead tofu, mushrooms and vegetables are used. It is open 8 am to 9 pm daily (closed 2 to 4 pm).

Dinh Y *(☎ 836 7715, 171B Đ Cong Quyen)*, just across the road from Thai Binh Market, is run by a Cao Dai family. The cheap and delicious vegie fare makes up for the lack of atmosphere.

Travellers Cafes

The streets of Đ Pham Ngu Lao and Đ De Tham form the axis of Saigon's budget eatery haven. Western backpackers easily outnumber the Vietnamese here, and indeed the locals have trouble figuring out the menus (banana muesli does not translate well into Vietnamese).

A long-running hang-out for budget travellers is ***Kim Cafe*** *(☎ 836 8122, 266 Đ De Tham)*. This is a good place to meet people, and you can arrange trips and get travel information at the Kim Travel tour office next door. An nearly identical set-up exists at the nearby ***Sinh Cafe*** *(☎ 836 7338, fax 836 9322, ⓔ sinhcafevietnam@hcm.vnn.vn, 246–248 Đ De Tham)*.

Saigon Cafe *(195 Đ Pham Ngu Lao)*, on the corner of Đ De Tham, is worthy of a plug and, along with ***Cafe 333*** (also on Đ De Tham) is where the largest numbers of expats congregate. ***Bin Cafe*** *(274 Đ De Tham)* is also popular.

Linh Cafe *(291 Đ Pham Ngu Lao)* is another great little place run by friendly people. You can also book tours here.

If you're feeling a bit spring-rolled out, head for ***Cafe Van*** *(☎ 836 0636, 169B Đ De Tham)*, on the corner of ĐL Tran Hung Dao. Also known as the *Sandwich Box*, this is a fine eatery serving up excellent meat pies, sandwiches, baked potatoes with all the fixings and Saigon's best chilli. It also offers takeaway and free delivery.

There is good cheap Italian food and great burritos at ***Margherita*** *(175/1 Pham Ngu Lao)*. ***Cappuccino*** *(222 Đ De Tham)* also does commendable pastas, and its neighbours ***Sasa Cafe***, ***Lucky Restaurant*** and ***Shanti Indian Restaurant*** are also worth checking out.

Lac Thien *(☎ 837 0080, 221 Đ Pham Ngu Lao)* was cloned straight from the trio of deaf-mute-run travellers restaurants up in Hué. The food is excellent.

For a good bowl beef noodle soup, look for ***Pho Bo*** *(96 Đ Bui Vien)*.

Other Cafes

The stylish ***Dong Du Cafe*** *(☎ 823 2414, 31 Đ Dong Du)* in the city centre dishes up great home-made ice cream, coffee and, if you're still hungry, a bit of Italian food.

For freshly baked pastries and bread downtown, try ***Paris Deli*** *(☎ 829 7533, 31 Đ Dong Khoi)*. There is a second branch *(☎ 821 6127, 65 ĐL Le Loi)* at the Saigon Centre. Both places do eat-in, takeaway and deliveries.

Some of the best real coffee in town is found at ***Java*** *(☎ 821 4742, 65 ĐL Le Loi)*, also in the Saigon Centre.

Chi Lang Cafe is a long-running indoor-outdoor coffee shop in the Dong Khoi area with park-like surroundings. It's right at the corner of Đ Dong Khoi and Đ Le Thanh Ton.

Food Stalls

Noodle soup is available all day long at street stalls and hole-in-the-wall shops everywhere. A large bowl of delicious beef noodles costs US$0.50 to US$1. Just look for the signs that say 'Pho'.

Sandwiches with a French look and a very Vietnamese taste are sold by street vendors. Fresh French *baguettes* are stuffed with something resembling pâté (don't ask) and cucumbers seasoned with soy sauce. A sandwich costs between US$0.50 and US$1, depending on what it's filled with and whether you are overcharged. Sandwiches filled with imported French soft cheese cost a little more. Baguettes a la carte cost about US$0.16.

Markets always have a side selection of food items, often on the ground floor or in the basement. Clusters of food stalls can be found in Thai Binh, Ben Thanh and Andong Markets.

The best noodle soup that I had was in the Ben Thanh Market itself. The food stalls inside the market were clean, the food fresh and the soup very tasty. It's also a fun place to eat because you quickly become the centre of attention.

John Lumley-Holmes

In Cholon there is good chicken noodle soup shop at ***Pho Ga Chu Sang*** *(204 Đ Hai Thuong Lan Ong)*. Just next door, ***Hong Phat*** *(206 Đ Hai Thuong Lai Ong)* serves equally good noodle soup with pork.

Self-Catering

Simple meals can easily be assembled from fruits, vegetables, French bread, croissants, cheese and other delectables sold in the city's markets and at street stalls. But avoid the unrefrigerated chocolate bars – they taste like they were left behind by the Americans in 1975.

Finding yourself daydreaming about Kellogg's Frosties, Pringle's potato chips, Twining's tea or Campbell's soup? A good place to satisfy these urges is ***Minimart*** *(101 Đ Nam Ky Khoi Nghia)* on the 2nd floor of the Saigon Intershop (just off of ĐL Le Loi). Prices here are as cheap as the street markets. It's open 9 am to 6 pm daily.

The ***Saigon Superbowl*** *(A43 Truong Son)*, near the airport in the Tan Binh District, offers Western-style mall culture, a supermarket and fast-food outlets.

Ice Cream Shops

Some of the best Vietnamese ice cream *(kem)* in Saigon is served at the three branches of ***Kem Bach Dang*** *(☎ 829 2707)*. Two are on ĐL Le Loi on either side of Đ Pasteur (Kem Bach Dang 1 is at 26 ĐL Le Loi and the other is at No 28). The third branch is at 67 ĐL Hai Ba Trung (on the corner of ĐL Le Loi). All three serve ice cream, hot and cold drinks and cakes at very reasonable prices. A US$1.50 speciality is ice cream served in a baby coconut with candied fruit on top *(kem trai dua)*.

There is excellent 'Franco-Vietnamese' ice cream at ***Fanny's*** *(☎ 821 1633, 29/31 Đ. Ton That Thiep)*, just east of D. Pasteur, on the south side of the street.

ENTERTAINMENT

Wartime Saigon was always known for its riotous nightlife. Liberation in 1975 put a real dampener on evening activities, but the pubs and discos have recently staged a comeback. However, periodic 'crack-down, clean-up' campaigns – allegedly to control drugs, prostitution and excessive noise – continue to keep Saigon's nightlife on the quiet side.

Sunday Night Live

Central Saigon is the place to be on Sunday and holiday nights (and lately Saturday nights as well). The streets are jam-packed with young Saigonese going *di troi* (cruising) on bicycles and motorbikes. Everyone is dressed in their fashionable best (often with the price tag still attached). The mass of slowly moving humanity is so thick on Đ Dong Khoi that you may have to wait until dawn to get across the street. It is utter chaos at intersections, where eight, 10 or more lanes of two-wheeled vehicles intersect without the benefit of traffic lights, safety helmets or sanity.

Near the Municipal Theatre, fashionably dressed young people take a break from cruising to watch the endless procession, lining up along the street next to their cycles. The air is electric with the glances of lovers and animated conversations among friends. Everyone is out to see and be seen – it's a sight you shouldn't miss.

Cinemas

Many Saigon maps have cinemas *(rap)* marked with a special symbol. There are several cinemas in the city centre, including ***Rap Mang Non***, on Đ Dong Khoi 100m from the Municipal Theatre. There is also ***Rap Dong Khoi*** *(163 Đ Dong Khoi)* and

Cong Nhan Cinema *(☎ 836 9556, 30 ĐL Tran Hung Dao, District 1).*

Water Puppets

This art really comes from the north, but in recent years has been introduced to the south, as it has been a relative hit with tourists. The venues to see water puppets in Saigon are the ***War Remnants Museum*** *(☎ 829 0325, 28 Đ Vo Van Tan)* and ***History Museum*** *(☎ 829 8146)*. Schedules change frequently, but shows tend to go on when a group of five or more customers has assembled.

Theatre

The ***Municipal Theatre*** *(Nha Hat Thanh Pho; ☎ 829 1249, 829 1584)* is on Đ Dong Khoi between the Continental and Caravelle hotels. Each week, it offers a different program, which may be Eastern European-style gymnastics, nightclub music or traditional Vietnamese theatre. There is typically some kind of performance at 8 pm. Refreshments are sold during intermission; public toilets are in the basement.

The huge ***Hoa Binh Theatre complex*** *(Nha Hat Hoa Binh, or Peace Theatre; 14 ĐL 3/2)* often has several performances taking place simultaneously in its various halls, the largest of which seats 2400 people. The complex is in District 10 next to the Vietnam Quoc Tu Pagoda. The ticket office (☎ 865 5199) is open from 7.30 am until the end of the evening show.

Evening performances, which begin around 7.30 pm, are usually held once or twice a week. Shows range from traditional and modern Vietnamese plays to Western pop music and circus acts.

Conservatory of Music

Both traditional Vietnamese and Western classical music are performed at the ***Conservatory of Music*** *(Nhac Vien Thanh Pho Ho Chi Minh; ☎ 839 6646, 112 Đ Nguyen Du)*, near Reunification Palace. Concerts are held at 7.30 pm each Monday and Friday during the two concert seasons (March–May and October–December).

Students aged seven to 16 attend the conservatory, which performs all the functions of a public school in addition to providing instruction in music. The music teachers here were trained in France, Britain and the USA, as well as the former Eastern Bloc. The school is free, but most of the students come from well-off families who can afford the prerequisite musical instruments.

Pubs

Saigon's widest variety of nightlife choices is in the central area around Đ Dong Khoi.

The stylish ***No 5 Ly Tu Trong*** *(☎ 825 6300)* is run by long-term Swiss expat, Heinz. Named for its address, the decor of this restored French colonial villa is stylish and sleek. Good music, tasty food and beer, pool and friendly staff all contribute to the pleasant atmosphere.

Another popular gathering spot for expats and travellers alike is the ***Underground*** *(☎ 829 9079, 69 Đ Dong Khoi)*, in the basement of the Lucky Plaza building. This spacious UK tube theme place has a gooc happy hour and excellent pizzas.

Sheridan's Irish House *(☎ 823 0973, 1 Đ Le Thanh Ton)* is a traditional Irish pul beamed straight from the backstreets o Dublin. For those seeking a naughtier edge ***Apocalypse Now*** *(☎ 824 1463, 2C Đ Th Sach)* has long led the pack. Music is lou and the patrons are from all walks of lif and apocalyptically rowdy.

The legendary imitation ***Hard Rock Caf*** *(24 Đ Mac Thi Buoi)* has music mellowe than the name suggests, but it's certainly popular spot.

The ***Tex-Mex Cantina*** *(☎ 829 5950, 2 Đ Le Thanh Ton)* features Mexican foo with a Texan twist. It's also notable for i pool tables.

Blue Gecko Bar & Restaurant has goo food, drinks and satellite TV – and yes, couple of odd geckos climbing the walls.

Wanna-be ranch hands should check o the ***Wild West Saloon*** *(☎ 829 5127, 33 Đ Hai Ba Trung)*, near the Saigon River in th centre. It's done up in a full-blown cowb motif.

When it comes to nightlife, Pham N Lao has a few hot spots. ***Allez Boo Bar*** *(1 Đ Pham Ngu Lao)*, on the corner of Đ I

Tham, is a dimly lit, bamboo-decorated place open to the backpacker street scene.

Long Phi Bar is one of the longest running Pham Ngu Lao pubs, and ***Bar Rolling Stones*** *(177 Đ Pham Ngu Lao)* and the ***Backpacker Bar*** *(167 Đ Pham Ngu Lao)* are also known for their late hours, loud music and party atmosphere. A short walk south-west on Đ Pham Ngu Lao is the slightly mellower ***Guns & Roses Bar***.

Nightclubs

Tropical Rainforest *(☎ 825 7783, 5–15 Đ Ho Huan Nghiep)* – called Mua Rung in Vietnamese – is done up in Amazonian rainforest-theme decor. It is one of the hottest dance spots in the city centre, and the US$4 cover charge entitles you to one free drink; the cocktail list features choices like 'Envy', 'Seduction' and 'Orgasm'. (You'll find it in the Dong Khoi map area, on the south side of D Ho Huan Nghiep, half-way between D Dong Khoi and Me Linh Square.)

Planet Europe *(A43 Truong Son)* is a flashy place out in the Saigon Superbowl (near the airport). Happy hour lasts from 6.30 to 9 pm.

The New World Hotel at 76 Đ Le Lai chips in with ***Catwalk*** *(☎ 824 3760)*. The disco is particularly big with Hong Kongers. The ***Saxophone Lounge*** *(☎ 822 8305)* is also here.

SPECTATOR SPORTS

Saigon Race Track

When South Vietnam was liberated in 1975, one of Hanoi's policies was to ban debauched, capitalistic pastimes such as gambling. Horse-racing tracks – mostly found in the Saigon area – were shut down. However, the government's need for hard cash has caused a rethink. The Saigon Race Track (Cau Lac Bo TDTT, ☎ 855 1205), which dates from around 1900, reopened in 1989.

Like the state lottery, the race track is extremely lucrative. But grumbling about just where the money is going has been coupled with widespread allegations about the drugging of horses. The minimum legal age for jockeys is 14 years; most look like they are about 10.

The overwhelming majority of gamblers are Vietnamese though there is no rule prohibiting foreigners from joining in. The maximum legal bet is US$2. High rollers can win a million dong (about US$90). Races are held Saturday and Sunday afternoons starting at 1 pm. Plans to introduce off-track betting have so far not materialised. However, illegal book-making (bets can be placed in gold!) offers one form of competition to the government-owned monopoly.

The Saigon Race Track is in District 11 at 2 Đ Le Dai Hanh.

SHOPPING

Arts & Crafts

In the last few years the free market in tourist junk has been booming – you can pick up a useful item like a lacquered turtle with a clock in its stomach or a ceramic Buddha that whistles the national anthem. And even if you're not the sort of person who needs a wind-up mechanical monkey that plays the cymbals, there is sure to be something that catches your eye.

Đ Dong Khoi has a reputation as the centre for handicrafts, but most shop owners drive a hard bargain. The Pham Ngu Lao area also has good pickings. For antiques, check out the selection at Indochine House, 29 Đ Dong Du, in the city centre.

Saigon is brimming with art galleries, and the following are just a sample:

Blue Space Gallery (☎ 821 3695)
1A Đ Le Thi Hong Gam, District 1 (inside the Fine Art Museum, Central Saigon map).

Saigon Gallery (☎ 829 7102)
5 Đ Ton Duc Thang, District 1
(centrally located on the Saigon waterfront).

Tu Do Gallery (☎ 823 1785)
142 Đ Dong Khoi, District 1
(a short stroll from the Rex Hotel).

Vinh Loi Gallery (☎ 822 2006)
41 Đ Ba Huyen Thanh Quan, District 3

Just opposite the Omni Hotel (on the way to the airport) is Lamson Art Gallery (☎ 844 1361), 106 Đ Nguyen Van Troi, Phu Nhuan District. This place sells high-quality, but relatively expensive, lacquerware, rattan, ceramics, woodcarvings and more. You can watch the artisans create their masterpieces and it's worth stopping by to have a look.

The Ho Chi Minh City Association of Fine Arts (☎ 823 0026), 218A Đ Pasteur, District 1, is where many aspiring young artists display their latest works. Typical prices for paintings are in the US$30 to US$50 range, but the artists may ask 10 times that.

The Home Zone (☎ 822 8022), 41 Đ Dinh Tien Hoang, near the corner of ĐL Le Duan, is an interesting place to look for locally made home furnishings.

Carved Seals

No bureaucracy, Communist or otherwise, can exist without the official stamps and seals that provide the *raison d'être* for legions of clerks. This need is well-catered to by the numerous shops strung out along the street just north of the New World Hotel (opposite side of the street and just west of Ben Thanh Market). In Cholon, you can find shops making these seals along Đ Hai Thuong Lai Ong.

Most Vietnamese also own carved seals bearing their name (an old tradition borrowed from China). You can have one made too, but ask a local to help translate your name into Vietnamese. You might want to get your seal carved in Cholon using Chinese characters, these are certainly more artistic (though less practical) than the Romanised script used by the Vietnamese today.

Clothing

At the budget end of the scale, T-shirts are available from vendors along ĐL Nguyen Hue in the city centre, or Đ De Tham in the Pham Ngu Lao area. Expect to pay about US$2 for a printed T-shirt, or US$3 to US$5 for an embroidered one.

Vietsilk (☎ 823 4860), 21 Đ Dong Khoi, sells ready-made garments, as well as embroidery and drawings on silk.

Women's ao dai, the flowing silk blouse slit up the sides and worn over trousers (see the 'Camau Saves the Ao Dai' boxed text in the Mekong Delta chapter), are tailored at shops in and around Ben Thanh Market or the Saigon Intershop area. There are also male ao dais available – these are a bit looser fitting and come with a silk-covered head wrap to match the top of the outfit. Places to buy ao dais include:

Ao Dai Si Hoang (☎ 829 9156)
36 Ly Tu Trong, District 1

Ao Dai Thanh Chau (☎ 823 1032)
244 Đ Dinh Tien Hoang. Famous with locals, though a bit far from the city centre.

Vietnam Silk (☎ 829 2607, fax 843 9279)
183 Đ Dong Khoi (opposite Continental Hotel)

For ready-made women's fashions try Thai Fashion at 92H Đ Le Thanh Ton, District 1. You might want to check out nearby Down Under Fashions at 229 Đ Le Thanh Ton. Both are centrally located in District 1, on D Le Thanh Ton.

There are numerous tailors' shops in central Saigon and also in Cholon; several upmarket hotels have in-house tailors.

Coffee

Vietnamese coffee is prime stuff and is amazingly cheap if you know where to buy it. The best grades are from Buon Ma Thuot and the beans are roasted in butter. Obviously, price varies according to quality and also with the seasons. You can buy whole beans or have them ground for no extra charge.

The city's major markets have the best prices and widest selection. We scored some top-grade caffeine in Ben Thanh Market, also the best place to find the peculiar coffee-drippers used by the Vietnamese. Get a stainless-steel one, which are easier to use than the cheaper aluminium ones. Also look in the market for a coffee grinder if you're buying whole beans.

Stamps & Coins

As you enter the main post office at 2 Cong Xa Paris, immediately to your right is a counter selling stationery, and also some decent stamp collections. Also as you face the entrance from the outside, to your right are a few stalls which have stamp collections and other goods such as foreign coin and banknotes. You can even find stuff from the former South Vietnamese regime. Price are variable: about US$2 will get you a respectable set of late-model stamps already mounted in a book, but the older and rarer collections cost more.

Many bookshops and antique shops along Đ Dong Khoi sell overpriced French Indochinese coins and banknotes as well as packets of Vietnamese stamps.

Markets

The street market which runs along Đ Huynh Thuc Khang and Đ Ton That Dam in the Dong Khoi area sells everything. The area used to be known as the Electronics Black Market until early 1989, when it was legalised. It's now generally called the Huynh Thuc Khang Street Market, although it doesn't have an official name.

You can still buy electronic goods of all sorts – from mosquito zappers to video cassette players – but the market has expanded enormously to include clothing, washing detergent, lacquerware, condoms, pirated cassettes, posters of Ho Chi Minh, Michael Jackson and Mickey Mouse, smuggled bottles of Johnny Walker, Chinese-made 'Swiss' army knives and just about anything else to satisfy your material needs.

Ben Thanh Market Saigon has a number of incredibly huge indoor markets selling all manner of goods. They are some of the best places to pick up conical hats and ao dai. The most central of these is Ben Thanh Market (Cho Ben Thanh). The market and surrounding streets makes up one the city's liveliest areas. Everything commonly eaten, worn or used by the Saigonese is available here: vegetables, fruits, meat, spices, biscuits, sweets, tobacco, clothing, hats, household items, hardware and so forth. The legendary slogan of US country stores applies equally well here: 'If we don't have it, you don't need it'. Nearby, food stalls sell inexpensive meals.

Ben Thanh Market is 700m south-west of the Rex Hotel at the intersection of ĐL Le Loi, ĐL Ham Nghi, ĐL Tran Hung Dao and Đ Le Lai. Known to the French as the Halles Centrales, it was built in 1914 from reinforced concrete; the central cupola is 28m in diameter. The main entrance, with its belfry and clock, has become a symbol of Saigon.

Opposite the belfry, in the centre of the traffic roundabout, is an equestrian statue of Tran Nguyen Hai, the first person in Vietnam to use carrier pigeons. At the base, on a pillar, is a small white bust of Quach Thi Trang, a Buddhist woman killed during antigovernment protests in 1963.

The Old Market Despite the name, this is not a place to find antiques. Rather, the Old Market is where you can most easily buy imported (black market?) foods, wines, shaving cream, shampoo etc. However, this is not the place to look for electronics or machinery (you have to go to Dan Sinh Market for these). There is a problem using the Vietnamese name for this market (Cho Cu), because written or pronounced without the correct tones it means 'penis'. Your cyclo driver will no doubt be much amused if you say that this is what you're looking for. Perhaps directions would be better – the Old Market is on the north side of ĐL Ham Nghi between D Ton That Dam and Đ Ho Tung Mau.

Dan Sinh Market Also known as the War Surplus Market, this is the place to shop for a chic pair of combat boots or rusty dog tags. It's also the best market for electronics and other types of imported machinery – you could easily renovate a whole villa from the goods on sale.

The market is at 104 Đ Yersin, next to Phung Son Tu Pagoda. The front part is filled with stalls selling automobiles and motorbikes, but directly behind the pagoda building you can find reproductions of what appears to be second-hand military gear.

Stall after stall sells everything from handy gas masks and field stretchers to rain gear and mosquito nets. You can also find canteens, duffel bags, ponchos and boots. Anyone planning on spending time in Rwanda or New York City should consider picking up a second-hand flak jacket (prices are good). But watch out for exorbitant overcharging of tourists looking for American War souvenirs.

Binh Tay Market Binh Tay Market (Cho Binh Tay) is Cholon's main marketplace (actually about one block away in District 6). Much of the business here is wholesale. Binh Tay Market is on ĐL Hau Giang about 1km south-west of Đ Chau Van Liem.

Andong Market Cholon's other indoor market, Andong, is very close to the intersection of ĐL Tran Phu and ĐL An Duong Vuong. This market is four storeys high and is packed with shops. The 1st floor has heaps of clothing, including imported designer jeans from Hong Kong, the latest pumps from Paris and ao dai. The basement is a gourmet's delight of small restaurants – a perfect place to pig out 'on a shoestring'.

GETTING THERE & AWAY

Air

Below is a selected list of Ho Chi Minh City's airline offices. To locate more international airlines, check the listings in The Guide or Time Out.

Cathay Pacific Airways (☎ 824 5405) 58 Đ Dong Khoi, District 1
Japan Airlines (☎ 821 9098) 115 Đ Nguyen Hue, District 1
Korean Air (☎ 824 2878, fax 824 2877) 34 Đ Le Duan, District 1
Lao Aviation (☎ 822 6990) 93 Đ Pasteur, District 1
Malaysia Airlines (☎ 829 2529, fax 829 9027) 132–134 Đ Dong Khoi, District 1
Royal Air Cambodge (☎ 844 0126, fax 842 1578) 343 Đ Le Van Sy, Tan Binh District
Singapore Airlines (☎ 823 1588, fax 823 1554) Suite 101, Saigon Tower Building, 29 ĐL Le Duan, District 1
Thai Airways International (☎ 822 3365, fax 822 3465) 65 Đ Nguyen Du, District 1
Vasco (☎ 842 2790, fax 844 5224) 114 Đ Bach Dang, Tan Binh District, Tan Son Nhat Airport
Vietnam Airlines (☎ 829 2118, fax 823 0273) 116 ĐL Nguyen Hue, District 1

Tan Son Nhat airport was one of the three busiest airports in the world during the late 1960s. The runways are still lined with lichen-covered, mortar-proof, aircraft retaining walls and other military structures.

You must reconfirm all reservations for flights out of the country. For more details on international air transport see the Getting There & Away chapter.

Domestic flights from Saigon are operated by both Vietnam Airlines and Pacific Airlines. See the Getting Around chapter for details on air fares, routes and schedules.

Bus

Cholon Station Intercity buses depart from and arrive at a variety of stations around Saigon. Cholon station is the most convenient place to get buses to Mytho and other Mekong Delta towns. It is at the very western end of ĐL Tran Hung Dao in District 5, close to Binh Tay Market.

Mien Tay Station Less convenient than Cholon station, Mien Tay station nevertheless has even more buses to areas south of Saigon (basically the Mekong Delta). This huge station (Ben Xe Mien Tay; ☎ 825 5955) is about 10km west of Saigon in An Lac, a part of Binh Chanh District (Huyen Binh Chanh).

Buses and minibuses from Mien Tay serve Bac Lieu (six hours), Camau (12 hours), Cantho (3½ hours), Chau Doc (six hours), Long Xuyen (five hours) and Rach Gia (six to seven hours).

Mien Dong Station Buses to points north of Saigon leave from Mien Dong bus station (Ben Xe Mien Dong; ☎ 829 4056), in Binh Thanh District about 5km from central Saigon on National Highway 13 (Quoc Lo 13), the continuation of Đ Xo Viet Nghe Tinh.

The station is just under 2km north of the intersection of Đ Xo Viet Nghe Tinh and Đ Dien Bien Phu.

There are services from Mien Dong to Buon Ma Thuot (15 hours), Danang (2[illegible] hours), Haiphong (53 hours), Nha Trang (1[illegible] hours), Hanoi (49 hours), Hué (29 hours), Pleiku (22 hours), Vinh (42 hours) Quang Ngai (24 hours), Qui Nhon (17 hours), Nam Dinh (47 hours) and Tuy Hoa (12 hours). Most buses leave daily from 5 to 5.30 am.

Tay Ninh Station Buses to Tay Ninh, Cu Chi and points north-east of Saigon depart from the Tay Ninh bus station (Ben Xe Ta

Ninh; ☎ 849 5935), in Tan Binh District west of the centre. To get there, head all the way out on Đ Cach Mang Thang Tam. The station is about 1km past where Đ Cach Mang Thang Tam merges with Đ Le Dai Hanh.

Vung Tau Just next to the Saigon Hotel and the mosque on Đ Dong Du is a bus stop for buses to Vung Tau. As this is not an official bus station, it could be suddenly moved, so inquire first.

Train

Saigon train station (Ga Sai Gon; ☎ 823 0105) is in District 3 at 1 Đ Nguyen Thong. Trains from here serve cities along the coast north of Saigon. The ticket office is open 7.15 to 11 am and 1 to 3 pm daily.

For details on the *Reunification Express* service see the Getting Around chapter.

Car

Inquire at almost any tourist cafe or hotel to arrange a car rental. Renting from a licensed agency is safer, albeit more expensive, but you needn't go to the most expensive places like Saigon Tourist. The agencies in the Pham Ngu Lao area generally offer the lowest prices.

Boat

For details on the Greenlines hydrofoil service to/from Ho Chi Minh City and the Mekong Delta, see the 'Hydrofoil' boxed text in the Mekong Delta chapter.

There is also a hydrofoil service to Vung Tao for US$10 each way (1 1/4 hours, US$10 for foreigners, half-price children). In Saigon, departures are from the Bach Dang Jetty on Đ Ton Duc Thang. Boats depart Saigon/Vung Tao six times daily between 6.30 am and 4.30 pm. For more information contact the Vina Express office at the jetty (☎ 821 5609). In Vung Tau you board the hydrofoil at Cau Da pier opposite the Hai Au Hotel (Front Beach). Vina Express (☎ 856530) has a Vung Tau office by the pier.

Cargo ferries to the Mekong Delta depart from a dock (☎ 829 7892) at the river end of ĐL Ham Nghi. There is daily service to the provinces of An Giang and Vinh Long and to the towns of Ben Tre (eight hours), Camau (30 hours; once every four days), Mytho (six hours; departs at 11 am) and Tan Chau. Buy your tickets on the boat. Simple food may be available on board. Be aware that these ancient vessels lack the most elementary safety gear, such as life jackets.

Organised Tours

There are surprisingly few day tours available of Saigon itself, though any local travel agent can come up with something in exchange for a fee. Hiring a cyclo for a half-day or full day of sightseeing is another interesting option, but be sure to agree on the price before setting out (most drivers charge around US$1 per hour).

There are heaps of tours to the outlying areas such as the Cu Chi Tunnels, Tay Ninh and the Mekong Delta. Some of the tours are day trips and other are overnighters. The cheapest tours by far are available from cafes and agencies in the Pham Ngu Lao area (see Travel Agencies earlier in this chapter).

GETTING AROUND

To/From the Airport

Tan Son Nhat airport is 7km from central Saigon. Metered taxis are your best bet and cost 55,000d to 60,000d (around US$4) between the airport and the city centre. You will be enthusiastically greeted by a group of taxi drivers after you exit the terminal; most are OK, but make sure that:

- The driver agrees to use the meter.
- The meter is switched on *after* you get in the car.
- The final fare does not go much over 60,000d to get to the city centre.

Be aware that taxi drivers will probably recommend a 'good and cheap' hotel, and deliver you to a hotel for a commission; if you don't know where you are going, this is not a bad system per se. Problems arise, however, when you ask a taxi driver to take you to a place which doesn't pay commission – the driver may tell you the hotel is closed, burned down, is dirty and dangerous, or anything to steer you somewhere else.

If you're travelling solo and without much baggage, a motorbike 'taxi' is an option for getting to/from the airport. Drivers hang out near the airport car park and typically ask around US$3 to go to the city centre. If you take a motorbike to Tan Son Nhat, you may have to walk the short distance from the airport gate to the terminal. Private cars can bring you into the airport, but must drop you off at the domestic terminal, only a one-minute walk from the international terminal.

To get to the airport, you can call a taxi (see the Taxi section later). Some cafes in the Pham Ngu Lao area do runs to the airport – these places even have sign-up sheets where you can book share taxis for US$2 per person.

Bus

Few tourists make use of the city buses, though they are safer than cyclos if less aesthetic. Now that Ho Chi Minh City's People's Committee has resolved to phase out cyclos, some money is finally being put into the badly neglected public transport system.

At present, there are only a few bus routes, though more undoubtedly will be added. No decent bus map is available and bus stops are mostly unmarked, so it's worth summarising the main bus lines, which are as follows:

Saigon–Cholon Buses depart from central Saigon at Me Linh Square (by the Saigon River) and continue along ĐL Tran Hung Dao to Binh Tay Market in Cholon, then return along the same route. The bus company running this route is an Australian joint venture – buses have air-conditioning and video movies and the driver is well dressed! All this for US$0.25. Buy your ticket on board from the female attendant.

Mien Dong–Mien Tay Buses depart from Mien Dong bus station (north-east Saigon), pass through Cholon and terminate at Mien Tay bus station on the western edge of town. The fare is US$0.40.

Taxi

Metered taxis cruises the streets, but it's often easier to phone for one. There are several companies in Saigon offering metered taxis and they charge almost exactly the same rates. Flagfall is around US$0.50 for the first kilometre and US$0.50 thereafter.

Your Friendly Taxi Driver

A minor warning – some airport taxi drivers like to play a little game when it comes to taking you to a hotel. They want the hotel to pay them a commission and they know which hotels pay commissions and which don't. If you want to go to a hotel which does not pay commissions then don't be surprised if the driver claims that place is very dirty, unsafe, expensive or even out of business.

Many backpackers simply ask the driver to take them to a given hotel in the Pham Ngu Lao area; however, when you arrive there the driver may insist on going inside the hotel first 'to check if there's any rooms'. If the hotel refuses to pay him, then he'll tell you that there are 'no rooms left'. Sometimes the hotels really are full, but you really have to go inside yourself and ask – don't *always* believe what your driver tells you.

Most hotels don't like this arrangement, but they are forced to go along with it – otherwise, they lose business. Even nastier is that some of the hotel owners go to the airport to make an agreement with the drivers – if they bring guests to their hotel, then the driver shares 50% of the first night's accommodation fee. With such a strong incentive, it's not surprising that many drivers at the airport try to shove a hotel name card into your hand and claim it's 'very good'.

All of the above applies also to cyclos, motorbikes and taxis parked at the train station.

The competitors include:

Ben Thanh Taxi	☎ 842 2422
Mai Linh Taxi	☎ 822 6666
Red Taxi	☎ 844 6677
Saigon Taxi	☎ 842 4242
Vina Taxi	☎ 811 1111

Cyclo

Cyclos can be hailed along major thoroughfares almost any time, day or night. In Saigon, many of the drivers are former South Vietnamese army soldiers and quite a few know at least basic English, while others are quite fluent. Each driver has a story of wa 're-education', persecution and poverty to tell (see the 'Life on the Streets' boxed text).

In an effort to control Saigon's rapidly growing traffic problems, there are presently 51 streets on which cyclos are prohibited to ride. As a result, your driver must often take a circuitous route to avoid these trouble spots, since the police will not hesitate to fine him. For the same reason, the driver may not be able to drop you off at the exact address you want, but will bring you to the nearest side street. Try to have some sympathy since it is not their fault. Perhaps the authorities would have served the city better by allowing the quiet and atmospheric cyclos carte blanche and forcing the smoke-spewing cars to take an alternative route.

Short hops around the city centre should cost around 5000d (US$0.40), and definitely no more than 10,000d (US$0.80); central Saigon to central Cholon costs about US$1.60. Overcharging is the norm, so negotiate a price beforehand and have the exact change ready. Rent a cyclo for US$1 per hour, a fine idea if you will be doing much touring; most cyclo drivers around the Pham Ngu Lao area can produce a sample tour program.

Enjoy cyclos while you can, as the municipal government intends to phase them out.

Xe Lam

Xe Lams (tiny three-wheeled vehicles otherwise known as Lambrettas) connect the various bus stations. There is a useful Xe Lam stop on the north-west corner of Đ Pham Ngu Lao and Đ Nguyen Thai Hoc where you can catch a ride to the Mien Tay bus station, for the Mekong Delta.

Honda Om

A quick (if precarious) way around town is to ride on the back of a motorbike *(Honda om)*. You can either try to flag someone down (most drivers can use the extra cash) or ask a Vietnamese to find a Honda om for you. The accepted rate is comparable to cyclos.

Car & Motorbike

Travel agencies, hotels and cafes are all into the car rental business. Most of the vehicles are relatively recent Japanese or Korean-made machines – everything from subcompacts to minibuses. However, it's occasionally possible to enjoy a ride in a vintage vehicle from the 1950s or 60s. Not long ago, boat-like classic American cars (complete with tail fins and impressive chrome fenders) were popular as 'wedding taxis'. Prestige these days, however, means a white Toyota. Nevertheless, some of the old vehicles can be hired for excursions in and around Saigon. You'll also see the occasional French-built Renault or Citroën. The former Soviet Union chips in with Ladas, Moskviches and Volgas.

If you're brave, you can rent a motorbike and really earn your 'I Survived Saigon' T-shirt. Many say this is the fastest and easiest way to get around Saigon and that's probably true as long as you don't crash into anything.

Motorbike rentals are ubiquitous in places where tourists congregate – the Pham Ngu Lao area is as good as any. Ask at the cafes.

A 50cc motorbike can be rented for US$5 to US$8 per day. Before renting one, make sure it's rideable, and if you are wise wear a helmet.

Bicycle

A bicycle is a great, if slow way to get around the city and see things. Bikes can be rented from a number of places – many hotels, cafes and travel agencies can accommodate you.

A good place to buy a decent (ie, imported) bicycle is Federal Bike Shop (☎ 833 2899), which has three locations: 139H Đ Nguyen Trai, 158B Đ Vo Thi Sau and 156 Đ Pham Hong Thai. Cheaper deals may be found at some of the shops around 288 Đ Le Thanh Ton (corner of Đ Cach Mang Thang Tam). You can also buy bike components: Czech and French frames, Chinese derailleurs, headlamps etc. A bicycle with foreign components costs about US$100. In Cholon, you might try the bicycle shops on ĐL Ngo Gia Tu just south-west of ĐL Ly Thai To (near An Quang Pagoda). In District 4 there are bicycle parts shops along Đ Nguyen Tat Thanh just south of the Ho Chi Minh Museum.

For cheap and poorly assembled domestic bicycles and parts, try the ground floor

Life on the Streets

Through the smoke and pollution, groups of battered old men lean against their cyclos – three-wheeled rickshaws, operated by pedal-power, with a seat attached to the front. Win, a veteran cyclo driver recently explained, 'It's hard to earn one's living. You have to bend in order to pedal and earn a little money'.

Before the American War many cyclo drivers were doctors, teachers or journalists, but like many of their friends they were punished for siding with the Americans. After the cease-fire, tens of thousands of them were stripped of their citizenship and sent to re-education camps for seven years or more. Over 20 years later, it is still impossible for them to return to the jobs they are qualified to do and, as most do not have an official residence permit (which means they cannot own property or a business), it's technically illegal for them to be in the city. Many of these men have never had families because they could not afford (or were not permitted by the government) a home to live in.

Around the restaurants, hotels, nightclubs and karaoke bars of central Saigon, it's hard to miss them in their worn clothes and tar-stained sandals, victims from years of being caught in the jagged chains of the cyclos. The comings and goings at hotels are a constant form of entertainment (and business) for Saigon's cyclo drivers. Nothing misses their sharp eyes. Their courteous propositions hide their desire to establish your first name and claim you as 'their property' while you're in Saigon. Once known, cries of your name across crowded streets will hound you as the determined drivers compete for your business.

of the Tax Department Store on the corner of ĐL Nguyen Hue and ĐL Le Loi.

For on-the-spot bicycle repairs, look for an upturned army helmet and a hand pump sitting next to the curb.

Bicycle parking lots are usually just roped-off sections of pavement. For about 1000d (US$0.08) you can safely leave your bicycle (bicycle theft is a big problem). When you pull up, your bicycle will have a number written on the seat in chalk or stapled to the handlebars. You will be given a reclaim chit (don't lose it!). If you come back and your bicycle is gone, the parking lot is supposedly required to replace it.

Boat

You can easily hire a motorised 5m boat to see the city from the Saigon River. There will always be someone hanging around looking to charter a boat – ask them to bring the boat to you, rather than you go to the boat (they can easily do this). Warning: there have been countless unpleasant incidents with bag snatching and pickpocketing at the docks at the base of ĐL Ham Nghi.

The price should be US$5 per hour for a small boat or US$10 to US$15 for a larger and faster craft. Interesting destinations for short trips include Cholon (along Ben Nghe Channel) and the zoo (along Thi Nghe Channel). Note that both channels are fascinating, but filthy – raw sewage is discharged into the water. Tourists regard the channels as a major attraction, but the government considers them an eyesore and has already launched a program to move residents out. The channels will eventually be filled in and the water diverted into underground sewer pipes.

For longer trips up the Saigon River, it is worth chartering a fast speedboat from Saigon Tourist. Although these cost US$2(per hour, you'll save money when you consider that a cheap boat takes at least five times longer for the same journey. Splitting the cost between a small group of travellers makes sense and it can be more fun boating with others. Although cruising the Saigon River can be interesting, it pales in comparison with the splendour of the canals in the Mekong Delta region (see the Mekong Delta chapter for details). One traveller wrote:

> We hired a small boat with driver and femal guide for US$5 for an hour for two people an were able to go up the Cholon Channel and se life on the waterfront. The bridges are too low fc

Life on the Streets

Cyclo drivers are, however, excellent city guides – they know every corner of the city and can give you a potted history of the key sites. Also, the front seat of a cyclo really is one of the best ways to see Saigon – but it does take some getting used to. In heavy traffic it's like riding a roller-coaster at a fairground; the traffic races towards you at startling speeds from every direction and, just when you think you are surely going to die, your cyclo driver slips into a gap that magically appears in the traffic, while you thank the gods that you are still in one piece.

Tourists love to reverse roles and have a go in the saddle, mistakenly thinking that it is easy to spend one's day cycling from place to place, but their opinions quickly change. In most cases they find the cyclos too hard to peddle and, if they advance at all, they don't get very far on the uneven, potholed roads.

The drivers' home is usually a street corner, which is made colourful and interesting by using wooden tables and small, multicoloured, plastic footstools which support them only inches off the ground. Their floor is broken up bits of pavement slabs and the 'drivers' drinks cabinet' (a street stall or two) nestles just behind them.

After a day's sightseeing, they might invite you to join them for either a whisky in a Coke bottle or the local beer Ba, Ba, Ba (pronounce it 'baa-baa-baa' slowly because in Vietnamese it can also sound like you are saying 'three old women'!). An evening with these guys is always worthwhile.

Juliet Coombe

regular tourist craft. It was extremely interesting to see how these stilt-house dwellers live. We were told that when the water level is low 'pirate boys' board the boats demanding money, but we had no problems. We were able to take many interesting photographs.

But another traveller had a different attitude:

Boat trips through the Ben Nghe Channel to Cholon are a bit of a rip-off. The pieces of plastic and the water-plants in the very dirty water make the motor stop every two or three minutes. This forces the boat owner to stop and do a cleaning job which takes much time. We spent 35 minutes drifting on 5km of stinking water without any protection from the rain. There are better places in Vietnam to do boat journeys, such as Cantho, Nha Trang, Hoi An and Hué, to name a few.

Since you hire boats by the hour, some will go particularly slowly because they know the meter is running. You might want to set a time limit from the outset.

Ferries across the Saigon River leave from the dock at the foot of ĐL Ham Nghi. They run every half-hour or so from 4.30 am to 10.30 pm. To get on these vessels, you have to run the gauntlet of greedy boat owners and pickpockets.

Around Ho Chi Minh City

CU CHI TUNNELS

☎ 08

The town of Cu Chi has now become a district of greater Ho Chi Minh City (Saigon), and has a population of 200,000 (it had about 80,000 residents during the American War). At first glance, there is little evidence here to indicate the intense fighting, bombing and destruction that went on in Cu Chi during the war. To see what went on, you have to dig deeper – underground.

The tunnel network of Cu Chi became legendary during the 1960s for its role in facilitating Viet Cong (VC) control of a large rural area only 30km to 40km from Ho Chi Minh City. At its height, the tunnel system stretched from the South Vietnamese capital to the Cambodian border; in the district of Cu Chi alone, there were over 250km of tunnels. The network, parts of which were several storeys deep, included innumerable trapdoors, specially constructed living areas, storage facilities, weapons' factories, field hospitals, command centres and kitchens.

The tunnels made possible communication and coordination between VC-controlled enclaves isolated from each other by South Vietnamese and American land and air operations. They also allowed the guerrillas to mount surprise attacks wherever the tunnels went – even within the perimeters of the US military base at Dong Du – and to disappear into hidden trapdoors without a trace. After ground operations against the tunnels claimed large numbers of US casualties and proved ineffective, the Americans resorted to massive firepower, eventually turning Cu Chi's 420 sq km into what the authors of *The Tunnels of Cu Chi* (Tom Mangold & John Penycate) have called 'the most bombed, shelled, gassed, defoliated and generally devastated area in the history of warfare'.

Today, Cu Chi has become a pilgrimage site for Vietnamese school children and Party cadres. Parts of this remarkable tunnel network – enlarged and upgraded versions of the real thing – are open to the public.

Highlights

- Crawl through the tunnels dug by the Viet Cong at Cu Chi.
- Observe the daily worship service at the colourful Caodai temple in Tay Ninh.
- Visit the bustling seaside resort of Vung Tau, or relax on the less-populated beaches at Long Hai or Hoc Coc.

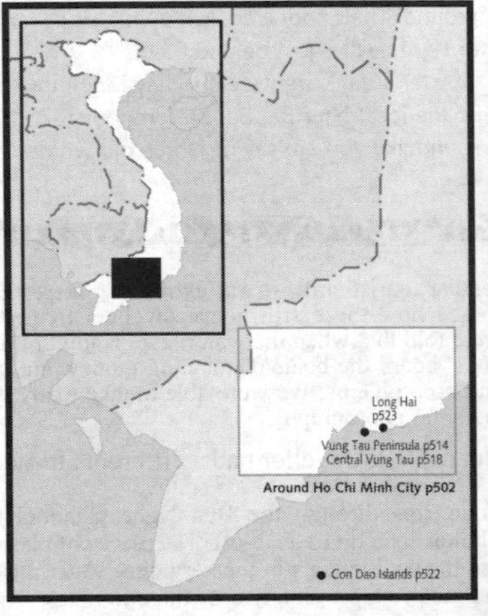

The unadulterated tunnels, though not actually closed to tourists, are hard to get to and are rarely visited.

There are numerous war cemeteries all around Cu Chi.

History

The tunnels of Cu Chi were built over a period of 25 years beginning in the late 1940s. They were the improvised response of a poorly equipped peasant army to its enemy's high-tech ordnance, helicopters, artillery, bombers and chemical weapons.

The Viet Minh built the first dugouts and tunnels in the hard, red earth of Cu Chi – th area is ideal for the construction of tunnels – during the war against the French. The excavations were used mostly for communication between villages and to evade French army sweeps of the area.

When the VC's National Liberation Front (NLF) insurgency began in earnest around 1960, the old Viet Minh tunnels were repaired and new extensions excavated. Within a few years the system assumed enormous strategic importance, and most of Cu Chi District and nearby areas came under firm VC control. In addition, Cu Chi was used as a base for infiltrating intelligence agents and sabotage teams into Saigon. The stunning attacks in the South Vietnamese capital during the 1968 Tet Offensive were planned and launched from Cu Chi.

In early 1963, the Diem government implemented the botched Strategic Hamlets Program, under which fortified encampments, surrounded by rows of sharp bamboo spikes, were built to house people 'relocated' from Communist-controlled areas. The first 'strategic hamlet' was in Ben Cat District, next door to Cu Chi. Not only was the program carried out with incredible incompetence, alienating the peasantry, but the VC launched a major effort to defeat it; the VC was able to tunnel into the hamlets and control them from within. By the end of 1963, the first showpiece hamlet had been overrun.

The series of setbacks and defeats suffered by the South Vietnamese government forces in the Cu Chi area rendered a complete VC victory by the end of 1965 a distinct possibility. Indeed, in the early months of that year, the guerrillas boldly held a victory parade in the middle of Cu Chi town. VC strength in and around Cu Chi was one of the reasons the Johnson administration decided to involve American combat troops in the war.

To deal with the threat posed by VC control of an area so near the South Vietnamese capital, one of the Americans' first actions was to establish a large base camp in Cu Chi District. Unknowingly, they built it right on top of an existing tunnel network. It took months for the 25th Division to figure out why they kept getting shot at in their tents at night.

The Americans and Australians tried a variety of methods to 'pacify' the area around Cu Chi that came to be known as the Iron Triangle. They launched large-scale ground operations involving tens of thousands of troops, but failed to locate the tunnels. To deny the VC cover and supplies, rice paddies were defoliated, huge swathes of jungle bulldozed, and villages evacuated and razed. The Americans also sprayed chemical defoliants on the area from the air and then, a few months later, ignited the tinder-dry vegetation with gasoline and napalm. But the intense heat interacted with the wet tropical air in such a way as to create cloudbursts that extinguished the fires. The VC remained safe and sound in their tunnels.

Unable to win this battle with chemicals, the US army began sending men down into the tunnels. These 'tunnel rats', who were often involved in underground fire fights, sustained appallingly high casualty rates.

When the Americans began using Alsatians trained to use their keen sense of smell to locate trapdoors and guerrillas, the VC put out pepper to distract the dogs. They also began washing with American toilet soap, which gave off a scent the canines identified as friendly. Captured American uniforms, which had the familiar smell of bodies nourished on American-style food, were put out to confuse the dogs further. Most importantly, the dogs were not able to spot booby traps. So many dogs were killed or maimed that their horrified army handlers refused to send them into the tunnels.

The Americans declared Cu Chi a free-strike zone: minimal authorisation was needed to shoot at anything in the area, random artillery was fired into the area at night, and pilots were told to drop unused bombs and napalm there before returning to base. But the VC stayed put. Finally, in the late 1960s, American B-52 bombers carpet-bombed the whole area, destroying most of the tunnels along with everything else around. The gesture was militarily useless by then: the USA was already on its way out of the war. The tunnels had served their purpose.

The VC guerrillas serving in the tunnels lived in extremely difficult conditions and suffered horrific casualties. Only about 6000 of the 16,000 cadres who fought in the tunnels survived the war. In addition, uncounted thousands of civilians in the area were killed. Their tenacity despite the bombings, the pressures of living underground for weeks and months at a time, and the deaths of countless friends and comrades is extraordinary.

The villages of Cu Chi have been presented with numerous honorific awards, decorations and citations by the government, and many have been declared 'heroic villages'. Since 1975, new hamlets have been established and the population of the area has more than doubled, but chemical defoliants remain in the soil and water, and crop yields are still poor.

For more details, you might want to take a look at *The Tunnels of Cu Chi* by Tom Mangold & John Penycate.

The Tunnels

Over the years the VC, learning by trial and error, developed simple but effective techniques to make their tunnels difficult to detect or disable. Wooden trapdoors were camouflaged with earth and branches; some were booby-trapped. Hidden underwater entrances from rivers were constructed. To cook, they used 'Dien Bien Phu kitchens', which exhausted the smoke through vents many metres away from the cooking site. Trapdoors were installed throughout the network to prevent tear gas, smoke or water from moving from one part of the system to another. Some sections were even equipped with electric lighting.

Presently, two of the tunnel sites are open to visitors. One is near the village of Ben Dinh and the other is at Ben Duoc.

Ben Dinh This small, renovated section of the tunnel system is near the village of Ben Dinh, 50km from Ho Chi Minh City. In one

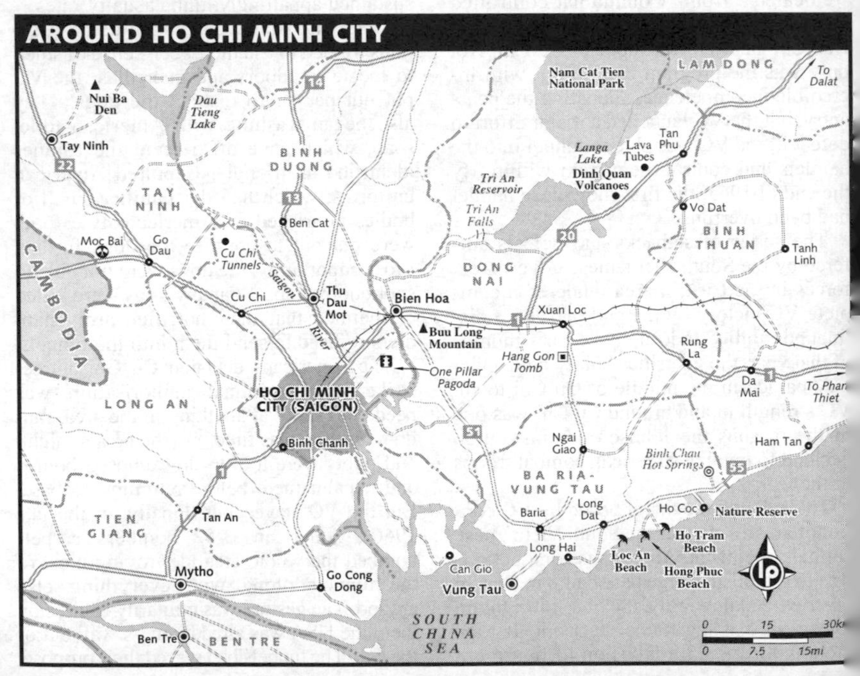

of the classrooms at the visitors centre, a large map shows the extent of the network (the area shown is in the north-western corner of Greater Ho Chi Minh City). The tunnels are marked in red, VC bases are shown in light grey and the light blue lines are rivers (the Saigon River is at the top). Fortified villages held by South Vietnamese and American forces are marked in grey, while blue dots represent the American and South Vietnamese military posts that were supposed to ensure the security of nearby villages. The dark blue area in the centre is the base of the American 25th Infantry Division. Most prearranged tours do not take you to this former base, but it is not off limits and you can easily arrange a visit if you have your own guide and driver.

To the right of the large map are two cross-section diagrams of the tunnels. The bottom diagram is a reproduction of one used by General William Westmoreland, the commander of American forces in Vietnam (1964–8). For once, the Americans seemed to have had their intelligence information right (though the tunnels did not pass under rivers, nor did the guerrillas wear headgear underground).

The section of the tunnel system presently open to visitors is a few hundred metres south of the visitors centre. It snakes up and down through various chambers along its 50m length. The unlit tunnels are about 1.2m high and 80cm across. A knocked-out M-48 tank and a bomb crater are near the exit, which is in a reforested eucalyptus grove.

Entry to the tunnel site costs US$4 for tourists, but is free for Vietnamese nationals.

Ben Duoc These are not the genuine tunnels but a full-fledged reconstruction for the benefit of visitors. The emphasis here is more on the fun fair, and tourists are given the chance to imagine what it was like to be a guerrilla. At this site there is even the opportunity to fire an M-16, AK-47 or Russian carbine rifle. This costs US$1 per bullet, but may be the only opportunity you'll ever get. It's recommended that you wear hearing protection.

Admission to the tunnels is US$4.

Cu Chi War History Museum

This museum is not actually at the tunnel sites, but rather just off the main highway in the central area of the town of Cu Chi. Sadly, the Cu Chi War History Museum (Nha Truyen Thong Huyen Cu Chi) is rather disappointing and gets few visitors.

It's a small museum and almost all explanations are in Vietnamese. One English explanation attached to a canoe reads:

> Mr Nguyen Van Tranh's boat. He now is living in hamlet Mui Con, Phuoc Hiep village. During the wars against the French colonialists and the American imperialists, he was using this boat for transporting food and weapons, as well as carrying revolutionary cadres to and fro.

There is a collection of some gruesome photos showing civilians who were severely wounded or killed after being attacked by American bombs or burned with napalm. A painting on the wall shows American soldiers armed with rifles being attacked by Vietnamese peasants armed only with sticks. A sign near the photos formerly read (in Vietnamese) 'American conquest and crimes', but this was changed in 1995 to read 'Enemy conquest and crimes'. Apparently, some effort is being made to tone down the rhetoric in anticipation of receiving more American visitors.

One wall of the museum contains a long list of names, all VC guerrillas killed in the Cu Chi area. An adjacent room of the museum displays recent photos of prosperous farms and factories, an effort to show the benefits of Vietnam's economic reforms. There is also an odd collection of pottery and lacquerware with no explanations attached. In the lobby near the entrance is a statue of Ho Chi Minh with his right arm raised, waving hello.

Admission to the Cu Chi War History Museum is US$1.

Getting There & Away

Cu Chi District covers a large area, parts of which are as close as 30km to central Ho Chi Minh City. The Cu Chi War History Museum is closest to the city, while the Ben Dinh and Ben Duoc tunnels are about 50km and 70km respectively from central Ho Chi Minh City

Unbearable Treatment

Perhaps the most disturbing part of the entire Cu Chi Tunnels tour – Vietnam's No 1 tourist attraction – is not the almost impossible confines of the narrow tunnels, nor the harrowing descriptions of the guerillas' lives within them, but the sight of a caged black bear by the requisite tourist shop. We have been inundated with readers letters expressing dismay and horror at the appearance of this poor animal, who spends its entire life clinging to the bars of a cage looking forlorn and depressed.

Like many other Asian countries, Vietnam does not share a great concern for the welfare of animals, and while the brains behind the Cu Chi exhibit undoubtedly feel that the bear is a positive addition to the site, they have failed to realise that not only does the presence of a caged bear have absolutely nothing to do with the general theme of the tunnels as a tourist attraction, it upsets many visitors who consider it an unnecessary cruelty.

So far, visitors have expressed their outrage through an unoffical boycott of the souvenir store – hardly a great sacrifice – but the authorities remain unperturbed. Countless tour groups still fork out $4 per person to visit the tunnels, and the bear remains.

We agree that the only way to effect any kind of change in the bear's pitiful circumstances is through economic pressure, and while writing to Vietnamese tourism authorities, your embassy or to environmental NGOs will help raise general awareness of the bear's condition, we suggest that you voice your concern directly to the tour company with whom you booked your tour. The greater the complaints, the greater the chances are that the tour companies will put pressure on the authorities at Cu Chi to do something about this shameful blot on what is otherwise a unique and fascinating tour.

by highway. There is a back road that cuts the commute quite significantly, though it means driving on bumpy dirt roads.

Organised Tours An organised tour is the best way to visit the Cu Chi tunnels and is not at all expensive. Most of the cafes on Đ Pham Ngu Lao run combined full-day tours to the Cu Chi tunnels and Caodai Great Temple for as little as US$4 (plus entry fees to the tunnels).

Bus All buses to Tay Ninh pass though Cu Chi, but getting from the town of Cu Chi to the tunnels by public transport is impossible – it's 15km, so you'll have to hire a motorbike. (See the Getting There & Away section for Tay Ninh later in this chapter for details.)

Taxi Hiring a taxi in Ho Chi Minh City and just driving out to Cu Chi is not all that expensive, especially if the cost is split by several people. For details on hiring a car or taxi, see the Ho Chi Minh City chapter's Getting There & Away and Getting Around sections.

A visit to the Cu Chi tunnel complex can easily be combined with a stop at the headquarters of the Caodai sect in Tay Ninh. A taxi for an all-day excursion to both should cost about US$40.

TAY NINH

☎ 066 • pop 41,300

Tay Ninh town, the capital of Tay Ninh Province, serves as the headquarters of one of Vietnam's most interesting indigenous religions, Caodaism. The Caodai Great Temple at the sect's Holy See is one of the most striking structures in all of Asia. Built between 1933 and 1955, the temple is a rococo extravaganza combining the perhaps conflicting architectural idiosyncrasies of a French church, a Chinese pagoda, Hong Kong's Tiger Balm Gardens and Madame Tussaud's Wax Museum.

Tay Ninh Province, north-west of Ho Chi Minh City, is bordered by Cambodia on three sides. The area's dominant geographic feature is Nui Ba Den (Black Lady Mountain), which towers above the surrounding plains. Tay Ninh Province's eastern border is formed by the Saigon River. The Vam Co River flows from Cambodia through the western part of the province.

Because of the once-vaunted political and military power of the Caodai, this region was the scene of prolonged and heavy fighting during the Franco–Viet Minh War. Tay Ninh Province served as a major terminus of the Ho Chi Minh Trail during the American War. In 1969 the VC captured Tay Ninh town and held it for several days.

During the period of tension between Cambodia and Vietnam in the late 1970s, the Khmer Rouge launched a number of cross-border raids into Tay Ninh Province, and committed atrocities against civilians. Several cemeteries around Tay Ninh are stark reminders of these events.

Information

Tay Ninh Tourist (☎ 822 376) is in the Hoa Binh Hotel on Đ 30/4.

Caodaism

Caodaism (Dai Dao Tam Ky Pho Do) is the outcome of an attempt to create the ideal religion through the fusion of the secular and religious philosophies of the East and West. The result is an eclectic potpourri that includes bits and pieces of most of the religious philosophies known in Vietnam during the early 20th century: Buddhism, Confucianism, Taoism, native Vietnamese spiritualism, Christianity and Islam.

The term 'Caodai' (literally, high tower or palace) is a euphemism for God. The hierarchy of the sect, whose priesthood is nonprofessional, is partly based on the structure of the Roman Catholic Church.

History Caodaism was founded by the mystic Ngo Minh Chieu (also known as Ngo Van Chieu, born 1878), a civil servant who once served as district chief of Phu Quoc Island. He was widely read in Eastern and Western religious works and became active in seances, at which his presence was said to greatly improve the quality of communication with the spirits. Around 1919 he began to receive a series of revelations from Caodai in which the tenets of Caodai doctrine were set forth.

Caodaism was officially founded as a religion in a ceremony held in 1926. Within a year, the group had 26,000 followers. Many of the sect's early followers were Vietnamese members of the French colonial administration. By the mid-1950s, one in eight southern Vietnamese was a Caodai and the sect was famous worldwide for its imaginative garishness, and the Caodai had established a virtually independent feudal state in Tay Ninh Province; they retained enormous influence in the affairs of the province for the next two decades. But in 1954, British author Graham Greene, who had once considered converting to Caodaism, wrote in the *Times* of London: 'What on my first two visits has seemed gay and bizarre (is) now like a game that had gone on too long'.

The Caodai also played a significant political and military role in South Vietnam from 1926 to 1956, when most of the 25,000-strong Caodai army, which had been given support by the Japanese and later the French, was incorporated into the South Vietnamese army. During the Franco–Viet Minh War, Caodai munitions factories specialised in making mortar tubes out of automobile exhaust pipes.

Because they refused to support the VC during the American War – and despite the fact that they had been barely tolerated by the Saigon government – the Caodai feared the worst after reunification. Indeed, all Caodai lands were confiscated by the new Communist government and four members of the sect were executed in 1979. However, in 1985 the Holy See and some 400 temples were returned to Caodai control.

Caodaism is strongest in Tay Ninh Province and the Mekong Delta, but Caodai temples can be found throughout southern and central Vietnam. Today, there are an estimated three million followers of Caodaism. Vietnamese who fled abroad after the Communists came to power have spread the Caodai religion to Western countries, though their numbers are not large.

Philosophy Much of Caodai doctrine is drawn from Mahayana Buddhism, mixed with Taoist and Confucian elements (Vietnam's 'Triple Religion'). Caodai ethics are based on the Buddhist ideal of 'the good

Ecocide

During the American War, the USA engaged in the deliberate destruction of the environment as a military tactic on an enormous scale. In an effort to stifle the operations of the Viet Cong, 72 million litres of the herbicides known as Agent Orange, Agent White and Agent Blue were sprayed on 16% of South Vietnam's land area (including 10% of the inland forests and 36% of the mangrove forests). It is said that the deforestation caused by spraying these chemicals would have been enough to supply Vietnam's timber harvesters for 30 years. The most seriously affected regions were the provinces of Dong Nai, Song Be and Tay Ninh.

The 40 million litres of Agent Orange used contained 170kg of dioxin, which is the most toxic chemical known, and is highly carcinogenic and mutagenic. Today, more than 20 years after the spraying, dioxin is still present in the food chain, though its concentrations are gradually diminishing. Researchers have reported elevated levels of dioxin in samples of human breast milk collected in affected areas, where about 7.5% of the population of the south now lives. Vietnamese refugees living in the USA who were exposed to Agent Orange have shown unusually high rates of cancer. The same goes for American soldiers, who filed a class action lawsuit against the US government to seek compensation.

Scientists have yet to conclusively prove a link between the residues of chemicals used by the USA during the war and spontaneous abortions, stillbirths, birth defects and other human health problems. However, the circumstantial evidence is certainly compelling.

person', but incorporate traditional Vietnamese taboos and sanctions as well.

The ultimate goal of the disciple of Caodaism is to escape the cycle of reincarnation. This can only be achieved by the performance of certain human duties, including first and foremost following the prohibitions against killing, lying, luxurious living, sensuality and stealing.

The main tenets of Caodaism include believing in one god, the existence of the soul and the use of mediums to communicate with the spiritual world. Caodai practices include priestly celibacy, vegetarianism, communications with spirits through seances, reverence for the dead, maintenance of the cult of ancestors, fervent proselytising and sessions of meditative self-cultivation.

Following the Chinese duality of yin and yang, there are two principal deities, the Mother Goddess, who is female, and God, who is male (a duality that somewhat complicates the belief in 'one god'). There is a debate among the Caodai as to which deity was the primary source of creation.

According to Caodaism, history is divided into three major periods of divine revelation. During the first period, God's truth was revealed to humanity through Laozi (Laotse) and figures associated with Buddhism, Confucianism and Taoism. The human agents of revelation during the second period were Buddha (Sakyamuni), Mohammed, Confucius, Jesus and Moses. The Caodai believe that their messages were corrupted because of the human frailty of the messengers and their disciples. They also believe that these revelations were limited in scope, intended to be applicable only during a specific age to the people of the area in which the messengers lived.

Caodaism sees itself as the product of the 'Third Alliance Between God and Man', the third and final revelation. Disciples believe that Caodaism avoids the failures of the first two periods because it is based on divine truth as communicated through the spirits that serve as messengers of salvation and instructors of doctrine. Spirits who have been in touch with the Caodai include deceased Caodai leaders, patriots, heroes, philosophers, poets, political leaders and warriors, as well as ordinary people. Among the contacted spirits who lived as Westerners are Joan of Arc, René Descartes

Ecocide

Those wishing to pursue this topic further might want to pay a visit to Tu Du Hospital on Đ Nguyen Thi Minh Khai in Ho Chi Minh City. There are hundreds of dead deformed babies preserved in bottles here, each one marked with the date of birth. The gynaecologists at the hospital speak good English and will tell you all about it if you show genuine interest. Please remember, though, that this is a hospital and not a tourist attraction.

Another environmentally disastrous method of defoliation involved the use of enormous bulldozers called Rome ploughs to rip up the jungle floor. Large tracts of forests, agricultural land, villages and even cemeteries were bulldozed, removing both the vegetation and topsoil. Flammable melaleuca forests were ignited with napalm. In mountain areas, landslides were deliberately created by bombing and by spraying acid on limestone hillsides. Elephants, useful for transport, were attacked from the air with bombs and napalm. By the war's end, extensive areas had been taken over by tough weeds (known locally as 'American grass'). The government estimates that 20,000 sq km of forest and farmland were lost as a direct result of the American War effort.

Overall, some 13 million tonnes of bombs – equivalent to 450 times the energy of the atomic bomb used on Hiroshima – were dropped on the region. This comes to 265kg for every man, woman and child in Indochina. If the Americans had showered the people of Indochina with the money all those bombs cost (the war cost US$2000 per person in Indochina), it's likely both the environment and the economy of Vietnam would be in much better shape.

William Shakespeare (who hasn't been heard from since 1935), Victor Hugo, Louis Pasteur and Vladimir Ilyich Lenin. Because of his frequent appearances to Caodai mediums at the Phnom Penh mission, Victor Hugo was posthumously named the chief spirit of foreign missionary works.

Communication with the spirits is carried out in Vietnamese, Chinese, French and English. The methods of receiving messages from the spirits illustrate the influence of both East Asian and Western spiritualism on Caodai seance rites. Sometimes, a medium holds a pen or Chinese calligraphy brush. In the 1920s, a 66cm-long wooden staff known as a *corbeille à bec* was used. Mediums held one end while a crayon attached to the other wrote out the spirits' messages. The Caodai also use what is known as *pneumatographie*, in which a blank slip of paper is sealed in an envelope and hung above the altar. When the envelope is taken down, there is a message on the paper.

Most of the sacred literature of Caodaism consists of messages communicated to Caodai leaders during seances held between 1925 and 1929. From 1927 to 1975, only the official seances held at Tay Ninh were considered reliable and divinely ordained by the Caodai hierarchy, though dissident groups continued to hold seances that produced communications contradicting accepted doctrine.

The Caodai consider vegetarianism to be of service to humanity because it does not involve harming fellow beings during the process of their spiritual evolution. They also see vegetarianism as a form of self-purification. There are several different vegetarian regimens followed by Caodai disciples. The least rigorous involves eating vegetarian food six days a month. Priests must be full-time vegetarians.

The clergy is open to both men and women (but women are prevented from reaching the highest levels), though when male and female officials of equal rank are serving in the same area, male clergy are in charge. Female officials wear white robes and are addressed with the title *huong* (perfume); male clergy are addressed as *thanh* (pure). Caodai temples are constructed so that male and female disciples enter on opposite sides; women worship on the left, men on the right.

All Caodai temples observe four daily ceremonies, which are held at 6 am, noon, 6 pm and midnight. These rituals, during which dignitaries wear ceremonial dress and hats, include offerings of incense, tea, alcohol, fruit and flowers. All Caodai altars have the 'divine eye' above them, which became the religion's official symbol after Ngo Minh Chieu saw it in a vision he had while on Phu Quoc Island.

Caodai Holy See

The Caodai Holy See, founded in 1926, is 4km east of Tay Ninh in the village of Long Hoa.

The complex includes the Caodai Great Temple (Thanh That Cao Dai), administrative offices, residences for officials and adepts, and a hospital of traditional Vietnamese herbal medicine where people from all over the south travel for treatment. After reunification, the government 'borrowed' parts of the complex for its own use (and perhaps to keep an eye on the sect).

Prayers are conducted four times daily in the Great Temple, though they may be suspended during Tet. It's worth visiting during prayer sessions (the one at noon is most popular with tour groups from Ho Chi Minh City), but take care not to disturb the worshippers. Only a few hundred priests participate in weekday prayers, but on festivals several thousand priests, dressed in special white garments, may attend. The Caodai clergy has no objection to your photographing temple objects, but you cannot photograph people without their permission, which is seldom granted. However, you can photograph the prayer sessions from the upstairs balcony, an apparent concession to the troops of tourists who come here every day.

It is important that guests wear modest and respectful attire (no shorts or sleeveless T-shirts) inside the temple. However, sandals are OK, since you have to take them off anyway before you enter.

Above the front portico of the Great Temple is the 'divine eye'. Americans often comment that it looks as if it were copied from the back of a US$1 bill (raising the question why a divine eye is on US currency). Lay women enter the Great Temple through a door at the base of the tower on the left. Once inside, they walk around the outside of the colonnaded hall in a clockwise direction. Men enter on the right and walk around the hall in an anticlockwise direction. Shoes and hats must be removed upon entering the building. The area in the centre of the sanctuary (between the pillars) is reserved for Caodai priests.

A mural in the front entry hall depicts the three signatories of the 'Third Alliance Between God and Man'. The Chinese statesman and revolutionary leader Dr Sun Yatsen (1866–1925) holds an inkstone, while Vietnamese poet Nguyen Binh Khiem (1492–1587) and French poet and author Victor Hugo (1802–85) write 'God and Humanity' and 'Love and Justice' in Chinese and French. Nguyen Binh Khiem writes with a brush; Victor Hugo uses a quill pen. Nearby signs in English, French and German each give a slightly different version of the fundamentals of Caodaism.

The Great Temple is built on nine levels, which represent the nine steps to heaven. Each level is marked by a pair of columns. At the far end of the sanctuary, eight plaster columns entwined with multicoloured dragons support a dome representing the heavens – as does the rest of the ceiling. Under the dome is a giant star-speckled blue globe with the 'divine eye' on it.

The largest of the seven chairs in front of the globe is reserved for the Caodai pope, a position that has remained unfilled since 1933. The next three chairs are for the three men responsible for the religion's law books. The remaining chairs are for the leaders of the three branches of Caodaism, represented by the colours yellow, blue and red.

On both sides of the area between the columns are two pulpits similar in design to the *minbars* found in mosques. During festivals, the pulpits are used by officials to address the assembled worshippers. The upstairs balconies are used if there is a crowd overflow.

Up near the altar are barely discernible portraits of six figures important to

Caodaism: Sakyamuni (Siddhartha Guatama, the founder of Buddhism); Ly Thai Bach (Li Taibai, a fairy from Chinese mythology); Khuong Tu Nha (Jiang Taigong, a Chinese saint); Laozi (the founder of Taoism); Quan Cong (Guangong, Chinese God of War); and Quan Am (Guanyin, the Goddess of Mercy).

Long Hoa Market

Long Hoa Market is several kilometres south of the Caodai Holy See complex. Open daily from 5 am to about 6 pm, this large market sells meat, food staples, clothing and pretty much everything else you would expect to find in a rural marketplace. Before reunification, the Caodai sect had the right to collect taxes from the merchants here.

Places to Stay

The main place in town where travellers can stay is the ***Hoa Binh Hotel** (☎ 822376/822383, Đ 30/4)*. Rooms with fan only are US$8, but most rooms are air-con and cost US$10 to US$20. The hotel is 5km from the Caodai Great Temple.

Another alternative is the ***Anh Dao Hotel** (☎ 827306, Đ 30/4)*, 500m west of Hoa Binh Hotel. Twin rooms cost US$12 to US$20.

Places to Eat

The ***Nha Hang Diem Thuy** (☎ 827318, Đ 30/40)* is a great restaurant with reasonable prices. *Tom can* (giant crayfish) are one of its specialities and, although they are not cheap, cost only a third of what you'd pay in Ho Chi Minh City.

One kilometre north of the Tay Ninh market, near the river, is the ***Hoang Yen Restaurant***, considered by locals to be the best in town.

Getting There & Away

Bus Buses from Ho Chi Minh City to Tay Ninh leave from the Tay Ninh bus station (Ben Xe Tay Ninh) in Tan Binh District and Mien Tay bus station in An Lac.

Tay Ninh is on Highway 22 (Quoc Lo 22), 96km from Ho Chi Minh City. (The road passes through Trang Bang, where a famous news photo of a severely burned young girl, screaming and running, was taken during an American napalm attack.) There are several Caodai temples along Highway 22, including one, under construction in 1975, that was heavily damaged by the VC.

Taxi An easy way to get to Tay Ninh is by chartered taxi, perhaps on a day trip that includes a stop in Cu Chi. An all-day return trip to both should cost about US$40.

NUI BA DEN

Nui Ba Den (Black Lady Mountain), 15km north-east of Tay Ninh town, rises 850m above the rice paddies of the surrounding countryside. Over the centuries, Nui Ba Den has served as a shrine for various peoples of the area, including the Khmer, Chams, Vietnamese and Chinese, and there are several **cave temples** on the mountain. The summits of Nui Ba Den are much cooler than the rest of Tay Ninh Province, most of which is only a few dozen metres above sea level.

Nui Ba Den was used as a staging ground by both the Viet Minh and the VC, and was the scene of fierce fighting during the French and American Wars. At one time there was a US army firebase and relay station at the summit on the mountain, which was later, ironically, defoliated and heavily bombed by American aircraft.

The name Black Lady Mountain is derived from the legend of Huong, a young woman who married her true love despite the advances of a wealthy mandarin. While her husband was away doing military service, she would visit a magical statue of Buddha at the summit of the mountain. One day, Huong was attacked by kidnappers, but preferring death to dishonour, she threw herself off a cliff. She then reappeared in the visions of a monk living on the mountain, who told her story.

The hike from the base of the mountain to the main temple complex and back takes about 1½ hours. Although steep in parts, it's not a difficult walk – plenty of old women in sandals make the journey to worship at the temple. At the base of the mountain, you'll have to fend off the usual crowd of very persistent kids selling tourist junk, lottery tickets and chewing gum – they'll pursue you up the mountain, but you can easily outpace them if you wear running shoes and don't carry a heavy bag. Things are much more relaxed around the temple complex, where only a few stands sell snacks and drinks and the vendors aren't pushy.

If you'd like more exercise, a walk to the summit of the peak and back takes about six hours. The fastest (and easiest) way to the top is on the newly installed cable car.

Visiting during a holiday or festival is a bad idea. Aside from the crowds, at such times the main gate is closed. This forces vehicles to park 2km away from the trailhead, which means you've got another 4km of walking added to the return trip. This extra walking eats up a good deal of extra time, making it difficult to complete the return trip from Ho Chi Minh City in one day.

Place to Stay

About 500m past the main entrance gate are eight A-frame ***bungalows*** where double rooms can be rented for US$8 to US$12.

ONE PILLAR PAGODA

The official name of this interesting pagoda is Nam Thien Nhat Tru, but everyone calls it the One Pillar Pagoda of Thu Duc (Chua Mot Cot Thu Duc).

The One Pillar Pagoda of Thu Duc is modelled after Hanoi's One Pillar Pagoda, though the two structures do not look identical. Hanoi's original pagoda was built in the 9th century, but was destroyed by the French and rebuilt by the Vietnamese in 1954. Ho Chi Minh City's version was constructed in 1958.

When Vietnam was partitioned in 1954, Buddhist monks and Catholic priests wisely fled south so that they could avoid persecution and continue to practice their religion. One monk from Hanoi who travelled south in 1954 was Thich Tri Dung. Shortly after his arrival in Saigon, Thich petitioned the South Vietnamese government for permission to construct a replica of Hanoi's famous One Pillar Pagoda. However, President Ngo Dinh Diem was a Catholic with little tolerance for Buddhist clergy, and he denied permission. Nevertheless, Thich and his supporters raised the funds and built the pagoda in defiance of the president's orders. At one point, the Diem government ordered the monks to tear down the temple, but they refused even though they were threatened with imprisonment for not complying. Faced with significant opposition, the government's dispute with the monks reached a stand-off. However, the president's attempts to harass and intimidate the monks in a country that was 90% Buddhist did not go down well and ultimately contributed to Diem's assassination by his own troops in 1963.

During the war, the One Pillar Pagoda of Thu Duc was in possession of an extremely valuable plaque said to weigh 612kg. After liberation, the government took it for 'safekeeping' and brought it to Hanoi. However, none of the monks alive today could say just where it is. There is speculation that the government sold it to overseas collectors, but this cannot be confirmed. Certainly, it belongs in a museum.

The One Pillar Pagoda (☎ 08-896 0780) is in the Thu Duc District, about 15km north-east of central Ho Chi Minh City. The official address is 1/91 Đ Nguyen Du. Tours to the pagoda are rare, so you'll most likely have to visit by rented motorbike or car.

CAN GIO

☎ 08

The only beach within the municipality of Ho Chi Minh City is at Can Gio, a swampy island where the Saigon River meets the sea. The island was created by silt washing downstream, with the result that the beach is hard-packed mud rather than the fine white sand that sun worshippers crave. Furthermore, the beach sits in an exposed position and is lashed by strong winds. For these reasons, Can Gio gets few visitors and the beach remains entirely undeveloped.

Before you scratch Can Gio off your list of places to visit, it's worth noting that the island does have a wild beauty of its own. Unlike the rest of Ho Chi Minh City, overpopulation is hardly a problem here. Th lack of human inhabitants is chiefly because the island lacks a fresh water supply.

The land here is only about 2m above sea level and the island is basically one big mangrove swamp. The salty mud makes most forms of agriculture impossible, but aquaculture is another matter. The most profitable business here is shrimp farming. The hard-packed mud beach also teems with clams and other sea life, which island residents dig up to eat or sell. There is also a small salt industry – sea water is diverted into shallow ponds and is left to evaporate until a white layer of salt can be harvested. Can Gio has a small port where fishing boats can dock, but the shallow water prevents any large ships from dropping anchor here.

From about 1945 to 1954, Can Gio was controlled by Bay Vien, a general who also controlled a casino in Cholon. He was something of an independent warlord and gangster, but former President Ngo Dinh Diem persuaded Bay Vien to join forces with the South Vietnamese government. Not long thereafter, Bay Vien was murdered by an unknown assailant.

Can Gio Mangrove Park

Can Gio Mangrove Park (Lam Vien Can Gio, ☎ 874 3069, fax 874 3068) is a 70,000-hectare mangrove forest formed by sediment deposits from the Dong Nai and Long Tau Rivers. The **Can Gio Museum**, also in the park, has displays on flora and fauna of the area, as well as exhibits relating to local war history. Near the museum is an area where hundreds of monkeys live. Feeding the monkeys is popular with tourists, but be *very* careful with your belongings; the monkeys here are well practiced at swiping bags, pens, sunglasses etc, and the chances of retrieval are next to none. These critters are more skilled than the 'motorbike cowboy' thieves in central Ho Chi Minh City!

There is an entrance fee to the park of 3000d (US$0.25).

Caodai Temple

Though much smaller than the Caodai Great Temple at Tay Ninh, Can Gio boasts a Caodai Temple of its own. It's near the market and is easy to find. We didn't see anybody around and it seems that you can just walk inside and photograph as you please. Of course, if you encounter any worshippers, be respectful and don't photograph them without asking first.

Can Gio Market

Can Gio has a large market, made conspicuous by some rather powerful odours. Seafood and salt are definitely the local specialities. The vegetables, rice and fruit are all imported by boat from Ho Chi Minh City.

War Memorial & Cemetery

Adjacent to the local shrimp hatchery is a large and conspicuous cemetery and war memorial (Nghia Trang Liet Si Rung Sac), 2km from Can Gio Market. Like all such sites in Vietnam, the praise for bravery and patriotism goes entirely to the winning side and there is nothing said about the losers. Indeed, all of the former war cemeteries containing remains of South Vietnamese soldiers were bulldozed after liberation – a fact that still causes much bitterness.

The Beach

The southern side of the island faces the sea, creating a beachfront nearly 10km long. Unfortunately, a good deal of it is inaccessible because it's been fenced off by shrimp farmers and clam diggers. Nevertheless, there is a point about 4km west of the market where a dirt road turns off the main highway to Ho Chi Minh City and leads to the beach. The road is easily distinguished by the telephone poles and wires running alongside it. At the beach, you'll find a forlorn shack selling food and drinks.

The surface of the beach is as hard as concrete and it is possible to ride a motorbike on it; however, this is not recommended, as it damages the local ecology. While the beach may seem dead at first glance, it swarms with life just below the surface, as the breathing holes in the mud suggest. You can hear the crunch of tiny clam shells as you stroll along the surface. The water here is extremely shallow, and you can walk far from shore, but take care

– there is a good deal of inhospitable and well-armed sea life in these shallow waters. Stingrays, stone fish and sea urchins are just some of the local residents who can and will retaliate if you step on them.

The hills of the Vung Tau Peninsula are easily visible on a clear day.

Places to Stay

Most visitors do Can Gio as a day trip, and for good reason – the hotels in town are total dumps. Moreover, they are usually full, so you need to call ahead if you intend to stay.

Guesthouse 30/4 *(☎ 8743022)* is very basic, but at least it's near the beach. Rates are US$6 for fan rooms, or US$11 with air-con.

Places to Eat

There are a few stalls around the ***market*** near the fishing port, but one look at the level of sanitation can eliminate your appetite without the need to eat anything at all!

The ***Filao Restaurant*** near Guesthouse 30/4 is a good place to eat local seafood.

There is one solitary ***food and drink stall*** next to the beach. Basically, all that's on the menu is Coca-Cola and instant noodles, but it beats starving. It might be prudent to bring some snacks and bottled water with you on the odd chance that the food stall is closed.

Getting There & Away

Car & Motorbike Can Gio is about 60km south-east of central Ho Chi Minh City, and the fastest way to make the journey is by motorbike. Travel time is approximately three hours.

Cars can also make the journey, but this is much slower because you need to make two ferry crossings. The large ferries that can accommodate cars are infrequent, averaging about one every hour. By contrast, small boats make these crossings every few minutes, shuttling passengers and motorbikes. These small boats are so cheap that you could even charter one if need be.

The first ferry crossing is 15km from Ho Chi Minh City at Binh Khanh (Cat Lai), a former US navy base. Small ferry boats cost about US$0.20 for a motorbike and two passengers. Cars must wait for the large ferry, which runs about once an hour; there is usually a long queue of vehicles.

The second, less-frequent ferry is 35km from Ho Chi Minh City and connects the two tiny villages of Dan Xay (closer to Ho Chi Minh City) with Hao Vo (on Can Gio Island). Motorbike riders can take a small ferry (US$0.35), which runs about once every 10 to 15 minutes. The car ferry is even less frequent, but there is a posted schedule.

The road is paved all the way from Ho Chi Minh City to Can Gio. Once you get past the first ferry, there is very little traffic and both sides of the road are lined with lush mangrove forests.

Boat There is one boat daily between Can Gio and Ho Chi Minh City. The boat departs from both places at approximately 5 to 6 am and the journey takes six hours.

There is also a small boat between Can Gio and Vung Tau. Departures from Can Gio are at 5 am, arriving in Vung Tau at 8 am. The boat departs from Vung Tau about noon, arriving in Can Gio three hours later. Occasionally, there is a later boat leaving Can Gio around 2 pm – make inquiries locally.

In Can Gio, you catch boats at the shipyards, which are built on an inlet 2km west of the Can Gio Market. In Ho Chi Minh City, you get the boat at the Bach Dang Jetty, on the shore of the Saigon River. In Vung Tau, you catch the boats from the beachfront market area opposite the Grand Hotel.

BUU LONG MOUNTAIN

Various tourist pamphlets and even local residents of Ho Chi Minh City will tell you that Buu Long Mountain is the 'Halong Bay of the south'. Considering Halong Bay is northern Vietnam's top scenic drawcard, you might be forgiven for thinking that Buu Long Mountain must be nothing short of stunningly beautiful.

Indeed, we were stunned when we visited Buu Long Mountain. Mostly, we were stunned that anyone would waste the time and admission fee to visit this place. Residents of Ho Chi Minh City indeed have a vivid imagination to call this another Halong Bay; residents of Halong Bay ought t

GREG ELMS

MASON FLORENCE

MASON FLORENCE

GARRETT CULHANE

CHRIS THOMAS

om Ho Chi Minh to the Honda Dream – socialist icons stand alongside the burgeoning fruits of pitalism.

GREG ELMS

Saigon's landmark Rex Hotel

JERRY ALEXANDER

Ho Chi Minh statue in the city centre

GREG ELMS

Bright lights, city nights in Saigon

GREG ELMS

The People's Committee Building (Hotel de Ville)

consider filing a defamation lawsuit against whoever invented that silly tourist slogan and wrote those pamphlets.

Nevertheless, if you're bored and want to enjoy some comic relief, it does no harm to visit Buu Long Mountain. The summit towers a big 60m above the car park. People may try to steer you off-course to visit the 'English-speaking monk', who will charge you a fee for speaking English to him.

The top of the mountain is marked by a pagoda. From this vantage point, you can look down and clearly see Long An (Dragon Lake).

Buu Long Mountain is 32km from central Ho Chi Minh City. It's 2km off the main highway after crossing the bridge that marks the border between Ho Chi Minh City and Dong Nai Province. The admission fee is US$0.40, plus an extra charge for bringing in a camera. Considering how little there is to see here, you might as well leave the camera at home. There are a few refreshment ***shops*** where you can buy cold drinks and noodles.

LONG AN

The shoreline along Long An (Dragon Lake) is dressed up with a few pavilions and decorative souvenir stands. To reach the lake, you have to descend Buu Long Mountain and pass through another gate, where you pay an additional admission fee. And for a small extra charge, you can paddle a boat around the slimy green waters in pursuit of the dragon that is said to live at the bottom of the lake. Although we didn't spot the dragon, we did find the boat ride an excellent way to escape the lottery ticket and postcard vendors.

TRI AN FALLS

Tri An Falls are an 8m-high and 30m-wide cascade on the Song Be (Be River). They are especially awesome in the late autumn, when the river's flow is at its greatest. Tri An Falls are in Song Be Province, 36km from Bien Hoa and 68km from Ho Chi Minh City (via Thu Dau Mot).

Further upstream is Tri An Reservoir (Ho Tri An), a large artificial lake, fed from the forest highlands around Dalat and created by the Tri An Dam. Completed in the early 1980s with Soviet assistance, the dam and its adjoining hydroelectric station supplies the lion's share of Ho Chi Minh City's electric power.

VUNG TAU

☎ 064 • pop 161,300

Vung Tau, known under the French as Cap St Jacques (it was so named by Portuguese mariners in honour of their patron saint), is a beach resort on the South China Sea, 128km south-east of Ho Chi Minh City. Sewage flowing down river from Ho Chi Minh City is a considerable source of pollution, and Vung Tau's four beaches are none too clean. Pollution from offshore drilling is another factor.

Vung Tau's beaches are easily reached from Ho Chi Minh City and have thus been a favourite of that city's residents since French colonists first began coming here around 1890. However, they are not Vietnam's nicest by any stretch of the imagination, largely because the city has cut down most of the palm trees in order to widen the roads.

Seaside areas near Vung Tau are dotted with the **villas** of the pre-1975 elite, now converted to guesthouses and restaurants for the post-1975 elite. In addition to sunning on the seashore and sipping sodas in nearby cafes, visitors can cycle around, or climb up, Vung Tau Peninsula's two mountains. There are also a number of interesting **religious sites** around town, including several pagodas and a huge standing figure of Jesus blessing the South China Sea.

Vung Tau is the headquarters of Vietsov-Petro, originally a joint Soviet-Vietnamese company, which continues to operate oil rigs about 60km offshore. There are still some Russian technicians around, though nowhere near the number that lived here in the 1980s.

Vung Tau became briefly famous to the world in 1973, when the last American combat troops in Vietnam left here by ship. However, a small contingent of American advisers, diplomats and CIA agents remained

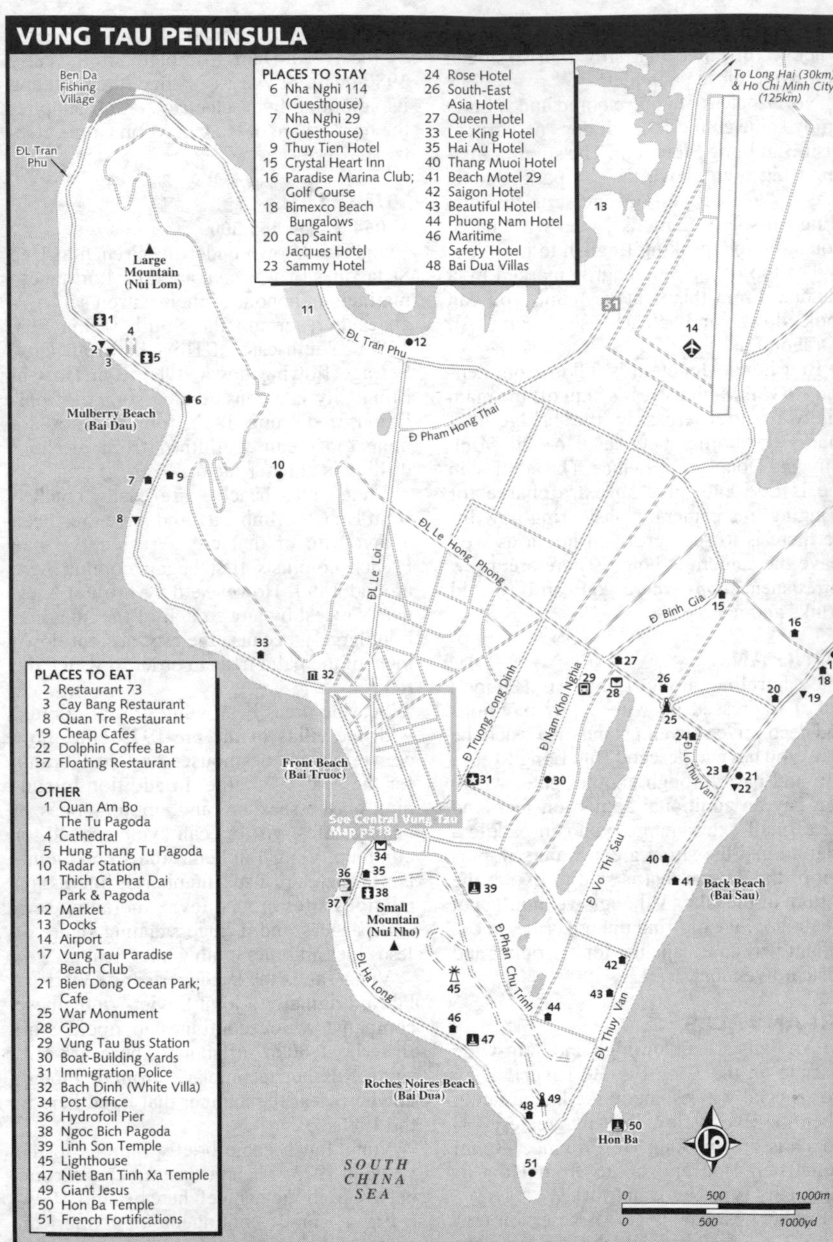

VUNG TAU PENINSULA
PLACES TO STAY
6 Nha Nghi 114 (Guesthouse)
7 Nha Nghi 29 (Guesthouse)
9 Thuy Tien Hotel
15 Crystal Heart Inn
16 Paradise Marina Club; Golf Course
18 Bimexco Beach Bungalows
20 Cap Saint Jacques Hotel
23 Sammy Hotel
24 Rose Hotel
26 South-East Asia Hotel
27 Queen Hotel
33 Lee King Hotel
35 Hai Au Hotel
40 Thang Muoi Hotel
41 Beach Motel 29
42 Saigon Hotel
43 Beautiful Hotel
44 Phuong Nam Hotel
46 Maritime Safety Hotel
48 Bai Dua Villas
PLACES TO EAT
2 Restaurant 73
3 Cay Bang Restaurant
8 Quan Tre Restaurant
19 Cheap Cafes
22 Dolphin Coffee Bar
37 Floating Restaurant
OTHER
1 Quan Am Bo The Tu Pagoda
4 Cathedral
5 Hung Thang Tu Pagoda
10 Radar Station
11 Thich Ca Phat Dai Park & Pagoda
12 Market
13 Docks
14 Airport
17 Vung Tau Paradise Beach Club
21 Bien Dong Ocean Park; Cafe
25 War Monument
28 GPO
29 Vung Tau Bus Station
30 Boat-Building Yards
31 Immigration Police
32 Bach Dinh (White Villa)
34 Post Office
36 Hydrofoil Pier
38 Ngoc Bich Pagoda
39 Linh Son Temple
45 Lighthouse
47 Niet Ban Tinh Xa Temple
49 Giant Jesus
50 Hon Ba Temple
51 French Fortifications
Ben Da Fishing Village
ĐL Tran Phu
Large Mountain (Nui Lom)
Mulberry Beach (Bai Dau)
To Long Hai (30km) & Ho Chi Minh City (125km)
51
ĐL Tran Phu
Đ Pham Hong Thai
ĐL Le Loi
ĐL Le Hong Phong
Đ Binh Gia
Đ Truong Cong Dinh
Đ Nam Khoi Nghia
Đ Lo Thuy Van
Front Beach (Bai Truoc)
See Central Vung Tau Map p518
Small Mountain (Nui Nho)
Đ Vo Thi Sau
Back Beach (Bai Sau)
ĐL Ha Long
Đ Phan Chu Trinh
ĐL Thuy Van
Roches Noires Beach (Bai Dua)
Hon Ba
SOUTH CHINA SEA
0 500 1000m
0 500 1000yd

in Vietnam for another two years – their moment on the world's centre stage came in 1975 during the rooftop helicopter evacuation from the US embassy in Saigon.

The local fishing fleet is quite active, though many Vietnamese fleeing their homeland by sea set sail from Vung Tau, taking many of the town's fishing trawlers with them. Vietnamese navy boats on patrol offshore ensure that the rest of the fleet comes home each day.

Vung Tau has long competed with Ho Chi Minh City to attract foreign 'sex tours' to Vietnam – massage parlours are ubiquitous. However, the AIDS epidemic has caused some soul searching and there has been a half-hearted crackdown on this lucrative industry.

Theft has increased in the area. Watch out for kids around the kiosks along Front Beach. Some may try to pick your pockets or snatch a bag. There are also Ho Chi Minh City-style motorbike cowboys.

Vung Tau is heavily commercialised and seems to be getting more so all the time. Despite this and a few other negative points, there is still plenty of sand, sun, surf, good food, draft beer and even a few budding discos. It's a party town and – for traffic-weary residents of Ho Chi Minh City – a welcome change of pace.

Orientation

The triangular Vung Tau Peninsula juts into the South China Sea near the mouth of the Saigon River.

Ben Da fishing village is in the north-west area of the peninsula. In the north-east is Vung Tau's airport, and most of the shops and places to stay and eat are scattered along the west coast.

Information

Money Vietcombank (☎ 859874), 27–29 Đ Tran Hung Dao, has foreign currency exchange and does cash advances.

Post & Communications There is a post office (☎ 852377) at 4 ĐL Ha Long, at the southern end of Front Beach, and another on ĐL Le Loi.

Immigration Police The immigration police operate out of the police station on Đ Truong Cong Dinh near the intersection with Đ Ly Thuong Kiet.

Beaches

Back Beach The main bathing area on the peninsula is Back Beach (Bai Sau, also known as Thuy Van Beach), an 8km stretch of sun, sand and tourists. Unfortunately, it's also the ugliest stretch of beach in Vung Tau, thanks largely to crass commercialisation. Basically, this is the land of concrete, car parks, hotels and cafes.

Front Beach Front Beach (Bai Truoc, also called Thuy Duong Beach) borders the centre of town. The trees, which are a rarity in Vung Tau, make it reasonably attractive, though the beach itself has become eroded and polluted. Shady ĐL Quang Trung, lined with kiosks, runs along Front Beach. Early in the morning, local fishing boats moor here to unload the night's catch and clean the nets. The workers row themselves between boats or to the beach in *thung chai* (gigantic round wicker baskets sealed with pitch).

Mulberry Beach Mulberry Beach (Bai Dau) stretches around a small bay nestled beneath the verdant, western slopes of Large Mountain (Nui Lon). The problem with Mulberry Beach is that there isn't a lot of sand – it's rocky with only a few small sandy coves and the water is not exactly pristine.

The large and unusual **open-air cathedral** here is very photogenic and a major drawcard for Vietnamese tourists. The nearby Pho Da Son Quan Am Bo The Tu Pagoda boasts an impressive standing statue of female Buddhist saint Quan Am Bo Tat.

Mulberry Beach is 3km from the town centre along ĐL Tran Phu. The best way to get there is by bicycle or motorbike.

On a clear day, you can look out from Mulberry Beach and see Can Gio, a low-lying palm-fringed island in the distance. There is a daily boat from Vung Tau's Front Beach to Can Gio (see the Can Gio section earlier in this chapter for details).

Child Prostitution & Sex Tourism

Over the last decade or so the Asian region has become notorious for its sex tourism industry. In Vietnam, the recent liberalisation of government policy has seen prostitution increase to levels not seen since the American War.

Thanks to the combination of poverty and regional sex industry cartels, more and more Vietnamese women and children are becoming sex workers; either trafficked overseas to meet international demand, or catering to a growing domestic market and local sex tourism operators.

Sex tourism in the South-East Asian region can be traced back to the American War when Bankok became a major centre for 'Rest and Recreation'. Since then sex tourism has taken off in the region.

According to the international group End Child Prostitution, Pornography and Trafficking (ECPAT) Australia, Vietnam's illicit sex industry is booming, and prostitutes are widely available throughout the country. Vietnam is also among the newest international sites for child prostitution (along with Cambodia, Laos, China and the Dominican Republic).

It is difficult to find reliable statistics on child prostitution in Vietnam, however a recent estimate suggested that around 30% of all sex workers were under the age of 16, and police reports show that sex crimes in general are steadily increasing.

Fear of contracting HIV/AIDS from mature sex workers has led to increasing exploitation of – supposedly as yet uninfected – children. This is perhaps the most disturbing element of the worldwide growth in the sex trade.

Many humanitarian groups consider the Internet to be one of the greatest tools for sex offenders to exchange information (for instance, the best destinations for sex tourism) and spread child pornography.

Local, regional and international nongovernment organisations are campaigning to raise awareness of trafficking and child prostitution, and to press for international cooperation in shutting it down. At least 23 countries have laws allowing the persecution of citizens at home for sex offences with children overseas, which is certainly a step towards combating this global phenomenon.

For more information see the 'Prostitution & Paedophilia' section in the Facts for the Visitor section, or check our the ECPAT Web site: www.ecpat.org.

If you would like to make a donation to agencies working to help victims of the sex industry see the 'NGOs in Vietnam' boxed text in the Facts for the Visitor section.

Hilary Rogers & Rachael Antony

Roches Noires Beach Roches Noires Beach (Bai Dua) is a small, rocky beach about 2km south of the town centre on ĐL Ha Long. This is a great place to watch the sun setting over the South China Sea. Road widening has made it treeless and new hotels are continually being built.

Pagodas & Temples

Hon Ba Temple (Chua Hon Ba) is on a tiny island just south of Back Beach. It can be reached on foot at low tide.

Niet Ban Tinh Xa, one of the largest Buddhist temples in Vietnam, is on the western side of Small Mountain (Nui Nho). Built in 1971, it is famous for its 5000kg bronze bell, a huge reclining Buddha and intricate mosaic work.

Thich Ca Phat Dai Pagoda & Park

Thich Ca Phat Dai, a must-see site for domestic tourists, is a hillside park of monumental **Buddhist statuary** built in the early 1960s. Inside the main gate and to the right is a row of small souvenir kiosks selling, among other things, inexpensive items made of seashells and coral (bear in mind the environmental impact of the production of shell and coral products). Above the kiosks, shaded paths lead to several large white cement Buddhas, a **giant lotus blossom**, and many smaller figures of people and animals.

The park is on the eastern side of Large Mountain at 25 ĐL Tran Phu and is open from 6 am to 6 pm. To get there from the town centre, take ĐL Le Loi north almost to the end and turn left on to ĐL Tran Phu. Alternatively you can follow the coastal road past Mulberry Beach.

Lighthouse

The 360° view of the entire hammerhead-shaped peninsula from the *hai dang* (lighthouse) is truly spectacular, especially at sunset. The lighthouse was built in 1910 and sits atop Small Mountain. The concrete passage from the tower to the building next to it was constructed by the French in response to Viet Minh attacks. A 1939 French guidebook warns visitors that photography is not permitted from here and, unfortunately, this is still the case over half a century and four regimes later.

The narrow paved road up Small Mountain to the lighthouse intersects ĐL Ha Long 150m south-west of the post office. The grade is quite gentle and could be done on bicycle. There is also a dirt road to the lighthouse from near Back Beach.

Giant Jesus

An enormous Rio de Janeiro-style figure of Jesus (Thanh Gioc), with his arms outstretched gazing out across the South China Sea, can be seen from the southern end of Small Mountain.

The 30m-high Giant Jesus statue was constructed in 1974 on the site of an old lighthouse built by the French a century before. The statue can be reached on foot by a path that heads up the hill from a point just south of Back Beach.

Unfortunately, Jesus is literally in a precarious position these days. Small Mountain continues to get smaller – the demand for rock and sand to build new hotels and highways means the southern slope of the mountain is being dug up and carted away. The digging has continued almost right up to the base of the statue's feet and there is the real possibility that a bad typhoon could send the whole structure toppling into the sea. Local Christians are reportedly unhappy at the prospect of their statue being made to walk on water and have protested the matter – so far to no avail.

Bach Dinh

Bach Dinh, the White Villa (Villa Blanche), is a former royal residence set amid frangipanis and bougainvilleas on a lushly forested hillside overlooking the sea.

Bach Dinh was built in 1909 as a retreat for French governor Paul Doumer. It later became a summer palace for Vietnamese royalty. King Thanh Thai was kept here for a while under house arrest before being shipped off to the French island of Réunion to perform hard prison labour. From the late 1960s to the early 1970s, the building was a part-time playground for South Vietnamese President Thieu.

The mansion itself is emphatically French in its ornamentation, which includes colourful mosaics and Roman-style busts set into the exterior walls. Inside, there is an exhibit of Chinese pottery (Qing Dynasty) salvaged from an 18th-century shipwreck near Con Dao Island.

The main entrance to the park surrounding Bach Dinh is just north of Front Beach at 12 DL Tran Phu. It is open from 6 am to 9 pm; admission is US$1.20.

Boat-Building Yards

New wooden fishing craft are built at a location which, oddly enough, is over 1km from the nearest water. The boat yards are on Đ Nam Ky Khoi Nghia, 500m south of Vung Tau bus station.

Golf Course

The Paradise Marina Club does not have a marina, but it does have an international standard golf course. For nonmembers, green fees are a 'trifling' US$97 per day. Membership costs US$20,000, but then green fees are reduced to just US$12 per day. At these rates, becoming a member will pay off provided you play golf here more than 235 times.

Small Mountain Circuit

The 6km circuit around Small Mountain (elevation 197m), known to the French as *le tour de la Petite Corniche*, begins at the post office and continues on ĐL Ha Long along the coastline. ĐL Ha Long passes Ngoc Bich Pagoda (which is built in the style of Hanoi's famous One Pillar Pagoda), Roches Noires Beach and a number of villas before reaching the tip of the Vung Tau Peninsula. The promontory, reached through a traditional gate, was once guarded by French naval guns whose reinforced concrete emplacements remain, slowly crumbling in the salt air.

Đ Phan Boi Chau goes from the southern end of Back Beach into town along the eastern base of Small Mountain, passing the century-old Linh Son Temple, which contains a Buddha of pre-Angkorian Khmer origin.

Large Mountain Circuit

The 10km circuit around Large Mountain (elevation 520m) passes seaside villas, Mulberry Beach, the homes of poor families living in old French fortifications and a number of quarries where boulders blown out of the hillside by dynamite are made into gravel by workers using sledgehammers. Blasting

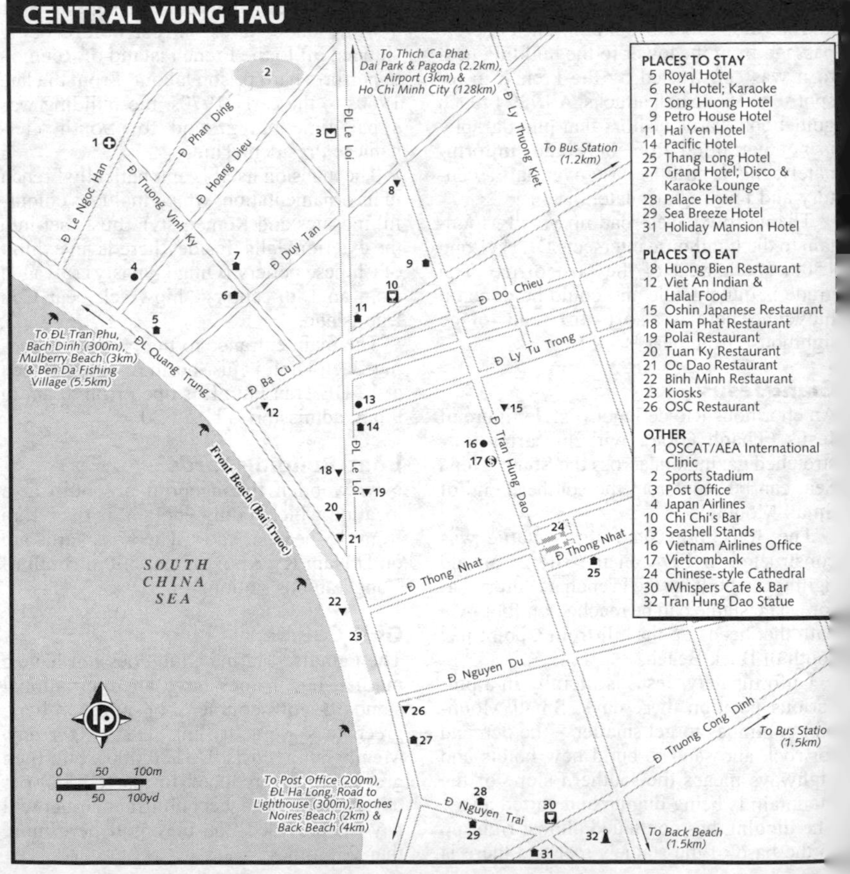

sometimes closes the road for a few hours. At the northern tip of Large Mountain is Ben Da fishing village. The village is notable for its large church and bad roads; from here a road leads up and along the spine of the hill to the *rada* (old radar installation).

On the eastern side of Large Mountain, which faces tidal marshes and the giant cranes of the VietsovPetro docks, is Thich Ca Phat Dai Pagoda and statuary park.

Places to Stay

During weekends and holidays, Vung Tau's hotels are usually booked out. Aside from price, the main consideration is finding a place at the beach you prefer.

Back Beach Cheapest is ***Beach Motel 29*** *(☎ 853481, 29 ĐL Thuy Van)*. Prices from Monday to Friday are US$5 with fan only, rising to US$10 with air-con.

At the northern end of Back Beach is the cosy A-frame ***Bimexco Beach Bungalows*** *(☎ 859916)*. The cheapest rooms with shared bathroom are US$8, or US$11 with private toilet. A room with air-con and bath costs US$16.

Close to the beach is the large ***Saigon Hotel*** *(☎ 852317, 72 ĐL Thuy Van)*. Only the old building, where rooms are US$12 to US$38, has sea views; in the new wing rooms are US$25.

Thang Muoi Hotel *(☎ 852665, fax 859876, 4–6 ĐL Thuy Van)* boasts an alluring, garden-like environment. Doubles with fan/air-con cost US$10/17.

The swish ***Cap Saint Jacques Hotel*** *(☎ 859 519, fax 859518, 2 ĐL Thuy Van)* is run by the Ministry of Construction; at least it shouldn't topple over. Rates are US$25 to US$48.

If you've got the cash, consider ***Beautiful Hotel*** *(☎/fax 852177, 100–2 ĐL Thuy Van)*. Twins are US$35 to US$50.

Nearby on Ngoc Tuoc Hill, ***Rose Hotel*** *(☎ 852633, fax 859 262)* has self-contained, brick A-frame cottages for US$17/20 for singles/doubles. All rooms have air-con, IDD phones and satellite TV.

Sammy Hotel *(☎ 854755, fax 854762, 33 ĐL Thuy Van)* is a snazzy high-rise chock full of modern amenities. Rooms cost US$50 to US$100.

Set back from Back Beach, the ***South-East Asia Hotel,*** aka Khach San Dong Nam A *(☎ 859412, fax 853630, 249 ĐL Le Hong Phong),* has decent rooms from US$15 to US$30.

A little further up the road, ***Queen Hotel*** *(☎ 858871, fax 859838, 28A ĐL Le Hong Phong)* charges US$15 to US$20.

Another reasonable spot off the beach is ***Phuong Nam Hotel*** *(☎ 852512, 8 Đ Phan Chu Trinh)*, which has rooms from US$18 to US$21.

Crystal Heart Inn *(☎ 854043, fax 854044, 143–5 Đ Binh Gia)* is its own little condo-village. Air-con rooms with rattan furnishings cost US$20 to US$40.

The long awaited ***Paradise Marina Club*** *(☎ 859687, fax 859695)* should be open soon. Eventually the complex will have 1500 rooms! Facilities will include a golf course, swimming pool and tennis courts. Prices have not been announced yet, but it's fair to say that this won't be for budget travellers.

Front Beach The ***Song Huong Hotel*** *(☎ 852491, fax 859862, 10 Đ Truong Vinh Ky)* was once a dorm for Russian experts (luckily, it's been renovated). Twins are US$20 to US$26.

At the far north end of the beach area, ***Lee King Hotel*** *(☎ 850223, fax 856219, 24–6 ĐL Tran Phu)* is a new and attractive place charging US$20 for well-appointed rooms with sea views.

The brochure of the grand ***Petro House Hotel*** *(☎ 852014, fax 852015, 89 Đ Tran Hung Dao)* reads, 'A haven for oil executives and discerning tourists'. Of course, it should at these prices: twins cost US$55 to US$65; suites cost US$85 to US$195.

Hai Yen Hotel *(☎ 852571, fax 852858, 8 ĐL Le Loi)* advertises a restaurant, cafe, dance hall, steam bath and Thai massage. Twins cost US$12 to US$17.

Pacific Hotel *(☎ 852279, fax 852391, 4 ĐL Le Loi)* is a clean and modern place. Room rates depend on whether or not you get a sea view. The price range is US$10 to US$14.

Hai Au Hotel *(☎ 852178, fax 856868, 100 ĐL Ha Long)* is a fancy place with tour-group amenities, including a swimming pool, private beach, barber shop, post office, disco bar and business centre. Standard rooms cost US$18 to US$30, but fancier suites are US$45 to US$59.

Holiday Mansion Hotel *(☎ 856169, fax 856171)* on Đ Truong Cong Dinh is a relatively small but well-kept place. Twins are US$25 to US$30.

Sea Breeze Hotel *(☎ 852392, fax 859856, 2 Đ Nguyen Trai)* is a nice Australian joint-venture hotel, with rooms from US$20 to US$30. There is an excellent Cajun-style restaurant on the ground floor.

Palace Hotel *(☎ 856265, fax 856878, ⓔ palacevt@hcm.vnn.vn, 1 Đ Nguyen Trai)* is a fancy place with a swimming pool and pleasant terrace café, and advertises, among other things, 'gentle receptionists'. Rooms cost US$39 to US$100.

Grand Hotel *(☎ 856164, fax 856088, 28 ĐL Quang Trung)* has a grand location just opposite the beach. Owned by the Oil Services Company, the hotel has a souvenir shop, steam bath, disco and Thai massage facilities. Singles with fan and attached cold bath are US$7, while twins with air-con are US$22.

Rex Hotel *(☎ 852135, fax 859862, 1 Đ Duy Tan)* is a high-rise with two restaurants, tennis courts and a nightclub. All rooms have air-con and a terrace, and cost US$35 to US$100. It's no relation to the upmarket Rex in Ho Chi Minh City.

Royal Hotel *(☎ 859852, fax 859 851, 48 ĐL Quang Trung)* has a glossy pamphlet promising that it is 'where the sunkissed beaches and cool sea breeze bring you into the exciting world of deep crystal blue sea'. The hotel is very classy and thoroughly air-conditioned; rooms cost US$46 to US$120.

The popular ***Thang Long Hotel*** *(☎ 852175, 45 Đ Thong Nhat)*, just across from a lovely cathedral topped with Chinese-style roof tiles, was being renovated at the time of writing.

Mulberry Beach There are several *nha nghi* (guesthouses) in former private villas along Mulberry Beach. This is the cheapest neighbourhood in the Vung Tau area, though no longer dirt-cheap as it once was. Most of the guesthouses have rooms with fans and communal bathrooms, and cost US$15 or less, but several upmarket places have air-con and baths.

Nha Nghi 29 *(☎ 834403, 73 ĐL Tran Phu)* is right on the seafront, but is a large concrete box. Rooms with air-con cost US$13.

A better choice is ***Thuy Tien Hotel*** *(☎ 835220, 84 ĐL Tran Phu)*, a newer place perched up on a hillside providing sea views. Doubles with air-con cost US$12, or US$15 for a triple.

Roches Noires Beach This is a new development area – the small guesthouses have been blown away recently and new tourist pleasure palaces are under construction. The first one to open its doors is the sparkling ***Neptune Hotel*** *(☎ 856192, fax 856434, 36C1 ĐL Ha Long)*. Rooms cost US$18 to US$40.

Maritime Safety Hotel *(☎ 856357, fax 856360, 110 ĐL Ha Long)* has rooms from US$20 to US$40.

Bai Dua Villas *(☎ 856285, fax 856281, 22 ĐL Ha Long)*, a 'village of villas', charges US$15 to US$30.

Places to Eat

Back Beach The northern end of Back Beach has excellent cheap ***cafes*** hidden among the few remaining palm trees. The ***Dolphin Coffee Bar*** is an attractive seaside cafe, and there is decent food served at the ***Bien Dong Ocean Park***.

Front Beach The ***kiosks*** lining the beach do cheap noodle dishes. Near the Grand Hotel, the ***OSC Restaurant*** serves decent Vietnamese fare and seafood.

At the end of Đ Thong Nhat, the pleasan[t] ***Binh Minh Restarant*** has good seafood.

Another place for excellent seafood i[s] ***Huong Bien Restaurant***, at the intersectio[n] of Đ Duy Tan and Đ Tran Hung Dao.

Closer to the seaside, there are severa[l] more places to eat, including the ***Nam Pha***

Restaurant, ***Polai Restaurant***, ***Tuan Ky Restaurant*** and ***Oc Dao Restaurant***.

There are good Indian curries and Halal food at ***Viet An***, near the corner of ĐL Quang Trung and Đ Ba Cu.

Oshin, nearly across from Vietnam Airlines on ĐL Tran Hung Dao, does authentic Japanese dishes.

Mulberry Beach Mulberry Beach chips in with a handful of waterfront seafood restaurants, including ***Restaurant 73*** *(73 ĐL Tran Phu)*, ***Cay Bang Restaurant*** *(69 ĐL Tran Phu)* and ***Quan Tre Restaurant***.

Roches Noires Beach Just north of Roches Noires, ***Floating Restaurant*** on the ĐL Ha Long waterfront has good food and a sweeping view of the sea.

Entertainment

Expat bars that get moving in the evening include ***Whispers Cafe & Bar*** *(☎ 856762, 438 Đ Truong Cong Dinh)* and ***Chi Chi's Bar*** *(☎ 853948, 236 Đ Ba Cu)*.

The ***Grand Hotel*** has a disco and karaoke lounge operating from 7 pm until midnight, and the ***Rex Hotel*** also has karaoke on the ground floor.

Getting There & Away

Bus The most convenient minibuses to Vung Tau depart from in front of the Saigon Hotel, on Đ Dong Du near the Saigon Central Mosque. Departures are approximately once every hour between 6 am and 6 pm. The 128km trip takes two hours and costs US$4. To return from Vung Tau, catch these minibuses at the petrol station or the Sea Breeze Hotel.

Vung Tau bus station (Ben Xe Khach Vung Tau) is about 1.5km north-east of the town centre at 52 Đ Nam Ky Khoi Nghia. There are non-express buses to Baria, Long Hai, Bien Hoa, Long Khanh, Mytho, Ho Chi Minh City and Tay Ninh.

Hydrofoil The best way to reach Vung Tau is by hydrofoil (adults/kids US$10/US$5, about 1¼ hours). One hydrofoil can carry 124 passengers.

Boats depart from Ho Chi Minh City and Vung Tao six times daily between 6.30 am and 4.30 pm. For more information contact the Vina Express office (☎ 08-821 5609) at the jetty.

In Ho Chi Minh City, departures are from the Bach Dang Jetty on Đ Ton Duc Thang. In Vung Tau you board the hydrofoil at Cau Da pier opposite the Hai Au Hotel (Front Beach). Vina Express (☎ 856530) has a Vung Tau office by the pier.

Getting Around

The best way to get around the Vung Tau Peninsula is by bicycle. These are available for hire from some hotels for around US$1 per day.

There is a place opposite the Rex Hotel that rents motorbikes. A 50cc bike costs US$5 per day.

Vicaren Taxi (☎ 858485) and Vung Tau Taxi (☎ 856565) are the duopoly suppliers of cabs with meters and air-con.

CON DAO ISLANDS

☎ 064 • pop 1,650

The Con Dao Archipelago is a group of 14 islands and islets 180km (97 nautical miles) south of Vung Tau in the South China Sea. The largest island in the group, with a total land area of 20 sq km, is the partly forested Con Son Island, which is ringed with bays, bathing beaches and coral reefs. Con Son Island is also known by its Europeanised Malay name, Poulo Condore (Pulau Kundur), which means 'Island of the Squashes'. Local products include teak and pine wood, fruits (grapes, coconuts and mangoes), cashews, pearls, sea turtles, lobster and coral.

Occupied at various times by the Khmer, Malays and Vietnamese, Con Son also served as an early base for European commercial ventures in the region. The British East India Company maintained a fortified trading post here from 1702 to 1705 – an experiment that ended when the English on the island were massacred in a revolt by the Macassar soldiers they had recruited on the Indonesian island of Sulawesi.

Under the French, Con Son was used as a prison for opponents of French colonialism,

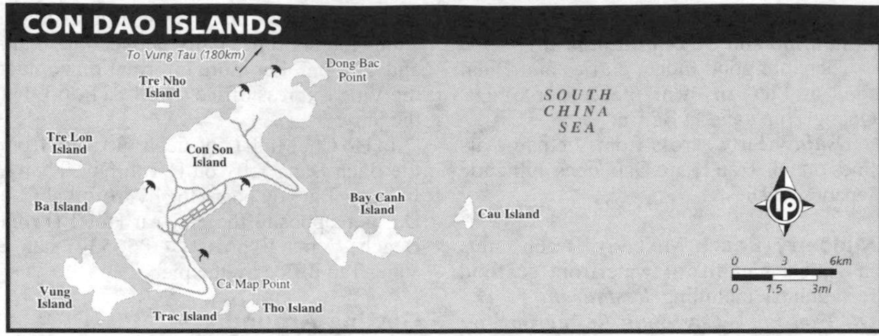

earning a fearsome reputation for the routine mistreatment and torture of prisoners. In 1954 the prison was taken over by the South Vietnamese government, which continued to take advantage of its remoteness to hold opponents of the government (including students) in horrifying conditions. The island's **Revolutionary Museum** has exhibits on Vietnamese resistance to the French, Communist opposition to the Republic of Vietnam, and the treatment of political prisoners. A ditch in which Communist Party members were dunked in cow's urine is open to the public.

These days most visitors to Con Son are package tour groups of former VC soldiers who were imprisoned on the island. The Vietnamese government generously subsidises these jaunts as a show of gratitude for their sacrifice.

Places to Stay

The ***Phi Yen Hotel*** *(☎ 830168)* rents air-con twins for US$18, or US$25 with a sea view.

Getting There & Away

Air Vasco Airlines flies three times weekly between Ho Chi Minh City and Con Son Island, but the flight is technically a charter and won't go if there are insufficient passengers. There are also flights (sometimes) available from Vung Tau to the Con Dao Islands.

In Ho Chi Minh City contact Vasco (☎ 08-842 2790, fax 844 5224), 114 Đ Bach Dang, Tan Binh District. The Vasco booking office (☎ 064-856100) in Vung Tau is at 27 ĐL Quang Trung.

Boat The 180km route between Vung Tau and Con Dao takes about 12 hours on a ship operated by the Vietnamese navy. Civilians can get permission to do this boat journey provided there is a reasonably large group making the trip. Inquire about the trip at the Oil Service Company & Tourism (☎ 852012, fax 852834), 2 ĐL Le Loi, Vung Tau.

LONG HAI

☎ 064

Tourism has turned Vung Tau into something of a circus, and many travellers crave a less developed seaside retreat. As a result, travellers are increasingly heading to Long Hai, 30km north-east of Vung Tau. Backpacker cafes can organise tours here, and it is also easy enough to travel to independently.

The western end of the beach is where fishing boats moor and is therefore none too clean. However, the eastern end is attractive, with a reasonable amount of white sand and palm trees. Some of the nicest municipal beach is in front of the Military Guesthouse. You can rent beach chairs here for US$0.80.

Annually, following the TET holiday (roughly from the 10th to 12th day of the second lunar month), Long Hai plays host to a major **fishermens' pilgrimage** festival where hundreds of boats come from afar to worship at Mo Co Temple.

Beside the beaches, there are several sites in the area well worth exploring. At Minh Dam, 5km from Long Hai, there are **caves** with historical connections to the French and American Wars. Nearby there is a **mountain**

top temple offering great panoramic views of the coastline.

Another 20km away at Dia Dao there are **underground tunnels** (similar, but on a smaller scale, to those at Cu Chi) dating from the American War.

Chua Phap Hoa is a peaceful pagoda set in a forest with lots of wild monkeys.

If you are heading to/from Highway 1 north of Long Hai, a great route is via the hot springs at Binh Chau, just 60km away from Long Hai. There are plenty more beaches to seek out as you make your way north or south on coastal Route 55.

Places to Stay – Budget

The friendly ***Dong Nai Guesthouse*** *(☎ 868421)* was recently renovated and looks good. Facilities include a tennis court and a swimming pool. Fan rooms are just US$3.50, or US$8 to US$11 with air-con.

Huong Bien Hotel *(☎ 868430)* offers beach bungalows hidden among the palm and pine trees. There are five bungalows with two rooms in each. Most rooms have fan and cold bath, and cost US$8. With air-con, rooms cost US$13.

Palace Hotel *(☎ 868364)* is an interesting place. It was originally built to accommodate Emperor Bao Dai, who had a taste for fancy beachside villas and had a chain of them erected in his favourite holiday spots. Bao Dai lost the franchise, but you can rent a rundown room here with fan and cold bath for US$8. Air-con (which even Bao Dai didn't have) and hot water will set you back US$11.

Military Guesthouse *(Nha Nghi Quan Doi, ☎ 868316)* has a good beach front location. Fan rooms in the main building cost from US$5. There are also two beach houses (recommended!) where rooms cost US$7. Air-con ups the tab to US$10 to US$14.

The Soviet-style ***Rang Dong Hotel*** *(☎ 868356)* is memorable chiefly for the karaoke that cranks up the decibels from

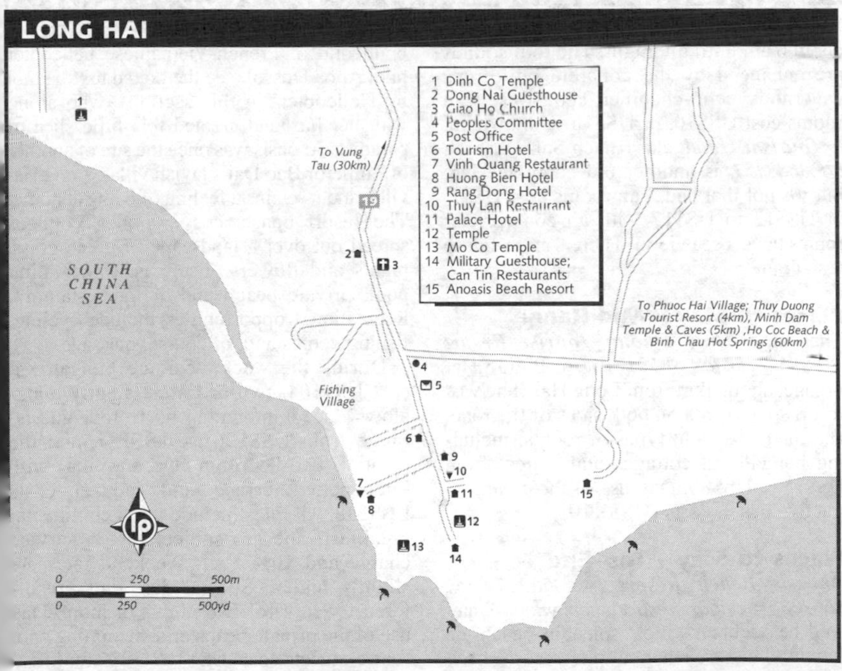

Spratly Spat

The Paracel Islands (Quan Dao Hoang Xa), 300km east of Danang, and the Spratly Islands (Quan Dao Thruong Xa), 475km south-east of Nha Trang, seem likely to be the source of future conflict between all the nations surrounding the South China Sea.

Several of the Paracel Islands, which historically have been only sporadically occupied, were seized by China in 1951. In the 1960s, a few islands were occupied by the South Vietnamese, who were driven out by Chinese forces in 1964, an action protested by both the Saigon and Hanoi governments.

The Spratlys, which consist of hundreds of tiny islets, are closer to Borneo than Vietnam. They have been claimed by virtually every country in the vicinity, including the Philippines, Malaysia, Indonesia, China, Taiwan and Vietnam. In 1988 Vietnam lost two ships and 70 sailors in a clash with China over the Spratlys. In mid-1992 Chinese military patrol boats reportedly opened fire several times on Vietnamese cargo vessels that were leaving Hong Kong, bringing trade between Vietnam and Hong Kong to a near halt. The explanation given was that China was trying to prevent smuggling.

Both archipelagos have little intrinsic value, but the country that has sovereignty over them can claim huge areas of the South China Sea – reported to hold vast oil reserves – as its territorial waters. China pushed tensions to a new high in 1992 by occupying one of the islets claimed by Vietnam, and by signing contracts with a US company (Crestone Corporation) to search for oil in the disputed areas. Vietnam returned the favour in 1996, by signing an oil exploration contract with a competing American company, Conoco. Also in 1996, the Philippine navy destroyed a small Chinese-built radar base on Mischief Reef in the Spratlys. The sovereignty of the islands remains unresolved.

about 6 am until midnight. The foul sounds are enhanced by the concrete building's cavernous echo-chamber acoustics. Fan rooms cost US$10, or US$16 with air-con.

Tourism Hotel, aka Khach San Du Lich (☎ *868312)*, is another old concrete slab, but it's not that bad. Fan rooms cost US$5, or US$12 to US$17 with air-con (pricier rooms have a sea view). There's an in-house restaurant.

Places to Stay – Mid Range

The large ***Thuy Duong Tourist Resort*** *(☎ 886 215, fax 886210)* is in Phuoc Hai village, about 4km from Long Hai. The vast resort sprawls out on both sides of the road, and there are eight types of rooms, including bungalows, cottages and suites, from US$15 to US$80. Day use of the clean, attractive beach costs (US$1.10).

Places to Stay – Top-End

Anoasis Beach Resort *(☎ 868227, fax 868228,* ⓔ *anoasisresort@hcm.vnn.vn)* may well be Vietnam's most splendid beachside retreat. This stylish boutique resort is the brainchild of French-Vietnamese helicopter pilot Anoa Dussol (see the boxed text 'Hanoi by Helicopter' in this section), who along with her husband created this little slice of paradise. Anoasis was once the site of another of Emperor Bao Dai's lavish villas, Long Hai villa, and it retains a feeling of being at home. The resort boasts cosy wooden cottages spread out over a landscape of green grass, plants and flowers. There is a swimming pool, private beach and a fine restaurant. Recreational opportunities include cycling, fishing, tennis and, of course, massage.

During the week, 'cottage bungalows' cost US$104, two-bedroom 'family bungalows' (accommodating up to four guests) range from US$126 to US$155, and the palatial, two-bedroom 'Ocean Villa' with kitchenette, terrace and jacuzzi costs US$248. All rates include a full continental breakfast, and are subject to 5% service charge and 10% VAT. Weekend rates are slightly higher. Special discounts are offered for stays of two nights or more. Day use of the private beach and swimming pool for nonguests costs US$10 (US$5 for kids).

Places to Eat
There is a cluster of good beachside restaurants called ***Can Tin 1, 2 and 3*** near the Military Guesthouse.

Across from the Palace Hotel, ***Thuy Lan Restaurant*** is also good (and clean), as is the seaside ***Vinh Quang Restaurant***, near the Huong Bien Hotel.

Getting There & Away
Long Hai is 124km from Ho Chi Minh City and takes about two hours to reach by car. There are some Long Hai–Ho Chi Minh City buses, though not many. Getting from Vung Tau to Long Hai is more difficult – you may have to rent a motorbike and drive yourself.

Getting around
Motorbike taxi drivers hang around all the likely tourist spots and will repeatedly offer you a ride whether you want one or not.

LOC AN BEACH
Heading north from Long Hai to Binh Chau you will see a turn-off onto Route 328 that leads 10km to Ho Tram Beach. This beach itself is disappointing, but about half-way there is a right-hand turn leading to a beautiful and seldom-visited beach at Ben Cat Loc An.

Places to Stay & Eat
If you follow the road a few kilometres to the beach, you will eventually reach a fork with signs posted for the two accommodation choices in the area.

The cheaper of the two is ***Thuy Hoang*** *(☎ 064-874223)*, where tiny A-frame beach bungalows cost just US$4 with shared toilet, or US$8 with a basic toilet inside.

The left fork will soon put you at ***Hong Phuc*** *(☎ 088-655176, fax 088-650542)*, which offers a slightly higher standard of beach cottage accommodation from US$9 to US$16.

Both of these places have ***restaurants*** serving good local seafood and cold beer.

HO COC BEACH
☎ 064

About 50km north-east of Long Hai is the remote and beautiful Ho Coc Beach. It's still a very undeveloped area, though the weekends bring crowds of Vietnamese tourists.

The area surrounding the beach is part of an 11,000-hectare rainforest designated as a nature reserve in 1975. Most of the larger wildlife was exterminated or relocated for safety reasons (most of the elephants were sent to Thailand under a government program), but plenty of birds and monkeys can be spotted in the forest. Guides for the walking trails can be hired for about US$4 a day (inquire at Hang Duong Ho Coc – see Places to Stay & Eat following).

Places to Stay & Eat
There are two accommodation choices right at the beach.

Khu Du Lich Bien Ho Coc *(☎ 878175, fax 871130)* consists of five little wooden A-frame bungalow that rent for US$7. Each bungalow has an attached bath with cold water only. The adjoining ***restaurant*** serves good seafood.

About 50m south down the beach is ***Hang Duong Ho Coc*** *(☎ 878145, fax 874146)*, which has cosy wooden cottages set back about 100m from the beach. Rooms cost US$8 and have attached bath (cold water only). There is also one larger cottage on the beach, where beds in the five-person room cost US$4 per person, or US$6 for a single room upstairs.

Getting There & Away
Public transport can be a little difficult, mainly because there isn't any. Some of the budget cafes in Ho Chi Minh City offer appealling day and overnight trips to Ho Coc. This also makes for a good (but very long) day trip on a motorbike. The 10km, unsealed road to Ho Coc takes you through the forest of the local nature reserve.

BINH CHAU HOT SPRINGS
☎ 064

About 140km from Ho Chi Minh City, and 60km north-east of Long Hai, is Binh Chau Hot Springs (Suoi Khoang Nong Binh Chau, ☎/fax 871130). There is a pleasant resort here, and for the most part tacky commercialisation is blessedly absent.

Hanoi by Helicopter

Since the late 1980s, thousands of Viet Kieu (Overseas Vietnamese) have returned to their homeland. Many have surmounted innumerable challenges, returning to what is still an insular and largely conservative society after so many years abroad. One of the most fascinating stories is that of Anoa Dussol-Perran, a gutsy French national who was born in Vietnam but left at the age of four with her adopted French parents.

A multitalented woman with a flair for getting the most out of life, Dussol-Perran developed a passion for flying helicopters, which she indulged whenever she could get away from her work in real estate. Although she had lived most of her life in France, she also was keenly aware of her Vietnamese heritage and in 1993 she made a momentous decision to return…in style.

She left Paris by helicopter in June, and three weeks and 41 stops later landed at Hanoi airport where she announced that she was going to set up a helicopter charter service. The local authorities were not impressed. They impounded her chopper and she was summoned to explain her actions in front of a none-too-sympathetic committee of government officials.

After nine months of legal wrangles, and cutting her way through miles of red tape, Dussol-Perran was finally able to obtain the proper documentation, and Vietnam's only female helicopter pilot set up the country's only privately run charter company.

However, it was not all smooth flying. A terrible crash a year later in the mountains around Dien Bien Phu cost the lives of two of her pilots, and Anoa had to struggle to keep the business afloat amid ever-worsening economic conditions, which saw business visitors to Vietnam – the mainstay of her clientele – overwhelmingly outnumbered by backpackers who stuck to terra firma. After three years, the sudden crash of the Asian economy finally put paid to her business and she closed the company.

Undaunted, Anoa decided her next project would keep her on firm ground and she scoured the country looking for the perfect spot to build a resort hotel. A year-long search brought her to Long Hai, today the site of the Anoasis Resort Hotel, which she runs in conjunction with her hotelier husband Ricardo. When she first came across the site – the tattered ruins of a palatial spread that once belonged to Emperor Bao Dai but was overgrown with jungle – she spent a number of nights sleeping rough (and alone) atop one of the villas to get a feel for the place. During one of these nights she was visited (or so she claims) by the ghostly apparition of a woman who told her that this site was her home, and that she should stay. Her search was over, and six months later construction of the resort began.

Despite the turbulence of her experiences since returning, Dussol-Perran has committed her future to Vietnam and has vowed to remain. Nevertheless, she refuses to be pigeon-holed about what projects she might entertain in the future. One thing is for sure, though, whatever she does, she will do it with her customary élan.

The main drawing card is the outdoor hot spring baths. All private baths are for rent, and each bath is on its own covered wooden platform, complete with a small changing room. The baths range from 37°C to 40°C, and the minerals in the water are said to be beneficial to your bones, muscles and skin, and are also said to improve blood circulation and mental disorders!

The baths come in different sizes and prices. A 3 sq metre-bath for two people costs 36,000d (US$2.50), a 5 sq metre-bath for up to five people costs 60,000d (US$4.30) and a 10 sq metre-bath for a party of 10 will set you back 96,000d (US$6.85). A dip in a large, shared swimming pool costs 6000d per person (US$0.40), or 2500d (US$0.18) for kids.

After your bath, the touristy thing to do is take a ride in an ox-drawn cart around the resort. Until recently there was wildlife in the area, including tigers and elephants, but it seems humans have nearly won the area over. In 1994, six elephants were captured near the springs, but after a few months of keeping them as pets they were turned over to the Ho Chi Minh City Zoo (seems the owners of the resort was unaware of how much it costs to feed six elephants). Nowadays, the only wildlife you are likely to spot are the ceramic lions, cheetahs and panthers that decorate the marshes around the springs.

To get to the hot springs, you have to walk down a wooden path. Be sure that you don't stray from the paths, as the earthen crust is thin here and you could conceivably fall through into an underground pool of scalding water! The hottest spring reaches 82°C, which is hot enough to boil an egg in 10 to 15 minutes. The Vietnamese all like to boil eggs in the cauldrons set aside for this purpose; you'll find a couple of small springs where bamboo baskets have been laid aside for just this purpose. Raw eggs are on sale for US$0.10 each.

Despite what you might hear, you should not drink the water here. However, at the time of writing, the management was planning to import a special European water filtration system to filter and distribute bottled mineral water across Vietnam.

There is an admission fee to the compound of 6000d (US$0.40). The resort has a hotel and an adjoining restaurant, and massage and acupuncture are also on offer.

Places to Stay

If you want to spend the night (in fact, it's not a bad place to stay), the only choice is the ***Hotel Cumi*** *(☎ 871131)*. There is a main hotel building, as well as three rustic *rong* (tree) houses. The rong houses have a double bed and shared bath only, and cost US$8. Rooms in the hotel have attached baths; with fan only it's US$9, and with aircon you'll pay US$12 to US$16.

Getting There & Away

The resort is in a compound 6km north of the village of Binh Chau. The road connecting Route 55 to Binh Chau used to be primarily mud and potholes. This changed in the early 1990s when the Australian government donated funds to build a new road. While you might question why Binh Chau was so favoured (do Canberra officials have an irresistible urge to visit hot springs?), you can't complain about the smooth ride.

Good highway or not, there is no public transport. You'll need a motorbike or car. If you choose the latter, perhaps you can find some travellers to share the expense.

The sealed road continuing north from the Binh Chau turn-off to Ham Tan peters out after about 2km, from where it's back to an unsealed, but smooth surface.

HAM TAN

Ham Tan is the new name for this place, but many locals still call it by its former name, Binh Tuy. Basically, it's a pleasantly secluded beach 30km north-east of Binh Chau Hot Springs. There is a small hotel here, but it's safe to say that visitors of any sort are infrequent. From Ham Tan, it's only another 30km north to National Highway 1.

HANG GON TOMB

South of the town of Xuan Loc is an ancient tomb that was excavated in the early 1990s. The tomb is about 2000 years old, but the intriguing thing about this place is that nobody knows who built it. The tomb contains ancient script that no one has been able to decipher or match the writing to any known ethnic group. UFO theorists and viewers of the *X-Files* should be enthralled with the place. The bodies of those entombed here were cremated, so there are no remains other than ashes.

Getting There & Away

There's no public transport available to Hang Gon tomb. The tomb is about 6km south of the intersection between National Highway 1 and the Baria highway, on the right-hand side of the road as you head south.

Mekong Delta

Pancake flat but lusciously green and beautiful, the Mekong Delta is the southernmost region of Vietnam. It was formed by sediment deposited by the Mekong River, a process which continues today; silt deposits extend the delta's shoreline at the mouth of the river by as much as 79m per year. The river is so large that it has two daily tides. At low tide in the dry season, boats cannot even move through the shallow canals.

The land of the Mekong Delta is renowned for its richness, and almost half of it is under cultivation. The area is known as Vietnam's 'bread basket', though 'rice basket' would be more appropriate. The Mekong Delta produces enough rice to feed the entire country, with a sizeable surplus.

When the government introduced collective farming to the delta in 1975, production fell significantly and there were food shortages in Saigon (although farmers in the delta easily grew enough to feed themselves). People from Saigon would head down to the delta to buy sacks of black-market rice, but the police set up checkpoints and confiscated rice from anyone carrying more than 10kg, in the aim of preventing 'profiteering'. All this ended in 1986, and farmers in this region have propelled Vietnam forward to become the world's second largest rice exporter after Thailand (also see the boxed text 'Rice Production').

Other products from the delta include coconut, sugar cane, fruits and fish. Although the area is primarily rural, it is one of the most densely populated regions in Vietnam – nearly every hectare is intensively farmed. An exception to this is the sparsely inhabited mangrove swamps around Camau Province, where the land is not very productive.

The Mekong River is one of the world's great rivers, and its delta is one of the world's largest. The Mekong originates high in the Tibetan plateau, flowing 4500km through China, between Myanmar and Laos, through Laos, along the Laos-Thailand border, and through Cambodia and Vietnam on its way to the South China Sea. At Phnom Penh (Cambodia), the Mekong splits into two main branches: the Hau Giang (the Lower River, also called the Bassac River), which flows via Chau Doc, Long Xuyen and Cantho to the sea; and the Tien Giang (Upper River), which splits into several branches at Vinh Long and empties into the sea at five points. The numerous branches of the river explain the

Highlights

- Take a boat trip through the countless canals that splinter from the end of the mighty Mekong River.
- Explore the delta's bustling floating markets.
- Discuss Buddhism with monks at elaborate Khmer pagodas.
- Homestay on one of the island fruit orchards around Vinh Long.
- Relax on the powdery white-sand beaches of remote Phu Quoc Island.

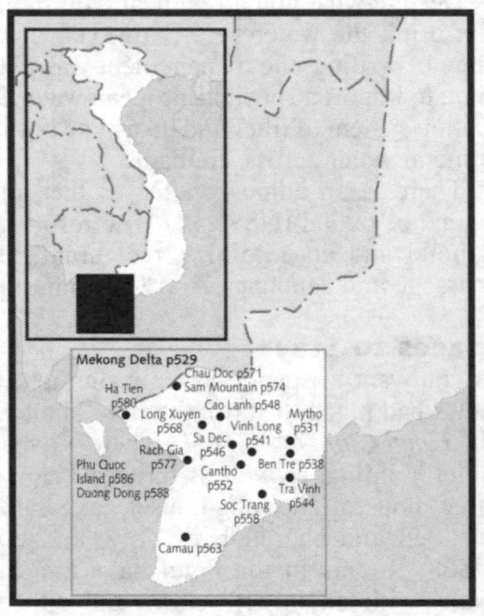

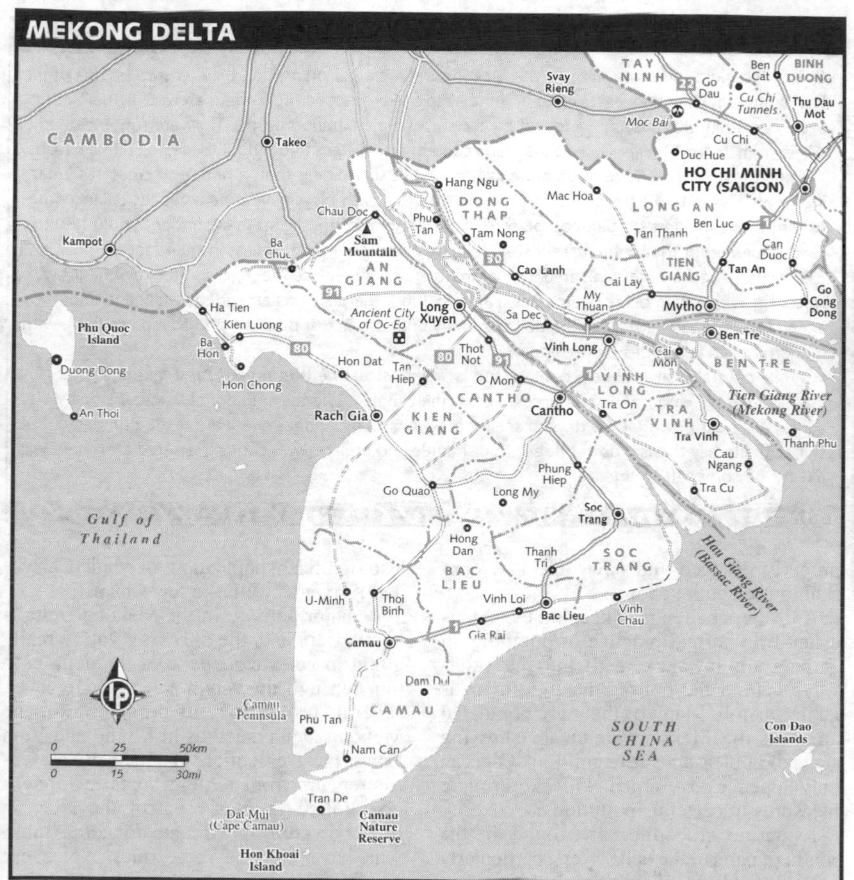

Vietnamese name for the Mekong: Song Cuu Long (River of Nine Dragons).

The water flow in the Mekong begins to rise around the end of May and reaches its highest point in September; it ranges from 1900 to 38,000 cubic metres per second depending on the season. A tributary of the river that empties into the Mekong at Phnom Penh drains Cambodia's Tonlé Sap Lake. When the Mekong is at flood stage, this tributary reverses its flow and drains into Tonlé Sap, thereby somewhat reducing the danger of serious flooding in the Mekong Delta. Unfortunately, deforestation in Cambodia is upsetting this delicate balancing act, resulting in more floods in Vietnam's portion of the Mekong River basin.

Living on a flood plain presents some technical challenges. Lacking any high ground to escape flooding, many delta residents build their houses on bamboo stilts to avoid the rising waters. Many roads are submerged or turn to muck during floods – all-weather roads have to be built on raised embankments, but this is expensive. The traditional solution has been to build canals and travel by boat. There are thousands of canals in the Mekong Delta – keeping them

Monkey Bridges – An Endangered Species

One of the most endearing sights in the Mekong Delta is a person making their way across one of the fascinating 'monkey bridges' *(cau khi)*. These simple, arch-shaped footbridges are usually built of uneven logs about 30 to 80cm wide and have only a simple bamboo railing. They are suspended anywhere from 2m to 10m above the canals, and connect tiny villages throughout the region to main roads.

At first glance the bridges look more like makeshift scaffolding than a bridge to cross. It's amazing to watch the locals traverse these narrow catwalks with bicycles and heavy loads balanced between their shoulders on bamboo poles. A fall from one of these tightrope bridges could result in serious injury, but the Vietnamese just glide across with ease (and smiles on their faces).

In 1998 the government initiated a program to gradually replace the region's monkey bridges with safer, 1m-wide wood plank overpasses. Later, in 2000, the plan was amended a new and improved agenda to do away with *all* of the delta's money bridges once and for all, and to replace them with modern concrete bridges by the end of 2000.

While naturally this will be a boon to the local infrastructure throughout the Mekong Delta, giving local people easier and safer access across the canals, sadly the traditional landscape will suffer a loss. It is clear now that the days of seeing these charming bridges everywhere are numbered, but still, with literally thousands of bridges to dismantle and replace, you can rest assured that there will always be some left to find.

properly dredged and navigable is a constant but essential chore.

A further challenge is keeping the canals clean. The normal practice of dumping all garbage and sewage directly into the waterways behind the houses that line them is taking its toll. Many of the more populated areas in the Mekong Delta are showing signs of unpleasant waste build-up. One can only hope the government will take stronger measures to curb this pollution.

Estuarine crocodiles are found in the southern parts of the delta rivers, particularly in the Hau Giang River. These creatures can be dangerous and travellers are advised to keep a healthy distance from them.

The Mekong Delta was once part of the Khmer kingdom, and was the last region of modern-day Vietnam to be annexed and settled by the Vietnamese. Cambodians, mindful that they controlled the area until the 18th century, still call the delta 'Lower Cambodia'. The Khmer Rouge tried to follow up on this claim by raiding Vietnamese villages and massacring the inhabitants. This led the Vietnamese army to invade Cambodia in 1979 and oust the Khmer Rouge from power. Most of the current inhabitants of the Mekong Delta are ethnic-Vietnamese, but there are also significant populations of ethnic-Chinese and Khmer as well as a few Chams.

A major activity in the Mekong Delta is boating. Indeed, the only way you're really going to get a close look at the delta is to tour through the canals by boat. However, several provincial governments in the Mekong Delta, such as in Mytho and Vinh Long, have essentially banned private entrepreneurs from renting boats to foreigners. Police regularly patrol the river in high-powered speedboats to catch those who have violated these rules. Not every provincial government is so restrictive, though – there are several places in the delta, Ben Tre for one, where you can simply rent a boat and go where you like.

Getting There & Away

Many travellers head to the delta by public bus (cheap but rough) or rented motorbike (good fun, though you can get lost among the maze of country roads).

The other way is by minibus tour. There are more than a few of these on offer, including many inexpensive trips that can be booked at the budget cafes in Ho Chi Minh City. However, before you book anything, do some crosschecking. Cheapest is not alway best – the cost largely depends on how far from Ho Chi Minh City the tour goes. This is not to say that you need to book a pricey tour, but sometimes 'rock bottom' means all you will get is a brief glance at the delta region. The standard of accommodation will be another determining factor.

With the May 2000 completion of the Australian-engineered My Thuan suspension bridge, one less ferry ride is necessary to reach the Mekong River, and travel time has been slashed by around an hour.

One of the quickest ways to get to the Mekong Delta from Ho Chi Minh City is by hydrofoil (see the boxed text on page 534-5).

MYTHO

☎ 074 • pop 169,300

Mytho, the quiet capital city of Tien Giang Province, is the closest city in the Mekong Delta to Ho Chi Minh City, and visitors on 10-day Vietnam tours come here for day trips to catch a glimpse of the famous river.

Being so close to booming Ho Chi Minh City, one would expect Mytho to have profited handsomely from the new economic reforms. Sadly, this is not the case – Mytho is

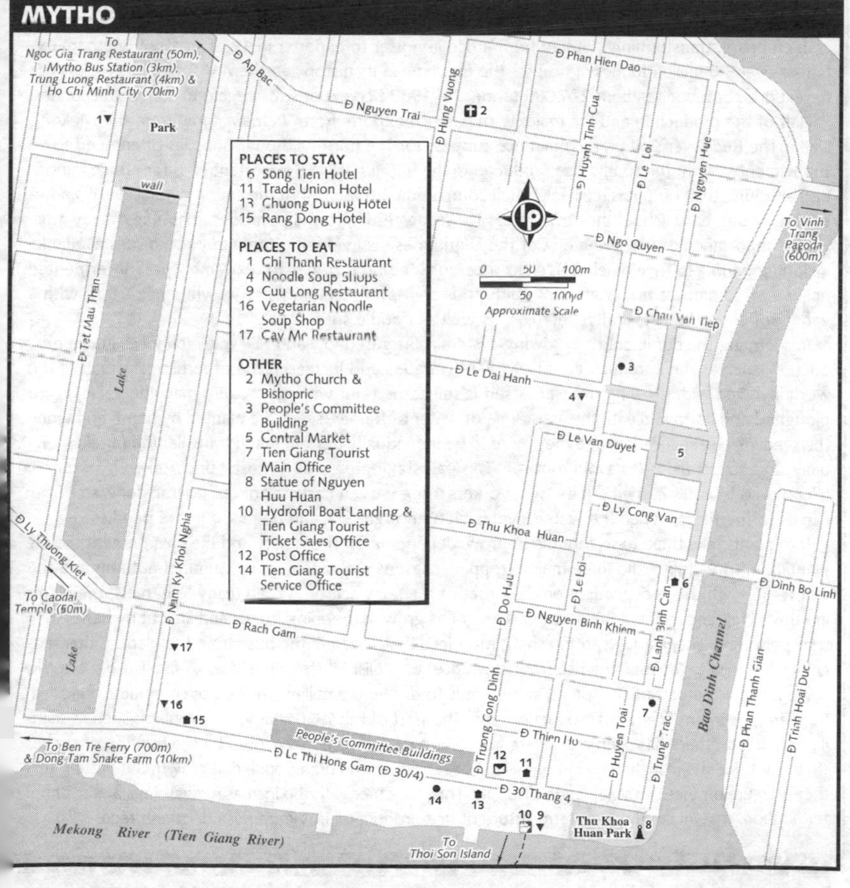

Rice Production

The ancient Indian word for rice, *dhanya*, meaning 'sustainer of the human race', is apt when describing the importance of rice to the Vietnamese.

A Vietnamese fable tells of a time when rice did not need to be harvested. Instead it would be summoned through prayer and arrive in each home from the heavens in the form of a large ball. One day, a man ordered his wife to sweep the floor in preparation for the coming of the rice, but she was still sweeping when the huge ball arrived and struck it by accident causing it to shatter into many pieces. Since then, Vietnamese have had to toil to produce rice by hand.

Rural Vietnam today is in many ways similar to what it would have been centuries ago: women in conical hats *(non bai tho)* irrigating fields by hand, farmers stooping to plant the flooded paddies, and water buffalo ploughing seedbeds with harrows.

Despite the labour-intensive production process, rice is the single most important crop in Vietnam, involving 70% of the working population. While always playing an important role in the Vietnamese economy, its production intensified considerably as a result of economic reforms, known as Doi Moi or 'renovation', in 1986. The reforms shifted agricultural production away from subsistence towards cash cropping, transforming Vietnam from a rice importer to exporter in 1989. In 1997, Vietnam exported over 3.5 million tonnes of rice; for the first time in its history, northern Vietnam had excess rice for export, contributing about 270,000 tonnes. In 1999 rice exports rose again to 4.5 million tonnes.

Half of the production and the majority of the rice exports from Vietnam come from the Mekong Delta. The Red River Delta is the main rice supplier for the north, although supplies often need to be supplemented from the south. Rice produced in the highlands is an important crop for ethnic minorities, although their output is relatively small compared with the rest of the country. Ironically, it's powerful rural cartels, which set their own prices for seeds, fertilisers and pesticides, that reap the rewards.

The importance of rice in the diet of the Vietnamese is evident in the many rice dishes available, including *banh xeo* (rice omelette), *chao* (rice porridge) and *ruou gao* (extremely potent fermented rice wine), to name a few. Vietnam's ubiquitous *com-pho* restaurants serve white rice *(com)* with a variety of cooked meats and vegetables, as well as noodle soup *(pho)*.

In Vietnam, the dominant rice growing system is 'irrigated lowland'. Despite advances in rice production, such as the introduction of new plant varieties and increased use of fertilisers, much of the work involved with growing the plant itself is still carried out without modern machinery. Fields are ploughed and harrowed with the assistance of water buffaloes, seeds are planted by hand, and when the seedlings reach a certain age they have to be individually uprooted and transplanted (again manually) to another field – to avoid root rot. This painstaking process is mostly undertaken by women. Irrigation is typically carried out by two workers using woven baskets on rope to transfer water from canals to the fields. When the water level is high enough, fish can be raised in the paddies.

Rice plants take three to six months to grow, depending on the variety and the environment they're planted in. In Vietnam, the three major cropping seasons are winter-spring, summer-autumn and the wet season, which are dependent on the onset of the rainy season. When ready to harvest, the plants are thigh high and in about 30cm water. The grains grow in drooping fronds and are cut by hand, then transported by wheelbarrows to thrashing machines that separate the husk from the plant. Other machines are used to 'dehusk' the rice (for brown rice) or 'polish' it (for white rice). A familiar sight at this stage is brown carpets of rice spread along roads to dry before milling. While rice continues to grow in Vietnam, the intensification of production since the start of the 1990s has led to problems such as salinity. In addition there has been a growing infestation of rice-field rats caused by the hunting of snakes (that hunt the rats). Unabated environmental degradation and high population growth are placing further pressure on Vietnam's staple grain supply. This, together with the increasing warnings against high fertilisation, may mean the long-term future of rice production in Vietnam is not guaranteed.

one of the poorest cities in the Mekong Delta, though it is said to have the richest government and one of the strictest police forces.

Mytho was founded in the 1680s by Chinese refugees fleeing Taiwan for political reasons. The Chinese have virtually all gone now, having been driven out in the late 1970s when their property was seized by the government. The economy – what's left of it – is based on fishing and the cultivation of rice, coconuts, bananas, mangoes, *nhan* (longans) and citrus fruit.

Orientation

Mytho, which sprawls along the bank of the northernmost branch of the Mekong River, is laid out in a fairly regular grid pattern.

The bus station is several kilometres west of town. Coming from the bus station, you enter Mytho on Đ Ap Bac, which turns into Đ Nguyen Trai (oriented west-east).

Parallel to the Mekong River is Đ 30 Thang 4, also written as Đ 30/4.

Information

Tien Giang Tourist (Cong Ty Du Lich Tien Giang, ☎ 872154, fax 873578) is the official tourism authority for Tien Giang Province. Its office is at 65 Đ Trung Trac, on the corner of Đ Rach Gam. For booking tours, however, head for its riverfront tourist service office (☎ 873184), at 8 Đ 30/4.

Nearby Islands

See Around Mytho for information about trips to nearby Phoenix, Dragon, Tortoise and Unicorn Islands.

Mytho Church & Bishopric

Mytho Church, a solid pastel-yellow building at 32 Đ Hung Vuong (corner of Đ Nguyen Trai), was built about a century ago. The stone plaques set in the church walls express *merci* and *cam on* to Fatima and other figures.

Today, two priests, two nuns and several assistants minister to most of Mytho's 7000 Catholics. The church is open every day from 4.30 to 6.30 am and 2.30 to 6.30 pm. Masses are held at 5 am and 5 pm, Monday to Saturday and 5 and 7 am and 5 pm on Sunday, with catechism classes in the late afternoon.

Caodai Temple

If you missed the one in Tay Ninh, Mytho has its own smaller Caodai Temple which is worth a look. It's on Đ Ly Thuong Kiet, between Đ Dong Da and Đ Tran Hung Dao.

Mytho Central Market

Mytho Central Market is an area of town along Đ Trung Trac and Đ Nguyen Hue that is closed to traffic. The streets are filled with stalls selling everything from fresh food and bulk tobacco to boat propellers. In an attempt to clear these streets, the local government has built a three-storey concrete monstrosity on the riverside, intending to relocate vendors inside. With the high rent and taxes, however, there have been very few takers, and the top two floors of the building remain empty.

Chinese District

The Chinese district is around Đ Phan Thanh Gian on the eastern bank of the Bao Dinh Channel. Though many people of Chinese decent remain, there is little else here to suggest that you're in Chinatown.

Vinh Trang Pagoda

Vinh Trang Pagoda is a beautiful and well-maintained sanctuary. The charitable monks here provide a home to orphans, disabled and other needy children.

The pagoda is about 1km from the city centre at 60A Đ Nguyen Trung Truc. To get there, take the bridge east across the river on Đ Nguyen Trai, and after 400m turn left. The entrance to the sanctuary is about 200m from the turn-off, on the right-hand side of the building as you approach it from the ornate gate.

Boat Tours

Boat trips are the highlight of a visit to Mytho. The small wooden vessels can navigate the Mekong (barely), but the target for most trips is cruising past pleasant rural villages through the maze of small canals. Depending on what you book, destinations usually include a coconut candy workshop, honey bee farm (try the banana wine!) and an orchid garden.

Hydrofoil Between Ho Chi Minh City and Mekong Delta

Greenlines operates a hydrofoil from Ho Chi Minh City (HCMC) to four cities in the Mekong Delta: Mytho, Cantho, Vinh Long and Chau Doc. You won't see much from inside these air-con water rockets, but the traffic-free ride takes far less time than travelling by road, leaving you more time to explore the areas you visit.

Victoria Resorts also offers chartered boat trips which link the Victoria Cantho and Chau Doc resorts in 2 ½ hours; stopovers can be arranged en route. Check out their Web site for details:www.victoriahotels-asia.com.

The following are the two different hydrofoil routes and schedules:

Route A:
Daily Service HCMC–Mytho–Cantho

city	departure time	city	arrival time
HCMC	7.30 am	Mytho	9.15 am
Mytho	9.30 am	Cantho	11.30 am
Cantho	1.30 pm	Mytho	3.30 pm
Mytho	4 pm	HCMC	5.30 pm

Route B:
Three Times Weekly Service HCMC–Mytho–Vinh Long–Chau Doc

Departures from HCMC on Tuesday, Thursday and Saturday

city	departure time	city	arrival time
HCMC	8 am	Mytho	9.50 am
Mytho	10 am	Vinh Long	10.50 am
Vinh Long	11 am	Chau Doc	1.30 pm

The Mytho People's Committee has a virtual monopoly over boat travel and their prices are so high that you need to be in a large group to make it economical. If you show up on your own and try to rent a boat, you'll have to pay at least US$23 for a two- to three-hour tour. If you sign up with a tour group in Ho Chi Minh City, it could work out at as little as US$7 per person, including bus transport between Ho Chi Minh City and Mytho. When comparing prices, check to see what you are actually getting – the tours can last anywhere from one to four hours (not including Ho Chi Minh City–Mytho travel time). Still, when you add up the costs, it would be nearly impossible to do it any cheaper on your own, though many travellers seem to prefer to do it that way.

There are also several private boat operators in Mytho defying the authorities by peddling local boat trips. They are indeed cheaper (most charge around US$5 per hour) than the 'official' rates, but they are also illegal and there is a chance you'll be pulled over and fined by the river cops. The best place to look for these freelancers is around the Cuu Long Restaurant or, ironically, just outside the gate of Tien Giang Tourist on Đ 30/4.

Places to Stay

Rang Dong Hotel *(☎ 874400, 25 Đ 30/4)* is privately run and one of the better cheap places in town. All rooms have air-con. Those with cold bath cost US$8 to US$11, and with hot water they are US$15.

Also popular with budget travellers is the ***Trade Union Hotel*** – also known as *Khach*

Hydrofoil Between Ho Chi Minh City and Mekong Delta

Departures from Chau Doc on Wednesday, Friday and Sunday

city	departure time	city	arrival time
Chau Doc	8.30 am	Vinh Long	10.30 am
Vinh Long	10.40 am	Mytho	11.30 am
Mytho	11.40 am	HCMC	1.30 am

In classic Vietnamese fashion, foreigners are charged more than double of what locals pay to ride the hydrofoils; children aged two to 12 pay half the adult fare. Ticket prices are as follows:

HCMC & Mytho	US$12
HCMC & Vinh Long	US$16
HCMC & Cantho	US$24
HCMC & Chau Doc	US$28
Mytho & Cantho	US$12
Mytho & Vinh Long	US$4
Vinh Long & Chau Doc	US$12

Greenlines ticket offices can be called locally where the boats arrive/depart:

HCMC Bach Dang Jetty (☎ 08-821 5609)
Mytho Lac Hong Park (☎ 073-872006)
Vinh Long Phuong Thuy Restaurant (☎ 070-823616)
Cantho Ninh Kieu Jetty (☎ 071-829372)
Chau Doc Victoria Hotel (☎ 076-865568)

For information and schedules on hydrofoil services to Vung Tao, see the Around Ho Chi Minh City chapter.

San Cong Doan – *(☎ 874324, 61 Đ 30/4).* River views are the attraction here. A single room with fan costs US$8, or you can have a room with air-con and refrigerator for US$11.

Song Tien Hotel *(☎ 872009)* is the largest hotel in town with fan rooms at US$6 and air-con rooms from US$10 to US$18.

The new ***Chuong Duong Hotel*** *(☎ 870875, fax 874250, 10 Đ 30/4)* is Mytho's most luxurious accommodation. This attractive building boasts a prime riverside location and there is good in-house restaurant as well. Rooms range from US$20 to US$30.

Another option to consider is overnighting on Unicorn Island; inquire at Tien Giang Tourist, or better yet, at the cafes in Ho Chi Minh City.

Places to Eat

Mytho is known for a special vermicelli soup, *hu tieu My Tho*, which is richly garnished with fresh and dried seafood, pork, chicken and fresh herbs. It is served either with broth or dry (with broth on the side). There are no speciality restaurants for trying hu tieu; it can be found at almost any eatery in town.

Right on the shore of the Mekong River, the ***Cuu Long Restaurant***, offers good views and decent food at reasonable prices. It's also a good place to meet private boat drivers.

Chi Thanh Restaurant *(☎ 873756, 279 Đ Tet Mau Than)* is another good spot for inexpensive Vietnamese fare, as is the ***Cay Me Restaurant*** at 60 Đ Nam Ky Khoi Nghia.

The ***noodle soup shops*** near the intersection of Đ Le Dai Hanh and Đ Le Loi are highly popular in the evening.

Search & Destroy

Only one major battle occurred in the Mekong Delta during the American War (in 1972 at Cai Lay, 20km from Mytho). Aside from that, all fighting in the delta during the war was confined to small-scale ambushes. Unfortunately for the Americans, the lush jungles, tall grass and mangrove swamps provided perfect camouflage for the Viet Cong (VC). The high civilian population density made it impossible for the Americans to use indiscriminate bombing, so it was necessary to send in ground-level 'search and destroy missions'. From the air, helicopter gunships raked the grasslands and jungles with machine gun fire. On the water, US forces used high-speed military boats to patrol the hundreds of canals crisscrossing the delta in an effort to intercept guerillas travelling by canoe to their sanctuaries.

For their part, the VC responded with booby traps, night-time raids, assassinations of 'uncooperative elements' and mines planted in the canals – essentially, the Communists controlled much of the delta at night. Both the Communists and the ARVN conscripted young men from the delta into their respective armies – it wasn't unusual for brothers to be fighting on opposite sides, often against their will. Desertions from both sides were high.

Caught in the crossfire, local villagers sensibly fled. By 1975, 40% of Saigon's population was from the Mekong Delta region.

Agent Orange was used to clear the mangrove forests of the delta in an effort to deny the guerillas sanctuary. Ironically, spraying the mangroves with defoliants may have backfired on the Americans. Obtaining food and supplies was one of the biggest headaches for the VC. Spraying the mangroves with Agent Orange caused the leaves of the plants to die, fall off and decay, providing a source of nutrition for shrimp which in turn were harvested by the VC. This provided the guerillas with a major short-term gain – they ate the shrimp and sold the surplus in the local markets to buy other supplies.

There is also good vegetarian noodle soup served in the ***shops*** at 36-44-46 Đ Nam Ky Khoi Nghia.

On the road entering Mytho from Ho Chi Minh City is the pleasant ***Ngoc Gia Trang Restaurant*** *(☎ 872742, 196 Đ Ap Bac)*. It's a bit pricey compared to the places in town, but has a lovely courtyard atmosphere and good set meals from around US$4 to US$12.

A few kilometres further out of town, by the gate marking the entry point to Mytho, the ***Trung Luong Restaurant*** *(☎ 855441)* has a nice garden, and the tour groups that stop here appreciate the clean toilets. The caged monkey, birds, and python, however, do not necessarily add to the charm.

Getting There & Away

Bus Mytho is served by buses leaving Ho Chi Minh City from Mien Tay bus station in An Lac, and also from the bus station in Cholon (US$0.75). Buses from Cholon have the added advantage of dropping passengers right in Mytho, as opposed to the bus station outside of town.

The Mytho bus station (Ben Xe Khach Tien Giang) is several kilometres west of town; it is open from 4 am to about 5 pm. To get there from the city centre, take Đ Ap Bac westward and continue on to National Highway 1 (Quoc Lo 1).

Buses to Ho Chi Minh City leave when full from the early morning until about 5 pm; the trip takes about two hours. There are daily bus services to Cantho (US$1.10, three to four hours), Vung Tau (five hours) and Tay Ninh (six hours).

Car & Motorbike By car or motorbike, the drive from Ho Chi Minh City to Mytho on National Highway 1 takes about 1½ hours.

Road distances from Mytho are 16km to Ben Tre, 104km to Cantho, 70km to Ho Chi Minh City and 66km to Vinh Long.

Boat For details on the Greenlines hydrofoil service to/from Mytho, see the boxed text 'Hydrofoil between Ho Chi Minh City and Mekong Delta' near the start of this chapter.

The car ferry to Ben Tre Province leaves from Ben Pha Rach Mieu station about 1km west of Mytho city centre near 2/10A Đ Le Thi Hong Gam (the western continuation of Đ 30/4). The ferry operates between 4 am and 10 pm and runs at least once an hour. Ten-person trucks shuttle passengers between the ferry terminal and the bus station.

Getting Around

Bicycle Bicycles can be rented from Tien Giang Tourist.

AROUND MYTHO

Dragon Island

A walk through the well-known longan orchards of Dragon Island (Con Tan Long) is pleasant. The lush, palm-fringed shores of the island are lined with wooden fishing boats; some of the residents of the island are shipwrights. There is a small ***restaurant*** on the island. Dragon Island is a five-minute boat trip from the dock at the southern end of Đ Le Loi.

Other Islands

The other two islands in the vicinity are Tortoise Island (Con Qui) and Unicorn Island (Thoi Son). For booking a trip to these islands or any of the others, it's cheapest to arrange a day tour from Ho Chi Minh City.

Dong Tam Snake Farm

There is a snake farm at Dong Tam, about 10km from Mytho towards Vinh Long. Most of the snakes raised here are pythons and cobras The snakes are bred for eating, for their skins and for producing antivenin. The king cobras are raised only for exhibit – they are extremely aggressive and are even capable of spitting poison; do not get too close to their cages. The regular cobras are kept in an open pit and will generally ignore you if you ignore them, but will strike if provoked. On the other hand, the pythons are docile enough to be taken out of their cages and 'played with' if you dare, but be warned the larger ones are capable of strangling a human.

Dong Tam also has a collection of mutant turtles and fish on display. The cause of their genetic deformities is almost certainly the spraying of Agent Orange during the American War, which was particularly intensive in forested parts of the Mekong Delta.

Other creatures exhibited here include sea turtles, deer, monkeys, bears, crocodiles, owls, canaries and other birds. (All the names and explanations of the creatures are in Vietnamese only.)

The snake farm is operated by the Vietnamese military for profit. It's open to the public and taking photos is encouraged. At your request, the staff will drape you with a large python to create that perfect photo for the loved ones back home. The ***restaurant*** at the snake farm includes cobra on the menu, and there is also a shop here where you can stock up on cobra antivenin.

The farm was formerly run by a retired Viet Cong (VC) colonel named Tu Duoc. He ran the place very efficiently, but after he died in 1990 facilities have gone steadily downhill. The cages look dirty, the animals neglected and the employees dispirited. It's certainly a sharp contrast to Bangkok's slick Snake Institute.

You'll need your own transport to get to Dong Tam Snake Farm. Coming from Ho Chi Minh City, continue for 3km beyond the turn-off to Mytho and turn left at the Dong Tam Junction (signposted). From the junction, follow the dirt road for 4km, turn right and continue for 1km until you reach the snake farm. To get there from Mytho, follow Đ Le Thi Hong Gam west along the river for around 7km and just beyond the Binh Duc Post Office turn right and follow the dirt road for 3km to the farm.

Admission is US$1.10.

BEN TRE

☎ 075 • pop 111,800

The picturesque little province of Ben Tre, just south of Mytho, consists of several large islands in the mouth of the Mekong River. The area gets few visitors because it's off the main highways. The provincial capital is also called Ben Tre, and is a friendly sort of place with a few old buildings near the banks of the Mekong.

Ben Tre is a good place for boat trips and, unlike Mytho, Vinh Long and Cantho,

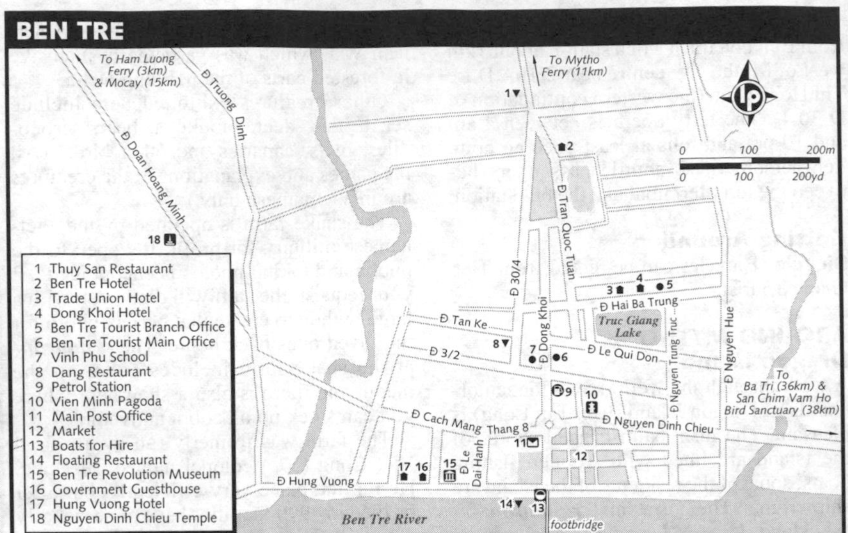

the People's Committee doesn't have a monopoly on the boat tour business, so prices have remained low.

Ben Tre Tourist (☎ 829618, fax 822440) is at 65 Đ Dong Khoi. There is also a branch office adjacent to the Dong Khoi Hotel.

Vien Minh Pagoda

Right in the centre of Ben Tre, this is the head office of the Buddhist Association of Ben Tre Province. Though the history of the pagoda is vague, the local monks say it is over 100 years old. The original structure was made of wood, but it was torn down to make way for the present building. Reconstruction took place from 1951 to 1958, using bricks and concrete.

A feature of this pagoda is a large white statue of Quan The Am Bo Tat (the Goddess of Mercy) in the front courtyard. The Chinese calligraphy adorning the pagoda was done by an old monk. None of the current monks can read Chinese, though some of the local worshippers can.

Truc Giang Lake

Truc Giang Lake, a small but pleasant lake fronting the Dong Khoi Hotel, is a place to play around in paddle boats. The surrounding park is too small for much strolling.

AROUND BEN TRE

Phoenix Island

Until his imprisonment by the Communists for anti-government activities and the consequent dispersion of his flock, the Coconut Monk (Ong Dao Dua) led a small community on Phoenix Island (Con Phung), a few kilometres from Mytho. In its heyday, the island was dominated by a fantastic open-air sanctuary that looked a bit like a cross between a cheaply built copy of Disneyland and the Tiger Balm Gardens of Singapore. The dragon-enwrapped columns and the multiplatformed tower, with its huge metal globe, must have once been brightly painted, but these days the whole place is faded, rickety and silent. Nevertheless, it's good kitschy fun – check out the model of the Apollo rocket set among the Buddhist statues! With a bit of imagination though, you can picture how it all must have appeared as the Coconut Monk presided over his congregation, flanked by elephant tusks and seated on a richly ornamented throne.

The Coconut Monk was so named, it is said, because he once ate only coconuts for three years; others claim he only drank coconut juice and ate fresh young corn. Whatever the story, he was born Nguyen Thanh Nam (though he later adopted Western name order, preferring to be called Nam Nguyen Thanh) in 1909, in what is now Ben Tre Province. He studied chemistry and physics in France at Lyon, Caen and Rouen from 1928 until 1935, when he returned to Vietnam, married and had a daughter.

In 1945 the Coconut Monk left his family to pursue a monastic life. For three years he sat on a stone slab under a flagpole and meditated day and night. He was repeatedly imprisoned by successive South Vietnamese governments, which were infuriated by his philosophy of achieving reunification through peaceful means. He died in 1990.

The Coconut Monk founded a religion, Tinh Do Cu Si, which was a mixture of Buddhism and Christianity. Representations of Jesus and the Buddha appeared together, as did the Virgin Mary and eminent Buddhist women. He employed both the cross and Buddhist symbols. The plaques on the 3.5m-high porcelain jar (created in 1972) tell all about him.

The Coconut Monk's complex is visible from the car ferry that runs from near Mytho to Ben Tre Province.

There is an admission fee of US$0.50; it would be nice to think this money is going to maintain the place. But, apparently, this is not the case – the island's adornments are falling apart and the place is becoming increasingly dilapidated. As one traveller lamented:

> The island is a great disappointment. It has faded almost into nothing. Beware of the cunning old chap claiming to be an ex-monk who drags you around the few sights at high speed and then demands you buy him an extortionate beer at the kiosk.
>
> **Sue Grossey**

The Mytho police will not permit you to visit this island using a private boat, so you will have to hire a government one for at least US$25. Another possibility is to hire a boat from Ben Tre Province, which is just across the river. In fact, Phoenix Island is in Ben Tre Province, which means that the Mytho police really don't have jurisdiction here. However, they can grab you going to and from the island even if they can't come onto the island itself. If you do first cross the river to Ben Tre Province, you can easily get a boat from there to Phoenix Island without the Mytho police being able to do anything.

Nguyen Dinh Chieu Temple

This temple is dedicated to Nguyen Dinh Chieu, a local scholar. It's in the Ba Tri District, about a 30-minute drive (36km) from Ben Tre. It's a very charming temple, excellent for photography.

Bird Sanctuary

The locals make much of the storks that nest at the local bird sanctuary, San Chim Vam Ho (☎ 858669), which is 38km from Ben Tre town. Ben Tre Tourist has speedboats that can make the round trip in about two hours, or slow boats that take about five hours. You can check the information and going rates at Ben Tre Tourist, and also compare against what the freelance boat operators are charging.

To get there overland, follow Đ Nguyen Dinh Chieu east out of town for 20km to Giong Tram. Turn left onto the windy, rural dirt road leading to Trai Tu K-20 (Prison K-20); you'll reach the prison after travelling 11km (you may see hundreds of prisoners out tilling the fields), and then turn right and drive the final 7km to Vam Ho.

Entry costs US$0.80.

Places to Stay

The bottom of the barrel is the ***Hung Vuong Hotel*** *(☎ 822408, 166 Đ Hung Vuong)*. Rooms with fan are US$6; air-con ups the tab to US$8 to US$12.

Just next door is the ***Government Guesthouse*** *(☎ 826134, 148 Đ Hung Vuong)*. Air-con doubles cost US$12, or US$15 with hot water. An air-con room for four with cold water costs US$20.

The ***Ben Tre Hotel*** *(☎ 822223, 8/2 Đ Tran Quoc Tuan)* has rooms with fan for US$7, while air-con rooms range from US$12 to US$15.

The ***Trade Union Hotel*** (☎ *825082, 50 Đ Hai Ba Trung)* is a decent place with fan rooms renting for US$16, or US$18 to US$20 with air-con.

Ben Tre's plushest accommodation can be found at the ***Dong Khoi Hotel*** (☎ *822240, 16 Đ Hai Ba Trung)*. All rooms have air-con. Doubles are US$20 to US$35. Take a peek at the hotel's gift shop – the souvenir spoons, chopsticks and coconut-wood ashtrays are certainly beautiful.

Places to Eat

The decaying ***Floating Restaurant*** is anchored on the south side of town near the market. The food is unremarkable, but you can't beat the location.

The ***Dang Restaurant*** and ***Thuy San Restaurant*** are two popular local joints worth checking out for Vietnamese fare, fresh river fish and seafood.

The ***Dong Khoi Hotel*** has the most upmarket restaurant in town. On Saturday night, a band entertains the guests.

There is also a big restaurant at the ***Hung Vuong Hotel***.

If you're travelling on the cheap, just head over to the market, which has plenty of ***food stalls*** where you can fill up for about US$0.50.

Getting There & Away

As this is an island province, crossing the Mekong River is a prerequisite for reaching Ben Tre. However, the ferry crossing is particularly slow – about 45 minutes each way.

Slow as it is, the Mytho–Ben Tre crossing is the fastest option. There are other possible ferry crossings further south but these are so slow and unreliable that you shouldn't count on them. Ferry crossings are much quicker if you're travelling by motorbike (as opposed to car) since there are numerous small boats that can take you across the river.

There are private vans that make the Ben Tre–Ho Chi Minh City run daily. These operate on no fixed schedule, so you'll need to inquire locally. Try asking around the market, or by the Vinh Phu school gate (where some vans leave from).

Getting Around

Ben Tre Tourist has a high-speed boat for rent, though it's not cheap at US$35 per hour. It can hold about eight people. Slower and larger boats can also be rented here, but other bargains can be negotiated at the public pier near the market. Here you can figure on about US$1.60 per hour, with a minimum of two hours cruising the local canals. Check with the boat drivers who hang around near the end of the footbridge.

VINH LONG

☎ 070 • pop 124,600

Vinh Long, the capital of Vinh Long Province, is a medium-sized town along the banks of the Mekong River, about midway between Mytho and Cantho.

Cuu Long Tourist (☎ 823616, fax 823357, 1 Đ Thang 5), which has a virtual monopoly on the local tourism market, is one of the more capable state-run tour outfits in the Mekong Delta. There is also a small booking office near the Phuong Thuy Restaurant which rents bicycles (US$2 per day) and motorbikes (US$8).

Cuu Long Tourism offers a variety of boat tours ranging from three to five hours, as well as overnight excursions. Tour destinations include small canals, fruit orchards, brick kilns, a conical palm hat workshop and the Cai Be Floating Market. Homestays at the orchards can also be arranged (see the boxed text 'A Home Away From Home', following).

As is the case in most of the Mekong Delta, if you're travelling independently you'll need to organise at least a few people to go with to make the prices of these tours reasonable.

Mekong River Islands

What makes a trip to Vinh Long worthwhile is not the town itself, but the beautiful small islands in the river. The islands are totally given over to agriculture, especially the raising of tropical fruits, which are shipped to markets in Ho Chi Minh City.

To visit the islands you will have to charter a boat through Cuu Long Tourist. Small boats cost US$25 per person for a three-hour journey – minimum of three people.

However, you may be able to negotiate a better deal. The tours include an English- or French-speaking Vietnamese guide.

One way to bypass the government monopoly is to take the public ferry (US$0.20) to one of the islands and then walk around on your own; however, this is not nearly as interesting as a boat tour since you will not cruise the narrow canals.

Some of the more popular islands to visit include Binh Hoa Phuoc and An Binh Island, but there are many others. This low-lying region is as much water as land, and houses are generally built on stilts. Bring plenty of film because there are photo opportunities in every direction you look.

Cai Be Floating Market

This bustling river market is worth including on a boat tour from Vinh Long. It runs from 5 am to 5 pm, but is best early in the morning. Wholesalers on big boats moor here, each specialising in one or a few types of fruit or vegetables. Customers cruise the market in smaller boats, and can easily find what they're looking for as the larger boats hang samples of their goods from tall wooden poles.

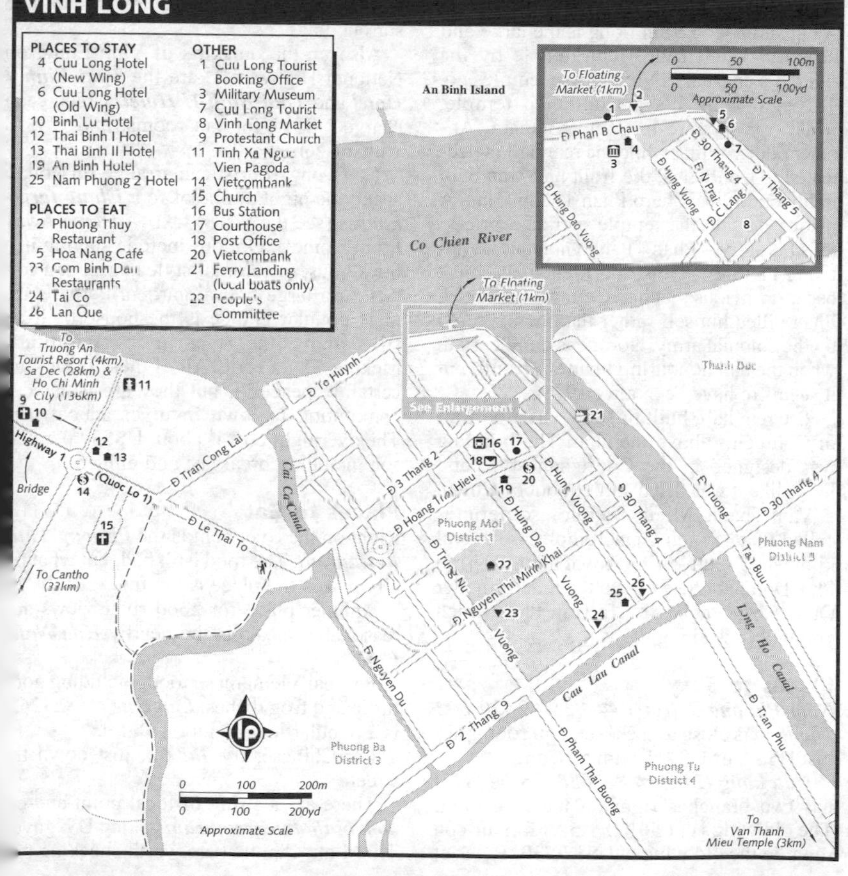

One interesting thing you won't see at other floating markets is the huge Catholic cathedral on the riverside – a popular and fantastic backdrop for photographs.

It takes about an hour to reach the market from Vinh Long, but most people make detours on the way there or back to see the canals or visit orchards.

Military Museum

It might not be up the standard of the military museums in Ho Chi Minh City and Hanoi, but there is a military museum (Bao Tang Quan Su) close to the Cuu Long Hotel.

Van Thanh Mieu Temple

A big surprise in Vinh Long is the large and beautiful Van Thanh Meiu Temple by the river. It's unusual as Vietnamese temples go. To begin with, it's a Confucian temple, which is very rare in South Vietnam. Another oddity is that while the rear hall is dedicated to Confucius, the front hall was built in honour of local hero Phan Thanh Gian. A plaque outside the temple entrance briefly tells his story – Phan Thanh Gian led an uprising in 1930 against the French. When it became obvious that his revolt was doomed, Phan killed himself rather than be captured by the colonial army. No-one is quite certain when the hall honouring Phan was built, but it seems to have been after 1975.

The rear hall, built in 1866, has a portrait of Confucius above the altar. The building was designed in the Confucian style and looks like it was lifted straight out of China.

Van Thanh Mieu Temple, sometimes called Phan Thanh Gian Temple, is several kilometres south-east of town along Đ Tran Phu. Don't confuse it with the much smaller Quoc Cong Pagoda on Đ Tran Phu, which you will pass along the way.

Places to Stay

Nam Phuong 2 Hotel *(☎ 821169, 20 Đ 2 Thang 9)* is close to the river. Fan rooms are just US$7, or US$11 with air-con.

Cuu Long Hotel *(☎ 823656, fax 823357)* has two branches right on the riverfront. The old wing is at 501 Đ 1/5. A fan/air-con room in the old wing is US$20/30. Rates at the new wing range from US$35 to US$45; all air-con rooms have satellite TV.

An Binh Hotel *(☎ 823190, 3 Đ Hoang Thai Hieu)* is nice enough, but not favoured by travellers because it's away from the scenic riverfront. Rooms with fan and outside toilet are US$10. Rooms with toilet and air-con are US$15 to US$25. Facilities include tennis courts and massage service.

Midway on the 8km stretch of road between Vinh Long and the My Thuan bridge is the ***Truong An Tourist Resort*** *(☎ 823161)*. It's a quiet place to stay if you don't mind being away from town. There are cottages here with rooms costing US$25. It's lovely to sit by the riverside and enjoy the parklike surroundings.

Also on the outskirts of Vinh Long, on National Highway 1, are the ***Thai Binh I Hotel*** and ***Thai Binh II Hotel***, which each charge US$15 for fan rooms, and US$18 with air-con.

Cuu Long Tourist can arrange for you to spend the night at one of four ***island farmhouses*** (see the boxed text 'A Home Away From Home'). Options include staying in a brick house, a colonial-style house, or a cottage in a large bonsai garden. Perhaps the most popular choice is the house built on stilts above the river in the traditional Mekong Delta style. All of these places are certainly peaceful, but they are isolated – commuting to town involves a boat trip. The overnight cost is about US$30 per person including breakfast and dinner.

Places to Eat

Right on the riverfront is the ***Phuong Thu Restaurant***. The food isn't bad, but what really makes the place is the fine view.

Another place for good river views and reasonable meals is the nearby ***Hoa Nam Café***.

For real Vietnamese food, including goo turtle and frog dishes, ***Lan Que*** *(☎ 82326*… is a popular local joint on Đ 2/9.

For Chinese, try ***Tai Co***, just down the street.

There are a string of local point-and-e… ***com binh dan restaurants*** along Đ Nguye… Thi Minh Khai that are worth checking o…

If great food at cheap prices is more important than scenery, check out the ***Vinh Long Market***. This is also a great place to try some delicious fruit, such as bananas, mangoes and papayas.

Getting There & Away

Bus Buses to Vinh Long leave Ho Chi Minh City from Cholon bus station in District 5, and from Mien Tay bus station in An Lac. Buses take about three hours and cost US$1.20. You can also get to Vinh Long by bus from Mytho, Tra Vinh, Cantho, Chau Doc and other points in the Mekong Delta.

Car & Motorbike Vinh Long is just off National Highway 1, 66km from Mytho, 33km from Cantho and 136km from Ho Chi Minh City.

Boat For details on the Greenlines hydrofoil service to/from Vinh Long, see the boxed text 'Hydrofoil between Ho Chi Minh City and Mekong Delta' at the start of this chapter.

It may also be possible to travel by cargo boat from Vinh Long all the way to Chau Doc (near the Cambodian border), but you should have a Vietnamese guide if you want to attempt this.

TRA VINH

☎ 074 • pop 70,000

Bordered by the Tien and Hau branches of the Mekong, Tra Vinh's location on a peninsula makes it somewhat isolated. Getting there is a straight up and back trip, because no car ferries cross the rivers here (motorbikes can be ferried by small boats). Western tourists are few, though there are several very worthwhile things to see here.

There are about 300,000 ethnic Khmer in Tra Vinh Province. At first glance, the Khmers might seem to be an invisible minority – they all speak fluent Vietnamese, and there is nothing outwardly distinguishing about their clothing or lifestyle. However, digging a little deeper quickly reveals that Khmer culture is alive and well in this part of Vietnam. There are over 140 Khmer pagodas in Tra Vinh Province, compared with 50 Vietnamese and five Chinese pagodas. The pagodas have schools to teach the Khmer language – most of the locals in Tra Vinh can read and write Khmer at least as well as Vietnamese.

Vietnam's Khmer minority are almost all followers of Theravada Buddhism. If you've visited monasteries in Cambodia, you may have observed that Khmer monks are not involved in growing food and rely on donations from the strictly religious locals. Here in Tra Vinh, Vietnamese guides will proudly point out the monks' rice harvest as one of the accomplishments of liberation. To the Vietnamese government, nonworking monks were parasites. The Khmers don't necessarily see it the same way, and continue to donate funds to the monasteries surreptitiously.

Between the ages of 15 and 20, most boys set aside a few months or years to live as monks (they decide themselves on the length of service). Khmer monks can eat meat, though they cannot kill animals.

There is also a small but active Chinese community in Tra Vinh, one of the few remaining in the Mekong Delta region.

Information

Tra Vinh Tourist (☎ 862559, fax 866768), 64–6 Đ Le Loi, has a monopoly here. The staff can book various trips to sites around the province, though the boat trips prove to be the most interesting.

Ong Pagoda

The Ong Pagoda (Chua Ong, also known as Chua Tau) is a very ornate, brightly painted building on the corner of Đ Dien Bien Phu and Đ Tran Phu. Rare for the Mekong Delta region, this is a 100% Chinese pagoda and is still a very active place of worship. The red-faced god on the altar is deified general Quan Cong (in Chinese: Guangong, Guandi or Guanyu). Quan Cong is believed to offer protection against war and is based on an historical figure, a soldier of the 3rd century. You can read more about him in the Chinese classic *The Romance of the Three Kingdoms*.

The Ong Pagoda was founded in 1556 by the Fujian Chinese Congregation, but has

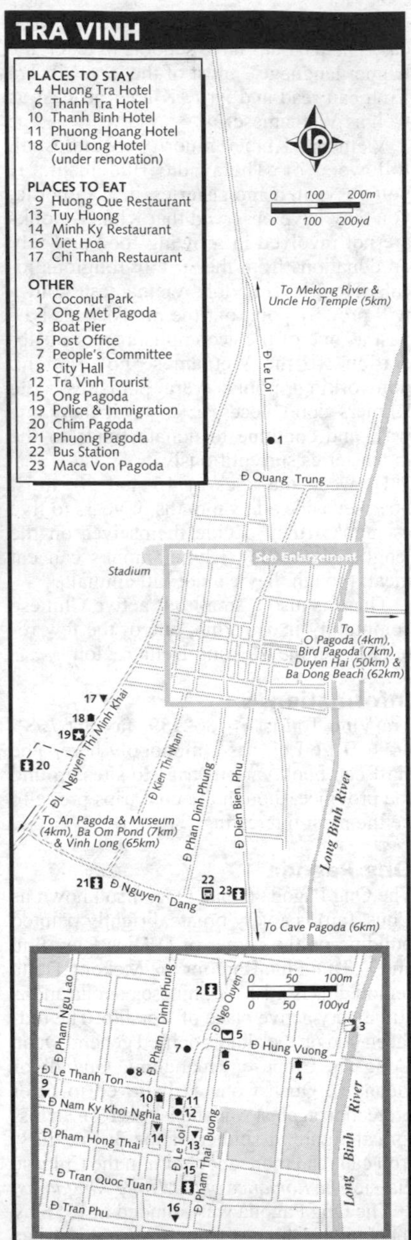

been rebuilt a number of times. Recent visitors from Taiwan and Hong Kong have contributed money for the pagoda's restoration, which is why it is in such fine shape.

Ong Met Pagoda

The chief reason for visiting this large Khmer pagoda is that it's the most accessible, being right in the centre of town. The monks at Ong Met Pagoda (Chua Ong Met) are friendly and happy to show you around the interior.

Chim Pagoda

An interesting monastery, Chim Pagoda (Chua Chim) sees few visitors because you have to wind your way along dirt roads to find it. It's actually just 1km off the main highway to Vinh Long in the south-west part of town. Probably the best way to get there if you don't have your own wheels is to get a local take you on a motorbike.

The friendly monks here claim that the pagoda was built 500 years ago, though the present structure is obviously much newer. There are about 20 monks in residence here.

An Pagoda & Museum

Four kilometres south-west of Tra Vinh town is An Pagoda (Chua An) and the Khmer Minority People's Museum – worth stopping in for a look.

Ba Om Pond

Known as Ao Ba Om (Square Lake), this is a spiritual site for the Khmers and a picnic and drinking spot for local Vietnamese. The square-shaped pond is surrounded by tall trees and is pleasant if not spectacular.

More interesting is the nearby An Vuong Pagoda (Angkor Rek Borei), a beautiful and venerable Khmer-style pagoda. There is also an interesting **museum** of Khmer culture (Bao Tang Van Hoa Dan Tac) on the far side of the lake (away from the highway), though nothing is labelled in English.

Ba Om Pond is 8km from Tra Vinh along the highway towards Vinh Long.

Uncle Ho Temple

Sometimes Vietnam throws something totally unexpected at you. Tra Vinh chips in

GREG ELMS

JOHN W BANAGAN

MASON FLORENCE

Water life: boating, fishing, and floating markets on the Mekong Delta.

RICHARD I'ANSON

RICHARD I'ANSON

RICHARD I'ANSON

Prepare to be overwhelmed by Cantho market, the Mekong Delta's biggest centre for market produce, much of which is transported by boat.

with the Uncle Ho Temple (Den Tho Bac), dedicated, of course, to late President Ho Chi Minh. Perhaps Tra Vinh's enterprising People's Committee was looking for a way to distinguish its fine town and put it on the tourist circuit. If so, it may have succeeded – although no monks have taken up residence, 'worshippers' continue to flock here (Communist Party brass arrive regularly in their chauffeur-driven limousines). A local tourist pamphlet calls the temple the 'Pride of Tra Vinh's inhabitants'. Ho himself would no doubt be horrified.

The Uncle Ho Temple is within the Long Duc commune, 5km north of Tra Vinh town.

Boat Tours

The narrow Long Binh River meanders southward from Tra Vinh town for over 10km before reaching a spillway. The spillway was built to prevent sea water from intruding at high tide. Otherwise, the salt would contaminate the river and kill the crops.

It is possible to hire boats from the pier on the east side of town to take you downstream to the spillway. Of course, Tra Vinh Tourist can also book you onto these trips, which typically take about 1½ hours by speedboat, longer for a slower boat.

Tours can also be arranged to Oyster Island (Con Ngao), an offshore mud flat that supports a small contingent of oyster farmers – of limited interest for most people. Tra Vinh Tourist offers trips for US$100 per boat regardless of group size, though you should be able to negotiate something cheaper with boat drivers at the pier.

Places to Stay

The ***Huong Tra Hotel*** *(☎ 862433, 67 Đ Ly Thuong Kiet)* is Tra Vinh's dingiest budget place. Fan rooms with shared toilet cost just US$3, and air-con with attached bath goes for US$6. It's fair to say you get what you pay for.

Slightly better, though still seedy, is the ***Thanh Binh Hotel*** *(☎ 864906, 1 Đ Le Thanh Ton)*. Fan/air-con rooms here cost US$5/9.

Rooms at the decent-looking ***Phuong Hoang Hotel*** *(☎ 862270, 1 Đ Le Thanh Ton)* all have private bathrooms. Single rooms with fan only are US$4 to US$6, while air-con doubles are US$7 to US$13.

Thanh Tra Hotel *(☎ 863621, fax 863769, 1 Đ Pham Thai Buong)* is where most tour groups are put up for the night. Rooms range from US$8 to US$27.

Cuu Long Hotel *(☎ 862615, 999 Đ Nguyen Thi Minh Khai)* was under reconstruction at the time of writing.

Places to Eat

One of the best places to eat in town is ***Viet Hoa*** *(☎ 836046, 80 Đ Tran Phu)*, run by a friendly Chinese family.

Another good place to look for is ***Tuy Huong*** *(8 Đ Dien Bien Phu)*.

Chi Thanh Restaurant *(105 Đ Nguyen Thi Minh Khai)* is a good place for local Vietnamese dishes.

Ditto for the ***Huong Que Restaurant*** *(16 Đ Nam Ky Khoi Nghia)* and ***Minh Ky Restaurant*** *(9 Đ Nam Ky Khoi Nghia)* nearby.

Getting There & Away

Tra Vinh is 65km from Vinh Long and 205km from Ho Chi Minh City. Either Vinh Long or Cantho would be logical places to catch buses to Tra Vinh.

AROUND TRA VINH

Chua Co

Chua Co is a particularly interesting Khmer monastery because the grounds form a bird sanctuary. Several types of storks and ibises arrive here in large numbers just before sunset to spend the night. Of course, there are many nests here and you must take care not to disturb them.

Chua Co is 43km from Tra Vinh. Travel 36km to Tra Cu, and then follow the sandy road for 7km to the monastery.

Luu Cu

Some ancient ruins are to be found at Luu Cu, south of Tra Vinh near the shores of the Hau Giang River. The ruins include brick foundations similar to those found at Cham temples. There have been a series of archaeological digs here and the site is now protected. Luu Cu attracts a large number of

French tourists. The site is 10km from the town of Tra Cu (36km from Tra Vinh).

Ba Dong Beach

This yellow-sand beach is not bad compared with other 'beaches' in the Mekong Delta, but the main attraction here is the peace and quiet (so far it has seen very few visitors). Tra Vinh Tourist (☎ 862559) recently built a ***restaurant*** and some simple ***bungalows*** by the beach – it is possible to stay overnight for US$5.

To get to Ba Dong Beach from Tra Vinh, head 50km along the paved road to Duyen Hai and follow the bumpy dirt road for 12km until you reach the beach.

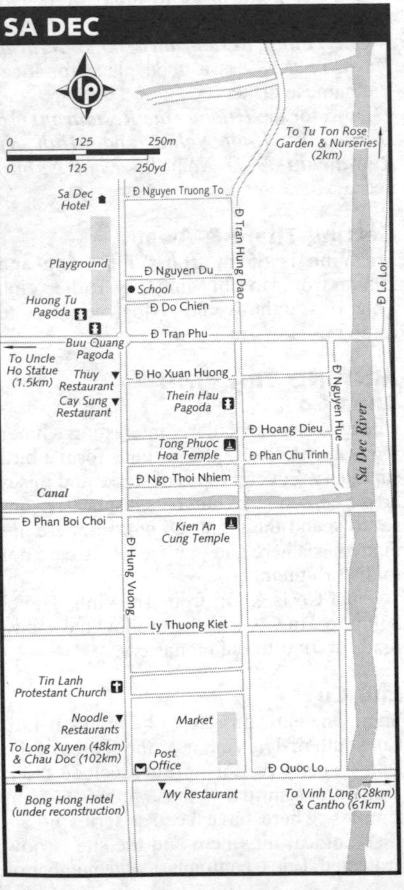

SA DEC

0 125 250m
0 125 250yd
To Tu Ton Rose Garden & Nurseries (2km)
Sa Dec Hotel
Đ Nguyen Truong To
Đ Tran Hung Dao
Playground
Đ Nguyen Du
School
Huong Tu Pagoda
Đ Do Chien
Đ Le Loi
Đ Tran Phu
Buu Quang Pagoda
To Uncle Ho Statue (1.5km)
Thuy Restaurant
Đ Ho Xuan Huong
Đ Nguyen Hue
Cay Sung Restaurant
Thein Hau Pagoda
Sa Dec River
Đ Hoang Dieu
Tong Phuoc Hoa Temple
Đ Phan Chu Trinh
Đ Ngo Thoi Nhiem
Canal
Đ Phan Boi Choi
Kien An Cung Temple
Đ Hung Vuong
Ly Thuong Kiet
Tin Lanh Protestant Church
Noodle Restaurants
Market
To Long Xuyen (48km) & Chau Doc (102km)
Post Office
Đ Quoc Lo
Bong Hong Hotel (under reconstruction)
My Restaurant
To Vinh Long (28km) & Cantho (61km)

SA DEC

☎ 067 • pop 101,800

The former capital of Dong Thap Province, Sa Dec gained some small fame as the setting for *The Lover*, a film based on the novel by Marguerite Duras. Among the Vietnamese, Sa Dec is famous for its many **nurseries** cultivating flowers and bonsai trees. The flowers are picked almost daily and transported fresh to shops in Ho Chi Minh City. The nurseries are a major sightseeing attraction for domestic tourists, not just foreigners.

Groups doing a whirlwind tour of the Mekong Delta often make a lunch stop here and drop in on the nurseries.

Huong Tu Pagoda

The Huong Tu Pagoda (Chua Co Huong Tu) is of classic Chinese design. A bright white statue of Quan The Am Bo Tat standing on a pedestal adorns the grounds. Don't confuse this place with the adjacent Buu Quang Pagoda, which is somewhat less glamorous.

Nurseries

The nurseries *(vuon hoa)* operate year-round, though they are stripped bare of their flowers just before Tet. You're welcome to have a look around, but don't pick any flowers unless you plan on buying them. Photography is certainly permitted – indeed, the flower farmers are quite used to it.

The nurseries don't belong to one person There are many small operators here, each with a different speciality. The most famous garden is called the Tu Ton Rose Garden (Vuon Hong Tu Ton), which has over 500 different kinds of roses in 50 different shades and colours.

Uncle Ho Statue

We're not being facetious – they really d call it 'Uncle Ho Statue' (Tuong Bac Ho) i Vietnamese. Ho Chi Minh didn't live in S Dec, but his father did. To commemorat this bit of historical consequence, a larg

A Home Away from Home

A homestay among the people of the Mekong Delta is an unforgettable experience and can give you a unique insight into the day-to-day lives of the local people.

The easiest ways to arrange such a visit are via hotels and cafes in Ho Chi Minh City or through Cuu Long Tourist in Vinh Long. However, independent travellers may be able to make arrangements with freelance agents at the An Binh boat station on arrival in Vinh Long. Rates are typically US$7 to US$10 per night.

Many of the homes that are open to Western visitors are on the banks of the Mekong River. When you reach the home of your host family, you should remove your shoes. Most families also prefer women to be well covered up.

In traditional houses, the sleeping area is open plan and has hammocks and wooden beds with mosquito nets hanging overhead (before the last rays of the sun disappear slap on plenty of repellent, as mosquitoes are rampant throughout the area).

A typical supper is the local favourite, elephant-ear fish, served bolt upright on a bed of greens with flourishes of carrots shaped as water flowers. The flesh of the fish is pulled off in chunks with chopsticks and wrapped into a rice paper pancake and dipped into sauce. This is accompanied by crispy spring rolls and is followed by soup and rice (Mekong rice is considered the most flavoursome in Vietnam).

After dinner some families exchange stories and songs over bottles of rice wine long into the night, while others cluster around the TV.

The morning starts as the first lights flicker across the water. Before breakfast, everyone takes a bath with the family. Splashing around in the muddy Mekong, fully dressed, can leave you feeling dirtier than when you started! After a hearty breakfast you say your goodbyes and head back to Vinh Long via the floating market.

The bulk of the local people make their living from growing fruit or cultivating rice, although some of the women work in small buildings making coconut sweets, spending their days boiling large cauldrons of sticky mixture, before rolling it out and cutting sections off into squares and wrapping them into paper for sale.

Juliet Coombe

statue of Ho Chi Minh (but not his father!) has been erected a few kilometres west of town. You'll need a motorbike to get out there, as it's probably too far for a *cyclo* unless you have a lot of time and patience. The statue is along the route to the nurseries, so you can take in both sights on the same journey.

Places to Stay

Not many foreigners overnight in Sa Dec because nearby Cao Lanh, Long Xuyen and Vinh Long all tend to siphon off the tourists. Still, Sa Dec is a pleasant, if not very exciting, place to spend an evening.

The main tourist accommodation is the ***Sa Dec Hotel*** *(☎ 861430)*. A room with fan costs US$10, while air-con rooms cost from US$20 to US$25. All rooms have baths.

At the time of writing, ***Bong Hong Hotel*** *(☎ 861301, 80 Đ Quoc Lo)* was being reconstructed.

Places to Eat

Across from the post office on Đ Quoc Lo, the ***My Restaurant*** is a backpackers' magnet.

Cay Sung Restaurant *(☎ 861749, 437 Đ Hung Vuong)* is new and has respectable Vietnamese fare.

Another local eatery is ***Thuy Restaurant*** *(☎ 861644, 439 Đ Hung Vuong)*. The food is also good, but the bizarre facial expressions on the fish in the big tank are even better!

Getting There & Away

Sa Dec, in Dong Thap Province midway between Vinh Long and Long Xuyen, is accessible by bus, minibus and car.

CAO LANH

☎ 067 • pop 139,100

Cao Lanh is a new town carved from the jungles and swamps of the Mekong Delta region. Its up-and-coming status has much to do with its designation as the provincial capital of Dong Thap Province. Boat tours of the bird sanctuaries and Rung Tram Forest are major attractions in this region.

Information

Tourist Offices Dong Thap Tourist (☎ 851547, fax 852 136), 2 Đ Doc Binh Kieu, deserves kudos for being helpful. This is the best place to inquire about boat tours of the surrounding area. There is a boat station branch office (☎ 821054) that handles boat tours from a landing in My Hiep Village.

Email & Internet Access There is an Internet service centre at the corner of Đ Doc Binh Kieu and Đ Hung Vuong.

War Memorial

The War Memorial (Dai Liet Si) off Highway 30 on the eastern edge of town is Cao Lanh's most prominent landmark. This masterpiece of socialist sculpture boasts a clamshell-shaped building displaying a large Vietnamese star alongside a hammer and sickle. In front of this are several large concrete statues of victorious peasants and soldiers brandishing weapons and upraised fists. The surrounding grounds are decked out with the graves of over 3000 VC who died in the American War.

Construction of the War Memorial began in 1977 and finished in 1984. There is no admission fee.

Nguyen Sinh Sac Grave Site

Another significant tomb is that of Nguyen Sinh Sac (1862–1929). Nguyen's main contribution to Vietnamese history was being the father of Ho Chi Minh. His large tomb (Lang Cu Nguyen Sinh Sac) occupies one

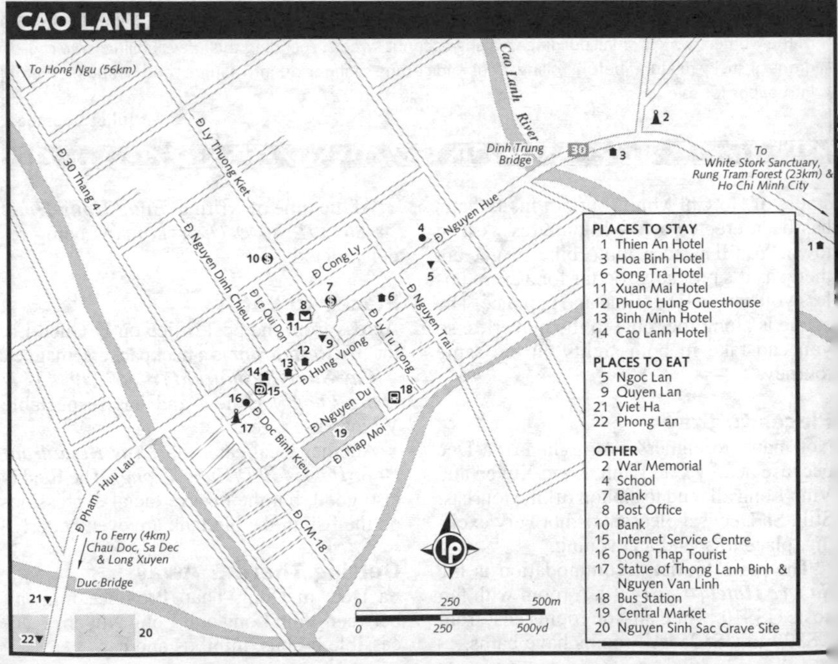

hectare, about 1km south-west of central Cao Lanh.

Although there are various plaques (in Vietnamese) and tourist pamphlets extolling Nguyen Sinh Sac as a great revolutionary, there is little evidence to suggest that he was involved in the anticolonial struggle against the French.

Places to Stay

The cheapest place in town is the ***Phuoc Hung Guesthouse*** *(☎ 851926, Đ Hung Vuong)*. Mr Hung is a friendly local school teacher. He charges from just US$3 to US$5 for very basic fan rooms. The one air-con room goes for US$9.

Just across the road, the ***Binh Minh Hotel*** *(☎ 853423, 147 Đ Hung Vuong)* is a new place with air-con rooms in the US$10 range.

Cao Lanh Hotel *(☎ 851061, 72 Đ Nguyen Hue)* is considerably older and grottier than the competition and is a definite candidate for renovations. Until that happens, rooms with fan and cold bath cost US$6. Air-con rooms with hot bath are US$10.

Xuan Mai Hotel *(☎ 852852, fax 853058, 2 Đ Le Qui Don)* is an excellent place behind the post office. All the rooms are equipped with air-con, hot water and even baths. Doubles cost US$18 to US$22.

Thien An Hotel *(☎ 853041)* is about 500m from the War Memorial towards Ho Chi Minh City. This new place is good value and a couple of the rooms have a view of the river. All rooms have air-con and attached hot bath, and range in price from US$10 to US$12.

Song Tra Hotel *(☎ 852504, fax 852623, 178 D Nguyen Hue)* has the city's most upmarket accommodation, and even features satellite TV. The price range is from US$25 to US$35.

Hoa Binh Hotel *(☎ 851469, fax 851218)* is on the east side of town on Highway 30, opposite the War Memorial. Try to book a room in the pleasant villa at the rear (convenient for the in-house beer garden!). Air-con rates range from US$18 to US$25. It also has satellite TV.

Places to Eat

If you're after something local, try ***Ngoc Lan*** *(208 Đ Nguyen Hue)*. We recommend the shredded frog, or better yet, the 'raw dish bowel'.

There is also good standard Vietnamese fare at ***Quyen Lan*** *(☎ 854917, 126 Đ Nguyen Hue)*, across from the post office.

On the road to/from the ferry, just south of the Duc Bridge, is ***Viet Ha*** *(☎ 851639)*, which serves good Vietnamese food.

Nearby, ***Phong Lan***, or the *Orchid Garden Restaurant*, is a tastier but slightly more expensive option.

In a pinch, there are decent restaurants in both the ***Song Tra Hotel*** and ***Hoa Binh Hotel***.

Getting There & Away

Aside from buses direct from Ho Chi Minh City, the easiest bus routes to Cao Lanh are from Mytho, Cantho and Vinh Long. The road between Cao Lanh and Long Xuyen is beautiful, but has few buses – you will probably need to hire your own vehicle to take that route.

Getting Around

The sights around Cao Lanh are best visited by river. Although you could possibly arrange something privately with boat owners, you'll probably find it easier to deal with Dong Thap Tourist. Fortunately, its rates are reasonable. There are too many different combinations of boat sizes and possible destinations to list them all, but a group of 15 people would be charged about US$2 per person for a half-day tour, including all transport. A group of five might pay US$5 each for the same thing. You may not be travelling with 14 companions, but it's not difficult to round up other travellers at the few hotels in town where everyone stays.

AROUND CAO LANH

White Stork Sanctuary

To the north-east of Cao Lanh is a bird sanctuary (Vuon Co Thap Muoi) for white storks. A white stork standing on the back of a water buffalo is the symbol of the Mekong Delta, and you probably have more chance of seeing a stork here than anywhere else. The sanctuary only covers two hectares, but the birds seem mostly undisturbed by the nearby farmers (who have been sternly warned not to hunt the storks).

The storks have grown accustomed to people and are fairly easy to spot, as they feed in the mangrove and bamboo forests in the area. They live in pairs and never migrate with the seasons, so you can see them at any time of the year. The birds live on fresh-water crabs and other tidbits that they catch in the canals.

There are no roads as such to the bird sanctuary, so getting there requires a trip by boat. Dong Thap Tourist can arrange this, though you may be able to arrange it elsewhere. A speedboat costs US$25 per hour, and the ride takes 50 minutes. A slow boat costs US$4 per person (with 20 people) and takes three hours to make the return journey. In the dry season, you have to plan your boat trip according to the two daily tides – at low tide the canals can become impassable.

Many travellers include a trip to White Stork Sanctuary with a visit to Rung Tram Forest.

Rung Tram Forest

South-east of Cao Lanh and accessible by boat tour is the 46-hectare Rung Tram Forest near My Long Village. The area is one vast swamp with a beautiful thick canopy of tall trees and vines. It's one of the last natural forests left in the Mekong Delta, and by now probably would have been turned into a rice paddy were it not for its historical significance. During the American War, the VC had a base here called Xeo Quit, where top-brass VC lived in underground bunkers. But don't mistake this for another Cu Chi Tunnels – it's very different.

Only about 10 VC were here at any given time. They were all generals who directed the war from here, just 2km from a US military base. The Americans never realised that the VC generals were living right under their noses. Of course, they were suspicious about that patch of forest, and periodically dropped some bombs on it just to reassure themselves, but the VC remained safe in their underground bunkers.

The location of the base was so secret that the wives of the generals didn't even know it. They did occasionally pay their husbands conjugal visits, but this had to be arranged at another special bunker.

When the US military departed from Vietnam in 1973, the VC grew bolder and put the base above ground. Attempts by the South Vietnamese military to dislodge the VC were thwarted – while the South was running out of funding and ammunition, the VC were able to build up their forces in the Mekong Delta and openly challenge the Saigon regime.

Access to the area is most popular by boat, and many visitors combine a visit with a trip to White Stork Sanctuary. A speedboat from Cao Lanh to Rung Tram Forest takes only a few minutes, but a slow boat takes around 30 minutes (depending on the tides). It is also possible now to reach the forest by road if you are travelling by car or motorbike.

Beware of the exceedingly mean red ants here – they are huge, fast and very aggressive.

Tram Chim Nature Reserve

Due north of Cao Lanh in Tam Nong (Dong Thap Province) is Tram Chim National Wetland Reserve (Tram Chim Tam Nong) notable for its eastern sarus cranes *(grus antigone sharpii)*. Over 220 species of birds have been identified within the reserve, but ornithologists will be particularly interested in the rare red-headed cranes, which grow to over 1.5m high. The birds nest here from about December to June. From July to November, they go on holiday to Cambodia, so you must schedule your visit to coordinate with the birds' travel itinerary if you want to see them. Also, the birds are early risers – early morning is the best time to see them though you might get a glimpse when the return home in the evening. During the day the birds are of course engaged in the important matter of eating.

Seeing these birds requires a considerabl commitment (time, effort and money), so it really a special-interest tour. Because you' need to be up at the crack of dawn, stayin in Cao Lanh doesn't work out too well – yc would have to head out at 4.30 am and trav in the dark over an unlit dirt road. This is not advisable, so you really need to stay at the government guesthouse in Tam Nong, which is much closer to where the birds are.

Tam Nong is a sleepy town 45km from Cao Lanh. The one-way drive takes 1½ hours by car, though this may be reduced to one hour when the currently abysmal road gets resurfaced. It is also possible to get there by boat. A speedboat takes only one hour, but costs US$25 per hour to rent. A slow boat (US$4 per person) can be arranged from Dong Thap Tourist, but the one-way journey takes four hours and requires 20 people to make it economically viable. From the guesthouse in Tam Nong, it takes another hour by small boat (at US$15 per hour) to reach the area where the red-headed cranes live and another hour to return. To this, add whatever time you spend (perhaps an hour) staring at your feathered friends through binoculars, and then the requisite one to four hours to return to Cao Lanh depending on your mode of transport. BYO binoculars.

The state-run ***guesthouse*** in Tam Nong is just before you cross the bridge heading into the town centre. It has 15 fan rooms that cost US$10. We found the guesthouse deplorable; not only were the rooms (and the sheets!) filthy, the place was absolutely overrun with thousands of bugs and the staff had no insecticide. If you're going to stay here, you may want to stock up on toxic chemicals in Cao Lanh, or try to score a can of bug killer in town.

Tam Nong shuts down early – if you want to eat dinner in town, make arrangements before 5 pm. One good restaurant is ***Phuong Chi*** *(☎ 067-827230, 537 Thi Tran Tram Chim)*, close to the market in the town centre. Meals can be served later if you book in advance, but you will have to pay extra.

There are heaps of mosquitoes in Tam Nong in the evening, so come prepared with insect repellent.

CANTHO

☎ 071 • pop 330,100

Cantho, capital of Cantho Province, is the political, economic, cultural and transportation centre of the Mekong Delta. Rice-husking mills provide a major local industry.

This friendly, bustling city is connected to most other population centres in the Mekong Delta by a system of rivers and canals. These waterways are the major tourist drawcard in Cantho – travellers come here to do economical boat trips.

Despite being the largest city in the Mekong Delta, Cantho seems to suffer from a growing Ho Chi Minh City complex. The city is being built up rapidly, and signs of urban degeneracy (like the street kids who now hover around the travellers cafes) are on the rise.

Information

Travel Agencies Cantho Tourist (☎ 821852, fax 822719), 18–20 Đ Hai Ba Trung, is the provincial tourism authority. The staff here are pleasant, speak English, French and Japanese, and are well equipped to serve tourists (this is the only Vietnamese tourist office we've found that can actually provide a map of its own city!).

Vietnam Airlines has a booking desk (☎ 824088) inside the office.

Money Foreign currency exchange can be done at Vietcombank (Ngan Hang Ngoai Thuong Viet Nam; ☎ 820445), 7 ĐL Hoa Binh.

Emergency The hospital is on the corner of Đ Chau Van Liem and ĐL Hoa Binh.

Munirangsyaram Pagoda

The ornamentation of Munirangsyaram Pagoda, at 36 ĐL Hoa Binh, is typical of Khmer Hinayana Buddhist pagodas, lacking the multiple Bodhisattvas and Taoist spirits common in Vietnamese Mahayana pagodas. In the upstairs sanctuary, a 1.5m-high representation of Siddhartha Gautama, the historical Buddha, sits under a *potthe* (bodhi) tree.

Built in 1946, the Munirangsyaram Pagoda serves the Khmer community of Cantho, which numbers about 2000. The Khmer monks hold daily prayers here at 5 am and 6 pm.

MEKONG DELTA

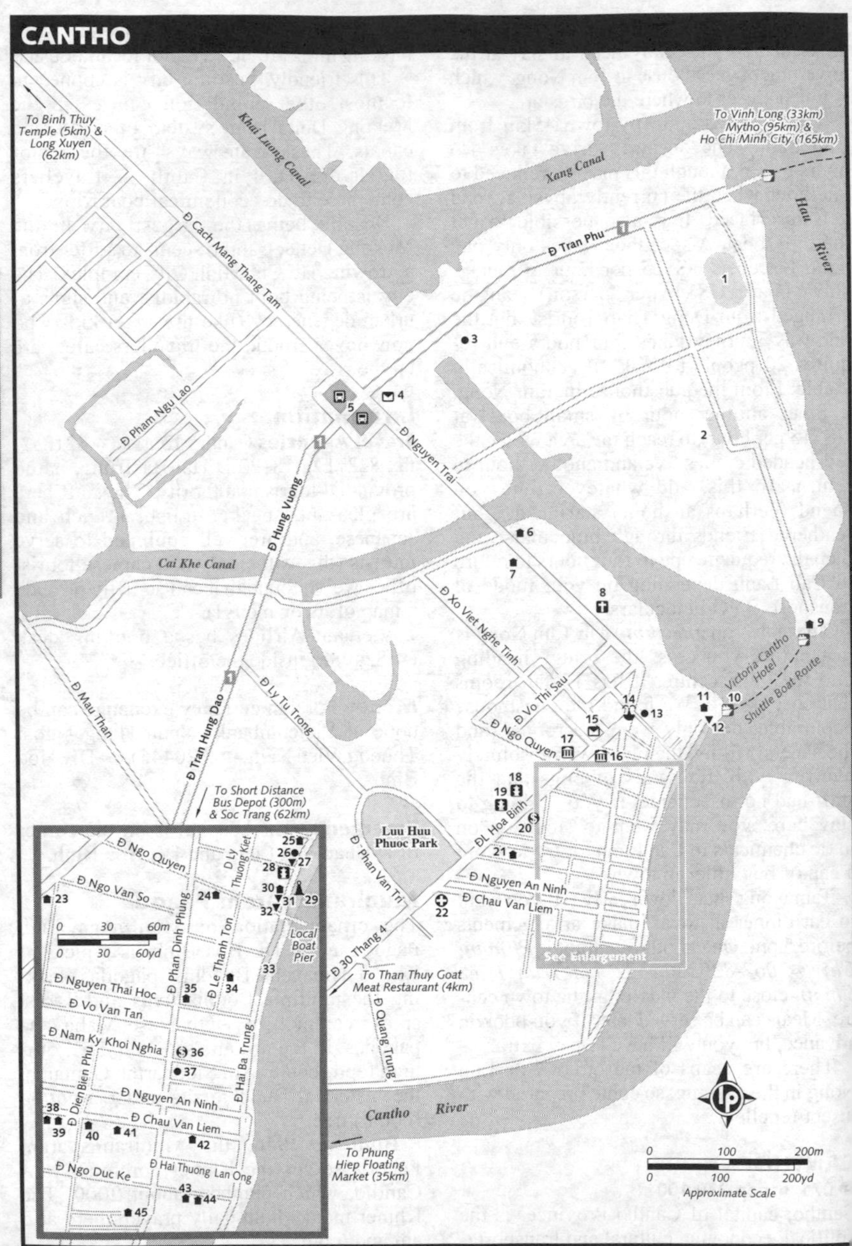
CANTHO
To Binh Thuy Temple (5km) & Long Xuyen (62km)
Khai Luong Canal
Xang Canal
To Vinh Long (33km) Mytho (95km) & Ho Chi Minh City (165km)
Hau River
Đ Tran Phu
Đ Cach Mang Thang Tam
Đ Pham Ngu Lao
Đ Nguyen Trai
Đ Hung Vuong
Cai Khe Canal
Đ Xo Viet Nghe Tinh
Đ Vo Thi Sau
Đ Ngo Quyen
Victoria Cantho Hotel
Shuttle Boat Route
Đ Mau Than
Đ Tran Hung Dao
Đ Ly Tu Trong
To Short Distance Bus Depot (300m) & Soc Trang (62km)
Luu Huu Phuoc Park
Đ Phan Van Tri
ĐL Hoa Binh
Đ Nguyen An Ninh
Đ Chau Van Liem
Đ 30 Thang 4
To Than Thuy Goat Meat Restaurant (4km)
Đ Quang Trung
See Enlargement
Cantho River
To Phung Hiep Floating Market (35km)
0 100 200m
0 100 200yd
Approximate Scale
Đ Ngo Quyen
Đ Ngo Van So
Đ Ly Thuong Kiet
Đ Phan Dinh Phung
Đ Le Thanh Ton
0 30 60m
0 30 60yd
Local Boat Pier
Đ Nguyen Thai Hoc
Đ Vo Van Tan
Đ Nam Ky Khoi Nghia
Đ Hai Ba Trung
Đ Dien Bien Phu
Đ Nguyen An Ninh
Đ Chau Van Liem
Đ Hai Thuong Lan Ong
Đ Ngo Duc Ke

CANTHO

PLACES TO STAY
6 Doan 30 Cantho Hotel
7 Guesthouse 101
9 Victoria Cantho Hotel
11 Ninh Kieu Hotel
21 Hau Giang A Hotel
23 Hoa Binh Hotel
24 Ngan Ha Hotel
25 Quoc Te Hotel
30 Tay Ho Hotel
34 Phan Trung Hotel; Fountain
35 Saigon-Cantho Hotel
38 Asia Hotel
39 Phong Nha Hotel; Photo Processing Shop
40 Tay Do Hotel
41 Cantho Hotel
42 Hau Giang B Hotel
43 Huy Hoang Hotel
44 Hotel-Restaurant 31
45 Hien Guesthouse

PLACES TO EAT
2 Local Cafes
12 Riverside Restaurant
27 Thien Hoa
31 Mekong; Nam Viet; Vinh Loi
32 Nam Bo

OTHER
1 Stadium
3 Cai Khe Market
4 Cai Khe Post Office
5 Long Distance Bus Depot
8 Church
10 Hydrofoil Boat Landing
13 Provincial People's Committee Building
14 Fountain
15 Main Post Office
16 Cantho Museum
17 Ho Chi Minh Museum
18 Vietnamese Pagoda
19 Munirangsyaram Pagoda
20 Vietcombank
22 Hospital
26 Cantho Tourist & Vietnam Airlines
28 Cantonese Congregation Pagoda
29 Ho Chi Minh Statue
33 Central Market
36 Indovina Bank
37 Local People's Committee Building

Cantonese Congregation Pagoda

This small Chinese pagoda (Quan Cong Hoi Quan) was built by the Cantonese Congregation. The original one was constructed on a different site about 70 years ago. The current pagoda was built with funds recently donated by Overseas Chinese. Cantho previously had a large ethnic-Chinese population, but most fled after the anti-Chinese persecutions of 1978–9.

The pagoda occupies a splendid location on Đ Hai Ba Trung facing the Cantho River.

Central Market

The Central Market is strung out along Đ Hai Ba Trung. The main building is at the intersection of Đ Hai Ba Trung and Đ Nam Ky Khoi Nghia. Many local farmers and wholesalers arrive here by boat to buy and sell. The fruit section, near the intersection of Đ Hai Ba Trung and Đ Ngo Quyen, is particularly notable and stays open into the late evening. Apparently the local authorities have plans to relocate this delightful market and built a modern shopping mall in its place. Clearly they are unaware that the lively, colourful scene here is a major boon for local tourism.

Ho Chi Minh Museum

This is the only museum in the Mekong Delta devoted to Ho Chi Minh, and it's a bit of a mystery why it was built here as Ho Chi Minh never lived in Cantho. If you are willing to overlook that small sticking point, there is no reason not to visit this large museum. It's inside a gated courtyard near the main post office on ĐL Hoa Binh. Opening hours are from 8 to 11 am, and 2 to 4.30 pm, Tuesday to Saturday. Entry is free.

Cantho Museum

The enormous Cantho Museum was under construction at the time of writing. It's easy to spot, located opposite the main post office.

Boat Tours

The most interesting thing to do in Cantho is take a boat ride through the canals and visit a floating market. The cost for this varies but is around US$3 per hour for a small paddle boat which can carry two or three passengers. You won't have to look hard for the boats – they will be looking for you. Just wander by the riverside near the market and you'll have plenty of offers. There is of course the option of booking through Cantho Tourist, but this leaves little room for negotiation. Most of the boats are operated by women.

Bring your camera, though keep it in a plastic bag when you're not actually shooting because it's easy to get splashed by the wake of motorised boats. The paddle boats only go on the smaller canals (they're actually more interesting), because the current is weaker.

Larger boats with motors can go further afield, and it's worth considering hiring one to make a tour of the Mekong River itself. You might check the going rates at Cantho Tourist, and then see what's on offer at the pier by the Ninh Kieu Hotel. For a three-hour tour of the canals and Cai Rang Floating Market expect to pay around US$9 for a small boat (one to four people), or US$12 for a larger one (five to 12 people). The cost of a five-hour boat trip to the Phong Dien Floating Market (one to ten people) is around US$16. The name of the game is negotiate.

For more on the area's floating markets, see the following Around Cantho section.

Places to Stay

Cantho boasts heaps of good accommodation possibilities – in fact the best in the Mekong Delta. Moreover, unlike in Mytho, the expensive places here are generally worth the money.

Places to Stay – Budget

A bona fide travellers' place is the tiny ***Hien Guesthouse*** *(☎ 812718, 118/10 Đ Phan Dinh Phung)*, tucked down a narrow alley a few minutes' walk from the city centre. The owner is a friendly local school teacher and is an excellent source of travel information about the area. Basic but clean rooms with floor-level mattresses cost just US$4/5 with fan for one/two people, or US$8 with air-con for two.

Huy Hoang Hotel *(☎ 825833, 35 Đ Ngo Duc Ke)* is another trendy spot for the backpacker crowd. Singles/doubles with fan are US$7/9, or US$11/14 with air-con.

Also popular is ***Hotel-Restaurant 31*** *(☎ 825287, 31 Đ Ngo Duc Ke)* nearby. Fan twins cost US$5, or you can ask for the air-con double for US$8. The restaurant here is recommended.

Phan Trung Hotel *(☎ 824477, 9 Đ Le Thanh Ton)* – also called the *NK* – is another choice in the budget realm. Fan rooms with shared bath cost US$4, or US$6 if you prefer your own private toilet. Air-con raises the tab to US$9 and US$13 respectively. The hotel boasts a full range of massage, sauna and karaoke for weary travellers.

Right on the riverfront, the friendly ***Tay Ho Hotel*** *(☎ 823392, 36 Đ Hai Ba Trung)* has fan rooms from US$6 to US$13, or US$15 to US$20 with air-con.

Phong Nha Hotel *(☎ 821615, 75 Đ Chau Van Liem)* is cheap, but is on a noisy street with many motorbikes. Singles/doubles/triples with fan cost US$4/5/8; triples with air-con are US$11.

The ***Hau Giang B Hotel*** *(☎ 821950, fax 821806, 27 Đ Chau Van Liem)* has rooms with fan and hot water for US$9, rising to US$15 with air-con.

Places to Stay – Mid-Range

The army-owned ***Doan 30 Cantho Hotel*** *(☎ 823623, 80A Đ Nguyen Trai)* at the northern end of town has some rooms with balconies and river views. There is an outdoor cafe on the riverside, and the hotel's private boat landing is convenient for boat trips. Standard rooms with fan/air-con cost US$10/18, and deluxe rooms with TV and fridge cost US$20. Rates include a simple breakfast.

Just across the street is ***Guesthouse 101*** *(☎ 825074, 101 Đ Nguyen Trai)*, also brought to you by the Vietnamese army. Rooms are arranged around a high-rise courtyard and are pleasant enough, but this place is less appealing than the Doan 30 Cantho. The tariff for fan only with cold bath is US$9, or US$16 to US$19 with air-con.

Asia Hotel *(☎ 822130, fax 812779, ⓔ asiahotel@hcm.vnn.vn, 91 Đ Chau Van Liem)* is a nice new place with large balconies. Rates for foreigners here range from US$20 to US$35, inclusive of tax, service charge and breakfast.

There is a similar standard at the nearby ***Cantho Hotel***.

Tay Do Hotel *(☎ 827009, fax 827008, 61 Đ Chau Van Liem)* is another spiffy place where air-con rooms with satellite TV range from US$27 to US$35. The rooms at the back are quieter, and cheaper.

Ninh Kieu Hotel *(☎ 821171, fax 821104, 2 Đ Hai Ba Trung)* is in a spacious compound within spitting distance of the hydrofoil boat landing, but it is looking a bit dark and gloomy these days. Room prices are US$25 to US$40.

Quoc Te Hotel *(☎ 822080, fax 821039, 12 Đ Hai Ba Trung)* is also known as the *International Hotel*. It's on the riverfront and is notable for its noisy karaoke bar. The expensive suites have an excellent view of the river, but the budget rooms are pretty bleak and not really worth the price. Rates here are from US$30 to US$48.

Ngan Ha Hotel *(☎ 822921, fax 823 473, 39–41 Đ Ngo Quyen)* is a private hotel in a convenient but noisy location. All rooms have air-con and hot bath, and cost US$12 to US$18 including breakfast.

Hau Giang A Hotel *(☎ 821851, fax 821806, 34 Đ Nam Ky Khoi Nghia)* is pleasant enough and attracts many travellers. Fan rooms cost US$15, or US$25 to US$30 with air-con. Rates include breakfast.

The three-star ***Saigon-Cantho Hotel*** *(☎ 825831, fax 823288, 55 Đ Phan Dinh Phung)* features a snazzy restaurant, a massage service, a sauna and karaoke. Rooms are fully equipped and cost US$30 to US$40 for singles, or US$39 to US$49 for doubles. Rates are inclusive of tax, service and breakfast.

After being held together with tape and glue for years, ***Hoa Binh Hotel*** *(☎ 820059, fax 810217, 5 DL Hoa Binh)* underwent extensive renovations in 1999 and has earned its three stars. Rooms have air-con, IDD phones and satellite TV. Standard rooms cost US$20 to US$24, superior rooms are US$32 or US$35, deluxe rooms are US$40 and suites cost US$58.

Places to Stay – Top End

Cantho's *créme de la créme* is the lovely ***Victoria Cantho Hotel*** *(☎ 810111, fax 829259, ⓔ victoriact@hcm.vnn.vn)*, Web site: www.victoriahotel-vietnam.com, located right on the riverfront. Garden-view rooms cost US$95, river-view rooms are US$110, and the eight spacious suites go for US$170; rates include tax and service. Facilities include two fine restaurants, an open-air bar, tennis courts and a swimming pool; even if you're not staying at the resort, it is worth coughing up US$5 for day use of the pool. The shuttle boat across the river is free.

Places to Eat

Along the Cantho River waterfront there are several cafe-restaurants, most serving Mekong Delta specialities such as fish, frog and turtle, as well as standard backpacker fare.

For superb European and Vietnamese cuisine in a delightful atmosphere, ***Nam Bo*** *(☎ 823908, 50 Đ Hai Ba Trung)* can fill the bill. It's housed in a thoughtfully restored, classic French villa, and the view of the local fruit market from the second-storey terrace can't be beat.

Others nearby on the riverfront strip include ***Mekong***, ***Nam Viet***, ***Vinh Loi*** and ***Thien Hoa***, all of which serve good food, and if you're lucky, a nip of snake wine. You'll find them just across from the huge silver Uncle Ho statue (which, incidentally, bears a curious resemblance to the Tin Man in *The Wizard of Oz*).

At the northern end of D Hai Ba Trung, ***Ninh Kieu Hotel*** boasts an attractive riverside restaurant with good views, and the nearby ***Quoc Te Hotel*** has an upmarket menu including deep-fried snake, turtle soup and some of the largest prawns you'll ever see.

Hotel-Restaurant 31 *(Đ 31 Ngo Duc Ke)* is cheap and excellent – some say it's got the best beef in the delta.

Restaurant Alley is an appropriate name for this place on Đ Nam Ky Khoi Nghia between Đ Dien Bien Phu and Đ Phan Dinh Phung.

There are about a dozen local ***restaurants*** scattered on both sides of the street.

And now for something different. ***Thanh Thuy*** *(☎ 840207, 149 Đ 30 Thang 4)* is a goat meat specialty restaurant run by a Frenchman named Christian – formerly a chef in Toulouse. The food is excellent and inexpensive; most dishes are in the US$2 to US$3 range. Try the curried goat, or if you're feeling brave, the goat scrotum hot pot. The restaurant (open from 10 am to 10 pm) is a few kilometres out of town, just beyond the local university. Look for the sign on your left, just beyond the junction with Đ Tran Hoang Na. You can easily reach it by bicycle or on a motorbike wagon (see Getting Around in this section) for about US$0.30.

Getting There & Away

Air Vietnam Airlines has had on-again off-again flights between Cantho and Ho Chi Minh City. At the time of writing, flights were off again. Currently, the only way to fly to Cantho is to charter an aircraft from Vasco Airlines (☎ 08-842 2790, fax 844 5224) in Ho Chi Minh City.

Bus Buses leave Ho Chi Minh City from Mien Tay bus station in An Lac and take five to six hours to reach Cantho.

The main bus station in Cantho is several kilometres north of town at the intersection of Đ Nguyen Trai and Đ Tran Phu. There is another short-haul bus depot about 300m south of the intersection of Đ 30/4 and Đ Mau Than, which is good for getting to/from Soc Trang and the Phung Hiep Floating Market.

Car & Motorbike By car or motorbike, the ride from Ho Chi Minh City to Cantho along National Highway 1 takes about four hours. There is one ferry crossing at Binh Minh (in Cantho). The Cantho ferry runs from 4 am to 2 am. Fruit, soft drinks and other food are sold where vehicles wait for the ferries. By regulation, only drivers can ride onto the ferries in their vehicles; passengers must walk on and off, and this can include a wait in the baking Mekong sun.

To get from ĐL Hoa Binh in Cantho to the ferry crossing, take Đ Nguyen Trai to the long-distance bus station and turn right onto Đ Tran Phu.

Boat For details on the Greenlines hydrofoil service to/from Cantho, see boxed text 'Hydrofoil between Ho Chi Minh City and Mekong Delta' near the beginning of this chapter.

Getting Around

To/From the Airport Assuming Vietnam Airlines restarts operations, Cantho airport is 10km south of the town centre along the road leading to Rach Gia. Transport by motorbike (about US$1.20) will be cheaper than taxi.

Xe Honda Loi Unique to the Mekong Delta, these makeshift vehicles are the main form of transport around Cantho. A *xe Honda loi* is essentially a two-wheeled wagon attached to the rear of a motorbike, creating what resembles a motorised cyclo, but with four wheels touching the ground rather than two. Fares around town should be about US$0.80, more for trips to outlying areas.

AROUND CANTHO

Perhaps the biggest drawcard of the Mekong Delta is its colourful **floating markets**. Unlike the floating markets you may have seen in Thailand, where small wooden boats thread narrow canals, most floating markets here are on the banks of wide stretches of river. Most open early to avoid the daytime heat, so try to visit between 6 and 8 am. The tides, however, are also a factor as bigger boats must often wait until the water is high enough for them to navigate.

Today, a number of the smaller, rural floating markets are disappearing, largely due to improved roads and access to private and public transport. Many of the larger markets near urban areas, however, are still going strong.

Rural areas of Cantho Province, renowned for their durian, mangosteen and orange orchards, can easily be reached from Cantho by boat or bicycle.

Cai Rang Floating Market

Just 6km from Cantho in the direction of Soc Trang is Cai Rang, the biggest floating market in the Mekong Delta. There is a bridge here that serves as a great vantage point for photography. The market is best before 9 am, and though some vendors hang out until noon, it's less lively by then.

Cai Rang can be seen from the road, but it is far more interesting to reach by boat. From the market area in Cantho, it takes about an hour by river, or you can drive to the Cau Dau Sau boat landing (by the Dau Sau Bridge), from where it only takes about 10 minutes to reach the market.

Phong Dien Floating Market

This is perhaps the best floating market in the Mekong Delta, as there are less motorised craft and more stand-up rowing boats around. It's less crowded than Cai Rang, and there are far less tourists. The market is at its bustling best between 6 and 8 am. Phong Dien is 20km south-west of Cantho, and most get there by road.

It is theoretically possible to do a whirlwind boat trip here, visiting the small canals on the way and finishing back at the Cai Rang floating market. This journey should take approximately five hours return from Cantho.

Phung Hiep Market

Until recently, the small town of Phung Hiep was notable for its eerie snake market. In April 1998, however, a new nationwide law banned the capture and sale of snakes in an effort to control the rapidly multiplying rat population which has been devastating rice crops (and flourishing due to a relative absence of snakes). Snake sellers throughout the country are now being forced to operate underground.

These days the snake cages that used to swell with cobras and pythons are empty, and Phung Hiep is back to being a regular (yet interesting) market. There is a small-scale floating market under the bridge and boats can be hired here for a tour along the river.

Phung Hiep is right on National Highway 1, and is 35km from Cantho in the direction of Soc Trang.

Vuon Co (Stork Garden)

Vuon Co is a 1.3-hectare stork sanctuary on the road between Cantho and Long Xuyen. It is popular stop for group tours, who come to view the thousands of storks that reside here. There is a tall wooden viewing platform, and the best times of day to see the birds are from 5 to 6 am, and again between 4 and 6 pm. Entry costs 2000d (US$0.25).

Vuon Co is in the Thot Not District, about 15km south-east of Long Xuyen. Look for a sign in the hamlet of Thoi An reading 'Ap Von Hoa'; coming from Cantho you will see the sign on the west side of the road, immediately after crossing a small bridge. The stork garden is a few kilometres off the main highway. You can walk to it in about 30 minutes, or hire a motorbike to take you there for about 5000d (US$0.40).

SOC TRANG

☎ 079 • pop 110,800

Soc Trang is the capital of Soc Trang Province, which has a 28% Khmer population. The town itself isn't much, but the Khmer have built some very impressive temples in the area. Furthermore, there is a very colourful annual festival (usually in December), and if you're in the vicinity at the right time, it's very much worth your while to catch it.

Soc Trang Tourist (☎ 821498, 822015, fax 821993), 131 Đ Nguyen Chi Thanh, is adjacent to the Phong Lan 2 Hotel. The staff are friendly enough, but speak next to no English and are hardly accustomed to serving walk-in tourists.

Kh'leng Pagoda

This stunning pagoda (Chua Kh'leng) looks like it's been transported straight out of Cambodia. Originally built from bamboo in 1533, it had a complete rebuild in 1905 (this time using concrete). There are seven religious festivals held here every year that are worth seeing – people come from outlying areas of the province for these events. Even at nonfestival times, Khmer people drop in regularly to bring donations and pray.

At the time of writing, 12 monks were residing in the pagoda. This place also serves as a base for over 150 student monks who come from around the Mekong Delta to study at Soc Trang's College of Buddhist Education across the street. The monks are friendly, and happy to show you around the pagoda and discuss Buddhism.

Khmer Museum

This museum is dedicated to the history and culture of Vietnam's Khmer minority. Indeed, it serves as a sort of cultural centre, and traditional dance and music shows are periodically staged here. You'll have to make inquiries about performances because there is no regular schedule; however, there's no doubt that something could be arranged for a group provided a little advance notice is given.

The Khmer Museum, just opposite Kh'leng Pagoda, is officially closed on weekends, but even during the week you may have to roust someone to let you in.

Clay Pagoda

Buu Son Tu, or 'Precious Mountain Temple', was founded over 200 years ago by a Chinese family named Ngo. Today the temple is better known as Chua Dat Set, which means 'Clay Pagoda'.

Unassuming from the outside, this pagoda is highly unusual in that nearly everything inside is made entirely of clay. These objects were hand-sculpted by the monk Ngo Kim Tong. From age 20 until his death at 62, Tong, a genius artisan, dedicated his life to decorating the pagoda. He made hundreds of statues and sculptures that adorn the interior today.

Entering the pagoda, visitors are immediately greeted by one of Ngo's greatest creations – a six-tusked clay elephant (which is said to have appeared in a dream of the Buddha's mother). Behind this is the centre altar, which alone was built from over five tonnes of clay. In the altar are a thousand Buddhas seated on lotus petals. Other highlights include a 13-storey Chinese-style tower over 4m tall. The tower features 208 cubbyholes, each with a mini-Buddha figure inside, and is decorated with 156 dragons.

Two giant candles have been burning here unceasingly since the clay artist died in 1970. To get an idea of how big these were to begin with (200kg and 260cm tall), there is another pair waiting to be lit when the current ones (expected to burn until 2005) are spent.

Though some of the stuff here is bordering on kitsch (our personal favourites are the lions with red light bulbs for eyeballs), the pagoda was not intended to be a Dalatesque tacky tourist theme park. It is an active place of worship, and totally different from the Khmer and Vietnamese Buddhist pagodas found elsewhere in Soc Trang. The resident monk, Ngo Kim Giang, is the younger brother of the artist and a delightful old man to chat with about the pagoda.

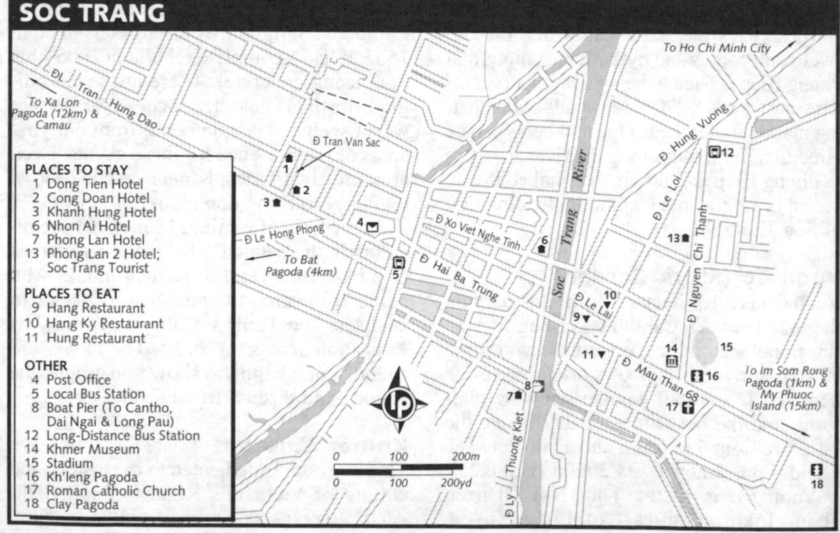

He speaks excellent French, but unfortunately very little English.

The Clay Pagoda is on Đ Mau Than 68, within walking distance of the town centre. Entry is free. Needless to say, the clay objects in the pagoda are highly fragile – do not touch.

Im Som Rong Pagoda

This large, beautiful Khmer pagoda was built in 1961 and is notable for its well-kept gardens. A plaque on the grounds honours the man who donated the funds to build the pagoda. There are many monks in residence here, who are very friendly.

Im Som Rong Pagoda is over 1km east of Soc Trang on the road to My Phuoc Island. When you reach the main gate it's a 300m walk along a dirt track to the pagoda itself.

Oc Bom Boc Festival

This is a Khmer name so don't bother trying to look it up in your Vietnamese dictionary. Once a year, the Khmer community turns out for longboat races on the Soc Trang River, an event that attracts visitors from all over Vietnam and even Cambodia. First prize is US$1500, so it's not difficult to see why competition is so fierce.

The races are held according to the lunar calendar on the 15th day of the 10th moon, which roughly means December. The races start at noon, but things get jumping in Soc Trang the evening before. Not surprisingly, hotel space is at a premium during the festival, and travellers without a prepaid hotel reservation will probably have to sleep in a car or minibus.

Places to Stay

A real budget place is ***Nhon Ai Hotel*** *(☎ 821974)*. Rooms with fan/air-con are US$4/5.

Though run down, ***Phong Lan 2 Hotel*** *(☎ 821757, 133 Đ Nguyen Chi Thanh)* is still an OK place to stay and notable for its massage and sauna service (US$4.50). A double with fan costs US$8, or US$10 to US$16 with air-con.

A fancier place is ***Khanh Hung Hotel*** *(☎ 821027, fax 820099, 15 ĐL Tran Hung Dao)*, boasting a large cafe with outdoor tables. A room with fan costs US$5. Air-con rooms range from US$9 to US$12. There is satellite TV, but it seems to only pick up Indian soap operas and movies.

Phong Lan Hotel *(☎ 821619, 124 Đ Dong Khoi)* is near the river. It's a bit pricey by Soc Trang standards – fan rooms are US$16, or US$21 to US$23 with air-con. If you're with a group, the hotel can arrange a traditional Khmer music & dance show.

Just opposite the Khanh Hung is the ***Cong Doan Hotel*** *(☎ 825614, 4 Đ Tran Van Sac)*, a state-run trade-union joint. It's very quiet, clean and not unreasonably priced – fan rooms cost US$10, or US$14 to US$18 with air-con and a fridge.

Places to Eat

One of the best places in town is the ***Hung Restaurant*** *(☎ 822268, 74–6 Đ Mau Than 68)*. It's open from breakfast until late into the evening and always seems to be busy.

Also popular is the ***Hang Restaurant*** *(☎ 822416, 2 Đ Le Lai)*. Neither of these places has English menus, nor prices written anywhere, so you will have to work it out like the Vietnamese.

Another spot worth a try for Vietnamese food is ***Hang Ky Restaurant*** *(☎ 820034, 1 Đ Le Loi)*.

AROUND SOC TRANG

Bat Pagoda

This is one of the Mekong Delta's most unusual sights, and now has become a favourite stopoff for both foreign and domestic tourists. The Bat Pagoda (Chua Doi) is a large monastery compound. You enter through an archway, and almost immediately you can hear the eerie screeching of the large colony of fruit bats that resides here. There are literally thousands of these creatures hanging from the fruit trees. The largest bats weigh about 1kg and have a wing span of about 1.5m.

Fruit bats make plenty of noise – in the morning the din is incredible, and so is the smell. The bats are not toilet trained, so watch out when standing under a tree or bring an umbrella. In the evening, the bats spread their wings and fly out to invade orchards all over the Mekong Delta, much to the consternation of farmers, who are known to trap the bats and eat them. Inside the monastery the creatures are protected, and the bats seem to know this – no doubt this is why they stay.

Locals tend to show excessive zeal in shaking the trees to make the bats fly around so that tourists can take photos – it's better to leave the poor things in peace – you can easily get a photo of the bats hanging off a branch if you have a good telephoto lens. The best times for visiting are early morning and at least an hour before sunset, when the bats are most active. Around dusk, hundreds of bats swoop out of the trees to go hunting.

The monks are very friendly and don't ask for money, though it doesn't hurt to leave a donation. The pagoda is decorated with gilt Buddhas, and murals paid for by Overseas Vietnamese contributors. In one room there's a life-size statue of the monk who was the former head of the complex. There is also a beautifully painted Khmer longboat here of the type used at the Oc Bom Boc Festival.

Behind the pagoda is a bizarre tomb painted with the image of a pig. It was erected in memory of a pig with five toenails (normal pigs have only four toenails). It died in 1996, but two other rare pigs with five toenails have survived and are being raised by the monks. These pigs are not for eating – they are pets.

Little kids hang around the front gate and beg from the tourists, but they aren't allowed inside the monastery grounds. We didn't give money but handed over a packet of biscuits – the kids devoured them as if they hadn't eaten in over a week. Perhaps they hadn't.

There is a ***restaurant*** just opposite the Bat Pagoda, but it does not serve bat meat.

The Bat Pagoda is about 4km west of Soc Trang. You can catch a motorbike taxi here, or easily walk there in under an hour. About 3km out of town towards the pagoda the road splits in two directions – take the right fork and continue for 1km.

Xa Lon (Sa Lon) Pagoda

This magnificent, classic Khmer pagoda is 12km from Soc Trang, towards Camau, on National Highway 1. The original structure was built over 200 years ago from wooden materials. In 1923 it was completely rebuilt, but proved to be too small. From 1969 to 1985, the present large pagoda was slowly built as funds trickled in from donations. The ceramic tiles on the exterior of the pagoda are particularly stunning.

As at other pagodas, the monks lead an austere life. They eat breakfast at 6 am and beg for contributions until 11 am, when they hold a one-hour worship. They eat again at noon and study in the afternoon – they do not eat dinner.

At present, 27 monks reside here. The pagoda also operates a school for the study of Buddhism and Sanskrit. The reason for studying Sanskrit, as the monks explained, is that all original books about Buddhism were written in this ancient language.

My Phuoc Island

A 15km journey east of Soc Trang brings you to the Hau River. From there it's a short boat ride to My Phuoc Island. It's an isolated spot very suitable for growing fruit. The local government tourist agency likes to bring foreigners here for tours of the orchards. You can do it yourself, though this is a little complicated since you'll need a motorbike to get to the river.

BAC LIEU

☎ 0781 • pop 129,300

Bac Lieu, the capital of southern Bac Lieu Province, is 280km from Ho Chi Minh City. Of the 800,000 people living in the province, about 8% are of Chinese or Cambodian origin.

The town has a few elegant but forlorn French colonial buildings, like the impressive Fop House (now being used as a community sports centre), but not much else.

Farming is a difficult occupation here because of saltwater intrusion, which means the town has remained fairly poor. The province is, however, known for its healthy longan orchards. The enterprising locals eke out a living from fishing, oyster collection and shrimp farming, as well as salt production (obtained from sea-water evaporating ponds that form immense salt flats).

For the Vietnamese, Bac Lieu's claim to fame is the grave site of Cao Van Lau (1892–1976), famed composer of *Da Co Hoai Long* (The Night Song of the Missing Husband). See the boxed text 'Da Co Hoai Lang', following.

Most foreigners give the tomb a miss, and instead use Bac Lieu as a springboard to reach the outstanding bird sanctuary outside of town, but if you're keen on seeing it, head out on Đ Cao Van Lau toward the bird sanctuary for about 1km, turn right and follow the dirt road for 150m to the grave.

Places to Stay & Eat

Most hotels in town are near the roundabout where the roads fork off to Soc Trang and Camau.

The ***Bac Lieu Guest House*** *(☎ 823815, 8 Đ Ly Tu Trong)* is a real budget special with fan doubles costing US$4, or US$6 or US$7 with air-con.

Bac Lieu Hotel *(☎ 822437, fax 823655, 4-6 Đ Hoang Van Thu)* is a snazzy new place where air-con rooms cost US$15 to US$25. There is a ***restaurant*** on the ground level, but you're better off looking outside the hotel for ***seafood restaurants***.

About 1km from the roundabout (in the direction of Soc Trang) is the ***Hoang Cung Hotel*** *(☎ 823362, 1B/5 Đ Tran Phu)*. Clean rooms cost US$10 with fan, or US$15 to US$20 with air-con.

AROUND BAC LIEU

Bac Lieu Bird Sanctuary

Five kilometres from town is Bac Lieu Bird Sanctuary (Vuon Chim Bac Lieu), notable for its 50-odd species of birds, including a large population of graceful white herons. This is one of the most interesting sights in the Mekong Delta, and is surprisingly popular with Vietnamese tourists. Foreign visitors are rare, probably because Bac Lieu is such an out-of-the-way place.

Whether or not you get to see any birds depends on what time of year you visit. Bird populations are at their peak in the rainy season – approximately May to October. The birds hang around to nest until about January, then fly off in search of greener pastures. There are basically no birds from February until the rainy season begins again.

Because of flooding, most travellers try to avoid the Mekong Delta during the rainy season, so you might want to aim for a December visit.

Although the drive is only 5km, the road

Dai Coa Hoaoi Lang (Night Song of the *Missing* Husband)

Composed in 1919 by Bac Lieu, this song is said to have inspired Vietnam's beloved *vong co* melodies. Following is the English translation.

Since my husband
Carried a sword and set off
I have been waiting for news of him
At night in my dreams
I look forward to receiving his news
And my heart aches
Though you live far away
You should not be unfaithful
Every night I long for news of you

In the daytime I am like a stone
Looking for my husband
Do you know, darling
That every night I am troubled with worries
When will we reunited?
Don't let our love fade
My only wish is that you have good health
And that one day you will return home
So we can live again as a couple

is in bad shape. The rest of the trek is through a dense jungle. There are lots of mosquitoes, so bring plenty of repellent. There is some mud to slog through – don't wear US$300 Italian shoes and white socks. Other things you should bring include bottled drinking water, binoculars, film and a camera (with a powerful telephoto lens, if you have one).

You pay the admission fee (US$0.80) when you reach the entrance of the bird sanctuary. You can (and should) hire a guide here – you'll probably get lost without one. Actually, the guides aren't supposed to take any money, so give them a tip (US$2 is enough) discreetly. Most guides do not speak English. Transport and guides can also be arranged at the sleepy Bac Lieu tourist office (☎ 822437, fax 823655), just next to the Bac Lieu Hotel. Hiring a guide here will cost you US$8.

Xiem Can Khmer Pagoda

Following the same road that takes you to the Bac Lieu Bird Sanctuary, drive 7km from Bac Lieu to reach this pagoda. As Khmer pagodas go, it's OK, but you can definitely see better ones in Tra Vinh or Soc Trang (not to mention Cambodia).

Bac Lieu Beach

The same road leading to the Bac Lieu Bird Sanctuary and Xiem Can Khmer Pagoda eventually terminates 10km from Bac Lieu at this beach (Bai Bien Bac Lieu). Don't expect white sand – it's basically hard-packed Mekong Delta mud. Quite a few shellfish and other slimy (and probably poisonous) things crawl around where the muck meets the sea. Tidal pool enthusiasts might be impressed. Locals may be willing to take you for a walk on the tidal flats where they harvest oysters.

Moi Hoa Binh Pagoda

This Khmer pagoda (Chua Moi Hoa Binh, also called Se Rey Vongsa) is 13km south of Bac Lieu along National Highway 1 (look to your left while driving to Camau).

The pagoda is uniquely designed, and chances are good that the monastery's enormous tower will catch your eye even if you're not looking for it. As pagodas in Vietnam go, it's relatively new, having first been built in 1952. The tower was added in 1990 and is used to store the bones of the deceased. There is a large and impressive meeting hall in front of the tower.

Most Khmer people in the area head for monastery schools in Soc Trang to receive a Khmer education. Therefore, very few students study at the Moi Hoa Binh Pagoda apart from the small contingent of student monks.

CAMAU

☎ 0780 • pop 173,300

Built on the swampy shores of the Ganh Hao River, Camau is the capital and largest city in Camau Province, which has a total population 1.7 million, and occupies the southern tip of the Mekong Delta. A wasteland for centuries, the area was first cultivated in the late 17th century.

Camau lies in the middle of Vietnam's largest swamp. The area is known for mosquitoes the size of hummingbirds – during the rainy season you might need a shotgun to keep them at bay. The mosquitoes come out in force just after dark and some travellers find they need to sit under a mosquito net just to eat dinner. The population of Camau includes many ethnic-Khmers Due to the boggy terrain, this area has the lowest population density in southern Vietnam.

Camau has developed rapidly in recent years, but the town itself is rather dull. The Camau police are also notoriously corrupt and renown for causing people trouble. The main attractions here are the nearby swamps and forests, which can be explored by boat Birdwatchers and aspiring botanists are reportedly most enthralled with the area. Unfortunately, high hotel prices, the long distance from Ho Chi Minh City and the vampire mosquitoes all conspire to keep the number of foreign tourists to a minimum

Still, the local tourist literature tries: 'Camau – people and nature still remain innocent, generous and of specialty fit stature'.

Information

Travel Agencies Camau Tourist (Cong Ty Du Lich Minh Hai, ☎ 831828), 17 Đ Nguyen Van Hai, can arrange interesting boat trips for two days and two nights to Nam Can, Dat Mui (Cape Camau), the Da Bac Islands and the U-Minh Forest.

Various other services include foreign currency exchange, boat rentals and visa extensions

Money Incombank, near the post office, can handle foreign currency exchange and cash advances for Visa and MasterCard.

Zoo

Officially labelled the 19th May Forest Park, is hardly provides a lush forest, rather, Camau's zoo 'shelters' a poorly maintained collection of miserable animals.

In the grounds of the zoo, along with a few noisy *cafes*, is a 'botanic garden', which looks rather like a half-acre patch of weeds. In short, there is nothing particularly inviting to see or do here.

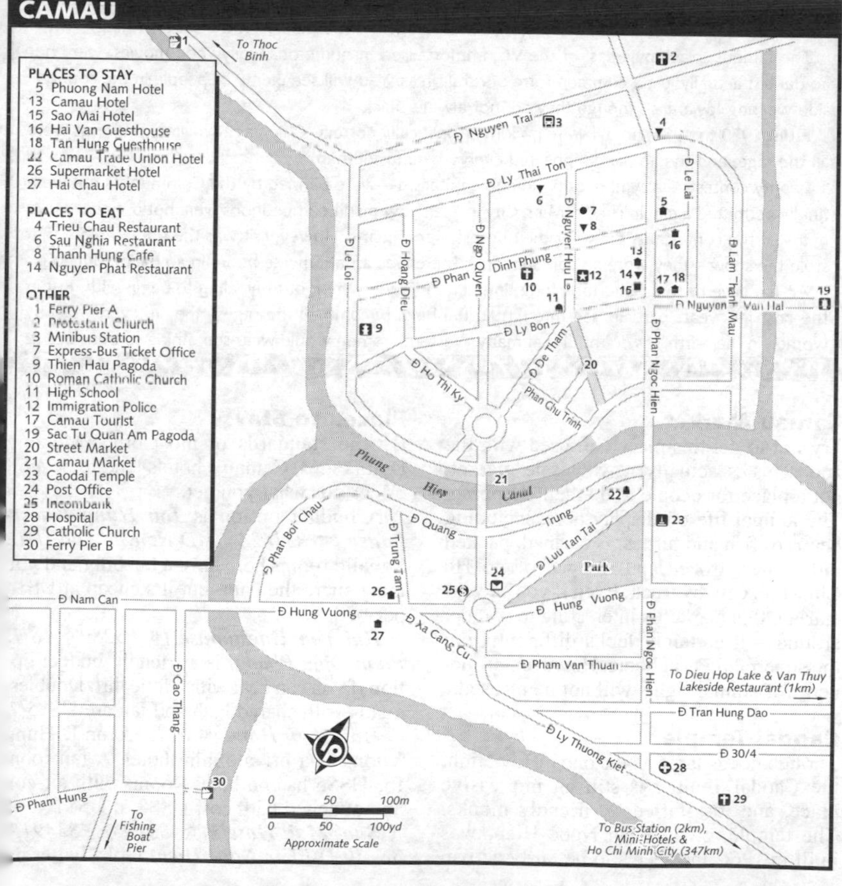

Camau Saves the Ao Dai

The graceful national dress of Vietnamese women is known as the *ao dai* (pronounced ow-zai in the north and ow-yai in the south). An ao dai consists of a close-fitting blouse with long panels at the front and back, which is worn over loose black or white trousers. The outfit was designed for the Vietnamese hot weather, and for that reason is much more common in the south, especially in Ho Chi Minh City and the Mekong Delta. Although ao dai are impractical for women doing stoop labour in the rice paddies, they are considered appropriate for office workers and students.

In years past, men also wore ao dai, but these days you are only likely to see this in traditional operas or musical performances. The male ao dai is shorter and looser than the female version. Before the end of dynastic rule, the colours of the brocade and embroidery indicated the rank of the wearer; gold brocade, accompanied by embroidered dragons, was reserved for the emperor. High-ranking mandarins wore purple, while lower-ranking mandarins had to settle for blue.

Ao dai are versatile and are even considered appropriate for funerals. Mourners usually wear either white or black ao dai (white is the traditional colour of mourning in Vietnam). More happily, ao dai can also be worn to weddings (bright colours with embroidery on the shirt is fitting).

The famous 'black pyjamas' of the VC, immortalised in numerous Hollywood movies, were not ao dai but actually just a common form of rural dress. You will see plenty of people in the countryside wearing 'pyjamas', though they are not always black.

From 1975 to 1985, ao dai were no longer politically correct. Chic baggy military uniforms were all the rage, and the ao dai disappeared everywhere in Vietnam.

Beauty contests – a symbol of bourgeois capitalism – were banned by the Communists but were finally permitted again in Ho Chi Minh City in 1989. Swimsuit competitions were not permitted, but many of the contestants did wear their best designer jeans. However, it was the Camau team that stole the show – they wore ao dai. Suddenly, there was a nationwide boom in ao dai production.

Ao dai have been around for a long time, and were anything but revealing to begin with. But in the past few years partially see-through ao dai have become all the rage – they're even worn by women in the north. It's doubtful that many Western women would wear something so translucent.

Camau Market

Try not to get this place confused with the zoo. This is actually a wholesale market, not a place for people to do their shopping. The animal life on display here, including heaps of fish and turtles, is cleaned, packed into crates, frozen and shipped off to Ho Chi Minh City by truck. Even if you're vegetarian, this market is interesting to wander around – it certainly looks different from the supermarkets at home. However, proponents of animal rights will not be pleased.

Caodai Temple

Though not as large as the one in Tay Ninh, the Caodai Temple is still an impressive place, and it's staffed by friendly monks. The temple, on Đ Phan Ngoc Hien, was built in 1966 and seems to be fairly active.

Places to Stay

By the standards of most other Mekong Delta cities, Camau's hotels tend to be a bit pricey for what you get.

A budget option is ***Tan Hung Guesthouse*** *(☎ 831622, 11 Đ Nguyen Van Hai)*. Squalid rooms here have a fan only and you must share the bath, but it's cheap at US$4 per bed.

Hai Van Guesthouse *(☎ 832897, 18 Đ Phan Dinh Phung)* is a friendly budget option if you can deal with a little dirt. Doubles/quads with shared bath and fan are US$5/7.

Hai Chau Hotel *(☎ 831255)* on Đ Hung Vuong is a private mini-hotel. A fan room for US$5 has no bath. Rooms with air-con and attached bath cost US$8 to US$11.

Sao Mai Hotel *(☎ 831035, 834913, 38–40 Đ Phan Ngoc Hien)* looks better on the outside than the inside. Fan rooms cost US$8, or with air-con you're looking at US$15 to US$25.

Conditions are better at ***Camau Hotel*** *(☎ 831165, fax 835075, 20 Đ Phan Ngoc Hien)*. Rooms with air-con cost US$15 to US$28, and include breakfast.

Camau Trade Union Hotel *(☎ 833245, 9 Đ Luu Tan Tai)* is almost opposite the Caodai Temple. Overpriced rooms with fan are US$15, or US$20 with air-con.

Phuong Nam Hotel *(☎ 831752, fax 834402, 91 Đ Phan Dinh Phung)* is an excellent place. All rooms have air-con and attached hot bath, and cost from US$13 to US$22. The more expensive rooms have satellite TV, and a complimentary breakfast is included.

Supermarket Hotel aka *Khach San Sieu Thi (☎ 832789, fax 836880)* is attached, as you may have guessed, to a large supermarket. Rates are US$20 to US$35 including breakfast.

There are a couple of very grotty-looking ***mini-hotels*** next to the bus station. Look for the signs that say *nha tro* (Vietnamese for 'dormitory'). The prices are the lowest in Camau, but these places are only for the desperate.

Places to Eat

Shrimp is Camau's speciality, which is raised in nearby ponds and mangrove swamps.

Between the Sao Mai and Camau hotels, ***Hong Ky Restaurant*** *(28 Đ Phan Ngoc Hien)* is an appealing option.

Other decent spots include ***Trieu Chau Restaurant*** *(243 Đ Ly Thai Ton)*, and the newer ***Sau Nghia Restaurant*** *(☎ 832913, 42 Đ Ly Thai Ton)*.

There is a cluster of small ***roadside restaurants*** on Đ Ly Bon, at the entrance to the street market. They are very cheap and the food is OK.

The friendly outdoor ***restaurant*** in the Camau Trade Union Hotel is not bad, and certainly more aesthetically pleasing than eating in the market.

You might also check out the ***restaurants*** in the Sao Mai, Camau and Phuong Nam hotels.

Finally, out on the Dieu Hop Lakeside, the indoor-outdoor ***Van Thuy Restaurant*** makes for a pleasant place to eat away from the city centre.

Getting There & Away

Bus Buses from Ho Chi Minh City to Camau leave from Mien Tay bus station in An Lac. The trip takes 11 hours by regular bus and eight hours by express bus. There are several daily express buses to Ho Chi Minh City leaving between 5 and 10.30 am.

The Camau bus station is 2.5km from the centre of town, along National Highway 1 towards Ho Chi Minh City. There is, however, an express-bus ticket office in town, on Đ Nguyen Huu Le, next to the Thanh Hung Cafe; if you arrive 20 minutes before departure to buy your tickets here, they will provide a free shuttle service out to the main bus station. Tickets cost US$3.50, but large backpacks may be subject to a ticket of their own.

A faster and more comfortable option to get back to Ho Chi Minh City is by express minibus. These leave from the minibus station (☎ 831874) at 121 Đ Nguyen Trai and cost US$11 per person. Call ahead for current departure times.

Car & Motorbike Camau is the end of the line for National Highway 1, the southernmost point in Vietnam accessible by car and bus. Drivers boldly attempting to drive the 'highway' south of Camau will soon find their vehicles sinking into a quagmire of mud and mangroves.

Camau is 178km from Cantho (three hours) and 347km from Ho Chi Minh City (eight hours).

Boat Boats run between Camau and Ho Chi Minh City approximately once every four days. The trip takes 30 hours and is certainly not comfortable.

Of more interest to backpackers is the boat from Camau north to Rach Gia (the boat docks in Rach Soi, about 10km from Rach Gia). This departs Ferry Pier B daily at around 5.15 am and takes about 10 hours. The cost is US$1.10, and motorbikes can be taken on board for another US$1.10. Hammocks rent for US$0.40. Ferry Pier B is also the spot where you can catch the speedboats heading south to Ngoc Hien.

Also popular are the boats to U-Minh Forest. These depart from Ferry Pier A. You'll have to do some negotiation to arrange a tour here. It's also worth asking at the hotels as they may arrange a whole group.

Getting Around

There are plenty of water taxis along the canal at the back of Camau Market. For longer trips upriver, larger longboats collect at the cluster of jetties just outside the market area. You can either join the throngs of passengers going downriver or hire the whole boat for about US$5 an hour.

AROUND CAMAU

U-Minh Forest

The town of Camau borders the U-Minh Forest, a huge mangrove swamp covering 1000 sq km of Camau and Kien Giang Provinces. Local people use certain species of mangrove as a source of timber, charcoal, thatch and tannin. When the mangroves flower, bees feed on the blossoms, providing both honey and wax. The area is an important habitat for waterfowl.

The U-Minh Forest, which is the largest mangrove swamp in the world outside of the Amazon basin, was a favourite hideout for the VC during the American War. US patrol boats were frequently ambushed here and the VC regularly planted mines in the canals. The Americans responded with chemical defoliation, which made their enemy more visible at the same time as doing enormous damage to the forests. Replanting efforts at first failed because the soil was so toxic, but gradually the heavy rainfall has washed the dioxin out to sea (where it no doubt poisons fish) and the forest is returning. Many eucalyptus trees have also been planted here because they have proved relatively resistant to dioxin.

Unfortunately, what Agent Orange started, the locals are finishing off – the mangrove forests are being further damaged by clearing for shrimp-raising ponds, charcoal making and woodchipping. The government has tried to limit these activities, but the conflict between nature and human developers continues. And the conflict will get worse before it gets better, because Vietnam's population is still growing rapidly.

The area is known for its birdlife, but these creatures too have taken a beating. Nevertheless, ornithologists will derive much joy from taking boat trips around Camau; however, don't expect to find the swarms of birds to be nearly as ubiquitous as the swarms of mosquitoes.

Camau Tourist offers all-day tours of the forest by boat. It costs US$135 per boat (maximum 10 people), though some bargaining is in order. You can also talk to the locals down at Ferry Pier A to see if you can find a better deal.

Bird Sanctuary

The Bird Sanctuary (Vuon Chim) is about 45km south-east of Camau. Storks are the largest and most easily seen birds here, though smaller feathered creatures also make their nests in the tall trees. Remember that birds will be birds – they don't particularly like humans to get close to them, and they leave their nests early in the morning in search of food. Thus, your chances of getting up close and have them hop onto your finger for a photo session are rather slim.

Camau Tourist offers a full-day tour by boat to the Bird Sanctuary for US$120 (one to 10 people).

NAM CAN

☎ 0780

Except for a minuscule fishing hamlet (Tran De) and an offshore island (Hon Khoai), Nam Can stakes its claim as the southernmost town in Vietnam. Few tourists come to this isolated community, which survives mainly from the shrimp-raising industry.

At the very southern tip of the delta is the **Camau Nature Reserve**, sometimes referred to as the Ngoc Hien Bird Sanctuary. It's one of the least developed and most protected parts of the Mekong Delta region. In this area, shrimp farming is prohibited. Access is only by boat.

At the southern end of the reserve is the tiny fishing village of Tran De. A public ferry connects Tran De to Nam Can. If you are obsessed with reaching Vietnam's southern tip, you'll have to take a boat from Tran De to Hon Khoai Island (see the Hon Khoai Island section, following).

If you're looking to visit another remote spot, you can hire a boat to take you to Dat Mui (Cape Camau), the south-western tip of Vietnam. However, few people find this worthwhile.

Places to Stay

There is only one hotel in Nam Can, so you'll have little choice unless you plan on ***camping***.

The ***Nam Can Hotel*** (☎ *877039*) has rooms that cost from US$15 to US$40.

Getting There & Away

A road connecting Camau to Nam Can is shown on most maps of Vietnam, but it's little more than wishful thinking. Basically, it's a muddy track which is underwater most of the time, though some have attempted it by motorbike.

The trip to Nam Can from Camau is best done by speedboat. These boats are readily available in Camau and take approximately four hours to do the journey.

From Nam Can south to Tran De takes another four hours.

HON KHOAI ISLAND

This island, 25km south of the southern tip of the Mekong Delta, is the southernmost point in Vietnam. Unlike the delta, which is pancake flat and intensively cultivated, Hon Khoai Island is rocky, hilly and forested. Unfortunately, getting there is fraught with hassles and few people bother. To begin with, the island is a military base, so travel permits are needed. To get these, apply in Camau at either the police station or Camau Tourist. More than likely, the police will refuse you anyway and you'll be referred to Camau Tourist. There is a small charge for this service.

The only place to stay on Hon Khoai Island is the ***military guesthouse***.

Getting There & Away

From Camau, you need to get yourself to Nam Can, where you change boats for Tran De; from Tran De you catch a fishing boat to Hon Khoai Island.

LONG XUYEN

☎ 076 • pop 238,100

Long Xuyen, the capital of An Giang Province, was once a stronghold of the Hoa Hao sect, founded in 1939. The sect emphasises simplicity in worship and does not believe in temples or intermediaries between humans and the Supreme Being. Until 1956, the Hoa Hao had an army and constituted a major military force in this region. The town's big claim to fame is being the birthplace of Vietnam's second president, Ton Duc Thang.

Today, Long Xuyen is a moderately prosperous town. There are a few sights around town, but for travellers its value is mainly as a transit point with good food, accommodation and a foreign exchange bank (change money here if you're heading to Chau Doc; there is no place in Chau Doc to exchange money). The market along the riverside is colourful and lively, and boats can be hired here for about US$4 per hour.

Information

The local tourist office (An Giang Tourist) is on Đ Nguyen Van Cung, beside the Long Xuyen Hotel. The staff can speak some English, and are courteous enough, but beyond providing you with a photocopied map of the town they are of little use to visitors.

Vietnam Airlines has a booking office in the Cuu Long Hotel.

Long Xuyen Catholic Church

Long Xuyen Catholic Church, an impressive modern structure with a 50m-high bell tower, is one of the largest churches in the Mekong Delta. It was constructed between 1966 and 1973, and can seat 1000 worshippers. The church is open for visitors from 4 am to 8 pm. Masses are held from 4.30 to 5.30 am and 6 to 7 pm Monday to Saturday and 5 to 6.30 am, 3.30 to 5 pm and 6 to 7.30 pm on Sunday.

Long Xuyen Protestant Church

Long Xuyen Protestant Church is a small, modern structure at 4 Đ Hung Vuong. Prayers are held on Sunday from 10 am to noon.

An Giang Museum

This sleepy little museum is a proud showcase of An Giang Province, featuring photographs and the personal effects of former president Ton Duc Thang. There are also some artefacts from the Oc-Eo site near Rach Gia (see Around Rach Gia later in this chapter) and displays detailing the history of this region from the 1930s to the present day.

The museum, also known as Bao Tang An Giang, at 77 Đ Thoai Ngoc Hau, is only open on Tuesday, Thursday, Saturday and Sunday, and only from 7.30 to 10.30 am (as well as 2 to 4.30 pm on Saturday and Sunday). Entry is free.

Cho Moi District

Cho Moi District, across the river from Long Xuyen, is known for its rich groves of banana, durian, guava, jackfruit, longan, mango, mangosteen and plum.

The women here are said to be the most beautiful in the Mekong Delta.

Cho Moi District can be reached by boat from the ferry terminal at the foot of Đ Nguyen Hue.

Places to Stay

If cheap is all that matters, ***Phat Thanh Hotel*** *(☎ 841708, 2 Đ Ly Tu Trong)* has fan rooms for US$3 to US$5, or US$8 for a double with air-con.

Prices and standards are similar next door at ***Thien Huong Hotel*** *(☎ 843152)* and at ***Binh Dan Hotel*** *(☎ 844557, 12 Đ Ly Tu Trong)*.

Two decent hotels worth considering are the ***An Long Hotel*** *(☎ 843298, 281 Đ Tran Hung Dao)* and the nearby, ***Thoai Chau 2 Hotel*** *(☎ 843882, fax 843220, 283A Đ Tran Hung Dao)*. Both of them charge US$4 for doubles with a fan, or US$8 to US$11 for air-conditioning.

Thai Binh Hotel II *(☎ 847078, 4–8 Đ Nguyen Hue A)* is privately owned and reasonably priced. Double rooms with fan and cold bath cost US$6, while singles/doubles/triples with hot water and air-con are US$8/11/16.

Xuan Phuong Hotel *(☎ 841041, 68 Đ Nguyen Trai)* rents doubles/triples/quads with fan for US$7/8/13, or US$9/10/16 with air-con.

An Giang Hotel *(☎ 841297, 40 Đ Hai Ba Trung)* is not bad. Singles/doubles with fan cost US$5/7. Air-con doubles cost US$9 to US$11, and triples with fan/air-con are US$18/19.

Long Xuyen Hotel *(17 Đ Nguyen Van Cung)* has rooms with fan and bath for US$7; with air-con they're US$9 to US$16. Optional life insurance is sold at reception for US$0.11 per day!

At ***Cuu Long Hotel*** *(☎ 841365, fax 843176, 15 Đ Nguyen Van Cung)* all rooms have air-con and hot water. Rooms with breakfast included cost US$14 to US$19; with no windows they're US$12.

Slightly out of the town centre, ***Thang Loi Hotel*** *(☎ 852637, fax 852568, 1 Đ Le Hong Phong)* is a big place with a good restaurant. Doubles/triples with fan cost US$9/10; doubles with air-con are US$12 to US$20.

Places to Eat

There is excellent vegetarian food at ***Bo De Duyen*** *(☎ 842432, 328/4 Đ Hung Vuong)*. The owner, used to be the head chef at the Long Xuyen Hotel. Even the *nuoc mam* sauce, normally made from fish, is made from fermented soy beans. Try the *banh xeo chay* (crepes), *hu tien* (noodle soup), *ho anh thanh* (fried wontons) or *cha gio* (spring rolls). The ***Xuan Phuong Hotel*** has a pleasant restaurant, and there are others in the ***An Giang***, ***Cuu Long***, ***Long Xuyen*** and ***Thai Binh*** hotels. There is a happening scene at the riverside ***cafes*** on Đ Pham Hong Thai.

Getting There & Away

Bus Buses from Ho Chi Minh City to Long Xuyen leave from the Mien Tay bus station in An Lac.

Long Xuyen bus station (Ben Xe Long Xuyen, ☎ 852125) is at the southern end of town opposite 96/3B Đ Tran Hung Dao. There are buses from Long Xuyen to Camau, Cantho, Chau Doc, Ha Tien, Ho Chi Minh City and Rach Gia.

Car & Motorbike Long Xuyen is 62km from Cantho, 126km from Mytho and 189km from Ho Chi Minh City.

Boat To get to the Long Xuyen ferry dock from Đ Pham Hong Thai, cross Duy Tan Bridge and turn right. Passenger ferries leave from here to Cho Vam, Dong Tien, Hong Ngu, Kien Luong, Lai Vung, Rach Gia, Sa Dec and Tan Chau. Boats to Rach Gia (US$0.80) take about nine hours, and leave at 6.30 and/or 8 am. You can also catch boats from here to Sa Dec at noon, taking about four hours and costing US$0.80.

From the An Hoa ferry terminal you can also catch boats to Cao Lanh and Sa Dec.

Getting Around

The best way to get around Long Xuyen is to take a *cyclo*, *xe dap loi* (a two-wheeled wagon pulled by a bicycle) or a xe Honda loi.

Car ferries from Long Xuyen to Cho Moi District (across the river) leave from the ferry terminal near the market every half-hour from 4 am to 6.30 pm.

CHAU DOC

☎ 076 • pop 99,700

Chau Doc is a riverside commercial centre not far from the Cambodian border. The city was once known for its dugout canoe races. Chau Doc has quite sizeable Chinese, Cham and Khmer communities, each of which has built distinctive temples that are worth a visit.

Be aware that there is *no* place to change travellers cheques or get cash advances in Chau Doc; you should take care of exchanging money elsewhere before you arrive (nearby Long Xuyen is a popular place to do this).

Chau Phu Temple

Chau Phu Temple (Dinh Than Chau Phu), on the corner of Đ Nguyen Van Thoai and Đ Gia Long, was built in 1926 to worship Nguyen Dynasty official Thoai Ngoc Hau, who is buried at Sam Mountain (see the Around Chau Doc section following). The structure is decorated with both Vietnamese and Chinese motifs. Inside are funeral tablets bearing the names of the deceased and biographical information about them.

Chau Doc Church

This small Catholic church, constructed in 1920, is across the street from 459 Đ Lien Tinh Lo 10 and is not far from Phu Hiep ferry landing. There are Masses Monday to Saturday at 5 am and 5 pm, and 7 am and 4 pm on Sunday.

Mosques

The domed and arched Chau Giang Mosque, which serves the local Cham Muslim community, is in the hamlet of Chau Giang. To get there, take the car ferry from Chau Giang ferry landing in Chau Doc across the Hau Giang River. From the landing, walk away from the river for 30m, turn left and walk 50m.

The **Mubarak Mosque** (Thanh Duong Hoi Giao), where children study the Koran in Arabic script, is also on the river bank opposite Chau Doc. Visitors are permitted, but you should avoid entering during the calls to prayer (five times daily) unless you are a Muslim.

There are other small mosques in the Chau Doc area. These are accessible by boat, but you'll probably need a local guide to find them all.

Floating Houses

These houses, whose floats consist of empty metal drums, are both a place to live and a livelihood for their residents. Under each house, fish are raised in suspended metal nets: the fish flourish in their natural river habitat, the family can feed them whatever scraps it has handy, and catching the fish does not require all the exertions of fishing. You can find these houses floating all around the Chau Doc area, and get a close-up look by hiring a boat (please be respectful of their privacy though).

Places to Stay – Budget & Mid-Range

The pleasant ***Thuan Loi Hotel** (☎ 866134, 18 Đ Tran Hung Dao)* commands a great location on the riverside. Doubles with fan cost US$6, or US$10 with air-con. The 3rd-floor terrace is a great place to watch life on the river go by.

***Guesthouse 44** (☎ 866540, 44 Đ Doc Phu Thu)* is a venerable favourite with backpackers, though it's definitely showing its age. Rooms with fan and cold bath cost from US$4 to US$7.

Moving downmarket, ***Cong Doan Guesthouse** (☎ 866477)* is grimy, loud, and has no air-con or private toilets, but charges just US$2 for singles, or US$4 for a double.

***Thai Binh Hotel** (☎ 866221, 37 Đ Nguyen Van Thoai)* is another real cheapie. Doubles with fan are US$3. A room for four people with private toilet costs US$11.

***Hotel 92** (☎ 866899, 92 Đ Nguyen Van Thoai)* is a good-looking place with only six rooms; all with cold baths. Its one fan room costs US$6, and air-con rooms are priced at US$9.

Ngoc Phu Hotel** (☎ 866484, 17 Đ Doc Phu Thu)* is a large and livable place. A room with fan is US$6, or US$10/12 for air-con doubles/triples. A similar standard prevails at the ***Hang Chau 2 Hotel on Đ Nguyen Van Thoai.

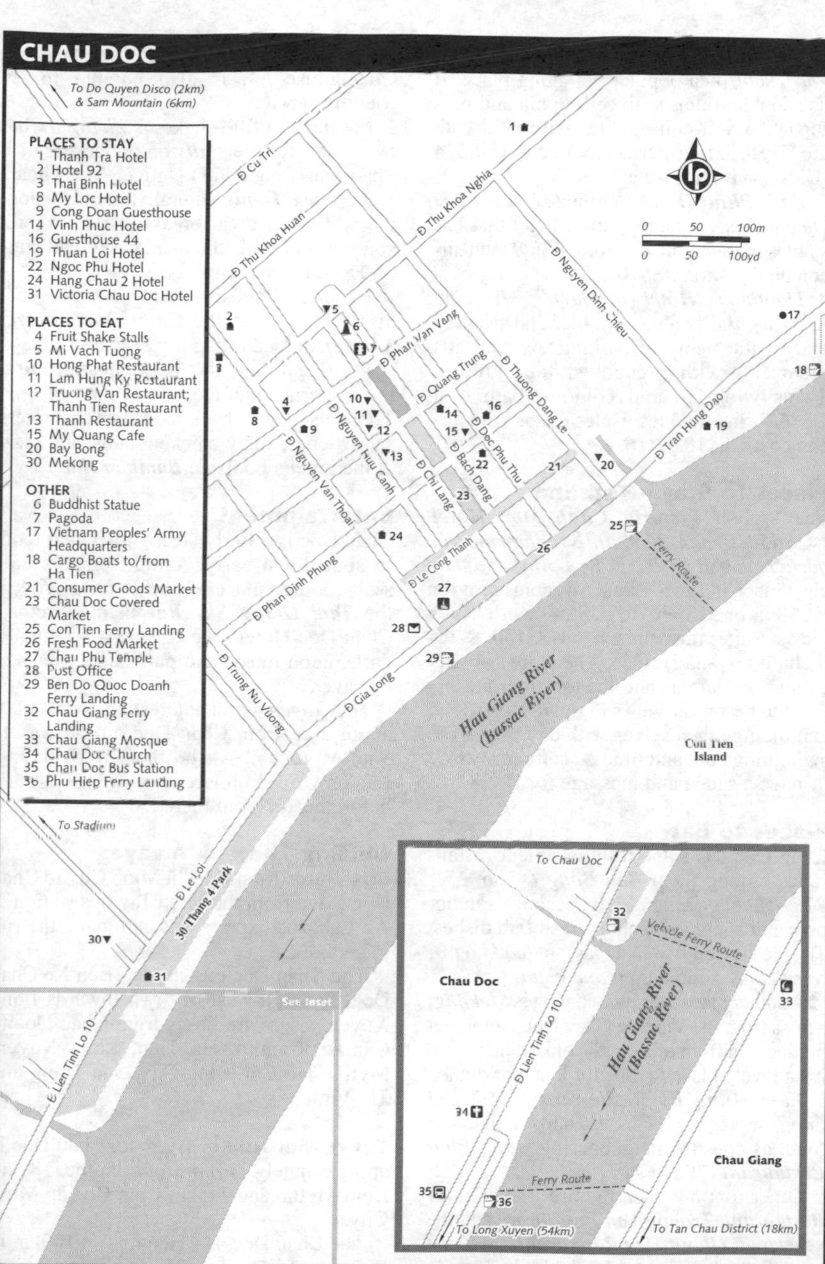
CHAU DOC
To Do Quyen Disco (2km) & Sam Mountain (6km)
PLACES TO STAY
1 Thanh Tra Hotel
2 Hotel 92
3 Thai Binh Hotel
8 My Loc Hotel
9 Cong Doan Guesthouse
14 Vinh Phuc Hotel
16 Guesthouse 44
19 Thuan Loi Hotel
22 Ngoc Phu Hotel
24 Hang Chau 2 Hotel
31 Victoria Chau Doc Hotel
PLACES TO EAT
4 Fruit Shake Stalls
5 Mi Vach Tuong
10 Hong Phat Restaurant
11 Lam Hung Ky Restaurant
12 Truong Van Restaurant; Thanh Tien Restaurant
13 Thanh Restaurant
15 My Quang Cafe
20 Bay Bong
30 Mekong
OTHER
6 Buddhist Statue
7 Pagoda
17 Vietnam Peoples' Army Headquarters
18 Cargo Boats to/from Ha Tien
21 Consumer Goods Market
23 Chau Doc Covered Market
25 Con Tien Ferry Landing
26 Fresh Food Market
27 Chau Phu Temple
28 Post Office
29 Ben Do Quoc Doanh Ferry Landing
32 Chau Giang Ferry Landing
33 Chau Giang Mosque
34 Chau Doc Church
35 Chau Doc Bus Station
36 Phu Hiep Ferry Landing
Đ Cu Tri
Đ Thu Khoa Huan
Đ Thu Khoa Nghia
Đ Nguyen Dinh Chieu
Đ Phan Van Vang
Đ Quang Trung
Đ Thuong Dang Le
Đ Tran Hung Dao
Đ Nguyen Huu Canh
Đ Nguyen Van Thoai
Đ Chi Lang
Đ Bach Dang
Đ Doc Phu Thu
Đ Le Cong Thanh
Đ Phan Dinh Phung
Đ Trung Nu Vuong
Đ Gia Long
Đ Le Loi
30 Thang 4 Park
Đ Lien Tinh Lo 10
Ferry Route
Hau Giang River (Bassac River)
Con Tien Island
To Stadium
See Inset
0 50 100m
0 50 100yd
To Chau Doc
Vehicle Ferry Route
Chau Doc
Chau Giang
To Long Xuyen (54km)
To Tan Chau District (18km)
MEKONG DELTA

My Loc Hotel *(☎ 866167, 51B Đ Nguyen Van Thoai)* is a popular yet aging place. It has double rooms with ceiling fan and bath for US$6. Air-con doubles with cold bath are US$8. A four-person room costs US$14 (US$17 with hot water).

Vinh Phuc Hotel *(☎ 866242, 12–14 Đ Quang Trung)* is a new mini-hotel that has singles with fan/air-con for US$6/8, and air-con doubles for US$10.

Thanh Tra Hotel *(☎ 866788, 77 Đ Thu Khoa Nghia)* is a clean, quiet and friendly place with plenty of parking. As such it's often full with prebooked tour groups. Twins with fan and cold/hot bath cost US$6/7, and doubles/triples/quads with air-con cost US$10/13/16.

Places to Stay – Top End

The stylish ***Victoria Chau Doc Hotel*** *(☎ 865010, fax 865020, ⓔ victoriachaudoc@hcm.vnn.vn, 32 Đ Le Loi)* is the fanciest place in town. Standard rooms rent for US$80, or US$90 to US$95 with river views. Suites raise the tab to US$150. Rates include tax and service. There are two excellent restaurants and the top-floor bar offers the best river views in town. Nonguests can indulge themselves with day use of the swimming pool and fitness centre for US$5, or have a sauna and massage for US$8.

Places to Eat

Chau Doc has some truly excellent restaurants, among them ***Bay Bong*** *(☎ 867271, 22 Đ Thuong Dang Le)*. It specialises in hot pots and soups, as well as fresh fish dishes. Try the stewed fish in a clay pot *(ca kho to)*, or sweet & sour soup *(canh chua)*.

Another place worthy of a plug is ***Mekong***, across from the Victoria Chau Doc Hotel. Set outdoors in front of a classic old French villa, it's a lovely place to dine for lunch or dinner.

Lam Hung Ky Restaurant *(71 Đ Chi Lang)* serves good Chinese and Vietnamese food, as does the neighbouring ***Hong Phat Restaurant*** *(79 Đ Chi Lang)*.

Other options nearby are the ***Thanh Restaurant, Truong Van Restaurant*** and the vegetarian ***Thanh Tien Restaurant*** (the name of the latter means to calm the body down).

The popular ***My Quang Cafe***, opposite Guesthouse 44, is also notable for its friendly service.

For the best fruit shakes *(sinh to)* in Chau Doc, look for the ***stalls*** on the corner of Đ Phan Van Vang and Đ Nguyen Van Thoai.

Mi Vach Tuong (literally, noodles along the wall) is a great breakfast *pho* (noodle soup) joint beside the local basketball court on Đ Thu Khoa Nghia.

Excellent, cheap Vietnamese food can also be found at the ***Chau Doc Covered Market***, spread out along Đ Bach Dang.

For fine dining, the ***Bassic Restaurant*** in the Victoria Chau Doc Hotel can't be beat. There also good snack food such as burgers, sandwiches, spicy chicken wings and pizza at the hotel's poolside ***Bamboo Bar***.

Entertainment

Chau Doc is a fairly sleepy town and tends to shut down early. Aside from the cafe scene, a nice place to pop in for a drink is the ***Tam Giang Sky Bar*** in the Victoria Chau Doc Hotel. The bar has a pool table, darts, good music and panoramic views of the river.

Do Quyen is an interesting local disco about 2km from Chau Doc on the way to Sam Mountain. At the time of writing, it was only open on weekends, so ask around before heading out there.

Getting There & Away

Bus Buses from Ho Chi Minh City to Chau Doc leave from the Mien Tay bus station in An Lac; the express bus can make the run in six hours.

The Chau Doc bus station (Ben Xe Chau Doc) is south-west of town towards Long Xuyen. There are buses from Chau Doc to Camau, Cantho, Ha Tien, Long Xuyen, Mytho, Ho Chi Minh City, Soc Trang and Tra Vinh.

Car & Motorbike By road, Chau Doc is approximately 117km from Cantho, 181km from Mytho and 245km from Ho Chi Minh City.

The Chau Doc–Ha Tien road is 100km in length and is now in decent shape. As you

Fish Farming

Fish farming constitutes some 15% of Vietnam's total seafood output, and is widely practiced in An Giang Province, in the region near the Cambodian border. The highest concentration of 'floating houses' with fish cages can be observed on the banks of the Bassac River in Chau Doc, near its confluence with the mighty Mekong.

The primary fish farmed here are two species of Pangasiidae (a member of the Asian catfish family), *Pangasius bocourti* and *P. hypophthalmus*. It is interesting to note that even with two tides a day here, there is no salt water in the river. Annually, around 15,000 tonnes of fish are exported, primarily to supply the European and American markets in the form of frozen white fish filets (about 5% makes it to Australia and Japan).

The two-step production cycle starts with capturing fish eggs from the wild, followed by raising the fish to a marketable size – usually about 1kg. Fish are fed on a kind of dough made by the farmers from cereal, vegetables and fish scraps. The largest cage measures 2000 cubic metres and can produce up to 400 tonnes of raw fish in each 10-month production cycle.

About 1000 people are directly employed by a giant processing plant in Long Xuyen (near Chau Doc). This ever-growing venture relies heavily on the production of wild seedlings – the seeds represent about 50% of the farmers' production cost. Since 1994 CIRAD (the French Institute for International Agronomic Research and Development) has been carrying out a project to develop an artificial reproduction method for the two Pangasiidae species. The first successful attempt was in 1995, and by 2000 production was up to 700 million larvae for each species. Further research is being conducted in Chau Doc on the nutrition and reproduction of the fish.

approach Ha Tien, the land turns into a mangrove swamp that is infertile and almost uninhabited. This area is a bit scary, especially with Cambodia just a few kilometres away. It's considered reasonably safe during the day, but it's not advisable to be out here after dark. The drive takes about three hours, and it's possible to visit Ba Chuc en route (see Ba Chuc later in this chapter). If you don't plan to drive yourself, *xe om* (motorbike taxi) drivers typically charge about US$6.

Boat For details on the Greenlines hydrofoil service to/from Mytho, see the boxed text 'Hydrofoil between Ho Chi Minh City and Mekong Delta' near the beginning of this chapter.

No-frills cargo boats run daily between Chau Doc and Ha Tien via the Vinh Te Canal; it's an interesting 95km trip. The waterway, which straddles the Cambodian border, is named after Vinh Te, the wife of Thoai Ngoc Hau, who built the canal. Departures are at 4 am and arrival time is roughly 5 pm; the unofficial foreigners' fare is US$5.

Getting Around

Boats to Chau Giang District (across the Hau Giang River) leave from two docks: vehicle ferries depart from Chau Giang ferry landing (Ben Pha Chau Giang), opposite 419 Đ Le Loi; smaller, more frequent boats leave from Phu Hiep ferry landing (Ben Pha FB Phu Hiep), a little further south.

Vehicle ferries to Con Tien Island depart from the Con Tien ferry landing (Ben Pha Con Tien) at the river end of Đ Thuong Dang Le; you can catch boats to Chau Giang and Tan Chau from the Ben Do Quoc Doanh ferry landing, opposite the post office on Đ Gia Long.

Private boats (rowed standing-up) can be hired from either of these spots for about US$5 per hour, and are highly recommended for seeing the floating houses and visiting nearby Cham minority villages and mosques.

Prices for all of the public ferries (US$0.04) are doubled at night; bicycles or motorbikes require their own ticket (about US$0.08).

AROUND CHAU DOC

Tan Chau District

Tan Chau District is famous all over southern Vietnam for its traditional industry, silk making.

The market in Tan Chau has a selection of competitively priced Thai and Cambodian goods.

To get to Tan Chau District from Chau Doc, take a boat across the Hau Giang River from the Phu Hiep ferry landing, and then catch a ride on the back of a motorbike taxi for the 18km trip to Tan Chau District.

Sam Mountain

☎ 076

There are dozens of pagodas and temples, many of them set in caves, around Sam Mountain (Nui Sam), which is about 6km south-west of Chau Doc out on Đ Bao Ho Thoai. The Chinese influence is obvious, and Sam Mountain is a favourite spot for ethnic-Chinese, both as pilgrims from Ho Chi Minh City and as tourists from Hong Kong and Taiwan.

Climbing the peak is of course the highlight of a visit to Sam Mountain. The views from the top are spectacular (weather permitting) and you can easily look out over Cambodia. There is a military outpost on the summit, a legacy of the days when the Khmer Rouge made cross-border raids and massacred Vietnamese civilians. The outpost is still functional, and the soldiers are quite used to tourists taking photos now; however, you should ply the soldiers with cigarettes and ask permission before taking photos of them or anything that could be considered militarily sensitive.

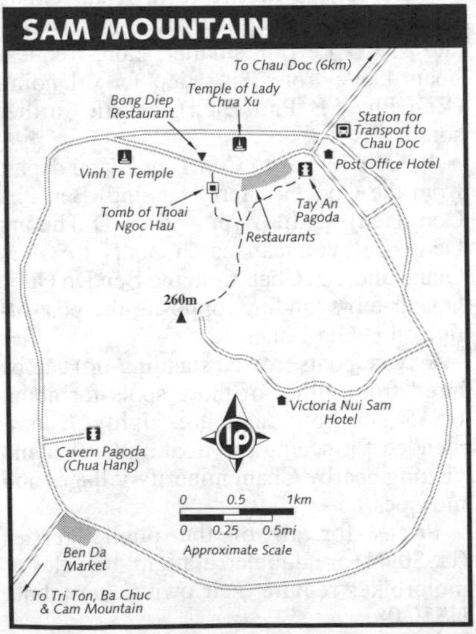

Walking down is easier than walking up, so if you want to cheat, have a motorbike take you to the summit. The road to the top is on the east side of the mountain. You can walk down along a peaceful, traffic-free trail on the north side which will bring you to the main temple area. The summit road has been decorated with amusement park ceramic dinosaurs and the like, perhaps a sign of abominations to come. But there are also some small shrines and pavilions, which add a bit of charm and remind you that this is indeed Vietnam and not Disneyland.

SAM MOUNTAIN

To Chau Doc (6km)
Temple of Lady Chua Xu
Bong Diep Restaurant
Station for Transport to Chau Doc
Post Office Hotel
Vinh Te Temple
Tay An Pagoda
Tomb of Thoai Ngoc Hau
Restaurants
260m
Victoria Nui Sam Hotel
Cavern Pagoda (Chua Hang)
0 0.5 1km
0 0.25 0.5mi
Approximate Scale
Ben Da Market
To Tri Ton, Ba Chuc & Cam Mountain

Tay An Pagoda Tay An Pagoda (Chua Tay An) is renowned for the fine carving of its hundreds of religious figures, most of which are made of wood. Aspects of the building's architecture reflect Hindu and Islamic influences. The first chief monk of Tay An Pagoda (founded in 1847) came from Giac Lam Pagoda in Saigon. Tay An was last rebuilt in 1958.

The main gate is of traditional Vietnamese design. Above the bi-level roof are figures of lions and two dragons fighting for possession of pearls, chrysanthemums, apricot trees and lotus blossoms. Nearby is a statue of Quan Am Thi Kinh, the Guardian Spirit of Mother and Child (see the boxed text 'Quan Am Thi Kinh' in the Ho Chi Minh City chapter).

In front of the pagoda are statues of a black elephant with two tusks and a white elephant with six tusks. Around the pagoda are monks' tombs. Inside are Buddha statues adorned with kitschy psychedelic disco lights.

Temple of Lady Chua Xu The Temple of Lady Chua Xu (Mieu Ba Chua Xu), founded in the 1820s, stands facing Sam Mountain not far from Tay An Pagoda. The first building here was made of bamboo and leaves; the last reconstruction took place in 1972.

According to legend, the statue of Lady Chua Xu used to stand at the summit of Sam Mountain. In the early 19th century, Siamese troops invaded the area and, impressed with the statue, decided to take it back to Thailand. But as they carried the statue down the hill, it became heavier and heavier, and they were forced to abandon it by the side of the path.

One day, villagers out cutting wood came upon the statue and decided to bring it back to their village in order to build a temple for it; but it weighed too much for them to budge. Suddenly, there appeared a girl who, possessed by a spirit, declared herself to be Lady Chua Xu. She announced that 40 virgins were to be brought and that they would be able to transport the statue down the mountainside. The 40 virgins were then summoned and carried the statue down the slope, but when they reached the plain, it became too heavy and they had to set it down. The people concluded that the site where the virgins halted had been selected by Lady Chua Xu for the construction of a temple, and it is here that the Temple of Lady Chua Xu stands to this day.

Another story relates that the wife of Thoai Ngoc Hau, builder of the Vinh Te Canal, swore to erect a temple when the canal, whose construction claimed many lives, was completed. She died before being able to carry out her oath, but Thoai Ngoc Hau implemented her plans by building the Temple of Lady Chua Xu.

Offerings of roast whole pigs are frequently made here, providing an interesting photo opportunity. The temple's most important festival is held from the 23rd to the 26th day of the fourth lunar month. During this time, pilgrims flock here, sleeping on mats in the large rooms of the two-storey guesthouse next to the temple.

Tomb of Thoai Ngoc Hau Thoai Ngoc Hau (1761–1829) was a high-ranking official who served the Nguyen lords and, later, the Nguyen Dynasty. In early 1829, Thoai Ngoc Hau ordered that a tomb be constructed for himself at the foot of Sam Mountain. The site he chose is not far from Tay An Pagoda.

The steps are made of red 'beehive' *(da ong)* stone brought from the south-eastern part of Vietnam. In the middle of the platform is the tomb of Thoai Ngoc Hau and those of his wives, Chau Thi Te and Truong Thi Miet. Nearby are several dozen other tombs where officials who served under Thoai Ngoc Hau are buried.

Cavern Pagoda The Cavern Pagoda (Chua Hang, also known as Phuoc Dien Tu) is about halfway up the western side of Sam Mountain. The lower part of the pagoda includes monks' quarters and two hexagonal tombs in which the founder of the pagoda, a female tailor named Le Thi Tho, and a former head monk, Thich Hue Thien, are buried.

The upper section consists of two parts: the main sanctuary, in which there are statues of A Di Da (the Buddha of the Past) and Thich Ca Buddha (Sakyamuni, the Historical Buddha); and the cavern. At the back of the cave behind the sanctuary building is a shrine dedicated to Quan The Am Bo Tat.

According to legend, Le Thi Tho came from Tay An Pagoda to this site half a century ago to lead a quiet, meditative life. When she arrived, she found two enormous snakes, one white and the other dark green. Le Thi Tho soon converted the snakes, who thereafter led pious lives. Upon her death, the snakes disappeared.

Places to Stay & Eat

The newly restored ***Post Office Hotel*** *(☎ 861666, fax 861600)*, also called the *Nui Sam Hotel*, is across the road from the Tay An Pagoda. It shares the building with the local post office, and you can take care of any philatelic needs in the lobby. Clean air-con doubles/quads cost US$22/27, and include breakfast at the in-house ***restaurant*** (one of the better places to eat in the area).

Victoria Nui Sam Hotel was under construction at the time of writing. We visited the site and saw several attractive stone cottages with red-tiled roofs well underway.

The hotel is located on the road leading to the summit of Sam Mountain, and is situated on a bluff with expansive views overlooking the plains into Cambodia.

BA CHUC

Close to the Cambodian border but just within Vietnam is Ba Chuc, otherwise known as the Bone Pagoda. The pagoda stands as a grisly reminder of the horrors perpetrated by the Khmer Rouge. Between 1975 and 1978, Khmer Rouge guerillas regularly crossed the border into Vietnam and slaughtered civilians. And this is to say nothing of the million or so Cambodians also killed.

Between 12 April and 30 April 1978, the Khmer Rouge killed 3157 people at Ba Chuc. Only two people are known to have survived. Many of the victims were tortured to death. The Vietnamese might have had other motives for invading Cambodia at the end of 1978, but certainly outrage at the Ba Chuc massacre was a major reason.

The two notable buildings at Ba Chuc are a temple and a 'skull' pagoda. The skull pagoda houses the skulls of the victims. This resembles Cambodia's Choeung Ek killing fields, where thousands of skulls of Khmer Rouge victims are on display. Near the skull collection is a temple that displays gruesome photos taken shortly after the massacre. The display is both fascinating and horrifying – you do need a strong stomach to visit.

To reach Ba Chuc, follow the unpaved road that runs along the canal from Chau Doc to Ha Tien. You need to turn off this main road onto Highway 3T and follow it for 4km.

RACH GIA

☎ 077 • pop 172,400

Rach Gia, the capital of Kien Giang Province, is a booming port-city on the Gulf of Thailand. The population includes significant numbers of both ethnic-Chinese and Khmers.

Fishing and agriculture have made the town reasonably prosperous. Access to the sea and the proximity of Cambodia and Thailand have also made smuggling a profitable business here. The Rach Gia area was once famous for the large feathers used to make ceremonial fans for the Imperial Court, but this is one industry that has little chance of being revived, despite economic liberalisation.

Visitors' main interest in Rach Gia is as an overnight stop on the way to Phu Quoc Island.

Information

Travel Agencies Kien Giang Tourist (Cong Ty Du Lich Kien Giang, ☎ 862081, fax 862111), at 12 Đ Ly Tu Trong, is the provincial tourism authority. It is opposite the Thanh Binh I Hotel.

Money Rach Gia is the last place you can change money before Ha Tien or Phu Quoc Island. Vietcombank (☎ 863427) is on the riverside, near the west end of Đ Hem Nguyen Trai.

Pagodas & Temples

Nguyen Trung Truc Temple This temple is dedicated to Nguyen Trung Truc, a leader of the Vietnamese resistance campaign of the 1860s against the newly arrived French. Among other exploits, he led the raid that resulted in the burning of the French warship *Espérance*. Despite repeated attempts to capture him, Nguyen Trung Truc continued to fight until 1868, when the French took his mother and a number of civilians hostage and threatened to kill them if he did not surrender. Nguyen Trung Truc turned himself in and was executed by the French in the marketplace of Rach Gia on 27 October 1868.

The first temple structure was a simple building with a thatched roof; over the years it has been enlarged and rebuilt several times. The last reconstruction took place between 1964 and 1970. In the centre of the main hall on an altar is a portrait of Nguyen Trung Truc.

Nguyen Trung Truc Temple is at 18 Đ Nguyen Cong Tru and is open from 7 am to 6 pm.

Phat Lon Pagoda This large Cambodian Hinayana Buddhist pagoda, whose name means Big Buddha, was founded about two centuries ago. Though all of the three dozen monks who live here are ethnic-Khmers, ethnic-Vietnamese also frequent the pagoda.

Inside the *vihara* (sanctuary), figures of the Thich Ca Buddha wear Cambodian- and Thai-style pointed hats. Around the exterior of the main hall are eight small altars.

The two towers near the main entrance are used to cremate the bodies of deceased monks. Near the pagoda are the tombs of about two dozen monks.

Prayers are held daily from 4 to 6 am and 5 to 7 pm. The pagoda, off Đ Quang Trung, is open from 4 am to 5 pm during the seventh, eighth and ninth lunar months (the summer season), but guests are welcome year-round.

Ong Bac De Pagoda Ong Bac De Pagoda, in the centre of town at 14 Đ Nguyen Du, was built by Rach Gia's Chinese community about a century ago. On the central altar is a statue of Ong Bac De, a reincarnation of the Jade Emperor. To the left is Ong Bon, Guardian Spirit of Happiness and Virtue; to the right is Quan Cong.

Pho Minh Pagoda A handful of Buddhist nuns live at Pho Minh Pagoda, which is on

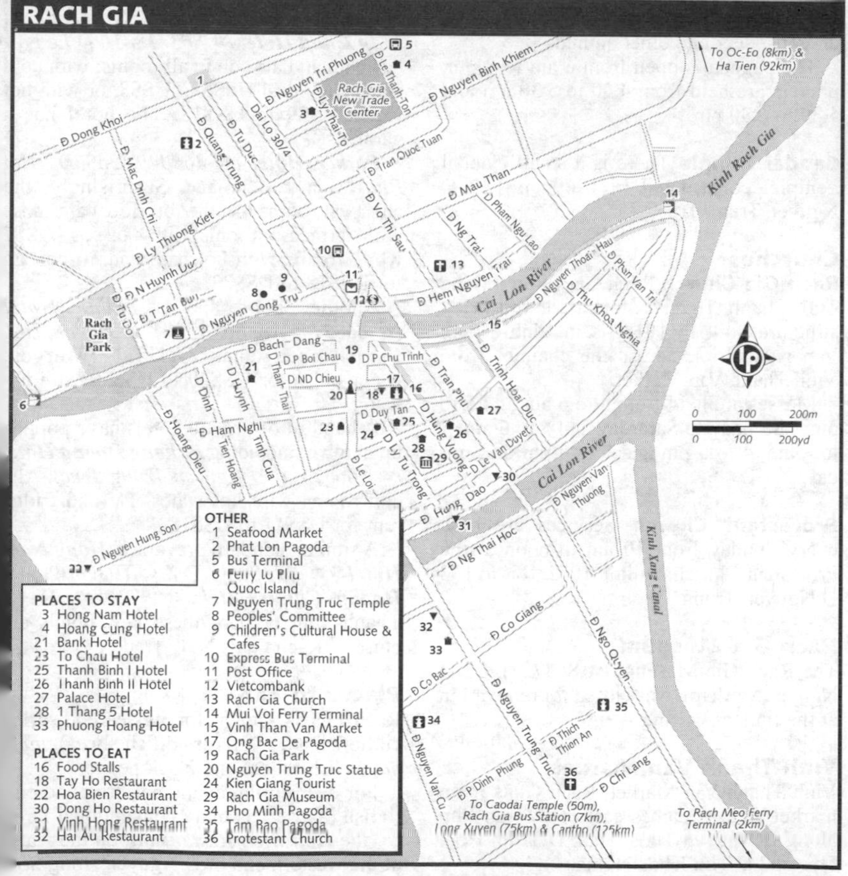

the corner of Đ Co Bac and Đ Nguyen Van Cu. This small pagoda was built in 1967 and contains a large Thai-style Thich Ca Buddha donated by a Buddhist organisation in Thailand. Nearby is a Vietnamese-style Thich Ca Buddha. The nuns live in a building behind the main hall.

The pagoda is open to visitors from 6 am to 10 pm; prayers are held daily from 3.30 to 4.30 am and 6.30 to 7.30 pm.

Tam Bao Pagoda This pagoda, which dates from the early 19th century, is near the corner of Đ Thich Thien An and Đ Ngo Quyen; it was last rebuilt in 1913. The garden contains numerous trees sculpted as dragons, deer and other animals.

The pagoda is open from 6 am to 8 pm; prayers are held from 4.30 to 5.30 am and 5.30 to 6.30 pm.

Caodai Temple There is a small Caodai Temple, constructed in 1969, at 189 Đ Nguyen Trung Truc.

Churches

Rach Gia Church Rach Gia Church (Nha Tho Chanh Toa Rach Gia), a red-brick structure built in 1918, is in Vinh Thanh Van subdistrict, across the channel from Vinh Thanh Van Market.

Masses are held from 5 to 6 am and 5 to 6 pm Monday to Saturday and 5 to 6 am, 7 to 8 am, 4 to 5 pm and 5 to 6 pm on Sunday.

Protestant Church Services are held every Sunday from 10 am to noon at the Protestant Church, built in 1972. It is at 133 Đ Nguyen Trung Truc.

Rach Gia Museum

The Rach Gia Museum (☎ 863727), 27 Đ Nguyen Van Troi, was closed for renovation at the time of writing.

Vinh Thanh Van Market

Vinh Thanh Van Market, Rach Gia's main market area, stretches east of Đ Tran Phu along Đ Nguyen Thoai Hau, Đ Trinh Hoai Duc and Đ Thu Khoa Nghia.

Places to Stay

Thanh Binh I Hotel *(☎ 863053, 11 Đ Ly Tu Trong)* is OK, though nothing to write home about. Rooms with fan cost US$4 to US$6. Each room has a cold bath/shower, but the toilet is down the hall.

Somewhat better, ***Thanh Binh II Hotel*** *(☎ 861921, 119 Đ Nguyen Hung Son)* has fan rooms with shared toilet for US$4 and US$5, or US$6 to US$8 with air-con.

1 Thang 5 Hotel *(☎ 862103, 38 Đ Nguyen Hung Son)* is named after International Workers' Day. Like the importance of the festival, the hotel has declined too and could use a renovation. It is cheap though, with air-con doubles from US$7 to US$11.

To Chau Hotel *(☎ 863718, 16 Đ Le Loi)* has bath and air-con in all rooms; with cold water they cost US$6 to US$8, or with hot water US$9 to US$18. The hotel has a garage.

Palace Hotel *(☎ 863049, 243 Đ Tran Phu)* is a good place. Surprisingly, the cheapest rooms (on the top floor) are those with terraces. Rooms with fan cost US$7 while rooms with hot bath and air-con go for US$18 to US$23.

Another good spot is ***Bank Hotel*** *(☎ 862214, fax 869877, 7 Đ Huynh Tinh Cua)*. Air-con rooms cost US$17 (with cold water only), or US$20 to US$29 with hot water.

A handful of private hotels have popped up in town, including ***Phuong Hoang Hotel*** *(☎ 866525, 6 Đ Nguyen Trung Truc)*. Air-con rooms with hot water, TV and fridge rent for US$11 to US$18.

A similar standard prevails at ***Hong Nam Hotel*** *(☎ 873090)*, Đ Ly Thai To, and ***Hoang Cung Hotel*** *(☎ 872655)*, Đ Le Thanh Ton; both of these new hotels are close to Rach Gia's New Trade Centre.

Places to Eat

Rach Gia is known for its seafood, dried cuttlefish, *ca thieu* (dried fish slices), *nuoc mam* (fish sauce) and black pepper.

For deer, turtle, cobra, eel, frog and cuttlefish (as well as more conventional fare) try the ***Hoa Bien Restaurant***, on the water at the western end of Đ Nguyen Hung Son

There is no sandy beach here, but the restaurant sets up lawn chairs for its customers to admire the view.

Tay Ho Restaurant *(16 Đ Nguyen Du)* serves good Chinese and Vietnamese food.

Dong Ho Restaurant *(124 Đ Tran Phu)* has Chinese, Vietnamese and Western dishes.

For standard Vietnamese dishes you might also try the ***Vinh Hong Restaurant***, by the Cai Lon River at the intersection of Đ Ly Tu Trong and Đ Tran Hung Dao, or the ***Hai Au Restaurant***, on the corner of Đ Nguyen Trung Truc and Đ Nguyen Van Cu.

Cheap, tasty Vietnamese food is sold from ***food stalls*** along Đ Hung Vuong between Đ Bach Dang and Đ Le Hong Phong.

Getting There & Away

Air Vietnam Airlines flies between Ho Chi Minh City and Rach Gia twice weekly; the same flight carries on to Phu Quoc Island (see Phu Quoc Island later in this chapter).

Bus Buses from Ho Chi Minh City to Rach Gia leave from the Mien Tay bus station in An Lac; the express bus takes six to seven hours. Night buses leave Rach Gia for Ho Chi Minh City between 7 and 11 pm and cost US$4.

The main Rach Gia bus station (Ben Xe Rach Soi) is 7km south of the city at 78 Đ Nguyen Trung Truc (towards Long Xuyen and Cantho). Buses link Rach Gia with Cantho, Dong Thap, Ha Tien, Long Xuyen and Ho Chi Minh City.

There is a second bus terminal (Ben Xe Ha Tien) closer to town on ĐL 30/4 that offers daily express services to Long Xuyen, Sa Dec and Ho Chi Minh City.

Yet a third bus terminal, this one by the Rach Gia New Trade Centre, is where you can catch buses to Hon Chong and Ha Tien.

Car & Motorbike Rach Gia is 92km from Ha Tien, 125km from Cantho and 248km from Ho Chi Minh City.

Boat Rach Gia Park at the western end of Đ Nguyen Cong Tru is where you catch the ferries across to Phu Quoc Island (see Phu Quoc Island later in this chapter).

Mui Voi ferry terminal (*mui* means nose and *voi* means elephant – so named because of the shape of the island) is at the northeastern end of Đ Nguyen Thoai Hau. Boats running from here make daily trips leaving at 8 am to Long Xuyen (US$0.80, 9 hours), Chau Doc and Tan Chau.

Boats for Camau leave at 5 am from the Rach Meo ferry terminal (☎ 811306), about 2km south of town at 747 Đ Ngo Quyen.

AROUND RACH GIA

Ancient City of Oc-Eo

Oc-Eo was a major trading city during the 1st to 6th centuries AD, when this area (along with the rest of southern Vietnam, much of southern Cambodia and the Malay peninsula) was ruled by the Indian-influenced empire of Funan. Much of what is known about Funan, which reached its height in the 5th century AD, comes from contemporary Chinese sources and the archaeological excavations at Oc-Eo. The excavations have uncovered evidence of significant contact between Oc-Eo and what is now Thailand, Malaysia, Indonesia, as well as Persia and even the Roman Empire.

An elaborate system of canals around Oc-Eo was used for both irrigation and transportation, prompting Chinese travellers of the time to write about 'sailing across Funan' on their way to the Malay peninsula. Most of the buildings of Oc-Eo were built on piles, and pieces of these structures indicate the high degree of refinement achieved by Funanese civilisation. Artefacts found at Oc-Eo are on display in Ho Chi Minh City at the History and Art museums, in Hanoi at the History Museum, and in Long Xuyen at the An Giang Museum.

Though there is in fact very little to see here, the remains of Oc-Eo are not far from Rach Gia. The nearest site is Cau Chau, a hill 11km inland that is littered with potsherds and shells. It's near the village of Vong The, which can be reached by 4WD, bicycle or motorbike from Hue Duc Village, a distance of about 8km. Head 3km toward Ha Tien, cross the local ferry and continue for 5km more. Oc-Eo is most accessible during the dry season. Special permission may be required to visit; for more information, contact Kien Giang Tourist. You might also inquire at the Hong Nam Hotel; ask for Mr. Duong Quang, a local English teacher who may be able to guide you to Oc-Eo.

HA TIEN

☎ 077 • pop 90,100

Ha Tien is on the Gulf of Thailand 8km from the Cambodian border. The area is known for its production of seafood, black pepper and items made from the shells of sea turtles. All around the area are lovely, towering limestone formations that give this place a very different appearance from the rest of the Mekong Delta. The rock formations support a network of caves, many of which have been turned into cave temples. Plantations of pepper trees cling to the hillsides. On a clear day, Phu Quoc Island is easily visible to the west.

Ha Tien was a province of Cambodia until 1708. However, in the face of attacks by the Thais, the Khmer-appointed governor, a Chinese immigrant named Mac Cuu, turned to the Vietnamese for protection and assistance. Mac Cuu thereafter governed this area as a fiefdom under the protection

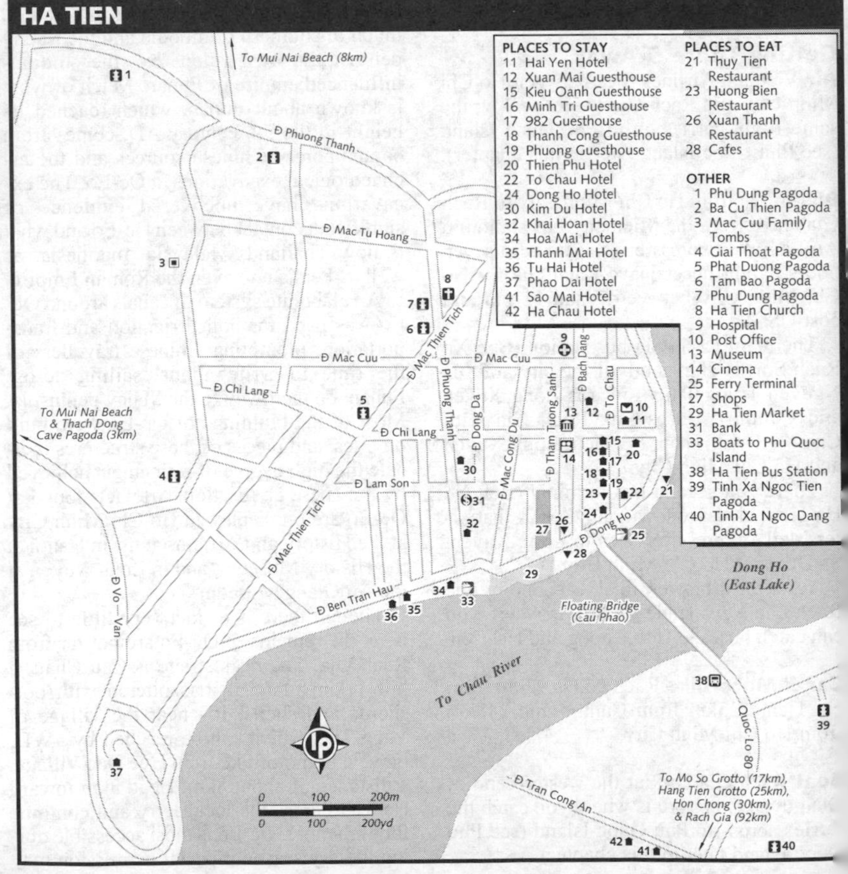

of the Nguyen Lords. He was succeeded as ruler by his son, Mac Thien Tu. During the 18th century, the area was invaded and pillaged several times by the Thais. Rach Gia and the southern tip of the Mekong Delta came under direct Nguyen rule in 1798.

During the Khmer Rouge regime, their forces repeatedly attacked Vietnamese territory and massacred thousands of civilians here. The entire populations of Ha Tien and nearby villages – tens of thousands of people – fled their homes. Also during this period, areas north of Ha Tien (along the Cambodian border) were sown with mines and booby traps, which have yet to be cleared.

Though the government has designated Ha Tien a 'frontier economic zone', the border crossing here is not yet open to tourists. Rumours are circulating, however, that it is just a matter of time.

Pagodas & Tombs

Mac Cuu Family Tombs The tombs (Lang Mac Cuu) are on a low ridge not far from town. They are known locally as Nui Lang, the Hill of the Tombs. Several dozen relatives of Mac Cuu are buried here in traditional Chinese tombs decorated with figures of dragons, phoenixes, lions and guardians.

The largest tomb is that of Mac Cuu himself; it was constructed in 1809 on the orders of Emperor Gia Long and is decorated with finely carved figures of Thanh Long (the Green Dragon) and Bach Ho (the White Tiger). The tomb of Mac Cuu's first wife is flanked by dragons and phoenixes. At the bottom of the ridge is a shrine dedicated to the Mac family.

Tam Bao Pagoda Also known as Sac Tu Tam Bao Tu, this pagoda was founded by Mac Cuu in 1730. It is now home to several Buddhist nuns. In front of the pagoda is a statue of Quan The Am Bo Tat standing on a lotus blossom in the middle of a pond. Inside the sanctuary, the largest statue on the dais is of A Di Da, the Buddha of the Past. It is made of bronze, but has been painted. Outside, the building are the tombs of 16 monks.

Near Tam Bao Pagoda is a section of the city wall dating from the early 18th century.

Warning!

Ha Tien itself is considered safe day or night; however, the rural areas north-west of town along the Cambodian border can be dangerous at night. In particular, this includes Mui Nai Beach. Khmer gangsters have slipped across the border at night on occasion to commit robberies or kidnap people for ransom.

Tam Bao Pagoda is at 328 Đ Phuong Thanh and is open from 7 am to 9 pm; prayers are held from 8 to 9 am and 2 to 3 pm. From the 15th day of the fourth lunar month to the 15th day of the seventh lunar month (roughly from May to August) prayers are held six times a day.

Phu Dung Pagoda This pagoda, also called Phu Cu Am Tu, was founded in the mid-18th century by Mac Thien Tich's wife, Nguyen Thi Xuan. It is now home to one monk.

In the middle of the main hall is a peculiar statue of nine dragons embracing a newly born Thich Ca Buddha. The most interesting statue on the main dais is a bronze Thich Ca Buddha brought from China, which is kept in a glass case. On the hillside behind the main hall are the tombs of Nguyen Thi Xuan and one of her female servants; nearby are four monks' tombs.

Behind the main hall is a small temple, Dien Ngoc Hoang, dedicated to the Taoist Jade Emperor. The figures inside are of Ngoc Hoang flanked by Nam Tao, the Taoist God of the Southern Polar Star and the God of Happiness (on the right), and Bac Dao, the Taoist God of the Northern Polar Star and the God of Longevity (on the left). The statues are made of papier-mache moulded over bamboo frames.

Phu Dung Pagoda is open from 6 am to 10 pm; prayers are held from 4 to 5 am and 7 to 8 pm. To get to Phu Dung Pagoda, turn off Đ Phuong Thanh at No 374.

Thach Dong Cave Pagoda Also known as Chua Thanh Van, this is a subterranean Buddhist temple 4km from town.

To the left of the entrance is the Stele of Hatred (Bia Cam Thu) commemorating the massacre of 130 people here by the Khmer Rouge on 14 March 1978.

Several of the chambers contain funerary tablets and altars to Ngoc Hoang, Quan The Am Bo Tat and the two Buddhist monks who founded the temples of Thach Dong Cave Pagoda. The wind here creates extraordinary sounds as it blows through the grotto's passageways. Openings in several branches of the cave afford views of nearby Cambodia.

Dong Ho

Dong Ho (*dong* means east; *ho* means lake) is in fact not a lake at all but an inlet of the sea. The 'lake' is just east of Ha Tien, and bounded to the east by a chain of granite hills known as the Ngu Ho (Five Tigers) and to the west by hills known as To Chan. Dong Ho is said to be most beautiful on nights when there is a full or almost-full moon. According to legend, it is on such nights that fairies dance here in the moonlight.

Ha Tien Market

Ha Tien has an excellent market along the To Chau River. It's well worth your while to stop here – many of the goods are imported (smuggled?) from Thailand and Cambodia, and prices are lower than in Ho Chi Minh City. Cigarette smuggling is particularly big business.

Places to Stay

Ha Tien's budget accommodation is very basic. Guesthouses charge around US$0.50 for a 'bed', or US$2 for a 'private' room (meaning you'll have a curtain to pull between you and your neighbour). These places include ***Phuong Guesthouse***, ***Thanh Cong Guesthouse*** and ***982 Guesthouse***, all on Đ To Chau.

Xuan Mai Guesthouse *(☎ 852470, 1035 Đ Bach Dang)* charges US$0.80 to sleep on a dorm mat and use the shared toilet, or US$5 for a private closet with bath. There is no air-con here.

Minh Tri Guesthouse *(☎ 852724, 22 Đ To Chau)* is a slightly better option with rooms from US$4 to US$6 (double the price if you want the air-con switched on).

Kieu Oanh Guesthouse *(☎ 852748, 20 Đ To Chau)*, next door, has a similar standard and prices.

Moving upmarket, ***Thien Phu Hotel*** *(☎ 851144, 684 Đ Chi Lang)* is a clean place. Fan rooms cost US$4 to US$6, or US$11 for a three-bed room that can sleep six.

The new ***Kim Du Hotel*** *(☎ 851929, fax 852119, 14 Đ Phuong Thanh)* is pleasant, and the in-house restaurant is good. Rates range from US$12 to US$21 for air-con rooms, including breakfast.

Another recent addition is the ***Hai Yen Hotel*** *(☎ 851580, 15 Đ To Chau)*, where the tariff is US$9 for air-con (add US$2 if you want hot water and a fridge).

Down by the riverside are two newer places, ***Thanh Mai Hotel*** and ***Tu Hai Hotel,*** both on Đ Ben Tran Hau. They look OK, but suffer from occasional gusts of stinky wind from shrimp drying on straw mats nearby. Both charge about US$5/10 for fan/air-con rooms.

The state-owned ***To Chau Hotel*** *(☎ 852148, Đ To Chau)* looks good. Air-con twins cost US$10, or US$13 for a triple room.

Dong Ho Hotel *(☎ 852141)* is another decent choice. Rooms with air-con, TV and fridge cost about US$10.

Khai Hoan Hotel *(☎ 852254, 239 Đ Phuong Thanh)* is a good place with air-con rooms for US$11.

Sao Mai Hotel *(☎ 852740)* is a nice friendly place. It's south of the floating bridge, on Đ Tran Cong An. Singles/doubles with air-con are US$9/11.

Next door is the similar ***Ha Chau Hotel*** *(☎ 852670)* with fan rooms for US$6, or rooms with air-con from US$9 to US$11.

In the far south-west of town, ***Phao Dai Hotel*** *(☎ 851849)* is a quiet place with fan rooms for US$6, or US$9 with air-con (add US$1 for TV).

Places to Eat

Ha Tien's speciality is an unusual variety of coconut that can only be found in Cambodia and this part of Vietnam. These coconuts contain no milk, but the delicate flesh is delicious. Restaurants all around the Ha Tien area serve the coconut flesh in a glass with ice and sugar. The Cambodians have long claimed that any place which has these coconuts is part of Cambodia, which served as one of the excuses for the Khmer Rouge attacks on this part of Vietnam.

Some of the best grub in Ha Tien is served at the friendly ***Xuan Thanh Restaurant***, opposite the market on the corner of Đ Ben Tran Hau and Đ Tham Tuong Sanh. This place has tasty food and the most salubrious surroundings in town.

Huong Bien Restaurant on Đ To Chau is also excellent.

Thuy Tien Restaurant has decent food, but most go for the scenic lakeside location on Đ Dong Ho.

Getting There & Away

Bus Buses from Ho Chi Minh City to Ha Tien leave from the Mien Tay bus station in An Lac; the trip takes nine to 10 hours.

Ha Tien bus station (Ben Xe Ha Tien) is on the other side of the floating toll bridge from the centre of town. Buses leave from here to An Giang Province, Cantho (5.50 am and 9.10 am), Vinh Long Province, Ho Chi Minh City (2 am) and Rach Gia (five times a day). The bus trip from Rach Gia to Ha Tien takes about five hours.

Car & Motorbike Ha Tien is 92km from Rach Gia, 95km from Chau Doc, 206km from Cantho and 338km from Ho Chi Minh City.

Boat Passenger ferries dock at the ferry terminal, which is not far from the To Chau Hotel near the floating bridge. Daily ferries depart for Chau Doc at 6 am and take around three hours. You can travel by boat all the way from Ho Chi Minh City to Ha Tien with a change of boats in Chau Doc, but it's a very long journey and the boats are anything but luxurious.

AROUND HA TIEN

There are numerous other islands off the coast between Rach Gia and the Cambodian border. Some local people make a living gathering precious *salangane*, or swifts' nests (the most important ingredient of that famous Chinese delicacy bird's-nest soup), on the islands' rocky cliffs.

Beaches

The beaches in this part of Vietnam face the Gulf of Thailand. The water is incredibly warm and calm, like a placid lake. The beaches are OK for bathing and diving, but hopeless for surfing.

Mui Nai (Stag's Head Peninsula) is 8km west of Ha Tien; it is said to resemble the head of a stag with its mouth pointing upward. On top is a lighthouse, and there are sand beaches on both sides of the peninsula. Mui Nai is accessible by road from both Ha Tien and from Thach Dong Cave Pagoda.

No Beach (Bai No), lined with coconut palms, is several kilometres west of Ha Tien near a fishing village.

Bang Beach (Bai Bang) is a long stretch of dark sand shaded by *bang* trees.

Mo So Grotto

About 17km towards Rach Gia from Ha Tien and 3km from the road, Mo So Grotto consists of three large rooms and a labyrinth of tunnels. Sadly, the local Morning Star cement factory has carted away a substantial amount of limestone and caused irreparable damage to the grotto. The cave is accessible on foot during the dry season and by small boat during the wet season. Visitors should take torches (flashlights) and a local guide.

Hang Tien Grotto

Hang Tien Grotto, 25km towards Rach Gia from Ha Tien, served as a hideout for Nguyen Anh (later Emperor Gia Long) in 1784, when he was being pursued by the Tay Son Rebels. His fighters found zinc coins buried here, a discovery which gave the cave its name, Coin Grotto. Hang Tien Grotto is accessible by boat.

Hon Giang Island

Hon Giang Island, which is about 15km from Ha Tien and can be reached by small boat, has a lovely, secluded beach.

HON CHONG

☎ 077

This small and secluded village beach resort has the most scenic stretch of coastline on the Mekong Delta mainland. It is a peaceful place (most of the year) and worth chilling out in for a few days – Hon Chong (also called Binh An) is seldom visited by foreign travellers.

The big attractions here are Chua Hang Grotto, Duong Beach and Nghe Island. Though a far cry from the stunning 3000-plus islands and grottoes of Halong Bay (see the North-East Vietnam chapter), the stone formations are indeed photogenic. Aside from three gargantuan eyesore cement factories spewing out smoke on the road from Ha Tien, the coastal drive there boasts some beautiful landscape.

Chua Hang Grotto

The grotto is entered through a Buddhist temple set against the base of a hill. The temple is called Hai Son Tu (Sea Mountain Temple). Visitors light incense and offer prayers here before entering the grotto itself, whose entrance is behind the altar. Inside is a plaster statue of Quan The Am Bo Tat. The thick stalactites are hollow and resonate like bells when tapped.

Duong Beach

This beach (also known as 'Bai Duong') runs north from Chua Hang Grotto and is named for its long-needled pine trees *(duong)*. The southern area can get busy with Vietnamese tourists (and their beloved karaoke), but otherwise the 3km stretch of coast is quite tranquil.

Although this is easily the prettiest beach in the Mekong Delta, don't expect powdery white sand. The waters around the delta contain heavy concentrations of silt (and recently, cement dust), so the beach tends to be packed hard and muddy once you're in the water. Still, the water is reasonably clear here and this is the only beach south of Ho Chi Minh City (excluding those on Phu Quoc Island) that looks appealing for swimming. The beach is known for its spectacular sunsets.

From the busy southern end of the beach (near Chua Hang Grotto), you can see Father and Son Isle (Hon Phu Tu) several hundred metres offshore; it is said to be shaped like a father embracing his son. The island, a column of stone, is perched on a 'foot' worn away by the pounding of the waves; the foot is almost fully exposed at low tide. Boats can be hired at the shore to row out for a closer look.

Nghe Island

This is the most beautiful island in the area, and is a favourite pilgrimage spot for Buddhists. The island contains a cave temple (Chua Hang) next to a large statue of Quan The Am Bo Tat, which faces the sea. The area where you'll find the cave temple and statue is called Doc Lau Chuong.

Finding a boat to the island is not too difficult, though it will be much cheaper if you can round up a group to accompany you. Inquire at the Hon Trem Guesthouse; a full-day, three-island boat trip costs around US$60, and the boat can accommodate 15 people. The boat ride to the island takes approximately one to two hours. There is also a speed boat for hire at the waterside Doi Xanh Restaurant, 4.5km from the Chua Hang Grotto back towards Ha Tien. The owner charges US$50/100 for a half/full day of island hopping. The boat can carry around 20 people.

At the time of writing, tourists were not permitted to stay on the island.

Places to Stay

A word of warning: The hotels are completely packed out when Buddhists arrive to worship 15 days before and one month after Tet. Another worship deluge occurs in March and April.

The first place you will see as you arrive in Hon Chong is the family-run ***Green House Guesthouse*** *(☎ 854369)*, perched on a knoll overlooking Duong Beach. Clean air-con rooms cost US$16 and meals can be arranged.

You could also consider staying at the state-owned ***Hon Trem Guesthouse*** *(☎ 854331, fax 862111)*, near the bend in the road, about 1km before the beach gate. It features air-con rooms in a large cottage for US$10, or in the main building for US$13. The hotel can prepare meals on request.

Phuong Thao Hotel *(☎ 854357)* is 200m beyond the Green House Guesthouse and has bungalow-style fan/air-con rooms for US$6/9.

Near the entrance gate to the Chua Hang Grotto, ***Huong Bien Guesthouse*** charges US$4 in a dorm, or US$8 for a fan double.

Binh An Hotel *(☎ 854332, fax 854338)*, 1km towards Chua Hang Grotto on the same road as the Phuong Thao Hotel, is a fine place. It's in a large quiet compound surrounded by a wall with gardens. All rooms have attached bath. The old-wing rooms are grotty, but cheap from US$6. Rooms in the new wing are much nicer and cost US$16.

The new ***My Lan Hotel*** *(☎ 759044, fax 759040)* was invested in by Overseas Vietnamese from Milan, Italy (hence its name My Lan). Fan rooms cost US$9, or US$13 with air-con.

Places to Eat

Aside from special orders prepared at your hotel, there are ***food stalls*** just by the entrance of Chua Hang Grotto. For a few dollars, you can point to one of the live chickens, which will be summarily executed and barbecued.

The ***Hong Ngoc Restaurant*** here is also recommended, and is a good place to sample delicious Ha Tien coconuts.

Getting There & Away

Chua Hang Grotto and Duong Beach are 32km towards Rach Gia from Ha Tien. The access road branches off the Rach Gia–Ha Tien highway at the small town of Ba Hon, which is just west of the cement factory at Kien Luong. Buses can drop you off at Ba Hon, from where you can hire a motorbike.

There is also direct bus service from Rach Gia to Hon Chong which takes four hours and costs US$1. It departs from the Ben Xe Ha Tien bus station on Đ 30/4 in Rach Gia at 10 am, and leaves again from Hon Chong (in front of the Huong Bien Guesthouse) to Rach Gia at 4 am.

PHU QUOC ISLAND

☎ 077 • pop 52,700

Mountainous and forested Phu Quoc Island is in the Gulf of Thailand, 45km west of Ha Tien, and 15km south of the coast of Cambodia. This tear-shaped island, which is 48km long and has an area of 1320 sq km, is ringed with some of the most beautiful beaches in Vietnam. There are fantastic views of marine life through transparent blue-green waters (though unfortunately there are no scuba diving operators on the island – as yet).

Phu Quoc is claimed by Cambodia; its Khmer name is usually rendered Ko Tral. Needless to say, the Vietnamese view it very differently, and to this end have built a substantial military base covering much of the northern end of the island. Phu Quoc is governed as a district of Kien Giang Province.

Phu Quoc Island served as a base for the French missionary Pigneau de Behaine during the 1760s and 80s. Prince Nguyen Anh, later Emperor Gia Long, was sheltered here by Behaine when he was being hunted by the Tay Son Rebels.

During the American War there was a little fighting here, but Phu Quoc Island was mainly useful to the Americans as a prison for captured VC.

Phu Quoc is not really part of the Mekong Delta, and doesn't share the delta's extraordinary ability to produce rice. The most valuable crop is black pepper, but the islanders have traditionally earned their living from the sea. Phu Quoc is also famous in Vietnam for its production of high-quality fish sauce *(nuoc mam)*.

The island is also known for Phu Quoc hunting dogs. The dogs have been a great success – with their help, the islanders have decimated most of the island's wildlife. These dogs are said to be able to pick up the scent of their master from over 1km away.

Phu Quoc has tremendous tourism potential, so far mostly unrealised. Transport difficulties, not to mention some of the best beaches being occupied by military bases, have contributed to keeping visitors away.

Rather than developing this island for tourism, the national government has been

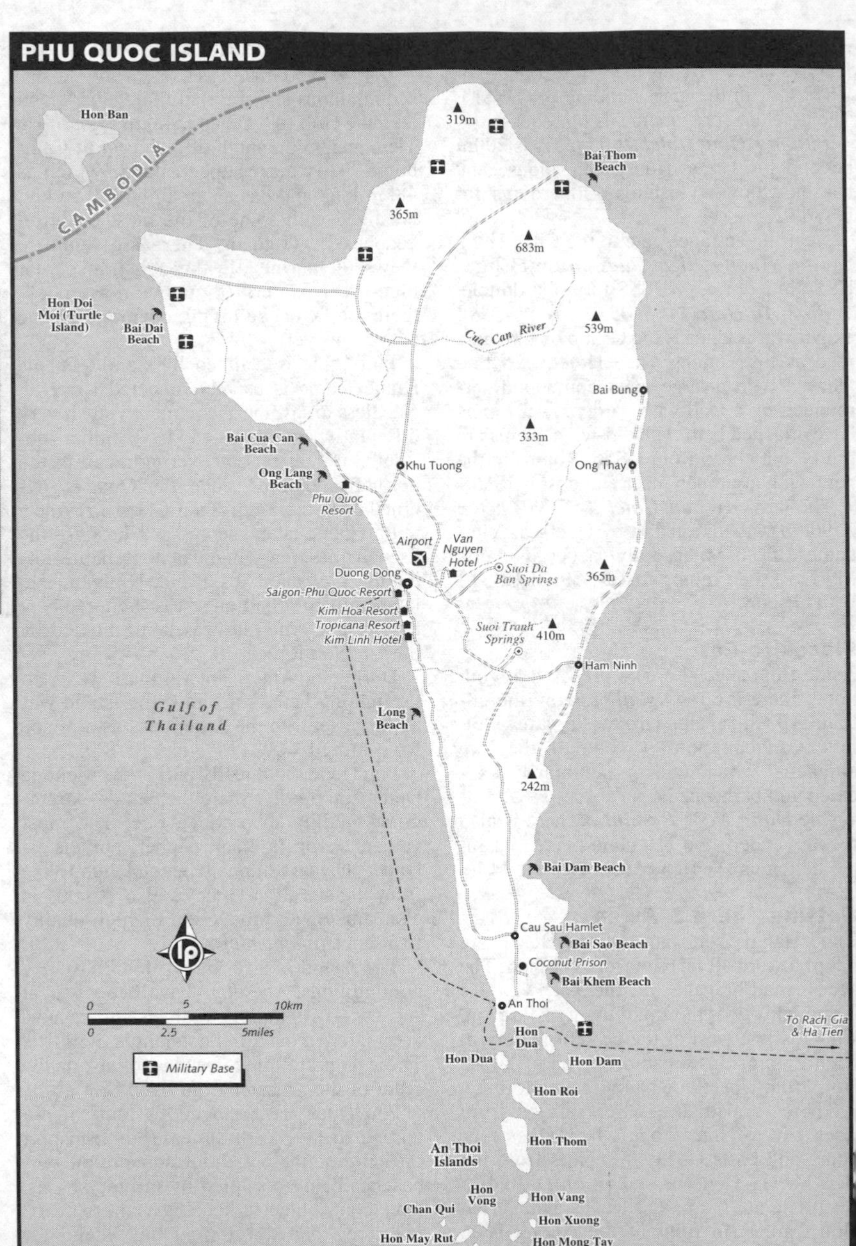
PHU QUOC ISLAND
Hon Ban
CAMBODIA
319m
Bai Thom Beach
365m
683m
Hon Doi Moi (Turtle Island)
Bai Dai Beach
Cua Can River
539m
Bai Bung
333m
Bai Cua Can Beach
Ong Lang Beach
Phu Quoc Resort
Khu Tuong
Ong Thay
Airport
Van Nguyen Hotel
Suoi Da Ban Springs
365m
Duong Dong
Saigon-Phu Quoc Resort
Kim Hoa Resort
Tropicana Resort
Kim Linh Hotel
Suoi Tranh Springs
410m
Ham Ninh
Gulf of Thailand
Long Beach
242m
Bai Dam Beach
Cau Sau Hamlet
Bai Sao Beach
Coconut Prison
Bai Khem Beach
An Thoi
0
5
10km
0
2.5
5miles
Military Base
Hon Dua
To Rach Gia & Ha Tien
Hon Dua
Hon Dam
Hon Roi
Hon Thom
An Thoi Islands
Hon Vong
Hon Vang
Chan Qui
Hon Xuong
Hon May Rut
Hon Mong Tay

contemplating a half-baked plan to turn Phu Quoc into 'another Singapore'. In other words, skyscrapers, high-tech industries and a container port are envisioned. The reasoning is that Singapore and Phu Quoc are both tropical islands and both are about the same size, so why shouldn't they have the same type of economic development? Both the Singaporeans and the World Bank have had a good laugh over this one. Less absurdly, the island could evolve into another Bali, assuming of course that no smokestack industries are introduced in pursuit of the Singapore fantasy.

Phu Quoc's rainy season is from July to November. The peak season for tourism is mid-winter, when the sky is blue and the sea is calm; however, when it's not raining, it's stinking hot (at least when the sun is up). Bring sunglasses and plenty of sunblock and be prepared to spend the afternoons at the beach or in the shade. Don't set out exploring the island unless you've got at least 2L of water in your day-pack or else you'll dehydrate.

Information

Travel Agencies Phu Quoc Tourist (☎ 846 318, fax 847125) has a sleepy office in central Duong Dong. The staff here sell pricey minibus and boat tours, but otherwise they can't do much for you that you couldn't accomplish through your hotel.

Most travellers get around the island by hired motorbike. There is only one real English-speaking motorbike guide on the island. 'Tony' was raised by a US military family and speaks a distinctive breed of Al Pacino English that could easily land him a role in the next sequel to *The Godfather*. He is easy to find (more likely he'll find you) or can be faxed on 077-846144, c/o Huynh Van Anh, if you want to prearrange something.

Money There is no place on the island to cash travellers cheques and the rate for changing dollars at the Agricultural Bank in Duong Dong is rotten. In other words, take care of all your money changing before you arrive. You can, of course, pay for almost anything with US dollars.

Duong Dong

The island's chief fishing port is Duong Dong, a town on the central west coast of the island. The airport and most of the hotels are here.

The town is not that exciting, though the markets are mildly interesting. The bridge nearby is a good vantage point to photograph the island's fishing fleet – you'll notice that the tiny harbour is anything but clean.

According to tourist brochures, the town's main attraction is Cau Castle (Dinh Cau). In fact, it's not so much a castle as a combination temple and lighthouse. It was built in 1937 to honour Thien Hau, Goddess of the Sea who protects sailors and fisherfolk. The castle is worth a quick look, and it does give you a good view of the entrance to the harbour.

Fish Sauce Factory

OK, so it's not your average sightseeing attraction, but some have enjoyed a visit to the distillery of Nuoc Mam Hung Thanh, the largest of Phu Quoc's fish sauce makers. At first glance, the giant wooden vats may make you think you've arrived for a wine tasting, but one sniff of the festering *nuoc mam* essence brings you right back to reality (it's actually not so bad after a few minutes).

Most of the sauce produced is exported to the mainland for domestic consumption, though a surprising amount finds its way abroad to kitchens in Japan, the USA, Canada and France.

The factory is a short walk from the markets in Duong Dong. There is no charge to visit, though you'd be best off taking a guide along unless you speak Vietnamese. Should you feel compelled to take a bottle of the stuff home to your loved ones as a souvenir, try the Hung Thanh retail shop, near the bridge in town.

An Thoi

The main shipping port is An Thoi at the southern tip of the island. The town is not blessed with scenic sights, though the market is worth a quick look. This is the embarkation point for Ha Tien and Rach Gia, or for day trips to the An Thoi Islands.

Beaches

Bai Dai in the far north-west and Bai Thom on the north-east coast are remote beaches and will require a motorbike ride of at least an hour over very bad roads. You can rest assured that neither beach is crowded.

Both are in military areas – the military opens these beaches to civilians on Sunday but you must leave your passport with the military receptionist while you're on the base. This is problematic since most hotels insist on taking your passport until you check out. In any event, do not try to sneak onto the beaches – make local inquiries and obey the rules.

Long Beach Long Beach (Bai Truong) is one long spectacular stretch of sand from Duong Dong southward along the west coast almost to An Thoi port (20km). The southern end of the beach is known as Tau Ru Bay (Khoe Tau Ru). The water is crystal clear and the beach is lined with coconut palms.

Long Beach is easily accessible on foot (just walk south from Duong Dong's Cau Castle), but you'll want a motorbike or bicycle to reach some of the remote stretches towards the southern end of the island. The beach around the Kim Linh Hotel is a particularly popular spot. There are a few bamboo huts where you can buy drinks, but bring water if you're planning a long hike along this beach.

Bai Khem The most beautiful white-sand beach of all is Bai Khem (Bai Kem), meaning 'cream beach'. The name is inspired by the creamy white sand, which resembles powdered chalk. The only shortcoming is that the beach lacks shade – there are no trees here.

The beach is in a cove at the south-eastern part of the island. This place is totally undeveloped because it's a military area, but civilians are permitted to enter. Turn off the main highway by the English sign saying

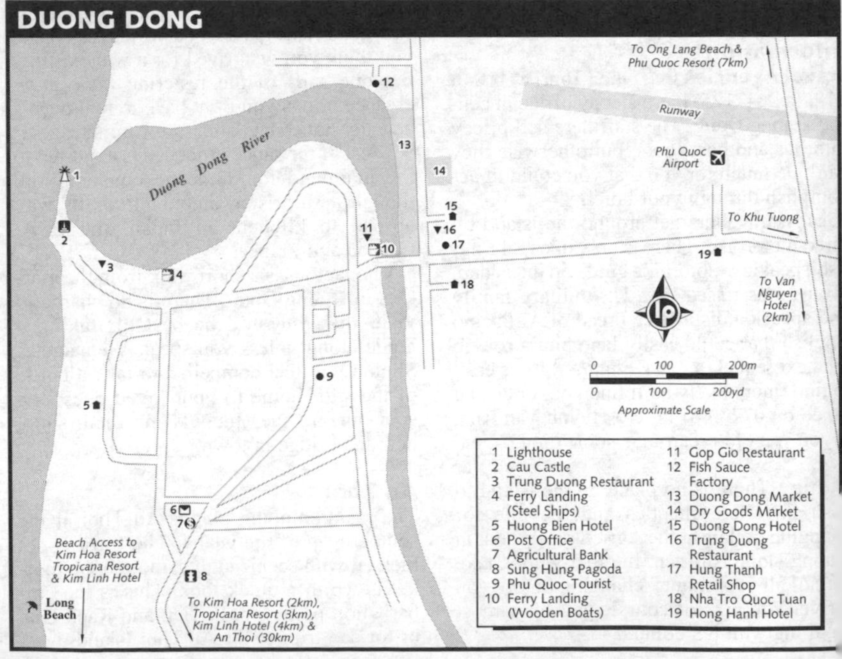

'Restricted Area – No Trespassing'. It's 28km from Duong Dong and 2km from An Thoi, so you'll almost certainly have to go there by motorbike or bicycle. You should lock the bike securely since you won't be able to watch it; however, bike theft is not a big problem in this remote spot.

Bai Sao & Bai Dam Along the south-east part of the island just north of Bai Khem are two other beaches, Bai Sao and Bai Dam.

Bai Cua Can This is the most accessible beach in the north-west. Bai Cua Can is 11km from Duong Dong, though it's a rather long dusty trip by motorbike.

Suoi Da Ban

Compared with the waterlogged Mekong Delta, Phu Quoc has very little surface moisture; however, there are several springs originating in the hills. The most accessible of these is Suoi Da Ban (Stony Surface Stream). Basically, it's a whitewater creek tumbling across some attractive large granite boulders. There are deep pools and it's pleasant enough for a swim. Bring mosquito repellent.

The stream is in the south-central part of the island. There is no admission charge, though there is a US$0.25 fee for parking a motorbike.

Forest Reserves

Phu Quoc's poor soil and lack of surface water have disappointed farmers for generations, although their grief has been the island's environmental salvation. About 90% of the island is forested, and the trees now enjoy official protection. Indeed, this is the last large stand of forest in southern Vietnam.

The forest is most dense in the mountainous northern half of the island. This area has been declared a Forest Reserve (Khu Rung Nguyen Sinh). You'll need a motorbike or mountain bike to get into the reserve. There are a few primitive dirt roads, but no real hiking trails.

An Thoi Islands

Off the southern tip of Phu Quoc are the tiny An Thoi Islands (Quan Dao An Thoi). These 15 islands and islets can be visited by chartered boat, and it's a fine area for sightseeing, fishing, swimming and snorkelling. Hon Thom (Pineapple Island) is about 3km in length and is the largest island in the group. Other islands here include Hon Dua (Coconut Island), Hon Roi (Lamp Island), Hon Vang (Echo Island), Hon May Rut (Cold Cloud Island), Hon Dam (Shadow Island), Chan Qui (Yellow Tortoise) and Hon Mong Tay (Short Gun Island).

Most boats depart from An Thoi on Phu Quoc, but you can make arrangements through hotels in Duong Dong. The Tropicana Resort has a large boat for charter that can make the trip directly from Long Beach. The Kim Linh also has two boats for day hire, one that can carry eight to 10 passengers (US$32), and a larger one that can carry 15 to 20 people (US$64).

Coconut Prison

Being an island and a marginal economic backwater of Vietnam, Phu Quoc was useful to the French colonial administration chiefly as a prison. The Americans took over where the French left off, and Phu Quoc housed about 40,000 VC prisoners.

The island's main penal colony was known as the Coconut Prison (Nha Lao Cay Dua) and is near An Thoi town. Though it's considered an historic site and plans are under way to open a museum here, it's still used as a prison. Not too surprisingly, few visitors come to check it out.

Places to Stay

Long Beach The aging ***Kim Linh Hotel*** *(☎ 846611, fax 846144)* remains the favourite of backpackers. It's often full, but the management tries to accommodate any overflow by renting out tents on the beach or allowing people to sleep in hammocks in the restaurant after it closes. Rooms cost US$10 to US$12 with fan, or US$15 with air-con.

A few hundred metres north is the newer ***Tropicana Resort*** *(☎ 847127, fax 847128)*. There are bungalows here with rooms renting from US$15 to US$30. Credit cards are accepted, and rates include breakfast and airport pick-up. There is an outdoor veranda-restaurant to watch the sunset from. Staff speak French and English.

A short walk from the Tropicana, the friendly ***Kim Hoa Resort*** *(☎ 847039, fax 846144)* has bungalows (US$15) and rooms (US$9 to US$13) near the beach. Here too there is a pleasant terrace restaurant. As a footnote, the proprietor here also owns a local fish sauce factory and can offer a tour to interested parties.

The snazzy ***Saigon-Phu Quoc Resort*** *(☎ 846510, fax 847163)* rents rooms in villa-type houses for US$27 (in a four-bedroom villa), or US$30 (in villas with two rooms). The rooms are attractive, and have a good vantage point. There is a swimming pool and a large restaurant on the property.

The government-run ***Huong Bien Hotel*** *(☎ 846113)* is a large, spiffy place on the west side of Duong Dong. It's right on Long Beach, but unfortunately not the nicer part. The hotel's name means 'fragrant sea', probably a reference to the sewerage discharged from the nearby Duong Dong fishing harbour. The rates range from US$10 to US$20.

Ong Lang Beach Ong Lang Beach, 7km north of Duong Dong near the hamlet of Ong Lang, is rockier and less beautiful than Long Beach, but is unquestionably less crowded and quieter.

The lovely ***Phu Quoc Resort*** *(☎ 091-91-9891, fax 846144)* has 10 wooden bungalows set in a vast open garden setting under the shade of cashew nut, palm and mango trees. The staff are friendly, and the restaurant is cosy. Rooms cost from US$10 to US$18, depending on the size. The resort is also known as Thang Loi (or Victory), as well as Ong Lang (named for the beach).

Duong Dong Most travellers prefer to put up at the beachside, though there are several options in the town if you're not bent on seafront property.

Directly across from the airport, ***Hong Hanh Hotel*** *(☎ 847187)* has clean double rooms for US$7/13 with fan/air-con.

Duong Dong Hotel *(☎ 846106)* is close to Duong Dong Market. The rooms are dark boxes, but the management is friendly. Doubles (shared bath only) cost US$6.

Slightly better is the nearby ***Nha Tro Quoc Tuan*** *(☎ 847552)*, which charges US$3 a room or US$5.50 with a private toilet.

Further away from the beach is the friendly ***Van Nguyen Hotel*** *(☎ 847133, fax 846229)*, a quiet place with gigantic rooms (all with bathtubs) and balconies overlooking the Duong Dong River. Fan rooms cost US$9, and air-con raises the price to US$15.

An Thoi Although few travellers care to stay in An Thoi township, it's worth considering if you arrive late on the ferry or will be taking the ferry early next morning. The only place in town is the ***Thanh Dat Guesthouse*** *(☎ 844022)*, which is also called *Nha Khach Phuong Tham*. Rooms cost US$8, and there's a dorm for US$2 per person.

Places to Eat

For atmosphere and fine food, check out the terrace restaurants at the ***Tropicana Resort*** or ***Kim Hoa Resort***.

For something a bit more local (and loud) try the outdoor ***beachside restaurants*** near the Kim Linh Hotel.

Near the ferry landing in Duong Dong, ***Gop Gio*** is a casual eatery that wins hands down for the freshest (and cheapest) seafood in town.

Another place to consider is the ***Trung Duong Restaurant***, across the river. There is a government-owned restaurant by the same name next to Cau Castle, but it's not very good.

There are heaps of cheap ***food stalls*** all around the market area in Duong Dong.

Getting There & Away

Air Vietnam Airlines has four flights weekly between Ho Chi Minh City and Duong Dong, Phu Quoc's main town. Some flights make a stop en route at Rach Gia, on the mainland.

A popular round trip between Ho Chi Minh City and Phu Quoc is overlanding through the Mekong Delta, taking a ferry to the island (or a flight for US$35) from Rach Gia, and when you're finally tanned and rested, taking the short one hour flight (US$53) back to Ho Chi Minh City.

Boat All passenger ferries departing and arriving at Phu Quoc use the port of An Thoi on the southern tip of the island.

There are ferries (☎ 863242) every morning between Rach Gia and Phu Quoc, which is a 140km trip. Departures are between 8 and 9 am, but vary somewhat due to the tides and passenger load. In any case, it's best to be there on the early side, not only to be assured passage, but to stake out a place to sit or lie down – avoid the cosy-looking platform over the engine unless you fancy being cooked! Stock up on snacks and water at the docks.

None in the fleet of boats (three vintage steel vessels and five more made of the wooden fishing boat variety) are very comfortable. They are usually packed with too many passengers (who string hammocks across every possible nook and cranny) and cargo (including noisy fighting cocks and other exotic animals). Although we haven't heard of any mishaps, concerned parties might consider flying. Boats cannot dock at Rach Gia when the tide is low – passengers and cargo have to be ferried offshore in a small shuttle boat.

The fare is US$4.25 and the ride to An Thoi takes about eight hours. Most travellers jump off here and catch a motorbike to Duong Dong. However, if you're not in a rush to reach your hotel by sundown, it's possible pay an extra US$1 (when you buy your ticket) and stay on board right up to Duong Dong. This takes another 1½ hours, plus about an hour waiting while the ferry unloads cargo in An Thoi, but you're likely to appreciate a moonlit cruise up the coast.

There are also on-again off-again boats to/from Ha Tien. When they're on, they depart Ha Tien at 9 am and the fare is US$3.

Getting Around

To/From the Airport Phu Quoc's airport is almost in central Duong Dong. Unless your luggage is really heavy, you can easily walk the few hundred metres to the centre of town, and if you're heading for one of the hotels on Long Beach, just walk down the beach from the Huong Bien Hotel.

The motorbike drivers at the airport will charge you about US$1 to most hotels, but are notorious for trying to cart people off to where they can collect a commission. If you know where you want to go, tell them you've already got a reservation.

Bus There is a skeletal bus service between An Thoi and Duong Dong. Buses run perhaps once every hour or two. There is a bus waiting for the ferry at An Thoi to take passengers to Duong Dong; the fare is US$0.80.

Motorbike You'll hardly have to look for the motorbike taxis – they'll be looking for you. Some polite bargaining may be necessary. For most short runs within the town itself, US$0.50 should be sufficient. Otherwise, figure on around US$0.80 for about 5km. From Duong Dong to An Thoi should cost you about US$2.

Motorbike rentals are available for US$10 per day. Add about another US$5 if you want a driver. This should be sufficient to get you anywhere on the island. If interested, just ask at your hotel.

There are no paved roads on the island, and after a day of motorbike riding you can expect to be covered from head to toe with dust.

Bicycle If you can ride a bicycle in the tropical heat over these dusty, bumpy roads, more power to you. Bicycle rentals are available through most hotels for about US$1 per day.

Language

The Vietnamese language (Kinh) is a fusion of Mon-Khmer, Tai and Chinese elements. Vietnamese derived a significant percentage of its basic words from the non-tonal Mon-Khmer languages. From the Tai languages, it adopted certain grammatical elements and tonality. Chinese gave Vietnamese most of its philosophical, literary, technical and governmental vocabulary, as well as its traditional writing system.

From around 1980 to about 1987, anyone caught studying English was liable to be arrested. This was part of a general crackdown against people wanting to flee to the West. That attitude has changed and today the study of English is being pursued with a passion. The most widely spoken foreign languages in Vietnam are Chinese (Cantonese and Mandarin), English and French, more or less in that order. People in their 50s and older (who grew up during the colonial period) are much more likely to understand some French than southerners of the successive generation, for whom English was indispensable for professional and commercial contacts with the Americans. Some southern Vietnamese men – former combat interpreters – speak a quaint form of English peppered with all sorts of charming southern-American expressions such as 'y'all come back' and 'it ain't worth didley-squat', pronounced with a perceptible drawl. Apparently, they worked with Americans from the deep south, carefully studied their pronunciation and diligently learned every nuance.

Many of the Vietnamese who speak English – especially former South Vietnamese soldiers and officials – learned it while working with the Americans during the war. After reunification, almost all of them spent periods of time ranging from a few months to 15 years in 're-education camps'. Many of these former South Vietnamese soldiers and officials will be delighted to renew contact with Americans, with whose compatriots they spent so much time, often in

Alexandre de Rhodes

One of the most illustrious of the early missionaries was the brilliant French Jesuit scholar Alexandre de Rhodes (1591–1660). De Rhodes first preached in Vietnamese only six months after arriving in the country in 1627, and he is most recognised for his work in devising *quoc ngu*, the Latin-based phonetic alphabet in which Vietnamese is written to this day. By replacing Chinese characters with quoc ngu, de Rhodes facilitated the propagation of the gospel to a wide audience.

Over the course of his long career, de Rhodes flitted back and forth between Hanoi, Macau, Rome and Paris, seeking support and funding for his missionary activities and battling both Portuguese colonial opposition and the intractable Vatican bureaucracy. In 1645, he was sentenced to death for illegally entering Vietnam to proselytise, but was expelled instead; two of the priests with him were beheaded.

For his contributions, Alexandre de Rhodes gained the highest respect from the Vietnamese (in the south, anyway), who called him *cha caả* (father). A memorial statue of de Rhodes stands in central Saigon.

very difficult circumstances, half a lifetime ago. Former long-term prisoners often have friends and acquaintances all over the country (you meet an awful lot of people in 10 or more years), constituting an 'old-boys' network' of sorts.

These days, almost everyone has a desire to learn English. If you're looking to make contacts with English students, the best place is at the basic food-stalls in university areas. But at times you might find yourself looking to avoid such contacts, as one foreigner commented:

> At a sightseeing spot I was approached by a group studying English in evening classes. They go in their spare time to tourist areas hoping to get a chance to talk with foreigners. Sometimes it gets a bit tiresome to cope with enthusiastic students with a very limited vocabulary, but I believe it is a must to be polite and never to be arrogant or rude. I observed that foreigners are often disrespectful towards Vietnamese, and that really annoyed me. Often the locals told me that foreigners are reluctant, evasive and also insulting when approached by Vietnamese students. I tried to explain to my counterparts that some travellers might be afraid when approached and surrounded by a group of strangers. I explained to them the paranoia caused by crime in the West, which they found surprising – they simply weren't aware of the problems of Western societies. When I told them openly of the negative aspects of my country, they immediately opened up to me too, telling off-the-record facts. Silly small talk is not what they are interested in, only the language barrier reduces conversations to that level. Better be prepared for questions about capitalistic societies: economics, law, the parliamentary system and so on.

Spoken Chinese (both Cantonese and Mandarin) is making a definite comeback after years of being supressed. The large number of free-spending tourists and investors from Taiwan and Hong Kong provides the chief motivation for studying Chinese. In addition, cross-border trade with mainland China has been increasing rapidly and those who can speak Chinese are well positioned to profit from it.

After reunification, the teaching of Russian was stressed all over the country. With the collapse of the USSR in 1991, all interest in studying Russian has ground to a screeching halt. Most Vietnamese who bothered to learn the language have either forgotten it or are in the process of forgetting it now.

Written Vietnamese

For centuries, the Vietnamese language was written in standard Chinese characters *(chu nho)*. Around the 13th century, the Vietnamese devised their own system of writing *(chu nom* or just *nom)*, which was created by combining Chinese characters or using them for their phonetic significance only. Both writing systems were used simultaneously until the 20th century – official business and scholarship was conducted in chu nho, while chu nom was used for popular literature. The Latin-based *quoc ngu* script, widely used since WWI, was developed in the 17th century by Alexandre de Rhodes (see the aside earlier in this chapter). The use of quoc ngu served to undermine the position of mandarin officials, whose power was based on traditional scholarship written in chu nho and chu nom, scripts largely inaccessible to the masses.

The Vietnamese treat every syllable as an independent word, so 'Saigon' is spelt 'Sai Gon' and 'Vietnam' is written as 'Viet Nam'. Foreigners aren't too comfortable with this system – we prefer to read 'London' rather than 'Lon Don'. This leads to the notion that Vietnamese is a 'monosyllabic language', where every syllable represents an independent word. This idea appears to be a hangover from the Chinese writing system, where every syllable is represented by an independent character and each character is treated as a meaningful word. In reality, Vietnamese appears to be polysyllabic, like English. However, writing systems do influence people's perceptions of their own language, so the Vietnamese themselves will insist that their language is monosyllabic – it's a debate probably not worth pursuing.

Pronunciation

Most of the names of the letters of the quoc ngu alphabet are pronounced like the letters of the French alphabet. Dictionaries are alphabetised as in English except that each vowel/tone combination is treated as a different letter. The consonants of the Romanised Vietnamese alphabet are pronounced more or less as they are in English with a few exceptions, and Vietnamese makes no use of the Roman letters 'f', 'j', 'w' and 'z'.

c	as an unaspirated 'k'
đ	(with crossbar) a hard 'd' as in 'do'
d	(without crossbar) as the 'z' in 'zoo' (north); as the 'y' in 'yes' (south)
gi-	as a 'z' (north); as 'y' (south)
kh-	as the 'ch' in German *buch*
ng-	as the '-nga-' sound in 'long ago'
nh-	as the 'ni' in 'onion'
ph-	as the 'f' in 'far'
r	as 'z' (north); as 'r' (south)
s	as 's' (north); as 'sh' (south)
tr-	as 'ch' (north); as 'tr' (south)
th-	a strongly aspirated 't'
x	like an 's'
-ch	like a 'k'
-ng	as the 'ng' in 'long' but with the lips closed
-nh	as the 'ng' in 'sing'

Tones

The hardest part of studying Vietnamese for westerners is learning to differentiate between the tones. There are six tones in spoken Vietnamese. Thus, every syllable in Vietnamese can be pronounced six different ways. For example, depending on the tones, the word *ma* can be read to mean 'phantom', 'but', 'mother', 'rice seedling', 'tomb' or 'horse'.

The six tones of spoken Vietnamese are indicated with five diacritical marks in written form (the first tone is left unmarked). These should not be confused with the four other diacritical marks used to indicate special consonants, such as the crossbar in **đ**.

The following examples show the six different tone representations:

Tone Name	Example	
dấu ngang	*ma*	'ghost'
dấu sắc	*má*	'mother'
dấu huyền	*mà*	'which'
dấu hỏi	*mả*	'tomb'
dấu ngã	*mã*	'horse'
dấu nặng	*mạ*	'rice seedling'

A visual representation looks something like this:

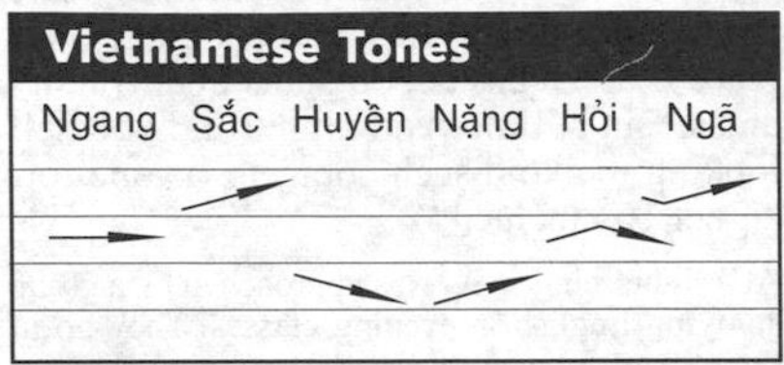

Grammar

Vietnamese grammar is fairly straightforward, with a wide variety of possible sentence structures. Nouns have no masculine/feminine or plural forms and verbs have only one form regardless of gender, person or tense. Instead, tool words and classifiers are used to show a word's relationship to its neighbours. For example, in the expression *con mèo (của) tôi* (my cat) *con* is the classifier, *mèo* is the noun, *của* means 'belong to' (and can be omitted), and *tôi* is the possessive adjective 'my'.

Questions are asked in the negative, as with *n'est-ce pas?* in French. When the Vietnamese ask 'Is it OK?' they say 'It is OK, is it not?'. The answer 'no' means 'Not OK it is not,' which is the double-negative form of 'Yes, it is OK'. The answer 'yes', on the other hand, means 'Yes, it is not OK' or as we would say in English 'No, it is not OK'. The result is that when negative questions ('It's not OK, is it?') are posed to Vietnamese, great confusion often ensues.

Proper Names

Most Vietnamese names consist of a family name, a middle name and a given name, in that order. Thus, if Henry David Thoreau had been Vietnamese, he would have been named Thoreau David Henry and would have been addressed as Mr Henry – people are called by their given name, but to do this without using the title Mr, Mrs or Mis is considered as expressing either great intimacy or arrogance of the sort a superior would use with his or her inferior.

In Vietnamese, Mr is *Ong* if the man is of your grandparents' generation, *Bac* if he is of your parents' age, *Chu* if he is younger than your parents and *Anh* if he is in his teens or early 20s. Mrs is *Ba* if the woman is of your grandparents' age and *Bac* if she is of your parents' generation or younger. Miss is *Chi* or *Em* unless the woman is very young, in which case *Co* might be more appropriate. Other titles of respect are *Thay* (Buddhist monk), *Ba* (Buddhist nun), *Cha* (Catholic priest) and *Co* (Catholic nun).

There are 300 or so family names in use in Vietnam, the most common of which is Nguyen (which is pronounced something like 'nwyen'). About half of all Vietnamese have the surname Nguyen! When women marry, they usually (but not always) take their husband's family name. The middle name may be purely ornamental, may indicate the sex of its bearer or may be used by all the male members of a given family. A person's given name is carefully chosen to form a harmonious and meaningful ensemble with their family and middle names and with the names of other family members.

For a more comprehensive guide to the language, get a copy of Lonely Planet's *Vietnamese phrasebook*. The following list of words and phrases will help get you started. Some variation exists between the Vietnamese of the north and the south – this is indicated by (N) and (S) respectively.

Pronouns

I	*tôi*
you (to an older man)	*(các) ông*
you (to an older woman)	*(các) bà*
you (to a man your own age)	*(các) anh*
you (to a woman your own age)	*(các) chi*
he	*cậu ấy/anh ấy* (N) *cậu đó/anh đó* (S)
she	*chị ấy/cô ấy* (N) *chị đó/anh đó* (S)
we	*chúng tôi*
they	*họ*

Greetings & Civilities

Hello.	*Xin chào.*
How are you?	*Có khoẻ không?*
Fine, thank you.	*Khoẻ, cám ưn.*
Good night.	*Chúc ngủ ngon.*
Excuse me. (often used before questions)	*Xin lỗi.*
Thank you.	*Cám ưn.*
Thank you very much.	*Cám ưn rất nhiều.*
Yes.	*Vâng.* (N) *Dạ.* (S)
No.	*Không.*

Useful Words & Phrases

change money	*đổi tiền*
come	*đến*
give	*cho*
fast	*nhanh* (N) *mau* (S)
slow	*chậm*
man	*nam*
woman	*nữ*
understand	*hiểu*
I don't understand.	*Tôi không hiểu.*
I need ...	*Tôi cần ...*

Small Talk

What's your name?	*Tên là gì?*
My name is ...	*Tên tôi là ...*
I like ...	*Tôi thích ...*
I don't like ...	*Tôi không thích*
I want ...	*Tôi muốn ...*
I don't want ...	*Tôi không muốn ...*

Getting Around

What time does the first bus depart?	*Chuyến xe buýt sớm nhất chạy lúc mấy giờ?*
What time does the last bus depart?	*Chuyến xe buýt cuối cùng sẽ chạy lúc mấy giờ?*
How many kilometres to ...?	*Cách xa bao nhiêu ki-lô-mét ...?*
How long does the journey take?	*Chuyến đi sẽ mất bao lâu?*
I want to go to ...	*Tôi muốn đi ...*

What time does it arrive? *Mấy giờ đến?*
Go. *Đi.*

hire a car *thuê xe hơi* (N) *muớn xe hơi* (S)
bus *xe buýt*
bus station *bến xe*
cyclo (pedicab) *xe xích lô*
map *bản đồ*
railway station *ga xe lửa*
receipt *biên lai*
sleeping berth *giường ngủ*
timetable *thời biểu*
train *xe lửa*

Around Town

office *văn phòng*
post office *bưu điện*
restaurant *nhà hàng*
telephone *điện thoại*
tourism *du lịch*

boulevard *đại lộ*
bridge *cầu*
highway *xa lộ*
island *đảo*
mountain *núi*
National Highway 1 *Quốc Lộ 1*
river *sông*
square (in a city) *công viên*
street *đường/phố*

north *bắc*
south *nam*
east *đông*
west *tây*

Accommodation

hotel *khách sạn*
guesthouse *nhà khách*

Where is there a (cheap) hotel? *Ở đâu có khách sạn (rẻ tiền)?*
How much does a room cost? *Giá một phòng là bao nhiêu?*
I'd like a cheap room. *Tôi thích một phòng loại rẻ.*
I need to leave at (five) o'clock tomorrow morning. *Tôi phải đi lúc (năm) giờ sáng mai.*

air-conditioning *máy lạnh*
bathroom *phòng tắm*
blanket *mền*
fan *quạt máy*
hot water *nước nóng*
laundry *giặt ủi*
mosquito net *mùng*
reception *tiếp tân*
room *phòng*
room key *chìa khóa phòng*
1st-class room *phòng loại 1*
2nd-class room *phòng loại 2*
sheet *ra trãi giường*
toilet *nhà vệ sinh*
toilet paper *giấy vệ sinh*
towel *khăn tắm*

Shopping

I'd like to buy ... *Tôi muốn mua ...*
How much is this? *Cái này giá bao nhiêu?*
I want to pay in dong. *Tôi muốn trả bằng tiền Việt Nam.*

buy *mua*
sell *bán*
cheap *rẻ tiền*
expensive *đắt tiền* (N) *mắc tiền* (S)
very expensive *rất đắt* (N) *mắc qua* (S)
market *chợ*
mosquito coils *hương đốt chống muỗi* (N) *nhang chống muỗi* (S)
insect repellent *thuốc chống muỗi*
sanitary pads *băng vệ sinh*

Time, Dates & Numbers

evening *chiều*
now *bây giờ*
today *hôm nay*
tomorrow *ngày mai*

Monday *Thứ hai*
Tuesday *Thứ ba*
Wednesday *Thứ tư*
Thursday *Thứ năm*
Friday *Thứ sáu*
Saturday *Thứ bảy*
Sunday *Chủ nhật*

Emergencies

Help!	*Cứu tôi với!*
I'm sick.	*Tôi bị đau*
Please call a doctor.	*Làm ơn gọi bác sĩ.*
Please take me to the hospital.	*Làm ơn đưa tôi bệnh viện.*
Thief!	*Cướp, cắp!*
Pickpocket!	*Móc túi!*
police	*công an*
immigration police station	*phòng quản lý người nước ngoài*

1	*một*
2	*hai*
3	*ba*
4	*bốn*
5	*năm*
6	*sáu*
7	*bảy*
8	*tám*
9	*chín*
10	*mười*
11	*mười một*
19	*mười chín*
20	*hai mươi*
21	*hai mươi mốt*
22	*hai mươi hai*
30	*ba mươi*
90	*chín mươi*
100	*một trăm*
200	*hai trăm*
900	*chín trăm*
1000	*một ngàn*
10,000	*mười ngàn*
one million	*một triệu*
two million	*hai triệu*
first	*thứ nhất*
second	*thứ hai*

Health

dentist	*nha sĩ*
doctor	*bác sĩ*
hospital	*bệnh viện*
pharmacy	*nhà thuốc tây*
backache	*đau lưng*
diarrhoea	*tiêu chảy* (N) *ỉa chảy* (S)
dizziness	*chóng mặt*
fever	*cảm/cúm*
headache	*nhức đầu*
malaria	*sốt rét*
stomachache	*đau bụng*
toothache	*nhức răng*
vomiting	*ói/mửa*

FOOD

Breakfast

pancake	*bánh xèo ngọt*
banana pancake	*bánh chuối*
pineapple pancake	*bánh dứa* (N) *bánh khóm* (S)
papaya pancake	*bánh đu đủ*
orange pancake	*bánh cam*
plain pancake	*bánh không nhân*
bread with ...	*bánh mì ...*
omelette	*trứng rán* (N) *trứng chiên* (S)
fried eggs	*trứng ốp la*
butter	*bơ*
butter & jam	*bơ mứt*
jam	*mứt*
cheese	*phomát* (N) *phomai* (S)
butter & cheese	*bơ phomát*
butter & honey	*bơ mật ong*
combination sandwich	*săn huýt*

Lunch & Dinner

noodles & rice noodles	*mì, hủ tíu*
beef noodle soup	*mì bò/phở bò* (N) *hủ tíu bò* (S)
chicken noodle soup	*mì gà/phở gà* (N) *hủ tíu gà* (S)
vegetarian noodle soup	*mì rau/mì chay*
duck, bamboo shoot noodle soup	*bún măng*
potatoes	*khoai tây*
french fries	*khoai rán* (N) *khoai chiên* (S)
fried potato & tomato	*khoai xào cà chua*
fried potato & butter	*khoai chiên bơ*

fried dishes	*các món xào*
fried noodle with chicken	*mì xào gà/hủ tíu xào gà*
fried noodle with beef	*mì xào bò/hủ tíu xào bò*
mixed fried noodle	*mì xào thập cẩm*
chicken	*gà*
roasted chicken	*gà quay/gà rô-ti*
chicken salad	*gà xeù phay*
fried chicken in mushroom sauce	*gà sốt nấm*
batter fried chicken	*gà tẩm bột rán/chiên*
fried chicken with lemon sauce	*gà rán/chiên sốt chanh*
curried chicken	*gà cà-ri*
pork	*lợn/heo*
skewered, grilled pork	*chả lợn xiên nướng/ chả heo nướng*
sweet & sour fried pork	*lợn xào chua ngọt/ heo xào chua ngọt*
roasted pork	*thịt lợn quay* (N) *heo quay* (S)
grilled pork	*thịt lợn nướng xả/ heo nướng xả*
beef	*thịt bò*
beefsteak	*bít tết*
skewered, grilled beef	*bò xiên nướng*
spicy beef	*bò xào sả ớt*
fried beef with pineapple	*bò xào dứa* (N) *khóm* (S)
fried beef with garlic	*bò xào tỏi*
grilled beef with ginger	*bò nướng gừng*
rare beef with vinegar	*bò nhúng giấm*
hot pot (hot & sour soup)	*lẩu*
beef hot pot	*lẩu bò*
eel hot pot	*lẩu lươn*
fish hot pot	*lẩu cá*
combination hot pot	*lẩu thập cẩm*
spring roll	*nem* (N) *chả giò* (S)
meat spring rolls	*nem thịt* (N) *chả giò* (S)
vegetarian spring rolls	*nem rau* (N) *chả giò chay* (S)
sour spring rolls	*nem chua*
pigeon	*chim bồ câu*
roasted pigeon	*bồ câu quay*
fried pigeon in mushroom sauce	*bồ câu xào nấm sốt*
soup	*súp*
chicken soup	*súp gà*
eel soup	*súp lươn*
combination soup	*súp thập cẩm*
maize soup	*súp ngô* (N) *súp bắp* (S)
vegetarian soup	*súp rau*
fish	*cá*
grilled fish with sugarcane	*chả cá bao mía*
fried fish in tomato sauce	*cá rán/chiên sốt cà*
sweet & sour fried fish	*cá sốt chua ngọt*
fried fish with lemon	*cá rán/chiên chanh*
fried fish with mushrooms	*cá xào hành nấm rơm*
steamed fish with ginger	*cá hấp gừng*
boiled fish	*cá luộc*
grilled fish	*cá nướng*
steamed fish in beer	*cá hấp bia*
shrimp/prawns	*tôm*
sweet & sour fried shrimp	*tôm xào chua ngọt*
fried shrimp with mushrooms	*tôm xào nấm*
grilled shrimp with sugarcane	*tôm bao mía* (N) *chạo tôm* (S)
batter fried shrimp	*tôm tẩm bột/ tôm hỏa tiễn*
steamed shrimp in beer	*tôm hấp bia*
crab	*cua*
salted fried crab	*cua rang muối*
crab with chopped meat	*cua nhồi thịt*
steamed crab in beer	*cua hấp bia*

squid	*mực*
fried squid	*mực chiên*
fried squid with mushrooms	*mực xào nấm*
fried squid with pineapple	*mực xào dứa* (N) *mực xào khóm* (S)
squid in sweet & sour sauce	*mực xào chua ngọt*
eel	*lươn*
fried eel with chopped meat	*lươn cuốn thịt rán/chiên*
simmered eel	*lươn om/um* (N/S)
fried eel with mushrooms	*lươn xào nấm*
snail	*ốc*
spicy snail	*ốc xào sả ớt*
fried snail with pineapple	*ốc xào dứa* (N) *ốc xào khóm* (S)
fried snail with tofu & bananas	*ốc xào đậu phu (đậu hủ) chuối xanh*
vegetarian	*các món chay*
I'm a vegetarian.	*Tôi là người ăn lạt.* (N) *Tôi là người ăn chay.* (S)
fried noodles with vegetable	*mì/hủ tíu xào rau*
vegetarian noodle soup	*mì/hủ tíu nấu rau*
fried vegetables	*rau xào*
boiled vegetables	*rau luộc*
vegetables	*rau*
fried vegetables	*rau xào*
boiled vegetables	*rau luộc*
sour vegetable	*dưa góp* (N) *dưa chua* (S)
fried bean sprouts	*giá xào*
vegetable soup (large bowl)	*canh rau*
salad	*rau sa lát*
fried vegetable with mushrooms	*rau cải xào nấm*
tofu	*đậu phụ/đậu hủ*
fried tofu with chopped meat	*thòt nhồi đậu phụ/ đậu hủ*
fried tofu with tomato sauce	*đậu phụ/đậu hủ sốt cà*
fried tofu with vegetable	*đậu phụ/đậu hủ xào*
rice	*cơm*
steamed rice	*cơm trắng*
mixed fried rice	*cơm rang thập cẩm* (N) *cơm chiên* (S)
rice porridge	*cháo*
specialities	*đặc sản*
lobster	*con tôm hùm*
frog	*con ếch*
oyster	*con sò*
bat	*con dơi*
cobra	*rắn hổ*
gecko	*con tắc kè/kỳ nhơng/ kỳ đà*
goat	*con dê*
pangolin	*con trúc/tê tê*
porcupine	*con nhím*
python	*con trăn*
small hornless deer	*con nai tơ*
turtle	*con rùa*
venison	*thịt nai*
wild pig	*con heo rừng*

Fruit

fruit	*trái cây*
apple	*trái táo* (N) *trái bơm* (S)
apricot	*trái lê*
avocado	*trái bư*
banana	*trái chuối*
coconut	*trái dừa*
custard apple	*trái măng cầu*
durian	*trái sầu riêng*
grapes	*trái nho*
green dragon fruit	*trái thanh long*
guava	*trái ổi*
jackfruit	*trái mít*
jujube (Chinese date)	*trái táo ta*
lemon	*trái chanh*
longan	*trái nhãn*
lychee	*trái vải*
mandarin orange	*trái quýt*
mangosteen	*trái măng cụt*
orange	*trái cam*
papaya	*trái đu đủ*
peach	*trái đào*
persimmon	*trái hồng xiêm*

pineapple	*trái khóm/trái dứa*
plum	*trái mận/trái mơ*
pomelo	*trái bưởi*
rambutan	*trái chôm chôm*
starfruit	*trái khế*
strawberry	*trái dâu*
tangerine	*trái quýt*
three-seed cherry	*trái sê-ri*
water apple	*trái roi đường* (N) *trái mận* (S)
watermelon	*trái dưa hấu*
fruit salad	*sa lát hoa quả* (N) *trái cây các loại* (S)
mixed fruit cocktail	*cóc-tai hoa quả*

Condiments

pepper	*tiêu xay*
salt	*muối*
sugar	*đường*
ice	*đá*
yoghurt	*sữa chua* (N) *da-ua* (S)
hot pepper	*ớt trái*
fresh chillis	*ớt*
soy sauce	*xì dầu* (N) *nước tương* (S)
fish sauce	*nước mắm*

DRINKS

coffee	*cà phê*
hot black coffee	*cà phê đen nóng*
hot milk coffee	*nâu nóng* (N) *cà phê sữa nóng* (S)
iced black coffee	*cà phê đá*
iced milk coffee	*nâu đá* (N) *cà phê sữa đá* (S)
tea	*chè* (N) *trà* (S)
hot black tea	*chè đen nóng* (N) *trà nóng* (S)
hot milk black tea	*chè đen sữa* (N) *trà pha sữa* (S)
hot honey black tea	*chè mật ong* (N) *trà pha mật* (S)
chocolate milk	*cacao sữa*
hot chocolate	*cacao nóng*
iced chocolate	*cacao đá*
hot milk	*sữa nóng*
iced milk	*sữa đá*
fruit juice	*nước quả/nước trái cây*
hot lemon juice	*chanh nóng*
iced lemon juice	*chanh đá*
hot orange juice	*cam nóng*
iced orange juice	*cam đá*
pure orange juice	*cam vắt*
fruit shake	*sinh tố/trái cây xay*
banana shake	*nước chuối xay*
milk & banana shake	*nước chuối sữa xay*
orange & banana shake	*nước cam/chuối xay*
papaya shake	*nước đu đủ xay*
pineapple shake	*nước dứa* (N) *khóm xay* (S)
mixed fruit shake	*sinh tố tổng hợp/ nước thập cẩm xay*
mango shake	*nước xoài xay*
mineral water	*nước khoáng* (N) *nước suối* (S)
lemon mineral water	*khoáng chanh* (N) *suối chanh* (S)
spring water (big/small)	*nước suối chai (lớn/nhỏ)*
tinned soft drinks	*thức uống đóng hộp*
Coca-Cola	*Coca Cola*
Pepsi	*Pepsi Cola*
7 Up	*7 Up*
tinned orange juice	*cam hộp*
soda water & lemon	*soda chanh*
soda water, lemon & sugar	*soda chanh đường*
beer	*bia*
Amstel beer	*bia Amstel*
333 beer	*bia 333*
BGI beer	*bia BGI*
Carlsberg beer	*bia Carlsberg*
Chinese beer	*bia Trung Quốc*
Halida beer	*bia Halida*
Heineken beer	*bia Heineken*
San Miguel beer	*bia San Miguel*
Tiger beer	*bia Tiger*
Tiger (large bottle)	*bia Tiger (chai to)*

HILL TRIBE LANGUAGES

The task of neatly classifying the different hill tribe groups of Vietnam is not an easy one. Ethnologists typically classify the Montagnards by linguistic distinction and commonly refer to three main groups (which further splinter into vast and complex sub-groupings). The Austro-Asian family includes the Viet-Muong, Mon-Khmer, Tay-Tai and Meo-Dzao language groups; the Austronesian family includes Malayo-Polynesian languages; and the Sino-Tibetan family encompasses the Chinese and Tibeto-Burmese language groups. Furthermore, within a single spoken language, there are often myriad varying dialectical variations.

The following words and phrases should prove useful when visiting members of the larger Vietnamese hill tribes. If you're planning on spending a lot of time within hill tribe areas, consider taking Lonely Planet's *Hill Tribes of South-East Asia phrasebook* with you. For more information on hill tribes and the areas they inhabit see the Population & People section in the Facts about Vietnam chapter.

Tay

Also known as the Ngan, Pa Di, Phen, Thu Lao and Tho, the Tay belong to the Tay-Thai language group.

Hello.	*Pá prama.*
Goodbye.	*Pá paynó.*
Yes.	*Mi.*
No.	*Boomi.*
Thank you.	*Đay fon.*
What is your name?	*Ten múng le xăng ma?*
Where do you come from?	*Mu'ng du' te là ma?*
How much does this cost?	*Ău ni ki lai tiên?*

H'mong

The H'mong are also known as Meo, Mieu, Mong Do (White H'mong), Mong Du (Black H'mong), Mong Lenh (Flower H'mong), Mong Si (Red H'mong). They belong to the H'mong-Dao language group, but their spoken language resembles Mandarin Chinese.

Hello.	*Ti nấu/Caó cu.*
Goodbye.	*Caó mun' g chè.*
Yes.	*Có mua.*
No.	*Chúi muá.*
Thank you.	*Ô chờ.*
What is your name?	*Caó be hua chan' g?*
Where do you come from?	*Caó nhao từ tuả?*
How much does this cost?	*Pố chở chá?*

Dao

Also known as Coc Mun, Coc Ngang, Dai Ban, Diu Mien, Dong, Kim Mien, lan Ten, Lu Gang, Ticu Ban, trai, Xa, this tribe belongs to the Mong Dao language group.

Hello.	*Puang tọi.*
Goodbye.	*Puang tọi.*
Yes.	*Mái.*
No.	*Mái mái.*
Thank you.	*Tỡ dun.*
What is your name?	*Mang nhi búa chiên nay?*
Where do you come from?	*May hải đo?*
How much does this cost?	*Pchiả nhăng?*

Glossary

A Di Da – Buddha of the Past
agent orange – toxic, carcinogenic chemical herbicide used extensively during the *American War*
am and duong – Vietnamese equivalent of Yin and Yang
Amerasians – children borne of unions between Asian women and US servicemen during the *American War*
American War – Vietnamese name for what is also known as the 'Vietnam War'
Annam – old Chinese name for Vietnam meaning 'Pacified South'
Annamites – term used by the French to describe the Vietnamese
ao dai – Vietnamese national dress
arhat – anyone who has attained nirvana
ARVN – Army of the Republic of Vietnam (former South Vietnamese army)

ba mu – 12 'midwives', each of whom teaches newborns a different skill necessary for the first year of life: smiling, sucking, lying on their stomachs and so forth
ban – village
bang – congregation (in the Chinese community)
bar om – or, 'karaoke om', literally 'holding' bars associated with the sex industry
Ba Tay – Mrs Westerner
binh dinh vo – traditional martial art performed with a bamboo stick
Black Flags – *Co Den*; a semi-autonomous army of Chinese, Vietnamese and hill tribe-troops
bonze – Vietnamese Buddhist monk
buu dien – post office

cai luong – modern theatre
Caodaism – indigenous Vietnamese religion
can – 10-year cycle
cay son – tree from whose resin lacquer is made
Cham – ethnic minority people descended from the people of Champa
Champa – Hindu kingdom dating from the late 2nd century AD
Charlie – US soldiers' nickname for the *VC*
Chuan De – Buddhist Goddess of Mercy (Chinese: Guanyin)
chu nho – standard Chinese characters (script)
chu nom – also *nom*, Vietnamese script
Cochinchina – the southern part of Vietnam during the French colonial era
Co Den – see Black Flags
Com Pho – rice-noodle soup; common sign on restaurants
cowboys – motorbike-borne thieves
crachin – fine drizzle
cu ly – fern stems used to stop bleeding
cyclo – pedicab or bicycle rickshaw

danh de – illegal numbers game
dau – oil
Di Lac Buddha – Buddha of the Future
dinh – communal meeting hall
DMZ – the misnamed Demilitarised Zone, a strip of land that once separated North and South Vietnam
doi moi – economic restructuring or reform
dong – natural caves
dong chi – comrade
DRV – Democratic Republic of Vietnam (the old North Vietnam)

ecocide – term used to describe the devastating effects of the herbicides sprayed over Vietnam during the *American War*

fengshui – see *phong thuy*
flechette – experimental US weapon; an artillery shell containing thousands of darts
fu – talisman
Funan – see *Oc-Eo*

garuda – Sanskrit term for griffin-like sky beings who feed on *naga*
ghe – long, narrow rowboat
giay phep di lai – internal travel permit
gom – ceramics

hai dang – lighthouse
han viet – Sino-Vietnamese literature

hat boi – classical theatre in the south
hat cheo – popular theatre
hat tuong – classical theatre in the north
Hoa – ethnic-Chinese, the largest single minority group in Vietnam
ho ca – aquarium
Ho Chi Minh Trail – route used by the *NVA* and *VC* to move supplies to guerrillas in the south
hoi – 60-year period (used in calendar)
hoi quan – Chinese congregational assembly halls
ho khau – residence permit needed for everything: to attend school, seek employment, own land, register a vehicle, buy a home, start a business etc
Honda Dream – most popular model of Honda motor-scooter sold in Vietnam
Honda om – motorbike taxi, also called *xe om*
huyen – rural district

Indochina – Vietnam, Cambodia and Laos. The name derives from Indian and Chinese influences.

kala-makara – sea monster god
kalan – a religious sanctuary
khach san – hotel
Khmer – ethnic-Cambodians
Khong Tu – Confucius
kich noi – spoken drama
Kinh – Vietnamese language
Kuomintang – or KMT, meaning Nationalist Party. The KMT controlled China around 1925–49 until defeated by the Communists.
ky – 12-year cycle (used in calendars)

lang – hereditary noble family who rules the communal land and collects the benefits of labour and tax through its use by locals
lang tam – tombs
Liberation – 1975 takeover of the South by the North; what most foreigners call 'reunification'
Lien Xo – literally, Soviet Union; used to call attention to a foreigner
linga – stylised phallus which represents the Hindu god Shiva
li xi – lucky money

MAAG – Military Assistance Advisory Group, set up to instruct troops receiving US weapons how to use them
mandapa – meditation hall
manushi-buddha – Buddha who appeared in human form
mat cua – 'watchful eyes', supposed to protect the residents of the house from harm
moi – derogatory word meaning 'savages', mostly used by ethnic-Vietnamese to describe hill tribe people
Montagnards – term meaning highlanders or mountain people, used to refer to the ethnic minorities who inhabit remote areas of Vietnam
muong – large village unit made up of *quel*

naga – Sanskrit term for a mythical serpent being with divine powers; often depicted forming a kind of shelter over the Buddha
nam phai – for men
napalm – jellied petrol (gasoline) dropped and lit from aircraft; used by US forces with devastating effect during the *American War*
NGO – nongovernment organisation
nha hang – restaurant
nha khach – hotel or guesthouse
nha nghi – guesthouse
nha-rong – large stilt house, used by hill tribes as a kind of community centre
nha tro – dormitory
NLF – National Liberation Front; official name for the *VC*
nom – see *chu nom*
nui – mountain
nu phai – for women
nuoc dua – coconut milk
nuoc mam – fish sauce, added to almost every dish in Vietnam
nuoc suoi – mineral water
NVA – North Vietnamese Army

Oc-Eo – Indianised kingdom (also called Funan) in southern Vietnam between 1st and 6th centuries
Ong Tay – Mr Westerner
Orderly Departure Program (ODP) – carried out under the auspices of the *UNHCR*, designed to allow orderly resettlement of Vietnamese political refugees
OSS – predecessor of the CIA

pagoda – traditionally an eight-sided Buddhist tower, but in Vietnam the word is commonly used to denote a temple
Phoenix Program – or Operation Phoenix; a controversial program run by the CIA, aimed at eliminating *VC* cadres by assassination, capture or defection
phong thuy – literally, wind water; used to describe geomancy; also known by its Chinese name, *fengshui*
Politburo – Political Bureau; about a dozen members overseeing the Party's day-to-day functioning with the power to issue directives to the government
POW – prisoner of war
PRG – Provisional Revolutionary Government, the temporary Communist government set up by the *VC* in the South. It existed from 1969 to 1976.
PTSD – Post-Traumatic Stress Disorder

quan – urban district
quel – small stilt-house hamlets
quoc am – modern Vietnamese literature
quoc ngu – Latin-based phonetic alphabet in which Vietnamese is written

rap – cinema
Revolutionary Youth League – first Marxist group in Vietnam and predecessor of the Communist Party
roi can – conventional puppetry
roi nuoc – water puppetry
ruou – wine
RVN – Republic of Vietnam (the old South Vietnam)

social evils – campaign to prevent evil ideas from the West 'polluting' Vietnamese society
song – river
son then – black
SRV – Socialist Republic of Vietnam (Vietnam's current official name)
Strategic Hamlets Program – an unsuccessful program of the US army and South Vietnamese government in which peasants were forcibly moved into fortified villages to deny the *VC* bases of support

Tam Giao – literally, triple religion; Confucianism, Taoism and Buddhism fused over time with popular Chinese beliefs and ancient Vietnamese animism
Tao – the Way; the essence of which all things are made
Tet – Vietnamese Lunar New Year
thanh long – dragon fruit
Thich Ca – historical Buddha (Sakyamuni)
thung chai – gigantic round wicket baskets sealed with pitch; used as rowboats.
thuoc bac – Chinese medicine
toc hanh – express bus
Tonkin – the northern part of Vietnam during the French colonial era; also name of a body of water in the north (Tonkin Gulf)
truyen khau – traditional oral literature

UNHCR – United Nations High Commission for Refugees

VC – Viet Cong or Vietnamese Communists
Viet Kieu – Overseas Vietnamese
Viet Minh – League for the Independence of Vietnam, a nationalistic movement which fought the Japanese and French but later became Communist-dominated
VNQDD – Viet Nam Quoc Dan Dang; largely middle-class nationalist party

xang – petrol
xe dap loi – wagon pulled by bicycle
xe Honda loi – wagon pulled by a motorbike
xe Lam – three-wheeled motorised vehicle
xe om – motorbike taxi, also called *Honda om*

yang – genie

Acknowledgments

THANKS

Many thanks to the travellers who used the last edition and wrote to us with helpful hints, useful advice and interesting anecdotes.

Warwick Abrahams, John Abrahamsen, Ralph Acosta, Garry Adams, Sean Adams, Charlie Addiman, Max Adrien, Anton Aendenroomer, Daniel Agar, Haroon Akram-Lodhi, Mary Aldred, Froukje Algera, Simon Aliwell, Gaynor Allen, Einar Anderson, Finn Andersson, Steve Andrews, Sallie Aprahamian, Richard Archer, Jan Arell, Jacopo Arpesani, Cathy Ashton, Richard Aspland, Richard Astley, Carolyn Ayers, Walt Bacak, Julie Balance, Bruce Baldock, Richard Baldwin, RA Balmanoukian, Ben Bangs, Hanneke Bannink, Vera J Barad, Chris & Ros Bardsley, Sheila Barnes, Kevin Barrows, Mandy Barton, Bhaskar Baruah, Lynne Bateman, Daniel M Battista, Susan Bauer, Clint Bauld, Zane Beallor, Gillian Beattie, Gladys Beatty, Sander Beekink, Max Beeson, Sonja Beierlein, John Belinski, Suzanne & Jon Benjamin, Tony Bennell, Michael Bennington, Dyanna Benny, P Berenguer, Yves Beretta, Steen Bergerud, Carel van der Bergh, A Bergmann, Annemiek Bergmans, Catherine Berryman, Melissa Beswick, Martin Biallowons, Harry Biddulph, James Bierman, Emma Birch, Michael K Birnmeyer, Fabio Biserna, Helen Black, Pam & Pax Blamey, Melissa Blanch, Jocelyn Blanchard, Adrian Bloch, Ron Blow, Miranda Blum, Poli Bodas, Markus Bohnert, Kelly & Ian Bolton, Franco Bondioli, Nicolas Bonner, Marc Bonnevle, Marc Bontemps, Chris Boomaars, Jessica Boon, Dennis Borg, Piet-Hein Bos, Peter Bottcher, Elizabeth Bowdrtch, Susan Boyd, RX & T Boyle, Michael Brand, Will Brant, Josiane Braver, GM Bray, J&P Brenchley, Jennie Brightwell, Lynda Britz, Graeme Brock, R Brodbeck, Bart van den Broek, Barbara Brons, Joan Brooking, Charlie Brooks, Paul Brown, Charles T Brumfield, Troels Brynskov, Robin Buckley, Garth Burgoine, Robert Burley, Thom Burns, Michelle Butler, Warren Calhoun, Nanci & Dick Calvert, Samantha Cameron, Adam Camilleri, Anne Cappodanno, Linden & Darren Caproli, Caterina Carbonara, Eduardo Cardellini Martino, Richard Carr, Partick Carter, Rusty Cartmill, Sindona Cassteel, C H Castelain, Lainie Chandler, Yvonne Chappell, Lawrence Chin, Lana Choi, W Christine, Marie Chrysander, Vilma R Cirimele, Barbara Clark, Barrie Clarke, Paul Clements, I Cliffe, Laurent Cnudde, Eduardo Coifman, Jill Cole, Tim Coles, L Collins, Marie Coloccia, Chris Conley, Pol Conway, Daniel Cook, Stephen Coombs, T&J Cooney, Gary B Cooper, Jim Cooper, Stanley Corbett, Tui Cordemans, Ray Corness, Bert Corte, Kevin Cosgriff, Siobhan Coshery, Paul J Costantino, Tony Coulson, Tara Cowell, Angela Cox, Katy Cox, Sam Crawley, Pat & Brian Croft, Siobhan Cunliffe, Julie Cunningham, I&Q Cutler, Ake Dahllof, Steve Daley, Dave Dallimore, Mirjam & Hans Damen, Paul R Danneberg, Alex Davis, Ian Davison, Robyn Dawkins, Dean Dawson, Kristen De, Chantal De bondt, William De Prado, Erik De Ryk, Yelle de Smet, Martin de Vries, Debbie Dear, Antoine Delage, Hilga & Jan Deloof, Emma Denton, Sharon DeQuine, Alex Derom, Martin Derry, John Devison, Enza Di Iorio, Scott Dickson, U Diehr, John Dobinson, Annabel Dobson, Nan Dodds, Alexandra Doerrie, Annie Dore, Michael Doud, Jacinta Drew, Brenda Drinkwater, Julian Druce, Francois Dutort, Noreen Duncan, Michael Dunphy, Jacob Dupont, Dr Christian Dupuis, Robin Dutt-Gupta, Frank Dutton, Mark Dworkin, Christian Dy, RW Earl, Sasha Earnheart-Gold, Delwyn Eason, Ann Eaton, Richard Edgell, Patrick Edington, Ellen Edmonds-Wilson, Kim Edwards, Michael Eisenstein, David Ellard, Louis Elliott, Joan & Bill Ellis, Steven Emmel, MJ Enderby, Sandra Engel, Mia Erkkila, Maureen Evans, M Evers.

Paolo Fabbro, Russ Facer, Jim Fairhall, Brian Farrelly, Moira Farrelly, Stuart & Carol Faulkner, Juliet Feibel, Christina J Felker, Peter Fellows, Bob Fenwick, Dean Fergie, Mel Ferguson, Brian Finch, Hanne Finholt, Taryn Firkser, Lesli Flaman, Lars Flateboe, T Fletcher, Enid Flint, Denise Flowerday, Peter Foggitt, Nikki Follis, Mathew Ford, Julie Foreman, Kent Foster, Andy Fox, Steven Franch Jensen, SM Franklin, Clare Freedman, Bill Fridl, Peter & Claire Frost, Walter Frost, Thilde Fruergaard, Mark Gadbois, Shari & Allen Gaerber, Alan & Eleanor Galt, Onne Ganel, James Garber, Russell Garbutt, Ines Garcia-Pintos Balbas, Dinah

Gardner, Christine & Simon Garrett, Ann Gates, Joan Gates, S Genest, Barbara Gibbs, Chris Gierymski, Rebecca Giles, Libby Gillingham, Steve Golden, Lorne Goldman, Dan Goldthorp, David Goode, Diane B Goodpasture, Albert Gordon, Andrew & Rachel Gordon, Scott Gordon, Audrey Gormley, Ana Goshko, John Goss, Cynthia Gough, Michelle & Nigel Gough, Dean Gould, Kellie Grace, Brian Graham, N Gray, Barry & Julie Green, M&I Griffiths, Sarah Grimson, Richard Groom, Sue Groom, Bruno & Martine Grosjean, Jacques Groulx, Isabella Gualano, Gilles Gut, D Gwilym-Williams, Gil Hahn, Shawn Hainsworth, Jenny Hall, Rachael Hall, Richard & Jenny Hall, Stephen Haller, Eammon Hamilton, Jan Hamilton, Steve Hammerton, Meredith Hamstead, Debbie Hanlon, Allan Hansell, John Hanson, Natasha Hanson, Inger Hansson, Peter Hardie, Ruth Harley, Pauline Harper, Valerie Harridge, Leslie-Jane Harrower, Donald Hatch, Ayana Haviv, Jonathan Hawke, Lucy Hayter, Andrew Heafield, Alexander Healy, P Healy, Gary Hedges, Marlies Heerdegen, Fran Hegarty, Henk F Heinekamp, Asa Hellstrom, Mary Helme, Carl Hemberg, Scott Hemphill, Jan Henning Scholz, Elisabeth Heraud, Inge Herbo, TE Hesse, Jeff Hill, R Hill, Tim Hill, Tanya Hines, Lewis Hitchcock, Brian Hjort, Niels & Bitten Hjorth, Le Hoang Quan, Sue & Tony Hoare, Luisa & Hanns Hoefer, Rachel Hoey, George Hoey Morris, Colin & Judith Holbrook, Andrew Holder, Bevan Holland, Sue & Brian Holley, Niels Hollum, Gaylene Holt, Debbie Hooglond, Jeff Hopkins, Allen Hoppes, Maura Horkan, Glenn Hornstein, Jonathon Horwitz, I Hoskins, Bruce Houldsworth, Martin Howard, Philip Howard, P Howard Useche, Merilyn Howorth, Susanne Hrinkov, Adrian Huber, C Huber, Petra Hubinette, Darril Hudson, Cathy & Doug Hull, Bernard Humbert, Anna Hung, Karin Hunger, Lee Hunt, Stephanie Hunt, Andy Hurst, Bui Huu Phuoc, Simon Hylson-Smith, Wyn Ingham, Sally Ingleton, Stephen Iremonger, Alice Iversen, Richard Iversen, Jerry Jackson, Larry W Jacobs, Aage Jacobsen, Christian Jacobsen, Britt & Kenneth Jademo, Christopher Jaensch, Christopher J James, Derrick James, H Javelle, David Jeffery, Ian Jenkins, Zena Jenkins, Henriette Radoor Jensen, Tine Jensen, Javier Jimenez, Anders Johansen, Rob John, W John Swartz, Ian Johnson, RF Johnson, Steve Johnson, Anne-Marie Johnston, Ce Johnston, Lee Johnston, Edward Jones, Ian Jones, John Jones, Peter D Jones, Wm Joseph Bruckner, Chris Jules, Richard Juterbock.

Jeffrey Kadet, Carolyn Kaltenbach, Peter Kapec, Paul Karalius, Bernhard Kasparek, Louis B Katz, Gina Kaye, Jens Kayser, Jonathan P Keeve, V Keks, Colette Kelly, K Kemmis-Betty, James Kennely, Charlotte Kenney, Tim Kerger, Margo Kerkvliet, Bill Kershaw, Jolanda Kersten, Luu Duc Khanh, Charlie Kime, C Kimme, Edwin Kirk, Susan Klock, David Kneser, Tracy Knights, Ingo Koeker, Danielle Koning, Maarten Kop, Maurice Koppes, Karin Kostel, Thomas Krag, Steven Kram, Naomi Kretschmer, Christian Kreuzer, Albert Kromkamp, Mike Krosin, Ann Krumboltz, Laszlo Kuster, Heidi Kuttler, Scott Laderman, Tara Lally, Sylvio Lamarche, John Lam-Po-Tang, Miles Lampson, Jane Lander, Jerry Landman, Mr Lane, Michael Lange, Jenni & Brett Lardner, Anne Larsen, Emma Latumahina, Vince Lau, Ian Laurenson, Christian Lauterburg, Linda Layfield, Nguyen Le Bac, Angela Lee, Annie Lee, Chris Lee, Dale Lee, Tim Lee, Brenda Lee Hill, Gan Lee Suan, Tim Leffel, Justin Leibowitz, John Arne Lein, Celia Leite, Hilde Lemaire, Tamhai Lenhu, Manfred Lenzen, Murray S Levin, Steven Li, Wolfgang Liebe, Cathy Lincoln, Stuart Lindsay, Will Linsdell, Amanda Lister, Michael Litt, M Littler, Debbie Lo, H Locke, Brian Locker, Bas Lodewijks, Wendy & Philip Lomax, Helen Longhammer, Lewis Lorton, Matt Love, Rebecca Loveless, Alex J Low, Annette Low, Hillary Lowe, Sam Lucero, Oanh Ly, Peter Lyden, Eric Lynn, Melissa Lysaght, Belinda Macgill, Madi Maclean, Mary MacNeill, Julia MacRae, Olivia Maehler, Dee Mahan, Stuart Malcolm, Linda Mallens, Mary Mallon, Marian Manders, Jim Manheimer, Amaya Manzano, Sancta Maria Orphanage, Louise Marks, Neal Marsden, Chloe Marshall, Judy Marshall, Keith Marshall, Kathy Martell, Patrick Martin, Philip Mason, David & Karen Mathieson, Steven Mathieson, Mrs & Mr Matropieri, Shisho Matsushima, Woods Mattingley, Claudia Maxelon, Keenan McAluney, Mrs & Mr McBride, Barrie McCormick, Kevin McCourt, Susan McGee, Tim & Meredith McGlone, Craig McGrath, Kevin McIntyre, Tom McLaren, Gary McLeod, Tony McLeod, Dallas McMaugh, Paula McNamara, Clifford C Raisbeck MD, Mike Medd, Christian Meier, Renee Melchert Thorpe, Spencer Melnick, Philip Merkle, Heather Merriam, Linda Merz, Cliff Meyer, Antoine Meyrignac, Dan Michaelis, Zenon Michniewicz, Alan Middlebrook, Peter Mijsberg, Gabriel Mikhael, Chad Miller, Gareth Miller, Jon Miller, Ron Miller, Steve Miller, Narelle Milligan, J Mindel, Michael Minen, Kim Mitchell, Steve Mitsos, Jock Moilliet, Rachel Moilliet, Kai Monkkonen, Laurence Monnier, Patina Monti, Tom & Shiela Mooney, Mike Morden, Liliane Morel, David Morgan, Lin Morgan, Nick Morgan, Valerie Morgan, Madeleine Morris, Lene Mortensen, Anne Mosher, Daniella Moss, Dave Mountain, Desmond Mow, Rory Mulholland, Andrea Munch, Natalie & Shane Mundy, Annie Murphy, Barry Murphy, J Murphy, Alastair Murray, Nick Murray, Paul Murray, Rod Myers, Dean Myerson, Teena Myscowsky, Amelie Nadeau, Craig Napier, Andrew Neale, Diane Nelson, Lucy Van Der Net, Steve Newcomer, Kerryn Newton, Scott Newton, Dr Truong Tan Nghiep, Nguyen Ngoc Chinh, Daisy Nguyen, Huy Nguyen, Thao Nguyen, Trung Nguyen, Hoang Thanh Nhan, C&B Nickel, Steven Nightingale, Ashok Nikapota, Kazuko Nishihara, Philip Nolan, Anders Nordstrom, Margaret Norman, Jane Norris, Kate Nulty, Shane Nunan.

Omer Nuriel, Jenna Oakley, Quinn Okamoto, Alex Olah, B Oliver, S Oliver, Per Olsson, Greetje Oolders, Mary Osborn, Jacob Page, B Page Leary, Damian Paine, Yudi Palkova, Jade Palmer, Kerryn Palmer, A Parienty, Janine Parker, Helen Parkin, Alejandro Parodi, Clem Parry, David Parry, Mel Parsonage, Steve Partridge, Helen & Lee Paterson, Mike Pattison, Fiona H Paul, Kelly Paxton, U Payern, Becky Payne, Diane & John Peake, Shirley Pearson, Linda & Gary Pedersen, Josep Penella, Benoit Perdu, Chris Peres, Matthew Perrement, Marc Perri, Tomas Persson, Marco Perucchi, Kelli Peterson, Harold Peulen, Ilona & Andreas pfeiffer, Vinh Pham, Mark Pickens, Cyril Piddington, Rodney Pinder, Sophie Pith, Roland Playford, Simon Poon, Clive Porter, James Porter, Judith Porter, Andreas Poulakidas, Bill Powell, Duncan Priestley, Sibille Pritchard, Mark Proctor, David Pryke, DC Purewal, R Rabenstein, Daniel Radack, Petra Raddatz, Marc Raderer, Marco Ragazzi, John Rainy, Clifford Raisbeck, Erin Rampling, Bruce Ramsey, Tine Rasborg, Elena Rasero, Jarmo Rautiola, Chad Raymond, Clive Reader, J Rebecca, Hans Rechseiner, Linda Reed, Dietrich Rehnert, Mady Reichliung, Pat Reiniz, Greg F Reinking, Eduard Reitsema, Rob Reynolds, Dan Rhodes, Adrian Rice, Clifford Rich, Manon Richard, PD Riches, C&D Riley, James Robert Bierman, Louise Roberts, Paul Robertson, Ken Robinson, Mark Robinson, Paul Robinson, Cindy Roche, Anne Rogers, Carrie A Rogers, Bill Rose, H Rose, Lou & Joan Rose, Helmut & Sabine Rosel, Marvin Rosen, Dan Rosenberg, Alison Ross, Matthew Ross, Neal Ross, Charles Round-Turner, Leanne Rowe, TherTse Rozijan, Jarek Rudnik, G Ruff, Nicolai Ruge, John Ruiz Jr, Pablo Ruiz Monroy, Ann Ryckaert, Klaus Rydahl Pedersen, Marianne Rynefeldt-Skog, Jutta Saas, Isabel Sabugueiro, Alexandra Saldy, A Salomaa, Richard Samwell, Larry Sapiro, Ineke van der Sar, Vincent Savage, Vicky Saville, Jevan Sayer, Paul & Margie Scarpignato, M Scattini, Andrea Schenk, Anja Schiffrin, Anthony Schlesinger, Gunnar Schmid, Martin Schmidt, Heiko Schmitz, Jochen J Schnell, K Schoenban, Ivan Scholte, Henning Scholz, Sune Schon, Ernst Schonmann, Ralf Schramm, Sara Schroter, M Schultes, Humez Sebastien, Christina & Martin Semler, Ron Settle, Bill Sharp, Daniel Shaw, Thersa Shaw, Betty Sheets, Phyl Shimeld, Greg Short, Ian Shrier, Chern Siang Jye, Jennifer Sild, Saverio Silva, EB Simonis-Warmersdam, David Simpson, Edward Simpson, Graham Simpson, Kaz Singer, J Slikker, Ken Sloane, Tyson Slocum, Peter Smith, Roger Smith, Sue Smith, Chad Smolinski, Max Smolka, Margaret Smyth, Audrey Sneddon, Jack Sneed, Patrick Sodergren, Ingeborg Solvang Olsen, JF Somers, Pranav Soneji, Richard Southern, Peter Spano, Stuart Spark, L Spashett, David Spencer, A Spiers, Henrik Sponholtz, Marielle Spreeuwers, Nick Spurgeon, Alice Steiner, Fiona Stephens, D Sternberg, Fiona & Dave Steward, J Stijnman, Marielle Stitzinger, Hans Van Der Stock, Lucy Stockoe, Bagus Sudiro, Ashley Sutherland, Pieter Swart.

Kevin Taggart, S Taliah, Lillian Tangen, Lisa Tapert, D Tapp, Simon Taskunas, JR Tattis, Lucy Taylor, Tansy Tazewell, Mikeal & Anna Teljstedt, Adam Tenbrink, Bob Tennent, Anette Terlutter, Albino TestonDiaz, Priscilla The, Anne-Marie Thepaut, Arleen Thomas, Mark Thomas, Nathan Thomas, JM Thomson, Tran Thuc-Uyen, Nell Todd, Adriana Totonelli, Margaret Traeger, Nathan Traller, Thanh-Tinh Tran, Henrik & Philippa Tribler, Peter Tse, Tatyana Tsinberg, Jim Turner, Lee Turner, Marc Turuow, JP Umber, Noam Urbach, Hartger van Brakel, Dreas van Donselaar, Judith Van Erp, Mieke van Heesewijk, Robert van Hooff, Pim Van Houten, Laurens van Kol, Dick van Kooten, Luc van Mechlan, Pascal Vanhove, Thanes Vanig, Carlos Velazquez, Daniel

Vellingiri, Med Vennlig Hilsen, Klaus Viitanen, Paul Virgo, Karin Vittrup, Antonio Vivaldi, Thanh Vo, Brandon R Vogt, Rob Vollmer, Freddy von Rabenau, NH & Rene Voyer, J&B Walker, Stuart Walker, Ian Wallach, Mark Wallem, Brian Wallis, Sondra Walter, Michael Ward, Jocelyn Warn, Ian Waters, David Watkins, Sandra Watkins, Mike Watson, Adam Waxman, P Wayne Frey, Michael Weaver, Sheila Webb, Daniel & Daniela Weizand, Nicholas Wellington, Julie Wenham, Ed Wenn, Jennifer West, Julie Westrupp, Natalie Wheatley, Annie White, Theresa White, H Whiting, Jennifer Whitson, Katharine Whittle, Joan & Mark Wierzba, Charles Wilding-White, Dr Annette Willems, Bev Williams, Carl Williams, Martin Williams, Grant Wills, Martin Winter, E Winters, Silke Wirtz, Joanna Wiseman, Tom Witt, John Wolf, Joyce Wood, Chris & Judy Woods, Fiona Woods, B Woods Mattingley, Penny Wright, Michael Wycks, Zbigniew Wysomierski, Donald Yap, Donald W M Yap, Chris Yarbrough, Angelina Yee, Tse Yin Lee, Elizabeth Yuan, Blaz Zabukovec, Ben Zabulis, Robert Zafran, Val Zogopoulos, LA Zook, Bianca Zubevich, J Zwaveling.

LONELY PLANET

ON THE ROAD

Travel Guides explore cities, regions and countries, and supply information on transport, restaurants and accommodation, covering all budgets. They come with reliable, easy-to-use maps, practical advice, cultural and historical facts and a rundown on attractions both on and off the beaten track. There are over 200 titles in this classic series, covering nearly every country in the world.

Lonely Planet Upgrades extend the shelf life of existing travel guides by detailing any changes that may affect travel in a region since a book has been published. Upgrades can be downloaded for free from **www.lonelyplanet.com/upgrades**

For travellers with more time than money, **Shoestring** guides offer dependable, first-hand information with hundreds of detailed maps, plus insider tips for stretching money as far as possible. Covering entire continents in most cases, the six-volume shoestring guides are known around the world as 'backpackers' bibles'.

For the discerning short-term visitor, **Condensed** guides highlight the best a destination has to offer in a full-colour, pocket-sized format designed for quick access. They include everything from top sights and walking tours to opinionated reviews of where to eat, stay, shop and have fun.

CitySync lets travellers use their Palm™ or Visor™ hand-held computers to guide them through a city with handy tips on transport, history, cultural life, major sights, and shopping and entertainment options. It can also quickly search and sort hundreds of reviews of hotels, restaurants and attractions, and pinpoint their location on scrollable street maps. CitySync can be downloaded from **www.citysync.com**

MAPS & ATLASES

Lonely Planet's **City Maps** feature downtown and metropolitan maps, as well as transit routes and walking tours. The maps come complete with an index of streets, a listing of sights and a plastic coat for extra durability.

Road Atlases are an essential navigation tool for serious travellers. Cross-referenced with the guidebooks, they also feature distance and climate charts and a complete site index.

LONELY PLANET

ESSENTIALS

Read This First books help new travellers to hit the road with confidence. These invaluable predeparture guides give step-by-step advice on preparing for a trip, budgeting, arranging a visa, planning an itinerary and staying safe while still getting off the beaten track.

Healthy Travel pocket guides offer a regional rundown on disease hot spots and practical advice on predeparture health measures, staying well on the road and what to do in emergencies. The guides come with a user-friendly design and helpful diagrams and tables.

Lonely Planet's **Phrasebooks** cover the essential words and phrases travellers need when they're strangers in a strange land. They come in a pocket-sized format with colour tabs for quick reference, extensive vocabulary lists, easy-to-follow pronunciation keys and two-way dictionaries.

Miffed by blurry photos of the Taj Mahal? Tired of the classic 'top of the head cut off' shot? **Travel Photography: A Guide to Taking Better Pictures** will help you turn ordinary holiday snaps into striking images and give you the know-how to capture every scene, from frenetic festivals to peaceful beach sunrises.

Lonely Planet's **Travel Journal** is a lightweight but sturdy travel diary for jotting down all those on-the-road observations and significant travel moments. It comes with a handy time-zone wheel, world maps and useful travel information.

Lonely Planet's eKno is an all-in one communication service developed especially for travellers. It offers low-cost international calls and free email and voicemail so that you can keep in touch while on the road. Check it out on **www.ekno.lonelyplanet.com**

FOOD & RESTAURANT GUIDES

Lonely Planet's **Out to Eat** guides recommend the brightest and best places to eat and drink in top international cities. These gourmet companions are arranged by neighbourhood, packed with dependable maps, garnished with scene-setting photos and served with quirky features.

For people who live to eat, drink and travel, **World Food** guides explore the culinary culture of each country. Entertaining and adventurous, each guide is packed with detail on staples and specialities, regional cuisine and local markets, as well as sumptuous recipes, comprehensive culinary dictionaries and lavish photos good enough to eat.

LONELY PLANET

OFF THE ROAD

Journeys, the travel literature series written by renowned travel authors, capture the spirit of a place or illuminate a culture with a journalist's attention to detail and a novelist's flair for words. These are tales to soak up while you're actually on the road or dip into as an at-home armchair indulgence.

The new range of lavishly illustrated **Pictorial** books is just the ticket for both travellers and dreamers. Off-beat tales and vivid photographs bring the adventure of travel to your doorstep long before the journey begins and long after it is over.

Lonely Planet **Videos** encourage the same independent, tough-minded approach as the guidebooks. Currently airing throughout the world, this award-winning series features innovative footage and an original soundtrack.

Yes, we know, work is tough, so do a little bit of deskside dreaming with the spiral-bound Lonely Planet **Diary**, the tearaway page-a-day **Day-to-Day Calendar** or a Lonely Planet **Wall Calendar**, filled with great photos from around the world.

TRAVELLERS NETWORK

Lonely Planet Online. Lonely Planet's award-winning Web site has insider information on hundreds of destinations, from Amsterdam to Zimbabwe, complete with interactive maps and relevant links. The site also offers the latest travel news, recent reports from travellers on the road, guidebook upgrades, a travel links site, an online book-buying option and a lively traveller's bulletin board. It can be viewed at **www.lonelyplanet.com** or AOL keyword: lp.

Planet Talk is a quarterly print newsletter, full of gossip, advice, anecdotes and author articles. It provides an antidote to the being-at-home blues and lets you plan and dream for the next trip. Contact the nearest Lonely Planet office for your free copy.

Comet, the free Lonely Planet newsletter, comes via email once a month. It's loaded with travel news, advice, dispatches from authors, travel competitions and letters from readers. To subscribe, click on the Comet subscription link on the front page of the Web site.

Index

Text

Bold indicates maps.

U

V

W

Boxed Text

Bold indicates maps.

MAP LEGEND

CITY ROUTES

Freeway	Freeway
Highway	Primary Road
Road	Secondary Road
Street	Street
Lane	Lane
	On/Off Ramp
	Unsealed Road
	One Way Street
	Pedestrian Street
	Stepped Street
	Tunnel
	Footbridge

REGIONAL ROUTES

Tollway, Freeway
Primary Road
Secondary Road
Minor Road

BOUNDARIES

International
State
Disputed
Fortified Wall

HYDROGRAPHY

River, Creek
Canal
Lake
Dry Lake; Salt Lake
Spring; Rapids
Waterfalls

TRANSPORT ROUTES & STATIONS

Train
Underground Train
Metro
Tramway
Cable Car, Chairlift
Ferry
Walking Trail
Walking Tour
Path
Pier or Jetty

AREA FEATURES

Building
Park, Gardens
Market
Sports Ground
Beach
Cemetery
Campus
Plaza

POPULATION SYMBOLS

CAPITAL	National Capital
CAPITAL	Provincial Capital
CITY	City
Town	Town
Village	Village
	Urban Area

MAP SYMBOLS

Place to Stay
Place to Eat
Point of Interest

Airport
Bank
Battle Site
Bus Terminal
Cave
Church
Cinema
Embassy
Golf Course
Hospital
Internet Cafe
Lookout
Monument
Mosque
Museum
National Park
Pagoda
Police Station
Post Office
Pub or Bar
Ruins
Swimming Pool
Spring
Telephone
Temple
Tomb
Tourist Information
Zoo

Note: not all symbols displayed above appear in this book

LONELY PLANET OFFICES

Australia
Locked Bag 1, Footscray, Victoria 3011
☎ 03 9689 4666 fax 03 9689 6833
email: talk2us@lonelyplanet.com.au

USA
150 Linden St, Oakland, CA 94607
☎ 510 893 8555 TOLL FREE: 800 275 8555
fax 510 893 8572
email: info@lonelyplanet.com

UK
10a Spring Place, London NW5 3BH
☎ 020 7428 4800 fax 020 7428 4828
email: go@lonelyplanet.co.uk

France
1 rue du Dahomey, 75011 Paris
☎ 01 55 25 33 00 fax 01 55 25 33 01
email: bip@lonelyplanet.fr
www.lonelyplanet.fr

World Wide Web: www.lonelyplanet.com *or* AOL keyword: lp
Lonely Planet Images: lpi@lonelyplanet.com.au